Mercer Commentary on the New Testament

D1121332

MERCER COMMENTARY ON THE NEW TESTAMENT

GENERAL EDITORS
Watson E. Mills
Richard F. Wilson

ASSOCIATE EDITORS
Roger A. Bullard
Walter Harrelson
Edgar V. McKnight

MERCER UNIVERSITY PRESS EDITOR
Edd Rowell

MERCER UNIVERSITY PRESS
Macon, Georgia

Ref.
BS
2341.25
.M47
2003

0-86554-864-1
MUP P271

Mercer Commentary on the New Testament
©2003 Mercer University Press
Macon, Georgia
Originally published as part of the *Mercer Commentary on the Bible*,
1995 by Mercer University Press

∞The paper used in this publication meets the minimum requirements of American National Standard for Information Sciences—Permanence of Paper for Printed Library Materials, ANSI Z39.48-1992.

Library of Congress Cataloging-in-Publication Data

Mills, Watson E., Richard F. Wilson, editors
Mercer Commentary on the New Testament / general editors Watson E. Mills,
Richard F. Wilson
p. cm.
1. Bible—Commentaries—New Testament.
BS491.2.M47   2003
220.7   20
94023638
NT

CONTENTS

140675

PUBLISHER'S NOTE

In 1995 Mercer University Press published the Mercer Commentary on the Bible, a one-volume commentary that was an award winning, critically acclaimed production. It was hailed for its conciseness and its scope. This was all the more amazing since it included the Apocrypha/Deuterocanonical books.

Eight years and 6,000 copies later, we are now issuing this commentary in two volumes, making it available in paperback for use in the classroom.

Please note three things.

1. You will notice many people in the contributor list wrote a commentary on a book that may be in the companion volume, rather than in the one you are holding. That list has been retained in its entirety and reproduced in each volume.

2. The same general articles have been reproduced in both volumes as in the original one-volume publication.

3. The pagination has been kept as in the original. In the Old Testament volume there will be nothing unusual. In the New Testament volume, however, please note that following the general articles that the page number of "939" is not a mistake.

As with all Mercer University Publications, we appreciate any feedback you wish to give.

Marc A. Jolley
Mercer University Press
12 June 2003

Foreword

The publication of the *Mercer Commentary on the Bible* represents the completion and fulfillment of the most challenging and important project ever undertaken by the Mercer University Press. This volume has been made possible through the generous support of the Warren P. and Ava F. Sewell Foundation, Inc., and by the encouragement, friendship, and support of Lamar Plunkett.

The *Commentary*, by intent and design, is a companion volume to the *Mercer Dictionary of the Bible*. Already in its fourth printing, MDB is serving thousands of Bible students in university and seminary classrooms, in a variety of Christian education settings in churches, and in private study and personal devotion. MDB has been cited as a "truly balanced, thorough, and useful reference work" (*Choice*). It is our hope and expectation that the *Commentary* will serve alongside MDB as a balanced, thorough, and useful guide to and through the Scriptures.

We come to the study of Scripture in a world of increasing religious conflict struggling alongside and within a culture that often dismisses altogether the relevance of religion. Our human situation calls upon us to enter the serious study of Scripture with renewed urgency so that we may understand what the Scriptures actually mean and how their meaning bears upon our living in a world of such dramatic religious pluralism. As we engage the Scriptures, it becomes apparent that we cannot appreciate or claim the depth and insight of Scriptures today unless we are prepared to probe the faith and witness from which our Scriptures sprang. It is from this desire and commitment to study, to understand, and to claim the relevance of Scripture for living that the *Commentary* has been born. The contributions of the sixty-three writers and editors of the *Commentary* come together as a celebration of both the compelling message of Scripture and the inexhaustible wellspring from which the message flows. As one scholar and teacher said of the 247 contributors to the *Dictionary*, the authors and editors of the *Commentary* also are "first-rate scholars who hold in effective relation their faith and their impressive critical learning." It is, we think, this creative tension—between the timeliness and timelessness of Scripture, between serious faith and sane scholarship—that also distinguishes the *Mercer Commentary on the Bible*. In "wholeheartedly and warmly" recommending MDB, *ADRIS Newsletter* observed that "the work is marked by integrity, balance, scholarship, and, above all, by love of the Bible." The *Mercer Commentary on the Bible* has the same markings.

The pedigree of MDB and MCB reflects the same heritage of faith and scholarship. The editors and contributors of both come from the ranks of the National Association of Baptist Professors of Religion, a fraternity of "teachers of Bible" and/or "teachers of religion." This community of scholars traces its beginnings to 1928 when the founding constitution defined its purpose as "the promotion of fellowship, the investigation of problems, and the formation of ideals in the field of religious education." Recently the NABPR resolved to reaffirm the connection of "our heritage . . . our faith . . . and our responsibility." In the *Mercer Commentary on the Bible*, as in MDB, heritage, faith, and responsibility have again been merged into a new and significant resource for serious Bible study.

At no time in history has it been more important than today that we hear and understand the compelling message of the Scriptures. The Bible's message has become garbled by conflicting and even opposing interpretations, sometimes from sources whose agenda is decidedly unscriptural if not antiscriptural. We earnestly hope that the *Mercer Commentary on the Bible* will take its place alongside MDB as a helpful and trustworthy guide beyond the morass of clamoring, often conflicting pronouncements *about* the Bible to the enduring truths *of* the Bible. Indeed, the publication of this work comes with the earnest hope that teachers and students alike can and will say of the *Mercer Commentary on the Bible* what Walter Brueggemann has said of the *Mercer Dictionary of the Bible*: "In the midst of current controversy about the Bible, this publication stands boldly for sanity, intelligence, and moderation."

R. Kirby Godsey
President, Mercer University

Dedication

Lamar Rich Plunkett

statesman, educator, benefactor, friend

Preface

In 1990 Mercer University Press in association with the National Association of Baptist Professors of Religion published the *Mercer Dictionary of the Bible*. The dictionary received the LMP Literary Award for best reference work published in 1990 (see *Publishers' Weekly*, 28 January 1991) and is now in its fourth printing. The *Mercer Dictionary of the Bible* (MDB) includes approximately 1,500 articles written by members of the NABPR. While firmly grounded in an initial and ongoing commitment to the scholarly community, with the publication of the dictionary Mercer University Press and the National Association of Baptist Professors of Religion undertook a new level of endeavor with regard to the development of scholarly religious literature. The *Mercer Commentary on the Bible* is another tangible result of a continuing commitment by both MUP and the NABPR.

The *Mercer Commentary on the Bible* (MCB) is a companion volume to the MDB. Thus the commentary has been conceived somewhat differently from other one-volume commentaries. A basic assumption was that MCB would not repeat information already contained in MDB since the two will be used in tandem; that is, the goal of creating companion volumes guided the work from the outset. Regular use has been made of specific terms already defined and discussed in MDB. Such references are easily identified since they appear in MCB in small capital letters. For example, when an author refers in the text to JUSTIFICATION, the reader knows that there is an article by that name in MDB. The number of introductory articles also is greatly reduced in comparison to other single-volume commentaries since the excellent work already produced in the MDB has been consciously taken into consideration.

The almost three million words of MDB and MCB spread over more than 2,200 large double-column pages do not claim to convey to the reader all one needs to know about the Bible. Rather, our hope is that the MDB and MCB will together provide accurate, relevant, and interesting information regarding the history, traditions, and interpretation of the literature collected in what we know as Scripture. Since both MDB and MCB are products of a professional community of scholars (the NABPR and MUP), they reflect a broad range of opinions and approaches to the critical issues involved in the study of the Bible. There has been a studied attempt *not* to require contributors to follow any specific school of interpretation. Likewise, every effort has been made to avoid pressing for a particular hermeneutical or theological position.

Neither the MDB nor the MCB are substitutes for the Scripture itself. To encourage study of the Scripture itself, both MDB and MCB reference a variety of tools, including thousands of specific references to the biblical materials, canonical and noncanonical. Further, these volumes do not pretend to supplant the more comprehensive standard Bible dictionaries or the multi-volume commentaries that are readily available to the serious student. Rather they seek to fill a real need for single-volume resources that are intended for use by both beginning and advanced Bible students in college, university, and seminary, as well as professional parish ministers and laypersons interested in serious study of the Bible. Our intention is that these two volumes begin and end with a classroom perspective without appearing "bookish." The editors and publishers of and contributors to these works are all either directly involved in teaching beginning and advanced Bible students or serve in support of those who are teaching; they are also involved in the life of the church. The needs of students, whether in formal academic settings or not, have shaped the structure and content of the *Mercer Dictionary of the Bible* and the *Mercer Commentary on the Bible*.

Abbreviations

We generally have followed the abbreviations for biblical books, apocrypha, and other extracanonical books as found in the widely used Society of Biblical Literature list. Bibliographies, where included, are necessarily brief. To save space, we give only the essential bibliographic information: the author's last name and initial(s), date, and the title of the work. Periodical citations include sufficient information to locate the reference, while encyclopedia and dictionary references include only the author, title, and referenced work (if arranged alphabetically; in cases where a reference work arranges articles in some other way, volume and/or page or column numbers are supplied).

Acknowledgments

With Mercer University Press and the National Association of Baptist Professors of Religion, we wish to acknowledge the generous support of Mr. Lamar R. Plunkett and the Warren P. and Ava F. Sewell Foundation, Inc., who have underwritten the publication of this volume. As a loyal Baptist and a distinguished educator himself, it is entirely fitting that this work bears the imprint of Mr. Plunkett's lifelong support of the work of Baptists and of Mercer University. We are honored to dedicate this work to him.

A project as large as this one is finally shaped by the efforts of more people than those listed as editors and contributors. In the final year of production Mrs. Nancy Stubbs, secretary for the Roberts Department of Christianity at Mercer University, has been tireless in her efforts to retype manuscripts as needed, and to enter corrections on computer disks that finally were used by editors and compositors. Her eagerness and cheerfulness has made a daunting task less so.

As the last months and weeks before publication slipped by, a small contingent from MUP joined the efforts to assure that the final volume would be as readable and free from typographical error as possible. Under the leadership of MUP Managing Editor R. Scott Nash, Jackie B. Riley, Nancy E. Hollomon, Vaughn CroweTipton, and Jon Peede logged untold hours of valuable assistance. We are grateful to them for their contributions.

Finally, we wish to acknowledge the continuing support and encouragement of the president of Mercer University, R. Kirby Godsey. His willing support of the Mercer University Press over the years is acknowledged and appreciated. We at Mercer are fortunate to be associated with an institution that respects and encourages the kind of scholarly endeavor reflected in the companion volumes, the *Mercer Dictionary of the Bible* and the *Mercer Commentary on the Bible*.

It is our hope that the *Mercer Commentary on the Bible* will be of real help in the larger world of biblical scholarship, and thus reflect well upon this great university.

Watson E. Mills
Richard F. Wilson
Mercer University
October 1994

Editors

WATSON E. MILLS, general editor, is Professor of New Testament Studies in the Roberts Department of Christianity at Mercer University, Macon, Georgia. He founded the Mercer University Press in 1979 and for twelve years served as its publisher. From 1984 until 1991 he was vice president for research and publication at Mercer University. He is a graduate of the University of Richmond (BA), the University of Louisville (MA), the Southern Baptist Theological Seminary (BD, ThM, ThD), and Baylor University (PhD). He has published widely, having written or edited more than twenty-five books and scores of articles. He is the editor of the *Mercer Dictionary of the Bible* and of the Mellen Intertextual Commentary series. He served for nineteen years as editor of *Perspectives in Religious Studies*, and for five years as the managing editor of *Religious Studies Review* and the *Bulletin of the Council of Societies for the Study of Religion*.

He served on the faculty at Averett College, Danville, Virginia from 1968 until 1979. He has been at Mercer University since 1979.

Mills was the executive officer of the Council of Societies for the Study of Religion (1985–1992) and executive secretary-treasurer of the National Association of Baptist Professors of Religion (1981–1992). He is a member of the Society of New Testament Studies, the Catholic Biblical Association, the Paul Seminar (Westar), and the Society of Biblical Literature.

RICHARD F. WILSON, general editor, is Associate Professor in the Roberts Department of Christianity at Mercer University, where he is also Dean of the Chapel. He is a graduate of Mississippi College (BA), and The Southern Baptist Theological Seminary (MDiv and PhD). He has completed additional studies at the University of Louisville, the University of Kentucky, and the University of Arizona. In the spring of 1994 he was visiting scholar at the International Baptist Theological Seminary in Buenos Aires, Argentina.

Prior to joining the faculty at Mercer in 1988 Wilson taught at Gardner-Webb College, where he also served as assistant academic dean for one year.

Since 1992 Wilson has served the National Association of Baptist Professors of Religion as the executive secretary-treasurer; from 1990 until 1992 he was the assistant executive secretary-treasurer of the NABPR. He is also a member of the American Academy of Religion, and the Society of Biblical Literature.

Wilson was a contributor and assistant editor for the *Mercer Dictionary of the Bible*. He also contributes to journals and other scholarly publications.

ROGER A. BULLARD, associate editor of the apocryphal and deuterocanonical works section, was educated at Union University (BA in English), the University of Kentucky (MA in Classics), Southeastern Baptist Theological Seminary (BD), and Vanderbilt University (PhD in Biblical Studies). From 1965 until 1994 he was on the faculty of Barton College (formerly Atlantic Christian College) in Wilson, North Carolina, where he was Professor of Religion and Philosophy. He has served as visiting professor at Southeastern Seminary and at Brite Divinity School.

He is an associate editor of the *Abingdon Dictionary of Living Religions* (now published as the *Perennial Dictionary of World Religions*). He served on the translation committee preparing the Old Testament and the Deuterocanonicals/Apocrypha of Today's English Version of the Bible and is the author of *The Hypostasis of the Archons: The Coptic Text with English Translation and Commentary* and *Messiah: the Gospel according to Handel's Oratorio*, as well as numerous articles and reviews.

Bullard is a member of the National Association of Baptist Professors of Religion, the Society of Biblical Literature, the American Association of University Professors, and the North Carolina Teachers of Religion. He has served as Corresponding Member of the Institute for Antiquity and Christianity, working on the Coptic Gnostic Project. He has received awards from the Christian Research Foundation, the American Council of Learned Societies, and the National Endowment for the Humanities.

WALTER HARRELSON, associate editor of the Old Testament section, is University Professor at Wake Forest University, and Distinguished Professor emeritus of Hebrew Bible at Vanderbilt University. His undergraduate studies were at Mars Hill College and the University of North Carolina, Chapel Hill, and his graduate studies were at Union Theological Seminary (New York), and the University of Basel. He taught at Andover Newton Theological School, and the Divinity School of the University of Chicago before coming to Vanderbilt in 1960, where he served for most of his academic career.

He is the author of seven books and has published extensively in biblical and theological encyclopedias, dictionaries, and periodicals. His most recent book (with Bruce M. Metzger and Robert C. Dentan) is *The Making of the New Revised Standard Version of the Bible*. A forthcoming book, written with Rabbi Randall M. Falk, deals with Jewish and Christian ethics.

He was vice chair of the committee that produced the New Revised Standard Version of the Bible; he served on two occasions as the rector of the Ecumenical Institute for Theological Research in Jerusalem; he has served as dean of the Divinity Schools of the University of Chicago and of Vanderbilt University; and he is currently assisting Wake Forest University in the creation of its new divinity school.

EDGAR V. MCKNIGHT, associate editor for the New Testament section, is the William R. Kenan, Jr. Professor of Religion at Furman University. He received his undergraduate education in Charleston, graduating from the College of Charleston in 1953. After professional and graduate studies at the Southern Baptist Theological Seminary (MDiv, 1956; PhD, 1960) and a brief appointment as chaplain at Chowan College in Murfreesboro, North Carolina, he joined the faculty of Furman University in 1963. At Furman he has taught in the departments of Classical Languages and Religion, chaired the Department of Classical Languages, served as associate dean of Academic Affairs, and was appointed to the Kenan chair in 1982. Early publications include a *History of Chowan College*; *Opening the Bible*; *A Guide to Understanding the Scriptures*; *What Is Form Criticism?*; and *Introduction to the New Testament*.

During his first sabbatical (1973–1974), McKnight studied philosophical theology with John Macquarrie of Christ Church, Oxford. Early studies and writings in the biblical field were thereby supplemented by work

in philosophical and theological hermeneutics. *Meaning in Texts: The Historical Shaping of a Narrative Hermeneutics* resulted from this work. A senior Fulbright professorship at the University of Tübingen in 1981–1982 provided opportunity for further study and writing in the relationship between biblical and literary studies. Two books grew out of this work: *The Bible and the Reader: An Introduction to Literary Criticism* and *Postmodern Use of the Bible*. McKnight is presently at work on a manuscript entitled "Theology and the Revolution in Biblical Studies."

EDD ROWELL is senior editor of Mercer University Press. He earned his AB in religious studies and languages at Howard College (Samford University) and his BD/MDiv at Southeastern Baptist Theological Seminary. From 1958 until 1980 he was pastor of Baptist churches in Alabama and Virginia. He has written numerous curriculum materials for the Sunday School Board and has contributed articles and reviews to a variety of journals. He was author of the two-volume study of Acts in the Bible Book Study Commentary series and of *Apostles—Jesus' Special Helpers* in the BibLearn series for children. He wrote the first unit for and was coeditor of the inaugural issue of Smyth & Helwys's *Formations Commentary* (1992). He was an assistant editor of and contributor to the *Mercer Dictionary of the Bible*. He was until 1993 an assistant editor of *Perspectives in Religious Studies*, and is advisory editor for the International Kierkegaard Commentary and advisory editor for the New Gospel Studies series. Rowell has been an instructor in the University College of Mercer University. He is a member of the Society of Biblical Literature and of the American Academy of Religion, an associate of the National Association of Baptist Professors of Religion, and an associate of the International Institute for the Renewal of Gospel Studies.

Contributors

Samuel E. Balentine
Professor of Old Testament
Baptist Theological Seminary at Richmond
Richmond, Virginia 23227

Jon L. Berquist
Assistant Professor of Old Testament
Phillips Graduate Seminary
Tulsa, Oklahoma 74104

Gerald L. Borchert
T. Rupert and Lucille Coleman Professor
    of New Testament Interpretation
The Southern Baptist Theological Seminary
Louisville, Kentucky 40280

Margaret Dee Bratcher
Associate Professor
Roberts Department of Christianity
Mercer University
Macon, Georgia 31207

Linda McKinnish Bridges
Associate Professor of New Testament and Greek
Baptist Theological Seminary at Richmond
Richmond, Virginia 23227

Edwin K. Broadhead
Whitley College
University of Melbourne
Pikeville Victoria 3052 Australia

J. Bradley Chance
Professor of Religion
Department of Religion
William Jewell College
Liberty, Missouri 64062

Charles H. Cosgrove
Associate Professor of New Testament
Northern Baptist Theological Seminary
Lombard, Illinois 60148

Kenneth M. Craig, Jr.
E. Lee Oliver Fagan Chair of Bible and Religion
Department of Religion and Philosophy
Chowan College
Murfreesboro, North Carolina 27855

Jerome F. D. Creach
Assistant Professor of Religion
Department of Religion and Philosophy
Barton College
Wilson, North Carolina 27893

James L. Crenshaw
Robert L. Flowers Professor of Old Testament
Duke Divinity School
Durham, North Carolina 27706

R. Alan Culpepper
Professor
Department of Religion
Baylor University
Waco, Texas 76798

Bruce T. Dahlberg
Professor of Religion and Biblical Literature
Smith College
Northhampton, Massachusetts 01063

Sharyn E. Dowd
Professor of New Testament
Lexington Theological Seminary
Lexington, Kentucky 40508

Joel F. Drinkard, Jr.
Professor of Old Testament
The Southern Baptist Theological Seminary
Louisville, Kentucky 40280

Paul D. Duke
Senior Pastor
Kirkwood Baptist Church
St. Louis, Missouri 63122

Robert C. Dunston
Professor and Chair
Department of Religion and Philosophy
Cumberland College
Williamsburg, Kentucky 40769

John I Durham
Pastor
Greenwich Baptist Church
Greenwich, Connecticut 06830

W. Hulitt Gloer
Professor of New Testament
Midwestern Baptist Theological Seminary
Kansas City, Missouri 64118

Carol Stuart Grizzard
Associate Professor of Religion
Pikeville College
Pikeville, Kentucky 41501

Thomas O. Hall, Jr.
Professor Emeritus
Department of Philosophy and Religious Studies
Virgina Commonwealth University
Richmond, Virginia 23284

Walter Harrelson
Distinguished Professor Emeritus of Hebrew Bible
Vanderbilt University
Nashville, Tennessee 37240, and
University Professor
Wake Forest University
Winston-Salem, North Carolina 27109

John H. Hayes
Professor of Old Testament
Emory University
Atlanta, Georgia 30322

E. Glenn Hinson
Professor of Spirituality, Worship, and Church History
Baptist Theological Seminary at Richmond
Richmond, Virginia 23227

Stephenson Humphries-Brooks
Associate Professor
Department of Religious Studies
Hamilton College
Clinton, New York 13323

Marie E. Isaacs
Head of the Department of Biblical Studies
Heythrop College
London University, England

John C. H. Laughlin
Professor and Chair
Department of Religion
Averett College
Danville, Virginia 24541

Claude F. Mariottini
Professor of Old Testament
Northern Baptist Theological Seminary
Lombard, Illinois 60148

Molly T. Marshall
Associate Professor of Christian Theology
The Southern Baptist Theological Seminary
Louisville, Kentucky 40280

Calvin Mercer
Associate Professor of Religious Studies
Department of Philosophy
East Carolina University
Greenville, North Carolina 27834

J. Ramsey Michaels
Professor
Department of Religious Studies
Southwest Missouri State University
Springfield, Missouri 65804

Watson E. Mills
Professor
Roberts Department of Christianity
Mercer University
Macon, Georgia 31207

John Joseph Owens
Professor Emeritus,
    Old Testament Interpretation
The Southern Baptist Theological Seminary
Louisville, Kentucky 40280

Mikeal C. Parsons
Assistant Professor
Department of Religion
Baylor University
Waco, Texas 76798

Jack G. Partain
Professor
Department of Religious Studies and Philosophy
Gardner-Webb University
Boiling Springs, North Carolina 28017

David Penchansky
Assistant Professor
Department of Theology
University of Saint Thomas
Saint Paul, Minnesota 55104

Leo G. Perdue
Professor of Hebrew Bible and Dean
Brite Divinity School
Texas Christian University
Forth Worth, Texas 76129

John B. Polhill
James Buchanan Harrison Professor
    of New Testament Interpretation;
Associate Dean of ThM/PhD Programs
The Southern Baptist Theological Seminary
Louisville, Kentucky 40280

Kandy M. Queen-Sutherland
Associate Professor
Religion Department
Stetson University,
DeLand, Florida 32720

Mitchell G. Reddish
Associate Professor and Chair
Religion Department
Stetson University
Deland, Florida 32720

Jeffrey S. Rogers
Dana Assistant Professor
Department of Religion
Furman University
Greenville, South Carolina 29613

Max Gray Rogers
Professor of Old Testament
Southeastern Baptist Theological Seminary
Wake Forest, North Carolina 27587

Edd Rowell
Senior Editor, Mercer University Press
Macon, Georgia 31207

John C. Shelley
Professor
Department of Religion
Furman University
Greenville, South Carolina 29613

David A. Smith
Professor Emeritus
Department of Religion
Furman University
Greenville, South Carolina 29613

Thomas Smothers
Professor of Old Testament
The Southern Baptist Theological Seminary
Louisville, Kentucky 40280

Marion L. Soards
Professor of New Testament Studies
Louisville Presbyterian Theological Seminary
Louisville, Kentucky 40205

Richard A. Spencer
Assistant Professor
Department of Foreign Language and Literature, and
Department of Philosophy and Religion
Appalachian State University
Boone, North Carolina 28608

Frank Stagg
Professor Emeritus, New Testament
The Southern Baptist Theological Seminary
Louisville, Kentucky 40280

Cecil P. Staton, Jr.
Publisher, Mercer University Press, and
President and Publisher
Smyth & Helwys Publishing Inc.
Macon, Georgia 31207

William P. Steeger
W. O. Vaught Professor of Bible and Chair
Division of Religion and Philosophy
Department of Religion
Ouachita Baptist University
Arkadelphia, Arkansas 71923

Charles H. Talbert
Wake Forest Professor of Religion
Wake Forest University
Winston-Salem, North Carolina 27109

Marvin E. Tate
John R. Sampey Professor of Old Testament
The Southern Baptist Theological Seminary
Louisville, Kentucky 40280

Joseph L. Trafton
Professor of Christian Origins
Department of Philosophy and Religion
Western Kentucky University
Bowling Green, Kentucky 42101

John H. Tullock
Professor Emeritus
Department of Religion
Belmont University
Nashville, Tennessee 37212

Dan O. Via
Professor Emeritus of New Testament
The Divinity School
Duke University
Durham, North Carolina 27708

James W. Watts
Assistant Professor
Department of Religion and Philosophy
Hastings College
Hastings, Nebraska 68902

John D. W. Watts
Senior Professor of Old Testament
The Southern Baptist Theological Seminary
Louisville, Kentucky 40280

Mona West
Academic Dean
Samaritan College
Lewisville, Texas 75067

John Keating Wiles
School of Law
University of North Carolina
Chapel Hill, North Carolina 27581

Richard F. Wilson
Associate Professor
Roberts Department of Christianity
Mercer University
Macon, Georgia 31207

Abbreviations

Periodicals/Journals

AASOR	*Annual of the American Schools of Oriental Research*
ADAJ	*Annual of the Dept. of Antiquities of Jordan*
AJA	*American Journal of Archaeology*
AnBib	*Analecta biblica*
Arch	*Archaeology*
AS	*Asiatische Studien*
ASORN	*ASOR Newsletter*
ATR	*Anglican Theological Review*
AUSS	*Andrews University Seminary Studies*
BA	*Biblical Archaeologist*
BAR	*Biblical Archaeology Review*
BASOR	*Bulletin of the ASOR*
BETL	*Bibliotheca ephemeridum theologicarum lovaniensium*
BHH	*Baptist History and Heritage*
BI	*Biblical Illustrator* (formerly SSLI)
Bib	*Biblica*
BibRev	*Bible Review*
BJRL	*Bulletin of the John Rylands University Library*
BJS	*British Journal of Sociology*
BL	*Bible und Leben*
BR	*Biblical Research*
BS	*Bibliotheca Sacra*
BT	*Bible Today*
BTB	*Biblical Theology Bulletin*
BTS	*Bible et terre sainte*
BYUS	*Brigham Young University Studies*
CBQ	*Catholic Biblical Quarterly*
CJ	*Concordia Journal*
Conc	*Concilium*
CQR	*Church Quarterly Review*
CSBSB	*Canadian Society of Biblical Studies Bulletin*
CTQ	*Concordia Theological Quarterly*
CTR	*Criswell Theological Review*
DA	*Dissertation Abstracts International*
DTT	*Dansk teologisk tidsskrift*
DR	*Downside Review*
EB	*Estudios biblicos*
ETL	*Ephemerides théologicae lovannienses*
ETR	*Études théologiques et religieuses*
EvQ	*Evangelical Quarterly*
ExpTim	*Expository Times*
GOTR	*Greek Orthodox Theological Review*
HAR	*Hebrew Annual Review*
HeyJ	*Heythrop Journal*
HR	*History of Religions*
HTR	*Harvard Theological Review*
HUCA	*Hebrew Union College Annual*
IEJ	*Israel Exploration Journal*
Int	*Interpretation*
IR	*Iliff Review*
ITQ	*Irish Theological Quarterly*
JAAR	*Journal of the American Academy of Religion*
JAOS	*Journal of the American Oriental Society*
JBL	*Journal of Biblical Literature*
JCS	*Journal of Cuneiform Studies*
JCU	*Judenten Christentum Urkirche*
JEA	*Journal of Egyptian Archaeology*
JJS	*Journal of Jewish Studies*
JLR	*Journal of Law and Religion*
JNES	*Journal of Near Eastern Studies*
JPH	*Journal of Presbyterian History*
JQR	*Jewish Quarterly Review*
JR	*Journal of Religion*
JRH	*Journal of Religious History*
JSJ	*Journal for the Study of Judaism*
JSNT	*Journal for the Study of the New Testament*
JSOT	*Journal for the Study of the Old Testament*
JSOTsup	JSOT supplement series
JSS	*Journal of Semitic Studies*
JSSR	*Journal for the Scientific Study of Religion*
JTC	*Journal for Theology and the Church*
JTS	*Journal of Theological Studies*
Jud	*Judaism*
KD	*Kerygma und Dogma*
NKZ	*Neue kirchliche Zeitschrift*
NovT	*Novum Testamentum*
NovTsup	NovT supplements
NTS	*New Testament Studies*
NTT	*Nederlands Theologisch Tijdschrift*
OTS	*Oudtestamentische Studien*
PEQ	*Palestine Exploration Quarterly*
PJ	*Perkins (School of Theology) Journal*
Proof	*Prooftexts*
PRS	*Perspectives in Religious Studies*
PRZ	*Patristic and Byzantine Review*
PSB	*Princeton Seminary Bulletin*
PTR	*Princeton Theological Review*
QDAP	*Quarterly of the Dept. of Antiquities of Palestine*
RB	*Revue biblique*
RE	*Review and Expositor*
RefR	*Reformed Review*
RevQ	*Revue de Qumran*
RHR	*Revue de l'historie des religions*
RL	*Religion in Life*
RQ	*Reformation Quarterly*
RSR	*Religious Studies Review*
Scr	*Scripture*
SecCen	*Second Century*
SJT	*Scottish Journal of Theology*
SLJ	*Saint Luke Journal*
SMS	*Syro-Mesopotamian Studies*
SR	*Sciences religieuses/Studies in Religion*
SSLI	*Sunday School Lesson Illustrator* (currently BI)

ST	*Studia theologica*
SVSQ	*St. Vladimir's Seminary Quarterly* (now SVTQ)
SVTQ	*St. Vladimir's Theological Quart.* (was SVSQ)
SWJT	*Southwestern Journal of Theology*
TJT	*Taiwan Journal of Theology*
TLZ	*Theologische Literaturzeitung*
Trad	*Tradition*
TRu	*Theologische Rundschau*
TS	*Theological Studies*
TT	*Theology Today*
TTE	*The Theological Educator*
TynBul	*Tyndale Bulletin*
UF	*Ugarit-Forschungen*
USQR	*Union Seminary Quarterly Review*
VC	*Vigiliae christianae*
VT	*Vetus Testamentum*
VTSup	VT supplements
WTJ	*Westminster Theological Journal*
ZAW	*Zeitschrift für die alttestamentliche Wissenschaft*
ZMR	*Zeitschrift für Missionskunde und Religionswissenschaft*
ZNW	*Zeitsch. für die neutestamentliche Wissenschaft*

HolmBD	*Holman Bible Dictionary*
HDB	*Hastings Dictionary of the Bible*
HDBsup	*Hastings Dictionary of the Bible* supplement
HDBrev	*HDB*, rev. 1-vol. ed.
IDB	*Interpreter's Dictionary of the Bible*
IDBsup	IDB supplementary volume
ISBE	*International Standard Bible Enc.*, 3rd rev. ed.
LionEB	*The Lion Encyclopedia of the Bible*
MDB	*Mercer Dictionary of the Bible*
NBD	*New Bible Dictionary*, 2nd ed. rev.
NCE	*New Catholic Encyclopedia*
NIBD	*Nelson's Illustrated Bible Dictionary*
NIDNTT	*New International Dictionary of NT Theology*
OComB	*The Oxford Companion to the Bible*
RGG	*Die Religion in Geschichte und Gegenwart*
TRE	*Theologische Realenzyklopädie*
UJEnc	*Universal Jewish Encyclopedia*
WBE	*Wycliff Bible Encyclopedia*
WDCE	*Westminster Dictionary of Christian Ethics*
ZPED	*Zondervan Pictorial Enclopedia of the Bible*

Reference Works

Annotated or Study Bibles

CASB	*Cambridge Annotated Study Bible* (NRSV)
CathSB	*The Catholic Study Bible* (NAB)
HCSB	*HarperCollins Study Bible* (NRSV)
HSB	*Harper's Study Bible* rev. ed. (NRSV)
JB	*The Jerusalem Bible* (JB)
NJB	*The New Jerusalem Bible* (NJB)
NIVSB	*The NIV Study Bible*
NOAB	*The New Oxford Annotated Bible* (RSV, NRSV)
OrthSB	*The Orthodox Study Bible* (NKJV)
OSE	*The NEB. Oxford Study Edition* (NEB)
OxSB	*The Oxford Study Bible* (REB)

Dictionaries and Encyclopedias

ADLR	*Abingdon Dictionary of Living Religions*
AEHL	*Archaeological Encyclopedia of the Holy Land*
AncBD	*Anchor Bible Dictionary*
CAH	*Cambridge Ancient History*
ComB	*A Companion to the Bible*, von Allmen
DBA	*Dictionary of Biblical Archaeology*
DBR	*The Dictionary of Bible and Religion*
DCB	*Dictionary of Christian Biography*
DNT	*Dictionary of the New Testament*
EAEHL	*Ency. of Arch. Excavations in the Holy Land*
EB	*Encyclopaedia Biblica*
EBD	*Eerdman's Bible Dictionary*
EBL	*Encyclopedia of Bible Life* (Harper's) 3rd ed.
EncBri	*Encyclopaedia Britannica*
EncJud	*Encyclopedia Judaica*
EncRel	*Encyclopedia of Religion*
EvDTh	*Evangelical Dictionary of Theology*
HBD	*Harper's Bible Dictionary*

Lexicons and Wordbooks

BAGD	Bauer/Arndt/Gingrich/Danker, *A Greek-English Lexicon of the N.T.*, revised edition
BDB	(Gesenius)/Brown/Driver/Briggs, *A Hebrew and English Lexicon of the Old Testament*
GELNT	*Greek-English Lexicon of the New Testament Based on Semantic Domains*
KB	Koehler/Baumgartner, *Lexicon in Veteris Testamenti libros.*
RdA	*Reallexikon der Assyriologie*
TDNT	*Theological Dict. of the NT* (ET of TWNT)
TDOT	*Theological Dict. of the OT* (ET of TWAT)
TWAT	*Theologisches Wörterbuch zum Alten Testament*
TWBB	Richardson, *Theological Wordbook of the Bible*
TWNT	*Theologisches Wörterbuch zum Neuen testament*

Commentaries

AmCNT	An American Commentary on the NT
AncB	Anchor Bible
AugCNT	Augsburg Commentary on the NT
BBC	*Broadman Bible Commentary*
BKAT	Biblischer Kommentar: Altes Testament
BNTC	Black's NT Commentaries (= HNTC [USA])
CBC	Cambridge Bible Commentary
CCHS	*A Catholic Comm. on Holy Scripture*, 1 vol.
DNEB	Die Neue Echter Bibel
EBC	*Eerdman's Bible Commentary* (=NBC)
EGT	The Expositor's Greek Testament
FOTL	Forms of the Old Testament Literature
HBC	*Harper's Bible Commentary*
Herm	Hermeneia
HNTC	Harper's NT Commentaries (= BNTC [UK])
HTKNT	Herders theologischer Kommentar zum N.T.

IB	*Interpreter's Bible*
ICC	International Critical Commentary
Interp	Interpretation. A Bible Commentary
IOVC	*Interpreter's One-Vol. Comm. on the Bible*
ITC	International Theological Commentary
JBC	*Jerome Biblical Commentary* (see NJBC)
JPSTC	JPS Torah Commentary
LBC	*The Layman's Bible Commentary*
MCB	*Mercer Commentary on the Bible*
MNTC	Moffatt New Testament Commentary
NAC	New American Commentary
NBC	*New Bible Commentary*, 3rd ed. (=EBC)
NCB	New Century Bible
NCCHS	*A New Catholic Comm. on H.S.*, new ed. CCHS
NICNT	New International Commentary on the NT
NICOT	New International Commentary on the OT
NIGTC	New International Greek Testament Commentary
NJBC	*New Jerome Biblical Comm.*, 1 vol. (rev. JBC)
NTD	Das Neue Testament Deutsch
OTL	Old Testament Library
SacPag	Sacra Pagina
Str-B	(Strack and) Billerbeck, *Kommentar zum N.T.*
TBC	Torch Bible Commentaries
THKNT	Theologischer Handkommentar zum N.T.
TNTC	Tyndale New Testament Commentaries
TOTC	Tyndale Old Testament Commentaries
WBC	Word Biblical Commentary
WmBC	*The Women's Bible Commentary*
WPelC	Westminster Pelican Commentaries

Essay Collections

AAR/SBLA	*AAR/SBL Abstracts* (SBLASP, AARASP)
BARead	*Biblical Archaeology Reader*
BZAW	Beihefte zur ZAW
BZNW	Beihefte zur ZNW
CHJ	*Cambridge History of Judaism*
CHB	*Cambridge History of the Bible*
SBLASP	*Society of Biblical Literature Abstracts and Seminar Papers* (now AAR/SBLA)

Series

CRINT	*Compendia Rerum Iudaicarum ad Novum Testamentum*
GBS/NT	Guides to Biblical Scholarship, NT series
HDR	Harvard Dissertations in Religion
LEC	Library of Early Christianity
NABPR/SS	NABPR Special Studies series
NHS	Nag Hammadi Studies
OBT	Overtures to Biblical Theology
SBLDS	SBL Dissertation Series
SBLMS	SBL Monograph Series
SBT	Studies in Biblical Theology
SJLA	Studies in Judaism in Late Antiquity

Pseudepigrapha

ApocAb	*Apocalypse of Abraham*
ApocBar	*Apocalypse of Baruch*
ApocMos	*Apocalypse of Moses*
ApocZeph	*Apocalypse of Zephaniah*
AscIsa	*Ascension of Isaiah*
AsMos	*Assumption of Moses*
(BibAnt	*Biblical Antiquities* = PsPhilo)
EpArist	*Epistle of Aristeas*
Hom	*Homilies*, Pseudo-Clement
JosAsen	*Joseph and Asenath*
Jub	*Jubilees*
Life	*Life of Adam and Eve*
LivProph	*Lives of the Prophets*
MartIsa	*Martrydom of Isaiah*
OdeSol	*Odes of Solomon*
PsPhilo	Pseudo-Philo, *Biblical Antiquities*
PssSol	*Psalms of Solomon*
Recog	*Recognitions*, Pseudo-Clement
SibOr	*Sibylline Oracles*
SyrMen	*Syriac Meander*
TMos	*Testament of Moses*
TSol	*Testament of Solomon*
T12Pat	*Testaments of the Twelve Patriarchs*
TAsher	*Testament of Asher*
TBenj	*Testament of Benjamin*
TDan	*Testament of Dan*
TGad	*Testament of Gad*
TIss	*Testament of Issachar*
TJos	*Testament of Joseph*
TJud	*Testament of Judah*
TLevi	*Testament of Levi*
TNaph	*Testament of Naphtali*
TReu	*Testament of Reuben*
TSim	*Testament of Simeon*
TZeb	*Testament of Zebulun*

New Testament Apocrypha

ActPet	*Act of Peter*, Berlin codex 8502
ActsJn	*Acts of John*
ActsPet	*Acts of Peter*
DialSav	*Dialogue of the Savior* (NH)
PistS	*Pistos Sophia*
POxy	*Oxyrhunchus Papyri*
ProtJs	*Protoevangelium of James*
SMark	*The Secret Gospel of Mark*

Dead Sea Scrolls and Related Texts

CD	(Cairo) *Damascus Document* (Zadokite Frag's)
1QapGen	*Genesis Apocryphon*
1QH	*Thanksgiving Hymns*, cave 1
1QM	*War Scroll*
1QpHab	*Pesher on Habakkuk*, cave 1

1QS	*Manual of Discipline*
1QSa	App. A to 1QS: *Rule of the Congregation*
4QAgesCreat	*The Ages of Creation*
4QFlor	*Florilegium*, cave 4
4QMMT	*Miqsat Ma'aseh Torah*, cave 4
4QPBles	*Patriarchal Blessings*
4QPEzek	*Pseudo-Ezekiel*, cave 4
4QpNah	*Pesher on Nahum*, cave 4
4QPssJosh	*Psalms of Joshua*, cave 4
4QMess	Aramaic "Messianic" text, cave 4
4QShirShabb	*Song of the Sabbath Sacrifice*, cave 4
4QTestim	Testimonia text, cave 4
4QTLevi	*Testament of Levi*, cave 4
11QMelch	*Melchizedek*, cave 11
11QPsª	Psalter (first copy), cave 11
11QPsᵇ	Psalter (ssecond copy), cave 11
11QPsApª	Apocryphal psalms (first copy), cave 11
11QTem	*Temple Scroll*, cave 11
11QtgJob	*Targum of Job*, cave 11

Nag Hammadi Codices

AcPet12	*Acts of Peter and the Twelve Apostles*
Allog	*Allogenes*
ApJas	*Apocryphon of James*
ApJohn	*Apocryphon of John*
ApocAdam	*Apocalypse of Adam*
1,2 ApocJas	*1,2 Apocalypse of James*
ApocPaul	*Apocalypse of Paul*
ApocPet	*Apocalypse of Peter*
Disc8-9	*Discourse on the Eighth and Ninth*
EpPetPhil	*Epistle of Peter to Philip*
GosEg	*Gospel of the Egyptians*
GosMary	*Gospel of Mary*
GosPhil	*Gospel of Philip*
GosThom	*Gospel of Thomas*
GosTruth	*Gospel of Truth*
HypArch	*Hypostasis of the Archons*
Mars	*Marsanes*
Melch	*Melchizedek*
NHC	Nag Hammadi Codices
Norea	*Thought of Norea*
OnBapA,B,C	*On Baptism* A, B, or C
OnEuchA,B	*On the Eucharist* A or B
OrigWorld	*On the Origin of the World*
ParaphShem	*Paraphrase of Shem*
PrThanks	*Prayer of Thanksgiving*
SentSextus	*Sentences of Sextus*
SophJC	*Sophia of Jesus Christ*
SteleSeth	*Three Steles of Seth*
TeachSilv	*Teachings of Silvanus*
TestTruth	*Testimony of Truth*
ThomCont	*Book of Thomas the Contender*
Thund	*Thunder, Perfect Mind*
TJob	*Testament of Job*
TreatRes	*Treatise on the Resurrection*

TreatSeth	*The Treatise of Seth*
TrimProt	*Trimorphic Protennoia*
TriTrac	*Tripartite Tractate*
ValExp	*A Valentinian Exposition*
Zost	*Zostrianos*

Tractates of the Mishnah and Talmud

BQam	*Baba Qamma*	Middot	*Middot*
Ed	*'Eduyyot*	Ned	*Nedarim*
Erub	*'Erubin*	Śab	*Šabbat*
GenR	*Genesis Rabbah*	Sanh	*Sanhedrin*
Git	*Gittin*	Taan	*Ta'anit*
Meg	*Megilla*	Yad	*Yadayim*

Miscellaneous Texts

ANEATP	*The ANE. An Anthology*, ed. Pritchard
ANEP	*Ancient Near East in Pictures*, ed. Pritchard
ANET	*Ancient Near Eastern Texts*, ed. Pritchard
ANESTP	*Ancient Near East. Supplementary*, ed. Pritchard
ApocNT	*The Apocryphal New Testament*, ed. James
ApocOT	*The Apocryphal Old Testament*, ed. Sparks
APOT	*Apoc and Pseudepigrapha of the OT*, ed. Charles
InscrGr	*Inscriptiones Graecae*
NTApoc	*The NT Apocrypha*, ed. Hennecke et al.
OTP	*OT Pseudepigrapha*, ed. Charlesworth
RST	*Ras Shamra Texts*

Apostolic Fathers

Barn	*Epistle of Barnabas*
1 Clem	*First Clement*
Did	*Didache*
IgnEph	Ignatius, *Epistle to the Ephesians*
Magn	Ignatius, *Epistle to the Magnesians*
Philad	Ignatius, *Epistle to the Philadelphians*
IgnRom	Ignatius, *Epistle to the Romans*
Smyrn	Ignatiue, *Epistle to the Smyrnaeans*
Vis	*Shepherd of Hermas, Vision(s)*

Other Ancient Authors

AdFam	Cicero, *Ad familares*
AdvHaer	Irenaeus, *Adversus omnes haereses*
AdvMarc	Tertullian, *Adversus Marcionem*
AgPrax	Tertullian, *Against Praxeas*
Anab	Xenophon, *Anabasis*
Ann	Tacitus, *Annals*
Ant	Josephus, *Antiquities of the Jews*
ApChOrd	*Apostolic Church Order*
Apol	Aristides, *Apologia*
Apol	Justin Martyr, *Apologia*
Apol	Tertullian, *Apologeticum*
AppWo	Tertullian, *Apparel of Women*
BJ	Josephus, *Jewish Wars*
CAp	Josephus, *Contra Apionem*
CCel	Origen, *Contra Celsum*

CEph	Jerome, *Commentary on Ephesians*	AV	Authorized Version (UK; =KJV)
CEzek	Jerome, *Commentary on Ezekiel*	Beck	*NT in the Language of Today*
ChrDoc	Augustine, *On Christian Doctine*	CCD	Confraternity of Christian Doctrine (RCC NT;
CIsa	Jerome, *Commentary on Isaiah*		see NCE; see also NCB = NAB)
CivDei	Augustine, *City of God*	CEV	Contemporary Eng. Ver. (NT w/Pss, Prov 1991)
2 Clem	*Second Clement*	CPV	Cotton Patch Version (Jordan, NT portions)
CMatt	Jerome, *Commentary on Matthew*	CTNT	*Centenary Trans. of the NT*
CMic	Jerome, *Commentary on Micah*	ERV	English Revised Version (rev. KJV; =RV in UK)
Cohort15	Pseudo-Justin, *Cohortatio 15*	GNB	*Good News Bible* (=TEV)
DePat	Tertullian, *De patientia*	JB	Jerusalem Bible (=annotated; see NJB)
DeVir	Jerome, *De viris illustribus*	KJV	King James Version (=AV in UK)
DivInst	Lactaantius, *Divinae institutiones*	Moffatt	*Holy Bible, a New Translation*
EccHist	Eusebius, *Ecclesiastical History*	NAB	New American Bible (RCC)
Ep	Augustine, *Epistles*	NASB	New American Standard Bible (=NASV)
EvGood	Philo, *Every Good Man Is Free*	NASV	New American Standard Version (=NASB)
ExcTheod	*Excerpts from Theodotus*	NCB	(New Confraternity Bible) =NAB
Frag	Heraclitus, *Fragment*	NCE	New Catholic Edition
Geog	Strabo, *Geography*	NEB	New English Bible (see REB)
Haer	Theodoret, *Haereticarum*	NIV	New International Version
Haer	Epiphanius, *Adversus lxxx haereses*	NJT, NJV	New Jewish Translation, NJVersion (=TNK)
Hist	Tacitus, *Historiae*	NJB	New Jerusalem Bible (rev. JB; =annotated)
Hist	Herodotus, *History*	NKJB	New King James Bible (=NKJV)
HLuke	Origen, *Homily on Luke*	NKJV	New King James Version (=NKJB)
HMatt	Chrysostom, *Homily on Matthew*	NRSV	New Revised Standard Version (rev. RSV)
HJere	Origen, *Homily on Jeremiah*	ONT	*Original New Testament*
Hyp	Philo, *Hypothetica*	PME	*NT in Modern English*
CJohn	Origen, *Commentary on John*	RV	Revised Version (usu. in UK; =ERV)
LAB	Pseudo-Philo, *Liber Antiquitatum Biblicarum*	REB	Revised English Bible (rev. NEB)
Lives	Suetonius, *Lives of the Twelve Caesars*	RSV	Revised Standard Version (rev. ASV/ERV)
MartPol	*Martyrdom of Polycarp*	TEV	Today's English Version (=GNB)
Mon2	Pseudo-Justin, *Monarchia 2*	TNK	TaNaKh (new JPS Hebrew Bible; =NJT =NJV)
NatHist	Pliny the Elder, *Naturalis historia*	Williams	*NT in the Language of the People*
Od	Homer, *Odyssey*		
OnAnt	Hippolytus, *On Antichrist*		
OnFF	Philo, *On Flight and Finding*		
Onom	Eusebius, *Onomasticon*		
OnPrin	Origen, *On First Principles*		
OpHist	Nicephorus, *Opuscula Historica*		
Pan	Epiphanius, *Panarion*		
Phaed	Plato, *Phaedrus*		
Plot	Porphyry, *Life of Plotinus*		
PraepEv	Eusebius, *Praeparatio Evangelica*		
PraescHaer	Tertullian, *De praescriptione haereticorum*		
Protrept	Clement of Alexandria, *Protrepticus*		
Ref	*Refutatio omnium haeresium*		
RomHist	Dio Cassius, *Roman History*		
Scorp	Tertullian, *Scorpiace*		
SpecLeg	Philo, *De Spelialibus Legibus*		
Strom	Clement of Alexandria, *Stromata*		
Trypho	Justin, *Dialogue with Trypho*		

English Versions

ASV	American Standard Version (USA ed. of ERV)
AT	An American Translation
	(aka "Goodspeed" and "Chicago Bible")

Biblical Texts

Old Testament

Gen	Genesis	Cant	Song of Solomon
Exod	Exodus	Isa	Isaiah
Lev	Leviticus	Jer	Jeremiah
Num	Numbers	Lam	Lamentations
Deut	Deuteronomy	Ezek	Ezekiel
Josh	Joshua	Dan	Daniel
Judg	Judges	Hos	Hosea
Ruth	Ruth	Joel	Joel
1,2 Sam	1, 2 Samuel	Amos	Amos
1,2 Kgs	1, 2 Kings	Obad	Obadiah
1,2 Chr	1, 2 Chronicles	Jonah	Jonah
Ezra	Ezra	Mic	Micah
Neh	Nehemiah	Nah	Nahum
Esth	Esther	Hab	Habakkuk
Job	Job	Zeph	Zephaniah
Ps/Pss	Psalms	Hag	Haggai
Prov	Proverbs	Zech	Zechariah
Eccl	Ecclesiastes	Mal	Malachi
(or Qoh	or Qoholet)		

Apocryphal and Deuterocanonical Books

Tob	Tobit
Jdt	Judith
Add Esth	Additions to Esther
Wis	Wisdom of Solomon
Sir	Ecclesiasticus, or Wisdom of Jesus Son of Sirach
Bar	Baruch
Ep Jer	Letter of Jeremiah
Pr Azar*	Prayer of Azariah and the Song of the Three Jews
(Song Thr*	Song of the Three Jews)
Sus*	Susanna
Bel*	Bel and the Dragon
1,2 Macc	1, 2 Maccabees
1 Esdr	1 Esdras
Pr Man	Prayer of Manasseh
Ps 151	Psalm 151
3 Macc	3 Maccabees
2 Esdr	2 Esdras
4 Macc	4 Maccabees

*(Pr Azar, Sus, and Bel are often treated as a composite unit: Add Dan = Additions to Daniel.)

New Testament

Matt	Matthew
Mark	Mark
Luke	Luke
John	John
Acts	Acts of the Apostles
Rom	Romans
1,2 Cor	1, 2 Corinthians
Gal	Galatians
Eph	Ephesians
Phil	Philippians
Col	Colossians
1,2 Thes	1, 2 Thessalonians
1,2 Tim	1, 2 Timothy
Titus	Titus
Phlm	Philemon
Heb	Hebrews
Jas	James
1,2 Pet	1, 2 Peter
1,2,3 John	1, 2, 3 John
Jude	Jude
Rev	Revelation

Miscellaneous

ABS	American Bible Society
app.	appendix(es)
ASOR	American Schools of Oriental Research
b.	born
B.C.E.	before the common/Christian era (=B.C.)
ca.	*circa*, approximately
C.E.	of/during the common/Christian era (=A.D.)
chap(s).	chapter(s)
cf.	*confer*, compare
d.	died
ed(s).	edition, editor(s), edited by
e.g.	*exempli gratia*, for example
esp.	especially
fl.	flourished
frag.	fragment
ft.	foot/feet
Gk.	Greek
Heb.	Hebrew
ibid.	*ibidem*, in that place, in the same place
i.e.	*id est*, that is
in.	inch(es)
JPS	Jewish Publication Society
km.	kilometer(s)
lit.	literally
log.	logion
LXX	Septuagint
m.	meter(s)
ms(s).	manuscript(s)
mg.	margin, marginal reading
mi.	mile(s)
MT	Masoretic Text (Heb. OT)
NABPR	National Association of Baptist Professors of Religion
NCC	National Council of the Churches of Christ in the USA (also NCC/USA)
NCCJ	National Council of Christians and Jews
NT	New Testament
OT	Old Testament
oz(s).	ounce(s)
r.	reigned, regnal period (dates for rulers)
par.	parallel(s)
Rab	Rabbinic interpretation
rev.	revised, revision, revised by
SBL	Society of Biblical Literature
UBS	United Bible Societies
v(v).	verse(s)
vs.	versus

The Nature of Scripture

Richard F. Wilson

In his 1983 presidential address before the Society of Biblical Literature, Krister Stendahl probed the topic "The Bible as a Classic and the Bible as Holy Scripture" (1984). The "and" in Stendahl's proposal is significant because he argues against all attempts to separate an understanding of the Old and New Testaments as "classics" of Western culture from the appropriation of those same bodies of literature as "Holy Scripture" for synagogues and churches throughout the last twenty-five centuries. The Bible is a classic of Western culture, Stendahl argues, precisely because it is revered as Scripture in communities of faith across the centuries. The reverence accorded Scripture precedes its status as a classic, or as Stendahl puts it: "it is its recognition that makes a classic a classic, not its inner qualities" (1984, 4). Failure to acknowledge the Bible as Scripture ignores the precise reason it has become a classic of Western culture. The Bible, with all its diversity of setting, genre, and confession, "*becomes important* for those to whom *the scriptures function* as the bearer of revelation" (Stendahl 1984, 5; emphasis added).

While the dominant emphasis of Stendahl's address is a challenge to biblical scholars to remember the confessional and revelatory nature of Scripture, there is nonetheless a serious challenge to *all* who pick up the books of the Old and New Testaments (and, if one is so inclined, the apocryphal and deuterocanonical writings) to remember that they are handling pieces of literature that are infused with the very identity of the communities of faith that undergird the synagogue and the church. The communities—ancient and contemporary—who "recognize" the revelatory function of Scripture both shape it and are shaped by their recognition of it. These books—the Old and New Testaments, and the apocryphal and deuterocanonical books for some—are more than literary survivors in the face of changing history. They are, by virtue of their status as Scripture, the shadows and echoes of communities of faith that stretch as far back as the time of ABRAHAM,

MOSES, DAVID, JEREMIAH, EZRA, Judas Maccabeus, JESUS, PAUL, JAMES, and JOHN.

They are, however, more than mere shadows and echoes. The Bible is the lifeblood and breath of the community of faith. Before the Bible became the Bible the stories and exhortations that fill its pages were the common language of memory in the community of faith. Rooted in the claim "A wandering Aramean was my ancestor" (Deut 26:5), and underscored with force in the Johannine confession on the lips of Thomas, "My Lord and my God!" (John 20:28), Scripture has become the mirror in which the community of faith glimpses its rich and diverse heritage, as well as its ultimate hopes. The two, heritage and hope, are different sides of the same coin. Any attempt to separate the history of the communities of faith in synagogue and church from the contemporary expressions of the people of God is a woeful perversion of the unity of God's revelatory presence in history. God is not solely revealed in history through literature; neither is God revealed in history merely in the life of the assembled body of those who seek God's presence. Both the community of faith and the literature of confession are required for a satisfactory foundation for understanding the Bible as Scripture.

In this essay we will explore the nature of Scripture in the context of the persistent reality of a community of faith that draws identity from the confession that the God of Abraham and Sarah shapes and transforms the community in each generation. Telling the stories of Abraham and Sarah, and the stories of all of those models of faithful pilgrims who came after them, is more than recounting the past. Telling the stories also is a way of enlivening the present. In the stories of Abraham and Sarah, and those like them, the community of faith experiences a unique opportunity to look backward and forward at the same time. Looking backward enriches the community's sense of heritage, which in turn stimulates the hope for a destination at the end of the pilgrimage. The writer of Hebrews captures the possibility of a simultaneous backward and forward perspective in the image of the runner in the arena: "Since we are surrounded by so great a cloud of witnesses, . . . let us run with perseverance the race that is set before us" (12:1).

Because the primary intent of this essay takes seriously the integral relationship between the community of faith and its confessional literature, there are three issues that will not receive the sort of detailed treatment some readers may expect. Readers will have to look elsewhere for in-depth discussions of the formation of CANON (Hinson 1990 offers a concise treatment), the structures of canon (there *is* more than one), and those thorny issues that surround the claims of the authority of Scripture (see Angell 1990). That is not to suggest that the history of the canon, the structures of canon, and the confessions of the authority of Scripture are not important. They are important indeed. Giving those issues only passing attention in this essay stems from the conviction that too much time and energy have been devoted to the historical and theological issues *about* the Bible at the expense of genuine explorations into the nature *of* the Bible.

James A. Sanders and Stanley Hauerwas are correct in their challenges to those in the academy and the church who would objectify Scripture as the focus of study rather than recognize the inseparable relationship between the Bible and the practicing community of faith. Sanders observes that "the Bible reaches its true stature in church . . . not in the university or even the pastor's study alone" (1987, xi). In his refreshingly confrontational manner Hauerwas claims that "fundamentalism and biblical criticism are both aberrations of the Christian tradition" because "both camps assume an objectivity of the text in order to the make the Bible available to anyone" (1993, 29, 36). To say that the Bible matures in the church recognizes that the nature of Scripture both draws from and feeds into the community of believers who, in each generation, attempt to see, experience, articulate, and model life lived in the presence of God.

Scripture by its nature is *more than* literature, although it is at least literature. Scripture by its nature is *more than* history, although it is at least history. Perhaps most important of all, Scripture by its nature is *more than* a guidebook for the community of faith when they are gathered for worship or dispersed throughout the larger communities from which they come. Scripture is at least a guide for worship, theology, and ethics, but it is no mere manual or "recipe

book" for the community seeking to live life in the presence of God.

Scripture in a Quilted Community

Most treatments of the formation of canon focus on the crises that prompted communities of faith to identify the core of the traditions that told them who they were, where they came from, and how they should live in relation to God, one another, and their world. The result is that Scripture becomes objectified as the end product of a relatively well-defined historical circumstance. As a corollary, attention and emphasis fall upon a significant person, or group, who exerts a power of influence over both the community and the literature it finally accepts as Scripture. For example, then, the name of Ezra is virtually synonymous with TORAH, and the name of IRENEAUS is inseparable from the collection of a fourfold Gospel.

The major motif of this essay argues against the dominance of such a patchwork of historical crises and charismatic leaders that effect the recognition of certain pieces or collections of literature as Scripture for the community. The patchwork exists, of course, and the historical events and personalities *do* deserve careful consideration. There is another side, however, that should receive primary consideration: the community of faith as it persistently exists through the ages. Conceive of Scripture as a richly crafted quilt, the sort of work grandmothers and aunts of days gone by invested months and years creating. The patchwork side of the quilt is clearly the more interesting with its variety of textures, patterns, and colors. If the quilt is a family project it also bears reminders of the traditions that give the family its identity. Without argument the patchwork side is the more interesting, but the other side—often a plain, but sturdy, seamless stretch of heavy flannel—is what gives the quilt its strength, its durability, and its usefulness.

An exploration into the nature of Scripture requires a primary acknowledgment of the community of faith that provides the constant context that holds together the changing history, diverse styles, and conflicting theologies found throughout the Bible. The authentic community of faith is the constant that gives Scripture its strength, durability, and usefulness precisely because it is the authentic community of faith that continually listens to and hears the words of Scripture as the word of God spoken afresh for each generation.

Textures in the Pentateuch. The first stop on the exploration of canon formation is usually the Water

Gate in Jerusalem during the days of Ezra and Nehe-miah (see Neh 8:1-8). The crisis of the EXILE, and then the return to Jerusalem and the struggle to rebuild the city walls and the Temple, had forced the community to ask the foundational questions of identity: Who are we? Where have we come from? and How do we relate to God, to one another, and to our world?

With Ezra's reading of the book of the law, which most readers of the Bible agree was very close to the Pentateuch as read today (Sanders 1972, 51), a closing date for the first division of the Hebrew Bible and Christian Scripture is established near the turn of the fourth century B.C.E. In the drama of the moment, however, it often seems that the great crowds that *heard and recognized* the event as the reading and hearing of the word of God are lost. The emphasis falls first of all upon the literature, and secondarily upon Ezra, frequently cited as the "Father of the Torah" or the "Father of Judaism."

But what of the community that heard and recog-nized the words as authoritative for their lives? Their hearing and recognizing the words as *more than litera-ture* and the stories of the Pentateuch as *more than history* is certainly the most enduring feature of this scrap of antiquity. An emphasis on the community who hears and recognizes Scripture may, perhaps, correct the imbalance of emphasis that has crept into discussions of Scripture. The literature and history of the Bible is not distinct from the life of the community that reveres it as revelatory; neither can the life of the community that reveres Scripture afford to separate it-self from the persistent questions asked through Scripture: Who are we? Where have we come from? and How do we relate to God, to one another, and to our world?

The other stops along the path of exploring the formation of canon look much like the first stop at the Water Gate in Jerusalem during the days of Ezra and Nehemiah. A major crisis catches the attention of the historian because of the way it forces a refocusing of the questions of identity for the community of faith. Through the adaptations of the identifying traditions in a new context, the stability of the community of faith—and its identity that allows it not only to survive but to flourish in the time of crisis—is once again secured. With the passing of the crisis a new division of sacred writings emerges as authoritative for the community.

Textures in the Prophets. The second division of the Hebrew Bible—the Prophets—takes its final shape in the prolonged crises of the growth of Hellenism in the second and third centuries B.C.E. There is wide-spread agreement that both the Former and Latter Prophets achieved literary stability as much as two cen-turies before they achieved canonical status. Happily there are no overpowering personalities to undermine the significance of the community of faith during this stage of development. The canonization of the Proph-ets lacks the sort of clear precipitating factors that make it easy to slight the significance of the commun-ity in the process. There is no Exile and no Ezra, as in the case of the Torah. There is no destruction of Jeru-salem and no so-called "Council of Jamnia," as in the case of the Writings. Neither are there a MARCION and an Ireneaus, as in the case of the Gospels; nor is there a letter from a powerful bishop of the church, as is the case for the remainder of the NT.

The emergence of the Prophets as Scripture is, therefore, an excellent place to look for the nature of Scripture in the combination of an active community of faith, its heritage and hopes, and the literature that sharpens its identity. Faced with the threat of assimila-tion into a very appealing Hellenistic world, it appears that the Prophets provided the means by which the community of faith was able to adapt its Torah faith to the present in a way that maintained the integrity of its Torah heritage.

The narratives of the Former Prophets (Josh-ua–Kings, but not Ruth; the Book of Ruth properly belongs with the Writings), for example, helped the community of faith understand how Torah faith could provide a bulwark against the cultural influences that surrounded them. Taking their cues from the stories of JOSHUA, the judges, ELIJAH and ELISHA, and the like, fourth-, third-, and second-century Jews in the SYNA-GOGUE apparently learned how to distance themselves, somewhat, from the Hellenists and their ways.

Both the Former Prophets and the Latter Prophets (Isaiah, Jeremiah, Ezekiel, and the Book of the Twelve) helped forge the Torah faith, with its focus on the role of Moses as the giver of God's law, into a Torah faith with a distinctly monarchical accent with David as the paradigm of God's presence in the midst of the people. The David narratives—the centerpiece of the Former Prophets—do not eclipse the covenants with Abraham and Moses that give the Torah its central identifying story. Rather the David narratives contemporize the community's identity as the people of God, giving a simultaneous glimpse of a rich heritage in the Davidic Kingdom and an exciting hope in the coming KINGDOM OF GOD. The Latter Prophets' point of departure in the David story as the clearest expression of the community's understanding of its relationship to God is a powerful illustration of how the Torah faith of the Exile was adapted in those communities of faith that survived and flourished in the centuries following the return to Jerusalem. Even the prophets of the Northern Kingdom, that is, AMOS and HOSEA, and the postexilic prophets' use of the Davidic ideal as the most appropriate way to understand the relationship between God and the people, whether in political or merely cultural terms, is testimony to the power and authority of the second division of the Hebrew Bible.

Without doubt the Maccabean Revolt (167–164 B.C.E.) drew upon the narratives of conquest found in the Books of Joshua, Judges, and Samuel. There the MACCABEES, and those that followed their leadership, found justification and authority for their resistance to the oppressive demands of the Syrians under the leadership of Antiochus IV. In the crucible of contemporary crisis the community of faith *heard and recognized* the word of God in a productive way. Their understanding of (the oral and) written traditions from their past transformed the meaning of Scripture into a foundational document that answered for them the questions: Who are we? Where have we come from? and How do we relate to God, to one another, and to our world?

Of course an exclusively political hearing and reading of the Torah and Prophets would cause problems for faithful Jews to follow, most notably the Zealots of the first century C.E. Nonetheless, adapting the traditions of the community of faith by recognizing the authority of another collection of literature alongside the Torah would serve to enrich an understanding of identify in the midst of a changing world.

Textures in the Septuagint. Alongside the emergence of the second division of the Hebrew Bible, the Prophets, some mention and discussion of the SEPTUAGINT (LXX) is needed. The LXX is a significant example of how the believing Jewish community attempted to adapt to the influences of Hellenism *without* being thoroughly assimilated. The language of the LXX, Greek, attests to the tensions in the community of faith that called it into existence. On the one hand they recognized that they were living in a world dominated by things Greek, language being the most pervasive example. On the other hand the community of faith continued to strain to *hear and recognize* their identi-

fying traditions, rooted in a Hebrew culture. In the LXX, members of contemporary communities of faith may glimpse reflections of earlier communities actively engaged in hearing, recognizing, and living according to the word of God in their midst.

From the middle of the third century B.C.E. until near the end of the first century C.E. the LXX functioned as Scripture for communities of faith, including those identified with the Jewish synagogues and, later, the early Christians and their churches. As had been the case before, this Scripture was the means through which the community *heard and recognized* the word of God in their midst as they attempted to answer the questions Who are we? Where have we come from? and How do we relate to God, to one another, and to our world?

Texture in the Writings. First-century JUDAISM, the soil from which Christianity sprang, thrived as a far-flung community of faith. Although members of that community participated in a variety of sociocultural settings from Rome, Corinth, Alexandria, throughout Asia Minor, Damascus, Jerusalem, and on to the East, they shared a common tradition that had been woven through the narratives, codes, and poetry of the Torah and the Prophets—and those other pieces of literature that filled out the LXX, many of which were included later in the Writings of the Hebrew Bible, the Christian OT, and the apocryphal and deuterocanonical works. That there was a common core tradition recognized as Scripture in spite of the deep and wide varieties among individual communities underscores the thesis of this essay. Both the community of faith and the literature of confession are required for a satisfactory foundation for understanding the Bible as Scripture.

By the end of the first century, however, the internal divisions of and the external threats to Judaism would result in a major transformation of the community of faith. Of the many faces of first-century Judaism—including those of SADDUCEES, PHARISEES, ESSENES, HERODIANS, ZEALOTS, and followers of "The Way" (see Acts 9:1)—only rabbinic Judaism, the legacy of the Pharisees, and Christianity survived. Remarkably, even with the demise of many expressions of Judaism, and the ultimate separation of the two that remained, the common core tradition recognized as Scripture remained intact. How could that be? Because the community of faith, even in disarray and fractured, continued to *hear and recognize* the word of God as it was used in the community. The community that preserved the traditions stretching back to the days of Abraham and Sarah was once again preserved to a large degree by those same traditions, now recognized as Scripture. The nature of Scripture is woven deep into the fabric of the community of faith. Only when the community uses the Scripture with integrity can it find out who it is *and* come to a genuine understanding of the nature of Scripture.

The common core of tradition found in the Torah and Prophets remained intact, but there were other developments in the community of faith that resulted in a reconsideration of the extent of the authoritative literature for its life. Until a generation ago those "other developments" at the end of the first century of the Common Era were finely focused around the destruction of the Temple in Jerusalem by the Romans in 70 C.E.

The standard explanation for the closing of the third and final division of the Hebrew Bible was the so-called Council of Jamnia. There a group of rabbis allegedly gathered to salvage what was left of their heritage. With the Temple gone all that remained were the Torah and the Prophets and collections of other literature (including the LXX). The outcome of the gathering was the "canonization" of the Writings.

The work of "canonical criticism" during the last twenty years has challenged the neat package of Jamnia in favor of an appreciation of the living community of faith that allows for a more fluid concept of canonization (see esp. Sanders 1987, 77–86). Thus the modern reader of Scripture may acknowledge that at some point during the end of the first and beginning of the second centuries of the Common Era the literature of the Hebrew Bible and the OT of Christian Scripture became a stable body of literature that could rightly be identified as Scripture. What is important to recognize is that no group of rabbis (or bishops) authorized the inclusion of the literature called Scripture. Rather, Scripture emerges in the context of the life of the community of faith as it seeks answers to the primary questions: Who are we? Where have we come from? and How do we relate to God, to one another, and to our world?

James Sanders rightly insists that "adaptability" is the "major characteristic" in the process of canon formation (1987, 22, 83). The traditions around which Scripture takes shape, primarily those of the EXODUS and of the Sinai COVENANT, are stable. Nonetheless, the life of the community of faith is focused and refocused in ever-changing ways. Its central traditions are interpreted in light of the dramatic changes that the community has faced throughout the centuries. With the emergence of the Prophets and the Writings the community of faith continues to find its identity in terms of the God who called Abraham and Moses, and who made a covenant with the people at SINAI. The Prophets and Writings do not eclipse the Torah faith. Instead they show how the community of faith adapted their Torah faith to a changing world.

The historical contexts that shaped the emergence of the three divisions of the Hebrew Bible span half a century; the literature itself was shaped over two millennia. The traditions of Abraham, Moses, and David that emerged as the central traditions of the community of faith that endured for those two thousand years provide the broad textures of both the Hebrew Bible and the Christian OT (the differences will be explored, in part, in the next section). Pressing the metaphor of the quilt, the primary motif of this essay, the textures of the Torah, Prophets, and Writings are the most obvious ones in the Bible. There are more, less dramatic, textures in the division of Christian Scripture called the NT. To those textures we now turn attention.

Textures in the New Testament. Paul the Apostle was what modern readers of the NT would call a "church planter." The letters he wrote, and those that were written under his influence, are specifically related to particular communities of faith, their particular circumstances, and their particular needs. Those letters are excellent reminders that the nature of Scripture is *always* directed to the needs of the community of faith. In the context of the NT, the particularity of the community of faith, then, is the constant feature of Scripture.

Perhaps contemporaneous with Paul—or at least in the next generation—another collection of letters circulated among the community of faith. These GENERAL LETTERS were not so tied to specific communities and were, therefore, broader treatments of the themes that demanded the attentions of the Christian church as it was being formed. By the end of the century there was also an apocalypse that many in the community looked to for hope and encouragement.

During the generation following Paul's activity as church planter and letter writer another type of literature emerged. The GOSPEL appeared in response to questions and confusion in the community about the Jesus story (see, e.g., Luke 1:1-4; John 20:30-31 and 21:20-25). That the broad community came to accept four distinct versions of the story (see below) is further evidence that the gospel genre was an important texture in the emergence of Scripture.

The NT as modern readers know it took its initial turn toward "canon" with the work of Marcion who, it seems, was the first to make a list of accepted writings for the Christian community. His selection of literature is well known—the Gospel of Luke, edited, and ten letters that bear the name of Paul (the PASTORAL EPISTLES were not included; some say Marcion did not know them), also edited—but what is sometimes lost in his wake is the widespread recognition of Pauline works. Because Marcion only identified the Gospel of Luke as authoritative for the community, most of the attention given to Marcion centers on the way his critics defended a broader collection of Gospels.

One of the most frequently noted critics of Marcion—and the Gnostics with whom he is associated—is Ireneaus, whose name is synonymous with the fourfold Gospel collection in the NT. Ireneaus did develop a rationale for seeing the Gospels of Matthew, Mark, Luke, and John as authoritative for the larger community, but in all likelihood his work was a reflection of the broad acceptance of the community of faith. Ireneaus did not establish the fourfold Gospels; he merely articulated one set of theological reasons behind a prior acceptance of those works (see *AdvHaer* 3.11.8).

The Pauline corpus never seems to have been disputed in the early communities of faith. Marcion included ten works; the MURATORIAN CANON includes them and the Pastoral Epistles. Later, in the *EccHist*, EUSEBIUS hesitated on five of the General Letters, but his hesitation was probably on the basis of the use of that literature in the community of faith. Eusebius was also ambivalent on the inclusion of the Revelation; again the ambivalence was a reflection of the attitudes of the community of faith. The point is that in the context of the early Christian church the community of faith seems to have directed in an obvious manner the acknowledgment of the literature that would, or would not, function as the authority of the community in that generation and for generations to come.

ATHANASIUS, bishop of Alexandria during the last half of the fourth century C.E. is credited with punctuating the canon of the NT. His Festal Letter of 367 included the first known enumeration of the twenty-seven pieces of literature currently included in the NT. Once again, however, it is significant to note that his work was directed to the community of faith as it was spread throughout the ROMAN EMPIRE of the day.

Athanasius did not create the canon. He did, however, reflect the ways the community of faith had been using the literature that modern readers call the NT.

The textures of Scripture underscore its particularity in communities of faith all the way from Ezra to Athanasius. The constant feature over that eight hundred years is a vibrant community of faith seeking to answer the important questions of Who are we? Where have we come from? and How do we relate to God, to one another, and to our world?

The nature of Scripture, then, is imbedded in the nature of the community of faith as it matured, was challenged, and revived. Scripture is the basic structure around which the community of faith finds refuge in changing times. Scripture cannot be divorced from the community and neither should it become an authority *above* the community. Rather Scripture should always be seen as the authority *within* the community of faith for every generation.

Scripture in a Diverse Community

In the foregoing section the textures that are apparent in Scripture were sketched in broad strokes, emphasizing that the textures themselves are clues to the nature of Scripture. Pursuing the motif of the quilt, the textures of Torah, Prophets, and Writings for the Hebrew Bible and Christian OT, and the textures of Epistles, Gospels, and Apocalypse for the Christian NT remind contemporary readers of Scripture that the Bible is inseparable from the history of the communities of faith that *heard and recognized* its words as the word of God in their midst.

Texture is only one part of the nature of Scripture. There are also present well-defined patterns and colors that allow the reader to see the rich diversity of the texts—and the communities—that comprise the Bible. This section of the essay will continue the motif of the quilt with specific attention given to the patterns and colors woven into the fabric of the community of faith and, subsequently, into the pages of Scripture.

Patterns in the Old Testament. For more than a century language derived from the so-called "documentary hypothesis" has had a place in discussions of the Pentateuch. While the initial assessment of literary diversity in the Torah was couched in terms of "documents" and, therefore, left the impression of individual authors or editors, "the process is now seen as communal" and "in terms of traditions which are linked to an ongoing community whose perceptions and understandings are related to their historical experience"

(Brueggemann 1976, 971–72). With a renewed perspective on the community of faith as a thriving organism with varied accents and emphases, the terms YAHWIST, ELOHIST, DEUTERONOMIST, and PRIESTLY WRITERS now point to the rich diversity within the community, rather than to competing voices within the community struggling to be heard. Such an emphasis upon diversity rather than competition makes it easier to understand how these varied patterns of expression can be found in the unified literature called Scripture.

In the same way the textures of Scripture provide glimpses of the community of faith in particular historical and political contexts, so too, the patterns of Scripture allow contemporary readers to observe and participate in the history and life of their forebears. Woven through the pages of the Pentateuch are the testimonies of the community of faith stimulated by five hundred years of continuity and change. The patterns of the Yahwist reflect life under the seemingly endless optimism that stamped the early days of Solomon's reign. That optimism is tempered by the cautions of the Elohist that flowed into Judah on the lips of refugees from the Northern Kingdom following its destruction by Assyria in 722 B.C.E.

The critical theological judgments that became vogue during the days of JOSIAH and his sweeping reforms of the nation punctuate the Pentateuch in the form of the Book of Deuteronomy. The Priestly writers offer a series of introductions and comments on the whole story of Abraham, Sarah, and their descendants from their perspective of hopeful theological reconstructions of faith that were forged in the period of the Exile.

Two features of the diverse patterns of the Pentateuch are particularly remarkable. Each underscores the primary place of the community of faith as the bearer of its own traditions, as opposed to the traditions being imposed upon the community by some force, whether that of a single charismatic leader or a powerful group within the community. First is the fact that these patterns are crafted around the same set of historic circumstances and events. The second is the fact that the patterns exist side by side without any apparent attempt to make the traditions uniform.

The stories of Abraham and Sarah illustrate the first point. Three episodes in the Genesis narratives provide shades of meaning to the idea of Abraham and Sarah as bearers of the covenant promise: the promise of COVENANT (Gen 15); CIRCUMCISION as the sign of the covenant (Gen 17); and the command to Abraham to

sacrifice Isaac as the point where the covenant faith of Abraham matures (Gen 22). The first episode bears the accent of the Yahwist; the second episode carries the perspective of the Priestly writers; the final scene conveys the cautions of the Elohist, cautions against confusing popular cultural practices and the word of God (von Rad 1972; cf. Westermann 1986). These three narratives from Genesis each make a confession about Abraham and Sarah as the bearers of the covenant promise that was important to the community of faith.

That these three episodes are found in the Book of Genesis with their distinct features intact is an illustration of the second point. Readers of these stories hear the unmistakable confession that covenants with God are "cut"; yet there is no attempt to regulate an understanding of "cutting the covenant." These stories are *unified* around the figures of Abraham and Sarah in relation to God, but there is no attempt to make the stories *uniform*. The diversity in the story of Abraham and Sarah reflects a diversity in the community of faith that sought in the Abraham story answers to the crucial questions: Who are we? Where have we come from? and How do we relate to God, to one another, and to our world? Those questions can have *unified* responses without having a *uniform* one.

Also significant in this trio of narratives is the point that the traditions they carry look back to the Abraham and Sarah story in order to clarify an identity in the present, and to find a point of departure from which to focus a hope for the future. The accents, or patterns, of three different moments in the life of the same community of faith are preserved. The accent of the Yahwist community from the tenth century does not drown out that of the Priestly writers of the fifth; neither of them eclipses the accent of the Elohist community from the eighth century. Pressing again the motif of this essay, these moments from three different periods in the life of the community of faith are held in place with their vibrant patterns and colors intact precisely by the continuity of the community, and its ability to adapt its understandings of its identity and purpose for each generation. The nature of Scripture is inseparable from the life of the community of faith. What gives the Scripture its strength, durability, and usefulness, then, is the willingness of the community of faith to *hear and recognize* the words of Scripture as the word of God in their midst.

The Pentateuch is the foundation for Scripture and for any understanding of the nature of Scripture. What is apparent in an examination of the Pentateuch is also applicable for the remaining literature that comprises an understanding of Scripture. The literature of the Bible reflects the diversity of the community of faith that *heard and recognized* the word of God in the stories of the patriarchs, the liberators (Moses, Joshua, and the judges), the kings, and the prophets. In each generation the narratives took on particular significance as Scripture when the people found in them identity and hope.

The Former Prophets do not present a uniform narrative of the work of God in the period preceding the establishment of the monarchy. The faithfulness of GIDEON (Judg 6–8), for example, stands in sharp contrast to the faithlessness of JEPHTHAH (Judg 10–12) and SAMSON (Judg 13–16). Likewise the narratives of SAMUEL and SAUL that surround the formation of the monarchy are ambivalent. On the one hand Saul appears as the perfect choice to lead Israel (1 Sam 9:1–10:16); on the other hand Saul is a dubious choice (1 Sam 10:17–27). Similar ambivalence is found throughout the episodes of DAVID and SOLOMON.

The Later Prophets also are unified around the themes of God's challenging presence in the midst of the people in changing times. Thus, for example, JEREMIAH's harsh interpretations of the Babylonian invasion of Jerusalem (Jer 29) finds a balance in the words of ISAIAH welcoming the returning exiles to Jerusalem (Isa 60). Both interpretations are included in Scripture, emphasizing the diversity of Scripture in response to changing circumstance of the community of faith. The Book of the Twelve includes the tirades of OBADIAH against Edom, promising destruction for its response to Judah's fall to Babylon; it also includes God's stinging rebuke to JONAH, and others like him, for taking glee in threats of destruction rather than seeking compassion and tolerance.

As is the case in the Pentateuch, the Prophets present a montage of narrative content, style, genre, and theology. These varying stories, the different manner in which they are told, and the wide range of theological emphases found in them draw attention to the community of faith once again. As it persisted across the ages the community was able to hear and recognize the word of God in its midst in a number of ways. That the richness of confessions within the community remains intact with all their patterns, colors, and accents still vivid is remarkable indeed. The nature of Scripture finds its greatest expression as it is stretched across the community of faith that continues to hear and recognize in Scripture the word of God.

Perhaps the starkest contrast within the OT literature comes when one compares the Writings to the Torah and Prophets. The themes introduced in the Book of Deuteronomy, and that also dominate the books of Joshua through Kings (recall, again, that the Book of Ruth is not included in the Prophets), are directly challenged by the WISDOM LITERATURE, especially the Book of Job and some of the Psalms. The deuteronomist is firm in the conclusion that suffering and defeat are the direct result of sinfulness, yet the writer of the Book of Job is adamant that Job is without sin (1:1, 8, 22 passim). Something happened in the community of faith that caused it to reconsider its conclusions about health and suffering, and success and failure. That "something" was probably the Exile; and so alongside the deuteronomic history there emerged a more reflective, poetic confession of the relationship between God and the community.

The Prophets also include a challenge to the notion that suffering is the result of sin and disobedience. How else are we to understand the Servant Songs that appear in Isa 40–55? But the thoroughgoing reversal of the dominant theology of the deuteronomist is most apparent in the Book of Job, and Psalms such as Pss 37, 49, and 73.

Five pieces of literature within the Writings specifically draw attention to the community of faith as it sought to hear and recognize the word of God it its midst, not only in a particular period of history, but in the recurring cycles observed in worship. These "festival scrolls," or *Megilloth*, are Song of Songs (read at Passover), Ruth (read during Pentecost), Ecclesiastes (read during Tabernacles or "Booths"), Esther (read during Purim), and Lamentations (read to commemorate the destruction of the Temple on the ninth of Ab, and on the Day of Atonement). Their presence in Scripture is a poignant reminder that the use of the literature of faith is inseparable from its status as Scripture. First of all these five scrolls found their way into the regular life of the community at worship; subsequently they were included in the canon.

What is remarkable about the *Megilloth* is its diversity. The Book of Ruth is as broadly tolerant of those outside of JUDAISM as the Book of Esther is intolerant. Likewise the Book of Ecclesiastes is as sanguine in the face of progress as the Book of Lamentations is passionate in the face of defeat. And the eroticism of the Song of Songs seems to have carried the unqualified confession of joy in the presence of the God of history who comes to the people in an unexpected manner. That these scrolls are included in the collection of the Writings is testimony to the rich colors and patterns found in Scripture. These scrolls are unified around the confession that God is at work it the community, but there is no effort to make the confession uniform.

Patterns in the New Testament. Turning to the NT one is struck by the sharp distinctions among the portrayals of the Jesus story, and those among the encouragements for the actual living of the Christian life. Even a casual reader of the Gospels is aware that the first three Gospels (usually identified as the Synoptics because they share a common perspective and chronology) see the Jesus story through a different lens than the writer of the Gospel of John. In the Synoptics Jesus has an intense and vigorous ministry that lasts no longer than eighteen months, and he dies in Jerusalem during his first visit there as an adult. By contrast, Jesus in the Gospel of John has a less intense ministry that allows him to make at least four trips to Jerusalem to celebrate the PASSOVER—thus the popular notion of a three-year ministry.

The diversity of perspective between the Synoptics and the Gospel of John is further evident in such features as the absence of narratives relating the TEMPTATION OF JESUS and the TRANSFIGURATION in the Gospel of John (which are key components in the Synoptics), and the absence of a clearly stated identity of Jesus as the Messiah in the Synoptics (which is the central, explicit confession of the Gospel of John [see John 20:30-31; cf. Mark 8:27-33 and par. where the title "Messiah" is cautiously shunted to the side]). The Gospels are unified around the figure of Jesus, but they do not present a uniformity in the telling of the Jesus story.

The remainder of the NT also reflects the diversity within the first broad community of Christians. While the Pauline materials dominate the collections of letters in the NT (some would even say that PAUL has overshadowed JESUS as the primary influence in the contemporary CHURCH) there are also the distinct patterns and colors that make the Book of James and the Johannine Letters, for example, so noticeable.

The Pauline materials are directed to that segment of early Christianity that came to the faith on a path other than historic Judaism (see, e.g., Gal 2:1-9; 1 Cor 6:9-11; Rom 9–11). Consequently, the content and tone of the Pauline letters establish a foundation for a community of faith less concerned with ritual demands than it was concerned with the liberating experience of

being justified by God's grace. Furthermore, the Pauline materials acknowledge the need to mature in one's thinking (see, e.g., 1 Cor 12–14). Thus through the letters that bear the name of Paul readers of Scripture glimpse the communities that heard and recognized Paul's confessions and encouragement as the word of God for them.

The reluctance in James to separate confessions of faith from faithful living is often placed in sharp contrast to the Pauline emphasis on "justification by faith." The conflict between James and Paul is more apparent than real: James is primarily interested in the *practice* of faith among confessing Christians, and Paul is interested in the *efficacy* of faith that leads to one's inclusion in the community of Christians (cf. Jas 2:17-18 and Eph 2:8-10). That both the Pauline material and James exist in the NT highlights the diversity of the community of faith. Clearly the community of faith was unified around the desire to model appropriate responses to the questions: Who are we? Where have we come from? and How do we relate to God, to one another, and to our world? Equally evident is that there was no effort to make the responses to those questions uniform. The acceptance of diversity takes precedence over any demand for uniformity.

Whereas the Pauline materials and the Letter of James probably reflect the same era (the 50s and 60s), the Johannine Letters (as well as the Gospel and the Apocalypse) belie a segment of the community of faith at least a generation later. The passing of time, especially beyond the significant threshold of the Roman destruction of Jerusalem in 70 C.E., establishes a context that is very different from the earlier days of broad tension between Christians from gentile and Jewish backgrounds. The Johannine Letters, as well as the Gospel of John (see esp. chap. 21), offer glimpses of a more narrowly defined community of faith beset with intramural squabbles about leadership and theological foundations (see Kysar 1992a and 1992b).

The Johannine materials underscore the diversity found in the NT less in their relationship to the rest of the literature than in the way they cohere. Within the confines of the Johannine collection, for example, the confessions about Jesus and the encouragement to live faithfully according to the model of Jesus (cf. John 13:31-35; 1 John 2:7-17; 3:11-24; 2 John 4-6) provide points of departure through which a particular community of faith is identified. The pattern established between "new commandment" and "love" is one of the sharpest patterns developed in the NT. The Johannine materials (and community) are clearly unified around such themes as new commandments and love—other themes also contribute to the coherence of the collection. In the broader collection of NT literature, however, there is no effort either to make Johannine perspectives conform to other patterns, or to reshape the Johannine collection in light of other collections. The confession of the Jesus story and encouragement for faithful living provide a unifying center without demanding a uniformity of confession and encouragement, not only for the Johannine materials, but for the whole NT.

Patterns in the Septuagint (and in the apocryphal and deuterocanonical works). Attention to the LXX as a precursor to the various canonical collections in contemporary Christianity (e.g., Eastern, Roman Catholic, and Protestant) is also an instructive glimpse at the diversity of the communities of faith that grew out of Hellenistic Judaism. The textures of the LXX have already been noted in relationship to the process of communities of faith accepting the Prophets and Writings as Scripture. What now captures our attention is the way that the LXX was transformed in the contexts of change within the communities of faith.

The LXX of the third century B.C.E. was a less than critical collection of diverse literature arranged in a manner that combines an interest in chronology and genre. The chronological impetus is reflected in the pattern of inserting the Book of Ruth between the Book of Judges and Kingdoms 1–4 (subsequently identified as 1–2 Samuel and 1–2 Kings), the inclusion of Judith, Tobit, and 1–4 Maccabees after Esther, and the longer versions of Jeremiah (the Additions to Jeremiah and the Letter of Baruch) and Daniel (the Prayer of Azariah, Susanna, and Bel and the Dragon). The attention to genre is seen in the insertion of Psalm 151 and the Prayer of Manasseh between Psalms and Proverbs, and the inclusion of the Wisdom of Solomon, Sirach, and another collection of psalms after the Book of Job.

The LXX included all of the pieces of literature that were subsequently identified as apocryphal or deuterocanonical. It also modelled an arrangement of texts that was ultimately accepted by the Christian community of faith, but rejected by the Jewish community of faith at the end of the first century C.E. (see Harrelson 1995).

More significant than the rearrangement of the texts of the Jewish Bible and the Christian OT (in its most narrow version) is the excision of certain books, such as the Maccabean literature, the additions to Daniel, Jeremiah, and Esther, and the poetic works of the Wisdom of Solomon and Sirach. Some segments of the community of faith apparently ceased to regard certain pieces of literature as Scripture. Even though the LXX functioned as Scripture for both Jewish and Christian communities during the second half of the first century, by the end of the century a retrenchment of the canon had occurred. In the synagogue Scripture was understood to be comprised of Torah, Prophets, and Writings; in the Christian churches Scripture was conceived along the lines of the LXX with or without the various additions of historical and poetic materials.

As James Sanders observes (1987), the canon is adaptable, even to the extent of being pared back. The emergence of the LXX in Hellenistic Judaism, its acceptance as Scripture in the synagogue and churches, and its subsequent downsizing by both Jews (by the end of the first century C.E.) and Christians (from the time of Jerome in the fourth century to that of Luther in the sixteenth [see Charlesworth 1992]) demonstrates, again, the relationship between Scripture and the communities that *heard and recognized* the literature as revelatory—or not!

That some pieces of literature were at one time considered Scripture by the community of faith, and later were assigned to the status of apocryphal and deuterocanonical works throws in sharp relief the boundaries between an authoritative collection of literature and the community (or communities) that regarded the literature "as the bearer of revelation" (Stendahl 1983, 5). The apocryphal and deuterocanonical works reveal the fluidity of the nature of Scripture as it was (and is) used in the broad center of faithful communities. Those communities that value the apocryphal and deuterocanonical works alongside the canons of the Old and New Testaments are part of the durable background that gives the patchwork of Scripture its stability. At the same time, however, those communities prove that there is no firm, impenetrable line to separate the communities and the literature they regard as revelatory.

Although it falls beyond the scope of this essay, it is important to note that vast collections of noncanonical literature have been used as supplements to Scripture by a variety of faithful communities through the centuries. The OT pseudepigrapha, the NT Apocrypha, the APOSTOLIC FATHERS, the DEAD SEA SCROLLS (which also contain canonical works), and the library discovered at NAG HAMMADI are the major examples of such supplemental literature. Interested readers would find exploration of the above-mentioned collections intriguing and instructive.

Scripture as Active Memory

The foregoing development of the nature of Scripture conceived through the metaphor of the quilt rests upon the conviction that the community of faith, as it has persisted through the centuries in synagogue and church, is both the preserver of the Word of God and the product of the Word of God. As the community has *heard and recognized* God's presence through Scripture, Scripture has emerged as the canon for the broader community of faith that spans time, geography, and cultures.

Leander Keck accurately draws attention to the relationship between Scripture and canon: "The Bible's standing in the church depends upon the church's experience of it as Scripture. When the Bible ceases to function as Scripture, as special, it ceases to be the canon and becomes instead a resource book on a shelf of great religious classics" (1983, 9). As noted above, all attempts to objectify Scripture—attempts to make the Bible a book on the shelf—undermine its mature nature. Critics who explore the historical, cultural, structural, and literary aspects of the Bible without also identifying the way Scripture functions in communities of faith through the centuries, fall short of understanding the true nature of Scripture. Likewise those who use the Bible as a tool to be used to corral the community, or as a weapon to wield against the opponents of the community, fail to experience the nature of Scripture. They fail to appreciate Scripture as the product of a persistent and diverse community of faith as reflected in synagogue and church over the last twenty-five centuries.

Attempting to objectify Scripture either as an esoteric focus of scholarship or as the devotional focus of the self-consciously religious finally ends with Scripture being read and used nostalgically. A nostalgic approach to Scripture is reductionistic at best and obscurantist at worst. The problem with nostalgia is twofold. First, what is wistfully recalled probably never actually existed. The Davidic Kingdom was not all peace and prosperity; the primitive church was not a paradigm of progress and harmony. Second, nostalgic forays are attempts to retreat rather than they are efforts to move forward.

The mature nature of Scripture is found in the way it stirs active memory in the life of the community of faith. In contrast to a nostalgic use of Scripture, the Bible as active memory confronts the multifaceted reality of the present even as it provides a lens through which the community of faith may glimpse the future. Nostalgia is that insidious inclination to be seduced by something dead and gone. The nostalgic impulse sucks the life breath out of the present and tries to blow it into the atrophied lungs of yesterday's corpse.

Memory, on the other hand, is the recognition that there is a continuity in what was alive and meaningful in the past and is still vibrant in the present. To preserve a memory is to broaden and deepen the very values that made life worth living in the past and to tap the same values for the present and future (cf. Buechner 1973, 58).

Scripture as active memory links the historic communities who *heard and recognized* the word of God in their midst with the contemporary community of faith in synagogues and churches who continues to *hear and recognize* the word of God in their midst. Scripture as active memory is at least literature and history, but it is more than that. Scripture as active memory is at least a guide for the community of faith, but it is more than that, too. The mature stature of Scripture emerges in the life of the community that acknowledges it as revelatory without thoroughly objectifying and externalizing it.

For Further Study

In the *Mercer Dictionary of the Bible*: APOCRYPHA, MODERN; APOCRYPHAL LITERATURE; APOSTOLIC FATHERS; BIBLE; BIBLE, AUTHORITY OF; CANON; DEAD SEA SCROLLS; NAG HAMMADI; REVELATION; TEXTS, MANUSCRIPTS, AND VERSIONS. In other sources: See the works cited, below, and P. Achtemeier, *The Inspiration of Scripture*; J. Barr, *Holy Scripture: Canon, Authority, Criticism*; J. Sanders, "The Strangeness of the Bible." *USQR* 42/1-2 (1988): 33-77; D. Tracy, *The Analogical Imagination*; J. Trafton, "The Importance of Noncanonical Literature," MCB.

Works Cited

Angell, J. William. 1990. "Bible, Authority of." MDB.

Brueggemann, Walter. 1976. "Yahwist." *IDBSup*.

Buechner, Frederick. 1973. *Wishful Thinking: A Theological ABC*.

Charlesworth, James H. 1992. "Old Testament Apocrypha," s.v. "Apocrypha." AncBD.

Harrelson, Walter. 1995. "The Hebrew Bible." MCB.

Hauerwas, Stanley. 1993. *Unleashing the Scripture*.

Hinson, E. Glenn. 1990. "Canon." MDB.

Keck, Leander E. 1983. "Scripture and Canon." *Quarterly Review* (Winter): 8–20.

Kysar, Robert. 1992a. "John, Epistles of." AncBD; 1992b. "John, Gospel of." AncBD.

Rad, Gerhard von. 1972. *Genesis*, rev. ed. OTL.

Sanders, James A. 1987. *From Sacred Story to Sacred Text*; 1974. *Torah and Canon*.

Stendahl, Krister. 1984. "The Bible as a Classic and the Bible as Holy Scripture." *JBL* 103/1:3-10.

Westermann, Claus. 1986. *Genesis 12–36: A Commentary*.

The Hebrew Bible

Walter Harrelson

The term "Hebrew Bible" is currently the most commonly used designation for the Christian Old Testament and the Jewish Bible. In the Jewish community the Hebrew Bible is also called by the acronym *Tanakh*, created by using the opening letter of the Hebrew names of the three parts of Jewish Scripture: *T* for the divine Law or Teaching (*Torah*), *N* for the Prophets (*Nevi'im)*, and *K* for the Writings (*Ketuvim*). Many Christians today look for terms more suitable than "Old Testament" to refer to the Scriptures of the Jews, since "Old" has often been understood to mean "old and outmoded." Terms other than "Hebrew Bible" that are suitable are "First Testament" (which then allows Christians to refer to the New Testament as the "Second Testament") and "Jewish Bible."

The problem is complicated further by the fact that the Christian community preserved as a part of its OT a number of works not found in the Bible of the Jews. These works, routinely called Apocrypha by Protestants (Roman Catholics regard most of them as "deuterocanonical" and Eastern churches include one to three more such books as [deutero]canonical), generally have had somewhat less standing than the books in the Jewish Bible, chiefly because they were *not* claimed as canonical by the Jewish community. Most Christian Bibles today, however, include these apocryphal writings, together with some (e.g., 3 and 4 Maccabees and Psalm 151) that were not included in Roman Catholic and Protestant Bibles. While the Apocrypha and other ancient Jewish literature are widely used in Jewish scholarship, they are not a part of sacred Scripture in the same way the oral Torah, found in the Talmud (see RABBINIC LITERATURE), is understood as authoritative. Some Christian communities continue to leave the apocryphal writings out of their CANON of sacred Scripture.

The *order* of the Jewish Bible and Christian OT is also distinct. Both communities agree that the first five books are Genesis, Exodus, Leviticus, Numbers, and Deuteronomy, the books that comprise the Jewish TORAH. The Jewish designation for the next block of books is, as we saw above, the "Prophets," which include two groups of books—the "former" or "earlier" prophets Joshua, Judges, 1–2 Samuel, and 1–2 Kings—and the "latter" or "later" prophets Isaiah, Jeremiah, Ezekiel, and the Book of the Twelve (Amos, Hosea, Micah, etc.). The final block of writings in the Jewish Bible is the (sacred) Writings: Job, Psalms, Proverbs; the small festal scrolls Ruth, Song of Solomon, Ecclesiastes, Lamentations, and Esther; and the late writings Daniel, Ezra and Nehemiah (treated as one book in ancient times), and 1–2 Chronicles.

In the Christian Bible, the collection is organized differently, an arrangement that began already in the Jewish community in Egypt. This Jewish translation of the Hebrew Scriptures into Greek (which began in the third century B.C.E.) is found today in the Christian Greek OT called the SEPTUAGINT. Its arrangement has continued to be used in virtually all Christian Bibles. The arrangement clearly shows the desire of the translators to organize the material by subject matter, with little attention being given to the chronological development of the literature. The Book of Ruth is placed after the Book of Judges because the story of RUTH and NAOMI is set in the period when the judges ruled. The Books of 1–2 Chronicles are placed directly after the Books of 1–2 Kings because they cover much of the same ground covered in 1–2 Kings. Ezra, Nehemiah, and Esther are placed at the end of the historical collection that includes Joshua, Judges, Ruth, 1–2 Samuel, 1–2 Kings, and 1–2 Chronicles because Ezra, Nehemiah, and Esther continue the story of Israel's history in EXILE and tell of the return from exile to Judah. The festal scrolls are placed with the other poetic and wisdom materials, and Daniel is included as one of Israel's great prophets because Daniel, too, receives oracles from God for the people of Israel.

This difference in arrangement has had consequences to this day. Since the early Christian community understood itself as having inherited God's promise made to Abraham and his descendants, it only made sense for their "Old Testament" to end with the promise of Elijah's return to usher in a definitive epoch in Israel's history (Mal 4:5-6). And since the Jewish community had only recently (66–70 C.E.) witnessed the destruction of Jerusalem and its temple with the loss of thousands of lives and the scattering of the Jewish people, it only made sense for Jewish scholars in the following decades to place at the end of their collection the Book of 2 Chronicles, which spoke of the edict of the Persian king CYRUS that allowed Jews in Babylonian exile to return to their homeland. Christians found that their "Old Testament" led directly into the world of the NT, while Jews could note that their Scripture ended with continuing confidence that God had not abandoned the people of the covenant. Just as God had brought their ancestors back from Babylonian captivity to reclaim the LAND, so God could be counted upon to bring deliverance to the faithful once more. The order of Scripture carries a message of its own.

The Torah

The term "Torah" means "guidance" or "teaching" as well as "Law." The fundamental teaching found in the first five books of the Torah is clear: God is the creator of all that exists, and God guides the course of human life through divine promises and demands. Human life itself is sheer gift of divine love, for God could and did manage even when there were no human beings to serve their appointed ends. But human life is purposive and good, and in the garden God enjoys the companionship of the first human pair, is grieved to see disobedience and wickedness break out, and takes steps, even through severe punishment, to direct the human community toward God's purposed ends.

This theme finds expression throughout all the parts of the Torah (see the commentary on each of the five books). The development can be followed as a divine promise on the way to realization but never fully realized. God's promise to ABRAHAM and to ISAAC and JACOB is concrete and practical: descendants, land, prosperity. The demand is that the people of the Covenant *be* a blessing to others even as they are blessed. The people of the COVENANT develop institutions, forms of worship, laws to regulate conduct, and procedures for rallying the tribes to defend the people against enemies. All of these are duly recorded in the complex literary traditions that comprise the Torah.

The whole is dominated by a few personalities, many of whom are portrayed in sagas that offer little by way of personal biography. Others, like MOSES and AARON and MIRIAM and JOSHUA, stand out in their individuality, their gifts and their failings evident. The society portrayed in the Torah is ostensibly in the control of the male population, but women keep breaking out of the encrusted patriarchy to claim dominant positions of leadership over and again. And God exercises restraint, unwilling to give up the choice of a people of God even though it often seems that the people are bent on flaunting the divine will and neglecting or perverting the divine promise.

As the Torah comes to an end, Moses is still in the land of Moab, where he is permitted to see the land of promise from afar. God buries Moses outside that promised land, hiding the location of his burial place from all (Deut 34:6). Even so, the Torah does not end tragically; Joshua has already been commissioned and prepared to take over. Although Moses—unlike Abraham and SARAH, Isaac and REBEKAH, and Jacob and LEAH and RACHEL—is buried outside the land that God is giving to the people of the covenant, still the story is not a tragedy. This extraordinary ending for the most sacred part of the Hebrew Bible, the Torah, makes clear that God's fulfilling of the Promise comes over time, comes through the agency of a *people*, and is not thwarted finally by human failings—even though it is clearly furthered by human fidelity and obedience. God remains sovereign over the divine promise.

We can see, therefore, that while the Torah was the product of centuries of experience, containing narratives, poems, lists, genealogies, priestly instructions, legal collections, and some circumstantial accounts of historical events, it is much more than the history of the beginnings of earth, of human life, and of the people Israel. The Torah offers an affirmation of faith: that everything that has being owes its being to the action and purposes of the one God; that the people of God are charged to live in covenant with the one God, seeing to it—under God's guidance—that divine blessing spreads over all the earth, reaching all of earth's peoples. Torah can be called the "gospel" of the Hebrew Bible.

The Former Prophets

It is generally recognized today that the Books of Joshua, Judges, 1–2 Samuel, and 1–2 Kings were brought together and recast to form a great historical account, the theme of which is the fate and fortunes of God's word of guidance, demand, and judgment. Much of the material is very ancient, handed down orally for some centuries, while other parts existed in written form and were brought together to form large literary unities long before the historical collection was made in the seventh century B.C.E.

The Book of Joshua has lists of tribal boundaries interwoven with lists of the major towns and cities of the various tribes. It also has vivid accounts of some battles against Canaanite cities and peoples, along with other generalizations about the course of battle. The book claims a total CONQUEST OF CANAAN, but then quickly notes that not all of the large Canaanite cities could, in fact, be captured. The actual course of Israel's settlement in Canaan may have involved some battles led by incoming Israelite tribes, but much of the land was claimed by peasants living in Canaan and oppressed by the city-state system of the time who got together, made common cause, and secured their freedom, joining forces with the Moses group later on.

The story that Joshua tells is a grim and bloody one. The tellers of the story were confident that God ordered the destruction of the population of Canaan and Israel's replacement of Canaan on the land. It is good to learn, from the Book of Joshua itself, that the settlement also involved peaceful treaty making, intermarriage, and a long and slow weaving together of the peoples and cultures and languages and religions of the population of Canaan.

In Joshua's farewell address (chap. 24) the point is made. Some among the Israelites continued to worship the traditional deities of Israel's ancestors in Mesopotamia, while others were worshipers of BAAL and Ashera and Anath, deities of Canaan. And still others worshiped God under the personal name YHWH, called the LORD. From this amalgam of religious customs, ideas, and traditions there developed our present account of the conquest of Canaan.

The Book of Judges personalizes the struggles for land and blessing and a secure place within Canaan. Again, the historian stylized the events, offering an account of how disobedience to the divine Word brought about historical disaster. Suffering under oppression by one or other of Israel's enemies, the people would cry out to God for help. God would raise up a deliverer, male or female, from one tribe or another, and with God's direction of affairs, the "judge" would prove victorious and the land would have rest once more. Here too we can see how God's promise is threatened, whether by Israel's failings or by the avarice of others, how human beings must do their part in preserving the promise, and how God stood

ready to intervene when called upon by the people of the covenant.

Some of the stories in Joshua and Judges (and elsewhere in the Bible) tell of wholesale slaughter done in the name of God. Such a religious teaching is not central to the religious understandings of the Hebrew Scriptures and is generally rejected by readers of the Bible today. The God of Jewish and Christian faith neither requires nor commends such acts of violence. The same must be said about the violence done to women (e.g., in the case of the concubine of the Levite from the tribe of Ephraim [Judg 19–21]).

The Books of Samuel and Kings introduce us to historical personalities who are more clearly etched than those of the earlier traditions. The difference probably lies with the coming of the Israelite kingship, which brought many baneful developments to Israel (distinctions of class and loss of personal freedom; a widening gap between the poor and the wealthy; new notions of deity that threatened the idea that God's special concern was with the lowly and the oppressed, etc.), but which also brought a richer and more sophisticated understanding of Israel's social and economic and religious world. In the Books of Samuel, for example, the struggle between SAMUEL and SAUL is told in such a way as to enable readers to see the strengths and weaknesses of both; neither is a hero, and neither is a villain. The same obtains in the portrayal of the struggles between Saul and DAVID. Was Saul a person promoted beyond his actual abilities, pathologically driven to maintain a position as king that he should simply have yielded to the better qualified David? Or was Saul a faithful worshiper of YHWH, determined not to adopt a form of royal life and leadership that would be religiously inappropriate, but taken advantage of by a much cleverer and more ruthless David, skilled in *using* the religious traditions to his own ends?

The remarkable fact is that the traditions justify our saying yes to both portrayals! Here we find profound discernment of the struggles and posturings and acts of heroism and of cruelty that take us into the political world of any time. Here, good and evil appear intertwined in all of Israel's leaders. And here too, the literary genius enables us to see our own world, and frequently our own selves, in these figures who also, in their distinctive ways, struggle with the promise of God for blessing and security and a purposeful destiny. A great leader, beloved by almost everyone, loses his sense of purpose when there are no more enemies to conquer. The remarkable political and economic and religious community that he has helped to form begins to disintegrate before his and our eyes. He would only need to rally in order to put an end to rebellion and corruption within his own family, but, alas, he has lost the will to do so. The greatness is still present, for God is with him; but the will to serve God is gone, and all else is thereby threatened.

The story continues in the Books of Kings, where occasional extended narratives (stories of ELIJAH, ELISHA, and MICAIAH SON OF IMLAH [1 Kgs 22] in particular) are woven into a rather subtle story-outline. The outline is about what happened to this kingship set up by David with such promise and with so much achieved. The narrator clearly sees things from a Judean vantage point, judging events in North Israel harshly, for the most part. But the historian is too honest to whitewash Judean events. Only two kings stand out as genuinely faithful to God (which is the author's chief criterion): HEZEKIAH and JOSIAH. The story ends with the last of Judah's kings in regular succession, JEHOIACHIN, who had been exiled to Babylonia along with much of the surviving population of Jerusalem, being released from prison and united with his family, apparently completely at the mercy of the foreign king. But the historian knows, as JEREMIAH also knew, that the promise of God has not run its course: "There is hope for your future, says the LORD" (Jer 31:17).

The Latter Prophets

Much of the treasure of Israelite literature and thought appears in the four prophetic collections called the Latter Prophets. The Book of Isaiah contains material composed over two and one half centuries, in all probability, all of it bearing Isaiah's name in the manuscripts. Isaiah's own words are found largely in the first thirty-two chapters, although these too have been supplemented by his disciples. But all of the sixty-six chapters claim the ISAIAH heritage and build upon it. If we think, then, of an Isaiah *tradition*, we can with confidence treat Isa 40–55 (a great literary masterpiece from the time shortly before the return of Jews from Babylonian exile, which began in the last half of the sixth century B.C.E.) as an exilic reclaiming of Isaiah's message and heritage. Similarly Isa 33 and 35 and Isa 56–66 are a rich reclaiming of Isaiah's message and heritage by disciples of Isaiah living in Judah (who associated themselves with the Isaiah tradition long after the prophet's death) in the period after the return from exile.

Isaiah of Jerusalem (last third of the eighth century B.C.E.) took with great seriousness both the demands of the covenant and its promises. In chapter after chapter, the Book of Isaiah affirms the divine glory and transcendence, calls on the community of Israel and its leaders to entrust their lives to God's care, even as they amend their ways and begin to practice the faith that they profess, and offers a variety of magnificent word pictures of what it will be like when God does bring the divine purposes and promises to their consummation. Much of the message of the prophet Isaiah and his followers has been captured in the liturgy and hymnody of synagogue and church. Whether the PROPHET is denouncing ISRAEL (Isa 1:2-20) or Israel's enemy ASSYRIA (Isa 10:5-19) or is offering promise to Israel and to the world (Isa 2:2-4; 9:1-7; 11:1-9), his words and images have gained a place in the consciousness of Jews and Christians that transcends the generations.

Jeremiah, too, has such a place in the religious consciousness of succeeding generations. This immensely long book (the longest in the Hebrew Scriptures) also was augmented by later disciples of the prophet, but there is much from the prophet himself and there is much *about* the prophet that can be taken to be historically reliable. Jeremiah's special contribution to Israelite religion is his lyrical account of the love with which God loved and still loves the people Israel. Even as the prophet denounces Israel and its leaders for acts of faithlessness, the prophet's own love for and identification with the people are unmistakable. He affirms with confidence that the exile to Babylon is not the end of God's dealings with Israel. Who can know, humanly speaking, how valuable for Israel's survival this faith of Jeremiah actually was? We have testimony that Jeremiah encouraged the first exiles from Jerusalem (598/7) to build houses, plant vineyards, settle in, and pray for the welfare of the land in which they were living as captives. Jeremiah was convinced that a faithful life could be lived in exile, but he also was fully convinced that God intended that the people of the Covenant return to the land promised to Israel's ancestors.

The prophet EZEKIEL apparently spent his entire career as a prophet among the Babylonian exiles, but his message was addressed to the entire community of Israel, those who were still in Jerusalem and Judah after he had been taken into EXILE, along with many other Israelite leaders, in 598/7 B.C.E., and those who were in exile with him. As the number of exiles swelled following Jerusalem's destruction in 587/6 B.C.E., Ezekiel's message included them as well, and it is remarkable to see how sharply his message changed after the fall of Jerusalem—from threats of divine punishment for sin to promises of restoration and a fresh start.

The message of Ezekiel is couched in rich and often strange symbolism. The prophet also uses strong and often violent language, denouncing the people as no prophet before him had done, while also making grand promises that seem to sweep aside any need for human repentance or amendment of life. The reasons for such sweeping language are not hard to identify. Ezekiel's own personality must surely have been a contributing factor, but in addition, Israel's desperate plight was largely responsible. Ezekiel had to convince those still living in Judah and Jerusalem that their having been spared in 598/7 was no indication that they were favored by God or that they could delay amendment of life.

Especially offensive to the priest Ezekiel were the non-Israelite religious rites being practiced in Jerusalem—in the name of the one God, YHWH. But he had to convince those in exile with him that God had not finished with Israel: the covenant with Israel and with David still held, although Ezekiel, like Isaiah and the other prophets, did much to transform the notion of kingship that was characteristic of ancient Near Eastern views. While God had not abandoned the promise made to David, new conquerors and potentates were not in God's plan and purpose, according to the prophets. A new kind of Davidic ruler was to come to Israel, one whose rule was characterized by justice for all and peace among the nations.

Ezekiel's speech and actions were forceful, graphic, and must often have been found to be offensive. He spoke of Jerusalem's beginnings as a result of a union of two different peoples (chap. 16). The result of the union was the birth of the child Jerusalem, abandoned beside the road, uncared for, left to die. It was God who came to do the duties of a midwife for Jerusalem (Jerusalem clearly includes the whole people Israel), to care for her, and eventually to return and claim Jerusalem as bride. The people's APOSTASY is the more shocking precisely because of these past demonstrations of the divine love.

But the future includes Israel's building up, reconstitution as a people, with God's Spirit breathed in to give life to all (Ezek 37). It includes the reconstitution of the very inner disposition and will of the people, as God removes the stony heart and inserts a heart of flesh (Ezek 36). And above all, it includes the transformation of the entire land, the resettlement of all the tribes, most of them in new locations, with the temple restored and its activities closely regulated, and with blessing and fertility extending throughout the entire land of the Promise (Ezek 40–48).

Many of the treasures of prophetic literature and thought are found in the collection called the Book of the Twelve (Prophets). Chief among these are the Books of Amos (the earliest of the twelve prophets), Hosea, Micah, Habakkuk, and Jonah. As the commentaries below will make clear, each has its distinct emphasis and setting within the life and faith of Israel.

AMOS is known for the rigor of his denunciation of the social and economic evils of Israel in his day and for the power and vitality of his language and imagery. While his message is addressed to North Israel in large part, his words are clearly intended for the whole people of God. As God's messenger, he pronounces divine judgment upon a faithless people, not for religious sins but for socioeconomic and political ones.

HOSEA too follows in that line, as does the prophet MICAH, but for Hosea the great crime is infidelity to God's searching and unrelenting love. God demands faithfulness of the people of the covenant, but God will go to the greatest of lengths to bring an errant people to faithfulness. Especially painful to the prophet was the corruption of the priests, the prophets, and other religious institutions.

HABAKKUK too has a distinctive word of faith tó utter. In the period when Judah was about to be destroyed by the Babylonians for their faithlessness to the covenant, the prophet pressed God to show how Israel's destruction can be fair. Is Israel *really* more evil than Assyria or Babylonia? Can God not find some way of bringing divine judgment on faithless Israel that is not itself an act of injustice? The prophet summons hearers to place their utter trust in God, anticipating new things in the near future.

And the Book of Jonah offers a critique of prophetic religion when that religion gets too rigorous and self-righteous, when prophets are bent upon seeing God's judgment fall upon the sinners of earth who deserve punishment. The whole narrative is designed to help hearers and readers feel the oppressive weight of a religious faith that demands that God stick to the divine demands, punishing sinners when they sin. The author's Jonah is a prophet who is never happier than when God brings deserved judgment upon sinners and sticks to the judgment. The problem presented by the Book of Jonah is that God keeps insisting upon finding ways to show mercy, compromising therefore the clean and rigorous judgment that means death to sinners and life to the righteous. The author knows well enough that *all* stand condemned, if God should insist upon exact retribution for human misdeeds (Ps 130).

The Writings

As we follow the order of the Hebrew Bible, we come next to the sacred Writings, all those books that do not belong with the Torah or the Prophets. This collection developed last, with the latest of the books (in their present form) perhaps taking that shape in the early second century B.C.E. (the Book of Daniel, e.g.). Here, we have the poetic and wisdom texts of the Septuagint (Psalms, Proverbs, Job, Song of Solomon, Ecclesiastes) plus the books placed in earlier collections of the Septuagint (Ruth, which follows Judges in the Septuagint, and the additions to the "Prophets": 1–2 Chronicles, Ezra, Nehemiah, and Esther, plus Lamentations and Daniel).

The Psalms contain actual prayers and praises of the people, given here with all their beauty, power, passion, and frequent expressions of hatred for enemies, disappointment in God, indications of self-satisfaction, and all the rest. Clearly, no one has sought to "edit" the collection to make it express only positive sentiments expressive of the love of God and neighbor that was Israel's mandate from the Torah.

Similarly, in the wisdom traditions, exalted pictures of Lady Wisdom and her part in the divine creation (Prov 8; see Sir 1 and 24, and Wisdom of Solomon) appear alongside practical guidance that often seems flat and banal. The wisdom collections appealed to common sense, held in general to the view that God's created universe operated on the basis of a divine *order* that could be depended upon. The wisdom collections offer perspectives and insights for all peoples, not just for the people of the covenant, and it was recognized by the wisdom teachers that this was so.

Two wisdom collections stand out because they seem not to fit the normal features of ancient Near Eastern wisdom. The first of these is the Book of Job, a powerful declaration of the truth, observable by all, that the claims made for a God of justice and fairness seem not to fit the actual experiences of human beings. The author of this seventh-sixth century B.C.E. classic seems to be affirming that God may indeed be just in governing the universe, but that the divine justice is by no means evident in public affairs. Righteous persons and groups suffer while lawless and cruel persons and groups often escape judgment for their misdeeds. But deeper than this observation is the question raised whether religion is not, after all, a bargain with God that the faithful strike, only to withdraw from the bargain if God does not deliver just what the worshipers believe is their due. Is there such a thing as devotion to God that is not based upon received or anticipated gain? Or is religion just another of the world's deals: one does certain things for God with the anticipation that God will return the favor. (The early theologians spoke of this by means of the Latin term *do ut des*: "I act in order that you [God] may act").

The resolution found in the Book of Job is itself mysterious. Does the deity accept Job's repentance once Job has experienced an actual vision of the deity (Job 42:1-6)? Or is the point of the author that there is the true and gracious and just God *behind* the notions of God that human beings create, a deity who lives and suffers with the faithful in their struggles but does not always miraculously intervene to spare them pain and the experiences of injustice and meaninglessness? It may be that the author of the Book of Job is pressing hearers and readers to trust their actual experience of God, an experience that is itself blessedness and peace and the promise of justice, even in the midst of personal and social injustices and evils.

The other book that stands out is the Book of Ecclesiastes, called in Hebrew *Qoheleth* ("the Preacher" or "the Assembler"—"the Teacher" in NRSV). This small book has much material that is like that found in the Book of Proverbs and in other wisdom collections, but throughout Ecclesiastes there is voiced the relentless insistence that human activities and strivings and accomplishments are but "vanity . . . a chasing after wind" (an image used at least nine times in the book). But here too at one point the author seems to show that God is engaging this vain world, along with human beings, bringing out of the struggles of life those features and meanings that are enduring. Ecclesiastes sees vanity all around, but the invitation to dig more deeply, to search for meaning (see 3:15), continues to be pressed upon hearers and readers. It is a powerful, prophetic book, shattering religious complacency.

The Types of Literature

The variety of OT literature is described in the commentary on the particular books. Here we need only point to the major features of that variety.

Among the oldest pieces are ancient victory hymns such as the Song of Miriam (Exod 15:21) and the larger Song of Moses (Exod 15:1-18) that precedes it. The Song of Deborah is probably of about the same age (Judg 5), and some of the poetic "blessings" of the tribes (Gen 49 and Deut 33) are also quite ancient. Akin to these are shorter blessings and long or short cursings, such as the blessings of Isaac on his sons (Gen 27:27-29 and 27:39-40), the taunt-song of LAMECH (Gen 4:23-24) that is almost a curse, and the self-curse of the tribes found near the end of the Book of Deuteronomy (Deut 27:15-26).

But by far the best known of the poetic pieces of the Hebrew Bible are the prayers and praises of the community (esp. the Book of Psalms), the wisdom collections, most of which are in the form of proverbs (see, e.g., the Book of Proverbs and the deuterocanonical Book of Sirach), and the prophetic utterances, many of which are poetic, covering a large variety of forms. The prophets made use of literary forms employed in legal proceedings, others used in the community's worship, some taken from the world of diplomacy and royal ceremonies, and many that came from daily life and work. In addition, they created new forms and often modified and transformed existing forms of speaking and writing.

Highly original speakers and writers in ancient Israel created distinct masterpieces, such as the poetry of the Book of Job, especially Job 3–27, 29–31, and 38:1–42:6, and the rich and often lyric poetry of Isa 40–55. Also original and distinctive are many of the classic narratives of the Hebrew Bible, among which the narratives of Genesis such as chaps. 16, 18, 22, and 24 stand out, as do some of the stories of the heroes and villains of the books of Judges, 1–2 Samuel, and 1–2 Kings. To these one must add the powerful stories of Ruth and Jonah, the love lyrics of the Song of Solomon (Song of Songs), and the iconoclastic wisdom collection known as Ecclesiastes.

But in addition there are those collections of laws, directions for the observation of religious rites, lists of the tribes and families of Israel, and accounts of the history of Israel and of Judah that make up the contents of much of the Hebrew Bible. There are also texts that portray the piety and faith of persons facing persecution (Esther and Daniel 1–6), and there are visionary portrayals of the fulfillment of God's purposes for the creation. In the prophetic collections these visions of the end of the age are still firmly rooted in history; they sketch out, with a variety of images, God's bringing to its intended purpose the life of Israel and of the nations of the world, on a transformed earth, and sometimes following severe judgment upon Israel for its faithlessness to the divine covenant.

Another kind of literature also describes the consummation of God's purposes—APOCALYPTIC LITERATURE. The second half of the Book of Daniel describes wars among the nations of earth that virtually wipe out all hostility to the divine will and purpose and prepare the way for God's blessing to fall upon the faithful people of God who will have been spared in the conflicts. Similar visions appear in Ezek 38–39 and Isa 24–27. This type of literature, widely represented in Jewish texts outside the canon of the Hebrew Bible but preserved in the canons of various Christian churches (texts such as the books of *Enoch*, parts of *4 Ezra*, and the *Testament of Moses*), is also found in NT literature (Mark 13 and par. and the Book of Revelation).

These two types of visions of the consummation of the divine purpose are both of great strength and value. The prophetic pictures of the end of the age offer the greater challenge to the community to public action, so that the structures of public life can be made to conform, here and now, more closely with the political and social structure that God purposes. Prophetic eschatology, that is to say, is a direct summons to social action on the part of the faithful community. Apocalyptic eschatology, too, is a summons to action, but this type of VISION of the triumph of God's purpose seems to arise in situations in which the social and political structures seem impervious to reformation and renewal. The community, even so, is not to lose heart, for what may be impossible to mortals is by no means impossible to God.

Actually, apocalyptic eschatology, as we know from our own day, can flourish in any kind of political community. The Christian community has continued to give a larger place to apocalyptic visions than the Jewish community has. Even the horrors of the Holocaust in Europe under Nazism did not issue in the adoption of an apocalyptic religious outlook among Jews. It is wise to acknowledge that the appeal of apocalyptic visions lies not only in external social and political circumstances; apocalyptic appeals to a distinct kind and quality of religious life, a reality that can appear and reappear quite apart from prosperity or adversity.

Literary and Theological Qualities of the Old Testament

The OT is a *literary* collection and should be treated as such. From the opening, sonorous lines of the creation story of Gen 1 to the circumstantial account of Israel's exile and promised return from exile in 2 Chronicles, we are dealing with a body of materials of varied literary forms and with varied tendencies and aims. It would be unwise to overlook this variety in our reading, just as it would be unwise to overlook this variety in a commentary on the entire Hebrew Bible. The first creation story (Gen 1) is intended to *teach* us, to make things clear, to avoid error and misunderstanding in interpretation. The second creation story (Gen 2) also teaches, but it does so by its captivating *story*, its delight in developing character, its show of the play of human emotions, its picture of how human beings, precisely when they are attempting to be creative and claim their place in God's world, ever so easily overstep the bounds and make grave difficulty for themselves. The story of the first human sin, similarly, tells us not only about the first sin; it tells us about the nature of sin as such. Human beings are *prompted* to fall into sin by realities and forces outside themselves (Gen 3, the snake stands for such forces). But they are also tempted *from within* to disobey the divine will. Human sin is a human act, but it also gets prompted by the very character of life in community, life on an earth for which humans are appointed to take responsibility.

Theological and literary strength and subtlety characterize the great narratives of the books of Genesis, Judges, and 1–2 Samuel as well. The story of Abraham's readiness to offer his son Isaac on one of the mountains in the land of Moriah (Gen 22) displays utter faithfulness, love, and trust—in God by Abraham, in his father by Isaac. The repeated clause "and they went, the two of them, together . . . " (Gen 22:6, 8) is at once heartbreaking and sublime.

And the complex and rich narratives of David reveal the grandeur and the baseness both of David himself and of those surrounding him.

But the literary qualities are equally important and impressive in wisdom texts (Job, Prov 8 and 31, Sir 39, 44–50, Bar 3–5), in prophecy (Isa 1, 35, 40–55, Jonah), in classic narratives of the later period such as Ruth, Esther, Tobit, Susanna, and Judith, and above all in the Psalms. In the treatment of particular books within this commentary, the attention of readers is called to some elements of this literary artistry and theological subtlety. But nothing takes the place of the reading of the Bible itself.

The Hebrew Bible and the New Testament

Christians through the centuries have resisted the temptation to lay aside the Hebrew Scriptures and claim the NT alone as their Bible. The story of the Hebrew Bible is Israel's story; it is also the story of the CHURCH. The Christian community has used various interpretive schemes to make this truth clear, some of which have contributed to Christian misunderstanding of Judaism and Christian mistreatment of the Jewish people. When the church has seen itself as the "new" Israel, the successor people to the people of the first covenant, it has been tempted to claim (against PAUL in Rom 9–11) that God has rejected Israel and passed the divine mission on to the church alone.

The NT writers, especially the authors of the Gospel of Matthew and the Letter to the Hebrews, underscore the continuities between JUDAISM and Christianity even as they assert the primacy of the new covenant over the old covenant. The author of Matthew stresses the continuing validity of the Torah, and the author of Hebrews shows how Jesus the HIGH PRIEST of a better covenant has brought to consummation the divine purposes for Israel and for the nations of earth.

The Book of Revelation draws heavily from Psalms and from prophetic texts to portray the consummation of God's work, which for this author centers in Jerusalem, the Zion of the last days spoken of so frequently by Israel's prophets. The representatives of the twelve tribes of Israel enter the heavenly Jerusalem through twelve gates that stand open continually, and so do the elect of God from all the nations and families of earth. In that city there is light eternal, for night is banished forever.

Conclusion

Theologically, the Hebrew Bible contributes richly to Christian understanding. It is *the* Bible of the earliest Christians, and its strong emphasis upon God's demand for public justice was surely presupposed by Jesus and by the earliest Christians. The OT teaching that God demands justice for all, care for the oppressed, the needy, and the stranger, and diligent care for the whole of the creation is a central part of Christian faith and morals. While the NT concentrates upon the new dimensions of the divine work in Jesus as the Christ, its message is inseparably linked, for Christians, to the literature, the history, and the thought of the people of Israel.

Christian Scripture is different from Jewish Scripture both in scope and understanding. But Christian Scripture has always included—to the great good of the Christian community—that part of Scripture called by Christians "The Old Testament."

For Further Study

In the *Mercer Dictionary of the Bible:* APOCALYPTIC LITERATURE; BIBLE IN WESTERN LITERATURE; CANON; LITERATURE, BIBLE AS; OLD TESTAMENT; ORAL TRADITION; POETRY; RABBININC LITERATURE; SEPTUAGINT; SOCIOLOGY OF THE OT; THEOLOGY OF THE OT; TORAH; WISDOM LITERATURE. In other sources: B. Anderson, *Understanding the Old Testament*, 4th ed; J. Blenkinsopp, *A History of Prophecy in Israel*; J. Crenshaw, *Old Testament Wisdom*; D. N. Freedman, ed.-in-chief, *Anchor Bible Dictionary*; N. K. Gottwald, *The Hebrew Bible: A Socio-Literary Introduction*. W. Harrelson, "Introduction to the Old Testament," in B. Anderson, ed., *The Books of the Bible*, vol. 1; A. J. Heschel, *The Prophets*; H. Ringgren, *Israelite Religion*; R. de Vaux, *Ancient Israel: Its Life and Institutions*.

A History of Interpretation

John H. Hayes

Inner-Biblical Interpretation

The earliest interpretation of biblical materials occurs within the Bible itself. This is especially the case if one considers the OT and NT together. Earlier texts are often reused, reinterpreted, reapplied, and reunderstood in later texts (often, of course, there is some difficulty in knowing which is earlier and which later). This reuse may be either overt, generally with some clear indication that earlier material is being used, or covert when allusion is made through borrowed image or verbal parallels.

In some cases the interpretation of a text will appear as a gloss, that is, as an explanatory note that has been added to aid the reader (it is, of course, difficult to know if the explanatory note was a secondary gloss or whether it belonged to the original stratum of a text). For example, Judg 1:10 speaks of Hebron and adds the statement "the name of Hebron was formerly Kiriath-arba." Numerous such glosses appear in the OT, where the intent is to elucidate and explain.

Interpretation sometimes involves a direct quotation of an earlier text. Daniel 9:1-2, 24-27 refers to the prophecy of Jeremiah concerning the seventy years of exile (see Jer 25:11-12; 29:10). The author of Daniel quotes Jeremiah as a respected text but offers an interpretation that assumes that the original prediction by Jeremiah contained a hidden meaning. The seventy years are then understood as referring to seventy *times* seven years. Here the reinterpretation of the earlier text is made so as to extend its frame of reference down to the time of the author of Daniel.

The numerous parallels between the laws in Deut 12–26 and other legal texts probably indicate that the author of Deuteronomy was reusing earlier legal collections. Many of the laws in this section have parallels in Exod 21–23. For example, the law on the Hebrew slave in Exod 21:11 is given a broader and a more humane application in Deut 15:12-18. Here the purpose would be a reapplication of an earlier law for later, changed conditions.

Most scholars assume that 1-2 Chronicles, where these overlap with the history in Samuel-Kings, is a retelling, a rewriting, of this earlier material (it may be that 1-2 Chronicles and Samuel-Kings both draw on a common source). The Chronicles material has different emphases (more priestly and religiously oriented) than the parallel texts in Samuel-Kings. This reuse of material would thus be intended to bring the presentation into line with a different portrayal of the history of Israel.

In the superscriptions to thirteen psalms (3, 7, 18, 34, 51, 52, 54, 56, 57, 59, 60, 63, 142), there are references to events in the life of David. All but one of the these (Ps 7) allude to events described in 1-2 Samuel. If these were added later as interpretive glosses then they serve two functions. On the one hand, the psalm material has been given a historical context against which it can be read and to which its sentiments can be related. On the other hand, a person reading the narratives about David could utilize the psalms to understand how David felt and reacted in the episodes.

Nehemiah 8:1-8 indicates that the law needed interpretation after a public reading. It is entirely possible that some of these early interpretations have found their way into the biblical texts themselves.

The prophets occasionally allude to stories and events also described in the Pentateuch. For example, Hos 9:10 seems to refer to Baal-peor about which there is a narrative in Num 25:1-18. Hosea 12:3-6 parallels Gen 25:26; 32:22-30; 28:11-17; and 35:5-8. Is Hosea alluding to and interpreting the Genesis accounts? Or do both draw upon common stories? Or has the pentateuchal material been composed to fill out the allusions in the prophetic references? We cannot be certain which is the case but clearly there are interplays between the texts and some element of intertextuality must be taken into consideration.

In the NT, the use of, quotation of, and allusion to OT texts and events becomes commonplace. There are hundreds of such quotations and allusions. The writers of the NT clearly wanted Jesus and the Christian movement to be seen in light of the OT. The early church understood the OT as divine word and Jesus and the new community as predicted in its contents.

Often a NT text will clearly indicate that some event or occurrence is a fulfillment of an OT passage. The clearest case is the Gospel of Matthew, which notes in eleven passages that something "fulfills what had been spoken."

At other times, OT texts are quoted to buttress an argument or a position. For example, Paul may conclude a point by quoting a biblical text (e.g., Rom 3:4) or even a collage of texts (see Rom 3:10-18).

In Stephen's speech in Acts, there is a retelling of much of the biblical story but obviously reinterpreted to present the history of Israel as one of constant rebellion. This is what might be called a Christian homily that applies the text to a contemporary audience.

Frequently the NT writers have Jesus dialoguing with Jewish leaders over the interpretation of some particular law (e.g., Mark 10:1-12, 17-31). In these episodes, Jesus is shown offering a rereading of the material. It is clear the early church wished to present Jesus as an interpreter of scripture whose interpretations agreed with the church's reading. In Luke 24:44-49, the resurrected Christ refers to "everything written about [him] in the law of Moses, the prophets, and the psalms." He is said to have "opened [their] minds to understand the scriptures."

Christians not only saw in the OT foreshadowings and predictions of Christ and the church but also the actual activity of the preexistent Christ. In 1 Cor 10:1-4, Paul not only describes OT events using the Christian symbol of baptism but he also identifies the "rock" in the wilderness from which the Israelites drank as Christ.

It was possible for Christians to deny the straightforward reference of an OT text in order to relate the text to new realities. According to Paul the reference to not muzzling an ox (Deut 25:4) does not really have to do with oxen but with whether Christians should receive payment for their services (1 Cor 9:3-10).

OT "prophecies" could be interpreted by Christians not only with reference to the first coming of Christ but also to the parousia or second coming. The son of man saying in Dan 7:13-14 was frequently used this way in the teachings attributed to Jesus.

Paul introduced terminology into his discussion of the OT that was greatly to influence later Christian interpretation. In places, he speaks of OT events as types or allegories (1 Cor 10:6, 11; Gal 4:21-26). Early events are viewed as types paralleling present realities and the account of these "were written down to instruct us" (1 Cor 10:11). In Gal 4:21-26, Hagar and Sarah are taken as allegories of the Jewish and Christian covenants or the present and heavenly Jerusalems. The obvious referent of the OT text is seen to contain a deeper, hidden reference.

Paul also spoke of the letter that kills and the Spirit that makes alive (2 Cor 3:6; cf. Rom 7:6). Although Paul here does not necessarily have reference to a twofold sense in a text, he nonetheless used terminology that could be so interpreted.

Early Jewish and Christian Interpretation

As noted above, Jewish and Christian interpretation of the Bible is already reflected in the Bible itself. Here we are concerned with a later phase in the process. The Jewish ordering of the Hebrew Bible—Torah, Prophets, Writings—already reflects an interpretive principle, namely, the TORAH takes precedence over all other biblical materials (the Christian shaping of the OT with the prophets at the end emphasized that the center of interpretation had shifted). The 613 commandments collected by the later rabbis are all drawn from the Torah and no prophet was said to be able to add to the Mosaic law. However, there grew up around the written law an oral law that was considered binding and was declared to have been given to Moses on Sinai. This presence of a dual law demonstrates that in Judaism the Torah was understood as both a closed entity and an expanding entity. What was authoritative was both the text *and* its traditional understanding. Judaism was thus a religion based on textual exegesis *and* interpretation. The interpreters, the scribes, raised their interpretations to the level of scripture.

Jewish rabbis recognized that interpretation of a text was necessary when it contained textual problems, was not clear, appeared to contradict other texts or traditional understanding, or needed clarification or supplementation to adapt it to changing conditions.

Examples of Jewish interpretation may be seen in the Aramaic translations of scripture (the targums) as well as in the Greek translation (especially of the Pentateuch but also in the Prophets), in the Mishnah where scripture is appealed to for substantiating a view or position, in the rewritten form of biblical materials, and in various types of commentaries (see RABBINIC LITERATURE). Since early Judaism, especially before 70 C.E., was not a homogeneous phenomenon, not all interpretation is identical.

The Qumran community was part of an eschatologically oriented Jewish sect which could read the scriptures much like the early Christians, namely, as a collection of oracles concerned with the founder and the present and future life of the community. The Temple Scroll from cave 11 represents a rewriting of the Pentateuch to incorporate the views of the sectarians. Among the Qumran scrolls are *pesharim* in which biblical texts are given an interpretation (i.e., its *pesher*) in terms of the community's beliefs (see PESHARIM, QUMRAN). Such *pesharim* could take the form of a running commentary on a book or commentary on a collection of texts. In the *pesharim* the biblical text is assumed to contain cryptic allusions to the future that concerned the sect. The Qumran community could also interpret scripture to formulate *halaka*, rules and regulations for observing the law.

Rabbinical Judaism whose schools produced the midrashim was less eschatologically oriented. In the midrashim, represented by such works as the *Mekhilta* of Rabbi Ishmael on Exodus, the *Sifra* on Leviticus, the *Sifre* on Numbers and Deuteronomy, and the *Pesiqta* of Rab Kahana on biblical readings for festivals and special days, one sees true commentary work that argues a case, offers divergent opinions, and sometimes leaves an issue or interpretation open. These commentaries contain both legal type material (*halaka*) and homiletical/narrative material (*aggada*). The former was intended to establish and aid in keeping the legal requirements while the latter was inspirational and edifying.

The Targums originated, as perhaps did the earliest Greek translations of the Torah, as translations into the vernacular so non-Hebrew speakers could comprehend the text. The Targums are often quite expansive and explanatory rather than literal translations.

As a rule, the material in the commentaries gives a straightforward interpretation of the text, especially in the legal portions although passages are often brought together on the basis of particular terms, general allusions, and incidental matters which might call another text to mind. The texts occasionally resort to typological and allegorical reading. This was especially the case with the Song of Songs where the two lovers were understood as God and Israel. The rabbis concluded that "the law speaks according to human language" (Babylonian Talmud *Berakoth* 31b) and that "no verse could ever lose its plain (*peshat*) sense" (Babylonian Talmud *Shabbath* 63a).

Various rules (*middot*) were formulated that were to be used in interpreting Torah. Seven such rules were attributed to Rabbi Hillel and thirteen to Rabbi Ishmael. These overlap somewhat and appear to be deductions drawn from how the rabbis already worked.

Of a totally different class were such Jewish exegetes as PHILO of Alexandria (ca. 20 B.C.E.–42 C.E.). Living in a thoroughly Hellenistic culture, Philo sought to harmonize Greek philosophy (Platonic and Stoic morality and natural philosophy) with the Bible. The scriptures were read as if they pointed to higher things; persons and events became symbols of other realities.

Early Christian interpretation, already reflected in the NT, drew upon both Jewish and Hellenistic exegetical techniques. The Greeks possessed a long tradition of reading Homer both grammatically and allegorically. Early Christian interpreters picked up on Paul's terminology and read the OT looking for types and allegories about Christ and the church. The apostolic writings, like the letter of Barnabas and 1 Clement, used typological exegesis as did JUSTIN MARTYR (ca. 100–ca. 165) and Melito of Sardis (late second century). In his *Dialogue with Trypho the Jew*, Justin sought to demonstrate the truth of Christianity on the basis of proof from prophecy.

In the course of the second century, what were considered variant forms of Christianity developed. One such was represented by MARCION (d. ca. 160) who put together a canon consisting of the Gospel of Luke and ten Pauline letters. Both the gospel and the letters were edited by Marcion to remove what he considered to be interpolations (a common practice among Hellenistic scholars). For Marcion these interpolations represented judaistic material. Since Marcion stressed the difference between the NT God of love and the alien deity of the OT, he rejected the Hebrew scriptures and anything Jewish. Marcion's position represented a dualism and the rejection of the OT as scripture, neither of which was acceptable to mainline Christians.

A second variant form of Christianity was represented by GNOSTICISM. Gnosticism read even the Christian texts, especially the Gospel of John, in the light of a doctrine of sin and salvation that the church found unacceptable.

In response to such threats, church leaders argued that scriptural interpretation is a prerogative of the church, and must be in agreement with accepted, traditional teaching (the rule of faith) and under the supervision of episcopal authority (see esp. IRENAEUS's *Against Heresies*).

The first major Christian treatise on biblical interpretation in found in book 4 of *On First Principles* by Origen (ca. 185–ca. 254). Origen advocated a multilevel reading of the scriptures although at times he vigorously defended the literal reading where others resorted to allegory. Drawing upon texts such as the Greek of Prov 22:20-21 and a tripartite anthropology, Origen argued that scripture has a body, soul, and spirit, a literal and a twofold spiritual sense. Some texts he argued contain no literal sense because their statements are absurd. Difficulties in the text have been placed there to challenge the interpreter. The spiritual meaning is intended to be appropriated by the Christians as they grow toward the heavenly world and as an aid in that growth.

Exegetes influenced by Origen (such as Gregory of Nyssa [ca. 335–395] and Didymus the Blind [d. 398]) laid great weight on the spiritual and allegorical reading of the text. In contrast to this Alexandrian school, exegetes in the region of Antioch were advocates of a more literal reading of the Bible, probably being influenced by Jewish exegesis, Aristotelian philosophy, and conservative Hellenistic grammarians. The most significant members of this school were Diodore of Tarsus (d. ca. 394) and Theodore of Mopsuestia (ca. 350–428). They argued that allegorical interpretation was without controls and emptied history of meaning. The Antiochians argued for what they called *theoria* which appears to have been spiritual truths that did not abrogate history. Theodore tried to prove that what Paul meant by allegory was *theoria*. Perhaps *allegoria* was oriented to spiritual knowledge while *theoria* was more morally based. The Antiochians greatly limited the number of messianic texts in the OT.

The two most influential early Christian interpreters were Jerome (347–420) and Augustine (354–430). Both stood somewhat midway between the Alexandrians and the Antiochians. Both produced many commentaries. (The fourth and early fifth centuries were the golden age of Christian commentaries. Only Cassiodurus [485–580] and Gregory the Great [540–604] produced notable commentaries in the sixth century.)

Jerome mastered Hebrew with the help of Jewish instructors and went back to the Hebrew to produce his translation of the OT. Augustine's *On Christian Doctrine* contains his fullest statements on biblical interpretation. He argued that the arts and other aids must be applied in the study of scripture and that one should know the original languages (though he didn't). For Augustine the primary purpose of scripture was to teach love and if the literal sense of a text was not edifying, then it must be taken nonliterally. Augustine's works, even his "literal commentary" on Genesis is filled with allegory.

The early Christian exegetes bequeated to the Middle Ages the view that the scriptures were a multilayered embodiment of all truth. Christian exegetes advanced various expressions to delineate the multifold levels of meaning in, and means for the understanding of scripture, sometimes threefold, sometimes fourfold. Jerome spoke of *historia*, *tropologica*, and *intelligentia spiritualis* (*Epistolae* 120.12); Gregory the Great, of *historia*, *significatio typica*, and *moralitas* (*Moralium libri Epistula missoria* 3); and Augustine, of *historia*, *allegoria*, *analogia*, and *aetiologia* (*De Genesi ad litteram* 1.1.1; and *De utilitate credendi* 3.5-9). Augustine's terminology—etiology and analogy—was never especially utilized either by himself or others (see Aquinas, *Summa Theologiae* Ia.1,10). Nevertheless, Augustine, along with Gregory, greatly influenced the medieval exegetes' search for more than one "higher" meaning in scripture. At the beginning of his unfinished literal commentary on Genesis, he wrote:

Four ways of expounding the Law are handed down by certain men who treat the Scriptures. Their names can be set forth in Greek, while they are defined and explained in Latin: in accord with history, allegory, analogy, and etiology. It is a matter of history when deeds done—whether by men or by God—are reported. It is a matter of allegory when things spoken in figures are understood. It is a matter of analogy, when the conformity of the Old and New Testaments is shown. It is a matter of etiology when the causes of what is said or done are reported. (*De Genesi ad litteram liber imperfectus*, 2.5)

The terminology and scheme of multiple meanings in scripture that were to become almost standard in medieval times was formulated by John Cassian (ca. 360–435):

[T]he practical side of knowledge is hived off among many professions and disciplines. The contemplative side is divided into two parts, namely, historical interpretation and spiritual interpretation.

Hence, Solomon, having listed the multiform grace present in the Church, goes on to say, "All those of her household are clothed twice over' (Prov. 31:21). Now there are three kinds of spiritual lore, namely, tropology, allegory, and anagoge. . . .

History embraces the knowledge of things which are past and which are perceptible. . . . What follows is allegorical, because the things which actually happened are said to have prefigured another mystery. . . . Anagoge climbs up from spiritual mysteries to the higher and more august secrets of heaven. . . . Tropology is moral teaching designed for the amendment of life and for instruction in asceticism. . . . And if we wish it, these four modes of interpretation flow into a unity so that the one Jerusalem can be understood in four different ways, in the historical sense as the city of the Jews, in allegory as the church of Christ, in anagoge as the heavenly city of God . . . , in the tropological sense as the human soul. . . . " (*Conferences*, 14.8)

In the later Middle Ages, this fourfold interpretation (the *Quadriga*) was expressed in a widely used rhyme first attested in the *Rotulus pugillaris*, an aid to preaching by the Dominican Augustine of Dacia (d. 1285).

> *Littera gesta docet; quid credas allegoria;*
> *moralitas quid agas; quid speres anagogia.*

> The letter teachs what happened;
>   allegory what to believe;
> morality how to behave;
>   anagogy what to hope for.

The Medieval Period

New impulses in Christian biblical studies were characteristic of the late eighth and most of the ninth centuries, the Carolingian period, and again beginning in the twelfth century. Jewish work on the scriptures during the early Middle Ages witnessed not only the completion of the work of the Masoretes but also extensive philological and commentary study of the Bible precipitated partially by the rise of the Karaites ("Scripturalists") in the eighth century and partially by the influence of Arabic grammarians and theologians/ philosophers.

The Bible was of course the central text in the medieval monasteries where its reading and exposition (*lectio divina*) nurtured and structured the life of the monks and centered around homiletical and meditative interests. The monastic focus was on the text as sacred page (*sacra pagina*) with its passive role toward the text through which God addressed the reader and hearer, shaping and forming the recipient in the search for divine wisdom and the beatific vision.

The most significant figure in Christian scholarship between late antiquity and the Carolingian era was the Venerable Bede (ca. 673–735). A native of Northumbria, Bede spent his life at the twin monasteries of Wearmouth and Jarrow where their founder Benedict Biscop (ca. 628–689) and his successor Coelfrid (d. 716) had accumulated an impressive library including Old Latin, Vulgate, and Latin-Greek texts as well as patristic and classical sources, and had produced manuscript copies of the Bible (e.g., *Codex Amiatinus*).

Bede wrote across a broad spectrum of subjects including commentaries on several OT and NT books (Gen 1–20; Samuel, Kings, Ezekiel, Ezra-Nehemiah, Song of Songs, Tobit, Luke, Acts, Revelation). His separate works on the tabernacle and the temple of Solomon texts represent the first time these materials were subjected to detailed commentary. Bede allegorized this material as prefiguring the church as the house of God. Bede apparently knew some Greek and utilized the *Laudian Acts*, a Latin-Greek bilingual text (see Gibson 1993, 22–23), in writing his retractions on his Acts commentary. His *De schematibus et tropis* was written to facilitate biblical studies and to offer help in reconciling difficulties in content. He described his primary work as follows:

> I have made it my business, for my own benefit and that of my brothers, to make brief extracts from the books of the venerable Fathers on Holy Scripture, or to add notes of my own to clarify their sense and interpretation.
>
> (*Ecclesiastical History* 5.24)

Although at points Bede displays exegetical originality and offers clarification of the fathers, he was heavily dependent upon patristic sources, drawing especially upon Ambrose, Augustine, Jerome, and Gregory the Great, whom he was the first to declare the four great doctors of the Latin church (in the prologue to his *In Lucae evangelium expositio*). His use of quotations of the fathers in running commentary anticipated the accumulation of patristic materials in the Carolingian period and subsequently.

The widespread reforms—political, religious, and educational—carried out by Pepin III (d. 768), Charlemagne (d. 814), and their successors greatly impacted biblical study. For the first time in church history, political and religious authorities cooperatively pushed for reform and improvement in the total educational enterprise. The Carolingian program, announced in the *Admonitio generalis* and *Epistola de litteris* called for the instruction of students in reading, chant, *computus*, and grammar with special attention to be given to the study and copying of the scriptures. Charlemagne recruited scholars widely to advise and supervise court and cathedral education life: the Italian Paul the Deacon (ca. 720–ca. 800), the Visigoth from Islamic Spain Theodulf of Orleans (ca. 750–821), and the Anglo-Saxon Alcuin (ca. 735–804).

Charlemagne's grandson Charles the Bald (d. 877) patronized the Irish philosopher John Scotus Erigena (ca. 810–ca. 877) who was made head of the palace school at Laon. An exceptional scholar of the Carolingian world, Erigena was noted for his knowledge of Greek and his translation of works by Maximus the Confessor, Gregory of Nyssa, and Pseudo-Dionysius. His direct approach to scripture, inquisitive mentality, and resort to the Greek text can be seen in his homily on the prologue and his commentary on the Gospel of John, his only exegetical works.

Several factors in the Carolingian renaissance are worthy of note. First, the production of texts of the Bible reached a new level. In addition to requisitioning books from elsewhere, especially Rome, Charlemagne expressed his desire for a grammatically and orthographically correct text of the Bible, just as his father Pepin had sponsored the production of a correct lectionary. St. Martin's monastery at Tours under Alcuin and his successors produced numerous biblical "pandects" and "gospelbooks," perhaps partially dependent upon the earlier work of Maurdramnus, abbot of Corbie (772–781). The pandects were massive folio lectern Bibles apparently based on a common text, although Alcuin and his disciples did not seek to produce a revision of the Latin text. Equally impressive are the texts produced under the direction of Theodulf with their smaller size and minuscular handwriting, obviously intended for scholarly use. Although Theodulfian manuscripts occasionally contain marginal variants, some in the psalms apparently based on the Hebrew, their texts are basically eclectic and all known copies show textual differences.

Second, aids to biblical study were also provided. Theodulf and Alcuin provided prefaces to the books of the Bible. Rabanus Maurus (780–856), in chapter 10 of book 2 of his handbook for clergy training (*De institutione clericorum libri tres*, ca. 819), provided a section outlining a program for biblical studies. Theodulfian Bibles included certain aids for biblical study: Isidore of Seville's *Chronica minora* containing an outline of world history to the seventh century C.E.; the second book of Eucherius of Lyon's *Instructiones* which offers explanations of various biblical names, places, and other facts and matters; Pseudo-Melito's *Clavis* which provided allegorical explanations and interpretations of biblical terminology; and Pseudo-Augustine's *Liber de divinis scripturis* which offered moral understanding of various biblical texts. These provided the interpreter with historical, allegorical, and tropological insights.

Third, Carolingian exegetes produced an exceptional number of biblical commentaries—the twenty or so volumes in J.-P. Migne's *Patrologia Latina* are far from exhaustive. Among the commentators were Alcuin, Rabanus Maurus, Paschasius Radbertus (ca. 790–865), Walafrid Strabo (ca. 808–849), Haimo (d. ca. 855), Heiric (ca. 841–ca. 885), Remigius of Auxerre (ca. 841–908), and John Scotus. For the first time in Christian history, there now existed full-fledged running commentaries on all the books of the Bible. No small role in this was played by Rabanus Maurus who produced commentaries on all the OT books except Baruch and on most of the NT. Two special factors should be noted about these commentaries. First, the Carolingian exegetes worked with an extraordinary veneration for the church fathers and treated their opinions about the meaning of biblical texts with what approached a dogmatic orthodoxy. Compilation, clarification, summation, and harmonization of patristic sources are thus typical of the commentaries. Which fathers are quoted often depended upon the availability of sources. Second, many of the commentaries were written at the requests and to meet the desires of particular patrons. Thus they display significant diversity in the handling of materials.

Two developments that were to culminate in the twelfth and thirteenth centuries have their roots in the Carolingian period. First, the glossing of biblical texts, a technique probably first used on classical secular texts, makes its appearance. Marginal notes, explanatory of the text and intentionally planned and executed by the scribe producing the biblical text, appear in manuscripts, especially of the psalter. Interlinear notations also appear in some manuscripts from the period but these were added by subsequent readers or later editors. The glossing of the Bible would reach its apex in the great *Glossa ordinaria* of the twelfth century. Second, although the use of questions and responses addressed to or arising out of the text was already present in the patristic period, this becomes more noticeable and begins to point to what would flourish in later scholastic exegesis.

Jewish biblical scholarship in the medieval period was both extensive and impressive. By the ninth century, the masoretes had completed their work of producing a pointed (voweled) text based on traditional pronunciation and interpretation. The masoretic text included not only vowel points but also accent markings and notes written in the margins, at the top and bottom of pages and at the end of books. These notes (the *masorah*) call attention to variant textual readings (the *kethiv* and *qere*), to the number of times an unusual word form occurs, and so on, as well as the number of words and letters in a book to aid in the correct copying of manuscripts. Three major schools of masoretes existed; the Tiberian and its system of vocalization and *masorah* became dominant.

The Muslim conquest of the Middle East in the seventh and eighth centuries brought many Jews into contact with an alien Semitic faith. Arabic-speaking Jews became conversant not only with the Islamic faith but also with Islamic science and philosophy where the thought of Aristotle was still known and influential. Jewish and Muslim dialogue over the Hebrew scriptures occurred and Hebrew studies were influenced by the work of Arabic grammarians.

In the mid-eighth century, a new Jewish sect arose, the Karaites ("scripturalists"), founded by Anan ben David. The Karaites argued that the Bible should be read and interpreted without reliance on, or even with the rejection of, the classical rabbinic interpretations. This "back to the Bible" movement argued for *sola scriptura* and sought to interpret scripture, without preconceived notions, though correlation of the Bible's contents.

Jewish response to these new impulses as well as a renewed interest in biblical studies in general found embodiment in the work of a number of outstanding scholars. Among the more philosophically oriented were Saadiah Gaon (882–942), Judah Halevi (ca. 1075–ca. 1140), and Moses Maimonides (1135–1204). Maimonides sought to reconcile biblical faith and human reason in a modified Aristotelianism. His *Guide for the Perplexed* (1190), which contains much biblical interpretation, was translated into Latin early in the thirteenth century and greatly influenced later Christian thought especially that of Albertus Magnus (ca. 1200–1280) and Thomas Aquinas (ca. 1225–1274).

Jewish biblical scholarship was especially cultivated in two regions, Spain-Provence and northern France (see Sarna 1971). The most famous French exegete was Rashi (Rabbi Solomon ben Isaac, 1040–1105) who drew upon rabbinic tradition but sought to expound the literal (*peshat*) meaning of the text. His commentaries remind one, at least in form, of the glossing of the Bible carried out by contemporary Christians.

Another important Jewish exegete was the Spanish Abraham Ibn Ezra (1089–1164) who travelled and wrote widely. In the introduction to his work *Sefer Ha-Yashar* (*The Book of the Upright*), a commentary on the Pentateuch, Ibn Ezra described five different types of Jewish biblical interpretation. These are widely assumed to reflect the various approaches to scripture taken by Jews in medieval times, but described of course from Ibn Ezra's distinctive perspective (see Jacobs 1973, from whom the translation is derived).

> The first method is lengthy and diffuse, remote from the souls of the men of our generation. If we use the illustration of a circle and place the truth at its center point, then this method can only be compared to the periphery of the circle, which goes round and round only to return to the place where it began. . . . Rabbi Saadiah, Gaon of the Exile, trod this path. . . . The same applies to Rabbi Samuel ben Hofni [d. 1034].

According to Ibn Ezra, these commentators interspersed their discussion of the text with long, extraneous treatises and digressions on all sorts of subjects only tangentially related to the text.

> The second method is that chosen by the distorters, albeit they are Jews. They imagine that they have reached the very point of the circle but in reality they have not the faintest idea where it is to be found. This is the way of the Sadducees [the Karaites] such as Anan [and others] . . . and the way of whoever does not believe in the words of the bearers of religious traditions. . . . Each of these men interprets the Bible as he sees fit and this applies even to the commandments and the laws. . . . How can anyone rely on their opinions . . . because you will not find a single precept explained fully in the Torah itself.

Here he argues against those who believe that scripture can interpret scripture adequately without recourse to traditional views.

> The third view is a way of darkness and obscurity. It lies entirely beyond the circle. This is the method of those who invent mysterious interpretations for all the passages in Scripture. It is their belief that the Torah and the precepts are riddles. . . . The words of the Torah are never less than straightforward. In one thing only are these people right. That is that every precept of the Torah, whether great or small, must be measured in the balance of the heart into which God has implanted some of His wisdom. Therefore if there appears something in the Torah which seems to contradict reason or to refute the evidence of our senses then here one should seek for the solution in a figurative interpretation. For reason is the foundation of everything. . . . the figurative meaning is evident on the surface.

Here Ibn Ezra is condemning those who read the text allegorically. Perhaps he would have included in this group the later qabbalists (cabalists).

> The fourth method is near to the point. A whole group of commentators have followed it. This is the method pursued by the sages . . . who are not over-much concerned with a balanced view but rely on the homiletical method.

Ibn Ezra describes those who engage in rabbinic exegesis of a midrashic-homiletical nature especially adaptable to preaching.

> My commentary is based on the fifth method. . . . First I shall investigate with all the power at my command the grammatical form of each word and then I shall explain its meaning to the best of my ability. . . . Also a correct interpretation does not involve any textual emendation. The Targum of the Torah in Aramaic is accurate. The authority of this work explains every difficulty. Even though he is addicted to the Midrashim we recognize that even more was he devoted to the true sense of the Hebrew language. . . . The plain meaning of a verse is not affected by its Midrashic interpretation for there are seventy faces to the Torah. . . . the bearers of the tradition, all of whom were righteous men, . . . with all the strength we have we must rely on the accuracy of what they say.

Ibn Ezra represents an approach that stresses the plain/literal sense which is to be modified only where such a reading would directly clash with the received tradition. For him, scripture is not a homogeneous whole consistent throughout. Thus one must use reason as well as the wisdom of the past sages, that is, grammatical focus, the cumulative tradition, and an intellectual independence of judgment must be combined.

Beginning in the twelfth century, new developments and emphases became characteristic of Christian biblical interpretation: an increased concern for the accuracy and authenticity of the text, an awakened interest in the original languages of the biblical text, a greater focus on the literal or historical reading of texts with a concomitant concern with the human authors, new developments in the manufacture of biblical texts, the production of new tools for study and employment of the biblical text, the introduction of scholastic methodology into the commentary tradition, as well as the development of new theological emphases.

Some of the reasons behind these new developments in Christian biblical study were similar to those that influenced forms of medieval Jewish interpretation. Renewed contact with ancient Greek philosophy, especially that of Aristotle, growth in the strength and number of monastic and cathedral schools and eventually the founding of universities, a greater utilization of the liberal arts (the *trivium*—grammar, rhetoric, and logic; and the *quadrivium*—arithmethic, geometry, astronomy, and music) in biblical study, the presence of heretics (e.g., the Cathari and the Waldenses), and other factors made their contribution.

Throughout the early Middle Ages, the Latin text produced by Jerome had been subject to various corruptions. Harmonizations with the Old Latin and changes and additions to bring the text into line with patristic readings had produced a very fluid and eclectic text. The Psalter, for example, circulated in various forms—the Old Roman and variations thereof, the Gallican, and Jerome's final revision (the *Hebraica veritas*) which was the least popular of all. Alcuin's and Theodulf's textual work was not an attempt to produce a critically corrected text but it did aid somewhat in creating a stabler text. John Scotus had compared the Latin text of John with Greek exemplars and some evidence exists for similar work on the psalter.

A new stage of textual comparison and revision is evident beginning in the early twelfth century. Odo (ca. 879–942) while abbot at St. Martin's prepared a quadruple psalter with the transliterated Greek paralleling the three Latin versions. The most thorough attempt to correct the Latin text was associated with the Cistercians and especially the work of Stephen Harding (d. 1134) early in the twelfth century and of Nicholas Manjacoria of Rome about mid-century. Both operated on the assumption that the fuller text is not necessarily the more original. Harding deleted material not found in the Hebrew. Subsequently in the thirteenth century various *correctoria* were circulated by the Dominicans and Franciscans.

Very few scholars in the Middle Ages were competent in Hebrew and Greek. Beginning in the twelfth century, interest in if not a thorough knowledge of Hebrew became rather widespread, more so than for Greek. Abelard (1079–1142) recommended to the nuns of the convent of the Paraclete that they study Hebrew, Greek, and Latin. The presence of Hebrew-speaking Jewish communities in many of the large medieval cities allowed Christians the opportunity for contact, conversation, and even instruction with Jews over the interpretation of the Hebrew scriptures. The existence of Hebrew-Latin psalters with commentary and the exegetical work on the psalms by Herbert of Bosham (fl. ca. 1160–1186) illustrate that some progress was made in this area. Robert Grosseteste (ca. 1175–1253) mastered Greek sufficently to translate numerous works into Latin including the *Testaments of the Twelve Patriarchs* and utilized the Greek texts of both testaments in his commentaries. The Council of Vienne (1311–1312) decreed, primarily to facilitate missionary activity and through the influence of Raymond Lull (ca. 1233–ca. 1315), that the study of Oriental languages—Arabic, Hebrew, and Aramaic—be established at the universities in Paris, Oxford, Salamanca, Bologna, and at the Roman court. Although the idea was supported by Popes Clement V (1305–1314) and John XXII (1316–1334), the goal of trilingual education was not realized until the sixteenth century.

A greater concern with the literal meaning of texts and the placing of texts within an original historical frame of reference become more noticeable in the literature of the twelfth and thirteenth centuries. A number of factors perhaps contributed to this development. The use of the *Quadriga* had of course always recognized the existence of the historical or literal sense or level in scripture and had certainly not ignored this completely. Paradoxically, at the same time that some scholars focused on the literal sense the allegorical reading was disseminated more widely than ever in lay circles through the preaching of the Domin-

ican and Franciscan mendicants, the appearance and widespread usage of preaching manuals (*Artes praedicandi*), and various forms of the *Bible moralisée* (probably of Parisian origin, early thirteenth century) and the so-called *Biblia pauperum* (probably of South German origin, mid-thirteenth century, one of the earliest books printed, ca. 1460).

A certain weariness with some allegorical readings becomes evident. Although no exact system of allegorical correspondences between OT events and characters and Christian figures and beliefs ever became standard, such allegorical reading as the widespread association of David with Christ, Bathsheba with the church, and Uriah with the devil was hard to justify for some interpreters. Alain of Lille (1120–1202) referred to the Bible as a "nose of wax," that is, something that could be shaped and used to fit one's conceptions and beliefs through allegory (this image appears frequently in the late sixteenth and seventeenth centuries).

Two clearly evident factors contributed to the focus on the literal. One was the increased contact between Jews and Christians. Acquaintance with Jews and Jewish interpretation with its concern for the *peshat* (plain or literate) level of reading and a subdued messianic emphasis forced Christians to recognize a more straightforward and less spiritual form of interpretation of the Hebrew scriptures than was traditional. The second factor was the introduction of Aristotelian thought into the mainstream of Christian scholarship in the late twelfth and thirteenth centuries. Aristotle's works on logic and dialetic with their emphasis on the univocality of language resisted the appeal to secondary levels of meaning in statements and argumentation. Further, the Aristotelian theory of causality with its concern for the analysis of efficient, material, formal, and final causes was highly significant. The adoption of this theory of causality led to a new form of prologue (*accesus*) in biblical commentaries and also to a sharper focus on the human author (the efficient cause) and the writer's method of treatment and organization of the material (the material cause; see Minnis 1988, 28–159; Minnis-Scott 1991, 197–276).

Hugh (ca. 1096–1141) and others associated with the abbey of St. Victor in Paris laid stress on the importance of history and the literal. Hugh's *Didascalicon* (late 1120s), a textbook on the arts and learning disciplines, in books 4–6, lays out a program of biblical study discussing such matters as the order in which biblical books should be read, how to read, the canon, and so forth, and throughout stresses the importance of the historical/literal level of meaning as an indispens-able foundation for interpretation. His pupil Andrew (d. 1175), more familiar with Jewish scholarship than Hugh, laid greater stress on the historical meaning, saw Jewish exegesis as reflective of the literal sense, and generally refused to offer a Christological/ecclesio-logical reading of OT texts. For example, he understood Isa 7:14 as referring to the prophet's wife (as did Rashi).

Others than the Victorines focused on the literal reading. Peter Lombard (ca. 1100–1160) exegeted the Pauline epistles in a literal fashion, often introducing historical considerations about Paul and his times into the discussion so as to relativize some of Paul's posi-tions (see Colish 1994; in his psalms exegesis, Lom-bard was more traditional). William of Auvergne (ca. 1180–1249) wrote on OT law and sought to understood the prescriptions in terms of their original function.

By the time of Aquinas (ca. 1225–1274), the nature and role of the literal sense of scripture had become a significant issue of controversy. In answering Andrew, Richard of St. Victor (d. 1173) had argued in *De Em-manuele* that the literal meaning of Isa 7:14 is its ref-erence to the Virgin Mary. In the opening sections of his *Summa theologiae* (Ia.1,9–10), Aquinas restates some of Augustine's positions: that words can signify things (the literal emphasis) and that these things can then signify other things (the spiritual emphasis) and that theological arguments and conclusions should be based on the literal.

> [A]ll meanings are based on one, namely, the literal sense. . . . nothing necessary for faith is contained under the spiritual sense that is not also conveyed through the literal sense elsewhere.

Aquinas argued that the literal sense is what the author intended but he also held that God is the ultimate au-thor of scripture which allowed for an open-endedness in interpretation so long as conclusions remained with-in the realm of traditional faith. Aquinas continued to find both literal and figurative meanings in OT texts, es-pecially those concerning ceremonial laws:

> The ceremonies of the Old Law had two causes: one, literal, in that they were directed to the wor-ship of God; the other, figurative, as directed to the prefiguring of Christ. . . . All the sacrifices of the Old Law were offered to prefigure this [Christ's] unique and principal sacrifice, the perfect prefig-ured by the imperfect. . . . And since the reason for the figure is to be drawn from what it figures, the

reasons for the figurative sacrifices of the Old Law are to be drawn from the true sacrifice of Christ. (*Summa theologiae* Ia2ae.102,3)

Since Christian interpreters were not content to read the OT without reference to its prefiguration, allegoriza-tion, and prophecy of the New, exegetes began to speak of a double literal meaning or a double inten-tionality of the author. In his psalms commentary based on Jerome's *Hebraica veritas* (written ca. 1317–1320) Nicholas Trevet spoke of the literal sense as the author's primary intention and the spiritual/mystical as a secondary intention. William of Nottingham (active at Oxford ca. 1312–1336) wrote of a double literal sense, the proper literal sense derived from the initial signification and a figurative literal sense derived from the metaphorical or secondary signification.

Nicholas of Lyra (ca. 1270–1349), knowledgeable in Hebrew and Jewish and Christian exegesis, and the most literalistic and ultimately the most influential of medieval exegetes, hypothesized a *duplex sensus litter-alis* for some texts, namely a reference to OT times and to NT realities. Nicholas produced a *Postilla litteralis* (with two prologues on hermenuetics, ca. 1322–1331) on the entire Bible (the first commentary to be printed, in 1471–1472, five volumes, and running into more than one hundred different editions and printings by 1600). Although Nicholas stressed the historical/literal sense and made critical observations throughout his work, he placed many interpretations into the literal category which had previously been understood as spiritual readings and also still held the view that much of the OT was literally Christological or ecclesio-logical in its signification. (Nicholas also wrote a spiritual commentary on scripture, the *Postilla moralis*, 1339.) The controversy over the nature and role of the literal sense of scripture was to continue on into the reformation period and later (see Froehlich 1977).

Several new developments in Bible production oc-curred in the medieval period (see Gibson 1993 and Gameson 1994). Generally, single biblical manuscripts contained only a portion of the text, most frequently divided according to the nine-volume pattern recom-mended by Cassiodorus (*Institutiones divinarum et saecularium Litterarum* I.11.3): Genesis-Ruth, six books of the Kings (1-2 Samuel, 1-2 Kings, 1-2 Chronicles), prophets, Psalms, wisdom literature, lives of great men and women (Job, Tobit, Esther, Judith, 1-2 Maccabees, Ezra-Nehemiah), four gospels, Pauline and Catholic epistles, and Acts and Revelation.

Few Latin pandects (*complete* Bibles, like the *Codex Amiatinus* from the eighth century) have survived from or were produced during the early Middle Ages. Following the productions of Alcuin and Theodulf, intended for lectern use, large display bibles were produced, especially in the late eleventh and early twelfth centuries, generally in two volumes and lavishly illustrated.

With the founding of the universities and the development of scholarly work on the scriptures, new efforts were made to produce a scholarly reference Bible. The result, to which many scholars and schools contributed, especially that at Laon, was the *Glossa ordinaria* (in nine or ten volumes) with carefully produced marginal and interlinear glosses derived primarily from the Latin fathers (see Gibson-Froehlich 1992). The *Glossa* reached its classic form in the second quarter of the twelfth century and remained rather stable thereafter. A product of the monastic scriptorium, the *Glossa* was intended for institutional libraries to be consulted and cribbed by the scholar. Manuscripts of the *Glossa* were produced for more than a century and the work was widely used until the shift to the use of Greek and Hebrew rendered it rather obsolete (no manuscript form in which all the volumes match in script and decoration is extant; the work was first printed in 1480–1481 and about a dozen different editions were produced by 1617). Various other glossed portions of the Bible were produced, the so-called *Magna glossatura* by Peter Lombard on the Psalms and the Pauline epistles being preferred over the *Glossa ordinaria*.

In the early thirteenth century, the production of biblical texts moved out of the monastic scriptorium and into secular workshops. The demands associated with higher education and university life created a sizeable market. In Paris and northern France, the so-called "Paris Bible" received wide circulation. Although varying somewhat in text and illumination, these one-volume Bibles utilized a thin parchment page and a small script. Placing all the books in a single volume necessitated a standard order and grouping for the biblical books. The Paris edition made the personal ownership of the Bible available to a wide audience—wealthy bourgeoisie, university teachers, and members of religious orders. A small or pocket-size, one-volume edition of the Bible, less than seven inches high, often containing a summary of the Christian faith expressed in selected biblical texts in an appendix, also appeared in the thirteenth century.

These were probably used by mendicant preachers and others defending and proclaiming the faith to heretics and outsiders.

New tools, in facts-reference works, for biblical study and use, were introduced in the late twelfth and thirteenth centuries. These were intended as guides for locating information rather than works for continuous reading. Several forms of biblical *distinctiones* were produced. This was a form of dictionary that listed various theological terms and subdivisions within the thought asssociated with the term. The term was provided with various supporting and illustrative biblical texts. These were of great aid to the preacher in preparing sermons.

A verbal concordance to the Bible, arranged alphabetically, was produced under the direction of Hugh of St. Cher (ca. 1195–1263) by the Dominicans at St. Jacques in Paris. This concordance used the chapter divisions current in Paris at the time, generally attributed to Stephen Langton (d. 1228). The enumeration of the chapters used Arabic numbers, adopted in Europe in the twelfth century. Since the enumeration of verses was not yet in use, chapters were divided into lettered sections (a-g). The concordance gave only the biblical references for words; later English Dominicans revised the work providing a sentence of context where terms occurred, thus giving the user the verbal contexts. The latter work was overly bulky, and late in the century a version with shorter contexts and with short chapters divided into only four units (a–d) was produced. At any rate, an indispensable tool for biblical study, the concordance, had come into being.

(Division of the NT into the verse divisions used today dates from 1551, when the printer-scholar Robert Estienne (Stephanus) published a Greek-Latin edition of the NT. The masoretic text of the Hebrew Bible was already divided into verses but not numbered. Estienne's 1555 Latin edition of the Bible, including the Apocrypha, utilized verse enumeration throughout. Rabbi Isaac Nathan (ca. 1440) had earlier produced a Hebrew concordance that used numbered verses for the masoretic text.)

A further tool that should be noted is the *Historia scholastica* of Peter Comestor (d. ca. 1179). This was a presentation of history from creation to the end of the Book of Acts that drew upon both biblical and patristic-classical sources. The work was one of the most widely used texts in medieval times. Comestor's work in a French translation was interlaced with the text of a French Bible to produce the *Bible historiale complétée* early in the fourteenth century. This work was also widely used and circulated.

The twelfth and thirteenth centuries saw the triumph of the scholastic approach to biblical studies and theology. The heavy utilization of logic and dialectic in theology by Abelard (1079–1142) and others led to a treatment of the scripture as *sacra doctrina*. Biblical expositors utilized the *quaestio* to address the text, which was then interrogated along the lines of the questions asked. Rather than merely interacting with the text, the scholastic method tended to subject the text to a series of inquisitions. This method of examining the text remained in use for years, reaching its apex in the enormous exegetical output of the Spanish Alfonso Tostado (ca. 1400–1455). (The approach is even found in modified form in Protestant exegetical works of the seventeenth century.)

Although most medieval theologians viewed their work as exposition of biblical faith, some like John Wyclif (ca. 1330–1384) and John Huss (ca. 1372–1415), wished to reform the church and the orders and did so by stressing biblical faith and life as the ideal. In his *De veritate Sacrae Scripturae*, *De ecclesia*, *De protestate Papae* (1377–1378), and *De apostasis* (ca. 1382), Wyclif maintained that the scriptures were the eternal exemplar of the Christian faith and should be used as the sole criterion of faith. He also concluded that the papacy and monastic orders were either ill-founded or without any foundation in scripture. Both Wyclif (and his followers, the Lollards) and Huss were persecuted by the church. Wyclif's followers rendered the Latin Bible into English. Wyclif's writings had great influence on Huss.

Renaissance and Reformation

New developments in the attitude toward and in the study of ancient texts, including the Bible, arose in the fifteenth century. These new developments, with many links to earlier attitudes, were part of what has been called the Renaissance or early humanism. Although this movement was complex and involved many areas of life, the focus here is on some literary dimensions, namely, the concern for and interpretation of ancient texts. Three general characteristics should be noted.

First, throughout the century, concerted efforts were made to recover texts from antiquity. This search for manuscripts was concerned not only to recover texts of works unavailable (and even unknown) at the time but also to recover source texts older than those from which contemporary editions were made.

Second, there was a desire to study ancient texts, including both the Bible and the church fathers, in their original form and language. This desire, even stated as a requirement, had been stressed by many important figures in the Middle Ages such as Roger Bacon (ca. 1220–1292) who made harsh criticisms of the contemporary Latin editions of the Bible and their deviations from the originals. The issue was now taken far more seriously and viewed not just as an idealized goal but as a potential that could be realized. Instruction in Greek was offered at Florence before the beginning of the fifteenth century and an increasing number of Christian scholars were learning Hebrew from Jews or Jewish converts (this of course became more difficult with the expulsion of Jews from most European countries).

Third, there was a new interest in encountering classical writings, including biblical and patristic texts, directly rather than reading than through a filter of glosses and comments. Such study of texts involved, on the practical level, a bypassing of tradition and traditional interpretations. Interpretation of a text had to start from the original and not from a translation. The characteristic slogan of the Renaissance, *Ad fontes*, "to the sources," expressed the view that later translations and commentaries were streams that flowed from the springs (sources) but that the purest waters were at the sources.

It was widely assumed at the time that the days when ancient texts were produced were better and more simplistic than the present. This produced a nostalgia about the past and the desire to "reproduce" classical times and the primitive church in the present as well as a critical attitude toward contemporary conditions and thought.

The growing interest in texts and their interpretation coincided with the development of the printing press utilizing movable type. In 1454(?), Johannes Gutenberg (ca. 1390–1468) printed a Latin Bible inaugurating the age of printed books. The printing press proved to be a major change agent in society and a great catalyst in biblical study (see Eisenstein 1979). The impact of the printing press was enormous.

First, it provided for a more rapid production of texts than previous manuscript workshops, in a standardized form, and at less cost. Second, availability of books and a reduced price meant that texts were distributed more widely. A teacher's influence, in the form of published lectures, could suddenly become widely known. Estimates suggest that Luther's writings sold more than 300,000 copies between 1517 and 1520. Third, private ownership of a book, especially of the Bible, allowed one to read the text and interact directly and subjectively with its content. Prior to the printing press, it is difficult to imagine Christianity as a religion of the book. Individualistic and subjective reading of the text embodied the possibility of practically everyone becoming their own interpreter. Fourth, printers and publishing houses were not only to encourage writing and even the creation of controversy so as to increase sales but also to function as clearing houses and educational institutions supporting research and writing and aiding in the collection and editing of texts. They became centers and gathering places for scholars. Printers themselves were often scholars and belonged to what came to be called the Republic of Letters (see below).

Two examples from the middle of the fifteenth century illustrate the nature and impact of textual work in biblical study. Giannozzo Manetti (1396–1459), eventually in the service of the king of Naples, put together a library of Jewish manuscripts, which later formed a part of the Vatican collection. Included were Hebrew manuscripts of the OT and works and commentaries by Rashi, Ibn Ezra, David Kimchi, and Gersonides. Manetti knew both Hebrew and Greek and prepared a new translation of the Psalter and the NT (neither ever published). He placed his Latin translation of the Psalter in parallel columns to the Gallican and *Hebraica veritas* of Jerome. His goal was to produce an accurate translation of the Bible, over against the widely used Latin Vulgate. Although his work was not published, Manetti illustrates the type of activity beginning to be undertaken.

Italian philologist Lorenzo Valla (1407–1457) compared several Greek manuscripts with the contemporary Latin translation and offered numerous instances where the Latin text did not adequately reflect the Greek. Valla's *Collatio Novi Testamenti* (1442/1443) was later, in his 1453/1457 rewrite, to be highly influential upon NT studies and especially upon Erasmus, who discovered a copy of Valla's manuscript in 1504 and edited and published it in 1505 as *Adnotationes in Novum Testamentum*. Not only was Valla a textual critic of the Latin Bible, but also a critic of ecclesiastical documents; his work, utilizing textual-historical criticism, on the so-called *Donation* of Constantine proved this document to be inauthentic. Valla criticized theologians who based their arguments on a Latin translation of the NT. If the Vulgate translation was faulty so might be theological conclusions based upon it.

In the last half of the fifteenth century, numerous publications made available biblical texts in Hebrew and Greek, but initially almost exclusively of the OT. The Hebrew psalter (with David Kimchi's commentary) was published in 1477, the Pentateuch (with the Targum Onkelos [see RABBINIC LITERATURE] and Rashi's commentary) in 1482, the prophets in 1485–1486, and the writings in 1486–1487. The complete Hebrew Bible appeared in 1488. In September 1481, Johannes Crastonus published the psalms in Greek with his Latin translation in parallel columns (the first biblical polyglot—actually a diglot—to be printed). In the preface Crastonus concluded that the text of Jerome's translation could no longer be established since the Vulgate text had become so contaminated.

Various forms of polyglots appeared early in the sixteenth century. Jacques Lefèvre (ca. 1455–1536) published *Quincuplex Psalterium* (1509), giving the psalms in five versions, and Agostino Giustiniani (1470–1536) published *Psalterium octaplum* (1516) which incorporated Hebrew, Greek, Arabic, and Aramaic versions of the psalms. (According to Giustiniani, Columbus's discovery of the New World fulfilled the prophecy of Ps 19:4.)

Pride of place as a scholarly tool was the *Complutensian Polyglot*, conceived in 1502 by Cardinal Ximenes de Cisneros (1436–1517) who had founded the trilingual university at Alcalà (Complutum) in Spain. Printed in 1514–1517, although not released until the early 1520s, the six volumes of this work contain the first printed edition of the Greek NT (completed 10 January 1514 but not published until 22 March 1520). For the Pentateuch, the Latin text is printed in a center column with the Greek (with interlinear translation) and the Hebrew versions on either side (see Gibson 1993, 84–85; in the preface Ximenes wrote: "Like Christ between two thieves"). Hebrew words in the text are coded to the Latin text and word roots are provided in the margin. The Aramaic targum with Latin translation is given at the bottom of the page (see Gibson 1993, 84–85). In addition to the text, the volumes offered various guides, word lists, and so forth, including the first Greek-Latin glossary of the NT. The value of the polyglot was not the aids it offered, mostly extracts and summaries of medieval material, but the parallel texts that allowed for comparative reading.

The humanist Desiderius Erasmus (ca. 1469–1536) was the first to publish an edition of the Greek NT

(*Novum instrumentum omne*, March 1516), but it was rushed to market and was not based on a very broad manuscript base.

Tools for learning the languages and using the Hebrew and Greek texts of the Bible were produced. Lascaris's Greek grammar appeared in 1495, to be followed by those of Theodore of Gaza (translated by Erasmus) in 1516, Melanchthon in 1518, Budé in 1520. The first significant Hebrew grammar published in Latin was Conrad Pellican's *De modo legendi et intelligendi Hebraeum* (1503 or 1504). This limited grammar was followed by Johannes Reuchlin's *De rudimentis Hebraicis* (1506), basically a translation and rewrite of David Kimchi's medieval grammar. The bulk of Reuchlin's work (pp. 32–451) consisted of a Hebrew-Latin dictionary. Reuchlin was recognized as one of the greatest humanistic scholars of his day and is remembered especially for his fight against elements in the church that sought the destruction of Jewish works, especially the Talmud.

The production of educational and scholarly tools for study of the Hebrew and Greek Bible texts was paralleled by efforts to produce reliable texts for the writings of the church fathers, which led to the recognition that many works had been falsely attributed.

Scholars such as Erasmus, Reuchlin, and Lefèvre, working with the new humanistic tools, produced new approaches to exegesis that were less dependent upon traditional views and were simultaneously the produce of direct engagement with the text in its original languages. Erasmus was highly critical of the scholastic method and of many traditions and practices of the church. These movements, it should be noted, had their origin and early development within Catholicism itself before the beginning of the Protestant Reformation.

The Protestant Reformation was engendered in the midst of this exciting and exhilarating period of academic and educational developments. The catalysts for the Reformation were indeed numerous: the need of the church for reform in both theology and practice; nostalgia for the idealized early days of Christendom; rising nationalism and regional consciousness; the inclinations and strengths of particular individuals; the recovery of Augustine's theology; and so forth. Certainly the new methods of Renaissance scholarship and the new approaches to the scriptures played a significant role. Luther welcomed the new "sacred philology." Most of the early reformers utilized and followed, to a lesser or greater degree, the same philological and linguistic tools and methods as their humanistic colleagues who remained within Roman Catholicism.

Certain positions were shared by practically all Protestants. (1) The church had drastically gone wrong at some point in its earlier history and departed from the original purity of the church reflected in the NT. They differed as to when this deviation from the true path had occurred. The magisterial reformation (Lutheranism and Calvinism) placed it after the early major church confessions. Others, like the Socinians and the more radical groups, placed the decay prior to the major church confessions, even at the close of NT history. Protestants were unanimously agreed that the Bible was the primary instrument for reforming the church and for returning it to its original purity.

(2) Theology and the church's institutional life should be based on the principle of *sola scriptura*. All theological doctrines and church and Christian practices should be rooted in and sanctioned by scripture, with scripture serving as its own interpreter, that is, interpretation of difficult texts should be done in light of other, clearer texts.

(3) The authoritative form of the Bible should be the Hebrew and Greek, with translations in the vernacular to be based on the original languages. (Many vernacular translations in various languages existed prior to the Reformation without church disapproval and often with church sanction, but these were made from the Latin.)

(4) People should have the right to read and interpret the Bible on their own. The individual's prerogative to interpret scripture was often played off against the authority of the pope and church councils.

(5) Most protestant reformers denied the multilevel reading of scripture and emphasized the literal sense, but the latter they generally understood as having a more Christological and ecclesiological dimension than would later be the case. The perspectives on the OT found in the writings of the NT were generally considered indicative of a literal reading. Many reformers, even Luther himself, continued to use allegorical and tropological readings and interpretations in making the connection between texts, especially those of the OT, and contemporary life and situations. This was also true of post-Reformation exegetes, who often spoke of the "spiritual" dimension of a text. The use of analogy between the text and the contemporary situation tended to become more common with the passage of time.

(6) The individual reader of the scriptures should personally encounter and engage the scriptures in an

existential manner, being directed by the Holy Spirit who had inspired the biblical writings in their original encodement. To some extent, this parallels the older monastic attitude toward the Bible as *sacra pagina*.

(7) The central doctrine of the Christian faith and the central thrust of the biblical materials were understood as "justification by faith" through the gracious act of God in Jesus Christ. Thus Luther distinguished among biblical writings, depending upon how much emphasis a certain work placed on Christology and justification by faith. For Luther, there was clearly "a canon within the canon" with Romans, Galatians, and the Gospel of John being the most favored NT books.

The sixteenth century witnessed an enormous output of biblical commentaries of diverse sorts (see Williams 1988). Martin Luther (1483–1546) and John Calvin (1509–64) were the most productive in this area. Luther, trained in medieval theology, wrote commentaries that expounded and narrated the faith, often with a great deal of anti-Catholicism incorporated. Calvin, educated in the humanistic disciplines, gave greater attention to the straightforward sense of the text and wrote commentaries with a distinctive modern cast (Calvin's first published work was a commentary on Seneca's *De Clementia* [1532] which he hoped would gain him a reputation over against Erasmus).

The humanist Erasmus worked with a somewhat reduced version of Christianity: he was interested in the *philosophia Christi* and in the Bible as *sacra littera*. His paraphrases of biblical texts sought to make the NT available in an easily digestible form (in spite of his emphasis on educating the common person, Erasmus wrote in Latin, hardly the language of everyday discourse).

Catholics such as Cardinal Cajetan (Thomas de Vio, 1469–1534), one of Luther's inquisitors in 1518, wrote numerous commentaries stressing the literal sense of scripture and seeking to show that the NT supported Catholic positions.

Protestants translated the scriptures into numerous vernacular languages, basing their translations on the Hebrew and Greek. Latin translations from the original languages were also popular among Protestant scholars and remained in use until well into the eighteenth century. After the Reformation was underway and especially after the Council of Trent, Catholics took a dim view of vernacular translations with their accompanying potential for private interpretation. An official edition of the Vulgate was issued under the authority of Pope Sixtus V in 1590 and reissued with more than 3,000 corrections as the Clementine edition by Pope Clement VIII in 1592.

Controversy over the nature, role, and interpretation of the Bible was a common staple of the sixteenth century. There was not only a Protestant-Catholic debate but also internal struggles within Protestantism. Luther, followed by the other reformers, accepted as the canonical OT only those writings found in the Hebrew Bible (but not in its order). Luther's decision was based partially on the fact that some doctrines (e.g., prayers and offerings for the dead) were taught in some of the deleted books with which he did not agree. To justify the shorter canon, the reformers appealed to the authority of Jerome (and some medieval writers) who had spoken of OT books not in the Hebrew canon as "Apocrypha."

The first defense and explanation of the Protestant canon was written by Andreas Bodenstein (Carlstadt): *De canonicis scripturis libellus* (August 1520; followed by a slimmer volume, *Welche Bucher biblisch seint*, November 1520). Carlstadt placed the books of the Bible into three categories, placing Hebrews, James, 2 Peter, 2-3 John, Jude, and Revelation (the *antilegomena* of Eusebius of Caesarea) into the third category and the last chapter of Mark and the Letter to the Laodiceans in the Apocrypha (he also argued on literary grounds that Moses could not have written the entire Pentateuch, a view already hinted at by Ibn Ezra). This subordination of certain previously contested NT writings was shared by many Lutheran reformers. Niels Hemmingsen (1513–1600) wrote in 1555:

> All these books of the New Testament are in the canon except Second Peter, Second and Third John, the Epistles of James and Jude along with the Apocalypse. Some also place the Epistle to the Hebrews outside the canon. (Steinmetz 1990, 188)

Books could thus be in the Bible without being canonical. The issue of the disputed books as well as Luther's attitude toward James ("a right strawy epistle") probably explains why no early Lutheran confession contains a separate section on the scripture with an enumeration of the biblical books. The fourth session of the Council of Trent (8 April 1546) set the Catholic OT canon once and for all by enumerating the books (including Tobit, Judith, Wisdom of Solomon, Ecclesiasticus, Baruch, and 1-2 Maccabees) and placing under anathema those who did not accept this list. Later, the Jewish convert to Christianity Sixtus Senensis coined the phrase "deuterocanonical" (secondarily canonical) with reference to these works (*Bibliotheca sancta*, 1566); this term has been widely used, especially in recent years.

Catholics and Protestants differed over who had the right to interpret scripture with the latter initially arguing for every person (at least those trained in the original languages). Catholics argued, prophetically, that such a broad endowment of the right to interpret would produce a plethora of interpretations and create divisiveness in the church. Again the Council of Trent declared authoritatively:

> In matters of faith and morals pertaining to the edification of the Christian doctrine, no one, relying on his own judgment and distorting the Sacred Scriptures according to his own conceptions, shall dare to interpret them contrary to that sense which Holy Mother Church, to whom it belongs to judge their true sense and meaning, has held and does hold, or even contrary to the unanimous agreement of the Fathers, even though such interpretations should never at any time be published.

To enforce its decree, the council declared that all publications "dealing with sacred matters" must be approved by the church (the basis for the later *Index librorum prohibitorum*).

The debate over "Holy Writ versus Holy Church" which had already troubled theological waters in the fourteenth and fifteenth centuries sharply divided Catholics and Protestants. Protestants argued for the priority of scripture and Catholics for the priority of the church and its tradition. Catholics argued that before any NT book was written, the church already was and that before the NT was written the faith was carried through the traditions and the oral proclamation. After lengthy debate, the Council of Trent denied the principle of *sola scriptura* but refused to declare that revelation comes partly through scripture and partly through tradition, opting instead for

> Truths and rules are contained in the written books and in the unwritten traditions which, received by the Apostles from the mouth of Christ Himself or from the Apostles themselves, the Holy Spirit dictating, have come down to us, transmitted as it were from hand to hand.

Catholics thus acknowledged that what is authoritative is the text and the faith which has grown up around the text, a view similar to that of Judaism and a position operative in practice for most "book religions."

It is interesting to note that Protestants soon created their own "tradition" by which the scriptures were to be read, namely, confessions of faith and theological treatises. In the preface to his *Institutes* (first edition, 1536), Calvin declared he had written the work so the reader of the Bible would know what to look for as one read. Most early English translations of the Bible were issued with extensive marginal notes, prologues, and summaries to guide the reader. Those in Tyndale's translation of the NT and Pentateuch (1520s) and in the complete Geneva Bible (1560) were strongly theological and highly influential. At the direction of King James, the authorized version of 1611 contained only marginal notes related to text and translation.

Protestants argued that the Bible was sufficiently clear to be understood by the normal reader (presumably in a vernacular translation) at least on all matters necessary for salvation. Many Catholics argued against this view and declared that the difficulties in understanding the scriptures should drive one to fideism and acceptance of the faith on the basis of the church's authority.

Protestants argued for the authority of the Hebrew and Greek forms of the scriptures but Catholics defended the Vulgate. The Council of Trent declared that

> the old Latin Vulgate edition, which has been approved for use in the Church for so many centuries, is to be taken as authentic in public lectures, disputations, and expositions, and that no one should dare or presume to reject it under any circumstances whatsoever.

Disputes within Protestantism over biblical interpretation occured early on in the movement. The mainline European reform movements could not agree on the nature of the Eucharist and whether the words of Jesus "this is my body" were to be interpreted literally or not (Catholics used this debate to show that Protestants did not read and believe the Bible literally). Socinians and others argued that the NT did not teach either a doctrine of the vicarious death of Jesus or a doctrine of the Trinity. For holding the latter position, Michael Servetus (1511–1553) was burned at the stake under Calvin's supervision on 27 October 1553. Sebastian Castellio (1515–1563) was forced out of Geneva, primarily over his humanist views and his conclusion that the Song of Songs was merely love poetry and should not be a part of the OT canon. In the annotations to his translation of the Bible into Ciceronian Latin (*Biblia Sacra Latina*, 1551) and his *De Haereticis* (1554) Castellio argued for unrestricted religious toleration and complete freedom of interpretation.

Already in the sixteenth century, there seem to have been people who did not share the general religious view that the Bible was the Word of God. Calvin and others allude to persons, whose voices have not been passed along, that denied the truthfulness of biblical content and challenged the religious opinion about the Bible. This disparagement of the Bible may explain the appearance of several harmonies of the gospels produced during the century, the first by Andreas Osiander (1498–1552). Others were published by Jansen, Codmann, Chemnitz, and Mercator. Most of these harmonies acknowledged an apologetic quality to their work—to defend the gospel accounts from those who repudiated their trustworthiness because of their contradictions and differences.

In 1646, Bishop John Wilkins (1614–1672), later to serve as secretary for the Royal Society, in his *Ecclesiastes, or a Discourse concerning the Gift of Preaching*, offered an extensive bibliography on the Bible. At the beginning he noted that the preacher should own two or three harmonizers, that is, works that showed how to overcome difficulties and problems in the text. At least at this time, it was assumed that the Bible properly understood could stand up against its despisers. It was not long thereafter that the Bible and its worldview would be put on the defensive.

Seventeenth and Eighteenth Centuries

In many respects, the seventeenth century represents the watershed in the interpretation of the Bible. In addition to the continued internecine warfare over biblical interpretation among Christians, new developments in science, philosophy, world exploration, and other areas presented challenges to the worldview derived from the Bible (travel books took second place to theology in popularity). In addition, study of the Bible itself presented scholars with the necessity to deal with the fact that the scriptures were not the unified document that had once been believed. On the one hand, some Protestant scholars took a rigid stance toward new assessments and expositions of the Bible and sought to defend the scriptures against Catholics and non-Christians through a highly developed form of scholasticism, a path that proved eventually to be a dead end (see Muller 1993 for a sympathetic treatment). On the other hand, more humanistic work on the scriptures, by both Catholics and Protestants, in the

tradition of Valla, Reuchlin, and Erasmus, made significant contributions to the field.

In the foreground of much research and publication throughout the seventeenth century was what was called the Republic of Letters (*Respublica litterarum*). This was an unorganized but self-conscious stratum of scholars that transcended national and confessional boundaries, interested in scholarship and new developments and discoveries. Theologians, jurists, scientists, philosophers, philologists, and persons interested in experimental science and world exploration made up its number. A network of correspondence in Latin kept the members informed of each other's work and in touch with one another.

The roots of this association may go back to humanist groups of the fifteenth century and the scholar-printers of the sixteenth and seventeenth centuries whose printing shops served as international houses, message centers, meeting places, and sanctuaries. Mutual cooperation and distribution of work as well as scholarly aid were characteristic of the group.

Throughout the century, two general conditions are noteworthy. First, there was a gradual erosion of the biblical worldview as the all-encompassing key for understanding human life and history. Accumulation of new knowledge expanded the biblical worldview to the breaking point. Second, after years of warfare and strife fought over the intricacies of theology and biblical interpretation, many sought to focus on the essentials of religion, on those doctrines on which all or most could agree, in hopes of creating more peaceful conditions. That is, a minimum of doctrine rather than a maximalist view gradually came to be stressed. Lord Herbert of Cherbury (1583–1648) in his *De Veritate* (1624) and subsequent writings argued that there are five essential inborn notions common to all religions: (1) there is a God, (2) who ought to be worshipped, (3) virtue and morality are the chief elements in service to the divine, (4) but since humans fail, repentance for sin is a duty, and (5) there is a future life of rewards and punishments. Near the end of the century, John Locke (1632–1704) concluded that, in the last analysis, Christianity could be reduced to one central tenet: belief in Jesus as the messiah.

Early in the century, the Galileo affair reflected the coming tensions that would occur between science and a worldview based on the Bible (see Blackwell 1991). In 1543, Nicolas Copernicus (1473–1543) had published his *De revolutionibus orbium coelestium* in which he advocated a heliocentric view of the universe. The full impact of his work was modified by Andreas Osiander (1498–1565) who attached a preface stating that Copernicus's views were proposed as a hypothesis, not as a statement of how things really were.

Utilizing the work of John Kepler (1571–1630) and his own astronomical observations, Galileo Galilei (1564–1642) proposed a heliocentric view of the universe as scientific fact. As part of his defense against the church which claimed his views were contrary to biblical teachings, Galileo wrote his famous *Letter to Madame Christina . . . Concerning the Use of Biblical Quotations in Matters of Science* (1615). Galileo argued that the primary purpose of the sacred writings was the service of God and the salvation of souls, not scientific facts and theories that are based on experimentation, observation, and reason: "The intention of the Holy Ghost is to teach us how one goes to heaven, not how heaven goes." Galileo proposed that some biblical statements should be taken allegorically or figuratively when they conflicted with scientific truths and that God was accommodating to human knowledge at the time in statements which imply a geocentric universe.

Galileo appealed to various church fathers and contemporary masters but especially to Augustine's *De Genesi ad literam* where Augustine had argued that one should not believe things inadvisedly perchance they later be proven to be untrue and that if something was disproved by most certain truth, then it was not holy scripture that ever affirmed it, but human ignorance that imagined it. In spite of his defense, Galileo was condemned. The church at the time interpreted scripture very literally (Josh 10:12-14—"the sun stood still and the moon stopped"—was the main text in the affair). Protestants did not have the same difficulties with the new astronomy.

Issues of world history and problems of chronology also moved outside the perimeters of the biblical worldview in the first half of the sixteenth century. Both Luther and Melanchthon as well as others had written on biblical chronology. Knowledge of other cultures and nonbiblical chronological schemes, however, began to create problems for understanding world history within biblical frames of reference. In 1632, J. d'Auzoles tabulated that there were 122 different interpretations of world chronology with seventy-nine different dates for creation ranging from 3083 to 6984 B.C.E. (*La sainte chronologie*). (Bishop James Ussher's [1581–1656] system with creation in 4004 B.C.E. was published in 1650–1654 in his *Annales Veteris et Novi Testamenti*). Simultaneous with the debates over chronology, the discovery of new worlds and people unmentioned in the Bible cast doubt on the accuracy of biblical contents. The issue of astronomy might be minor since the Bible never discusses the topic directly, but history and chronology were different matters. Biblical interpretation had to respond to outside impulses.

The Frenchman Isaac de la Peyrère (ca. 1596–1676) sought to meet the growing dilemma and offered an explanation of the origin of peoples and nations not mentioned in the Bible in his *Men before Adam. . . . By which are prov'd that the first men were created before Adam* (1655) which had circulated in manuscript form in the 1640s. Peyrère's theses were that Adam was not the first human but the tribal ancestor of Israel, Noah's flood was a local affair, and the Pentateuch was a hodgepodge of materials not written by Moses in its entirety. The work became widely known, appeared in an English translation in 1656, and introduced the polygenetic anthropology of pre-Adamic humans into Western thought (see Popkin 1987).

The Englishman Thomas Hobbes (1588–1679) published his *Leviathan* in 1651, offering an analysis of the Bible, how it should be used in politics, and suggestions about its study, especially in the third part (books 32–43). Hobbes concluded that it should be the prerogative of the sovereign power to set the contents of the canon for the realm and to serve as its ultimate interpreter. Hobbes argued that the authorship and antiquity of the biblical writings cannot be determined by tradition. The issue must be guided by the evidence drawn from the books themselves, "and this light, though it show us not the writer of every book, yet it is not unuseful to give us knowledge of the time, wherein they were written." On this basis, he concluded that anachronistic statements indicate that Moses did not produce the Pentateuch but probably only what the Bible says he wrote, namely, Deut 12–26, a book later discovered by Hilkiah the priest which was the basis for Josiah's reform (2 Kgs 22–23). Hobbes thus argued that good biblical study should bypass traditional views and reach decisions on the basis of internal evidence. Neither Galileo, nor Peyrère, nor Hobbes were biblical scholars per se, yet their concerns were issues interpreters soon had to face.

One issue that was of great concern and discussion in the Republic of Letters in the seventeenth century was the origin and date of the Hebrew vowel points. The debate had surfaced earlier, in 1538, when the

Jewish scholar Elias Levita (ca. 1468–1549) published his *Massoreth ha-Massoreth* which was translated into Latin the following year by the great Christian semiticist Sebastian Münster (1489–1522). Levita's work denied the widely assumed theory of the antiquity of the pointing and argued that the vowel points dated from post-Talmud times (after 600 C.E.). The issue first agitated Jewish scholars. Levita was answered by Azariah de Rossi (ca. 1514–1577) in 1574. At the turn of the century, the issue came to occupy Christians.

The reason the matter was of concern to the church had to do with the inspiration of the biblical text and the question of which OT text had the greatest claim to antiquity and authenticity. If the vowels were added as late as Levita claimed, then it was assumed they represented a late human addition to the text. Also if they were this late, then the Catholic Vulgate was translated from an older and thus more authentic text than the Masoretic text. Matters were further complicated when Pietro della Valle brought to Europe in 1616 a copy of the Samaritan Pentateuch, written in ancient Hebrew characters but without vowel points and differing from the Masoretic text at about 6,000 points.

Catholics seized on the argument that the Septuagint text and Jerome's Vulgate were really older than the Masoretic text and that the Protestant OT (the Hebrew text) was a later and likely a corrupt text. The debate raged for years (see Laplanche 1986). The antiquity of the vowel points was argued by many Protestants especially Johann Buxtorf (1564–1629) and his son (1599–1664). The lateness of the pointing was defended especially by Louis Cappell (1585–1658), an Arminian Protestant. Cappell, in his *Arcanum punctationis revelatum* (published anonymously in Holland by Thomas Erpenius in 1624) and *Critica sacra* (1650) established his case conclusively. *Critica sacra* was published through the efforts of the Catholic scholar Jean Morinus (1591–1659). For the first time since the Reformation, real scholarly cooperation in biblical study crossed Christian confessional boundaries. A new movement was underway: biblical criticism.

(The use of the term "criticism" with reference to the study, evaluation, and correction of texts came into widespread usage in the late sixteenth century, primarily in regard to nonbiblical classical texts. In his *History of the Royal Society*, 1667, Thomas Sprat could already write that "we have had enough of criticism"—but he had an axe to grind.)

In spite of Cappell's work conservative Swiss Protestants included belief in the antiquity and inspiration of the vowel points in the *Formula Consensus* (1675) and ruled (in 1678) that no one could be licensed to preach without publicly declaring a belief in the integrity of the Hebrew text and the divinity of the vowel points.

Two trajectories characterize mid-seventeenth biblical interpretation. On one hand, from the point of scholarship, it was one of the most productive periods in history. The Paris Polyglot, adding the Samaritan Pentateuch and an Arabic version, was produced during 1629–1645, in ten mammoth volumes (the Antwerp Polyglot [1569–1572, eight volumes] had added the Syriac NT). The London Polyglot, the finest ever produced, appeared in six volumes in 1655–1657 (there is a commonwealth and a royalist edition varying only in the preface and the time of binding). This included the Hebrew, Greek, Vulgate, Syriac, Ethiopic, Arabic, and Persian versions with Latin translations as well as the Samaritan Pentateuch, various Targums, and readings from Codex Alexandrinus (acquired by the British in 1627) along with various aids. Companion volumes to the London Polyglot included Castell's Heptaglot lexicon (two volumes, 1669) and the *Critici sacri* (nine volumes, 1660) which provided a commentary and annotations on the entire Bible (Apocrypha included) drawn from scores of sixteenth- and seventeenth-century commentators and several dozen dissertations on diverse topics, texts, and problems. Matthew Poole produced his *Synopsis criticorum* in 1669–1674 (five volumes) a recasting and supplementation of the *Critici sacri* which brought the number of commentators excerpted to about 150. In addition, the famous annotated Bible, generally associated with the Assembly of Divines, appeared in 1651.

Four of the most famous British interpreters published during this period were Edward Pococke (1604–1691) who published major commentaries on three of the minor prophets and was the first scholar to utilize Arabic extensively as an interpretive aid; John Lightfoot (1602–1675) who published numerous works on the Bible, being the first person to draw extensively on rabbinic literature to elucidate the NT (in his *Horae Hebraicae et Talmudicae*, six volumes, 1658–1678, and still in print); Henry Ainsworth (1560–1622) whose translation and commentary on the Pentateuch, Psalms, and Song of Songs appeared in 1639; and Henry Hammond (1605–1660) who published *A Paraphrase and Annotations upon all the Books of the New Testament* (1653), a widely used and respected volume and the first to raise Gnosticism as an important issue in understanding the NT. Bishop James Ussher's (1581–1656) study of the letters of Polycarp and Ignatius appearted in 1644 and his *Annales Veteris et Novi Testamenti* in 1650–1654. The work of the Dutch scholar Hugo Grotius (1583–1645), *Annotationes* to the entire Bible (six volumes, 1641–1650), employed all the humanistic tools and offered a historical reading of the Bible drawing upon innumerable ancient sources while still respecting scriptural authority. Probably no period in history has witnessed such scholarly achievements in the field. Biblical criticism had come of age.

On the other hand, the period of the English revolution and the Commonwealth (1640–1660), when press censorship was lifted, witnessed the use of the Bible to support practically every conceivable political and social form of life and behavior (see Hill 1993). Radical Millenarianism was rampant (Joseph Mede's *Clavis Apocalyptica* appeared in 1627). Quakerism and the appeal to the "inner light"—even over against the Bible—emerged. Oliver Cromwell (1599–1658) read his career in light of Psalm 110. John Milton (1608–1674) sought to reason away the NT prohibition against divorce (*The Doctrine and Discipline of Divorce*, 1643), and worked on his heterodox *De doctrina Christiana* (published posthumously) which contains more than 8,000 biblical references and declares in regard to biblical interpretation:

> No one else can usefully interpret for him, unless that person's interpretation coincides with the one he makes for himself and his own conscience. . . . Every man is his own arbitrator. . . . All things are eventually to be referred to the Spirit and the unwritten word. (*Complete Prose Works of Milton*, 6:583–90)

The doctrine of "the priesthood of the believer" had been stretched to its limit and applied to biblical interpretation. Biblical authority came out of the period somewhat shattered.

Two seventeenth-century figures, the excommunicated Dutch Jewish philosopher Baruch Spinoza (1632–1677) and the French Catholic Oratorian Richard Simon (1638–1712), have generally been considered precursors of the modern phase of biblical study. Spinoza wrote in the wake of the Cartesian revolution in philosophy and placed reason and philosophy above religion and faith as the arbiter of truth. In his *Tractatus theologico-politicus* (1670), he considered the Bible to be a humanly produced book which must be studied like any other book and its truths

assessed by reason. Spinoza explained biblical miracles as extraordinary events whose causes were unknown to the observers. Spinoza outlined a program of biblical studies: (1) knowledge of the original languages (he also wrote a Hebrew grammar and pointed to the Hebraic quality of NT Greek); (2) analysis of each book; (3) the Bible must be interpreted by the Bible (which for Spinoza allowed one to critique speculative conclusions about the Bible and its authority); (4) knowledge of the environment and intention of the author ("who was the speaker, what was the occasion, and to whom were the words addressed"); and (5) investigation of all that has happened to every book in the Bible (i.e., its transmission, corruption, copyist's errors, etc.).

For Spinoza, the Bible contains truths that could have been discovered through reason; it has a very persuasive character and is often imaginative literature; and the laws of the Torah were intended for a specific time for people in their childhood. He considered much of the OT to have been edited late, in the time of Ezra and afterward. Although Spinoza's book was almost universally condemned, banned, and placed on the Index of Forbidden Books, the work and his philosophy were highly influential.

Oratorian Richard Simon published an enormous amount of literature as well as a new translation of the NT: critical histories of the OT and the NT and the versions, and biblical commentators. His most influential work was *Histoire critique du Vieux Testament* (already printed in 1678 but most copies were destroyed by the censor; second edition, 1685). One of Simon's goals in this work was to prove to Protestants that the Hebrew OT (and all versions and translations) and its text were too unreliable and uncertain to be the basis of the faith, thus affirming the long-held Catholic view. Simon was caustic in his assessment of other commentators, even the patristic fathers (which got him into trouble with his church and order). Simon not only denied that Moses was the author of the Pentateuch but also proposed a theory regarding its origin along with the historical books: public scribes recorded events and happenings and their records served as the basis of the biblical books. Practically all of Simon's works were translated into English shortly after being published.

By the end of the seventeenth century, the historical-critical method (the quest for the *sensus historicus*) was reasonably well developed (though not necessarily widely accepted) resting on the following presumptions. (1) The Bible is a book of antiquity separated from the present both chronologically and conceptually. (2) The Bible should be studied and read like any other book, that is, in a straightforward fashion. Individual books or groupings of books must be read on their own, not filtered through the Bible as a whole or church/synagogue tradition (John Locke wrote "an essay for the understanding of St. Paul's Epistles, by consulting St. Paul himself"). (3) A biblical text is the product of a human author(s) living in a particular time and place. (4) The form and content of a text reflect and are intelligible only in light of the author's conceptions, intentions, and beliefs, which are conditioned by the time and context of the original writer's and readers' environment and thought world. (5) The authenticity and validity of the Bible or a biblical text depend, in no small measure, on how they and their content measure up to the canons of human thought and reason. (6) The causes and nature of events in the Bible must be understood in terms of historical analogy, what was possible then is possible now and vice versa (the latter perspective was more hinted at than declared).

The eighteenth century witnessed the Bible and biblical worldview under attack and, before the century was over, even ridiculed, as had not been the case since the days of Celsus, Porphyry, and Emperor Julian the Apostate (Muslim attacks on the Bible in the Middle Ages had been pointed but superficial). The broad movement behind this attitude toward the Bible (and "revealed" religion in general) was what has been broadly called Deism. The Deists sought greater liberty in civil life, increased freedom to publish without censorship, and the right, as Spinoza had already said, to "think what one likes, and say what one thinks." Deists denied the particularistic favoritism implied in all religions based on "special" revelation and argued for belief in a deity that treated all humans alike. The movement drew upon (1) the thought of Lord Herbert, Hobbes, and Spinoza; (2) the classics, especially the Greek skeptics with their critiques of religion; (3) Latitudinarian thinkers and theologians like Isaac Newton (1642–1727), John Locke (1632–1704), Samuel Clarke (1675–1729), and Archbishop John Tillotson (1630–1694) who sought to reconcile faith and reason and the new science, a movement that found embodiment in the famous Boyle Lectures; (4) certain elements in Calvin and Calvinism (Deism has been described as Calvinism without the anxiety, tears, and determinism); (5) the philosophy of Francis Bacon's (1561–1626)

empiricism with its desire to undertake "a total reconstruction of the sciences, arts, and all human knowledge, raised upon proper foundations"; and (6) the methods of Protestant anti-Catholic polemic (which had challenged such topics as the mystery of transubstantiation and continuing miracles in the church) which were then applied to the Protestant faith and primitive church, and to the biblical literature. Deism expounded a religion of nature ("Adamic religion") which was assumed to have been based on reason, was morally oriented and monotheistic, and had been perverted by the priestly hierarchy with innumerable superstitions to keep the common lot in ignorance, bondage, and servitude to the advantage of the priestly caste (see Byrne 1989). With the end of English government press censorship in 1696, the publication of deistic works became more widespread.

Before his suicide, Charles Blount (1654–1693) published something of a Deist Manifesto outlining the seven essential articles of natural religion. In 1696, John Toland (1670–1722) published *Christianity not Mysterious* in which he denied that either God or revelation were beyond human comprehension. By 1698, English Deism had become so widespread that Charles Leslie (1650–1722) wrote *A Short and Easy Method with the Deists, wherein the Certainty of the Christian Religion is demonstrated by Infallible Proof from Four Rules, which are Incompatible to any Imposture that ever yet has been, or that can possibly be.* Leslie outlined a method for the evidential-factual investigation of biblical events seeking to show how their historicity could be affirmed by appealing to certain characteristics of the events, their public nature, and their attestation in publicly available documents deriving from the time of the events. Something like Leslie's arguments has been a staple of much British biblical scholarship ever since.

The three issues related to biblical studies most attacked by the Deists were the fulfillment of prophecy, biblical miracles, and the Protestant understanding of the early church. The following are some of the representative works. Anthony Collins (1676–1729) published *A Discourse on the Grounds and Reasons of the Christian Faith* (1724) and *A Scheme of Literal Prophecy Considered* (1725) in which he argued that OT prophecies could be seen as fulfilled in Jesus and the early church only if understood allegorically, a common method of exegesis in the Judaism of Jesus' day. Thus there was no miraculous fulfillment of predictions to support the authenticity and uniqueness of the Bible and Christian faith but only an exegetical method.

The issue of OT prophecies and their fulfillment had been one of the basic elements in Christian apologetics and a hotly debated issue at the turn of the century. William Whiston (1667–1752) who succeded Newton as Lucasian professor of mathmatics at Cambridge had written *Accomplishment of Scripture Prophecies* (1708) arguing that prophecies had but one fulfillment but ended up arguing that the OT prophetical texts had been corrupted by the Jews thus explaining the differences between OT predictions and NT fulfillments. Thomas Woolston (1669–1731) wrote a series of discourses and defenses of these (in the 1620s) challenging the historicity of the gospel miracles (see Burns 1981). Woolston and other deistic writers discussed the gospels as theological statements, not factual reports.

Eventually the resurrection of Christ, the central NT miracle, became the center of debate. Thomas Sherlock (1678–1761) defended its historicity (*Tryal of the Witnesses of the Resurrection of Jesus*, 1729) and Peter Annet (1693–1769) offered the challenge (*The Resurrection of Jesus Considered*, 1743; *The Resurrection Reconsidered: The Resurrection Defenders Stript of All Defence*, 1745). Annet pointed to the difficulties in reconciling the gospel accounts of the resurrection to the fact that even witnesses may be deceived, and claimed that in any case "a historical fact [even a miracle] is not part of true and pure religion, which is founded only on truth and purity. That it [true religion] does not consist in the belief of any history."

The Deists, especially Toland (*Nazarenus, or Jewish, Gentile, and Mahometan Christianity*, 1718) and Thomas Morgan (d. 1743; *The Moral Philosopher*, three volumes, 1737–1740), offered a reconstruction of early church history. In the beginning, there was Jesus and his followers with a simple message ("purest morals," "reasonable worship," and "just conceptions of Heaven and Heavenly Things"). This movement was perverted by the introduction into the church of elements of Jewish ceremonial and Gentile mystery. Morgan formulated the issue in terms of a Pauline proclamation of Jesus as universal savior in conflict with a group represented by Peter and others which was strongly influenced by exclusivistic Jewish elements. Although Jewish Christianity prevailed for a time, Gentile and Jewish Christians eventually combined in the time of Christian persecution to produce what became Catholic Christianity, with the more strongly Pauline elements going over to Gnosticism.

The NT writings cover up this movement and contain corruptions and additions to bring them into line with developing thought.

If the reformers may be said to have concluded that medieval theologians and scholasticism had misunderstood biblical religion, the Socinians and radicals that all later theologians had misunderstood the Bible, and the Latitudianarians that the early creeds had misunderstood the NT, then the deistic movement may be said to have advocated the view that the NT writers had misunderstood Jesus. The way was now open for not only a detailed examination of the biblical writings in terms of the history of the early church and Christian thought but also for the study of the historical Jesus and the relationship of these writings to him.

The writings of the Deists themselves were representative of what might be called "coffee house" theology—disorganized, evocative, personalized, argumentative. (Coffee was first introduced into Europe in the year that Luther "nailed" his theses to the Wittenberg church door. The first coffee house opened in England at Oxford in 1650. Such houses became centers of dialogue and diatribe.) None of the English Deists held academic positions. Most were free floaters. Only Conyers Middleton (1683–1750) had university connections—he was librarian at Cambridge.

Deism was far more influential on the continent than in England. Most of their works were translated into French and German. Throughout most of the century European theology and biblical studies drew their stimulus from England. A massive nineteen-volume biblical commentary was produced by the Germans (1749–1770) consisting solely of translations from English in order to bring German scholarship abreast of work in England (initially edited by D. R. Teller). No deistic work was included, because no English Deist wrote commentaries or any systematic treatise on the Bible.

A movement that developed contemporaneously with Deism was Pietism, part of a transdenominational phenomenon represented in Judaism by Hasidism, in Catholicism by the Jansenists, and in Protestantism by the Moravian Brethen and Methodism. Within the German church the movement had its beginning in the publication of *Pia Desideria* (1675) by Philipp Jakob Spener (1635–1705) who sought revival of the church through biblical piety. Biblical study was fostered in frequent devotional meetings. The university of Halle and A. H. Francke (1663–1727) became rallying points for the movement which stressed the *sensus spiritualis* and the subjective, experiential reading of the text illumined by the Holy Spirit. Pietism produced a number of significant contributors to biblical studies, since its focus on the interpreter freed one to engage in even critical work on the text.

J. A. Bengel (1687–1752) published an edition of the Greek NT (1734) noting variant readings among texts of the NT in a critical apparatus (the first such critical apparatus was in Estienne's Greek NT, 1550). Bengel's commentary on the NT, *Gnomon Novi Testamenti* (1742) proved to be a classic. Textual criticism in which variant readings among Greek manuscripts were noted tended to relativize any doctrine of an inspired text as well as the widely held view that God would not allow his word to be corrupted in its transmission. John Mill (1645–1707) had published a Greek NT in 1707 with about 30,000 variant readings drawn from about one hundred manuscripts. J. J. Wettstein (1693–1754) published a still-valuable Greek NT (two volumes, 1751–1752) with a critical apparatus using *sigla* for the various texts and detailed exegetical notes (neither Mill nor Wettstein were pietists but NT textual criticism owed much to Pietism).

Two works published in 1753, one by a Frenchman and the other by an Englishman, marked new departures in biblical studies. Jean Astruc (1684–1766), physician at the court of Louis XV and professor of medicine at the royal college in Paris, published *Conjectures sur les Mémoires originaux dont il paroit que Moyse s'est servi pour composer le Livre de la Genèse*. Astruc, at least in his stated intent, set out to explain how Moses composed the book of Genesis and how it came to be in the corrupted form we possess, so as to silence biblical detractors. He divided the material in Genesis into a number (primarily four) of sources that Moses used in putting together the book. Moses used sources since he was no eyewitness to the events before his day. Astruc divided the sources primarily on the basis of the names used for God (Yahweh and Elohim). Source criticism of the Pentateuch was thus introduced into biblical studies.

Between 1741 and 1750, Robert Lowth (1710–1787), Oxford professor of poetry, delivered a series of lectures on Hebrew poetry that was published in 1753 as *De sacra poesi Hebraeorum* (English translation in 1787). Lowth argued that much of the OT was poetry (Psalms and Prophets especially) and must be understood aesthetically. His emphasis fell on literary appreciation of the Hebrew poetic genius which he identi-

fied with the work of the Holy Spirit. Lowth's work exerted enormous influence, especially in Germany.

Beginning in the second half of the eighteenth century, German scholarship came increasingly to dominate biblical studies. The emphasis on natural theology, reason, and the downplaying of revelation that undergirded English Deism had found expression in Germany in the work of Christian Wolff (1679–1754) who sought to synchronize reason and revelation. Historical criticism erupted in Germany in radical but scholarly form, being heavily dependent on ideas derived from English Deists.

After writing a dissertation defending the orthodox interpretation of prophecy and its fulfillment (1731), H. S. Reimarus (1694–1768) fell under the sway of rationalistic natural theology. At his death, Reimarus left behind a major work, partially published anonymously in 1774–1778 by G. E. Lessing (1729–1881). Reimarus reached radical conclusions about such events as the Exodus from Egypt as described in the Bible but his most controversial positions concerned the nature of Jesus' ministry and the resurrection. According to Reimarus, Jesus taught a natural, rational, and practical religion but saw himself as the messiah of a coming political realm, which of course never came into being. Following this failure, the disciples stole the body of Jesus, proclaimed his resurrection, and then edited his teachings to have Jesus proclaim his death and resurrection and his coming kingdom as a heavenly, spiritual realm. This alteration in the message of Jesus and the fabrication of the resurrection allowed the disciples to preserve their vocations as travelling clerics (again the perversion of the truth by the established hierarchy). Reimarus stressed that what was preached about Jesus was not identical with what Jesus preached and he felt that the differences among the gospels, particularly with regard to the resurrection, meant that they must all be false (therefore falsified).

At the same time that radical criticism was beginning to be openly published, the Bible was subjected to radical ridicule by extreme Deists such as Voltaire (1694–1778) and Thomas Paine (1737–1809). For both, the Bible, through not necessarily the real teachings of Jesus, was a collection of supersititions, incongruities, primitive mentality, and priestcraft.

In this context, one must understand the flowering of historical criticism in the late eighteenth century as not only the continuation of the mainstream of philological, textual, and historical criticism which had begun in the Renaissance but also as a major apologetic activity aimed at offering more reasonable discussion of the Bible and explanations of its problems than that of its despisers. The so-called historical-critical method, generally traced to the eighteenth century, is frequently presented as an attempt to undercut the Bible's authority, to bring it into line with modern thought, and to free biblical study from dogmatic dominance. In some respects, just the opposite is probably a more accurate description. The practitioners of the method were primarily Protestant scholars; they were not anti-biblical although their work was frequently anti-Catholic and anti-Jewish (see Moore 1921) and often at variance with traditional Christianity.

The second half of the eighteenth century witnessed the production of the first systematic introductions to the Bible, generally to the two testaments separately. These works discussed such matters as the development of the canon, origin and character of the individual books, and the history of the text. Such works took into account and subjected to judgment traditional views and opinions on these matters. J. D. Michaelis's (1717–1791) introduction to the NT appeared in 1750 (fourth edition, two volumes, 1788; English translation, four volumes, 1793–1801, with supplementation by Herbert Marsh [1757–1839]). The Englishman Nathaniel Lardner (1684–1768) in his *The Credibility of the Gospel History* (seventeen volumes, 1727–1757) had collected patristic evidence in defending traditional dates, circumstances, and authorship as well as on problem texts, providing scholarship with an invaluable resource. The first major OT introduction was published by J. G. Eichhorn (1752–1827; three volumes, 1780–1783, with subsequent editions). Eichhorn also published introductions to the Apocrypha (1795) and the NT (two volumes, 1804–1812). In these manuals, practically all the major issues of biblical interpretation were raised. Later work would restate the questions and/or provide different solutions to the problems or view the problems slightly differently. Radical solutions were already part of the discussion before the end of the century. Reimarus's work provides one illustration. Another is Edward Evanson (1731–1805), an English Unitarian, who, in *The Dissonance of the Four Generally Received Evangelists* (1792) and other works, argued that the only genuine first-century NT writings were Luke-Acts (minus interpolations), 1-2 Corinthians, Galatians, Philippians, 1-2 Thessalonians, 1-2 Timothy, Titus, Philemon, and the Apocalypse (minus the letters to the seven churches). All the rest were spurious second-century documents. An edition of the NT was published in 1807 containing only what Evanson had declared authentic.

The Nineteenth Century

As in previous centuries, a wide variety of biblical interpretations were practiced during this period. The older form of Protestant orthodoxy was continued (and lived on into the twentieth century as the so-called "Princeton School"). Pietistic and devotional use persisted as did mystical reading. Most movements cut across the boundaries of Jewish, Catholic, and Protestant categories. In general, orthodox, pietistic, and mystical reading of the Bible continued patterns and practices already long in existence. Here only new developments in biblical criticism can be noted.

Biblical criticism was to a large extent the domain of German Protestantism during the century (see Rogerson 1988). Following the French Revolution (1789), England was very resistant to European currents. Only a few isolated British scholars were open to German scholarship until well past the half century mark. The Catholic Alexander Geddes (1737–1802) and Hebert Marsh were two of the exceptions.

The program outlined by Charles Leslie in the fight against the Deists was used by British scholars against the new developments in German thought. The works of William Paley (1743–1805), *Horae Paulinae* (1790) and *View of the Evidences of Christianity* (1794), typify this view. In the United States, a circle associated with Theodore Parker (1810–1860) and the New England Unitarians accepted and publicized German scholarship for a short time but the group itself made no lasting contribution to biblical interpretation. In Judaism the development of the "Science of Judaism" (*Wissenschaft des Judentums*) beginning in the 1820s gradually moved some Jewish research into the mainstream of biblical interpretation.

In OT studies, the pivotal issue was the source analysis of the Pentateuch, already inaugurated by Astruc and developed by Eichhorn. (Theories that the Pentateuch was composed of numerous unrelated fragments or that it was composed of one major document with extensive supplementation were advocated but not widely followed.) Once the idea of source analysis became an operating principle, then the sources had to be delineated on the basis of some criteria, the sources had to be related to each other, and in some fashion associated with the history of Israel.

The pivotal figure in early eighteenth-century OT studies was W. M. L. de Wette (1780–1849). In his 1805 dissertation on Deuteronomy, he isolated Deuteronomy from the rest of the Pentateuch, argued that it was the latest stratum, and hinted at its association with Josiah's reform (2 Kgs 22–23). In two contributions on introduction to the OT (1806–1807), he sought to demonstrate that 1-2 Chronicles are much later than Samuel-Kings (whose narrative they retell so as to show that the full Mosaic law was operative from the time of David and Solomon) and that they were unreliable as documents for reconstructing the history of Israel. (A comparable move in NT studies was the treatment of the Gospel of John with its self-assertion of Christology by Jesus as an unhistorical source.)

The pentateuchal material was gradually divided into four sources, later called Priestly (P), Elohistic (E), Yahwistic (J), and Deuteronomic (D). After the differentiation of sources, the major question was their literary and chronological relationship. The idea that the priestly material (P) was the latest stratum was discussed in lectures by Edward Reuss (1804–1891) in 1833–1834, suggested in books written by Wilhelm Vatke (1806–1882) and J. F. L. George (1811–1873) in 1835, and then argued by K. H. Graf (1815–1869), Abraham Kuenen (1828–1891), and others in the 1860s. Involved in the problem of the relationship of the sources were the questions of the nature of early Israelite life and religion and the relationship of the prophets to OT law.

In 1878, Julius Wellhausen (1844–1918) published his *Prolegomena to the History of Israel* and laid out in convincing style the evidence supporting the following conclusions.

(1) the three pentateuchal law codes (in J(E), D, and P) are to be related to the history of Israel as reconstructed from the OT historical and prophetical books (minus 1-2 Chronicles); (2) this history suggests that the J(E) law code belongs to the middle monarchic (preclassical prophetic) period, D to the time of Josiah's reform, and P to the exilic period; (3) early Israel was a society that lived without written law, in freedom and only according to custom; (4) the major prophets preceded the ceremonical law and introduced the elements of morality and divine universalism into Israelite life; and (5) the law with its stifling quality is characteristic of postexilic times and Judaism in general (Wellhausen's Lutheranism, anti-Judaism, and romanticism are all reflected in the tone of his writings if not in his use of evidence).

Source and historical criticism were also applied to other books in the Hebrew Bible. The Book of Isaiah was divided into two halves following chap 39, and assigned to the eighth and sixth centuries BCE respectively. The Book of Daniel was dated to the time of the Maccabean revolt (ca. 165–164 B.C.E.) and so on.

The early practitioners of the historical-critical approach to the OT in Britain and the United States lost their posts or suffered church sanction, W. Robertson Smith (1846–94) in Britain and Charles Augustus Briggs (1841–1913) in America. By the end of the century, the English-speaking world had made something of a truce with the historical-critical method even if not with all its conclusions. The appointment of the moderate critic S. R. Driver (1846–1914) at Oxford and his reverent attitude toward the Bible helped the movement gain general acceptance.

Comparative texts from other cultures, first Egyptian and then Mesopotamian, led to the recognition of how much cultural and literary sharing there was between Israel and its neighbors. Babylonian creation and flood stories and law codes showed striking parallels to the Bible, so much so that "pan-Babylonianism," a movement tracing much in the Bible to Babylonian influence arose and climaxed in the *Bibel-Babel* (Bible-Babylon) controversy. Archaeological activity in Palestine exposed the artifacts of Israelite culture, and relating the "evidence of the spade" to biblical events became and remains a major field of inquiry.

The nineteenth-century preoccupation with history and the reading of the scriptures in terms of the original author-reader context led to a temporary demise in the writing of OT theologies, their place being taken by histories of Israelite and Hebrew religion.

In NT studies, the nineteenth century was especially preoccupied with the authentiticy and dating of NT writings, the relationship among the gospels, and the quest for the historical Jesus. The dominant figure for much of the century was F. C. Baur (1792–1860), the founder of the Tübingen School.

Baur inherited the view—from J. S. Semler (1725–1791) who in turn was influenced by Thomas Morgan—that the early church was a scene of conflict between Jewish and Gentile sentiments or the Pauline and Petrine parties (first advocated by Baur in an article in 1831). Party strife eventually resulted in a synthesis that became Catholic Christianity. Baur's pro-Pauline and anti-Catholic sympathies were combined with a Hegelian dialectic. In 1835, a vintage year in biblical scholarship, Baur published his work challenging the Pauline authorship of the pastoral epistles (not a view previously unheard of since Eichhorn ·had finally come to this position). Eventually Baur challenged all the letters attributed to Paul except Galatians, 1-2 Corinthians, and Romans. Acts was viewed by the Tübingen school as late, an attempt to downplay the conflict between Peter and Paul. The gospel of John was considered inauthentic (so already K. G. Bretschneider [1776–1848] in 1820) and placed in the middle of the second century as a synthesizing work. Matthew and Revelation were placed early as representative of Jewish, exclusivistic Christianity.

The relationship of the four gospels to each other was related both to the issue of the date and authenticity of the books as well as the quest for the historical Jesus. Generally church tradition had assumed the gospels were written in the order in which we have them, with Mark being an epitome of Matthew (a view probably falsely attributed to Augustine by Martin Chemnitz [1522–1586]). In 1782, J. B. Koppe (1750–1791) challenged the view of Matthew's priority and that Mark was a summary based on Matthew. Since J. J. Griesbach (1745–1812) had published his Greek NT text of the first three gospels in parallel columns (1774) there had been no doubt that some sort of relationships existed between these three (the synoptic) gospels. Various theories had been proposed and continued to be supported: all three synoptic gospels depended on oral tradition; a primitive (written or oral), probably Aramaic, gospel lay behind all three; various fragments of tradition were utilized independently; and the three depended upon each other in some way (e.g., Mark copied Matthew). Marcan priority as the solution to the synoptic problem was proposed by G. G. Wilke (1786–1854) in 1838 and eventually defended by H. J. Holtzmann (1832–1910) in 1863 along with idea that Matthew and Luke shared a common sayings source (traditionally designated "Q"). It was widely argued that the Gospel of Mark provided access to the Jesus of history.

The nineteenth-century quest for the historical Jesus reached its crisis point in the *Leben Jesu* (two volumes, 1835) of D. F. Strauss (1804–1874). Strauss ignored the Gospel of John and argued that the synoptic gospel portraits of Jesus are based on myths that express the sentiments of his early followers and their rereading of OT texts. Jesus is taken as a person who is the symbolic reflection of the unity between divinity and humanity. Very little can be known about the actual person of Jesus of Nazareth. The answers to and critiques of Strauss were numerous.

In spite of Strauss's work, the output of "lives of Jesus" was enormous (see Schweitzer 1910 and Pals 1985). Conservative, liberal, and pietistic "biographies" were written. Some opted to focus only on the "Christ of faith," that is, Jesus as presented in the gospels.

Near the end of the century, the Catholic Modernist Movement, saw several scholars, including Marie Joseph Lagrange (1855–1938) and Alfred F. Loisy (1857–1940), adopting the historical-critical approach to the scriptures. Pope Leo XIII had given encouragement to the study of the Bible in the encyclical *Providentissimus Deus* (18 November 1893). The movement was suppressed in 1907 by Pope Pius X, but a new day was dawning for Catholic biblical scholarship.

The Twentieth Century

Stimuli for much biblical study in this century have their roots in the last two decades of the nineteenth century. (1) First, the widespread liberalism that viewed the kingdom of God in terms of morality and community (e.g., Albert Ritschl [1822–1889]) and the preaching of Jesus as emphasizing certain central general ideas (the father of God, brotherhood of humanity, and infinite value of the individual; e.g., Adolf Harnack [1851–1930]) was already breaking down. (2) The apocalyptic orientation of the early church and also of the historical Jesus was beginning to be stressed. The last half of the nineteenth century witnessed the recovery of nonbiblical apocalyptic literature. In 1892, Johannes Weiss (1863–1914) wrote *Jesus' Proclamation of the Kingdom of God* (English translation, 1971) arguing that Jesus' preaching was consistently eschatological, a proclamation of the imminent appearance of the transcendent kingdom of God. (3) The rise of the history-of-religions school (*Religionsgeschichtliche Schule*) in the 1880s led to a focus on religion as a historical phenomenon understandable only in light of its origin and roots. Comparative religious phenomena and literature, not modern doctrinal concepts, it was argued, must be utilized to understand Christianity without appeal to special revelation. (4) New emphasis on the role of the community in the creation and shaping of literature and the role of literature in social contexts was replacing focus on individuality so characteristic of much of nineteenth-century thought. (5) Study of literature in terms of genre analysis rather than in terms of authorship was current in the general study of literature and was beginning to make headway into biblical study.

In 1906, Albert Schweitzer (1875–1965) published his *Quest of the Historical Jesus* (English translation, 1910) in which he presented a thoroughly eschatological Jesus while critiquing all earlier efforts at reconstruction. According to Schweitzer, only the spirit of the historical Jesus can challenge modern man; the historical Jesus cannot be made to fit into modern times.

> The study of the Life of Jesus has had a curious history. It set out in quest of the historical Jesus, believing that when it had found Him it could bring Him straight into our time as a Teacher and Saviour. It loosed the bands by which He had been riveted for centuries to the stony rocks of ecclesiastical doctrine, and rejoiced to see life and movement coming into the figure once more, and the historical Jesus advancing, as it seemed, to meet it. But He does not stay; He passes by our time and returns to His own. What surprised and dismayed the theology of the last forty years was that, despite all forced and arbitrary interpretations, it could not keep Him in our time, but had to let Him go. He returned to His own time, not owing to the application of any historical ingenuity, but by the same inevitable necessity by which the liberated pendulum returns to its original position. (Schweitzer 1910, 399)

Schweitzer felt he had written the obituary for the quest, but time has shown that he succeeded only in writing another life of Jesus. Nonetheless Schweitzer's "Jesus" was indicative of new impulses in biblical study.

Two methodologies dominated biblical scholarship in the first half of the century: form criticism and the history of tradition. Both disciplines share an emphasis on the importance of tradition and the community in the formation, structuring, and production of biblical writings (although not done consciously, this move represented an acceptance of the older Catholic position that before the Bible there was the believing community and tradition). A name associated with both methods is Hermann Gunkel (1862–1932). Gunkel was concerned with both genre (form) analysis and how material develops from its earliest oral phase to final canonical form. Gunkel argued that the biblical material can be classified into genres according to its mood and thought, stylistic features and linguistic structure, and its *Sitz im Leben* (the life situations in which the

material originated and was used). He believed the earliest genres could be isolated—short story, psalm (various types), law, wise saying, etiology, and so on—and that a history of tradition or literature, how the genres developed, could be written. Gunkel was also very much interested in early cultures and comparative literature and thought.

Form criticism became a significant factor in NT studies through the work of Martin Dibelius (1883–1947), K. L. Schmidt (1891–1956), and Rudolf Bultmann (1884–1976). The analysis of the material of the NT into various genres raised questions about the role of the church in shaping and creating tradition, about what could be traced back to Jesus, and about the structure of the gospels and whether this had any relationship to the actual course of events in the life of Jesus or was a theological construct.

In OT studies, the history of tradition became a special concern of a circle associated with Albrecht Alt (1883–1956). Martin Noth (1902–1968) and Gerhard von Rad (1901–1971) investigated how Israel's traditions originated and developed. Noth was concerned with the impact of the approach for understanding the history of Israel and von Rad for writing a theology of the OT in terms of the use and reinterpretation of traditions.

The most controversial development in NT study was Bultmann's program of demythologization. Bultmann argued that the biblical thought world and much of its content presuppose a mythological worldview that is in sharp contrast to contemporary thought. Bultmann argued that this mythological worldview should be transposed into an existentialist key so the texts can address the contemporary human understanding. For Bultmann, only the fact of the human existence of Jesus was necessary as a historical datum. For him, the life and preaching of Jesus was part of the Jewish background to Christianity since Jesus was, as Wellhausen had earlier noted, a Jew not a Christian.

In the wake of Bultmann's work, a new quest of the historical Jesus was pursued. The focus of this endeavor was to understand the movement from what Jesus preached and taught to what was preached and taught about Jesus. (A so-called third quest for the historical Jesus has begun in the 1990s.)

Nonbiblical texts and archaeological data have played a greater role in biblical studies in the twentieth century than ever before in history. New textual discoveries such as the Ugaritic texts, the Qumran (Dead Sea) Scrolls, and the Nag Hammadi texts have supplied scholars with new material. In addition, Hellenistic papyri, Eygptian and Mesopotamian texts, as well as Syro-Palestinian inscriptions can now be utilized in understanding the Bible. Palestine has become one of the most excavated areas in the world and people like W. F. Albright (1891–1971) and his students and Israeli scholars especially have worked to integrate this material.

Comparative study of ancient Near Eastern materials has led to seeing common patterns or at least analogous beliefs and practices that Israel and the early church shared with other cultures. The Myth and Ritual School in England and the Uppsala School in Scandinavia have highlighted these parallels. Gnosticism and its relationship to NT writings and early church life raises a similar set of issues.

Since the 1930s, Protestants and Catholics have concerned themselves with biblical theology, with formulating an approach that would allow a systematic presentation of the theology of the individual testaments and the Bible as a whole. Various methods and schemes have been employed. In spite of the failure of biblical theologians to arrive at a commonly shared approach and description, the effort has contributed to a better understanding of the biblical materials.

A distinctive feature of twentieth-century biblical interpretation has been its ecumenical dimension. The first half of the century saw the *Wissenschaft des Judentums* mature. Pope Pius XII's encyclical *Divino*

Afflante Spiritu (30 September 1943) gave greater freedom to Catholic scholars, a movement extended at the Second Vatican Council (1962–1965). Catholics, Protestants, and Jews now study the Bible, often cooperatively, utilizing similar methods and often arriving at similar conclusions.

A second new feature of bibical study is the diversity of methods employed. In the last four decades of the century, a great variety of interests and approaches have characterized biblical study. The old historical-critical paradigm that stressed the original historical sense of the text as the center of interpretation has last its dominance. New developments in literary analysis, sociocultural concerns, linguistics, and philosophy have made their impact on biblical interpretation. Thus one can approach the text with a wide variety of methods and questions realizing that interpretation is a multilevel and complex phenomenon. No one single approach is assumed to exhaust the text. In addition to the old fields of textual, source, form, and historical criticisms, new criticisms are now part of the scene—redaction, structural, reader response, rhetorical, canonical—each concerned with different emphases and goals. Simultaneously, the Bible is read with sensitivity toward and advocacy of the concerns of various social groups; thus we may now include liberation, third-world, feminist, and black hermeneutics among the many modern "schools" of biblical interpretation.

For Further Study

In the *Mercer Dictionary of the Bible*: BIBLE AND WESTERN LITERATURE; HERMENEUTICS; INTERPRETATION, HISTORY OF; LITERATRURE, BIBLE AS; PATRISTIC LITERATURE. In other sources: (See also works cited, below.)

General. P. R. Ackroyd et al., eds., *Cambridge History of the Bible*, 3 vols.; L. Diestel, *Geschichte des Alten Testamentes in der Christlichen Kirche*; *Enchiridion biblicum. Documenta ecclesiastica Sacram Scripturam spectantia*, 4th ed.; F. W. Farrar, *History of Interpretation*; R. M. Grant and D. Tracy, *A Short History of the Interpretation of the Bible*; F. E. Greenspahn, ed., *Scripture in the Jewish and Christian Traditions: Authority, Interpretation, Relevance*; C. Kannengiesser, ed., *Bible de tous les temps*. 8 vols.; D. E. Nineham, ed., *The Church's Use of the Bible: Past and Present*; D. Norton, *A History of the Bible as Literature*. 2 vols.

Inner-Biblical Interpretation. G. L. Archer and G. C. Chirichigno, *O.T. Quotations in the N.T.: A Complete Survey*; D. A. Carson and H. G. M. Williams,

eds., *It is Written: Scripture Citing Scripture*; D. Daube, *The N.T. and Rabbinic Judaism*; C. H. Dodd, *According to the Scriptures: The Sub-Structure of N.T. Theology*; E. E. Ellis, *The O.T. in Early Christianity*; M. Fishbane, *Biblical Interpretation in Ancient Israel*; L. Goppelt, *Typos: The Typological Interpretation of the O.T. in the New*; A. T. Hanson, *Living Utterances of God: The N.T. Exegesis of the Old*; D. H. Juel, *Messianic Exegesis: Christological Interpretation of the O.T. in Early Christianity*; B. Lindars, *N.T. Apologetic: The Doctrinal Significance of the O.T. Quotations*; J. Weingreen, *From Bible to Mishna: The Continuity of Tradition*.

Early Jewish and Christian Interpretation. J. Barton, *Oracles of God: Perceptions of Ancient Prophecy in Israel after the Exile*; J. Braverman, *Jerome's Commentary on Daniel: A Study of Comparative Jewish and Christian Interpretation of the Hebrew Bible*; G. J. Brooke, *Exegesis at Qumran: 4Q Florilegium in Its Jewish Context*; J. C. Endres, *Biblical Interpretation in the Book of Jubilees*; R. M. Grant, *Heresy and Criticism: The Search for Authenticity in Early Christian*

Literature; G. M. Hahneman, *The Muratorian Fragment and the Development of the Canon*; R. P. C. Hanson, *Allegory and Event: A Study of The Sources and Significance of Origen's Interpretation of Scripture*; M. P. Horgan, *Pesharim: Qumran Interpretations of Biblical Books*; J. L. Kugel and A. G. Rowan, *Early Biblical Interpretation*; B. de Margerie, *Introduction a l'histoire de l'exégèse*. 3 vols.; M. J. Mulder, ed., *Mikra: Text, Translation, Reading and Interpretation of the Hebrew Bible in Ancient Judaism and Early Christianity*; J. Neusner, *What is Midrash?*; D. Patte, *Early Jewish Hermeneutic in Palestine*; H. G. Reventlow, *Epochen der Bibelauslegung*, vol. 1, *Vom Alten Testament bis Origenes*; M. Simonetti, *Biblical Interpretation in the Early Church: An Historical Introduction to Patristic Exegesis*; H. L. Strack and G. Stemberger, *Introduction to the Talmud and Midrash*; T. H. Tobin, *The Creation of Man: Philo and the History of Interpretation*; J., W. Trigg, *Biblical Interpretation*; G. Vermes, *Scripture and Tradition in Judaism*; D. Winston, ed., *Philo of Alexandria*.

Medieval Period. A. Berlin, *Biblical Poetry through Medieval Jewish Eyes*; W. Chomsky, *David Kimhi's Hebrew Grammar (Mikhlol)*; I. Contreni, "Carolingian Biblical Studies," *Carolingian Essays*, ed. U.-R. Blumenthal; N. van Deusen, ed., *The Place of the Psalms in the Intellectual Culture of the Middle Ages*; R. K. Emmerson and B. McGinn, eds., *The Apocalypse in the Middle Ages*; G. R. Evans, *The Language and Logic of the Bible: The Earlier Middle Ages*; H. Feld, *Die Anfänge der modernen biblischen Hermeneutik in der spätmittelalterlichen Theologie*; B. Fischer, *Lateinische Bibelhandschriften im frühen Mittelalter*; K. Froehlich, "'Always to Keep the Literal Sense in Holy Scripture Means to Kill One's Soul': The State of Biblical Hermeneutics at the Beginning of the Fifteenth Century," in *Literary Uses of Typology from the Late Middle Ages to the Present*, ed. E. Miner; A. Funkenstein, *Theology and the Scientific Imagination from the Middle Ages to the Seventeenth Century*; H. Hailperin, *Rashi and The Christian Scholars*; B. Holtz, B., ed., *Back to The Sources: Reading The Classic Jewish Texts*; F. Kropatschek, *Das Schriftprinzip der lutherischen Kirche I: Die Vorgeschichte: Das Erbe des Mittelalters*; W. Lourdaux and D. Verhelst, eds., *The Bible and Medieval Culture*; de Lubac, H., *Exégèse Médiévale: Les quatre sens de l'écriture*. 4 vols; R. E. McNalley, *The Bible in The Early Middle Ages*; A. J. Minnis, *Medieval Theory of Authorship: Scholastic Literary Attitudes in the Later Middle Ages*. 2nd ed.; A. J. Minnis and A. B. Scott, *Medieval Literary Theory and Criticism ca. 1100-ca. 1375: The Commentary Tradition*, rev. ed.; J. S. Preus, *From Shadow to Promise: O.T. Interpretation from Augustine to the Young Luther*; H. Rost, *Die Bibel im Mittelalter*; H. Schüssler, *Der Primät der Heiligen Schrift als theologisches und kanonistisches Problem im Spätmittalter*; U. Simon, *Four Approaches to the Book of Psalms: From*

Saadiah Gaon to Abraham Ibn Ezra; B. Smalley, *Medieval Exegesis of Wisdom Literature: Essays by Beryl Smalley*, ed. R. E. Murphy; *Studies in Medieval Thought and Learning: From Abelard to Wyclif*; *The Study of the Bible in the Middle Ages*, 3rd ed.; and *The Gospels in the Schools ca. 1100-ca. 1280*; P. C. Spicq, *Esquisse d'une historie de l'exégèse latine du moyen age*; K. Walsh and D. Wood, eds., *The Bible in The Medieval World: Essays in Memory of Beryl Smalley*.

Renaissance-Reformation. D. C. Allen, *The Legend of Noah: Renaissance Rationalism in Art, Sciences and Letters*; J. H. Bentley, *Humanists and Holy Writ: N.T. Scholarship in the Renaissance*; G. R. Evans, *The Language and Logic of the Bible: The Road to Reformation*; O. Fatio and P. Fraenkel, eds., *Histoire de l'exégèse au XVI* siècle*; J. Friedman, *The Most Ancient Testimony: Sixteenth-Century Christian-Hebraica in the Age of Renaissance Nostalgia*; E. A. Gosselin, *The King's Progress to Jerusalem: Some Interpretations of David during The Reformation and Their Patristic and Medieval Background*; K. Hagen, *Luther's Approach to Scripture as Seen in His "Commentaries" on Galatians 1519-1538*; A. McGrath, *The Intellectual Origins of the European Reformation*; J. Pelikan, *Luther the Expositor: Introduction to the Reformer's Exegetical Writings*; W. Schwarz, *Principles and Problems of Biblical Translation: Some Reformation Controversies and Their Background*; D. C. Steinmetz, ed., *The Bible in the Sixteenth Century*; G. H. Tavard, *Holy Writ or Holy Church: The Crisis of the Protestant Reformation*.

Seventeenth and Eighteenth Centuries. W. Baird, *A History of N.T. Research*, vol. 1, *From Deism to Tübingen*; A. Barnes, *Jean Leclerc (1657-1736) et la république des lettres*; S. G. Burnett, *The Christian Hebraism of Johann Buxtorf (1564-1629)*; H. Chadwick, *Lessing's Theological Writings: Selections in Translation with an Introductory Essay*; M.-H. Cotoni, *Exégèse du Nouveau Testament dans la philosophie française du dix-huiteme siecle*; J. Drury, *Critics of the Bible 1724-1873*; H. W. Frei, *The Eclipse of Biblical Narrative: A Study in Eighteenth and Nineteenth Century Hermeneutics*; D. Freiday, *The Bible: Its Criticism, Interpretation and Use in 16th and 17th Century England*; R. C. Fuller, *Alexander Geddes 1737-1802: Pioneer of Biblical Criticism*; G. L. Jones, *The Discovery of Hebrew in Tudor England: A Third Language*; E. G. Kraeling, *The O.T. Since the Reformation*; H.-J. Kraus, *Die Biblische Theologie. Ihr Geschichte und Problematik*; H.-J. Kraus, *Geschichte der historisch-kritischen Erforschung des Alten Testaments*, 3rd ed.; W. G. Kümmel, *The N.T.: The History of the Investigation of Its Problems*; R. H. Popkin, *The History of Skepticism from Erasmus to Spinoza*; R. H. Popkin and J. E. Force, *Essays on the Context, Nature, and Influence of Isaac Newton's Theology*; R. Preus, *The Inspiration of Scripture: A Study of the Seventeenth Century Lutheran Dogmaticians*; G. Reedy, *The*

Bible and Reason: Anglicans and Scripture in Late Seventeenth-Century England; H. G. Reventlow, *The Authority of the Bible and the Rise of The Modern World*; H. G. Reventlow, et al. (eds.), *Historische Kritik und biblischer Kanon in der deutschen Aufklärung*; D. Ritschl, "Johann Salomo Semler: The Rise of the Historical-Critical Method in Eighteenth-Century Theology on the Continent," *Introduction to Modernity: A Symposium on Eighteenth-Century Thought*, ed. Robert Mollenauer; K. Scholder, *The Birth of Modern Critical Theory: Origins and Problems of Biblical Criticism in the Seventeenth Century*; E. S. Shaffer, *"Kubla Khan" and the Fall of Jerusalem: The Mythological School in Biblical Criticism and Secular Literature 1770-1880*; L. Stephen, *History of English Thought in the Eighteenth Century*, 2 vols.; B. Willey, *The Seventeenth Century Background: Studies in the Thought of the Age in Relation to Poetry and Religion.*

Nineteenth Century. C. Brown, *Jesus in European Protestant Thought 1778-1860*; J. W. Brown, *The Rise of Biblical Criticism in America, 1800-1870*; J. E. Carpenter, *The Bible in the Nineteenth Century*; T. K. Cheyne, *Founders of O.T. Criticism*; R. E. Clements, "The Study of the O.T.," in *Nineteenth Century Religious Thought in the West*, ed. N. Smart et al., 3 vols.; H. Detering, *Paulusbriefe ohne Paulus? Die Paulusbriefe in der holländisehen Radikalkritik*; S. J. De Vries, *Bible and Theology in the Netherlands: Dutch O.T. Criticism under Modernist and Conservative Auspices, 1850 to World War I*, 2nd ed.; G. B. Glover, *Evangelical Nonconformists and Higher Criticism in the Nineteenth Century*; E. Krentz, *The Historical-Critical Method*; M. C. Massey, *Christ Unmasked: The Meaning of The Life of Jesus in German Politics*; J. C. O'Neill, "The Study of the N.T.," in *Nineteenth Century Religious Thought*, ed. N. Smart et al. 3 vols.; J. C. O'Neill, *The Bible's Authority: A Portrait Gallery of Thinkers from Lessing to Bultmann*; R. A. Riesen, *Criticism and Faith in Late Victorian Scotland: A. B. Davidson, William Robertson Smith, and George Adam Smith*; J. W. Rogerson, *O.T. Criticism in the Nineteenth Century: England and Germany*; J. W. Rogerson, *W. M. L. de Wette, Founder of Modern Biblical Criticism: An Intellectual Biography*; R. J. Thompson, *Moses and the Law in a Century of Criticism since Graf.*

Twentieth Century. J. Barton, *Reading the O.T.: Method in Biblical Study*; H. Boers, *What is N.T. Theology?*; R. E. Clements, *A Century of O.T. Study*, rev. ed.; E. J. Epp and G. W. MacRae, eds., *The N.T. and Its Modern Interpreters*; H. F. Hahn, *The O.T. in Modern Research*, 2nd ed.; J. H. Hayes, *Introduction to Old Testament Study*; D. A. Knight and G. M. Tucker, eds., *The O.T. and Its Modern Interpreters*; I. H. Marshall, ed., *N.T. Interpretation*; R. Morgan (with J. Barton), *Biblical Interpretation*; S. Neill and T.

Wright, *The Interpretation of the N.T. 1861-1986*; O. C. Ollenburger, et al., eds., *The Flowering of O.T. Theology*; J. K. Riches, *A Century of N.T. Study*; H. G. Reventlow, *Problems of Old Testament Theology in the Twentieth Century*; H. G. Reventlow, *Problems of Biblical Theology in the Twentieth Century*; R. Smend, *Deutsche Alttestamentler in Drei Jahrhunderten.*

Works Cited

Blackwell, R. 1991. *Galileo, Bellarmine, and the Bible.*

Burns, R. M. 1981. *The Great Debate on Miracles: From Joseph Glanville to David Hume.*

Byrne, P. 1989. *Natural Religion and the Nature of Religion: The Legacy of Deism.*

Colish, M. L. 1994. *Peter Lombard.* Two volumes.

Eisenstein, E. L. 1979. *The Printing Press as an Agent of Change.*

Froehlich, K., ed. 1984. *Biblical Interpretation in the Early Church.*

Gameson, R. G., ed. 1994. *The Early Medieval Bible: Its Production, Decoration, and Use.*

Gibson, M. T. 1993. *The Bible in the Latin West.*

Gibson, M. T., and K. Froehlich, eds. 1992. *Biblia Latina cum Glossa Ordinaria: Facsimile Reprint of the Editio Princeps by Adolf Rusch of Strassburg, ca. 1480.* Four volumes.

Hill, C. 1993. *The English Bible and the Seventeenth Century Revolution.*

Jacobs, L. 1973. *Jewish Biblical Exegesis.*

Jordan, M. D. and K. Emery, eds. 1992. *Ad Litteram: Authoritative Texts and Their Medieval Readers.*

Laplanche, F. J. M. 1986. *L'Ecriture, le sacré et l'histoire. Erudits et politiques protestants devant la Bible en France au XVIIᵉ siecle.*

Moore, G. F. 1921. "Christian Writers on Judaism," *HTR* 14:197-254.

Muller, R. A. 1993. *Post-Reformation Reformed Dogmatics.* Vol. 2. *Holy Scripture: The Cognitive Foundation of Theology.*

Pals, D. 1982. *The Victorian "Lives" of Jesus.*

Popkin, R. H. 1987. *Isaac La Peyrère (1596-1676): His Life, Work, and Influence.*

Rogerson, J., C. Rowland, and B. Lindars. 1988. *The Study and Use of the Bible.*

Sarna, N. M. 1971. "Hebrew and Bible Studies in Medieval Spain," in *The Sephardi Heritage*, ed. R. D. Barnett.

Schweitzer, A. 1910. *The Quest of the Historical Jesus.*

van Rooden, P. T. 1989. *Theology, Biblical Scholarship, and Rabbinical Studies in the Seventeenth Century: Constantijn L'Empereur (1591-1648) Professor of Hebrew and Theology at Leiden.*

Williams, A. 1948. *The Common Expositor: An Account of the Commentaries on Genesis 1527-1633.*

Biblical Theology

Molly T. Marshall

Biblical theology is that discipline that articulates the message of Scripture, the ways of God with creation and humanity, in its own historical setting. Unlike systematic, philosophical, or dogmatic theology, biblical theology does not utilize categories drawn from the church's historic faith, systems of philosophy, or conciliar formulations or creeds. Rather, biblical theology seeks to understand the message of the BIBLE, which itself arises from varied voices in a wide range of historical contexts.

This form of theology necessarily includes exegetical, hermeneutical, and systematic (in terms of an orderly exposition of the biblical materials) dimensions; however, in its contemporary dress biblical theology often utilizes auxiliary disciplines such as literary criticism and sociology.

The question of the theological unity and diversity of the teachings of Scripture has made biblical theology a much debated enterprise, and establishing the central theme or forging agreement about key integrating motifs has been difficult. Thus, theologies of the whole Bible are rare; indeed, as Reventlow (1986) has observed, a " 'biblical theology' has yet to be written." Usually a scholar has attempted to treat the Hebrew Scriptures or the New Testament, or perhaps some body of literature within these testamental frameworks.

The contemporary status of biblical theology is fraught with conflicting perspectives concerning a terminal or healthy prognosis for the discipline. Representative of the former perspective are scholars such as Childs (1970), Barr (1976), Strecker (1991), and Reventlow (1986) who argue the discipline is in crisis (or at least is methodologically muddled) and needs a radical recasting. A more promising diagnosis is offered by Smart (1979), Mauser (1991), Trible (1978), and Reumann (1991), who see many creative possibilities on the horizon. The last few decades have witnessed the fragmentation of a once coherent if diverse movement that emerged during the 1940s and figured prominently in the period following the Second World War. The wide consensus concerning the tasks and methods of biblical theology that claimed scholars earlier in this century is no longer valid.

In this article, this development is charted by a brief history of the roots of biblical theology, a survey of the chief characteristics of the Biblical Theology Movement, an analysis of its decline due to tensions and methodological problems, and perspectives on the possibility of recovering or reorienting biblical theology in the present. Because many essays and monographs have been devoted to analyzing this movement (see the bibliography), this treatment will focus more on new approaches and trends in biblical theology.

The Historical Roots of Biblical Theology

The roots of biblical theology can be traced to the Reformation, or, perhaps, to the forerunner of the Reformation, John Wyclif (some scholars have even pointed as far back as the writings of IRENAEUS or Origen). For Wyclif the whole Bible was to be understood as the sole criterion of doctrine, a radical departure from the Medieval Schoolmen. Clearly, biblical teaching was not equal to ecclesiastical dogma in early Christianity and the Middle Ages.

The Reformers' renewed attention to biblical exegesis evoked understandings that conflicted with the magisterial tradition of the CHURCH, leading to one of the Reformation's overarching watchwords, *Sola Scriptura*. Yet neither the Reformers nor their followers produced a biblical theology. Instead, the subordination of the Bible to dogmatic theology (collections of texts under doctrinal headings) continued, now in the form of Protestant Orthodoxy. The Pietist Philipp Spener (1635–1705) in his *Pia Desideria* (*Pious Desires*, 1675) challenged this dogmatic control, urging a simple openness to the Bible that would allow it to function as the basis and norm for all theology.

The Enlightenment fostered powerful intellectual forces that called forth a major reorientation in biblical and theological study. As a new historical consciousness took form, eighteenth-century theologians began to call for a critical study of the Bible for its own sake, not as simply a ready compendium of proof texts for the dogmatic teaching of the church. In his inaugural address at the University of Altdorf in 1787, Johann Philipp Gabler (1753–1826) distinguished between *biblical* and *dogmatic* theology. Biblical theology, according to Gabler's rationalist program, is

> of historical origin, conveying what the holy writers felt about divine things; on the other hand, there is dogmatic theology of didactic origin, teaching what each theologian . . . philosophizes rationally about divine things.

Gabler is not suggesting that pure biblical theology can serve all needs for doctrinal teaching, but Scripture must not be interpreted through the dogmatic lens. His line of demarcation between historical and theological study of the Bible has been difficult to secure, as subsequent writings have demonstrated.

Gabler wanted the Bible to serve as the foundation of all theology. He argued that the Bible did not contain theology in the sense of a rigorous second-order reflection; rather, it offers religion that he understood to be the ordinary conceptions, beliefs, and teachings of persons responding to the divine revelation in their specific historical settings. He envisioned biblical theology as a purely historical discipline that should correct the errors of dogmatic theology. This clear delineation between biblical and dogmatic theology set forth by Gabler did not result in cooperation within these areas of study—the goal he desired—but rather in an ever-widening chasm between them until the emergence of the Biblical Theology Movement.

William Wrede (1859–1906) followed the impulse of Gabler's distinction to its logical conclusion. Wrede argued in 1897 in his little book *Concerning the Task and Method of the So-called New Testament Theology* that biblical theology as it pertains to the NT should not be bound to the dogmatic category of "canon." Further, the NT ought not be interpreted as a doctrinal system. This contention led to the development of the history-of-religions school that examined a variety of religious traditions without giving a privileged status to the religion of the NT. Historians of religion such as Wernle, Bousset, and Weiss, to mention only a few, interpreted the history of faith in Christ in the broad framework of the religious environment surrounding Christianity. Sources for this study included in addition to the NT writings extrabiblical materials from the early centuries. Rudolf Bultmann's magisterial *Theology of the New Testament* (1949, 1953; ET 1951, 1955) demonstrates the full flowering and perhaps final example of this approach.

As might be expected, reactions against the history-of-religions approach were voiced by scholars concerned for the theological meaning of the Bible for the church. About the turn of the century Adolf von Schlatter (1852–1938), an able representative of this conservative reaction, resisted the separation between historical and dogmatic work, contending that while a person of faith may approach these tasks as methodologically distinct, he or she cannot (and should not) bracket out the presuppositions that such faith contains. It is a chief responsibility of the Christian scholar to work out of a theological method that is not imposed by the culture.

Schlatter did not presume that the Scriptures provided theology in the strict sense of the term, but in his judgments more could be found than the simple ethical religion purported by the *Religionsgeschichtliche Schule*. The interpreter could not escape theological questions. In what way, for example, is the truth conveyed by the Scriptures in an earlier historical setting relevant for the Christian today? In many ways Schlatter anticipated some aspects of neoorthodoxy and the contemporary understanding in Gospel studies of the inseparable intertwining of the historical and theological materials, yet his own biblical theology remains in the fetters of dogmatics.

The Biblical Theology Movement

Robert C. Dentan (1963) suggests three factors that contributed to a move beyond the history-of-religions and liberal approaches of the late nineteenth and early twentieth centuries: (1) a loss of faith in evolutionary naturalism; (2) a reaction against the purely historical method that claimed complete objectivity and presumed the adequacy of the "bare facts" to convey historical truth; and (3) the recovery of the idea of revelation.

Identifying biblical theology as the "biblical companion" to dialectical theology, James Barr (1976) sees in these concomitant movements a strong reaction to the biblical interpretation of liberal theology that was ostensibly controlled by the History of Religions School. In neoorthodox theology and biblical theology the convergence of theological concern with renewed biblical study is evident.

The Distinctiveness of Biblical Thought

Biblical theology has characteristically been opposed to any philosophical system as the interpretative framework in which Scripture must be understood. Along with avoiding categories that Scripture itself does not provide, biblical theology has resisted the systematic impulses of dogmatic theology that follows the Lombardian order in *Sententiarum libri IV* (*Four Books of Sentences*, ca. 1148–1151), a theological method foreign to the Bible.

Biblical theology places considerable emphasis upon the distinctive Hebraic thought patterns and view of history found in the Bible. It considers Greek thought an alien and corrupting influence on the semitic structure found in Scripture. On the one hand, considering the NT apart from its sociocultural and religious setting in contradistinction to the history-of-religions approach heightened the distinctiveness of Christian faith; but on the other hand, it diminished the contribution that an understanding of context often makes to informed hermeneutics and theological construction.

The Unity of the Bible

Biblical theology assumes the unity of the Bible although individual scholars have construed this unity in disparate ways. An abiding problem has been the relationship between the testaments—a problem that has contributed to the almost insuperable task of writing a theology of the whole Bible. Christian scholars have at times sacrificed the original meaning and integrity of the Hebrew Scriptures in their historical situation in their haste to appropriate them for the church's teaching under the lordship of Christ, or they have regarded the OT as inferior revelation that has little consequence for theology and doctrine.

The relationship between the OT and the NT has been configured by biblical theologians in the following representative approaches (see the useful surveys by Barr [1976], Reventlow [1986], and Hasel [1984]).

Salvation-History. The model of an ongoing salvation history is an attempt to embrace both testaments under the theme of the continuity of God's redemptive activity. Under this rubric the tradition-history method of OT scholar Gerhard von Rad (1962, 1965) saw the historical traditions of the faith of Israel in an ineluctable process of reinterpretation in new contexts. The traditions of the OT logically lead into the NT, for the view of history in the biblical writings is open to a future.

Starting from a NT perspective, Oscar Cullmann (*Chrsit and Time*, 1945; ET 1949, [3]1962) offered a different approach. He argued that the center of God's saving acts was the Christ-event that is itself in continuity with the salvation-history of the OT where God acted through key events.

Typology. The typological approach was revivified by the Biblical Theology Movement through the efforts of scholars such as von Rad and Leonard Goppelt. Long thought to have been made obsolete by historical-critical studies, biblical theologians returned to a method prized by exegetes of the early church. Patterns or types are said to occur in the OT that prefigure some truth connected with Christianity.

Goppelt insisted that the typological approach of the OT in the NT (as the key method of interpretation and theological understanding) showed "the New Testament's consciousness of its own place in redemptive history." Roman Catholic theology has shared this interest in the typological method. Jean Daniélou (1960) argued for typology as a means of a spiritual reading of Scripture. He extended his exegetical work to both testaments since typology may be seen within the OT itself as well as in the NT's method of interpreting Scripture.

Sensus Plenior. Catholic scholarship has debated a third method of relating the OT and the NT during the decades following the Second World War. The *Sensus Plenior* or "fuller meaning" approach suggests that because Scripture is inspired by God there is a deeper meaning in the texts than any human author can know. This meaning can only be discerned in light of further revelation. Thus the whole Bible exists in an organic relationship and is best understood when related to the Christ event. This concept sought to interface traditional interpretations with renewed biblical study, for example, Isa 7:14 was discerned by Matthew (1:23) to be referring to the virgin birth.

Promise and Fulfillment. A fourth means of postulating the unity of Scripture is found in the scheme of promise and fulfillment. This could take the form of examining the "messianic promises" of the OT that find their fulfillment in the life of Jesus Christ. Biblical theologians using this method are not of one mind about whether the OT only points beyond itself to future actualization of prophecy or if there is a provisional level of fulfillment within the OT itself. Further, in what way can the biblical interpreter claim final fulfillment in the activity of Jesus, the expectation of the kingdom of God, and eschatological hope?

The Superiority of the Old Testament. A rather novel approach has been offered by A. A. van Ruler (1971), a Reformed theologian, who argued for the superiority of the OT. The integrating motif of the Bible is the theocratic Rule of God demonstrated in concrete earthly circumstances, which he maintains is evident in the OT. The NT's "spiritualization" of the Rule not only diminishes the robust character of the Reign of God, but cannot stand alone. Without Israel's understanding of their identity as the people of God, the land, the posterity, and supremely the Sovereign Rule of God, as found in the OT, the story of Jesus has no grounding. Indeed, van Ruler warns against doing violence to the OT by trying to find Jesus Christ within its pages; rather, one should read it to, for example, legitimate his messiahship, not to conscript it as a Christian text.

Word Studies

Bible dictionaries and word studies have been characteristic of biblical theology, and at times word studies have been *equated* with biblical theology. The Kittel-Friedrich ten-volume NT dictionary (1933–1976; ET 1964–1976), which features rich studies of Hebrew and Greek words, is the abiding fruit of this movement. Although the conception of language upon which this work was based (and its adherence to a salvation-history orientation) has been severely criticized, the word studies continue to shape the prospects for biblical theology.

Popular approaches included studying all the Hebrew names for God or the titles ascribed to Jesus as a means of discerning the theological content of texts. This atomistic method of interpretation neglected the narrative character of the biblical material and the interthematic connections within Scripture.

Revelation in History

Articulating a fully orbed understanding of revelation has been of chief interest to the Biblical Theology Movement. The emphasis on history as the locus for revelation has allowed biblical theologians to steer between a fundamentalist notion of the Bible as the deposit of doctrine and the liberal notion that Scripture merely reflects the progressive religious consciousness of a particular group of people. Selectively appropriating biblical material to reinforce the notion of the Hebrew view of history, scholars accentuated revelation through history. This perspective presupposes a special stream of saving history within the larger flow of world history, and the mighty acts of God were accessible only to those participating in the salvation history of Israel and the church.

Yet the construct of two realms of history seems to imply that while God is especially at work in "holy history" the rest of history (as well as nature) is marked by its exclusion from the redemptive activity of God. Further, the inaccessibility of this revelation to canons of historical criticism as put forward by the influential Ernst Troeltsch has rendered dubious the coherence of the idea of revelation in history, as the sustained work of Wolfhart Pannenberg manifests.

The Decline of Biblical Theology

Many reasons are cited for the dissipation of the Biblical Theology Movement (at least in its particularly American form), some of which have already been noted. Brevard Childs (1970) suggests that unresolved methodological problems led to the cracking of the walls and the erosion of the foundation of the movement. Central to Childs's critique of biblical theology is its "problem with the Bible."

There has been a prevailing uncertainty and awkwardness about how to use the Bible because of the lack of interface between historical criticism and theological interpretation. Consequently, locating biblical theology courses in the seminary curricula proved problematic. For example, in what way should these courses relate to biblical studies and to systematic theology?

The continuing separation of the study of the OT from the NT further retarded biblical theology. Beyond formal theological education, biblical theology did not serve congregational life effectively either. Childs argues that no "new genre of preaching" emerged and the claims for the "mighty acts of God" in history seemed overdrawn for the conventional life of the church. The relevance of the Bible for the life of modern Christianity was contestable—the nadir of what the Biblical Theology Movement has promised.

Fissures in the foundational affirmations of biblical theology concerning the significance of words studies, the concept of history, the Hebrew-Greek dichotomy, the distinctiveness of the Bible over against its environment, and the unity of the Bible, led to destructive divisions and decline. John Reumann (1991) observes a similar demise of the popularity of Barthian theology, for which biblical theology had a close affinity. Their common repudiation of philosophy and hostility to historical context could not withstand new developments in theological studies, and they were left behind.

Barr (1976) has maintained that biblical theology lacked a scientific method that could sustain its enterprise. Word studies and linguistic analysis came closest to such a method, but much of the work of biblical theologians was done in reaction to the guiding assumptions and critical tools of earlier liberal scholarship. Setting their work over against these academic forebears, they failed to justify their own approach adequately. Concepts such as the "Word of God," God's "mighty acts," or even "history" were left only vaguely defined or a common understanding was merely assumed.

Contemporary Perspectives on Biblical Theology

The period from about 1970 forward has seen a resurgence in biblical studies among Roman Catholics, following the direction set by Vatican II. Two contemporary Roman Catholic scholars, Karl Rahner and Edward Schillebeeckx demonstrate their conviction that dogmatic theology cannot avoid engaging in biblical theology. The theological content of the biblical writings must be joined with the larger Christian tradition, yet remain the *norma non normata* for theology and the Church. The Church's traditional emphases on canon and authority were easily compatible with renewed attention to the canonical shape and form of Scripture, and lectionary reform ensued.

Other significant methodological contributions to biblical theology have come in the form of new interest in the sociocultural context of the biblical writings (something of a return to the history-of-religions approach) as well as the social location of those who are reading the texts. This latter aspect, "reader-oriented" criticism, has been particularly accentuated by liberation and feminist theologians.

The current epoch is characterized by a paradigm shift from the *historical* era to the *literary* era in biblical studies. New methods drawn from literary criticism have fulminated a variety of new directions in biblical theology. Narrative criticism, rhetorical approaches, and structuralism are calling attention in a fresh way to the nature of the biblical story.

In 1973 Walter Brueggemann and John R. Donahue initiated a new monograph series entitled Overtures to Biblical Theology. In the series foreword they wrote: "The certainties of the older biblical theology *in service* of dogmatics, as well as of the more recent biblical theology movement *in lieu* of dogmatics, are no longer present" (Brueggemann 1977, xi). Hence, there

is great variation in the blueprints for constructing the bridge between the biblical texts and a coherent theological program (which is a strength); though some remain under construction, these bridges are proving that they can bear the weight of biblical theology.

In the remainder of this article, a brief overview of selected new methods will be offered. Distinctive approaches, each has significant implications for the promise of biblical theology for the future.

Feminist Hermeneutics

A "feminist biblical theology" has been emerging over the past two decades among Jewish and Christian scholars. Although there are pluriform critical strategies being employed among those who refuse to see the Bible as irredeemably misogynistic, the following methodological assumptions shape this new approach.

First, feminist biblical theology is conceived of as "advocacy" scholarship; feminist scholars believe descriptive treatments do little to further the liberation of women, a group regularly marginated in the Bible and society. Critics of this approach charge these scholars with subjective bias, coming to the biblical texts with a particular agenda; their response is that there is no neutral scholarship and biblical studies heretofore have been shaped by androcentric biases and concerns of mostly male students of Scripture. Feminist scholars are quite intentional about their purpose of studying the Bible in order to find liberating insights concerning God's intention for women. They cannot leave their own experience of "otherness" in a society where men have been the primary interpreters of reality behind as they pursue their exegetical and theological work.

Second, a critical feminist hermeneutics allows the reader to hear again the biblical stories of mostly silent women within patriarchal cultures. Through historical reconstruction of Christian origins (Elisabeth Schüssler Fiorenza 1983), discerning a "prophetic-liberating tradition" within Scripture (Rosemary Radford Ruether 1983), or careful linguistic and literary work (Phyllis Trible 1978; Mary Ann Tolbert 1983), the Bible is allowed to sing its song of God's care for the oppressed. This "reclamation project" is necessary for many for whom Scripture has become "unholy" (Trible's term). Numerous recent monographs and articles have focused on individual women of the Bible as well as their social and political circumstances.

Third, feminist approaches to biblical theology involve both a "hermeneutics of suspicion" and a "herme neutics of consent." The former prompts the interpreter to bring new questions to the biblical material, for example, why was Abraham's son Isaac spared while Jephthah's daughter—whose name we do not know—was not? What does this say about the status of women among the people of God and God's seeming legitimation of such oppression? The latter coordinate, a "hermeneutics of consent," privileges the biblical material as the horizon of the Christian community's faith and experience, and seeks to discern its dimensions of authority in the life of the church, and particularly in the lives of contemporary women.

Feminist approaches are rapidly changing the terrain traversed by biblical theologians. Burgeoning literature by feminist scholars reflecting creative interpretation and theological construction is making the pursuit of biblical theology both livelier and more complex. As a specialization within the larger field of liberation theology, feminist biblical theology gives voice to the urgent message of God's justice for the oppressed and forsaken found in the Bible.

The Jewishness of Jesus

Some recent scholars have suggested that a third "quest" for the historical Jesus is underway presently, the quest for the "Jewish Jesus." Yet this quest does not depend upon earlier historical methods that sought to unearth "bare facts" untainted by confessional or theological material. The map for this quest is charted by a new alliance with social sciences that offers a new perspectival window on the social setting and patterns of first-century JUDAISM. A new confidence about the possibility of learning a great deal about the life of Jesus accompanies these new methods.

The current interest in the Jewishness of Jesus is framed by the larger discussion of the relationship of Judaism to Christianity. Thus both Jewish (Pinchas Lapide 1983; David Flusser 1991; Geza Vermes 1973) and Christian (Marcus J. Borg 1987; Robert Funk 1975; E. P. Sanders 1985) scholars are contributing new insights to biblical studies that presage significant theological interpretation of a textual world they share.

How direct was Jesus about claiming messiahship? What was Jesus relationship to his people and to the official structures of Judaism? What was the purpose of Jesus' ministry within Judaism? How does the death of Jesus relate to his messianic status? Questions such as these are receiving new scrutiny and correcting certain biases with which biblical theologians in the Christian tradition have worked. Too often Christian

exegetes have been preoccupied with who Jesus was for Christianity rather than the prior question of Jesus' relationship to Judaism. A perjorative attitude toward and ignorance of Judaism has eviscerated much Christian scholarship of balanced perception. Indeed, the remarkable revival of interest in Jesus by Jewish as well as Christian scholars gives new depth to theological understanding of the Scriptures as a whole.

Theology in Canonical Context

A key response to the conundrum of the Biblical Theology Movement was a renewed interest in the meaning of canon for theology. Several methodological avenues vector out from this method: interest in biblical narrative, the literary character of the Bible, the canonical shaping of texts in their final form, intertextual reading, and the role of the canon in the church. The canon as the only appropriate context for doing biblical theology is due to its authoritative status because of the church's theological decision, according to Childs (1993), a foremost pioneer in this method.

Comprehensive in its treatment of Scripture, this strategy employs the whole Bible: both parts of the canon comprise the church's book. Hence, no "center" or "canon within the canon" can function as the hermeneutical key. Theology of the OT is treated as a Christian discipline because the Hebrew Scriptures are permanently joined to the NT by the church; likewise, the NT cannot be understood if severed from its place in the canon.

Important to this approach is an intertextual reading of the biblical materials. Worship, with its use of the lectionary, and doctrine, with its construal of texts drawn from the whole Bible, reflect the close relationship that biblical theology must forge with dogmatic theology.

Narrative theology owes its primary orientation to the emphasis on the final form of the text as proposed by this method. Rather than conducting an archaeological dig to discern the history behind the text, narrative theology reclaims an emphasis of the Reformers, that is, the perspicuity or the self-evident sense of Scripture for the community of faith. The literary-narrative shift promises to garner continuing attention.

Actualizing Interpretation

A final approach seeks to widen the aperture of vision for those pursuing biblical theology that they might address the present-day significance of their historical findings. The primary advocate of this method,

Heikki Räisänen (1990; although many others share his basic concern), seeks to repristinate Gabler's concern that *historical* and *theological* tasks be assigned to two different stages of work, but that both be done by *biblical* theologians. Averring that the unwieldy separation of the historical and theological tasks seen, for example, in Krister Stendahl's article on "Contemporary Biblical Theology" in *IDB* (1962), was doomed to failure, Räisänen contends for an approach that will allow biblical theology to actualize its constructs in a way that benefits universal human intellectual and religious needs. Biblical theology must not be a sequestered academic pursuit with primary attention devoted to the life of the church.

Biblical theology cannot rest with the descriptive task, yet what is its proper relationship to creeds, church tradition, and contemporary developments in Christian thought? Moreover, are there aspects of the theological task in which biblical theology has a normative role for humanity as a whole? These questions are probed by an actualizing interpretation that reflects on the biblical material from an ecumenical and global point of view. Perhaps the continuing vitality of the discipline is in large measure dependent upon such breadth of concern.

Conclusion

Biblical theology has changed graphically since its inception a little more than 200 years ago. Remarkable strides in the critical study of Scripture have sparked new insights into the biblical message; usually the trends have followed the larger cultural and theological trends in the academy and church.

The Biblical Theology Movement that held the field during the middle of this century has ended. Although a few scholars want to revive its major concerns (and a few more long for its unbridled confidence), biblical theology today is marked by vigorous new strategies and a bit more humility about the possibility of a holistic biblical theology.

Some of the same problems lurk as contemporary scholars attempt to relate the historical and theological components of the discipline to the contemporary church's need for dogmatic teaching. The diversity of Scripture wards off simple or forced harmonization, and its rich pluralism points beyond itself to the richness of divine revelation, indeed, to the mystery of God. Nevertheless, biblical theology remains a necessary and foundational partner for constructing a theological vision for the waning of this century and the beginning of the next. New means of access to these ancient texts are allowing them to speak their messages afresh.

For Further Study

In the *Mercer Dictionary of the Bible*: BIBLE; BIBLICAL THEOLOGY; CANON; FEMINIST HERMENEUTICS; HERMENEUTICS; THEOLOGY OF THE NT; THEOLOGY OF THE OT. In other sources: See the works cited below and H. Boers, *What Is N.T. Theology?*; H. Gese, *Essays on Biblical Theology*; L. Goppelt, *Theology of the N.T.*; W. Harrington, *The Path of Biblical Theology*; J. Lawson, *The Biblical Theology of St. Irenaeus*; R. Morgan, *The Nature of N.T. Theology*; P. Stuhlmacher, *Historical Criticism and Theological Interpretation of Scripture*; M. Tate, "Promising Paths toward Biblical Theology," *RE* 78/2 (1981): 169–85.

Works Cited

Barr, James. 1976. "Biblical Theology." *IDBSup.*

Borg, Marcus J. 1987. *Jesus: A New Vision.*

Brueggemann, Walter. 1977. *The Land: Place as Gift, Promise, and Challenge in Biblical Faith.* OBT.

Childs, Brevard S. 1970. *Biblical Theology in Crisis.* 1993. *Biblical Theology of the Old and New Testaments.*

Cullmann, Oscar. 1945; ET 1949, ³1962.

Daniélou, Jean. 1960. *From Shadows to Reality.*

Denten, Robert C. 1963. *Preface to Old Testament Theology.* Rev. ed.

Flusser, David. 1991. "Jesus, His Ancestry, and the Commandment of Love," in *Jesus' Jewishness*, ed J. H. Charlesworth.

Funk, Robert. 1975. *Jesus as Precursor.*

Hasel, G. F. 1984. "Biblical Theology Movement," *Evangelical Dictionary of Theology.*

Lapide, Pinchas. 1983. *The Resurrection of Jesus: A Jewish Perspective.*

Mauser, Ulrich. 1991. "Historical Criticism: Liberator or Foe of Biblical Theology," in Reumann 1991, 99-113.

Rad, Gerhard von. 1962. *Old Testament Theology.* Vol. 1. 1965. *Old Testament Theology.* Vol. 2.

Räisänen, Heikki. 1990. *Beyond New Testament Theology.*

Reumann, John, ed. 1991. *The Promise and Practice of Biblical Theology.*

Reventlow, Henning Graf. 1986. *Problems of Biblical Theology in the Twentieth Century.*

Ruether, Rosemany Radford. 1983. *Sexism and God-Talk: Toward a Feminist Theology.*

Ruler, Arnold Albert van. 1971. *The Christian Church and the O.T.*

Sanders, E. P. 1985. *Jesus and Judaism.*

Schüssler Fiorenza, Elisabeth. 1983. *In Memory of Her: A Feminist Theological Reconstruction of Christian Origins.*

Smart, James D. 1979. *The Past, Present, and Future of Biblical Theology.*

Strecker, Georg. 1991. "The Law in the Sermon on the Mount, and the Sermon on the Mount as Law," in Reumann 1991, 35–49.

Tolbert, Mary Ann. 1983. "Defining the Problem: The Bible and Feminist Hermeneutics," *Semeia* 28: 113–26.

Trible, Phyllis. 1978. *God and the Rhetoric of Sexuality.* OBT.

Vermes, Geza. 1973. *Jesus the Jew.*

The Importance of Noncanonical Literature

Joseph L. Trafton

Scholars frequently use the expression "noncanonical literature" to refer to specific groupings of Jewish and Christian writings that are not included in the biblical CANON. This article focuses on the five main groupings—the OT Apocrypha, the OT Pseudepigrapha, the Dead Sea Scrolls, the NT Apocrypha, and the Nag Hammadi library—and their importance for understanding the canonical literature.

Classification of Noncanonical Literature

The OT Apocrypha is a relatively fixed collection of Jewish writings found in the OT canons of Roman Catholic and Eastern Orthodox Christianity but not of Protestants. Roman Catholics call the books "Deuterocanonical"—secondarily canonical, or added later to the canon. The Deuterocanonical books are Tobit, Judith, Additions to Esther, Additions to Daniel (including Prayer of Azariah and the Song of the Three Jews, Susanna, and Bel and the Dragon), Wisdom of Solomon, Ecclesiasticus (Sirach), Baruch (or 1 Baruch), Letter of Jeremiah (=Baruch chap. 6), 1 Maccabees, and 2 Maccabees. The Greek Orthodox Church adds 1 Esdras, Psalm 151, Prayer of Manasseh, and 3 Maccabees, with 4 Maccabees in an appendix. The Russian Orthodox Church adds 1 Esdras, 2 Esdras, Psalm 151, and 3 Maccabees. The Roman Catholic canon places Prayer of Manasseh, 1 Esdras, and 2 Esdras in an appendix without implying canonicity.

The OT Pseudepigrapha is a modern collection of documents of primarily Jewish origin based mainly on the OT and frequently attributed (falsely) to OT figures. Most of the books were written between 200 B.C.E. and 200 C.E., although some were later. Many of them have been reworked by Christians, and some probably were composed by Christians. The separation of Jewish and Christian elements in many of these writings is a longstanding problem in Pseudepigrapha studies. The Pseudepigrapha are sometimes classified by literary form into APOCALYPTIC LITERATURE (e.g., *1 Enoch, 2 Enoch, 4 Ezra, 2 Baruch, 3 Baruch, Apocalypse of Abraham, Apocalypse of Zephaniah*, and *Apocalypse of Elijah*), testaments (e.g., *Testaments of the Twelve Patriarchs, Testament of Job, Testament of Abraham, Testament of Moses*, and *Testament of Solomon*), expansions of the OT and legends (e.g., *Letter of Aristeas, Jubilees, Martyrdom of Isaiah, Joseph and Asenath, Life of Adam and Eve, Pseudo-Philo, Lives of the Prophets, 4 Baruch*, and *Jannes and Jambres*), wisdom and philosophical literature (e.g., *Ahiqar* and 4 Maccabees), and prayers, psalms, and odes (e.g., Prayer of Manasseh, *Psalms of Solomon*, and *Odes of Solomon*), but such a classification is not precise.

The DEAD SEA SCROLLS is a vast collection of more than 800 ancient Jewish manuscripts discovered beginning in 1947 in caves along the DEAD SEA. These scrolls are the remains of a library that belonged to a group of sectarian Jews, probably ESSENES, who lived by the Dead Sea at a site called Qumran from ca. 141 B.C.E. to 68 C.E. In addition to containing the oldest known Hebrew OT manuscripts and portions of previously known apocrypha (apocryphal psalms, Letter of Jeremiah, Tobit, and Sirach) and pseudepigrapha (*Jubilees, 1 Enoch*, and *Testaments of the Twelve Patriarchs*), the scrolls contain other pseudepigrapha (e.g., *Genesis Apocryphon, Book of Giants, Book of Noah, Testament of Amram, Words of Moses, Samuel Apocryphon, Prayer of Nabonidus*, and *Pseudo-Daniel*), sectarian documents, including rules (e.g., *Manual of Discipline, Rule of the Congregation, Damascus Rule, War Rule, Temple Scroll*, and *Miqsat Ma'aseh Torah*), poetical-liturgical texts (e.g., *Thanksgiving Scroll, Angelic Liturgy, Blessings, Words of the Heavenly Lights*), and documents concerned with biblical interpretation (e.g., commentaries or *pesharim* on Isaiah, Habakkuk, Nahum, Hosea, Micah, and Psalm 37; *Florilegium* and *Testimonia*; *Patriarchal Blessings*; and *Melchizedek*), and miscellaneous writings (e.g., *New Jerusalem* and *Copper Scroll*).

The NT Apocrypha is a modern collection of writings composed by Christians between the first and fourth centuries C.E. They are about, or are pseudonymously attributed to, NT figures. These books are generally modeled after the literary forms found in the NT: there are apocryphal gospels (e.g., *Gospel of Peter*, *Infancy Gospel of Thomas*, *Protevangelium of James*, and *Gospel of Nicodemus*), apocryphal acts (e.g., *Acts of Peter*, *Acts of Paul*, *Acts of John*, *Acts of Andrew*, and *Acts of Thomas*), apocryphal letters (e.g., *3 Corinthians*, *Letter to the Laodiceans*, *Pseudo-Titus*, and *Letter of Barnabas*), and apocryphal revelations (e.g., *Apocalypse of Peter*, *Apocalypse of Paul* [ANT], and *Apocalypse of Thomas*).

The NAG HAMMADI library consists of thirteen codices discovered in 1945 near Nag Hammadi, Egypt. These codices, which date from the fourth century C.E., are the remains of a library that apparently belonged to a Christian monastery at nearby Chenoboskian. The codices contain fifty-two tractates, forty of which were unknown prior to this discovery. Most of the documents reflect the viewpoints of the syncretistic religious movement known as GNOSTICISM. Some are neither Jewish nor Christian (e.g., *Discourse on the Eighth and Ninth*, *Three Steles of Seth*, *Zostrianos*, and *Allogenes*); one, *Apocalypse of Adam*, is Jewish. Most, however, are Christian: there are gospels (e.g., *Gospel of Truth*, *Gospel of Thomas*, *Gospel of Philip*, and *Gospel of the Egyptians*), acts (e.g., *Acts of Peter and the Twelve Apostles* and *Letter of Peter to Philip*), letters (e.g., *Treatise on the Resurrection* and *Eugnostos*), and apocalypses (e.g., *Apocalypse of Peter*, *Apocalypse of Paul* (NH), *First Apocalypse of James*, and *Second Apocalypse of James*), as well as dialogues (e.g., *Sophia of Jesus Christ* and *Dialogue of the Savior*), "secret" books (e.g., *Apocryphon of James* and *Apocryphon of John*), and other miscellaneous writings (e.g., *Hypostasis of the Archons*, *On the Origin of the World*, *Exegesis on the Soul*, and *Teaching of Silvanus*).

Contributions
of Noncanonical Literature

Generally speaking, Jewish noncanonical literature fills in the gap between the OT and the NT, often called the "intertestamental period." These writings are cru-

cial for understanding JUDAISM of the era. Their primary importance for the study of the Bible is, therefore, as background material for the NT. Christian noncanonical literature is, with a few possible exceptions, later than the NT writings. These documents are very important for discerning certain nuances in the development of Christianity in its early centuries. They can also shed light on the NT, but the question of dating is always problematic, since most were composed later. The contributions of noncanonical literature to the study of the Bible can be grouped under four headings: historical events, religious movements, religious concepts and practices, and literary features.

Historical events

While the works of the first-century Jewish historian JOSEPHUS constitute the most important single source for knowledge of Jewish history between the OT and the NT, information about some historical events can be gleaned from the noncanonical Jewish writings.

The most important historical works in this literature are 1 and 2 MACCABEES. First Maccabees is the main source for reconstructing the history of the Jews in Palestine between 167 and 134 B.C.E., the period of the Maccabean Revolt and its immediate aftermath, and of the beginnings of the Hasmonean dynasty of Jewish kings. Second Maccabees traces the revolt only to 161 B.C.E. but gives a much more extensive account of the events leading up to the Maccabean period (ca. 180–167 B.C.E.). Although not without theological tendencies, these books together are indispensable for understanding this critical period in the history of the Jewish people. Some scholars, for instance, read the Book of Daniel as a response to the Maccabean crisis; if such an approach is valid, then a knowledge of the period is necessary for understanding Daniel. But the events of the Maccabean era are also important for the study of the NT. Although the right of self-determination gained by the Jews during the Maccabean Revolt had given way to Roman rule by the time of Jesus, the Jews' remembrance of their heroic ancestors encouraged at least some of them to work toward throwing off the Roman yoke, as the Maccabees had liberated themselves from the Seleucids 200 years earlier. Such thinking is reflected in the NT (cf. Luke 23:19; Acts 5:36-37) and resulted in the revolt against Rome in 66–70 C.E., with its disastrous consequences for the Jewish people.

Third Maccabees is obviously misnamed since it has nothing to do with the Maccabees. Rather, it narrates two crises faced by the Jews during the reign of Ptolemy IV Philopator of Egypt (221–204 B.C.E.), the first taking place in Jerusalem and the second in Alexandria. Whether these events actually occurred is not known.

The *Letter of Aristeas* purports to tell how the Hebrew Torah was translated into Greek in Alexandria during the reign of the Egyptian king Ptolemy II (285–247 B.C.E.)—by seventy-two Jewish scholars in seventy-two days. Although *Aristeas* is quite tendentious theologically and is probably not to be trusted as a factual account, it is nonetheless true that sometime during the last century or two before the Christian era, some Jews, perhaps in Alexandria, translated the Hebrew Scriptures into Greek. This translation, known as the SEPTUAGINT (LXX) was used by most of the NT writers when quoting the OT.

The *Letter of Aristeas* is a good example of the character of many, if not most, of the noncanonical writings: they are less valuable for *history* than they are for *tradition*. We learn from them not so much what actually happened as what people apparently *believed* to have happened.

Most of the Pseudepigrapha, for example, claims to *add to* the stories about OT figures. A good example is *Enoch*. Enoch is mentioned only briefly in the OT in a genealogy in Gen 5. Yet he is said not to have died because he "walked with God" (v. 24). Because he was seen as such a righteous man, pious Jews began to construct stories about him—stories, they felt, to develop and extend the minimal references to him in the Book of Genesis. The results are three long books, *1, 2,* and *3 Enoch*, not to mention speculations about Enoch in other writings.

Other perceived gaps in the OT narrative are addressed in other writings. What did Adam and Eve do *after* the fall? Read the *Life of Adam and Eve*. What was Abraham like *before* God called him? Try the *Apocalypse of Abraham*. How did Joseph meet his Egyptian wife? *Joseph and Asenath* tells the story. Why was Satan so upset with Job? The answer can be found in *Testament of Job*. The list goes on and on, and so do the traditions about OT figures.

What is the value of these traditions for understanding the Bible? Little, as far as the OT reader is concerned. These books are certainly interesting, but their date is so much later than the events they relate that it is improbable that they add any historical facts to the OT narratives. The writings, however, do provide a sharp contrast to what is actually *present* in the OT

narratives and, hence, how limited our knowledge about certain OT individuals and events really is.

The NT writers, on the other hand, were familiar with at least some of these traditions. The Book of Jude, for example, alludes to an extracanonical account of the death of Moses (v. 9), presumably a lost fragment of *Testament of Moses*, and provides a direct quotation of "Enoch" from *1 Enoch* 1:9 (vv. 14-15). The naming of the two Egyptian magicians who opposed Moses as JANNES AND JAMBRES (cf. the *Damascus Document*) is reflected in 2 Tim 3:8-9. The legend of Isaiah being sawn asunder (*Martyrdom of Isaiah*; *Lives of the Prophets*) is echoed in Heb 11:37.

In a similar way the noncanonical Christian writings provide numerous extracanonical traditions about Jesus and the disciples. The *Protevangelium of James*, for example, relates the story of Mary's birth, childhood, and eventual marriage to Joseph (a widower with children), culminating in a detailed account of the birth of Jesus (in a cave). The *Infancy Gospel of Thomas* describes Jesus' childhood from age five to age twelve. It presents the child Jesus performing numerous miracles—some of which are rather absurd (e.g., bringing clay sparrows to life). The *Gospel of Nicodemus* (also known as *Acts of Pilate*), provides a detailed account of the trial of Jesus and of Jesus' DESCENT INTO HELL. The *Gospel of Peter*, presents, after an otherwise straightforward account of the crucifixion, a vivid narration of the resurrection of Jesus, complete with a talking cross exiting the tomb.

Books such as *Gospel of Thomas*, *Gospel of Mary*, and *Dialogue of the Savior* claim to give "secret" teachings of Jesus. The apocryphal acts purport to trace the journeys of the apostles, with Thomas going all the way to India. Throughout these narratives, miracles abound, especially the raising of the dead. In the *Acts of Paul* even a talking lion is baptized. Only John is spared a martyr's death (*Acts of John*): Andrew is crucified (*Acts of Andrew*), Paul is beheaded (*Acts of Paul*), Peter is crucified upside down (*Acts of Peter*).

As in the case of the Pseudepigrapha, the dating of these documents raises serious doubt about their overall historical reliability. Yet their dates (typically second to third centuries C.E.) are not so far removed from the events themselves as to make it impossible that kernels of historical truth may be reflected in these otherwise legendary narratives. For instance, the notion that Jesus was born in a cave is also attested by the early second-century church father JUSTIN MARTYR, and it is certainly possible that Thomas, for example, went to India, or that John died in Ephesus of old age. How many, if any, such kernels remain, especially in the apocryphal acts, is unknown. As with the traditions about OT figures, these stories primarily serve to throw into sharp relief for the NT reader what is actually present in the NT narratives and, in many cases, how restrained the NT accounts actually are.

Some scholars believe the situation is more encouraging for at least some of the apocryphal gospels. The *Gospel of Thomas*, for example, is a collection of 114 sayings purportedly given by Jesus to Thomas. Some of these sayings are found—albeit sometimes in different (some scholars would say "earlier") forms—in the canonical Gospels. For example, *Gospel of Thomas* contains the parable of the sower (Matt 13:1-9) and the parable of the wheat and the tares (Matt 13:24-30), but both are without Jesus' interpretation (cf. Matt 13:18-23, 37-43). Some scholars have used this observation to support a longstanding argument that these interpretations in the canonical Gospels are not authentic, but were composed by the early church. It is also possible that the interpretations are authentic, but the community that produced the *Gospel of Thomas* did not find them to their liking and, hence, excluded them.

Also, *Gospel of Thomas* contains some sayings that sound like some of the sayings found in the canonical Gospels. For example, the kingdom of heaven is compared to a woman carrying a jar of meal; the handle breaks, the meal pours out behind her, and it is not until she reaches her house that she discovers her jar to be empty. Some scholars argue, then, that *Gospel of Thomas* contains authentic sayings of Jesus not found in the NT. If so, it would be potentially a very important document for recovering the teachings of Jesus.

On the other hand, *Gospel of Thomas* in its present form does contain a number of strange sayings that have been attributed to Gnostic or ascetic sources. Furthermore, the earliest extant manuscript of *Gospel of Thomas* dates from ca. 200 C.E. Thus, to project some early version of this document back to the first century C.E. (i.e., early enough to contain independent authentic traditions of Jesus) is highly speculative. Such a speculative approach, however, is precisely what is employed by those scholars who wish to propose that the apocryphal gospels contain independent historical material for studying the life and teaching of Jesus.

The most ambitious proposal of this type is that of J. D. Crossan, who classifies the traditions about Jesus into four chronological strata (Crossan 1991, 427–34). A simplified version of his scheme, focusing on the relative positions of the canonical and noncanonical gospels, follows. The first stratum (30–60 C.E.) contains the first edition of *Gospel of Thomas*, *Egerton Gospel*, two fragmentary papyrus gospels, *Gospel of the Hebrews*, the sayings gospel Q, a collection of miracles now embedded in Mark and John, an apocalyptic source behind Matt 24, and a cross gospel now embedded in *Gospel of Peter*. The second stratum (60–80 C.E.) includes *Gospel of the Egyptians*, *Secret Gospel of Mark*, Mark, another fragmentary papyrus gospel, the second edition of *Gospel of Thomas*, a dialogue collection now embedded in *Dialogue of the Savior*, and a signs gospel now embedded in John. The third stratum (80–120 C.E.) contains Matthew, Luke, and the first edition of John. The fourth stratum (120–150 C.E.) includes the second edition of John, *Apocryphon of James*, *Gospel of the Nazareans*, *Gospel of the Ebionites*, and *Gospel of Peter*. If Crossan's analysis is correct, then a number of apocryphal gospels (although admittedly some are quite fragmentary) are at least as important as, and in some cases even more than, the canonical Gospels for reconstructing the life and teachings of Jesus.

To be sure, Crossan's hypothesis is highly speculative. While other scholars affirm, in varying degrees, the significance of certain apocryphal gospels for shedding light on the historical Jesus, many more would agree with C. H. Talbert's cautious assessment of these writings: "It seems safe to say that, with the possible exception of the Coptic *Gospel of Thomas*, they provide us with no authentic traditions of words or deeds of Jesus, except insofar as they reproduce the canonical tradition" (Talbert 1990, 41).

Religious Movements

Noncanonical literature also provides important information concerning the diversity within both early JUDAISM and the early Church.

Readers familiar with the NT Gospels are well aware that Judaism at this time was characterized by a certain party spirit. The Gospel writers refer frequently to Sadducees and Pharisees, and occasionally to Herodians (e.g., Mark 3:6). Scholars have sometimes sought to identify certain noncanonical Jewish writings with a particular Jewish group. Sirach, for example, a collection (in a form resembling that of the Book of Proverbs) of the teachings of a second-century B.C.E. Jewish scribe named Jesus ben Sira, has sometimes been viewed as a proto-Sadducean book. The *Psalms of Solomon*, a first-century B.C.E. collection of eighteen psalms that clearly reflect the perspective of a particular group of Jews, and Judith, a captivating (though fictitious) story about the heroic exploits of a beautiful widow by the same name, have often been attributed to the Pharisees.

But scholars increasingly have come to recognize that the classic identification of Jewish parties into four groups that is based on Josephus—SADDUCEES, PHARISEES, ESSENES, and ZEALOTS—is probably an over-simplification of a very complex situation. Rather than assign documents to one of these four groups, scholars are more apt to speak more generally: 1 Maccabees, for example, is pro-Hasmonean, while *Psalms of Solomon* is anti-Hasmonean. Other writings. especially the apocalypses, apparently reflect the views of un-named Jewish groups.

The point is that the noncanonical Jewish literature gives ample evidence of a rich diversity within early Judaism; many groups existed and left their mark on the literary remains of this period.

Yet there is one sect of Jews that seems to come into much clearer focus through at least some of this literature: the Essenes. Most scholars believe the DEAD SEA SCROLLS represent the library of an Essene community. Indeed, the discovery of the scrolls has led some scholars to suggest that virtually all of the noncanon-ical Jewish literature was composed by the Essenes, but this suggestion has little to commend it. Yet the discovery of fragments of *Jubilees, 1 Enoch*, and *Testaments of the Twelve Patriarchs* among the scrolls, combined with certain parallels between some of their teachings and those of the scrolls, makes it likely that these three documents, at least, are proto-Essenic writings.

Veiled references in the scrolls suggest that the ori-gins of the sect centered around differences with the Temple leadership. The key figure in the early history of the Essenes was the Teacher of Righteousness, an otherwise unnamed individual who gave the sect direc-tion and focus in its early stages. The Essenes believed God had revealed to the Teacher of Righteousness the mysteries concerning the Law. Thus, he alone could properly interpret the Law; other Jews misunderstood it. Led by the Teacher of Righteousness, who was him-self a priest, the sect rejected the Temple cult in Jeru-salem as it was currently practiced and probably even the ruling priesthood as being illegitimate. Guided by the command in Isa 40:3 to prepare a way for the Lord "in the wilderness" (cf. Matt 3:3), the sect removed itself to the desert area by the Dead Sea to await the final war, from which, with God's help, they as the true Israel would emerge victorious and after which they would restore the sacrificial cult and proper priest-hood to Jerusalem.

The Essenes saw themselves as the "sons of light"; outsiders were the "sons of darkness," from whom they were called to separate. The community was governed by stringent entrance procedures, a detailed code of conduct, and a strict organizational hierarchy under the leadership of the priests. The sectarians had a communal lifestyle, sharing property and work, study-ing the Law, and meeting together for discussion of community matters and for ceremonies. Worship was an important aspect of communal life; the sect under-stood itself as participating in the angelic worship of God. Especially significant was the sacred meal. Cere-monial washings for purification were routine, and em-phasis was placed on the use of the solar calendar, rather than the lunar calendar of official Judaism. Un-able to offer sacrifices in the defiled Jerusalem Tem-ple, the community viewed prayer and obedience as acceptable offerings. Other aspects of personal piety included a deep sense of human frailty and sinfulness and thanksgiving to God for his GRACE and ELECTION.

A number of concepts in the scrolls have striking NT parallels. The centrality of a founding Teacher re-minds one of Jesus. The sacred meal calls to mind the LORD'S SUPPER (cf. 1 Cor 11:17-34). Aspects of the organizational structure (elders, overseer) are reminis-cent of that found in the Pastorals. The dependence on God's grace has been linked by some to justification by faith in Paul. The teaching that God created Two Spirits in which people must walk—the Prince of Light/Angel of Truth/Spirit of Truth and the Angel of Darkness/Spirit of Falsehood (cf. 1 John 4:6)—and that those led by the Two Spirits are characterized by cer-tain attitudes are reminiscent of Gal 5:19-23. Other NT parallels, just to note a few, include the identification of the sect as the Way (cf. Acts 9:2) and as the com-munity of the new covenant (Luke 22:20; 2 Cor 3:6; Heb 8:7-13), the use of Isa 40:3 to justify a movement "in the wilderness" (cf. Mark 1:2), and a number of similarities between *War Rule* and certain parts of Revelation, including the idea of a final war depicted in cosmic terms (cf. Rev 12:7; 16:13-16; 19:11-21), songs celebrating the defeat of the enemy (cf. Rev 18), an interest in the role of trumpets (cf. Rev 8–9) and in precise specifications and precious stones (cf. Rev 21:12-21), and a significant role for the archangel Michael (cf. Rev 12:7).

While the Essenes are not mentioned in the NT (some would see them, however, in the HERODIANS) such parallels have resulted in far-reaching speculation regarding "connections" between the scrolls and Christianity. But most conjectures of any direct link (e.g., that JESUS and/or JOHN THE BAPTIST were at one time a part of the sect) have little support. On the other hand, it is quite possible Jesus knew about the Essenes.

The closest parallel in pre-Christian Judaism, for example, to the command to hate one's enemies (opposed by Jesus in Matt 5:43-44 with a directive to love one's enemies) is found in *Manual of Discipline*, where members of the community are commanded to love the sons of light and to hate the sons of darkness. It is also possible that certain NT writers, in particular John, might have been influenced by Essene beliefs.

Noncanonical Christian literature testifies to the diversity within the early Church. The apocryphal acts, for example, promote a celibate lifestyle, even among husbands and wives. In the *Acts of Thomas*, for example, Jesus appears to a bride and groom on their wedding night and convinces them to refrain from consummating their marriage. In the *Acts of Paul* Paul is banished from Iconium for teaching women not to marry. Although later than the NT, they remind one of the ascetic groups opposed in Col 2:20-23 or in 1 Tim 4:3.

Some of the apocryphal acts also promote a docetic view of Jesus, that is, that he was not really human, but only appeared to be so. In the *Acts of John*, for example, "John" observes that Jesus would change his appearance and that he never left a footprint. Important to the docetic perspective was the affirmation that Jesus, since he was not human, did not really die on the cross. In the *Acts of John*, while Jesus is appearing to be crucified, he appears to John in a cave on the Mount of Olives and reveals to John that he is not in fact experiencing anything that will be said about his crucifixion. John thus descends from the mountain and laughs at the those who "witness" the crucifixion (cf. *SecTreatSeth*). Such a perspective is combatted in 1 John 4:2-3 and 2 John 7, and, perhaps, in John 1:14.

The *Pseudo-Clementine Homilies* and *Recognitions* testify to a rather conservative Jewish-Christian movement, perhaps the Ebionites, in the second and third centuries C.E., somewhat reminding one of the Judaizers in Acts and Galatians. Also Jewish-Christian, though perhaps not all relating to the same movement, are *Gospel of the Hebrews*, *Gospel of the Ebionites*, and *Gospel of the Nazareans*.

But the group about which the noncanonical Christian writings provide the most information is GNOSTICISM. The NAG HAMMADI library, in particular, consists mostly of Gnostic texts. Gnosticism itself was a diverse movement. Indeed, some of the Nag Hammadi tractates have been identified with Valentinian Gnosticism (e.g., *Apocryphon of James*, *Gospel of Truth*, *Tripartite Tractate*, *Gospel of Philip*, and *A Valentinian Exposition*), others with Sethian Gnosticism (e.g., *Apocryphon of John*, *Hypostasis of the Archons*, *Gospel of the Egyptians*, *Apocalypse of Adam*, *Three Steles of Seth*, *Zostrianos*, *Melchizedek* [NH], *Thought of Norea*, *Marsanes*, *Allogenes*, and *Trimorphic Protennoia*), while others cannot at present be connected with any known Gnostic sect (e.g., *Gospel of Thomas* and *Thunder, Perfect Mind*).

Yet the various Gnostic sects shared certain basic beliefs, most importantly a world-rejecting outlook and an emphasis on knowledge (i.e., *gnosis*, the Gk. word from which the term "Gnosticism" derives) as the means to salvation. Gnostics believed that the Creator-god of the material world is an inferior, even evil, spiritual being who has created an inferior, evil world. This Creator-god, in collaboration with his various, and equally evil, spiritual cohorts, conspires to keep humans trapped in ignorance of the higher spiritual realm. The Creator-god's evil designs are ultimately thwarted when beneficent spiritual beings of this higher realm send an emissary (Christ, in Christian forms of Gnosticism) into the lower world to bring the *gnosis* that illuminates and liberates. The Gnostic systems that incorporated these basic beliefs were highly complex, typically going to great lengths to name and to describe the various spiritual entities, both good and evil.

The extent to which the NT writers encountered some form of Gnosticism is difficult to determine. Scholars have proposed that Gnosticism is opposed, for example, in Luke-Acts, the Corinthian letters, Ephesians, Colossians, 2 Peter, and Jude. First and Second Timothy seem particularly open to such an interpretation. The false teaching opposed in these letters is characterized by a concern with "myths" (1 Tim 1:4; 4:7; 2 Tim 4:4), "genealogies" (1 Tim 1:4), "disputes about words" (1 Tim 6:4; 2 Tim 2:14, 23), "speculations" (1 Tim 1:4; 6:4), "knowledge" (1 Tim 6:20), "meaningless talk" (1 Tim 1:6), and "profane chatter" (1 Tim 6:20; 2 Tim 2:16). The false teachers teach false doctrines (1 Tim 1:3; 4:1; 6:3), which include the prohibition of marriage and of certain foods (1 Tim 4:3) and the belief that "the resurrection has already taken place" (2 Tim 2:18). A number of these features—for example, the specific doctrinal teachings (cf. *Treatise on the Resurrection*), the interest in myths and genealogies (cf., e.g., *Apocryphon of John, Hypostasis of the Archons, On the Origin of the World, Thought of Norea, Sophia of Jesus Christ, Tripartite Tractate,* and *A Valentinian Exposition*), and the concern for "knowledge"—suggest that the false teaching might have been an early form of Gnosticism. However, some of the more characteristic aspects of later Gnosticism are lacking, and other explanations have been offered. Since the Gnostic writings date from the second century C.E. and later, a large part of the problem is determining the extent to which Gnosticism was present, if at all, during the first century. Perhaps further analysis of the Nag Hammadi texts will help to clarify these questions.

Religious Concepts and Practices

The OT was written in Hebrew and Aramaic. The fact that the NT was composed in Greek is itself testimony to significant changes that took place in JUDAISM during the centuries after Alexander. As evidenced by the widespread use of the Greek language, there was a certain penetration into Judaism of Greek ideas and practices, a process known as Hellenization. The extent to which Jews adopted Greek ideas and practices differed from place to place and even from Jew to Jew, but it was widespread, nonetheless.

The noncanonical Jewish writings testify, in various ways, to the process of Hellenization. Second Maccabees recounts in some detail Hellenistic inroads into Jewish culture, such as the establishment of a gymnasium for Jewish youth to participate in Greek athletic contests, in Jerusalem prior to the Maccabean Revolt. Fourth Maccabees, an imaginative retelling of a series of Jewish martyrdoms already recorded in 2 Maccabees, employs Stoic ideas in an attempt to demonstrate that inspired reason, guided by the Law, is supreme ruler over the passions. The Wisdom of Solomon, a wisdom book written to strengthen the faith of Jews living in Egypt, affirms such Greek concepts as the preexistence and the immortality of the soul and employs the Greek method of allegorical interpretation. Allegorical interpretation is also used extensively in the *Letter of Aristeas*, where the Jewish dietary laws are understood to refer to universal human virtues and vices. The Jewish composers of the *Sibylline Oracles* adopt both a Greek literary form (epic

hexameter) and figure (the prophetess Sibyl) to set forth a series of oracles on the future of the world.

Many more examples of Hellenization in Jewish noncanonical writings could be given, especially in the ethical sections of these documents. But these are sufficient to indicate that the Hellenization of Judaism is something of which the NT reader must be aware. Both Jesus and his disciples encountered and conversed with gentiles. Thus, they must have been able to speak not only Aramaic, the common language of Palestinian Jews at that time, but also Greek. Furthermore, certain early Christians, apparently associated with Jerusalem synagogues populated by Jewish immigrants from Hellenistic regions, were known as "the Hellenists" (Acts 6:1). Paul demonstrated his ability to interact with Greek culture through both his preaching (Acts 17:22-32) and his letters; indeed, the extent to which Paul's theology was influenced primarily by Jewish or by Greek thought has been long debated. Scholars typically view the author of Hebrews as a Jewish Christian trained in Hellenistic rhetoric and learning. The list could continue, but the point is clear: the interaction between Judaism and Hellenism is an important part of the background of the NT.

Another area where noncanonical Jewish literature is important for the study of the NT is that of the religious practices of the Jews. In John 10:22-23 Jesus is in the Temple during the FEAST OF DEDICATION. An examination of the OT reveals no such feast. The reason is that the feast has it roots not in the OT, but in the Maccabean Revolt. As part of his policy of Hellenization of the Jews, the Seleucid king Antiochus IV profaned the Temple by desecrating the altar with sacrifices to Zeus in December 168/7 B.C.E. Three years later, the Maccabees, following their initial victories, reconsecrated the Temple and established the annual Feast of Dedication (also called Hanukkah, which means "dedication"). The story is told in 1 and 2 Maccabees.

In the Gospels and Acts the Jewish practice of almsgiving is assumed (e.g., Matt 6:1-4; Acts 10:2, 4). Although the OT contains numerous exhortations to provide for the poor (e.g., Exod 23:10-11; Lev 19:9-10; Deut 24:29-22), there is perhaps no finer example of a Jew who cared for the poor than Tobit (see also Job in *Testament of Job*), whose inordinate burden to help the needy leads to his own blindness and sets the stage for God's resolution of the plight of two pious families in Tobit. This delightful story, more than any mere exhortation, gives a vivid picture of the high esteem in which almsgiving was held among Jews.

A major aspect of Judaism in any period is OT interpretation. The noncanonical Jewish writings reveal a variety of methods used by Jews to interpret the scriptures during the intertestamental period. The use of allegorical interpretation in the Wisdom of Solomon and the *Letter of Aristeas* has already been mentioned. This method is also found among the DEAD SEA SCROLLS, especially in the *Damascus Rule*. Allegorical interpretation looks beyond the literal meaning of a text to some supposed "symbolic" meaning. In the *Letter of Aristeas*, for example, animals with a cloven or divided hoof symbolize the separation of human actions for good rather than evil. Allegorical interpretation became a favorite method of OT interpretation in the early Church, as exhibited, for example, in the *Letter of Barnabas*, and was occasionally used in the NT (e.g., 1 Cor 10:4).

One of the most striking characteristics of the Dead Sea Scrolls is the distinctive manner of interpreting the OT found in many of the scrolls. Members of the Dead Sea sect (probably Essenes) believed the OT books were full of mysteries that were fulfilled in the history of the community. The meaning of these mysteries was hidden until God revealed them to the founder of the sect, the Teacher of Righteousness, and some of his followers—hence the need for *pesher*, or interpretation. One approach to such interpretation was the production of continuous commentaries, called *pesharim*, on OT books, including Habakkuk, Micah, Psalms, Isaiah, Hosea, Nahum, and Zephaniah. The commentaries are filled with enigmatic historical allusions to figures related to the history of the sect and thus illustrate the sect's method of viewing the OT as fulfilled in itself. Another interpretive strategy of the sect was to collect and interpret OT passages in accordance with a particular theme. The *Testimonia*, for example, seems to be an anthology of messianic texts, the *Florilegium* an amalgam of eschatological texts and interpretations, and *Melchizedek* a collection of OT texts and interpretations centering around the mysterious OT person of the same name (cf. Gen 14:18-20; Heb 5:10; 6:20–7:17).

Similarities between the interpretive strategies found in the Dead Sea Scrolls, especially the *pesharim*, and those found in the NT are obvious. On a number of occasions Matthew, for example, introduces a citation from the OT with an expression to the effect that an event took place "to fulfill what had been spoken through the prophet . . ." (e.g., Matt 1:22-23; 2:15, 17-18, 23). At the opening of his public ministry in Luke, Jesus interprets in a Nazareth synagogue Isa 61:1-2 as being fulfilled in himself (Luke 4:16-21). Similar passages can be found throughout the NT. To be sure, no NT writer wrote a continuous commentary on an OT book, as did the writers of the scrolls, but it is clear that the NT writers employed a strategy similar to that of the Essenes by interpreting much of the OT as having been fulfilled in the events relating to Jesus and the early Church. Some scholars have even proposed that, like the anthologies among the scrolls, collections of key OT texts viewed as relating to Jesus were drawn up by and circulated among the early Christians.

No treatment of OT interpretive strategies in the noncanonical literature would be complete without some mention of the method of interpretation used in certain Gnostic texts (e.g., the *Apocryphon of John, Hypostasis of the Archons*, and *On the Origin of the World*). The most startling feature of the approach of these texts to the OT is that they turn the early chapters of Genesis on their head, so to speak. In accordance with the Gnostic view of the universe, they understand the Creator-god as evil, the serpent as good, and the "Fall" of Adam and Eve as a positive step towards overcoming the Creator-god's evil schemes. The relevance of this rather bizarre method of reading the OT for studying the NT is primarily one of contrast: the NT writers understood Genesis quite traditionally (cf. Rom 5).

The noncanonical literature also sheds light on certain Jewish institutions. Throughout the Gospels and Acts there are references to scribes, or teachers of the Law. Paul studied under one such teacher, Gamaliel (Acts 22:3; cf. 5:34). Sirach presents in some detail the teachings of such a scribe, Jesus ben Sira, who devoted himself to the study of Wisdom and the Law, and who shared his learning with his students. The Gospels and Acts also testify to the preeminence of the priesthood, and especially the high priest, in Jewish life. Second Maccabees recounts the growing influence (and politicization) of the high priesthood prior to the Maccabean Revolt. The transferral of the high priesthood to a new family, the Hasmoneans, during the revolt (cf. 1 Maccabees) and the results for Temple worship are harshly criticized in the *Psalms of Solomon*. Similarly, the strong priestly concern running throughout the sectarian Dead Sea Scrolls (cf. especially *Miqsat Ma'aseh Torah*) suggests that the sect probably had its origins in a dispute over the priesthood and Temple worship in the middle of the second century B.C.E. All of this provides insight not only into the NT narratives, but also into certain theological developments in the NT, such as the portrayal of Jesus as the superior high priest in Hebrews or the identification of Christians as priests in 1 Pet 2:9 and Rev 1:6; 5:10; 20:6.

Examples such as the one just given indicate that it is the conceptual world of the NT that is most illuminated by noncanonical literature. The following survey is by no means exhaustive, but is merely suggestive of the kinds of conceptual parallels to the NT that can be found in these writings.

In 2 Cor 12:1-4 Paul speaks of being "caught up to the third heaven," which he identifies as "Paradise." In Rev 4:1-2 John is invited to come up into heaven; he does so "in the Spirit" and spends the time of the rest of the book there. While there are precedents for this in the OT (e.g., Ezek 1; Isa 6), such heavenly travel becomes a major motif in the noncanonical literature. Journeys through the heavens are made, for example, by Enoch (*1, 2,* and *3 Enoch*), Abraham (*Apocalypse of Abraham* and *Testament of Abraham*), Isaac (*Testament of Isaac*), Jacob (*Testament of Jacob*), Levi (*Testament of Levi*), Isaiah (*Ascension of Isaiah*), Baruch (*3 Baruch*), Ezra (*Greek Apocalypse of Ezra* and *Vision of Ezra*), Sedrach (*Apocalypse of Sedrach*), Zephaniah (*Apocalypse of Zephaniah*), Peter (*Apocalypse of Peter*), and Paul (*Apocalypse of Paul* [ANT] and *Apocalypse of Paul* [NH]). But the heavens are also sometimes numbered: there are three (*Apocalypse of Sedrach* and *Apocalypse of Paul* [ANT]), five (*3 Baruch* and *Apocalypse of Zephaniah*), seven (*2 Enoch* [short recension], *Apocalypse of Abraham, Testament of Levi, Ascension of Isaiah*), eight (*Hypostasis of the Archons* and *On the Origin of the World*), or even ten (*2 Enoch* [long recension]; *Apocalypse of Paul* [NH]). As in 2 Corinthians, *Paradise* is in the third heaven (*2 Enoch* and *Life of Adam and Eve*).

John's apocalyptic vision begins with his observance of the worship directed by the "twenty-four elders" and the "four living creatures" towards "the one who sits on the throne" and towards the "Lamb" (Rev 4:8–5:14). In other writings, the seer often experiences the heavenly worship that the angels direct towards God (cf. also from Qumran the *Angelic Liturgy* and the *Blessings* [*1QSb*]). Some scholars have proposed that visions of angelic worship are part of the problem underlying Colossians (cf. Col 2:18).

John also sees a great white throne, where people are judged by what they have done, as recorded in "books," and by the absence of their names from "the book of life" (Rev 20:11-19). Other heavenly travelers record some striking depictions of judgment. In the *Testament of Abraham*, for example, the heavenly judge is Abel, and the one keeping the record of people's deeds is Enoch (recension B; cf. *Jubilees, Ascension of Isaiah, 2 Baruch*, and *4 Ezra*). Individuals are judged in two ways: their righteous deeds are weighed on a balance scale against their sins (cf. *1* and *2 Enoch, Apocalypse of Zephaniah*) and their works are tested by fire (cf. 1 Cor 3:12-15). In the *Apocalypse of Zephaniah* it is two groups of angels who write down the deeds of people: the angels of God record the good deeds and the angels of the accuser the sins, so that the accuser might accuse the dead at the judgment. This latter scenario serves as a striking background for the portrayal of Jesus both in Revelation, where by his blood he casts down the accuser of his followers (12:10-11), and in Colossians, where he nails to the cross the bond that stood against Christians, thereby disarming the principalities and powers (2:13-15). As for *the book of life*, it is mentioned, for example, in *Jubilees, Joseph and Asenath, Apocalypse of Zephaniah*, and *Testament of Jacob.*

Another striking feature of Revelation is its frequent references to angels, including a climactic battle waged by Michael and his angels against the devil and his angels (12:7-9). Angels appear elsewhere in the NT (e.g., Matt 1–2; Luke 1 [Gabriel] and 2) and are mentioned, for example, by Paul and the author of Hebrews. In the noncanonical writings there is a great interest in angels, especially Michael (the *War Scroll, 1* and *2 Enoch, Apocalypse of Abraham, Testament of Abraham, 3* and *4 Baruch, Joseph and Asenath, Apocalypse of Sedrach, Life of Adam and Eve, Sibylline Oracles, Testament of Moses, Ascension of Isaiah, Testament of Jacob*, and *Testament of Solomon*), who in *1 Enoch* is identified, along with Gabriel, Raphael, and Uriel, as one of the four archangels (cf. *Sibylline Oracles*). In Tobit the angel Raphael even (in disguise) accompanies Tobias on his journey.

The NT writers also speak often of Satan, and demons are plentiful in the Gospels. Several noncanonical books seek to explain the origins of the evil angels. In the *Life of Adam and Eve*, for example, the devil explains that he was cast out of heaven for refusing to worship Adam. *First Enoch* opens with a lengthy narrative of how a group of angels, called the Watchers, who desired human women, took them as wives, and produced malevolent giants as offspring (cf. Gen 6:1-4). This story, to which Jude alludes (6), was widely known (cf. *Genesis Apocryphon, 2 Enoch, Jubilees, Apocalypse of Abraham, Pseudo-Philo, Sibylline Oracles, 2 Baruch, Testament of Naphtali, Testament of Reuben*).

A favorite name for the devil in this literature is Beliar/Belial (*Damascus Document, Manual of Discipline, War Scroll, Thanksgiving Hymns, Jubilees, Sibylline Oracles, Lives of the Prophets, Martyrdom of Isaiah, Testament of the Twelve Patriarchs*; cf. 2 Cor 6:15). Speculations about demons and their roles continued after the NT period, as can be seen in the *Testament of Solomon*, a legendary work about Solomon's building of the Temple that describes in considerable detail the astrological signs and characteristic activities of various demons over which Solomon gained mastery through a magic ring.

The NT writers do not always blame sin upon the evil one. Paul, for example, can argue that humans are responsible for their own sins (e.g., Rom 1–2; Eph 2:1-3; Col 1:21), but he can also point the finger at Adam (Rom 5; cf. 1 Cor 15:21-22). Eve even receives the blame in 1 Tim 2:14. *Fourth Ezra* also affirms the effect of Adam's sin upon his descendants by infecting them with an evil heart (cf. *3 Baruch*), while *2 Baruch* explicitly rejects such a notion, affirming the individual's free choice (cf. *Sirach*). Sirach and the *Life of Adam and Eve* stress the role of Eve. The deep sense of personal sin over against God's grace that pervades Paul's thought finds parallels in some of the Dead Sea Scrolls such as *Manual of Discipline* and *Thanksgiving Hymns*. While the importance of repentance is affirmed in many documents (e.g., *Testament of Abraham* and *Joseph and Asenath*), the most beautiful example is the Prayer of Manasseh, a short prayer of confession for individual sin combining trust in the forgiving mercy of God with confidence in the efficacy of heartfelt repentance.

The NT writers emphasize the hope of the resurrection of the body (e.g., 1 Cor 15; 1 Thes 4:13-18), to be followed by eternal life (e.g., Matt 25:46; John 3:15-16; Rom 5:21). The noncanonical books typically share the hope of resurrection (e.g., 2 Maccabees, *Life of Adam and Eve, 1* and *2 Enoch, Testament of Abraham, Testament of Benjamin, Testament of Judah, Pseudo-Philo, Sibylline Oracles, Psalms of Solomon, Testament of Job, 4 Ezra, 2 Baruch*, and *Lives of the Prophets*), although some of the more Hellenized

Jewish writings focus on the immortality of the soul (e.g., 4 Maccabees, Wisdom) and the Gnostic writings understand the resurrection in spiritual terms (e.g., *Treatise on the Resurrection*). Eternal life is affirmed as well (e.g., *2 Enoch, Testament of Abraham, Joseph and Asenath*, and *Pseudo-Philo*). On the other hand, the reality of death is nowhere more graphically portrayed than in the *Testament of Abraham*, a legendary account of Abraham's death in which God sends Michael to prepare Abraham for his death. Abraham refuses to go. Eventually, God sends personified Death, who comes to Abraham in great glory and youthful beauty. Abraham refuses to follow him as well. At Abraham's request, Death reveals himself in all his ugliness and horror. Abraham still resists. Finally, Death tricks Abraham, and Abraham dies. There is no more fitting context in which to read Paul's celebration of death being swallowed up in victory (1 Cor 15:54-55) than *Testament of Abraham*.

In the NT detailed descriptions of heaven are relatively few. The most extensive is Rev 21:1–22:5, which vividly depicts a glorified "new" Jerusalem, complete with the tree of life. In the noncanonical writings there are numerous pictures of the state of the righteous in heaven (e.g., *1* and *2 Enoch, Apocalypse of Zephaniah, Testament of Jacob, Apocalypse of Peter* [ANT], and *Apocalypse of Paul* [ANT]), including portrayals, often in even greater detail than in Revelation, of a glorified Jerusalem and Temple (e.g., Tobit, Sirach, *Sibylline Oracles, 4 Ezra, 2 Baruch*, and *New Jerusalem* [5Q15]; cf. *Temple Scroll*), the latter of which is conspicuously missing in John's picture (Rev 21:22). There is also frequent mention of the tree of life (4 Maccabees, *Life of Adam and Eve, 1* and *2 Enoch, Testament of Levi, Jubilees, Pseudo-Philo, 4 Ezra*, and *Apocalypse of Sedrach*).

The NT writers are even more restrained when in comes to depicting hell, a concept only hinted at in the OT. There are a few pictorial references to fire (e.g., Matt 3:12; 13:42; 18:8; Mark 9:48; Rev 20:10-15), as well as to outer darkness, with weeping and gnashing of teeth (e.g., Matt 8:12). But elsewhere the focus is more generally on the wrath of God (e.g., John 3:36; Rom 5:9) or eternal punishment (Matt 25:46) and/or exclusion from God's presence (2 Thes 1:8-9). Eternal punishment of the wicked is assumed in many of the noncanonical writings (e.g., Judith, 4 Maccabees, and Wisdom), and fire is a standard part of the picture (e.g., in *1* and *2 Enoch, Testament of Isaiah, Testament of Jacob, Joseph and Asenath, Jannes and*

Jambres, Sibylline Oracles, 2 Baruch, 4 Ezra, Greek Apocalypse of Ezra, and *Vision of Ezra).* But some Jewish and especially Christian writers were more than eager to provide a graphic description of the place where sinners are punished (e.g., *Apocalypse of Zephaniah, Testament of Isaiah, Testament of Jacob, Greek Apocalypse of Ezra, Vision of Ezra, Acts of Thomas, Apocalypse of Peter* [ANT], *Apocalypse of Paul* [ANT], and *Book of Thomas the Contender).* The *Apocalypse of Peter* (ANT) is an excellent example of such a document. In this second century C.E. writing Jesus purportedly gives Peter a lengthy tour of hell, followed by a brief tour of heaven. In hell Peter sees sinners being punished in accordance with their sins: blasphemers, for example, hang by their tongues over a blazing fire, while murderers are cast into a pit full of poisonous snakes. Such pictures of hell had, through later authors such as Dante, a great influence on the development of the Christian concept of hell.

Leading up to the end of the age, the NT writers sometimes predict a series of eschatological woes (e.g., Mark 13; 2 Thes 2; Rev). In 2 Thes 2 these woes include the lawless one, and in Rev 13 the beast, popularly called the Antichrist. Noncanonical writings also predict eschatological plagues (e.g., *Apocalypse of Abraham, Sibylline Oracles, 4 Ezra, 2 Baruch, Testament of Moses, Martyrdom of Isaiah, Apocalypse of Elijah, Greek Apocalypse of Ezra, Epistula Apostolorum,* and *Apocalypse of Thomas),* and several Christian documents speculate on the Antichrist (*Martyrdom of Isaiah, Apocalypse of Elijah,* and *Greek Apocalypse of Ezra).* The *Apocalypse of Elijah,* for example, describes Antichrist as skinny-legged, with a tuft of gray hair at the front of his bald head, eyebrows reaching to his ears, and a leprous spot on the front of his hands. The *Sibylline Oracles* and the *Martyrdom of Isaiah* portray him in terms of the Nero-redivivus myth, which was a rumor widely circulated in the late first century C.E. to the effect that the Roman emperor Nero would return from the dead. Some scholars view this myth as standing behind certain passages in Revelation (e.g., Rev 13, 17).

Central to the NT, of course, is the affirmation that Jesus is the Messiah or Christ. Closely connected with this affirmation is that Jesus is the long-awaited son of David (cf. 2 Sam 7:12-16; Isa 9:2-7; 11:1-16; Jer 33:14-18; Ezek 34:23-24), that is, the king (e.g., Matt 1:1; Acts 2:30-31; Rom 1:3; Rev 1:5). One of the characteristics of Judaism in the intertestamental period is the reemergence of the hope for the Messiah

after several centuries of domination by foreign powers. Not all Jews were looking for a Messiah: books such as Tobit, for example, exhibit a staunch hope for a glorified Jerusalem, without any reference to a Messiah. But other writings depict, in varying ways, the Messianic hopes of at least some Jews.

The Dream Visions section of *1 Enoch,* probably written in the late 160s B.C.E. against the backdrop of the Maccabean Revolt, presents the figure of a conquering ram. The expectation is clearly one of military leadership. In *Psalms of Solomon* (first century B.C.E.), the psalmist looks forward to the day when Messiah, the son of David, will come and rid the nation of its enemies and restore Jerusalem to its proper place (cf. *Sibylline Oracles* and *2 Baruch).* Yet the psalmist does not really see the Messiah as a military leader: his trust will be in God, not in horse or rider or bow. Rather, the psalmist, building on Ps 2 (cf. Rev 19:15) and Isa 11 (cf. Rev 22:16), sees him as king, judge, and shepherd. The *Testaments of the Twelve Patriarchs* (first century B.C.E.), especially *Testament of Levi* and *Testament of Judah* affirm a dual Messianic expectation: the kingship from Judah and the priesthood from Levi, with the kingship being subject to the priesthood (cf. *Jubilees).*

The most unusual picture of Messiah is found in *4 Ezra* (end of the first century C.E.). The Messiah, identified as "my [God's] son," will be revealed for a 400-year period of rejoicing (cf. Rev 20:4-6), after which he, along with everyone else, will die. He will also free the remnant of God's people by destroying their enemies through the execution of final judgment according to the standard of the Law.

The Messianic hope found in the Dead Sea Scrolls is extremely complex, testifying perhaps to changing Messianic views over the 200-year history of the sect. Like the *Testaments of the Twelve Patriarchs,* the *Manual of Discipline* (and presumably *Rule of the Congregation* and the *Damascus Document)* anticipates two Messiahs: a priestly Messiah and a royal Messiah, with the priestly Messiah given preeminence. *Patriarchal Blessings* speaks of a single, royal Messiah, who is identified further as the Branch of David. An eschatological Branch of David is also in view in *Florilegium,* where he is associated with the Interpreter of the Law, and in *Pesher on Isaiah. Manual of Discipline* speaks further of the coming of the Prophet (cf. *Testimonia); Damascus Document* and *Blessings* (i.e, *1QSb)* speak of the appearance of the Prince of the Congregation; and *Testimonia* speaks of the Star of

Jacob and the Scepter of Israel. The precise relationship among these figures is not clear. By contrast, *Melchizedek* views MELCHIZEDEK as the key figure in the final jubilee (cf. Lev 25; Luke 4:16-21) who will restore and make atonement for the sons of light and will execute God's judgment against Belial and his lot (cf. Heb 5:5–7:28).

Given the immense publicity the Dead Sea Scrolls have received and the sensationalistic claims often propounded in connection with them, it is necessary to make a few more observations about them here. First, despite claims to the contrary, there is no evidence that the Dead Sea sect viewed the Teacher of Righteousness as the Messiah, believed him to have met a violent death, or awaited his return at the end of time.

The Teacher of Righteousness and Jesus are indeed similar in certain ways—for example, each founded a movement and each claimed to provide the proper interpretation of the Law (cf. Matt 5–7)—but the differences are equally striking. Second, although there is a fragmentary text that mentions "the Son of God" (*4Q246*), it is not clear whether the text is speaking of a Messianic figure or an evil ruler, such as Antiochus IV. Third, the so-called "pierced Messiah" text (*4Q285*) probably refers not to the slaying of a Messianic figure, but to that of an enemy of the sect.

The most-common self-designation used by Jesus in the Gospels is SON OF MAN (e.g., Matt 9:6). In the "Similitudes of Enoch" section of *1 Enoch* there is extensive development of the concept of the Son of Man as an exalted figure who will come to execute judgment, long recognized for containing striking parallels with the Gospels. The evidence from the Dead Sea Scrolls, however, indicates that this section was not originally part of *1 Enoch*. Whether or not it was written before the coming of Jesus and thus serves as background material for the Son of Man concept in the Gospels, therefore, is uncertain.

John, Paul, and the author of Hebrews affirm the involvement of the preexistent Christ in the creation of the universe (John 1:12; Col 1:15-16; Heb 1:1-2). Such an affirmation is based upon the personification of Wisdom in the OT and the belief that Wisdom was involved in creation (Prov 8; cf. *Wisdom*). Over against those Jews who came to identify Wisdom with the Law (e.g., *1 Baruch* and Sirach), these NT writers instead identified Wisdom with Christ.

The NT writers make much of the importance of Jesus' death in providing atonement for sins. While 2 Maccabees implies that the suffering of martyrs atones for the sins of the nation, 4 Maccabees makes the connection explicit, using the words "ransom" (cf. Mark 10:45) and "atoning sacrifice" or "sacrifice of atonement" ("expiation" in RSV; cf. Rom 3:25).

As already indicated, the portrayal of Jesus as the authoritative interpreter of the Law is similar to that of the Teacher of Righteousness. Indeed, a number of interesting parallels to the teachings of Jesus can be discovered in the intertestamental Jewish writings. For example, the Golden Rule (Matt 7:12) is found in a negative form ("What you hate, do not do to anyone") in the *Letter of Aristeas* and in Tobit. The commands to love God and to love others (Matt 22:37-40) are combined in the *Testament of Issachar* and the *Testament of Daniel*.

The equating of lust with adultery (Matt 5:28) is found in the *Testament of Issachar* and the *Testament of Benjamin*. Tobit, the *Testament of Joseph*, and *2 Enoch* all have passages reminiscent of Jesus' comments in the parable of the sheep and the goats concerning being hungry, naked, in prison, and the like (Matt 25:35-36). The teaching of two ways, a narrow path leading to life and a wide one leading to destruction (Matt 7:13-14), is found in the *Testament of Abraham* (cf. *2 Enoch*). Many more examples could be given.

Such parallels show, on the one hand, the Jewishness of Jesus and his teachings. But they also provide a context in which the distinctiveness of Jesus' teachings becomes clearer. For example, Jesus' positive restatement of the Golden Rule (*In everything do to others as you would have them do to you*—Matt 7:12) marks a very different orientation to living than that of the negative form: the one is active and focuses on what is desirable, the other is passive and focuses on what is undesirable.

A number of other interesting parallels to the NT in noncanonical literature can be noted briefly. Hostility to the Samaritans (cf. John 4:9) is exhibited in Sirach. First Maccabees draws attention to the long absence of prophets among the Jewish people (cf. the coming of JOHN THE BAPTIST). The ability to speak angelic languages (cf. 1 Cor 13:1) is described in a strange passage in the *Testament of Job*. *Joseph and Asenath* on several occasions mentions the bread of life and the cup of immortality (cf. the LORD'S SUPPER). The *Lives of the Prophets* testifies to the veneration of Jewish heroes of old (cf. Matt 23:29). In addition, there are numerous parallels between John and the *Odes of Solomon*, James and Sirach, and Revelation and 2 Esdras.

Literary Features

Noncanonical literature provides background for understanding various literary genres used in the NT. For example, Luke 1–2 and Revelation contain a number of songs in poetic form. Writings such as the *Apocryphal Psalms*, the *Psalms of Solomon*, *Thanksgiving Scroll*, *War Rule*, and *Manual of Discipline* provide a context for recovering Jewish poetic techniques and conventions in this period. Also, books such as the *Testaments of the Twelve Patriarchs* and the *Testament of Job*, with their emphasis on the moral teaching contained in the last words of their purported authors, give cause for viewing 2 Timothy and 2 Peter as "testaments." The *Gospel of Thomas*, with its collection of Jesus' sayings apart from a narrative framework, provides an example of what Q, the sayings source widely supposed by scholars to have been used by Matthew and Luke, might have been.

Probably the best example of the value of noncanonical writings for understanding literary genre is Revelation. More important than the ongoing scholarly debate as to whether Revelation is "prophecy" or "apocalyptic" is the recognition that the literary and conceptual world in which Revelation resides is that of the apocalyptic writings (e.g., the *War Scroll*, *1* and *2 Enoch*, *Sibylline Oracles*, *Apocalypse of Zephaniah*, *Apocalypse of Abraham*, *4 Ezra*, and *2* and *3 Baruch*) and the apocalyptic sections of other writings (e.g., *Testaments of the Twelve Patriarchs* and *Testament of Moses*). These writings are filled with visionary experiences, not to mention symbolic language, not unlike that found in Revelation.

For example, in *4 Ezra* the seer has a vision, described at length, of an eagle, with twelve feathered wings and three heads, rising from the sea "with ten horns and seven heads," that comes to reign over the earth. Though the details differ, the vision bears similarities to John's vision of the beast rising from the sea (Rev 13). The vision is explained to the seer cryptically, as is John's vision in Rev 17. In another vision the seer observes a man against whom an innumerable multitude gathers to make war. The man holds no weapon of war, but rather sends forth from his mouth a stream of fire, a flaming breath, and a storm of sparks, which together incinerate his enemies. This vision bears a striking resemblance to the vision in Rev 19 of the rider on the white horse who comes with the armies of heaven; the kings of the earth and their armies gather together to make was against him,

but he slays them with the only weapon he bears—a sword coming out of his mouth. What is noteworthy about the vision in *4 Ezra* is that the seer is given a *figurative* interpretation of the vision, that is, it is a vivid picture not of a literal war but of final judgment meted out by the Messiah. Such an interpretation is entirely plausible for Rev 19 (v. 11: *in righteousness he judges and makes war*). Nevertheless, the point is that only by immersing oneself in similar literature of the time can one grasp the literary conventions John employed and understand the way he used language.

Another literary feature that characterizes much of the noncanonical literature is pseudonymity: the self-attribution of a writing to someone who was not actually the author. In noncanonical but scripture-related literature, such attribution of course was usually to biblical characters such as Enoch, Abraham, Moses, Ezra, Peter, or Paul. Reasons for pseudonymity were varied—for example, to lend authority to a writing or to attribute ideas to the biblical character who inspired them. At one time or another, some scholars have proposed most of the NT books as being pseudonymous, yet the authenticity of all of the NT books, even those widely viewed as pseudonymous, such as the Pastorals and 2 Peter, continues to be defended by many scholars. The issue of pseudonymity raises a further theological question: does pseudonymity disqualify a book from being useful and/or inspired? Many scholars would answer that it does not. Others would disagree, arguing that while a pseudonymous writing might indeed be useful for understanding the beliefs and perspective of its actual author, pseudonymity is by definition deception and, therefore, eliminates a book from being inspired; thus, they would argue, no canonical writing is, in fact, pseudonymous. In any event, the practice of pseudonymity was widespread during the biblical period and provides the necessary literary and historical, if not theological, context for such a discussion.

To read the noncanonical literature is to enter into the worlds of intertestamental Judaism and postapostolic Christianity. Some of the writings provide a backdrop against which the NT should be read; others throw the OT and NT into relief by showing how ideas and movements developed *after* the canonical books were composed. Some of the writings are difficult; some are informative; and some are simply fun to read. Serious readers of the Bible will want to introduce themselves to the vast, and fascinating, realm of noncanonical literature.

For Further Study

In the *Mercer Dictionary of the Bible*: APOCALYPTIC
LITERATURE; APOCRYPHAL ACTS; APOCRYPHAL LITERATURE;
CANON; DEAD SEA SCROLLS; GNOSTICISM; NAG HAMMADI;
TESTAMENTS, APOCRYPHAL.

In other sources: R. H. Charles, ed., *Apocrypha and
Pseudepigrapha of the Old Testament*, 2 vols.; J. H.
Charlesworth, ed., *The Old Testament Pseudepigrapha*,
2 vols., and *The Old Testament Pseudepigrapha and
the New Testament*; J. Dart, *The Jesus of Heresy and
History: The Discovery and Meaning of the Gnostic
Nag Hammadi Library*; J. K. Elliott, ed., *The Apocry-
phal New Testament*; E. Hennecke and W. Schnee-
melcher, eds., *New Testament Apocrypha*, 2 vols.;
B. M. Metzger, *An Introduction to the Apocrypha*;
G. W. E. Nickelsburg, *Jewish Literature between the
Bible and the Mishnah*; J. M. Robinson, ed., *The Nag
Hammadi Library*, rev. ed.; E. Schürer, *The History of
the Jewish People in the Age of Jesus Christ*, vol. 3,
rev. and ed. G. Vermes, F. Millar, and M. Goodman;
H. F. D. Sparks, ed., *The Apocryphal Old Testament*;
G. Vermes, *The Dead Sea Scrolls in English*, 3rd ed.

Works Cited

Crossan, J. D. 1991. *The Historical Jesus: The Life of
a Mediterranean Jewish Peasant*.

Talbert, C. H. 1990. "Apocryphal Gospels," MDB.

The Bible and the Church

Paul D. Duke

The force of fundamentalism in recent years has set the agenda for much of our conversation concerning the BIBLE. The results have been tragic. Believers who are not biblicists have fallen into defensive positions with regard to the Scriptures. Leaning hard against the onslaughts of a fundamentalism that claims too much for the Bible and at the same time too little, we have insisted much on what the Bible is not. To our great harm, the energy spent on these denials has become energy largely lost to the real work of coming to terms with what the Bible must be for us. Denouncing the worship of the book, we are distracted from sufficient hearing of what the book would say. In Abraham Heschel's words, "we have so much to say *about the Bible* that we are not prepared to hear what the Bible has to say about us" (Heschel 1972, 171).

To be sure, these are idolatrous times, requiring us to declare faithfully what the Bible is *not*. It is not God. It is not a perfect book bearing pure and perfect disclosures of God. It is not without the contingencies of particular cultures and times. It is not without the real limits of human knowledge, speech, and imagination. The Bible is not a monolithic code of belief and behavior, whose every discrete text is uniformly inspired. It is not equivalent to the living Word of God. Recent reports to the contrary, the Trinity has not expanded to name the Bible the Fourth Person of the Godhead, nor has Holy Scripture replaced Holy Spirit as the Third. The Bible performs its servant work and witness well beneath the majesty of God, the lordship of Christ, and the power of Holy Spirit.

To say these things, however, is without any virtue. It is a very small thing indeed, though the times require it, to name what Scripture is not. Beyond these purely preliminary delineations lies the vast and proper labor of attending to Scripture's word, granting it the reverence of our offered minds, immersing ourselves in its story, meditating on its precepts, discerning its patterns, preaching its claims, praying its prayers, receiving its correction, permitting it to give steady and authoritative shape to the individuals and communities of faith that we are becoming.

The Relationship of Community and Scripture

The relationship between the Bible and the faith community is one of absolute and subtle interdependence. Neither exists without the other. The community came first, of course. Both Israel and the CHURCH were given birth well before their distinctive Scriptures developed. These Scriptures were composed by the community, for the community, to bear witness to the community's experience of God, to address specific moments and needs within the community's history. Furthermore, the community chose which of its writings to include in its CANON, and which to exclude. Having chosen, the community ever since has exercised the right to interpret these texts, making choices in the location of meaning and nuance, often assigning relative values to different texts, interpreting some passages in the light of others. In these ways it can be asserted that the Bible very much belongs to the church.

In other ways, however, it must be affirmed that the church belongs to the Bible. Although the Scriptures flowed from the community, the same divine initiative that was the impetus of the community was also the impetus of the Scriptures. The Bible not only bears witness to the community-creating initiatives of God, it continues to call forth, to critique, to correct, to give new existence and shape to communities of faith. As surely as the church made its Scripture, so Scripture makes the church. Samuel Terrien expressed the relationship in this way:

The church did not really "canonize" her own canon. She officially recognized that the Scripture was canonical because it already constituted for her a test, a standard, a norm, a critique. Both the church and the Bible are different and complimentary manifestations of the Word. The Bible remains the record of the church's origin, the "yardstick" of her fidelity. It is the Bible that judges the church, not the contrary. In the testimony of the Bible, the church finds the cloth of her worship, the substance of her thought, and the nerve of her action.

(Terrien 1962, 81)

The church then lives under biblical authority. The Scriptures, composed, canonized, and interpreted by the community, speak decisively to the community, whose experience again and again affirms that in these words is heard the Word of the Living God.

The church fails its heritage, however, if its submission to Scripture's word is slavish. There is a distinct liberty in the life we live under Scripture's authority. This liberty stems, on the one hand, from the fact that the Bible is so big. With so many different layers, traditions, times, and voices represented in Scripture, there is no question of simple obedience to each chapter and verse. The vast and variegated fabric of Scripture requires us instead to interpret, to locate the crucial within Scripture's witness, and having submitted ourselves to the crucial, to wrestle—in freedom, honesty, and humility—with those texts that are in apparent tension with it. This is our necessary freedom under the authority of so big a Bible.

Our liberty stems, on the other hand, from the fact that as big as the Bible is, God's living Word is bigger. We live in "a new covenant, not of letter but of spirit; for the letter kills, but the Spirit gives life. . . . and where the Spirit of the Lord is, there is freedom" (2 Cor 3:6, 17). God is free to do a new thing, and the Christ who came not to abolish the law but fulfill it, has embodied the freedom of God both to fulfill Scripture's promise and to surpass what Scripture can foresee. As John Barton says,

The tension between the new faith and the old Scriptures therefore is . . . part of the essence of Christianity from the beginning. Christians are people who have a book, in order to be able to proclaim their freedom from it; yet the character of that freedom is deeply shaped by the book from which they have been freed, and it is the God who gave the book who also gives the freedom.

(Barton 1988, 9–10)

The enormous challenge to the church is to find its submission to Scripture in ways that do not forfeit the real freedom of the Gospel, and to find its freedom under the real authority of Scripture's word.

The Functions of Authority

Perhaps we do well to understand Scripture's *authority* for the community in terms of Scripture's *functions* in the community. How do we experience Scripture authoritatively?

We do so first in the experience of Scripture's function as the church's *memory*. The Bible tells the story that tells us who we are. We are cherished people, created good in God's image to live as partners with God in creation. We are tragic people, self-absorbed and deceived, refusing freedom, forfeiting vocation, enslaved by death. We are fortunate people, recipients of GRACE, God's amazing initiative to set us free, most decisively given in the life, death and resurrection of JESUS, the Word made flesh. We are empowered people, led by the Holy Spirit to live glad and prophetic lives, bearing witness to God's peace. We are expectant people, looking in hope for the final triumph of God's purpose.

This story of creation, fall, redemption, Pentecost, and consummation is the story of who we were, who we are, who we shall be. Hearing the Scriptures restores our memory. We learn our names. We locate ourselves in the story of God, and so recover our purpose. This recovery takes place in hearing the Bible's stories as our own stories. We are ABRAHAM and SARAH, called to forsake security for an impossible promise. We are slaves oppressed by PHARAOH, we are Pharaoh oppressing slaves, we are MOSES seized by God to call Pharaoh to justice and slaves to freedom. We are ZACCHAEUS up a tree. We are Peter shattered by failure and forgiveness. We are Mary Magdalene blinded by tears, stumbling over smiling angels. We are John of Patmos hearing heaven's final laughter.

But the church's memory resides not only in the stories. We remember ourselves also in Scripture's hymns and prayers, in its oracles and pronouncements, and powerfully in its commandments, which give gracious boundaries and definition to our life together. The function of commandment as a guarantor of faithful memory is strikingly illustrated in a text addressed to the kings of Israel. The king "must not acquire many horses for himself" and "he must not acquire many wives for himself, or else his heart will turn away; also silver and gold he must not acquire in great quantity for himself" (Deut 17:16-17). These limits having been given, the text goes on:

When he has taken the throne of his kingdom, he shall have a copy of this law written for him. . . .

It shall remain with him and he shall read in it all the days of his life, so that he may learn to fear the LORD his God. . . . (Deut 17:18-19)

The text, knowing kings to be forgetful, requires the king to read daily the commandment that tells him who he is and who he is not. The church lives under the same danger and the same restorative instruction. In Scripture's law, as in its story, the church may find and nourish its memory.

In a related way the Bible functions as the church's fiercest *critic*. The community is always tempted to domesticate its Bible, perverting it into false comfort, reading selectively and conveniently by a dishonest assumption of ownership. The fact is that from the beginning these writings functioned confrontationally against the communities to whom they were given.

I hate, I despise your festivals,
and I take no delight in your solemn assemblies. . . .
But let justice roll down like waters,
    and righteousness like an everflowing stream.
(Amos 5:21, 24)

Not everyone who says to me, "Lord, Lord," will enter the kingdom of heaven, but only the one who does the will of my Father in heaven. (Matt 7:21)

It may safely be said that no church can read Scripture honestly and be comfortable with it. Nor has Scripture ever been comfortable with us, for never has the community of faith been fully faithful. As Leander Keck has said,

New Testament Christianity must not be confused with early Christianity; in fact, Christianity according to the New Testament is a fundamental critique of the early Christianity that was actually developing. Precisely the same point must be made for much of the Old Testament. Old Testament faith and religion is not the same as Israelite faith and religion, but a series of critiques of it.
(Keck 1978, 94–95)

The adversarial relationship of the Bible to the church is a central and nonnegotiable function, for the church is both a community of sinners and the inevitable institutionalizing of the community's sins. We cannot hope to be fully faithful. Being human, we will be idolatrous, often in ways we cannot see. At the very least we can confess it, and in humility grant to the Bible its authority to question us, to accuse us and call us to repentance. Our racism, our militarism, our abuse of the poor, our violence against the earth, all our failures of faith, all our idolatries, especially the ones we commit inside the temple—God rages in Scripture against them all. No reformation of the church has ever come that did not begin with a new hearing of Scripture's sharp correction. The church has little hope for itself unless the church's book remain the church's critic.

A third experience of Scripture's authority lies in the discovery of the Bible as the church's *voice*. The church is in need not only of a saving word to hear, but of a proper word to say. Scripture offers both. Not only bearing God's word to our ears, it places our own truest words on our tongues.

We may not know our own hearts but the Scriptures do. We are mute with fears we cannot name, sorrows we cannot grasp, unarticulated sins, unutterable longings and joys. Uncannily, Scripture names them. The Bible astonishes us by its keen articulation of our hearts, and so liberates us to be truthful, and so teaches us to pray. The Psalms, called by Calvin "the anatomy of all parts of the soul," are the centerpiece of this articulation. Here we learn how to sigh, how to rage, how to ask our darkest questions of God, how to confess, how to sing, how to be silent.

To find the human voice of Scripture is, of course, to discover voices other than our own. We may not have numbered ourselves among the poor, the outcast, the ones who suffer unjustly; but Scripture supplies for them the clearest voice of all and invites the whole church to take up their voice. The Bible speaks for all who are denied a voice in the world. Some of these "little ones" are members of the household of faith, many are not; regardless, Scripture speaks for them. In this respect the Bible is far more than the church's book, "the Bible is everybody's book" (Merton 1970, 28, 39). Its agenda is not the church but the whole of creation (Brueggemann 1978, 143). The church finds its faithfulness in learning from Scripture to speak with and for all creation.

This cannot be done apart from finding also in Scripture our voice for speaking *to* the world. This is commanded: we are witnesses, we are advocates, we have news. In the words of the prophets to the nations, in the words of the apostles to the councils and the crowds, in the words of Jesus to the poor, to the powerful, to the lost, we have our mandate and our pattern for lifting a voice to the world. The Bible is far more than what the church needs to hear. It is what the church needs to say (see Craddock 1985, 26).

A fourth way of describing Scripture's authoritative function is to speak of the Bible as the church's *vision*. Our human confusion is characterized by distorted visions of our neighbors and ourselves, the creation and the Creator. Incorrigible idol-makers, we are hemmed in by false images. We may improve our speech to be "politically correct," we may adjust our outward behaviors to be circumspect and civil, but if our minds are filled with deep and ancient, distorted images, we are in Jesus' words, "like whitewashed tombs" (Matt 23:27).

Here is the taproot of all prejudice, anxiety, and distorted desire: we see neighbor, world, ourselves, and God in false images. "But if your eye is unhealthy, your whole body will be full of darkness" (Matt 6:23).

Scripture's gift is to offer a world of alternative images. The Bible gleams with new pictures of God and humankind. To stand together before these pictures, to gaze on them steadily, to let them recast our speech and our imaginations is to be in time reformed. No transformation of human consciousness occurs apart from replacing old mental pictures with new ones. Immersion into Scripture's world may grant such a transformation, for "the Bible is a lens through which all of life is to be discerned" (Brueggemann 1978, 154).

Through the lens of Scripture we come to see ourselves no longer as owners, competitors, animals, or angels, but as fortunate guests, forgiven transgressors, trusted partners in a sacred vocation. We come to see other persons no longer as the enemy, the problem, or the object, but as neighbors and kin, honored embodiments of the actual Christ. We come to see the future not as fate, but as a new city, a great feast, the triumph of a great love. And though always through a glass darkly, we see more and more of God: true father, mother, lover, friend, servant, host, enthroned in the heavens, hung from a cross, heartbreaking splendor, ineffable light.

With this slow dawning of new vision comes light enough to walk by. Scripture becomes a real source for daily discernment, reliable guidance in the habits and choices that lead to life. The Gospels of Matthew and Luke relate a powerful paradigm for the church as described in the experience of Jesus. In the wilderness tempted by the devil, who sets before him false images and idolatrous choices, Jesus locates his alternative way again and again in quotations from Scripture. By this light he sees his way.

> Your word is a lamp to my feet
> and a light to my path. (Ps 119:105)
> . . . in your light we see light. (Ps 36:9)

We may speak of a final function of Scripture's experienced authority in the church: the Bible as *communion*. We have said unequivocally that the Bible is not God, nor does it merit our worship. It is a book, and the book itself may not rightly be called holy. But the church has had good reason to call these writings Holy Scripture, for in reading and reflecting on Scripture's word, the church has found itself again and again encountered by the Holy One. Not by any abstract doctrine of inspiration, but by the testimony of long experience, the church gives thankful witness that the Bible is a meeting place. Always on its own terms, not ours, never automatically or predictably, still the Bible bears us in time to a presence. When the community of faith brings itself to Scripture in humility and constancy, when this open book is met with open minds and hearts, the Spirit often speaks, and we are on holy ground.

In this respect we have warrant to speak of the sacrament of Scripture as a mediating instrument of the presence of God (see Wainwright 1980, 178–81). Like the sacrament of the table, which likewise brings us to our memory, our critic, our voice, our vision, and our communion, the sacrament of the word may nourish us and transform us. It is an outward and visible sign of an inner, invisible grace. The church reads the Scriptures with reverence ("This is the word of the Lord") and with gratitude ("Thanks be to God"), for the Bible is an instrument of the real presence of God among us.

The Bible in the Church's Worship

Because the Bible serves these authoritative functions in the church, the book is opened, read, and proclaimed whenever the community gathers for worship. Scripture itself provides the forms of our worship, the pattern of our prayers, the substance of our preaching, and much of the very language we employ in the worship of God. Being in particular the church's memory and the church's voice, the Bible is the church's book of worship.

It should go without saying that Christian worship will include times for Scripture, without added commentary, to be publicly read. The liturgical churches follow ancient tradition in the reading of an OT lesson, an Epistle lesson, a Gospel lesson, and a Psalm in each service of worship. Some churches, however, read Scripture hardly at all in their worship, with tragic results. It is common in these churches to attend worship and hear nothing of Scripture itself, apart from a few verses read by a preacher as introduction to the sermon. The Bible itself urges: "Give attention to the public reading of Scripture" (1 Tim 4:13).

The reason for separate, sustained reading of the Bible in worship is that Scripture makes its own witness, "independent of current interpretation and application" (Wainwright 1980, 168). These are the ancient words heard by the ancient communities of faith and by every generation that has followed them. They are the words that have preceded us, waiting all these centuries to speak to our new situation. To read them in the hearing of the congregation, entirely apart from the sermon, is to recognize that Scripture stands apart from its interpretation. It is to grant space for the Bible to function as the critic of the church, the judgment of God on our worship and practice. Such reading also permits the Spirit to make its own witness within the hearts of the hearers, who may understand and apply the word in ways the preacher cannot begin to know.

Because of the weight of Scripture's word, careful attention will be given to the manner of its public reading. The readings should most often be done by laypersons, since the Bible is not the clergy's but the community's book. It should be read clearly, simply and without haste. Dietrich Bonhoeffer suggested that "the situation of the reader of Scripture is probably closest to that in which I read to others a letter from a friend," showing an attentive regard for the friend's word and conveying it as the friend's word, not one's own. In any way to call attention to the self instead of the word "is to commit the worst of sins in presenting the Scriptures" (Bonhoeffer, 1954, 56).

Then comes the word-event called preaching. That the sermon should rise from and be formed by biblical texts is not accepted by all who preach. Fortunately for the church, however, biblical preaching has been widely renewed in recent years. The disciplines of biblical scholarship and homiletics have been engaged in the most fruitful new conversations and mergers. New resources are abundant to assist pastors in the preaching of sermons that are faithful to the forms and intentions of biblical texts.

Because Scripture is the church's memory, its critic, its voice, its vision, and an instrument of its communion with God, the sermon should impart Scripture's word. The people did not come to church to learn what was on the minister's mind, they came hoping for some glimpse, however brief, of God. They are hungry for a Word. Preachers desiring to be "relevant" may be tempted week by week to shuttle from one psychological or political issue to another, hoping at best to tie in a text at the end. They may manage to be interesting and even helpful, but they will not have preached, nor will they have been relevant. Attending to Scripture reveals what is relevant to God. Biblical preaching will invariably speak to the issues of the day. But only by beginning with Scripture do we discern which questions are God's questions. Only by proceeding from Scripture do the people discern their relevant agenda from the prior word that has preceded them, foreseen them and called them to a purpose.

Which texts shall be preached? Some preachers are fastened to a narrow strip of Scripture. Like MARCION, their canon includes little but PAUL. Or perhaps they have settled into the Synoptics. Or perhaps again, they choose texts from all over the canon, but only those texts that can serve—or be forced to serve—two or three endlessly recapitulated themes. Though it is natural enough for preachers to preach most what they know best, it is crucial that they learn the discipline of preaching from the full range of Scripture's witness—texts and themes from all parts of the canon. Otherwise preaching is not biblical. It is precisely the nature of Scripture to be a vast and variegated witness, bearing in its numerous perspectives and even in its tensions with itself, the many colors of real life, the many names and faces of God.

Preaching from the lectionary can assist in this discipline. The ancient practice of preaching from assigned texts, which over the course of the church year celebrates the many themes of Scripture's whole story, has been newly embraced by a great many congregations and preachers. Among other gifts, the lectionary can add a keen sense of the vital relationship between the Bible and the church, as an ever-growing portion of the church stands before the same texts on the same day. Not all preachers will use the lectionary. A full and faithful proclamation of Scripture's witness can be made without it. Many wonderful texts can only be preached without it. Preachers who do not use the lectionary should only be sure that their preaching includes texts that they themselves would not naturally choose, but that are in some sense imposed upon them.

As a servant of the word, the preacher will give faithful, scrupulous attention to the study of the texts to be preached. This is work, and it is indispensable work. The discipline of study will include coming to terms with the historical setting of the text, the function of its literary form, the meaning of its words, its intended work among those to whom it is addressed. Without any display of this scaffolding of scholarship, the sermon should take its purpose and its shape from these real structures and movements within the text. Biblical preaching does not consist of repeated quotations from the Bible, but of faithfully pursuing the intentions of biblical texts.

It should always be clear that proclamation is not so much the function of the preacher as of the community. The whole church shares in the partnership of preaching, and a congregation can be invited in many ways to enter into the preacher's conversations with a text, to share in the ownership of the sermon. It should certainly be clear that the church's preaching is in complete continuity with what the Bible itself has been from the beginning. The Bible began as preaching. Most of its units are thoroughly oral in form, shaped by preaching and intended to be heard in worshiping communities. Furthermore, the texts not only bear witness to received tradition; they proceed, as preaching does, to interpret and apply the tradition. In its preaching the church continues what Scripture has always been and what it will always invite: a witness to the gracious initiatives of God and a struggle to interpret and apply this news for living in the world, an enfleshment of the word again and again.

The Bible in the Church's Study

It is not enough for the church to hear and proclaim Scripture in its weekly worship. Because it is the community's book, the community seeks regular times and ways to open it together, to question and be questioned by it, to exchange insights, to grapple with its implications for ordinary life.

We are speaking of what is often called the church's ministry of Christian education. Like preaching, this enterprise has often missed its mark, drifting into pedantic, moralistic little Sunday School lessons, closer to indoctrination than to communal conversation and study. But also like preaching, the field of Christian education has experienced a recent renewal in many sectors of the church. The communal study of Scripture is a vital source of the church's life and health. Recent research has found, in fact, that "effective Christian education is the most powerful single influence congregations have on maturity of faith" (Roehlkepartain 1990, 496).

Scripture insists on this enterprise. The great commandment to "love the LORD your God with all your heart, and with all your soul, and with all your might" (Deut 6:5) is instantly followed by a homely call to communal reflection and study:

> Keep these words that I am commanding you today in your heart. Recite them to your children and talk about them. . . .　　　　　　　(Deut 6:6-7)

The purpose is transformation. By keeping Scripture's word in the community's conversation, by inquiring of it, recalling it to each other, pressing it against the ongoing issues of the day and the ordinary circumstances of our lives, we bind it to our heads and hands and write it on our gates. We are altered. Annie Dillard has written of her experience as a child at church camp and Sunday school.

> I had miles of Bible in memory: some perforce, but most by hap, like the words to songs. There was no corner of my brain where you could not find, among the files of clothing labels and heaps of rocks and minerals, among the swarms of protozoans and shelves of novels, whole tapes and snarls and reels of Bible. . . .
> Why did they spread this scandalous document before our eyes? If they had read it, I thought, they would have hid it. They did not recognize the lively danger that we would, through repeated exposure catch a dose of its virulent opposition to their world.　　　　　　　(Corn 1990, 28, 35)

Scripture can be privately read and studied, of course; but there is particular and irreplaceable value in communal study. Rising out of communities, the Bible remains a community book. Its implications are best discerned among and between believers and seekers. In communal study we can be delivered from some of our personal predispositions to a text, corrected or confirmed in our understandings and regularly surprised by meanings and applications we could never have guessed. The Spirit interprets Scripture to us through the word and experience of the sister and brother.

> The Bible speaks to us today, as in the past, not by means of a miracle, not by means of audiovisual magic, but by communal effort.
> 　　　　　　　(Visotzky 1991, 10)

Communal study will therefore maintain an openness to all questions and perspectives. Naturally the community arrives at a certain consensus of meanings that holds idiosyncratic or exotic readings in check. But no question is disallowed. Every perspective is heard and weighed. The church has much to learn from the ancient rabbis, who gloried in multiple readings of texts and rejoiced in the Torah as a gem with at least seventy facets in every word (Visotzky 1991, 228). The Bible gives multiple perspectives on itself. It asks a thousand questions of itself. So the community gathers to hear Scripture afresh by hearing each other's questions, insights, hunches, and stories. In this pooling of light the church finds more of its way.

The Bible in Devotion

The community imparts the word to the individual, but in doing so does not relieve the individual of the necessity of a personal confrontation with the word. In fact, the community relies on each member to attend privately to Scripture. This is so because each member of the community is a priest, personally accountable to the word and personally accountable to exert the word's witness in the community. Each member reads the Bible for the sake of her own soul and for the sake of the church.

For this reason we encourage one another to the daily practice of reading and meditating on Scripture. This need not be considered a legalism. It is a transforming discipline, a sacred duty and privilege. It is not the quest for a certain daily devotional feeling. On many days it yields little feeling at all. It is simply a commitment over time to saturate the mind with Scripture's word, to let it penetrate the heart and have new openings to extend itself in one's thought and behavior.

Among our many aversions to this discipline is that the Bible's words may already be familiar to us. Why devote time to reading words that we know? This is, of course, an illusion. It is precisely our familiarity with Scripture's words that most often keeps us from knowing them. "Let us not be too sure we know the Bible just because we have learned not to be astonished by it" (Merton 1970, 27). There are ways to reopen our minds to amazement, there are new insights and fresh applications to be discovered.

[The Bible] is still at the very beginning of its career, the full meaning of its content having hardly touched the thresholds of our minds; like an ocean at the bottom of which countless pearls lie, waiting to be discovered, its spirit is still to be unfolded. Though its words seem plain and its idiom translu-

cent, unnoticed meanings, undreamed-of intimations break forth constantly. . . . Today it is as if . . . we had not even begun to read it.

(Heschel 1955, 242)

The Bible does not yield its secrets to casual, perfunctory reading. Layers of meaning will also be lost to those who read only with the intellect. The place of critical thinking in the study of Scripture, as we have seen, is crucial. But for Scripture to speak in its fullness, another kind of reading is required. This is meditative reading, reading that takes place in the shape of prayer.

Jewish piety has a long tradition of meditation upon the words of Scripture, as do the Roman Catholic and Orthodox Christian communities. More recently, Dietrich Bonhoeffer did Protestants a great service by calling them, in the tradition of Luther, to the practice of such meditation. He urged not only an ongoing regimen of daily reading from the Bible, but also the choice of a shorter text for use in meditation throughout each week. The text is read again and again. It is surrounded with reflective silence and pondered prayerfully. The thoughts it generates are written down, the prayers it invokes are prayed; the word is kept.

Ponder this word in your heart as Mary did. That is all. That is meditation . . . ponder this word in your heart at length until it is entirely within you and has taken possession of you.

(Bonhoeffer 1986, 32–33)

Whether or not Bonhoeffer's particular method is employed, the regular practice of some form of personal reflection on biblical texts is worthy and is commended by Scripture itself (e.g., Ps 1:2; 119). Much of the Bible is meant to be prayed or to be read on the verge of prayer. Those who permit Scripture's word to bear them into prayer and meditation will have joined in a vital portion of the conversation that Scripture means to have with us.

On this subject a particular word belongs to pastors and others whose profession entails much public use of Scripture. We of all persons are subject to a disinclination to hear Scripture for ourselves. Having labored to hear it and speak it for others, we grow weary and set it aside. Having handled it too often for our professional purposes, we are embarrassed to face it and hear it tell us who we are. As George McDonald said, "Nothing is so deadening to the divine as an habitual dealing with the outsides of holy things" (Doberstein 1986, 248).

We are not only among those who are most at risk, we are also among those whose need to be corrected and formed by Scripture is most urgent. In what profession does ego insinuate itself more insidiously than in ours? And who holds more power to lead the people into making idols than Aaron the priest? Our profession is dangerous, both to ourselves and to the church. Thomas Merton once suggested that the phenomenon of "unconscious revolt against the Bible" on the part of pastors and priests probably accounts for "much that is rigid, callous, inhuman, fanatical in the religious sphere" (Merton 1970, 17–18).

So the pastor, not looking for a sermon, not imagining how a text might be used in the work, will sit before the Scriptures to hear them honestly, correctively, intimately. This appointment may grant many unforeseen gifts to a minister, not the least of which may be a new measure of freedom from the tyrannical grip of the church itself. We who interpret the Bible most often must permit it to interpret us to ourselves and lead us to the offering of our own most secret and saving prayers.

The Bible in the Formation of the Church's Life

We have spoken of Scripture's capacity to give shape to the church. As in the first creation story of Genesis, where the universe is created by a Word, so this same Word—not equivalent to Scripture but borne by it to open hearts—continues to create the church and give it new shape for its vocation in the world.

Clearly the Bible's capacity to give better shape to human lives and institutions is in no way automatic. It is entirely possible in reading the Bible to feel confirmed in one's own preferences and bigotries. Some of the meanest people on earth read the Bible every day and find themselves justified. Most of the cruellest movements in the history of the Western world have taken Scripture as their warrant. Dedicated servants of the Nazi regime, assisting cheerfully in the death camps, could open their Bibles daily and see no contradiction. Baptist deacons in the American South could pose for a photograph by the body of a lynched man, holding Bibles in their hands. Endless is the church's capacity to neglect, pervert, and demonize the Scriptures.

The Bible may be very much like a mirror: self-righteousness looking in will see self-righteousness looking back. In this respect Scripture can be a peculiar instrument of God's wrath upon its readers. In Karl Barth's words,

> The Bible gives to every man and to every era such answers to their questions as they deserve. We shall always find in it as much as we seek and no more. (Barth 1956, 32)

Nothing we can say about the Bible's capacity to transform us can overlook the equal capacities of our own intransigence.

Throughout the church's history, however, where individuals and communities have stood before the Scriptures in humility and openness, an answering power has given a better shape to character, behavior, and life. Scripture's own pattern in speaking of itself says very little of what it *is*, but a great deal about what it *does*. It is not so much a book with a status as with a function. More than repositories of truth, these texts have intensions. "My word . . . will *accomplish* that which I purpose" (Isa 55:11).

There is a kind of organic force ascribed to Scripture, the power of planted seed to stir and grow to a conquering profusion. "Welcome with meekness the implanted word that has the power to save your souls" (Jas 1:21). It is understood as "useful for teaching, for reproof, for correction, and for training in righteousness" (2 Tim 3:16)—*useful*, a "low-key word, strikingly contrasted with what has been made of this text in later times" (Barr 1980, 119), pointing us again to the pragmatic servant-function of Scripture to do real work among us.

We do not learn Scripture for the sake of learning Scripture. The church reads, proclaims, studies, and meditates on Scripture so that these words may do the long and steady work of forming us into communities that embody more of the Christ in the world. Stanley Hauerwas has spoken of the church as a "Story-Formed Community" (Hauerwas 1981, 9–35). Learning Scripture's story, submitting to its pressure and promise, we are formed by it. We are sculpted to the cruciform. Our vocation of character, our ethics and relationships, our evangelical and prophetic mission to the world take their shape as we give ourselves into the hands of Scripture. Witness the definitive shaping force exerted by the biblical story of the exodus upon the African-American churches in the 1960s. Similarly, churches in Latin America, Africa, and Eastern Europe have given striking recent examples of how cruciform communities, shaped by biblical memory and hope, may bear revolutionary witness to their time. Scripture takes hold of the church and shapes it toward Christ that the church may take hold of and give shape to the world.

For the Bible to serve this function we must, above all, take seriously it's strangeness, its tensions with us. Many of its precepts are frankly alien to our sensibilities. Many of its voices and figures—supremely Jesus himself—are baffling to us. Our inclination to soften these tensions, to flatten these bewildering and often offensive voices to a more manageable, falsely coherent system of faith, must at all costs by rejected. Scripture cannot form the church unless the hard words of Scripture are permitted to press against the church. Confronted by difficult words on such subjects as sexuality, marriage and divorce, war and peace, rich and poor, church and state, believers are free under the Holy Spirit to interpret these texts, to struggle with them and argue with them, to note where they may be culturally tinged, to place them ultimately under the higher lordship of Christ. We are not free to dismiss them. The tensions of Scripture within itself and with us must be felt, honored, and permitted to press against the church. By this submission the community and its members are formed for their vocation.

Encountered and amazed by the living God, the ancient church wrote words bearing witness to what it had seen and heard, expressing in many voices and forms the implications of its news. When today's church reads the ancient church's book as our book and as a book of God—granting it diligent study, reverent reflection, and obedient service—the Encounter recurs. Again and again the church is met and amazed.

For Further Study

In the *Mercer Dictionary of the Bible*: BIBLE; BIBLE AND LIBERATION MOVEMENTS; BIBLE AND WESTERN LITERATURE; CANON; CHURCH; CHURCH AND LAW; HERMENEUTICS; INTERPRETATION, HISTORY OF; LITERATURE, BIBLE AS. In other sources: See works cited, below.

Works Cited

Barr, James. 1980. *The Scope and Authority of the Bible*.

Barth, Karl. 1956. *The Word of God and the Word of Man*.

Barton, John. 1988. *People of the Book? The Authority of the Bible in Christianity*.

Bonhoeffer, Dietrich. 1954. *Life Together*. 1986. *Meditating on the Word*.

Brueggemann, Walter. 1978. *The Bible Makes Sense*.

Corn, Alfred, ed. 1990. *Incarnation: Contemporary Writers on the New Testament*.

Craddock, Fred B. 1985. *Preaching*.

Doberstein, John W., ed. 1986. *Minister's Prayer Book*.

Hauerwas, Stanley. 1981. *A Community of Character*.

Heschel, Abraham Joshua. 1955. *God in Search of Man*. 1972. *The Insecurity of Freedom*.

Keck, Leander E. 1978. *The Bible in the Pulpit*.

Merton, Thomas. 1970. *Opening the Bible*.

Roehlkepartain, Eugene C. 1990. "What Makes Faith Mature?" *The Christian Century* (9 May): 496–99.

Terrien, Samuel. 1962. *The Bible and the Church*.

Visotzky, Burton L. *Reading the Book: Making the Bible a Timeless Text*.

Matthew

Stephenson Humphries-Brooks

Introduction

Christians approach Matthew as a catechetical manual, as a source book for homily, and as a guide to faith and practice within contemporary Christian communities. Scholars use Matthew as a historical text that informs us about Jesus of Nazareth, the structure of faith of an early Christian author, and/or the faith and practice of an early Christian community of the Mediterranean world in the first century C.E. Moreover, the Matthean depiction of Jesus influences the development of ethical and legal systems in Western culture.

In the following commentary the process of investigation and interpretation begins and ends with the text. Matthew prompts significant questions for a contemporary critical audience broadly conceived.

The Text of the Gospel of Matthew

The Plot of Matthew. We tend to read Matthew as containing an organized series of episodes about Jesus. We find a "plot" of his life complete with complication, climax, and denouement. The series of episodes implies some causal relationship from one event to the next. For example the information that Jesus is adopted into the Davidic royal line by Joseph (1:1-21) helps us to make sense of the visit of the MAGI and the attempt by HEROD to destroy the one born *king of the Jews* (2:1-18).

The plot of Matthew does not directly violate normal historical expectations. In general the sequence of the plot of Matthew conforms to causal and temporal sequence, that is, no events occur out of their normal order. We can easily summarize the plot of Matthew: Jesus is born and adopted into the royal line of Israel. He escapes a murderous plot by a rival king. He is baptized and immediately tempted by Satan. He begins a career of preaching the arrival of the kingdom of heaven. He teaches, performs miracles, recruits disciples. The religious leaders become his enemies. He arrives in the capital city and one of his own disciples betrays him. He is tried and put to death by crucifixion for blasphemy and political sedition. He is buried and resurrected.

Characters and Characterization in Matthew. The episodes that form the plot of Matthew focus on the actions of JESUS, who is the main character. The text depicts Jesus by commentary from the narrator, by Jesus' actions, by commentary from other characters, and finally and most importantly by what Jesus says. The picture that emerges of Jesus is that he is the SON OF GOD, the SON OF MAN. During the process of his story he also becomes invested with all authority and power, a claim the narrator makes for him implicitly by calling him *Emmanuel, . . . God-with-us* (1:23). Jesus himself explicitly claims such power after the resurrection (28:18).

The development of the divine power and authority of Jesus throughout his life occurs in conjunction with a downward trend in Jesus' mundane fortunes. Initially, Jesus appears as a claimant to the throne of David. He is a legitimate threat to Herod and the rulers of Jerusalem. As an adult he takes up residence as a free householder of an urban area, CAPERNAUM (4:13; 9:1). His disciples, also, are depicted as free householders. Contrary to this depiction, Jesus identifies himself as homeless (8:20). At the CRUCIFIXION the text avoids referring to MARY as his mother and names instead only his brothers as her sons, thereby emphasizing his homelessness (27:56; cf. 13:55). At the same time Jesus becomes not only the preacher and teacher of the kingdom of heaven, but also its chief citizen. Ironically, he is crucified as *King of the Jews* (27:37) the same title under which Herod seeks his death. Jesus, therefore, is not depicted as Christ or Messiah in historical terms.

We are led by the Gospel to evaluate other characters according to Jesus' actions and words. With regard to social status as understood in the ancient

Mediterranean world three major types of characters appear: powerful urban elites; the free of the cities; women, children, and other supplicants. Repeatedly characters of different status interact in specific episodes. Matthew contains episodes interwoven into the plot to show how characters with lower status displace those with higher status as more dependable witnesses to the kingdom of heaven. Those characters associated with the urban elite oppose Jesus. They are not part of the kingdom of heaven. The disciples remain ambiguous as to their future faithfulness to Jesus. Only women, children, and other supplicants, those of the lowest status according to mundane social-historical perception, appear as faithful witnesses to Jesus (Humphries-Brooks 1991).

The treatment of other characters and character groups is consistent with the treatment of Jesus in the plot of the Gospel. Only as a homeless and marginal person does Jesus become fully empowered; only homeless and marginal people fully perceive and act on the faith that arrives with the kingdom of heaven.

The Speeches of Jesus. The text begins with a carefully plotted series of episodes associated with the birth and early career of Jesus (1:1–5:1). Similarly the conclusion to the Gospel (26:1b–28:20) contains a carefully recounted series of episodes concerning the PASSION, death, and resurrection of Jesus.

In the midsection of Matthew, however, narrative plot becomes less significant as attention shifts to speeches and PARABLES (5:1–26:1a). These serve several functions in the context of the plot of Matthew: 1. They focus attention on the character and person of Jesus; 2. They make the "once-upon-a-time" ministry of Jesus contemporary with every new performance of the text; 3. They describe the kingdom of heaven; 4. Therefore, they provide the vantage point from which all characters and episodes in Matthew are to be judged. We cannot fully understand Matthew by merely understanding the causal sequence of Jesus' life. Rather, we must perceive Matthew as a whole and use information provided in the speeches of Jesus to interpret the activity of those characters described by the plot.

The author asks us by this arrangement of the narrative to pay less attention to the continuous unrolling of the life of Jesus, and more attention to associations in the narrative that reveal the kingdom of heaven. The work must be read as layers, or perceived like a building, "architectonically" (Davies 1964, 14). We become, therefore, actively involved with the text

as we construct meaning from it. This perception makes it impossible to read or interpret according to one-dimensional thematic- or plot-oriented outlines. In this commentary, we follow the text as it shifts from plot to speech. The divisions proposed by the outline and commentary are governed by a concern to describe the reading experience for us as a critical contemporary audience. Such divisions do not necessarily reconstruct the experience of the text for the original ancient audience, nor do they attempt to recover the conscious intent of the author who probably did not compose according to an outline.

By disrupting our attention from plot, the speeches and parables of Jesus present a view of the kingdom of heaven as disruptive to perception of the historical .world. They invite us, as they invited the ancient audience of the Matthean community, to see the presence of the kingdom of heaven in the world.

Major Themes in Matthew

Based on this analysis the single underlying and organizing theme of the Gospel of Matthew is the arrival of the kingdom of heaven in history and its effect on normal experience. Matthew makes apparent that the mystery of the kingdom of heaven is not limited to or encapsulated by the person of Jesus, but requires a discernment of God's will from the perspective of the kingdom proclaimed by Jesus. In the final analysis, Matthew is not a christological or ecclesiological document, but a *theological* one; its focus is on God.

The kingdom of heaven becomes the major term used to describe the power of God on earth in Matthew. It possesses its own justice, a justice that is unique in terms of politics, ethics, economics, and status orientation. The kingdom of heaven comes into conflict with the historical world familiar to us and represented in the plot of the Gospel as well.

The totality of Matthew exposes a world fractured and restructured by conflict and struggle between the kingdom of heaven and the kingdoms of the world. Clearly those kingdoms are claimed by the power of EVIL represented by a variety of titles including "Satan," "the Devil," "Beelzebul," and "the Evil One." Matthew assumes that the world possessed by evil powers can only be overcome by the intervention of God independent of normal human individuals, institutions, and political structures. God's intervention takes on real political form in the life and teaching of Jesus, which bears witness to and invites discernment of the kingdom of heaven and the battle currently engaged.

The conclusion to that conflict will be one of judgment and the removal of evil from the world by God.

Therefore, the kingdom of heaven always takes its bearings from God's end to time rather than from the discernment of God's purposes through past events. The value of persons in its justice is based upon God's righteousness that includes a balance between GRACE and judgment. Matthew depicts God's righteousness at odds with normal political existence because such human justice is in the control of evil.

The worldview of Matthew accords with views expressed in early Christian and Jewish APOCALYPTIC LITERATURE. It has its roots in the prophetic tradition of JUDAISM and in modes of thought that come from a combination of traditional Hebrew culture with Hellenistic thought. Unlike the Jewish and Christian apocalyptic tradition out of which it arises, however, Matthew abandons the view of God as divine warrior who opposes the institutionalized violence of oppressive regimes with invasions of heavenly death-dealing hosts. Consistently, Jesus in Matthew resists the use of violence to combat violence. Rather, the antidote to death in Matthew comes in the resurrection of Jesus by God.

The Composition of the Author

The Gospel of Matthew recounts the significant events of Jesus' life in such a way that those who read it know that these events are not regarded by the author as fictions or fabrications. One of the most popular genres of the ancient world is biography. Ancient biographers seek to reveal to their audiences the essential truth about a person through actions and speech (Talbert 1988). But further, by encountering the truth about a particular person, the audience becomes educated into the universal truths that inform action in the world. An ancient audience, therefore, anticipates that Matthew will educate them not only about the person, Jesus, but through him about their own appropriate action in the world.

The accurate depiction of historical event remains of paramount importance for most modern biographers. For the ancient biographer, including the author of Matthew, the unveiling of truth that cannot be contained in the merely historical is of paramount importance. After all history is mere appearance: biography lays bare essence not otherwise apparent. Therefore, Matthew contains only a selection of the events of Jesus' life told in such a way as to effect a change in the audience. The following commentary is guided by the thesis that the author of Matthew constructs a biog-

raphy because it most effectively educates the church community into the way of life that characterizes the kingdom of heaven. As such, Matthew, even though it may not prove to be historical in the modern sense, may not be regarded as fiction. For the author and for the original audience, witness to the kingdom of heaven in the life of Jesus is not entertainment, but a matter of life and death.

The author uses both direct quotations from and allusions to the scriptures of Judaism (after about 150 C.E. Christians refer to these as the "Old Testament"), particularly the divisions known as the Law and the Prophets. On at least twenty-two occasions Matthew contains direct quotations from the Prophets. In seventeen of these instances the quotation is introduced by a formula, for example, *All this took place to fulfill.* Additional quotations from and allusions especially to the Law may be found throughout Matthew (see Brown 1977, Gundry 1967, and Stendahl 1968).

While citations from the Jewish scriptures appear in Matthew, at no point does the text explicitly cite or give evidence of other early Christian writings. This may mean that at the time Matthew was composed, no other Gospels were regarded as "scripture" by the author or the Matthean community. Most scholars think, however, that the author knew at least two early Christian writings. One, the Gospel of Mark, provided the majority of the episodes and their arrangement for the author. The second, a collection of sayings of Jesus at least partially in written form provided the sayings and parables found both in Matthew and Luke. Scholars refer to this source as Q.

In addition to these two sources of information the author has access to a broad assortment of traditions handed on within the community for which Matthew was written. These may have included narratives about Jesus, such as the birth account, sayings of Jesus, and parables not otherwise attested in the Gospels. Generally, such material is referred to as "M" by scholars and may have been in both oral and written form (see Brooks 1987).

The familiarity with the Jewish scriptures demonstrated from the text of Matthew allows us to suppose that those writings, particularly the Law and the Prophets, had a significant literary influence on the author and the Matthean community. Furthermore, the adoption of a popular genre, biography, known to all Greek-speaking audiences of the Mediterranean world indicates that the author and community live and work within the broader culture of their day. The Gospel of

Matthew is a hybrid of diverse cultural traditions focused through the inspired creative genius of an individual.

The author carefully and subtly arranges and uses the sources and traditions available from the history of the church community for which Matthew was written. In that sense, to the extent that we read Matthew as a self-contained textual world, we are subject to the intent of the author. We also, because we bring to the text our own preconceptions and perceptions, may see implications in the text that the author did not consciously intend. To that extent we participate in the revelatory superfluity of the text. The commentary will be guided by both aspects of the text. We shall, however, remain within the confines of the text by seeking to interpret only that which may be found in Matthew. To offer a critical interpretation means to offer an interpretation that accounts for the text as written, not as we wish it.

From about the middle of the second century onward, major churches thought that the Gospel of Matthew was written by MATTHEW, a disciple of Jesus. The sources that report this opinion, however, are suspect and we do not know the identity of the author of the Gospel. Since we do not know who the author is, in our commentary we will simply speak of "the author" and of the book by its shortened traditional title "Matthew." The story of the call of the tax collector in 9:9 refers to the man by the name *Matthew*. Since the parallel passage in Mark 2:13-14 calls the tax collector "Levi" this passage may indicate a conscious change on the part of the author that shows that the disciple Matthew played an important role in the founding of the community.

Speculation on the personal history of the author depends exclusively on the interpretation of implicit and perhaps tenuous evidence in the text itself. It has been suggested that the author was a converted Jewish RABBI or scribe, or that the author was a non-Jewish convert to a Jewish-Christian community, or that the author was a member of a "school" of scribes within a Jewish-Christian community.

While almost all recent scholarship refers to the author as "he," we can be no more sure of the gender of the author than of the author's name. Many women in the Mediterranean basin of the first century possessed the education necessary to write the Greek found in Matthew. We know from other early Christian writings that women occupied high places in early Christian communities. The Gospel itself indicates the consistent and faithful witness of key women to Jesus. Such a motif in the Gospel leads us to suspect that women played important roles in the formation and transmission of the Matthean tradition. There is no secure historical means to determine the gender of the anonymous or pseudonymous author of a NT book from its content.

Internal evidence makes it probable that Matthew was written after the destruction of the Temple of Jerusalem in 70 C.E. Matt 22:7 apparently contains an allusion to this event. IGNATIUS, writing between 110 and 115 C.E. is the first writer to quote Matthew. Other less-clear indications may help us to further limit the date of composition. Matthew's use of Mark may be helpful. Mark (according to most scholars) was composed no earlier than 67 C.E. Some time must have elapsed during which Mark was used by and commented on in the community of Matthew. The modifications to Mark noticeable by a comparison with Matthew would indicate some significant duration of use and commentary within the community, perhaps by a scribal school. Further, as we shall see below, the history of the community implied by the text would indicate a separation of the community from the synagogues of its city that would best fit in the decade between 90 and 100. These considerations would suggest that Matthew was composed sometime between 90 and 105 C.E.

The Matthean Community

Perhaps no other question has exercised recent interpreters so much as the question of the social, historical, and religious configuration of the community of Matthew. We shall summarize here the view that emerges from and informs the following commentary (see Kingsbury 1988, 147–60).

The Greek of Matthew indicates that the community was most likely urban. While at times the Greek of the text is semitic in flavor or style, there is little indication that the audience was bilingual, knowing both Greek, the *lingua franca* of the Mediterranean world, and Aramaic, the language of rural Syria and Palestine. The semitic nature of the Greek would fit well, however, with the Greek spoken and written by residents of a major city of the eastern Mediterranean, such as Antioch in Syria. When we add to the linguistic observations the evidence from Ignatius of Antioch who first quotes the Gospel, then a good working hypothesis is that the community of Matthew was to be found in Antioch of Syria (modern Antakya, Turkey) in the last decade of the first century.

The community was relatively well-off and enjoyed material prosperity. Jesus and the disciples are characterized as ministering to cities and being resident householders in cities. The word "city" is used no fewer than twenty-six times in Matthew. The text also refers to a wider variety and larger amounts of money than those that occur in Mark or Luke (Kingsbury 1988, 152-3).

The religious configuration of the community remains problematic, probably not least because our understanding of ethnic relationships, of which religion is a part, remains fragmentary for the ancient Mediterranean world. We may venture the following suggestions.

The community for which the author writes is Jewish with regard to its authoritative scripture. We know from Jewish documents of the third to sixth centuries that early the Law or Torah: (Genesis–Deuteronomy) and the Prophets (Joshua–Kings [excluding Ruth]) were recognized as canonical.

Matthew also shows high regard for the Temple in Jerusalem (5:23-24; 23:16-21). Further, we detect no animosity toward the Temple cultus per se, although appropriate Temple worship and use is advocated. Therefore, with regard to the religious institution of the Temple, Matthew seems to represent some segment of Judaism in the first century.

The author portrays the PHARISEES as a powerful religious elite in control of the synagogues. The text of Matthew constantly refers to "their" synagogues in a pejorative sense. The corresponding institution ordained by Jesus is not "our" SYNAGOGUE but rather the *ekklēsia* (gathering, community). Further, the community may not use synagogue titles of respect for each other (23:8-12). Finally, 10:16-23 and 23:34-36 indicate the strong possibility that the some members of the community or their predecessors have suffered persecution at the hands of synagogue authorities. Such considerations indicate that the community of Matthew does not associate with the Jewish synagogues of its city.

Furthermore, the community recruits members who are not originally from Judaism, that is, "gentiles." The resurrected Lord sends the disciples out to all of humanity or the *nations* (28:16-20). There may be other references in the text to non-Jewish proselytes within the community as well (e.g., 6:7-8; 23:15). We may conclude that the community of Matthew was

composed of Jewish-Christians and their gentile converts who had a positive regard for the Jewish scriptures and Temple, while constituting themselves outside of the local synagogue(s) of their city (see Brown 1983). The community had its own means of internal organization including provisions for the reception of new members.

From the perspective of the study of religions, a community that both identifies with a dominant established tradition and separates itself from other institutions representative of that tradition may be considered a sect. As the commentary explores, this sect holds to specific beliefs about its founder, Jesus. With regard to its adherence to the person of Jesus Christ, then, this Jewish sect may also be called CHRISTIAN.

The text contains few indications about the terms used within the community for community members. The term "Christian" does not occur. Nor does the text ever refer to the community as the "New" or "True" Israel. Terms of equality dominate, however. Jesus speaks of "brothers," "children," and "little ones" when referring to members of the community. We may suspect, however, that two groups are recognized as given special gifts by God: prophets and teachers (scribes [Kingsbury, 1988, 158]). While these two groups probably possess specific gifts appreciated by the community, they are not associated with special church office or privilege.

There are indications that some from these groups are trying to assert hierarchical preeminence at the time of the publication of the Gospel. They do this by invoking traditions about the preeminence of PETER and THE TWELVE. Matthew was written in part as a corrective to these tendencies. It reasserts the egalitarian tradition of the community and denies the sanction of Jesus to those who would assert authoritative doctrinal or interpretative power over the community members. The commentary explores the religious perspective of the author and the sect from which the author and text emerge and to which it speaks.

The author sought to bear witness to the events of Jesus Christ and by the composition of the Gospel to give the audience a perspective that would inform the faith and practice of their religious community. The text, therefore, gives evidence of both perceptions the author had of the intended original audience and conventions operating at an unconscious level. These perceptions and conventions interest us because we wish to understand and be informed by the beliefs and practices of our ancient forebears.

Having begun with the text of the Gospel of Matthew, however, we consider also the appropriation of this faith into our own historical moment. This happens first and foremost because we take seriously the claim of the Gospel to bear witness to Jesus Christ and his revelatory value for the real world. We undertake, therefore, to understand the faith to which the Gospel of Matthew bears witness and to ask how we might responsibly receive and understand the meaning of the Gospel text for our own lives.

Theologically, therefore, we will accept as our interpretative starting point the claim of Matthew that God has manifested God's self in the life of Jesus of Nazareth and ask what that might say to our own historical moment.

For Further Study

In the *Mercer Dictionary of the Bible*: DEMON IN THE NT; GOSPEL; GOSPELS, CRITICAL STUDY OF; JOHN THE BAPTIST; KINGDOM OF GOD; MATTHEW; MATTHEW, BOOK OF; MIRACLE STORY; PASSION NARRATIVE; Q; REDACTION; RESURRECTION IN THE NT; RHETORICAL CRITICISM; SCRIBE IN THE NT; SLAUGHTER OF THE INNOCENTS; SON OF GOD; SON OF MAN; SYNOPTIC PROBLEM; TEMPTATION OF JESUS; TRANSFIGURATION.

In other sources: J. C. Anderson, "Matthew: Gender and Reading," *Semeia* 28 (1983): 3-27; H. D. Betz, *Essays on the Sermon on the Mount*; R. E. Brown and J. P. Meier, *Antioch and Rome*; W. D. Davies and D. Allison, *A Critical and Exegetical Commentary on the Gospel according to Saint Matthew*, ICC; D. Garland, *Reading Matthew: A Literary and Theological Commentary on the First Gospel*, Reading in the New Testament Series; D. R. A. Hare, *Matthew*, Interp; D. Harrington, *The Gospel of Matthew*, SacPag 1; J. D. Kingsbury, *Matthew As Story*, 2d ed; A.-J. Levine, *The Social and Ethnic Dimensions of Matthean Salvation History: "Go nowhere among the Gentiles . . ."* (*Matt. 10:5b*), Studies in the Bible and Early Christianity 14; U. Luz, *Matthew 1–7: A Commentary*; J. P. Meier, *The Vision of Matthew. Christ, Church, and Morality in the First Gospel*; D. Patte, *The Gospel According to Matthew: A Structural Commentary on Matthew's Faith*; D. Senior, *The Passion of Jesus in the Gospel of Matthew* and *What Are they Saying about Matthew?*; F. Stagg, *Matthew*, BBC.

Commentary

The following outline indicates shifts between plot and speech and provides a guide to the dominant strategies for reading the text. The heading of each section comes directly from the text itself. The outline may be read, therefore, as a summary of and guide for the reading of the Gospel. Within the major divisions of plot and speech, the outline and commentary try to emulate the structure and language of Matthew as closely as practical and possible. Such an organization will allow for easy reference to the text of Matthew as we proceed. An outline, however, may be used only as a constructive entry point into the text for our generation of readers. The commentary seeks to open up new interpretations, not offer the final word or closure on previous ones.

The commentary presumes that our discussion will proceed with the Gospel of Matthew open before us so that we may hear the voice of the author constantly correcting and informing us as part of the interpretative enterprise.

An Outline

I. Plot: The Book of the Birth of Jesus Christ, 1:1–5:1
   A. An Account of the Genealogy of Jesus the Messiah, 1:1-17
   B. The Birth of Jesus the Messiah Took Place, 1:18-25
   C. In the Time of King Herod, Wise Men Came, 2:1-25
   D. John the Baptist Appeared, 3:1-17
   E. Jesus Was Led Up by the Spirit to Be Tempted by the Devil, 4:1-11
   F. Now When Jesus Heard That John Had Been Arrested, 4:12–5:1
II. Speech: Jesus Began to Speak, and Taught Them, 5:2–7:27
   A. Then He Began to Speak 5:2-16
   B. Do Not Think That I Have Come to Abolish, 5:17-48
   C. Beware of Practicing Your Righteousness, 6:1-34
   D. Do Not Judge, 7:1-23
   E. Everyone then Who Hears, 7:24-27
III. Plot: When Jesus Had Finished Saying These Things, 7:28–10:4
   A. The Crowds Were Astounded, 7:28-29

Plot: The Book
of the Birth of Jesus Christ, 1:1–5:1

The first sentence of Matthew is ambiguous as to the intention of the book and immediately gives us clues to the multidimensionality of meanings in the Gospel (see Brown 1977, 45-232 for a thorough treatment of the Matthean infancy narrative). The translation, "A book of the birth of Jesus Christ," presents a literal rendering of the Greek into English. Does the phrase refer to the entire Gospel, or only to the first section ending at 2:23, or should we understand the phrase to refer only to 1:1-18 and accept the more restrictive interpretation offered by the NRSV? The translation offered by the NRSV also raises the question of how to understand the use of the term *christos* in Matthew. Should we understand this title to be a general surname for Jesus or does it bear the specific political implications associated with the Davidic monarchy? As we read this section, we become aware of the multilayered conflict between the kingdoms of the world and the kingdom of heaven. It establishes the major themes that will be further developed as the Gospel proceeds.

An Account of the Genealogy of Jesus the Messiah, 1:1-17

The genealogy introduces Jesus as the Messiah who comes from the line of DAVID and ABRAHAM. The Greek *christos* rendered by the NRSV according to its Hebrew/Aramaic equivalent as *Messiah* means "anointed" in reference to the king of Israel. While "Christ" becomes the surname of Jesus in Christianity quite early, it retains its reference to political power. The narrator uses the term as a proper name for Jesus only here and in 1:18 (see also 1:17). The genealogy establishes that Jesus is the legitimate, albeit adopted, heir to David's throne (v. 16). The genealogy points out the historical claim that Jesus is a royal, messianic figure who, like David, might establish rule over Israel.

The genealogy also establishes a tie between Jesus and non-Israelite proselytes. It begins with Abraham. He is the ancestor of all of Israel and therefore of David. He also is the first convert to the God of Israel and may be seen as the patron of all proselytes.

Furthermore, the genealogy refers specifically to four ancestral women. *Tamar* (v. 3) is regarded as an Aramean in some traditions (Jub 41:1). *Rahab* and *Ruth* (v. 5) are non-Israelites who marry into Israel. And in v. 6, *Uriah*, a Hittite, is named to identify *Bathsheba*, the mother of *Solomon*, thereby emphasizing her relationship to non-Israel.

In addition to the concern with non-Israelites the presence of these particular women in a patrilineal genealogy points to the faithfulness of God to justice for the marginal. TAMAR must seduce her father-in-law Judah in the disguise of a prostitute as a means of gaining justice under the rule of levirate marriage (Gen 38:26). RAHAB, a prostitute, hides the spies of Israel from the king of Jericho. She expresses faith in the God of Israel (Josh 2:12; see 6:17-25). RUTH and NAOMI gain social justice from the patriarchy of Bethlehem by deftly reminding the next-of-kin of the obligations to justice that go along with property possession in Israel (Ruth 3:1–4:6). They gain security over against the greed of a patriarchally organized society that would condemn them to penury. Finally, BATHSHEBA is taken

by David in an adulterous union (1 Sam 11:1–12:25). The story shows her as powerless in the face of the king's lust. David, God's anointed, is alone responsible for the adultery and murder that results. Later, she presses for Solomon's inheritance of the throne.

Each of these women either explicitly or tacitly express their faith in God. In the cases of Tamar and Bathsheba the direct injustice of patriarch and king comes to the fore. These common elements coupled with the absence of the more well-known royal mothers, for example, Sarah, Rebecca, or Rachel, indicate that the genealogy is designed to persuade the reader that sexual relations as preferred by patriarchal society frequently do not serve the purposes of the God of justice. We may look for faithfulness and righteousness to emerge not from the political and ethical center that stands for correct order but from the chaotic and questionable fringes.

The Birth of Jesus the Messiah Took Place, 1:18-25

1:18-19. His mother Mary had been engaged. These verses provide a narrative transition to a carefully written scene of a dream annunciation to JOSEPH. Joseph is a *righteous man* (v. 19). These words may refer to his piety in legal observance. They also align Joseph with the characterization of Jesus (3:15) and children of the kingdom of heaven elsewhere in the Gospel (see especially 5:20 and 6:33). Furthermore, such terms and Joseph's characterization accord with the appropriate behavior of a member of the messianic lineage as depicted in Isa 9:6-7.

1:20-21. An angel of the Lord appeared. In the dream annunciation Joseph is clearly instructed about the circumstances of Jesus' conception and as to Joseph's future action in adopting Jesus as his legal heir. Jewish law, similar to both Greek and Roman law, provided that by naming the child the father claimed all the rights and duties of legal paternity. Joseph does as he is instructed and thereby becomes the first character in the Gospel to be shown to fulfill the will of God.

1:22-23. All this took place to fulfill. The text introduces a quotation from a prophet with the phrase *All this took place to fulfill*. The following quotation comes from Isa 7:14. A Greek form of the text is quoted which has the term VIRGIN rather than the Hebrew form which has a word meaning any young woman who has reached puberty. The Hebrew text makes no comment on the previous sexual activity of the woman. By introducing this reading, the author directs attention to the unusual nature of the conception of Jesus.

By the placement of this scene after the genealogy, the author provides a new perspective that distances Jesus from the royal lineage of Messiah. At the end of the genealogy the author sets the stage by referring to Joseph as *the husband of Mary,* rather than as Jesus' father. The author also suggestively refers to the one *called the Messiah* (1:16). This designation proves inadequate for Jesus. In 1:23 the citation designates Jesus not as Messiah, but as *Emmanuel.* At least a portion of the original audience must not have understood Hebrew, since the author explains the meaning of the name as *God with us.*

The presentation of the genealogy and adoption of Jesus in Matthew serves several functions. It shows the unusual relationship of Jesus to the royal household of David. It links Jesus with the tradition of incorporation of non-Israelites into Israel. God works in unusual ways in order to extend the message of Israel's God to non-Israelites. It reminds us of stories about God's dealing with Israel for the sake of God's justice in behalf of the marginal outside of the social and political structures controlled by the patriarchy.

The genealogy also focuses attention on women as bearers of faith. The virginal conception along with the presence of the four women in the genealogy emphasizes God's power manifested through faith for the sake of God's justice and righteousness. Women of abused status bear in their bodies the signs of faith that come into the world from God. The virginal conception disjoins Jesus from the normal royal patrilineage.

In the Time of King Herod, Wise Men Came, 2:1-25

2:1-12, 16-18. He was frightened. The interaction of characters in these episodes constitutes a major means by which the text forms the audience's judgment about Jesus and the world into which he is born. The text depicts Herod along with the entire city of Jerusalem as frightened at the announcement of the birth of Jesus, who is the only character identified as *King of the Jews* in Matthew. The *chief priests and scribes of the people* (v. 4) are the male religious and political leaders who reside in Jerusalem and who have power to advise Herod. They use their education to deduce, by scriptural interpretation, that the Messiah comes from BETHLEHEM. Finally, this information is used by Herod as the basis for his attempt to murder

Jesus which results in the murder of all children in and around Bethlehem (v. 16). The combination of political power and scriptural interpretation results in the annihilation of innocent children who have no power in this world of the urban political elite. There are no records of Herod's murder of the children in Bethlehem outside of this text.

The wise men remind us that Jesus even as a child draws foreigners, non-Israel, to himself. The idea of wise men, magi, or astrologers from the East, perhaps priests of Zoroastrianism or Mithraism, has particular appeal to the Greek-speaking Mediterranean audience of the first century, who tend to regard things Eastern with both fascination and fear. Abraham was also from the East (Gen 12:4).

2:13-15. An angel of the Lord appeared to Joseph. The dream of Joseph and the departure to Egypt align Joseph with the patriarch Joseph who also descended into Egypt and was noted for his dreams and interpretations (Gen 37:1–47:28). Jesus escapes the plot of a murderous king, reminiscent of the plot by PHARAOH to kill the male children of the Israelites (Exod 1:22). Clearly the story of the descent into Egypt and return is shaped by a desire to align the story of Jesus with Jewish tradition of the EXODUS from Egypt.

2:19-23. When Herod died, The concluding verses provide the motivation for the removal to Nazareth and also provide yet another scene of the opposition of the political rulers of Jerusalem to Jesus. By the conclusion of this section, those associated with the powerful elites of Jerusalem are characters not to be trusted; indeed, they are intent on the destruction of Jesus.

Furthermore, the author aligns Jesus in important ways with the common history of Israel both in terms of explicit commentary by the prophets and in terms of story reminiscent of important events in Israelite history. The action of Archelaus is perfectly understandable as the response of earthly kings to an earthly threat to their throne from David's heir. The virginal conception and angelic appearances indicate that the point at issue is to understand Jesus from the perspective of God and not in normal political and social terms. Joseph adopts God's perspective and becomes the father who protects and nurtures rather than owning his family.

John the Baptist Appeared, 3:1-17

3:1-12. Repent for the kingdom of heaven has come near. John the Baptist looks and acts like ELIJAH or ELISHA. Both prophets are noteworthy for their opposition to the royal household of AHAB. Both function as warriors in behalf of the God of Israel (1 Kings 17–21; 2 Kings 1–13). John announces judgment not based on ethnic identity, as the PHARISEES and SADDUCEES suppose, but according to action by those who follow God's will. Admission into the kingdom of heaven does not depend on ethnic identity or religious status. The kingdom of heaven as judgment arrives in the ministry of John and will continue into Jesus' ministry. The kingdom of heaven invades the world for the purpose of judgment.

3:13-17. Jesus came from Galilee to be baptized by John. John preaches the arrival of the kingdom of heaven. The term *kingdom of heaven* indicates the actualizing of the foreshadowing in birth and dreams in the previous sections. Jesus by his baptism associates with a kingdom configured differently from the kingdom of Herod.

Verse 15 epitomizes the content of the previous verses: the kingdom of heaven contains righteousness or justice. Here, Jesus shows himself as servant of the righteousness that belongs to the kingdom of heaven. His character arises out of the will of God. His behavior provides the antinomic and determinative opposite to that of the Pharisees and Sadducees. In the same way that the events of Jesus' birth have been shown to fulfill the will of God expressed in the prophets, the action of Jesus as an adult also fulfills God's will.

The text may imply that Jesus' baptism is one of repentance (v. 6). God approves of his action by announcing Jesus' sonship. Jesus correctly perceives the kingdom of heaven and its justice. Here the text introduces for the first time Jesus' own awareness of his divine sonship by virtue of a visionary experience from the heavens and direct communication by a voice.

Jesus Was Led Up by the Spirit to Be Tempted by the Devil, 4:1-11

The scene bears similarities to the wanderings of Israel in the DESERT recounted in Exodus, Numbers, and Deuteronomy. Unlike Israel, however, Jesus successfully resists temptation to sin and indicates clearly the nature of his ministry and proclamation (Meier 1979, 59–62).

The temptation occurs in three scenes culminating dramatically in the temptation to possess universal political power (4:3-4, 5-7, 8-11). In each scene *the devil* speaks first followed by a quotation of Jesus from the Law (Deut 8:3; 6:16; 6:13 at vv. 4, 7, 10). The devil is shown to be a powerful and intelligent individual learned in techniques of scriptural argumentation.

In the final scene, vv. 8-10, Satan asserts that he owns the kingdoms of the world. Jesus does not dispute the point, but rather responds with a quotation from the Law that places the issue on the theological grounds of the lordship of God. Two points emerge from this scene. First, evil powers possess and control the mundane political process. Second, the coming of the kingdom of heaven means that a new politics arrives, one overseen by God. We meet here a view derived from Jewish apocalyptic perspectives as found for example in Isaiah 56–66, Zechariah, Daniel, and 1 Enoch (Hanson 1979). The underlying view is one of a world in antinomic conflict (see Martyn 1985).

The scene opens up a multi-dimensional drama being worked out in the life of Jesus. What appeared to be a political power play between the urban elite of Herod's household and the adopted son of David is the universal struggle between the kingdoms of the world ruled by Satan and the kingdom of heaven. The two dimensions mutually inform and interact with each other throughout Matthew.

Now When Jesus Heard That John Had Been Arrested, 4:12-5:1

4:12-17. He made his home in Capernaum. Jesus resettles to CAPERNAUM as a householder. The citation in vv. 15-16 refers to the same prophetic context as the citation in 1:23 (Isa 9:1-2) and reconfirms Jesus' status as God-with-us. It also emphasizes that Jesus' ministry begins both in traditional Israelite tribal territory (Zebulun, Naphtali) and among non-Israelite peoples (*Galilee of the Gentiles*, v. 15). The ministry is set amidst ethnic diversity. Within this context, Jesus begins the same proclamation as John (3:2). This episode is framed by the notation of John's arrest and the repetition of his preaching. Such framing suggests that the ministry and destiny of John serves as a model for the ministry and destiny of Jesus.

4:18-22. He saw two brothers. The following episode illustrates the immediate fulfillment of the citation of v. 15. Jesus recruits his first followers. They are depicted as male Israelite householders like himself. The Greek names PETER, ANDREW, JAMES, and JOHN show by comparison with the name ZEBEDEE, the father of James and John, the cultural diversity of the generation who will constitute the disciples.

4:23–5:1. Jesus went throughout Galilee. The third episode illustrates the PROPHECY of 4:16. Jesus' actions define him not as a mundane political revolutionary, but as witness to and embodiment of a kingdom whose concern is healing and *good news of the kingdom* (v. 23). For the first time in Matthew we encounter the term "gospel" (NRSV mg.). In 9:35 and 24:14, as here, it is the *good news of the kingdom.* Good news, the preaching of Jesus (and John?) therefore belongs to the kingdom of heaven. According to the prophecy of v. 16, this gospel means the elimination of death. The place names imply that Jesus' activity attracts not only Israelites but also non-Israelites as well. Both *Syria* (v. 24) and the *Decapolis* (v. 25) are composed of non-Israelite territory and non-Jewish populations. From the beginning of his ministry Jesus heals and preaches to both Jewish and gentile crowds.

Matthew 5:1 may be read either as the first verse of the next literary section or as the conclusion to the previous plot section. Since we are organizing our commentary according to shifts in reading strategy, 5:1 is the last plot notation until 7:28-29. These two inclusive sentences establish for the reader that Jesus speaks both to the disciples and the crowds. Hence the content of the following speech is directed at a universal and multicultural audience. The teaching may be read as representative of Jesus' proclamation. Unlike the preaching of 4:23, the following teaching takes place outside of the confines of the synagogue.

Speech: Jesus Began to Speak, and Taught Them, 5:2–7:27

Explicitly, the SERMON ON THE MOUNT focuses attention on the content of the kingdom of heaven with emphasis on the righteousness that belongs to that kingdom (5:20; 6:1; 6:34). Implicitly, the speech also reveals more to us about the character of Jesus and his relationship to the kingdom of heaven.

The sermon on the mount introduces a new literary technique that is used throughout the Matthean speeches and parables. The narrated story that frames the sermon consistently occurs in the past tense, while the speech itself is stated in the present tense as direct discourse. Because the speech takes up considerable space, our temporal orientation becomes dehistoricized. We experience the sermon as the direct address of Jesus to us. By this technique the text of Matthew invites the reader to take up Jesus' perspective as definitive.

Then He Began to Speak, 5:2-16

5:2-12. Blessed are the poor in spirit. The form of these verses corresponds closely with blessings found in the wisdom writings of JUDAISM (cf. Pss 1:1; 32:1;

41:1; 119:1-2; 128:1; Sir 25:7-11). They have distinct characteristics that mark them, however, as peculiar to the tradition about Jesus. First, vv. 4, 5, 6, 7, 8, and 9 contain a statement of reward in the future in their result clause. By comparison, vv. 3, 10, and 11, which refer to the kingdom of heaven as reward, are present tense. It becomes apparent that these blessings are set in a time that is different from and yet impinges upon the current historical moment. The kingdom of heaven is a present possession and a future reward for God's children. These blessings then, are eschatological and apocalyptic in nature.

Each of the BEATITUDES represents the reality of the kingdom of heaven as opposed to the normal experience of historical reality. The first clause of each beatitude mentions a group of people who, in the ancient world, are not considered at the center of political, religious, or social power. By completing the list with two beatitudes concerning persecution, Jesus makes it clear that these blessings describe the destiny of God's children within the kingdoms of the world. Their comfort is and will be in the kingdom of heaven (v. 12). The beatitudes define the kingdom of heaven from the perspective of God's future.

The time and content of the kingdom flows backwards from an assured future into the oppressive kingdoms of the present. This backward flow may be seen as the epistemological crux of interpretation for understanding the kingdom of heaven in Matthew.

5:13-16. You are the salt of the earth. The concluding verses to this section summarize the current status of God's children and imply a subtle warning about the results of failure to fulfill that status by the negative comparisons involved. Verse 16 also identifies the work of the children of God with that described for Jesus by 4:16.

Do Not Think That I Have Come to Abolish, 5:17-48

5:17-20. I have come not to abolish but to fulfill. Jesus in v. 17 adopts self-consciously the perspective given by the narrator of the Gospel when citing prophetic passages and when constructing scenes alluding to the Law or Prophets. The following commandments are to be read as expressing the apocalyptic-eschatological filling up of canonical tradition. Verse 17 implies a polemic against a group of opponents that holds that Jesus is guilty of the abolition of God's will as expressed in the Law. Based on v. 20 we may suspect that the group is the scribes and Pharisees. In response to this position, Jesus does not argue, he asserts. He at no point in the subsequent commandments submits his judgment to the structures of scriptural exegesis.

Verse 18 suggests that the Law has a temporal limit at the juncture of the ending of heaven and earth. Jesus later confirms that this temporal limit will be reached (24:35). What transcends the temporal limits of history, however, are the words of Jesus. In this sense they displace the Law, regarded by significant portions of first-century Judaism as eternal. In Matthew the Law may be conceived as limited and bounded by history and therefore subject to the evil powers that are brought to light by the arrival of the kingdom of heaven.

Verse 19 poses the most perplexing problem for interpretation in this paragraph. The reference of *these* is not absolutely clear. It may refer backward to the commandments of the Law indicated by the phrase *not one letter, not one stroke* (v. 18), but that reading is grammatically difficult since no plural noun occurs in the phrase. Or, alternatively, it may refer forward to the subsequent commands of 5:21–7:27. This second reference, while not a common construction, is grammatically possible and may make the best sense of the composition of the speech as a whole.

Jesus uses a form that suggests a curse and a blessing for those who break or keep these commands. The blessing is enhanced status in the kingdom of heaven. The curse is not exclusion from the kingdom, as we might expect, but simply a lower status in the kingdom. If this verse refers to the commands of Jesus, then v. 19 makes clear that the following commands are not entrance requirements but the characteristics of children of God already in the kingdom.

Verse 20 provides a polemical summation and perhaps an indication of the opponent group envisioned by the statement of v. 17. The verse calls to mind 3:7 where the Pharisees were first introduced as those who appeal to their ethnic identity as a means of ensuring their acceptability to God as children of Abraham. Here they are apparently a group who possess some form of recognizable "righteousness" or "justice" that is insufficient for entry into the kingdom of heaven. Verses 17-20 establish a clear division between the presentation of the commands of Jesus and the interpretation of the Law by the Pharisees. The character of this excessive righteousness becomes the focus of the remainder of the speech.

5:21-48. You have heard that it was said. In this section five statements use an antithetical formula on the pattern of 5:21 (Brooks 1987, 74–7). In addition, 5:31 contains a shortened form of the formula that functions to relate the saying on DIVORCE to the previous antithesis on ADULTERY. The saying on divorce occurs as a subpoint to the broader structure of this section. Each of these antitheses is composed of three elements: (1) the thesis, *You have heard that it was said*; (2) a scriptural citation or paraphrase; (3) the antithesis, *But I say to you*. The phrase *to those of ancient times* in the theses of vv. 21 and 33 refers to those who received the written Law on Sinai. The citation of scripture from the Law that follows each thesis in (2), supports this identification.

Since the formula refers to the scene of the giving of the Law on Sinai, then we should recall that scene. In Exodus Moses acts as the spokesperson between God and the people. Exodus 20:1 makes clear that the DECALOGUE is spoken by God.

The implication of Jesus' claim is contained in the third part of each saying. *But, I say to you* shows that he is the originator of what follows. By referring to written Law, rather than ORAL TRADITION or a rabbi's opinion, Jesus emphasizes his identification with God and his independence from the confines of the institutions of normal religion. Official teachers teach with the support of group authority, sanctioned by official and historical institutions, and seek to interpret canonical texts harmoniously. Jesus, on the other hand, appeals to no group authority, has the support of the tradition of no official historical institutions, and interprets the Mosaic Law antithetically.

In three of the sayings that follow this pattern, the antitheses on MURDER, adultery, and love of neighbor, Jesus extends and radicalizes existing interpretation of the Law. In the remaining three, on divorce, oaths, and talion, he utters new commands that may be seen by those outside the kingdom to revoke the plain meaning of canonical Law (Meier 1976, 131–61). Jesus as God-with-us takes his bearings not from Sinai but from the future of the kingdom that is now present. He further commands fellow members of the kingdom to do likewise. Fulfillment for the Gospel of Matthew means perception of the righteousness of God from the perspective of God's future, not the historical past.

Beware of Practicing Your Righteousness, 6:1-34

6:1. For you have no reward. Jesus continues the theme of righteousness begun in 5:20. Unfortunately, this connection is blurred in the NRSV translation *practicing your piety*. The Greek word is the same word translated as *righteousness* in 3:15, 5:20, and 6:34. The Gospel makes no distinction between what we might call acts of piety and other ethical acts.

6:2-18. So whenever you give alms. Jesus discusses almsgiving, PRAYER, and FASTING. Jesus' teaching alters significantly but does not preclude public worship. He offers specific restrictions and a theological principle: that which can be understood as rewardable by public acclaim should be avoided. Matthew 6:2-18 is unique to Jewish and Christian documents of the first century in its designation of God as *your Father who sees in secret.* The inclusion of these teachings here may be motivated out of a polemic against what the author regards as inappropriate worship forms within the community. The attempt seems to be to separate the community's worship from synagogual practice and from non-Jewish types of worship habits being brought into the community by gentiles (vv. 7-8). Jesus' injunctions prohibit the assignment of status to members of the community by virtue of their financial donations, laudatory prayers, or works of pious observance. Thereby, this teaching on righteousness implies social equality between all children of God. Any judgments on individual righteousness are left only to God.

6:19-21. Do not store up treasure on earth. Jesus completes the description of God's righteousness begun antithetically in vv. 1-18. This saying describes the dualism between heaven and earth that determines the allegiance of the heart based upon the storing of treasure.

6:22-23. The eye is the lamp of the body. Jesus describes an interaction between LIGHT and DARKNESS that can result in failure to see. These verses also unify physical and moral perception (Betz 1985, 85). Hence we cannot talk about a physical and spiritual dualism because the kingdom of heaven as indicated by Jesus' speech in Matthew regards the material, physical cosmos as coextensive with the spiritual cosmos. Division occurs not along spiritual/physical lines but along the lines demarcated by light-darkness, good-evil.

6:24. No one can serve two masters. Jesus contrasts two figures as competing lords: God and Mammon (Gk.). Mammon, that is, *wealth*, is depicted as a lord who rules over the things of the earth and (by parallel relation with v. 23) associates with evil and darkness. A person's place within the realm of one lord determines allegiance and the truth of perception.

6:25-34. Do not worry about your life. Jesus concludes with a more precise discussion of this interactive dualism. Verse 25 centers attention on the au-

thority of Jesus, who describes the world as it is to true sight.

Verses 26-32 describe first the created order as apparent to usual mundane perception. By the use of the terminology *his righteousness,* v. 33 makes explicit the connection between the kingdom of God and the righteousness of God. In order for God's righteousness and God's kingdom to be realities that are sought, they must not only be possessions of God but also available for possession by others. Therefore, *his righteousness* indicates that one is to seek both the kingdom and the righteousness that belong to God and comes as a gift from God, the Lord who grants true sight.

The guarantee that follows in v. 34 is not based on the theological idea of the continuity of God with creation, but rather on the radical discontinuity between God and the world, which is in the possession of evil powers. Verse 34 presupposes that the outcome of the confrontation has already occurred in God's future, or kingdom of heaven. It presumes that this confrontation issues in the final victory of God. Once again is visible the remarkable truth that time flows from future to present in the text of Matthew. The righteousness of God is thus both the presupposition and end for the disciple.

The apocalyptic instruction given through Jesus becomes a powerful education. It does not provide the terms of admission into God's rule. Rather it draws the disciple more deeply into the mystery of the kingdom which is a new creation by God and in which the disciple is found. Jesus describes the boundary line between God's kingdom and the kingdom of evil that rules the world. The world thinks possessions and the reduction of anxieties about material security are prime issues in life. The children of the kingdom of God know what lord they serve and recognize that the righteousness that comes from God is their only pursuit. They are guaranteed on the basis of the power-infused authority of Jesus as God-with-us that they will find this righteousness. They are free from the anxieties of this world (see further Humphries-Brooks 1989).

Do Not Judge, 7:1-23

7:1-6. For with the judgment you make you will be judged. Jesus warns against judgment of another within the community. "Brother" is used regularly in Matthew to indicate other members of the community. The Greek word need not refer only to males and the NRSV uses the word *neighbor*. Jesus advises self inspection for HYPOCRISY.

Verse 6 indicates that as readily as Jesus prohibits judging for the sake of exclusion or hierarchy, he also enjoins care over the dispensation of those things that belong to God's kingdom to those incapable of appropriating them. There seems to be an ideological distinction here that may refer to problems of mission. Verses 1-5 refer to intracommunity relationships while v. 6 refers to relationships with those of the outside. It may also refer to those within the community who in the past have proven unworthy or unteachable from the perspective established by Jesus in the Gospel.

7:7-14. Ask and it will be given you. By comparing the positive behavior of broken humanity with God's infinite grace, the saying promises the resolution of judgment between good and evil in the future of God out of which and to which the kingdom of heaven moves. The community must wait in anticipation of that final fulfillment guided by the rule of mutual care embodied in v. 12.

Taken alone, the statement *in everything do to others as you would have them do to you; for this is the law and the prophets,* would miss the reference in the text of the sermon to the inbreaking of the kingdom of heaven, which Jesus claims is the fulfillment of the Law and the Prophets (5:17). The fulfillment is not salvation built out of the ethical systems of the past somehow summarized in a wise saying like v. 12, but rather it is grace that comes from the future into the present as apocalyptic-eschatological event.

7:13-14. Enter through the narrow gate. Verse 12 is situated between the grace of God artfully referred to by a short narrative in vv. 7-11 and the judgment of God clearly demarcated by the saying on the narrow gate in vv. 13-14. This tension reflects a fundamental theological insight in Matthew. The Gospel of Matthew represents throughout its text the problems of life as a child of the kingdom between the CRUCIFIXION and the PAROUSIA. At stake is the child's education to the insight that privilege and status come not from human will or action but only from God.

7:15-23. Beware of false prophets. Jesus warns against false prophets who appeal to his name as a means of validating their mighty words and works. These warnings indicate the probability that the Matthean community experienced divisions created by some type of early preachers and miracle workers. Verse 20 reminds the audience of the charge of John the Baptist in 3:8 to the Pharisees and Sadducees.

Apparently, these false prophets are to be understood as a phenomenon parallel to the religious leaders of Jesus' day. They are hypocrites when tested against the content of the commands of Jesus that provide the greater righteousness referred to by 5:20. Jesus, however, remains consistent in his advice. Warning is given, the audience is to recognize them when they come (v. 20). They are to be known by tests of orthopraxy, not orthodoxy, but no action against such individuals is to be taken.

Everyone Then Who Hears, 7:24-27

The concluding simile emphasizes the urgency of the sermon. The speech takes on the significance of life and death. The idea of foundation upon rock will be later exploited by Jesus in 16:13-23 in response to the confession of Simon Peter.

The sermon on the mount becomes the perspective by which all subsequent and previous narrative should be judged. Further, the text is so structured here and throughout the sermon as to press upon the audience the urgency to interpret their own personal and corporate histories from the same perspective. In short, the text presumes that its readers are children of God, members of the kingdom of heaven.

Plot: When Jesus Had Finished Saying These Things, 7:28–10:4

Both Israelites and non-Israelites emerge from the crowds as the suppliants of Jesus. By the end of the section, however, the crowds are narrowly conceived of as Israelite. This careful description of the narrowing of Jesus' ministry exclusively to Israel provides the setting for the speech of 10:5-42 and the plot of chaps. 11–12.

The arrangement of episodes in this section also follows a careful pattern of three sets of three miracle stories divided by three sections that describe Jesus' disciples (Meier 1979, 67–73). The content of each episode shows unnamed suppliants as better examples of faith than the disciples. Careful attention to the details of these miracles demonstrates that the speech or behavior of the suppliant frequently reveals to Jesus the faith of the individual and provides the opportunity for the exercise of Jesus' power.

The Crowds Were Astounded, 7:28-29

Jesus has *authority*. The underlying Greek concept more closely relates to what we might call directed, intelligent power. It is power appropriate to God-with-us (cf. 1:23). The word will be repeated again at the conclusion of the Gospel (28:16).

The crowds have been present all along to hear the sermon. The description of the kingdom provided by Jesus is presented not only to the disciples but to all. Verse 29 compares the speech of Jesus to that of normal human traditioners. The term *their scribes* implies that the crowds are part of Israel's institutions. Nevertheless, the following miracle stories include non-Israelite supplicants who emerge from the crowds.

When Jesus Had Come Down
from the Mountain, 8:1-17

This section is composed of three healings: the leper, the centurion's slave, and the mother-in-law of Peter. The stories highlight the faith of the supplicants. The clearest pattern occurs in the healing of the centurion's slave. In vv. 9-13 the text depicts in detail the faith of the centurion by direct speech. The status of the centurion as non-Israel and the status of the ill slave give precise detail to the text and evoke Jesus' amazement. The plot shows Jesus as being educated into the will of God with regard to non-Israelites and slaves. The character, Jesus, perceives the faith of the centurion by his speech.

The centurion, like the leper before him, addresses Jesus as "Lord." Based upon what we have learned from the discussion of lordship in 6:19-34 as well as the use of this term of Jesus only in a confessional sense throughout the whole of the Gospel, we may understand that the use of the term is a sign of faith. The scene shows Jesus applying the perception of the kingdom of heaven to actual events within his ministry.

While the account of the healing of Peter's mother-in-law is not as detailed as the accounts of the two other healings, we may infer that Jesus perceives faith in her, or (on the pattern of the slave) in her behalf.

Now When Jesus Saw Great Crowds, 8:18-22

The kingdom overturns obligations of property and paternity, two of the most revered institutions of the ancient Jewish and non-Jewish world. Jesus addresses the scribe in v. 19, thereby tying the verse to the scribes in 7:29. Further, a disciple, which one we are not told, is given the even more severe injunction in v. 22. We are left not knowing the reaction of either character. We may presume that the disciple is also involved in the following episode.

Jesus himself denies his own status and identifies here for the first time with the homeless and fatherless, that is, those unprotected by the normal social and religious structures of the day. He implies that his disciples must do the same.

And When He Got into the Boat, 8:23-9:8

8:23-27. A windstorm arose on the sea. The miracle of the stilling of the storm provides important contrasts with the previous set of miracles. Unlike the supplicants, the disciples do not emerge from the crowd. Since we do not know the decision reached by the disciple in the previous episode, we cannot yet judge whether Jesus' disciples, like himself, will renounce their status as free householders. Identical to the leper and the centurion, they address Jesus as "Lord." But their address is interpreted by Jesus to mean that they are of *little faith*. Surprisingly Jesus finds faith in great measure among the nameless with little or no status, while the faith of his disciples by comparison is untrustworthy and meager. By asking about the nature of the humanity of Jesus in v. 27, the disciples provide the question which will be answered by the two subsequent miracles. Each depicts more fully the nature of faith and the person of Jesus and his authority.

8:28-34. Two demoniacs met him. The element of faith seems missing altogether in the story of the Gadarene demoniacs. But the demoniacs place this story on a different footing from the others by addressing Jesus as SON OF GOD, the first humans to do so in the Gospel. This story boldly depicts a direct exorcistic battle between the Son of God and the demonic realm. It is therefore an appropriate story here because it prepares for the claim to power by Jesus in the subsequent story.

Unlike the parallel story in Mark, two demoniacs rather than one are mentioned. The text may be constructed in this way under the influence of the Jewish legal provision that requires two witnesses to any act (Deut 19:15). The witness to the Son of God recognizes him by non-human power. In this case, those enslaved to evil recognize their liberator, but fear him as conqueror.

In the ancient understanding, different sorts of demons lived in different places. Some lived in water, others in the air, or on land. All were regarded as striving for power over some host creature. The demons, by asking to be allowed to go into the SWINE, seek to trick Jesus into allowing them to continue their lives. They do not fool Jesus, however. The story might well have elicited humor from the Matthean community if a significant portion were ethnically

Jewish and therefore regarded the swine as unclean animals.

The text leaves it to the reader to surmise the townspeople's motivation for asking Jesus to leave. One possible motive that is consistent with the Matthean view of material possession would be that they feared further property destruction. The sanity of two demoniacs is less important than a herd of swine to these people. They do not recognize the presence of God and God's righteousness and do not seek it. The fact that this event occurs in the DECAPOLIS, a collection of non-Jewish cities, also may serve to emphasize that not all mission to the gentiles was necessarily successful. It may constitute part of Jesus' motivation for limiting the mission to Israel in 10:5.

9:1-8. Some people were carrying a paralyzed man. The contrast between the supplicants and the disciples continues in the last miracle of this trio, the healing of the paralytic (9:2-8). The supplicants form the model for faith as opposed to the anti-model provided by the disciples.

Jesus recognizes the faith of the paralytic's friends and heals him. The faith of a group of unknowns becomes the positive model to which we may compare the faith of the disciples. The story also becomes the occasion for Jesus to initiate a dispute with the scribes. Verse 5 makes clear that Jesus has provoked his opponents into an error of theological judgment by forgiving the man's sins. God in the healings of Jesus makes whole a created order broken and diseased by sin, an instrument of evil. Healing is the grace of God expressed through the SON OF MAN as a sign that the power of evil is coming to an end.

As Jesus Was Walking Along, He Saw Matthew, 9:9-17

9:9-13. He got up and followed him. By singling out the tax gatherer by name, the Gospel directs attention to the fact that the kingdom is composed of sinners. Sinners, or the unrighteous are, therefore, those who exceed the righteousness of the PHARISEES (5:20). The author repeatedly ironizes the religious self-consciousness of this group thereby exposing the claim to religious status as part of condemnable hypocrisy.

9:14-17. The disciples of John came to him. The disciples of John concur with the Pharisees in the religious observance of FASTING. Jesus interprets fasting as mourning the unrighteous state of the world prior to the coming of the day of the Lord. The conclusion of Matthew promises Jesus' presence to the end of the

age (28:20). Verse 15 indicates, therefore, that the children of the kingdom continually experience the presence of the bridegroom so that signs of mourning such as fasting are inappropriate. This verse adds to the understanding of religious observance begun in 6:1-18 and may suggest that even the type of fasting envisioned by 6:16-18 is unnecessary. The apocalyptic-eschatological context of the audience is the time after the crucifixion and before the coming of the Son of Man to judge, but the wedding feast continues in its celebration because Jesus remains with his community (see also 18:20).

Viewed from the perspective indicated by v. 15, the *both* of v. 17 refers to the *new wine* and *fresh wineskins*. Jesus indicates the radical disjuncture of the kingdom with religious forms that precede it or oppose it historically.

While He Was Saying These Things, 9:18-34

9:18-26. A leader came in and knelt before him. The placement of the story of the woman with hemorrhages within the story of the leader's daughter highlights the contrast of the faith of the woman with the unfaith of the crowds (vv. 22, 25). Matthew lets us infer that Jesus *seeing her* recognizes her faith and comments on it. The Greek text of Matthew does not contain *of the synagogue* (v. 18). The author probably did not intend for this civic leader to be understood as part of that institution. This accords with the overall characterization of Jesus' ministry as moving outside of the confines of traditional synagogue authority and with a general antipathy to the synagogue. The reading of the NRSV in v. 18 seems to be an unfortunate confusion of the Matthean story with the similar story in Mark 5:36.

9:27-31. Two blind men followed him. The idea of seeing as an essential metaphor for faith continues in the story of *the two blind men*. Here Jesus perceives their faith by direct question (v. 28).

9:32-34. A demoniac was brought to him. The following miracle indicates the division that Jesus creates within Israel. It fulfills to some degree the apocalyptic statement of 9:17. The crowds are amazed, while the Pharisees explicitly assign his power to the realm of evil.

Then Jesus Went about All the Cities and Villages, 9:35–10:4

The division described narratively in 9:32-34 now receives direct comment by Jesus in vv. 35-38 and is followed by his own reaction to the situation of a divided Israel in 10:1-4. The two scenes are written in such a way as to relate closely to each other, therefore, we have chosen to include 10:1-4 as the conclusion to the previous plot narrative.

Matthew 9:35 restates 4:23 and acts as an inclusionary summation but unlike 4:23 focusses exclusively on Israel. The text adds the observation that the crowds have no leadership (v. 36). The gathering opposition of the synagogue authorities summarized by their indictment of Jesus in the previous episode shows that they have an unsound eye and cannot discern the kingdom. Therefore, Jesus directly addresses this problem discovered within Israel by summoning THE TWELVE for the first time (10:1-4).

Speech:
These Twelve Jesus Sent Out, 10:5-42

Go Nowhere among the Gentiles, 10:5-15

Jesus' ministry as depicted from 4:23 has included both Israel and non-Israel. The sending of the disciples exclusively to Israel is in response to Jesus' discovery of the blindness of its leaders not to a preordained plan of salvation first to Israel and then to non-Israel.

The specific nature of the mission spelled out in vv. 7-8 corresponds precisely to the ministry of Jesus depicted in 4:23–9:35. The disciple reproduces what has been learned observing the master. The prohibition of accepting payment (vv. 8b-10) demands ministry in identification with the homeless SON OF MAN (8:20). Finally, this ministry carries with it both grace and judgment as indicated by vv. 13-15.

See, I Am Sending You out like Sheep, 10:16-23

From v. 16 onward the speech takes on significance beyond the events narrated in the text of the Gospel. Jesus foretells judicial action at the synagogue level and trial by non-Israelite leaders (vv. 17-20). Within the text, however, the disciples are never so treated. Therefore, we may suspect that this prediction applies to some time after the crucifixion and prior to the PAROUSIA. The Matthean community either knows of those who have undergone persecution or anticipates it. Such a mission results in the direct dissolution of family ties.

The limitation of the time frame of the mission to Israelite cities in v. 23 to the time prior to the coming of the Son of Man may indicate that the mission to Israel continues even in the time of the Matthean community. The coming of the Son of Man is clearly de-scribed in Matt 24 and that arrival is different from the beginning of the end time that arrives with the CRUCIFIXION and resurrection of Jesus.

A Disciple Is Not above the Teacher, 10:24-42

10:24-25. If they have called the master Beelzebul. These verses continue the shift of focus for the audience begun by the mention of the Son of Man in v. 23. The reference to *Beelzebul* shows that the conflict with the Pharisees in history is nothing other than a portion of the world-encompassing conflict between the kingdom of heaven and the kingdoms of the world (see 9:34; 12:24). Therefore, the trials depicted in 10:17-23 should be reread not only in reference to the particular politics of sectarianism in the ancient world, but also as a sign of the apocalyptic conflict initiated by the preaching of Jesus and the ministry of his disciples.

10:26-31. Have no fear of them. The following verses depict from various angles the reality of this apocalyptic conflict. An alternative translation of the beginning of this verse reads, "Do not fear them, for there is nothing hidden that will not be *apocalypsed.*" The following verses direct attention to appropriate allegiance during the apocalyptic hour. Hope is grounded in the justice and mercy of God as the juxtaposition of judgment and grace makes clear in vv. 28-31; Jesus provides images of God as both righteous judge and caring parent.

10:32-38. Everyone who acknowledges me. Jesus relates the problem of the disintegration of households in normal historical existence to the creation of a new family in the kingdom of heaven. The conflict initiated by the arrival of the kingdom results in both death to normal patriarchal structures and death for the individual. The series begins in v. 35 with relationship to the father and concludes in a manner consistent with the teaching in 9:21-22. The image of cross-bearing in v. 38 results in the conundrum of v. 39. The problem of this paradoxical teaching can be solved only by applying what we learn from the whole of Matthew. Jesus shows that the disciple must identify with Jesus' own destiny in terms of crucifixion and resurrection. The antinomic opposition to death is life given from God.

10:40-42. Whoever welcomes you. Jesus discusses reward as a paradoxical concept. It refers both to the reward of God within God's kingdom as well as the destiny of the prophets and the righteous placed at the mercy of the kingdoms of the world (see 23:29-39). Children of the kingdom cannot avoid the conflict. The conclusion in v. 42 introduces the idea that the emissaries of Jesus have in their OBEDIENCE the sanction of the judgment of the kingdom. It also directs attention to *these little ones*. The reference must be to those supplicants seeking healing from the disciples with the same faith as the supplicants in Matt 8-9. Hence, the rule of justice employed by Jesus as God-with-us (cf. 1:23) in the apocalyptic moment is one of service to those who are at the margins and have no advocate, save God.

Plot and Speech: Now When Jesus Had Finished, 11:1–12:50

With this section the text fully manifests the ambiguity between plot and speech narration in the Gospel of Matthew. Two major movements of plot can be discerned: (1) Jesus teaches and preaches *in their cities* (11:1-30); (2) Jesus disputes with the Pharisees (12:1-50). The activity of Jesus combined with dialogue and brief speeches indicates that the gospel comes to the nation Israel and that both its people and its leaders reject it. The urban mission of Jesus within Israel fails.

The text directs us to perceive within these historical events the confrontation with the kingdom of evil brought about by Jesus. The confrontation becomes apparent through Jesus' interpretation of event. With this section, the strategy of speeches enters into the middle of the strategy of plot in the same way as the kingdom moves into the world. Literary pattern represents world palingenesis (Wilder 1982, 34).

He Went on to Teach, 11:1-30.

11:1-6. He went on to proclaim in their cities. John sends disciples to Jesus to determine if he is the Messiah. Jesus does not affirm the title but answers by a recapitulation of his ministry (vv. 4-6). The language of Jesus echoes Isa 61:1-2, a passage that refers to a prophetic, not messianic, anointing and ministry. The conclusion in v. 6 establishes the basis for reproach and judgment against the cities and against the Pharisees in the following episodes. We are not told of John's reaction to Jesus' reply, rather this episode provides the opportunity for the speech of Jesus that follows.

11:7-30. Jesus began to speak to the crowds. These verses comprise one extended speech by Jesus addressed to the urban Israelite crowds (vv. 7, 20). The first section (vv. 7-19) serves to differentiate the ministry of Jesus from that of John. Verse 11 appears

to consign John to the mundane historical plane and to separate him to some degree from those in the kingdom of heaven. Notwithstanding this indication, however, vv. 12-14 show that he is the initiator of the presence of the kingdom of heaven in the historical world and the recipient of the first attacks of violence by those who serve the kingdoms of the world. We should read v. 12 in the context of the arrest, imprisonment, and eventual beheading of John by Herod, who belongs to the urban power elite reckoned throughout Matthew as servants of evil (3:12; 11:2; 14:1-12). Verse 12 interprets the two-level battle observable in the realm of mundane historical existence interpenetrated by the powers of evil aligned against the power of God. In this context, v. 14 indicates that John is a new type of emissary not to be confused with the *prophets and the law* (v. 13).

Verses 16-19 conclude this first section by interpreting the crowds as like children whose whims cannot be satisfied. In the illustration religious and cultural practices related to weddings and funerals are invoked (Jeremias 1972, 160–62). Even though John adopts the perspective that the arrival of the kingdom is a time of repentance and mourning, while Jesus adopts the perspective of the wedding feast, neither the judgment nor the grace of God is acceptable to the crowds.

Therefore, Jesus condemns the cities for their lack of repentance in vv. 20-24. Following this general condemnation Jesus makes clear that only the least powerful of status groups receive the apocalypsis of God. The word translated by the NRSV as *infants* should better be understood from context as the direct antonym to the *wise and intelligent* (v. 25), that is, uneducated and naive. Along with v. 27 this passage makes clear what has been implicit throughout the ministry of Jesus: those who manifest faith to Jesus do so by the gift of God's gracious will and Jesus responds by revealing God to the faith that comes from God.

The idea of education links vv. 28-30 with the preceding section. Jesus addresses the uneducated and naive and offers them a particular education that results in rest. Jesus does not characterize the apocalyptic-eschatological message of the kingdom as difficult or impossible.

Jesus Went through the Grainfields on the Sabbath, 12:1-50

12:1-14. His disciples began to pluck heads of grain. After the aside to those chosen from among the least, we view the unfaith and condemnation of the greatest, the leadership represented by the Pharisees. In two scenes they initiate disputes over proper SABBATH observance (12:1-8; 9-14). In each case Jesus invokes an emergency situation to claim the overturning of mundane sabbath observance as the will of God. The emergency alluded to in these stories is the arrival of the kingdom of heaven. The Pharisees, on the other hand, remain on the side of historical perception with the result that they make plans to kill Jesus.

12:15-21. Many crowds followed him. The narrator interrupts the disputes with the Pharisees with a citation of Isa 42:1-4. The quotation shows that the future of the kingdom of heaven lies with the gentiles. The interruption recalls earlier sections of Matthew that imply that non-Israel is included in the mission of Jesus. In this regard it may well be that v. 15 refers to "many" who follow him (instead of *many crowds*) and that we are to understand this as a reference to predominantly non-Israelite groups. Reliable ancient manuscripts do not contain the word "crowds," which in this section of Matthew has been used to refer to Israelites. Verse 16, therefore, indicates that during this special period of Jesus' ministry, the mission to non-Israel should remain secret.

12:22-45. By Beelzebul this fellow casts out demons. The concluding episode in this series of disputes with the Pharisees exposes once and for all their allegiance to and determination by the powers of evil. Jesus responds to their accusation by an extended speech (vv. 25-45). Jesus is in the business of destroying the kingdom of Satan (vv. 25-28). Underlying the story of the strong man bound (v. 29) is an apocalyptic perspective of the world possessed by evil powers. Jesus interprets his role as miracle worker as robbing those powers of their control over human beings. The Pharisees oppose such activity as impious because it violates the sabbath. By refusing to recognize the power of God in the action of Jesus, religious leaders judge themselves. By accusing Jesus, the Pharisees reveal their true origin. Such misnaming of powers is unforgivable (vv. 32; 33-37).

Verses 38-45 pronounce the eschatological judgment of the Son of Man against the Pharisees. The sign of Jonah indicates the time between the death and resurrection of Jesus. It also links Jesus in his death to the Son of Man, who will judge. The references to Nineveh and the queen of the South enhance the theme of the discovery of faith among non-Israel and women begun in the genealogy.

The story of the unclean spirit indicates that those whose origin is in the power of evil rather than in God, condemn themselves to a descending cycle of absorption into the realm of Satan (vv. 43-45). What begins as religious propriety may end in acts of evil. The religious leaders are this type of person. They oppose Jesus on the historical and religious plane and in doing so dwell more and more radically and enslave themselves more and more surely to the kingdom of Satan until there is no escape. Their plot to kill Jesus referred to in 12:14 is only the historical manifestation of the power that controls their lives and destiny.

The speech concludes with positive instructions about Jesus' own household (vv. 46-50). By the use of terminology derived from family relationships, Jesus throughout Matthew develops a model of the community of the kingdom of heaven that is both similar to and distinct from patriarchal families. The will of God determines the reality of family relationships rather than allegiances based on blood or ethnic ties. Consistently in Matthew all status markers normal in human society are transcended or negated by participation in the kingdom of heaven.

Speech: He Told Them Many Things in Parables, 13:1-52

Two small movements of plot divide this speech into four episodes in which Jesus' speech is directly addressed to two different character groups (Bauer 1988, 131). In addition, the four episodes are interrupted by a citation of scripture by the narrator. The integration of plot with speech represents the permeation of the current historical process by the kingdom of heaven. Matthew 13:52 states the purpose of the speech: to train scribes for the kingdom of heaven. As we explore this speech, therefore, we need to be aware that here we have evidence of the process of training for the kingdom as well as its content.

A Sower Went out to Sow, 13:1-9

The scene of the first parable by Jesus in Matthew links it closely with the preceding narrative. Jesus addresses the parable to the crowds. Given the previous section of narrative, the setting implies that these crowds are predominantly Israelite. The emphasis of the parable seems to fall on the miraculous production of the seed (v. 8).

Why Do You Speak to Them in Parables?, 13:10-23

13:10-17. To you it has been given. The PARABLES divide the disciples from the crowds. Israel has been judged first by the miracle-working activity of Jesus and now is being judged by the parables. The judgment of parable-telling comes in revealing the fact of nonperception of the kingdom of heaven (v. 13). Further, Jesus himself interprets this judgment as a fulfillment of the prophetic judgment of Isa 6:9-10, a prophecy that specifically indicts the rulers and people of Jerusalem for their refusal to repent. The parables act as an eschatological sealing of the consciousness of the people for judgment by God.

13:18-23. Hear the parable of the sower. While the parable appears to emphasize the miraculous gift of an excessive harvest, Jesus provides to the disciples a specific key to interpret the parable at a deeper level: the different types of soils represent different types of people and their response to the word. In each case the opposition to the word is connected to the kingdom of Satan. Verse 19 connects it to the *evil one* himself. Verse 20 connects it to persecution; the source of persecution is not only human institutions but also the lord served by those institutions. Verse 22, which identifies the cares and wealth of the world as the seduction away from the word, may be read with reference to 6:24 and understood to indicate that wealth is under the control of Mammon (cf. 6:24), a servant of the *evil one* as well.

According to Jesus, the key to understanding the parable is the ability to see a two-level conflict in the present moment. The conflict on the surface may appear to be a historical one: normal worldly cares, greed, and persecution destroy one's attention to the word of salvation to humans. But more, all of these are weapons in the struggle of the kingdom of the evil one against the incoming kingdom of heaven. This understanding cannot be deduced from the parable itself, which emphasizes the miraculous growth of the kingdom, but only from the proper perspective provided by Jesus to those to whom the secrets of the kingdom have already been given. The trained scribe adopts the apocalyptic perspective of Jesus in order to properly interpret the parables at all levels.

He Put before Them Another Parable, 13:24-34

Jesus addresses the three parables that follow the interpretation to the crowds once more (v. 34). Since they are addressed to the crowds composed of urban Israel who are being judged by the parables, no interpretation of these parables is provided. We shall wait to offer an interpretation of these parables from Jesus' perspective when the text returns to these parables at v. 36.

This Was to Fulfill 13:35

The narrator interrupts the development of the parable speech of Jesus with an interpretative citation of prophetic scripture. The citation comes from Ps 78:2 and is traditionally attributed to ASAPH who according to 2 Chr 29:30 was a seer or prophet. According to Ps 78:2-4 the parable reveals what previously has been hidden. In Matthew, Jesus uses parables on the one side to judge the crowds and on the other to instruct the disciples and through them all members of the kingdom of heaven.

Then He Left the Crowds, 13:36-52

13:36-43. Explain to us the parable. Jesus explains in allegorical fashion the parable of 13:24-30. The key to interpretation remains an apocalyptic-eschatological perspective. Judgment is reserved for the Son of Man who is both the sower of good seed and the judge at the end of the age. The interpretation of Jesus makes clear that his ministry to Israel as the Son of Man forms the basis for justice in the final time. The justice of God assigns proper place to those found as children of the kingdom or children of the evil one at the end time.

13:31-32. The kingdom of heaven is like a mustard seed. At this point we return to the earlier parables (13:24-34), since we now have a pattern of interpretation established by the presentation of the text. While Jesus himself does not provide an interpretation, the text presumes that we can provide one based upon the method of Jesus. The parable of the mustard seed, therefore, may be interpreted as referring to the planting of the kingdom of heaven through the ministry of Jesus. The result is an unexpected home for the homeless (v. 32).

13:33. The kingdom of heaven is like yeast. The parable of the leaven breaks the pattern of its group of parables since planting is not involved. Jesus is compared to a woman, or perhaps the female character is God. The emphasis falls on the miracle of leavening. The image indicates the active nature of God's kingdom through Jesus. As the depiction of the miracles of Jesus in Matthew makes clear, the kingdom of heaven is not simply beset and beleaguered by the Evil One and its children, it also is in the business of claiming territory for itself.

13:44-45. The kingdom of heaven is like treasure. This pair of parables emphasizes the inherent and almost irrational value of the kingdom; the emphasis in both falls on the activity of the individual in selling all that he has for the sake of the treasure of the kingdom. Jesus provides a parabolic expression of the activity he advocated in 6:19-34. The theme will be further developed in 19:16-29.

13:47-50. The kingdom of heaven is like a net. The final parable of the speech returns to the theme of eschatological judgment already emphasized by the parables of the sower and the weeds among wheat. Here, presumably since Jesus is speaking only to the disciples and through them to the audience, parable and apocalyptic-eschatological interpretation occur together.

13:51-52. Have you understood all this? The parable discourse concludes with a dialogue between Jesus and the disciples. Verse 52 marks the purpose of the discourse as the training of scribes for the kingdom of heaven. The simile invites an apocalyptic-eschatological reading, first, because of its place within the parable chapter. The reversal of normal historical sequence in the phrase *what is new and what is old* points in the same direction. The perspective induced by the speeches of Matt 13 begins with the new: the inbreaking of the kingdom of God into the world. God's arrival creates a division within humanity through the parables of Jesus. Humans are being judged by the ministry of Jesus who is already the coming Son of Man. From the Matthean perspective, the division of humanity occurs for the first time in the life of Jesus. The final process of judgment will not be complete until some point in the historical future.

Plot and Speech: When Jesus Had Finished These Parables, 13:53–17:27

The plot focuses on the reaction to Jesus' person and message on the part of three groups of characters: crowds, Pharisees, and disciples.

He Came to His Hometown, 13:53-58

NAZARETH rejects Jesus and on the basis of this lack of faith he performs no miracle (v. 58). The story implies that the rejection comes out of the townspeople's association with the synagogue. They seek to understand Jesus as part of a human household, com-

posed of his mother and brothers (v. 55). By depending on a social perspective, the people of Jesus' hometown become offended at him. According to Jesus, national identity, ethnicity, and association with family prohibits the perception generated by God's kingdom (v. 57). After this episode, Jesus moves outside of normal social and religious institutions for the proclamation of his message.

Herod the Ruler Heard about Jesus, 14:1-12

HEROD the ruler along with his wife Herodias brings about the death of JOHN THE BAPTIST. Herodias's daughter, unnamed by the narrator, has no real power vis-à-vis her mother. She is both an object of her stepfather's lust and the means to accomplish Herodias's murderous intent. The story does not portray the daughter as culpable for her actions. She extends the Matthean theme of the victimization of children begun in the infancy narrative. The text exposes the stupidity of male pride and the false valuing of personal status by showing Herod's adherence to a frivolous oath (see 5:37) and acquiescence to her unjust request so as to preserve his personal power in the eyes of those assembled. Among the kings of the world, children, especially female children, become tools instead of persons.

Jesus Withdrew to a Deserted Place, 14:13-21

The miracle of the feeding of the five thousand and the walking on the water occur together in all four Gospels. The association probably was influenced by the similar stories about MOSES, ELIJAH, and ELISHA found in the Jewish scriptures. Matthew, however, contains its own peculiar emphases. The focus in each story becomes the disciples and their faith.

Whereas previous miracles have emphasized the marginality of the supplicants, this miracle by its setting depicts the advent of the kingdom as outside of the cities, synagogues, and households of Israel. The enactment of the feeding miracle before the crowds reflects compassion. The crowds' eagerness to follow Jesus and the presence among them of the sick implies that Jesus recognizes faith from their action.

The disciples and their response become the focus by virtue of their request of Jesus. The disciples reflect a lack of faith since they judge according to mundane historical needs and satisfaction of those needs (cf. Patte, 209–11). Jesus' blessing directed toward the heavens draws attention to the power of God expressed through the miracle.

Jesus Made the Disciples
Get into the Boat, 14:22-36

The first scene depicts Jesus walking on the water to the disciples who as a group fail to recognize him and take him to be a ghost. The motif of their lack of discernment implicit in the previous story becomes explicit.

Peter acts both as an individual and as a representative of the Twelve. Jesus recognizes and emphasizes his lack of faith (v. 31). His behavior remains consistent with the previous behavior of the disciples in a similar situation at 8:26. The author depicts Peter throughout the Gospel as undependable and doubting.

The Pharisees and Scribes
Came from Jerusalem, 15:1-20

Jesus condemns the PHARISEES for substituting their will for God's will. Jesus regards their interpretation as opposed to God's commandments. Verses 6-9 indicate that such a tradition is a human, not divine, institution and imply that their tradition antithetically opposes the word of God. For Jesus the word of God means the will of God revealed to be righteous and just in the eschatological time of Jesus' ministry. The function of the parable like those of Matt 13 must be to judge the crowd.

Beginning with v. 12, Jesus interprets the parable of 15:11. The scene shows that the disciples have not understood the speech of Matt 13, nor have they understood the actions of Jesus. They as yet lack faith that comes from the perspective of the kingdom. In Matthew faith and understanding appear to be two aspects of the same gift from God.

Jesus Left That Place
and Went Away to Tyre and Sidon, 15:21-39

15:21-28. A Canaanite woman started shouting. The use of *Canaanite* rather than SYROPHONECIAN as in Mark 7:26 emphasizes that the woman comes from an ethnicity traditionally an enemy of Israel worthy of extermination (see Josh 12:20). The story of the Canaanite woman shows that Jesus himself can initially fail to perceive faith and thereby refuse access to the kingdom to those to whom he was sent. Jesus, an Israelite man, allows himself to be duped by the appearance of this supplicant as a woman and a non-Israelite.

Jesus refuses to hear her petition and strives to silence her by ignoring her (v. 23a). But the woman demands a hearing for her daughter's need. The disciples become upset at her noisy importunity and plead for Jesus to *send her away* (v. 23b). The male householders strive to silence the supplicating woman and assign her to the margins.

At v. 24 Jesus finally engages in conversation with her after reiterating his statement of mission in the same words as 10:5. Matthew depicts Jesus' earlier mission up to that point as universal. During that mission Jesus recognizes and heals women supplicants from Israel as well as men of both Israel and non-Israel (Matt 8–9). Here, for the first time, Jesus confronts a non-Israelite woman.

Jesus' journey to TYRE AND SIDON indicates an intention to transcend the borders of the Israelite homeland with his mission. Therefore, on the basis of the previous behavior of Jesus and the development of plot in this section, we might anticipate that here Jesus himself will move beyond the ethnic and national boundaries imposed since 10:5. Such a return would confirm the earlier indications in Matthew of a universal mission.

The speech and action of Jesus do not accord with either his own actions or speeches elsewhere and therefore disconfirms our expectations. The woman, however, proves to be a better theologian than Jesus. She willingly identifies her utter abasement as a crumb-lapping dog and refers to the "Lords' table" from which she begs scraps. This phrase is usually translated as *masters' table* thereby referring to the people of Israel who are also understood as the *children* in Jesus' response of v. 26. Such a reading is difficult within the larger context of Matthew since the narrative previously condemned the people and leadership of Israel as unrepentant.

The woman appears, at one level, to argue a truism—dogs eat crumbs from their masters' table. At a second level, however, the woman's statement implies a confession of faith. In Matthew the singular *Lord* occurs as a confessional title used by supplicants of Jesus. Jesus recognizes in this title the presence of faith. The woman uses this form of supplication in vv. 22, 25, 27. By using the plural the woman shows that she recognizes not only Jesus but also God as her lord. She understands the table as the table of the final banquet presided over by God and the SON OF MAN, that includes all despite accidents of ethnicity. Her interpretation accords with Jesus' own interpretation of the faith of the centurion in 8:10-13. Her understanding can come only from God.

Jesus pronounces her faith and heals her daughter. The author does not shrink from showing Jesus as learning from a woman of an inappropriate ethnicity. Both status as woman and as non-Israel are highlighted in order to show the apocalyptic faith that comes from the kingdom of heaven and that destroys all historical claims to prerogatives within the kingdom. Even Jesus in this Gospel can be educated by such faith.

15:29-39. He passed along the Sea of Galilee. The following episodes show Jesus re-initiating a self-conscious ministry to gentiles after the education by the woman (cf. Gundry 1982, 317–22). Galilee has already been associated with the gentiles in 4:13-18. The healing ministry and the feeding miracle apparently take place on the eastern shore of the Sea of Galilee in the general area of the DECAPOLIS. *Magadan* (v. 39) is on the western shore. The sentence *And they praised the God of Israel* (v. 31) indicates clearly that the crowds are non-Israel. Jesus fulfills the prophecy of Isa 61:1-2 specifically for a non-Israelite crowd. The miracle of the feeding of the four thousand contrasts with the earlier feeding of the five thousand performed for a predominantly Israelite crowd.

The Pharisees and Sadducees Test Jesus, 16:1-12

Within the plot of Matthew this episode repeats in an abbreviated form the episode found in 12:38-42. Therefore, the episode offers another opportunity for Jesus to condemn the religious leadership. He does so as the Son of Man who will die. Implied is the eschatological perception that the crucifixion and resurrection of Jesus function not only to include children in the kingdom of heaven, but also to judge. Matthew presents Jesus as Son of Man who judges: first, during his historical ministry to the cities of Israel; second, by his death and resurrection; and third, in his PAROUSIA. Such a rich conceptualization of the Son of Man indicates the fluidity with which the author discerns the movement of time and event along spatial axes. The future of God erupts in Matthean narrative where God wills it regardless of the clocks of historical causality. Such thought here and elsewhere proves disorienting to those of us accustomed to narratives that express a worldview that privileges historical sequence and causality. The disciples represent the historical viewpoint as well. They lack faith (v. 8) and perception (v. 11). They finally gain some understanding (v. 12).

Jesus Asked His Disciples about the Son of Man, 16:13–17:23

The previous episodes introduce an extended section composed of three episodes in which Jesus directly teaches the disciples about his person and destiny. Jesus connects the titles, Son of God and Son of Man. Peter and the other disciples with him fail to understand Jesus. Ultimately, they are pronounced faithless. Ironically as Jesus reveals himself fully to them the disciples' own lack of faith becomes apparent.

16:13-27. You are the Messiah. To Peter, first, and then later to all of his disciples, Jesus gives power of interpretation and adjudication (16:19 and 18:18). This development is surprising, since PETER and THE TWELVE have yet to be shown to be trustworthy.

Peter—whom Jesus calls *rock* (for the foundation of the community in the eschatological moment)—is given power to *bind* and *loose*, which is understood to be the power to interpret the kingdom of heaven on earth. He is the chief scribe in a school of scribes.

In what sense Peter or Peter's confession constitutes the *rock* on which the community is built remains ambiguous in the text. The ambiguity may be due to the fact that the following scene de-centers and uproots Peter and his tradition from any claim to authoritative hegemony over the Matthean community.

The bestowal of authority is followed immediately by the condemnation of Peter (vv. 21-23). The juxtaposition creates ironic tension. In v. 23 Jesus places Peter in the same relationship to the kingdom of heaven as the powerful urban elites. He is to be found with Satan aligned against God. As elsewhere in Matthew, Jesus knows this not by superhuman insight but by what Peter says. Peter expresses misperception—the wrong epistemology—in v. 22. The condemnation of Peter indicates that the confession of v. 16 is only partial and inadequate from the viewpoint of Jesus and the author. Indeed it is dangerous. Jesus is not the Messiah that Peter would like, the David who will restore Israel to its national independence, but rather he is the Son of God and Son of Man who judges and who dies for the entire world. Peter seeks the kingdom of humans dominated by the evil one and opposed to the kingdom of heaven whose agent is God-with-us. Peter is christologically, theologically, and politically in error.

17:1-21. Jesus took with him Peter and James and his brother John. The section demonstrates who Jesus is and the disciples' failure to understand his identity as the Son of God who is also the Son of Man who will suffer. This failure of perception results in their condemnation as *faithless and perverse* (v. 17).

The implicit comparison between Jesus and MOSES and ELIJAH established in the miracles of the feeding and the walking on the water becomes explicit here. In addition the themes of the lack of faith and understanding of Peter and the other disciples continue. Peter wants to engage in a building program (v. 4) rather than listen and must be silenced from heaven by the same words heard at Jesus' baptism. Jesus supersedes the authority of Moses and Elijah. Their appearances here may represent the impending end of time. Both were regarded by some segments of Judaism as returning from heaven in the final days prior to the DAY OF THE LORD (cf. Mal 4).

As in the previous section, a warning about the earthly destiny of the Son of Man follows direct revelation from God about who Jesus is as the Son of God (v. 9). The disciples again indicate their lack of insight because they ask about Elijah, rather than addressing the more apparent issue of the identity and destiny of Jesus (vv. 10-12).

Verses 14-21 conclude this section and focus attention on the disciples' lack of faith. Jesus condemns them as a group in terms almost identical to the condemnation of the Pharisees and Sadducees in 16:4. Supplicants, however, have faith. The disciples cannot heal because of their little faith (v. 21).

17:22-23. As they were gathering in Galilee, Jesus said. These verses contain a concluding teaching about the Son of Man in Galilee. They provide an inclusion with 16:13 in which Jesus answers his own question of his identity and destiny. Furthermore, the episode is written so that when we come to the gathering of the eleven disciples in Galilee after the resurrection (28:16-20) we will be immediately reminded of the disciples and their distress at Jesus' prophecy. As is shown in the teaching about the Son of Man who must suffer and die, the disciples lack the faith to understand Jesus and his destiny. The faithless disciples gathered in Galilee are greatly distressed. Later in Galilee some will doubt (28:17).

The Children Are Free, 17:24-27

The episode singles out Peter. Jesus frees the children of the kingdom from religious obligation and sees the Temple tax as imposed by the kings of the earth. A historical problem is addressed, as well as the true origin and allegiance within the kingdom. The miracle places the provision in the hands of God and conforms to the teaching on Mammon in 6:19-34. Hence the plot of Matthew provides concrete examples of the principles articulated in the speeches of Jesus that describe the constitution and politics of the kingdom.

Verse 27 makes clear that violent resistance must not be the course of action for the child. To refuse to pay would align Jesus with political seditionists that might use the power of Mammon withheld from the Temple officials for the purpose of bringing down the kings of the world. Implicit here is the theological and political principle that the means can never justify ends. The use of worldly power necessarily brings enslavement to the powers of the world.

Speech: Who Is the Greatest in the Kingdom of Heaven? 18:1-35

Matthew 13:52–17:27 contains little or no plot advancement. Therefore, the movement to the fourth extended speech by Jesus fuses without disruption into the preceding section. The immediately preceding episode provides an excellent introduction to the speech since it highlights children as free within the kingdom and the world. Literarily, the speech represents an artistic use of both dialogue and parable. It is organized into two parts. The first answers, *Who is the greatest in the kingdom of heaven?* (vv. 1-5). The second explores the question of how the *little ones* are to be treated (vv. 6-35). The weight of the speech rests on the last point. Thereby, Jesus shifts the attention of the audience from rank in the kingdom to service and relationship within the community or *ekklēsia*.

Matthew infuses ecclesiology with theology. Unlike the narrative section that precedes it, direct reflection on the person of Jesus, christology, is absent or at best only implied in the fact that he is the speaker. Rather, the entire focus is on the kingdom of heaven, the master who deploys it, and the relationship of the children of that kingdom in their historical gathering to one another. In this speech Jesus teaches about living in mundane human community as children of God. Politics becomes focussed through ethics.

He Called a Child, 18:1-5

Jesus presents for the first time an expanded teaching on the understanding of status within the kingdom. While Jesus has used diminutive terms such as "children," "little ones," and "naive ones" in prior contexts, he here presents a coherent view.

In Matthew children are characters of the lowest and most vulnerable status. They never speak in Matthew. Herod murders them. Those who are healed are healed at the request of adults of higher status. If we understand the daughter of Herodias to be still a child, then we must also recognize sexual abuse implied as an aspect of children's status in Matthew. No children, except Jesus himself, receive names in Matthew.

This representation accords well with the place of children in the ancient world. While there is some evidence for the romanticization of children in the art and literature of Hellenistic culture, such ideas appear to have had little effect on the treatment of children. Infanticide, for example, was advocated by many moral philosophers as a means of eliminating unwanted or handicapped children. How common the practice was, we have no way of knowing. Similar to our society, children in the ancient world have minimal civil rights and remain completely under the domination of their fathers. Children are regarded as naive, uneducated, and foolish. No philosopher or wise man would seek to emulate them. Jesus appears to be unique in the ancient world in his valuation of children as exemplars for the life of a community.

These points should help reveal to us the uncomfortable irony that the ancient audience would likely feel at this episode. The disciples are free male householders who receive the instruction of Jesus. They should be the wise and pious models of the kingdom. Jesus instructs them to become like the child. The aspiration to humility runs opposite to the desire for knowledge and maturity. The kingdom of heaven requires the direct reversal of status aspirations.

If You Put a Stumbling Block before One of These, 18:6-35

Jesus constructs an answer to a question not asked by the disciples. By this rhetorical device he shifts attention to the question of relationships within the kingdom of heaven and its specific historical manifestation, the community. These verses fall into three sections: vv. 6-9; 10-14; 15-35. The extensive discussion of the last section indicates the emphasis of the speech that moves from the general conceptuality of the kingdom to the specifics of individual religious communities. As we interpret these verses we should remember that the teaching of vv. 2-5 shows that we should presuppose a community in which all members have the status of children and therefore no hierarchical roles may be assigned.

18:6-9. Woe to the world. Jesus warns against being the cause of temptation to other members of the kingdom in graphic terms of eschatological judgment.

18:10-14. Take care. Jesus offers the positive alternative to this negative behavior. The shepherd's behavior in the parable beginning in v. 12 constitutes foolishness. By leaving the ninety-nine on the mountain he endangers his entire livelihood. Seen from the perspective of the kingdom, however, the shepherd represents God's care for the lost.

18:15-35. If another sins against you, The third section follows logically and forcefully on these first two principles. Verses 15-20 apply in a practical case the principle enunciated by the parable. The reader of the English text has the disadvantage of a language that makes no formal distinction between you (pl.) and you (sing.). In Greek, however, there is a clear distinction. Verses 15-17 in Greek use you (sing.). Hence, they should be read as referring to the behavior of the one wronged toward the one doing the wrong. The conclusion of the process in v. 17 allows for the entire community to be brought together to settle the dispute. The outcome of the process, should it not result in reconciliation, is that the sinner be regarded as a gentile *tax collector*. Given the depiction of these groups in Matthew as those most likely to hear the message of the gospel then the offended party is being instructed to consider the sinning community member as a mission field for the gospel. Matthew provides no basis for the practice of excommunication or exclusion from the community by a hierarchical collegium, group of elders, or those who appeal to the traditional lineage of the apostles (cf. Thompson 1970).

Verses 19-20 support this interpretation. They return to the use of the you (pl.) in reference to the disciples and/or the community envisioned as the audience of the speech. This "you" group is the group described earlier in v. 4 as having the status of children. Hence, claim to status privilege would remove one from the presence of either the Father or Jesus and withhold divine sanction for the decision of the community. Verse 20 indicates the presence of Jesus as God-with-us (cf. 1:23) to guarantee the status-free structure of the community. In this context, Jesus bestows anew the privilege of judgment and interpretation earlier granted to Peter. This time, however, the unity of the speech makes it clear that such privilege depends upon the perception by the disciple of her/his own dependence on God and equal status before God with all other members of the community. The view of the historical church that emerges from Matt 18 therefore is a congregation of equals whose access to God and Jesus depends upon their continued affirmation of their nonhierarchical, noncentric status.

Peter presses the teaching further. Does he genuinely desire a mathematics of GRACE? If so, then he adopts a casuistic stance already condemned by Jesus in the Pharisees. He displays a behavior appropriate only to the leadership of their synagogues, not to the leadership of the community. The parable that Jesus tells to conclude this speech indicates the theological basis of equality among all children in the kingdom. It should be read according to the apocalyptic-eschatological method taught in Matt 13. From the perspective of God's judgment, the child of the kingdom should extend to those sinning against itself the same mercy extended by God to the child, otherwise it condemns itself to the judgment of God. The child of the kingdom must be merciful, as God is merciful, must be perfect as God is perfect, or it transgresses the delicate balance between grace and justice advocated so eloquently by Jesus. Such a balance can be seen only from the eschatological perspective of God's future coming in the Son of Man, whose apocalypse is now in Jesus.

Plot and Speech: When Jesus Had Finished Saying These Things, 19:1-29

In the following episodes Jesus eliminates claims to special religious and social privileges claimed through Israelite custom and law by the male heads of households.

Some Pharisees Came to Test Him, 19:1-12.

19:1-9. Is it lawful for a man to divorce? Jesus protects women from invidious impoverishment by males and conforms to the overall concern of the text for the marginal. The scene applies the apocalyptic-eschatological perspective to the problem of DIVORCE. Jesus concerns himself only with the practice of men unilaterally divorcing their wives as provided by Mosaic Law. He does not discuss the relatively modern phenomenon of a mutual decision to dissolve a household.

By combining quotations from Gen 1:27 and 2:24, Jesus reveals the intention of God at creation to be for males to leave their family and property for their wives. This matrilocality constitutes the opposite of property relationships of the first century. The law that allows for divorce was given by Moses, not God, be-

cause of the formation of patriarchal marriages after the advent of SIN. Even within the current patrilocal practice, a man who has undertaken responsibility for a household may not abandon it, according to Jesus. Male householder property rights that include possession of their wives come not from God, but from humans.

Only in the case of *unchastity* (v. 9) may men unilaterally dissolve their marriages. The exception is obscure since the Greek word used refers to almost any sort of undesirable sexual activity. It may refer to marriages discovered to be incestuous by first-century Judaism but allowable in the non-Jewish world (see 5:31; Meier 1976, 147–50; Baltensweiler 1967, 88–100). Therefore, the exception might refer particularly to problems among non-Jewish proselytes within the Matthean community.

19:10-12. It is better not to marry. The disciples apparently find the elimination of their privileges in marriage so harsh as to be almost unbearable. Jesus, having eliminated the preeminent place of the Israelite male as disposer of household property including women, further indicates that maleness is not essential for inclusion within God's kingdom. Infertile, phallically disempowered males may be as blessed by God as others. Such a teaching contradicts directly the prescriptions of the Law that refuse a EUNUCH access to the congregation of Israel (Deut 23:1). Such prescriptions reserve full righteousness before God only for "normal" phallically capable males. Jesus aligns himself, rather, with the prophetic tradition of Isaiah that foresees the eschatological time as a time when eunuchs will enter the congregation of Israel (Isa 56:3-5). Jesus sees that time as now. Therefore, women and nonmales hold as high a position of privilege in the kingdom as males.

Then Little Children Were Being Brought to Him, 19:13-15

The immediately preceding episode shows the disciples to be fixed on their own privilege as male householders so as to exclude the marginal. In this episode, in spite of the instruction of Matt 18, they still are unable to accept and act upon the kingdom as proclaimed by Jesus. Therefore, he must instruct them again in speech that eloquently testifies to God's concern for the powerless. "Suffer the little children to come unto me and forbid them not for of such is the Kingdom of heaven" (KJV). By its forceful simplicity the theological and social radicality of this verse eludes its appropriation by the original readers and by all subsequent readers of Matthew.

What Good Deed Must I
Do to Have Eternal Life?, 19:16-29

The third episode concludes a consideration of the situation of the male householder in the kingdom of heaven. Two conversations occur: one, between Jesus and a young man (vv. 16-22); the second, between Jesus and the disciples led by Peter (vv. 23-29).

19:16-22. Why do you ask? In the first conversation, the dispersal of material wealth for the poor is placed at the end of a discussion of righteousness according to the Law. Jesus' statement in v. 21 epitomizes the demand of God given through Moses in Deut 15:4-5. This scripture describes the sabbatical year of the remission of debts in Israel. God guarantees that there will be no poor "if only you will obey the Lord your God by diligently observing this entire commandment that I command you today" (see also Lev 25). In the historical field, the keeping of the Law, as indicated by the claim of vv. 18-20, must include the elimination of the poor in Israel. The continued presence of the poor should be regarded as a sign of the unrighteousness of those who have possessions. The young man cannot go this far (v. 22).

19:23-29. It will be hard for a rich man. More than the historical field emerges here. The teaching of 6:19-34 illuminates the underlying cause of the young man's failure as being in the lordship of Mammon. Only the powerful lordship of God can overcome economic investiture. The disciples recognize that the problem exists not only for the extremely wealthy but for householders such as themselves (v. 25). Their reply to the teaching parallels their response in 19:10. They resist applying the perspective of the kingdom to their own status.

Peter seeks to identify himself and his brother disciples with the homelessness of Jesus (v. 27). Nevertheless he remains fixated on hierarchical privilege ensured by eschatological reward. Jesus' answer deftly avoids promising material hierarchy by leaving unspecified the nature of the hundredfold reward (v. 29; cf. Mark 10:30).

Verse 28 seems to promise the power of judgment to the apostles at the PAROUSIA. The immediate context strongly circumscribes understanding this verse as guaranteeing privilege. The parable that follows (20:1-16) further arrests the plot and opens a window into the organization of the kingdom as a uniform field in-

fused by God's justice and grace. Should we not also read irony here, since the disciples are given power over only the judgment of Israel patriarchally arranged in tribes. This patriarchy is no longer valid in the kingdom in which only the Son of Man exercises universal judgment (Matt 24–25).

Speech: But Many Who Are First
Will Be Last, 19:30–20:16

The parable compares the kingdom of heaven to a *householder who*. According to the interpretative perspective taught in Matt 13, we should understand the householder either to be God or Jesus as the Son of Man/Son of God. Jesus draws on prophetic teaching tradition by reference to the figure of the *vineyard* as a figure of Israel's relationship to God (Isa 5).

The householder promises those hired at nine o'clock to pay *whatever is just* (v. 4). The question of righteousness thereby becomes the focus of the parable. Verse 8 provides the setting for the conflict with which the parable ends. It provides those hired first with the opportunity to see the act of payment. This act of payment defines within the plot of the parable what is just.

No hierarchy of merit exists among the workers at the conclusion of the parable. Jesus depicts economic relationships within the kingdom of heaven as a uniform field of power whose nature is utterly nonhierarchical. The choice implied in v. 13 is whether or not to remain in the harvest field.

Verse 15, "Am I not allowed to do what I want with what is mine? Or is your eye evil because I am good?" (author trans.) refers to teaching by Jesus found in 6:23 where the same phrase *your eye is evil* denotes a connection between physical sight and moral judgment. The author ends the parable with a question about the appropriate judgment to be made.

In v. 16 Jesus echoes 19:30. In what way did the last become first and the first last? Clearly, it was not in the reward granted: all are equal. Rather, v. 16 forces us to reread v. 8, to stand with those hired first, and to decide about the justice of the kingdom of heaven.

The last receive their wages for the day. A *denarias* constitutes the amount necessary to sustain a worker and family for one day. According to the theological economy of the Gospel of Matthew, physical sustenance is guaranteed by God in the kingdom of heaven. Matthew 6:19-33 indicates that more than this causes anxiety that emanates not from God, but from the kingdom of Satan. The first hired, along with the disciples and the audience of the Gospel, are invited to see the justice of God, and choose.

Plot: While Jesus Was Going Up to Jerusalem, 20:17–21:27

The Son of Man Will Be Handed Over, 20:17-28

20:17-19. They will condemn him to death. The episode begins with Jesus' prediction of his death and resurrection as the Son of Man and concludes with his interpretation of his death as a servant, the Son of Man, who gives his life for many. Jesus emphasizes the complicity of both the chief priests and scribes along with the Roman ruler in v. 19. The elite of Jerusalem who sought to kill Jesus as a child will accomplish their intention shortly. The prediction of the resurrection completes the prediction theologically and in parallel with v. 28 shows the result of the service of the Son of Man. In Matthew, the crucifixion and resurrection are always held together as one event of salvific significance.

20:20-23. The mother of the sons of Zebedee came. The reference to the rulers in v. 25 reminds us of the historical plane infused by evil powers. The action of the mother of the Zebedee brothers coincides with this historical emphasis by presuming that there will remain a hierarchical organization in the kingdom. Her presence here indicates perhaps the presence of those other than the male disciple band during the ministry of Jesus. She will reappear in the narrative at the foot of the cross. She, unlike her sons who abandon Jesus prior to his death, learns the meaning of kingdom and service.

20:24-28. When the ten heard it they were angry. The disciples also are in grave danger of hoping for a hierarchy in the kingdom of heaven that mirrors the hierarchy in the kingdoms of the world. Jesus predicts a nonhierarchical, noncentered system with no special privileges afforded to the disciples except service and death. Here the historical destiny of the Son of Man becomes the epistemological key for the disciples to understand the destiny of the children of the kingdom.

As They Were Leaving Jericho, 20:29-34

Two blind supplicants emerge from the crowds and form an ironic counterpoint to the blindness of the disciples in the previous scene. The last healing before entering Jerusalem emphasizes that these two suppli-

cants, unlike the inhabitants and rulers of Jerusalem, see and follow Jesus. They not only form a counterpoint to the blindness of the disciples, but they also function as witnesses against the city of Jerusalem.

When They Had Come near Jerusalem, 21:1-27

21:1-17. You will find a donkey tied and a colt. The quotation from Zech 9:9 has shaped the emphasis in vv. 2 and 7 that *two* animals are brought and ridden. The image evoked by the text makes Jesus into a sort of circus rider. We may doubt whether an ancient author intended to propose a difficult if not impossible physical act. Rather, concern to show the precise fulfillment of prophecy may override more mundane considerations.

The literal fulfillment of the prophecy results in the perception of Jesus as the Davidic Messiah by the crowds (v. 9). Zechariah's prophecy, however, refers not to the triumphal entry of the Davidic monarch but rather to the arrival of the Lord God at the endtime (Zech 9:14-17). Using ZECHARIAH, the narrator makes clear that the crowds misunderstand Jesus' entry as a messianic act. The crowds also misunderstand him to be a PROPHET (v. 11). Rather, the entry into Jerusalem constitutes the final arrival of God in power to usher in the endtime.

Verses 12-17 continue to characterize Jesus as the arrival of God in the Temple. He claims rulership over his Temple both by his words and action (vv. 12-13). He heals in the Temple as a sign of the presence of God. Verses 15-16 emphasize the objection of the Temple leadership to the cries of *children*. Jesus' response taken from Ps 8:2 identifies himself as God. The entry into Jerusalem and cleansing of the Temple constitute the episodes in which Jesus' status as God-with-us in the eschatological time becomes fully apparent. Jesus by action and scriptural reference proclaims who he is.

21:18-22. He was hungry. The withering of the FIG TREE functions within the plot of this section as a sign of the impending judgment against Jerusalem. It also provides another opportunity for the disciples to perceive faith. The disciples are challenged to faith by the sight of the tree.

21:23-27. By what authority? Jesus forces the urban elites to choose between the sources of John's authority. They refuse because of political considerations. Jesus' argument implies that since John is the lesser of the two, if they do not understand John, they cannot understand him.

Speech:
What Do You Think?, 21:28–22:14

The previous episodes have made clear that Jesus is God. The continued BLINDNESS of the rulers of Jerusalem results, therefore, in the following three parables of judgment. Not since the parables of Matt 13 has Jesus developed an extended speech composed of parables and interpretation. Three parables occur: two sons (21:28-31a); vineyard (21:33-41); and wedding banquet (22:1-14).

The first two parables receive immediate interpretations. The parable of the two sons receives a direct interpretation by Jesus that judges the chief priests and elders of the people for their failure to respond to the way of righteousness proclaimed by John (21:31b-32; 3:7-10). Jesus provides an interpretation to the second parable by scriptural citation. This parable of the vineyard understood from an allegorical eschatological-apocalyptic perspective refers proleptically to Jesus' own death. The reaction of the chief priests and Pharisees in vv. 45-46 makes this interpretation apparent.

The final parable of the wedding feast contains within it elements that specify it as an ALLEGORY of apocalyptic judgment. Therefore, it is not followed by an interpretation. In v. 7 the rage of the king involves a destruction of the city of the murderers and probably refers to the actual destruction of Jerusalem in 70 C.E. Verses 11-14 recount the judgment against those within the banquet indicating that those within the kingdom are also liable to judgment.

The section builds to a forceful conclusion. The parables refer allegorically to the judgment of God that has already arrived. The author expects the audience to see the judgment of God against the urban ruling elite of Jerusalem for the rejection of John the Baptist and for the death of Jesus in the destruction of Jerusalem in 70. At some future date the judgment of God will be completed, including judgment of members of the kingdom. The same understanding of God's justice in the final days will be restated in the final speech of Jesus in Matt 23-26.

Plot and Speech:
Then the Pharisees Went
and Plotted to Entrap Him, 22:15-46

The return to plot in this section shows three arguments in which Jesus silences the PHARISEES and SADDUCEES.

Is It Lawful to Pay Taxes
to the Emperor, or Not?, 22:15-22

In the first episode the Pharisees seek to entrap Jesus as a political seditionist. His reply operates at two levels. First, it affirms that economic systems rely on the political authority for their daily functioning. Therefore, taxes belong to that authority. On a second level, however, the response relativizes such political authority. The coin bears the emperor's image. The unspoken question of theological importance therefore would be, what bears the image of God? According to Gen 1:27, humans, male and female, bear God's image. Jesus' response implicitly lays the claim of God to humanity as God's own. The answer fits with the Matthean view that the kingdoms of the world are under the sway of the evil one who controls Mammon. Political claims over human beings are contrary to the will of God who by creation confirms God's Lordship over humanity. In a real sense, Jesus' answer is seditious. Governments regularly claim power over human lives and bodies.

Some Sadducees Came to Him, Saying
There Is No Resurrection, 22:23-33

The episode of the Sadducees' challenge to the idea of resurrection accords with the depiction of JOSEPHUS, a Jewish historian of the first century, of the Sadducean sect (*BJ* 2.164–66). They deny the resurrection from the dead based on the fact that it is not recorded in the Pentateuch, the only scripture that they hold as authoritative. Jesus interprets Exod 3:6, a central confessional passage in the Pentateuch, from within his power as God to refer to the resurrection. The Sadducees are silenced.

When the Pharisees Heard
That He Had Silenced the Sadducees, 22:34-46

The final episode of silencing of Jesus' opponents occurs in two parts: vv. 34-39 and vv. 41-46. In the first the Pharisees receive an answer directly from the Law (Deut 6:5; Lev 19:18). Jesus' interpretation remains clearly within the traditions of Judaism.

Jesus then turns the tables on the Pharisees and asks for their own interpretation. The quotation comes from a psalm attributed to David (Ps 110:1). Jesus regards David as the speaker, therefore, the implication is that David refers both to God (the first Lord) and also to the Messiah (the second Lord). Therefore, David adopts the same theological position as we noted of the Canaanite woman in Matt 14. The Messiah must be regarded as prior to, not descended from, David. From the perspective of Matthean christology, the conundrum presented by Jesus can be resolved only by seeing Jesus as God-with-us.

Speech: Then Jesus Said to the Crowds and to His Disciples, 23:1–26:1

The speech blends almost without seam into the preceding narrative and emphasizes in discourse form what has already been portrayed through emplotment. The Matthean literary technique shows the full leavening of the historical with the mythopoeic. The kingdom of heaven interprets and alters the causality of history through the action and speech of God-with-us.

We should avoid the tendency to fragment this speech into discreet components. Rather, its literary organization functions within the world of the text to describe the judgment of various political-religious groups and institutions. Like the parables found in 21:28–22:14, the speech also refers to events known to the Matthean community. That referentiality serves to guide possible interpretations of the text.

The Scribes and the Pharisees Sit on Moses' Seat, 23:1-36

Jesus condemns the leaders of the SYNAGOGUE who interpret Mosaic Law. He accuses them both of improper action and improper interpretation of the Law (vv. 2-28). The community should avoid titles of respect and hierarchy adopted from the synagogue (vv. 8-12). Such hypocrisy, Jesus implies, results in unbelief that leads to murder of the righteous emissaries of God, both in the past and in the future (vv. 29-36). The future emissaries include prophets, sages, and scribes sent by Jesus who will be persecuted and killed by the religious institutions led by the Pharisees (v. 34). Such behavior results in bloodguilt that will be judged within a generation (v. 36).

Jerusalem, Jerusalem, the City That Kills the Prophets, 23:37–24:26

Jesus associates the Pharisees and scribes of the synagogues with the guilt of the city of Jerusalem. The condemnation of Jerusalem provides a transition to the prophecy of the judgment of the Temple (24:1-28). Jesus dwells on the details of some form of military campaign against the city emphasizing that this aspect of judgment (while necessary) is not the coming of the Son of Man or Messiah (vv. 5-8; 15-26). Jesus' view-point conforms closely to the view of the Hebrew prophets who understand the judgment of God to come upon the unrighteousness of Israel/Judah particularly by foreign military action against Jerusalem. God uses mundane historical power to God's own purposes of justice.

The destruction of the Temple and Jerusalem will be accompanied by persecution and by false prophets (vv. 9-14). Jesus counsels endurance to the end including active continuation of his own ministry beyond the confines of Israel to the whole world. Only upon the completion of this universal mission will the end come.

After the Suffering, 24:27-35

Jesus briefly describes the coming of the Son of Man to gather the children of the kingdom. Here the theological perspective moves beyond prophetic conceptualities like those of the previous section to apocalyptic-eschatological modes of thought. The endtime is not conceived in a messianic fashion as the reconstruction of mundane political structures through the power of a righteous king supported by God. Rather, the entire cosmos is involved (v. 29) in an event that obliterates historical reality and continuity (v. 35). Jesus provides no details except the enigmatic statement that all will take place before *this generation* passes away (v. 34). The reference may be to those who read the Gospel, rather than to the disciples per se.

But about That Day and Hour No One Knows, 24:36–25:30

The section of sayings that follows continues the emphasis on avoiding idle speculation and begins a call to watchful attentiveness. Jesus warns against counting days and hours implying that such preoccupation distracts from watchful, faithful attentiveness (vv. 36-44). The issue is so important that Jesus tells three parables illustrating the principle. Each parable addresses the community of believers. Each grows in length and intensity. Failure results in expulsion from the kingdom (25:30).

When the Son of Man Comes, 25:31-46

Jesus depicts the final universal judgment by the Son of Man. The metaphor of the sheep and the goats is used; nevertheless, this section is not a parable but a direct vision of the final judgment. The principle of judgment invoked by the Son of Man is to identify the presence of Jesus with supplicants, the marginal, indicated by the *least of these*. The Gospel shows this group to be the women, children, and other supplicants among whom faith is consistently found in the Gospel. The idea of the Son of Man hidden among these is consistent with the idea of God as one who sees in secret (6:1-18). The result of failure to perceive the presence of God in the marginal, silent ones including the homeless, imprisoned, and sick is eternal punishment (v. 46).

When Jesus Had Finished
Saying All These Things, 26:1

Only with the concluding transitional sentence do we recognize the full importance of this section. It concludes the sayings of Jesus in Matthew. It announces the arrival of the judgment of God through the Son of Man in the world.

The concluding formula asks the reader to reconsider the entirety of the preceding section in the terms of the total context of Matthew. We must not read this text as a bifurcation of salvation-history into an "us-them" perspective on God's actions with Israel first and then Christianity. Rather, the text makes the radical claim that holds institutions accountable for their historical refusal of the gospel of the kingdom. It portrays a universal people of God composed of both Jews and non-Jews whose response to the kingdom determines, individually and not ethnically, their destiny in the judgment of God's day.

Matthew identifies the enemies of Jesus as the leadership and people specifically and historically aligned with the kingdoms of the world. The text portrays their judgment already to have been accomplished by the destruction of their city and shrine of ethnic, political, and religious identity. Such a portrayal arises as a prophetic vision from within the traditions of Judaism, not as an externally imposed historical analysis. For Matthew the judgment falls not on Jews as a family (Gk. *genos)* or race (Gk. *ethnos)*, but upon the leaders of national religious institutions. This leadership has opposed the arrival of the kingdom from the birth of its proclaimer and Lord. For the Matthean community this judgment begins with the crucifixion of the Son of Man and ends with the destruction of Jerusalem by the Romans in 70.

Matthew also portrays a universal judgment of the world at some indefinite and incalculable time. This judgment will separate evildoers from the children of the kingdom based upon their faithful action toward the marginalized among whom Jesus dwells. The insis-

tence that faith comes first and foremost from the least is raised to the principle of eschatological justice. Both the mercy of God and the righteousness of God cohere in the scene of final judgment.

Matthew reserves for the community the strongest warning to watchfulness in three parables. Failure in preparation may lead even the most well-intentioned into outer darkness. If we ask what the members of the community are to engage themselves in while watchfully waiting, these parables integrate with the prediction that the proclamation of the gospel must go first to the world. The community in word and deed bears witness to the kingdom of which they are a part. Members cannot smugly await final salvation while the world tears itself asunder.

Therefore, the final speech of Jesus locates its anticipated audience between the destruction of Jerusalem in 70 and the manifestation of the Son of Man at the final judgment. We should not make the mistake of associating the apocalyptic-eschatological viewpoint of the text as indicating an expectation of the chronologically imminent return of the Son of Man. Matthew ties the judgment directly to the witness-bearing mission of the community. Historically seen the chronological duration of that witness is of no consequence to the urgency of an apocalyptic-eschatological expectation of the kairotic imminence of the kingdom of heaven. The mercy and righteousness of God are always and everywhere imminent. The vision of God's grace and justice cannot be limited by historical causation.

Plot: The Son of Man Will Be Handed Over to Be Crucified, 26:2–28:20

Each section of the PASSION NARRATIVE contains episodes that allow the audience to view the actions of various characters or character groups in relationship to Jesus. Their faithfulness, doubt, or opposition becomes apparent as they respond to the unfolding of Jesus' faithfulness to the will of God as he suffers, dies, and is resurrected.

The Passover Is Coming, 26:2-16

26:2. The Son of Man will be handed over. The Gospel of Matthew portrays Jesus, especially in his passion, to be aligned with the events that befall him. These are the last things and they are overseen by the will of God. The disciples are reminded once again of the impending death by crucifixion of the Son of Man.

26:3-5. They conspired to arrest Jesus. *The chief priests and elders of the people* previously in collusion with Herod were unsuccessful in destroying the child Jesus (2:4). Now they will be successful in collusion with PILATE, but not before Jesus has completed his mission. Their plot is left incomplete for the moment since they require stealth.

26:6-13. A woman came to him. The episode returns to the disciple band and provides a contrast between the faith of the marginal and the little faith of the inner circle. *Simon the leper* (v. 6) does not appear elsewhere in the Gospel of Matthew, but he recalls the leper healed by Jesus at the beginning of his ministry (8:1-4). An unnamed woman shows that she has understanding superior to the disciples concerning the person and destiny of Jesus. They should apply the understanding given by Jesus previously that he is about to die (most recently at 26:2 and also at 16:21; 17:22-23; 20:17-19). No prediction to the woman occurs in Matthew. The text allows the inference that she has this knowledge by divine will. In addition Jesus links her act inextricably with the proclamation of *this good news* (v. 13).

26:14-16. One of the twelve went to the chief priests. With the action of Judas, the plot to arrest and kill Jesus is completed. By inserting the anointing at Bethany between the two episodes of plotting, Matthew allows reflection on the disciples' lack of faith in perceiving the divine will and on the collusion of one of their band with the opposition. Among the Gospels, only Matthew develops the story of JUDAS and does so as one of a pair of negative examples of discipleship. The other is PETER. Money motivates Judas.

On the First Day of Unleavened Bread, 26:17-75.

26:17-19. My time is near. Jesus shows his alignment with God's will and control over his destiny by directing the preparations for his last Passover with his disciples. In identifying *my time* Jesus in Matthew uses the Greek word *kairos* rather than *chronos* indicating thereby a time of fulfillment and new beginning (Senior 1985, 60).

26:20-30. One of you will betray me. Jesus shows for the first time that he knows that he will be betrayed. Judas reveals himself to Jesus as the betrayer. In a typical Passover meal of the first century, all of the disciples are likely to have dipped their hand into the same bowl. The notation in v. 23, therefore, only indicates that Jesus knew that one of the Twelve would betray him, not which one.

Even in the face of this knowledge and with Judas presumably still present Jesus interprets his own death for his disciples using the bread and cup as parabolic symbol. In Matthew no specific interpretation of the bread as body is given, rather the interpretation of the cup as *blood of the covenant, which is poured out for many for the forgiveness of sins* (v. 28) stands as interpretation of the entire symbolic act. By declaring this act an interpretation of his impending death, Jesus combines the ideas of the covenant-making sacrifice with the image of the sin offering also found in Jewish ritual and tradition. The combined force of the religious symbol contextualized into the life of Jesus, God-with-us (cf. 1:23), remains a mystery that transcends sacrificial or covenantal religious symbolization and interpretation.

Jesus adds to this complex religious experience by making the celebration of his death a promise of the final banquet within the coming kingdom of heaven. The performance of this parable in the midst of the twelve disciples in spite of their unfaith and even betrayal holds open the promise of forgiveness. Set within the action of Peter and Judas, the words of Jesus take on particular poignancy. The use of the plural *you* in v. 29 may well imply that even the betrayer will be found in the kingdom.

26:30-35. You will all become deserters. In the face of the promise of v. 29, Jesus predicts the desertion of all of the disciples (v. 31). This is followed by a denial by Peter and all of the disciples who emphasize their willingness to die with Jesus. While Peter is depicted as an individual disciple, the text makes us aware that his behavior characterizes the disciples as a group.

26:36-56. Sit here while I pray. Such characterization continues into the next episode in GETHSEMANE (vv. 36-46). The disciples, Peter and the sons of Zebedee are especially mentioned, are unable to watch and pray with Jesus. Jesus' admonition to *stay awake and pray* (v. 41) associates this episode with his previous instruction on the coming of the Son of Man (24:36-25:30) and further develops the implication that his death means the eschatological coming of the Son of Man. Verse 46 directly links the fate of Jesus with the fate of the Son of Man.

The narrator reminds us that Judas is *one of the twelve* yet again at his arrival in v. 47. In this episode, Judas aligns himself not only with the power of money but also with the power of violence to which Jesus has been opposed throughout Matthew. This alignment even afflicts the disciple band, presumably one of which (v. 51) initiates armed resistance against the arresting officials. Jesus repudiates the use of violence to protect his life and mission (Senior 1985, 86). He remains consistent with his own teaching throughout the Gospel. Additionally, he repudiates the traditional Jewish and Christian anticipation of the intervention of Yahweh God as a warrior in behalf of the righteous. Such an understanding is deeply embedded in the Hebrew traditions of the EXODUS (e.g., Exod 14-15) and is heightened in the apocalyptic traditions of Isaiah, Zechariah, and Daniel. While 26:52-54 closely parallels Rev 13:10, the overarching apocalyptic vision expressed in Matthew clearly refuses the solution of divine warfare advocated by the apocalyptic tradition of the Book of Revelation. Jesus, while recognizing the warrior aspect of God, declares such a solution to be aside from the will of the Father (vv. 52-56). The Matthean depiction of the crucifixion remains consistent with such a vision. For the Matthean apocalyptic view, directly informed as it is by the suffering of the Son of Man who is God-with-us, the antidote to the structured and legal power of political violence is not retributive violence. Both are rooted in evil. The antinomic opposition to death is resurrection, not death and blood, however justified, in return.

26:57-75. Those took him to Caiaphas. The final episode of the section recounts an interrogation at the house of the high priest, CAIAPHAS. The procedure was not a normal judiciary procedure of the SANHEDRIN according to what we know of such procedures in the first century. Caiaphas swears an oath in order to get Jesus to speak, contrary to the teaching of Jesus (5:33-37). Jesus answers by declaring the immediate arrival of the Son of Man. The scene shows that the end of the age and the PASSION of Jesus are considered as one event by Matthew. Matthew does not locate the coming of the Son of Man purely at the end of history, but sees the end of history as already present in the historical moment of Jesus' passion. Such a view strains narration, dependent as it is on sequential reading.

The actions of Peter invite comparison with those of the HIGH PRIEST since they follow immediately and conclude the scene. Peter, questioned three times, denies knowledge of Jesus concluding with an OATH in v. 74. By this action Peter aligns himself against Jesus and with the same power that informs the oath-taking actions of Jesus' opponents. He is portrayed in the narrative as in grave danger of joining them in their opposition. His weeping at the remembrance of Jesus' prediction is left ambiguous by the narrator. It should not be taken as showing more than an emotional response to his own failure (cf. Senior 1985, 95–102).

When Morning Came, 27:1-56

27:1-10. Judas repented. While Peter's weeping remains opaque, the conclusion to the story of Judas reveals more about Judas' inner motivations. The episode of Judas interrupts the movement from the high priest's house to the trial by Pilate. The scene stresses the guilt of the religious leadership and the innocence of Jesus, as well as Jesus' obedience to God's will indicated by a citation of prophecy (cf. Kingsbury 1988, 88).

Judas sees his error in the condemnation of Jesus and declares that Jesus is innocent. Judas declares his sin (v. 4). The narrator states that Judas, *repented*. By returning the money he acts on that new perception. The word translated *repented* (v. 3) also occurs in the parable of the two sons in 21:29, 32 to indicate the change of mind of the first son who later is judged to do the will of the father. Typically the author uses a different Greek word to mean "repent" (3:2, 8, 11; 4:17; 11:20, 21; 12:41). Judas indicates his frame of mind both by what he says and what he does.

The suicide of Judas constitutes an antitype to the innocent death of Jesus who also is "hung" in crucifixion. Both may be seen as condemned to a death under the curse of the Law according to Deut 21:23. The portrayal remains ambiguous, however, since Judas is the only disciple to "change his mind." While he is not present to witness the resurrection, we are only left to wonder whether his doubt was removed by what he saw (v. 3). No other disciple is portrayed as recognizing the innocence of Jesus and acting to ameliorate his own denial.

27:11-26. Jesus stood before the governor. The charge before Pilate shifts to political sedition. Pilate completes the work begun by Herod and eliminates the adopted Davidic heir. While the opponents of Jesus believe him to be *King of the Jews*, Jesus himself will not confirm their viewpoint. The ascent of Jesus to messianic kingship in Matthew is a result of his opponents' charges. His descent to identity with marginal and homeless people comes through his own fulfillment of the roles of SON OF MAN and SON OF GOD according to the righteousness of the kingdom. Only Jesus of all the male characters in the Gospel succeeds in this self-emptying (cf. Phil 2:5-11). Such emptying earns him the condemnation of the leaders.

Counterpoint to Pilate's behavior is that of his wife (v. 19). She affirms the innocence of Jesus at his trial. She knows his innocence from a dream. In Matthew the only other dreams mentioned occur to Joseph and the magi in the infancy narrative. Her dream is a revelation of divine will to which Pilate will not listen. The unnamed woman knows the truth.

The action of the crowds in vv. 24-25 has been used in the history of Christian interpretation to condemn Jews as "Christ killers." Such a view exceeds the text and misses the viewpoint of Matthew, rooted as it is in Israelite prophetic tradition. In this climactic scene, the Gospel makes clear that Jerusalem, its leaders and people, reject Jesus. The author crafts this scene in accord with what we have already observed in Matt 23–25. The destruction of Jerusalem by the Romans in 70 constitutes for the author the judgment of God against Jerusalem, its rulers and people, in retribution for the crucifixion of Jesus as the Son of Man, Son of God, the unrecognized God-with-us (cf. 1:23). The event coincides rather precisely with a "generation" if we accept ca. 30 C.E. as the death date of Jesus. In Jewish tradition forty years usually is regarded as a generation (see Senior 1985, 116–22).

The Gospel indicates a continuing mission to all in 28:16-20 as well as perhaps to any cities of Israel remaining post-70 (see 10:23); it does not depict a salvation-historical rejection of Israel or of the Jews by God. It does not even depict condemnation for all of Israel for the crucifixion of Jesus. Rather the condemnation remains specific.

27:27-30. The soldiers took Jesus. Matthew depicts with great care and circumspection the brutal torture of Jesus by the Praetorian guards. The episode shows the control Pilate has over the crucifixion and emphasizes the political nature of Jesus' condemnation. The title *King of the Jews* is emphasized; other titles are excluded. Herod's fear of political sedition by a messiah culminates in Rome's derision of the same pretender.

27:32-44. This is Jesus, King of the Jews. The text shows Jesus as the legal heir to David's throne, therefore, the ruling elite correctly see him as a historical threat. We know, however, that the threat to the mundane order runs deeper because Jesus is not the Davidic Messiah of historical anticipation, but rather is the Son of Man, Son of God, God-with-us who undercuts and robs the kingdoms of the world of their power rooted in violence, death, and injustice. Jesus is a threat because in his person and proclamation he embodies the lordship of God and God's kingdom. The ruling center rightly seeks to kill him in order to preserve their power undergirded by the evil whose face takes shape in hypocrisy and violence. These percep-

tions come to the fore in the taunts of the bandits, religious leaders, and bystanders. They combine traditional titles of the Davidic monarch and deride Jesus as Son of God and King of Israel.

27:45-54. Darkness came over the whole land. Five responses to Jesus' death occur. First, the earth responds with darkness. Second, Jesus responds with the theological question of abandonment to the power of death. Third, the bystanders respond by seeking to drug him and provide more time for their jeers. Fourth, God responds by initiating the turn of the ages, opening the tombs. Fifth, the CENTURION responds by the affirmation of Jesus' divine sonship.

The climax of the plot of Matthew occurs in this scene. Jesus' own cry and death raise the question of God's response and dependability. Jesus' statement of mind in his final moment reveals the pernicious evil of death. God's resurrection proleptically indicated in vv. 52-53 is the cause for recognizing Jesus' emptying on the CROSS transformed into life for all by God's will. Death is not further education for Jesus, but rather is regarded in the text as annihilating even his perception of relationship to the God to whom his life bears witness. In Jesus' death the kingdom of God arrives in power to liberate from death those who have fallen asleep. The answer to Jesus' question is the resurrection from God.

27:55-56. Many women were also there. The women followers of Jesus receive introduction. They, parallel to THE TWELVE, have followed him from Galilee. They also witnessed the events narrated previously in Jesus' life. Two are named. Mary Magdalene does not appear previously in Matthew. The second Mary almost certainly is the mother of Jesus (see 13:55; Gundry 1982, 579). She is not named as his mother in order to preserve the emphasis in the text on Jesus as a homeless and householdless person. These two women provide consistent witness to the life, death, burial, and resurrection of Jesus. Mary, the mother, can bear witness to his identity from birth.

When It Was Evening, 27:57-66

Two episodes contrast faithful followers with the opponents. Missing are the eleven disciples. In v. 57 JOSEPH of Arimathea, *a rich man* and *a disciple*, is said to have provided for Jesus' burial. He apparently was drawn through the eye of the needle by God (19:23-26). Unlike the Twelve who had left everything (19:27) Joseph aligns himself as a marginal follower of Jesus, as do the two Marys who watch the tomb.

In opposition to the faithfulness of Joseph and the Marys, the political and religious opponents post their own guard. The text by this juxtaposition emphasizes the difference between centralized violent guarded authority and marginal faithful watchfulness.

After the Sabbath, 28:1-15

Two episodes emphasize the resurrection of Jesus as part of the eschatological turn of the ages and the proper response to the event. The Marys are consistent witnesses to the biography of Jesus on the historical plane. Also to them comes the revelation of God's resurrection of Jesus (vv. 2-3). The angelic messenger sends the women to re-include the eleven who have denied Jesus (vv. 5-7). The eleven will see him in Galilee. The Marys see him immediately: *Suddenly Jesus met them and said, 'Greetings!' And they came to him, took hold of his feet, and worshipped him* (v. 9). Their response to the resurrection provides a model with which we may compare subsequent responses.

The response of the chief priests to the account of the guards provides a negative foil to the Marys. They use the power of money to silence the news of the resurrection. Their disinformation continues to deceive the Jews to the author's own day. This deception may be emphasized here because it has a negative impact on a continuation of a mission to JUDAISM by the Matthean community.

Now the Eleven Disciples
Went to Galilee, 28:16-20

The final scene of Matthew opens the story of Jesus as God-with-us (cf. 1:23) into an all-powerful future. It also leaves open the future of the eleven and with them the orientation of the audience of the Gospel.

The appearance to the eleven completes the episode begun with the appearance to the women and should be read as a third response to the resurrection. We understand that the women faithfully fulfilled their mission. The response of the eleven also directly parallels that of the women, *when they saw him, they worshipped him, but some doubted* (v. 17; emphasis added). This verse is constructed so as to continue the irony that has attended the characterization of the disciples throughout the narrative. The only character said to doubt previously in the plot is Peter (14:31). The verse also reminds us of the pattern of each episode of *little faith* on the part of the disciples (8:26; 14:31; 16:8; 17:20) and each episode of faith and

worship on the part of the marginalized. The disciples have never been shown to be effective interpreters, teachers, or missionaries within the text. The text, therefore, will not allow for the conclusion that in 28:19 the authority of Jesus is transferred to the disciples. Nor does it clearly rehabilitate them as faithful apostles after their abandonment of Jesus.

The scene as written subverts and destroys any claim by the disciples and/or their institutional heirs to patriarchal or hierarchical authority over gentiles, women, children, or other supplicants within the community. The text remains true in its emplotment and characterization to a vision of the kingdom of heaven that de-centers, de-marginalizes, and in short abandons all -archic, -centric structures with their attendant systems of status.

The audience and not the disciples becomes *scribes trained for the kingdom* (13:52). The work involved in the commission of 28:19-20 is left to those who accept the role and education provided them by Matthew. They behave not like the disciples, but like the faithful of the margins.

Nevertheless, the eleven are not assimilated to the character of the Pharisees. They are left as ironic example. The commission does not transfer Jesus' authority to them. Rather, Jesus remains with them (v. 20), while reserving his own complete power to himself to the end of the age. His story may not be closed by any but God's power expressed through Emmanuel, God-with-us (cf. 1:23).

Works Cited

Baltensweiler, H. 1967. *Die Ehe im Neue Testament.*

Bauer, David R. 1988. *The Structure of Matthew's Gospel: A Study in Literary Design.* Bible and Literature series 15.

Betz, Hans Dieter. 1985. "Matthew 6.22-23 and Ancient Theories of Vision," in *Essays on the Sermon on the Mount,* 71–87.

Brooks, Stephenson H. 1987. *Matthew's Community: The Evidence of His Special Sayings Material.* JSNTSup 16. (*See also* Humphries-Brooks, Stephenson.)

Brown, Raymond E. 1977. *The Birth of the Messiah.* 1983. "Not Jewish Christianity and Gentile Christianity but Types of Jewish/Gentile Christianity," *CBQ* 45:74–79.

Davies, W. D. 1964. *The Setting of the Sermon on the Mount.*

Gundry, Robert H. 1967. *The Use of the Old Testament in St. Matthew's Gospel, with Special Reference to the Messianic Hope*. 1982. *Matthew: A Commentary on His Literary and Theological Art*.

Hanson, Paul D. 1979. *The Dawn of Apocalyptic*. Rev. ed.

Humphries-Brooks, Stephenson. 1989. "Apocalyptic Paraenesis in Matthew 6:19-34," in *Apocalyptic and the New Testament. Essays in Honor of J. Louis Martyn*, ed. Joel Marcus and Marion L. Soards, 95–112. JSNTSupp 24. 1991. "Indicators of Social Organization and Status in Matthew's Gospel," SBLSP 30:31–49.

Jeremias, Joachim. 1972. *The Parables of Jesus*. Second ed.

Kingsbury, Jack Dean. 1988. *Matthew As Story*. Second ed.

Martyn, J. Louis. 1985. "Apocalyptic Antinomies in Paul's Letter to the Galatians," *NTS* 31:410–24.

Meier, John P. 1976. *Law and History in Matthew's Gospel. A Redactional Study of Matt 5:17-48*. AnBib 71. 1979. *The Vision of Matthew: Christ, Church and Morality in the First Gospel*.

Patte, Daniel. 1987. *The Gospel according to Matthew: A Structural Commentary on Matthew's Faith*.

Senior, Donald. 1985. *The Passion of Jesus in the Gospel of Matthew*.

Stendahl, Krister. 1968. *The School of St. Matthew and Its Use of the Old Testament*. Second ed.

Talbert, Charles H. 1988. "Once Again: Gospel Genre," *Semeia* 43:53–73.

Thompson, William G. 1970. *Matthew's Advice to a Divided Community. Matt 17:22–18:35*. AnBib 44.

Wilder, Amos Niven. 1982. *Jesus' Parables and the War of Myths: Essays on Imagination in Scripture*, ed. James Breech.

Mark

Sharyn E. Dowd

Introduction

Of the more than twenty extant gospels, Mark is one of the four that was finally included in the CANON of the early church. Its traditional title "The Gospel according to Mark" did not come from the hand of the author, but was added to a copy of the manuscript during the second century C.E. The name and gender of the author, the date and place of composition, and the intended audience are all unknown.

Mark in Context

Before Mark there was no genre of literature known as "gospel," a term that means "good news." The author of Mark (another term for the author in this commentary is "the evangelist") was not inventing a new genre, but writing a biography of Jesus. Like many ancient biographies, Mark was written not to provide a list of facts about Jesus of Nazareth, but to interpret the significance of the life, death, and resurrection of *Jesus Christ, the Son of God* (1:1). Thus, this biography is a kind of narrative theology. It proclaims Christian faith in the form of a story.

Mark is a popular ancient biography. That is, it was not stuffy elite literature written in elevated language, but a lively story written in a popular style that was easy to read, much like paperback novels today. Of course, the author did not invent the stories; they had been handed down through preaching and teaching in the early Christian communities. What the evangelist did was to arrange the material in its present order and retell the story of Jesus so those who heard the story read aloud would understand how committing themselves to Jesus and his way would affect their lives.

Books were expensive in the ancient world, and not everyone could read, even if books had been easily accessible. It is likely that the Gospel of Mark was intended to be read aloud and heard by an audience of gathered Christians, rather than read privately by one person.

The structure of Mark is distinguished by various kinds of repetition. Repetition is useful in helping the listening audience keep track of the story. For example, in 3:10 the audience hears that people could be healed by touching Jesus. In 5:24b-34 an example is given of a woman who actually was healed by touching Jesus' clothes. Then in 6:56 the audience is reminded again that even touching Jesus' clothes was enough to bring healing to people. Repetition reinforces the point.

Other kinds of repetition found in Mark are the INCLUSIO and the CHIASM. The inclusio is simply a frame. The same information or phrase that begins a unit of material is repeated at the end. This A-B-A form is familiar to us because of its use in many musical compositions.

The chiasm is similar except that the repetition is more extensive. Not only do the first and last parts match each other, but the second and next-to-last also match, and so on. Chiastic structures can be as short as a sentence (*The sabbath was made for humankind, and not humankind for the sabbath*, 2:27), or as long as several pages. These patterns of repetition and other literary devices were used by ancient authors to indicate where thought units began and ended. The chapter divisions now found in the NT were added in the thirteenth century C.E. and often do not reflect the actual literary shape of the text.

Some ancient authors did not like for the sections of a work to be joined end to end like blocks in a row. They preferred that the sections overlap, like links in a chain. The author of Mark was one such author. That is why the outline that begins this commentary may look strange to modern eyes. The reader will notice that one section begins at a point before the end of the previous section. These "hinges" or "hooks" in the structure of the Gospel will be pointed out in the outline and in the commentary.

Mark is a popular biography written from the presuppositions of the apocalyptic worldview, so although it is not an apocalypse like the Book of Revelation, it is in a sense apocalyptic literature. The evangelist believed that in the ministry of Jesus, God's kingdom or reign was breaking into history. The resurrection of Jesus was the beginning of the end. Soon the forces of Satan would be defeated for good and Jesus would return for his *elect*, or "chosen ones" (13:27). The apocalyptic presuppositions of the Gospel of Mark are the reason for the prevalence of conflict and even the language of warfare in the story. Jesus is the divine warrior who does battle with the enemies of God who afflict God's creation with illness, demonic possession, and temptation.

Mark is a popular biography written from within an apocalyptic worldview with a feeling of urgency. Therefore, the author uses every means available to persuade the Christians who hear the story to remain faithful. Two of these means are Jewish scriptural interpretation techniques and Hellenistic rhetorical techniques.

Even though God has done something radically new in Jesus, the evangelist is certain that everything about Jesus is in perfect continuity with the way that God has dealt with people in the past. Everything in the Gospel of Mark is interpreted in terms of the way it fits in with the OT. The author's favorite OT books seem to be Isaiah, Daniel, and the Psalms, although others are used as well to help explain the meaning of Jesus' story.

In ancient Greek schools pupils like the author of Mark learned rhetorical techniques, that is, appropriate ways of proving a point or persuading an audience. Studying how the NT writers used these techniques and adapted them to suit their material is called RHETORICAL CRITICISM. Some of these techniques will be discussed in the commentary.

The Gospel of Mark can be very helpful to the church today not only because of *what* it tells us about the theological significance of what God has done in Christ, but also because of *how* it combines a variety of cultural and literary traditions into an intricate and interesting whole in the service of that good news.

This commentary is intended as a reading guide to the Gospel of Mark. It has been deliberately written in such a way that it will make no sense to the reader who does not have a Bible open alongside the commentary. No commentary can be a substitute for the Bible itself.

For Further Study

In the *Mercer Dictionary of the Bible*: APOCALYPTIC LITERATURE; APOCRYPHAL GOSPELS; DISCIPLE/DISCIPLESHIP; ESCHATOLOGY IN THE NT; GENRE, CONCEPT OF; GENRE, GOSPEL; GOSPEL; GOSPELS, CRITICAL STUDY OF; INCLUSIO; KINGDOM OF GOD; MARK, GOSPEL OF; MARK, LONG ENDING OF; RHETORICAL CRITICISM; SON OF GOD; SON OF MAN; SYNOPTIC PROBLEM; TWELVE, THE; WOMEN IN THE NT; WORSHIP IN THE NT.

In other sources: W. Harrington, *Mark*; E. S. Malbon, "Narrative Criticism: How Does the Story Mean?" *Mark and Method*, ed. Anderson and Moore, 23–49.

Commentary

An Outline

Prologue, 1:1-15

The prologue is held together by a frame or INCLUSIO in 1:1-3 and 1:14-15. Both ends of the inclusio contain the word *good news* (εὐαγγέλιον) followed by an ambiguous prepositional phrase (good news of/about Jesus Christ, v. 1; good news of/about God, v. 14). Although there are a number of scriptural allusions in the prologue, the author of Mark names only Isaiah (v. 2). This makes it clear that the evangelist is interpreting the story of Jesus in terms of the theology of Isaiah, particularly the portion often called Deutero-Isaiah (chaps. 40–55).

Jesus' announcement in v. 15 echoes the prophetic promise that the time of slavery and bondage is filled up and the time of God's favor is on the way (Isa 40:1; 49:8). The good news is that God reigns (Isa 52:7). This message is first announced by a voice crying in the wilderness, *Prepare the way of the Lord*! (v. 3; Isa 40:3 LXX). Thus, the ministry of Jesus is interpreted as a new exodus from bondage into freedom, like the new exodus from exile announced by Isaiah.

But the audience of Mark will soon learn that like Isaiah, Jesus speaks to people who have deaf ears and hardened hearts. He enacts God's liberating power in the presence of people whose eyes see only dimly or not at all (4:12; 8:17-18; Isa 6:9).

Within the frame provided by vv. 1-3 and vv. 14-15, there are three smaller units, each of which emphasizes the activity of the Spirit in connection with the ministry of Jesus: vv. 4-8, 9-11, 12-13. The frame and the inner sections are knit together by repeated words and phrases: *messenger(s)* (1:2, 13); *in the wilderness* (1:3, 4, 12); *baptize/baptizer/baptism* (1:4, 5, 8, 9); *Jordan* (1:5, 9); *son* (1:1, 11); *proclaim* (1:7, 14); *repent/repentance* (1:4, 15).

John Announces the One
Who Will Baptize in the Spirit, 1:4-8

In this unit John the baptizer announces that although he immerses in water, the coming stronger one will immerse in the Holy Spirit. This will be necessary, the audience may surmise, because John's water baptism does not effect the reversal of mindset (μετά-νοια, usually translated "repentance") to which he calls the inhabitants of Judea. Although they confess their sins, the narrative is silent about any change of mind and heart. That there is none is made evident by the blindness, deafness, and hardness of heart with which Jesus' message is greeted in the subsequent narrative. Only the transforming baptism in the Holy Spirit, promised but not narrated in the Gospel of Mark, will effect a change to God's way of thinking (8:33) and result in bold witness (13:11).

In this first appearance in the story, John wears the costume of ELIJAH (v. 6; 2 Kgs 1:8). This identifies him as the forerunner promised in Mal 3:1; 4:5 (v. 2; 9:11-12) and prepares for his persecution by a scheming queen (6:17-29; 9:13).

Jesus Is Baptized in the Spirit, 1:9-11

The baptism scene establishes Jesus' God-given identity for the information of the audience of the Gospel. In Mark, John does not share Jesus' vision of the descending Spirit (v. 10; cf. John 1:32), nor does the voice from heaven make a public announcement (cf. Matt 3:17). Thus, only Jesus and the audience understand that Jesus' baptism legitimates him as PROPHET, servant, and anointed royal SON OF GOD. The bystanders at the story level see only a country boy from Galilee joining in the mass confession and baptism in the Jordan River.

It does not occur to the author of Mark, as it does to the author of Matthew, that Jesus' baptism as one of the crowd requires the explanation that Jesus had no sins to confess (cf. Matt 3:14-15). On the contrary, the Markan Jesus identifies with the sin of his people even as he accepts his call to the prophetic vocation (Isa 6:5). In this way, the baptism prefigures the passion: "He was counted among the lawless" (Isa 53:12 LXX).

Sight (v. 10) is reinforced by hearing (v. 11). The voice from heaven, like the narrator (vv. 2-3), quotes scripture; again the evangelist emphasizes the continuity between the good news and the old, old story of God's self-revelation in the past. The heavenly voice quotes a combination of Ps 2:7 ("You are my son"—God's word to the Davidic ruler) and Isa 42:1b ("my chosen, in whom my soul delights"—God's word to the servant).

But there is another, more disturbing element: the word *beloved* (v. 11) which comes not from the psalmist nor from the prophet but from Gen 22:2. This is the story about a brush with death of another "beloved son"—Isaac. For Jesus there will be no ram in the thicket; he will give his life to redeem others (10:45).

The Spirit Thrusts Jesus
into Battle with Satan, 1:12-13

Here the narrator introduces the conflict that will drive the plot of the Gospel: the cosmic conflict between Jesus, God's agent, and Satan, leader of the resistance to God's reign. Later in the Gospel, Satan will be identified with Beelzebul, the chief of the demons (3:22-27). The exorcisms, which will begin in 1:21-27, will demonstrate that Jesus was the victor in this desert encounter.

In ancient thought, human beings who could remain unharmed in the presence of wild animals were believed to be the recipients of divine favor and protection; Romulus, the founder of Rome, was believed to have been saved from starvation by a wolf. In the Israelite wisdom traditions, it was the righteous sage who was protected against wild animals (Ps 91:11-13). According to Isa 11:6-9, all humanity will be at peace with the animals in the reign of God, when "a shoot shall come out from the stump of Jesse" upon whom "the spirit of the Lord shall rest" (11:1-2). Thus, the narrative logic is complete when, immediately after the wilderness testing scene, the Markan Jesus announces that God's reign is imminent (1:14-15).

Ministry in Galilee
and in Gentile Territory, 1:14–8:30

The first major section of the Gospel is an interpretation of the in-breaking reign of God in Jesus' ministry of teaching, exorcism, healing, and forgiveness. The section begins with Jesus' initial proclamation of God's reign in 1:14-15 and concludes with Peter's identification of Jesus as the one anointed to bring in God's reign (8:27-30).

The portrait of Jesus presented by the evangelist combines elements of the OT prophetic traditions, Davidic kingship motifs, and Hellenistic understandings of the wandering teacher/philosopher and his band of followers. This enabled both gentiles and Jews in the audience to grasp the significance of Jesus and his revelation of God.

Paradigmatic Beginning
of Jesus' Ministry, 1:14–3:12

The section 1:14–8:30 is made up of three overlapping subsections: 1:14–3:12, 3:7–6:30, and 6:14–8:30. These develop the audience's understanding of Jesus progressively, beginning with a paradigmatic depiction of the various aspects of his ministry in 1:14–3:12. This subsection may be outlined as follows: Introductory summary of Jesus' message (1:14-15); Calling the first disciples (1:16-20); Jesus' power over illness and demonic oppression (1:21-45); Jesus' authority to forgive sins and interpret scripture (2:1–3:6); Concluding summary of Jesus' healings and exorcisms (3:7-12).

1:14-15. Introductory summary of Jesus' message. Returning to Galilee after his baptism and encounter with Satan in the Judean desert, Jesus begins to proclaim "the good message of God" (τὸ εὐαγγέλιον τοῦ θεοῦ, v. 14). The deliberate ambiguity informs the audience that God's message, proclaimed by Jesus, originates with God and is a message about God. Specifically, it is a message about the kingdom of God, that is, God's reign or sovereignty, which has come near (ἤγγικεν).

This is an eschatological message, because, although God is the rightful sovereign over all creation, God's sovereignty is presently contested by evil and its human agents. In Jesus' ministry the reign of God that will soon be fully present is experienced in a preliminary way by those who encounter Jesus. His teaching and ministry of power prefigure the final defeat of all opposition to God's sovereignty and show what life will be like when God reigns unopposed (Boring 1987, 131).

The appropriate response to this proclamation is repentance and trust (v. 15). The two are related; only the one who trusts that God, and not evil, is ultimately in control is prepared to undergo the change of mindset and attitude signified by the imperative *Repent!* Those who persist in holding a human outlook rather than adopting God's view of reality (8:33b) are not ready to trust the good news that God reigns.

1:16-20. Calling the first disciples. The author of Mark does not narrate the call of each individual named in the list of disciples (3:16-19). The call story at the beginning of the Galilean ministry is meant to characterize the summons to all disciples: they are to follow Jesus, who will cause them to fish for people (v. 17).

In this story the Markan Jesus does not behave in the way that was most typical of rabbis or philosophers in antiquity. Jewish rabbis and most pagan philosophers did not recruit followers. Rather, those who wanted to learn sought out a teacher and requested permission to become a disciple. However, the Greek writer Diogenes Laertius repeats two call stories that are similar to the story in Mark 1:16-20.

In one story the philosopher Socrates encounters Xenophon in an alley and asks him where various kinds of food can be bought. Xenophon answers correctly. Socrates then asks where people can become good and honorable. When Xenophon does not know the answer, Socrates says to him, "Then follow me and learn."

The second story concerns Zeno, the founder of Stoicism. He is portrayed as sitting in a book shop reading Xenophon's biography of Socrates. Impressed with the life of the great philosopher, Zeno asks where men like Socrates might be found. At that moment Crates, a disciple of Socrates was passing by, so the bookseller pointed to him and said to Zeno, "Follow that man." Zeno then became Crates' disciple.

The similarities with the Markan call story are: (1) people are engaged in the daily activities of life with no thought of seeking a teacher; (2) a teacher suddenly attracts their attention; (3) there is an imperative summons to "follow"; and (4) they respond by becoming disciples.

It is likely that the author of Mark chose this model over the more common one in which the student seeks a teacher because this summons/response pattern conforms more closely with the theology of the OT. In the

OT God takes the initiative, calling into a covenant relationship people who are going about their business with no thought of being called by God. This is true of Abraham (Gen 12:1-4), Jacob (Gen 28:10-17), Moses (Exod 3:1-6), and Israel as a people (Deut 6:21-25).

The initiative of God is also an important feature of prophetic call stories (Amos 7:14-15; Jer 1:5). Isaiah speaks of Israel as "called" by God (42:6; 49:1). The Markan Jesus calls disciples in a way that conforms to the biblical understanding of the way God relates to the chosen people.

The specific promise of the Markan Jesus is that those who had been catching fish would now catch human beings (v. 17). Again the evangelist is drawing upon a metaphor that would have been familiar to both the Jewish and the gentile members of his audience. The analogy of fishing was used in the Israelite wisdom tradition as well as in Greek educational philosophy to speak about the way in which people were lured by the bait of the teacher's ideas and thus were prevented from wasting their lives in meaningless pursuits.

Greeks hoped to be caught in the nets of the gods rather than being snared by the evil spirits that were also out fishing for people. The Hebrew prophets spoke of Israel's enemies as God's fishers, gathering in the people of Israel for judgment—a judgment designed to lead to their repentance and return to covenant faithfulness (Ezek 17:19-21; Jer 16:16). So when Jesus' disciples go out to heal and to preach that people should repent (6:12) they are fulfilling Jesus' promise that they will become fishers for people.

1:21-45. Healings and exorcisms. This section and the one that follows it are both organized in the literary form of the chiasm, sometimes called a "concentric" or "ring" composition:

A Jesus makes a demon "go out from" a man.
    Jesus contrasted with the scribes, 21-27
    B Jesus' reputation goes from a synagogue
        into "all Galilee," 28
        C Simon's mother-in-law
           is healed by Jesus, 29-31
           D Summary: healings and exorcisms,
               Jesus' identity, 32-34
        C' Simon interrupts Jesus' prayer, 35-38
    B' Jesus goes into synagogues in "all Galilee," 39
A' Jesus makes leprosy "go off of" a man.
    Jesus contrasted with the priests, 40-45.

The parallel elements will be considered together.

In A (vv. 21-27) Jesus casts a demon out of a man in the Capernaum synagogue. The response of the people is noteworthy. They exclaim, *What is this? A new teaching—with authority! He commands even the unclean spirits, and they obey him.* In this way the evangelist makes the point that Jesus' teaching includes not only what he says, but also what he does. His teaching and his healings and exorcisms form a unified whole. One is not more normative than the other.

In A' (vv. 40-45) the disease the Bible calls LEPROSY seems to have been thought of as demonic in character, at least in an early stage of the transmission of this story. Three elements in the story are more characteristic of exorcism stories than of healing stories: (1) Jesus' anger in v. 41 (see note *n* in the NRSV) and in v. 43; (2) the verb "cast out" (ἐξέβαλεν) in v. 43; (3) the report of the result of Jesus' action in v. 42 (*Immediately the leprosy left him*; cf. v. 26: "it [the demon] went out of him").

In both stories Jesus' authority and power are contrasted with those of the religious establishment. He has authority that they do not have and he can make a leper clean, whereas they can only give official recognition to the cure that has already taken place.

The hostility toward Jesus that becomes explicit in 2:1–3:6 is prepared for by these two stories. Jesus' behavior disrupts the established lines of teaching authority and the traditional ways of dealing with uncleanness. He should have become ritually unclean when he touched the leper; instead, the leper became clean. Because healing leprosy was understood as something that only God could do (2 Kgs 5:7) this story makes it clear that Jesus' power and authority are not his but God's. As *the Holy One of God* he has indeed *come to destroy* the demons and illnesses that afflict humankind (1:24). But he will be persecuted because his authority comes from God and not from the religious establishment.

In B (v. 28) Jesus' reputation goes out *throughout the surrounding region of Galilee.* This notice prepares for B' (v. 39), when Jesus himself goes into synagogues *throughout Galilee.*

Simon, the first disciple Jesus called (v. 16), plays a role in both C (vv. 29-31) and C' (vv. 35-38). In vv. 29-31 the Markan Jesus heals Simon's mother-in-law. She responds by "serving" (v. 31). It is customary in a healing story for the last element in the story to constitute some kind of proof that the person has indeed been restored to health. But in this story, the nameless woman's service has another point; it is the mark of a

true follower of Jesus, as James and John will be reminded in 10:45.

Simon appears again in C' (vv. 35-38), where he and his companions seek Jesus, who has slipped out of CAPERNAUM before dawn to pray. Like so many sincere activists in today's churches, Simon sees no point in wasting time in prayer when there are hurting people back in Capernaum to be helped. The contrast in the story is between Simon's human-centered concerns and Jesus' focus on God as the source of his direction and his power to heal. Jesus is not lacking in compassion, but he demonstrates the importance of putting priority on the discovery and the doing of God's will. In this case, his assignment is not to continue healing people in Capernaum, but to move out into other areas.

The central part of the chiasm (vv. 32-34) sums up the healing and exorcistic activity of Jesus, which the individual stories are intended to illustrate. Jesus attracts large numbers of the sick and demon-possessed and restores them to wholeness. Here for the first time the evangelist introduces a theme that will become increasingly problematic as the story progresses: the issue of Jesus' identity: *He would not permit the demons to speak, because they knew him* (v. 34).

Indeed the demons do know him; the one in v. 24 knows that he is *the Holy One of God* and that he has *come to destroy* the demons. The disciples, however, do not do as well as the demons; they puzzle over Jesus' identity and fail to understand him despite their close association and private instruction. Indeed, the last words on the lips of any disciple in the Gospel are "I don't know the person of whom you are speaking" (14:71, author trans.).

Since the audience of the Gospel has been fully informed about Jesus' identity since 1:1, the disciples' confusion and Jesus' puzzling commands to silence create a tension and expectation that contribute to the movement of the narrative.

By the end of the section Jesus' fame has spread so widely that he *could no longer go into a town openly* (v. 45) without being overwhelmed by the numbers of people coming to him.

2:1–3:6. Controversies. The previous section demonstrated Jesus' authority and power over demons and illness—an authority that was superior to that of the religious establishment. In this section, which is also arranged chiastically, the author of Mark tells five controversy stories which demonstrate Jesus' authority to forgive sins and to interpret scripture in nontraditional ways.

Jesus' authority to forgive sins is linked by the evangelist with his specific concern for sinners, rather than for righteous people who seek no forgiveness. According to Mark, protecting and enforcing religious law is not the focus of Jesus' ministry. Jesus and his followers, past and present, serve a God who is interested in reconciling sinners, feeding the hungry, and healing the sick.

This focus puts Jesus in conflict with religious people whose power depends upon identifying and ostracizing sinners. At first their opposition is limited to private criticism (2:6), but by the end of the section they are plotting to destroy Jesus (3:6).

It is important to note that the author of Mark does not criticize Jews or Jewish leaders as such. That is to say, Mark does not sanction anti-Semitism. Rather, like the OT prophets, the evangelist points out that God's reign runs counter to the claims of all who attempt to preempt God's sovereign authority, even those who claim to represent God. The section may be outlined as follows (Dewey 1980):

A Healing of paralytic. Controversy plus healing
    [call of Levi (2:13-16) echoes 1:16-20
      and prepares for 2:15-17], 2:1-12
    B Controversy over eating. Jesus and his disciples
      eat with the wrong people, 2:15-17
      C Controversy over fasting (not eating), 2:18-22
    B' Controversy over eating. Jesus' disciples acquire
      food in the wrong way, 2:23-28
A' Healing of withered hand.
    Controversy plus healing, 3:1-6

The parallel passages will be discussed together.

A (2:1-12) and A' (3:1-6) lay the groundwork for the two trials of Jesus and establish his innocence ahead of time. In 2:7 the scribes accuse Jesus of blasphemy (cf. 14:64) because he exercises God's prerogative to forgive sins. They are correct that only God can do this, but they miss the point. The audience realizes that Jesus is not blaspheming because his authority comes from God.

It is not illegal on the SABBATH to command a person to stand up in the SYNAGOGUE and stretch out his hand (3:1-5). Jesus has done nothing wrong (cf. 15:14). His opponents are the guilty ones because they plot to commit murder, which is not legal on any day of the week. Jesus saves life (3:4); for this he will die.

B (2:15-17) and B' (2:23-28) emphasize God's initiative toward human beings. The community whose life is centered on fellowship with Jesus is a community of sinners and their religious practice represents God's provision for their benefit, not their attempt to please God.

The call of Levi (2:13-16) is important preparation for the controversy over eating with sinners because tax collectors (publicans) were not only regarded as dishonest, but were also despised as collaborators with the Roman overlords. Revolutionary groups who might have applauded Jesus' association with the poor peasants would have been appalled by his association with the running dogs of Roman imperialism.

But the Markan Jesus is not captive to ideological categories. The only requirement for his company is to understand oneself as a sinner—no better than the lowest form of human being one can imagine. "If you don't consider yourself to be in that category," the Gospel writer says, "then don't count yourself among the associates of Jesus."

If the point of Christian community is *not* to avoid sinners, then the point of sabbath observance is *not* to be religious, but rather to meet human need. *The sabbath was made for humankind, not humankind for the sabbath* (2:27). Furthermore, Jesus, the Son of Man, is lord even over the sabbath and over the scriptures, which he interprets to prove his point: David broke religious laws to feed his hungry troops (1 Sam 21:1-6). The Gospel writer cites David's act during the days of ABIATHAR, which poses a problem for careful readers of the Bible.

Right in the center of the chiastic structure is the controversy over fasting (2:18-22). In an oblique reference to the CRUCIFIXION, the Markan Jesus speaks of a time when he (the bridegroom) will be *taken away* (v. 20). That will be the time for fasting.

The discussion about fasting leads into a pair of sayings on the relationship between the old and the new. The good news that Jesus brings is by its very nature disruptive of old patterns. New and flexible structures are necessary, because the fermentation of the gospel will soon destroy containers that are rigid and fragile.

Taken together, 1:21-45 and 2:1–3:6 present a complete overview of Jesus' ministry, which the evangelist regards as normative for the church in his own day. The church is about the business of teaching, healing, casting out demons, building a community of sinners, and meeting human needs. Jesus' authority to interpret scripture overrides that of the old establishment and creates new wineskins flexible enough to allow for the gospel's disruptive bubbling.

But it is not a cheap victory. It will cost Jesus his life and it will cost his followers every shred of security and self-righteousness.

3:7-12. Conclusion. The large section 1:14–3:12, which establishes the basic pattern of Jesus' ministry, concludes with a summary in 3:7-12. The return to the sea with the disciples (3:7) forms an INCLUSIO with the original calling of the disciples by the sea (1:16).

There Jesus had promised to make the former fishermen into fishers for people. Here the audience learns that Jesus himself is a successful people-fisher; not only has he attracted crowds from Galilee, but people have come from long distances after hearing about him.

The summary reemphasizes Jesus' ministry of healing and exorcism and reminds the audience that although the demons knew Jesus' true identity as Son of God, Jesus did not permit them to make him known to others.

Extension of Jesus' Ministry and Intensification of Conflict, 3:7–6:30

3:7-12. Introduction. This summary serves not only to conclude the previous section, but also to introduce places and ideas that will be important in the second and third major sections of the ministry in Galilee and gentile territory.

The crowd that follows Jesus includes people from Galilee, Judea, Jerusalem (which is in Judea), Idumea (home territory of the Herodians), the territory east of the Jordan River, and the region around TYRE AND SIDON (Phoenicia). Information that sick people were pressing around Jesus attempting to touch him prepares for the story of the hemorrhaging woman (5:25-34).

The mention of Tyre and Sidon prepares for Jesus' visit there in 7:24-30 and explains to the audience why the SYROPHOENICIAN woman expected Jesus to be able to exorcise her daughter. According to Mark, gentile followers of Jesus had spread the word in their home territory about the miracles they had seen in Galilee.

The boat that will become the platform for Jesus' teaching in 4:1 and the means by which he himself ventures into gentile territory in 5:1 is introduced in 3:9. The material in 3:13–6:30 may be outlined as follows:

A Disciples appointed ("sent out ones,"
   sent out, 3:14), 3:13-19
   B Misinterpretation by family
      and religious leaders, 3:20-35

C Jesus' words and deeds heard and seen
   but not always understood, 4:1–5:43
   1. Jesus' words (collection of parables),
      4:1-34
   2. Jesus' deeds (collection of miracle
      stories), 4:35–5:43
B' Misinterpretation by associates in home town,
   6:1-6
A' Disciples *sent out* ("sent out ones," 6:30), 6:7-13

3:13-19. Disciples appointed. As Baptist translator Helen Barrett Montgomery points out, the word translated "apostle" in most English Bibles actually means "missionary" or "one sent out" (1924, Mark 3:14, n. 1). Thus the material in 3:13–6:30 is framed by an emphasis on Christian mission (3:13-19 and 6:7-13, 30).

But the author of Mark is careful to make clear that mission *follows* a period of developing a relationship with Jesus:

And he appointed twelve (whom he also named
missionaries) in order that
   (1) they might be with him and in order that
   (2) he might commission them
      (a) to proclaim and
      (b) to have authority to cast out the demons
and he appointed the twelve (author trans.).

In the ancient world it was thought that a disciple could not properly carry out the instructions of the teacher without first spending a great deal of time in the teacher's presence. The Gospel of Mark applies this insight to Christian formation.

The active ministry of the disciples is patterned after that of Jesus himself: proclamation (cf. 1:14) and spiritual warfare (cf. 1:21-27, 34, 39; 3:11-12), speech and action. Neither is optional and one may not be substituted for the other. It is worth noting that the authority of the disciples extends only to demons. They are given no authority over other followers of Jesus.

In Mark, THE TWELVE named in chap. 3 do not constitute an inside group of disciples who have special privileges. The size of the group called "disciples" or "followers" of Jesus varies from scene to scene in Mark, and includes, besides the twelve named here, Levi (2:14), *many* tax collectors and sinners (2:15), Mary Magdalene, Mary the mother of James and Joses, Salome (15:40), Bartimaeus (10:52), and the Gethsemane "streaker" (14:51). The greatest privilege bestowed in the Gospel seems to be the gift of "the mystery of the reign of God" (4:11 author trans.), and that gift is said to have been given to a group larger than the twelve. Thus, "twelve" should be understood as symbolic of the new people of God; the number corresponds to the twelve tribes of Israel in the OT. It does not delineate an exclusive group.

3:20-35. Misinterpretation by family and religious leaders. In this unit, a controversy with the scribes is framed by the misunderstanding of Jesus by his family of origin and their replacement by "those who do the will of God" (author trans.). Since the controversy involves two charges by opponents, to which Jesus responds in reverse order, the result is a chiastic structure (Robbins 1989, 172, n. 27):

A Jesus' family comes to seize him, 20-21
   B Accusation 1: He has Beelzebul, 22a
      C Accusation 2: By the prince of demons
         he casts out demons, 22b
      C' Refutation 2: Satan would not
         cast out demons, 23-27
   B' Refutation 1: Saying Jesus has an unclean spirit
      is blasphemy, 28-30
A' Jesus' true family consists of those
    who do the will of God, 31-35

In 3:21, members of Jesus' family respond to the crowds that he is attracting by coming out to seize him because in their opinion Jesus is out of his mind (ἐξέστη, lit. "standing outside [himself]"). In 3:31, however, the evangelist turns the tables; now the family is standing outside (ἔξω στήκοντες) by contrast with those who are seated around Jesus on the inside.

The Markan Jesus explains that his kin are not those who are related to him by blood, but those who are related to him by sharing his purpose: doing the will of God. The message to the audience is twofold: (1) Sometimes even one's own relatives will think one crazy for doing the will of God; (2) Those whose relatives misunderstand their Christian commitment find a new family in the Christian community, just as Jesus did (cf. 10:29-30).

When the scribes accuse Jesus of having Beelzebul and of using that demon's power to perform exorcisms, the audience would have understood that they were accusing Jesus of practicing magic. Magicians were believed to have gained control of spirits that they could call upon to do their bidding. Spells and incantations were used to force the gods and spirits to do the will of the magician or witch who was casting the spell.

When an ancient miracle worker was accused of practicing magic, his defense often was to claim that he had not used incantations, but had prayed. He was not, after all, a magician trying to force the gods to do his will, but a pious person who did only the will of the gods. So when the author of Mark portrays Jesus and his followers as those who "do the will of God" he is relying upon a commonly accepted line of argument to make his point.

Further, the Markan Jesus responds to his opponents by pointing out that it would be inconsistent for Satan, the ruler of demons, to allow his power to be used to cast out demons. Finally, the audience is reminded of the real source of Jesus' power—the Holy Spirit that came into him at his baptism (1:8, 10). The scribes' false attribution of the work of the Holy Spirit to Satan is not an innocent mistake. It is an unpardonable sin.

As the scene closes Jesus and his associates are inside and those who misunderstand and oppose him are standing outside. This contrast between insiders and outsiders, which seems so clear-cut in this passage, will become increasingly problematic as the story progresses.

4:1-34. Jesus' words (parables). The parable chapter is the first of only two long speeches by the Markan Jesus. The other is the apocalyptic discourse in chap. 13. In fact, both speeches are primarily about eschatology. In chap. 4 the author of Mark combines PARABLES and sayings from the Jesus tradition to explain why the proclamation of God's reign is meeting with resistance and to assure the audience that despite the present apparent lack of progress, God's reign will eventually burst forth in amazing fruitfulness.

A secondary and related concern of chaps. 4 and 13 is a warning against apostasy. This is regarded by the evangelist as a danger even for those who have experienced God's grace mediated through Jesus.

The author of Mark has arranged the material into a carefully constructed chiastic arrangement (Marcus 1986, 221):

A Narrative introduction, 1-2
  B Seed parable (public teaching), 3-9
    C Statement about hiddenness
      (private teaching), 10-12
      D Allegorical explanation of parable
        (private teaching), 13-20
    C' Statements about revelation
      (private teaching), 21-25
  B' Seed parables (public teaching), 26-29, 30-32
A' Narrative conclusion, 33-34

According to this arrangement, all three seed parables are addressed to the crowd that assembles in 4:1 and is left behind in 4:36. This public teaching frames the private teaching to "those around him with the twelve" (v. 10, author trans.). The private teaching, while it picks up the agricultural images of the parable in the allegorical explanation (vv. 13-20), also introduces images drawn from domestic life: lamp, basket, bed, lampstand, house, and measure (vv. 21-25).

Agricultural images were commonly used by Hellenistic writers to teach lessons about education and improvement of character. They were used in the OT and in apocalyptic Judaism to teach about God's will and God's coming reign. The Markan Jesus combines these emphases, but alters the images to suit his purposes.

The seed parables (vv. 3-9, 26-29, 30-32) make three points:

(1) The ultimate success of God's reign is inevitable, despite present appearances to the contrary. Although much seed falls on unproductive soil, the good soil will yield a harvest abundant beyond all imagination.

(2) God's reign is the result of what God does, not the result of what human beings do. All the farmer has to do is sow the seed. Everything else is outside his control. This is a marked contrast with Hellenistic emphases upon the importance of human effort in producing a good "harvest," but it coincides with the apocalyptic idea that in the drama of history God is the primary actor and human beings merely respond to God's initiative.

(3) God's reign is inclusive, but not imperialistic. The parable of the mustard seed speaks of God's reign as a plant with large branches that shelter the birds of the air. In Dan 4:10-17 the BABYLONIAN EMPIRE is portrayed as a large tree; in Ezek 31:3-14 the same image is used for ASSYRIA. The author of Ezek 17:22-24 regards that image as appropriate for the glorious Messianic kingdom that was expected after the humiliation of the exile. But the Markan story deflates all this grandiosity by comparing God's reign, not to a mighty cedar, but to a humble mustard bush. It doesn't look like much, but it provides shelter for all who flock to it (Waetjen 1989, 108–109).

The sayings on hiddenness and revelation (vv. 10-12, 21-25) have presented a challenge to interpreters over the centuries. In the Markan context, three points are being made:

(1) Just as Isaiah's words were meant to prevent understanding and repentance, so Jesus' parables prevent understanding and repentance by those "outside" who oppose God's reign (vv. 10-12).

(2) Concealment is not the last word. *There is nothing hidden, except to be disclosed; nor is anything secret, except to come to light* (v. 22).

(3) Those who have been "given the secret of God's reign" (v. 11, author trans.) had better not be complacent. They need to pay attention to the insight they have (v. 24). This includes not only the disciples in the story, but the audience of the Gospel as well.

The central emphasis of the passage falls on the allegorical interpretation of the first seed parable. The Markan Jesus says that understanding this parable is critically important for understanding all the parables (v. 13).

The parable itself pointed to the ultimate success of God's reign. The interpretation explains why the present circumstances are so difficult and why so much seed fails to bear fruit. The explanation is a typically apocalyptic one: God's reign is temporarily opposed by Satan and his forces.

In the first case, Satan snatches away the word before it takes root. This is a reference to people who, although they hear the message, do not even begin as followers of Jesus.

The second and third cases are about people who begin as followers of Jesus, but fail to follow through in discipleship. Some are unable to withstand *when trouble or persecution arises on account of the word* (v. 17) and some are distracted by the concerns of the present age (an apocalyptic term), the seductive power of wealth, and the desire for "things" other than the "things of God" (8:33, author trans.). APOSTASY, according to Mark, can be a response either to difficulties or to comfortable circumstances.

When Christians encounter opposition and persecution, or when they see converts lost to the seductive addictions of increased ease and affluence, they are not to be discouraged. This is all part of the ministry to which they are called. Their part is to keep sowing. The rest is up to God.

4:35–5:43. Jesus' deeds (miracle stories). The unit of parables is followed by a unit of miracle stories. Like the parables, the miracles proclaim the reign of God and are a source of misunderstanding for some. Jesus' words are heard, but not understood; his deeds are seen, but not perceived (cf. 4:12).

The miracle stories are grouped in two pairs:
A Conquest of demonic storm, 4:35-41
   Setting: on the sea, on the way to gentile territory

Beneficiaries: male disciples
Level of threat: the disciples fear
    that they are about to die
A' Conquest of demons in GERASA, 5:1-20
    Setting: near the sea, in gentile territory
    Beneficiary: male gentile
    Level of threat: the demoniac lives among the dead
B Healing of hemorrhaging woman, 5:24b-34
    Setting: Jewish territory
    Beneficiary: female; ritually unclean;
      ill for 12 years
    Level of threat: she is in the process of dying
      (life is draining away)
B' Raising of Jairus' daughter, 5:21-24a, 35-43
    Setting: Jewish territory
    Beneficiary: female; ritually unclean corpse;
      twelve years old
    Level of threat: she is already dead
      when Jesus arrives

The confidence that God's unlimited power is at work in Jesus is called "faith" in these miracle stories (5:34). The evangelist puts them here not merely to record Jesus' past activity, but to encourage those who hear the stories to resist paralyzing fear (4:40; 5:36) and to maintain confidence in God's power to overcome evil, sickness, and death.

In the first pair of stories Jesus' role as divine warrior against evil is emphasized. The storm that Jesus and his disciples encounter on the Sea of Galilee is interpreted in the narrative as an attempt by demonic forces to keep Jesus from invading gentile territory (5:1-20). In order to make sense of the Markan Jesus' movements back and forth across the sea, the reader should consult a map of the area (MBD, plate 23). Jesus "rebukes" the storm (4:39) in the same way that he addresses the demons (1:25, 3:12). Like the demons, *the wind and the sea obey him* (4:41). The sea represents the forces of chaos and death, over which Jesus, the life-bringer, exercises control.

But the disciples are still in the dark, asking, "Who then is this?" The demons know, the audience knows, but even those who have been given the mystery of the reign of God fail to perceive the meaning in what they see.

Having resisted the onslaught of the sea demons, Jesus lands in gentile territory and immediately encounters more demons in a militant mood. A whole legion of them are tormenting a man whose days of living death are passed *among the tombs and on the*

mountains (5:5). Like Pharoah's army, however, these enemy troops rush into the sea and are drowned (5:13). Again the victory goes to the divine warrior. Chaos becomes order and wholeness (5:15).

But again Jesus' saving power is seen by blind eyes. The Gerasenes see the loss of the pigs and send Jesus away. Before he goes, he commissions the former demoniac to tell *how much the Lord has done for him* (5:19). The man's response has two effects: (1) By preaching (κηρύσσειν, cf. 1:14, 3:14), he does what disciples are supposed to do. He becomes one who makes the deeds of the Lord "known . . . among the nations" (Isa 12:4); (2) His proclamation equates the merciful activity of the Lord with the ministry of Jesus (5:20). The answer to the disciples' question, "Who then is this?" is "Jesus is the Lord."

In the second pair of stories the setting shifts from gentile to Jewish territory and the emphasis shifts from cosmic combat to healing, but the boundary-crossing character of Jesus' ministry is still apparent. Having crossed geographical boundaries to release a gentile from bondage, Jesus now crosses traditional purity boundaries to restore life to two suffering women.

Neither woman is ritually "clean" when Jesus encounters her. According to Torah, vaginal bleeding renders a woman unclean (Lev 5:19-30) and all corpses are unclean (Num 19:11-21). In these stories the theme first sounded in the cleansing of the leper (1:40-45) is repeated. Although Jesus should have become unclean by touching the bleeding woman and the dead girl, exactly the opposite happens. His touch restores both women to health and to states of ritual purity.

Both Jairus and the bleeding woman are portrayed positively as having faith in Jesus' healing power. Jairus is called upon to "keep on believing" (5:36, author trans.) for an even greater miracle than healing after his daughter is pronounced dead before Jesus' arrival.

Jairus is a leader of the synagogue—a religious and social insider. He has a right to ask for help and he does so directly, but not arrogantly. Rather than flaunting his social and religious status, he humbles himself (5:22-23), an attitude that Jesus will praise in 9:35, 10:41-45.

The anonymous woman, by contrast, has been a religious and social outsider for twelve years, experiencing neither the worship of God nor human embrace. She has no right to jeopardize Jesus' ritual status by touching him. However, she refuses to be defined by her situation and takes bold action on the basis of what she has heard about Jesus (5:27; cf. 3:10).

Whereas the parables emphasize assurance of the *final* victory of God's reign, this unit of MIRACLE STORIES promises *present* help for those who call on Jesus with confidence in his power.

6:1-6. Misinterpretation by associates in hometown. This second instance of misinterpretation of Jesus' miracle-working activity by intimate associates corresponds to 3:20-35 in Mark's chiastic outline of 3:13–6:30. Like the scribes (3:22), the people of Nazareth raise questions about the source of Jesus' power and wisdom. They recognize that Jesus is doing miraculous things and that he has been given extraordinary wisdom (v. 3), but they do not see in these phenomena the inbreaking of the reign of God. They do not admit that God is the source of Jesus' power.

They point to Jesus' ordinary occupation; he is a carpenter, not a scribe or a rabbi. He does not come from a traditional family; they call him *son of Mary* (v. 3) rather than the traditional "son of Joseph" (cf. Luke 4:22; John 6:42). The hometown boy is getting something from somewhere, but where? No one suggests God.

The evangelist comments, *they took offense at him* (ἐσκανδαλίζοντο ἐν αὐτῷ). This phrase can mean two things in Mark. In 4:17; 9:42-47; and 14:27 it means to be caused to abandon allegiance to Jesus after beginning as a disciple. Here, however, it is used of nonfollowers and means that the people of Nazareth were prevented from becoming Jesus' disciples.

The people of Nazareth are like the seed that fell beside the path: they never take root at all. Their opinions of who Jesus is prevent their seeing God at work in his miracles. Jesus is amazed by their unbelief.

In the miracle stories (4:35–5:43), to "have faith" means to have confidence in Jesus' power. Here the evangelist expands the definition beyond that. To recognize that Jesus has power is not enough; it is necessary to recognize that Jesus' power and wisdom come from God, and from no other source.

The conclusion of this scene is strangely paradoxical. The evangelist says that *[Jesus] could do no deed of power there* and then says *he laid his hands on a few sick people and cured them* (v. 5). The reason for this odd sentence is that the author of Mark wants to summarize his complex view of the relationship between faith and miracles.

On the one hand, confidence in Jesus' power (faith) is basic if the Christian community expects to experience that power in its life and ministry (5:34, 36; 9:23; 10:52). On the other hand, there are no absolute conditions that can limit God's freedom to act in sovereign power. Even when faith is inadequate, grace may extend miraculous help (4:35-41; 6:5; 9:24-27).

The Markan Jesus summarizes the misunderstanding of Nazareth with a traditional proverb: *Prophets are not without honor, except in their hometown, and among their own kin, and in their own house* (v. 4). Many Christians have found it so.

6:7-13, 30. Disciples sent out. The large section 3:13–6:30 concludes with Jesus' sending out of the disciples to do the ministry to which he had appointed them at the beginning of the section (3:13-19). Having now been with Jesus (3:14b) and observed his ministry of word (4:1-34) and deed (4:35–5:43), the disciples are ready to be sent out in pairs to proclaim repentance and to exercise Jesus' authority over the demonic spirits. They also bring God's healing to the sick.

There is no hint here of the kind of dispensationalist understanding of miracle that came to characterize the church in later generations. The author of Mark believes that Jesus' followers are to replicate his ministry. They do not do this alone, but with others. There are no superstars or lone rangers.

Finally the evangelist stresses accountability. Mark 6:30 is not merely a narrative conclusion. It suggests that disciples will give an account of their faithfulness to the one who sent them out.

In Mark 6:8-11 the Gospel writer sets out instructions for missionaries. They are allowed to have a walking stick and a pair of sandals, which are all they need to get from one place to another. They are not allowed to carry bread, money, a begging bag, or an extra tunic. For the necessities of life they will have to depend on God and God's people. Like the Israelites who lived from one day's supply of manna to the next, they are radically dependent on God's providential care.

The rejection that missionaries encounter is not regarded as a surprising development, but as an expected outcome. The response is to be neither discouragement nor vindictive reprisal, but continued ministry elsewhere. The result is not the problem of the sowers. All they have to do is sow.

Jesus' Ministry Removes Barriers between Jews and Gentiles, 6:14–8:30

This third and final subsection of 1:14–8:30 picks up and expands the theme of the inclusion of the gentiles that was introduced in 5:1-20. The section is framed by identical speculations about Jesus' identity:

Is he John the baptizer reincarnated? Is he Elijah, the forerunner of the Messiah? Is he some other prophet? (6:14-16; 8:27-30).

In chap. 6 the question of Jesus' identity is left hanging, but the question of whether his opponents will succeed in destroying him (3:6, 3:19) is clarified in a chilling flashback. The execution of John the baptizer suggests that the prospects are grim for those who run afoul of Herod and his partisans.

Beginning at 6:31, Jesus feeds and heals first Jews (6:31-56) and then gentiles (7:24–8:10). Between the ministry to Jews and the ministry to gentiles, a discussion with Pharisees over the proper understanding of religious defilement (7:1-23) prepares for the move to the gentiles in 7:24.

The section closes with summaries illustrating the failure by Jesus' opponents (8:11-13) and by his disciples (8:14-21) to perceive the significance of his ministry. The arrival at Bethsaida in 8:22 marks the end of the sea crossings that began in 4:35; the story of the blind man healed in two stages (8:22-26) prepares for the discipleship section 8:22–10:52, which ends with the only other healing of blindness in Mark (10:46-52).

6:14-29. Death of John the baptizer. The execution of John the baptizer by Herod Antipas is confirmed by Josephus (*Ant* 18.5.2), who understood it as an attempt to prevent John's organizing a political revolution. Mark's macabre interpretation of the episode is designed to foreshadow the passion of Jesus and perhaps also to suggest future suffering for his followers, who have just been sent out on their first assignment.

It is important to notice the artistry of this story, which is one of the more obvious of the Markan "sandwiched" narratives. The story is told between the sending of the disciples in vv. 7-13 and their return in v. 30. After the disciples have been sent out, the narrator informs the audience that "King Herod heard of it, for Jesus' name had become known."

Herod's participation in the speculation about Jesus' identity prepares for the narrative flashback of vv. 17-29. Herod's own conclusion is that Jesus' power is due to the fact that he is a reincarnation of the executed prophet. This failure to identify God as the source of Jesus' power has already been labeled "unbelief" by the evangelist (6:1-6).

The Markan account of the circumstances leading to John's death is the longest and most melodramatic that has been preserved. It is also replete with OT allusions. By calling Herod the tetrarch a "king" and by making John's criticism of Herod's immoral marriage

(Lev 18:16, 20:21) the reason for his imprisonment, the evangelist identifies John with the long line of prophets who rebuked kings (1 Sam 15:17-29; 2 Sam 12:1-15; 2 Kgs 20:16-18; Jer 38:14-23) and of martyrs who upheld the law in the face of royal opposition (2 Macc 6:18–7:42; 4 Macc 5–18).

The primary prophet that the author of Mark has in mind, however, is Elijah, with whom he identifies John elsewhere in the Gospel (1:6-7; 9:11-13). In this story Herodias plays Jezebel to John's Elijah. But whereas Jezebel was unsuccessful in eliminating Elijah, Herodias succeeds in destroying John.

The involvement of the young daughter is a particularly chilling detail. Textual variants make it uncertain whether the evangelist regards her as the daughter of Herodias only, or also of Herod (see NRSV v. 22, mrg). Commentators usually assume that the dance was erotic, although this is likewise uncertain. What is plain, however, is that she is put by the evangelist into the same age group as Jairus's twelve-year-old daughter. The same word (κοράσιον) is used for both. One little daughter is restored to life; one participates in a grisly murder. It is the child who adds the detail of the platter. John's head is the final course in this macabre banquet (Anderson 1992).

John's headless body is claimed by his disciples and laid in a tomb. When Jesus' time for burial comes, however, his disciples will be nowhere to be found.

6:30-56. Ministry to Jews. This section has three parts: the feeding miracle (vv. 31-44), the sea-walking story (vv. 45-52), and a series of healings (vv. 53-56). The first and third take place on the western side of the Sea of Galilee, that is, in Jewish territory. The three-part series opens and closes with references to the crowds that surround Jesus and the disciples (v. 31 [cf. 3:19]; vv. 54-56).

In the first of two feeding miracles in the Gospel, Jesus is portrayed as the faithful shepherd promised to Israel in the prophetic and APOCALYPTIC LITERATURE (Ezek 34:23; Jer 23:4; PssSol 17:40). Because both Moses (Exod 3:1) and David (1 Sam 16:11) had been shepherds, the shepherd became a metaphor for the religious and political leaders of Israel and also for Yahweh, Israel's ultimately faithful shepherd.

The prophets criticized Israel's leaders for being irresponsible shepherds (Isa 56:11-12; Jer 23:1-2; Ezek 34:1-10), or for leaving the people unprotected, without a shepherd (Ezek 34:5; cf. Num 27:17; 1 Kgs 22:17; cf. Isa 53:6). Through the prophets, Yahweh promised to replace the unworthy shepherds, either by shepherding the people himself, or by raising up a faithful shepherd, usually a Davidic leader (Ezek 34:11-16; Jer 23:3-6; Isa 40:11; 49:9b-10).

By invoking these images in v. 34, the author of Mark proclaims the good news that the eschatological shepherd has arrived to provide for the needs of God's people. As their shepherd, Jesus teaches the crowds (v. 34b), provides them with food (v. 42; cf. Ezek 34:2, 8; Isa 40:11; Ps 23:2), and heals their sick and injured (vv. 53-56; cf. Ezek 34:4). There is also an implicit criticism of the religious leaders who oppose Jesus; they are the irresponsible shepherds condemned by the prophets.

The desert setting of the feeding miracle (vv. 34-35) reminds the audience of the Isaian theme of the New Exodus (Mark 1:3) and of God's miraculous provision of manna during the original Exodus. Both this story and its gentile counterpart (8:1-10) foreshadow the last meal Jesus will share with his disciples. There, as in the feeding stories, Jesus takes bread, pronounces a thanksgiving or a blessing, breaks the bread, and gives it to his disciples (14:22). Not only is the hunger of the crowd satisfied, but the leftovers fill twelve large baskets typically used by Jews for carrying loads. The number twelve further reinforces the Jewish cultural setting. Interestingly enough, the disciples, who have just returned from a mission on which they were forbidden to take bread (v. 8), manage, when pressed, to produce five loaves and two fish (v. 38).

After the feeding the Markan Jesus sends the disciples across the sea toward Bethsaida on the *other side* (v. 45), that is, in gentile territory. Jesus dismisses the crowd and, like Moses and Elijah before him, retires to the mountain to meet with God.

It soon becomes apparent, however, that without Jesus' leadership the disciples are not going to make it to gentile territory; again they are meeting with opposition, as in 4:35-41. Seeing this, the Markan Jesus again demonstrates his superiority over the hostile sea power by striding across the sea (vv. 47-52), an activity attributed to God in Job 9:8 and Isa 43:16. His intent was to walk ahead of them—to guide them, like a good shepherd, to their destination. However, the disciples do not recognize him and cry out in fear.

Continuing the imagery of the New Exodus, the narrator has Jesus identify himself with the self-designation of Yahweh, "I am" (Exod 3:14, Isa 41:4, 43:10-11). Thus the author of Mark provides the audience with a defintive answer to the question raised by the disciples in the previous sea-rescue story: *Who then is*

this? (4:41). The promise of deliverance is reinforced by an echo of Deutero-Isaiah's *Do not be afraid* (v. 50; cf. Isa 43:10, 43; 45:18; 51:2). Sadly, none of this clarifies things for the disciples, who remain "utterly astounded."

Their astonishment reveals that they have missed the exodus allusions completely. They *did not understand about the loaves* (v. 52—the renewal of provision in the wilderness), or about Jesus' being the eschatological shepherd who takes care of his own, or about the way being made for God's people through the sea and the desert, or about Jesus' revelation of the character of God and God's reign in his person and ministry.

Worse yet, the narrator informs the audience that, like Jesus' opponents (3:5) and *those outside* (4:10-12, alluding to Isa 6:9-10) their hearts have been hardened. Despite their having been chosen and sent out on a successful mission, despite their having just participated in Jesus' own miraculous ministry, the disciples seem to be in danger of becoming outsiders. The narrator leaves the audience no room for complacency.

The trip to gentile territory aborted, Jesus and the disciples disembark at Gennesaret on the Jewish shore and are immediately surrounded by people seeking healing (vv. 53-55). As their shepherd, it is Jesus' responsibility to heal them (Ezek 34:4) and he does so. Echoing 3:10 and 5:24b-34, the narrator reports that people were healed merely by touching Jesus' clothes (v. 56).

This series of three episodes repeats the pattern seen throughout the Gospel in which Jesus' ministry has three components: teaching, healing, and domination of the demonic powers. The pervasive image throughout this series is the Jewish expectation of the eschatological shepherd who will feed, heal, and lead his flock to safety through watery chaos and threatening wilderness. The next section of the Gospel redefines membership in this eschatological flock.

7:1-23, Redefinition of clean/unclean, Coming immediately after the teaching, feeding, and healing of the Jewish crowds, this section prepares for the mission to the gentiles by challenging the understanding of defilement represented as that of the religious establishment and by asserting Jesus' authority to replace ritual boundaries with ethical ones. The Markan Jesus does not eliminate the notion of impurity; rather, he redefines it.

The literary structure follows the pattern set in 3:20–4:34: a controversy with authorities from Jerusalem is followed by a parable and its private interpretation to the inquiring disciples. The controversy (7:1-13) appears to be over the validity of the oral law. At a deeper level, it is about the way in which human sinfulness uses religion as a way of avoiding confrontation with God.

The parable (vv. 14-15) and its interpretation (vv. 17-23) deny the polluting character of nonkosher foods and insist that impurity is caused by behaviors that destroy human community. That this material was understood by some early readers as a literary parallel to the parables in chap. 4 is indicated by the addition of v. 16: "Let anyone with ears to hear listen," which is a scribal attempt to achieve conformity with 4:9, 23.

Whether or not one must perform ritual hand rinsing before eating (vv. 1-5) must not have been a burning issue for Christians at the time the gospel was written, since the evangelist finds it necessary to explain the practice in a long parenthesis (vv. 3-4). The religious leaders want to know why Jesus' disciples do not observe the oral traditions *of the elders* prescribing such cleansing rituals (v. 5). Jesus' answer is given in chiastic form (Gundry 1993, 349):

A Biblical citation from the prophets
(Isa 29:13, LXX) with application, 7:6-7
B Accusation: *You abandon the commandment of God and hold to human tradition*, 7:8
B' Accusation: *You have a fine way of rejecting the commandment of God in order to keep your tradition*, 7:9
A' Biblical citation from the law of Moses
(Exod 20:12; 21:17) with application, 7:10-13

The Markan Jesus asserts that the oral tradition was not, as its proponents thought, a way of guaranteeing faithfulness to God's will by building a fence around Torah. Instead, people had found a way to put religion to their own use; a veneer of religion covered a complete reversal of God's explicit commandment. Instead of honoring mother and father by providing for them, the subject of Jesus' illustration uses a religious vow to put the resources the parents need out of their reach.

Since the evangelist has to explain the meaning of *corban* (v. 11) and the handwashing issue to the audience, it is unlikely that he is attacking Jewish practices familiar to and controversial among Christians or defending Christians against Jewish opponents. Rather, the author may be critiquing the tendency within the Christian community itself to prefer the practice of religion over obedience to God. Human traditions and lip service substitute for wholehearted self-surrender, as Isaiah said so well.

The parable about inside and outside (vv. 14-15) and its interpretation (vv. 17-23) complete the unit. The Markan Jesus begins as he did in 4:3 by addressing the crowd with the command, *Listen!* What follows is a change of subject from the previous discussion. There the issue was *how* one might eat; here it is *what* one may eat. The parable demands an explanation since the *word of God* so important to Jesus in v. 13 explicitly forbids the ingestion of foods that *defile* a person. Furthermore, the second claim of the parable seems to contradict Torah, which teaches that defecation does not defile the defecator (Gundry 1993, 354-55). Again, as in chap. 4, the disciples' question provides the opportunity for the evangelist to explain to the audience.

Everything turns upon an assumption that is not stated directly until v. 21, but ultimately derives from the Isaiah quotation: it is the human heart that is the locus of purity and defilement. What goes in through one's lips and down into one's stomach cannot defile because (as Torah teaches) its evacuation into the latrine does not cause impurity in the person. That which does not involve the heart does not pollute. But although what comes out of the intestines does not pollute, what comes out of the heart certainly does.

Lists of vices like the one in v. 21 are common in Hellenistic discussions of ethics (cf. Epictetus, *Diss* 2.16.45) and appear frequently in the NT (Rom 1:29-31; 1 Cor 6:9-10; Gal 5:19-21; Eph 5:5; Rev 21:8; 22:15). Everything on Mark's list is destructive of human relationships and is condemned by the OT. The Markan Jesus thus does not deny the authority of scripture, but he does revoke the food laws in favor of Isaiah's emphasis on the importance of the attitude of the heart toward God. In the evangelist's view, devotion to God results in right relationships with other human beings.

To make sure the audience does not miss the point, the author points out parenthetically that in this statement, Jesus "made all foods clean" (author trans.). Again Jesus is seen to speak *as one having authority* by contrast with the scribes (1:22). Having made all foods clean in this section, the Markan Jesus proceeds in 7:24-30 to make all persons clean as well.

7:24–8:9. Ministry to gentiles. Like 6:31-56, which described Jesus' ministry to Jews, this section consists of three stories: exorcism of a Syrophoenician woman's daughter (vv. 24-30), restoration of hearing and speech to a man (vv. 31-37), and the feeding of 4,000 in the DECAPOLIS (8:1-9). Whereas the first panel *began* with a feeding miracle, this panel *ends* with one. Both sections witness to Jesus' power to heal disease and to defeat demonic powers.

The transition from the previous material in 7:1-23 is marked by a change of setting. Jesus goes alone into Phoenicia, not to preach or to heal, but to escape (v. 24). His vacation is cut short, however, by an "uppity" woman who invades his private space with a request for help (Wahlberg 1975, 13). The narrator has prepared the audience for this story by making certain that there were people from Tyre and Sidon present in 3:7-12 to benefit from Jesus' healings and exorcisms; the audience is to understand that the woman has "heard about him" from other gentiles who have encountered the power of Jesus.

The evangelist's description of the woman specifies the three ways in which she is unworthy to make demands on Jesus: She is female, a Greek (probably meaning "pagan" by religion), and a Syrophoenician by race. Like the Jewish father Jairus, this pagan mother bows at Jesus' feet and makes her request. She wants her daughter whole.

The Markan Jesus responds with the mission strategy that everyone knew was the right one: Jew first, then gentile (Isaiah; Luke–Acts; Rom 1:16; 2:9-10). It isn't right, he says, to take the bread from the table of the descendants (τέκνων, v. 27) and toss it out (βαλεῖν) to the dogs. Like any Palestinian Jew, the Markan Jesus is portrayed as thinking that all urban dogs are scavengers who run wild in the streets; Jews did not have house dogs. It would be unthinkable to deprive the descendants of Abraham of their due in order to minister to gentile dogs.

The woman responds out of a different cultural context. For her it is not a matter of sequence but of simultaneity. "In our culture," she explains, "the children (παιδίων, v. 28) and the house dogs eat at the same time" (Dufton 1989, 417). By changing the cultural context, the woman appeals to the experience of her people; they were receiving the benefits of Jesus' ministry before he ever left Galilee. They went to him before he came to them. There is enough healing for everyone all at the same time. No one need be deprived or made to wait.

By replacing the word for descendants (implying those entitled to an inheritance, 12:19) with the word Jesus will later use to describe those who are included *despite* their lack of status (9:37, 10:14), the woman completes her rhetorical coup and wins the argument

(Grimes 1991). The woman's effective sermon (λόγος, cf. 2:2, 4:33) achieves its goal; the unclean spirit leaves her daughter. Having made clean all foods in the previous section, the Markan Jesus now makes clean all races and peoples. It is worth noting that according to Mark, this anonymous woman won a place at the table not merely for her daughter, but for every gentile Christian who reads these words.

Mark next displays his lack of interest in geography by having Jesus travel north to Sidon in order to arrive in the region of the Decapolis, southeast of Phoenicia on the eastern (gentile) side of the Sea of Galilee. Here Jesus heals a deaf man, one who, although he has ears, cannot hear (8:18, cf. 4:9, 12, 23). This suggests that the spiritual deafness Jesus continues to encounter may ultimately be overcome as well.

Having made it possible for the man to hear and also to speak, Jesus promptly commands him and the witnesses to the miracle to keep silent, but to no avail. Like the Jewish leper, these gentiles ignore Jesus' instructions and proclaim (κηρύσσειν, 1:45, 7:36) his mighty works. Their words echo Gen 1:31 LXX and Isa 35:5-6. In the Gospel of Mark, even the gentiles quote the Law and the Prophets to announce the good news of God's eschatological reign.

There is no change of scene at the beginning of the story of the feeding of the 4,000; the gentile setting of 7:31-37 remains the same. What has changed is the cast of characters; the disciples have rejoined Jesus after missing every previous encounter with gentiles. Sadly, they have learned nothing from their earlier experience and repeat their despairing question, *How can one feed these people with bread here in the desert?* (8:4). Although the audience might have forgiven them for not expecting a miracle the first time, this time their dismay is inexcusable.

Jesus, however, is unperturbed by the disciples' anxiety about scarcity and again lays claim to their meager supplies. The Syrophoenician woman turns out to be right after all. When everything the disciples have is given to Jesus, he transforms it into enough to feed the whole crowd of undeserving gentiles without depriving the disciples at all. They collect enough leftovers to fill seven baskets large enough to hold a man (σπυρίς, 8:8, Acts 9:25).

This story brings the third subsection of 6:31–8:9 around to where it began—with the feeding of the 5,000 in 6:31-44. By this time everyone must surely have eyes to see and ears to hear the truth about Jesus and the inauguration of God's reign. The summaries with which the section concludes indicate that the this is *not* the case.

8:10-30. Conclusion of the Galilean ministry. The ministry of Jesus in Galilee and in gentile territory closes with three scenes that summarize the major themes of 1:14–8:9: words and deeds, controversy and opposition, blindness and deafness, scarcity and bread. The failure to hear, see, and understand that the audience has come to expect from the "outsiders" who oppose Jesus has by this time clearly become a problem for the "insiders" as well.

The last Galilean encounter with opponents (vv. 10-13) is bracketed by trips across the sea. In v. 10 Jesus and his disciples leave gentile territory and cross over to Dalmanutha. The place is unknown, but the encounter with Pharisees suggests a Jewish setting. Besides, the concluding boat trip, which begins in v. 13, is a crossing *to the other side* and the boat lands at Bethsaida on the eastern (gentile) side of the sea. Thus the setting of 8:11-12 is a Jewish one.

There are few surprises here. The audience already knows that the Pharisees and the Herodians are plotting to kill Jesus (3:6). The Pharisees are often associated with the scribes (7:1) who have been Jesus' opponents from the beginning (2:6, 16, 24).

The Pharisees' request for a sign is not equivalent to the requests for healing and exorcism that have been made to Jesus so far in the narrative. The evangelist makes this clear in two ways.

(1) They ask for a *sign* (v. 11), rather than making a specific request for a specific need. Mark's word for miracles that are portrayed in a positive light is δύναμις, "powerful act" (6:2, 5, 14; 9:39); σημεῖα, "signs," on the other hand, are understood negatively as acts done to establish one's identity or status (13:22). That is what the Pharisees request here: a sign *from heaven* as proof that Jesus is someone they should take seriously.

(2) Their motive is revealed to the audience by the omniscient narrator who knows everyone's motives in the story: they ask in order to put Jesus to the test (v. 11). Since the activity of "testing" Jesus has already been identified as the program of Satan (1:13), it is clear that the Pharisees remain opposed to Jesus' mission.

Jesus' refusal to give a sign makes two points that are theologically important to the evangelist:

(1) The miracles in the Gospel are not to be understood as "signs." They prove nothing about Jesus' identity or status. This will become even more clear

when the audience learns that *false* messiahs perform signs in order to prove who they are (13:22).

(2) The opponents' request for a sign from heaven shows that they have not understood that every aspect of Jesus' life is "from heaven." They do not recognize that God is the ground and source of Jesus' ministry (cf. 3:20-35; 6:1-6).

The last of the three boat scenes in the Gospel (vv. 14-21) brings to a climax the disciples' incomprehension. In 4:35-41 they had asked, *Who then is this?* and Jesus had asked, *Have you still no faith?* In 6:45-52 the disciples had failed to recognize Jesus and he had answered their previous question with the divine self-definition, "I am." The narrator had remarked that *they did not understand about the loaves, but their hearts were hardened* (6:52).

In this final scene it becomes clear that the disciples still do not understand about the loaves. Even after two miraculous feedings they are worried about their scarcity of bread. This is more than the Markan Jesus can tolerate, and he fires questions at them faster than they can answer: *Why are you talking about having no bread? Do you still not perceive or understand? Are your hearts hardened? Do you have eyes, and fail to see? Do you have ears, and fail to hear? And do you not remember?* (vv. 17-18). Even his review quiz on the number of baskets of leftovers after each feeding leaves them baffled.

The audience comes to the chilling realization that indeed the disciples are deaf and blind, indeed their hearts are hardened. Worse yet, these are the characteristics of *those outside* (4:10-12; Isa 6:9-10). If the disciples are to be counted among the outsiders, who is left on the inside? And how can one be sure of remaining inside, when the boundaries seem so fluid?

Finally in v. 22 Jesus and the disciples arrive in gentile Bethsaida, their destination ever since 6:45. There, Jesus heals a man of a particularly stubborn case of blindness. The story is narrated in such a way as to provide a parallel to 7:31-37 (the healing of a deaf man): Jesus arrives (7:31; 8:22a); people bring to him an afflicted person and beg Jesus to touch him (7:32; 8:22b); Jesus takes the person aside and performs some healing action (7:33; 8:23); the healing is confirmed (7:35; 8:25b); and Jesus attempts to conceal the healing from public notice (7:36; 8:26). After the devastation of vv. 14-21 these two stories hold out hope that Jesus may yet be able to heal the disciples' spiritual blindness and deafness as well.

The issue of Jesus' identity closes the large section 6:14–8:30. Is Jesus John the baptizer come back to life? Is he Elijah? Is he some other prophet? Just when it appears that the disciples have found the right answer (*You are the Messiah, v. 29*), the audience learns that there is more to messiahship than anyone bargained for. With that unsettling revelation, the evangelist begins the third major section of the Gospel.

On the Way, 8:22–10:52

The healing of the blind man at Bethsaida (8:22-26) and the story of Peter's confession at Caesarea Philippi (8:27-30) both have dual functions in the structural plan of the Gospel. Their functions in the narrative of the Galilean ministry have already been discussed, and we now turn to a study of the third major section of the Gospel in which the Markan Jesus teaches his disciples about the community implied by God's reign and about the role of suffering in Jesus' life and in the lives of his followers. Of course, the teachings of Jesus in this section have become the vehicle by which the evangelist teaches *his* audience on these topics.

We have already seen how Mark takes over Isaiah's imagery of sight and hearing, blindness and deafness. The material in 8:27–10:45 is framed by two stories about the healing of blindness—the only two such stories in this Gospel. Within this frame there is a narrative introduction (8:27-30) that sets the stage for the section. The subsequent material is arranged in three units of similar structure but differing length: 8:31–9:29; 9:30–10:31; and 10:32-45.

Each of these units begins with a prediction of Jesus' suffering and death (PASSION prediction). The prediction is followed by a response by disciples indicating that they do not understand the significance of what Jesus is telling them. This provides the Markan Jesus with an opportunity to engage in further teaching about the nature of discipleship.

The author of Mark has already indicated that although the disciples have eyes, they cannot see (8:18). Even though they have been given the secret of the reign of God, they have not perceived or understood it because their hearts are hardened (4:11; 6:52; 8:17). The teaching on the way to Jerusalem is Jesus' attempt to penetrate their blindness with the light of understanding. To indicate that purpose the evangelist begins the teaching section with the story of the healing of a blind man.

This is the only healing story in any Gospel that suggests difficulty or partiality in achieving the result.

Jesus puts saliva on the man's eyes and lays his hands on him, then checks to see how the healing is going: *Can you see anything?* (v. 23). The man reports partial sight (8:24). Jesus lays his hands on his eyes again and this time the man *looked intently and his sight was restored, and he saw everything clearly* (v. 25). This two-stage healing prepares for the encounter with the disciples that follows it.

That encounter takes place *on the way* to the villages of Caesarea Philippi. Of the sixteen references to "the way" (ὁδός) in Mark, half are concentrated between 8:27 and 11:8. In this section "the way" is the way to the cross, which becomes clear for the first time in the passion predictions. It is also *the way of the Lord* about which Isaiah wrote in the citation that began the Gospel (1:2-3). This way out of bondage into freedom, this second Exodus is a way the disciples are going to find especially distasteful. But then Isaiah also wrote, "My plans are not like your plans nor are your ways like my ways (ὁδοί, LXX), says the Lord."

Introductory Narrative, 8:27-30

This is the moment the audience of Mark has been waiting for. In 4:41 the disciples had asked, *Who then is this, that even the wind and the sea obey him?* In 6:50 Jesus had answered their question: *I am* (cf. Exod 3:14; Isa 43:10, 25; 45:18; 51:12). But their concern over bread in the last boat scene (8:14-21) showed that they were still blind to what they had seen.

Now the Markan Jesus asks them directly about his identity, beginning with what others are saying (v. 27). The speculations are those heard in Herod's court back in 6:13-15. Then comes the question that has challenged would-be disciples in the centuries since Mark first wrote it: *But who do you say that I am?* (v. 29).

Peter, speaking for the other disciples as he so often does in Mark, replies, *You are the Messiah* (v. 29; "Christ" is the Greek word for the messianic role or office). The audience breathes a sigh of relief. At last the disciples have seen the light. But Jesus interrupts the applause with a command to silence: *He sternly ordered them not to tell anyone about him* (v. 30). The audience knows that Peter is right (1:1), but apparently there is more to learn about who Jesus is before the news can be spread.

First Passion Prediction Unit, 8:31–9:29

The evangelist places the first passion prediction immediately after Peter's confession and Jesus' command to silence in order to show that before Jesus can be proclaimed as the Messiah, the component of suffering must be integrated into the messianic role.

Jesus' suffering is interpreted as a necessary part of the coming of God's eschatological reign by the use of the word translated *must* (δεῖ) in the NRSV (v. 31). The inbreak of God's reign can be seen in Jesus' miracles and exorcisms, but before its final consummation Jesus will have to be killed and to rise from death. By contrast with his usual mode of speech *in parables*, the passion prediction is crystal clear (v. 32).

Peter, as the representative of all the disciples, rejects the necessity of the passion. Jesus' retort means that to reject the necessity of suffering is to identify with Satan, Jesus' cosmic opponent (1:13; 3:22-27). The critique of Jesus' opponents in 7:6-13 here becomes the critique of the disciples: they are substituting human values and attitudes for the values and attitudes characteristic of God. From God's point of view there is no contradiction in a suffering healer, a victimized rescuer, a dying life-bringer. That the disciples see a contradiction indicates that they are looking with human half-sight. Like the blind man at Bethsaida, they need a second touch before they can see clearly.

Having added the component of suffering to the definition of messiahship, the Markan Jesus proceeds to add it to the definition of discipleship in 8:34–9:1. To follow behind the miracle worker is not enough; followers will deny themselves and accept the instruments of their own execution. Real life is found in losing one's life for the sake of Jesus and his good news. The desire for self-protection is the surest way to lose everything.

The concept of self-denial here must be interpreted in the context of the Gospel of Mark. It does not mean giving up certain pleasures or desires. It does not mean adopting the posture of a doormat by abandoning all sense of self. It means, rather, abandoning all claims to self-definition and accepting God's program for and God's claim upon one's life.

This is what the Markan Jesus does in 14:36. He has a will of his own, but he chooses God's will instead. In 14:62 Jesus denies himself publicly by the paradoxical act of boldly *claiming* his God-given identity and role. As a result, he takes up his cross and saves his life by losing it. Peter, by contrast, becomes the example of one who tries to save his life by denying *his* God-given identity and role as a follower of Jesus. For a Christian to deny herself, then, is to have the courage to be who she truly is. A Christian who tries to protect himself from persecution as a follower

of Jesus denies Jesus and loses the ground and center of his life.

Denying Jesus, or *being ashamed* of him and his teaching, has serious consequences. Of such a person Jesus will *be ashamed* when he comes as eschatological judge (8:38), and that judgment will be very soon (8:39). It is clear that the evangelist finds it necessary to issue a strong warning about the consequences of apostasy during persecution.

The next scene in this unit is the transfiguration. Exodus symbolism is again prominent: Moses, a high mountain, a cloud, the shining appearance of God's messenger, the building of tabernacles (9:5, NRSV *dwellings*). Along with Moses the lawgiver appears the prophet Elijah, with whom the evangelist has linked John the baptizer (1:2-8; 6:17-29).

John (Elijah) was present at Jesus' baptism, the first time the voice from heaven spoke (1:9-11). On that occasion Jesus received the Holy Spirit's presence and power for his ministry of teaching, healing and exorcism. Now the voice from heaven speaks again in the presence of Elijah and Moses to confirm the necessity of Jesus' humiliation and suffering just announced in 8:31. The *beloved son* will die (cf. Gen 22:2). At the baptism the voice was addressed only to Jesus; now the voice addresses the disciples: *Listen to him!* But this is not a message they are able to hear.

On the way down the mountain Jesus again enjoins silence *until after the Son of Man had risen from the dead* (9:9). The disciples raise the question about Elijah's coming as the forerunner (Mal 4:5). Indeed he has come, says Jesus, and you see what happened to him! (6:17-29).

The final story in the first passion prediction unit is the healing of the demon-possessed boy (9:14-29). Here the author of Mark has two points to make: (1) God's miraculous power and human confidence in that power are inextricably linked, and (2) God's power is not an impersonal force to be manipulated, but a gift to be prayed for. In order to make these two points, the evangelist uses this story of a botched exorcism to criticize the father and the crowd for their lack of faith and to criticize the disciples for their prayerlessness.

Having been disappointed once, the father is understandably skeptical and desperate: *If you are able to do anything, have pity on us and help us* (9:22). But in Mark, Jesus' *ability* to help is never at issue; the leper was right when he said, *If you choose, you can . . .* (1:40). So Jesus answers, *If you are able!—All things can be done for the one who believes* (9:23). Still desperate and still honest, the father cries out, *I be-lieve; help my unbelief* [by healing my son]! (9:24). To this request Jesus immediately responds.

Faith is needed for miracles in Mark, but some-times miracles are needed to awaken faith in Jesus' power (Dowd 1988, 107-14).

But the father's lack of faith is not the whole story. When the disciples get Jesus alone *in the house*, where all private teaching takes place, they ask the reason for their failure (9:28). Jesus' answer is that *this kind* of demon comes out only for those who cultivate the habit of prayer (as Jesus himself does 1:35; 6:46). Dis-ciples do not give orders to God as magicians in the ancient world were known to do; rather, they make re-quests out of the quality of their relationship with God.

Second Passion Prediction Unit, 9:30–10:31

This unit is carefully organized, with a number of overlapping structures. After the passion prediction and the disciples' failure to understand (9:30-32), the teaching material that follows is held together by an in-clusio: *Whoever wants to be first must be last* (9:35) and *Many who are first will be last, and the last will be first* (10:31).

Within this frame, two major subjects are dealt with. First the Markan Jesus holds out hope for the powerless in 9:33–10:16. This material has its own frame: receive children (9:33-37) and receive God's reign as a child (10:13-16). The second topic is hope for the powerful (10:17-27); their salvation is impossi-ble for humans but possible for God (10:27).

The last item in the unit is a conversation between Jesus and his disciples on the rewards awaiting those who give up everything to follow Jesus (10:28-31). This conversation concludes with the saying on last/first that closes the frame on the entire unit.

The material in 9:30-50 is set in Galilee. The movement from the mountain of transfiguration south toward Jerusalem has begun. The second passion pre-diction introduces for the first time in the disciples' hearing the notion that Jesus will be betrayed. The au-dience, of course, has known of the betrayal and the identity of the betrayer since 3:19. The disciples do not understand and are afraid to ask questions (9:32).

All the teaching in chap. 9 takes place *in the house* in Capernaum. It begins with Jesus' awareness of an argument among the disciples (9:33) and ends with his admonition that they have peace among themselves (9:50). According to the narrator, the argument was about who was the greatest; this gives the Markan

Jesus the opportunity to emphasize that the values of God's reign are the reverse of those of this age. The one who serves everyone else is the greatest.

Jesus follows up by identifying with one of the "last" of society—a child. To welcome a powerless child is to welcome Jesus himself. The high infant mor-tality rate in antiquity contributed to the marginaliza-tion of children. Perhaps fewer than half lived to their fifth year (Wiedemann 1989, 16). They had only re-cently come from the divine realm and were likely to leave this life at any time; thus, they were not fully human beings.

On the other hand, this marginal status conferred on children a certain mystery. They were thought to be closer to the gods than adults and sometimes even their casual utterances were regarded as omens. (The best-known instance of this belief occurs in Augus-tine's account of his conversion, *Conf.* 8.12.) This con-text enables the evangelist to portray Jesus as designat-ing children as the bearers of his presence when they are welcomed in his name.

The phrase "in your/my name" links this story with the one that follows. Although the disciples want to limit exorcism in Jesus' name to their own group, the Markan Jesus insists that all who minister wholeness in his name are to be recognized as *for us* (v. 40). The use of *the name* makes it clear that the issue here is not the ultimate status of non-Christians who do good works; rather, the issue is openness toward the minis-try of Christian groups other than one's own. But any-one (even a non-Christian) who shows mercy toward the Christian community will be rewarded (9:41; cf. Matt 25:31-46).

Calling attention back to the child in his arms, the Markan Jesus pronounces an ominous warning against influencing a believing child (or any new Christian?) to commit apostasy (v. 42). On the topic of apostasy in general, the sayings in vv. 43-48 make it clear that "it is better to enter life having renounced certain cher-ished acts than to go into hell having done it all with-out restraint" (Via 1985, 18). Self-fulfillment is not to be equated with "entering into life," and self-indul-gence may lead to self-destruction.

In 10:1 the scene shifts even further south. The mention of Judea anticipates the setting of chaps. 11–16. At this point the Pharisees reenter the picture and raise the question about divorce. The Markan Je-sus explains that the Mosaic permission of divorce was not an expression of God's intent, but reflected the situ-ation of fallenness and human *hardness of heart*.

The appeal to creation serves Mark's eschatology; God's reign, which is breaking through in Jesus' ministry, restores the possibility of relationships as they were intended in the beginning. The conversation with the disciples (vv. 10-12) changes the status of women from victims to responsible moral agents. No longer merely passive in marriage and divorce, they too must take responsibility for their decisions and actions. It should be noted that the evangelist believes divorce and adultery can be forgiven. The only unpardonable sin is blasphemy against the Holy Spirit (3:29).

The second reference to children portrays the disciples as still unable to get the point. Just as in the second feeding story, they have learned nothing from their previous experience. Despite 9:37 they try to prevent children from having access to Jesus (Tannehill 1977, 401). Jesus now says that the childlike are the primary citizens of God's realm (v. 14) and that everyone who enters God's realm must enter *as a little child* (v. 15).

This is "not an invitation to childlike innocence and naivete but a challenge to relinquish all claims of power and domination over others" (Fiorenza 1983, 148). God's reign cannot be achieved or earned; it must be received in the way that children in antiquity received what they needed for life. According to the Markan Jesus, people enter the reign of God, not in a proud triumphal procession, but in complete vulnerability, with no claim to any rights or status. It was not what the disciples had in mind.

Their amazement that it is humanly impossible for a rich person to enter God's reign (v. 26) reflects the relationship between wealth and religion in which prosperity was regarded as a blessing from God and therefore a sign of righteousness (Deut 28:1-14; Prov 13:25; 15:6; 37:25-26). In the world of Greco-Roman polytheism, wealth made it possible to persuade the gods with fine sacrifices and to be initiated into a variety of mystery religions (Apuleius, *The Golden Ass*).

The fact that Jesus expects a rich and religious person to renounce all the possessions and righteousness that he has acquired (v. 21) shocks the rich man and the disciples. They want to know who *can* be saved, if not this one. Jesus' answer is consistent with his earlier sayings about the advantage of the powerless. Humans cannot achieve salvation; God gives it away for free. Those who are accustomed to living on handouts will find it easier to enter God's reign than those who are accustomed to paying their own way. But God can do anything—even save a rich person (v. 27).

Peter misses the point about having no claim and attempts to convert his abandonment of possessions into an asset (v. 28). This gives the Markan Jesus an opportunity to recapitulate the theme of 3:31-35. The family that has been lost as a result of Christian conversion is replaced by the Christian community in the present and eternal life in the future (vv. 29-30).

This new family is radically different from the old, however, because it includes no fathers. In antiquity, the father had almost absolute control over the other members of the family. Control from above by a person who has power over others is repudiated by the vision of Christian community articulated by the Markan Jesus. God is the only father (8:38; 14:36; 11:25). The fatherhood of God in the context of Markan theology has the same function as the kingship of God: it guarantees a church made up of equals. God rules precisely in order to make sure that no one else does.

The evangelist cannot resist one wry addition to the list of blessings Christians receive *in this age*. Along with the new family, houses, and fields come persecutions (v. 30). Besides, *many who are first will be last, and the last first* (v. 31). For Peter, the disciple who was called first, this could be construed as a warning.

Third Passion Prediction Unit, 10:32-52

Much shorter than the previous two units, this one nevertheless begins with the longest and most detailed of the three passion predictions; it is virtually an outline for Mark 14:43–16:8. "The way" has taken Jesus and his disciples almost to Jerusalem and all of the instruction Jesus has given his followers so far has not made a dent in their amazement and fear (v. 32).

The placement of vv. 35-40 immediately after the passion prediction results in dramatic irony. The story about the request of James and John is narrated in such a way that the audience sees them stepping up briskly, as though they had been waiting impatiently for Jesus to stop talking. Their request is a boorish *non sequitur* after Jesus' solemn recitation of the tortures about to be inflicted on him.

In the first passion prediction unit the Markan Jesus had spoken about his coming in glory as eschatological deliverer (8:31, 38; 9:12). Peter's acclamation of him as the Messiah (8:29) was qualified, but not rejected, and the heavenly voice at the transfiguration alluded to one of the royal psalms (9:7; Ps 2:7). The narrative suggests that although James and John had no under standing about the passion (9:32) or the resurrection

(9:10), they had understood the part about glory and royalty and were determined to participate in it. They ask to be seated next to Jesus *in your glory* (v. 37).

Jesus begins his response with a warning: *You do not know what you are asking* (v. 38). Indeed they do not, for the positions they request on Jesus' right and left will be the positions of two crucified criminals (15:27). Taking up their vision of royalty, Jesus then reminds them that those closest to the king have to drink from his cup; if the wine is poisoned, they share the death intended for the ruler (v. 38; cf. Gen 40:1-13; 41:9-13; Neh 1:11b–2:1; Xenophon, *Cyropaedia* 1.3.9, Suetonius, *Claudius* 44.2).

There may be a pun on the word "baptize" in v. 38, since one of the meanings of the verb was "to destroy (e.g., a person by drowning, or a ship by sinking)" (Beasley-Murray 1990, 85). James and John apparently understand the question in the sense of ritual washing and answer brashly, *We are able* (v. 39). The gospel song based on their reply perpetuates their naivete.

As it turns out, their quest is frustrated. Jesus can guarantee martyrdom for James and John, but not glory (v. 40). The prediction of their martyrdoms here suggests that their blindness and self-seeking will finally be replaced by faithfulness.

The anger of the other disciples upon learning that the two brothers were seeking special privileges gives the Markan Jesus an opportunity to teach about the upside-down values of Christian leadership (vv. 41-45). The community is not to be modeled on secular Roman ("gentile") structures. The teachings of 9:35 and 10:31 are recapitulated for emphasis: The one who wants to be great must be a servant; the one who wants to be first must be the slave of all.

In v. 45 the evangelist provides the christological rationale for this role reversal. Christian leaders must be servants because *the Son of Man came not to be served but to serve, and to give his life a ransom for many.* The first half of this saying interprets the ministry of Jesus up to this point as "service." All of his miracles and exorcisms, his teaching with authority, his winning arguments with the religious leaders, were done not to call attention to his status or power, but to serve. This is the point most often missed by interpretations of Mark that attempt to set miracle working and service in opposition to each other. They are synonyms, not opposites.

The second half of the saying points forward to the passion narrative. The word usually translated "ransom" here has the general meaning of a price paid for the release of a slave or prisoner of war. It is one of at least three understandings of the efficacy of Jesus' death that the author of Mark has incorporated into his Gospel. As we will see, the PASSION NARRATIVE is based primarily on the theme of the suffering righteous man, derived from the thought of ancient Israel and developed in the Hellenistic Jewish wisdom literature. To this general picture the author of Mark adds the metaphors of (1) covenant sacrifice (14:24) and (2) liberation from bondage (10:45).

The related verb, meaning "redeem," "ransom," or "set free," is important in the theology of Deutero-Isaiah, although the noun used in Mark 10:45 appears only once (45:13). Isaiah connects the concept of ransom/redemption/liberation with the interpretation of the return from exile as a second Exodus (41:14; 43:1, 14; 44:22-24; 51:11; 52:3; 62:12; 63:4, 9). Since this Isaian theme is central to Mark's theology, it is possible that the evangelist intends the saying to be understood as a metaphor for the freedom from bondage that will be effected by Jesus' death. This would be an understanding of the cross that would correspond with the freedom experienced by the human beneficiaries of Jesus' ministry of exorcism. The powerful one who has served by healing the broken bodies and psyches of humanity will also effect their ultimate freedom by giving his life.

The "way" section of Mark ends with the story of Bartimaeus, which closes the frame on the entire section, but is also linked explicitly with the previous request of James and John. Like the brothers, Bartimaeus brings a request. Jesus asks him exactly the same question he asked James and John: *What do you want me to do for you?* (10:36, 51). The repetition signals the audience that the misguided ambition expressed in the previous story is about to be corrected. Bartimaeus asks for the one thing that all the characters in Mark need most—sight. Jesus heals him with a word; the contrast with the two-stage healing of the blind man at Bethsaida is dramatic.

Bartimaeus's response to his healing is the response Jesus has been calling for throughout this section of the Gospel. As soon as he can see, he begins to follow Jesus *on the way* to Jerusalem, the place of crucifixion. To see aright is to walk the way of the cross unflinchingly. This vision and faithful response however, is not a human achievement. It is a divine miracle.

Ministry and Passion in Jerusalem, 11:1–16:8

The healing of Bartimaeus on the way out of Jericho marks the end of the "way" section. The rest of the narrative is set in Jerusalem and its environs. This final division of the Gospel falls into two parts. The passion and resurrection narrative (14:1–16:8) is preceded by a literary unit focused on Jesus' actions and sayings in and about the Temple (11:1–13:37).

Jesus and the Temple, 11:1–13:37

This unit of deeds and words is bracketed by references to the Mount of Olives. In 11:1-11 Jesus leaves the Mount of Olives and enters Jerusalem and the Temple; in 13:1-37 Jesus leaves the Temple, predicting its destruction, and goes to the Mount of Olives, where he delivers an apocalyptic discourse on the coming of the Son of Man.

The material between Jesus' entry into and exit from the Temple begins with two stories about Jesus' actions (the fig tree incident and the expulsion of the merchants and moneychangers, 11:12-25). This is followed by a series of teachings and controversies (11:27–12:44).

11:1-25. Deeds. This section is marked by a continual shift in location between Bethany and the Jerusalem Temple, whereas the setting for all the controversy and teaching material in 11:27–12:44 is the Temple itself. Of course, even this action material is not devoid of teaching, as the Markan Jesus interprets his actions to his opponents and to his disciples.

Jesus' power and authority are the primary emphases of the narrative of his initial actions in Jerusalem. The finding of the colt for the ride into Jerusalem (vv. 1-6) and the similar story of the finding of the room for the final meal (14:12-16) demonstrate Jesus' powers of prediction and his authority to requisition what he needs. Now that he has three times redefined his messiahship by combining access to divine power with vulnerability to rejection and death, the Markan Jesus has no need to conceal his identity as the one who inaugurates the reign of God.

The acclamation of the disciples in chiastic form (vv. 9b-10: hosanna, blessed, blessed, hosanna) is based partly on Ps 118:26. This psalm portrays a procession of thanksgiving to the Temple and emphasizes national sovereignty and defeat of Israel's enemies. Here translated into an apocalyptic mode, the psalm fragment is incorporated into a shout of welcome for the eschatological savior promised by Isaiah (33:22). Both Jewish and gentile members of Mark's audience would have recognized this as a procession to celebrate a victory, but unlike the group of disciples pictured in the narrative, the audience would have appreciated the irony of the scene. Whereas Roman triumphal processions ended with the execution of the prisoners of war, this one will end with the execution of the victor.

Only in Mark is Jesus' provocative action in the Temple sandwiched between the beginning and the end of the strange story of the withered fig tree. Unlike his modern interpreters, the author of Mark was completely unconcerned about the propriety of Jesus' destroying a helpless tree. The evangelist is interested in the way in which the destruction of the fruitless tree foreshadows the destruction of the Jerusalem Temple which, in his view, had also failed to bear the expected fruit.

Although Isaiah had written that the Temple was to be "a house of prayer for all the gentile nations" (56:7, author trans.), the Temple hierarchy had made it into a "robbers' hideout" (v. 17, author trans.) where they huddled together, claiming the protection of the holy place. This had been Jeremiah's complaint in his famous Temple sermon (7:11), from which the Markan Jesus quotes. The objection is not that dishonest merchants are cheating the public. The word λῃστῶν means not cheats, but muggers or pirates, who use their "hideouts" not for robbing people but for evading detection and punishment.

The author of Mark interprets Jesus' actions not as a cleansing or reform of the Temple, but as a cancellation of Temple worship altogether. The Markan Jesus makes it impossible, not only for proper sacrificial animals to be procured and money changed for the Temple taxes, but also for the priests to carry through the Temple the vessels necessary to perform the rituals. Because the gentiles had been excluded from prayer in God's house, God's authoritative representative signals the end of all prayer in the Temple.

This, however, requires a reinterpretation of the conditions for effective prayer. Like all ancient religions, JUDAISM had a tradition of understanding the temple of the deity as the place where petitions were sure to be granted (1 Sam 1:1-29; 2 Kgs 19:14-37; 2 Macc 3:24-40). If the Temple, the holy place where God is especially present, is rejected, how can the followers of Jesus expect their prayers to be effective?

The answer comes with the reassurances about prayer in vv. 22-25. There are two conditions for effective prayer: faith (vv. 22-24) and forgiveness (v. 25). To *have faith* means to maintain the confidence that God is able to do what is otherwise impossible (9:23; 10:29). This faith is not "saving faith" but certainty about a worldview that early Christians shared with Hellenistic Jews and adherents of Neopythagorean philosophy. By contrast, the Platonists held that some things were impossible for the gods and the Epicureans argued that the gods did not intervene to perform miracles in response to human prayer.

But confidence in God's power must be combined with the clean slate provided only by God's forgiving disciples' sins. The catch is that in order to be forgiven, they will have to forgive each other (v. 25).

The evangelist replaces the holy place with the holy people who forgive and are forgiven and who stubbornly maintain their Christian worldview in the face of the philosophical alternatives. This is the ideal. But the Markan Jesus has already shown that God reserves the option of providing miraculous assistance to those who have inadequate faith (4:40; 8:4; 9:24). In Mark, the power of God overcomes even human unbelief.

11:27–12:44, Words in the Temple. In this teaching section, set in the Temple, the evangelist places a three-part discussion of theology and ethics between two three-part discussions which focus on christology (A—11:27-33; 12:1-9, 10-12; B—12:13-17, 18-27, 28-34, A'—12:35-37, 38-40, 41-44). The section begins with Jesus walking around in the Temple like a peripatetic philosopher (11:27) and ends with Jesus sitting to teach his disciples like a Jewish rabbi (12:41). These two postures correspond to the types of argumentation used throughout the section. Thoroughly Jewish modes of scriptural exegesis are combined with thoroughly Hellenistic rhetorical ploys, and all are set into an apocalyptic frame of reference.

The first christological subsection (11:27–12:12) makes the point that like the Davidic king who celebrates victory over his enemies (Ps 118), Jesus will be vindicated by God. His rejection and death are not the last word. The stone the builders rejected has become the cornerstone of the new temple, replacing the fruitless Jerusalem Temple. This new temple, the Christian community, is the house of prayer for all the gentiles that the previous Temple had failed to become. Thus, Isaiah's apocalyptic vision of the inclusion of the gentiles in the people of God is fulfilled in the Christian community (Isa 2:2-3; 56:6-7; Marcus 1992, 111-29).

Subsection A begins with a conversation with Jesus' opponents that links the teaching section with the series of actions that preceded it. The religious leaders confront Jesus over the issue of his authority to suspend the Temple cult. The audience, of course, knows the right answer to the leaders' question and Jesus' counterquestion: both John's and Jesus' authority came not from human beings, but from God (1:11; 9:7). Jesus' opponents are caught in the trap of their own cowardice, but their answer, *We do not know* (11:33), is ironically true. Indeed, their ignorance and blindness mark them as *those outside* (4:10-12).

The confrontation with the opponents continues as Jesus takes the initiative in the parable of the vineyard (12:1-9). Developing the imagery of Isa 5:2, the Markan Jesus takes an accusation that Isaiah directed against the whole people of Israel and focuses it specifically on the religious leaders. As interpreted by the Psalm quotation in 12:10-12, the parable becomes another prediction of Jesus' rejection, death, and vindication.

Subsection B consists of three encounters arranged in a chiastic structure with a central focus on the reality of the resurrection (Donahue 1982). This issue is dealt with in the conversation with the Sadducees (12:18-27). The form of Jesus' response is the rhetorical device known as an enthymeme (a syllogism in which one of the members is implied rather than stated):

Major premise (implied): God speaks accurately in scripture.
Minor premise: In scripture God speaks of the dead in the present tense (Exod 3:6).
Conclusion: The dead live in the presence of God. Resurrection is true.

The centrality of the resurrection is bracketed by conversations dealing with the ethical implications of theological claims. In 12:13-17 the Markan Jesus uses another enthymeme to escape a rhetorical trap designed to get him in trouble either with the people, who disliked paying Roman taxes, or with the Romans who demanded the payment. The implied major premise is: Ownership is established by the seal imprinted on something. Since the denarius bears Caesar's image, it is to be given to Caesar. What then is to be given to God? Obviously, that which bears God's image, that is, human beings (Gen 1:26-28). They are preeminently the "things of God," which must be surrendered completely to God. It is this self-giving to

God that characterizes the Markan Jesus, as 14:32-42 will make strikingly clear.

The question about the great commandment (12:28-34) completes the theological discussion. The stress is on monotheism and its implications. God was contrasted with Caesar in 12:13-17; here the obligation to love God with the entire self is combined with the obligation to love one's neighbor as oneself. The scribe who recognizes that Jesus' emphasis accords with the theology of Deutero-Isaiah (45:21, "There is no other god besides me") is not far from the eschatological reign of God foreseen by the prophet and inaugurated in Jesus' ministry.

By having the scribe cite the prophetic critique of sacrifice without obedience (1 Sam 15:22; Hos 6:6; Mic 6:6-8) the evangelist delivers a final blow to the Temple system. Its fruitlessness is conceded by one of its own scholarly elite. After this coup, no one puts any more questions to the Markan Jesus (12:34b).

In subsection A', the initiative shifts. Now it is Jesus' turn to ask the questions. He turns the conversation back to christology by making the point that the expectation of a royal Davidic messiah is inadequate. Although the evangelist clearly makes Davidic claims for Jesus with his use of Pss 2, 118, and 110, Jesus' messiahship is both more and less than the title *Son of David* suggests. Whereas the Davidic messiah was merely a human ruler who would defeat human enemies, Jesus is the divine warrior who defeats the demonic powers and ushers in God's reign. Unlike the expected Davidic messiah Jesus' victory is won by losing—by humiliation and death (Marcus 1992, 130-50).

The theme of judgment on the religious leaders is sounded again in 12:38-40. The scribes who *devour* widows' houses (Isa 1:17, 23; 10:2; Ezek 22:25) clearly do not live by the standard advocated by one of their own number in 12:32-33 (Beavis 1989, 102). By contrast, the widow in 12:40-44 performs the exemplary action. Like Jesus, she gives God everything she has, even "her whole life" (12:44, author trans; cf. 12:17, 30). This giving of one's life recalls 10:45. The widow gives all she has to live on; Jesus will give his life to set God's people free.

13:1-2. Transition. Having been in the Temple since 11:27, the Markan Jesus now leaves the Temple and predicts its destruction: *Not one stone will be left here upon another*. What was implicit in 11:15-17 here becomes explicit. This closes the section of teaching in the Temple and prepares for the following teaching *opposite the temple* (13:3).

13:3-37. Words opposite the Temple (the apocalyptic discourse). This second long speech by the Markan Jesus has a number of common features with the parable discourse in chap. 4. Both assume the cosmic conflict myth so fundamental to apocalyptic thought. Both contain repeated admonitions to pay attention (4:3, 9, 23, 24; 13:5, 9, 23, 33, 35, 37). Both use parables from nature (4:3-9, 26-32; 13:28-29), and both contain allegorical applications of parabolic material to discipleship (4:13-20; 13:34-37, Donahue 1988, 61).

It is characteristic of both speeches that an extended discourse punctuated by second-person-plural imperatives tends to blur the distinction between the addressees at the story level and the audience of the Gospel as a whole. The "you" of the teaching material reaches out to include the listeners in any subsequent time (Tannehill 1980, 141).

The scene in chap. 13 is the Mount of Olives. The cast of characters is exactly the same as that of the first scene of the Galilean ministry (11:16-20): Jesus, Peter, James, John, and Andrew. The only function of the disciples in this scene is to ask two questions. They are not mentioned again.

The disciples' questions are: (1) When will these things happen? and (2) What will be the sign? They are portrayed as regarding the destruction of the Temple, which Jesus has just predicted, as a catastrophic event that would surely be preceded by a significant omen. They understand themselves as insiders who are entitled to be let in on the secret (cf. 4:11).

Jesus, however, has more important information to impart. He never mentions the Temple again; rather, he begins to talk about false and true signs of the eschatological consummation of God's reign. Although he is answering a question the disciples have not asked, he takes up the two issues they have raised in reverse order, beginning with how to recognize the sign of the end (vv. 5-27) and moving to the issue of the time of the end (vv. 28-37).

The Markan Jesus first explains that no historical event can be read as a sign of the eschaton (vv. 5-23). This material is arranged chiastically:

A Danger of deception, 5-6
  B Prediction of future events, 7-8
    C Persecution and mission, 9-13
  B' Appropriate response to future events, 14-20
A' Danger of deception, 21-23

The section begins and ends with warnings that there will be deceivers who will make messianic claims for themselves and others and perform miracles in order to lead Christians astray (vv. 5-6, 21-23). Their apocalyptic interpretations of events are to be ignored (vv. 21, 23).

B and B' describe historical and natural events that might be misinterpreted as signs of the end (vv. 7-8) and prescribe the proper way to respond to such difficult times (vv. 14-20). Christians must always be ready to move quickly in times of crisis. Attachment to possessions will have to be put aside and even the most natural relationships will pose a problem (vv. 15-17). But although the suffering will be terrible, God is in control and will provide for God's chosen people. The right response is prayer and trust (vv. 18-20).

The center of the chiasm focuses on the persecution of the church (vv. 9-13). Like Jesus, Christians will be handed over, betrayed, brought to trial, and put to death. They are not to be afraid, because the Holy Spirit will enable them to bear witness. In the midst of their persecutions, they must continue to preach the gospel to the gentiles, because this is part of the divinely ordained prelude to the end (v. 10). *The one who endures to the end will be saved* (v. 13).

Scholars usually assume that the events described in vv. 5-23 were already taking place at the time of the writing of the Gospel. Jesus is portrayed as speaking in the past about events in the future, which is the evangelist's present. It is likely that the audience of the Gospel is facing some of the things described in this section. Some may already be in the past. But there is no way of knowing that all the events in this description are past or present. The evangelist may anticipate that some of these difficulties lie ahead for the church and may wish to prepare them to respond appropriately.

After an extensive discussion of events that are *not* signs of the end, the Markan Jesus turns to the real sign of the end: the coming of the Son of Man on the clouds, amid cosmic upheaval, to gather the elect from all over the earth (vv. 24-27). When they see Jesus coming for them again, they will know that the end is about to take place; no natural or political disasters that take place before that are to distract them from their mission.

As for the question of "When?" the Markan Jesus takes care of that in short order. This brief section (vv. 28-37) begins and ends with a parable. The parable of the fig tree makes the point that when the disciples see "these things" (i.e., the coming of the Son of Man, vv. 24-27), they will know that he is *at the very gates* (v.

29). In other words, when you see it happening, you will know that it is happening, and not before!

This is reinforced by repeated reminders that *you do not know when* (vv. 33, 35). In fact, no one knows except the Father. The futility of calculation based on "signs of the times" could not be more dramatically portrayed. But if "biblical prophecy" workshops are not appropriate, neither is complacency. The parable of the returning landlord (vv. 34-36) emphasizes the suddenness of the arrival of the eschaton. Since you do not know, be ready and alert at all times. The final exhortation is addressed explicitly to the audience: *What I say to you I say to all: Keep awake* (v. 37).

Passion and Resurrection Narratives, 14:1–16:8

Jesus' death in Mark. In their struggle to interpret the humiliation and crucifixion of Jesus, early Christians made use of a variety of biblical and cultural resources. Ancient people, both Jews and pagans, knew that life was often unfair. The individual psalms of lament preserved the complaints of the righteous person who suffered unjustly at the hands of enemies. In Plato's *Republic* (361e-362a), Socrates is challenged by dialogue partners who suggest that the truly righteous person will "hold his course unchangeable, even unto death," having "to endure the lash, the rack, chains," and "finally, after every extremity of suffering, he will be crucified." That the execution of just persons was not merely a theoretical possibility is made clear by the interpretations of Socrates' own death at the hands of the state (Plato, *Apology, Phaedo*; Xenophon, *Memorabilia*).

But human beings recoil from the notion that the death of the upright is meaningless. The psalmist cries out for vindication. The Isaian Servant Songs interpret the death of the servant as vicarious suffering for the sins of others. The author of the Wisdom of Solomon transforms the victims into the judges of their persecutors (4:16–5:2). The Greeks made heroes of kings and soldiers who died to save the lives of others. The Maccabean martyrs are portrayed as giving their lives to atone for the sins of their compatriots (2 Macc 7:38; 4 Macc 6:28-29).

The Gospel of Mark draws upon a number of these biblical and extrabiblical patterns to interpret the death of Jesus as a necessary part of God's eschatological victory over all that enslaves and distorts human life. Although blameless, Jesus is unjustly condemned and crucified. His death redeems enslaved humanity (10:45) and seals a covenant (14:25) that brings even gentiles into the people of God. Vindicated in the resurrection, he leaves the tomb empty as he leads his followers on the way of mission and martyrdom.

The overall organization of the Markan passion narrative is controlled by chronology; within that framework the individual episodes are carefully crafted for rhetorical and theological effect. The sense of speed and energy so characteristic of the Galilean ministry is replaced by a series of solemn notices of the passing of time (14:1, 12, 17; 15:1, 26, 33, 34, 42) as the evangelist tolls the agonizing final hours of Jesus' life.

The story of the anointing woman (14:3-9) has two literary functions in the outline of the Gospel. With the story of the widow's offering (12:41-44), it forms a frame (INCLUSIO) around the apocalyptic discourse in chap. 13. In both cases, women are praised for their actions, which point forward to Jesus' giving of his life and to his burial. The women are contrasted with the religious leaders, who exploit them (12:40) and oppose Jesus (14:1-2).

With the story of the three women who go in search of Jesus' corpse to anoint it for burial (16:1-8), the story of the anointing woman in 14:3-9 forms a frame around the passion narrative. Her act makes theirs unnecessary. Jesus has already left the tomb and is on the way to Galilee.

14:1-11. Plot and anointing. The story of the anointing woman is sandwiched into the narrative about the plot to kill Jesus (vv. 1-2, 10-11; cf. Ps 10:7-8; Wis 2:12). Judas provides the missing link that will enable the religious leaders to "arrest Jesus by stealth" away from the crowds.

Having redefined the concepts of clean and unclean verbally in 7:1-23, Jesus now acts on that redefinition by having dinner in the house of an "unclean" leper. In an act reminiscent of the OT prophets, a woman comes in and anoints Jesus' head, signifying his royal authority (2 Kgs 19:1-3; 1 Sam 10:1; 1 Kgs 1:38-49; Ps 133:2). Like many of Jesus' own words and actions, the woman's deed is misunderstood by those present; they criticize her extravagance.

But Jesus defends the woman and reinterprets her action as an anointing for burial. Just as Peter's confession of Jesus as the Messiah had to be reinterpreted in terms of the passion, so the woman prophet's confession of Jesus as the Messiah by her action requires reinterpretation. The royal anointing becomes a burial rite. It is the only anointing that the Markan Jesus will receive, since by the time his women disciples arrive at the tomb with their spices, Jesus will be gone.

14:12-31. The Last Supper. The preparation for the Passover meal again confirms Jesus' foreknowledge of events (cf. 11:1-6). The two sent ahead to prepare are joined in v. 17 by Jesus and THE TWELVE, suggesting that the evangelist wanted to make clear that attendance at this important meal was not limited to the group named in chap. 3.

Jesus predicts his betrayal by one of those at table with him (Ps 41:9). The disciples are portrayed as claiming innocence in the form of a question that implies a negative answer: *Surely, not I?* (v. 19). Jesus' response reflects the apocalyptic viewpoint that all is happening in accordance with God's plan (v. 21a) and human beings are nevertheless culpable for their opposition to God's elect (v. 21b).

Ignoring the symbolic actions usually associated with Passover meals, the narrator introduces new symbols. The broken bread is Jesus' body; the cup of wine is his blood. The reference to covenant sacrifice (v. 24; cf. Exod 24:8; Zech 9:11) points backward to God's faithfulness in the past. The reference to the messianic banquet in "the reign of God" (v. 25, author trans.) points forward to eschatological vindication and celebration in communion with God (Isa 25:6).

On the way to the Mount of Olives, Jesus predicts the apostasy of all his disciples and their reunion with him in Galilee (vv. 27-28; cf. Zech 13:7-9; 14:4). Their tentative *Surely, not I?* of moments before now becomes a bold assertion of loyalty even to the point of death (v. 31b). But by this time the audience is more inclined to believe Jesus. If he says that the disciples will flee and Peter will deny him three times, that is what the audience expects.

14:32-42. Gethsemane. This scene is carefully constructed. The prayer of Jesus is at the center. Leading up to the prayer, three verbs of motion (vv. 32a, 33, 35a) are followed by three requests by the Markan Jesus: to the larger group of disciples (v. 32b), to Peter, James, and John (v. 34), and finally to God (v. 35b).

The prayer itself expresses confidence in God's power (*for you all things are possible*) and makes a direct request (*remove this cup from me*). Thus the evangelist shows that Jesus follows his own instructions; he has faith and he asks for a miracle every bit as stupendous as tossing a mountain into the sea (11:22-24). He asks to be spared the cross, after having repeatedly acknowledged its necessity in the preceding narrative. But now in his practice of prayer the Markan Jesus adds something that was not in his earlier teaching about prayer: submission to the will of God. This is what distinguishes the Markan Jesus from the numerous other miracle workers and magicians of antiquity; he does God's will, not his own.

After the prayer, Jesus returns to find his disciples sleeping. They have fallen into the trap about which he warned them in the parable of the absent landlord (13:34-36). Again, as at the transfiguration, they do not know how to respond (v. 40; cf. 9:6).

It is important to notice that the Markan theology of prayer does not *substitute* submission to God's will for petitionary prayer. The two are combined as the Markan Jesus wrestles with God three times *saying the same words* (v. 39). Finally he wakes the sleeping disciples in time to confront Judas and his lynch mob.

14:43-52. Arrest. With the arrival of the arresting party, Jesus' predictions begin to be fulfilled in rapid-fire succession. He is betrayed by Judas (cf. 14:18) into the hands of the religious leaders (cf. 10:33). Despite their boasting of a few hours before (14:27), all his disciples desert Jesus to save themselves (8:34-38). Mark emphasizes the complete abandonment of Jesus by repeating the *all* of 14:31b in v. 50. The story of the terrified youth who flees naked has two functions: it reminds the audience that the group that attended the supper and followed Jesus to Gethsemane was larger than "the twelve" and it makes a graphic comment on the cowardice and shame of the flight of the disciples. Nowhere in Mark is there any suggestion that the young man is to be identified with the author of the Gospel.

14:53-72. Sanhedrin trial/denial of Peter. The evangelist weaves together the story of the Sanhedrin TRIAL OF JESUS, which takes place inside the residence of the high priest, and the story of Peter's denial, which is set outside in the courtyard. He narrates the introduction to the trial scene (15:53), then the introduction to the denial (15:54), proceeds with the trial narrative (15:55-65), and then completes the denial story (15:66-72). This emphasizes the point that these events are to be understood as occurring simultaneously, even though they must be narrated sequentially.

From this point forward the passion narrative is riddled with dramatic irony. Jesus' enemies bungle their plot against him because their false witnesses (Pss 27:12; 35:11) cannot get their stories straight. Ironically, though, their *false* testimony is true; although the Markan Jesus has not said that he will destroy the Temple and replace it with one *not made with hands* (v. 58), that is in fact exactly what will happen. The

Christian community will replace the Temple as the *house of prayer for all the nations* (11:17).

Since the opponents fail in their attempt to condemn him, Jesus has to condemn himself. In order for his commission from God to be fulfilled, Jesus has to give true testimony about himself, which the Sanhedrin then misinterprets as blasphemy. Here the evangelist brings together all the aspects of Jesus' identity. In response to the high priest's question, *Are you the Messiah, the Son of the Blessed One?* (v. 61, a reverent Jewish circumlocution for "God"), Jesus answers with the divine self-designation, *I am* (v. 62; cf. Isa 43:10, 45; 43:25; 45:18; 51:12; cf. Wis 2:13-20a), and adds the Danielic image used already in 8:38–9:1 and 13:26—the Son of Man coming on the clouds (Dan 7:13-14). All this identifies the one who will shortly die the most shameful possible death in the company of criminals.

By thus identifying himself correctly, Jesus "denies himself," doing God's will rather than his own. As a result, he will take up his cross, saving his life by losing it. Meanwhile, out in the courtyard, Peter is denying Jesus, forfeiting everything by attempting to save his own life. And the evangelist arranges for Peter to fulfill Jesus' prophecy of his denial in excruciating detail at the exact moment that Jesus is being mocked by the Sanhedrin as a false prophet (14:65; cf. Isa 50:6).

But in his denial, Peter ironically tells the truth. The fact is that he does not really *know this man* (v. 71). He never has. He breaks down in tears. Having "been ashamed" of Jesus, he has put himself into the category of those of whom the eschatological judge will ultimately *be ashamed* (8:38). Peter "the Rock" is rocky soil indeed (4:16-17).

15:1-15. Trial before Pilate. This section of the passion narrative begins with Jesus' being "handed over" to Pilate (15:1) and ends with his being "handed over" by Pilate to the crucifixion squad (15:15). The unit is held together by the vocabulary of "binding" (15:1, 7) and "releasing" (15:6, 9, 11, 15; Robbins 1992, 1165-67). The title "King of the Jews" is heard first on the lips of Pilate (15:2, 9, 12) then in the taunts of the soldiers (15:18), and finally on the lips of the religious leaders (15:32). Although the evangelist has spoken of God's kingship, and implied Jesus' kingship by the titles "Messiah" (one who is anointed) and "Son of God," he does not allow Jesus to be called "king" openly except by his enemies. They do not know how right they are because they cannot imagine a king who reigns from a gallows and triumphs by dying in public disgrace.

Jesus, the one who calls God "Abba" (father, 14:36) has been falsely arrested as though he were a rebel bandit (14:48). The crowd chooses death for the one who restored life to others, while a genuine rebel bandit who has committed murder (15:7) goes free. "Barabbas," ironically, means "son" (*bar*, cf. Bartimaeus, 10:46) of the "father" (*abba*, cf. 14:36).

15:16-20a. Mocking. This short unit highlights the humiliation of Jesus and the irony of the kingship motif. It is arranged chiastically:

A Jesus is led into the courtyard, 16
  B Jesus is clothed and crowned as a king, 17
    C The soldiers mock Jesus in speech:
      "Hail, King of the Jews!" 18
    C' The soldiers mock Jesus in actions:
      knelt down in homage, 19
  B' Jesus is stripped and clothed
    in his own clothes, 20a
A' Jesus is led out of the courtyard, 20b

15:20b-25. Crucifixion. The repetition of the verb "to crucify" marks the beginning and end of this unit (vv. 20b, 24, 25). Simon, an African from Cyrene with a Jewish name (probably to be understood as having come to Jerusalem for Passover), is conscripted to carry Jesus' cross. He thus becomes the first of those who pick up the cross and follow Jesus (cf. 8:34). His sons Alexander and Rufus (typical gentile names) must have been well known to the original audience of Mark, since Simon is identified for the audience by association with his sons' names.

The soldiers' offer of myrrhed wine is further mockery; this drink was a delicacy (Pliny, *NatHist* 14.15.92-93). It would have served as a numbing agent as well, which is why the Markan Jesus refuses it; he follows his own advice to stay alert (13:37; Gundry 1993, 944, 956). Jesus is then crucified naked while the soldiers gamble for his clothing, the mere touching of which had once conferred healing (5:27-29; 6:56; cf. Ps 22:18).

15:26-32. Ridicule of Jesus on the cross. This section is tied together by repetition. The mocking inscription on the cross, *"The King of the Jews"* (v. 26), is picked up by the religious leaders when they ridicule Jesus as *Messiah, King of Israel* (v. 32a). Those crucified with Jesus are mentioned in v. 27 and v. 32b (cf. Isa 53:12). Jesus is *blasphemed* (NRSV mg.) by passersby, "mocked" by the religious leaders, and *taunted* by the revolutionaries on his regal right hand and left

hand (cf. 10:37; Ps 22:7-8; Wis 2:17-20). Twice he is invited to save himself (v. 29, 30).

Again Jesus' enemies say more than they know. They articulate the paradox of the passion with the words, *He saved others; he cannot save himself* (v. 31). Only by not saving himself can Jesus save the *many* for whom his life is given as ransom (10:45) and with whom God initiates a covenant in his blood (14:24). If anyone is ever to see and believe it is essential that Jesus *not* come down from the cross now (v. 32a).

15:33-39. Death of Jesus. The darkness recalls Isa 13:9-10; 50:3. Jesus' first loud cry (and the only word from the cross in Mark) is the beginning of Ps 22. Having begun his references to this psalm in 15:22 with Ps 22:18 and moved backward to Ps 22:6-7 in 15:29-30, the narrator ends at the beginning of the psalm with a cry of desolation rather than with the victorious note on which the psalm ends (Robbins 1992, 1175-80).

These last words of Jesus are a prayer, but they contrast sharply with his prayer of submission in 14:36. The evangelist apparently believes that there is no contradiction between commitment to doing the will of God and the anger and abandonment one feels when God's will leads to unbearable suffering and Godforsakenness. The Markan Jesus models the expression of honest anger in the prayers of the faithful.

But like everything else that he has said, these words of the Markan Jesus meet with misunderstanding. Bystanders think that he is calling on Elijah rather than on God (v. 35). Not only that, but Elijah's role is interpreted in terms of his miracle-working power, whereas the Gospel of Mark understands Elijah/John the baptizer as Jesus' predecessor in rejection and suffering (6:14-29; 9:11-13).

The offer of sour wine recalls Ps 69:21: "for my thirst they gave me vinegar to drink." The irony of the misunderstanding is heightened for those members of the audience who would have been familiar with the next verses of Ps 69: "Let their eyes be darkened so that they cannot see" (23a). The three hours of darkness mirror the spiritual blindness of those who see Jesus without understanding and cannot comprehend his words, his actions, or the significance of his passion (Marcus 1992, 183-84).

Jesus' death is portrayed in such a way as to recall the moment of his baptism. The spirit that went into Jesus then (1:10, τὸ πνεῦμα . . . εἰς αὐτόν) now bursts forth from the dying Jesus (15:37, 39, ἐξέπνευσεν) with a loud cry. At the same time, a portent occurs at the Temple inside the city walls. There was an ornate tapestry hanging in front of the outer doors of the Temple, on which, according to JOSEPHUS, "was portrayed a panorama of the heavens" (BJ 5.5.4.212-14). This tapestry is ripped apart (ἐσχίσθη) from above by unseen hands (15:38), just as the heavens had been ripped apart (σχιζομένους) at the baptism (1:10) prior to the descent of the Spirit into Jesus (Ulansey 1991).

The tearing of the Temple tapestry has two functions in Mark: (1) it portends the destruction of the Temple that had been prophetically enacted by the Markan Jesus in 11:15-16 and explicitly predicted by him in 13:2; (2) it minimizes the significance of that destruction by interpreting the death of Jesus as the release of the divine Spirit into the world. No longer is the presence of God to be found in a special way in the Temple; instead, the apocalyptic inbreaking of God's reign, inaugurated by Jesus' victory over the demons, is now marked by the pouring out of that same eschatological Spirit into the world as it struggles to give birth to the new creation. Before his own martyrdom, John had prophesied that Jesus would "baptize in the Holy Spirit." The Markan crucifixion account shows that the baptism in the Holy Spirit that empowers the church for ministry and bold witness (13:11) is made possible by the death of Jesus.

The response of the centurion to Jesus' death is a "confession" only in the ears of Mark's audience. On the level of the story it is a sarcastic comment on the lips of a jaded professional executioner who has just watched one more peasant revolutionary die calling on his God: "Oh sure—*that's* a son of Zeus all right!" (v. 39; Fowler 1991, 205–208). His attitude is the same as that of the others at the foot of the cross: if Jesus had really been anybody special, he would have been translated to heaven before dying such a shameful death (Origen, *CCel* 2.68).

Ironically, however, the centurion represents all the gentiles who will hear the gospel and make a sincere confession as a result of Jesus' death (13:10; cf. Isa 52:15; 2:1-4; 56:6-8). Their inclusion has already been prefigured in the proclamation of the gentile man whom Jesus freed from demonic oppression (5:20) and in the insistence of the gentile woman that Jesus is the "Lord" at whose table even the *dogs* will be satisfied (7:24-30).

15:40-47. Burial. This unit is framed by the description of Jesus' female disciples who watch (from a safe distance) as he is crucified and buried (v. 40, 47). These women are followers of Jesus and participants in the servanthood that he has described as the essence of his mission (v. 41; cf. 1:31; 10:45). They do not come forward to bury him, however.

John's disciples had taken his decapitated corpse and laid it in a tomb (6:29) but there is no one to perform this service for Jesus except one of the enemies who condemned him. Joseph is portrayed as a pious but misguided member of the Sanhedrin (v. 43; not a secret disciple as in Matthew and John) who buries Jesus out of adherence to the requirements of Torah. Deuteronomy 21:22-23 specifies that a criminal who has been impaled must be buried before sundown, lest the land be defiled (Brown 1988, 236). The fact that Joseph is still *waiting expectantly* (v. 43) for God's reign shows that he has missed the whole point; God's reign began to burst into existence before his very eyes, but he condemned the messenger (not dissenting from the verdict as in Luke). Now he tosses Jesus' body into a nearby tomb (not his own tomb or a new tomb as in Matthew, Luke, and John) without even washing it, let alone anointing it for burial.

16:1-8. Empty tomb. After his burial, the Markan Jesus is neither seen nor heard again, although his message is conveyed to the women by the young man at the empty tomb. Mark is the only canonical Gospel that narrates no appearances of the risen Jesus. The spurious later additions to the Gospel show how unsatisfactory this decision was to subsequent readers of the text. Later editors would add stories of appearances, creating the long ending of Mark that continues to puzzle devotional and scholarly readers alike.

It would be a mistake, however, to conclude that since the resurrection is not narrated the evangelist wished to emphasize the absence of Jesus between the resurrection and the eschaton. The Markan miracle stories provide abundant evidence that the author of Mark wanted to encourage beleaguered Christians to have confidence in the presence and power of the risen Lord in the midst of their difficulties (e.g., 4:35-41). The abrupt ending is deliberate, but it puts the emphasis on mission rather than on the absence of Jesus.

At the beginning of chap. 16 the women followers of Jesus are seen belatedly making their way to the tomb to anoint Jesus' body. They are not expecting a resurrection, despite Jesus' repeated predictions, but at least they are still on the scene, unlike the men, whose absence is highlighted by the women's conversation about who is going to do the heavy work of rolling away the "very large" stone from the entrance to the tomb (vv. 3-4).

After this conversation, the rest of the narrative is framed by the women's entering the tomb in v. 5 and exiting the tomb in v. 8. In the tomb they encounter a young man in white, whose numinous quality is established by his resemblance to the transfigured Jesus (9:3). The response of these three disciples, like that of the three disciples at the transfiguration, is fear (16:5; cf. 9:6), but the messenger begins with the greeting, "Fear not!" (v. 6, author trans.).

Stating the obvious, he continues: "You are looking for Jesus of Nazareth, the crucified one. He has been raised (cf. Isa 52:13). He is not *here*" (v. 6, author trans.). Seeking for Jesus is never the right response in Mark (cf. 1:37); following Jesus is. So the messenger now shifts into the imperative mood: "Go tell his disciples (even Peter!) that he is leading you into Galilee; *there* you will see him, just as he told you" (v. 7, author trans.).

Several things are significant about this message. First, the message is delivered in indirect discourse and uses the second person plural. This makes it clear that the women are among those who are to go to Galilee; the messenger does not say, "Tell his disciples that he is leading them into Galilee; there they will see him just as he told them."

Second, the encounter with Jesus that is promised in the message is an example of unmerited grace based solely on the earlier promise of Jesus (*just as he told you*, v. 7). Nothing accounts for the inclusion of the apostate disciples in the community of the resurrection except for Jesus' promise to them in 14:28. Persistently blind, deaf, and hard of heart, they proved themselves "ashamed of Jesus" when the chips were down and by every criterion operative in the narrative so far they should be counted among the outsiders who have no part in God's reign. Even Peter is included, his denial forgiven.

The amazing grace according to Mark is that even those who fail all the tests articulated by the Markan Jesus may yet hear the reconciling call of the Risen Lord and be given another opportunity to follow him on his way. And this good news is "just as it is written in the prophet Isaiah," (cf. Mark 1:2), where the author of Mark had read

Fear not, for I have ransomed you; I have called you by name; you are mine. . . . I will say, "Lead my sons from far away and my daughters from the end of the earth—everyone who is called by my name. For I created [them] for my glory and I formed them and made them. I led out the people

who are blind, yet have eyes, who are deaf, yet have ears . . . I, I am the Lord and besides me there is no savior" (Isa 43:1-11, LXX).

The message is given to the women disciples who flee in fear and silence. That, of course, made no difference, since everyone knew that if the women had told about the resurrection, they would not have been believed (Luke 24:10-11). But somebody must have met Jesus on the way of ministry and martyrdom because the story has just been told again. The abrupt ending of the Gospel of Mark leaves no one else to bear witness to the Risen but unseen Lord except the audience of the story's most recent telling. And that is as it should be.

Works Cited

Anderson, Janice Capel. 1992. "Feminist Criticism: The Dancing Daughter," *Mark and Method*, ed. J. C. Anderson and S. D. Moore, 103–34.

Beasley-Murray, G. R. 1990. "Baptism," MDB.

Beavis, Mary Ann. 1989. *Mark's Audience.*

Boring, M. Eugene. 1987. "The Kingdom of God in Mark," *The Kingdom of God in Twentieth-Century Interpretation*, ed. W. Willis.

Brown, Raymond E. 1988. "The Burial of Jesus (Mark 15:42-47)," *CBQ* 50:233–45.

Dewey, Joanna. 1980. *Markan Public Debate.* SBLDS 48.

Donahue, John R. 1982. "A Neglected Factor in the Theology of Mark," *JBL* 101:563–94. 1988. *The Gospel in Parable.*

Dowd, Sharyn. 1988. *Prayer, Power, and the Problem of Suffering.* SBLDS 105.

Dufton, Francis. 1989. "The Syrophoenician Woman and Her Dogs," *ExpTim* 100:417.

Fiorenza, Elisabeth Schüssler. 1983. *In Memory of Her.*

Fowler, Robert M. 1991. *Let the Reader Understand.*

Grimes, Betty J. 1991. "The Syrophoenician Woman," M.Div. paper, Lexington Theological Seminary.

Gundry, Robert H. 1993. *Mark.*

Marcus, Joel. 1986. *The Mystery of the Kingdom of God.* SBLDS 90. 1992. *The Way of the Lord.*

Montgomery, Helen Barrett. 1924. *The New Testament in Modern English.*

Robbins, Vernon K. 1989. "Rhetorical Composition and the Beelzebul Controversy," *Patterns of Persuasion in the Gospels*, by B. L. Mack and V. K. Robbins, 161–93. 1992. "Psalm 22 in the Markan

Crucifixion," *The Four Gospels 1992*. Festschrift Frans Neirynck. BETL 100.

Schüssler-Fiorenza, Elisabeth. *See* Fiorenza, Elisabeth.

Tannehill, Robert C. 1977. "The Disciples in Mark: The Function of a Narrative Role," *JR* 57:386–405. 1980. "Tension in Synoptic Sayings and Stories," *Int* 34:138–59.

Ulansey, David. 1991. "The Heavenly Veil Torn: Mark's Cosmic *Inclusio*," *JBL* 110:123–35.

Via, Dan O, Jr. 1985. *The Ethics of Mark's Gospel*.

Waetjen, Herman C. 1989. *A Reordering of Power*.

Wahlberg, Rachel Conrad. 1975. *Jesus according to a Woman*.

Wiedemann, Thomas. 1989. *Adults and Children in the Roman Empire*.

Luke

J. Bradley Chance

Introduction

Luke is the third Gospel in the NT. Like the other Gospels it describes the life and teachings of Jesus of Nazareth. Unlike the other Gospels it has a sequel attached to it, the Acts of the Apostles. That both Luke and Acts, commonly referred to simply as Luke-Acts, were written by the same person can be seen by comparing the prologues of each work. The employment of geography to structure the story depicts God's universal offering of salvation. The centrality of JERUSALEM in the narratives serves to remind the reader of God's promises to Israel. The movement of the story in Acts "to the ends of the earth" (Acts 1:8) gives expression to God's salvific concern for everyone, everywhere.

Luke and the Other Gospels

Luke shares much in common with the other two synoptic Gospels, Mark and Matthew, leading interpreters to conclude that some type of direct literary relationship exists between them. Since the nineteenth century, biblical scholars have generally agreed that the Gospel of Mark was employed as a source both by the authors of Luke and Matthew. In addition, interpreters argue that both Luke and Matthew employed a source called Q which consisted primarily of sayings of Jesus. A significant minority of biblical scholars rejects this "two-document hypothesis," arguing that Luke's primary source was the Gospel of Matthew. Luke also shares certain affinities with the Fourth Gospel, such as the somewhat similar story found in Luke 5:4-9 and John 21:5-11 about a miraculous catch of fish. Few scholars have concluded, however, that there existed a direct literary relationship between these two gospels.

Authorship

IRENAEUS (ca. 180 C.E.) expresses the common view of the church fathers concerning the authorship of Luke-Acts: "Luke, too, the companion of Paul, set forth in a book the Gospel as preached by him" (*Adv-Haer* 3.1, 1). Colossians 4:14 and Phlm 24 do refer to a certain Luke, implying that he was an occasional associate of PAUL. Irenaeus also viewed the so-called "we sections" of Acts (cf. Acts 16:10) as the author's indication of his close relationship with Paul (*AdvHaer* 3.14, 1). Modern interpreters note that neither the Gospel nor Acts offers any explicit word concerning the author's identity. Furthermore, the author of Luke-Acts seems to offer a very different portrait of Paul than that offered by Paul himself in his letters. In fact, the author of Acts shows no awareness that Paul was even a prolific letter writer. This evidence leads many scholars to reject the conclusion that the author of Acts was a companion of Paul, much less the specific person named Luke. Some current interpreters have reasonably defended the traditional identification of Luke as the author of Luke-Acts (e.g., Fitzmyer 1981, 35-51). The issue cannot be resolved, so it is best not to base one's interpretation of the narrative on any particular hypothesis concerning the actual identity of the real author. "Luke" is a name used primarily for convenience.

Date and Place of Composition

Luke's description of the fall of Jerusalem (19:43-44; 21:20; cf. the much more general reference in Mark 13:14), leads most interpreters to conclude that Luke was composed after the fall of Jerusalem (70 C.E.). The fact that Luke shows no knowledge of Paul's letter writing activity suggests a date of composition 100 C.E., before the approximate time when Paul's letters began to circulate as a collection. Any author as informed as Luke claims to be (Luke 1:1-4) would surely have known of such a collection. Hence, one may suggest a date of composition between 70 and 100 C.E. No one knows the place of composition, although many suggestions have been offered, both by ancient and modern readers of Luke-Acts.

Genre

Knowing the genre of an ancient text can guide the modern reader in reading the text as an ancient might have. Regrettably, modern scholars can reach no consensus concerning the genre of Luke and Acts. Do they represent separate genres, with the Gospel showing affinities with ancient biography (Burridge 1992) and Acts looking something like an ancient historical novel (Pervo 1989)? Does Luke-Acts represent a type of ancient history (Aune 1987)? Ancient biography (Talbert 1988)? Clearly, the subject of the Gospel is Jesus, allowing the conclusion that readers are reading an ancient biography. But Jesus is a character within a larger story describing God's dealings with Israel and the rest of the world; hence, readers should not hesitate to look for a bigger story within this story about Jesus.

For Further Study

In the *Mercer Dictionary of the Bible*: APOSTLE/APOSTLE-SHIP; APOSTLES, ACTS OF THE; DISCIPLE/DISCIPLESHIP; ESCHATOLOGY IN THE NT; GOSPELS, CRITICAL STUDY OF; HOLY SPIRIT; KINGDOM OF GOD; LORD'S SUPPER; LUKE; LUKE, GOSPEL OF; PASSOVER; Q; REDACTION; SON OF GOD; SON OF MAN; SOURCE CRITICISM; SYNOPTIC PROBLEM; TRAVEL NARRATIVE; TWELVE, THE; WOMEN IN THE NT; WORSHIP IN THE NT.

In other sources: D. E. Aune, *The N.T. in Its Literary Environment*; R. A. Burridge, *What Are the Gospels? A Comparison with Graeco-Roman Biography*; J. A. Fitzmyer, *The Gospel according to Luke I-IX*, AncB; R. Pervo, "Must Luke and Acts Belong to the Same Genre?" *SBLSP* (1989): 309-16; C. H. Talbert, "Once Again: Gospel Genre," *Semeia* 43 (1988): 53-73.

Commentary

An Outline

Prologue, 1:1-4

Luke is the only one of the four Gospels to begin with a formal, literary prologue. This prologue has a number of characteristics found in the formal prologues of other ancient biographies, historical narratives, and even fictional works. First, one finds a statement concerning the author's awareness of earlier, similar works ("many have undertaken to compile a narrative," 1:1 RSV). This may be a reference to Mark and Q, assuming the two-document hypothesis. Luke may have known of other narratives. Second, a statement of the contents of the work (*events that have been fulfilled among us*, v. 1) and a plan of presentation (*to write an orderly account for you*, v. 3). Third, a statement rehearsing the author's qualifications (vv. 2-3). Such statements were often rhetorical attempts to gain the reader's confidence rather than literal records of the author's research techniques. Fourth, a statement of purpose (v. 4). Fifth, identification of the addressee (*Theophilus*, v. 3). Finally, a very good literary style, which is discernable even in most English translations. Regrettably, the prologue offers no help in identifying specifically the author of the narrative, since it lacks what was a common feature of prologues: the author's name.

Although readers learn nothing of the author's identity, the text does imply some things about the author. First, he uses a masculine participle in the word translated as *investigating* (v. 3) to describe himself. Second, he makes no claims to having been an eyewitness, but rather describes himself as the recipient of tradition which goes back to *eyewitnesses and servants* (v. 2). Third, the author presents himself as informed and educated. Such an impression is made not only by what he says about how carefully he has investigated everything, but the very style of the prologue itself. It is clear that the author is calling the reader to take the forthcoming narrative seriously.

The prologue also implies certain things about the reader, whom the author identifies as *Theophilus*. If this were an actual person, his identity is unknown. Luke may be addressing the gospel to any "lover of God," which is what the name literally means. Regardless, the text assumes a reader who has had some previous instruction in the Christian tradition. The text also assumes an inquisitive reader who wishes to be better informed and who desires to *know the truth* (v. 4) about these matters. The very use of a formal prologue, inviting readers to compare this narrative to other works of history and biography, implies readers who would appreciate a narrative about Jesus and his followers written from a cultured, even cosmopolitan perspective.

In short, any reader, ancient or modern, who assumes the role of the reader implied by the text will approach the narrative as an informed, inquisitive, and cosmopolitan reader sympathetic with the Christian tradition. That is the perspective that shall be employed in the following commentary.

Preparing the Way, 1:5–4:13

In this first section of the narrative Luke will provide a context in which readers can understand the public ministry of Jesus. Hence, the "way" is not only being prepared for Jesus, but for the reader. This narrative of preparation indicates that Jesus' story finds its roots in the story of the OT, the story of Israel and Israel's God. Jesus' story is the realization of the hopes of Israel and the promises made by God to Israel's ancestors, Abraham, Isaac, and Jacob. Further, this coming salvation will be not only for Israel's glory but will offer revelation to the gentiles also.

John's public preaching announces that the time of the Lord's coming is at hand, placing the people of Israel and the reader at the edge of the time of the actual realization of the promises and hopes. Jesus' BAPTISM and testing by the devil offer some real insight into the profound significance of the work he is about to accomplish.

Preparation through Announcement, 1:5-56

Like the Gospel of Matthew, Luke begins his "narrative concerning the things which have been fulfilled among us" (author trans.) with an account of the birth of Jesus. Each of them likely constructed their infancy narratives on the basis of limited yet common traditions for the purpose of conveying to their readers something of the purpose and significance of Jesus' life—a common function of ancient biographical birth accounts. (See Fitzmyer 1981, 305-309.)

Readers of Luke's birth narrative should note in Gabriel's announcements to ZECHARIAH and MARY similarities with birth announcements of OT worthies (such as ABRAHAM), including the presence of an ANGEL, a message about the child, and sometimes even human questioning (cf. Gen 16:7-13; 17:1-22; Judg 13:3-20). These OT allusions, combined with a literary style reminiscent of the LXX, the Bible of Luke's readers, and the primary setting of Jerusalem and the Temple, places Luke's story and, hence, his readers into the world of the OT.

1:5-25. Announcement to Zechariah. Zechariah and ELIZABETH are introduced as stock, pious characters out of the OT, being described as righteous, blameless, and of priestly descent. Even their childless state puts them in company with OT heroes like Abraham and SARAH. During his priestly service Zechariah receives the vision of Gabriel concerning John's birth. Like heroes who have preceded them, Zechariah and Elizabeth will have a child late in life. This child will also resemble OT heroes, especially Elijah (1:16-17). Comparison with ELIJAH raises a note of expectation: the Lord is coming! Israel must be prepared! (cf. Mal 4:5-6).

Zechariah is struck dumb as an immediate and concrete sign to address his skepticism. It also renders Zechariah unable to offer the priestly blessing to the people waiting outside, perhaps implying that the old way of receiving the blessing of God is about to pass away. The story ends with a clear word that the announcement has come true—Elizabeth has experienced the favor of God.

1:26-38. Announcement to Mary. This angelic announcement also refers to a wondrous birth—but it is even more wondrous than that of John. Mary's child will be conceived by the power of the HOLY SPIRIT.

While John was compared to the great prophet Elijah, Jesus is called *the Son of the Most High* and will sit on the throne of DAVID and *reign over the house of Jacob forever* (vv. 32-33). Long awaited hopes for the messianic king are finally going to be realized. Gabriel's talk of the Holy Spirit, denoting the dynamic presence of God, Elizabeth's conception, and his concluding words, *nothing will be impossible with God* (vv. 35-37), serve to indicate the direct intervention of God into the story of the people of Israel. Mary's obedient response (v. 38) offers a model for all who experience God's favor (v. 28) to emulate.

1:39-56. Announcement of the mothers. When the two relatives meet, Elizabeth, being filled with the Holy Spirit, offers Mary a blessing. Mary is blessed because she is an instrument of God, bearing the Lord as *the fruit of [her] womb* (v. 42), and because she has responded to God by believing (having faith in) the word spoken to her (v. 45). The stirring of John in Elizabeth's womb and her filling with the Spirit confirm once again the power and immediate presence of God.

Mary offers up a hymn of praise (the MAGNIFICAT, vv. 46b-55), making explicit what has been intimated in the narrative: God is accomplishing great things. Specific blessings are coming Israel's way in fulfillment of God's promises to Israel's ancestors. Among these blessings is a great reversal of stations (vv. 51-53) commonly associated with the messianic age.

Preparation through Wondrous Births and Childhoods, 1:57–2:52

1:57-66 The circumcision and naming of John. The angelic announcement now finds fulfillment. John's circumcision continues the theme of Jewish piety (v. 59). In obedience to the vision (v. 13), Zechariah confirms Elizabeth's statement that the child shall be named "John" (vv. 60-63). His tongue is then loosed, evoking praise from him and fear from the neighbors and relatives (v. 65). Exciting expectations are raised among the people as they ask *what then will this child become?* (v. 66).

1:67-80. The Benedictus. Zechariah, filled with the Spirit, answers their question through *prophecy* in vv. 68-79. Zechariah repeats an important theme of Mary's Magnificat: God is fulfilling promises made of old to Israel's prophets (v. 70) and ancestors (vv. 72-73). Themes of deliverance abound: *redeemed, mighty savior for us, saved from our enemies, rescued from the hands of our enemies.* John, as *prophet of the Most*

High, shall prepare the Lord's ways offering *knowledge of salvation, the forgiveness of their sins* (v. 77), leading to *the dawn from on high* to break in and offer *light to those . . . in darkness,* and *the way of peace* (vv. 78-79). But Israel, and the reader, must wait until the day when John appears *publicly to Israel* (v. 80).

2:1-20. The birth of Jesus. Luke is aware of the tradition that Bethlehem was the place of Jesus' birth. He uses a vague reminiscence of a census around the time of Jesus' birth as a means of explaining how Joseph and Mary came to be in Bethlehem. What confuses interpreters is the fact that the *registration . . . taken while Quirinius was governor of Syria* (v. 2) occurred in 6 C.E., long after "the days of King Herod" (1:5, d. 4 B.C.E.). Luke notes that Joseph, Mary's fiancee, was a descendant of David and Bethlehem was ·the city of David (v. 3) to emphasize the point that Jesus is to be the one to inherit *the throne of his ancestor David* (1:32).

The announcement to and visitation of the shepherds (vv. 8-20) allows for a number of important themes to be reiterated or introduced. The angelic announcement, which includes a *sign* (v. 12), indicates the activity of God. Shepherds as the recipients of this *good news of great joy* denote the lowly whom God is lifting up (1:52). Jesus is specifically identified as *a Savior* and *the Messiah* (v. 11). Just as expectations were raised among the people regarding John, all who hear the shepherds' report are *amazed* (v. 18). The shepherds' *glorifying and praising God* (v. 20) represents appropriate response to the great thing God is accomplishing.

2:21-40. The presentation of Jesus. The piety of Jesus' parents is made evident as they circumcise Jesus, name him in obedience to the angelic vision (v. 21), and do all that is necessary *according to the law of Moses* (v. 22). The favored status of the lowly, the poor, and humble (cf. 1:51-53) is reinforced by notification that Jesus' parents offer the sacrifice of those who are poor (v. 24. cf. Lev 12:8).

SIMEON too embodies pious characteristics, being guided by the Spirit, *righteous and devout, looking forward to the consolation of Israel* (v. 25). His hope is fulfilled as he is permitted to see Jesus. His words of praise introduce a new element into this story: this salvation is for "all of the peoples"—glory for Israel, *revelation to the Gentiles* (v. 32). Even Mary and Joseph *were amazed at what was being said about him* (v. 33), inviting readers to pause and reflect on what was so amazing about what Simeon has just said: even the gentiles will benefit from this savior! But then Simeon offers a final, ominous word: *the falling and rising of many in Israel* is coming. Jesus will be *a sign that will be opposed*. Even Mary will not be spared this dividing sword (v. 35). ANNA, a PROPHET, further shows how the truly pious of Israel recognize the significance of Jesus and what he has to offer those *looking for the redemption of Jerusalem* (v. 38).

2:41-52. Jesus at the Temple. This final story serves to foreshadow Jesus' ultimate obedience to God (v. 49), even over family (cf. Mary's experiencing the sword of division, v. 35), and his authority as an interpreter of God's law. The latter is evidenced by the astonishment of *teachers . . . at his understanding and his answers*. A final note (v. 52) confirms the favored status of Jesus.

Preparation through John's Preaching, 3:1-20

3:1-6. Historical introduction. The historical details offered by Luke serve to root the story of Jesus in world history. *The fifteenth year of the reign of Emperor Tiberius* is most likely 28/29 C.E. Pontius PILATE, who governed Judea 26–36 C.E., will play a role in Jesus' trial (chap. 23), as will HEROD (*ruler of Galilee* 4 B.C.E.–39 C.E.). Philip, Herod's brother, and Lysanias play no role in the story. Verse 2 leaves the impression that Annas and CAIAPHAS jointly held the office of high priest. Annas, the father-in-law of Caiaphas, actually held the office from 6–15 C.E. Caiaphas was the actual ruling high priest during Jesus' ministry (18–36 C.E.). Neither Annas nor Caiaphas appears by name anywhere else in Luke's story, but Luke must have one of these in mind when he refers to Jesus' hearing at the *high priest's house* (Luke 22:54).

This detailed introduction also provides for John the kind of historical introduction that is found in OT prophetic books (cf. Isa 1:1; Jer 1:1-3). This is a most fitting introduction since John has already been referred to as *prophet of the Most High* (1:76). John prepares the way by *proclaiming a baptism of repentance for the forgiveness of sins* (v. 3). Luke does not interpret the connection between baptism, repentance, and forgiveness. Perhaps he understood John's baptism as a kind of foreshadowing of (preparation for) Christian baptism (cf., e.g., Acts 19:1-7). John had already been introduced as one whose work would involve repentance, or turning (1:16-17), and forgiveness of sins (1:77). Now he is carrying out that role. The quotation from Isa 40:3-5 (vv. 4-6) is longer than that offered in

either Matthew or Mark and emphasizes the cosmic and universal significance (*all flesh shall see the salvation of God*; cf. 2:32) of what is about to happen.

3:7-17. The preaching of John. John's preaching focuses on three issues. Verses 7-9 make clear the necessity of repentance in the face of the eschatological wrath that is coming. Talk of wrath might seem surprising, but both Mary (1:51-53) and Zechariah (1:71-73) have already spoken of reversals that are necessary to set the world right. Despite such declarations as 1:55 and 1:73, John makes clear that repentance is needed even from the children of Abraham.

Verses 10-14 offer specific examples of repentance—a radical change of priorities, values, and ethical behavior. The fact that even *tax collectors* and *soldiers* are depicted among *the crowds that came out to be baptized by him* indicates that all are afforded the opportunity to prepare themselves for the coming of the Lord.

Verses 15-18 begin with people wondering whether this one *might be the Messiah*. The crowds clearly recognize the eschatological implications of John's message. Their inquiry leads John to point their attention to another: *one who is more powerful than* he is coming. Readers know that this is Jesus. John proclaims that this mighty one will carry out the baptism of salvation (*Holy Spirit*) or damnation (*fire*), dividing humanity into wheat and chaff. Recall Simeon's prophecy concerning the *falling and rising of many in Israel* (2:34).

3:18-20. The imprisonment of John. Neither Matthew (4:12; cf. 14:3-4) nor Mark (1:14a; cf. 6:17-18) informs the reader of John's arrest until after Jesus had been baptized. In Luke, however, John exits the stage prior to Jesus' baptism when Herod throws John in prison because he openly preached against Herod's marriage to his brother's wife. (JOSEPHUS confirms this fact, although he states that Herod feared the political implications of John's preaching [*Ant* 18.5.2].) The way has now been prepared for the Lord.

Preparation through Jesus' Baptism and Temptation, 3:21–4:13

Although the way has been prepared for Jesus through the proclamation of repentance and forgiveness, Jesus must be prepared through divine commissioning and a period of testing.

3:21-22. The baptism of Jesus. Unlike Matthew (3:13-17) and Mark (1:9-11), Luke does not state that

John baptized Jesus; in fact, he leaves exactly the opposite impression. Rather, Luke speaks of Jesus' baptism in an almost parenthetical statement associating Jesus' baptism with that of *all the people*. Luke offers no clues that Jesus was in need of repentance and forgiveness. But such identification prepares for the special ministry of Jesus to outcasts and sinners of Israel.

Luke notes that the Spirit descends upon Jesus while he is praying. The eschatological mission that is about to commence requires prayer and the enabling of the Spirit. No hint is given that any other than Jesus heard the voice confirming the identity of Jesus as God's *Son, the Beloved* with whom God is *well pleased* (contra? Matt 3:17). Informed readers would catch the allusion to Ps 2:7, a psalm of enthronement in which the LORD declares "you are my son," and recall the promise made to Mary (1:32). They would also note the allusion to Isa 42:1, an oracle concerning God's servant who receives God's spirit "to bring forth justice to the nations" (ἔθνη), and recall Simeon's prophecy that Jesus would be *a light for revelation to the Gentiles* (ἔθνη, 2:32).

3:23-38. The genealogy of Jesus. Matthew also offers a genealogy of Jesus (Matt 1:2-16), although it is not the same genealogy. The genealogies of Matthew and Luke, like other ancient genealogies, served to make a statement about the identity of Jesus. From Luke's genealogy one learns that through Joseph, Jesus' legal father (*the son [as was thought] of Joseph*, [v. 23]), Jesus is indeed of the line of David, although, interestingly, not of the royal line (cf. v. 32; Jesus is descended from David's son Nathan, not Solomon). Perhaps Luke was aware of specific prophecies such as those found in Jer 22:24-30; 36:30-31, stating that the Davidic dynasty would end with JEHOIACHIN (Coniah in Jer 22:24), son of JEHOIAKIM (cf. esp. Jer 22:30). Further by tracing Jesus' genealogy back to ADAM and God (v. 38) the genealogy also "serves to explain in still another way the relation of Jesus . . . to God and to the human beings he has come to serve" (Fitzmyer 1981, 498). The genealogy reinforces the impression made by the baptism story: that Jesus identifies with "all the people" and is God's son.

4:1-13. The temptation of Jesus. Luke's narration of the temptation, or testing, of Jesus is most similar to the account found in Matt 4:1-11 (cf. Mark 1:12-13), although the order of temptations is not the same. Luke introduces the temptation narrative by twice noting Jesus' close association with the *Holy Spirit* (v. 1), stating that Jesus was *full of the Holy Spirit*, and

that he *was led by the Spirit in the wilderness*. Recall that Luke has closely juxtaposed the descent of the Spirit and the affirmation of Jesus' sonship in 3:22 and has just concluded the genealogy of Jesus with the phrase *son of God* (3:38). This allows the conclusion that it is Jesus, in his role as Son of God, who is being led by the Spirit into the wilderness. Twice Jesus' adversary begins his challenges to Jesus by saying *if you are the Son of God* (vv. 3, 9), confirming that, indeed, this narrative is primarily about Jesus and his work as God's Son.

The reason for Jesus' pilgrimage to the wilderness is clearly stated: Jesus *for forty days . . . was tempted by the devil* (v. 2). By portraying the time of testing as extending throughout the time of the forty days (contra Matt 4:1-3), Luke portrays a most intense and significant struggle.

The reference to *forty days* might be nothing more than a way of indicating an extended duration of time. One would not be reading too much into the text to find some sort of symbolic significance. For example, Moses and Elijah, two great figures of the OT whose names will often appear in Luke's narrative (and they will even appear as characters in the action! [cf. 9:28-36]), also experienced a period of forty days of solitude from other people at significant periods in their lives (cf. Exod 24:18; 1 Kgs 19:8). Perhaps Luke wishes the reader to compare the work of Jesus to the important influence of these great men of old.

The number *forty* might also allude to the forty years of testing in the wilderness experienced by Israel during the exodus. In all three temptations, Jesus' retorts to the devil consist of quotations from Deuteronomy. In the first (v. 4) Jesus quotes Deut 8:3. In Deut 8:2, Moses refers explicitly to Israel's testing for "forty years in the wilderness" and Israel's experiencing hunger and being fed with manna "in order to make you understand that one does not live by bread alone." Jesus' second retort to the devil (v. 8) quotes Deut 6:13, found in a context referring to Israel's impending possession of the land. It is emphasized that God gave Israel the land and Israel should, therefore, serve only God (cf. Deut 6:10-15). Notably, Jesus rebuffs the devil's offer to give him *all the kingdoms of the world* if Jesus will only worship him (vv. 5-7) with a quotation from the OT found in a context emphasizing that it is *God* who gives the land. It is also relevant that Ps 106, which rehearses the rebellious story of Israel in the face of God's mercy, notes that one of Israel's iniquitous acts "in the wilderness" was the false worship offered to the calf (Ps 106:14, 19-20). Jesus, unlike Israel, does not succumb to the temptation of false worship. In the final retort, v. 12, Jesus quotes Deut 6:16. Moses specifically commanded Israel, "Do not put the LORD your God to the test, as you tested him at Massah." Psalm 106:14b also states that Israel "put God to the test in the desert." Collectively, these rejections of the devil's tests show that Jesus accomplished in the wilderness what Israel could not. Such an impression cannot help but leave the reader sensing that indeed good times may be ahead for Israel. Where Israel had failed in the past, Jesus, the one who brings God's salvation prepared *for glory to [God's] people Israel* (2:32), succeeds. And yet, such reminders of Israel's failings might leave the reader feeling ambiguous. If Israel failed before, might failure come again?

Although informed readers can easily detect a comparison between Jesus and Israel, they cannot overlook the fact that this narrative is about a direct conflict between Jesus, the Spirit-anointed Son of God, and the devil. Luke does not need to introduce the devil; informed readers know who he is. He is Satan (cf., e.g., 10:18; 11:18; 13:16), Beelzebul, the ruler of demons (11:15), and even the ruler of *all the kingdoms of the world* (v. 5).

This, the last story told before Jesus begins his public ministry, makes clear that the way that has been prepared is a way that involves conflict of the most serious proportions. Jesus' nemesis will be Satan himself. To be sure, Jesus wins this round: *when the devil had finished every test, he departed from him* (v. 13). Luke has made clear to the reader that the Spirit-anointed Son of God is more powerful than Satan. But this battle is not over, for the devil *departed [only] . . . until an opportune time.* As subsequent stories will make clear, Satan, this ruler of demons, has allies everywhere.

The Galilean Ministry of the Spirit-Anointed Prophet, 4:14–9:50

This second section of Luke's narrative hurls Jesus into action and into confrontation with the allies of Satan. The first pericope sets the tone of the entire section and for Jesus' ministry: it will be a ministry of liberation, or release. In parts one (4:14–6:16) and three (7:1–9:50) of this section, Jesus' ministry of liberation comes primarily through his and his followers' actions. In part two (6:17-49) he offers his liberating word in the sermon on the plain.

Release to the Captives, 4:14–6:16

4:14-30. The rejection at Nazareth. Luke prefaces the story of the Nazareth incident with a summary statement (vv. 14-15) of Jesus' public ministry, leaving the impression Jesus has been at work for some time. This summary of Jesus' activities differs from that of Matt 4:13-17 and Mark 1:14b-15, both of which make explicit reference to Jesus' proclamation of the "kingdom of God." This has led some to believe that Luke does not wish to emphasize the eschatological significance of Jesus' work. The remainder of chap. 4 challenges this conclusion.

Luke's story of Jesus' Nazareth rejection is longer than the accounts found in Matt 13:54-58 and Mark 6:1-6a. The length of the story and Luke's use of this story to inaugurate Jesus' public ministry indicate its significance. The text from which Jesus reads (Isa 61:1-2a; 58:6) refers to familiar issues, especially *the Spirit of the Lord*, and *anointed* (having same Gk. root as the word "Christ"). Since readers already know Jesus to be the "anointed one" (2:11) and "full of the Spirit" (4:1), they will associate this text with Jesus and the work he is going to perform.

Captives and *oppressed* (v. 18) describe similar types of people. The words translated *release* and *go free* represent the same word in Greek (ἄφεσις). Reference is being made to the "setting free," the liberation, of oppressed persons. Such liberation is juxtaposed with references to bringing *good news to the poor, recovery of sight to the blind*, and proclaiming *the year of the Lord's favor* (vv. 18-19). Thus, several important issues pertaining the upcoming ministry of Jesus, particularly preaching and healing, are set in an overall context of liberation.

The eyes of all . . . were fixed on him (v. 20). Something significant is happening. Jesus declares that *today this scripture has been fulfilled in your hearing.* Thus, it is not surprising that *all spoke well of him and were amazed at the gracious words* (v. 22). Of course, readers know that Jesus is not merely *Joseph's son* (v. 22). Still readers share with the audience the expectation that liberation is coming, and wonder just what kind of liberation. Just who are the oppressed and the captives?

Jesus does not warmly receive the reaction of his hometown audience. He predicts that his people will quote Jesus the proverb, *Doctor, cure yourself* (v. 23), which he then interprets and applies specifically: *Do here also in your hometown the things we have heard you did at Capernaum* (v. 23). Despite an initially positive response, relations will cool. Such cooling has to do with Jesus' hometown citizens wanting to make sure that no other town receives anything that they do not. There are evidenced here hints of possessiveness and even jealousy.

Jesus' next words offer further interpretation, applying to himself the title prophet and stating that he will not be accepted by his own. Rejection, however, does not stop the prophet from doing his work. Elijah had certainly experienced rejection from his own, being the object of AHAB's and JEZEBEL's wrath requiring that he flee for his life (1 Kgs 19). Yet his prophetic work continued even in the midst of such struggle as indicated by his being sent to a non-Israelite widow (1 Kgs 17). ELISHA, upon whom the spirit of Elijah had come to rest (2 Kgs 2:15), further demonstrated that God's blessings were not reserved for Israel in that he healed the Syrian Namaan (2 Kgs 5).

The application to Jesus' own situation is clear: he will experience rejection from his own—but that will not stop him from performing the liberating work to which God has called him. He will move on from NAZARETH. In the larger setting of Luke-Acts readers may also sense something of an ominous foreshadowing: will Jesus ultimately be rejected by Israel just as he has predicted that he will be rejected by his hometown? If so, readers are assured that such rejection will not stop the liberating work of God. Elijah and Elisha went to the others—so can Jesus.

The reaction of Jesus' hometown is violent beyond reason. The very hint that God's blessings will not be halted by the rejection of his messenger drives the people to fury. Their violent protest against the prophecy that they will reject Jesus leads them to do precisely what Jesus predicted: *they drove him out of town* and tried to *hurl him off the cliff* (v. 29). Already the "rising and falling of many in Israel" has begun. Jesus' first public word to Israel has shown him to be the *sign that will be opposed* (2:34).

4:31-44. The liberating work of God's reign. Luke offers four pericopes that quickly demonstrate precisely the kind of liberation Jesus was talking about in Nazareth.

The first is 4:31-37. Jesus' word in 4:23 has prepared readers for something significant to happen in Capernaum. This pericope fulfills the expectation. The significant thing that happens is Jesus' confrontation with an *unclean demon* (v. 33), clearly an ally of the devil. The demon, speaking for himself and his band

of fellow hosts of Satan, sums up the essence of the conflict: *Have you come to destroy us?* (v. 34) Jesus' answer is clear as he *rebuked him* and thereby demonstrated his *authority and power* to command *the unclean spirits, and out they come!* (v. 36) Jesus' liberating ministry has begun.

Jesus' liberating work continues as he assaults not only demons but disease (vv. 38-39). The clause, he *rebuked the fever* (v. 39), recalls how he had earlier *rebuked* the demon (v. 35). The connection with Jesus' announced ministry of "release" (4:18) is found in the statement that the fever *left her*, which literally is translated "it released her." The *service* Peter's liberated mother-in-law renders to them demonstrates that she is indeed well. A deeper meaning is suggested in that the word used for service (διακονέω) is often used of "Christian service" (e.g., Luke 22:24-27). Those liberated by Jesus are liberated for service to him and others.

The third pericope (4:40-41) again juxtaposes Jesus' healings and exorcisms. Readers are told that Jesus *rebuked* the demons, not permitting them to reveal his identity as *the Messiah* and *Son of God*. No specific clue is given as to why Jesus will not permit such revelations. Perhaps Jesus wishes to define these titles on his own terms.

In the final pericope (4:42-44) of this section, Luke uses a phrase he has not yet used: *the kingdom of God*. Finally, readers know what all this is about. The proclaiming of *good news to the poor* and *release to the captives* (4:18), the rebuking of demons and disease, even the head-to-head encounter with the devil in the wilderness—all of these come under the straightforward clause: *to proclaim to good news of the kingdom of God* (v. 43). The reign of God himself is coming—and with it comes liberation from that which has oppressed and held captive God's people. CAPERNAUM has enjoyed these blessings. Capernaum must learn what Nazareth failed to learn: these blessings are not only for them. Jesus must proclaim this good news in *other cities also*.

5:1-11. Calling disciples. Luke introduces the story by referring to the pressing *crowd*, a mass-character already introduced (cf. 4:42). This is one of the many references portraying the masses as responding favorably to Jesus (cf. 5:15; 6:17; 7:11, et al.).

The story indicates the work of Jesus will involve the help of others, of whom *Simon* and *James and John, sons of Zebedee*, are the first chosen. Luke introduced Simon rather abruptly in 4:38. It is clear that he has seen the many mighty works of Jesus, works that point to Jesus' authority and power (cf. 4:36). The miraculous catch of fish offers one more demonstration of Jesus' power, a power to which Simon responds in amazement (v. 9). *He fell down at Jesus' knees, saying, "Go away from me, Lord, for I am a sinful man"* (v. 8). The call of Jesus transcends the sinful human condition. In spite of Peter's condition as a sinner Jesus calls him to *be catching people* (v. 10), a peculiar phrase literally rendered "catching alive." Surely, the implication is that Simon will be catching people alive for the kingdom of God (4:43). Simon and his companions respond with total allegiance: *they left everything and followed him* (v. 11).

5:12-16. Healing of a leper. Luke offers another example of the liberating power of Jesus. Here Jesus heals a man inflicted with a disease that ostracized him from the community of the people, due to uncleanness (Lev 13:45-46). The leper, therefore, desires to be made clean (5:12). Jesus' concern to restore the leper to community is shown in his command that the leper go immediately to the priest to *make an offering for your cleansing*, an offering that resulted in restoration to the community (cf. Lev 14:2-9). The liberating power of Jesus has genuine communal and sociological concern.

Luke now offers a series of controversy stories, extending from 5:17 through 6:11. In these stories, Jesus will continue to manifest his power and authority through the miracles by which he confronts oppressive disease. Jesus will also demonstrate his authority through confrontation with a new set of characters, the religious authorities. These people offer a different, yet no less real, kind of oppression of human beings: scrupulous religion.

5:17-26. The forgiveness of sins. Luke sets the stage for the next story by introducing the *Pharisees and teachers of the law* (v. 17). Readers would associate them with religious authorities, an association reinforced by reference to their being *from Jerusalem*. Notification of the presence of the crowd (v. 19), whom Luke has already shown to be positively disposed to the work of Jesus, raises a question as to whether the religious leaders will also respond positively to Jesus' work.

Luke sets readers up for another healing miracle, stating that *the power of the Lord was with him to heal* (v. 17). The story then takes a strange turn. When the paralytic is presented to Jesus, he declares, *"Your sins are forgiven"* (v. 18). Two things become clear. One,

the religious leaders react negatively to Jesus' word of forgiveness. Readers know the power of the Lord to be with Jesus (cf. 5:17; 3:21-22; 4:1); the leaders obviously do not. Their reaction is quite the opposite of the crowd who *glorified God* (v. 26). The division of Israel has begun! Ironically, in their skepticism the leaders ask what is a crucially important question: "Who is this man . . . ?" (author trans.) Two, readers are invited to consider that the power of Jesus to liberate from demons and disease can also liberate people from sin. The word used for "forgiveness" shares the same Gk. root as the word for "release" found in 4:18. "Release from sins" is part of a much larger ministry of liberation—the liberation from the oppressive grip of the devil from which the kingdom of God has come to release humanity. Jesus associates this dimension of the liberation with the title *Son of Man*, thereby answering his opponents' question.

5:27–6:11. Controversy with the religious leaders. Luke now offers a number of dramatic controversies. Jesus' word of forgiveness in the preceding pericope sets the stage for this story of calling a notorious sinner (a tax collector) to follow Jesus (5:27-32). The *Pharisees and their scribes* (5:30) are both equally scandalized by this act of Jesus. Jesus employs another physician proverb (cf. 4:23) to make clear that the invitation of sinners to repentance is why he has come, implying that the liberation from sin that Jesus offers requires a genuine change of heart and mind in the life of the sinner.

The following PARABLES offered by Jesus (5:33-39) make clear that this way of offering God's liberating power is something radically new. Jesus has not come to confirm the old ways of piety and religion, such as fasting, but to bring a joyful new way of life that calls for celebration. The seemingly innocuous metaphors about cloth and patches, wine and wineskins, illustrate a most ominous principle: the new and the old won't mix—indeed they cannot mix.

The incident of plucking grain on the SABBATH (6:1-5) demonstrates the *Pharisees'* brand of religiosity. Jesus appeals to the story of David (1 Sam 21:1-7) to declare that human need takes precedence over legal scruples. Speaking again of the *Son of Man* he declares himself (implicitly) to be lord even of the Sabbath. Luke seems to be presenting Jesus as the one whose authority alone as the lord of the Sabbath allows for this radically new understanding of Sabbath law, rooted in Jesus' unique and authoritative interpretation of scripture.

Luke concludes this section with one final Sabbath controversy (6:6-11). The intensity of the conflict between Jesus and the religious leaders may have led readers to wonder just how far these leaders might go to stop Jesus. Verse 11 invites readers to assume the worst. Could it be that even these religious leaders, like demons and disease, are on the side the devil? Luke leaves readers wondering.

6:12-16. Naming of the apostles. Luke concludes this section by completing the circle of those whom he is calling to "catch people." That this is to be the mission of the *apostles* (v. 13), these men whom Jesus will "send out," is suggested by the fact that Simon, whom Jesus specifically called to "catch people" (5:10) heads the list. The number twelve is reminiscent of the twelve tribes of Israel, suggesting that Jesus' liberating work does indeed involve a renewal and possibly redefinition of Israel. The statement that JUDAS *became a traitor* is particularly ominous in light 6:11. Will the leaders and Judas form some alliance?

Proclaiming the Favorable Year of the Lord, 6:17-49

In the preceding section, Jesus has demonstrated the liberating power of God through miracle and confrontation. In this section, the sermon on the plain, Jesus offers the liberating word.

6:17-19. Introduction. Here Luke introduces two important details: notification of the audience and a reminder of the eschatological context. The audience consists of the apostles (*them*), *a great crowd of his disciples* v. 17; (Jesus' followers are not limited to the circle of the apostles), and *a great multitude of people*. *People* is almost a technical term denoting "the people of Israel." It is often synonymous with the "crowd(s)" (cf. 5:19). Conspicuous by their absence is the Jewish leadership. The eschatological context is noted with reference to healing and exorcisms. This word of Jesus is to be heard within the context of his ministry of liberation.

6:20-26. The beatitudes and woes. Beatitudes are words of blessing that announce the happy condition of someone. They are not exhortations. The first beatitude, for example, does not say, "Be poor and God will give you the kingdom." Rather, the poor, the hungry, the sorrowful, and the despised and excluded are pronounced as blessed now because of what God will offer in the future: the kingdom, satisfaction, joy, and reward in heaven (cf. 1:52b, 53a). Present blessing on the basis of God's future action is no numbing

opiate for the masses. Recall the demonstrations of Jesus' power already manifested. God's reign is already breaking in to set right a corrupt world whose *kingdoms, authority,* and *glory* now lay in the hand of the devil (cf. 4:5-6). For those who have no claim or stake in the kingdom of this age, the liberation of God's kingdom comes.

For those who have staked their claim in the *kingdoms of the world* (cf. 4:5)—the rich, the satiated, the happy-go-lucky, and the respected (cf. 1:51b, 52a, 53b)—God's action brings *woe*. The demonic grip on the world is already being loosened—the sandy and shifting foundation of that world is being washed away (cf. 6:49). Indeed, *woe to you* who have staked your lives on this!

6:27-42. Response to God's initiative. God's action now, serving as a foretaste of his action to come, requires response. At the heart of that response is the command, *Be merciful, just as your Father is merciful* (v. 36). The one who benefits from God's merciful reclamation of his world and its inhabitants from the grip of evil must extend that mercy to others.

Such mercy manifests itself primarily in two ways. First, one is to love radically, even one's enemies (vv. 27-31), and without the expectation of reciprocity (vv. 32-35a). The word of Jesus offers concrete (although not casuistic or exhaustive) illustrations of such radical love. It involves the love of enemies (might this be how, in God's reign, enemies are conquered? [cf. 1:71, 74]), prayer for the abusive, turning the other cheek, giving both to the one who would beg and the one who would take, and even loving the one who has no intention of returning such love. The shock of Jesus' examples is no doubt intentional, leading the reader to "feel" just how radical the expectations of God's mercy really are. Such expectations, however, are grounded in the fact that God *is kind to the ungrateful and the wicked* (v. 35b). Readers cannot help but ask whether God's mercy to them has been as radical as loving those who despise, abuse, and take advantage of them.

The second concrete way that one exhibits the mercy received is to refuse to judge and condemn, and to extend forgiveness and generosity (vv. 37-38). Being merciful as God is merciful does not justify being the judge as God is the judge. Such refusal to judge does not mean refusal to acknowledge and address the corrupting evil of the present age. To conclude this is to forget the eschatological context of the sermon (cf. 6:17-19). It does require, however, that one's concern with sin and corruption begin with the logs that obscure one's own vision, not the specks that one is so sure pervert the vision of one's neighbor.

6:43-49. Concluding parables. The first concluding parable (vv. 43-45) teaches that the kind of good *fruit* required of those called to be *children of the Most High* (v. 35) can only come from good trees. Verse 45 interprets the metaphor, indicating that Jesus is talking about *the good person [who] out of the good treasure of the heart produces good.* Transformed persons and hearts are the prerequisites to the response demanded of the kingdom. The whole of this Gospel clearly implies that such transformation is possible only in light of the merciful liberation Jesus has come to offer. In short, God is the source of this "goodness" (cf. 18:19). Nonetheless, as the second concluding parable (vv. 46-49) indicates, a life built on the solid foundation which can survive the onslaught of God's discerning judgment, is the life of one who *hears my words, and acts on them.* Obedience, not just good intentions (what many call a "good heart") is demanded.

Release to the Oppressed, 7:1–9:50

This section provides further illustration of Jesus' ministry of liberation. In this section Jesus will encounter and conquer demons, disease, and even death. As these encounters progress, characters in the story will address the central question: Who is Jesus?

7:1-10. The centurion's slave. Jesus returns to Capernaum having finished offering his words of liberation to the *people.* He hears of a *centurion,* a gentile. Simeon's words about Jesus being *a light for revelation to the Gentiles* (2:32) come to mind. Unlike Matthew's version, Jesus does not deal with the gentile directly, but through intermediaries, Jewish leaders and the gentile's friends. Perhaps Luke views this as representative of the indirect way gentiles of his time encounter Jesus. The Jewish elders appeal to Jesus on the basis of the centurion's merits saying, *"He is worthy of having you do this for him"* (v. 4). However, when the centurion speaks for himself, through friends he sent to Jesus, he says, *"I am not worthy to have you come under my roof"* (v. 6). The centurion bases his request entirely on his simple faith that the *word* of Jesus carries with it *authority.* The centurion shows by this simple statement that he recognizes what Jesus has been demonstrating since the initiation of his ministry: he is the one with the authority to vanquish the corrupting powers within the world (cf. 4:36; 5:17, 24; 6:19). Jesus' statement indicates that such recognition

is exactly the appropriate response to Jesus. *Not even in Israel have I found such faith* (v. 9). Faith in the absolute power and authority of Jesus over evil is what renders such power effective (cf. 5:20).

7:11-17. Jesus confronts death. While this story offers Jesus' greatest challenge yet, Luke makes clear that compassion for the plight of a widow, now without a son, is what moves Jesus to act. This woman could now look forward only to an anxious existence in a world where orphans and widows served as proverbial models of the oppressed (cf. Jas 1:27). The story reminds readers that behind the awesome power that vanquishes evil is the love of God. Through his characters, Luke comments on the larger implications of the event. The people recognize that *a great prophet has risen among us* (cf. Jesus' own words [4:18-24]). Further, the crowd recognizes that *God has visited his people* (RSV cf. 1:78; "the dawn from on high has visited us" [author trans.]). The conquering of death shows clearly that the oppressive forces of evil and corruption are being conquered.

7:18-23. The Baptist's question. John is in prison (3:19-20), so he asks his question to Jesus through his *disciples.* The question, *Are you the one who is to come?,* is reminiscent of John's declaration of 3:16: *one who is more powerful than I is coming.* John predicted that this powerful one would separate the wheat from the chaff (3:17). John's question now can only imply that he does not recognize that Jesus is accomplishing the mission of this "powerful one" of 3:17. Jesus' response is a summary of his healing activity (v. 22; cf. Isa 35:5,6; 61:1; Luke 4:18). This summary, combined with Jesus' blessing of those who do not take offense at him, certainly communicates a positive response to John. Readers know these activities of Jesus to be demonstrations of his authority over evil. Readers also should recognize that the division Jesus is creating in Israel, manifested to this point primarily by the different responses to him by the masses and the leaders, is the realization of John's prediction that Jesus would separate the wheat from the chaff.

7:24-30. Jesus' view of John. Jesus invites his audience to consider the role of John. He is a prophet, but more than a prophet. Jesus reviews the role of John already spoken of by Luke. He is the *messenger* sent *to prepare your way before you* (cf. 1:17, 76: 3:4). John is more than a prophet, for he is a prophet whose role was itself a fulfillment of prophecy (cf. Mal 4:5). Yet John, as great as he is, pales in significance when compared to that for which his primary role was to prepare the people: the reign of God. The least of those who share in the reign of God are greater than the best of those who prepared the way for it. So much greater is the time of fulfillment than the time of promise. Verses 29-30 note the division created by John's preaching, a division between the masses and the leaders continued by Jesus. "The people . . . justified God" (RSV); the leaders "rejected the purpose of God" (RSV).

7:31-35. This generation. Luke introduces a new term to denote those opposed to Jesus and his work: *this generation*. In this pericope *this generation* denotes those who are like spoiled children who reject both the strict asceticism of John and the openness of Jesus. In this context, *this generation* denotes *the Pharisees and the lawyers* (v. 30). To be contrasted with *this generation* are the *children of wisdom*. These "children" by whom "wisdom is justified" (RSV) clearly denote the "the people" who "justified God" (7:29). *This generation* is clearly a group to which one does not wish to belong.

7:36-50. The sinner and Simon. The sinner woman and Simon the Pharisee offer concrete illustrations of the two types of people spoken of in the previous episode. No duplicity is hinted at in Simon's invitation to Jesus. Still, in the end, Simon refuses to acknowledge that Jesus is a prophet (v. 39), for Jesus allowed the sinner to touch him. By this lack of acknowledgment Simon showed himself to be one of "this generation" who rejected Jesus because he showed himself to be *a friend of tax collectors and sinners* (7:34). On the other hand, the sinner woman's act of heartfelt affection showed her to be one who "justified God," that is, "to acknowledge the rightness of [God's] call in John and Jesus and to repent and be forgiven" (Talbert 1986, 85).

Jesus' parable about the two debtors indicates that the operative principle in this story is that great forgiveness renders great love. In short, the woman is not forgiven because she treats Jesus lavishly. She treats Jesus lavishly because she has experienced the "release from sins" (v. 48). She has been a recipient of the ministry of liberation, which serves as the hallmark of Jesus' work in Luke (Luke 4:18-19). *Her sins, which were many, have been forgiven, hence she has shown great love.* The following statement, *But the one to whom little is forgiven, loves little,* can only be directed at Simon who has demonstrated "little love" for Jesus. The question of Simon's guests, *Who is this who even forgives sins?* echoes the question of other

Pharisees in 5:21. The woman who has experienced "release," salvation, and *peace* shows by her *faith* in Jesus that she knows the answer to the detractors' question.

8:1-21. The word of the kingdom. Luke sets the stage by reiterating and expanding upon some themes already introduced, reminding readers that Jesus is preaching the *kingdom of God* and is accompanied by *the twelve*. Yet he also has other followers, *some women who had been cured of evil spirits and infirmities* (vv. 1-2). Talk of Jesus' healing reminds readers of the nature of Jesus' kingdom work: liberation from the corrupting powers of evil. Inclusion of women among his followers offers an expanded definition of Jesus' followers. He has come to liberate all persons and to call all persons to follow him.

The parable of the sower and its interpretation (vv. 4-15) serves to explain how the preaching of the kingdom of God brings division among the people. Verses 9-10 offer a partial explanation. As offensive as it may appear to modern readers, these verses declare that the will of God stands behind this division. To the disciples *it has been given to know the secrets of the kingdom of God.* Such "giving" can only come from God. The others are described as *looking* although *they may not perceive* and *listening* although *they may not understand* (v. 10). Jesus is offering a loose quotation of Isa 6:9. This prophet, to whom Jesus has already compared himself (4:18-19), was called to preach to a people whom God knew would not heed his word. Jesus too has been called to preach to a people, not all of whom will perceive or understand, for Jesus has been *destined for the falling and the rising of many of Israel* (2:34).

Verses 11-15 provide further explanation as to why many reject the *seed* that is *the word of God.* Satan and his hosts hinder the planting, nurturing, and growth of the seed. For some, *the devil comes and takes away the word from their hearts.* For others faith lasts only until *a time of testing comes* and they *fall away.* Luke 4:2 and 13 imply the devil to be the source of such *testing.* Other people *are choked by the cares and riches and pleasures of life.* One who suspects the devil to be behind such life-killing concerns is correct (cf. Acts 5:1-3). The seed of the word proves fruitful only in those who *hold it fast in an honest and good heart.* Jesus here is speaking of the same kind of person about whom he spoke in 6:45.

Verses 16-18 exhort those who possess the *secrets of the kingdom of God* (8:10) to share the light of revelation that has been offered them. The world must continue to hear that God's victorious reign is breaking in. This is how one must *listen* to the word preached. A good example of the kind of persons about whom Jesus is talking are his *mother and his brothers* (v. 19), for such *are those who hear the word of God and do it* (v. 21). Readers are invited to recall how Mary responded obediently to the Lord, *according to [his] word* (1:38) and proclaimed openly his mighty works of salvation (1:46-55).

8:22-25. Rebuking the forces of chaos. This is the first of four miracles that make up a unit prior to the pericope of the sending forth of the twelve (9:1-6). Together they offer powerful testimony to the authority and power of Jesus over the forces of evil—a power and authority he will soon share with his followers.

This appears initially to be a story about Jesus' power over nature. Luke may wish the reader to discern a deeper meaning. The *windstorm [that] swept down on the lake* placed Jesus' disciples in *danger*, leading them to believe that they were *perishing*. In response Jesus *rebuked the wind and raging waves. Rebuked* is the same word used in 4:35, 39 where Jesus "rebuked" a demon and a fever. Luke might be intimating that even "forces of nature," which modern persons interpret in the context of the naturalistic laws of nature, can also be used by the "forces of evil" to harm people.

Jesus' question to his disciples, *Where is your faith?*, implies that if they truly trusted Jesus as the one who could "release" people from the threatening grip of evil, they would have realized that even the demonically manipulated forces of nature could be subdued by their *master*. Their concluding question, *Who then is this?*, shows that even those to whom *the secrets* have been given (8:10) can manifest a lack of perception like those of *this generation* (cf. 7:31, 49).

8:26-39. The Gerasene demoniac. Jesus has entered gentile territory, as evidenced by the presence of a *herd of swine* (v. 32). Jesus' first miracle in Jewish territory was an exorcism (4:31-37). So it is in gentile territory. This case of demon-possession seems particularly acute (cf. vv. 27, 29), suggesting that Satan's grip on the non-Jewish world was even tighter than his grip on Jesus' homeland.

The demons fear being sent *back into the abyss* (v. 31), which would spell the end of their earthly dominion. Jesus tricks them by granting their request to be sent into the swine. However, the swine *rushed . . . into the lake and drowned* (v. 33). The drowning of the demon-possessed swine in the lake results in the return of the demons to the abyss, for large bodies of water, such as lakes, were considered the entrance into the abyss (cf. vv. 22-25).

Again, Jesus offers release from the oppressive forces of the devil; as in Jewish territory, his work creates division. The *people of the surrounding country . . . asked Jesus to leave them* (v. 37). The one who had been *healed* (v. 36; lit. "saved"; cf. 7:50) wished to remain with Jesus. Jesus, however, commands that he return to his home and *declare how much God has done for you* (cf. 8:16). Luke states that he *proclaimed . . . how much Jesus had done for him*. Although anachronistic trinitarian thinking is not to be assumed, Luke clearly invites the reader to acknowledge that Jesus' work is actually God's work.

8:40-56. Jairus's daughter and the hemorrhaging woman. These two intertwined miracle stories conclude this section. Jesus has returned to Jewish territory, as evidenced by the presence of *Jairus, a leader of the synagogue.* Verse 42 indicates that the *crowds,* who have tended to respond positively to Jesus, are back on the scene as well.

On the way to Jairus' house, *a woman who had been suffering from hemorrhages for twelve years* and who had been unable to find help from doctors approached Jesus from behind *and touched the fringe of his clothes* (v. 43-44). This woman would have been considered as living in a perpetual state of uncleanness (cf. 4:12-16; Lev 15:25-27) and not welcome in the community. When touched, Jesus discerns *that power had gone out from* him (v. 46) and demands to know who touched him. In fear, the woman confesses what she had done. Jesus' statement is, in the Gk. text, exactly the same as that offered to the sinner woman who dared to approach him: "Your faith has saved you. Go in peace" (v. 48, author trans.; cf. 7:50). The trust that brings salvation manifested in "release from sins" also brings salvation manifested in being released from uncleanness. The ministry of liberation continues.

Upon arriving at the ruler's house, it is announced that Jairus' daughter is dead. Jesus can liberate from this evil as well: "Only believe and she shall be saved" (v. 50, author trans.). Again, "faith" and "salvation" are explicitly juxtaposed. The cynical skepticism of the crowd, offering notice to readers that the crowds do not fully trust in Jesus as one might hope, does not dissuade him. Taking his closest disciples and the girl's parents, he enters the house and raises her from the dead. His command to silence (v. 56) indicates that this mighty deed was in response to faith, not to convince the skeptics.

Four miracle stories have spoken clearly of "faith" (8:25, 48, 50) and "salvation" (8:36, 48, 50). The kind of salvation Jesus has come to offer is becoming increasingly clear: liberation from *all* forms of evil demonic oppression. The power that unleashes Jesus' liberating power is faith. THE TWELVE who have been with Jesus for the events of this entire chapter (cf. 8:1) are now ready to share in the work of Jesus.

9:1-6. The sending out of the twelve. *The twelve* have been with Jesus since 6:12-16. They have witnessed the mighty deeds of liberation. Now they share in that mission as Jesus gives them *power and authority over all demons and to cure diseases* (v. 1). The work that they do, like that of Jesus, is *to proclaim the kingdom of God* (v. 2). Jesus will not do his work alone. They travel without provision showing that those who accomplish the work of Jesus accomplish it by faith.

9:7-9. Herod's question. This brief notice serves three functions. One, it informs readers of the Baptist's fate—he is dead. Two, it raises the question of the precise identity of Jesus, an issue readers have seen before (cf. 5:21; 7:49; 8:25). Three, it raises an ominous note in that the one who had killed the Baptist now wants to see Jesus.

9:10-17. Feeding of the five thousand. *The apostles* have returned and *told Jesus all they had done. The crowds* are also back on the scene (v. 11). Readers are offered still another reminder of what the mission of Jesus is all about: he *spoke to them about the kingdom of God, and healed those who needed to be cured.*

Having established the audience and the eschatological setting and context, Luke narrates the miraculous feeding. One should not hunt only for symbolic meaning, as though the actual feeding of people in need of literal food is not at all the issue. Still, it seems that *the crowds* who have *followed him* (v. 11) are hungry for more than just bread—after all, one does not live by bread alone (4:4). One cannot ignore the language of the last supper (cf. vv. 16; 22:19) or the Lukan interest in the "breaking of bread" as an expression both of Christian fellowship (Acts 2:42, 46; 20:7) and recognition of fellowship with the risen Lord (24:30-31, 35). The fact that the apostles assist with the distribution of the food conjures up post-Easter images of Christian community as well. In short, a Christian reader (cf. 1:4) would recognize in this incident a foreshadowing of the spiritual nourishment that was to come in the context of the "breaking of bread." It is this spiritual hunger that the Messiah has come to fill (v. 17; 6:22). This too is a very real part of the liberating reign of God.

9:18-36. Recognizing Jesus. If in Luke's narrative world recognition of the risen Lord comes in the context of the *breaking of bread* (cf. 24:35), it is no surprise that after Jesus first breaks bread in the narrative (9:16), his disciples explicitly come to recognize who Jesus is. Readers too will learn some new things.

First, Peter confesses Jesus to be *the Messiah of God* (v. 20), something readers have known for some time. Second, Jesus, in defining his role as Messiah, talks in terms of his death and resurrection as the *Son of Man* (v. 22). Jesus' language is quite strong: *The Son of Man must undergo. . . .* The Greek word for *must* (δεῖ) is almost a Lukan code word to denote "divine necessity." The "Son of Man" has functioned in other capacities to this point (5:24; 6:5; 7:34). The implication is that this death and resurrection will play a decisive role in the work of liberation. Third, *the Son of Man* is spoken of by Jesus as the glorious judge of the end time. Fourth, after Jesus, Peter, James, and John ascend to the mount of transfiguration, the glory of Jesus is revealed even now to these men (v. 32). Luke may wish to emphasize that the glorious Son of Man to come is *this* Jesus whom the disciples are now following. Fifth, Moses and Elijah appear with Jesus and speak of his departure, which he was about to accomplish (lit. fulfill) at Jerusalem (v. 31). The OT, which these two so thoroughly embody, finds its realization in Jesus and in some significant event he is to fulfill in Jerusalem. Finally, God himself speaks to the disciples to identify Jesus: *This is my Son.* This provides the warrant for the concluding exhortation: *Listen to him* (v. 35). Readers will later learn from Acts 3:22-23 that this Jesus is the "prophet like Moses" to whom one must listen or "be utterly rooted out of the people."

The disciples also learn about following Jesus. Just as they have been called and sent out to share in his work of liberation (cf. esp. 9:1-6), so too they are called to share in his life of self-denial (vv. 23-24).

Luke has portrayed Jesus as the minister of the liberating power of the reign of God. Readers might expect that this climactic section offering the strongest testimony thus far concerning the identity (MESSIAH, SON OF MAN, SON OF GOD) and work (death and resurrection, exodus at Jerusalem) of Jesus might very well have some connection with this mission of God's liberating kingdom. Such a connection seems warranted, even if not fully explained, given the specific declaration of Jesus in the middle of this section: *some standing here . . . will not taste death before they see the kingdom of God* (v. 27).

This tantalizing declaration is followed by the experience of Peter, James, and John on the mountain where they not only behold Moses and Elijah, but experience the direct and immediate presence of God. This raises expectations that the disciples have come to the highest and best possible moment in their relationship with Jesus. Such expectations are shattered in the very next scenes.

9:37-50. Failing disciples. The conclusion to this section (4:14–9:50) ends on a low note. This disappointing conclusion is made even more noticeable by the "high notes" resonating from the preceding scenes.

The first scene, vv. 37-43, depicts the followers of Jesus as unable to use the power they had only recently been given (cf. 9:1) to heal the demoniac child. Jesus' response, *you faithless and perverse generation,* which has the disciples in view, is particularly strong for two reasons. One, *this generation* is a term already used by Jesus to denote those who *rejected God's purposes* (cf. 7:30-31). Two, the miracle stories that have preceded chap. 9 have emphasized the importance of faith in the actualization of Jesus' liberating power (cf. 8:48, 50). The disciples lack this faith and hence are unable to accomplish the ministry assigned to them.

Jesus reiterates his upcoming rejection (9:43b-45). Jesus' introduction, *"Let these words sink into your ears"* (v. 44; cf.8:18), highlights the significance of his words. *But they did not understand this saying; its meaning was concealed from them* v. 45). Not only do the disciples fail in doing what Jesus has given them authority to do, they have not at all grasped what lies at the heart of his mission of liberation. Luke does not say who or what concealed the meaning from them, but in light of the parable about the devil and his means of robbing people from the fruition of the planted word (8:12-14), one may suspect demonic foul play.

The disciples do not understand the role of self-denial to which Jesus had earlier called them (vv. 46-48; cf. 9:23-25), for on the heels of Jesus' speaking of his own rejection, they argue *as to which one of them was the greatest* (v. 46). Jesus must repeat his exhortation to self-denial, using a child as an illustration.

Finally, the disciples do not recognize that the work of Jesus is about the conquering of evil, not merely

being associated with the inner circle which *follow[s] with us* (v. 49). The fact that the unknown exorcist was doing what the disciples themselves could not do (cf. 9:37-43a) and thereby accomplishing the work of the Spirit-anointed Son of God, is not within the purview of the disciples' perception.

The Anointed Prophet's Journey to Jerusalem, 9:51–19:44

The transfiguration scene of 9:28-36 sets the stage for this upcoming journey. There Moses and Elijah spoke of Jesus' "exodus which he was about to fulfill in Jerusalem" (9:31; author trans.). This section narrates the journey to that city. Later the voice of God spoke to the disciples of Jesus declaring, *"This is my Son . . . listen to him!"* (9:35; cf. Acts 3:22-23). The low notes on which Luke ended the previous section indicate that they have much listening to do. Hence, this journey section is rich with sayings material that the Son offers to his disciples, as well as the crowds and even his adversaries. On this journey, "Israel" will have opportunity to listen to God's Son, the Spirit-anointed prophet like Moses.

Beginning the Journey, 9:51–10:42

9:51-56. Rejection of the Samaritans. This pericope twice states that Jesus' *face was set toward Jerusalem,* the goal of Jesus' journey. For the prophet to "set his face against" something implies judgment (cf. Ezek. 21:2). On the surface, the Samaritans' rejection of Jesus is explained by the long-standing antipathy between Jews and Samaritans (cf. Neh 4:2-9; John 4:9). In the context of the story, Jesus' rejection by the Samaritans places the whole journey to Jerusalem under the ominous cloud of rejection. Jesus' refusal *to command fire to come down from heaven* (vv. 54-55) to destroy the Samaritans for their rejection, however, makes clear that rejection of Jesus is not unforgivable or irreversible. The fact that Jesus *rebuked* (cf. 4:35, 39; 8:24) his disciples for suggesting such irreversible judgment implies the ungodly, even demonic, character of such a sentiment.

9:57-62. Following Jesus. "Following" and its demands are the themes of this pericope (vv. 57, 59, 61). One is called to *follow* the *Son of Man,* whose mission is defined by rejection (v. II 58; cf. 9:22, 44). One is called to a thorough-going commitment to the *kingdom of God,* even at the expense of essential family duty or loyalty, such as burying one's father or bidding *farewell* to one's family. Since following Jesus involves a decision to enter into the fray against the devil himself who will stop at nothing to hinder fruitful discipleship (8:11-14), commitment must be unequivocal.

10:1-16. Mission of the seventy. As the previous pericope implied, Jesus is willing to gather new disciples as he journeys to Jerusalem (9:57), and to specify the demands of such discipleship as well. Jesus has now gathered *seventy others* as followers and is sending them out on a mission similar to that of the twelve (cf. 9:1-6).

Only Luke has a mission of the seventy (some ancient mss. read "seventy-two"). The instructions to the seventy echo the instructions Jesus gives to the twelve in Matt 9:37-38; 10:7-16. The seventy might symbolize the traditional seventy nations (cf. Gen 10), foreshadowing the mission to the nations. They may be similar to the seventy elders whom Moses appointed (cf. Num 11:16-25), comparing Jesus to Moses (cf. Acts 3:22-23). The focus of their mission is to be the same as that of Jesus and the twelve: *cure the sick* and proclaim that *the kingdom of God has come near* (vv. 9-11). The authority of the seventy is emphasized as Jesus declares that *whoever listens to you listens to me* and, ultimately, whoever *rejects you rejects me and . . . the one who sent me.*

Such an authoritative message demands response. Thus Jesus lays forth the consequences of rejecting the messengers and their message in a series of woes (v. 13) and explicit threats of judgment (vv. 14-15). The particularly harsh words directed at CAPERNAUM (v. 15) where Jesus has spent so much time (cf. 4:31-42; 7:1-10) convey that repentance is required especially of those blessed with witnessing Jesus' ministry (cf. 13:26-27).

10:17-24. Return of the seventy. Having returned, the seventy joyfully report what readers already knew: the work of healing and proclamation subjected *even the demons.* Jesus reports a vision that interprets what the subjection of the demons means: the fall of Satan from heaven (cf. Rev 12:7-9). Such a fall is not the final defeat of Satan. In fact, such a *fall from heaven* can portend intensified struggle here on earth (cf. Rev 12:10-17). In this struggle Jesus' followers have been given *authority to tread on snakes and scorpions; and over all the power of the enemy* (vv. 19-20). More importantly, Jesus' followers should rejoice in the assurance of their final salvation, their names having been *written in heaven* (v. 20; cf. Rev 3:5).

In vv. 21-22 *these things* refer to this demise of Satan. Jesus' prayer states that the impending fall of Satan is not apparent to all. Failure of the *wise and intelligent* to recognize the significance of the present time serves only to show that they are not among the *infants* (cf. 7:35) to whom God, in his *gracious will,* has chosen to *reveal* these things. The affirmation of v. 22, reminiscent of the language of John's Gospel, indicates that recognizing the meaning of *these things* is dependent on revelation from *the Son.* Apart from following Jesus in the work of the kingdom (cf. 9:57-62), *these things* shall remain *hidden.*

Verses 23-24 show *the disciples* to be among those privileged to *see* and *hear* what the worthies of old only hoped for. One, however, must "perceive" as well as *see,* and "understand" as well as *hear* (cf. 8:10).

10:25-37. The lawyer's challenge. Luke introduces this scholar of the Jewish law negatively, explicitly stating that he wished *to test* Jesus, an activity attributed to the devil (cf. 4:2, 13). Like the devil who tested Jesus, the lawyer knows his scripture. He can answer rightly what one must *do to inherit eternal life:* love God wholly and one's neighbor. The lawyer, however, wishes to limit his definition of *neighbor* (v. 29). Luke's statement that he wished *to justify himself* echoes 7:29-30, where Jesus contrasted the crowds who "justified God" with the "Pharisees and lawyers" who "rejected the plan of God."

The parable of the good Samaritan is Jesus' response to the lawyer. Two points are clear. One, Jesus substitutes the broadest possible definition of neighbor for the lawyer's attempt to offer a restrictive definition. One is to be neighbor to any who must be shown *compassion* (v. 33, RSV) and *mercy* (v. 37). Two, by making a non-Jew the hero of the parable, over even the Jewish priest and Levite, Jesus suggests that doing what the law requires to inherit eternal life is not the exclusive privilege of the Jews (cf. 3:7-8). God's offering of eternal life is for all (cf. 2:31-32; 3:6) and attempts to limit God's saving grace to one's own group will be rebuffed by Jesus (cf. 4:24-30; 5:30-32).

10:38-42. Mary and Martha. The universalistic concern of Luke extends to women (cf. 8:1-3). This story continues that theme while offering commentary on the notion of "service" (RSV; NRSV reads *tasks,* v. 40). Given the choice between "serving" and sitting at the feet of *the Lord* and "hearing his word" (lit. trans.), Mary has chosen the latter. Jesus explicitly states that she *has chosen the better part.* Women too can hear the word. Martha is described as *distracted by many things.* These many distracting things are described earlier as "much serving" (v. 40; RSV). The word used for service is used elsewhere by Luke to denote Christian ministry (cf. 22:26; Acts 1:17, 25; 6:1-4). Luke does not wish to belittle such "service" (cf. the good Samaritan), but this story reveals that *there is need of only one thing*: "hearing the word." Service not rooted in such hearing becomes busy work. Yet, one who truly "hears" will serve (cf. 6:47; 8:21).

Understanding the Present Time, 11:1–13:35

As the Spirit-anointed prophet like Moses makes his way toward Jerusalem offering the word to which Israel should listen, he will devote a major portion of his teaching to the issue of the eschatological significance of his work and response to that work.

11:1-13. Teaching on prayer. Prayer has empowered Jesus during his ministry of eschatological liberation (cf. 4:21; 5:16; 9:18; et al.). *His disciples* need to pray as well.

The Lord's prayer. Disciples are charged to approach God even as Jesus does, as *Father* (cf. 2:49; 10:21-22), implying a direct and intimate approach to God. The prayer presents five petitions.

The first, "let your name be made holy" (author trans.), requests that God act so as to establish before all his sovereignty and holiness. An ancient Jewish prayer captures the sense: "Exalted and hallowed be his great name in the world which he created according to his will" (Marshall 1978, 457).

Two, *your kingdom come* (v. 2). This petition is no empty plea, for even now Jesus and his disciples are proclaiming and demonstrating that the "kingdom of God is drawing near" (cf. 10:9).

Petition three requests the provision of daily sustenance. Luke 9:3-5 and 10:8 inform readers that such sustenance comes from the hands of God's people. Luke 4:4 and 9:12-17 offer reminders that essential sustenance is not confined to literal "bread alone."

The fourth petition, *forgive us our sins*, (v. 4) asks God to make effective for his disciples the "releasing" benefits (cf. 4:18; 5:17-26) of God's salvation (cf. 7:48-50). Disciples must remember that God releases "because we ourselves release everyone owing us" (author trans.), for disciples must be merciful just as their *Father is merciful* (cf. 6:36).

The final petition acknowledges the reality of *trial* (v. 4; lit. "testing," cf. 4:2, 13; 8:13; 10:25) that will come the way of the disciple. "The kingdom of God is caught up in a struggle of powers. . . . This is not a struggle for humans to enter armed only with their 'free will'" (Tiede 1988, 214).

Verses 5-13 exhort persistence in prayer. The parable about the friend (vv. 5-8) is not saying that God responds only to nagging. This is an argument "from the lesser to the greater." If a friend, merely wanting to be left alone, will respond to one's request, surely God will respond to the requests of those who call him "Father." A similar message is conveyed by vv. 11-13.

The concluding statement that *the heavenly Father [will] give the Holy Spirit to those who ask him* (v. 13) is most appropriate in the Lukan context. Prayer focuses on the KINGDOM OF GOD and what is needed from God to engage in the struggle of the kingdom (cf. vv. 2-4). The greatest power for this struggle is that of the Spirit, which empowers Jesus himself.

11:14-36. Controversy over Jesus' power. Reference to the HOLY SPIRIT in the preceding verse sets the stage for this conflict over the source of Jesus' power in exorcising demons. Jesus' antagonists charge that he is in league with Beelzebul. These antagonists are *some of . . . the crowds* (vv. 14-15), which is not a good sign, since to this point the crowds have generally responded well to Jesus. *Others*, presumably from *the crowds* as well, wish *to test* Jesus by *demanding* a *sign from heaven* (cf. 4:9-12). Testing is the work of the devil (cf. 11:4) and that too does not bid well for the crowds.

Jesus rebukes their charge (vv. 17-23) and their demand for a sign (vv. 29-36). He rebukes the charge, first, by pointing out its obvious absurdity. Satan would not be casting out his own demons (vv. 17-18). Second, Jesus declares that his exorcisms demonstrate that *the kingdom of God has come to you.* Further, such works demonstrate that Satan, the *strong man, fully armed*, is being *attacked, overpowered*, and *plundered* (vv. 21-22). Jesus concludes his defense with an emphatic demand for total allegiance in this eschatological struggle: *whoever is not with me is against me* (v. 23).

Before responding to the sign-seekers Jesus offers a warning. Verses 24-25 assume that exorcised demons can return and make matters worse. "It is not sufficient to cast out demons if there is no acceptance of the kingdom whose presence is attested by the expulsion of demons" (Marshall 1978, 479). Hearing and obeying the word of God is the only sure cure, which, if applicable even to Jesus' mother, is surely applicable to everyone else (vv. 27-28). Such hearing and obeying of God's word is linked with hearing and obeying Jesus and his message of the kingdom (cf. 6:46-49; 9:26-27).

Jesus addresses *the crowds* demanding a sign in harsh terms (vv. 29-32). He identifies them with *this generation*, the term used by Luke to denote those who reject God' purpose (cf. 7:30). Non-Israelites, like the *queen of the South* who listened *to the wisdom of Solomon* and the *people of Nineveh [who] repented at the proclamation of Jonah*, know how to respond to God. The Jewish crowds are now confronted with something much greater than either of these OT figures or events: *the kingdom of God has come to you!* (v. 20). In the face of this, *this generation* (cf. above commentary on 7:31-35) is headed for judgment and condemnation.

Jesus concludes with a collection of sayings having to do with light, a general metaphor for that which pertains to God (vv. 33-36). He exhorts the crowds to have a healthy eye, which denotes one who "focuses his or her eye on God alone" (Garrett 1991, 99). Most especially the crowds are exhorted to *consider whether the light in you is not darkness* (v. 35), that is, whether they have a vision of life which is so perverse (such as imagining that "Satan is divided against himself" [v. 18]) that, in fact, *your body is full of darkness* (v. 34). At this juncture, the crowds stand in peril of eschatological judgment.

11:37-54. Controversy with Pharisees and lawyers. Luke has just identified the crowds with *this generation*, the generation epitomized by the PHARISEES and lawyers (cf. 7:30-31; 11:50-51 [Moessner 1989, 92-114]). Jesus has exhorted the crowds not to live in utter darkness. Now Luke uses Pharisees and lawyers to illustrate a kind of "light" that is, in fact, "darkness" (cf. 11:35).

The Pharisees (vv. 37-44) demonstrate "darkened light" in their meticulous concern for external piety, such as cleaning *the outside of the cup and of the dish* (v. 39) and tithing *mint and rue and herbs* (v. 42) at the expense of *those things that are within* (v. 41) and more important matters such as *justice and the love of God* (v. 42). Thus, *inside you are full of greed and wickedness* (v. 39), i.e., their bodies are *full of darkness* (v. 34).

The lawyers (vv. 45-48), the scholars of the Law and Prophets, show their concern for the law through their interpretations and teachings. In fact, they *only load people with burdens hard to bear* (v. 46). They claim to honor the prophets because they have built tombs for them, a boast Jesus turns on them: *you . . . approve the deeds of your ancestors* by building these tombs (vv. 47-48).

The judgment pronounced on *this generation* (vv. 50-51) is unequivocal. It will *be charged with the blood of all the prophets shed since the foundation of the world*. From the first murder recorded in Hebrew scriptures (Abel, Gen 4:8), to the last (Zechariah, 2 Chr 24:20-22), *it will be charged against this generation*. When one considers that *all*, not only Jewish leaders, but the "crowds" (cf. 11:29-32) and even the disciples (cf. 9:37-43) have been linked with *this generation*, things are looking quite gloomy indeed. In the face of this gloom, Luke's closing comment, that *the scribes . . . and Pharisees* now *began to be very hostile toward* Jesus (v. 53; cf. 6:11), borders on wry understatement.

12:1-12. Warnings to the disciples. Jesus has just offered a harsh judgment against *this generation*, epitomized by the Pharisees. Jesus has also identified both the crowds and the disciples with *this generation*. It is fitting, therefore, that as *the crowds gathered by the thousands* Jesus would tell *his disciples* to *"beware of the yeast of the Pharisees, that is, their hypocrisy"* (v. 1; see Moessner, 1990).

Verses 2-3 state that there will eventually come total disclosure of one's cover-ups, secrets, and whispers. Judgment *is* coming. Do not be associated with *this generation*, for its inner *greed and wickedness* (11:39) will be exposed. This exhortation anticipates the clear call of Peter to the masses of Jerusalem in Acts 2:40: "Save yourselves from *this* corrupt *generation*" (emphasis added).

Verses 4-7. The eschatological fray into which Jesus' followers are called to enter can bring death. Jesus calls upon his *friends* in the struggle to remember to whom ultimate allegiance, even *fear*, belongs. *Fear of him who . . . has authority to cast into hell* exhorts the disciple to stand firm before *those who kill the body*. The realization that one's total allegiance belongs to the one who does not even forget the sparrow or who has *counted the hairs of your head* can bring a deeper comfort which warrants the exhortation, *do not be afraid*.

Verses 8-12. The one who calls the disciples *my friends* (v. 4) is also the one who will come as the eschatological judge, *the Son of Man*. As the SON OF MAN, Jesus will judge according to whether one has *acknowledged* or *denied* him *before others*, presumably *the synagogues, the rulers, and the authorities*. Denial of Jesus, speaking *against the Son of Man, will be forgiven* (cf. 22:31-34, 61-62). Blasphemy *against the Holy Spirit*, however, *will not be*. Clearly, Luke has a post-Easter understanding of the Spirit in view here, given the statement *the Holy Spirit will teach you [the disciples] at that very hour what you ought to say.* The disciples do not receive the Spirit until after Easter (cf. Acts 2:1-4). In this context, to blaspheme against the Spirit is to persist in rejecting and opposing the gospel message spoken by God's Spirit-inspired people. "As long as that obstinate mindset perdures, God's forgiveness cannot be accorded . . . " (Fitzmyer 1985, 964).

12:13-34. Concern over possessions. The word of Jesus offered in 8:14 has already warned that an improper view of riches can choke the word. Here he offers a more detailed word about possessions.

Verses 13-21. *Someone in the crowd* misunderstands the nature of Jesus' authority, thinking that Jesus is concerned to offer judgment over matters of the *family inheritance.* Rather, Jesus warns the crowd to be on guard against greed that can distort one's perception of what life truly consists. The parable of the rich fool illustrates the folly of those who think life *consists in the abundance of possessions* and the storing *up of treasures for themselves but are not rich toward God* (v. 21). In the end, he has absolutely nothing.

Verses 22-31. Using arguments from the lesser (*ravens, lilies*) to the greater (people), Jesus offers assurance that God does care about the basic needs of life. Still, Jesus requires acceptance of the principle that *life is more than food, and the body more than clothing* (v. 23). Most importantly, one is to *strive for [God's] kingdom.* The promise that *these things will be given to you as well* must be heard rightly (*pay attention to how you listen!* [cf.8:18]). This is no carte blanche. To strive for the kingdom involves following the rejected Son of Man (9:58) into the fray of battle that can lead even to death (12:4). Only when heard in such a context is this promise heard rightly.

Verses 32-34. What is involved in being *rich toward God* (v. 21) and striving *for his kingdom* (v. 31) is a radical detachment from one's possessions. Possessions only bind one to an age that is passing (cf. 1 Cor 7:31). Detachment allows one to receive "the kingdom from your Father and to make for yourselves treasure in heaven" (author trans.). What one treasures reveals what type of *heart* one has (cf. 6:45; 8:15).

12:35-59. Eschatology: future and present. This subsection offers three parables (vv. 35-48) dealing with the future and three clusters of sayings, including one parable, dealing with the significance of the present time (vv. 49-59).

The three parables dealing with the future all involve the theme of readiness. One must be ready for the future coming of the *master* (vv. 36, 43), that is, *Son of Man* (v. 40), for when he comes he will bring judgment. Luke's readers know this master/Son of Man to be Jesus and the subject to be the PAROUSIA.

Verses 41-48 show that these warnings of readiness are not just *for us [but] for everyone.* All disciples, not just the inner circle of Jesus' time, need to hear these exhortations to readiness. This last parable not only speaks of readiness, but helps to define it. Readiness consists of the disciples being faithfully *at work* when the master arrives. The *manager* or *slave*, who represents the disciple, *who knew what his master wanted, but did not prepare himself or do what was wanted, will receive a severe beating (v. 47).* In the parable itself, doing *what was wanted* is described as giving the other slaves *their allowance of food at the proper time.* This is a metaphorical reference to responsible discipleship that is defined for readers by the teachings of Jesus in this entire journey section. The parable concludes with an explicit warning to *everyone to whom much has been given: much will be required* (v. 48). With the privileged call of discipleship comes responsibility.

Verses 49-59 focus on the eschatological significance of the present time. The present time is not significant just because the master or Son of Man is coming at some point in the future. The present is significant because the reign of God is breaking in even now.

Verses 49-53 offer a word on the intensity and importance of Jesus' present mission: it brings the *fire* of judgment *to the earth.* It is a mission—a *baptism*—which consumes him completely: *what stress I am under until it is completed!* (v. 50). The judgment Jesus brings involves *division* (cf. 2:34-35 [the *falling and rising of many in Israel*]; 3:16-17 [the separation of the wheat and the chaff]; 7:29-35 [the *children of wisdom* vs. those who *reject the plan of God*]). Such division reaches into the intimacy of the *household.* In the present time one must decide to gather with Jesus or to scatter, to be for Jesus or against him (cf. 11:23).

Verses 54-59. This chapter began with a warning to Jesus' disciples in the presence of the crowds to beware of the *yeast of the Pharisees* (12:1). These verses continue Jesus' warning to *the crowds.* He calls them *hypocrites*—which is the very *yeast of the Pharisees* (12:1). Apparently the crowds are being overcome by the pervasive influence of *this generation* (cf.7:31-35). They must come to see the present time as a time for radical decision. They can *interpret the appearance of the earth and sky*, but they cannot see *the present time* as a time for decision that carries eternal significance. It is the time prophets and kings had longed to see (10:24). It is the time of Satan's demise (10:18). *The kingdom of God has come to you!* (11:20).

This generation is on its way to court (vv. 57-59). One must come to terms with one's *accuser* before one gets to the judgment bench. In short, one must come to terms with Jesus now. It will be too late once one is *dragged before the judge.*

13:1-9. The need to repent. The preceding talk of judgment and decision leads to the issue of repentance. In vv. 1-5 the essential message is that all need to repent. Persons cannot take comfort in the fact that life is going relatively well for them, that they have escaped the sword of Pilate or the catastrophe of falling buildings. Jesus indicates here that such fortune or lack of misfortune does not denote one's innocence before God: *No, I tell you; but unless you repent, you will all perish just as they did.*

The theme of repentance is continued with the parable of the fruitless fig tree (vv. 6-9). Trees that do not bear fruit are cut down. Readers recall echoes of John's preaching about *bearing fruits worthy of repentance* and trees not bearing good fruit being *cut down and thrown into the fire* (3:8-9). In this parable the fruitless tree is given a brief reprieve—it is given one more year to bear fruit. The implication is that the time is short.

13:10-17. Healing on the sabbath. Two important themes are reiterated. One, Luke offers a clear reminder of what is so significant about this present time: it is time when those bound by Satan are set free from his bondage (cf. 4:1-44). Two, the story reiterates the theme of division. The *leader of the synagogue*, whom Jesus identifies with the *hypocrites*, the Pharisees and *this generation* (cf. 11:50–12:1), is trying to persuade *the crowd* to his point of view. He is spreading the "yeast" of "hypocrisy" (cf. 12:1). His view is that strict, external sabbath observance takes precedence over human need. This is the kind of religiosity Jesus has condemned in 11:37-44. In this story, *the entire crowd* sides with Jesus. Is the crowd heeding Jesus' warning and call to repentance (13:5)?

13:18-21. Parables of the kingdom. Talk of the release from the bonds of Satan leads logically *(he said therefore)* to talk of the kingdom of God. Both parables are contrast parables—the point of the parable is found in contrasting the beginning with the end result.

Jesus' healings and even resuscitations, impressive as they are, hardly justify the claim that God reigns totally and Satan is now completely bound. True. What one sees now is but the beginning, the *mustard seed* which will *become a tree*; the little bit of *yeast* that will leaven the whole *three measures of flour*. The comparison of the kingdom with *yeast* invites contrast between the leaven of the kingdom and that of the Pharisees (cf. 12:1). The parable affirms that, in the end, the leaven of the kingdom will prevail.

13:22-30. Further warnings. After offering a reminder of the "journey theme" and what is so central to this journey (*Jesus* was *teaching as he made his way to Jerusalem* [v. 22]), Luke presents Jesus giving more warnings to his listeners. Verses 24-27 prevent one from being too optimistic about the ultimate response of the crowd to Jesus (contra 13:17). The door leading to salvation is *narrow* and although *many . . . will try to enter*, they *will not be able*. Reflection upon the "demands of discipleship" makes clear why (cf. 9:57-62). When judgment day comes, having been in the presence of Jesus (as are the crowds, Jewish leaders, and even disciples as he journeys to Jerusalem) will not be sufficient. When the festive banquet of the kingdom begins (vv. 28-30) *you* will be *thrown out*, while *people* from all over the world *will·eat in the kingdom of God*. Jesus could hardly offer a more dire warning to his audience: some of these who have been *the first* to hear this word of the kingdom *will be last* when judgment comes.

13:31-35. The Pharisees warn Jesus. The way that Pharisees have been presented to this point (cf. esp. 11:37-44; 12:1) hardly allows readers to view their motives as above suspicion. They bear bad news. HEROD, who killed John (8:9), now wishes to kill Jesus. Jesus' work of liberation (exorcisms and cures) will not be deterred, for his mission is driven by divine necessity. (The *must* of v. 33 translates the Gk. δεῖ [see comment on 9:18-36]). The reference to *today, tomorrow, and . . . the third day/next day* should not be taken literally—that Jesus' work will be completed within the next seventy-two hours. Such wording points to the deliberateness of God's plan.

Jesus' work of liberation culminates in JERUSALEM, where the prophets are destined to die (vv. 33b-34). Jesus' "exodus" (9:31) and being "taken up" (9:51) will occur in the city which *kills the prophets and . . . those who are sent to it* (cf. Jer 26:20-23). Jesus falls short of explicitly predicting his death there, but readers will get the point. Sadly, Jesus wishes *to gather your children together* but *you are not willing.* Consequently, "your house is abandoned" (author trans.). "House" may refer either to the city, the temple, or the leadership—the meaning is still the same. The irony is that the word translated "abandoned" is the same Gk. word translated as "release" or "forgiveness" in many significant texts (4:18; 5:20; 7:48; 11:4). Jesus came to offer "release"; Jerusalem's response ensures "abandonment." Jesus concludes with a curious prophecy about what must happen before Jerusalem will *see* him. Is Jesus talking about literal sight, or more in-depth sight (cf. 8:10; 19:38)?

The Leaven of the Pharisees, 14:1–16:31

Jesus has warned his audience of disciples and crowds to beware of the Pharisees' leaven (12:1), the quintessential example of *this generation* (cf.7:31-35). This section is devoted primarily to an exposure of that corrupting yeast and some of the consequences of yielding to it.

14:1-24. Dining with the Pharisees and lawyers. Luke wastes no time in continuing his indictment of these Pharisees and their allies, the lawyers. Jesus is on his way to eat with them, but their invitation should not fool readers. They want to *watch him closely.* Such watching is motivated by sinister intentions: *to catch him in something that he might say* (see 11:54). On the way, Jesus performs a sabbath healing which again exposes the contrast between Jesus' and the Pharisees' notion of what is *lawful.* The Pharisees are not persuaded by Jesus' rhetorical question. They have learned only that they cannot successfully challenge him. Jesus' question of v. 5, reminiscent of 13:15-16, reminds readers that this healing is ultimately about liberation of people from the bonds of evil.

Verses 7-14. Noting how the Pharisees jockey for *the places of honor* (vindicating Jesus' charge of 11:43), Jesus offers a parable that puts their lack of humility into the proper perspective. On the level of social decorum, the jockeying of the Pharisees was most inappropriate (cf. Prov 25:6-7). Verse 11 gives this parable about the public humiliation of the arrogant a more general application. Yet talk of the proud being humbled and the humble being exalted gives the whole scene an eschatological application (cf. 1:51-53; 6:20-26; 13:29-30). These Pharisees show themselves to belong to the proud and mighty whom God's judgment will bring down.

Jesus presses his point further, still using the meal setting as context for his teaching. He encourages *the one who had invited him* (a Pharisee, 14:1), to invite to his *banquet* those who cannot reciprocate (*the poor, crippled, lame, and blind*). This is consistent with what Jesus taught earlier in 6:30, 34. Why should one do such a thing? Because *you will be repaid at the resurrection of the righteous.* Nothing in the story indicates that Jesus' host would consider inviting such people, implying that he does not show concern for those whom Jesus, God's Spirit-anointed prophet, shows concern. Such lack of concern further implies that the Pharisee does not belong to "the righteous" destined for resurrection.

Verses 15-24. A guest catches the eschatological allusions of Jesus and pronounces a blessing on those *who will eat bread in the kingdom of God.* Jesus' parable about *someone [who] gave a great dinner* offers a rather direct message: only those who respond positively to the invitation to the banquet of the kingdom will participate in that banquet. Jesus and his followers have thus far in Luke's Gospel made reference to the reign of God some twenty times, as early as 4:43 and recently as 13:29. Yet the Pharisees and their kind (*this generation*) have yet to say yes to the invitation. Who is saying "yes"? The kind one would not think of inviting to a banquet in the first place: *the poor, crippled, blind, and lame* (v. 21; cf. 14:13) and those who reside in the *roads and lanes* (v. 22). These social outcasts represent not only literally those whom Jesus is inviting to share in the kingdom's blessing (cf. 7:22), but the spiritual outcasts as well—the tax collectors and sinners—whom Jesus also invites (cf. 5:27-32). The concluding line of the story serves as Jesus' closing line to his Pharisaic hosts: *none of those who were invited will taste my dinner* (v. 24). Why? The parable gives the answer: they chose not to come.

14:25-35. Counting the costs. The audience changes from Pharisees to *large crowds . . . traveling with him.* The crowds' being with Jesus offers another hopeful sign that they will heed Jesus' warning concerning the Pharisees' leaven (12:1). Jesus refuses to soften his message, however: the door into salvation is narrow (13:24) and he does the crowds no favors not to spell out clearly the demands if they are to continue to travel with him.

Jesus demands loyalty beyond family and even self (vv. 26-27). Literal hatred of anyone is not consistent with the message of Luke's Jesus (cf. 6:27; 10:27-28). The strong language confronts the crowds (and the reader) with how thorough and radical the demand of Jesus is. Are the crowds willing to risk what Jesus

Idemands? Just as one does not begin to *build a tower* unless one is sure that he can finish the project; just as a king does not go to war unless he is sure that he can successfully oppose the approaching army, one should not pick up the cross (v. 27) unless one is ready to follow through with total commitment—and that includes that one *give up all [one's] possessions.* Would-be disciples who turn back after putting their hands to the plow (cf. 9:62) are worth less than worthless salt that one would not even throw on the dungheap (vv. 34-35). Although Luke's Jesus would want to take the masses "under his wing" as he would even Jerusalem (cf. 13:34), he will pull no punches with them to persuade them to follow.

15:1-32. Pharisees and scribes oppose the mercy of God. The Pharisees and scribes show their contempt for Jesus' association with the spiritual equivalent of those types whom they would *not* invite to *their* banquets (cf. 14:13). While the *tax collectors and sinners* wish *to hear* Jesus, the Pharisees and scribes *were grumbling and saying* that Jesus *welcomes sinners and eats with them.* They have raised this objection before and Jesus has before responded to their objection (5:29-32). Now Jesus offers three parables that not only address why he associates with such types but that challenge their attitudes as well.

The parables of the lost sheep (vv. 3-7) and the lost coin (vv. 8-9) carry the same message. Both the shepherd and the woman value highly what is lost. Such extraordinary concern is indicated by shepherd's willingness to *leave the ninety-nine in the wilderness and go after the one that is lost* and the care he shows the sheep, laying *it on his shoulders.* Concern is shown in the way the woman searches for the lost coin (lighting the lamp and sweeping the house). To be sure, the parables end with a word about repentance—but repentance is preceded by persistent searching on the part of characters who represent God. Why would God take the initiative to look for sinners in the way depicted by these parabolic characters and react with such joy over their repentance? The reader must supply the only possible answer. God is merciful (cf. 6:36).

The parable of the prodigal son (vv. 11-32) offers insight into three different characters, each easily representing characters in Luke's story. The father, so anxious and willing to forgive the erring son, provides a glimpse of the mercy and love of God. Clearly the father was mistreated by his younger son who literally could not wait until he was dead to inherit his *share of the property* (v. 12). In receiving back his son with

joyous celebration—the best robe, rings, sandals, and veal (v. 22-23)—he portrays the God who *is kind to the ungrateful and the wicked* (see 6:35).

The younger son illustrates well that as much as God may take the merciful initiative (as demonstrated by the first two parables), sinners are not really passive sheep or inanimate coins. The younger son *came to himself* (v. 17) and resolved to confess his sin before his father (v. 18). The parable expresses no interest in the motives of the son. One can argue that he was seeking his own best interest—being a slave is better than eating pig slop. The father, however, is not interested in pure motives. He is interested in receiving the lost. That too is merciful.

The elder son illustrates the *grumbling* Pharisees and scribes (v. 2). He begrudges the father's forgiveness of the younger brother (whom the elder brother can only bring himself to call *this son of yours*, v. 30). What is further exposed in his conversation with his father is how baseless the elder brother's fear and jealousy is. The father loves the obedient son no less simply because he also loves the son who was lost: *Son, you are always with me, and all that is mine is yours* (v. 31). Thus his son simply has no good reason not to *rejoice* because *this brother of yours was dead and has come to life.* Likewise, the Pharisees and scribes who are opposed to God's sharing of his love with those who need his forgiveness have no good reason either.

16:1-15. The dishonest manager and wealth. The primary audience of this section is *the disciples*, although *the Pharisees* (v. 14) are also present. The portion of the story has three sections. Verses 1-8a present the parable of the dishonest manager. Verses 8b-13 offer general application of the meaning of the parable. Verses 14-15 offer specific application to and judgment of the Pharisees.

The parable of the dishonest manager is confusing to many because *the master commended the dishonest manager because he had acted shrewdly* (v. 8). What impresses the master, despite the fact that he will still have to fire the manager, is that the manager, when faced with the prospect of being turned out into the streets either to *dig* ditches or *to beg*, devised a plan to protect himself. He took a course of action to ensure that *people may welcome [him] into their homes* once he was dismissed. What the manager did, of course, was to reduce the amount due from his master's debtors. Whether the manager was stealing one last time from his master by fixing the books or merely writing off his own healthy commission is not clear nor that significant. The point is that he used money to lay a foundation for the future.

In vv. 8b-15 Jesus invites the disciples to use wealth as a means of laying a foundation for the future—the ultimate future. Surely if *the children of this age* can do this, *the children of light* can. Just as the dishonest manager used wealth that people might welcome him into their homes (v. 4), Jesus exhorts the disciples to use *dishonest wealth* (lit. "unrighteous mammon," used here to denote "money") *that they* [probably a circumlocution for God] *may welcome you into the eternal homes.*

Jesus continues his application in vv. 10-13. Verse 10 makes clear that the issue here is *faithful* use of that to which one has been entrusted. On this earth, God entrusted his children to deal with money (*dishonest wealth*). If they cannot deal responsibly with that, *who will entrust you with true riches?*, which probably denotes spiritual wealth. If disciples cannot be *faithful with what belongs to another*, an allusion to money that is "on trust from God" (Marshall 1978, 623), *who will give you what is your own?*, an allusion most likely to *treasure in heaven* (see 12:33). Verse 13 indicates that what is at stake in the way one uses money is the issue of whether one is truly devoted to God or something else. Unfaithful use of wealth, of which the upcoming parable offers an excellent illustration, renders one a *slave* to *wealth* and a despiser of God.

The Pharisees, described as *lovers of wealth*, ridicule such a notion. By their own response they show where their loyalties lie. They are people more concerned to *justify* themselves (cf. 10:29) than God (cf. 7:29-30). Thus, what they value *is an abomination in the sight of God* (v. 15). No wonder theirs is a leaven which must be utterly avoided!

16:16-18. The law and the prophets. Hans Conzelmann (1982, 157-69) argued that v. 16 served as the key to Luke's view of history: phase one was the period of the *law and the prophets*, which *were in effect until [and including the time when] John came. Since then*, phase two, the proclamation *of the kingdom of God* by Jesus, is in effect. Phase three, the era of the church, will begin with the outpouring the Spirit. Conzelmann drew the lines too sharply between the old and the new. As Jesus himself says in the very next verse *the law* is still very much in force; in fact *it is easier for heaven and earth to pass away* than for even one *stroke . . . in the letter to be dropped.*

Verse 18 illustrates just how much in force it is! In fact, the demand of the law, interpreted in the context of the kingdom of God, is intensified. *Adultery* is no longer confined to "sleeping with another person's spouse." It includes even the perverse legal niceties people use to justify breaking a marriage covenant.

With respect to the *kingdom of God*, Jesus says that *everyone tries to enter it by force.* Perhaps a better translation is the NRSV marginal note: *everyone is strongly urged to enter it.* This kingdom is something to which one *must* respond. The consequences for not entering the kingdom are disastrous, as the next parable clearly shows.

16:19-31. The rich man and Lazarus. This is a fitting parable to conclude this section aimed at the Pharisees' corrupting brand of religion. The audience is still the disciples (16:1), to whom the parable offers warning, and the Pharisees to whom the parable offers judgment as lovers of money (16:14).

The rich man, traditionally known as Dives (Latin for "rich man"), clearly does not use his wealth in such a way so as to be "welcomed in eternal homes" (16:9). After reading this parable, no one is left wondering just what Jesus meant by not being "faithful with dishonest wealth" (16:11). Ignoring the plight of the poor and oppressed, whom Jesus and the kingdom have come to liberate, is to oppose the liberating work of the kingdom and to be against Jesus (11:23).

The words of ABRAHAM in vv. 29 and 31 allude back to Jesus' comments concerning the law and the prophets in 16:16-17. The implication is that one who truly "hears" (listen, NRSV) *Moses and the prophets* will know that such contemptuous use of wealth is eternally damnable. The message of the kingdom is not adding anything new to the Law and the Prophets, nor is it diminishing this aspect of the Law's and the Prophets' demand for justice. Dives, as an example of one who embodies the Pharisees' love of money, offers clear reason to the disciples and readers why the leaven of the Pharisees must be utterly avoided.

Verse 31 offers an ironic allusion to the resurrection of Jesus. People who cannot "hear" the message of the Law and the Prophets will not be convinced even by one rising from the dead (cf. Acts 13:26-41). This concluding word offers a harbinger of the ultimate reaction of the Jewish leadership to the message of the kingdom—and an ominous warning as to what side of the eternal *chasm* they and people like them will end up on.

Persistence for the Journey to Come, 17:1–18:30

The disciples are not the exclusive focus of this section, but they are certainly the primary focus. Furthermore, many of Jesus' words concern issues that would be facing the church of Luke's time—the time of the church's journey.

17:1-10. Demands and duty. Verses 1-4 offer two difficult demands for life among disciples. Verses 1-2 acknowledge that *occasions for stumbling* will come. Jesus requires that disciples not be the ones to *cause one of these little ones* (other followers) *to stumble*. The second demand, vv. 3-4, requires disciples to forgive—offer "release" to (cf. 4:18)—those who sin against them and *turn back* (meaning "repent"). Disciples share in the liberating work of the kingdom is by the offering of forgiveness to others.

Such demands require faith (vv. 5-6), even for *apostles*. The Greek construction of Jesus' answer *does* assume such faith—little as it may be (contrary to NRSV). Only a little faith is needed to accomplish great things, such as watching out for and forgiving others.

Verses 7-10 offer a parable making clear that when disciples *have done all that [they] were ordered to do* it is not cause for self-adulation, for they *have done only what [they] ought to have done*.

17:11-19. The ten lepers. Luke offers another story of healing, the meaning of which readers are now accustomed to hearing: faith in Jesus brings salvation (v. 19, lit., "your faith has saved you"). It is important that such words are pronounced on a *Samaritan foreigner*.

First, v. 11 refers to Jesus being *on the way to Jerusalem* and *going through the region between Samaria and Galilee*, which recalls 9:51 where Jesus, on his way to Jerusalem, was rejected by the Samaritans. Here Jesus pronounces the same word of salvation upon a Samaritan that he has pronounced on Jews earlier (cf. 7:50; 8:48). The fact that this Samaritan *turned back* (v. 15, same Gk. word found in 17:4), allows Jesus to illustrate how *he* responds to those who "turn back": he offers salvation. Second, this Samaritan's *praising God* serves to foreshadow the response that Samaria would give to the gospel later in Acts (Acts 8:5-25).

17:20-37. The kingdom of God and seeing the Son of Man. The question of *the Pharisees* (vv. 20-21) concerning *when the kingdom of God was coming* lets Luke reiterate that the power of God's reign is already active in the world *among you* (v. 21). ("Within you"

[NIV, NRSV mg.] assumes an inner-spiritualistic view of God's reign that does not do justice to the kind of reign Luke's Jesus proclaims.) The Pharisees' inability to see the kingdom reveals their blindness (cf. esp. 11:14-36).

Attention is turned again to the disciples and *the days of the Son of Man* (v. 22; cf. vv. 24, 26). The subject here is the PAROUSIA. The coming of the Son of Man, like the reign of God, is not something that one can localize *there* or *here*. Unlike the reign of God, whose presence in the world can be missed, the coming of the Son of Man cannot be missed, for it is like the *lightening* flash which *lights up the sky from one side to the other*. Thus disciples need not be distracted by over-zealous cries that the Son of Man is already *there* or *here* (cf. 2 Thes 2:1-2). To silence any speculation that Jesus' current ministry represents the *days of the Son of Man*, Jesus reminds the disciples that he must first *be rejected by this generation*. Such words remind readers of the severe judgment Jesus has already pronounced on this *generation* (cf. 11:49-52).

Verses 26-37 envisages the judgment on the generation that rejects the Son of Man. The judgment will fall with complete surprise as *in the days of Noah* and *the days of Lot*. Verses 31-32 offer images of persons facing catastrophe. There is no time to gather one's possessions! No time to look back! One must escape to safety! These vivid illustrations show that in the *days of the Son of Man* (v.22) there will be no escape: *one will be taken and the other left*. Only those who were willing to *lose their life* for the sake of Christ (cf. 14:26-27) and the kingdom of God (cf. 18:29) *will keep* their lives. Where will those be who are left? *Where . . . the vultures will gather*—as food for the birds (v. 37).

18:1-14. Persistent and genuine prayer. The stark images of judgment make Jesus' following comments on prayer most appropriate. Jesus' question of 18:8, *When the Son of Man comes, will he find faith on earth?*, indicates that these words on prayer should be heard in the context of the preceding words on the *days of the Son of Man* (17:22). The Greek construction implies that the question is asked in an anxious frame of mind, betraying the seriousness of the question. Only each disciple, and each reader, can answer the question for him or herself. Hard times are coming. Will the disciple endure? Only by prayer.

The parable and application of the widow (vv.1-8) offers another example of Jesus arguing from the lesser to the greater (cf. 11:5-8). If an *unjust judge . . .*

will grant her justice simply not to be bothered, surely God *will . . . grant justice to his chosen ones who cry to him day and night.* Indeed, he will do it *quickly.*

The parable of the Pharisee and tax collector (vv. 9-14) is directed at persons *who trusted in themselves that they were righteous and regarded others with contempt.* Fittingly, Jesus uses a Pharisee as the example of that kind of person. Yet the words are not addressed only to Pharisees. Disciples in the journey to come need to beware of such a disposition. Jesus has come to invite sinners and the many types of social outcasts to repent and share in the reign of God (5:32; 14:21). In his mercy God is anxious to receive such persons (cf. chap. 15). The one who recognizes this, such as the tax collector of this parable, is the one who will go *down to his home justified.*

18:15-17. Jesus and the children. This story illustrates that *disciples* were not (or are not) immune from holding others in contempt, as they *sternly ordered* people not to bring their *infants* to Jesus. Jesus does not call upon *the little children* to repent or to become disciples, but he does command that people *let* (lit. "release"!) *the little children come to him . . . for it is to such as these that the kingdom of God belongs.* While the story does affirm God's love of *even infants,* it is also about the spirit with which one must receive the kingdom—*as a little child:* complete trust in the care and mercy of God—like the tax collector of the preceding parable.

18:18-30. A final word on wealth. Wealth is an important issue to Luke (cf. e.g., 6:30, 34; 8:3, 14; 12:13-34; 14:33; 16:1-14, 19-31). It is fitting, therefore, that this section, which offers teachings for the journey to come conclude with a word on the topic. This final word offers three sub-sections: the story of the rich ruler (vv. 18-23), Jesus' interpretation (vv. 24-26), and Jesus' final word to Peter (vv. 28-30).

Jesus' response to the appellation *Good Teacher* (v.18) should be viewed neither as a denial that he is good nor as a coy way of identifying himself with God. His response reminds the ruler and readers that all that is genuinely good, including *eternal life,* is found in *God alone.* The ruler wants to know what he must *do to inherit eternal life.* Jesus has heard the question before (10:25). Here, as there, Jesus looks to the law. The ruler insists that he has *kept all these [commandments] since [his] youth.* Jesus insists that *there is still one thing lacking.* This ruler is bound by his possessions. Hence, Jesus requires of him what he said in 12:33 that he requires of all disciples: *sell your*

possessions, and give alms. Make . . . for yourselves . . . an unfailing treasure in heaven. The ruler counts the costs and realizes that the price of eternal life is too high.

Jesus' interpretation assumes what he has tried to make clear throughout the Gospel. *Total* surrender to him is necessary: family, life, and possessions (14:26-33). The sad fact is that the rich are too blessed for their own good. They have so much to surrender. Thus, it is *hard . . . for those who have wealth to enter the kingdom of God!* (v.24). It is *hard* for everyone. Family, life, and even meager possessions are humanly impossible to abandon. *What is impossible for mortals is possible for God* (v.26). This echoes what the angel said to Mary (1:37). God does not force his possibilities on people. One must respond to what he makes possible even as Mary did: *let it be with me according to your word* (1:38).

Peter reminds Jesus that he and the disciples *have left [their] homes and followed* Jesus (cf. 5:11). The word translated *homes* is literally "our own things" and is used in Acts to denote friends (4:23; 24:23), financial resources (4:32; 28:30), and homes (21:6). The disciples are not perfect, but they have left it all behind to follow Jesus. He promises them *much more in this age* ("perhaps a reference to the new family in the church" [Talbert 1986, 173]) and *in the age to come eternal life.* A most fitting promise to end a section offering guidance to disciples for the "journey to come."

Approaching Jerusalem, 18:31–19:44

This last portion of the "journey to Jerusalem" begins with a final prediction of the passion of Jesus in Jerusalem (18:31-34) and ends with Jesus approaching and weeping over the city (19:41). In between, some important events and words performed and spoken in Jericho are narrated (18:35-19:28).

18:31-34. The passion foretold. This is the fourth PASSION prediction in Luke (cf. 9:22, 44-45; 17:25). It is by far the most detailed and specific: Jesus will die in Jerusalem in order to accomplish *everything that is written about the Son of Man by the prophets.* As horrifying as the Jerusalem events will be, they are according to the plan of God. The disciples do not understand (cf. 9:45), and Luke seems purposefully mysterious as to the cause. More important than who or what has *hidden . . . what he said . . . from them* is whether they will ever come to see.

18:35-43. The first Jericho story: healing a blind man. It is not accidental that word of the disciples' lack of understanding sets the stage for a story about a blind man. In this story readers encounter one who can see who Jesus is and what he is all about. The blind man hails Jesus as *Son of David*, a designation of Jesus as the Messiah (cf. 1:32, 69). He also knows the mission of this *Son of David*: to show *mercy* (cf. chap. 15). He approaches Jesus with the kind of *faith* that others have demonstrated before and Jesus pronounces a word with which readers have become familiar: literally, *your faith has saved you* (v. 42; cf. 7:50; 8:48, cf. v. 50; 17:19). The blind man has come truly "to see" as evidenced by his reaction: he *followed him, glorifying God.* Perhaps *the people* as well are seeing more clearly, for *all the people, when they saw it, praised God.*

19:1-10. The second Jericho story; Zacchaeus. This too involves a man who wanted *to see who Jesus was.* Unlike the blind man, Zacchaeus is restricted by more than his physical limitations—his profession as a *chief tax collector* who *was rich* makes him an example of the rich whom it is virtually impossible to save (cf. 18:23-26). Zacchaeus, this *Son of Abraham*, however, is willing to let go of that which binds him to this age. Like the daughter of Abraham whom Jesus released from the bondage of Satan (cf. 13:16), Jesus releases Zacchaeus. Unlike the rich ruler who was *sad* (cf. 18:23), Zacchaeus bears *fruits worthy of repentance* which characterize the true *children of Abraham* (cf. 3:8). For Zacchaeus declares, *Half of my possessions . . . I will give to the poor; and if I have defrauded anyone of anything, I will pay back four times as much* (v. 8; cf. 3:12-13).

The reaction of *all who saw it*, presumably the same people who just moments ago were praising God (cf. 18:43), is identical to the reaction of the Pharisees and scribes when they saw Jesus associating with tax collectors and sinners (cf. 15:1-2). In both instances there was grumbling (v. 7; cf. 15:2). Jesus' mission as the *Son of Man* is *to seek out and save the lost.* Will the masses ever come to see this?

19:11-28. The third Jericho story; the parable of the pounds. Luke indicates that the parable is prompted by the fact that *he was near Jerusalem, and because they supposed that the kingdom of God was to appear immediately* (v. 11). The parable as a whole informs readers that the kingdom of God did not appear with Jesus' arrival in Jerusalem. Talbert is perhaps correct that "in Luke's church . . . some disciples were regarding events in Jerusalem (Jesus' resurrection and ascen-

sion) as the PAROUSIA. In response the evangelist is saying 'not yet'" (Talbert 1986, 178).

There are three main characters, *a nobleman, slaves,* and *citizens of his country,* all of which are open to allegorical interpretation, representing, respectively, Jesus, his disciples, and the Jews who reject him. The parable directs attention away from the false notion that the *kingdom of God* appeared with Jesus' arrival in Jerusalem and redirects attention to the future.

The *nobleman* is going away for a while *to get royal power for himself and then return* (v. 12). In the meantime his *slaves* are given equal amounts of responsibility, represented by the *ten pounds* given to *ten of his slaves,* presumably one to each. They are to *do business with these until I come back. . . . When he returned, having received royal power* (vv. 14-15), he summoned the slaves to see what they had done with the pounds for which they had been given responsibility. The overall message is clear: those who used fruitfully what the nobleman had given them are rewarded; those who did not will not be rewarded. In fact, even what they have will be taken away. The message is harsh, but it is quite consistent with the message heard throughout the Gospel: following Jesus requires total commitment and dedication.

The citizens reject *the nobleman* because they *do not want this man to rule over* them. Their punishment was most harsh *when he returned.* He calls these citizens *these enemies of mine who did not want me to be king over them* and orders that they be slaughtered in his presence (v. 27).

Luke concludes bluntly: *After he had said this, he went on ahead, going up to Jerusalem* (v. 28). This journey section is about to come to a close. Israel, consisting of disciples, crowds, and the Jewish leadership have had opportunity to hear the word of God's Son (cf. 9:35). This concluding parable makes clear the consequences of not hearing.

19:29-40. Descending the Mount of Olives. Jesus' preparation to enter the city of Jerusalem is introduced by the story of the disciples' securing a colt for him. The impression left is that some sort of supernatural prescience on Jesus' part is involved. This impression reinforces the notion that what lies ahead in Jerusalem is according to some larger plan. As Jesus descends down the Mount of Olives he is greeted by the cry of *the whole multitude of the disciples.* Their cry, *Blessed is the king who comes in the name of the Lord* (v. 38), is a clear echo of 13:35 where Jesus said that Jerusalem would not see him until it offered a similar cry.

Two things stand out. One, it is not Jerusalem that makes this cry. Only the disciples do. Jerusalem has not offered the cry Jesus says it must if it is truly to "see" him. In fact, *the Pharisees*, the closest representatives to "Jerusalem" in this story, want Jesus to rebuke his disciples into silence. Jerusalem, it seems, does not "see" who Jesus really is. Will it ever? Two, the disciples hail Jesus as *the king*. This harks back to 19:27. These disciples are not like the citizens of that parable who did not want the nobleman to be their king. Like the blind man of Jericho (18:35-43), the disciples have come to see who Jesus is. No one else seems to. This does not bid well for the citizens of Jerusalem, but it does seem that at least a portion of Israel, the disciples, has listened to the SON OF GOD during the journey to the city (cf. 9:35).

19:41-44. Jesus weeps over Jerusalem. Jesus has still not reached Jerusalem, but as he approached it *he wept over it*. Jerusalem, unlike the disciples who cried *Peace in heaven!* (19:38), does not "see" *the things that make for peace;* in fact, *these things are hidden from [its] eyes* (v. 42). The consequences are devastating: Jerusalem and its inhabitants will be destroyed. "God has visited his people" (author trans. of 7:16b) in Jesus, but Jerusalem, the city of God's people, *did not recognize the time of [its] visitation* (v. 44).

The fate of Jerusalem and its people now seems a foregone conclusion. Jesus had earlier said that *this generation* would be charged with the blood of the prophets (cf. 11:49-50), including, it seems, the blood of the prophet Jesus (cf. 13:33-35a). Luke 17:25-37 envisaged the judgment to come to *this generation* that rejects the Son of Man.

Apparently, part of the punishment of *this generation* will include judgment against Jerusalem and its inhabitants as *they will crush you [Jerusalem] to the ground, you and your children within you* (v. 44). There seems only one means of escape: to separate oneself from *this generation* and accept Jesus as king. That will not save Jerusalem, but at least one might save oneself. Upon entering Jerusalem Jesus will present the word one more time to all the people of Israel. How will they respond?

Exodus from Jerusalem, 19:45–24:53

With the arrival of Jesus at the Temple (19:45), Jesus arrives in Jerusalem. He can now fulfill the exodus from this city about which MOSES and ELIJAH had spoken (9:31). There are three steps to fulfill this exodus: one, Jesus' teaching of *all the people* of Israel in the Temple (19:45–21:38); two, Jesus' passion, the *hour of darkness* (cf. 22:53; 23:44); three, Jesus' *entrance into glory* (24:26).

The Temple Ministry, 19:45–21:38

19:45-46. The cleansing of the Temple. Before Jesus can teach from the Temple, he must possess it. He must transform this place, intended as a *house of prayer* (Isa. 56:7) but *made* into *a den of robbers* (Jer 7:11), that it might be worthy of the king's (19:38) presence.

19:47-48. The opening notice of Jesus' teaching. Luke 19:47-48 and 21:37-38 mark the beginning and ending of this section. Both passages state that every day *he was teaching in the temple* and that his audience was "all the people." Luke consistently uses "people" to denote "Israel" (cf. 1:68) and, thus, in a sense Jesus, the Messiah, is teaching "Israel" in its holy Temple, calling it to a decision.

Here Luke presents a division between *all the people* and *the chief priests, scribes, and the leaders of the people*. The Pharisees have disappeared. It is clear that their role is now assumed by these representatives of Jerusalem leadership—the officers of the SANHEDRIN, or ruling assembly (cf. 22:66), who are *looking for a way to kill him*. The people of Jerusalem failed to welcome Jesus as the king. Now, if they will only remain on the side of Jesus and opposed to their leaders, perhaps they can escape the fate of Jerusalem (19:41-44) and *this generation* (11:49-52; 17:25-37).

20:1-8. Jesus' authority. The Jerusalem leadership begins its attack on Jesus by questioning the source of his *authority* to do *these things*, referring to seizing the Temple and teaching the people from it. This is a legitimate question for the religious leadership to ask, assuming they are sincere in their question. Jesus asks them to decide the source of John's authority—and, implicitly, his own. Was it human or divine? They deliberate, not because they are really interested in the issue itself (although as the leaders of Israel they certainly should be!), but only for jaded, political reasons. Is there any way to win this bout with Jesus? They decide they cannot win and retreat, exposing their insincere motives in asking the question. Having exposed their motives, Jesus is under no obligation to answer their question.

20:9-19. Parable of the tenants. Jesus goes on the offensive against his opponents (v. 19), offering a parable and interpretation. The parable, vv. 9-16, is open to allegorical interpretation, with the *vineyard* representing Israel (cf. Isa 5:1-7), *the owner* representing God, *the tenants* representing the Jewish leadership, and *the son* representing Jesus. The meaning is clear: the Jewish leadership rejects all of God's messengers, including even his son, whom they kill. As a consequence, God will *destroy those tenants [the leaders] and give the vineyard [Israel] to others* (v. 16). Israel is *not* destroyed—only its leaders! Who are the others? (cf. 22:28-30).

The people, to whom Jesus is telling the parable, react in horror (*Heaven forbid!*, v. 16), recognizing the ominous tone of his message. Jesus drives his message home, quoting from Ps 118:22 and Isa 8:14-15. He is the *stone* the *builders* (the leaders) will reject. He will be vindicated; he will *become the cornerstone*. In addition, he will become a stone that will trip up and crush those who opposed him. The option of the people seems clear: do not side with *the builders*!

20:20-26. Taxes to Caesar. The *spies*, sent from the leadership, possess the pseudo-righteousness of the Pharisees (NRSV *honest*; lit. "righteous"; cf. 18:9). They flatter Jesus (v. 21) with words they do not mean, but with words which are, nonetheless, absolutely true. Their goal is to place Jesus in the untenable position of either loosing credibility *in the presence of the people* by advocating payment of taxes, or placing himself in legal jeopardy with the *authority of the governor* by advocating refusal to pay taxes.

Jesus' answer (v. 25) does not speak of divided loyalties, but of legitimate obligations. Jesus does not deny the legitimacy of giving the Roman emperor back his due of his own money, money that, ironically, not Jesus but only his opponents carry in their pockets. One must give to God what is God's due. Readers should recall 10:27-28. God's due is total love and devotion. Such total devotion does require that when obligations to human beings conflict with loyalty to God, one must "obey God rather than any human authority" (as Peter proclaims in Acts 5:29).

20:27-40. The question of the resurrection. Some *Sadducees* now try to challenge Jesus. The *chief priests* and perhaps even some of *the elders* of 20:1 would have been aligned with this aristocratic, conservative party of Jewish society. Apparently they want to force Jesus either into rejecting the idea of resurrection, an idea to which the Sadducees did not adhere, or into advocating marital infidelities in the afterlife. Either way, he will loose credibility with the people.

They appeal to the Jewish law of Levirate marriage, wherein a widow married the brother of her dead husband (Deut 25:5-6). The Sadducees set up a comical situation, seeming to require Jesus to approve either of bigamy *in the resurrection*, with the woman now having seven husbands for eternity, or of multiple divorces, a practice Jesus has already forbidden (16:18).

Jesus responds, first, by rejecting the assumptions of the Sadducees who wrongly believe that life in *that age* is a continuation of life in *this age* (vv. 35-36). *Marriage* is a divinely sanctioned rite of *this age* to perpetuate the human race (cf. Gen 1:28). It is not necessary for the *children of the resurrection* for *they cannot die anymore*. Second (vv. 37-38), Jesus affirms the idea of resurrection by appealing to the Torah (Exod 3:6), the portion of scripture which the Sadducees recognized as authoritative. He asserts that God would not refer to himself as the God of Moses' ancestors if they were dead at the time God spoke to Moses, for God *is not God of the dead, but of the living*. Hence, the three ancestors must have been *living*. Thus, *the dead are raised*.

Even *some of scribes* had to acknowledge that Jesus was right (v. 39). Verse 40 indicates that attempts to *question* Jesus are finished. Will the leadership give up or resort to other means to kill Jesus?

20:41-47. Jesus' conclusion. In vv. 41-44, Jesus addresses the question of authority raised in 20:2. Jesus acts on the authority of *the king* (19:38) and the Messiah (2:11; 9:20), the son of David (1:32, 69; 18:35-43). How is Jesus this son of David? Ps 110:1 provides the answer. Jesus is rightly understood as the Messiah and son of David when he is understood as the one who is also David's Lord, who sits at the *right hand* of God until his *enemies* are subdued. By this kingly authority Jesus does *these things* (cf. 20:2).

Earlier Jesus warned the disciples in the presence of the crowd to *beware of the yeast of the Pharisees* (12:1). In vv. 45-47, Jesus, *in the hearing of all the people*, offers a word of warning *to the disciples* to *beware of the scribes*. His description of the scribes is similar to what he said about the Pharisees (cf. 11:43; 14:7). The people and the disciples must beware of all elements of the Jewish religious leadership: the Pharisees, the scribes, and the chief priests and elders. It is they who evict *widows* while they *say long prayers*, and who are destined for *the greater condemnation*.

21:1-4. The widow's offering. Having just spoken of widows, Luke now tells a story about a widow's offering. While the rich contribute to the Temple *out of their abundance, the poor widow* contributes *out of her poverty.* While Jesus may admire her devotion, readers might well wonder how this woman who *has put in all she had to live on* will now live at all. One way that the Temple has become a *den of robbers* (19:46) is by taking the last of the poor's pennies, knowing that they will soon be evicted.

21:5-38. The destruction of Jerusalem and the end of the world. This speech must be read carefully, for it is presented to two audiences *in the story* and an audience *outside the story.* The audience outside the story is Luke's readers. For them, the destruction of the Temple is a past event (70 C.E.) and they would read from that perspective. One audience in the story is Jesus' disciples (20:45). The other audience in the story is the people who call Jesus *teacher* (v. 7). In Luke's Gospel, "only non-disciples refer to Jesus by the title 'teacher'" (Chance 1988, 135–36). Hence, readers of Jesus' words cannot ignore that Jesus is speaking not only to disciples outside and inside the story, but to non-disciples, the people of Jerusalem, inside the story as well. Careful reading is required to maintain a proper focus.

21:5-7. The destruction foretold. The *some* who are with Jesus who speak *about the temple,* includes both the disciples (20:45) and *some* of *all the people* whom Luke describes as *spellbound by what they heard* (19:48). Mention of the Temple prompts Jesus to predict its destruction and to address the question *when will this be?*

21:8-19. Coming catastrophes and persecution. In the story, Jesus is presenting to his audience predictions of what will come prior to destruction of the Temple: the rise of false messiahs, predictions that the *time is near,* political, economic, and even natural upheavals as well as *dreadful portents and signs from heaven.* Luke's readers know these to be past events. The Jewish historian JOSEPHUS wrote of such things occurring before the destruction of Jerusalem (*Ant* 18.4.1; 20.5.1; 20.8.6; *BJ* 6.5.3-4).

Verses 12-19 are directed to the disciples in Jesus' story audience, for they speak of persecutions to come to Jesus' followers *before* the destruction of the Temple and the events of vv. 8-11 (cf. v. 12a). Luke will write of these persecutions in Acts.

21:20-24. The destruction of Jerusalem. These words are addressed to both of Jesus' story audiences, the disciples and the people. After the events of vv. 8-19 *you [will] see Jerusalem surrounded by armies.*

Jesus then begins to talk in the third person about those who will actually experience the destruction of Jerusalem. This allows Jesus' words to apply to any who might live in Jerusalem and its environs when Jerusalem's *desolation has come near,* not just the story audiences. Jesus' words make clear that the destruction of Jerusalem exhibits the *days of vengeance* and speaks *wrath against this people.* Both elements of Jesus' audience must know that the destruction of Jerusalem is God's emphatic word of judgment against *this people.* The gentiles will trample God's holy city, but only *until the times of the Gentiles are fulfilled* (cf. Dan 8:1-14). Both elements of Jesus' audience hear that Jerusalem's trampling is of limited duration. What will happen to Jerusalem, and more importantly its people, after this?

21:25-28. The Son of Man and your redemption. From v. 25 through the remainder of Jesus' speech, Luke's readers and Jesus' story audience are on equal footing, for they are both hearing Jesus speak of things yet-to-come. Great cosmic and natural upheavals will create *distress among the nations* and *foreboding.* Then *they will see "the Son of Man coming."* They probably denotes everybody, the *people* of v. 26 (lit. "humans" [ἄνθρωποι]).

With the coming of the Son of Man comes the end (17:22-37). With the coming of this end comes *your redemption.* Hence, when *these things* [the events of vv. 25-26] *begin to take place* "you" can know that *your redemption is drawing near.* What is the antecedent of "your"? Jesus' story audience consists of both disciples and the people of Jerusalem. Is Jesus promising the people of Jerusalem, as well as the disciples, that when *the times of the Gentiles are fulfilled* (v. 24) they will experience redemption? Might this be the time when Jerusalem will declare, *Blessed is the one who comes in the name of the Lord*? (13:35b)?

21:29-33. Concluding predictions. Jesus offers *them a parable.* "Them" denotes immediately his two story audiences and implies his reading audience. In this parable the same message of v. 28 is reiterated: *the kingdom of God is near* when *you see these things taking place.* Verse 33 offers an emphatic affirmation of the sure authority of Jesus' words. Verse 32 is saying more than all these things will happen before Jesus' contemporaries die. *This generation* denotes those who reject the Son of Man (cf. 17:25) who will experience severe judgment (cf. 11:49-51). *This generation* will not escape the *days of vengeance* (21:22) or the *great distress* and *wrath* (21:23). It shall by no means disappear from the stage until all these things have come upon it.

21:34-38. A final warning. Jesus concludes with a word to his audiences to stay on the alert so that *that day* (the "day of the Son of Man," cf. 17:24; 21:27) will not be one's undoing. Prayer will not allow one to avoid the hard times that are coming, but will allow one *to escape* the judgment that will fall upon *the whole earth* and *to stand before the Son of Man.* Jesus' disciples (both inside and outside the story) must continue in their faithfulness to obey his exhortation. The thus-far uncommitted people must decide whose side they are on.

The comments on 19:47-48 also apply to 21:37-38. What opened in chap. 19 comes to a close in chap. 21.

The Hour of Darkness, 22:1–23:56

This section tells of Jesus' PASSION. The other Gospels tell broadly the same story, with the other two synoptics being most similar to Luke (cf. Matt 26:1–27:66; Mark 14:1–15:47; John 13:1–19:42). John's is much longer in part because of the great attention given to Jesus' discourses (cf. esp. chaps. 14-17). Many interpreters believe a PASSION NARRATIVE to have been one of the earliest connected narratives to be composed by Jesus' early followers. Some argue that Luke had access to two passion narratives: Mark's and an independent narrative (see Fitzmyer 1985, 1359-68).

Luke began the story of Jesus' ministry by telling of direct confrontation between Jesus and the devil (4:1-13), described as a period of "testing." Now Satan reemerges as a direct player in the action (22:3), marshaling his allies of darkness (22:53) in this final time of "testing" (22:46). During this passion story, the three sets of characters with whom Jesus has been dealing in the preceding narrative, disciples, crowds (people), and the Jewish leadership, will have to make firm choices whether they are for or against Jesus (cf. 11:23).

22:1-6. The plot to kill Jesus. *The chief priests and scribes* still seek to kill Jesus (cf. 19:47). There is no question whose side they are on in this struggle. *The people* are not on their side in this plot (cf. 19:48), for an *opportunity* must be found for the leadership to catch Jesus *when no crowd was present.* Sadly, *Judas, one of the twelve,* will provide this *opportunity.* Will all the disciples side with evil? Judas' plot offers a warning that any can be corrupted by the leaven of the Pharisees (cf. 12:1) and join forces with *this genera-*

tion (cf. 17:25). *Satan* is directly involved in creating the *opportunity* to betray Jesus—the *opportune time* he has been waiting for since 4:13. The conflict of the two kingdoms (cf. 11:18-20) is about to reach a critical moment.

22:7-13. Preparing the Passover. The time for the sacrifice and preparation of *the Passover lamb* was the afternoon of 14 Nisan (March/April). The story displays Jesus' prescience (cf. 19:29-34), implying that things are unfolding according to plan.

22:14-23. The last supper. There are some significant textual critical issues in this passage (see NRSV mg.). The commentary below follows the NRSV text.

The Passover meal was eaten the evening after preparation. The Jewish day goes from sundown to sundown, hence, sundown brought the 15th of Nisan. Verses 15-16 imply that Jesus did not share the meal with his disciples, but only led in their eating of it. He declares that he *will not eat it until it is fulfilled in the kingdom of God.* He makes a similar statement about drinking with the disciples (v. 18). Jesus has given notice that the reign of God is already here (cf. 11:20; 17:21). He recently spoke of the reign that is to come (21:31) with the coming of the Son of Man (21:27). It is this reign to which Jesus primarily refers. Jesus promises his disciples that they will eat and drink together at the kingdom's table (cf. 13:28-29).

In vv. 19b-20 Jesus offers an interpretation of the *bread* and *cup* that need not await fulfillment in the kingdom of God to be meaningful. He speaks of the giving of his body and pouring out of his blood *for you* and *the new covenant.* Jesus' mission to inaugurate the reign of God, manifested in the offering of liberation ("release/forgiveness" [cf. 4:18; 5:20] and "salvation" [cf. 7:50]), will include his dying. Jesus' many predictions of his death have implied that. Jesus' relating of his death to *the new covenant* strongly implies that this death is most significant in the accomplishment of his ministry of liberation.

In vv. 21-23 Luke conveys that the tragic plot of Jesus' enemies will succeed. But Jesus' words also make clear *the Son of Man is going as it has been determined,* assuring readers that God is in control of the action.

22:24-34. The flawed, yet faithful, disciples. Readers have read the many attempts on the part of Jesus to lead his disciples into a mature following. The betrayal by Judas (cf. vv. 21-22) reminds readers that even one of the twelve can fall away. The dispute that arises concerning who *was to be regarded as the greatest* shows that even the balance of the disciples have much to learn. Having just spoken of his own death, Jesus calls upon the disciples not to pattern themselves after gentile lords. Rather they are to take their cues from Jesus who is among them *as one who serves.*

The disciples must learn the proper way to lead, for Jesus is conferring upon them *a kingdom.* This promise assures the disciples and the readers that despite their failings the disciples will share rule with Jesus in his kingdom *judging the twelve tribes of Israel.* Why? It is because they are *those who have stood by [Jesus] in [his] trials* (lit. "testing" cf. 4:13). Jesus does not expect perfection. He does demand faithfulness in standing with him in the trials that come in the struggle with evil.

Despite their failures, the disciples have, to this point, stuck with Jesus. Following his resurrection, Jesus will ascend to his throne and begin his reign as Messiah (cf. Acts 2:34-36). It is in this context that the apostles *will sit on thrones* (v. 30) and lead Israel—at least that portion of Israel which comes to recognize Jesus as Messiah and saves itself from "this corrupt generation" (cf. Acts 2:40).

The sad dialogue with Peter (vv. 31-34) communicates that Satan will harass the apostles. Their hitherto "standing" with Jesus will begin to unravel. Even those who want to be faithful will fail. Jesus' prayer will prevent the total failure of faith. When Peter has *turned back* (cf. 17:3-4) he will *strengthen [his] brothers.* Readers will discover in Acts just how effective a leader Peter becomes.

22:35-38. Two swords. Jesus' question of v. 35 refers back to 10:4. *But now,* points to a change of circumstances. The disciples, as they "stand by" Jesus (22:28), are about to enter into the thickest flack in the fray against evil. They must take full provisions, including a *sword.* This makes clear how intense the struggle is to become. The reference to the *sword* is metaphorical, although the disciples take Jesus literally. *It is enough* is Jesus' rebuke of their philistine interpretation. Verse 37 appeals to Isa 53:12 and prepares readers for 23:32.

22:39-46. Prayer in the time of trial. Jesus and the disciples are about to enter *the time of trial* (lit. "testing"). Will the disciples stand with Jesus during the upcoming testing as they have to this point (cf. 22:28)? Testing is not something anyone should want to endure. Thus Jesus exhorts his disciples to pray that they might *not come into* such a *time* (cf. 11:4). Prayer

is the best "provision" (cf. 22:36) one has for the struggle to come. Jesus himself prays a prayer of deliverance (v. 42). Verse 43 is textually questionable (see NRSV mg.), but offers a valid interpretation of why one must pray: it offers *strength.* Prayer for deliverance must include the willingness to do God's will, not one's own (v. 42). The disciples, *sleeping because of grief,* do not rise to the occasion. Satan's sifting (cf. 22:31) has begun. They may not continue to stand with Jesus. Readers recall hopefully the promise Jesus made in 22:32.

22:47-53. The arrest of Jesus. *Judas,* who has chosen to side with evil in the struggle against evil, leads *a crowd* to arrest Jesus. Verse 52 defines the *crowd: chief priests . . . the temple police, and the elders.* The disciples *strike with the sword* indicating that they do not grasp that prayer is how they are to engage the enemy in this present time of testing.

The Jewish leaders come to arrest Jesus *as a bandit.* Yet it is they, not Jesus, who have made the Temple a *den of robbers* (19:46, same Gk. word). Such blatant hypocrisy is to be expected, for they have assumed the role of the hypocritical Pharisees (cf. 12:1). More importantly, the Jewish leadership, being led by Judas, whom Satan is leading (22:3), are now explicitly in league with Satan, *the power of darkness* (cf. Acts 26:18). The arrest and subsequent execution of the Son of God is evil's finest *hour.* It will also be evil's undoing.

22:54-65. Peter's denial. Satan's sifting (22:21) continues. As Jesus was led to *the high priest's house* (cf. 3:2 for possible identity), *Peter was following,* but only *at a distance.* Peter's threefold denial shows that he completely fails as a thoroughly loyal disciple willing to give his life for Jesus (cf. 22:33).

Readers should recall that Jesus has promised a kingdom to his disciples because they have "stood with him" (22:28-29). They should also recall the many radical demands that Jesus laid upon those who wished to follow him (cf. esp. 9:23-26, 57-62; 12:49-53; 14:25-35). Throughout this passion narrative, one can hardly be impressed by how the disciples have "stood" or how faithfully they have devoted their lives to Jesus. If, indeed, Jesus does follow through on his promise to give the disciples a kingdom, it will be through no merit of their own. At this point readers may recall Jesus' word that he has prayed for Peter that his faith will not fail utterly. He demands repentance, to be sure (cf. *once you have turned back* [22:32]), but it is Jesus' action on behalf of his disciples that will restore and sustain them. The message of radical mercy rings through. Perhaps Peter realized this as *he wept bitterly.*

The abuse of Jesus (vv. 63-65) shows the utter contempt of Jesus' opponents as they mockingly encourage Jesus to *prophesy!* Readers catch the irony in that they have just witnessed a prophecy of Jesus come to realization as *the cock crowed.*

22:66-71. Hearing before the assembly. *The assembly* is the SANHEDRIN, the Jewish high court. This assembly as depicted in Luke has little interest in justice. In 20:20 the leadership schemed to secure politically incriminating testimony from Jesus. Getting Jesus to acknowledge his messianic status is similarly motivated. He refuses to cooperate.

Verse 68 alludes to 20:1-8, a narrative exposing the duplicity of the Jewish leadership which explains why they *would not believe* even if Jesus did answer their inquiry. He does affirm, however, that the Son of Man will assume royal power (*the right hand of God*). Readers know Jesus is talking about himself. Jesus' questioners suspect so, given the follow-up question of v. 70. Jesus' implicit affirmation gives them grounds to pursue legal action, although as the subsequent narrative will show they will have to offer a most twisted interpretation of Jesus' admission if they hope to get the governor to pass sentence.

23:1-5. The first hearing before Pilate. The charge concerning *taxes* is simply false (cf. 20:20-26). The charge of claiming to be the *Messiah* is a half-truth at best. Jesus has made no explicit claim, and certainly he has not portrayed himself as the kind of *king of the Jews* that PILATE would be interested in executing. Pilate quickly dismisses the charges before *the chief priests and the crowds.* The latter have perhaps arrived expecting to hear Jesus' teaching (cf. 21:38). The *they* of v. 5 who respond to Pilate are likely the chief priests who insist that Jesus *stirs up the people.* This charge gives Pilate further reason to execute their enemy Jesus.

23:6-12. Hearing before Herod. Readers recall that HEROD, having killed JOHN THE BAPTIST, had been wanting to see Jesus (9:9) and was seeking to kill him (13:31). Even corrupt Herod, after *he questioned him at some length* and heard *the chief priests and the scribes . . . vehemently accusing him* found nothing worthy of execution and *sent him back to Pilate* (vv. 9-11). On *that same day* they became *friends.* It is a perverted friendship, rooted in their willingness to appease the Jewish leadership. Although Herod did not recommend

execution, he is held fully accountable for his complicity in Jesus' death in Acts 4:25-28.

23:13-25. The second hearing before Pilate. Again, the leadership and the people are present. Pilate, however, seems more interested in addressing his comments to the leadership, reminding them of the charges they had made against Jesus earlier in the day: *this man . . . was perverting the people.* Since Pilate cannot find *this man guilty of any of your charges against him* he will flog Jesus *and release him* (vv.14-17).

Then they all shouted out together, "Away with this fellow!" Who are *they*? The leadership and the people, or the leadership who had been making the charges against Jesus? Luke is not clear. Whether *the people* at this juncture join the leaders of *this generation* (cf. 7:31-35) in demanding Jesus' crucifixion or simply acquiesce out of fear, the consequences are the same, as subsequent pronouncements by Jesus (23:27-31) and his followers (Acts 3:14-15) make clear: they are guilty. The implications of 11:23 become clear: *Whoever is not with me is against me.* The people have shown themselves not to be "with Jesus." Their failure, like that of the disciples, cannot be excused—it can only be forgiven. The early chapters of Acts will tell of the apostles preaching to the people offering. them the opportunity to repent and be forgiven (Acts 2:38) and to separate themselves from "this corrupt generation" (Acts 2:40).

23:26-31. The walk to crucifixion. Luke again is unclear concerning the identity of the *they* who *led him away.* Romans? Jewish leaders? Jewish people? Luke distinguishes *a great number of the people* from those taking Jesus away to crucify him. Yet even those bemoaning Jesus' fate will not escape the punishment to befall *the daughters of Jerusalem* and their *children.* Terrible days are coming when even death would be better than life—clearly a reference to Jerusalem's destruction (cf. 19:43-44; 21:6, 20-24). The enigmatic saying of v. 31 means "If this kind of violent thing can happen to an innocent man (the *green wood*), imagine what will happen to a guilty city and its people (*dry wood*)."

23:32-56. The crucifixion of Jesus. This scene has three sections: the mocking of Jesus by the Jewish leaders and the soldiers (vv. 32-38); the two criminals (vv. 39-43); the death and burial of Jesus (vv. 44-56).

Verses 32-38. The scoffing and mocking of Jesus by *the leaders* (Jewish) and *the soldiers* (gentiles; cf. 18:32) centers around the spectacle of a supposed *Messiah* and *King of the Jews* not being able to *save* himself. The Jews and the gentiles share in the ridicule of the Lord's anointed (Acts 4:25-28). *The people stood by, watching*, not sharing in the ridicule of Jesus. The later sermons of Acts will condemn them, nonetheless (Acts 3:12-15).

Readers know Jesus to be the savior (1:69; 2:11) and Messiah (2:11; 9:20) and have seen him demonstrate his saving power over sin (7:48-40), disease (8:43-48), even death (8:49-50). Jesus accomplishes his saving mission through his self-giving. Luke may offer no explicit doctrine of the atonement, but the emphasis Jesus himself places upon his rejection and death as the divinely necessitated culmination of his earthly work as the Son of Man and prophet (see comments on 9:18-36; 13:33-34) allows readers to know that this death does play a role in his work of liberation and salvation. To mock him is to show that one simply does not understand "the plan of God" (cf. 7:30).

The first sentence of v. 34 may not be original (see NRSV mg.). But it is fitting here. Jesus offers ("release/liberation"; cf. 4:18)—saving others even as they mock him for saving others while he cannot save himself. It also prepares for Acts 3:17.

Verses 39-43. One *criminal* joins the scoffers. The other criminal implies his recognition of Jesus as the Messiah as he requests that Jesus remember him *when [he] comes into [his] kingdom*. Jesus' promise assures him of salvation, and even sooner than the criminal expected: *today. Paradise* was a common term to denote heaven and its blessings (2 Cor 12:4; Rev 2:7). The Messiah demonstrates his saving power as he dies, even as the scoffers scoff.

Verses 44-56. Reference to the failing of *the sun's light* recalls Jesus' word concerning *the power of darkness* (22:53). Jerusalem will pay a heavy price for aligning itself with darkness. The tearing of *the curtain of the temple* (v. 45) serves as an omen that the Temple will be destroyed, adding weight to what Jesus had predicted (19:43-44; 21:6). Jesus' last words show his trust in the *Father*, Jesus' favorite designation for God in the Gospel, even from childhood (cf. 2:49).

Luke narrates a number of reactions. The CENTURION, representing the mocking soldiers of 23:36, recognizes Jesus as *innocent* (Gk.: righteous). Jesus' opponents had thought they were "righteous" (18:9; 20:20 [NRSV "honest"]), but their brand of righteousness killed the one who truly was righteous. Does the centurion's response hold out hope for the gentiles?

The people react in gestures of mourning, *beating their breasts* (v. 48). The time for *weeping for themselves and their children* has begun (cf. 23:27-30). The phrase translated *returned home* is literally "turned back," sharing the same Greek root as a word Jesus has related to repentance (cf. 17:3-4), yet the verb does not actually mean "repentance." Their reaction is ambiguous. Is there hope for them?

THE TWELVE (eleven?), if present at all, are buried away in the anonymity of Jesus' *acquaintances* (v. 49). Theirs and the women's response to the scene (watching from a distance) is really no less ambiguous than that of the people. The report of the women's going to prepare spices is touching, but it also makes clear that they did not grasp Jesus' own predictions of his resurrection. Is there hope for Jesus' followers?

Joseph of Arimathea, *a member of the council*, is described most positively as *good and righteous*. His action is also the most courageous, having gone *to Pilate* to ask for *the body of Jesus*. It is made clear that he did not consent to the *plan and action* of the *council* (vv. 50-56). Readers might find some comfort in knowing that not all the Jewish leadership is utterly corrupt. Is there hope even for them?

Representatives from all groups involved in the execution of Jesus, Jewish and gentile, are present. Yet it is curious how Luke has presented them: the apostles are anonymous at best; the representative from the Jewish leadership—Joseph—is *good and righteous*. These last scenes of Jesus' passion are unsettling enough to dissuade readers from thinking that what happens in the story of Jesus is predictable. Glimmers of hope are offered for all the representative characters, especially when one remembers the prayers of Jesus on behalf of the "sifted" followers (22:31-32) and those who mocked and watched (23:34-46).

Entering into Glory, 24:1-53

For background discussion of the resurrection narratives and the resurrection of Jesus, see Fitzmyer 1985, 1533-43.

As readers reach the end of a story they look for resolution of issues raised in what has preceded (Parsons 1986, 201-204). Having arrived at the end of the story, Luke will now need to bring some closure to his story. Review of previous sections of the narrative recalls the issues of the story in need of resolution.

First, Jesus has come to offer redemption to Israel in fulfillment of scriptural promises, with clear hints of inclusion of the gentiles into God's salvation. There will be division among the people (1:5–4:13).

Second, Jesus has come to offer liberation ("release") to the captives and the oppressed. This section makes clear that Satan, later called *the power of darkness* (22:53), is behind this oppression. Jesus' shorthand expression for this liberation from Satan's power is *the reign of God* (4:16–9:50).

Third, Jesus is the PROPHET, indeed the Son of God, to whom Israel must listen (9:35). As he journeys to JERUSALEM, ISRAEL, consisting of disciples, the people, and the leadership, the last represented primarily by the Pharisees, are given ample opportunity to hear him. The leadership is hostile. The people vacillate. The disciples stay with Jesus, but they lack understanding. Despite these evidences of division among Israel, to all have been applied the negative appellation *this generation* (9:51–19:44).

Fourth, in Jerusalem Jesus called Israel to decision. No reader can be impressed by the response of any element of Israel in the passion narrative. With the death of Jesus, one must ask, will there be redemption in fulfillment of scriptural promises, liberation from the power of darkness, and a positive hearing of the word of Jesus by Israel? Readers, anticipating the resurrection, know that if resolution is to come it must come from the resurrected one.

24:1-12. The empty tomb. The women, later identified in v. 10, come to the tomb on Sunday (*the first day of the week*) morning. They have come for the wrong reason, to anoint a dead man, but *they did not find the body*. The description of *the two men in dazzling clothes* implies angelic beings (cf. 24:23). They announce the resurrection and recall the prediction that Jesus himself had made (v. 6; cf. 9:22). With Jesus alive expectations of resolution are raised. The women *told all this to the eleven* but they thought it *an idle tale*. PETER does go to inspect the tomb, however (v. 12, although this text is disputed [see NRSV mg.]). He is amazed, but does not see Jesus. So far, no resolution of any issues.

24:13-35. The road to Emmaus. It is still Sunday (v. 13). Hopes for resolution are raised as *Jesus himself* proceeds to walk with two persons journeying to EMMAUS. *But their eyes were kept from recognizing him* (v.16); a phrase hauntingly reminiscent of what Jesus had said of Jerusalem (19:42). Hopes for resolution are quickly taken away.

The conversation of CLEOPAS and his companion reminds readers of issues in need of resolution: Will there be redemption for Israel in fulfillment of scriptural promises? They certainly do not think so (cf. v.

21). The unrecognized Jesus is emphatic that the suffering of the Messiah is part of the fulfillment of the scriptural promises, although the two do not see it and the reader is even left clueless as to exactly how. Still, it is clear that the resurrected Jesus affirms the fulfillment of scripture. This hope is not to be abandoned.

What of the work of liberation and the reign of God? The fact of Jesus' resurrection, which by the end of the story, even the characters come to recognize, affirms the effectiveness of the liberating power of God. Jesus' act of taking, blessing, breaking, and giving bread is reminiscent of 22:19. In that context Jesus had said he would *not eat . . . until it is fulfilled in the kingdom of God*. What readers are witnessing is hardly the fulfillment of the kingdom of God; Luke 21:25-33 has made clear that such will accompany the coming of the Son of Man *in a cloud with power and great glory*. Still the picture of the resurrected Jesus breaking bread with his followers instills confidence that bread will be broken again when it is fulfilled in the kingdom of God. Here one may not find the realization of the reign of God, but one does find justification to hope for such realization.

What of the response of Israel? The disciples respond affirmatively; once *their eyes were opened* (v. 31), Jesus *appeared* to them (v. 34), and *had been made known* (v. 35) to them. Response, even after being "sifted by Satan" (22:31), is possible, but it can come only at the initiation of the resurrected Lord. Will the rest of Israel have opportunity to respond to this resurrected one? Comments concerning the leadership are thoroughly negative, leaving little hope (v. 20). What of the people? They are not explicitly indicted in v. 20, but neither is any explicit word offered to indicate that they will respond to the word of Jesus. The final phrase, stating that Jesus *had been made known to them in the breaking of the bread* (v. 35), might offer a clue that recognition of Jesus apart from life in the community of faith is not possible, for in Acts "breaking bread" serves to denote Christian fellowship at the table of the Lord (cf. 22:30; Acts 2:42, 46; 20:7, 11).

24:36-53. Appearance and exodus. It is now Sunday evening (cf. vv. 29, 33, 36). Jesus' appearance to the group (vv. 36-42) affirms for them and the readers the reality of his resurrection. Jesus invites them to *touch* him and to see his *flesh and bones*. He even eats *in their presence* (v. 43) to confirm the reality of his resurrection.

Jesus' pronouncement of *peace be with you* (v. 36) recalls the disciples acclamation of peace when Jesus approached Jerusalem (19:38) and especially the angelic announcement of 2:14. There the angels promised peace due to the birth of the Messiah. In this scene, Jesus fulfills this hope. He had wanted to offer such peace to Jerusalem, but it could not see it (19:42). This appearance reinforces resolution of the issue concerning the response of the disciples to Jesus. At least this part of Israel sees who this Jesus is.

In vv. 44-49, numerous issues are offered resolution, although new expectations are also raised. Jesus affirms again that, indeed, *everything written about [him] in the law of Moses, the prophets, and the psalms must be fulfilled.* Jesus affirms that the story of his passion itself was *written* in the scriptures. This story readers have just read is the realization, or at least an integral part of the realization, of the fulfillment of Israel's scriptures.

Still readers are not told exactly what scriptures are fulfilled. But Jesus *opened their minds to understand the scriptures.* This assures readers that the resurrected Lord can lead believers to see to exactly how the "Jesus story" fulfills "scripture's story." In Acts, readers will have several opportunities to hear the scriptures interpreted and to see how exactly Jesus fulfills the scriptures.

The ministry of liberation, or "release," is addressed explicitly in the charge Jesus makes to his followers. This work of liberation, which included in Jesus' ministry the offering of *forgiveness* (or "release") *of sins* is to continue (v. 47). In fact, this very continuation of the ministry of liberation is itself said to be part of the fulfillment of what *is written* (v. 46). What is more, this proclamation of *repentance and forgiveness of sins* will begin *from Jerusalem.* Jerusalem and its people (even its leaders?) will hear the message of repentance and be offered the opportunity to experience the liberation they rejected just a few days before. The proclamation will not stop in Jerusalem. It shall be offered to *all the nations* (same Gk. word as "gentiles").

Will redemption come to Israel as she once again is given opportunity to hear the message? Jesus' predictions about the destruction of Jerusalem create tension. Is there a way that redemption, liberation, and forgiveness can still come to Israel if, indeed, Jerusalem must fall? Will the nations (gentiles) respond positively? These questions are not answered. But Luke approaches the conclusion with hopeful expectations.

Finally in this section, Luke raises the expectation that the mission in which he is calling his disciples to engage will be assisted by something promised by the *Father* himself that Jesus will send: *power from on high.* Attentive readers will recall such texts as 3:16; 11:13; 12:12. Less attentive readers will have to wait until Acts to find out what Jesus is talking about.

In vv. 50-53, Jesus' exodus (departure [cf. 9:31]) and "taking up" (9:51) are to be realized. The journey of Jesus is coming to an end. Before he leaves he offers his followers a priestly blessing, *lifting up his hands.* The Temple may be destined to fall someday (and from the perspective of Luke's readers it has fallen), but the blessing of God's anointed will not be impeded by the lack of a Temple and priesthood, just as the existence of a Temple and priesthood cannot insure blessing (cf. 1:22).

The brief description of Jesus' ascension *up into heaven* allows readers to experience and witness the realization of Jesus' bold claim before his oppressors in 22:69: *the Son of Man will be seated at the right hand of . . . God.* Jesus has been vindicated.

The disciples return *to Jerusalem* whence the continuing mission of liberation will commence, *continually in the temple blessing God.* Jerusalem and the Temple will fall one day. But for now, the Temple has been cleansed by the Messiah (19:45-46) and is a most fitting place for his people to congregate.

Luke ends the story where he began it: in the holy city and sanctuary of Israel, the people of God. As readers prepare to turn the page to begin Luke's second book—the Book of Acts—this closing scene calls them back to the opening scenes and to hopes raised by such characters as Mary, the mother of Jesus, and Zechariah, the father of the Baptist, but perhaps expressed best by Simeon, the righteous man longing for the consolation of Israel. *My eyes have seen your salvation . . . a light for revelation to the Gentiles and for glory to your people Israel* (2:30-32).

Works Cited

Aune, David E. 1987. *The New Testament in Its Literary Environment.*

Burridge, Richard A. 1992. *What Are the Gospels? A Comparison with Graeco-Roman Biography.* SNTSMS 70.

Chance, J. Bradley. 1988. *Jerusalem, the Temple, and the New Age in Luke–Acts.*

Conzelmann, Hans. 1982 [1960]. *The Theology of St. Luke.*

Fitzmyer, Joseph A., S.J. 1981, 1985. *The Gospel according to Luke*. 2 vols. (pages numbered consecutively). AncB.

Garrett, Susan R. "'Lest the Light in You Be Darkness': Luke 11:33-36 and the Question of Commitment," *JBL* 110/1 (1991): 93-105.

Marshall, I. Howard. 1978. *Commentary on Luke*, NIGTC.

Moesnner, David P. 1989. *Lord of the Banquet: The Literary and Theological Significance of the Lukan Travel Narrative*; 1990. "The 'Leaven of the Pharisees' and 'This Generation': Israel's Rejection of Jesus according to Luke," *Reimaging the Death of Jesus*, ed. Dennis D. Sylva, 79–107.

Pervo, Richard I. 1989. "Must Luke and Acts Belong to the Same Genre?" SBLASP, 309-16.

Parsons, Mikeal C. 1986. "Narrative Closure and Openness in the Plot of the Third Gospel: The Sense of Ending in Luke 24:50-53," SBLASP.

Talbert, Charles H. 1986. *Reading Luke: A Literary and Theological Commentary on the Third Gospel*. 1988. "Once Again: Gospel Genre," *Semeia* 43:53-73.

Tiede, David L. 1988. *Luke*. AugCNT.

John

Gerald L. Borchert

Introduction

The fourth Gospel is one of the most fascinating books in the Bible. Its poetic-like stories have engulfed many, and a number of its verses are among the most familiar in scripture. Although its vocabulary is simple and verges on being redundant, the Gospel is one of the most complex compositions in the Bible in terms of the interweaving of theological themes. It is like a complex symphony that periodically repeats earlier themes with refreshing variations so that the reader is caught in the awe-inspiring work of a masterfully sophisticated artist.

John and the Synoptics

When one reads John after reading one of the Synoptics (Matthew, Mark, or Luke), one has the feeling of being in familiar territory. Yet, in spite of the similarities, it is strangely different. JESUS certainly performs miracles (in John called "signs"), but, except for the multiplication of bread and the walking on the water in chap. 6, the sign stories are all different. There is a great catch of fish in chap. 21 that reminds the reader of Luke 5, but it takes place after the resurrection in John so that scholars have a field day trying to work out the relationship between the two stories.

In terms of organization the Synoptics have Jesus moving from GALILEE to JUDEA to die, whereas John moves Jesus at will between the two regions. It is likely this Gospel's movement of Jesus is more reflective of what actually happened, but we are not quite sure. The question of the cleansing of the Temple points to the problem. Because the story appears in John near the beginning of the Gospel (chap. 2) and in the Synoptics in the final stages of Jesus' life, many readers automatically begin to think there are two cleansings of the Temple. But there is only one in any one Gospel. This fact raises the important question of organization in John.

Organization of the Gospel

When many readers are asked "How long did Jesus live?" the normal reply is thirty-three years. The reason is that they take the thirty years of preparation from Luke 3:23 and then go to John and count the number of Passovers recorded there. But to count Passovers in this manner is to misunderstand this Gospel (Borchert 1993).

The Gospel of John is organized according to cycles, and PASSOVER is a key to understanding John's cycle-thinking. The Gospel begins with a prologue (1:1-18, probably written after the Gospel was finished as an introduction to the Gospel) that relates Jesus to God and to the very beginning of time. Then there is a series of short stories (1:19-52) that introduces Jesus in terms of a variety of titles including MESSIAH, SON OF GOD, and King of Israel, with the focal designation being *the Lamb of God who takes away the sin of the world!* (1:29, 36). That lamb is meant to be understood as the world's Passover Lamb.

This introductory chapter is followed by a series of three cycles in which Passover plays a significant role. The Cana cycle (chaps. 2–4) has at its heart the Passover and the cleansing of the Temple (2:13-25). The Festival cycle (chaps. 5–11) after an introduction to feast thinking (chap. 5) moves from Passover (6:4) to Passover (11:55). Chapter 12 serves as a saddle text between the public ministry of Jesus and his private ministry to his disciples. The setting is just before the Passover (12:1). The farewell cycle (chaps. 13–17) begins with an announcement of Passover (13:1), and these chapters seek to prepare the disciples for Passover and the coming of a new era.

The Passover sequence is drawn to a conclusion in the death story (chaps. 18–19) with the dying of the perfect Passover lamb on the specific day of Preparation when the Passover lambs were killed (19:14, 31).

The resurrection stories (chaps. 20–21) then move the reader beyond Passover to the new era of the spirit-led community (20:22) of Jesus Christ (Borchert, *John*).

The Context of the Gospel

Behind this Gospel lies a community of faith that tradition situates in EPHESUS. Its history cannot be fully detailed but its BELOVED DISCIPLE (13:23; 19:26; 20:2; 21:20) may have been the unnamed disciple of JOHN THE BAPTIST (1:35-40).

Some time during its formative period, as J. Louis Martyn (1979, 37–62) has forcefully argued, members of the community undoubtedly encountered hostility from the SYNAGOGUE. Whether they moved from Israel first to Antioch or immediately to Ephesus is not certain. Neither is it clear whether their numbers included SAMARITANS, as might be argued from John 4:39-42.

The hostility with the synagogue seems clearly behind the story of the blind man (9:22, 34, 40) as well as the entire argument of Jesus in 8:31-59 and the warning in 16:2-4. Whether the *Birkath ha-Minim* (the curse of the heretics that was inserted into the Jewish benedictions) is directly related to this community, it is clear that the context of hostility is very similar. In this context, the reader cannot help but be reminded of the Christian evaluation of the Jews as the "synagogue of Satan" in the Apocalypse (Rev 2:9; 3:9).

The entire Gospel seems to be written from the perspective of the way Jesus filled the expectations of the OT. He is viewed, for example, as the new Temple (2:19-21), the successor to the hope of the lifted-up serpent (3:14), the interpreter of SABBATH (5:9-18), the true bread from heaven (6:48-51), the living water of Tabernacles (7:37-38), and the true shepherd king expected in Ezek 34 and Jer 23 (John 10:1-30). Such views undoubtedly raised the ire of many Jews.

Authorship

The traditional view has been that John the son of Zebedee was the author of this Gospel. Such a view was enunciated by Irenaeus in the second century C.E. (*AdvHaer* 3.1.1) and maintained until the late eighteenth and early nineteenth centuries. The theology then was challenged by some as being later dualistic and Platonic thinking (e.g., D. F. Strauss). Some began to point to the probability that the Gospel was written by a second-century disciple of the apostle (19:35; 21:25; e.g., H. Paulus). The next stage in thinking was that a school or community was responsible for the

Gospel (e.g., J. B. Lightfoot) and this theory received an expanded treatment recently by Culpepper (1975).

Clearly the epilogue is suggestive in terms of authorship because three parties are there identified. The first is the disciple or witness (21:24), the second is the church or community that authenticates the work (e.g., *we*, 21:24), and the third party is the *I* (21:25) who appears to be the writer of at least the last two verses and probably more. The text itself, therefore, indicates a multiplicity of persons involved in the writing and transmission of this Gospel. The Beloved Disciple, however, is clearly viewed as the source of the tradition or basis for the message. In this commentary the designations evangelist and John are used interchangeably, recognizing the complex nature of the issue.

Date

The traditional date for the writing of the Gospel has been the decade of 90–100 C.E. This date had been called into question by some who supposed the theology was second-century. The discovery of a fragment of the Gospel in Egypt (containing 18:31-33, 37-38, and housed in the Rylands Library in Manchester), which probably dates from the early second century, has resulted in the earlier date being resubstantiated.

Theology

This Gospel was early regarded as a very special work. Clement of Alexandria designated it as the "spiritual gospel." That name has adhered to it throughout the centuries. Even before Clement, however, Gnostic mythologizers and spiritualizers found it to be a powerful vehicle for their distorted message (see Borchert 1981, 249). Indeed works like the Gospel of Truth (*Evangelium Veritatis*) found at NAG HAMMADI and reputed to have been written by Valentinus made use of the Gospel of John. Moreover, Gnostic spiritualizers like Heracleon were the first commentators on the Gospel.

Such facts have led some to suspect the Gospel to be marginally heretical. Its theology is certainly lofty and its CHRISTOLOGY is among the most elevated in the NT. The Gospel does not begin with the birth of Jesus but with the LOGOS/WORD at the beginning of time. But while the christology is elevated, it is important to see that on the basis of the purpose of John the Jesus of this Gospel cannot be an adoptionistic, nonsuffering, alien messenger from without. The Jesus of this Gospel is very real, very human but also God-directed and divinely empowered. He is truly a God-man.

His concern is for his suffering community and for leading people from one stage of believing to the next. In John, Jesus is the divine-human rescuer of faithless, doubting people. He, the creator of the world (1:3), has come to his own people and place and has been rejected (1:9-11) but he continues to build a community from those who will believe (1:12), the purpose for which John wrote his Gospel (20:30-31).

In reaching this purpose the evangelist has interwoven many great themes. Those themes include seeing, believing, knowing, light, darkness, life, death, truth, hour, signs, judgment, love, "I am," freedom, bread, water, and a host of others. Each theme can make for interesting research studies and each can be developed as windows into the nature of the Gospel.

The careful reader will also discover that this Gospel can be studied on various levels so that its wells of insight seldom run dry. It is a work that is loved by many new Christians although they may not understand what it means to *eat the flesh of the Son of Man* (6:53). It will challenge the minds and hearts of the most mature believer. It is indeed a book that is used by the Spirit of God to touch the world.

For Further Study

In the *Mercer Dictionary of the Bible*: BELOVED DISCIPLE, THE; CHRISTOLOGY; FEASTS AND FESTIVALS; GNOSTICISM; GOSPELS, CRITICAL STUDY OF; INCARNATION; JESUS; JOHN THE APOSTLE; JOHN THE BAPTIST; JOHN, GOSPEL AND LETTERS OF; LAMB OF GOD; LAZARUS; LOGOS/WORD; MESSIAH/CHRIST; MIRACLE STORY; PHARISEES; RESURRECTION IN THE NT; SIGNS AND WONDERS; WOMEN IN THE NT; WORSHIP IN THE NT. In other sources: G. R. Beasley-Murray, *John*, WBC; G. L. Borchert, *John*, NAC; R. E. Brown, *The Gospel according to John*, AncB; D. A. Carson, *The Gospel according to John*; J. Charlesworth, ed., *John and the Dead Sea Scrolls*; E. Haenchen, *John*; R. Schnackenburg, *The Gospel according to St. John*.

Commentary

An Outline

Introduction, 1:1-51

The Gospel of John is one of the most fascinating documents in the NT. While it may appear to be simple in vocabulary and style, it is one of the most highly organized and sophisticated works in the Bible (Borchert 1981, 249). Although scholars suggest some variations in detail concerning organization, most agree in the primary divisions of the book, with a major-segment break at either chap. 12 or 13. My particular contribution (Borchert 1987, 86–152; and Borchert, *John*) is the view that the Gospel was written in cycles (the Cana cycle, chaps. 2–4; the Festival cycle, chaps. 5–11; the farewell cycle, chaps. 13–17) framed by other sections that provide special developmental emphases (the prologue, 1:1-18; stories of witness, 1:19-51; transition to death, chap. 12; the death story, chaps. 18–19; the resurrection stories, chap. 20; and the postscript, chap. 21). Moreover, the book hangs together as a magnificent testimony to Jesus, *the Lamb of God who takes away the sin of the world* (1:29), and provides a model of authentic life for the community of believers.

The Purpose, 20:30-31

To understand the thought and goal of John, one would do well to begin with the first ending of the book—its purpose statement. This purpose statement is formulated to provide readers with a window into what has been written. There it is said that

> Many other signs, indeed, Jesus did before his disciples that are not recorded in this book, but these are recorded that you might believe that Jesus is the Christ, the Son of God, and that in [the genuine act of] believing you might have life by [or in the power of] his name (author trans.).

From this statement it is evident that the evangelist expects a response from the reader. Clearly nothing less than active believing in Jesus which issues in a new way of living is adequate to encompass what this Gospel intends for its readership (Borchert 1987, 91). True life is the goal, authentic believing is the means, and relationship to Jesus (the SON OF GOD) is the basis. Furthermore, this purpose statement also indicates some of the most important themes that permeate the Gospel such as the understanding of signs, the importance of believing and life, the nature of Jesus, the importance of names and confession, and the significance of discipleship. In addition, readers of this Gospel should be alert to repetitive themes, words, phrases, and questions that arise in the Gospel. Attending to them should bring a new vitality to the study of this magnificent book. But all study should be related to the evangelist's purpose for the book and should result in a personal response involving one's own life. Only in such a context will the purpose be realized.

The Prologue, 1:1-18

The Gospel begins with one of the most profound statements concerning Jesus in the NT. The lofty CHRISTOLOGY is scarcely approximated elsewhere except perhaps in Heb 1:1-13 or Col 1:15-20. Moreover, its poetic-like style has led scholars to speculate on whether it was originally a poem or a hymn (e.g., J. Sanders 1971, 20–24; R. Brown 1966, 3–4). Some have sought to find a core document in Aramaic (Burney 1922, 40) while others like Bultmann have thought they found its roots in a gnostic logos hymn (1971, 23–28). Käsemann has countered that it was probably an early Christian hymn that was incorporated into the Gospel (1969, 138–67). Whatever may have been its roots, as it stands it has been thoroughly Johnninized in the editing process.

1:1-5. The eternal Word. In contrast to the synoptic Gospels, the evangelist begins at *the beginning* and builds upon the first and sixth orders of the creation account in Gen 1. He does not repeat those earlier presuppositions but identifies the *Word* ($\lambda\acute{o}\gamma o\varsigma$) with the very beginning and with God's divine selfhood, not in terms of subjugation of the *Word* but in a pattern of mutual interaction (Newman and Nida 1980, 8). The *Word* here is to be understood as a persona of God, not "a god" of subordination as argued by the Jehovah's Witnesses (see Metzger 1953).

In the prologue the contrast between the Greek verbs for "being" ($\mathring{\eta}\nu$) and "becoming" ($\mathring{\epsilon}\gamma\acute{\epsilon}\nu\epsilon\tau o$) is very crucial. The verb for "being" is used in vv. 1, 2, 4, 8, 9, 10, and 15 and refers to an existence without precondition, whereas the second word is used in vv. 3, 6, 10, 14, and 17, and implies moments within history. The *Word* in v. 1, however, is not a mere philosophical term to be identified simply with divine rationality as in Philonic speculation or Jewish Wisdom literature (cf. Dodd 1958, 274–75). Instead, it is to be understood as an early stage in the Trinitarian formulation concerning the various *personas* of God.

Not only is the preexistence of the *Word* here clearly implied, but it is also asserted that the *Word* has been active in the entire process of creation (v. 3). Indeed, the *Word* is here identified with the age-old quest of human beings for the essence of life (v. 4) and this pre-life-existing one is designated as the light-giver whose light is unquenchable (v. 5).

Many scholars today reject the translation of *overcome* ($\kappa\alpha\tau\acute{\epsilon}\lambda\alpha\beta\epsilon\nu$) in v. 5, arguing that the idea here could hardly be related to the ancient struggle between light and darkness—viewed as a conflict picture, symbolic of the warfare between good and evil (Beasley-Murray 1987, 32; Brown 1966, 8; Schnackenburg 1987, 1:245–49). My suggestion (*John*) is that there is a conflict to be understood here related to the rejection or nonreception ($\pi\alpha\rho\acute{\epsilon}\lambda\alpha\beta o\nu$) of the *Word* (cf. v. 11). For John the coming of Jesus divides persons and realities, and the underlying postresurrection perspective in the entire Gospel means that evil and rejection will not triumph (Borchert, *John*, and 1988, 502).

1:6-8. John the witness. The next three verses are prose and focus attention on *John* (the baptizer or *witness*). They function like a window from the lofty, poetic stance of the hymn on the *Word* down to the human context of witness, which is the first subject of concern following the lofty prologue. As such these verses provide a clear contrast: namely, John the witness is not to be considered in the same category or on the same level as the *Word* (cf. also 1:15), a view some of John's disciples apparently could not accept (John 3:25-30; see Borchert, *John*). Yet the designation of John as a witness is not to be considered a minor matter because witness, as J. Boice (1970, 31–38) argued, is a major theme in the Gospel. John the witness, like many persons in the Gospel, is more than an ancient person. He is an exemplar or representative.

1:9-13. Receiving the light. The *Word* is next identified as authentic light and linked to the idea of "the coming one," a designation derived from OT texts such as Zech 9:9 and used to identify the coming of the Messiah (cf. 4:25). According to the evangelist, however, although the *true light* entered the world in the midst of those who should have been expecting him, the tragic reality was that the *Word* encountered rejection rather than reception. This theme of rejection is often repeated in the Johannine stories of Jesus. But the evangelist is quick to assert that, despite rejection by many, those who believed are named the children of God not because of human lineage, desire, or power but because they have received the active *Word* of God.

1:14-18. The Incarnation and its implications. The second appearance of λόγος (*Word*) in the prologue signals the changed state of the *Word*'s work. In the first stage the emphasis was upon creation. The second stage, the work of the coming one, is redemption. In the language of the TENT OF MEETING in the EXODUS story, the evangelist describes the "enfleshment" of the *Word* in "tent" (σκηνόω) terminology. The *Word* is said to have actually "presenced" itself among humans. The idea of tent here implies no mere gnostic appearance theology. Instead, the meaning is that the *Word* actually entered the historical context and *became* (ἐγένετο) *flesh* or truly human. INCARNATION theology is one of the basic theses of historic Christianity.

As Israel experienced the glory of God at the wilderness tent (Exod 40:34), so both John (*we*, v. 14) and the early witnesses experienced divine glory in the enfleshed *Word* (Borchert, *John*). This sense of divine presence and glory was given to the world in God's

"only" (μονογενής, see Moody 1953, 213–19) son. In him was vested divine "fullness" (πλήρωμα), a term later used by the Gnostics to describe their godhead. But here the fullness of the *Word* is said to be the source for the Christian experience of abundant *grace* (v. 16). Such grace (a term used only in the prologue of John) is contrasted directly with the divine gift of law that came through Moses (remember: law is also gift).

Then in v. 17 the *Word* is finally named: *Jesus* Christ, the divine-human agent of grace and truth. Truth or authenticity is one of the major themes in John and is a mark of both Jesus and his genuine followers. Clearly no one has ever seen the full semblance of God. But Jesus—the only SON OF GOD, whose intimacy with God the Father is described by the term "bosom" (v. 18; *heart* NRSV)—has portrayed, detailed, or narrated (ἐξηγήσατο) the nature of God for the world. With this idea of portrayal, the evangelist concludes the prologue of his Gospel (see Borchert, *John*) and sets the stage for the introduction of Jesus by John, the witness.

The Baptizer's Witness, 1:19-28

Each of the canonical Gospels focuses on John the Baptizer prior to introducing the ministry of Jesus. This means that for the early Christians the work of the Baptizer was seen as a strategic signal for the beginning of the Gospel (cf. Mark 1:1). In this Gospel the Baptizer almost appears to be an intruder into the prologue. Yet for the evangelist the Baptizer is no intruder. Everything in this Gospel treats the Baptizer as an ideal model of witness. There is no suggestion here of doubt concerning Jesus by the Baptizer (as in Matt 11:3). His disciples may have doubts (3:26), but not John.

1:19-23. Questioning of John. Without further introduction, John is set in a defense posture by the investigating committee of Jews (the term *Jews* in this Gospel is applied primarily to adversaries; see Freeman 1991). In successive questions he is asked whether he is MESSIAH (cf. 1QS 9.1), ELIJAH (cf. Mal 4:5), or the *prophet* (cf. Deut 18:15). When these questions fail to elicit the anticipated response, the next question posed is a demand for self-definition. As a former lawyer, I usually ponder both such questions and their answers. Many scholars have noted that these questions reflect the confusing nature of the messianic expectations of the time. But it is also important to draw attention to the fact that the first two of John's answers are similar to Peter's first two answers in his denial, namely, *I am not* (οὐκ εἰμί, v. 21). As such these answers are a direct contrast to the constant affirmation in this Gospel of Jesus as "I am" (ἐγώ εἰμι, see Borchert, *John*). The clarity of the final "no" gives rise to John's self-definition as a non-self-centered "voice" of witness. Using Isaiah's reference to the unevenness of Israel's natural geography, the Baptizer calls his hearers to prepare a new highway of reformation.

1:24-28. Criticism and John's response. Undeterred by the Baptizer's call for preparing a new way, the PHARISEES questioned his right to testify. To set this story in the context of the time of writing it is important to remember that the Pharisees were major opponents of Christian witnesses. Other parties such as the SADDUCEES are not mentioned because they had vanished with the destruction of Jerusalem. The Baptizer's response then can be viewed from two perspectives: the time of Jesus and the time of the early Christians. Moreover, the Baptizer's words are a proclamation of the presence of true authority in their midst and an assertion of his own personal unworthiness even to be a slave (one who touches feet) of this worthy one.

Three Cameos of Witness, 1:29-51

The next three witness stories form a unit that emphasizes seeing and finding the Messiah who is identified by a series of names such as the LAMB OF GOD, SON OF GOD, teacher or RABBI, CHRIST, King of Israel, and SON OF MAN. Each segment begins with the notation *the next day* indicating the interrelationship of these three pericopes.

1:29-34. Witness to the Lamb. The Passover in John is not merely a time designation. It is a theological organizing principle for the Gospel (see Borchert 1993) and it is introduced by the Baptizer/Witness when he identifies Jesus as *the Lamb of God who takes away the sin of the world* (v. 29). To his earlier statements of self-humiliation or unworthiness the Baptizer here added his admitted lack of full understanding by his confession that he did not know the Lamb until he gained insight through the descent of the Spirit upon Jesus.

Some scholars take pains to seek a harmonization with Luke's infancy accounts of the relationship between the mothers of Jesus and the Baptizer by suggesting that the latter's solitary life may explain the text (see e.g., Brown 1966, 65). But "knowing" in John is not mere acquaintance. Recognizing Jesus for who he is takes spiritual insight (Borchert, *John*). When spiritual insight comes then there follows both the ability to distinguish between mortal and spiritual realities (baptism with water vs. the Holy Spirit) and the willingness to confess that Jesus is the *Son of God* (v. 34; a better translation than "elect of God" as in some texts).

Readers of John should not interpret the descent of the Spirit upon Jesus as an adoptionistic view whereby Jesus becomes Son of God, but as a divine witness to the Baptizer concerning the existing divine nature of Jesus. Readers should also note that the confirming voice from heaven at the baptism in the Synoptics (e.g., Mark 1:11 and par.) is reserved in John for the personal confirmation of Jesus' Passover death (John 12:28-30). They should likewise note that nowhere in John is the Baptizer said to baptize Jesus. Such a reference would have run counter to the evangelist's goal of arguing against the views of the remaining disciples of the Baptizer who had not understood the Baptizer's mission of witnessing to Jesus (see John 3:25-30).

1:35-42. Witness to the first disciples. The next stage of witness involved the turning over of the Baptizer's disciples to Jesus by the announcement to them that Jesus was God's Lamb. ANDREW and an unnamed disciple (some suggest Philip) responded and followed this Lamb. Bultmann reminds us that upon seeing them, Jesus began his transforming invitation with a simple question: "What do you want?" (Bultmann 1971, 99–100). This dialogue, I would argue, is crucial because "Where are you remaining [abiding]?" (v. 33, author trans.) initiates one of the great themes of discipleship in John and the response *come and see* (v. 39) identifies another of those themes (Cullmann 1953).

What this Gospel teaches us concerning the making of disciples is that witness and invitation are far more important than argument and apologetics. That is the pattern with Andrew who found PETER. It was the same with PHILIP who found Nathaniel in the next pericope. The theme of finding is important in these two pericopes because the witnesses not only find the prospects but also say they have found the expected one. The irony in the stories is that while disciples may say they find Jesus, it is not Jesus who is lost or unknowing.

Readers will also note in this pericope several interpretive statements: Rabbi means teacher, Messiah means Christ, and Cephas means Peter (today, we would probably say "Rocky"). These and other notations in the Gospel indicate that the intended readers were probably unfamiliar with Jewish or Hebrew/Aramaic terminology and needed guidance from an interpreter.

1:43-51. Witness to Nathaniel. The theme of finding again forms the background of this story. But here Nathaniel is introduced with a protest or argument: *Can anything good come out of Nazareth?* The response of Philip is not argument but witness: *Come and see* (v. 46).

Jesus recognized in Nathaniel (v. 47) as he did in Simon (v. 42) that which was authentic, and he named him an Israelite without guile (a contrast to the pre-Jabbok Jacob, Gen 32:27-28). In answer to Nathaniel's puzzlement—*Where did you get to know me?* (v. 48)—Jesus identified him as a serious student seeking God's way (for studying under a FIG TREE, cf. Str-B 2:371).

When Nathaniel responded to Jesus with some exalted titles of messianic expectation (*Son of God* and *King of Israel* v. 40), Jesus virtually said that you are just at the beginning of understanding who I am. Instead of prediction, however, Jesus pointed back to the strategic dream of JACOB (Gen 28:10-17) and identified himself both as a new BETHEL ("house of God") and as *Son of Man* (a favorite self-designation of Jesus which involves a number of theological possibilities from the embodiment of humanity to an apocalyptic figure). With this self-witness of Jesus these cameos both reach their conclusion and provide an introduction to the actions of Jesus in the Cana cycle.

The Cana Cycle, 2:1–4:54

The five stories that form this cycle move the reader's mind from Galilee and Cana to Jerusalem, then with ever widening ripples of the darkness of the Judean context to the acceptance of Jesus by the rejects of SAMARIA, and then back to the more open setting of GALILEE (4:47, 54). The cycle also moves from the first (beginning) sign to the second sign, both of which take place in Cana and are the only signs in the Gospel designated by numerical order.

The First Cana Sign: Water to Wine, 2:1-12

The attentive reader should learn quickly that this wonderful little wedding story which is cited in some wedding services is fraught with a number of interpretive pitfalls that can easily distract from the main points of the pericope. Briefly reviewing some of these

traps, the reader should note that *the third day* (v. 1) is not a sequential time designation following the three "next days" of chap. 1. Moreover, Jesus did not mistreat his mother when he called her *Woman* and added "What is it between me and you?" (v. 4, author trans.). And for those troubled by Jesus turning water into wine (οἶνος), it is a non sequitur to argue that such wine has no alcoholic content. It is also illegitimate to use this text as an authorization by Jesus for or against drinking alcohol today or as an authorization for or against a certain kind of wedding pattern.

2:1-4. A troubled wedding ceremony. In this story the mother of Jesus apparently had an important relationship with those in charge of the wedding party in which embarrassment was on the horizon either because of something such as inadequate planning or lack of funds to cover the long celebration (perhaps a week or longer, cf. Tob 8:19; 11:18). Typical of any Jewish mother in such a tense situation, the mother of Jesus began to use her parental relationship to solve the crisis of another relationship. It was at this initial stage that Jesus reminded her that he was not to be some magical solution or amulet to prevent disaster from striking, nor was she the one who directed his life. He was directed by a divine purpose or *hour* (v. 4, a theme of John).

2:5-10. Water to wine. His mother (she is not called Mary in this Gospel) quickly caught his meaning and redirected her attention from Jesus to the servants with the words *Do whatever he tells you* (v. 5). The message is clear: humans, including his mother, cannot use Jesus (or God) for their purposes. Instead, God uses persons to bring about the divine purpose.

The six large *stone water jars* used for purification in this story probably contained nine gallons each (Newman and Nida 1980, 59). A great deal of water! When the changed water was carried to the banquet master (who was responsible for keeping the guests happy), he was confused by the quality of the wine at this late point in the festivities. He *knew* nothing of the involvement of Jesus and could only judge that something strange had occurred.

2:11-12. The sign. While the banquet master viewed the results as strange, the evangelist reflected that the incident served as a *sign* (not "miracle" as in KJV) to the disciples. Indeed it was the beginning (or a key) to signs because in it Jesus *revealed his glory* (v. 11 a Johannine theme) and the disciples believed. In this strange act, the disciples saw something more than water and wine, and it led to commitment.

The pericope ends with a brief pause in the action as Jesus spends a few days with his family (mother and brothers—not cousins) and friends before the storm of the next pericope.

The Temple Cleansing, 2:13-25

Many persons with mindsets focused on chronology become sidetracked with comparisons here between John and the Synoptics and argue either for the priority of the Synoptics or of John, minimizing the theological concerns of both (cf. Brown 1966, 117–19). The alternative is to argue for two cleansings of the Temple, but such an approach is a construct of the interpreter, and no Gospel has two such cleansings. The problem is a presupposition that insists on turning the Gospels into pedantic prose/chronological reports and fails to allow a great literary figure like the Johannine evangelist to write the way he wishes. Instead, this story seems to serve the evangelist in a way similar to the literary or dramatic vehicle called *in medius res* ("in the thing's middle") where decisive moments are transported to the beginning of a story to involve readers immediately in the trauma of the story (see Borchert, *John*). Such does not minimize history and chronology but allows both to serve the purpose of theology and witness.

2:13-17. Jesus' confrontation in the Temple. The story opens with the strategic notation that it was PASSOVER time (see Borchert, *John*) *and Jesus went up to Jerusalem* (always "up" in the minds of the Jews). The time was the significant celebration of God's deliverance or salvation. Rather than being focused on God and worship, however, the Temple here is pictured as a combination of a noisy bank or exchange ("tables," the Greek term for banking) and a farmer's market. This misuse of God's house irritated Jesus, and he reacted with zeal by forcefully stopping all business transactions (not a "namby-pamby" Jesus).

2:18-22. The meaning of the act. The attack on the Temple business brought a demand from the Jews for an explanation or *sign* (a Johannine theme). Jesus' response was a three-day prediction concerning his death and resurrection. The Jewish reaction of forty-six years in building the Temple is significant because this story would then be dated at ca. 27 C.E., since the Temple rebuilding began ca. 20–19 B.C.E. (Josephus, *Ant* 15.11.1).

The entire conversation is important because it is packaged in a play on words for Temple. In vv. 14 and 15 ἱερόν means the "Temple complex" with its courts, whereas ναός (vv. 19, 20, 21) means "sanctuary" and is here used not of a building but of Jesus' body. This text also supplies an important post-resurrection perspective for this Gospel (v. 22), a fact that should be remembered by all readers of John (see Borchert 1988, 502–503).

2:23-25. The nature of believing. The evangelist adds a crucial postscript to this Temple confrontation by referring again to Passover and by reminding readers that Jesus does not accept everyone's believing because he knows human nature. The distinction about true and authentic believing is not a linguistic nicety of Greek, as some have suggested, but a matter of commitment to Jesus (cf. Carson 1981, 249–50n.37).

This postscript or summary statement is, like the entire Gospel, written from a holistic or post-resurrection view of the work of Jesus. The responses to him are reckoned from such a perspective. Thus, when one encounters the plural word *signs* (v. 23; cf. 3:2) before the *second sign* at 4:54 and when one meets a variety of believing responses so early in the Gospel, one should be alerted to the necessity of reading this Gospel from a holistic or post-resurrection point of view.

Nicodemus and Teaching on Salvation, 3:1-21

The pericope involving Nicodemus contains some of the best-known verses in the Bible. It is also the first of John's longer units that combine to form superb teaching vehicles.

3:1-4. The opening exchange. In the introduction Nicodemus is described as a significant Jewish Pharisee who was recognized as a ruler (ἄρχων) or member of the Jewish high council (SANHEDRIN), composed of the high priest and his seventy advisers (cf. 7:44-52). He came to Jesus by night (not merely a time notation in John but also a reflection of a spiritual state).

His polite assessment, based upon his supposed knowledge of Jesus' role with God, received a startling response. He was told in no uncertain terms that he needed to be born ἄνωθεν ("again" or "from above") or he would not experience the KINGDOM OF GOD. His initial knowledge vanished with his question: how could he as an adult re-enter the tiny womb of his mother? It was illogical.

3:5-10. Clarification and confusion. Jesus' response to Nicodemus' question of logic was to present two levels of discourse based on the word ἄνωθεν. Nicodemus understood the term to signify *again* (implying an earthly context), while Jesus meant that the new-ness or birth was *from above* (a spiritual context; cf. 3:31). *Spirit* and *flesh* are thus regarded as different realms.

Spiritual (new) birth here is identified with the combination symbol of water and the spirit. *Spirit* should not be capitalized in v. 5 as in NRSV because it usually results in the "and" being treated disjunctively (cf. Harris 1971, 3:1178, and Carson 1991, 191–96). This combination reflects the interconnection between the water of cleansing and newness of heart or new spirit in the OT (e.g., Ezek 36:24-27). Some scholars would argue that this verse reflects a baptismal con-cern and I have so argued, but the major focus of the text is not on an event or a sacrament/ordinance but upon spiritual life. Bultmann dismisses the baptismal question completely by attributing the words "water and" to a later ecclesiastical redactor (1971, 139). But such is unnecessary, if one understands the OT roots.

Flesh (σάρξ) in John refers to the realm of human-ity with all its weakness and mortality. The word here is not per se antagonistic to God as is the expression "according to the flesh" in Paul, which implies that a person has made this existence the center of life (cf. Rom 8:4-8). Here the spirit (πνεῦμα) is used to desig-nate the empowerment of weak humanity by the Spirit of God (v. 6).

The expression "spiritual birth" thus should not lead the believer to puzzlement (v. 7) because an en-lightened person should perceive the two levels of dis-course, illustrated here by the fact that spirit and wind are the same word (πνεῦμα). Yet a teacher like Nico-demus, if he could not perceive the two levels, would remain confused (vv. 9-10).

3:11-13. The witness of the Son of Man. Clarifica-tion of human confusion concerning divine realities is possible only through the in-breaking of Jesus as the divine witness who descended to earth from the heav-enly realm. No one else than the SON OF MAN, accord-ing to John, has been able personally to bring such a firsthand account of heaven to the realm of earth. This Son of Man figure, however, is *not* to be identified as a nonhuman, nonsuffering gnostic alien messenger from outside our realm but as the divine one who truly became human and suffered the passover death for the world.

3:14-15. Jesus and the Mosaic serpent. The work of this Son of Man is thus identified as a healing agent, like the bronze serpent that Moses had fashioned and set on a pole in the wilderness epic of the poisonous snakes (Num 21:4-9). When the bronze snake was raised and the people looked upon it, healing came to the stricken. So believing in the *lifted up* Jesus (cf. also John 8:28 and 12:32, a symbol primarily of his death but not unrelated to his resurrection/exaltation) provides the agency for healing or salvation, here called eternal life.

The expression *eternal life* (ζωὴ αἰώνιος) is a particularly important Johannine theme that is used only once in the LXX (Dan 12:2) to render the rare OT idea of "life to the end of the age" or possibly "life of eternity." In John the qualitative nature of such life is stressed, although the long duration of such life is not to be dismissed.

3:16-18. Eternal life and judgment. These three verses contain one of the best known theological sum-mations concerning salvation in the Bible. While many have memorized 3:16, however, I have consistently insisted that the three verses belong together in pro-viding a proper theological balance (e.g., Borchert 1987, 104–105). The middle verse (17) states God's intention or purpose in sending his only son: not for destruction but for salvation. In v. 16 both the encom-passing, self-giving love of God for the world is asserted and the necessary human response of believ-ing is defined. Then in v. 18 the harsh reality of the situation is acknowledged: namely, believing provides the rescue whereas failure to believe means condemna-tion—not merely in the future but already in the pres-ent. This dark side of the gospel is an *integral part* of the message of salvation.

In sending his "one and only Son" (3:16; cf. Moody 1953), however, God made clear that his intention was not destruction. The God of the entire Bible is a loving and caring God whose concern is acceptance and salvation (v. 17). But there is pathos in the divine sacrifice that was illustrated beautifully on the human level in Abraham's near sacrifice of his "only" son Isaac (Gen 22:1-14). Yet the cost of human salvation was far more significant because the price was the life of God's only Son.

3:19-21. Actions, the measure of life. Love and hate, like believing and unbelieving, are action words in John. They define the nature of a person's life like the motifs of obedience and disobedience. According-ly, as in the Book of James, this Gospel is concerned about the evidence of Christian life (v. 21). The one who acts authentically is associated with light, but the one who does evil hates light because it reveals the dark side of one's life.

The Baptizer and Salvation, 3:22-36

The Baptizer, as witness, here takes center stage for a final time. Scholars often debated the sequence of events in this Gospel, particularly since in the Synoptics the Baptizer was imprisoned before the Galilean ministry began and Jesus had in the Gospel of John performed a sign in Cana at 2:1-11. Unlike the Synoptics, however, Jesus in John moves with regularity between south and north, leading some like Bultmann to posit displacements in segments of the Gospel. Schnackenburg (1987, 1:380–96) places 3:31-36 before 3:13 to combine the salvation discussions, but I find most displacement theories including this one unconvincing because of the failure to recognize the evangelist's totalistic perspective of time.

3:22-24. Jesus and John's baptizing. The notations at v. 22 and 4:1-2 are the only places in the Gospels where Jesus and his disciples are said to be associated with baptism prior to the resurrection. Many questions therefore arise as a result of these statements, including the question of the significance of such baptism at this stage and its relation to the baptism of John.

The assertion that John had not yet been imprisoned in v. 24 indicates that the evangelist is clearly aware of chronological issues and is making a point. Perhaps the reference to the two baptisms of Jesus and John is here made in the context of John's forthcoming imprisonment because some of his disciples (vv. 25-30) had not understood the differences in the two baptisms indicated in 1:33. In any case, Jesus is said to have been baptizing in the territory of Judea and John is identified with Aenon meaning "a place of springs" near a town called Salim meaning "a place of peace." The identification of these places is not certain, although some possibilities include a northeast DEAD SEA site and a place near SHECHEM.

3:25-30. Concerns of the Baptizer's disciples. A dispute over water purification arose between the disciples of the Baptizer and a Jew (Loisy 1921, 71, speculated that the original may have been "and of Jesus"). The reason was consternation over the popularity of Jesus. Seeking consolation, John's disciples confronted their teacher with his diminishing status. True to his earlier stance, however, John reminded them of his former witness (cf. 1:19-28) and asserted that Jesus' calling was given from heaven (a typical Jewish circumlocution for God). Then he confirmed his witness by identifying Jesus symbolically with a bridegroom and his own role as the friend of the bridegroom, whose task was to listen for the bridegroom's expression of joy in the marriage (for marriage customs see Str-B 1:45–46 and 500–502).

Acts 19:1-5 (cf. 11:16) provides evidence that the Baptizer's disciples apparently were still active at a later time. It is doubtful, however, as some have suggested that a direct connection can be made between the Baptizer and the later Mandeans (cf. Borchert, John).

3:31-36. Summation concerning the Son. The evangelist then unites the stories of Nicodemus and of the Baptizer in a reaffirmation of two levels of discourse. Only the one from above can provide authentic witness concerning divine reality. The tragedy is the general lack of acceptance (no one, a literary hyperbole) of this witness from above (v. 32). But fortunately some do accept (cf. 1:11-12) and by their acceptance here have confirmed, sealed, or certified the authenticity of this divine witness.

While God has sent many on missions (including the Baptizer), the Son is God's model for mission (having the Spirit without limitation v. 34). Into his hand the Father "has given" (a timeless perfect) all things (v. 35). Such an assertion does not mean that the Father has abandoned the world but that in the love of God there is epitomized the unity of purpose between Son and Father. Accordingly, believing (πισ-τεύων εἰς) the Son provides the assurance of life eternal, whereas disobeying (ἀπειθῶν) the Son guarantees the horrifying reality of God's abiding (μένει) wrath (v. 36). There is thus no room for sitting on the fence concerning Jesus because of the present reality of judgment (cf. also 3:18).

The Samaritan Woman:
An Unlikely Witness, 4:1-42

This pericope is one of the most fascinating in the Gospel. It not only challenges certain set prejudices of some religious people but it offers insights for ministry such as evangelism (Borchert 1976, 62).

4:1-6. Transition and introduction. This section may provide some rationale for the departure of Jesus to GALILEE via SAMARIA, namely: Pharisaic suspicion because of his popularity (4:1-3, cf. 4:44). But the use of ἔδει ("It was necessary" [author trans.], 4:4) in John may suggest once again that Jesus was moving according to the divine plan (cf. the use of hour in 2:4). This section certainly serves to correct any possible misconception that Jesus was a baptizer (only his disciples did so). In addition, it supplies a general description of the setting for the encounter. The meeting place was at the ancient town well near *Sychar* (a site not identified but probably on the slope of Mt. Ebal across from Mt. Gerizim) and near land owned by Jacob and Joseph (Gen 48:22). Sources of water were often places of meeting (cf. Gen 24:10-15; 29:1-12). The time was *about noon* (v. 6).

4:7-9. The meeting and the first exchange. The unusual circumstances are quickly defined: a Samaritan woman seeking to draw water during the heat of the day and a tired Jewish man asking her for a drink. It was the kind of setting that would cause heads to turn.

In fact, the encounter was unusual for the woman. Jesus did not fit the pattern and she sought an explanation to his request for a drink. SAMARITANS were rejected by Jews as half-breeds, a people with mixed origins (cf. Ezra 9–10), resulting from the settlement patterns of the Assyrians after the fall of SAMARIA in 722 B.C.E. (2 Kgs 17:6, 24). Their temple was later ruthlessly destroyed by the Jewish Hasmonean king John Hyrcanus (128 B.C.E.) and relations with the Jews continued to deteriorate until a major engagement in 52 C.E. (cf. Josephus, *Ant* 20.118–136). Although the temple was not rebuilt, Samaritans have continued even today to hold their Passover celebrations on that site.

While Jesus was resting, the disciples were engaged in a shopping tour. The quest was for food, acceptable food in Samaria. They probably settled on some bread and fruit (allowable items) after their search.

4:10-15. The second exchange: on water. Picking up the water themes from previous chapters that focused on baptism and water into wine, water now becomes the subject of the two levels of discourse. The woman was concerned with water and Jesus offered her *living water* (v. 10). Her mind, however, remained fixed on the earthly plane but her question in v. 12 (*Are you greater than our ancestor Jacob?*), although anticipating a negative response, provided Jesus the necessary opening to move the conversation back to the eternal realm.

The point is that water here temporarily quenches thirst, but the water of Jesus results in *eternal life* (v. 14). Yet the woman was stuck in the concerns of worldly tasks and asked for help to ease her burden (v. 15). She was in for a surprise.

4:16-19. The third exchange: the woman's life. The response of Jesus was to address her life and relationships. Although she tried to bypass the issue, Jesus spelled out her story in greater detail. The only way to avoid the issue was to change the subject to Jesus and

focus on his perceived wisdom (*a prophet*), then ask him some questions. It was a sure way to discussion.

4:20-26. The fourth and fifth exchanges: ecclesiastical and theological issues. What better way is there to create religious tension than to ask which is the best place to worship, especially since the Jews had destroyed the Samaritan temple? Carson, however, apparently thinks such an explanation is too psychological (1991, 221–22). But I think there is more to the story than Carson sees because Jesus did not fall into the trap of a changed subject. Instead, he once again turned the discussion from the level of earthly institutionalism (v. 21) to the realm of the divine goal (*hour*) for worship and to God who is the subject of such worship (v. 23-24). Moreover, he reminded the woman that proper worship, like salvation, is a matter of divine revelation (*from the Jews*) and not a human construct concerning a God who is unknown (v. 22). It was a stinging rebuttal of Samaritan worship.

The woman's next response (v. 25) is intriguing because she has been moved in her concern to speak of the future era. Yet it is not entirely clear if she is using messianic talk to counter the rebuttal of Jesus by reminding him of a higher source for information (i.e., the Messiah) since she had already politely acknowledged him as *a prophet*. Or is this statement her honest anticipation? One thing seems clear: she had not yet connected Jesus with the Messiah or the coming of the messianic age.

That connection Jesus quickly made is an important self-identification. English readers of most translations may not recognize that the Greek at v. 26 is ἐγώ εἰμί (*I am*), the primary thematic self-designation of Jesus for his role as God's anointed one (Messiah) in this Gospel.

4:27-30. The disciples' interruption and the woman's witness. The return of the disciples signals the end to this part of the story. Their surprise which is indicated by their confused thinking (v. 27) only confirms the unusual nature of Jesus' conversation with the woman. Jewish men seldom talked to women in public. Yet here he was speaking with a Samaritan woman, and one not having the best reputation.

But the evangelist wanted readers to understand that the woman's concern had shifted from the mundane realm of the water pot (she left it) to the realm of messianic visitation. The Greek text says she sought out the "men" of the town and informed them she had met a man *who told me everything I have ever done* (v. 29). I wonder if *people* (v. 28) in the RSV and NRSV

is the best translation? It seems that some of the implications for the initial interest which the men had in
Jesus may be lost in these versions. But her question—*He cannot be the Messiah, can he?*—certainly
had its desired effect because they left the city to meet
Jesus (vv. 29-30).

While Craddock (1982, 36–37) makes a point that
her believing was hardly ideal, I would insist that her
story must be seen in the context of how John organized the Cana cycle through increasing stages of more
adequate patterns of believing. Here she carries her
understanding of Jesus to the point of telling others
what she is thinking.

4:31-38. The disciples miss the point. While the
woman had moved from the mundane level in her
thinking to that of messianic expectation, the disciples
were stuck in the physical realm of food (vv. 31, 33).
So Jesus tried to raise the level of their thinking from
the mere search for food to the quest for nourishment
that comes by fulfilling their calling of doing the will
of God. He modeled for them the concern that satisfied his hunger (v. 34) and he challenged them to
accept their role of harvesting *fruit for eternal life* (v.
36).

The *four months* mentioned in the proverbial statement of v. 35 is generally regarded as the shortest time
between the last of the seeding season and the start of
harvest. Jesus was thus calling for his disciples to
recognize that the messianic era of reaping had
dawned. The evangelist, as Morris argues (1986,
150–51), undoubtedly considered this message also to
be an urgent call for the church to evangelization,
especially since he included the notation for the disciples that reaping is a crucial task even when the reaper
had not been the sower (v. 38). Yet both sower and
reaper can rejoice together at the harvest (v. 36) because the division of labor here does not exclude the
sower from the returns of harvest as many ancient
proverbs might suggest (cf. Beasley-Murray 1987, 64
and Brown 1966, 182–83), but both laborers are seen
as partners with God in this important work of ingathering.

4:39-42. The Samaritans' belief and confession.
The conclusion to this magnificent story indicates both
the openness of Jesus to the rejects of the world (he
stayed with them for *two days*, dispensing with propri-
etary living patterns of status and purity) and the fact
that such rejects could make the most important confession in the Cana cycle. The Samaritan rejects came
to discover Jesus through the witness of a rejected
woman and then to confess him as *the Savior of the
world* through direct encounter (v. 42). The motif of
Savior in the OT is used of God (e.g., Isa 12:2 and
43:3, cf. Luke 1:47) and not elsewhere in the Gospels
of the preresurrected Jesus, except in the prediction of
the angel (Luke 2:12). It is a familiar Christian confession following the resurrection (e.g., Acts 5:31; Phil
3:20; 2 Pet 1:11). Since the designation was used by
Jews of God and by others of Hellenistic deities and
even the Roman emperor, the Christians' use of the
term for Jesus was probably one of their identifying
marks.

This confession signals for readers of the Gospel
the great scope (i.e. *the world*) of the mission of Jesus
and agrees with the intention of God in blessing Abraham (Gen 12:3). While Jesus told the Samaritan woman that *salvation is from the Jews* (v. 22, the historical
womb of God's blessing), this village of rejects discovered that God really loves *the world* (3:16) and *all
who receive* Jesus can become children of God (1:12).

4:43-45. Transition to Galilee. These verses serve
as one of the typical "saddle" or "shoulder" texts between pericopes in a similar way that "saddles" unite
mountain peaks in a mountain chain. The evangelist
uses this saddle to move attention from Samaria to
Galilee and to remind readers that Galileans are not
unaware of what had been taking place in Jerusalem at
the Passover.

The Second Cana Sign:
Healing the Official's Son, 4:46-54

By focusing on Cana in Galilee for the second sign
(only two are numbered by John) the first and second
signs serve as an INCLUSIO (contrary to Beasley-Murray)
whereby the stories in chaps. 2 to 4 form a unit. The
first story identifies the role of signs in believing
(2:11) and the second argues for a new level of believing that questions the very need for signs (4:48).

The second sign is in the form of a healing story
with a twist. A person (a boy) is seriously ill and a
request is made for healing (in this case by the father).
Jesus then responds and the person is made well. But
unlike the healing of the centurion's servant in the
Synoptics (Matt 8:5-13; Luke 7:1-10), the royal official here (probably an administrator or soldier in the
service of the Herodian dynasty or the Roman Caesar)
begs for Jesus to come to his home. In the synoptic
story the centurion begs for healing but he tells Jesus
it is not necessary to come to his home. There Jesus
greatly commends such gentile faith (e.g., Luke 7:9).

Here, however, Jesus must tell the father to go because his son is living (v. 50). This word of Jesus then engenders believing in the father, even though he is unable to see the reality of the healing. But when the father confirms the healing, he again and for the first time his house are said to believe (v. 53).

This pericope thus is important because it may suggest a Johannine view of stages in believing. Certainly when people in John believe, they are usually called to the next stage of believing (Brown and Carson think they can distinguish such levels by variants in the Greek form of "believe," but such linguistic distinctions should not be pushed in John). This story also seems to foreshadow the kind of believing without seeing to which Thomas is called at the end of the book (20:29).

The Festival Cycle, 5:1–11:57

Many patterns of organization have been suggested for chaps. 4–12 of this Gospel. Bultmann has chaps. 7–10 as a unit; Brown has chaps. 5–10; Carson has two segments involving chaps. 5 to 7 and 8 to 10; and Sloyan has chaps. 5 to 7 and 8 to 12. Beasley-Murray, Morris, and Schnackenburg eschew finding a unit principle and settle for much smaller sections from chaps. 4 to 12. Bultmann and Schnackenburg are impressed by some topical and geographical variations in the stories and advocate theories of displacement to settle their uneasiness with these chapters.

Aileen Guilding proposed a theory that the Gospel had been organized as a festival lectionary (1960). While her overall theory found little acceptance, her focus on the Jewish festivals sparked renewed attention by some commentators on the festival context of several chapters. Brown in particular highlights the festivals in chaps. 5 to 10. I suggest (Borchert 1993) that chaps. 5–11 are a festival cycle with an introduction involving the overarching Jewish festival of Sabbath (chap. 5) and a cycle running from Passover (chap. 6) to Passover (chap. 11). The focus of this cycle is on the growing hostility that led inevitably to the Passover death of Jesus.

In this section the Jews are frequently mentioned. It is important for the reader to realize that the context in which this Gospel was written was one of persecution of Christians by the Jews, similar to that suggested by Rev 2:9 and 3:9. But such historical realities must not be made the basis for hatred of any group today.

The Sabbath and the Healing at Bethesda, 5:1-47

The festival cycle opens with a notation concerning a feast of the Jews (v. 1) but it remains undesignated except that it soon becomes evident that the issue focuses not on that unnamed feast per se, but on a SABBATH conflict. This conflict quickly touches many other underlying concerns like Jesus' authority, identity, and relationship to the Father as well as themes such as hour, judgment, life, and witness. As Sabbath became for the Jews a pervasive, haunting factor in their lives (witnessed by its importance in the Mishnah), so the Sabbath controversy was important for the evangelist. Yet it is used only in the festival cycle and serves the evangelist as one of the factors leading to the inevitable death of Jesus.

Some scholars are not satisfied here to discuss Sabbath alone and seek to posit possibilities for this feast such as PENTECOST, TABERNACLES, etc. I think the focus here falls on Sabbath, but it is intriguing to note that the evangelist speaks of "the great day of the Sabbath" (19:31, author trans.) in connection with Passover. The problem for most commentators is that they are concerned with filling in the chronology of John and fail to realize the cyclical pattern of John that focuses on Passover.

5:1-9a. The healing of the paralytic. When Jesus went up to Jerusalem he visited the pool area below the Temple where the helpless dregs of society existed in a pathetic state. While most people avoided the area, Jesus went out of his way to visit the place and found a paralytic who had experienced the wilderness of abandonment for thirty-eight years (equal to the time of Israel's wilderness experience from Kadesh to the brook Zared, cf. Deut 2:14).

The man's response to Jesus' question concerning healing revealed his hopelessness. His only expectation was a trust in a myth concerning angelic visitations to the pool (vv. 3b-4 are later additions to the text). His hopelessness was highlighted by the fact that he thought God was not interested in the most helpless. Jesus did not argue with his erroneous presupposition or his theological perspectives about receiving healing. Instead, Jesus merely told him to get up, pick up his bed roll, and be on his way. Healing was the immediate result.

5:9b-16. Sabbath controversy. The next statement that this day was the Sabbath strikes the reader with the force of a bomb. The opponents pounce on the helpless man who has just experienced the unbelievable joy of entering the promised land of a new existence. They focus not on his healing but on his breaking of their carefully articulated Sabbath rules, formulated to support the TORAH principle in Exod 31:12-14. The bewildered man can only defend himself by quoting his healer's words, even though he did not know who he was (vv. 12-13). The evangelist, however, reminds us that Jesus did not simply leave victims to the wolves but *found* them (v. 14, cf. 9:35; cf. also the theme at 1:41ff.).

The warning of Jesus not to *sin any more* is not to be understood here as a reference to a direct cause and effect relationship between sin and illness. That issue is treated at 9:2ff. Here Jesus is alluding to sin and judgment, which are treated in the next section (5:24). While Jesus had evidenced a self-giving-healing spirit, the healed paralytic (in contrast to the healed blind man of chap. 9) may have displayed a spirit of self-preservation in reporting to the Jews. In any case, the result was that Jewish sabbatarians turned their hostility on Jesus.

5:17-18. Jesus' first response: Sabbath. The response of Jesus confronted these sabbatarians and led to a new charge. Carson (1991, 247–48) notes that the rabbis would basically agree with Jesus that providence demands that God should continue to work on the Sabbath. The issue for the rabbis is that humans are not God. That, of course, is the question. So, if God continues to work positively on the Sabbath and Jesus' works are the works of God, then why are his works not legitimate? The battle was joined when Jesus called God his Father. The Jews recognized the equation immediately. Now the charge was not merely Sabbath breaking but also blasphemy.

5:19-24. Jesus' second response: relationship to the Father. The double ἀμήν (*truly*) signals again that two crucial statements are being made in this section. While the Jews have focused on equality, Jesus had highlighted his dependency on the Father. That dependency would be the means by which humans would come to understand the Son's role in the giving of life and the rendering of judgment. In that context there would come a recognition of the relationship between Father and Son. Moreover, obedience is not defined by Jesus in relation to rules such as observation of the Sabbath, but in terms of dynamic life patterns involving honoring the Son (v. 23) and believing (v. 24). Such obedient response is the basis for gaining the assurance of eternal life and avoiding judgment.

5:25-29. Jesus' third response: the two resurrections. In these responses the questioners have almost faded into the background as the evangelist's interest is directed only to the words of Jesus. The double ἀμήν once again announces a significant statement. The previous response identified a division between life and judgment. In this response the announcement is sounded concerning the coming of the decisive hour and the future eschatological separation between life and judgment represented in the idea of two resurrections.

Bultmann (1971, 258–61), who is committed to a perspective of realized eschatology, finds such futuristic suggestions to be "dangerous" editorial additions to the early message. But the perspective of the text is that both present and future are genuine realities. Yet these realities are intertwined because present hearing (obedience) leads to the resurrection of life. Moreover, the idea of resurrection from the evangelist's understanding was hardly a mere spiritual experience. For Jews the resurrection meant dealing with dead bodies and that is the reason why John has no hesitation in including a reference to persons emerging from tombs (v. 28). The point of the discussion is that Jesus' opponents and the evangelist's hearers are being clearly warned that relationship to Jesus has immense eschatological consequences.

5:30-47. Jesus' fourth response: witnesses to his authority. The statements in vv. 30 and 31 seem to presuppose challenges both to Jesus' authority in judgment and the validity of his God-directed claims. The responses on the part of Jesus are a forthright denial of his self-seeking and the articulation of a four-fold testimony supporting his claims.

The first witness he called was John the Baptizer. He chose John not because he wished to rely on human testimony but because such a testimony might help lead humans to salvation (v. 34). The second testimony is rated by Jesus at a higher level than the first, namely, his works. These works he was doing in accordance with the Father's will and the Jews could hardly deny their existence (v. 36).

The third witness he called was the Father. What does the evangelist mean by such a statement? It was a type of shorthand. Was it some voice from heaven (e.g., 12:28) or a sense of divine presence (e.g., 11:41-42)? Greater clarity would help. But the difficulty of using the Father as a witness for them was immediately apparent to Jesus and he highlighted it. They could not accept such a witness because, unlike the prophets, they had not heard God speak. Moreover, unlike Isaiah (Isa 6:1) or Jacob at Jabbok (Gen 32:30), they had no vision of him or sense of his form. But perhaps most devastating of all was that they who claimed to uphold the Torah did not have God's *word* inwardly resident in them (vv. 37-38).

The mention of God's word provides the fourth and final witness: *the scriptures*, to which they by profession had committed themselves (v. 39). Here Jesus forthrightly condemns them because of their refusal to accept him (v. 40) and recognize the testimony of the texts they supposedly defended. Human religious confirmation of his role, however, was not required by Jesus (v. 41) because humans are confused in their offering of praise (vv. 43-44). So Jesus asserted that the religious leaders should clearly realize that he did not need to play the roles of both accuser and judge concerning them. Their accuser would be none other than Moses on whom they said they relied but failed in fact to believe (vv. 45-46).

Passover and the Exodus Motif, 6:1-71

The crossing of the sea (v. 1) and the coming of people out to a lonely mountainside (v. 3) formed a picture-perfect setting for reflecting about Jesus and the EXODUS. Accordingly, it should be no surprise that in this chapter the linkage of a miraculous feeding and a control of the sea is compared to the experience of MOSES in the wilderness.

It should also be no surprise that in such a context the evangelist announces it was PASSOVER time (v. 4). Even within the Passover Haggada today, in the introduction before the pronouncing of the "three words" and the "Halelya," two of the great "benefits" that are rehearsed are the control of the sea and the feeding of manna (see e.g., Fisch 1965). Likewise, when detailing God's great mercies both the Psalmist (Ps 78:13-30) and Paul (1 Cor 10:1-4) link these two events of water control and food supply as crucial for remembrance.

It is most likely, therefore, that as the early Christians told the stories of their Lord, bread and water miracles from his earthly life were also recited. Thus, when Mark first set the gospel in written form, it was quite natural that these two events would be narrated in a related context (Mark 6:30-52). Another highly significant event for Mark was the decisive point of discipleship in which Mark includes a confession by Peter (Mark 8:27-30). John brings all of these elements together in his development of this strategic Passover

chapter and hints at the fact that the death of Jesus (flesh and blood) will be a key to eternal life (v. 54).

6:1-13. The distribution of food. In the unfolding of the text, following the crossing of the Sea of Tiberias (the Roman designation usually called Galilee, but also Gennesaret in Luke 5:1 [from the Heb. *kinnereth*], because it had the outline of a lyre), Jesus is pictured as sitting on a mountain side (v. 3), reminiscent of an ancient dispenser of divine wisdom. The linkage with the Mosaic experience at SINAI may be in mind (cf. Matt 5:1).

The feeding is introduced by Jesus questioning PHILIP (the company logician) concerning resources. Philip's answer was that the crowd was so large (5,000) that even 200 days' pay would have been insufficient to feed them. ANDREW (the company helper) found a small amount of food among the crowd (five barley loaves and two dried fish), but for Jesus it was sufficient (total, seven; cf. also the seven loaves and a "few" fish in feeding 4,000 of Mark 8:6-7). Thus, when Jesus acted, everyone had enough (v. 11).

Indeed, there was so much remaining that the disciples (Brown 1966, 233, wonders whether they are synonymous with the Twelve) collected twelve baskets of bread. The number twelve is symbolic for the people of God. This story was of such significance to early Christians that it is the only miracle per se reported in all four Gospels. The sea miracles vary, but their impact is the same. For John the bread miracle served as an important sign and became the basis for the following discourse.

6:14-15. The people's messianic expectations. In the minds of the Jews awaiting the MESSIAH, this act of feeding spurred the people's messianic hopes. Their immediate reaction was that this Jesus had to be the long expected *prophet* like Moses (Deut 18:15; cf. John 1:21). The additional reference to the one *who is to come* (v. 15) was, as Mowinckle has argued, also viewed as a messianic designation (1954, 213–41, 295–321, 385–93).

The expectations of the people were ignited to such an extent that they were ready to give Jesus the throne of DAVID and force the realization of their hopes (v. 15; cf. Jer 23:5; Ezek 34:23). But Jesus instead took to the mountains again because their understanding and timing were both skewed.

6:16-21. Walking on water. This pericope begins with a note that night and darkness fell. Such designations in John are usually theologically instructive (cf. 3:2 and 13:30), especially here since a storm arose and the disciples were caught in the middle of the sea (which was between five and seven mi. wide; cf. Josephus, *BJ* 3.10.7; 506). Despite the conditions, Jesus calmly walked on the sea. The Exodus symbolism is hard to miss.

No doubt the evangelist regarded this appearance as a Christophany (like the appearances of God in the OT) for here are present both the familiar sense of fear and the calming words, *Do not be afraid* (v. 20). While the expression "I am" ($\dot{\epsilon}\gamma\dot{\omega}$ $\epsilon\dot{\iota}\mu\iota$) may be interpreted as a simple self-identification (*It is I*, as in many translations), the reader familiar with John cannot help but connect these words with God's revelation to Moses (Exod 3:14).

The joy of the disciples then replaced their fear as Jesus entered the boat. Moreover, their goal of reaching a safe harbor was immediately realized. Jesus thus is like the God of the OT who brings his people from a stormy sea to a safe haven (Ps 107:23-32).

6:22-25. The people sought Jesus. While the geography is a little vague, these stories suggest that the feeding may have taken place on the east side of the sea where there are hills (less likely is the traditional northeast side). The boats came from the west side (TIBERIAS) and the people took their boats from *near* the feeding place and found Jesus on the northwest side (CAPERNAUM). The people's query of Jesus concerning his coming to that place set the stage for a discourse on the sign of bread.

6:26-34. The sign of bread. The familiar Johannine double $\dot{\alpha}\mu\dot{\eta}\nu$ (*truly*) formula once again introduces a key perspective. The people were following because of the physical food, not because they recognized the *signs* (v. 26). The KJV incorrectly reads "miracles" here. The nature of the sign is to point beyond miracle to the one who nourishes to eternal life. When one understands such a sign, one should perceive the relationship of the acts of the *Son of Man* (Jesus' self-definition, cf. 1:51) to the works of the Father.

The response of unperceiving Jews, however, was tragic. Their request for a sign that would lead them to believe thus inspired yet another double-level Johannine insight framed, as Borgen (1965) has argued, like a midrashic interpretation of Exod 16:15, etc. They missed the point because their desire was for a return to a physical preservation model like that of manna in the wilderness (v. 31). But the bread was not merely a gift from a deliverer like MOSES; it had been given by God. The real gift of God's bread was not physical; it was life *come down from heaven* (v. 33). The misun-

derstanding inherent in their subsequent request for continual supplying of such bread (6:34) introduces an "I am" discourse.

6:35-40. Jesus' proclamation: the bread of life. The self-identification of Jesus as *I am the bread of life* (v. 35) is made here, but the motif of eating is expanded to include drinking (important for the next section). This affirmation merges into a discussion of separation and preservation. The opponents of Jesus are judged as unbelieving. But those whom the Father gives to Jesus will not be castaways (vv. 37, 39). Instead, they will have eternal life and experience resurrection in *the last day* (vv. 39-40). This concept of the resurrection on the last day is defuturized in Bultmann (1971, 233) but would have been perfectly understandable to a futuristically oriented Jewish Christian audience of the first century.

6:41-48. Reaction and defense. The reaction of the Jews is by John defined in Exodus terminology: "murmured" (NRSV, *complained*). The text implies they understood that he was claiming divine descent and mission. As a result they launched into a discussion of his family tree, which they said they knew (v. 42). The irony is obvious. Jesus responded in terms of his relationship to the Father and the eschatological hope of those drawn to him by God (v. 44). His response was based on the proclamation of the prophets that in the messianic era God's people would be instructed by God (cf. Isa 54:13; Jer 31:33-34).

Employing another double $\dot{\alpha}\mu\dot{\eta}\nu$ saying, he then identified their concern for physical bread and their earthly messianic hope with the hopeless state of those who perished in the wilderness even though they ate physical MANNA. But those who are nourished by *the living bread*, Jesus said, would have eternal life (v. 51). The problem for them was that such bread was his *flesh*.

6:52-59. Identification of flesh and blood. This identification of bread and flesh was too much for the Jews to swallow. The response of Jesus was another double $\dot{\alpha}\mu\dot{\eta}\nu$ saying that linked the inward acceptance (eating) of his sacrificial death (flesh and blood) to the reception of eternal life and resurrection on the last day (v. 54). The Jews, however, were stuck in the physical realm of reality with their fathers who ate manna and died (v. 58).

This section has been the focus of much theological discussion concerning the relationship to the LORD'S SUPPER. Brown (1966, 287–93), for example, sees it as the Johannine "institution," whereas Carson (1991,

295) thinks that the use of "flesh" rather than "body" argues against such a primary eucharistic sense. It is impossible in this space to detail the arguments on this matter but our attention should be kept on the major focus of the passage: namely, the familiar Johannine theme of receiving Jesus (cf. 1:12). That the evangelist probably saw in the supper a symbolic representation of the reception of Jesus is quite likely. But it is a question of what gives birth to what in John. This Gospel is certainly very symbolic. The issue is: Is sacrament a primary focus here?

6:60-71. Reaction of the disciples. The reader of John may be confused here by the designation *disciples* in this passage because disciples are said here to be troubled by Jesus' saying and, like the wilderness people, they murmured (v. 60). Indeed, Jesus said, they did not believe (v. 64) and in fact they departed and no longer walked with him (v. 66).

The insertion of the distinction between flesh and spirit in this context (v.63) is a reminder that the evangelist frequently employs words with two levels of meaning as he did when he used the term *believe* at 2:23-24. The confession of Peter and the mention of Judas is here a clear indication of this double level in discipleship.

The mention of Jesus choosing Judas Iscariot (vv. 70-71) must not be made the basis for a theology of reprobation (election or determinism to destruction). The text does not say that Jesus determined Judas to be a devil-man. The designation Iscariot is not totally clear. He may have been a man (*ish*; or the son of a man) from Kerioth or one of the "sicarii" (revolutionary knife men). But John will not let the reader forget the dark side of this disciple in contrast to the self-sacrifice of Jesus.

Tabernacles and the Motif of Deliverance, 7:1–9:41

This section of the Festival cycle involves the popular (Josephus *Ant* 8.100) post-harvest Feast of Booths or Tabernacles. If the Messiah were to come, it would be expected that he would put in an appearance in the month of Tishri, the most celebrated month of the Jewish year. The month started with the joyous celebration of the New Year on the first and second. It was followed on the tenth by the most sacred day of *Yom Kippur* (Day of Atonement) and it was climaxed with the joyous celebration of Tabernacles on the fifteenth to the twenty-second when the faithful devo-

tees left their houses and dwelt in booths as a reminder of God's preservation and deliverance.

This section, which highlights controversy, begins with the issue of timing concerning the adoption of Jesus' messianic role (7:1-13) and the reaction he engenders (7:14-36). The focus then moves to Jesus as water (7:37-39) and returns to the question of Jesus' messiahship (7:40-52). It moves next to Jesus as light (8:12) and returns again to his messiahship in terms of the question of his origin and purpose (8:13-29). Then it moves to the question of freedom (8:31-32) and leads to an outright confrontation on lineage and bondage (8:33-59). The evangelist then illustrates the importance of both light and deliverance in the story of the blind man (9:1-34) and concludes with Jesus' verdict about the parties in the dispute (9:35-41).

The pericope of the adulterous woman (7:53–8:11) is a fascinating story that wound up as a somewhat disconnected segment in the framework of the message of Tabernacles, and will be treated in an appendix at the end of the commentary. This style of treatment is no reflection on the worthiness of the story or its legitimacy to be regarded as a canonical pericope.

7:1-13. The brothers' question of messiahship at Tabernacles. The mood of this section is set by the opening notation of hostility. The issue is focused by the demand of the brothers (Mary's other children, not cousins) that Jesus adopt their time frame for his messianic revelation at Tabernacles (v. 3). The dialogue that follows is somewhat reminiscent of Jesus' rejection of his mother's timing (2:4).

Many readers become confused by the fact that Jesus said he was not going up to the feast (v. 8) when he did so almost immediately (v. 10). Like many other issues in John, the reader needs to recognize the two levels of discourse that are taking place. Jesus' timing is PASSOVER not TABERNACLES, and his role is not that of conquering hero but of dying Messiah. It was not Jesus' time for public show (v. 4) but for personal ministry (vv. 4, 10). Expectation concerning Jesus was obviously very high at this feast (vv. 11-12) although fear muted some open expression of it (v. 13). That Jesus could not help but engender public reaction (v. 26), however, does not change the fact that for John the actual public work of Jesus is his hour of glorification (12:31-32; 17:1).

7:14-36. Reactions to Jesus' messiahship. The appearance of Jesus in a teaching mode raised a question immediately. The *am ha'erez* (the "people of the land," who worked with their hands like carpenters and fishermen) were not trained in the technicalities of religious dialogue. Their insecurity in religious discussion would be obvious. Yet to the surprise of his hearers, Jesus (who was one of them) assumed the authority to teach (v. 15). Indeed, he claimed divine authority (v. 16) and criticized his opponents (the Jewish leadership) for not obeying Moses.

Their intention was to kill him (v. 19) because he healed on the Sabbath (v. 23; cf. 5:18). Of course, the argument could have turned on the rabbinic interpretations of the priority of Sabbath laws (Exod 31:12-17) over murder laws (Exod 20:13) but here they denied any intention to kill him. Indeed, they categorized him as a misguided, demon-possessed lunatic (v. 20). But Jesus did not accept their designation and attacked their motives and their Sabbath law logic by reference to circumcision (v. 22). The point was to critique their lack of tenderness for hurting people (vv. 23-24).

This open confrontation on religious logic with the religious elite raised for the people the issue of his role and their theories of an unknown origin for the Messiah. The questions of *where?* (origin, v. 27) and *where?* (goal, v. 35) are an undercurrent in this Gospel and once again John employs an ironic double-level meaning for the word *know* (v. 27) to focus attention on who Jesus is.

The leadership's answer to this threat was an attempt to silence this religious interloper by dispatching their guard to seize him (7:32).

7:37-39. Jesus and the water ritual. When the Jewish people moved in large numbers from the rural areas to the cities, the festive experiences of harvest were not as significant. But following long dry summers, cisterns were usually depleted and urbanites prayed for the coming of rain. The PHARISEES (mostly urbanites) promoted the addition of rain prayers in the celebration of Tabernacles (cf. Zech 14:16-19; *m. Sukk.* 5:1). The SADDUCEES generally had resisted this insertion as revisionist and conflict over this matter came to a head in the time of the Sadducean high priest and king, Alexander Janaeus, who poured the water offering at his feet. A rapprochement with the Pharisees was gained by his successors and the water ritual was retained. While the festival was eight days in length (including a Sabbath climax) the water ritual was conducted for seven days. On the seventh day the priests brought water seven times from the pool of Siloam. It may be that the evangelist means this seventh day by his designation *the last day* (v. 37) or perhaps he means the solemn Sabbath that followed.

The evangelist here draws together several themes in reflecting on Jesus at this event. Water in the OT is linked with the people's expectation of salvation (Isa 12:3; 55:1). Also, as life-sustaining water flowed from the rock (Exod 17:6), so life-giving water comes from Jesus (v. 38; cf. the visions of the future in Ezek 47:9-12 and Rev 22:1-2). Moreover, the evangelist notes that such a life-enhancing experience is to be connected with the coming of the Spirit following the glorification of Jesus (v. 39).

There is a minor textual variation in vv. 37 and 38. The NRSV, which links believing and drinking and forms a parallelism, is to be preferred over the earlier RSV rendering.

7:40-52. Evaluations of Jesus' messiahship. Division of opinions followed. Some affirmed him and answered positively the questions directed at John the Baptist (cf. 1:20-21). Some were frustrated by their theories concerning his origin. Others wanted to be rid of him. The guard returned empty-handed, stunned by the power of his words (v. 46). But the authorities and Pharisees remained undeterred. Their arrogant question (Had any of them believed? v. 48) was for the evangelist a double-edged irony when compared to their opinion of the stupid *crowd* (v. 49). Even the logic of fairness proposed by *Nicodemus* (v. 50-51) was rebuffed by their intolerance and name-calling. The issue for them was closed.

8:12. The light. The joyousness of the ritual of lights, which was accompanied by singing and dancing and which permeated the seven festival days of Tabernacles, was a reminder of God's leading of the people by fire in the darkness of the wilderness (Exod 13:21). Here the *I am* saying affirms the role of Jesus in lighting the darkness for his followers.

8:13-29. Return to the conflict: A legal argument. The rejection of Jesus' messiahship is again raised by a Pharisaic charge of bearing witness to himself, a charge Jesus preemptively argued in 5:30-47. In this passage, however, the issue of "whence" and "whither" (origin and goal; v. 14) are brought to center stage in the context of truth or authenticity.

The scene here is reminiscent of a legal argument. The opponents have rendered their verdict by rejecting Jesus (v. 15). His rebuttal was that he was not yet at the judgment stage (cf. v. 26), but if he were to render a verdict, it would be true because of his divine connection (v. 16). Instead, he was at the witness stage and while he provided the required two witnesses (cf. Deut 19:15) their problem was that they did not know the Father who functioned as his confirming witness. Moreover, their failure to regard him made it impossible for them to know the Father (v. 19). This testimony is certainly a tight one, but it is not necessarily convincing to the unconvinced.

On the other hand, the opponents were unable to carry out the sentence attached to their verdict because of a fundamental Johannine thesis: the *hour had not yet come* (v. 20). So the conflict continued.

There is no question, however, that Jesus understood that the opponents' desire for his death would be fulfilled. But it was not to be interpreted as their victory. Rather it was a divinely directed departure (v. 21) or "lifting up" (v. 28) that would bring a verdict on them: namely, they would die in their sin (v. 21). Yet Jesus did supply a verdict. They would not be able to join him in his realm above (vv. 22-23) because the basis for entrance to that realm was believing that he was the *I am* (v. 24; cf. Exod 3:14).

The dialogue that follows confirms the fact that Jesus and the Jews were operating on different wave lengths (v. 27). While the text of v. 25b is not entirely clear, the remaining verses indicate that recognition and condemnation would follow upon his death.

8:30-59. The conflict continues: truth and freedom. The notation in the midst of the conflict that many believed (v. 30) is followed by a statement that to those who believed Jesus issued his famous logion concerning truth and freedom (v. 32). The result was an immediate defensive response on the part of those addressed, involving both an assertion of kinship with father Abraham and a denial of any bondage experience (v. 33). These verses thus provide an illustration or commentary on 2:23-25 and the fallacy of much human believing.

Because the logion in v. 32 is frequently removed from its context and used as a justification for academic education, it is well to remember that knowing truth here is not related to academic information. The point is knowing Jesus. Moreover, freedom is not mere liberty; it is freedom in Christ and freedom from sin (vv. 34-36).

These "believers" are thus not to be categorized as legitimate disciples because their reliance for acceptance was built upon human descent patterns (father Abraham, vv. 37, 39) and their style of life was linked to those who would kill Jesus (vv. 37, 40). True believing in Jesus and true children of God would reflect the attitude of loving Jesus (v. 42). Instead, Jesus judged them harshly as *liars* and as children of the

devil (v. 44). Accordingly, Jesus asked them to respond to two underlying questions: (1) Who can bring a verdict of sin upon Jesus? and (2) Why did they not in fact believe (v. 46)?

Their reaction was predictable. Like the priests and Pharisees who dismissed Nicodemus with a name (cf. 7:52), these "believers" categorized Jesus as a despised Samaritan (cf. 4:9) and as one possessed of a demon (v. 48). This interaction between Jesus and the so-called "believers" raised the issue of honor and shame (v. 49) in that society (for discussion, see e.g. Malina 1981, 25–50), a reality that runs extremely deep, particularly in many non-Western cultures.

The response of Jesus was another double ἀμήν (*truly*) saying, this one concerning obedience and death (v. 51). The promise of no death was for his opponents the proof of his authenticity. Even Abraham died. Who did he think he was? *Greater than . . . Abraham* (v. 53)? This question, like the woman's concerning Jacob (4:12), was seen by the evangelist to provide the coup de grace for his argument. Abraham acknowledged the priority of Jesus and not the reverse (vv. 56-58). The second double ἀμήν saying here (v. 58) is fascinating because it explodes our natural reasoning concerning time and reminds the reader that Jesus is the *I am*.

Such a response was too much for his opponents and although they would have stoned him, he departed and left them with their frustrations (v. 59).

9:1-12. Healing a blind man. The Tabernacles motif is brought to a climax with the story of the blind man. The connection with Tabernacles and chap. 8 is assured by the repetition of the *I am* saying concerning the light of the world (v. 5; cf. 8:12). The story is thus to be regarded as an illustrative outworking of earlier issues.

The question of theodicy (God's goodness and power in the face of evil) serves as the starting point of the story. It was raised by the disciples who sought a simplistic rationale to the problem OF BLINDNESS (v. 2). They were not unlike the pessimistic friends of JOB and they certainly had hardly digested the message of Ezek 18:20 concerning blame and the role of parents. But here was a man born blind. Who was to blame for this tragedy? Rather than agreeing to their easy solutions of blame, Jesus shifted the discussion to the grace of God in the face of human need (v. 3) and called attention to the shortness of his mission by reference to the theme of light and darkness (vv. 4-5).

Then he put mud cakes on the man's eyes and sent him to wash at Siloam ("sent," vv. 6-7). Following his healing the neighbors were filled with questions (vv. 8-9) and he was called upon to answer their queries concerning this strange happening (vv. 10-12).

9:13-34. A predetermined controversy. Verses 13 and 14 serve as early warning signals in the story that trouble was on the horizon. Bringing the man to the Pharisees had all the earmarks of a kangaroo court and the notation that it was Sabbath is like a prediction of doom (cf. 5:9b).

The interrogation began with a simple question about what happened (v. 15). It quickly led to a division of opinion concerning the relative weights to be attached to Sabbath and healing in the evaluation process (v. 16). So the man was asked for his judgment about the healer. His response that the healer was a *prophet* would seem on the surface to be a minimally safe assessment (v. 17). But for judges who have predetermined the case and who are unimpressed by a caring, merciful spirit, such logic carries little or no casuistic force in an argument.

Instead, the interrogation sought for a reason to debunk the impressive miracle. First, they questioned the authenticity of the man's former blindness. So they called for a confirmation from his parents about his blindness and for an explanation of his transformed state (vv. 18-19). The parents were of little help in the debunking process. Moreover, in seeking to avoid excommunication from the synagogue the parents refused to become involved and referred the interrogators back to their son as fully capable of answering for himself (vv. 20-21).

Next the interrogators tried to set the parameters for the man's answers so they could accept his present state and reject the healer (v. 24). But the man refused their theological gymnastics by reminding them of the legitimacy of the miracle (v. 25). So they began their questioning again. The exasperated man then questioned both their motives (v. 27) and their evaluation (vv. 30-32) concerning the healer. His logic proved impeccable because healing and a good God belong to the same side of reality and are not opposites as the interrogators were trying to make him believe.

These teachers (who relied on Moses and did not know who sent this healer) refused to accept correct teaching, called the man a name (sinner), dismissed his testimony, and excommunicated him (v. 34). The relationship of this story to the early Christians who were designated heretics (*minim*) and excluded from the synagogue would hardly be missed by the early readers.

9:35-41. The verdict of Jesus. The verdict of the interrogators and their dismissal, however, was followed by the searching Jesus who *found* (v. 35, cf. 1:43 and the ironic uses in 1:41, 45) the abandoned man and began a brief, alternative interrogation geared to his acceptance.

The man's witness to the Pharisees had been firm although he had not seen his healer. Now he had the chance to behold the *Son of Man* and confirm his belief (vv. 35-37). Forged in the context of deliverance and defense and faced with his God-sent healer, his confession became a firm *I believe* and his worship of Jesus (v. 38) has stood as unique in this Gospel's pre-resurrection stories of Jesus. He is a model of faith and commitment to the fulfillment of the messianic hope (cf. 4:23-26).

Accordingly, Jesus as judge judged the parties. In his coming as light to the world the blind were enabled to see and those who thought they saw became blind (vv. 39-41). The verdict was clear.

Dedication and the Motif of the Shepherd, 10:1-42

The Gospel is filled with many symbolic ideas, ironic statements, and double-level presentations. But in this long symbolic or parabolic chapter the evangelist for the first time identifies his treatment as figurative (παροιμία; cf. 16:25, 29). This mashal or extended parable provides several insightful portrayals of who Jesus is and his relationship to his followers. Moreover, he is symbolically contrasted with his opponents and the pseudoservants of God.

The chapter begins with a portrayal of Jesus as shepherd (vv. 1-6) which merges into a more involved picture of him as both door or gate and shepherd (vv. 7-18) which then leads to a familiar theme of division (vv. 19-21). In the heart of the discussion the note is sounded that it was the feast of Dedication at the Temple (vv. 22-23) that celebrated the cleansing of the defamed altar and Temple in the time of Judas Maccabeus, who himself became a messianic symbol. The discussion, accordingly, moves to the messianic role of Jesus as shepherd and his relationships with both believers and unbelievers as well as with the Father (vv. 24-30). It concludes with the attempt to stone Jesus which results in his departure across the Jordan (vv. 31-42).

10:1-6. Jesus the shepherd. The double ἀμήν introduces a new section and a new series of *I am* sayings focusing on the role of Jesus as the Messiah (cf.

10:24). The first picture is of Jesus as a shepherd leader, who fits the prophetic picture of the coming messianic shepherd-king like DAVID (Jer 23:5-6; Ezek 34:23-24). To watch shepherds leading (cf. vv. 3-4) sheep in Israel today with a song or tune even in urban areas points to the intimacy of relationship between shepherd and sheep that is often missed in the hard driving patterns of much contemporary life. Thieves and strangers cannot participate in such a close relationship and the evangelist points his judgmental finger at the opponents of Jesus with the words *they did not understand what he was saying to them* (v. 6).

10:7-18. Jesus as door and shepherd. The second double ἀμήν saying adjusts the focus slightly to describe Jesus as *the gate* or door of the sheepfold (v. 7). Many sheepfolds were built of rock walls but without gates. So once the sheep were safely inside, the shepherd took his position at the entrance serving as the guard.

The shepherd who is thus symbolized as the means of safety and security for the sheep is contrasted to thieves (v. 10) and wolves (v. 12) who plunder, devour, and devastate the flock. The implication would have been very clear in that day because the prophets likened the leaders of God's people to such destructive portraits (cf. Jer 23:12; Ezek 34:3-5).

The shepherd is likewise contrasted to the hired servant (v. 12) who received pay for work but was hardly invested in the sheep. Thus, when danger threatened, the paid worker was more concerned with payment and self-survival than with the security of the sheep (v. 13; cf. Ezek 34:8b-10).

The good shepherd, however, was invested so much in the sheep that he was ready to die for the sheep (vv. 11, 17). The picture of the dying shepherd is clearly to be associated in John with the dying *Lamb of God that takes away the sin of the world* (1:29), an image that coordinates with the fact that the goal of the death and resurrection for Jesus reaches beyond the Jews to the whole world (v. 16). The death and resurrection are here clearly implied (vv. 17-18) and the death is to be understood as Jesus' authoritative self-sacrifice and certainly not in terms of the power of world authorities over Jesus. The meaning is one of divine control and timing even in death.

10:19-21. Division. By now the reader is familiar with the theme that Jesus caused division (cf. 1:11-12). His words brought hostile reactions so that he was identified by many as demon possessed (v. 20; cf. 7:20; 8:48; etc.). Yet his works often caused others to evaluate him differently (10:21, 32-33; cf. 2:23; 4:48; 7:31; 9:32-33; etc.).

10:22-30. Dedication and the messianic question. On the twenty-fifth of Kislev 164 B.C.E., a new festival of Hanukkah (Dedication) was inaugurated into the Jewish year that celebrated the rededication of the Temple after the Syrians of Antiochus IV (Epiphanes) desecrated the Temple by slaughtering a pig on the altar and by setting up a statue of Zeus in the Temple. The defeat of the Syrians, the liberation of Jerusalem, and the cleansing of the Temple under the Maccabees electrified Jewish messianic dreams. These dreams of a messianic state bubbled into sporadic uprisings until they were crushed by the Roman destruction of Jerusalem in 70 C.E. and finally put to rest by the defeat of Bar-Kochba (135 C.E.).

These dreams were undoubtedly behind the question of the Jews concerning the possibility of Jesus being the *Messiah* (Christ, v. 24). But a shroud may be cast over the question by the fact that John announced it was Dedication and *it was winter* (v. 23). Obviously, Dedication came in winter time, but time designations in John often have theological import. Could it be that John was again thinking on two levels? In any case, their request that he should speak *plainly* (v. 24) is set in contrast to the "figurative" nature (10:6) of most of this chapter.

The response of Jesus to their request has the earmarks of frustration with their unwillingness to accept his words and to recognize the divine origin of his works (v. 25). The issue was not one of having information concerning Jesus but of being his sheep and believing the reality to which his words and works witnessed (vv. 26-27).

The reintroduction of the shepherd motif serves an important function in this argument. After operating on the thesis that his sheep knew him and heeded his voice (cf. 10:3-4, 14), Jesus moved their thinking from the level of safety in the sheepfold to safety and security in terms of eternal life of the believer and security from the powers of destruction (v. 28). This verse has often been used as a proof text in discussions of the security of the believer and sometimes linked with theories of predestination (here *given me* v. 29) to advocate concepts like "eternal security." It is important to recognize both that the term "eternal security" is a multi-meaning construct that does not appear in the Bible, and that any theory of security must take seriously the warnings of God and the idea of "following" the shepherd (v. 27—see Borchert 1987).

For the believer, life and security are gifts of God which are vested in the unified leading of the shepherd and the Father (vv. 27-30).

10:31-42. The hostile reaction. The identification of Jesus with the Father (10:30) once again raised the ire of the Jews (v. 31; cf. 5:18). Stoning for them was the answer (cf. 8:59). The Romans were in charge of capital punishment cases, but mob violence was frequent in the uneasy context of Judea. The charge here of blasphemy (v. 33; using God's holy name) was not technically satisfied (m. Sanh. 7:5) but mobs are hardly concerned with technicalities.

Jesus' defense (v. 34) was to cite a passage from Ps 82:6 where others are called gods (the meaning of that text is not clear but it may refer to sons of God at Sinai, corrupt judges who act like gods, or angelic beings). The purpose of the citation was to challenge their judgment patterns by reference to their indisputable source of argument, *the scripture* (v. 35). The reference to *law* here (v. 34) is obviously not to be understood technically as the written five books of Moses but as a general reference to scripture.

Jesus' concern was to help them understand his role in the overall work of God. So in the context of Dedication he referred to himself as *the Father's* consecrated (or *sanctified*) one, *sent* on mission by the Father (v. 36; cf. 17:17-19). He then turned to remind them that he was not blaspheming as the Son of God. He called them to think about his works as a basis for understanding his words of identification with the Father (vv. 37-38).

His defense, however, failed to convince them because they could not accept the premise of the relationship of Jesus and the Father (v. 38). Instead, they once again attempted to arrest him, but they were unsuccessful (v. 39). Accordingly, he left Judea and crossed the Jordan. He stayed in the area where John the Baptizer began his witness. People there, in contrast to Judea, *believed in him* (vv. 40-42).

A Climactic Sign and the Passover Plot, 11:1-57

In this strategic chapter the Festival cycle has come full circle. Beginning with a SABBATH introduction (chap. 5) the evangelist leads the reader from PASSOVER (6:4) to Passover (11:55) and from a desire to kill Jesus (5:18) to the decisive death plot (11:47-53). As the earlier Cana cycle began (2:11) and ended (4:54) with miraculous signs, so this cycle that has five signs begins (5:8) and ends (11:43) with miraculous events.

Unlike the portraits of Jesus in the Synoptics where the cleansing of the Temple is viewed as the last straw for the Jewish opposition, the event in John that welded the opposition into its climactic verdict (v. 50) is the raising of LAZARUS. The story of Lazarus (vv. 1-44) and the Passover plot (vv. 45-57) are thus intimately bound together in a stirring conclusion to the Festival cycle.

11:1-16. The setting: The death of Lazarus and reactions of the disciples. The story begins with the introduction of a sick man, Lazarus, and his two sisters from BETHANY (probably a town on the eastern ridge of the Mount of Olives, a short distance from Jerusalem). Mary is further identified, prior to the event, as *the one who anointed* Jesus (v. 2; cf. 12:3). This note provides perspective later when the reader learns that the anointing was for his burial (12:7).

The message the sisters sent to Jesus, *he whom you love is ill* (v. 3), has led Filson (1963, 22–25) to speculate that the BELOVED DISCIPLE and thus the author of this Gospel was Lazarus. While this argument is intriguing, it has been accepted by very few scholars. However, it does point out that speculation is always with us.

The reaction of Jesus that the sickness is *not to* (πρός) *death* but *for God's glory* (v. 4) may seem to the reader to conflict with the statement that *Lazarus is dead* (v. 14). But the author, who is in control of the story, employs the earlier statement as a window into the development of the story so that the reader will realize that Jesus is in control of the situation and that the events of the story will lead to the glorification of the *Son of God* (v. 4).

This window can be helpful in understanding both the actions of Jesus and the reactions of his followers. It may seem from a modern perspective that Jesus' love for Lazarus and his sisters (v. 5) cannot be coordinated with his delay of *two days* in coming to them (v. 6). Indeed, later Martha and Mary seem to express such a feeling (11:21, 32).

The disciples on the other hand were relieved to be outside of Judea and had no desire to return. So when Jesus announced to them an intention to return (v. 7), resistance seized their minds and they reminded him of the Judean threat of stoning (v. 8). The sermonette of Jesus about walking in the daylight hardly calmed their troubled hearts (vv. 9-10). When, therefore, Jesus told them he was going to awaken the sleeping Lazarus, they pled that he would not do anything rash because sick and sleeping people recover and wake up (v. 12).

His announcement that Lazarus was dead stunned them and they failed to hear his words that the situation would ultimately support their believing (v. 15). THOMAS, the model of earthly realism, voiced their hopelessness in the decision. But it was hardly the perspective of a coward. It was the voice of resignation in the face of a perceived reality, the acceptance of hopelessness for what it seemed to be. It was a willingness to die (v. 16). History has generally treated Thomas superficially. But the foundations for the major confession in this Gospel (20:28) can already be seen in the realism of the man popularly called "doubter."

11:17-44. The dialogues with the grieving and the work of Jesus. This scene opens with Lazarus already *in the tomb four days* (v. 17). Hope even for any word from the deceased was thus totally gone because, in popular thinking, the spirit no longer hovered around the tomb but departed for SHEOL (the place of the dead) on the third day.

As Jesus made his way towards his friends, a grieving Martha met him with the emotion-filled words *if you had been here . . . but even now . . .* (vv. 21-22). Those words indicate her strong belief in the power of Jesus but also reflect her sense of hopeless resignation. The words of Jesus, *Your brother will rise again,* were met with a strong affirmation of her trust in Jewish resurrection theology (vv. 23-24). The rejoinder of Jesus that he is the resurrection and the agent against death was met by Martha with an affirmation of belief in his messiahship and his descent from God.

The last statement represents the third time within a few verses that the title SON OF GOD is used (10:36; 11:4, 27) and indicates a definite movement in the Johannine message that earlier employed SON OF MAN as Jesus' self-designation (cf. 9:35). The linkage was of course already suggested in the Nathaniel pericope (1:49, 51).

Because the confession of Martha is such a strong theological statement, preachers using this chapter may tend to conclude their sermons with the high note of 11:27. But that is not the end of the story. Indeed, when one adds Martha's reaction at the tomb "Lord . . . he stinks" (NRSV, *there is a stench,* v. 39), it becomes quite clear that Jesus and Martha have been talking on two different levels of reality. Confession and belief do not always match.

Sandwiched between the two segments of the Martha story is a pericope about the hopeless state of Mary and the mourners. In spite of Martha's theological assertions nothing had changed. Indeed, Mary re-peated the first hopeless statement of Martha *if you had been here* (v. 32; cf. 11:21). The text says that when Jesus saw her and the mourners weeping and beheld the situation at the tomb of Lazarus, "Jesus wept" (RSV, cf. NRSV, *Jesus began to weep,* v. 35).

Many interpreters accept the mourner's view of the weeping Jesus (vv. 36-37), but I am not so sure that an interpretation of mere "love" for Lazarus is fully sufficient to explain the weeping of Jesus. The mourners thought that all was lost (*kept this man from dying,* v. 37) but Jesus was hardly a helpless mourner. It is, therefore, not unlikely that their lack of comprehension (failing to understand the power that could open blind eyes could also touch a dead man) greatly contributed to the emotion of Jesus. Indeed, the next event begins to confront their puny presuppositions.

The events that followed are a study in contrast. Jesus' command to remove the stone (it is not clear here whether the tomb stone was a slab or a roller) brought forth Martha's protest against the stench. But Jesus was undeterred. In fact he gently censured her for her lack of believing in his role of bringing the glory of God (v. 40). The prayer of Jesus here begins with the typical Johannine address, *Father,* and moves to Jesus' concern for his mission (vv. 41-42; cf. 12:27-28 and esp. comments at chap. 17). But his prayer is not for his benefit (10:42). The cry of Jesus to the dead man and the command to release the resuscitated Lazarus was a stunning example of the power of Jesus to deal with human presupposition and doubt and at the same time to give incredible meaning to the theological formulations of Martha.

The story is a masterpiece of narrative writing. It is a reminder that theological answers can be very shallow in life application. It is, moreover, a story that moves the reader to the conclusion of the Festival cycle and towards the end of the public ministry of Jesus. Unlike the other stories in the cycle, however, most of the theological dialogue here precedes the act of Jesus.

But it must be added that not all the dialogue precedes because the Festival cycle has a major focus on conflict and up to this point the story has involved only the friends of Jesus. The foes of Jesus and the conflict dialogue are introduced next as the raising of Lazarus is seen as the climactic event that stirred the Passover plot (v. 53).

While many believed, some reported the event to the Pharisees (v. 45). The council members (SANHEDRIN) were frustrated by the implications of Jesus and they sought to avoid the possibility of confrontation with the Romans and the loss of their power and devastation of the nation (vv. 47-48). This section of the story is filled with irony (cf. Duke 1985, 86–89), especially when the reader remembers that the Gospel was written after the fall of Jerusalem (70 C.E.). The protective efforts of the Jews, from the Johannine perspective, proved to be futile.

Indeed, the argument of the high priest (which for the evangelist was the equivalent of an *ex cathedra* statement, v. 51) was also laced with irony. The high priest declared that saving the people would take the death of one man (10:50). It was a typical argument of the end justifying the means but for the evangelist it was an insight into the gospel of salvation. Moreover, the words of Jesus were not limited to the nation but were for all of God's scattered children (v. 52).

This section like several others in John may raise for readers questions of historicity: e.g., how did the author know the mind of the high priest? Such a question has been answered both skeptically and positively. Some posit a witness such as Nicodemus reporting the incident. In general, however, such discussions are attempts to use silence and are best recognized as speculation.

The Passover, the time of cleansing, was on the horizon (v. 55). The orders for the arrest of Jesus had been issued (v. 57). Jerusalem was in a state of upheaval and excitement (v. 56), but Jesus had departed from there and stayed with his disciples on the edge of the desert (v. 54). It is not entirely clear where this town of *Ephraim* was located. It may have been in the hill country between Jerusalem and the Jordan River but in spite of speculation, no archaeological confirmation has yet been made.

The Festival cycle is thus concluded. The remainder of the Gospel involves the outworking of Passover in the death and resurrection of Jesus.

The Anointing and Entry into Jerusalem, 12:1-50

Positioned between the Festival cycle and the Farewell cycle is the strategic chapter which announces the forthcoming death of Jesus. For mountain climbers it functions like a saddle that unites peaks of mountains and provides the opportunity to move from one place to another. In that sense this chapter contains elements of both what has been said and what is yet to be said. It is one reason why scholars have sometimes wrestled with the relationship of chaps. 11–13.

Most scholars begin a new section with chap. 13 because of the summary type section at 12:44-50, but chap. 12 should not be totally divorced from chap. 13 any more than it should be completely segmented from chap. 11. Chapter 12 is a literary conjunction and should be treated as such. But it is more than a conjunction between chaps. 11 and 13; it also is a preparation for chap. 18 and the death story.

This chapter is the work of a literary genius because of the multiplicity of cords that are being struck. In this chapter is the familiar story of the entry into Jerusalem and the several reactions that are raised by it (vv. 12-22). But the entry story is sandwiched between the anointing scene (vv. 1-11) and the Johannine Gethsemane-like scene (vv. 23-36a), both of which give the entry scene the ominous sense of a dirge. The chapter then concludes with two summations, one on believing (vv. 36b-43) and another on judgment (vv. 44-50).

12:1-11. The anointing for death. The opening announcement that it was six days before Passover sets the stage for the interpretation of this chapter as a window into the death of Jesus. Verses 1 and 10, which refer to Lazarus, underline the fact that the raising of Lazarus was viewed by the evangelist as a crucial event in the coming death of the Passover lamb.

The mention here of Martha and Mary together with brief references concerning their activities (vv. 2-3) is intriguing because the Johannine statements are quite consistent with the picture presented in Luke 10:38-42, the only other pericope in the NT where the sisters are mentioned together. In the Lukan context Martha is busy in the serving role and Mary is at Jesus' feet listening to his teaching. Here Martha is serving a meal and Mary is at the Lord's feet anointing him. In both stories Mary is commended for her activity (v. 7; cf. Luke 10:42).

It is also intriguing that the name Lazarus appears elsewhere in the NT only in the Lukan pericope with the rich man (Luke 16:19-31), although in Luke he was not a dead man but a helpless beggar who was full of sores. Dual texts like these involving the sisters and Lazarus make scholars ask questions concerning possible links between Johannine and Lukan traditions, at least at the oral or pre-canonical stage of the texts.

The anointing material has been variously translated into English as an "ointment" (KJV, RSV) or perhaps better a *perfume* (NRSV, TEV) since the emphasis seems to fall on its smell (v. 3c). The vial of *nard* or "spikenard" (KJV) used here was probably a plant oil extracted from the root (and "spike") of the Indian nard plant. The point here is its expensiveness (v. 3a) since the vial was valued by Judas as the equivalent of a year's wages (v. 5: *three hundred denarii* is of course one denarius per day for about six working days per week for a year, less the festival days).

The contrast here is between the self-giving Mary and Judas Iscariot (see comment at 6:70-71), whom John designates as the thieving treasurer of the band. While it could be argued with Judas that the anointing was a waste of resources that could have been used on the poor (v. 6), in censuring Judas Jesus was not rejecting the needs of the poor (v. 8). Instead, Jesus regarded the breaking of the fragrant vial as a symbol of his forthcoming burial (v. 7; cf. the commendation at Mark 14:8-9). It was an anointing fit for a king (cf. the elaborate burial spicing of the body at 19:39-41).

The scene closes with an expanded death plot that includes Lazarus (v. 10) because of the dead man's living testimony. The reference to departing and believing (v. 11) may have been viewed by the evangelist as a foretaste of the conflict which the early Christians would have with the synagogue and the subsequent departure of believers from their Jewish cradle.

12:12-22. The entry to Jerusalem and the reactions. While many Christians refer to the Palm Sunday event as a "triumphal entry," the designation scarcely does justice to the Johannine perspective. There is no question that the crowd was excited. The people shouted *Hosanna!* (v. 13), which is either an exclamation of salvation or an emotional petition for salvation (cf. Ps 118:25). The attached blessing makes it clear that the people were ready to install Jesus as *King of Israel* (v. 13; cf. Nathaniel's similar messianic exclamation 1:49). *The one who comes* (v. 13) from Ps 118:26 was viewed as a messianic designation and the early Christians regarded the entrance on a donkey to be a fulfillment of Zech 9:9. It was for the crowd the hoped-for beginning of the messianic age and the Lazarus event seemed to confirm their hope (vv. 17-18).

The disciples are pictured as being in the event but as those who were trying to piece together the strange puzzle of Jesus. Their problem was that they did not yet have the key of his death and resurrection (his glorification) so it did not yet make sense (v. 16).

The Pharisees were exasperated. The world seemed to be changing around them and they could not integrate Jesus into their socio-theological structures. The events were passing them by and they did not like it (v. 19).

The Greeks (Ἕλληνες, not merely Greek-speaking Jews) are next introduced (v. 20). The obvious implication is that the gentiles are interested in meeting ("seeing") Jesus. Andrew, the helper, and Philip, the programmer (cf. 14:8), are called upon to deal with this new situation (vv. 21-22; cf. 6:5-9). The mission of Jesus was expanding and they needed his direction (v. 22). The request of the Greeks, however, was not in fact answered in this story. Instead, it is as though the coming of the Greeks is merged into the Gethsemane-like experience recorded in the Synoptics (cf. Matt 26:36-39 and par.). Did the evangelist view it as the signal for the next stage of the story and part of the overall purpose of the gospel? It certainly seems so because Jesus declared in John 12:23 that his hour had come.

12:23-36a. The agony of Jesus and his purpose. The evangelist drew together the anointing and entry scenes into an integrated focus with the announcement that the hour had arrived for the glorification of the *Son of Man* (v. 23). Moreover, he provided another double ἀμήν *truly*) saying involving the dying of a grain of wheat to make it absolutely clear that the glorification of Jesus had to involve his death (v. 24).

But the metaphor of the seed contains an important Johannine statement of reversal. The dying of seed brings multiplication of life (v. 24). In the same manner losing or gaining eternal life actually is rooted in a reversal (v. 25) and following Jesus is indelibly linked to being a servant (v. 26).

Nevertheless, such reversal is often costly for it can be an agonizing experience, one that involved pain for Jesus. Avoidance of pain is a human desire and even Jesus wrestled with such avoidance (v. 27, *save me from this hour*). Yet, recognizing God's hand in pain was the method and model of Jesus. His prayer of yielding to the will of the Father and accepting his divinely given purpose in life (see also Borchert, "Prayer") was answered by an assuring voice from heaven.

Because the Synoptic scenes of the BAPTISM of Jesus (cf. Mark 1:9-11, and par.) and the TRANSFIGURATION (Mark 9:2-8 and par.) have been eliminated in John, the evangelist employed the confirming voice from heaven as an assurance that Jesus' acceptance of his death was affirmed in heaven (v. 28). The statement that the voice was not for his sake (v. 30), however, is somewhat confusing in the light of the fact the crowd thought it thundered (v. 29). It is a little speculative to argue that the evangelist was here making a distinction between the crowd and the disciples who heard. But it seems clear that he is once again clarifying for the reader that Jesus was not in danger of choosing the wrong way.

With this decisive moment concluded, Jesus declared that judgment-time had arrived together with the defeat (driving out) of the world ruler (v. 31), the deeper mystery about which C. S. Lewis wrote in his tale of Aslan (1950). The lifting up of Jesus (his death) was the hope of life for all (vv. 32-33; cf. 3:14-15). But the death of the Messiah did not fit the crowd's messianic expectations (v. 34) because they did not understand the deeper mystery of victory beyond death. Light was now with them for a short while. Their task was to believe the light so that they might become the children of light (vv. 35-36a).

12:36b-50. Summations; believing and judgment. The seven signs of the two cycles have been concluded and the final sign (the death and resurrection of Jesus) has been unequivocally introduced. But the reality was that the people would not believe (v. 37) and so the evangelist brings his story of Jesus' public ministry to a close with Jesus hiding himself from the people (v. 36b; cf. 8:59).

This rejection must have been hard for John to accept but he provided a rationale for such a rejection by including a composite text from sections of Isaiah (vv. 38-40; cf., e.g., Paul's use of such a florilegium in Rom 3:10-18).

The rationale here began with the haunting questions of who and why earlier addressed in Isa 53:1, a text frequently used by early Christians (cf. Rom 10:16). The answer, as Isaiah reflected in his call (6:6-9), was understood and determined by God alone. While Isaiah referred to both hearing and seeing problems of the people, the focus here is on seeing (v. 40), undoubtedly because of the Johannine emphasis on signs (v. 37).

The concept of God's hardening in this proof text (v. 40), as Beasley-Murray (1987, 216) has well observed, should not be made a basis for a view of reprobation (see notes at 6:70-71 and 10:27-28). The OT can speak at the same time of God hardening Pharaoh's heart (e.g., Exod 7:13) and of Pharaoh hardening his own heart (Exod 8:15, etc.). The tension between God's work and human reaction is never fully resolved in the Bible and must remain a mystery. Here John says *they did not believe* (v. 37) and at the same time *many, even of the authorities, believed* (v. 42). The broad sweep of Johannine categorizations may

disturb some Western readers but the point is that the tension must always be understood in John.

But the evangelist added that believing by itself is not adequate because some believed yet failed to confess openly their loyalties to Jesus because they yielded to human pressures and affirmations rather than seeking divine acceptance (vv. 42-43; cf. 2:23-25). Such a situation brought forth a concluding analysis from Jesus: believing in him is the equivalent of believing in the one who sent him (v. 44) and such believing is enlightening in a dark world (vv. 45-46). Failure to hear and keep (obey) his word will result in judgment (v. 48), although that was certainly not the purpose of Jesus' coming (v. 47; cf. 3:17). Both the Father and Jesus have been of one purpose, namely the provision of eternal life (vv. 49-50).

The Farewell Cycle, 13:1–17:26

Scholars have long recognized that in chaps. 13–17 Jesus was preparing his disciples for his departure. Moreover, Leon Morris (1971, 610) and other writers have designated these chapters as the "Farewell Discourses," but these chapters are clearly more than discourses.

The cycle begins with the reminder that it was almost time for the PASSOVER and that Jesus' hour of destiny had come. This cycle is therefore epitomized in an act that has become the model of the self-giving love of Jesus for his disciples (chap. 13). The cycle ends with a prayer that epitomizes both Jesus' self-giving love for his disciples who must live and witness in a hostile world and the assuring expectation that his followers would be with him (chap. 17). Between these two "book-end" segments the evangelist placed some very tender discussions concerning the disciples' perceived sense of abandonment (chap. 14) but also Jesus' promise of the supportive Paraclete (chaps. 14–16). These three middle chapters then frame a central magnificent mashal or parable concerning the vine and the branches (15:1-11) and a crucial reminder of the importance of the love command (15:12-17) introduced earlier (13:34-35). This central segment thus forcefully illustrates the relationship between Jesus and his followers.

The Footwashing
and Authentic Discipleship, 13:1-38

This chapter is regarded by many as a model of Christian discipleship. It is also a strategic introduction to the farewell cycle.

13:1-11. Jesus, the footwashing, and Judas. The story opens with the notation again that it was almost Passover. The dull ring of those words is joined by the reminder that the hour of darkness had arrived. Judas, the devil's agent, was about to act (vv. 1-2). The evangelist makes sure that the reader knows that the events were not unexpected for Jesus.

In the midst of this fateful time one would expect a dirge, yet a melody of "love" is sharply sounded (v. 1). Love is a theme used in chaps. 13–21 four times more frequently than in chaps. 1–12. Here love is portrayed by Jesus in the moving scene of laying aside his clothes and taking up the slave's towel. He assumed the demeaning role of washing the disciples' feet (a role usually reserved for the lowest gentile slaves, women, and people of little status; cf. Str-B 1:121).

This act was undoubtedly repulsive to the disciples. Peter voiced the common shock in his halting words (v. 6) "Lord, *you* are washing my feet?" (author trans.) Peter's response to such an idea was equivalent to "Stop!"

The reply of Jesus was virtually: "No washing of your feet, then no part in me!" That answer sent another shock wave through Peter. He did not know the meaning. Understanding would come later because the act was a symbolic prediction (v. 7).

Peter immediately changed his tune from refusal to a request for a bath or a shower (vv. 8-9). It is a humorous note of good intention that misses the point. A bath was not the issue (v. 10). Bath terminology is here symbolic of the OT concern for CLEAN/UNCLEAN (purity). In many OT contexts uncleanness is linked to sinfulness (cf. Lev 16:16-30; Ps 51:2; Isa 1:16, 64:6; Zech 13:1).

It was not, therefore, the amount of water nor the number of body parts being washed that counted with Jesus. He was concerned with the nature of a person. Moreover, the issue is probably not even BAPTISM as some have thought, although it may be a related idea. The cleansing of Christ is the issue.

The disciples were cleansible, but one of them was not (v. 11). The evangelist never whitewashes Judas. He was the devil's agent, and the verdict was firm (vv. 2-18, 26-27). For John, Judas was bad news because as a friend he *lifted his heel against* Jesus (v. 18; cf. Ps 41:9). He was certainly numbered among the *chosen* (v. 18; cf. 6:70), but he was, nonetheless, a traitor.

13:12-20. The meaning of the event. The actions of Judas like the denials of Peter (cf. 13:38), however, did not take Jesus by surprise. For John all these events are within Jesus' messianic mission. They are viewed as fulfilling scripture and said to have contributed to believing that Jesus was indeed the *I am* (v. 19; cf. Exod 3:14).

The disciples' designations of Jesus as *Teacher* and *Lord* (v. 13) were fundamentally correct but incomplete. Jesus was their master and instructor, but they also needed to understand that self-giving humility was a mark of Jesus. Indeed, it was also to be a mark of his followers (vv. 14-15).

Accordingly, two double ἀμήν (*truly*) sayings were added to remind readers of the need to accept this servant role (vv. 16-17) and to receive both Jesus and anyone sent by him (v. 20). In these sayings the evangelist has again developed a dual level of discourse. Here one can sense John has in mind both the settings in the life of Jesus and that of the readers of this Gospel. Receiving a sent one is clearly an illusion to the post-resurrection work of Jesus' followers.

13:21-30. The painful tragedy and Judas. This section opens with the pain of Jesus (v. 21; cf. 12:27) and with a double ἀμήν saying concerning betrayal (v. 21). The announcement created confusion among the disciples, and Peter sought clarification (vv. 22, 24).

The evangelist uses the event to introduce one of his famous contrasts between PETER and the BELOVED DISCIPLE. Here the Beloved Disciple reclines next to Jesus at an oriental style meal (vv. 23-24; cf. 20:4; 21:7, 20-22). As in other cases Peter seems to emerge "second best," perhaps reflective of some struggle between the early Johannine community and others. But these statements in John are not a denigration of Peter as much as a positioning of him.

The identification by the dipped morsel (probably bread or perhaps some Passover herbs, v. 26) was also the effective signal for Judas to accept his role as the instrument of the devil (v. 27). The restraining power of God was removed from him and Satan took over. Therefore, there was no necessity for further delaying his tragic work (v. 27). The meaning of the signal, however, was not yet clear to the other disciples who assumed he was engaged in some economic enterprise (v. 29). But the evangelist understood that this event was decisive. Judas' departure finally brought the tragedy of "night" (v. 30; cf. 12:35-36).

13:31-35. The new command. Segovia (1991, 59) and others think the first unit of the discourses begins at this point. Perhaps, but this section also serves as a summation of the introduction to the farewell cycle and as a window into the discourses.

The coming of the hour (v. 1) had brought the imminent glorification of the SON OF MAN (v. 31). The departure of Judas signaled the coming "departure" of Jesus (v. 33). In this context Jesus enunciated for his disciples (*little children*, v. 33; cf. 1 John 2:1) one of his most famous statements: the new commandment of love. Love was to epitomize his followers and was to be the means by which everyone would recognize them as disciples of Jesus (vv. 34-35).

This command is one of the core statements of Christianity because the mark of discipleship was not formulated in terms of a statement of faith but in terms of a way of living. In the history of the church the last day of Jesus with his disciples is remembered in the celebration of MAUNDY THURSDAY (a name derived from a defective form of the Latin *mando*, "I command," in honor of this crucial saying of Jesus). The mandate of discipleship applies more than once a year.

13:36-38. Peter's denial foretold. The announcement of Jesus' departure (13:33) drew from Peter the question: *Where are you going?* (v. 36). This question formed the foundation for Peter's strong assertion of faithfulness and Jesus' prediction of Peter's threefold denial (vv. 37-38). It also served the evangelist as the introduction to the next chapter with Thomas's question and Jesus' discussion of going away (14:1-11, 18). Moreover, it undoubtedly influenced the second-century C.E. story of the return of Peter to face death in Rome when according to one tradition Jesus appeared as Peter was fleeing and asked, *Quo vadis?* ("Where are you going?"; see *ActsPet* 35; cf. Brown 1970, 607–608).

The Question of Anxiety and Loneliness, 14:1-31

Chapter 14 is the first of the three central discourse chapters of the farewell cycle. The focus in these chapters is on the disciples' relationship to God and to others. In this chapter the evangelist seeks to confront the disciples' fear and anxiety from loneliness. Also woven into the discussions here are the first two of five Paraclete sayings.

This chapter breaks naturally into four sections involving the departure of Jesus (vv. 1-3, previously introduced in 13:33 and 36), questions of Thomas and Philip concerning the way to the glorified Jesus and the Father (vv. 5-11), the relationship of believing, working, and asking through Jesus (vv. 12-14), and the promise of the Paraclete's presence in loneliness and frustration (vv. 15-31).

14:1-3. Departure and preparation for the future. The chapter begins with two crucial commands: one negative—"Don't let your troubled hearts (wills) control you"—and one positive—"Commit yourselves to (believe in) God and me" (author trans., v. 1). The reason given for heeding these exhortations is that in God there is security. God's home has many secure dwelling places, and the role of Jesus was to prepare for our future (vv. 2-3).

14:4-11. Questions of our destiny. Jesus' comment that the disciples now know their destiny with him (v. 4) brought utter confusion among them. Thomas, like Nicodemus, had difficulty in thinking about the realm of God (v. 5; cf. 3:12). He wanted a road map to his destiny. The *I am* saying of Jesus concerning *way, truth,* and *life* (v. 6) failed to clarify the situation because the disciples really did not understand the relationship of Jesus to the Father. Philip's practical request for a genuine vision of the Father (v. 8) revealed that the key to their understanding was still missing. Later Thomas would know the key (20:28), but not before the resurrection.

Seeing Jesus did not yet mean for them having a vision of God (vv. 9-10). So Jesus once again reminded them of his works (v. 11).

14:12-14. Elements of discipleship. Having mentioned his works, Jesus turned the conversation to discipleship. Believing was basic to accepting the disciples' work on behalf of Jesus. Indeed, they would expand his ministry (*do greater works*; v. 12) after his departure if they were properly attuned to him (*ask in my name*; v. 14). Such asking was not merely repeating Jesus' name in prayer, but asking according to his nature. God would thus be glorified in their working for Jesus (v. 13).

14:15-31. The coming of the Paraclete. While talk of Jesus' departure left them feeling empty and lonely, Jesus was not abandoning them (v. 18). He had been their companion; now they would have *another Advocate* (v. 16; one who would stand alongside of them). This term *Advocate* (or Paraclete) includes various meanings such as support, counsel, comfort, and exhortation. The disciples would not be orphaned because the authentic Spirit (of Truth) would be an internal resource for them (v. 17).

The distinction between *with* and *in* (v. 17) must not be made the basis of two levels of Christian life, as argued in some charismatic discussions concerning the Spirit. Rather, it is to be related to John's historical view of the coming of the Spirit and John's understanding of transformation (e.g., the nature of external and internal knowing and believing God). *On that day* (v. 20) they would understand (*know*) internally the relationship between Jesus and the Father and the true meaning of obedience (keeping Jesus' commands) which is rooted in love (vv. 20-21; cf. the love command in 13:34).

Living in the love of God and obediently loving others (cf. the two great commands of Mark 12:28-31 and par.) is the basis for sensing the divine presence in one's life. Such presence dispels loneliness (vv. 18, 21-24). The purpose of the first ADVOCATE/PARACLETE saying is thus to clarify the nature of God's presence in the disciples' life.

The second Advocate/Paraclete saying is built upon the first. In theophanies (appearances of God), angelophanies, and christophanies of the Bible, the presence of God usually brings a sense of fear and the need for a calming word of assurance (cf., e.g., Judg 6:22-24; Matt 14:26-27; see Thornton and Borchert, 1989).

The word of assurance normally is "Don't be afraid," or "Peace/Shalom." Here Jesus offers his shalom—a peace unlike that which the world can offer. It is a message not to be afraid or troubled by this new sense of presence and the departure of Jesus (vv. 27-28).

The role of the Advocate/Paraclete in the lives of Jesus' followers would be that of instructor to help them live in a hostile world (vv. 26, 30). The idea of instruction is deeply rooted in the OT faith. The Torah or Law was the center of instruction (Deut 6:4-9). Paul then argued that the Law's instructional value was to lead to Christ (Gal 3:24). Here the Spirit's, i.e., the Advocate/Paraclete, instructional role is to remind the disciple of Jesus (v. 26).

The pain of Jesus' departure was not to be magnified. Instead, the disciples were to rejoice at this new stage in God's unfolding work and in the fact that God's enemy (*the ruler of this world*) is not ultimately in control (vv. 28-30). Indeed the departure would turn out to be a witness to the world (v. 31).

The chapter ends with a note *Rise, let us be on our way* (v. 31). Some scholars have suggested that this note indicates that chaps. 15–17 are an insert. Others would argue that 15–17 take place in the garden (18:1) or somewhere between the site of the last supper and the garden. Perhaps the easiest answer is that it was a note retained from an earlier stage in the editing process and is one of the few literary seams in the Gospel (cf. Brown 1970, 656–57).

The Vine and the Branches, 15:1-17

In the midst of the painful discussion of farewell involving the disciples' fears and Jesus' promises of the Paraclete, the evangelist has inserted the captivating *mashal* or allegory of the vine and the branches together with the powerful reminder of the love command, both of which focus on the intimate relationship between Jesus and his followers.

This beautiful poetic passage contains the second *mashal* of John. The other in chap. 10 also focuses on Jesus' relationship to his disciples and pictures Jesus as the good shepherd. The opponents of Jesus are there likened to thieves, wolves and hired servants. Here are portrayed various aspects of authentic (true) and inauthentic discipleship in vineyard terminology.

Scholars hold varying opinions on the relationship of this section of the Gospel to the Lord's Supper or Eucharist. Its placement within the farewell cycle certainly is related to the death (glorification) of Jesus. The linkage of the love command here (v. 12) with the command in the footwashing scene (13:34) is hard to miss. But it is probably safe to conclude that the *mashal* per se was probably not eucharistic in orientation and should only be seen secondarily as such (for the contrary see: Beasley-Murray 1987, 269 and Brown 1970, 672–74).

15:1-11. Discipleship and the allegory of the vine. The vineyard had long been a symbol of Israel, God's people (cf. for example Isa 3:14; 5:1-7; Ps 80:8-18). Here the vineyard keeper is pictured as God the Father. Jesus is the authentic vine and his followers are branches (vv. 1-2). Genuine disciples know they are utterly dependent on Jesus and his word for cleansing (v. 3), fruitfulness (vv. 4, 8), and a proper understanding of their identity (v. 5). Failure to live in the vine is devastating in its implications (v. 6) but abiding in the vine is the key to prayer (v. 7, cf. 14:13), the glorification of God, and authentic discipleship (v. 8).

Such abiding is defined in terms of love (v. 9) and obedience (v. 10). Both are modeled on the relationship between Jesus and the Father. Indeed, such abiding should lead to the joy of the Lord becoming evident in the life of the disciple (v. 11).

15:12-17. Love and chosen disciples. The command to *love one another* announced at 13:34 is forcefully repeated here and identified with a call for the sacrificial death of the disciples (vv. 12-13). The strong summons undoubtedly reflects not only the circumstances in the farewell of Jesus but also the evangelist's context of a persecuted community. To love one another is the glue that enables the Christian community to stand together in times of suffering.

But this love is more than comradeship. It is rooted in the identification of the disciple with Jesus. Therefore, the evangelist includes the reminder that dying disciples are not merely obedient slaves but are participating friends in the mission of Jesus (vv. 14-15). Moreover, they are not self-directed actors but chosen and appointed agents of Jesus. Their mission is to bear fruit that lasts (v. 16).

Two important principles emerge in this central section of the cycle. First, divine chosenness or election in the Bible is not to privilege but to mission. God chooses not for the person's own benefit but to serve God's desire to bless the world (cf. Abraham's call in Gen 12:1-3). To reject the mission is tantamount to rejecting the call.

Second, the theme of "abiding," "remaining," or "lasting" is foundational in the Bible for inheritance or salvation texts. Accordingly, all assurance texts have a stated or implied warning or condition attached to them (cf. John 15:4, 6; 3:18). Thus, the promises made to successive patriarchs or kings are renegotiated between God and each generation. Moreover, each warning text has a stated or implied promise or assurance attached to it because God's intention is not the destruction of the world but the hope of salvation for all humanity (cf. 15:7, 10-11; 3:17).

It is in this context of the tension between assurance and warning that texts concerning asking God (or prayer) must be understood (15:7, 16; 14:14). God is not an unthinking Santa Claus-like figure supplying endless human desires or prayers. If such were the case, he certainly would have supplied the request of Jesus to avoid "the cup" of death (cf. Mark 14:36). God loves us and desires to commune with us but to pray in the name of Jesus is to accept the Lord's nature in our lives when we pray (cf. Borchert 1970).

The Question of Anxiety and Persecution, 15:18–16:33

This second major section dealing with the anxiety of the disciples is like a reversal or mirror image of chap. 14, except that the focus shifts from loneliness to world hatred. The earlier section ended with an announcement of the world ruler's limited power (14:30) and this section begins with world hatred and persecution (15:18-25). The earlier section began with Jesus confronting the anxiety of the disciples' loneliness

over his departure (14:1-11) and this section ends with Jesus confronting their anxiety over his departure, the forthcoming persecution, and their superficial understanding of the implications of what was to happen (16:16-33).

Embedded in both sections is a reminder that they are to pray or to ask for divine help concerning their situations (14:13; 16:23-24). Both sections also contain Paraclete sayings: two in the first part (14:16-17; 14:26-27) and three in this second part (15:26; 16:7-11; 16:12-15). These three chapters thus form an INCLUSIO framed around the central *mashal* and love command (15:1-17).

15:18-25. World hatred and persecution. The world in this farewell section is viewed from a negative, anti-Jesus perspective (cf. 3:16 where the world was viewed as the place of mission). Because the disciples have become identified with Jesus' select group, they stand over against this orientation of the world and thus receive the same hatred that was directed at Jesus (vv. 18-19).

The dual setting of the Gospel is once again in mind—for example, the life of Jesus and the early church. The maxim concerning *master* and *servant* is again used to recall the pattern. Not only were the disciples to be like their teacher in their life of service (13:13-16; cf. Luke 6:40), but here it is clear that the disciples would also not be able to avoid the hostility directed at their Lord (v. 20; cf. Matt 10:24). Persecution of the disciples and the church was therefore inevitable because the enemies would not accept (*do not know*) Jesus (v. 21).

Moreover, the hatred of Jesus meant the enemies also despised and did not know God the Father (vv. 21, 23). But they would not be excused for their sinful actions because their rejection of Jesus and his works preempted any defense on their part (vv. 22, 24; cf. the testimony section in 5:30-47). The unjustified nature of their hatred is supported here by a quotation from Ps 69, which early Christians viewed as messianic (v. 25 and Ps 69:4; cf. Ps 35:19. Note also the use of Ps 69:9 in John 2:17). *Law* (Torah) is the general use of the term for the OT. The enemies in mind here are Jewish persecutors but the early Christians would have expanded this negative orientation of world to include other persecutors as well (see Brown, 1979).

15:26–16:15. Three more Paraclete sayings. To face the world's hostility Christians are again reminded of their resource: the Paraclete or Spirit (cf. 14:15-31). The disciples' task was/is that of witness in the midst of hostility, but their witness was not self-induced or self-motivated. They had been with Jesus from the start of his ministry and were to bear witness to him (v. 27). In this third Paraclete saying Jesus indicated that their support for witness would be the Paraclete or Spirit of truth that was to be sent by Jesus and to come from the Father.

During the centuries when Christians were formulating the early creeds a dispute arose between the Eastern and Western churches about whether the Spirit proceeds from the Father "and the Son" (Lat. *filioque*). While much ink has been spilled over this Trinitarian formulation, it is best not to view the statement in v. 27 as involving a concern for relations within the Godhead per se. As Schnackenburg (1987, 3:118-19) has argued, it is a mission statement of the Spirit that in parallel form involves both Jesus and the Father. The point is that the Paraclete is intimately involved in the witness of Christians.

The concern of the evangelist was that Christians who were faced with persecution, death, and exclusion from the synagogues would be tempted to "abandon," "stumble," "fall away," "become scandalized" (σκανδαλίζω) by the persecution (16:1-2). Such persecution was in the time of the evangelist not merely a vague threat; it was a reality. In the Apocalypse of John one can sense the scope of that threat because there the synagogue is called "a synagogue of Satan" (Rev 2:9 and 3:9; cf. the *birkath ha-minim* or so-called Jewish curse of the Nazarenes and heretics in the twelfth benediction [see Martyn 1979]). The Christian community was under attack and the evangelist wanted to remind the members (16:4) that Jesus understood their plight and that, like their Lord, Christians also would have their hour. But in that hour of danger they had a God-given resource to prevent their capitulation.

The fourth Paraclete saying is introduced by another statement concerning Jesus' departure, the disciples' accompanying sorrow (16:5-6; cf. 14:1-11), and the promise of consolation (16:7; cf. 14:18). Here the coming of the Paraclete is said to be an advantage. Certainly the statement does not suggest superiority of the Spirit to Jesus but the meaning probably implies that the extent of the personal ministry of Paraclete in the world is to expand the implications of the coming of Jesus.

In this fourth saying the threefold role of the Spirit in the world is outlined. The governing term (ἐλέγχω) that introduces *sin and righteousness and judgment* is multidimensional (16:8). Its meanings include "ex-

pose," "convict," demonstrate," "correct," and "convince." Obviously in using such a word with these three roles, the evangelist implies that the Paraclete is prepared to use Christians in confronting all orientation to evil in the world. In so doing the Paraclete will expose the world's sinfulness, identify the standards of righteousness in Jesus, and judge all sin as connected with Satan, the prince of evil (16:9-11). The role is a powerful one.

The fifth and final Spirit statement (Paraclete is not used here but follows by implication) involves future counsel or direction for the disciples. Recognizing that it was impossible to spell out everything, the function of the Spirit in relation to the disciples themselves was to be that of guide (16:13). But the guide would not operate independently of the revelation in Jesus. Indeed, in all communication the Spirit would glorify Jesus and in so doing affirm the unity between Jesus and the Father (16:13-15).

16:16-33. Confronting the implications of Jesus' departure. Following upon the sorrow of the disciples (16:6) and the last two Spirit sayings, Jesus' mention of *a little while* in reference to both not seeing him and seeing him, especially in the context of going to the Father, left the disciples confused (vv. 16-18). In response Jesus replied with the first of two double ἀμήν (*truly*) sayings. Sorrow would come to them, but it would be followed by joy (v. 20).

The combination of pain followed by joy is like the delivery process for a woman concluding in the birth of a child (v. 21). The mention of birth pangs immediately brings to mind the idea of the birth pangs of the Messiah. Israel developed a sense of hope and an expectation of deliverance in the midst of their experiences under foreign rulers. Grist for the idea was supplied by important texts such as Isa 66:5-14 and Mic 4:9-10; 5:2-3. In v. 22 the event does not signify joy at the birth of the Messiah but joy at the resurrection of Jesus and his ascent to the Father (cf. v. 17) following the painful experience of the crucifixion.

In the light of such an anticipated victory the second double ἀμήν saying is employed to remind the disciples that the Father takes seriously the prayers of Jesus' followers (v. 23). God's desire is to respond to Christians so that they will be filled with joy (v. 24; but for further perspective on asking in the name of Jesus see the discussions at 15:16 and at 14:14 and 15:7).

The pattern of Jesus in his ministry was to describe his life and work in word-pictures. With the coming of the hour, however, the disciples would have the key to understanding Jesus' mission and such figurative patterns would be unnecessary (v. 25). They would understand prayer and the relationship between Jesus and the Father at that point (vv. 26-28).

But the disciples jumped to the conclusion that they had the key before the crucial events (v. 29). Clearly they perceived that Jesus was God-sent (v. 30). Yet they still did not have the kind of perception that Jesus was seeking. Accordingly, Jesus announced that they would abandon him (vv. 31-32). While Jesus would not abandon them (cf. 14:18), their perception did not result in commitment. Yet Jesus did not give up on them. He reminded the disciples that he (*in me*) was the source of authentic *shalom* (*peace*; v. 33). The world was not the basis for peace. It provided the opposite, namely persecution or trouble. But the disciple should not despair because the disciples' Lord has *conquered the world* (v. 33).

The Great Prayer, John 17:1-26

In recent years many scholars have commented on this great prayer (see Borchert, "Prayer"). Some (such as Schnackenburg, Malatesta, and Black) have emphasized structural analysis based on theological or linguistic studies and many have focused on the theme of unity. Some have divided the text into three parts following Westcott, and others have opted for a four-part division.

In an earlier study on prayer, I showed that chap. 17 breaks naturally into seven petitions all except one of which follow the Johannine formula of invoking the *Father* (πάτερ). This formula is also present in other prayers in the Gospel (cf. 11:41; 12:27, 28). Also similar is that each of the petitions, no matter what the context, deals with some aspect of Jesus' mission. Although the invocation *Father* is used only six times (vv. 1, 5, 11, 21, 24, and 25), there are actually seven petitions because of the interconnection of the prayers. Taken as a whole the chapter is a magnificent summary not only of the farewell cycle but of the entire Gospel.

17:1-3. The first petition. The lifting up of Jesus' eyes and the announcement that the hour had come following the first *Father* signals the conclusion to the farewell cycle. The emphasis in vv. 2 and 3 is really a restatement of the mission of Jesus and the purpose statement for the Gospel in 20:30-31.

17:4-8. The second petition. The emphasis on *finishing the work* and "the glory before the world be-

gan" (author trans.) is a clear reminiscence of the "Word" who was "at the beginning" intimately related to God (1:1) and was the "only" Son who came to make God known (1:14, 18). The petition in 17:5 for the restoration of glory (cf. 1:14) is striking. Also striking is the fact that 17:7-8 concerning the disciples' receiving, knowing, and believing Jesus and his words echoes the key verses of the prologue (1:10-12) as well as the major emphasis of the Cana cycle—seen in the disciples at Cana (2:11), the crucial perspective on believing after the Temple incident (2:23-25), Nicodemus (3:12), the Samaritans (4:42), and the official (4:48-49).

17:9-19. The third and fourth petitions. *I am asking* or "I pray" (v. 9) begins a new emphasis on the situation of the disciples in a hostile world. The strong invocation *Holy Father* (v. 11) together with the repeated request for protection (vv. 11-15) in the *name* of God appears to be an allusion to the OT idea of power in the name of God and to the idea that God's name must never be spoken irreverently (e.g., Exod 20:7). The perceived hostility in these verses echoes the repeated hostility to Jesus in the festival cycle with the paralytic (5:18), the bread of life (6:41 and 70), the statement on truth (8:41-48), the blind man (9:24), the good shepherd (10:31-33), and Lazarus (11:45-50). Evil or *the evil one* is real (v. 15) and the disciples need the protection of God to survive.

The fourth petition, which does not include the invocation "Father," is a prayer for holiness or sanctification (v. 17) that picks up the holiness idea in the earlier invocation (v. 11). The use of *holiness* terminology is exceedingly rare in this Gospel and the only other use is in the good shepherd *mashal* (10:36; it is also used in 1 John 2:20 in a conflict situation). The purpose of the disciples on mission here (v. 18) is similar to that at 10:36.

17:20-26. The fifth, sixth, and seventh petitions. Again the words *I ask* signal a shift of emphasis (v. 20). These last three petitions are related to the farewell cycle but in fact go beyond them.

The prayer for oneness (v. 21) immediately reminds one of the central *mashal* of the vine and the mission of fruit bearing (15:5), which is mirrored in the purpose of the world believing in the one who was sent (vv. 21, 23). Moreover, the *through their word* reminds one of the post-Thomas expectation concerning those who will have to rely for believing on testimony (v. 20; cf. 20:29). The theme of love is also very significant here (v. 23) and reminds one of the command to love (13:34; 15:12) and the questions to Peter (21:15-17; cf. Peter's earlier scene in 13:37-38).

The sixth petition is the wish for the disciples to share in the glory of Jesus. The words *where I am* (v. 24) are exactly the same words as in 14:3, which emphasize the future the disciples can expect.

The final petition begins with the invocation *Righteous Father* and forcefully distinguishes the world from Jesus and his followers (vv. 25-26). The petition is intriguing because it remains unexpressed, but the interpretation seems clear. The only two places in the entire Gospel where the righteousness motif is used are here and at 16:10 of the farewell cycle where the role of the Paraclete is again introduced because Jesus is going *to the Father* (13:1; 14:6, 12, 28; 16:10, 17, 28; 20:17).

The task of the Paraclete there (16:8-10) was to define for the sinful world the nature of righteousness in and through the followers of Jesus. It is significant, therefore, that the nature of the community that should provide the standard for the world's judgment is here (v. 26) defined not in theological formulas but in terms of the love of the community.

Thus in bringing the farewell cycle to a close the evangelist ends where he began in chap. 13 with the model of Jesus' love lived out in the lives of his followers.

The Death Story, 18:1–19:42

The death story of John is one of the most fascinating pieces of NT literature. Throughout the story Jesus is portrayed as serenely in control of everything from the betrayal and arrest (18:1-11) to the mock trial before Annas (18:12-14, 19-24), the denials of Peter (18:15-18, 25-27), the skillfully crafted seven scenes before Pilate that move in and out of the praetorium (18:28–19:16), the crucifixion and death scenes (19:17-37), and finally the burial (19:38-42).

All the actors in the story pale in comparison to the king of Israel (Jesus). He is in charge of his own death and everyone connected with it. The skill of the evangelist is evident throughout the story; irony is a great tool that makes the portrait of Jesus stand out in bold relief when compared to the hollow characters who think they are in charge of his death.

In this story there is no kiss of Judas (cf. Mark 14:45), no washing of the hands of Pilate (cf. Matt 27:24), no carrying of the cross by Simon of Cyrene (cf. Mark 15:21), no identification of the two who were crucified with him (contrast Mark 15:27 and Matt 27:38 with Luke 23:32, 39-43), no acknowledgement of sin by Judas and report of his death (contrast Matt 27:3-10 with Acts 1:16-20), no cry of forsakenness or tearing of the Temple veil (cf. Mark 15:33-38, etc.), and no centurion's confession of the Son of God (cf. Mark 15:39). It is not that these events did not happen, but that for John the focus is upon Jesus' control of his death and the guilt of all the world before the enthroned king on the cross. Jesus as king is the central figure in this story and everything points towards his yielding of his spirit in death as the sacrificial LAMB OF GOD.

18:1-11. The garden scene. Separating the Mount of Olives and the Temple Mount runs the Kidron Valley. At the base of the Mount of Olives still today lies a garden that tradition marks as the place of the arrest of Jesus. But in John the scene is pictured in a unique manner.

The soldiers are there with Judas. Indeed, the *detachment* is designated by John (vv. 3, 12) in Greek as a σπεῖρα, normally used to refer to a battalion or cohort of at least 600. The leader is called a χιλιάρχος, a rank just under that of a general in the Roman army (v. 12). The picture is clearly intended to be one of imperial force coming out against Jesus, and to this political force was added the power of the religious establishment (v. 3). But the irony is that with all their human weaponry this great force needed lanterns and torches to find their way (v. 3), a reminder that night had come (13:30) and they did not know where they were going (cf. 12:35; 11:9-10).

The story is ironic in another way because it was Jesus who asked them: "Whom do you seek? (v. 4, author trans.)" The powerful ones were on a search-and-seize mission but it was Jesus who identified himself. And the identification words of Jesus echo the identification of God to Moses (Exod 3:14): "I am." The devil-man, Judas, is merely mentioned (vv. 2, 5) and then melts into the background. He does not identify Jesus in John. The evangelist wanted the reader to realize that Jesus was in control, even of his arrest. When therefore the religious leaders and powerful soldiers heard the self-identification of Jesus, they were rendered absolutely helpless in his presence (v. 6). Worldly power met supreme power, and human power faded.

It was Jesus who then gave the human pawns permission to arrest him but not before he cared for his disciples (vv. 8-9). Yet brash Peter had to act for the disciples. Impressed with these events, Peter determined he would try to rescue Jesus (only in John do we learn that the disciple is Peter, v. 10). The puny sword of Peter could damage a human ear but it could not deter a divine mission. The cup of death was the will of God. Inconsistent Peter was in the way of the divine mission and Jesus censured him. But Peter would still have his chance to prove his commitment.

18:12-27. The mock priestly trials and Peter's denials. For John the verdict had already been delivered by CAIAPHAS, the reigning high priest. The verdict was death, a sacrificial death (vv. 13-14; cf. 11:49-52). The trial therefore was a sham.

It was conducted by *Annas . . . the father-in-law of Caiaphas* (v. 13) whom John also designates as *the high priest* (v. 19). While Annas was no longer technically the high priest because he had been deposed in 15 C.E. by the Roman general Valerius, he continued to be the power broker of the high priestly family, acting through his sons, son-in-law, and grandson. The power-hungry corruption of the high priesthood was well known at this time and Ananais, the high priest at the time of Paul (cf. Acts 23:2), was so despised that the Jews themselves assassinated him before the fall of Jerusalem.

The arguments before Annas in John are little more than a late-night interrogation and are a contrast to the openness of Jesus' teaching in the synagogues and Temple (v. 20). The blow to Jesus by the high priest's servant could be explained as a defense of God's prince (Exod 22:28). But such a defense was firmly challenged by Jesus' own question concerning unjust punishment and false witnesses (v. 23). The interrogation became a standoff between justice and injustice so Jesus was shuttled to Caiaphas, the high priest (v. 24).

Alternating with these interrogation scenes, the evangelist inserts Peter's denial scenes. Both scene-patterns take place at night—the interrogations are inside while the denials are outside. The denial scenes take place in the context of *a charcoal fire* (ἀνθρακία, a term used only here at v. 18 and at 21:9). The three-fold denial of Peter will later be paralleled in chap. 21 by a threefold question of love and service.

The responses of Peter in these denial scenes are striking when contrasted with the response of Jesus in the garden. Jesus had responded *I am* (ἐγώ εἰμι, vv. 5-6), but Peter responded to his question of commitment and identity with *I am not* (οὐκ εἰμί, vv. 17, 25). The implications are enormous. The disciple was ready to fight but would not accept the way of Jesus. But in his third response even his willingness to fight is shown

to be a mere shadow, for Peter, when confronted with his own slashing of the servant in the garden, denied even that involvement. The denial was thus complete and the cock immediately crowed (v. 27), fulfilling Jesus' prediction indicating that Peter's commitment was a matter of hollow words (13:36-38).

18:28–19:16. The mock trial before Pilate. The setting was the praetorium or Roman judgment hall, and the scenes once again alternate between inside and outside. The Jewish leaders, who had already determined Jesus' guilt even before the trial (v. 31; cf. 11:50), desired to maintain their ritual purity by remaining outside the gentile court at PASSOVER time (v. 28). The irony for John is clear because the lamb was being readied for Passover and the leaders were responsible for the fact that he was delivered (παραδίδωμι, v. 30; the same word frequently used of Judas, the betrayer) to be killed (v. 32).

The next scene shifts as PILATE, the procurator or prefect, entered the praetorium to question Jesus. Judea was a subdivision of the imperial province of Syria and unlike the senatorial provinces imperial provinces were viewed as hostile to Rome. The question of treason and rebellion was always a concern in such provinces.

From Pilate's viewpoint the question *Are you the King of the Jews?* (v. 33) was directed at determining the possibility of such a treasonable situation. The dialogue that ensued over Jesus' kingship left Pilate asking *What is truth?* (v. 38) and Jesus affirming his kingship but redefining the nature of such kingship (v. 37).

The third scene moves outside again and reveals a frustrated Pilate who found that Jesus was hardly a political rebel as Pilate had been led to believe. Accordingly, he sought to release Jesus because in his judgment Jesus was innocent. Realizing the determination of the Jews to condemn Jesus, however, Pilate tried the gimmick of a tradition or custom established for the Jews at Passover in releasing a confirmed criminal (v. 39). He gave them what seemed an easy choice—a hardened criminal BARABBAS, a thief who had no doubt robbed some of them, or the seemingly facile preacher Jesus. His strategy failed, and they chose Barabbas.

The fourth scene reveals Pilate's next strategy. Inside the fortress his troops whipped Jesus and played their mocking kingly game with him. Then in the fifth scene Pilate brought Jesus out to the hostile crowd, hoping that the sight of the beaten Jesus ("Behold the man," 19:5 KJV) might engender sympathy. But the crowd had tasted blood and wanted more. *Crucify him*, they shouted, to which Pilate finally responded, *Take him*. Yet he added his evaluation of innocence (v. 6; cf. 18:38; 19:4). Political expediency was carrying the day.

But the Jews countered Pilate's declaration of innocence with their own judgment that he was guilty of blasphemy because he declared himself to be the *Son of God* (v. 7). That announcement stunned Pilate who wanted a "time-out." Yet as Garland (1988, 491) and others have indicated, the Jews' reliance on the law to condemn Jesus set the stage for their own condemnation. They broke the law in their unjust pursuit of Jesus' death and ultimately in their affirmation of Caesar as their only king (v. 15).

Pilate's time-out forms the sixth scene. At this point his fear at the breach of the Roman peace by a mob uprising was countered by his fear of the unknown, and he reentered the praetorium to requestion Jesus (v. 8). His question, couched in the Johannine theme of origin, brought nothing but silence from Jesus. Pilate retorted by reminding Jesus of his power to condemn and to free, but Jesus finally broke the uneasy silence with a reminder that Pilate was not the source of power. Dispensing power was in the hands of God but guilt was the result of human action. So the theme of the deliverer is once again brought to focus and it serves as a forewarning to Pilate (v. 11).

The seventh and final scene took place before the Jews. It began with Pilate's renewed attempt to release Jesus but it was countered by the Jewish threat to identify Pilate as a foe of Caesar and a supporter of treason (v. 12). The threat proved effective and brought Pilate to the judgment seat to render the verdict.

Scholars today debate whether the *Pavement* (*lithostratus*, v. 13) was at the Herodian Palace on the west side of Jerusalem near the Jaffa Gate or at the Tower of Antonio to the north of the Temple (see Mackowski 1980, 91–111). While a few translations suggest that Pilate sat Jesus on the judgment seat in a defiant act, most translations correctly have Pilate seated to begin the final phase. To think that a Roman puppet would turn over his seat to a Jewish peasant seems highly unlikely.

The time of this event is duly noted by the evangelist, namely, *the day of Preparation . . . about noon*. The time is significant for John and it is repeated (19:14, 31) because the *day of Preparation* was the day for killing the Passover lambs. In the Synoptics the day of crucifixion is merely related to Passover, but theologically for John the death of Jesus has to be related specifically to the slaying of the lambs. Because of the apparent differences in such time statements, scholars have sought to reconcile John and the Synoptics by a number of arguments, including an argument based on the differences in the calendar of official Judaism and the calendar of the ESSENES. Such attempts usually prove to be fruitless. What is clear in John is the theological nature of the time designations.

In the final trial scene Pilate made one last attempt to free Jesus, but he was rebuffed by the ultimate Jewish hypocrisy: *We have no king but the emperor* (i.e., Caesar, v. 15). Throughout Israel's history it was ·God that was to be their king (cf. 1 Sam 8:7). So finally Pilate also joined the deliverers and handed Jesus over to be crucified (v. 16). Judas, the Jews, and Pilate are all guilty.

19:17-27. The crucifixion of the king. John simply notes that Jesus bore his own cross to the place of the skull and was crucified between two others. While Luke mentions Simon of Cyrene and the death confession of one of the criminals (Luke 23:26, 40-42), John's focus is on Jesus and the cross itself. Charges of condemned victims were nailed to their crosses. The charge against Jesus was treason because he was *the King of the Jews* (v. 19).

For John two facts were important. The charge was written in three languages: Hebrew, the language of the chosen people; Latin, the language of Roman authority and government; and Greek, the language of international commerce (v. 20). So the evangelist regards the charge as in fact a confession to the whole world concerning the kingship of Jesus. Moreover, while the Jews sought to modify the charge/confession to that of a pretender, John sees the weakling Pilate as finally having a backbone (vv. 21-22).

The conclusion is obvious: Pilate is not in control of this death. He has indeed finally received strength to stand against the Jews so that the integrity of the death scene is maintained. Jesus was indeed *the King of the Jews*.

The evangelist highlights two groups around the cross for attention. The soldiers in disposing of the clothing of Jesus are seen as fulfilling scripture (cf. Ps 22:18).

The women are briefly mentioned as a means to introduce Jesus' mother and *the disciple whom [Jesus] loved*. Traditionally that disciple was regarded as John.

The thesis of Filson (1963, 22) that the disciple was Lazarus has little support. As the eldest son, Jesus cared for his mother and in this text Jesus made his choice (vv. 26-27). The implications were significant. The Johannine community was special and Jesus cared for his own.

19:28-37. The death of the lamb. Two more statements from the cross bring to a conclusion the death of the lamb. The *I am thirsty* (v. 28) reminds the reader that the death scene was real and the *It is finished* (v. 30) accentuates the fact that the death was part of God's intention to bring Jesus to this hour. With this last statement Jesus *gave up his Spirit.* The point is clear: people were not ultimately in charge of the death of the lamb.

With the ending of *the day of Preparation* (and the killing of the Passover lambs), the Jews sought to ready the land ritually for SABBATH by having the crucified ones quickly dispatched. But surprisingly, the soldiers found the Passover lamb was already dead and there was no need to break Jesus' legs. John sees that fact to be very significant because the lamb died without blemish (Exod 12:46; Num 9:12). Yet he was appropriately stabbed, a fact that must have reminded the evangelist of some allusions to a pierced Messiah (cf. Zech 12:10).

But when he was pierced there came out *blood and water* (v. 34). Some writers and preachers who are opposed to ideas of Johannine symbolism have often been tempted to interpret blood and water as mere signs of death. But to a symbolic writer like John *blood and water* carry multifaceted meanings related to salvation, including but not limited to the ordinances or sacraments of the church.

The fact that the evangelist makes a special note to the effect that these symbols or signs are testimonies and are important for believing (v. 35) immediately reminds the careful reader of the purpose statement of the Gospel (20:30-31).

19:38-42. The burial of the king. The picture presented in this burial is that of a king. He was buried in *a new tomb* (v. 41) with the appropriate bindings and a hundred (Roman) pounds of spices (seventy-five by modern measure), sufficient to bury a king. The attendants, Joseph and Nicodemus, were undoubtedly among the PHARISEES who believed in the resurrection but who were still somewhat fearful of the Jewish leadership. With the burial of the king, the story seemed to be finished. But everyone was in for a big surprise.

The Resurrection Stories, 20:1-29; 21:1-23

The great PASSOVER had taken place; the lamb was slain; the king had died. No more would the theme of Passover be mentioned in this Gospel. A new day was ready to dawn. The night was ready to pass away. The stories of the resurrection in John are thus the stories of the transition into the new era.

In the Synoptics the appearance stories are set either in Galilee (in Matthew, except 28:9-10, and apparently in Mark) or in the Jerusalem area (in Luke). In John the main appearances occur in Jerusalem (chap. 20) but in the postscript the context is Galilee (chap. 21). The stories in John are unique although they are not different in kind from those in the Synoptics.

Chapter 20 contains three stories: the story of Mary Magdalene (20:1-2, 11-18), the episode of the two disciples visiting the tomb (20:2-10), and the appearances to the disciples and Thomas (20:19-29). Chapter 21 is a threefold story of the miraculous catch of fish, the breakfast, and the restoration of Peter (21:1-23).

20:2-10. The visit of the two disciples to the tomb. Although the resurrection stories begin with the note that Mary is the first one to the tomb, the story quickly shifts to the two disciples: Peter and the disciple whom Jesus loved (v. 2). The comparison between the two disciples that began at 13:23-24 is peculiar to John.

After being informed by Mary that the tomb was open, the BELOVED DISCIPLE outran Peter and first saw the tomb with the empty grave wrappings (vv. 4-5). Why he did not enter has been variously interpreted by commentators from a sense of reverence to waiting for Peter. Ecclesiologies often determine perspectives. But in spite of the order of entrance the text indicates that other disciple *saw and believed* (v. 8). This text is the only statement in the canonical Gospels where it is said that the empty tomb was a sufficient basis for belief. In all other cases the basis was the appearance of Jesus. What stage of believing was implied here is not quite clear because the evangelist seems anxious to move the people in the narratives from one level of belief to the next. Clearly he suggests that they did not yet fully understand the scriptural warrant for Jesus' resurrection (v. 9).

20:1-2, 11-18. Mary Magdalene. After her initial visit to the tomb and the notification to the disciples that the tomb was empty (vv. 1-2), Mary returned to the tomb weeping (v. 11). Then after the appearance of angels in the tomb she conversed with someone (who seemed to be a gardener, v. 15) about her sorrow and the missing body. But all the pain vanished with one word: *Mary!* He spoke her name and everything was changed (v. 16).

She grabbed at him and uttered the intensive word *Rabbouni!* But Jesus stopped her with the words, *Do not hold on to me* (v. 17). The reason given by the risen Lord is that he had not yet ascended. This statement has led a few commentators and preachers to pose an ascent and then a descent so that Jesus could be later touched. Such thinking is a complete misunderstanding of the text. Assurance of Christ's presence and support does not come via his physical presence (see Borchert 1987, 142). Mary wanted to hold on to him but such was not possible. Instead she had to leave him and carry her testimony to others (v. 18).

20:19-29. The disciples and Thomas. It was again *evening* and fear still plagued the disciples as they gathered on the *first day of the week* (v. 19). But they were in for a shock. Locked doors like a shut tomb did not deter the risen Jesus. He entered their room and like the theophanies or angelophanies of the OT the appearance of Jesus was accompanied by his word of *Peace* (vv. 19, 21) and followed by a commission to carry the message of forgiveness to others (v. 23).

Interpreters of this text must not concentrate on the "retaining" aspect here any more than they should concentrate on the "binding" aspect of the Matthean statement at Caesarea Philippi (Matt 16:19; 18:18). The role of the authentic rabbi (and believer) was to bring persons into a proper relationship with God.

The breathing on the disciples and the command to receive the Holy Spirit is the Johannine summation of the pentecostal promise (v. 22; cf. Luke 24:49, 51; Acts 1:8, etc.). Interpreters of these stories should avoid detailed, Tatian-like (as found in the DIATESSARON), Western attempts to fit these stories into neat packages. The testimonies are authentic messages concerning God's Son and our faith. They stand as faithful statements of the evangelists. For this reason Tatian was never accepted as a substitute for the Gospels.

While the disciples who were gathered on the first day of the week received a blessing, Thomas missed the first church service. When he heard the report, he stoutly refused to accept the word of testimony from others without the authentication of the nail holes and the stab wound (v. 25).

But the next Lord's Day, that is, *the first day of the week* (v. 19), he was at the service. Eight days later is

one week later according to our system of reckoning where the first day is not counted (v. 26). Again Jesus entered and gave his "peace" or "shalom to those gathered. The ecclesiastical implications are obvious. The church meets each Lord's Day to receive the peace of the risen Lord.

Thomas had challenged the other's testimonies. At this gathering his failure to believe was challenged by Jesus' offer to touch his wounds. The experience was more than convincing for Thomas, and he uttered what has come to be Christianity's premier confession of faith: *My Lord and my God!* (v. 28). But the doubter turned confessor was nonetheless reminded that the church that would thereafter be built upon testimony would not have the same opportunity for verification. Thus a blessing was issued by the risen Lord to those who would believe "without seeing" (v. 29).

21:1-23. The epilogue, a triple story. The first segment of this story once again begins at night but this time it is in Galilee. The disciples decided to return to fishing and as in Luke 5:1-11 they toiled all night without success. At daybreak Jesus appeared on the shore and suggested to these seasoned fishermen that they try the other side of the boat (v. 6). The result was a large catch of fish. The BELOVED DISCIPLE first recognized the Lord and informed Peter (v. 7). Once again the comparison is made. And once again Peter, the second best, impetuously dashed off to see Jesus.

This story has been the subject of considerable form analysis and comparison with the Lukan story. These two texts are the only two places where a miraculous catch is recorded. Some argue that it is the same story with Luke being a transposed resurrection narrative. But some also suggest that part of the story is not unlike Peter walking on the water in Matt 14:28-33. Such suggestions have led to speculation that the entire story may be a construction from segments of other stories.

Others have asked about the significance of the number of fish. Some have suggested that maybe the author thought there were 153 varieties of fish in the sea or 153 language patterns at the time of the evangelist's writing, both of which might be the symbol of the worldwide scope of the Christian mission. Clearly this text is the subject of a great deal of speculation and analysis. While the story can stand on its own, further reflection may be helpful (see Brown 1970; Bultmann 1963; Schnackenburg 1987, v. 3).

The second part of the story takes place on land. The *charcoal fire* (v. 9) is a reminder of the one burning when Peter denied Jesus three times (cf. 18:1-8). In this story the risen Lord had prepared a meal of fish and bread (clearly reminiscent of the feeding of the five thousand at Passover time in the pre-resurrection era; cf. 6:1-14). The statement that Jesus *took the bread and gave it to them* as well as *the fish* (v. 13) is related to the words of the church's supper. The point is that in this event the disciples recognized that it was *the Lord* (v. 12), a theme related to the breaking of bread in the Lukan EMMAUS story (Luke 24:30).

The third part of the story involves the threefold question to Peter in his restoration. That threefold question of the Lord involved Peter's love. Would his relationship to others get in the way of his love for Jesus? It had done so on the horrible night of his betrayal. It was therefore review time. When Peter answered three times that his love for Jesus was primary, Jesus gave him a commission to feed the flock (vv. 15, 16, 17), a commission that Peter faithfully passed on to subsequent church leaders (cf. 1 Pet 5:2).

In preaching on this text some ministers become enamored with linguistic discussions about *love*. But the point of Peter's grief is not primarily a linguistic nicety. The text indicates that Peter was grieved because Jesus asked *the third time, "Do you love me?"* (v. 17). The third time was a haunting reminder that Jesus was right and he was wrong in his boast of commitment to Jesus (cf. John 13:37-38).

But when Peter's restoration was completed, the story was not ended because his boast of dying for Jesus (13:37) was accepted by the Lord. He would indeed die for Jesus, the stretched out death of crucifixion (v. 18).

Yet like all of us Peter was still Peter. If he were to die, what about the BELOVED DISCIPLE (vv. 20-21)? That question, Jesus told Peter, was totally irrelevant to him. His task was to follow Jesus (v. 22).

But that question was relevant for the Johannine community because some thought that Jesus said the Beloved Disciple would not die (v. 23). Obviously that disciple was either dead by the time the Gospel was being circulated or very near death. So the correction of false theories needed to be made.

Conclusions, 20:30-31 and 21:24-25

This Gospel contains two conclusions, the first at the end of chap. 20, which originally was intended to serve as the conclusion to the book, and the second at the end of chap. 21, which concludes the epilogue and expands the force of the earlier conclusion.

20:30-31. The first ending. As indicated earlier, these verses in fact contain a summary purpose statement for the entire book and tie together a number of the major themes of the Gospel. So complete did Loisy consider the work to be at the end of chap. 20 that he wrote: "The book is complete, quite complete" (1921, 514). The first twenty chapters—despite the displacement theories of Bultmann, the organizational weavings of MacGregor and Morton, and the structural arguments of Fortna—appear to be a continuous theological argument of the evangelist. This conclusion is therefore a masterfully tied knot that encircles these twenty chapters.

21:24-25. The second ending. While the epilogue should definitely be viewed as an afterthought or a postscript, it is important to recognize with Westcott (1889, 359) that there is no textual support for thinking that the other twenty chapters ever circulated without this epilogue. It was from the earliest times an attachment to the text. In theology and style the epilogue is truly Johannine.

In form this ending has two parts: an authentication and a conclusion. The authentication is a community-written testimony (*we know,* v. 24) that this Gospel represents the genuine witness of the disciple who stands behind the written text. The conclusion is an affirmation of the selective nature of materials included in the Gospel and the hyperbolic statement reflects the writer's (*I,* v. 25) grand opinion that the selection is drawn from a vast resource of material concerning Jesus.

The *I* of v. 25 may imply that the writer is a recorder who differs from the witness of v. 24. But this final verse stands as a striking invitation to discover the magnificent testimony of John that is drawn from an immense storehouse of information concerning Jesus, the word of God come in human flesh (1:14).

Appendix.
The Woman Taken in Adultery, 7:53–8:11

This pericope has been regarded by most textual analysts as an insertion into the Johannine Gospel. In style, form, and content it was hardly written by the author of the other parts of the Gospel. But that does not mean it should not be considered canonical. Early Christians were convinced that it was a reflection of an authentic Jesus tradition.

The major question seemed to be where it should be placed. Some manuscripts contain it here in the context of Johannine conflict stories but other manuscripts have it after Luke 21:38 and before the plot to kill Jesus. While it is more like the Lukan stories that emphasize the care of the Lord for the unfortunate, the setting at the end of Luke 21 is also a misfit. The best solution is to regard the pericope as an independent story going back to Jesus.

Adultery was regarded as a violation of the will of God in accordance with the seventh statement of the TEN COMMANDMENTS (Exod 20:14). But a double standard had emerged that held women more liable than men. This story reflects that same double standard because the woman's partner was not brought forward by the condemning men.

Jesus recognized the double standard and the Pharisees' attempt to entrap him in his care for the helpless (v. 6). His response therefore was aimed at the self-righteousness of the accusers (v. 7). When he disposed of those self-righteous ones and was alone with the woman, he addressed her in a forgiving spirit without dismissing the reality of her sin (v. 11).

The pericope is thus an excellent example of Jesus' firm confrontation of hypocritical self-righteousness and caring salvation of sinners who need to find transformation.

Works Cited

Beasley-Murray, G. R. 1987. *John*. WBC.

Black, D. 1988. "On the Style and Significance of John 17," *CTR* 3:141–59.

Boice, J. M. 1970. *Witness and Revelation in the Gospel of John*.

Borchert, G. L. 1981. "The Fourth Gospel and Its Theological Impact," *RE* 78:249–58. 1987. *Assurance and Warning*. 1988. "The Resurrection Perspective in John," *RE* 85:501–13. 1993. "Passover and the Narrative Cycles in John," *Perspectives in John*, ed. M. Parsons and R. Sloan, 303–16. Forthcoming. *John*. NAC. Forthcoming. "Prayer in John 17," in *Prayer in Biblical Research*.

Borgen, P. 1965. "Bread from Heaven," NovTsup.

Brown, R. E. 1966, 1970. *The Gospel according to John*. AncB. 1979. *The Community of the Beloved Disciple*.

Bultmann, R. 1963. *The History of the Synoptic Tradition*. 1971. *The Gospel of John*.

Burney, C. F. 1922. *The Aramaic Origin of the Fourth Gospel*.

Carson, D. A. 1991. *The Gospel According to John*.

Craddock, F. 1982. *John*. Knox Preaching Guides.

Culmann, O. 1953. *Early Christian Worship*.

Culpepper, R. A. 1975. *The Johannine School*. SBLDS 26. 1983. *Anatomy of the Fourth Gospel*.

Dodd, C. H. 1958. *The Interpretation of the Fourth Gospel*.

Duke, P. 1985. *Irony in the Fourth Gospel*.

Filson, F. 1963. *John*. LBC.

Fisch, H., ed. 1965. *Haggada*.

Fortna, R. 1988. *The Fourth Gospel and Its Predecessor*.

Freeman, C. H. 1991. "The Function of Polemic in John 7 and 8," Ph.D. diss., The Southern Baptist Theological Seminary.

Garland, D. E. 1988. "John 18–19: Life through Jesus' Death," *RE* 85:485-99.

Guilding, A. 1960. *The Fourth Gospel and Jewish Worship*.

Harris, M. 1971. "Prepositions and Theology in the Greek NT," *NIDNTT*, 1171–1215.

Haenchen, E. 1984. *John*. Herm.

Käsemann, E. 1969. "The Structure and Purpose of the Prologue to John's Gospel," *NT Questions of Today*, 138–67.

Lewis, C. S. 1950. *The Lion, the Witch and the Wardrobe*.

Loisy, A. 1921. *Le Quatrieme Evangile*.

MacGregor, G., and A. Morton. 1961. *The Structure of the Fourth Gospel*.

Mackowski, R. M. 1980. *Jerusalem, City of Jesus: An Exploration of the Traditions, Writings, and Remains of the Holy City from the Time of Christ*.

Malatesta, E. 1971. "The Literary Structure of John 17," *Bib* 52:190–214.

Malina, Bruce. 1981. *The NT World: Insights from Cultural Anthropology*.

Martyn, J. L. 1979. *History and Theology in the Fourth Gospel*.

Metzger, Bruce M. 1953. "The Jehovah's Witnesses and Jesus Christ: A Biblical and Theological Appraisal," *TT* 10:65–85.

Moody, D. 1953. " 'God's Only Son': John 3:16 in the RSV," *JBL* 72:213–19.

Morris, L. 1971. *The Gospel according to John*. NIGNT. 1986–1990. *Reflections on the Gospel of John*. 4 vols.

Mowinckle, Sigmund. 1956. *He That Cometh*.

Newman, B., and E. Nida. 1980. *A Translator's Handbook on the Gospel of John*.

Sanders, J. T. 1971. *The NT Christological Hymns*. SNTSMS 15.

Schnackenburg, R. 1987. *The Gospel according to John*.

Segovia, F. 1991. *The Farewell of the Word*.

Sloyan, G. 1988. *John*. Interp.

Thornton, Edward E., and Gerald Borchert. 1988. *The Crisis of Fear*.

Westcott, B. F. 1887 [1954]. *The Gospel according to St. John*.

Acts of the Apostles
Mikeal C. Parsons

Introduction

The Acts of the Apostles is the only book that presents the story of the early church in the apostolic age. As such it is a foundational document for understanding the life and work of the earliest Christian communities much as the four Gospels are the foundational documents for understanding the life and work of JESUS of Nazareth. The placement of Acts in the NT CANON between the fourfold gospel and the collection of Pauline epistles is reflective of its function in the canon: Acts is a bridge between the time of the founder of the community and the time of his first followers.

Authorship

Early Christian tradition argues that Luke the physician, the traveling companion of PAUL (see Col 4:14; 2 Tim 4:11; Phlm 24), was the author of Acts (see Irenaeus, *AdvHaer* 3.14). Although this traditional view still has its ardent supporters (see Fitzmyer 1981, 35–51), many scholars today are skeptical about identifying the author of Acts with any certainty. Since Cadbury, appeals to the "medical language" of Acts to support the traditional view of Lukan authorship is neither fashionable nor persuasive. Even the view that Luke and Acts were written by a gentile author has met strong resistance by those who view the conflict in Acts as an inter-Jewish problem. The identity of the author will probably remain a point of contention, but accepting an anonymous author in no way detracts from the message of the book. The name "Luke" is used throughout this commentary as a matter of convenience to refer to the implied author of Acts without any assumptions about the identity of the real author.

Relationship between Luke and Acts

Acts is the sequel to the Gospel of Luke. As such, one document is best read in light of the other, much like the fourth Gospel is best understood in the light of the Johannine Epis tles. That Luke and Acts were writ-ten by the same person seems indisputable; to argue that these two writings comprise a single, continuous narrative (represented by the hyphenated title "Luke-Acts"), however, is to make too much of the evid ence. There is no manuscript evidence that these two writings ever existed as one document in a "precanoni-cal" form. In fact, the longer Western text of Acts supports the notion that the writings enjoyed basically independent reception in the early church and were probably composed as discrete, although interrelated, narratives. In other words, the separation of Luke from Acts in the NT canon is not simply the result of a "botched" job by the "canonical" editors, but rather an accurate reflection of the independent character of each writing. Maintaining the individual character of each Lukan writing allows the reader to see both the similarities and the differences between the Gospel of Luke and the Acts of the Apostles.

Date and Place

Most scholars assume Acts was written after the third Gospel and near the end of the first century C.E., although the date assigned ranges from as early as pre-70 C.E. to as late as 150 C.E. The concerns reflected in Acts are similar to those of the Pastoral Epistles and tend to support a late first-century date. ACHAIA, CAESAREA, ANTIOCH, and more recently EPHESUS have been suggested as the locale of the Lukan community. Still others argue there was no one "Lukan community" but that Luke was addressing Christians in various locales. As with authorship, however, the questions of date and place remain unsettled; furthermore, a detailed understanding of those issues is essentially irrelevant for purposes of interpretation.

Genre and Literary Forms

The form of a writing helps interpret its content. Unfortunately, the genre of Acts is a much disputed issue. The book contains features often found in ancient biography, history, and novel, and scholars variously assign Acts to one of those forms. Although the overall genre of Acts is difficult to establish, understanding the constituent literary forms may be helpful in the reading process. The speeches, travel narrative (including the WE-SECTIONS), miracle stories (including "punitive" miracles), stories of edification, and summary statements all share literary conventions typical of other ancient literature, al though Luke has given his material a distinctive Christian "spin." Whatever sources were at Luke's disposal, the Book of Acts reflects an author in control of his materials. Above all, Acts is a story and employs literary conventions typical of ancient narrative.

For Further Study

In the *Mercer Dictionary of the Bible*: APOSTLE/APOSTLE-SHIP; APOSTLES, ACTS OF THE; BARNABAS; CHRISTOLOGY; FELLOWSHIP; HOLY SPIRIT; JAMES; JERUSALEM COUNCIL; LUKE; LUKE, GOSPEL OF; MIRACLE STORY; PAUL; PETER; PHILIP; RESURRECTION IN THE NT; ROMAN EMPIRE; SEVEN, THE; STEPHEN; TWELVE, THE; WE-SECTIONS; WOMEN IN THE NT. In other sources: J. Chance, "Luke," *MCB*; J. Fitzmyer, *The Gospel according to Luke I–IX*, AncB; R. Funk, *The Poetics of Biblical Narrative*; S. Garrett, *The Demise of the Devil: Magic and the Demonic in Luke's Writings*; D. Gill, "The Structure of Acts 9," *Bib* 55:546–48; E. Haenchen, *The Acts of the Apostles*; G. Krodel, *Acts*, AugCNT; J. Polhill, *Acts*, NAC.

Commentary

An Outline

The Sense of a Beginning, 1:1–5:42

The Beginning of the Church, 1:1-26

The opening chapter of Acts refers to the previous story of the founder of the earliest Christian communi-

ty, Jesus of Nazareth, and sets the stage for the emergence and spread of that community. Acts 1:1-14 orients the reader to the story, and the remainder of chap. 1 (vv. 15-26) tells of the defection of Judas and the selection of his successor.

1:1-14. Introduction. Acts contains a brief, retrospective summary that describes the contents of the third Gospel (vv. 1-2). A prospective outline of the contents of Acts is given in v. 8 (this pattern is one of several used in narrative writings in antiquity: see, e.g., Polybius, *Hist* 2.1.4-8; 3.1.5–3.3.3; Philo, *Life of Moses* 2). Significantly, the outline is given by Jesus and is couched in the narrative as a promise.

The ascension account in Acts (vv. 6-11) follows the form of Greco-Roman assumption stories, while its terminology is heavily dependent on the assumption story of ELIJAH (2 Kgs 2:1-12). Just as ancient assumption stories accentuate the elevated status of their subjects, the ascension of Jesus underlines his exaltation. It is the fitting conclusion to the ministry of Jesus (so Luke 24:50-53); and here, it makes the life of the church both possible and intelligible. The ending of the story of Jesus then serves as the appropriate beginning of the story of the church.

Although after chap. 1 Jesus is absent as a character from the narrative of Acts (but see Acts 7:56), his influence throughout the rest of the narrative is profound. The name of Jesus occurs no less than sixty-nine times in Acts. He is at the center of the church's controversy with the Jews. He guides the church in its missionary efforts; he empowers the disciples to perform miracles. The ascended and exalted Christ, although absent as a character, is present throughout the narrative.

The ascension is significant for Luke's story and theology, but these opening verses actually focus on the response of the disciples to Jesus. This second section (vv. 6-11) contains two parts, and each one concludes with a reproof of the disciples (vv. 7, 11a) followed by a promise to them (vv. 8a, 11b; see Talbert 1984, 6–7). Despite the reproaches, the fact that both dialogues end with promises to the disciples invites a favorable judgment of the disciples by the audience.

In the summary of vv. 12-14, Luke lists the disciples who have gathered together in the *room upstairs*. The names of the disciples in Acts 1 are the same as those in Luke 6:13-16, although the order is slightly different. The list of followers is extended in Acts to include women and the family of Jesus. To mention women in ancient genealogies is unusual. Mary, the mother of Jesus, stands as a bridge figure between the women who followed Jesus (see Luke 8:2; 23:49, 55; 24:10) and the family of Jesus, who, except for James, receive no further mention in the text. The omission of Judas's name from the list, of course, prepares the reader for the report of his death and the choice of his replacement.

1:15-26. The death of Judas and the election of Matthias. Before Luke narrates the fulfillment at Pentecost of Jesus' promise that the disciples will be empowered by the Holy Spirit, Luke addresses what was for him a problem of the first magnitude. The circle of THE TWELVE has been broken and must be restored.

Peter stands in the midst of the believers to address this problem (v. 15). The situational irony of this first apostolic speech in the post-Easter community should not be lost. The irony is created by the similarities in the pre-Easter actions of JUDAS and PETER. Judas betrayed Jesus (Luke 22:47), thus fulfilling Jesus' prophecy (Luke 22:21-22). Peter denied knowing Jesus three times (Luke 22:54-62), thus fulfilling Jesus' prophecy (Luke 22:34). The actions of both Judas and Peter were associated with the work of Satan (Luke 22:3; 22:31). And so in Acts v. 15, we have the ironical predicament of the one who denied Jesus standing up to retell the story of the one who had betrayed him.

Before leaving v. 15, we should note the narrator's use of a narrative aside to address the reader directly about the size of the assembly gathered with Peter: *together the crowd numbered about one hundred twenty*

persons. The number is significant since 120 is not only a multiple of the Twelve but also because 120 males were required to constitute a local Jewish SANHEDRIN or council (Sanh 1.6). Luke may be arguing that the early church is also a "properly constituted" community according to Pharisaic standards. Regardless, it is clear that in this newly formed community, women also count (see v. 14; also Luke 8:1-3; 23:49).

Peter's speech (vv. 16-22) turns upon the OT quotation cited in v. 20. The first half of the quotation taken from Ps 69:26 deals with the demise of Judas; the second half, a citation of Ps 109:8, addresses the election of Judas's successor. The double use of the verb for divine necessity ($\delta \epsilon \hat{\iota}$) in vv. 16 and 21 is the narrative clue for dividing the speech into these two parts.

Peter depicts the defection of Judas and his subsequent judgment in the language of economics (Johnson 1977, 179–81). Judas does not repent and return the betrayal money (contra Matt 27:3-5), but rather purchases a farm (v. 18). This purchase not only stands in contrast to the believers who sold their farms and laid the proceeds at the apostles' feet (see 4:32-35); it also is juxtaposed to Peter who, along with James and John, "left everything" to follow Jesus (see Luke 5:11). Judas's purchase of property is a symbol of his apostasy from the circle of the Twelve.

Ironically, Judas dies on this same property. There is no hint of suicide here (as in Matt 27). The death is apparently the result of divine judgment, and the field is called the *Hakeldama, that is, Field of Blood* (v. 19). And just as the purchasing of a field symbolized Judas's defection, so also the fact that his property is doomed to perpetual desertion (v. 20) is a sign of his judgment.

Joseph and Matthias are put forward as apostolic candidates, and the assembly prays for divine guidance in the selection process. Matthias is chosen as the replacement. Note the play on words throughout this scene: Judas has forfeited his "share" ($\kappa\lambda\hat{\eta}\rho\sigma$) in the apostolic ministry and gone to his own "place" ($\tau\acute{o}\pi\sigma$). In contrast, the "lot" ($\kappa\lambda\hat{\eta}\rho\sigma$) now falls to Matthias, and he takes his "place" ($\tau\acute{o}\pi\sigma$) alongside the eleven in the apostolic ministry. The scriptures are fulfilled, the circle of Twelve is reconstituted, and the stage is set for Pentecost.

Pentecost, 2:1-47

The Holy Spirit descended on Jesus at the outset of his public ministry (Luke 3:22; 4:1; 4:14). Now the Holy Spirit comes upon the disciples at the inauguration of their public ministry. The disciples are worthy successors of Jesus.

2:1-13. The miracle of Pentecost. All narratives have gaps in the telling of a story, and what a narrator decides *not* to say is sometimes as important as what is said. The story of Pentecost is such a story. The story itself fills a gap created when Jesus instructs the disciples to stay in the city for an indeterminate length of time until they *receive power when the Holy Spirit has come upon* them (1:8). In v. 1 the length of time is fifty days. That time has not been idle time for the disciples: they spend forty days being instructed by the risen Lord about the kingdom of God (1:3) and an unspecified time electing Judas's replacement.

But gaps still remain within the story itself. In this Pentecost narrative, the reader encounters rather large lacunae over the nature of the miracle of glossolalia and the overall background against which the passage should be read. How one chooses to fill those gaps will determine in large measure the interpretation assigned to this particular passage.

What is the nature of the miracle recorded in Acts 2? The coming of the Spirit is joined by two manifestations: a loud noise and *tongues, as of fire.* But the function of these audial and visual signs in this narrative is unclear. When the apostles speak "in other tongues" (v. 4 RSV; NRSV *languages*) are they speaking in ecstatic, unintelligible speech (see 1 Cor 12–14), or are they speaking in the languages of the many foreign peoples gathered together there? There is evidence for both interpretations. Those gathered there heard in their own languages (vv. 6-7); but others mistook the disciples as drunk (v. 13), suggesting that, at least for some, the apostles' speech was unintelligible. The weight of the evidence seems to favor a miracle of hearing, but the "correct" interpretation is perhaps finally undecidable. Such rich ambiguity may underscore the multilayered understanding that Luke himself had of this event.

In the Pentecost narrative, the reader, standing at a crossroads, is faced with choosing among these various options. The road signs are few, and the exegetical path one chooses will determine the direction of interpretation when one encounters the next crossroad. Reading the passage against these various backgrounds at times sheds new light; at other times, such choices perpetuate certain misreadings.

Whichever of these paths the interpreter chooses to follow, one often-neglected emphasis of this passage remains constant. Alongside the theme of the Holy Spirit empowering the disciples (Acts 1:4) is the countertheme that Pentecost also hints at the benefits of waiting, of being patient (Luke 24:52; Acts 1:8, 12; 2:1). So Pentecost celebrates both an empowered church as well as a patient God who endures the church's abuse of that power. Filling the interpretive gap left by the Pentecost narrative with an emphasis on the patience of waiting disciples and a faithful God also picks up on a major point of the text from Joel, which serves as the basis for Peter's sermon.

2:14-40. Peter's Pentecostal sermon. Peter's interpretation of the Pentecost experience is almost three times longer than the narrative detailing the event itself. The speech divides into two main parts (vv. 17-21; 22-36), with an introduction (vv. 14-16) and conclusion (vv. 37-40).

Peter stands again (see 1:15-22) to strengthen the brothers and sisters (vv. 14-15). The narrator's introduction (v. 14a) anchors the speech firmly within the narrative framework of 2:1-13. The linguistic connections are strong. Peter raises his *voice* (φωνή, v. 14) in harmony with the *sound* (φωνή, v. 6) that had drawn the multitudes to the company of believers in the first place. Furthermore, the word Luke uses to describe the address of Peter to the crowd is the same word used to describe the inspired speech the Spirit gave to the believers who were speaking in "other tongues" (see 2:4). Not only are the "tongues" at Pentecost divinely inspired, but Peter's interpretation of that event is likewise authoritatively inspired.

The introduction to the speech itself is a response to the exasperated question some of them were posing to one another, *What does this mean?* (v. 12). If Peter rejects the mockery of some that the believers are drunk (v. 15; see v. 13), he also affirms the understanding of others that the believers are rehearsing the *God's deeds of power* (v. 11). This citation of Joel 2:28-32 (LXX 3:1-5) functions as the bridge both to what precedes and follows it.

Note first the inclusive nature of this citation. This community Joel speaks about and that Peter says is realized in the earliest Christian community is remarkably inclusive. It is gender inclusive: *your sons and your daughters* (v. 17); *my slaves, both men and women* (v. 18). It is age inclusive: *your young men* and *your old men* (v. 17). And if we are to take seriously the opening of this citation (*all flesh,* v. 17), then this community is also destined to be ethnically inclusive.

The Joel citation has been modified by the addition of several significant terms and phrases. That this new community itself is an eschatological sign is underscored by the change from "after these days" in the LXX text of Joel (cf. Joel 2:29) to *in the last days* found here in Acts. That this sermon is inspired speech is further underscored by the addition in v. 17 of *God declares*. Peter had assumed the role of the narrator in this speech, but quickly yields the floor to Joel who in turn defers to God. The effect of these narrative layers—Luke said that Peter said that Joel said that God said—is to reinforce the utterly reliable and authoritative character of the speech here. This point is made again by the next Lukan addition to the quotation at the end of v. 18: *and they shall prophesy*. This promise is fulfilled not only in the Pentecost event; Peter is fulfilling it himself in this very speech.

The last element added to the Joel citations, *signs* (v. 19), is perhaps the most significant addition. The phrase "wonders and signs" or SIGNS AND WONDERS becomes something of a refrain throughout the first half of Acts. It first recurs in the context of this very speech when Peter refers three verses later to *Jesus of Nazareth, a man attested to you by God with deeds of power, wonders, and signs . . .* (v. 22). Jesus is the primary referent to the prophecy that God would work wonders and signs as eschatological portents of the coming Day of the Lord.

But Jesus is not the only referent. Later in this chapter we find wonders and signs being done through the apostles (cf. 4:30; 5:12). Stephen, one of THE SEVEN Hellenists selected to assist the Twelve (see 6:1-6), is himself described as one who *did great wonders and signs among the people* (6:8). Stephen next describes Moses as *having performed wonders and signs in Egypt, at the Red Sea, and in the wilderness for forty years* (7:36). Philip also works *signs* (8:6—note the absence of "wonders"). Finally, the Lord grants *signs and wonders to be done* by the hands of Paul and Barnabas (14:3; see 15:12).

Signs and wonders, then, accompany the ministries of the leaders of God's community in unbroken succession, from Moses to Jesus, to the Twelve, to Stephen and Philip the Hellenists, and to Paul and Barnabas, the leaders of the gentile mission. Luke demonstrates that the early church has been more faithful to the tradition of Moses than other groups making the same claims. Membership in this radically inclusive community is restricted in only one way: *Then everyone who calls on the name of the Lord shall be saved* (v. 21). The identity of this "Lord" is explored in the second part of this sermon (vv. 22-36), and the call to

"be saved" is the focus of the invitation at the end (vv. 37-41).

Acts 2:22-36 is marked with several appeals for attention that serve as indicators of rhetorical shifts. This part of the speech forms the following chiastic structure (Krodel 1986, 83):

> A the kerygma, 22-24
>   B proof from scripture, 25-28
>   C interpretation of scripture, 34a
>   D exaltation of Jesus and the
>   mediation of the Holy Spirit, 32-33
>   C' interpretation of scripture, 29-31
>   B' proof from scripture, 34b-35
> A' the kerygma, 36

The heart of the Pentecost sermon is to be found in vv. 32-33. Peter identifies the unnamed Christ as Jesus (v. 32), which distinguishes early Christian messianic exegesis from that of Jewish contemporaries. The identification is further strengthened by the use of resurrection language. David foresaw and spoke of the *resurrection of the Messiah* (v. 31) who is *this Jesus God raised up* (v. 32a).

These verses also serve to link the speech with the Pentecost narrative and its interpretive framework provided by the Joel citation. The reference to the *promise* Jesus *received from the Father* (v. 33) recalls the Pentecost event; v. 33 identifies that promise as the *Holy Spirit*. That Jesus *poured out this that you both see and hear* (v. 33) echoes the Joel prophecy ("I will pour out my Spirit," Joel 2:28) and explicitly interprets Pentecost as a miracle of both sight and sound.

The conclusion of Peter's sermon (vv. 37-39) is interrupted by the audience who are cut to the heart and ask Peter and the rest of the apostles, *Brothers, what should we do?* (cf. Luke 3:10). Peter then offers a soteriological conclusion to his sermon: *Repent, and be baptized every one of you in the name of Jesus Christ so that your sins may be forgiven* (v. 38a). He also promises that they too will receive the "gift which is the Holy Spirit" (v. 38b, author trans.). This promise (see v. 33) is not only for Peter's audience, but for their children and *for all who are far away* (v. 39). The final phrase of Peter's speech, *everyone whom the Lord our God calls to him*, takes the last phrase of the Joel citation (v. 21=Joel 2:32) and turns it on its head. The invitation to salvation is reciprocal: "Everyone who calls on the name of Lord" will be those "whom the Lord our God calls to him."

2:41-47. Narrative summary. Luke concludes this section with the first of a series of long summary statements. Some summaries, such as Acts 1:12-14, are brief (see 6:7; 8:14; 9:31-32; 11:19-20); others, such as vv. 41-47, are longer and more detailed (cf. 4:32-35; 5:12-16). These summaries are quite common in the early chapters of Acts and serve a double purpose. They divide the narrative into segments but serve also as connective tissue or "narrative glue," shaping the episodes into a continuous account.

The summary begins and ends with reference to the numerical growth of the community (vv. 41b, 47b). In between, the narrator depicts the shared life of the community, which for Luke is the life of the Spirit. The believers who accepted the word and were baptized, now devote themselves to the teaching of the apostles, to the shared life, to the breaking of bread, and to prayer. These four elements characterize the life of the Spirit and are illustrated by the examples given in vv. 43-47.

The Healing of a Lame Man, 3:1–4:31

This section is clearly set off from the rest of Acts by narrative summaries on either side (2:41-47; 4:32-35). The passage itself displays a certain internal coherence and is divided into four segments or scenes that are marked by shifts in space, time, and/or participants (Funk 1988, 83). While these changes in time, setting, and characters provide clear rhetorical markers for dividing the text into four scenes, these segments are also united by several thematic links. The theme of healing is found in every scene, either with specific reference to the lame man at the Beautiful Gate (3:7, 16; 4:9-10, 22) or to healing in general (4:30). Likewise, references to "the name of Jesus" are found throughout this stretch of narrative on the lips of Peter (3:6, 16; 4:10, 12), the religious leaders (4:7, 17, 18), and the community of believers (4:30).

3:1-10. Scene 1. At the Beautiful Gate. The opening verses (vv. 1-2) particularize the general description of the community of believers found in the preceding narrative summary. Two of these apostles, PETER and JOHN, are going to worship in the Temple on a specific day at a specific time, three o'clock in the afternoon, the hour of prayer. With the setting, time, and characters in place, the stage is set for a specific *sign* of healing (2:43; see 4:22).

This beggar sits at the Beautiful Gate of the Temple doing the only thing he knows to do: he begs for alms. But to his surprise, he receives the mercies of God. *I have no silver or gold*, Peter responds, *but what I have I give to you; in the name of Jesus Christ of Nazareth, stand up and walk* (v. 6). The name of Jesus Christ is introduced into this story for the first time and will remain the focus of attention throughout this stretch of narrative. The lame man's feet and ankles are made strong, and Peter and John, like Jesus before them (Luke 5:17-26) and Paul after them (Acts 14:8-18), command the lame to walk, confirming and extending the programmatic ministry of Jesus (Luke 7:22).

The once-lame man leaps and praises God (echoing Isa 35:6; see also Luke 7:22). A third group of participants now enter the scene, *all the people*, who recognize the man as the one who sat for alms (vv. 9-10). For the second time, the Beautiful Gate of the Temple is mentioned. With this second reference to the gate, one wonders if the narrator may be less interested in its specific locale and more interested in working a wordplay between the repetition of *hour* (ὥρα, *hour of prayer*, v. 1) and the Beautiful (ὡραῖα) Gate. Within the semantic domain of this word is the meaning "opportune moment" or "timely" (see Rom 10:15 quoting Isa 52:7). Could the narrator be hinting that this ninth hour (three o'clock in the afternoon), the hour of prayer, is the "timely" moment of opportunity for this lame man who sits begging, ironically, at the Gate of Opportunity?

3:11-4:4. Scene 2. In Solomon's Portico. The change in locale from the Beautiful Gate to Solomon's Portico indicates a scene change (v. 11). The pattern of Pentecost is repeated here: a miraculous event (vv. 1-10; cf. 2:1-4) draws a crowd (v. 11; cf. 2:5-12) and Peter delivers a speech (vv. 12-26; cf. 2:14-40).

The outer frame of the first half of Peter's speech (vv. 12-16) deals with the healing of the lame man (vv. 12, 16) which is interpreted by the inner frame, a traditional christological kerygma (vv. 13-15). This kerygmatic statement is arranged in a chiastic pattern:

A *The God of Abraham, the God of Isaac,*
    and the God of Jacob . . .
        has glorified his servant Jesus, 13a
  B *whom you handed over and rejected*
      in the presence of Pilate, 13b
    B' *But you rejected the Holy and Righteous One*
      . . . and you killed the Author of life, 14-15a
A' *whom God raised from the dead,* 15b

The loaded christological titles, *servant, Holy and Righteous One,* and *Author of life,* along with this traditional kerygma, provide the foundation for the correct interpretation of the healing of the lame man. Some observers of this sign might conclude that Peter and John through their *own power or piety . . . made him walk* (v. 12), but Peter denies this interpretation and argues rather that "the faith that is through Jesus has given him this perfect health in the presence of all of you" (v. 16).

And now, friends is the rhetorical clue that marks the beginning of the second half of Peter's sermon (vv. 17-26). Here Peter extends an invitation to repentance undergirded by various citations of and allusions to scripture. He begins by acknowledging that his audience, although culpable for the death of Jesus, *acted in ignorance, as did also your rulers* (v. 17). Still, this ignorance produces a guilt that stands in need of repentance (v. 19).

The call to *repent, therefore* is accompanied by the promise of a number of benefits (vv. 19-22). These benefits carry with them the responsibility to listen to the prophet like Moses (v. 22). The addition in v. 22 of the words *tells you* in this quotation from Deut 18:15-20, is a rhetorical device the Lukan Peter employs to sharpen the challenge to his audience. The speech ends on a salvation-historical note: God, having raised up his servant (see v. 12), *sent him first to you* (v. 26), hinting at least at the gentile mission that will soon follow in Acts led by Peter himself (see Acts 10).

In the concluding verses to this scene (4:1-4), new participants are introduced—priests and the captain of the Temple and the SADDUCEES—who take Peter and John into custody for "teaching the people and proclaiming that in Jesus there is the resurrection of the dead" (v. 2). It is late, so their interrogation will have to wait until tomorrow. The major temporal break between the first two scenes and the last two does not occur, however, before the narrator reports in a brief aside that *many of those who heard the word believed; and they numbered about five thousand* (v. 4). Even in the face of danger, the community of believers continues to add to its numbers.

4:5-22. Scene 3. Before the Sanhedrin. The next two scenes take place on the following day, and a formidable group of religious leaders gather for the interrogation of Peter and John (v. 6). The apostles are set in their midst, and the inquiry by the leaders links with Peter's previous speech: *By what power* (see 3:12) *or by what name* (see 3:16) *did you do this?* (v. 7). Before recording Peter's response, the narrator reports that Peter was *filled with the Holy Spirit* (v. 8), thus fulfilling Jesus' words of encouragement that

when his followers are oppressed "the Holy Spirit will teach you at that very hour what you ought to say" (Luke 12:12). Peter, then, recapitulates his previous speech, echoing the traditional christological kerygma: the one "whom you crucified, whom God raised from the dead" (v. 10; see 3:13, 15); reiterating the rejection of Jesus by his audience: *This Jesus is the stone that was rejected by you, the builders* (v. 11; see 3:13-14); and underscoring the fact that the healing was through *the name of Jesus Christ of Nazareth* (v. 10; see 3:16).

Peter introduces a new element into his summary; he identifies the healing as a *good deed*, or "benefaction" (v. 9). Later in Acts, Peter will characterize the healing ministry of the earthly Jesus with the same word (10:38). This is the technical word associated with the benefactor/client system so prominent in the social structures of the ancient Greco-Roman world. Benefactors gave support, financial and otherwise, to individuals, groups, and sometimes whole cities. In return the recipients of such benefaction pledged and gave their loyalty to these benefactors (Danker 1982). The disciples here have taken over the role of benefactor, and, like Jesus, that which they have to give— wholeness of life—is far more precious than the typical benefits of *silver and gold*.

Unable to rebuke Peter and John because the lame man stood beside the apostles as empirical proof of the truth of Peter's words, the religious leaders order them out of the council (SANHEDRIN) and discussed what they should do. This scene heightens in tension when the council reaches the conclusion to issue a restraining order to the apostles (v. 17).

The apostles are called back in and warned *not to speak or teach at all in the name of Jesus* (v. 18). They respond with the boldness the SANHEDRIN has already observed: *we cannot keep from speaking about what we have seen and heard* (v. 20). The narrator depicts Peter and John speaking these words in unison (v. 19), highlighting the unity of the apostolic witness. The Sanhedrin further threatens them and then releases them, unable to follow through on their threats because of the people (v. 21).

This scene ends with a reference to the healing event of 3:1-10 (v. 22). The reader learns that the lame man was more than forty years old, although the narrator does not disclose the significance of that reference. Is he old enough to be a reliable witness to the event? Does his age underscore the miraculous nature of the healing of this one who had been *lame from birth* (3:2)? The reader must fill this gap.

More significant, perhaps, is the reference to this event as a *sign of healing* (v. 22) linking this miracle closely to the *wonders and signs* done through the apostles (2:43). The Sanhedrin had just acknowledged that this healing was *a notable sign* (v. 16). Earlier Peter had made the connection between this man who had been *healed* (σῴζω, v. 9) *by the name of Jesus Christ* and his soteriological conclusion that *there is no other name under heaven given among mortals by which we must be saved* ("saved" = σωθῆναι, v. 12). The use of this word, which bears the double meaning of "heal" and "save," suggests that this healing story is more permeated with soteriological content.

The healed lame man has become the paradigm of salvation through Jesus' name in Acts. Just as the blind man who regains his sight in John 9 is a model disciple in the fourth Gospel where believing is symbolized as a kind of seeing, so the lame man who walks in Acts 3 is the symbol of salvation in a story where journey narratives occupy much narrative space, and where the Christian movement is referred to simply as "the Way" (see 9:2; 19:9, 23; 22:4; 24:14, 22).

4:23-31. Scene 4. Reunited with friends. The finale to this episode is set in some unnamed place in Jerusalem where the apostles return to *their friends* (Gk. "their own") and recount to them what the reader already knows about the threats of the chief priests and elders. This recapitulation prompts the community to pray with one voice to God in a show of solidarity with their beleaguered colleagues.

The prayer (vv. 24b-30) begins with an invocation of the Sovereign Creator. Psalm 2 is then interpreted in light of the passion of Jesus. The kings (HEROD and Pontius PILATE) and rulers (by inference the Sanhedrin, see 4:5) gathered with the gentiles and the peoples of Israel against the Lord and his Anointed. Of course, even these acts are according to God's hand and plan that God *predestined to take place* (v. 28; see 2:23).

But this psalm is also interpreted in light of the present circumstances of the believers. The believers pray that the Lord will *look at their threats* and grant to his servants *to speak your word with all boldness* (v. 29). The final verse of the prayer is a precis of many of the issues already addressed in this episode: *While you stretch out your hand to heal, and signs and wonders are performed through the name of your holy servant Jesus* (v. 30), with emphasis placed on the role of Jesus as the power source for the wonder-performing servant.

The entire episode is brought to a close in v. 31. The place in which they were gathered was shaken, and they were filled with the Holy Spirit (recalling Pentecost, 2:1-4). The first part of their petition, to speak *the word of God with boldness*, is fulfilled. In fact, this theme of speaking the word of God with "boldness" or "openness" (παρρασίας) is another dominant theme not only in this episode (see vv. 13, 29, and here in v. 31), but throughout the Book of Acts (see 2:29; 9:28; 13:46; 14:3; 18:26; 26:26; 28:31). Such boldness will surely be needed, as in the next episode the believers face conflict both within and without the community.

Tensions Within and Without, 4:32–5:42

Attention is turned again by way of a narrative summary (4:32-35) to the shape of this company of believers. Two case studies follow, providing positive and negative examples of how believers dealt with their possessions and commitments within the community. The final episode, 5:12-42, depicts the life of the community from an outsider's perspective. Here many of the themes found in 3:1–4:31 are repeated: the apostles are found healing the sick (5:12-16; cf. 3:1-10), which prompts the religious authorities to arrest them again and to bring them before the Sanhedrin for their second interrogation (5:17-42; cf. 3:11–4:22, see Tannehill 1990, 59–79). As the community is marked by unity and tension within, so it is characterized by similar challenges from without.

4:32–5:11. Tensions within. In 4:32-35, Luke reiterates the point of emphasis of the summary in 2:41-47. But this summary also provides an interesting variation to the themes found in chap. 2. Now, the believers took the proceeds from their sales and *laid it at the apostles' feet* (v. 35). To assume the posture of being at another's feet is a gesture of submission in the OT (Josh 10:24; 1 Sam 25:24, 41; 2 Sam 22:39; Pss 8:7; 110:1). Luke also employs this language of being at another's feet as a symbol of submission (Luke 7:38, 44, 45, 46; 8:35, 41; 10:39; 17:16; 20:43; Acts 2:35; 10:35; 22:3). So here in v. 35, laying the proceeds at the apostles' feet is more than just a way of taking care of an administrative detail. As Luke Johnson has noted: "When the believers lay their possessions at the Apostles' feet, therefore, they were symbolically laying themselves there, in a gesture of submission to the authority of the Twelve" (Johnson 1977, 202). In just such an act of submission, Barnabas lay his gift at the apostles' feet (vv. 36-37—see further comment on Barnabas at 11:19-30; 12:25).

Not everyone submitted themselves to the authority of the apostles, as the story of ANANIAS and Sapphira indicates (5:1-11). This story is linked linguistically to the previous two scenes by the words *at the apostles' feet* (v. 2) and depicts a negative example of community life. Ananias and Sapphira sell a piece of property, but they mock the community's Spirit of unity, and they usurp the authority of the apostles when they lay only a part of the proceeds at their feet.

Peter assumes the role of prophet when he confronts Ananias with the conspiracy (v. 3). Like Judas, Ananias has fallen prey to Satan (v. 3; cf. Luke 22:3), and like Judas, Ananias will not live to enjoy the material gains of his deceit (v. 5; see 1:17-18). Although Ananias has not lied verbally, the act of conspiracy itself was a *lie to the Holy Spirit* (v. 3).

Peter's remaining questions suggest that Ananias and Sapphira were not required to dispose of their property in this way, but could have retained authority over it (v. 4). But by taking this duplicitous action, they usurped the authority of the apostles. The offense was not simply against the community, Peter argues; it was against God. The problem was not simply a human one; it had serious spiritual dimensions, and as Ananias soon found out, serious repercussions. Upon hearing Peter's words, *he fell down and died* (v. 5).

After the disposal of Ananias and an interval—the narrator tells us—of *about three hours* (v. 7), Peter confronts Sapphira in what resembles a legal trial. The story drips rich with irony because the reader has knowledge Sapphira does not possess: the conspiracy is broken. Unknowingly Sapphira compounds the conspiracy with a verbal lie. Yes, she tells Peter, they sold the land *for such and such a price* (v. 8).

Peter's role as prophet becomes even more active when he predicts that this one who with her husband conspired against the community and God would now suffer the same fate as he (v. 8). And the final note of irony: Sapphira falls dead at Peter's feet. She who had feigned to lay her possessions at the apostles' feet now literally does fall at Peter's feet. The submission to apostolic authority she failed to give in life, she now gives permanently in death.

This grizzly story fulfills the threat of Peter's earlier sermon: *everyone who does not listen to that prophet will be utterly rooted out of the people* (3:23). No wonder that a *great fear seized the whole church and all who heard of these things* (v. 11).

5:12-42. Tensions without. This third and final summary (vv. 12-16), which describes the Jerusalem church, in several ways recalls a previous episode (3:1–4:31). First, there is the setting of Solomon's Portico that was the site of Peter's speech and the apostles' arrest (3:11–4:4). Second, the other half of the believers' prayer that *signs and wonders* be performed (4:30) is now fulfilled when the narrator reports: *Now many signs and wonders were done among the people through the apostles* (v. 12). Finally, the healing of one man in chap. 3 has now been generalized so that people carried their sick into the streets (vv. 14-15) where the apostles continue their benefaction (see 4:9), and *they were all cured* (v. 16). And, of course, the narrator does not miss an opportunity to record that *more than ever believers were added to the Lord, great numbers of both men and women* (v. 14). This summary is, however, distinct from the previous two in at least one important way. In contrast to the previous summaries (2:41-47; 4:32-35), "which looked inward at the internal life of the community, Luke's new summary looks outward at the public effect of the apostles on the Jewish people" (Krodel 1986, 124).

The public character of this summary scene is presumed in the closing episode of the chapter, vv. 17-42. The reader now learns of another response to the apostles than that of the people who *held them in high esteem* (v. 13). The high priest and the party of the Sadducees were *filled with jealousy* (v. 17). This response also explains further the timidity of the people who dared not join the believers (v. 13).

There is also remarkable redundancy between vv. 17-42 and Acts 4:1-22 (Tannehill 1990, 59–79). Both include the arrest of the apostles, their appearance before the Sanhedrin, short speeches that highlight the apostolic witness to Jesus and their commitment to obey God rather than the Sanhedrin, deliberation by the Sanhedrin out of the presence of the apostles, and the decision to release the apostles with the warning not to preach in Jesus' name. But variations in detail between these two accounts serve to heighten the tension of the narrative between the believers and the religious establishment. How will the church respond to these challenges from without?

In this closing episode, the conflict broadens: all of the apostles are placed in prison, not just Peter and John (cf. 4:3). This scene also adds the new dimension of divine intervention with an ironic twist. The narrator winks at the reader when he reports that the apostles are released from prison by an "angel," whose very existence the Sadducees deny (see 23:8). On the next morning, the officers find the prison guards standing watch over an empty cell (v. 23). The liberated apostles are found teaching in the Temple as they were instructed to do (v. 20), and they are quietly returned to the Sanhedrin (vv. 25-26).

The stage is set for the second interrogation (vv. 27-32). The old charge of teaching *in this name* (v. 27; cf. 4:7) is coupled with a new reaction by the Sadducees to the accusation that the apostles' teaching is intended to *bring this man's blood on us* (v. 28). The stakes have been raised considerably since the last confrontation. Peter responds with a confession similar to the one he made at the first interrogation (see 4:19): *We must obey God rather than any human authority* (v. 29). What had been a conditional sentence becomes a divine imperative, and the duet of Peter and John now becomes an apostolic chorus led by Peter.

They then employ the christological kerygma typical of the previous speeches (2:23-24, 36; 3:13-15; 4:10): *The God of our ancestors raised up Jesus, whom you had killed by hanging him on a tree* (v. 30). But rather than calling down this man's blood upon the Sadducees as the high priest had feared, the apostles argue that the exalted Jesus is the Leader and Savior who gives repentance and forgiveness of sins (v. 31). The speech concludes with the apostles reaffirming in unison their role as witnesses along with *the Holy Spirit whom God has given to those who obey him* (v. 32).

The apostles' insistence on the culpability of the religious leaders in Jesus' death, the need for Israel's repentance, and the reference to the gift of the *Spirit* (in which the Sadducees also did not believe—see 23:8) now not only annoys the Sadducees (see 4:2), but enrages them to the point of contemplating murder (v. 33). GAMALIEL, a PHARISEE member of the Council who was *respected by all the people*, swiftly stands and orders the apostles taken outside. In this tense moment, he offers a brief speech marked by restraint and caution. Citing the historical examples of Theudas and Judas the Galilean who were leaders of revolutionary movements that *came to nothing*, Gamaliel advises the council that *if this plan or this undertaking is of human origin, it will fail; but if it is of God, you will not be able to overthrow them* (vv. 38-39).

Of course, Luke's reader already knows from the divine intervention, the miraculous healings, and other signs and wonders, that *this plan* and *this deed* are, indeed, *of God*. The only conclusion to be drawn from

the narrator's point of view is that the Sanhedrin has already been found opposing God (v. 39). An angel had intervened earlier on behalf of the apostles in freeing them from prison; now the agent of intervention is a human one, a Pharisee, who compels by the wisdom of his argument.

So the Sanhedrin took Gamaliel's advice and released the apostles (v. 40). Again, the religious leaders charge them not to speak in the name of Jesus (see 4:18), but the conflict is heightened as the threats turn into beatings. Once again, the apostles boldly defy the Sanhedrin's instructions, and every day in their expressions of corporate worship, publicly in the Temple and privately at home (see 2:46), the apostles *did not cease to teach and proclaim Jesus as the Messiah* (v. 42). This plan and this deed must surely be of God.

Problems and Personalities, 6:1–12:25

The first five chapters of Acts focus on the action in and around Jerusalem, and the second half of Acts (chaps. 13–28) narrates the spread of the gospel by focusing on the places where the apostle Paul and his companions travel. These middle chapters, however, explore personalities more than places. The adventures of STEPHEN, PHILIP, PAUL, PETER, and BARNABAS fill these pages. Of course, the success of the gospel in overcoming problems in the community is still the underlying theme that holds these stories together (see the INCLUSIO formed by the references to the spreading of the word of God in 6:7 and 12:24), but this middle division provides perhaps the best justification for the title assigned to this work in the second century, the "Acts of the Apostles."

Stephen: His Witness and Death, 6:1–8:3

6:1-7. Structures and the spirit. This first scene serves two purposes: to provide another example of how conflict in the early Christian community is resolved (and schism thus avoided) and to introduce Stephen and Philip into the narrative.

To fulfill the first purpose, Luke employs a narrative pattern remarkably similar to the OT form for choosing auxiliary leadership (Exod 18 and Num 27): (1) statement of the problem—a grumbling among the Hellenists that Greek-speaking Jewish-Christian widows were being excluded from table fellowship (vv. 1-2; cf. Exod 18:14-18; Num 27:12-14); (2) the proposed solution—the apostles thus propose that they continue to devote themselves to *serving the word* (v. 4b) and that the newly appointed auxiliary leadership be responsible to *wait on tables* (vv. 2c-3; cf. Exod 18:19-23; Num 27:15-17); (3) requisite qualifications for new leadership—they are to be *of good standing, full of the Spirit and of wisdom* (v. 3), and, judging from their Greek names, they came from the part of the church that had complained about mistreatment of some of its constituency (v. 3b; cf. Exod 18:21; Num 27:18-21); (4) *setting apart the new leader ship*—the Seven are set apart by prayer and the laying on of hands (vv. 5-6; cf. Exod 18:25; Num 27:22-23; on this pattern, see Talbert 1984, 29).

This unit ends with a second reference to the way *the number of the disciples increased greatly in Jerusalem* (v. 7; cf. v. 1). The point is further emphasized by the notice that "the word of God grew" (author trans.: on this phrase, see the comments below, at 12:24). The narrator goes on to add that *a great many of the priests became obedient to the faith* (v. 7). The upshot for Luke, of course, is that despite the conflicts that threaten the unity of the fledgling community, the church is able to solve its problems and continues to grow.

6:8–7:1. The controversy. The tensions between the followers of Jesus and the leaders of the Jewish community, recounted in Acts 4 and 5, now continue with the story of Stephen, one of THE SEVEN. Stephen, whom the narrator again reminds the reader is *full of grace and power* (v. 8) and *wisdom and the Spirit* (v. 10) performs signs and wonders like the apostles before him (4:30). Stephen is soon engaged in a dispute by some diaspora Jews (originally from various places, but probably belonging now to one synagogue; cf. v. 9) who stir up the people and bring him before the Council (v. 12).

The scene before the Sanhedrin parallels (and intensifies) the encounters of the apostles with the Council with one significant variation. In the previous conflict scenes, the "people" sided with the apostles (cf. 4:21, 5:26; see Tannehill, 84); here the people are stirred up against Stephen, thus removing the buffer that had previously protected the apostles. Instead, the scene now more closely parallels the arrest and trial scene of Jesus. Like Jesus, Stephen is led into the Sanhedrin (v. 12; Luke 22:66); and the people are stirred first against Jesus, now against Stephen (see Luke 23:13-25).

The tension has escalated here in Acts to unprecedented proportions. Only during the ministry of Jesus had such tensions been previously experienced, a fact that only intensifies the suspense for the readers.

The charge of blasphemy against Stephen (see Luke 5:21) is specified by false witnesses: Stephen had proclaimed that Jesus would destroy the Temple and change the customs of Moses. Stephen will ultimately address both these charges (see comments on the speech below). The charges do not die with Stephen; they will resurface later against Paul (21:28). In response to the high priest's question regarding the validity of the charges, Stephen speaks.

7:2-53. The speech. The speech of Stephen is the longest in Acts and is very important for understanding the nature of the conflict in the Jewish community about the role and purposes of Jesus. The speech is not a comprehensive retelling of Jewish history; in fact, it is very selective. Nor is the story a dispassionate, neutral account; it is revisionist history from a Christian perspective. As is the case in so many discourses, both oral and written, the purpose of Stephen's recounting Israel's history comes into focus only at its conclusion. At the end of the speech, Stephen accuses his listeners of *opposing the Holy Spirit, just as your ancestors used to do* (v. 51). Specifically, just as the ancestors had persecuted the prophets, so now their descendants had betrayed and murdered the Righteous One whose coming the prophets had foretold (v. 52). Both ancestors and contemporaries had rejected the law they had received. In short, Stephen argues that the death of Jesus fit into the overall pattern of rejection that was characteristic of Israel's history. All that goes before this part of the speech leads, in one way or another, to this climax.

The speech itself is organized into five parts: (a) the story of Abraham, vv. 2-8; (b) the story of Joseph and the patriarchs, vv. 9-16; (c) the story of Moses in three parts of forty years each, vv. 17-29, 30-34, 35-43; (d) the story of the tent and the Temple, vv. 44-50; and finally (e) the invective against Stephen's listeners, vv. 51-53. In the speech, Stephen at times will quote the LXX, summarize its content, or at least in one significant instance, expand the story with more explicit details. All of the parts fit together to make up Stephen's Christian interpretation of Jewish history.

MOSES receives more attention in the speech than any other OT character. His life is divided into three periods of forty years each (see above). Although Jesus is not explicitly mentioned until v. 52 (and even there not by name), the retelling of Moses' story has striking similarities to the story of Jesus. These parallels are most clearly seen in the first and last units (vv. 17-29 and 35-43). In Stephen's reconstruction, the infancy and childhood of Moses is parallel with that of Jesus. Moses was beautiful before God (v. 20; cf. Exod 2:2); Jesus was in favor with God (Luke 2:52). Moses was instructed in wisdom (v. 22) as was Jesus (Luke 2:52). As an adult Moses, like Jesus, was "powerful in words and deeds" (v. 22; cf. Luke 24:19; Acts 2:22).

In the last unit (vv. 35-43), the parallels continue. Both Jesus and Moses (and Stephen—see v. 8) performed signs and wonders (v. 36; see 2:22). Both Moses and Jesus are prophets. The typology is made explicit in Moses' words to the Israelites, *God will raise up a prophet for you from your own people as he raised me up* (v. 37).

This theme of Jesus as the *prophet like [Moses]* (see 3:22) is the most important parallel and lies at the heart of the Stephen speech. The ignorance of the people regarding Moses' call (v. 25) and their subsequent rejection of him (v. 35) foreshadow the rejection of Jesus by the people (v. 52).

The rejection of God's representatives is no less than a rejection of God himself. That is the point made at the end of the episode about Moses. Not knowing what had happened to Moses (v. 40), the people turn to idolatry, making a calf and sacrificing to it (v. 41). God then turns away from them and gives them up to their idolatry (vv. 42-43). The people have not only rejected Moses; they have rejected God.

The Moses' episode also contains Stephen's first response to his accusers that Stephen had claimed that Jesus would change the *customs that Moses handed on to us* (6:14). The rhetoric of Stephen's argument indicates that the Jewish leadership, not the followers of Jesus, are responsible for abandoning Moses and the law (v. 39; cf. v. 53). From Stephen's (i.e., Luke's) perspective, the Christian community is the "true Israel," i.e., the group within Judaism that is authentically preserving the customs of Moses as they reflect the purpose and destiny of what it means to be the people of God.

The second charge against Stephen, that he claimed that Jesus would destroy *this place* (6:14, i.e., the Temple), is addressed in the next unit (vv. 44-50). Here Stephen's complaint is not against the existence of the Temple per se, but rather against the view that God's presence is limited to a particular place. To worship God in "this place" was not to be understood as limiting God's self-disclosure to the Temple. Although Stephen does not make explicit the consequences for violating the purposes of the Temple as he

did the claim that God would judge the people's misunderstanding of Moses and his *customs* (6:14; cf. vv. 42-43), Luke's readers no doubt understood this invective against the background of the destruction of the Temple. Luke, then, in Stephen's speech, is not only drawing on the content of OT history, he is employing the familiar pattern of the Deuteronomistic history of disobedience, punishment, call to repentance, and restoration to make sense of the Temple's destruction. The people had defied the purpose of Temple worship and suffered then the destruction of that institution.

The climax of the speech, as we noted above, occurs here at the end. Both ancestors and contemporaries were guilty of *forever opposing the Holy Spirit* (v. 51). They had rejected the prophets from Moses to Jesus, they had an inadequate understanding of where and how they were to worship, and they had rejected the laws and customs of Moses. They had not kept the things that had been *ordained by angels* (v. 53), and now they were about to reject the one whose *face was like the face of an angel* (6:15).

7:54–8:3. The martyrdom. The speech results in the stoning of Stephen (reminiscent of the stoning of NABOTH in 1 Kgs 21:8-13). Earlier in the Pentecost sermon, Peter had leveled similar accusations against his listeners that *cut to the heart* (2:37) and led to their repentance. Here those whose hearts and ears are *uncircumcised* (7:51) harden their hearts and cover *their ears* (v. 57) and drag Stephen out of the city to stone him, with one Saul aiding and abetting them.

Actually this violent action only occurs after Stephen has recounted his vision of *the Son of Man standing at the right hand of God!* (v. 56). The term SON OF MAN, occurs only here outside the Gospels, and the curious detail that the Son of Man is standing rather than sitting (see Luke 22:69) may be taken in a juridical sense where Jesus stands as in advocacy for Stephen before God.

The last words of Stephen continue the parallels with Jesus begun in 6:8-15: *Lord Jesus, receive my spirit*, spoken by Stephen in 7:59 is reminiscent of Jesus' word from the cross: "Father, into your hands I commend my spirit" (Luke 23:46); and Stephen's final words, *Lord, do not hold this sin against them* (v. 60), echo Jesus' prayer: "Father, forgive them, for they do not know what they are doing" (Luke 23:43). Stephen, like Jesus in the third Gospel, dies the death of an innocent martyr and thus takes his place as yet another example of a prophet who, because he spoke of *the coming of the Righteous One* (7:52), is the victim of *stiff-necked people* who continue to persecute the representatives of God (7:51).

Luke concludes this section (8:1-3) with the notice that this persecution was not limited to Stephen, but was against the whole Jerusalem church (v. 1). Chief among those persecuting the church is one Saul who by dragging the believers to prison (v. 3; cf. Luke 21:12) is inadvertently contributing to the growth of the Word, as the next unit indicates.

Philip: A Man on Mission, 8:4-40

Philip is the other member of the Seven who, with Stephen, plays a major role in the story. With Philip's ministry, the gospel enters the area of the Samaritans. In chap. 8, he is the focus of two very important episodes and is in dialogue with two of the most interesting characters in Acts: SIMON MAGUS and the ETHIOPIAN EUNUCH.

8:4-25. Philip and Simon: miracles vs. magic. From the second century, Simon has been characterized as the first Gnostic and archrival to Christianity (Justin, *Apol* 1.26.1-3; 1.56.2; *Trypho* 120; Irenaeus, *AdvHaer*, 1.23). The text of Acts, however, is silent on the final destiny of Simon, and unfortunately these later reflections have preoccupied most interpreters of Acts 8. Comments here will be limited to what can be gleaned from the narrative of Acts itself (see Garrett 1989, 61–78, for a detailed exposition).

One of Luke's purposes in recording Philip's encounter with Simon was to respond to charges that the signs and wonders performed by early Christian missionaries were indistinguishable from the magical practices of antiquity. Luke concedes (contra later apologists) that outwardly there are similarities between Christian miracle workers and magicians, but then argues that the similarities are only superficial: at a deeper level there are profound differences between "Christian miracles" and "pagan magic." Luke makes this point forcefully in the Simon Magus episode.

On first reading there are striking parallels between the acts of Philip and Simon. Only closer reading of the text demonstrates the fundamental difference between the two: Simon's deeds point to himself in an act of self-aggrandizement; Philip's signs point to the kingdom of God and corroborate his proclamation of the Christian gospel. In fact, the opening passage about Philip ties his words and deeds very closely together: *The crowds with one accord listened eagerly to what was said by Philip, hearing and seeing the signs that*

he did (v. 6). What was the content of this message? Luke fills it out later in the narrative claiming that Philip *was proclaiming the good news about the kingdom of God and the name of Jesus Christ* (v. 12).

So to preach the gospel for Philip was to proclaim (1) that Jesus was the "Christ," the one God had anointed for *doing good and healing all who were oppressed by the devil* (as Peter would put it in 10:38); (2) that the KINGDOM OF GOD, inaugurated in the ministry of Jesus, would be completed when all of Christ's enemies—surely including Satan himself—had been brought into submission at Christ's feet (cf. 2:34); and (3) that this proclamation "in the name of Jesus" would issue forth in the forgiveness or liberation from sin and Satan's authority to the power of God. In other words, "Philip's message about the Christ, the Kingdom of God, and the name of Jesus was implied also to be a message about release from Satan's authority" (Garrett 1989, 65). Hence, Philip's signs and wonders—the healings and exorcisms—were outward signs reinforcing his message: Satan is being overcome, and the kingdom of God is being established.

In contrast to Philip, the deeds of Simon Magus were performed only to bring glory to himself. In a flashback (v. 9), the readers learn that Simon had been amazing the Samaritans with his magic and that they have designated him as the *power of God* (vv. 9-11). This claim stands in direct contrast to Luke's depiction of Jesus. From Luke's perspective, *the power of God* (v. 10) was in Jesus, or upon Jesus, or with Jesus, but the power of God was always distinct *from* Jesus. That Simon does not reject this title (as Paul and Barnabas do in Acts 14:11-15) but rather encourages it through his magic, places him in the tradition of the "false prophets" who throughout Jewish history, and now in Christian history, reject the way of God (now most clearly revealed in the ministry of Jesus and his followers) in favor of idolatry (cf. Luke 6:22-23; Acts 7:51-52). As such, Simon is depicted as an agent of Satan who is an opponent to God and the "true prophets" of Christianity. Nonetheless, this section ends with Simon believing, being baptized, and being constantly amazed (cf. v. 11) at *the signs and great miracles* of Philip (v. 13).

The sincerity of Simon's conversion has long been questioned because of this closing climactic scene. The opening notice (vv. 14-17) that the Jerusalem apostles prayed for the new believers and that they received the HOLY SPIRIT *after* their BAPTISM stands in contrast with the sequence in Acts 2:38 and argues against basing any *rigid* doctrine of the relationship between baptism and the gift of the Spirit on Acts.

More important, however, is Luke's report that Simon tried to buy the Holy Spirit from the apostles (v. 18). This detail confirms the earlier impression that Simon is portrayed as a false prophet, an agent of Satan. Magicians practiced their art for money, and as Hermas noted, the false prophet "accepts rewards for his prophecy, and if he does not receive them he does not prophesy" (*Man* 11:12). Although it is true that here Simon is offering money and not receiving it, clearly if he is willing to pay money for the use of the Spirit, he will later accept payment when he employs its power. In contrast, Peter makes it clear that the apostles would never take money for what they do (see 3:6). "Thereby Luke demonstrates that the Christians do not share one of the most widely recognized traits of practitioners of magic" (Garrett 1989, 70).

The fate of Simon is ambiguous. The language of Peter's curse is reminiscent of OT curses of idolatry (see esp. Deut 29:17-19). Either Simon is to repent of his wickedness, i.e., his idolatry, or he (and his money!) is to be condemned to eternal destruction at the judgment (vv. 20-22). Although he has supposedly entered the Christian community, Simon is still in *the chains of wickedness* (v. 23), i.e., still under the authority of Satan, and has not fully experienced Philip's message of liberation from sin. Simon beseeches Peter and John to pray for him that he might be spared this judgment. Luke perhaps does not know the fate of Simon and thus leaves the conclusion uncertain. More important to Luke is the fact that in this encounter Satan and his agent have been overcome, and the path is cleared for the preaching of the gospel in Samaria. So Peter and John (one of the two who had earlier offered to call fire down to consume the Samaritans! Luke 9:54) do indeed proclaim *the good news to many villages of the Samaritans* (v. 25).

8:26-40. Philip and the Ethiopian eunuch: What hinders me? The next pericope involving Philip is foundational to Luke's theology and certainly is the most exotic in its details. Philip is characterized as a prophet and preacher, and his entrance and exit in the story is reminiscent of ELIJAH and EZEKIEL (1 Kgs 18:12; 2 Kgs 2:16; Ezek 11:24). The story also echoes another foundational story in Luke and Acts: the two on the road to EMMAUS (see also the parallels with Luke 4:16-30 and Acts 13:13-43). Just as Jesus opens the scriptures to CLEOPAS and his companion, so Philip explains Isa 53:7-8 to the eunuch. Both Jesus and Philip make quick exits from the story (Luke 24:31; Acts 8:39). Finally the two stories relate to the two ordinances of the church—the Emmaus story to the LORD'S SUPPER and the Ethiopian eunuch episode to Baptism. Also noteworthy are the parallels between this episode and the other three conversion stories recorded in this immediate context: the conversion of the Samaritans (8:4-13), the conversion of Paul (9:1-31), and the conversion of CORNELIUS (Acts 10:1–11:18). Most striking is the way Luke intensifies the element of divine intervention and providence in the last three episodes as the Spirit directs Philip, Paul (and Ananias), and Peter (and Cornelius; for other parallels with the Cornelius episode, see Tannehill 1990, 110–11).

Another way of understanding the meaning of the passage is by probing its form. Most scholars agree that a chiastic structure shapes the unit, although they disagree about its details. At the heart of any structure, however, lies the citation from the OT and the eunuch's questions. The quotation of Isa 53:7-8 is the only time in Luke or Acts when the narrator quotes the OT directly, apart from the lips of an individual character. Philip uses this OT text to tell *the good news about Jesus* (v. 35).

This kind of messianic exegesis was not as unusual as is sometimes thought. In first-century Judaism, interpreters were using a method of messianic exegesis to interpret the Hebrew scriptures, often providing messianic interpretations of scriptures that originally were not messianic prophecies. The messianic exegesis of Christians was not unique because they saw the Messiah foretold in the scriptures (their Jewish contemporaries saw that as well); the uniqueness lay in the fact that they believed this Messiah had already come in the person of Jesus Christ. Convinced of the truth of Philip's message, the eunuch lets forth with the refrain of an unhindered gospel that runs throughout Acts: *Look, here is water! What is to prevent me from being baptized?* (v. 36; cf. 10:47; 28:31). How is it, though, that the story of the Ethiopian eunuch bears witness to this "unhindered" gospel?

The answer may be found in the very description of this new convert: the Ethiopian eunuch. Implicit in each of those words are two very important characteristics. First, he is an Ethiopian, which informs the readers of the geographic and ethnographic significance of this conversion. Ethiopia was viewed by people of antiquity as lying at the southernmost end or limit of the earth (see e.g., Homer, *Iliad* 23.205–97; Herodotus, *Hist* 3.114–15; Strabo, *Geog* 1.2.27–28;

2.2.2). Thus the conversion of an Ethiopian represents "the symbolic (and partial) fulfillment of Acts 1:8c of mission to 'the end of the earth' " (Martin 1989, 120). Second, it is also well documented in ancient literature that skin color was an Ethiopian's most distinctive feature. Homer (*Odyssey* 19.244-48), Herodotus (*Hist* 2.29-32; 3.17-24; 4.183, 197), and Seneca (*Naturales Questiones* IV A. 218), among others, all refer to the dark skin of the Ethiopians. What is the ethnographic significance of the Ethiopian's conversion? Clarice Martin (1989, 114) argues that "the story of a black African . . . from what would be perceived as a distant nation to the south of the empire is consistent with the Lukan emphasis on 'universalism,' a recurrent motif in both Luke and Acts, and one that is well known."

The Ethiopian is also a eunuch, from which the readers infer two additional items. He is, first of all, an outsider, since Deut 23:2 forbids a castrated person from entrance into the assembly of the Lord and probably precluded even proselyte status. In the Acts passage, he has just returned from Jerusalem where he had gone to worship and was, no doubt, relegated to the outermost chambers of the Temple. For Luke, then, the Ethiopian eunuch is a God-fearing gentile and, as such, is the first gentile convert to Christianity. Commentators who resist this conclusion normally do so to preserve Cornelius as the first gentile convert and Peter as the founder of the gentile mission. The significance of Cornelius notwithstanding, the conversion of the Ethiopian eunuch is Luke's report of how, through Philip, the gospel reached the "end of the earth" and the gentile mission was initiated. Again, the reader is put in the superior position of knowing more about the story of the early church's progress than any of its characters.

Philip in these two stories is depicted as a man on mission. He is pressing the boundaries, with the apostles scrambling to keep up. He preaches the gospel, and Samaritans and a representative from the "ends of the earth" are converted. Evidently, it will take the Jerusalem church some time before it comes to the same position and then only through the insistence of the apostle to the gentiles, Paul. Later, Paul finds Philip in Caesarea (21:8) where the narrator left him. But now Philip is not alone; he has four unmarried daughters *who had the gift of prophecy* (21:9), and no doubt Philip's encouragement to exercise it. Not only is Philip's adventuresome spirit reaffirmed for the reader, but his openness to the fresh winds of God's Spirit has been passed on to another generation.

Paul: His Conversion and Call, 9:1-31

It would be difficult to overestimate the significance of the conversion of Paul for the narrative of Acts or, indeed, the course of early Christian history. Acts 9 is the first of three accounts in Acts of Paul's conversion (see chaps. 22 and 26). The accounts are slightly different in detail and tone (see the comments on chap. 22 for a discussion of the variations), but the repetition of the event indicates its importance for Luke. The passage in Acts 9 is not only about the conversion of Paul; it is also the narration of his call and commission to become the "apostle to the gentiles." As such, it shares similar formal features with other commissioning stories, both within Luke and Acts (e.g., Luke 1:5-25, 26-38; 2:8-20; 24:36-53; Acts 5:17-21; 10:1-8, 9-23; 16:9-10; 18:9-11; etc.) and throughout the biblical narratives (see e.g., Gen 17:1-4; Exod 3:1–4:16; Judg 6:11-24; 1 Kgs 19:1-19a; Matt 28:1-8; Mark 16:1-8; John 20:19-23; see Hubbard for other references and a list of the formal features associated with the commissioning story). Acts 9 then is about the conversion of Paul from a persecutor of Christ to one persecuted for Christ and Paul's call to be apostle to the gentiles.

9:1-25. Paul in Damascus. The unit is organized into two parts. The first part describes the events in and around DAMASCUS; the second details Paul's preaching ministry in JERUSALEM. The following chiastic arrangement for this first unit has been suggested (see Talbert 1984, 40):

A Paul plots against the Christians in Damascus, 1-2
  B Paul sees the vision, is blinded, and fasts, 3-9
    C Ananias sees a vision,
        is commissioned to go to Paul, 10-14
      D Paul's mission is foretold by Christ, 15-16
    C' Ananias goes to Paul, reports his vision, 17
  B' Paul's sight is restored,
      he is baptized and eats, 18-19a
A' Paul preaches Christ in Damascus,
    the Jews plot to kill him, 19b-25

Paul reappears in the opening verses of chap. 9. He was last mentioned in 8:3 where he was *ravaging the church*. Here in chap. 9 he is still *breathing threats and murder against the disciples of the Lord* (v. 1) and seeks permission to extend his persecution beyond Jerusalem to Damascus. The description of Paul here recalls Stephen's invective against those who *are forever opposing the Holy Spirit* (7:51-52).

Paul is not the only character to receive a vision in this episode; the Lord also visits Ananias, a disciple in Damascus (vv. 10-14). This "double vision" provides for Paul a (reluctant) deliverer from his blindness. Ananias's vision also supplies the content of Paul's call (vv. 15-16). In the CHIASM above, these verses lie at the heart of the passage and should be taken as its primary focus. Two points are made: (1) Paul is to be an *instrument whom I* [Christ] *have chosen to bring my name before Gentiles and kings and before the people of Israel* (v. 15) and (2) that Paul *must suffer for the sake of my name* (v. 16). Paul's call to the gentile mission cannot be separated from his call to suffer. His entire ministry throughout Acts is characterized by a mission in which he experiences rejection and persecution (cf. 13:46-47; 20:19-21; 22:15-18). As such, he stands in the long line of persecuted prophets that extend from Moses to Jesus and more recently to Stephen. But Paul does not have to wait until his "first" missionary journey to experience this suffering. His first preaching tour in Damascus ends with a narrow escape from his persecutors in a basket.

9:26-31. Paul in Jerusalem. This emphasis on the suffering character of Paul's ministry continues in this next episode of Paul in Jerusalem. The events in Damascus and Jerusalem are almost exact parallels (Gill 1974, 547-48).

Damascus	Jerusalem
Ananias hesitates to believe that Paul has been converted, 13-14.	The disciples fear Paul, "not believing that he is a disciple," 26.
The Lord reassures him, 15-16.	Barnabas reassures them, 27.
Ananias goes to Paul, cures, and baptizes him, 17-192.	
Paul is *with* the disciples in Damascus, 19b.	"Paul was *with* them going in and out at Jerusalem," 28a.
Paul preaches immediately in the synagogues, 20-22.	Paul speaks freely in the name of the Lord, 28b-29a.
The Jews plot to kill Paul, 23-24.	The Hellenists try to kill him, 29b.
Paul escapes, 25.	Paul escapes, 30.

Gill has commented on the significance of this parallelism: "The Jerusalem episode acts out for a second time the theme of preaching and persecution which Luke has placed as a heading over the whole chapter" (Gill 1974, 548). The zealous persecutor of Christ and his church has become the zealous missionary persecuted in Christ's name and for his church.

Peter: His Words and Deeds, 9:32–11:18

The next three scenes, the healing of AENEAS, the raising of Tabitha, and the conversion of Cornelius, may all be grouped under the larger heading "the acts of Peter." Theologically, all three stories serve to underscore the inclusive nature of the gospel, as well as to reveal further the complex character of PETER. Pairing stories of men and women is typical of Luke. Further, to join two shorter stories with a longer third one to make basically the same point is not uncommon to Luke. In fact, these stories are similar to Luke 15 where we have the two briefer stories of the lost sheep and the lost coin standing alongside the much longer story of the lost sons—with all three describing the joy in the kingdom when that which was lost is found. As with these three parables, readers can also detect the movement in these three stories in Acts to open the gospel to all persons.

9:32-43. Peter's raising of Aeneas and Tabitha. While evidently on a preaching tour, Peter encounters a paralyzed *saint* in Lydda who had been bedridden. Now for the second time (see Acts 3:1-10), Peter heals a lame man. The story is bare and unadorned with details; the narrator gets right to the point. Peter informs Aeneas that "Jesus Christ heals you; get up and make your bed!"

The reader is led to empathize more deeply with Tabitha and her mourners in the next scene. Tabitha (which the narrator tells us means DORCAS or "Gazelle") is described as one who is *devoted to good works and acts of charity* (v. 36—cf. the description later of Cornelius in 10:1 of the next episode). The products of her benevolence are made explicit when the widows who are mourning her death show to Peter *the tunics and other clothing Dorcas had made while she was with them* (v. 39). Quite possibly, they are wearing the garments (the verb is in the middle voice; for the widows to lose Dorcas was to lose their benefactor.

Once again, the problem of helpless Greek-speaking Jewish-Christian widows resurfaces in the narrative (cf. 6:1). Peter orders everyone outside (like Jesus, see Luke 8:51) and commands, *Tabitha, get up* (again reminiscent of Jesus' words in Mark 5:41). She, too, is raised, and he presents her alive to the saints and widows (v. 41).

These two stories share much in common: they echo the ELIJAH-ELISHA cycles of 1–2 Kings, as well as events in the career of Jesus (Acts 9:32-35 = Luke 5:18-26; Acts 9:36-43 = Luke 8:40-56). Further, unlike most healing stories in Luke and Acts, the healed persons here are named (contra Luke 5:17-26; 11:14-23; 18:35-43; Acts 3:1-10; 14:8-18). Both Aeneas and Tabitha are healed through divine power (vv. 34, 40). In their respective locales, both healings result in many conversions to the faith (vv. 35 and 42).

Finally, the raising of a lame man and the resuscitation of a dead woman are more similar than might appear at first glance. In the ancient Mediterranean world, the body was divided into three symbolic zones: (1) the heart-eyes, which is the zone of emotions and thoughts; (2) the mouth-ears, which is the zone of self-expressive speech; and (3) the hands-feet, which is the zone of purposeful action (Pilch 1991, 204). Aeneas's healing obviously falls into the zone of purposeful action. But resuscitations are also related to this zone; the dead can perform no purposeful act (Pilch 1991, 205). Thus, both healings share in the same symbolic zone; Aeneas and Tabitha are healed so they can resume their places as contributing members of the Christian community and walk in *the Way* (9:2).

10:1–11:18. The conversion of Cornelius and Peter. Many scholars focus in this story on the significance of the conversion of CORNELIUS and his household for the spread of the gospel to the gentiles in Acts. This episode does represent a critical turning point in the narrative of Acts. Equally as important, though, is the conversion of Peter to a new point of view, namely, that salvation knows no human boundaries and that *God shows no partiality* (v. 34). The chapter divisions here (as in many other places in scripture) are misleading. The episode actually divides into seven scenes (see Haenchen 1971, 357–59), interrelated by much repetition (the vision of Cornelius is reported four times; Peter's vision is twice related; and all of chap. 11 is basically a summary of chap. 10).

Scene 1. 10:1-8. Cornelius's vision in Caesarea. Cornelius, a centurion (see Luke 7:1-10), is favorably described by Luke as a *devout* man who practiced traditional Jewish piety in almsgiving and prayer, although he was himself a gentile "God-fearer." In this opening scene, Cornelius has a vision in which he is told his prayers and alms have been heard and accepted (v. 4) and that he should send to Joppa for a certain Simon Peter. Without further question, Cornelius complies by dispatching two personal servants and a soldier to fetch Peter. Throughout the narrative the activities are directed from above (cf. chap. 9), but that does not mean there is no human response to this divine activity. Rather, the pattern here is that the divine revelations or epiphanies of both Cornelius and Peter are incomplete (Tannehill 1990, 129) and are only understood after further reflection and interaction with other human characters. Revelation here is depicted in contextual and interrelational terms, which means that both Cornelius and Peter have to move with the light they have before they can receive further illumination.

Scene 2. 10:9-16. Peter's vision in Joppa. Peter, like Cornelius, experiences a vision while at prayer (v. 10). This vision, too, is incomplete. Three times Peter is shown a sheet with all kinds of animals on it and is commanded to eat. Three times he refuses, claiming, *By no means, Lord, for I have never eaten anything that is profane or unclean* (v. 14). Is he thrice resisting temptation (cf. Luke 3) or thrice denying his Lord (cf. Luke 23)? The final response of the heavenly voice makes Peter's resistance clear: *What God has made clean, you must not call profane* (v. 15). What remains unclear is the subject of this vision. Is Peter to disregard Jewish dietary laws or is something else at stake?

Scene 3. 10:17-23a. Cornelius's men in Joppa. While Peter is wondering about the vision, Cornelius's emissaries arrive in JOPPA. The puzzled Peter is still obedient enough to respond to the Spirit's call to go with these men *without hesitation* (v. 20) or "without discrimination" (author trans.). Peter takes the first step in understanding his vision by extending hospitality to these gentile visitors and giving them a night's lodging.

Scene 4. 10:23b-33. Peter in Caesarea. The vision comes more into focus with Peter's visit to CAESAREA. After correcting Cornelius's mistaken assumption that Peter is a god (vv. 25-26), Peter takes the next step in correctly interpreting his vision when he sees the crowd of gentiles gathered in Cornelius's house and says, *You yourselves know that it is unlawful for a Jew to associate with or to visit a gentile* [Peter now has done both], *but God has shown me that I should not call anyone profane or unclean* (v. 28; cf. the restrictions of *Jub* 22:16; *JosAsen* 7:1).

Sociologists use the term "map" to designate "the concrete and systematic patterns of organizing, locating, and classifying persons, places, times, actions, etc. according to some abstract notion of 'purity' or order" (Neyrey 1991, 278). Peter understands that the vision of the sheet is not just about what can or cannot be eaten, that is, a cultural "map of the body"; but more importantly it addresses the question of who is and is not clean, i.e., the question of a radically new cultural "map of persons." Just as Stephen proposed a new map of holy places (which did not limit "holy space" to the Temple), so Peter is being directed to draw a new cultural map of people which was radically inclusive and gave gentiles a place on the map. The issue of the vision is not whether gentiles can be included in salvation: Peter has heard Jesus say as much (Luke 24:47) and has himself preached it (Acts 2:39; 3:25-26). The obstacle for the Jewish Christian to launch the gentile mission is gentile uncleanness that obstructs Jewish-gentile social relationships. The vision of the sheet now removes that obstacle.

Scene 5. 10:34-43. Peter's speech. After Cornelius recounts his vision (vv. 30-33, now for the third time), Peter responds to Cornelius's invitation to address the assembly. His speech falls into three parts: the introduction (vv. 34-36), the kerygma (vv. 37-41), and the conclusion (vv. 42-43). Peter's conversion to this new perspective of gentile cleanness is completed in the opening line of this speech: *I truly understand that God shows no partiality* (v. 34).

The next two verses are grammatically troublesome, and their meaning is obscured by both RSV and NRSV. Perhaps the best way to understand these verses is reflected in the following translation:

> Truly I perceive that God shows no partiality, but in every nation anyone who fears him and practices righteousness is acceptable to him. This [namely, the statement just made] is the word which he sent to the children of Israel, preaching good news of peace through Jesus Christ—He is Lord of all (vv. 34b-36, cited by Krodel 1986, 196).

This translation makes "He is Lord of all" the centerpiece of the thought unit rather than a disruptive or intrusive phrase (in parentheses in RSV). Both God (who "shows no partiality") and Jesus (who is "Lord of all") support Peter's perspective on the radically inclusive nature of the Gospel. The kerygma that follows (vv. 37-41) characterizes Jesus' ministry as one of benefaction, a particularly appropriate image for a gentile audience familiar with patronage and especially the audience in Cornelius's house who no doubt had personally enjoyed the benefits of Cornelius's benefaction.

Peter ends his speech (vv. 43-44) by returning to the theme of universality: *everyone who believes in him receives forgiveness of sins through his name.*

Scene 6. 10:44-48. The gentile Pentecost. Before Peter could finish speaking (v. 44), a second Pentecost occurs: the Holy Spirit falls on these gentiles. As in the first Pentecost, the gift of the Spirit is con firmed for the "circumcised believers" when *they heard them* [the gentiles] *speaking in tongues and extolling God* (v. 46). Peter strikes a major theme of Acts again when he asks, "Is anyone able to hinder the water for baptizing these who have received the Holy Spirit just like us?" (author trans.). The answer for Luke is, of course not. Just as earlier nothing could hinder the Ethiopian eunuch from being baptized (8:36) and later not even prison could hinder Paul from preaching the gospel (28:31), so now the barrier of gentile uncleanness could no longer hinder the inclusion of gentiles into the kingdom although it would indeed be the subject of one more debate (see chap. 15).

Scene 7. 11:1-18. Reporting to the Jerusalem church. The conversion of Cornelius and his household, as noted earlier, is important not because Cornelius is the first gentile converted in Acts (that honor belongs to the Ethiopian eunuch), but because his is the first gentile conversion publicly acknowledged by the Jerusalem church. Most of chap. 11 is a recapitulation (with some interesting variations) of the events reported in chap. 10. Most important are the opening verses that set the context: Peter is asked to defend his actions, not of ordering these gentiles to be baptized, but of eating with the "uncircumcised," i.e., of rewriting the "cultural map" of persons (see above). After recounting the incident (again the repetition points out the significance of this event for Luke), Peter asks, *Who was I that I could hinder God?* (v. 17; on "hinder" see the comments on scene 6 above). The question is not intended to be rhetorical, and the silence is finally broken when these Jewish Christians from Jerusalem praise God saying, *Then God has given even to the Gentiles the repentance that leads to life* (v. 18).

The issue of gentile inclusion in the church is by no means resolved, as Acts 15 demonstrates, but at least Peter's conversion is as complete as that of Cornelius and his household. For Peter, at least, as far as Jews and gentiles were concerned, God *has made no distinction between them and us* (15:9).

Barnabas, Peter, and Herod: Contrasting Examples, 11:19–12:25

In Luke's version of the last supper, a dispute arose among the disciples as to who was to be regarded as the greatest. In Luke 22:25-26, Jesus says, "The kings of the Gentiles lord it over them; and those in authority over them are called benefactors. But not so with you; rather the greatest among you must become like the youngest, and the leader like one who serves." In a sense, this episode (Acts 11:19–12:25) provides an exegesis by example of the saying in Luke 22. The contrasts between displays of divine and earthly power are striking.

11:19-30; 12:25. Barnabas and the church at Antioch. Luke presents the fledgling church at ANTIOCH as a case study of the mission of the early church. The church at Antioch receives considerable attention from Luke. It is established just after the conversion of Cornelius. Antioch was primarily a "Hellenistic city" (although there was a significant Jewish population of between 25,000 and 50,000). Antioch's population of 500,000 to 800,000 ranked it third largest in the Roman Empire (Polhill 1992, 268–69). The church was founded by Hellenists who *were scattered because of the persecution that took place over Stephen* (v. 19). Although some Hellenists spoke only to Jews, Christians from Cyprus and Cyrene evangelized the gentiles in Antioch. These Hellenistic Jewish-Christians who themselves had grown up in the gentile environment of the dispersion were sensitive to the cultural back ground of the Antiochenes and spoke not of Jesus as the Jewish Messiah, but rather proclaimed *the Lord Jesus* (v. 20), a title more familiar to those gentiles.

After the church was established and then encouraged and confirmed by BARNABAS and PAUL (vv. 22-26), the church at Antioch had the opportunity to minister to the believers in the church at Jerusalem, a clear sign that those first missionaries encouraged mission not only *to* but *with* the Antiochenes.

The Antiochenes' sensitivity to the plight of Judea is remarkable for several reasons. First, the famine was not confined to Judea, but rather evidently Antioch itself was gripped by famine during this time (ca. 46–47 C.E.). Second, the city of Antioch had experienced numerous disasters itself over the past one hundred years that must have left their mark on the collective memory of the inhabitants. In the midst of their own suffering, the Antiochene Christians reached out to those in need, not out of plenty but out of want.

Barnabas embodies this spirit of generosity so characteristic of the Antiochene Christians. When the disciples decide to send relief *to the believers living in Judea,* they send it by the hands of Barnabas and Saul (vv. 29-30). Like Saul (Acts 7:58), Barnabas makes a cameo appearance before assuming the center stage of

the gentile mission (4:36-37; see Acts 11, 15). He provides a concrete example of those believers who demonstrated their commitment to the apostles' authority by laying the proceeds from the sale of his property at the apostles' feet (4:35).

The narrator supplies several interesting details about Barnabas; he is a LEVITE (who in the OT had no portion in the land!—see Deut 12:12; 14:29) and a native of Cyprus. But the most important detail is that the apostles have given him a surname, Barnabas. That the apostles have given this name is another indication that Barnabas has submitted himself to the authority of the apostles.

> By having one of the two great leaders of the gentile mission express submission to the Twelve by receiving from them a new name and laying his goods at their feet, Luke is subtly but effectively creating an image in the reader's mind: the image of the Gentile mission under the authority of the Twelve (Johnson 1977, 202).

Also noteworthy is the translation the narrator provides for Barnabas's name, *Son of encouragement* (4:36). The significance lies less in the etymology of the Aramaic than it does in the role Barnabas will play later in this story. Barnabas is a sign both of submission to the apostles and of encouragement to fellow believers. While the Jews plot to kill Saul and the believers are afraid of him and doubt that he is a disciple (9:23-27), Barnabas takes the risk of befriending Saul, bringing him before the apostles, and confirming Saul's Damascus-road experience before them (9:27). When the church in Jerusalem hears about Greeks who had *turned to the Lord* in Antioch (vv. 19-21), they send Barnabas to Antioch, and he "encouraged [see 4:36] them all to remain faithful to the Lord with steadfast purpose" (v. 23, author trans.).

But Barnabas's submission to apostolic authority is not blind loyalty. When he turns his attention to the gentile mission, he is sent out, not by the apostles, but by the Holy Spirit (13:4; see also 13:43, 46, 50). The active role of Barnabas in the Apostolic Conference (chap. 15) is direct testimony to the way in which he (and Paul) held respect for the apostles' authority in tension with submission to the guidance of the Holy Spirit. This Barnabas who is (not blindly) loyal to the apostles and a continuing source of encouragement to the community (see also 15:36-40) stands in sharp contrast not only to the story of Ananias and Sapphira, but to the following story about Herod.

12:1-24. Herod: unmasking the powers. With the note of true Christian benefaction ringing in their ears, the readers are introduced to the manufactured benefaction of a tyrant, HEROD. In between is sandwiched the story of Peter's deliverance from prison. This chapter is one of the most delightful in Acts, but it is not only entertaining; it is also profitable, for it demonstrates Luke's understanding of the nature and locale of true power.

In the opening scene (vv. 1-5), Herod (whom the first- and twentieth-century reader might mistakenly identify as the wicked king of the Gospels) had JAMES, John's brother, *killed with the sword* (v. 2). Seeing this curried the favor of the Jews, Herod determines to serve them Peter as well. Perhaps aware of Peter's reputation as an escape artist (see 5:19-26), he places Peter under close watch around the clock (v. 4).

In an aside, the narrator notes that the arrest of Peter occurred during the PASSOVER (v. 3). This detail is important for several reasons. First, it accounts for the reason Peter did not immediately suffer the same fate as John; Herod wished to avoid a tumult of the people (see v. 4). This setting also parallels this deliverance scene with the passion of Jesus, which also occurred during the festival of Unleavened Bread (Luke 22:1, 7). (By now, the reader has noted the frequency with which the experience of the church parallels the experiences of Jesus.) Finally, the setting creates the biting irony of Peter in chains during the very festival that celebrated the deliverance of Israel from bondage in Egypt (see Pervo 1990, 41). This should not be surprising to the readers since Luke in his first volume had already described the passion of Jesus as an "exodus" (Luke 9:31).

The Passover setting, then, is very important in understanding the next scene, the deliverance of Peter from prison (vv. 6-11). The Exodus imagery continues, particularly in Luke's choice of language: *the night before* (v. 6; Exod 12:12); *Get up quickly* (v. 7; Exod 12:11); *put on your . . . sandals* (v. 8, Exod 12:11); *the Lord has rescued* (v. 11; Exod 18:4, 8-10). As in the Cornelius episode, everything is directed "from above" by an angel of the Lord who gives specific instructions to Peter even on how to dress himself. Peter's passivity is emphasized by the fact that he thought what was happening was another vision (cf. chap. 10), not realizing the reality of the situation. He does at least respond again to the call, *Follow me* (v. 8). Clearly, this is the story of Peter's divine deliverance from bondage (like the Israelites), not his escape.

Realizing finally the reality of his deliverance, Peter goes to the house of Mary, mother of John Mark, where the believers have gathered to pray (v. 12). This scene is filled with drama, punctuated with irony and comic relief. Peter encounters a second gate, only this time it does not open miraculously (cf. v. 10). Vulnerable to anyone who might see him, Peter knocks and a maidservant named *Rhoda* or "Rose" comes to answer. In Luke and Acts, this is Peter's second encounter with a maidservant (cf. Luke 22:56-57), neither of which is very successful. Rhoda is so overjoyed at recognizing Peter's voice that she runs inside to tell the others, leaving Peter standing at the gate (v. 14). The believers who presumably had gathered to pray for Peter (see vv. 5, 12) refuse to believe that their prayers have been answered. Rather, they inform Rhoda that she is out of her mind and suggest that what she has seen is not Peter but his ghost. This is evidently another sign that they did not trust that God would deliver Peter since, in popular Jewish tradition, it was believed that a person's "guardian angel" often appeared immediately following the person's death. As Polhill remarked, "They found it easier to believe that Peter had died and gone to heaven than that their prayers had been answered" (1992, 282). Like the two on the road to Emmaus, these believers refused to believe female testimony (cf. Luke 24:22-23).

But Peter continues to knock, and finally they open the gate and find him there, much to their amazement (v. 16). After recounting his rescue, Peter asks them to tell these things to James (presumably the brother of Jesus) and the believers. This is the key verse in this scene since it marks the beginning of the changing of the guard in the Jerusalem church from Peter to James, a transition that will be completed in chap. 15. Peter then departs, and Herod's frustrated search for Peter ends in the death of the guards from whom he escaped (vv. 18-19). With this note, attention turns again to Herod.

Already Herod has killed the other James, imprisoned Peter with the intentions of putting him to death, and executed the four squads of guards (a total of sixteen men) who had watched over him. Now he cuts off food supplies from the people of Tyre and Sidon (in Phoenicia) because he is angry with them for some unspecified reason (v. 20). After negotiations between the king and the Phoenician citizens brokered by the king's personal servant Blastus result in reconciliation, a celebration is held for the king to receive the people's praise for his benefaction (which, of course, is only necessary because of Herod's own vindictiveness). His speech garners the people's favor, and he is hailed as a god (v. 22). When Herod accepts this praise without protest and without giving "glory to God," he receives his own tap from an angel (v. 23; see v. 7) and meets the fate he intended for Peter. Like other tyrants (according to Josephus, *Ant* 19.343-52), Herod dies a grisly, worm-infested death.

The story of Peter is the second of three rescues from prison, and the demise of Herod is the third punitive miracle where the opponent of God is struck down (see JUDAS and ANANIAS and SAPPHIRA). These stories "unfold in inverse symmetry" (Pervo 1990, 43). The result is that the earthly powers, here represented by Herod, are unmasked for the impostors they are, and the power of God is demonstrated through the Antioch church, Barnabas, and Peter. Like the seed sown on good earth (see Luke 8:4-15), the *word of God* (meant here by Luke as figurative language to refer to the church) *grew* in the face of opposition and continued to produce a remarkable yield, just as it did at the beginning of this section (v. 24; see 6:7).

Paul's Mission to the Gentile World, 13:1–19:41

This next major division of Acts narrows its vision from the activities of the Twelve and the Seven to focus on the gentile mission of PAUL and his apostolic company. To speak of these chapters as Paul's "three missionary journeys" is inaccurate since Luke himself never refers to Paul's campaigns in such fashion. In fact, only Paul's first "foray" into the gentile world (13:1–14:28) has the character of an intentional journey, in this case a round trip beginning in and returning to Antioch. The second section revolves around the controversy surrounding Paul's missionary efforts and its resolution (15:1-35). The next three sections focus on Paul in MACEDONIA (15:36–17:15), the Achaian cities of ATHENS and CORINTH (17:16–18:17), and EPHESUS (18:18–19:41). The shift then is from persons (chaps. 5–12) to places (chaps. 13–19), but the spread of the gospel remains the central theme.

Paul's Initial Missionary Campaign, 13:1–14:28

13:1-12. Commissioned and tested. This scene begins with the commissioning of Paul and Barnabas by the church at Syrian Antioch (vv. 1-3). Two things are noteworthy about this opening. First is the diversity of the Antiochene church evidenced by this short list: SIMEON or Niger, a black person, perhaps from North Africa; Lucius, who is originally from CYRENE and perhaps among those broad-minded enough to evangelize among the gentiles (see 11:20); and Manaen, who is of aristocratic Jewish stock, having been brought up in the court of Herod Antipas (see Luke 3:1; Acts 4:27). Barnabas and Saul are also counted as prophets in this list. The second important feature is the role of Holy Spirit in the commissioning. Luke wants it clear that just as the Holy Spirit was involved in the beginning of Jesus' public ministry, the Antiochene church sets Saul and Barnabas apart only under the direction of the Holy Spirit (v. 3).

The parallel between Paul and Jesus continues in the next scene (vv. 4-12). Saul and Barnabas are sent out by the Holy Spirit (v. 4) after their commissioning, as was Jesus (see Luke 4:1). For the second time in Acts, a Christian missionary confronts a magician (see Acts 8). Here the opponent is Bar-Jesus, known also as ELYMAS, a *Jewish false prophet* (v. 6). Elymas, who is in the service of a leading Roman official—Sergius Paulus—fears that Sergius might be persuaded to turn to the Christian faith by Paul and Barnabas so he opposes them (vv. 7-9). Elymas is closely related to Satan in Paul's curse where he is called *a son of the devil* and an *enemy of all righteousness*. He is also described as being *full of all deceit and villainy* (v. 10).

The confrontation here is between Paul, a true prophet full of the Holy Spirit, and Bar-Jesus, who seeks to make *crooked the straight paths of the Lord* (v. 10)—thus undoing the work of another true prophet, JOHN THE BAPTIST. It is nothing less than a confrontation between the Holy Spirit and the devil and echoes the conflict between Jesus and Satan at the beginning of Jesus' public ministry (Luke 4). Paul's curse of blindness on Elymas is especially fitting: as an idolater who serves as an agent of Satan, Elymas is cursed to the darkness from which he has come (see Deut 28:28-29; 1 QS 2:11-19).

Note also the irony here: Paul, who has himself just made the transition from darkness to light (see chap. 9), now pronounces a curse of "mist and darkness" that causes Elymas to search for *someone to lead him by the hand* (v. 11). The point of this scene for the ministry of Paul is crucial: Like Jesus, Paul has demonstrated his authority over the forces of Satan and thus has proven himself worthy of the mission set before him. The conversion and commission of Paul that began in chap. 9 is now complete, and perhaps this explains why from this point on, Saul is consistently referred to as Paul (see v. 9). With the fulfillment of his change in status from one who opposed.God to one who now serves him comes a change in name (see Garrett 1989, 85). That the church also gains a prominent convert in Sergius Paulus is a nice by-product of this encounter, but by no means the central focus.

13:13-52. Paul's speech at Pisidian Antioch. This next scene has three parts: (1) the setting (vv. 13-16), (2) the speech (vv. 17-41), and (3) the aftermath (vv. 42-52). After a whistle stop in Perga, Paul and his company come to Antioch of Pisidia. As would prove to be his pattern in Acts, Paul enters the synagogue on the Sabbath (v. 14). After the reading of scripture (see Luke 4), Paul is given the opportunity to speak and delivers the first of the major addresses in Acts (cf. Acts 17:22-31; 20:18-35).

Paul's inaugural speech (vv. 17-41) is remarkably similar to Jesus' inaugural address in Luke 4 and Peter's first major speech recorded in Acts 2 (see Tannehill 1990, 160). All three speeches use scripture to interpret the mission (Luke 4:18-19; Acts 2:17-21; 13:47) and include gentiles in God's salvation (Luke 4:25-28; Acts 2:39; 13:45-48). The speech itself narrates God's promises to Israel (vv. 16b-25), the fulfillment of those promises in Christ (vv. 26-37), and an invitation and warning (vv. 38-41). Each of these units is introduced with a form of direct address (You Israelites . . . [v. 16b]; my brothers . . . [v. 26]; my brothers [v. 38]). These direct addresses make it clear that Paul is addressing Jews (you Israelites) and those who are deeply interested in Judaism (others who fear God).

The first part of the speech (vv. 16b-25) is similar to Stephen's speech in that it recounts Israel's history; its focus however differs by concentrating not on Israel's rebelliousness, but rather on God's faithfulness. After this brief summary of Israel's history from the ancestors to David, the central claim of the section is made in v. 23: Of this man's [David's] posterity God has brought to Israel a Savior, Jesus, as he promised. Paul then cites the words of John the Baptist as corroborating evidence to support his claim that God's faithfulness has climaxed in Jesus.

That Jesus is the fulfillment of God's promises to Israel is worked out in more detail in the second part of Paul's speech (vv. 26-37). Having appealed to the content of Jewish history (vv. 17-22) and the witness of John the Baptist, Paul now employs two favorite scriptures (Pss 2, 16) and the rules of Jewish messianic interpretation (see comments on Acts 8). But Christian messianic exegesis once again takes a startling turn (see 3:20); this Messiah, whom God promised and to

whom the scriptures point, has already come in the person of Jesus (vv. 32-33).

The conclusion of the sermon is twofold. First, Paul extends an invitation for the hearers to receive the forgiveness of sins that can come only through Jesus, not through the Law of Moses (vv. 38-39). He also issues a prophetic warning (quoting Hab 1:5, cf. 1QpHab 2:1-10) that to reject Paul's message is to reject God's salvation and to be condemned to play the part of scoffers whose fate it is to perish (v. 41).

Immediately following the sermon, the people urge Paul and Barnabas to return the next Sabbath, and in the meantime the people follow these Christian missionaries who continue to exhort them (vv. 42-43). The rest of this unit falls into two parallel scenes (vv. 44-48; 49-52) summarizing Paul's ministry in Antioch (see Talbert 1984, 59; Krodel 1986, 246–47).

A The gathering of the whole city
   to hear the word of the Lord, 44
  B The rejection of unbelieving Jews, 45
    C Response of Paul and Barnabas:
      turning to the Gentiles, 46-47
     D The Gentiles rejoice, 48
A' The word of the Lord
   spread throughout the region, 49
  B' Unbelieving Jews stir up persecution
    against Paul and Barnabas, 50
    C' Response of Paul and Barnabas:
      shaking off the dust from their feet, 51
     D' The Disciples are filled with joy, 52

This pattern of (1) the proclamation of the gospel that leads to (2) division among those listening, (3) rejection by the unbelievers, (4) withdrawal by the Christian missionaries, and, finally, (5) Luke's report of the progress despite the opposition continues to the end of Acts. It will be repeated in the very next scene of Paul and Barnabas in Iconium.

14:1-28. Paul in Iconium, Lystra, and elsewhere. The description of the scene in ICONIUM (vv. 1-7) prevents the readers from reducing Paul's ministry to the simple formula of rejection by the Jews and success among the gentiles (Tannehill 1990, 176). Rather, Luke reports that a great number of both Jews and Greeks became believers (v. 1). Likewise, both Jews and gentiles persecute the apostles (v. 5) who withdraw to the surrounding country and continue to preach the good news (vv. 6-7). Paul's words in 13:46-47 are not to be understood in any rigid sense; division is not always along ethnic lines, certainly not in Iconium. The division is not between Jews and gentiles, but between those who hear the word and accept and those who reject the message and persecute the messengers.

In LYSTRA, Paul heals a man lame from birth (vv. 8-10; cf. Acts 3:1-10). As a result, the crowds cried out that *the gods have come down to us in human form* (v. 11), specifically Zeus (Barnabas) and Hermes (Paul). This story echoes an ancient legend no doubt familiar to the ancient reader that Zeus and Hermes had once visited the region of Phrygia and Lycaonia but had not been recognized nor warmly received until they came upon an elderly couple Baucis and Philemon (see Ovid, *Metamorph.* 8.626). Perhaps the hasty conclusion reached here by the Lycaonians was an attempt to avoid making the same mistake twice.

In sharp contrast to Simon Magus (Acts 8) and Herod (Acts 12), Paul and Barnabas are quick to deny their newly acquired divinity. In a quickly composed speech that anticipates the AREOPAGUS address (Acts 17), Paul is still barely able to restrain the people from honoring them with sacrifice. This turmoil gives way quickly to more serious trouble when Jews from Antioch and Iconium who have been pursuing Paul and Barnabas persuade this fickle crowd to join them in stoning Paul, dragging him outside the city, and leaving him for dead (v. 19). Suffering for Christ's name, foretold to Ananias in an epiphany (9:16), now becomes a painful reality. Surrounded by the support of other disciples, Paul gets up and continues his ministry in DERBE. This symbolic death and resurrection bear witness again to the "unhindered" nature of the gospel.

Luke quickly narrates the story of how Paul and Barnabas retrace their steps, and this episode ends in Syrian Antioch where it began, forming a literary inclusio (vv. 21-28). On this first missionary endeavor, Paul had fulfilled his calling first revealed to Ananias that Paul would *bring* [Jesus'] *name before Gentiles and kings and before the people of Israel* and that *he must suffer for the sake of* [Jesus'] *name* (9:15-16). So in Antioch, they reported to the church how God *had opened a door of faith for the Gentiles* (v. 27). Very shortly, however, some in the church would seek to close that door or at least severely limit its access.

The Conference in Jerusalem, 15:1-35

Acts 15 stands at the center of the Book of Acts both literarily and theologically. Finally the issue of gentile inclusion into the family of God is addressed and resolved. The episode is structured in four scenes: a description of the nature of the conflict (1-5); the debate in Jerusalem focusing on the three speeches by Peter, Paul, and Barnabas, and James (6-21); the solution (22-29); and the report to Antioch (30-35).

15:1-5. The conflict. The success of Paul and Barnabas reported in Acts 13 and 14 prompts some unnamed individuals to come down from Judea to Antioch to assert the official position of the Jerusalem church: *Unless you are circumcised according to the custom of Moses, you cannot be saved* (v. 1). *No small dissension and debate* (v. 2) between them and Paul and Barnabas resulted, and delegates were sent to Jerusalem to resolve the matter.

Verse 2 introduces the major players: the circumcision party (whom Luke refers to as *believers who belonged to the sect of the Pharisees* [v. 5]) which has no individual spokesperson but rather speaks as a group; the apostles, represented by Peter; and the elders, represented by James. The only group missing are the Hellenists, and Luke may intend for the reader to understand that Paul and Barnabas have been appointed by the Antioch church to represent their concerns (v. 2; cf. 13:1). The issue is stated sharply by the sect of the PHARISEES: GENTILES cannot become Christians without first becoming JEWS, that is, they must be circumcised and observe the Law of Moses.

15:6-21. The debate. The other representatives are then allowed to present their position. Peter speaks first. By recounting briefly the Cornelius story (without mentioning his name), Peter appeals to his own experience to justify including without restrictions the gentiles within the family of God. Two points are of special interest in Peter's speech. First, Peter's argument is not a mere autobiographical argument from personal experience; it is a theological argument (Tannehill 1990, 184). The speech throughout de scribes what God was doing in those events. God is the subject of most of the verbs and participles in this speech: God made a choice; God knows the human heart; God testified to them (gentiles); God gave them the Holy Spirit; God cleansed their hearts; God has made no distinction between them and us (vv. 7-9). The upshot is that God, not Peter (or Paul), is responsible for the inclusion of the gentiles. In light of this appeal to divine mandate, Peter's question, *Why are you putting God to the test by placing on the neck of the disciples a yoke that neither our ancestors nor we have been able to bear?* (v. 10), reduces the assembly from *much debate* (v. 7) to *silence* (v. 12).

The other point of emphasis in Peter's speech is on justification by grace through faith. The speech ends with these words: *we believe that we will be saved through the grace of the Lord Jesus, just as they will* (v. 11; cf. v. 9). The emphasis is, of course, a very common theme in Paul's letters (cf. e.g., Gal 3:15), but it is also found in the message of the Lukan Paul. At the end of his synagogue speech in Antioch, Paul asserts "everyone who believes is justified" (13:38-39, author trans.). Peter then represents the most liberal position on this issue: gentiles need only to believe in order to be saved. Salvation is an act of God's grace, not the result of human effort.

After Paul and Barnabas support Peter by relating the *signs and wonders that God had done through them among the Gentiles* (v. 12), James, representative of the Jerusalem elders, addresses the assembly. As Peter had offered a theological argument for gentile inclusion on the basis of his personal experience, James offers a theological argument based on another source of authority—scripture. James begins his speech with a reference to Peter's speech: *Simeon has related how God first looked favorably on the Gentiles to take from among them a people for his name* (v. 14). The Greek word for "people" is used in Luke almost exclusively for the Jews, but here it unmistakably identifies believing gentiles with God's chosen "people."

James argues further that the inclusion of gentiles into the people of God was foretold by the prophet Amos. James's interpretation of Amos 9:11-12 rests on the LXX version of that passage, which claims that the house of David will be restored *so that all other peoples may seek the Lord—even all the Gentiles over whom my name has been called* (v. 17; cf. Amos 9:12 where the sense is very different). Since no mention is made in Amos of the gentiles being circumcised or obeying the Mosaic law, James concludes that scripture confirms Peter's experience that the gentiles should not have to become Jews in order to become Christians: *we should not trouble those Gentiles who are turning to God* (v. 19).

James does, however, go one step further toward compromise with the sect of the Pharisees by suggesting that the council write to the gentiles, instructing them to observe certain dietary laws (v. 20). The council is persuaded by James's words and decides to communicate its decision to the gentile believers in Antioch, Cilicia, and Syria (15:23). But what exactly have they decided? Is this last addition by James a soteriological requirement or social compromise? In other words, has James removed circumcision only to substitute dietary laws as a requirement for gentile sal-

vation, or is he addressing a social problem of how gentiles and Jews are to live together peaceably in the church? A closer examination of the decree itself and the context of Acts in general may help resolve this question.

15:22-29. The solution. The four requirements demanding abstention from food offered to idols, from sexual immorality, from meat of strangled animals, and from blood (possibly based on Lev 17:8–18:18) are repeated in the letter composed for gentile consumption. The immediate context of the letter suggests these requirements should not be viewed as necessary for salvation, since the letter has been sent to correct those *certain persons who have gone out from us, though with no instructions from us,* and who *have said things to disturb you and have unsettled your minds* (v. 24). Further, these four requirements are "all basically ritual requirements aimed at making fellowship possible between Jewish and Gentile Christians" (Polhill 1992, 331). This view is supported by other clues in the text. In 16:1-3, Timothy (whose mother is Jewish and father Greek) is circumcised by Paul, not to insure his salvation, but to remove any obstacle that would hinder fellowship with the Jews with whom he came into contact. These regulations are recalled again in 21:21, where Paul is accused of leading Jews living among gentiles to *forsake Moses.* The situation has changed: "The problem is no longer the demands being made on Gentiles to become Jews but the pressure being felt by Jews to conform to a Gentile way of life" (Tannehill 1990, 191). The problem is still basically a social one of fellowship between Jewish and gentile Christians.

15:30-35. The report distributed. The appointed delegation—Paul, Barnabas, Judas BARSABBAS, and SILAS—depart, and the letter is delivered to the church at Antioch. It achieves the desired results: the congregation read it and *they rejoiced at the exhortation* (v. 31). The gentile mission has won a significant dispute; and, equally important for Luke, the church has resolved another major dispute in an orderly and peaceable fashion. Once again, church unity has been restored, and Paul and Barnabas can return to the task of teaching and proclaiming the word of the Lord (v. 35).

Paul in Macedonia, 15:36–17:15

15:36–16:10. Paul and the Apostolic company. Following the conference, Paul proposes to Barnabas that they retrace the steps of their first missionary campaign to see how the fledgling churches are faring (v. 36). This plan does not materialize because of a dispute about whether John Mark should accompany them. Again the conflict produces a positive result. The division actually leads to a multiplication of missionary efforts: Barnabas and Mark sail to Cyprus; and Paul and Silas travel through Syria and Cilicia, *strengthening the churches* (v. 41).

Paul's choice of traveling companions, Silas (15:40) and Timothy (16:1-3), deserves further comment. Timothy's mother was a Jewish Christian (on his circumcision, see comments on 15:22-29 above), and he himself *was well spoken of by the believers in Lystra and Iconium* (16:2). As a companion of Paul, he insured that the concerns and interests of these newly founded churches would be well represented. Silas, along with Judas, was one of the *leaders* of the Jerusalem church (15:22) who had been chosen to bear the apostolic decree to the gentile churches. In Antioch, Silas had shown his mettle by saying much *to encourage and strengthen the believers* (15:32). In fact, Luke identifies him as a *prophet*. Rather than exclude the Jerusalem church from further participation in the mission because they were on the losing side of the debate, Paul chooses to include Silas in his apostolic company. Silas, therefore, embodies the Jerusalem church's commitment to support the Jewish-gentile mission of Paul (see Tannehill 1990, 196).

So when Luke reports that *they went from town to town,* delivering the accord reached by apostles and elders in Jerusalem (16:4), it is significant that the *they* includes both a member of one of these diaspora churches and a member of the Jerusalem congregation. As a result of such strategy the churches grew daily both qualitatively (*in the faith*) and quantitatively (*in numbers* [16:5]).

Despite these positive references, Luke does not avoid reporting the limitations and failures of Paul's mission. With Paul and his company traveling as it were by trial and error, Luke twice reports that Paul was forbidden by the Spirit, first from speaking the word in Asia (16:6) and next from entering into Bithynia. The floundering mission is finally given focus in Troas when Paul experiences a vision (cf. chap. 10) in which a Macedonian man pleads with Paul to travel to Macedonia to *help us* (16:9). Guided now by the conviction that the campaign had divine endorsement, Paul sets sail for Macedonia (16:10).

Actually, the text says *we immediately tried to cross over to Macedonia* (16:10). Here Luke introduces the first of several so-called WE-SECTIONS, where the narrator seems to become a participant in the story.

The use of first-person narration is important because: "Geographically, it is prominent in the Aegean coastal region, but not limited thereto. Thematically, it emphasizes major moments and events. Literarily, the 'we' brings readers into the story. Its intimacy makes this story *our* story" (Pervo 1990, 56). The use of the first person, then, signals that important events are about to follow.

16:11-40. Conversions and imprisonments. The reader is certainly not disappointed, for what follows is another household conversion story (vv. 11-15; cf. Acts 10–11), an exorcism (vv. 16-24), and the third rescue from prison (vv. 25-40). Paul and his companions pass quickly through Samothrace and Neapolis to Philippi, *a leading city of the district of Macedonia and a Roman colony* (vv. 11-12), where they encounter some women at prayer, the most notable of whom is LYDIA (vv. 13-14). The story of Lydia actually frames this unit (vv. 13-15, 40).

The reader learns several things about Lydia: she is a *worshiper of God* (like Cornelius, a devout gentile who had not yet fully converted to Judaism [cf. 10:2]) and a dealer in purple cloth from Thyatira, which indicates that she is a rich businesswoman (v. 14). After she and her household are converted, she adopts the role of a gracious Christian hostess and patroness (see Rom 12:13; Heb 13:2; 3 John 5-8) in opening her home to and sharing her possessions with Paul and his company.

During their time with Lydia, Paul and his companions encounter a slave girl with *a spirit of divination* whose fortune-telling was very lucrative for her owners (v. 16). She rightly identifies the missionaries as *slaves of the Most High God, who proclaim to you a way of salvation* (v. 17). After *many days* of this, Paul commanded the spirit to leave the girl, reminiscent of Jesus's exorcisms (v. 18; cf. Luke 4:34; 8:28).

With the departure of the spirit went also the fortune of the slave-girl's owners. Once again, the material effect of the missionaries efforts leads to adverse results. The owners drag Paul and Silas into the marketplace before the authorities and hide their rage at economic loss behind political charges that will stick: *These men are disturbing our city; they are Jews and are advocating customs that are not lawful for us as Romans to adopt or observe* (vv. 20-21). The crowds join in, and the local authorities acquiesce. Stripped and flogged, Paul and Silas are thrown into prison where they are put in the innermost cell, what we would call the dungeon (vv. 22-24).

The next scene resembles a rescue-from-prison scene, but there is a significant difference. Prayers, hymn singing, and an earthquake lead not to the rescue of Paul and Silas from prison, but rather the deliverance of the Philippian jailer and his household to salvation. When the jailer awakens to discover the prison doors opened, he draws his sword to take his own life before the local authorities can (cf. 11:18-19). But Paul interrupts; the earthquake had opened the prison doors and unfastened the prisoners' fetters, but Paul and Silas were still there (vv. 27-29). Trembling, the jailer asks, *Sirs, what must I do to be saved?* (v. 30). Paul and Silas respond with the kerygma in a nutshell, *Believe on the Lord Jesus, and you will be saved, you and your household* (v. 31). In the middle of the night these words come true. Both parties receive cleansing waters—one for wounds, the other for baptism—and a symbolic Lord's Supper follows as the jailer sets food before them (vv. 32-34). Like Lydia, the jailer demonstrates the authenticity of his faith by acting as the proper host.

The scene has come to a proper denouement with the conversion of the jailer, but Luke has one more important detail to report. Only now in the story does the reader learn that Paul and Silas have been illegally beaten and imprisoned—they are Roman citizens (v. 37). This disclosure of citizenship comes too late in the story to offer protection, but it does set the stage for later encounters with political authorities when Paul's Roman citizenship becomes important again (22:25). This scene ends where it began, in Lydia's house (v. 15) with Paul and Silas strengthening the brothers and sisters there.

17:1-15. Conflict in Thessalonica. Paul and Silas's journeys next take them to THESSALONICA where there is a Jewish synagogue (v. 1). Luke reminds us that it was Paul's custom to speak in the synagogue; he has not yet abandoned the Jewish mission. His message is strikingly similar to the message of the risen Christ in Luke 24 (Tannehill 1990, 206): Paul "opens" the scriptures (*explaining and proving,* v. 3a; see Luke 24:32); he speaks of the necessity of the Messiah's suffering (v. 3b; Luke 24:26, 46). The result is that a few of the Jews were converted as well as *a great many of the devout Greeks and not a few of the leading women* (v. 4).

The notice given to these women converts is interesting. Although Luke has consistently given attention to the role of women in the Christian community (e.g., 1:14; 5:14; 8:12), they receive even greater attention in chaps. 16–18 (see 16:13-14, 16; 17:4, 12, 34; 18:2, 18, 26). The notice of leading women in the Macedonian churches is "very much in keeping with inscriptional evidence that in Macedonia women had considerable social and civic influence" (Polhill, 361). Even more important for the role of women in these churches, no doubt, was the gospel of freedom and radical inclusion that Paul preached.

A familiar pattern emerges in Acts 17:5-8. The Jews become jealous and join with some *ruffians* to form a lynch mob against Paul and Silas. When their searching fails to turn up Paul, they settle for Jason and some other believers instead (v. 6). Knowing that religious differences will matter little to the city authorities, they hurl political charges again (see 16:21), claiming the Christians *have been turning the world upside down* and that they *are all acting contrary to the decrees of the emperor saying that there is another king named Jesus* (vv. 6-7; see 1 Thes 1:1-20; 5:3). The officials are disturbed, but choose only to fine Jason and the others before releasing them (v. 8).

Meanwhile, Paul and Silas are carried off to Beroea where they repeat the pattern of going to the synagogue (v. 10). Luke reports that these Beroean *Jews were more receptive than those in Thessalonica* (v. 11). Whereas in Thessalonica only *some* Jews believed, Luke reports that in Beroea *many of them believed,* along with *not a few Greek women and men of high standing* (v. 12). Although the Beroean Jews are receptive, the Thessalonian Jews are equally persistent; they come to Beroea and again stir up the crowds (v. 14; cf. 14:19-20). And again, believers intervene, accompanying Paul ultimately all the way to Athens (v. 15). These believers receive instructions from Paul that Silas and TIMOTHY (who had been left behind, v. 14) are to join him as soon as possible, and they depart (v. 15).

Paul in Achaia, 17:16–18:17

This next episode takes place in the region of ACHAIA. In Athens, Paul gives his only missionary speech addressed to a gentile audience. As such it stands as a model for preaching to the gentiles. Paul next spends an extended period of time in Corinth. Both of these cities were well known in the ancient world. ATHENS, although it had faded from its period of prominence (4th–5th century B.C.E.), was still highly regarded as the cultural and intellectual center of the ROMAN EMPIRE, and CORINTH had emerged as the largest, most cosmopolitan city in Greece. Thus, in Achaia

Paul continues his pattern of evangelizing in significant urban centers.

17:16-34. Paul in Athens. The scene in Athens is divided into three parts: the setting leading up to the sermon is described in some detail (vv. 16-21); the sermon itself is the centerpiece of the episode in Athens (vv. 22-31); and the scene ends with a report of the responses to Paul's message (vv. 32-34).

While waiting for Silas and Timothy to join him, Paul has the opportunity to see Athens. Rather than being impressed by its magnificent art and architecture, Luke reports that Paul was "infuriated" (author trans.) to see the city full of idols (v. 16), a point Paul will address in his sermon. Again Paul follows the normal pattern of arguing with the Jews in the synagogue, but Luke goes on to say that he also engages in debate with people, especially Epicurean and Stoic philosophers, in the marketplace or agora (v. 17).

The EPICUREANS and STOICS represented two of the leading philosophical schools of the day. The Epicureans were committed to an ethical system that tolerated the existence of gods, but gave them no vital role. The Stoics were pantheists who held a more dynamic view of the gods, believing that the divine "spark" was present in all of creation. Paul will allude several times in his speech to certain views of these philosophers.

Evidently, Paul had not been terribly successful in communicating his views, for his audience assumed that he, too, was a pantheist presenting his view about Jesus (which in Greek is grammatically masculine) and his consort "Anastasia" ("Resurrection," which in Greek is grammatically feminine). Before he was through, however, Paul would dispel any notions that he was a polytheistic thinker.

Enamored with intellectual fads (see Demosthenes, *Oration* 4:10), the Athenians took Paul to the AREOPAGUS to present his new ideas (vv. 19-21). There is some debate whether Luke means that Paul was taken to a hill located beneath the acropolis and above the agora called the Areopagus (see, e.g., the KJV "Mars Hill") or whether he had in mind the court known by that name (an analogy is "Wall Street," which may refer either to the place or the stock exchange named after the street).

Internal evidence, such as the conversion of Dionysus, a member of the court of Areopagus (v. 34), suggests that Paul addressed the court of the Areopagus (which by this time was probably meeting in the *Stoa Basileios* or Royal Portico) in the northwest corner of the agora (Polhill 1992, 368). This view is further supported by the possible parallel that the ancient reader might have drawn between Paul's experience and the trial of Socrates. The accusation that Socrates had "introduced" other new gods (Plato, *Apologia* 24B) may be echoed in the description of Paul "introducing" a *new teaching* (v. 19) that had earlier been identified as *foreign divinities* (v. 18). Paul, of course, escapes here the fate of Socrates, and one does not have to posit a formal trial before the Areopagus to acknowledge the parallels with Socrates' trial.

The Areopagus sermon is the fullest and most dramatic speech of Paul's missionary career (vv. 22-31). Anticipated by the shorter address in Lystra (14:15-17) and consistent with the kerygma Paul presents to the gentiles in his letters (cf. Rom 1; 1 Thes 1), this address provides a window into how Paul dealt with the gentiles in other places. The speech itself is composed of five couplets following a chiastic pattern (see Polhill 1992, 37).

A Introduction: evidence of the ignorance
    of pagan worship, 23-24
  B The object of true worship
     is the one Creator God, 25-26
    C Proper relationship between humanity
      and God, 26-27
  B' The objects of false worship are the idols
     of gold, silver, or stone, 28-29
A' Conclusion: the time of ignorance
    is now over, 30-31

The sermon begins with a typical convention of ancient rhetoric, the *captatio benevolentia*, in which the speaker attempts to curry the favor of his audience with a compliment. Here Paul says, *Athenians, I see how extremely religious you are in every way* (v. 22). His evidence is taken from his tour of the city, during which he has seen an altar with the inscription *"To an unknown god"* (see Pausanias 1.1.4; Philostratus, *Life of Apollonius of Tyana* 6.3.5). But within the compliment is an implicit criticism, *What . . . you worship as unknown* [or perhaps in ignorance], *this I proclaim to you* (v. 23). The Athenians had been worshiping an object not a personal God, a "what" not a "whom."

Paul then claims that this unknown God is none other than the Creator God (vv. 25-26). There is no other god worthy of worship; indeed, Paul would argue, there is no other God. Although Paul does not quote scripture, his monotheism is biblically grounded (e.g., Paul's description that God *does not live in shrines made by human hands* (v. 24)—cf. 1 Kgs 8:27;

also Acts 7:48-50), as is his language used to speak of God creating all nations *from one ancestor* (presumably Adam) as well as the human response to search for God (vv. 26-27).

What Paul does quote, however, is not the OT, but rather the Stoic philosopher Aratus: *For "in him we live and move and have our being"; as even some of your own poets have said, "For we too are his offspring"* (v. 28). Here then is the basis for Paul's attack on idolatry that follows: since humans are God's offspring and in the true image of God, then no image *formed by the art and imagination of mortals* could possibly be anything other than a distortion of the image of the one, true God (v. 29).

Paul concludes his sermon by announcing that the time of ignorance is over. God will no longer *overlook* this ignorance (cf. 14:16; Rom 3:25); now is the time for repentance (v. 30). Just as God had made all the nations *to inhabit the whole earth* from *one ancestor* (v. 26), so God will judge the world through *a man* whom God appointed (cf. Rom 5). That this man is Jesus is confirmed when Paul says that God raised him from the dead (v. 31).

The sermon gets mixed reviews (vv. 32-34). The resurrection is viewed as "folly" by some of the Greeks in Paul's audience (v. 32; cf. 1 Cor 1:23), but to view the Areopagus speech as a failure would be a mistake. Some pledge to hear Paul speak again (v. 32); others, Dionysius and Damarius among them, became believers. Neither Paul nor the gospel failed in Athens; only those who heard the good news and did not respond in faith have failed.

18:1-17. Paul in Corinth. In the opening section (vv. 1-4), Paul leaves Athens and travels to Corinth. There he meets PRISCILLA AND AQUILA who had recently come to Corinth from Italy where they and other Jews had been expelled by the emperor Claudius (cf. Suetonius, *Life of Claudius* 25.4). Like Paul, they were tentmakers (v. 3). Paul stayed and worked with them (see Acts 20:34; cf. 1 Cor 4:12; 1 Thes 2; 2 Cor 11:7), while continuing to follow his customary pattern of trying to persuade Jews and gentiles that Jesus was Messiah (v. 4).

The rest of this passage preserves three "type scenes," defined as "when a basic situation, with similar characters and plot elements, recurs several times in a given literature" (Tannehill 1990, 202, 221–29). The first type scene is a kind of "synagogue rejection" that occurs three times in Acts and in which Paul turns to the gentiles in the face of Jewish rejection. The first

such scene takes place in Pisidian Antioch (13:44-47); the third occurs in Paul's speech to the Jews in Rome (28:23-28; cf. also 19:8-9; 22:17-21). In each instance, Paul makes a speech in which he announces that from that point on he is turning to the gentiles (13:46; 19:6; 28:28). Why does Paul continue to preach to the Jews in the face of such resistance? His prophetic act of shaking the dust off his feet (cf. 13:51; Luke 9:5) combines with his prophetic words *Your blood be on your own heads* (v. 6; cf. Ezek 33:4) and his symbolic shift from the synagogue to the house of a believer, Titius Justus, to demonstrate that Paul is fulfilling his responsibility as witness to the Jews. The Jews are responsible for their reaction. In fact, individual Jews continue to convert (witness Crispus the synagogue ruler and his household in this very scene, v. 8). Paul is obligated only to present the gospel; he cannot coerce converts.

The second type scene is that of a "divine commissioning" (see Tannehill 1990, 223). This scene was familiar to the readers from their reading of the OT (Exod 3:2-12; Josh 1:1-9; Jer 1:5-10; Isa 41:10-14) and Acts (5:17-21; 9:10-18; 16:6-10; 27:23-24). The scene consists of a confrontation (v. 9a, *The Lord said to Paul in a vision*), the commission to undertake a task (v. 9b, *speak and do not be silent*), reassurance (esp. prominent here in vv. 9-10, *Do not be afraid . . . for I am with you, and no one will lay a hand on you to harm you*), and a conclusion where the commissionee usually fulfills the assigned task (v. 11, *He [Paul] stayed there a year and six months, teaching the word of God among them*). Paul can continue his mission in the confidence that the Lord is present with him. The reality of this presence is felt in the next scene.

The third type scene has been identified as a scene of public accusation before an official, here Gallio (vv. 12-17). Twice already the reader has encountered this pattern (16:19-24; 17:5-7; cf. also 18:23-41) that has three elements (Tannehill 1990, 202): (1) Christians are compelled to appear before an official person or body (v. 12); (2) they are accused of wrongdoing, political or religious (v. 13); (3) the outcome is reported (vv. 14-17). This scene differs from the others in the outcome because, rather than being beaten and imprisoned (16:19-24) or fined (17:5-7), Paul is acquitted and SOSTHENES, the official of the synagogue, is beaten instead. Perhaps the difference in outcome is due to the fact that in the first two "public accusation" scenes, the charges are political; here they are religious—*This man is persuading people to worship God in ways that are contrary to the law* (v. 13)—giving Gallio an excuse to pay *no attention to any of these things* (v. 17). In any case, this scene proves the truthfulness of the previous unit: at least in Corinth no one will lay a hand on Paul.

Paul in Ephesus, 18:18–19:41

The final episode (18:18–19:41) of this division (chaps. 13–19) focuses on the city of Ephesus. The unit is organized into the following scenes: (1) Paul visits EPHESUS, JERUSALEM, and ANTIOCH (18:18-23); (2) the baptism of John (18:24–19:7); (3) Paul and the sons of Sceva (19:8-20); (4) Paul's resolve (19:21-22); and (5) the riot in Ephesus (19:23-41).

18:18-23. Paul visits Ephesus, Jerusalem, and Antioch. The first scene is transitional and could as easily be included at the end of the preceding section. Paul returns to Antioch where he began these missionary endeavors (15:35-41), but he also makes a quick stop in Ephesus where he leaves Priscilla and Aquila and enters into a quick debate with the Jews in the synagogue there (v. 19). Along the way, Paul shaves his hair to fulfill a vow (a Nazirite vow?—see Num 6:1-21), signifying that he continues to be a practicing Jew despite charges otherwise (see Acts 21:21). Paul also stops in Jerusalem to greet the church (v. 22); the tie between the gentile mission and the Jerusalem church remains unbroken. This passage then looks back to Antioch where Paul began his missionary career and forward to Ephesus where he will spend his last three years as a free man.

18:24–19:7. The baptism of John. The connection between the next two scenes, 18:24-28 and 19:1-7, may not be immediately obvious. In the first, Luke does a rare thing by shifting the spotlight away from Paul to APOLLOS. Apollos is described in glowing terms. He is *an eloquent man, well-versed in the scriptures. . . . instructed in the Way of the Lord* (vv. 24-25). He "spoke being fervent in the Spirit" (author trans.), and *taught accurately the things concerning Jesus* (v. 25). The only thing lacking is that Apollos *knew only the baptism of John* (v. 25).

Here then is the point of contact with the next unit (19:1-7) where Paul encounters some disciples in Ephesus who likewise have only experienced the baptism of John (v. 3). In both cases, "those knowing or having experienced John's baptism have their knowledge (18:26) or experience (19:4-6) completed by the associates of Paul (18:26) or by Paul himself (19:6)" (Talbert 1984, 81).

Nonetheless, there are significant differences in these two stories. Apollos is depicted much more favorably than the "disciples" encountered by Paul. The disciples were not only limited to the baptism of John; they had not heard that there was a Holy Spirit! (19:2). Apollos, on the other hand, spoke, "being fervent in the Spirit" (18:25). Further, these Ephesian disciples had to be instructed about the meaning of John's baptism for the coming of Jesus, while Apollos, limited as he was to John's baptism, is still able to teach *accurately the things concerning Jesus* (18:25). Further, with a little fine-tuning instruction from Priscilla and Aquila (note a woman instructing an evangelist here in a post-Pauline document, cf. 1 Tim 2:12), Apollos is able to secure a letter of recommendation from the Ephesians to continue his ministry in Corinth (18:27-28; 19:1).

These contrasts explain why the Ephesian disciples needed to receive baptism in the name of Jesus and the gift of the Holy Spirit (confirmed again by glossolalia, cf. 2:21-24; 10:44-48) while Apollos did not, even though both knew only the baptism of John.

19:8-20. Paul and the sons of Sceva. In this scene, the pattern of synagogue rejection continues. After three months, Paul's sermons in the Ephesian synagogue are met with such resistance by the Jews that he leaves and takes up residence elsewhere, in this case, the lecture hall of Tyrannus, where he preaches both to Jews and Greeks (18:8-10). As in the portrayal of Philip, Paul's healing ministry (vv. 11-12; cf. 8:6-7; also 5:15) confirms his message. By healing illnesses and casting out unclean spirits, Paul confirms the Christian kerygma that the authority of Satan has been overturned (on this passage, see Garrett 1989, 89–99).

Now for the third time (see Acts 8, 13), a Christian missionary confronts a practitioner of magic. In Ephesus, *some itinerant Jewish exorcists tried to use the name of the Lord Jesus over those who had evil spirits* (v. 13). The language used to describe the activities of these *seven sons of a Jewish high priest named Sceva* (v. 14) echoes magical practices of antiquity, especially "exorcist" and "adjure." That these exorcists are using the formula *the Jesus whom Paul preaches* probably implies that they, like Simon Magus, have mistaken Christian miracles for feats of magic. Thus they try to use Jesus' name in a way typical of magical technique, but Luke makes it clear that Jesus' name is not some magical name vulnerable to manipulation. Rather there is a close tie between Jesus' authority and the authority of the one calling upon his name. In Acts

16:16-17, e.g., the spirit in the slave girl recognizes Paul and his companions as *slaves of the Most High God*. But here the evil spirit replies to the sons of Sceva, *Jesus I know, and Paul I know; but who are you?* (v. 15). The demon does not know them, i.e., does not acknowledge their authority, and therefore refuses to obey them. Instead, the demon becomes master over them, sending them out of the house *naked and wounded* (v. 16). "The seven sons failed to mobilize Jesus' power because they lacked the authority to invoke his holy name, and so the demon remains in control" (Garrett 1989, 94).

The defeat of the sons of Sceva makes the accomplishments of Paul's exorcisms even more impressive, a fact not lost on the Ephesians (vv. 17-19). This incident demonstrates that the name of Jesus cannot be manipulated and therefore is worthy of praise (v. 17). Further, these Jews and Greeks had already heard the word of the Lord (v. 10) and seen the defeat of Satan confirmed in the healing ministry of Paul (vv. 11-12); now they reckon with the fact that magic itself is obsolete. "The magic books are useless now—emblems of a defeated regime—and so must be burned" (Garrett 1989, 95). The value of the books burned (*fifty thousand silver coins*) has been reckoned as having a current market value of about $1 billion.

The burning of the magical books is not to be viewed as an act of believers who had secretly practiced magic until now, but rather as part of the act of repentance on the part of those who, as a result of this incident, forsake their belief in and practice of magic and become believers. Thus, Luke uses language—"extol" and "awestruck"—that is intimately associated with conversion (cf. 9:31; 10:46). Furthermore, as noted earlier (see on 12:24), the phrase that concludes this section, *the word of the Lord grew mightily,* is one way Luke refers to the addition of believers to the church (see also 6:7, 12:24). Ironically, the victory of the demon over Sceva's sons is actually a defeat for the devil, because both sides serve Satan. Satan's kingdom is divided and thus doomed (Luke 11:18), and the Word of the Lord continues to grow.

19:21-22. Paul's resolve. In the next unit composed of only two verses (vv. 21-22), Luke anticipates the rest of Paul's ministry as it is recorded in Acts. Paul resolves in the Spirit (v. 21) to go through Macedonia and Achaia (see 20:1-12), to visit Jerusalem once again (see 21:15-38), and finally to go to Rome (see 28:14-16). The language is quite strong; Paul says that he *must* see Rome, a word characteristically used in

Acts to describe divine purpose. As such it is reminiscent of Jesus' resolve to go to Jerusalem (Luke 9:51). Although suffering is not mentioned explicitly, there is good reason to see here that the parallels between Jesus' journey to Jerusalem and Paul's journey to Rome include the dimension of suffering. For Paul, this insight becomes clearer the farther he journeys (20:22-24), but here we have the first step taken by Paul in understanding his divine destiny to travel to Rome.

19:23-41. The riot in Ephesus. Although Paul is largely absent from this scene, he remains at the center of controversy. The unit opens with one DEMETRIUS, a silversmith who made shrines of ARTEMIS, the Asian mother goddess of nature, addressing his fellow artisans. Demetrius has accurately perceived that Paul's invectives against idols would be bad for business (v. 26). To this economic argument, Demetrius adds a religious one: *the temple of the great goddess Artemis will be scorned, and she will be deprived of her majesty that brought all Asia and the world to worship her* (v. 27).

Even here, economics is not far beneath the surface; the temple of Artemis was a central pillar in the financial structures of Asia (Dio Chrysostom, *Oration* 31.54) as well as one of the seven wonders of the world bound to beef up the tourist industry in Ephesus.

Demetrius is successful in stirring up the crowd who drag GAIUS and Aristarchus, two of Paul's companions, into the theater. In the midst of mass confusion and shouts of *Great is Artemis of the Ephesians!* Paul is urged by some officials of Asia, who were friendly to him, to stay clear of the theater (v. 31). Finally, Alexander, a Jew, stepped forward to *make a defense before the people* (v. 33). Did Alexander intend to disassociate the Jews from the Christians or to defend Jewish rejection of idols? We will never know, but the crowd at least identifies this Jew with the Christian rejection of idols and drown him out in a verbal filibuster, resuming their chant: *Great is Artemis of the Ephesians!* (v. 34).

A speech by Demetrius began the riot; finally a speech by the town clerk ends it (Tannehill 1990, 243). With appropriate rhetorical flourish (cf. Acts 17:23), the town clerk begins by identifying with the point of view of the crowds, speaking of the *great Artemis* whose statue *fell from heaven* and whose temple is entrusted to the keeping of the city of the Ephesians (v. 35). In Gamaliel-like fashion, he points out the innocence of Gaius and Aristarchus and that the danger to the Ephesians was not Paul, but rather *the danger of being charged with rioting* (v. 40).

This scene shares similarities with previous public accusations (in chaps. 16, 17, and 18). Here, as in the first scene in Philippi, the accusers are gentiles (Jews are accusers in Thessalonica and Corinth, see Tannehill 1990, 202–203), making it a mistake to view opposition to the Christian movement as only and characteristically Jewish. The scene also bears remarkable similarity to the riot in the Jerusalem Temple (21:27-36). Especially similar is the reason for the riot in both instances: "Members of an established religion are protesting the effect that Paul's mission is having on their religion and its temple" (Tannehill 1990, 242). The riot subsides, order is restored, and Paul is prepared to make his final journey to Jerusalem and Rome (Acts 20–28).

Paul's Farewell Journey, 20:1–28:31

This last division of Acts (20–28) narrates Paul's farewell journey. For much of this part of the story Paul is under arrest, and the narrative is punctuated with Paul's defense speeches.

Paul's Last Journey to Jerusalem, 20:1–21:16

This first section describes the beginning of Paul's journey to Jerusalem (20:1-16), recounts his farewell address to the Ephesians (20:17-38), and records the resolve of Paul to continue to Jerusalem despite several warnings otherwise. Throughout the section, Paul exchanges good-byes with those whom he thinks he will never see again.

20:1-16. The beginning of the farewell journey. After the riot in Ephesus has been quieted, Paul gathers the disciples, encourages and bids them good-bye, and heads for Macedonia (vv. 1-6). Paul is accompanied by seven named companions who represent various areas of the gentile mission. Perhaps the number "seven" not only indicates a certain completion or fullness of the apostolic company, but represents the gentile mission itself (cf. the "seven" appointed to represent the concerns of the "Hellenists" in Acts 6). Yet another of Paul's companions reappears here when the narrator employs the first-person narration, the second such "we-passage" in Acts (cf. 16:17). This farewell ministry is characterized by the continued opposition of the Jews to Paul's witness (v. 3) and Paul *had given the believers much encouragement* (v. 2).

This encouragement is given further detail in the next scene (vv. 7-12). Paul's companions, separated at

Philippi, are reunited in Troas, where they stay for a week (v. 6). Paul meets with the believers there on Sunday to share in the Lord's Supper, to *break bread* as Luke preferred to call it (v. 7; see Acts 2:42, 46). Since this was his last message to these believers, Paul continues to preach until midnight (v. 7). A young man named EUTYCHUS ("Lucky") has the misfortune of falling asleep and then falling out of a window of the upstairs room where they had met (v. 9). Pronounced dead by the time Paul gets to him, Paul takes the boy in his arms (cf. 2 Kgs 4:34) and announces that *his life is in him* (v. 10). Like Jesus (Luke 7:11-17) and Peter (Acts 9:36-42) before him, Paul now restores to life one who was presumably dead.

This story has a symbolic dimension: in the context of Paul's passion Luke places a story that foreshadows the resurrection power of the gospel to overcome death. Along these lines, the seemingly irrelevant detail about the *many lamps* in the meeting place (v. 8) may be read both literally, as an explanation of why, in the face of heat and lack of oxygen, Eutychus went to the window, and symbolically, as a contrast between the meeting room where the Word of God was proclaimed and the Lord's Supper as a place of light (13:47; 26:18, 23) and the place of death and darkness where Eutychus falls when he falls asleep. Eutychus's story is an exegesis by example of Paul's later admonition to the Ephesians to "stay awake" (author trans.) in his absence (v. 31). They may not be so fortunate as Eutychus ("Lucky"), who had Paul to reverse the misfortunes of his lack of moral diligence.

The story ends with Luke's report that the Troas believers were "not a little encouraged" (v. 12, author trans.), picking up on the word used to describe Paul's ministry throughout Macedonia and Greece (v. 2). The encouragement here derives from the integrity between Paul's *word* through preaching and sacrament (v. 11) and his *deed* in raising Eutychus.

The episode ends with a brief summary of Paul's travels from TROAS to MILETUS (vv. 13-15). The readers learn that a temporal goal has been added to Paul's spatial goal: he hopes to be in Jerusalem by the day of Pentecost (v. 16). He also chooses not to stop in Ephesus (because he dreaded the grief of leaving that Christian community again?) but rather sends for the leaders of the community to join him in Miletus (v. 16).

20:17-38. Paul's farewell address to the Ephesians. Sandwiched between the report of the arrival (v. 17) and departure (20:26-38) of the Ephesian elders is the speech given by Paul to them (vv. 18-35). Before examining the structure and content of the speech itself, it may help the reader to place the speech in several contexts. First in the context of Acts, this speech is the third by the Lukan Paul. The first in Antioch of Pisidia (Acts 13:16-41) is addressed to Jews; the second is the Areopagus speech delivered to the Greeks in Athens (17:22-31). The audience partly determines the shape and content of those first two speeches, and this is no less true for this last speech addressed to the Christian leaders from Ephesus who had gathered in Miletus to hear Paul. This speech serves as a window on the problems not only associated with the Ephesian church during Paul's day, but also with the problems faced by Luke's community in a post-Pauline time period. Luke's story about the time of Paul now gives way to Paul's story about Luke's time. As such, this speech has much in common with the Pastoral Epistles (1, 2 Timothy; Titus) that, like Acts, evidently address ecclesiastical problems in a post-Pauline situation. These problems will be given more attention in the exploration of the speech itself.

In form, the speech shares many similarities with the ancient genre of the farewell address. Farewell speeches were common in late Judaism (Gen 49; Josh 23–24; 1 Sam 12; Tob 14; *AsMos*; *T.12 Patr.*) and early Christianity (Mark 13; John 13–17; Luke 22:14-38; 2 Tim 3:1–4:8; 2 Pet) and shared certain constituent elements: (1) the assembling of the speaker's family and/or friends; (2) notice that the speaker is about to leave or die; and (3) a speech that exhorts the listener to emulate desired behavior and predicts events that will follow the speaker's departure/death (Polhill 1992, 423). The Miletus address reflects all these features.

The speech itself defies neat organization, although Talbert (1984, 85) has offered the following helpful proposal (here slightly modified). The speech divides into three parts (18b-27; 28-31a, 31b-35), each with its own chiastic or concentric structure:

1. Defense and Prediction, 18b-27
   A Paul's review and defense of his past ministry with the Ephesians, 18b-21
      B Paul's prediction of his future suffering— marked by "and now," 22-24
      B' Paul's prediction of his death— marked by "and now," 25
   A' Paul's defense of his past ministry, 26-27
2. Exhortations and a Prediction, 28-31a
   A Exhortation to elders to watch over the church, 28

B Prediction that heresies will arise, 29-30
   A' Exhortation to elders to "stay awake," 31a
3. Exhortation and a Blessing, 31b-35
   A Paul's past exhortation, 31b
      B Paul's present blessing, 32
   A' Paul's past example, 33-35

At the heart of this speech lie the predictions that heresies will arise (vv. 29-30). These predictions function at two levels; a narrative level in which the predictions are fulfilled within the course of Acts, and a historical level in which these predictions have already come to pass in Luke's community. Thus, within the narrative itself there is good reason to view those external opponents (*savage wolves will come in among you*, v. 29) as Jews, such as the ones who in the very next episode (21:27-28) are found in opposition to the church (note that in 21:27 these Jews are identified as being from Asia, strengthening this argument), and the internal opponents as Jewish Christians or gentiles influenced by Judaism (21:20-21). There is also ample historical evidence for heresy in Ephesus at the end of the first century (see Eusebius, *EccHist* 3.32.7-8). The crisis faced here is how, in the face of internal and external pressures, to insure that the Christian traditions are preserved in the passing from one generation to the next.

21:1-16. Warnings to avoid Jerusalem. With tears and farewells, Paul and his company set sail again. After passing through Cos, Rhodes, and Patara, they land at Tyre to unload the ship's cargo (vv. 1-3) and stay there seven days. *Through the Spirit* the believers at Tyre gave Paul his first warning *not to go on to Jerusalem* (v. 4), probably because they, like Paul, knew that suffering and persecution were awaiting him there (cf. 20:23). Still, in spite of this weighty testimony to the contrary, Paul persists in continuing his journey to Jerusalem (vv. 5-6).

After a brief stop in Ptolemais, Paul and his company arrive in Caesarea and encounter several characters already familiar to the readers. They stay in the home of Philip the evangelist (see Acts 8) who has *four unmarried daughters who had the gift of prophecy* (v. 9). While it is unclear whether Paul will make it to Jerusalem by Pentecost, it is clear that already in Caesarea he is seeing evidence of the fulfillment of Pentecost prophecies, in this case, that both *sons and . . . daughters shall prophesy* (Acts 2:17).

Paul also meets with the prophet AGABUS who had prophesied a famine in Judea (11:27-30). Through

Agabus, the Holy Spirit again describes the persecution awaiting Paul in Jerusalem (cf. 20:23). Like an OT prophet, Agabus combines a prophetic sign, binding his own hands and feet with Paul's belt, with a prophetic warning: *This is the way the Jews in Jerusalem will bind the man who owns this belt and will hand him over to the Gentiles* (v. 11). This time, the believers, not the Holy Spirit, interpret this sign as a warning to Paul not to continue the journey to Jerusalem.

In the face of this third prediction of his passion (20:23; 21:4, 11), Paul remains resolute: *I am ready not only to be bound but even to die in Jerusalem for the name of the Lord Jesus* (v. 13). Unlike Peter who made a similar promise (Luke 22:33) but failed to fulfill it (at least in the narrative of Luke), Paul remains true to his oath. Seeing they could not persuade him otherwise, the believers pray that *the Lord's will be done* (v. 14). In language that echoes Luke 22:42, Paul is depicted here as facing his own Gethsemane, where he, like Jesus, finally prays, "Lord not my will, but yours be done."

This scene ends with some of the disciples from Caesarea escorting Paul and his company to the house of Mnason of Cyprus with whom they lodged in Jerusalem (v. 16).

Paul in Jerusalem, 21:17–23:35

21:17-40. Paul's arrival and arrest in Jerusalem. Paul and his companions are warmly received by the Jerusalem believers (v. 17), and on the next day, Paul meets with James and the Jerusalem elders (v. 18). In a scene reminiscent of the Jerusalem conference (Acts 15), Paul recounts what *God had done among the Gentiles through his ministry* (v. 19). The Jerusalem elders, in turn, invite Paul to see *how many thousands of believers there are among the Jews* (v. 20). But herein lies the problem: the Jewish believers have been told that Paul was teaching Jews living among gentiles to forsake Moses and abandon Jewish customs (v. 21).

This is the third church conflict involving Jewish-gentile relations (see Tannehill 1990, 268). First the question of baptizing gentiles was resolved in Acts 11. Then the controversy over requiring gentiles to be circumcised was addressed in Acts 15. The problem before the church now has to do with pressure, real or perceived, on Jewish Christians to forsake their Jewish customs, values, and practices. Paul is at the center of this problem because as leader of the gentile mission, he is creating a social situation that is not particularly supportive of Jewish Christians who wish also to honor their Jewish heritage. As the gentile mission continues to be successful and the Jewish population in the church becomes more and more of a minority, this problem intensifies.

The solution proposed by James and the elders is for Paul to demonstrate tangibly his support for Jewish Christians to live as Jews (v. 23). Paul is to join four Jewish believers who are under a vow in going through a seven-day rite of purification in the Temple (vv. 23-24). This will provide the evidence needed to dispel the rumors about Paul. Further, they argue, this solution in no way compromises the agreement reached at the Jerusalem conference regarding the gentiles (v. 25). Paul, despite all the Spirit's previous warnings of persecution and suffering, agrees and engages in the very public act of Temple purification (v. 26).

While Luke reports nothing of the response by Jewish believers to Paul's acts, he has much to say about the reaction of the Jewish community. Jews from Asia, who had seen Paul in the Temple and had also previously seen the gentile TROPHIMUS from Ephesus with Paul, jump to the conclusion that Paul has defiled the Temple by taking Trophimus into it (vv. 27, 29). Thus they stir up the crowd milling around the Temple charging that Paul is *the man who is teaching everyone everywhere against our people, our law, and this place* (v. 28)—charges similar to the ones leveled against Stephen (cf. 7:13). These Asian Jews incite a riot that would rival the one Paul had just endured in Ephesus. Paul was dragged from the Temple, and the Temple doors ominously were shut, never to be open to Paul again (v. 30).

Only the intervention of a Roman tribune prevents Paul from meeting his death (vv. 31-32). Paul is arrested and bound (cf. Agabus's prophecy in v. 11), and efforts by the tribune to learn Paul's identity are thwarted by the uproar of the crowd (v. 34). Instead, the pursuing mob becomes so violent that Paul has to be carried away by Roman soldiers in the midst of shouts of *Away with him!* (v. 36), the very cry of the crowds who called for Jesus' death (Luke 23:18).

While Jesus went to his death with no defense speech, Paul requests to address the crowd (vv. 37, 39). The tribune is surprised to learn that Paul speaks Greek, for he had mistakenly supposed that Paul was an Egyptian insurrectionist (v. 38). Paul identifies himself to the Roman tribune as a Jew from a leading city and then stands to clarify his identity to the Jewish mob (v. 40).

22:1-29. Paul addresses the crowd and the Roman tribune. Paul gestures for the crowd to be silent, but when they hear him speaking in their own language they become even more quiet (v. 2). Paul's speech addresses three issues: his Jewish piety and former life (vv. 1-5), his conversion (vv. 6-12), and his divine commission to go to the gentiles (13-21).

In the first unit (vv. 1-5), Paul again follows the conventions of ancient rhetoric and tries to identify with his audience: he is a pious Jew. He makes this point by (1) speaking in Hebrew (probably here meaning Aramaic), (2) addressing the audience as *brothers and fathers* (v. 1), (3) claiming immediately to be a Jew (v. 3), (4) recounting his impeccable Pharisaic education at the feet of Gamaliel (v. 3; cf. 5:34-38), (5) claiming to share a zeal for God with his audience (v. 3), and (6) appealing to the high priest and the whole council of elders as witnesses to his persecution of the church (vv. 4-5).

This affinity with his audience continues as Paul recounts his conversion experience in the form of a commissioning story, a form familiar to an audience steeped in the similar stories found in scripture (vv. 6-11). This is the second time Paul's conversion is narrated in Acts (see Acts 9:1-18), and there are both significant similarities and differences between the two accounts (and the third to be related later in chap. 26). Many of the differences may be explained by the fact that the audience with whom Paul is trying to relate to is Jewish (see Polhill 1992, 459–61 for a discussion of other differences). The dialogue between Paul and Jesus in the two accounts is nearly verbatim (compare vv. 7-8 with 9:4-5). The addition of *of Nazareth* to Jesus' name (v. 8) is appropriate for such a Jewish audience. Likewise, the description of Ananias as a pious Jew (v. 12) rather than a devout Christian (as in 9:10) again helps Paul establish his Jewishness with this Temple mob.

Also important in explaining the differences is the fact that Paul, not an omniscient narrator (as in chap. 9), is recounting the story, and thus Paul relates events as they unfolded to him. Hence the commission to go to the gentiles comes to Paul (vv. 17-21) and not to Ananias (9:15-16).

Again, Paul, like a good Jew, is praying in the Temple when Jesus commands him, *Go, for I will send you far away to the Gentiles* (v. 21). The brief mention of Stephen's stoning (where Paul was present, giving his approval, v. 20) prepares the readers for the response of the crowd.

Once Paul mentions the gentile mission, the mob is stirred against him again, throwing off their garments, tossing dust in the air, and shouting, *Away with such a fellow from the earth! For he should not be allowed to live* (vv. 22-23). In that sense, Paul's *defense* (as he calls it in v. 1) is a failure; his efforts to prove his "Jewishness" to the crowd finally give way to his conviction that he is called to be apostle to the gentiles.

Once again the tribune intervenes and decides to get to the bottom of this conflict by literally beating the answers out of Paul (v. 24). But just before he is to receive lashes, Paul reveals to the centurion what the reader already knows (see 16:37), namely, that Paul is a Roman citizen (v. 25), and flogging a Roman citizen was simply not an acceptable practice (see, e.g., Cicero, *Verrine Orations* 2.5.66). Paul has not purchased his Roman citizenship as did the tribune (who probably mentions the fact out of suspicion that Paul is lying); even better, he is a citizen by birth. Realizing he has bound and nearly flogged a Roman citizen, the tribune looks for an alternative plan for finding out the nature of the differences between Paul and the Jews.

22:30–23:11. Paul before the Sanhedrin. The tribune convenes a meeting of the SANHEDRIN and places Paul before them to speak (22:30). Paul begins with the assertion, *Brothers, up to this day I have lived my life with a clear conscience before God* (23:1). He is saying, in effect, that he has been obedient to his calling to the gentile mission (cf. 26:19). The high priest simply cannot accept that Paul's mission is indicative of his obedience to God and so orders Paul struck on the mouth (v. 2). Paul immediately responds with a sharp retort, *God will strike you, you white-washed wall! Are you sitting there to judge me according to the law, and yet in violation of the law you order me to be struck?* (v. 3). When observers point out to Paul that he has insulted the high priest (v. 4), Paul's tone changes rapidly, *I did not realize, brothers, that he was high priest; for it is written, "You shall not speak evil of a leader of your people"* (v. 5). The reader who notes a little irony here is probably not mistaken: Paul did not recognize the high priest (for whose organization he previously worked) because he was not acting like one might expect the leader of the people to act.

Paul then notices that both Sadducees and Pharisees are present on the council, and he attempts to redirect the focus of the debate from whether or not Paul is an observant Jew to a weighty theological issue, the question of the resurrection of the dead. Paul is really attempting to do more, however, than simply start a controversy among members of the Sanhedrin. Rather, his concern about *hope and resurrection* raised here continues to be an important theme throughout the defense even when it no longer creates controversy (see 24:15, 21; 28:20; see Tannehill 1990, 286–87). Nonetheless, Paul's words about resurrection here do spark a debate between the Sadducees who deny the doctrine of resurrection (as well as the existence of angels and spirits) and the Pharisees who affirm it. Note that Paul is speaking about a final eschatological resurrection of the dead (plural), not specifically of the resurrection of Christ. The Lukan Paul is seeking to emphasize the similarities between Christianity and segments of Judaism and thus lay the groundwork for more explicit claims later about the resurrection of Jesus (26:23). The Pharisees proclaim Paul's innocence (v. 9), much as Pilate, Herod, the penitent thief, and the centurion pronounced Jesus innocent (cf. Luke 23).

Once again, the tribune, fearing for Paul's safety, has him delivered back to the barracks. This scene ends with Paul as the recipient of yet another nocturnal christophany: *That night the Lord stood near him and said, "Keep up your courage! For just as you have testified for me in Jerusalem, so you must bear witness also in Rome"* (v. 11). The reason for the divine necessity for Paul to go to Rome is made clear: he is to *bear witness* there as he has in Jerusalem.

23:12-35. An ambush avoided. The resolve of the Jerusalem Jews against Paul is demonstrated by the next scene in which forty Jews take a solemn oath neither to eat nor drink until they had killed Paul (v. 12). They approached the Temple establishment (Sadducean chief priests and elders) with a plan to take Paul by ambush (the absence of the more sympathetic Pharisees from this conspiracy is noteworthy).

The plan is thwarted by Paul's nephew, his sister's son. The young man reports the conspiracy first to Paul and then to the tribune with detailed accuracy (vv. 16-21). The tribune again acts decisively in Paul's behalf. After ordering Paul's nephew to tell no one of their conversation, the tribune orders an impressive guard (200 soldiers, seventy horsemen, and 200 spearmen) to transport Paul to Caesarea where the procurator FELIX resides (vv. 23-24). In addition, the tribune drafts a letter to be delivered to Felix.

This letter is interesting for both its form and content. In form, the letter follows the threefold salutation typical of ancient letter writing: the sender, the recipient, and the word of greeting. For the first time, the readers learn the tribune's name, CLAUDIUS LYSIAS (v. 26). Lysias is a complex character. He has acted decisively in Paul's behalf, thrice intervening in life-threatening situations (21:31-36; 23:10; 23:23-25). He has also been persistent in his investigations to learn the facts about Paul, and he has been willing to accept new information about Paul (to believe that he was an Egyptian insurrectionist, to accept that he was a Roman citizen, and now to believe the reports of Jewish conspiracy to kill Paul). But his letter reveals that Lysias also is willing to rearrange and suppress the facts to put himself in a better light. In the letter to Felix, Lysias suggests that he intervened in Paul's behalf after learning that he was a Roman citizen (v. 27). If this account were true, Paul presumably would not have been bound. But the reader knows that Lysias had at first thought Paul was a revolutionary and learned of Paul's citizenship only *after* he had placed him in chains and nearly had him flogged. Lysias's self-assurance in decision making is marred with interests of self-protection. Other political figures encountered later will demonstrate a similar complexity in character.

Both Paul and the letter are safely delivered to Felix (vv. 31-33). After learning that Paul is from Cilicia and within his jurisdiction, Felix promises to give Paul a hearing when his accusers arrive. Meanwhile Paul is kept under house arrest in Herod's headquarters (v. 35).

Paul before Felix, Festus, and Agrippa, 24:1–26:32

This section is filled with legal scenes and defense speeches. Here Paul confronts the political establishment—the Roman officials Felix and FESTUS and the Jewish king AGRIPPA. But a close reading of these passages reveals that Paul is not the only one "on trial": he is joined by the Christian gospel. Paul not only defends himself; he bears witness to the Christian faith whether before the Jews, the Roman PROCURATOR, or even Caesar himself.

The political establishment presents a less than consistent picture. On the one hand, the Romans protect Paul and testify to his innocence. On the other, they are willing to distort the facts in order to portray themselves in the most favorable light—this is true of Lysias, Felix, and Festus. Both Felix and Festus withhold justice from Paul, despite his innocence, in their desire to "do a favor for the Jews" (see 24:27). Each episode is examined in more detail below.

24:1-27. Paul before Felix. When Ananias and some of the elders arrive in Caesarea some five days after Paul, they bring with them their own attorney, TERTULLUS, who uses his persuasive skills in oration to present the case against Paul to Felix (v. 1). There are several interesting points about Tertullus's speech. The *captatio benevolentia*, in which Felix is praised, is nearly as long as the formal complaint lodged against Paul (vv. 2-4). Further, this section of praise is excessive. Tertullus uses all the right phrases to curry Felix's favor. Felix has brought much *peace* to the Jews (v. 2). He has enacted reforms that grew out of his *foresight* or "providence" (v. 2). And, Tertullus continues, all Jews everywhere and in every way are grateful to Felix for his benevolence (v. 3). The reader who knows the facts of Felix's reign, flawed as it was with countless rebellions by disgruntled Jews, however, will see through this poorly veiled attempt to influence Felix through flattery (see Tacitus, *Ann* 12:54; Josephus, *Ant* 20.181-182).

When Tertullus finally gets to the charges against Paul, the reader notes that the accusation has taken a decidedly political direction from the complaints lodged earlier in 21:21. Here Tertullus combines the charge that Paul is profaning the Temple (v. 6) with the more serious charge, from Felix's point of view, that Paul is a *pestilent fellow* who is *an agitator among all the Jews throughout all the world, and a ringleader of the sect of the Nazarenes* (v. 5). This charge of sedition would not be taken lightly by Felix, in light of the previous Jewish riots in Felix's territory of Judea (see Josephus, *BJ* 6.124-28). Tertullus concludes his speech by inviting Felix to examine Paul for himself, but Tertullus does not supply any supporting evidence or witnesses for his accusations (a point Paul will capitalize on in his rebuttal). The best Tertullus can do is produce other Jews who simply maintain the truth of his charges (v. 9).

Rather than conduct his own investigation at this point, Felix nods to Paul (v. 10) to present his defense, which he does (v. 10-21). Like Tertullus, Paul begins with a *captatio benevolentiae*, but Paul limits his "praise" to the simple acknowledgement that Felix's experience as *judge over this nation* ought to qualify him to judge the veracity of the charges brought against Paul (v. 10). Paul counters Tertullus's sweeping and ambiguous charges with a detailed narration of the events of twelve days ago. Paul had no past history of inciting people to riot (v. 12); Paul had come to Jerusalem to worship, not stir up a rebellion (v. 11).

His accusers have no way of making their case stand up under scrutiny (v. 13).

After this string of denials, Paul is willing to make a confession: he is a member of *the Way,* what the Jews call a *sect,* and as such, Paul confesses, he worships *the God of our ancestors, believing everything laid down according to the law or written in the prophets* (v. 14). Such a confession could hardly be found objectionable to Paul's opponents.

Paul then goes on to point out that he shares a hope in the resurrection of the dead with his accusers (Sadducees notwithstanding). Then in vv. 17-19, he responds to Tertullus's charge that he had tried to desecrate the Temple (v. 6). To the contrary, Paul was conducting himself as a pious Jew, bringing alms, making sacrifice, and completing the rite of purification—all without any disturbance (v. 18). The uproar, Paul claims, was caused by Jews from Asia who are not even at the trial to bring their charges firsthand (v. 19).

Paul concludes his speech by making explicit the true nature of the charge against him. His crime, he says, *was this one sentence that I called out while standing before them, "It is about the resurrection of the dead that I am on trial before you today"* (v. 21). Paul is not guilty of political sedition or even violation of Jewish law. What is at stake here is the *resurrection of the dead*—the "fundamental issue that unites Pharisaic Judaism with Christianity and divides non-Christian Judaism" (Krodel 1986, 441).

Felix's decision to postpone judgment until Lysias arrives appears at first reading to be a cautious and reasonable choice by a competent judge: he is, after all, *rather well informed about the Way* (v. 22). Felix even gives Paul some freedom under a loosely designed house arrest and arranges to hear him again (v. 23). But this initial favorable impression of Felix changes quickly.

Felix and his Jewish wife Drusilla (on the infelicities of this marriage, see Josephus, *Ant* 20.139-44) hear Paul *speak concerning faith in Jesus Christ* (v. 24). However offensive such talk may have been to the Jewess Drusilla is left to the imagination of the reader. What does disturb Felix is Paul's discussion of *justice, self-control, and the coming judgment* (v. 25). Felix's own inadequacy in the area of self-control is revealed in his hope to receive bribe money from Paul, a desire that motivates frequent conversations between Felix and Paul. His lack of justice is demonstrated when he leaves Paul in prison for two years in order *to grant the Jews a favor* (v. 27). "Thus Roman justice is undermined by an unjust administrator" (Tannehill 1990, 302).

25:1-12. Paul before Festus. The change in administration from Felix to Festus raises new hope that justice may be done for Paul. This hope is sustained when Festus refuses to grant a favor to the Jews against Paul, a favor they no doubt had come to expect from the Roman procurator through their dealings with Felix. Underlying the request to transfer Paul to Jerusalem was the old plot to ambush him along the way (v. 3). Festus replies that Paul would stay in Caesarea and if they had any accusations against Paul, those with authority should travel there along with Festus and present them personally before him (vv. 5-6).

In little more than a week, both Festus and the Jews have arrived to hear Paul (v. 6). Unsubstantiated charges are once again hurled against Paul (v. 7). And within these eight or ten days, Festus has evidently learned the political necessity of doing favors for the Jews (v. 9; see Tannehill 1990, 306-307) and asks Paul if he wishes to go to Jerusalem for trial. Paul's response is no little shock: rather than a simple yes or no, Paul once again maintains his innocence and appeals to Caesar for his trial (v. 11). That Paul is aware that he can receive no fair trial at the hands of Festus is hinted at in his words, "No one can *grant* me as *a favor* to them [the Jews]," echoing the narrator's statement that Festus wished "to grant the Jews a favor" (author trans.).

Historically, Paul's appeal to the emperor, the *provocatio*, is shrouded in mystery. Whether Paul thought he could have a fairer hearing before the emperor (then Nero) than before Festus is probably less important than his desire to fulfill his destiny to bear witness to the gospel before the emperor in Rome (19:21; 23:11; 27:24). Festus and his council, sensing an opportunity to rid themselves of a difficult case, formally ratify Paul's request with the terse judgment, *You have appealed to the emperor; to the emperor you will go* (v. 12).

25:13-26:32. Paul before Agrippa. After a few days, King Agrippa and his sister, Bernice, arrive to greet the newly appointed Festus (v. 13). Festus uses this opportunity to involve Agrippa in the proceedings against Paul, and more importantly, to offer a public defense of his own actions. In these two speeches by Festus (25:14-22 and 24-27), Luke subtly discloses Festus's hypocrisy without explicitly labeling it as such (see Tannehill 1990, 310–15). Like Lysias and Felix before him, Festus tries to put his public image

in the best light possible. His concern for justice that permeates his speech is notably absent from the narrator's account (25:1-12). His summary of the events surrounding Paul are decidedly biased toward his own self-interests. Festus correctly reports that he refused to turn Paul over to the Jews without a proper trial (25:16), but he glosses over his real purpose in proposing a Jerusalem trial for Paul (to gain the favor of the Jews, 25:9) by claiming that he *was at a loss how to investigate these questions* (25:20). Agrippa responds by requesting an audience with Paul, which Festus promptly arranges (25:22).

In his second address, however, Festus continues his distortion. First he exaggerates the pressure he is under from the Jews. He claims that the *whole Jewish community . . . both in Jerusalem and here* [Caesarea], petitioned him (25:24), while the narrator indicates only *the high priests and the leaders of the Jews* brought charges against Paul (25:2). Despite this (albeit exaggerated) pressure, Festus claims that Paul *had done nothing deserving death* (25:25). But when Paul had appealed to Caesar, there was nothing Festus could do but grant the request. If one takes Festus's remarks at face value, then Paul's request is incomprehensible. If, however, his speeches are understood as a cover-up, then Paul's appeal to Caesar to escape the incompetence if not corruption of this judge is even more understandable.

The decision to send Paul to Rome relieves one problem but creates another. Festus is no longer responsible for rendering a judgment in Paul's case, but he must specify the charges against Paul in a letter to the emperor. Perhaps his motivation to include Agrippa in the process is grounded in the desire to have someone to share the responsibility should the emperor determine the charges against Paul are of no substance, but rather are due to the incompetence of the local administration. Whatever the reason, Paul's address before Agrippa is "his most important speech before his most distinguished audience. The King Agrippa scene is as close as we shall get to seeing a speech before the king at Rome" (Pervo 1990, 87).

Indeed, Paul's speech in this scene allows him to fulfill the words of Jesus directed at his followers: "You will be brought before kings and governors for my name's sake" (Luke 21:13). The speech falls into five parts: (1) the *captatio benevolentiae* in which Paul (again following convention) curries the favor of Agrippa (26:2-3), (2) a summary of his Jewish background and credentials (26:4-8), (3) his work as persecutor of Christians (26:9-11), (4) a recounting of his conversion that here has more of the character of a prophetic call or commissioning (26:12-18), and (5) a brief summary of his missionary activity (26:19-23). The speech climaxes with Paul's assertion that the *Messiah must suffer* and be *the first to rise from the dead* (26:23). Paul's defense speech has a thorough christological grounding.

Festus interrupts Paul's speech at this point and accuses him of being *out of your mind* (26:24). For the first time in this scene, Paul addresses Festus, but only to make the point that Agrippa is fully aware of the things about which Paul speaks. None of the things associated with the Christian community has been *done in a corner* (26:26); rather Paul has made his case publicly in the marketplace and in the synagogues.

Agrippa replies to Paul's question about whether he believes the prophets with a sharp retort: *Are you so quickly persuading me to become a Christian?* (26:28). Paul concludes his defense with an object lesson: *Whether quickly or not, I pray to God that not only you but all who are listening to me today might become such as I am* [i.e., a follower of Jesus]—*except for these chains* (26:29).

But Agrippa has heard enough and rises to leave with Festus and Bernice. He does not depart without making this observation, *This man is doing nothing to deserve death or imprisonment* (26:31), and for the fifth time Paul's innocence is declared (see 23:9, 29; 25:18-19, 25). By now, the response that Paul could have been set free if he had not appealed to the emperor (26:32) sounds more than a little lame. The readers have no reason to think that Festus and Agrippa would have released Paul, regardless of his innocence or his appeal. The voyage to Rome begins.

The Sea Voyage to Rome, 27:1–28:31

In the last unit of Acts, the long-awaited journey to Rome is narrated. Luke returns to his use of first-person narration in these chapters, and much of the material shares common features with other sea voyage stories: shipwreck, narrow escapes, suspense, conflict, and high drama. This unit falls into two parallel panels, with the first and last being the most detailed.

A Paul journeys to Malta, 27:1-44
 B Paul in Malta, 28:1-10
A' Paul journeys to Rome, 28:11-16
 B' Paul in Rome, 28:17-31

Of course, Paul's voyage to Malta is determined by where he and his companions are washed ashore while his voyage to Rome has been an intentional destination for much of the second half of Acts. These units are examined in more detail below.

27:1-44. To Malta. The journey begins in Caesarea when Paul is entrusted to the custodial care of a centurion named Julius, who shows kindness to Paul (vv. 1-3). Verses 1-12 are both a prologue and a summary: in eight verses Luke describes Paul and the others on board setting sail for Italy and stopping at four different ports along the way, culminating with Paul's warning not to continue past *Fair Havens*. The storm (vv. 13-38) and shipwreck (vv. 39-44) are narrated in detailed and technical nautical language.

In a way typical of sea-voyage stories, Luke describes a variety of settings through which Paul and his fellow prisoners, the sailors, and Julius and his fellow soldiers pass: Sidon, Myra (in Lycia), Cnidus (or nearby), Fair Havens (on Crete), and Malta. In the process, they pass near several other cities, regions, or islands: Cilicia and Pamphylia, Lasea, Phoenix, Cauda, and Syrtis. But the one setting that remains constant throughout this voyage is the sea (both the Mediterranean and the Adriatic), and this setting is the most important for understanding the significance of this passage.

In both ancient Jewish and Greek literature, the sea was viewed sometimes as an evil or hostile place of chaos and confusion, sometimes as a vehicle through which divine forces punish wickedness. Homer tells how Odysseus's crew was killed in a shipwreck as punishment for destroying Helios's cattle (*Odyssey* 12.127-41, 259-446). In Chariton's *Chaereas and Callirhoe*, evil persons are drowned at sea and the just are spared (3.3.10, 18, 3.4.9-10; cited by Talbert 1984, 101). In the OT, God uses the sea to reverse creation and judge evil humanity (Gen 6–8); God uses a sea to destroy the Egyptians and rescue the Israelites (Exod 14); God employs a storm to persuade a recalcitrant prophet to speak (Jonah 1). The same view is held in postbiblical Judaism. In the Babylonian Talmud (*B.Mes.*, 58b-59), Rabbi Gamaliel is spared from the raging sea only after declaring his innocence before God (see Talbert 1984, 102).

Thus, both Greek and Jewish readers would understand the potential disasters involved here. If Paul perishes at sea, he is no doubt guilty of the charges leveled against him; if he is spared, then he is honored with divine vindication. The closing note to this section, where Paul and his traveling entourage are brought safely to land, reveals God's evaluation of Paul and his mission (v. 44).

Luke also uses this sea voyage with all its colorful details and rich imagery to depict the symbolic death and resurrection of Paul, much as he narrates the imprisonment and release of Peter in Acts 12. Both prison and shipwreck are common metaphors for death in antiquity. Night, the disappearance of heavenly luminaries (v. 20; cf. Luke 23:44-45), and the loss of hope (v. 20; cf. Luke 24:21) all echo the passion of Jesus and allude to Paul's symbolic death. On the other hand, references to daylight, the third day (21:19), a shared meal (vv. 33-35; cf. Luke 24:30-31), and Paul's deliverance from the tomb of the sea (v. 44) all point to a kind of symbolic resurrection.

Luke also deepens the characterization of Paul as a Christian benefactor through a description of his words and deeds. Two are especially noteworthy. After taking harbor in *Fair Havens* (v. 8), Paul predicts the dangers that lie before him and his fellow travelers: *Sirs, I can see that the voyage will be with danger and much heavy loss, not only of the cargo and the ship, but also of our lives* (v. 10). Like a prophet of old, Paul's words are ignored by his audience (vv. 11-12), and finally under divine direction he modifies his original prophecy to assure his companions that *God has granted safety to all those who are sailing with you* (v. 24). Still, Paul's heroic role as leader and visionary is strengthened by these words of prophetic insight, not to mention that Paul alone is granted direct discourse throughout this passage.

Equally important is the scene described in vv. 33-35 where Paul urges his companions to take food. The eucharistic symbolism of this passage is quite apparent: *After he had said this, he took bread; and giving thanks to God in the presence of all, he broke it and began to eat* (v. 35; cf. Luke 22:19). While perhaps not strictly bespeaking an observance of the Lord's Supper since most of the company are not believers, this meal anticipates deliverance in some sense similar to the promise of deliverance present in the Lord's Supper. This position is supported by the repeated references to "salvation" or "deliverance" throughout this section (vv. 20, 31, 34, 43, 44; 28:1, 4), no doubt "a reminder to a Christian reader that the same God who delivered the storm-tossed voyagers from physical harm is the God who in Christ brings ultimate salvation and true eternal life" (Polhill 1992, 527).

28:1-10. In Malta, Paul and all his companions are delivered safely from the shipwreck and find themselves on the island of Malta. Here the theme of Paul's vindication continues. Just as nature was understood to be a vehicle of divine vindication or retribution, so also was the animal kingdom (see *t.Sanh.* 8:3; *y.Ber.* 5:1; cited by Talbert 1984, 102). Paul survived the shipwreck, but will he survive the bite of the viper who fastened itself to Paul's hand while he gathers firewood (vv. 2-4)? The natives think not, assuming the snakebite is punishment for some heinous crime such as murder and that Paul is being punished by the Greek goddess of "Justice" (v. 5). But once gain, Paul is vindicated by God, and, unharmed, he shakes the serpent into the fire. By now there is no need to correct for the reader the native's misperception that Paul is a god (v. 6; cf. 10:25-26; 14:11-15).

The final act of Paul on Malta also confirms his role as a righteous representative of a beneficent God. When the leading man of the island, Publius, falls ill, Paul cures him *by praying and putting his hands on him* (v. 8). In return, Paul the Christian benefactor is the recipient of great honor and provisions at the hands of the Maltese. Christians, Luke seems to say, have no corner on hospitality and benefaction.

28:11-16. To Rome. After three months of winter, Paul and company set sail again. Three days in Syracuse, one day at Rhegium, and they join a community of believers in Puteoli where they lodge for a week. Paul next travels to Rome and takes the decisive step in fulfilling the earlier theophanic prophecy (*Do not be afraid, Paul; you must stand before the emperor*, 27:24). Having literally survived hell and high water (symbolized by the Satanic serpent and the storm at sea), Paul and crew finally come to Rome (see Pervo 1990, 92). The scene ends with a reminder that Paul, despite his immediate past heroism, is still a prisoner: *When we came into Rome, Paul was allowed to live by himself, with the soldier who was guarding him* (v. 16).

28:17-31. In Rome. The end of a book is no less important than its beginning. Luke chooses to end this narrative neither with a confrontation between Paul and the emperor, nor with a narration of Paul's martyrdom, but rather by focusing on Paul's dialogue with the Roman Jews. The closing scene is organized into three parts: Paul's first (vv. 17-22) and second (vv. 23-28) encounters with the Jews, and the final summary statement about Paul's ministry in Rome (vv. 30-31).

In the first encounter with the Roman Jews, Paul recounts the events of Acts 22–26. In so doing, Luke preserves what is most important for his readers to retain from that long stretch of narrative and speeches. Most important is Paul's claim that he *had done nothing against our people or the customs of our ancestors* (v. 17). Further, his appeal to Caesar did not mean that Paul intended to bring a charge against the Jewish nation (v. 19). To the contrary, Paul insists that *it is for the sake of the hope of Israel that I am bound with this chain* (v. 20). Throughout this speech, Paul maintains that he has remained a loyal Jew and that his mission to the gentiles is not based on an anti-Jewish foundation. The Jews respond by saying that they would like to hear more of Paul's thinking, especially regarding the Christian *sect* that is spoken against everywhere (v. 22).

In the second encounter with the Roman Jews, a familiar pattern emerges: Paul is first heard favorably by the Jews, is then resisted, and finally turns to the gentiles (see 13:42-48; 18:5-7; 19:8-10). Once again, his proclamation of Jesus divides his audience: *Some were convinced by what he had said, while others refused to believe* (v. 24). In his parting statement to them Paul quotes Isa 6:9-10, a harsh indictment of the dullness of ears, eyes, and heart of the Jewish people. Individual Jews may continue to believe, but Israel as a nation, at least at the time of Luke's writing, has rejected the new thing God has done in and through Christ Jesus. Now for the third and final time, Paul turns to the gentiles and thus opens up the *salvation of God* to all who would come (v. 28; cf. 13:46; 18:6).

The Book of Acts ends with the notice that Paul spent the next two years living under house arrest at his own expense (v. 30). Mention of *two years* in Acts often refers to periods of special blessing (see 18:11; 19:10; see Talbert 1984, 104; although cf. 24:27). The last claim of the book is that Paul preached the kingdom of God (cf. 1:6) *without hindrance* (v. 31), or "unhindered." The focus subtly shifts from Paul the messenger to the message he is proclaiming, the Christian gospel.

Frank Stagg has persuasively demonstrated that this final word—unhindered—sums up the message of Acts: the Gospel has overcome all human-made prejudice and every geographical, social, ethnic, gender, and theological barrier (Stagg 1955). In this regard, Pervo's words are apropos: "Luke's own last word is a perfect summary of his writings, a one-word closure, i.e., at the same time, an opening, a bright and invigorating bid to the future, an assurance that 'the ends of the earth' is not the arrival at a boundary, but realization of the limitless promises of the dominion of God" (Pervo 1990, 96).

The gospel is unhindered because of the sovereignty of God who ultimately insures its triumph in the face of adversity. But from Luke's perspective, this "unhindered" gospel remains an "unfinished" gospel. The gospel is unfinished because of the grace of God who ultimately insures that its completion can occur when all have had the opportunity to hear about the "kingdom of God" and the "Lord Jesus Christ." Unfettered yet unfinished, the gospel can only be completed when the readers finally take up the challenge to fulfill the prophecy uttered at the beginning of the first of Luke's two volumes proclaimed by John the Baptist (who also quotes the words of the prophet Isaiah): "all flesh shall see the salvation of God" (Luke 3:6).

Works Cited

Danker, Frederick. 1982. *Benefactor: Epigraphic Study of a Graeco-Roman and N.T. Semantic Field.*

Fitzmyer, Joseph A. 1981. *The Gospel according to Luke I–IX.* AncB.

Funk, Robert. 1988. *The Poetics of Biblical Narrative.*

Garrett, Susan R. 1989. *The Demise of the Devil: Magic and the Demonic in Luke's Writings.*

Gill, David. 1974. "The Structure of Acts 9," *Bib* 55:546–48.

Haenchen, Ernst. 1971. *The Acts of the Apostles.*

Krodel, Gerhard. 1986. *Acts.* AugCNT.

Johnson, Luke T. 1977. *The Literary Function of Possessions in Luke-Acts.* SBLDS 39.

Martin, Clarice J. 1989. "A Chamberlain's Journey and the Challenge of Interpretation for Liberation," *Semeia* 47: 105–35.

Neyrey, Jerome H. 1991. "The Symbolic Universe of Luke-Acts: 'They Turned the World Upside Down'," in *The Social World of Luke-Acts: Models for Interpretation*, ed. Neyrey, 271–304.

Pervo, Richard I. 1990. *Luke's Story of Paul.*

Pilch, John J. 1991. "Sickness and Healing in Luke-Acts," in *The Social World of Luke-Acts,* 181-209.

Polhill, John B. 1992. *Acts.* NAC.

Stagg, Frank. 1955. *The Book of Acts.* 1990. "Apostles, Acts of the," MDB.

Talbert, Charles H. 1984. *Acts.* Knox Preaching Guides. 1990. "Luke, Gospel of," MDB.

Tannehill, Robert C. 1990. *The Narrative Unity of Luke-Acts.* Vol. 2. *The Acts of the Apostles.*

Romans

Dan O. Via

Introduction

Across the centuries the Christian church has found Paul's letter to the Romans to be one of its richest theological resources.

Genuineness, Unity, and Place in the Canon

Genuineness and unity. Scholars have generally concluded that PAUL was in fact the author of the whole original letter as established on the basis of the best manuscripts. Although the argument is inevitably somewhat circular, Romans is held to be in broad agreement with the other letters considered to be genuine writings of Paul in style, vocabulary, and thought. We shall see below that in light of the textual (i.e., manuscript) evidence there has been debate about whether the original letter was composed of chaps. 1–14, 1–15, or 1–16.

One should note that there have been some exceptions to the general consensus that Paul is the author of the whole original letter and that the letter is a coherent unity. Three examples will be mentioned. Rudolf Bultmann argued that Romans contains several later glosses (2:1; 2:16; 6:17b; 7:25b; 8:1; 10:17; 13:5) (Bultmann 1967). Walter Schmithals maintained that our Romans is composed of two earlier letters of Paul plus some fragments. According to Schmithals, letter A contained Rom 1:1–4:25; 5:12–11:36; 15:8-13, and letter B consisted of 12:1-21; 13:8-10; 14:1–15:4a, 7, 5-6; 15:14-32; 16:21-23; 15:33 (Schmithals 1975, 180, 189). Gloss and partition theories are not supported by ms. evidence.

Perhaps the most radical challenge to the genuineness and unity of Romans came from J. C. O'Neill, who argued that not only had short marginal comments of others been taken into the text but also editors had supplemented the text with substantial interpolations. Among the extensive sections that O'Neill denied to Paul are 1:18-32; 2:1-16; 2:17-29; 5:12-21; 7:14-25; 9:1-29; 10:16–11:36; 12:1–15:13 (O'Neill 1975, 14, 41–42, 49, 53, 96, 131–32, 155, 177, 192). O'Neill strained hard to explain why the manuscript evidence does not support his position (O'Neill 1975, 14–15) and generally based his argument on three questionable presuppositions: (1) that Paul always argued in a single-mindedly logical line and that, therefore, any inconsistencies have to be attributed to someone else; (2) that an author (Paul) is more likely to be consistent than a commentator; and (3) that Paul always used terms in the same sense.

Canonical Location. The individual title "To the Romans" suggests that Paul's letters became widely known as parts of a collection with a comprehensive title something like "The Letters of Paul." The most plausible explanation for this collection is that Paul's associates began a continuing "Pauline school" that sought to preserve and extend his influence. The first clear evidence for the existence of the Pauline collection, however, is provided by the second-century semignostic MARCION, whose arrangement places Romans after Galatians and 1 and 2 Corinthians (Knox 1982, 356–57; Gamble 1985, 41).

While Marcion gives us the first definite evidence, it seems probable that the collection originated earlier, in the late first or early second century. Had Marcion's collection been the first one, there would likely have been "orthodox" suspicion of Paul. But there is no indication of second-century hostility to Paul except from heterodox Jewish Christianity. Moreover, the reference of IGNATIUS (early second century) to "Paul in every letter" suggests that he knew a Pauline collection. The order of letters in this early collection was based on the length of the letters, but there seem to have been two editions of the collection based on the fact that length was assessed in different ways. In both cases the order ran from longest to shortest. The first approach regarded all letters to a given community as one unit and produced the order 1–2 Corinthians, Romans, Ephesians, 1–2 Thessalonians, Galatians, Philippians, Colossians (Philemon?). The second approach considered each individual letter as a separate unit and produced the order Romans, 1 Corinthians, 2 Corinthians, Ephesians, Galatians, Philippians, Colossians, 1 Thessalonians, 2 Thessalonians, (Philemon?) (Gamble 1985, 40–45; Knox 1982, 356–57).

Place of Writing and Date

Place. As Paul draws to the conclusion of the letter, he tells his readers that he has evangelized the Mediterranean world from JERUSALEM to ILLYRICUM (roughly the former modern Yugoslavia and Albania) and therefore has no more place to work in the East (15:19, 23). He hopes to extend the preaching of the gospel to Spain and to visit Rome on his way there (15:23-24, 28), but first he must go to Jerusalem to carry the money that he has collected in MACEDONIA and ACHAIA for the poor among the Jerusalem Christians (15:25-26).

Where is he as he writes? CORINTH is the most likely place. In the CORINTHIAN CORRESPONDENCE Paul is also concerned about the offering to be sent from the gentile churches of Achaia and GALATIA to Jerusalem, and he contemplates that he may make the trip to Jerusalem himself (1 Cor 16:1-4; 2 Cor 8:1-14; 9:1-5). In addition, PHOEBE, whom he recommends and who may be the bearer of the letter, is a deacon in the church of CENCHREAE, the port of Corinth (16:1-2). Beyond that GAIUS, his host (16:23), may well be the Gaius of 1 Cor 1:14, one of Paul's Corinthian converts. And ERASTUS (16:23) also could be loosely associated with Corinth (Acts 19:21-22; 2 Tim 4:20).

Date. Paul was apparently in Corinth three times, and Romans would have been written during the third of these sojourns. That means the writing occurred late in his life. The three-missionary-journey scheme in Acts would call for dating the letter late in the third journey (Acts 20:1-3). While the Acts format may contain individual items that are historically accurate, the scheme as a whole, and especially its stress on Paul's dependence on Jerusalem, is historically suspect. Nevertheless, Paul's letters confirm that he was a travelling missionary and suggest that he wrote Romans late in his career.

The one certainly datable event during Paul's missionary activities is the proconsulship of the Roman GALLIO in Corinth, whose tenure in office lasted from the spring of 51 to the spring of 52. During his first stay in Corinth Paul was haled before Gallio, according to Acts 18:12-17, by hostile Jews. It is plausible to suppose that the third visit to Corinth, the occasion for writing Romans, was sometime around 55 or 56.

Manuscript Evidence and Destination

Paul did not found the church in Rome and had not visited it prior to the writing of the letter. Why did he write this letter to Rome? Did he in fact write it *to Rome*? It seems altogether probable that the original letter was addressed by Paul directly to the Roman church, but that contention has not gone unchallenged.

One reason for challenging an original Roman destination is that the words "in Rome" are omitted in 1:7, 15 in a few manuscripts of a Western textual type. If this omission were the original reading, then it might be argued that Paul wrote the letter as a circular one, not intended for any one particular church. But the evidence is strongly in favor of including "in Rome" in the text. The great preponderance of manuscript evidence supports it. Romans 1:13 shows that the letter is written to a particular church that he has wanted to visit but has thus far been prevented from visiting. It can also be demonstrated that Romans as a whole can be rather specifically connected with a particular situation in the church at Rome.

The major textual problem in Romans is that the final doxology (16:25-27) appears in several different places in the manuscript tradition. The doxology itself is probably post-Pauline (see commentary), but it must have been composed quite early, and its placement bears on the question of the various versions of Romans that circulated in the early church. The complex manuscript tradition supports the following six configurations:

(1) 1:1–16:23 + doxology
(2) 1:1–14:23 + doxology + 15:1–16:23 + doxology
(3) 1:1–14:23 + doxology + 15:1–16:24
(4) 1:1–16:24
(5) 1:1–15:33 + doxology + 16:1-23
(6) 1:1–14:23 + 16:24 + doxology

(Metzger 1975, 534)

The evidence suggests that at an early date three versions of Romans were in circulation: Rom 1–14, Rom 1–15, and Rom 1–16. Each will be briefly assessed.

Romans 1–14 is probably not the original. The manuscript evidence is weaker than it is for the other alternatives, and the thought of 15:1-13 shows no break with that of chap. 14. A tradition going back to

ORIGEN says that Marcion cut off chaps. 15–16, and we can understand why he might have. He would have wanted to remove the personal material in 15:14-33 and chap. 16. And his antipathy for the OT would have prompted him to excise 15:1-13 as he did chaps. 4 and 9–11 (Manson 1991, 9–11).

A somewhat stronger case can be made for Rom 1–15 as the original. Only one manuscript supports it (the PAPYRUS P[46] which shows the concluding doxology after 15:33), but it is the oldest Greek manuscript of Paul (ca. 200) and represents the early Alexandrian text, generally considered the best. Moreover, Rom 16 with its many greetings to named individuals and its biting criticism of false teachings in 16:17-20a seems very different in content from chap. 15. The preceding factors have generated some arguments that Rom 16 was a separate letter of Paul and that it was sent to EPHESUS, not Rome. (1) Paul knows more people than he would have known in Rome, but he would have had many friends in Ephesus where he had a long ministry. (2) Some of the people greeted in Rom 16 are explicitly connected with ASIA, the province surrounding Ephesus: Prisca and Aquila (Acts 18:24-26; Rom 16:3), Epaenetus (Rom 16:5). (3) Paul knows some of these people too well for them to belong to a church he has never visited. For example, he knows who have house churches meeting in their homes (16:5, 15) and knows the identity of household groups (16:10, 11). (4) Rom 16:17-20 is inappropriately sharp for the Roman situation but could have been directed to a church like Ephesus where Paul had long worked. (5) Rom 15:33 has the solemn tone of a conclusion (Kümmel 1965, 222–26; Knox 1982, 364–68; Manson 1991, 12–13).

Similar arguments can be used to support the view that Paul wrote all of Rom 1–16 to Ephesus and 1–15 to Rome (Manson 1991, 11–13).

On the other side arguments have been brought forward against a connection between Rom 16 (or 1–16) and Ephesus and against the independence of chap. 16. (1) While there are other examples of letters composed primarily of greetings, there seems to be no other case in the Pauline corpus of combining letters to more than one church. (2) Inscriptions support the currency of the names Urbanus, Phlegon, Persis, and Asyncritus in Rome in the first century but not in Ephesus. (3) Paul seems not to have singled out individuals for greetings in churches that he did found. (4) Rom 15:33 is not a characteristic Pauline conclusion. Typically the peace wish (Rom 15:33) preceded (Gal 6:16; 1 Thes 5:23)

the concluding benediction, which always makes reference to grace, an element lacking in Rom 15:33 (Lampe 1991, 216–17; Gamble 1977, 53–54, 84, 90; Ziesler 1989, 21). It should be pointed out, however, that this is not a strong argument because it could be held that an original fifteen-chapter version of Romans contained a grace benediction following 15:33.

John Knox maintained that the arguments for Ephesus and Rome cancelled each other out and that neither should be regarded as the destination of Rom 16. Rather that chapter was written after Paul's time by someone in the Roman church in order to claim Paul's authority in the fight against false teaching (Knox 1954, 364–68). Knox's position has a good bit to commend it. However, the strongest manuscript evidence places the final doxology at the end of chap. 16. Moreover, in recent years additional arguments have been articulated in favor of connecting Rom 16 with the situation of the Roman church and of regarding that chapter as an integral part of Paul's original letter to the Romans. That is now the consensus position (Donfried 1991a, lxx).

These arguments in support of it may here be considered: (1) Paul might well have known many people in the Roman church because Jewish Christians expelled from Rome by the edict of CLAUDIUS (see next section), whom Paul met in Ephesus (and elsewhere), could have returned to Rome after Claudius' death. (2) Movement was easy in the ROMAN EMPIRE. (3) Paul need not actually have known all whom he greeted. (4) Rom 16:1-2 does resemble a letter of recommendation, but there are other examples of notes of recommendation within the conclusions of longer letters. (5) Other letters of Paul display the same concluding structure: (a) travel plans (1 Cor 16:5-9; Rom 15:22-29); (b) recommendation of a third party (1 Cor 16:10-11, 15-18; Rom 16:1-2); (c) final greeting (1 Cor 16:19-21; Rom 16:3-16) (Gamble 1977, 47–51, 85, 87, 89; Donfried 1991b, 48–49). (6) As for 16:17-20 the sterner tone may suggest that Paul realizes there are other issues in Rome than the ones he had addressed or he may have outside infiltrators in mind. Changes of tone within Paul's letters are not unusual (1 Cor 16:22; Phil 3:2, 18-19; 1 Thes 2:15-16), and in any case his addressing the readers here as "brothers" shows that his posture is not strongly polemical (Ziesler 1989, 23; Lampe 1991, 219; Wedderburn 1991, 15; Gamble 1977, 52).

Paul's purpose for the multiple greetings is to support the individuals who are named but even more to undergird his own credibility by associating himself with these people whom the Roman church knows and trusts. This would be important to do in a church that he did not establish (Lampe 1991, 219; Gamble 1977, 48, 92).

We have seen that it is quite plausible to suppose that Paul knew a number of people in the Roman church and that he knew at least some of them well and was in close touch with them. That would be because mobility was high in the Roman Empire and mail communication was quick and easy—seven or eight days between Corinth and Rome. Paul then could have had a good deal of specific knowledge about the situation of the church at Rome.

Occasion and Purpose

A good case then can be made for connecting Romans closely to a specific situation in the Roman church. But Paul's own situation and the one that he addresses in Rome both have many aspects, and the purposes that motivate his writing of the letter are more than one.

In assessing the occasion and purpose we have to take account not only of the situation in Rome but also of Paul's own situation and experiences. How do his successes, hardships, and conflicts in Galatia, Corinth, Ephesus, and elsewhere and his sense of having completed the evangelization of the East affect his posture? What impact do his intentions to visit not just Rome but also Jerusalem and Spain have on the content of the letter? And we must consider the character of the letter itself. While it is not at all a full, constructive statement of Paul's theology, it is relatively systematic and tightly argued. Whether or not it was Paul's intention to write such a letter, that nevertheless defines its nature. And while a convincing case can be made that the letter addresses a particular situation in Rome, it is by no means immediately obvious in what precise ways that situation is reflected in the letter.

Sometimes those who argue for a close relationship to a precise historical setting speak as if the only two alternatives are that the letter either is totally conditioned historically or is a timeless theological compendium unrelated to a specific setting. But that is not an adequate grasp of our interpretive task. The letter *is* historically conditioned. Thus the two real alternatives become is its meaning exhausted by its historical connectedness or does the meaning both reflect and transcend the setting? The more probable alternative is that the historical situation affects the meaning but does not account for everything in it.

Because the historical and theological context is complicated and the precise relationship of the letter to the Roman situation is not obvious, many have found the governing key to the meaning and purpose of Romans in some other factor: (1) it is a general theological treatise; (2) it reflects *Paul's* situation; (3) it has the imminent trip to Jerusalem primarily in view; (4) it is controlled by the hope of a mission to Spain. No one of these alone is an adequate explanation for the letter, but each must be considered for what it contributes to our understanding of it.

(1) According to Anders Nygren, Paul in Romans is dealing with a great theological issue on which hangs human life itself. It would be a misunderstanding of Romans and a constriction of its meaning to try to interpret it in the light of the accidental circumstances of the Roman setting, of which Paul had very little knowledge anyway (Nygren 1949, 4–8). Günther Bornkamm in a famous article held that while Paul had only a general knowledge of the Roman church, the letter grew out of the specifics of *Paul's* situation and is not a timeless theological treatise. However, Bornkamm ended up asserting that Romans lifts Paul's theology above the moment of definite situations and conflicts and into the sphere of the eternally and universally valid (Bornkamm 1991, 20, 21, 28). This unexpected turn in Bornkamm's argument shows how hard it is to confine the meaning of Romans within any specific historical situation.

(2) That Romans is to be explained not in light of the Roman situation but in light of Paul's own was also argued by T. W. Manson. Paul sums up the position that he had reached as a result of his controversies in Galatia and Corinth over the relationship of law to gospel (Manson 1991, 14–15). Robert Karris sees Romans as dealing with theological and ethical issues in the light of solutions to problems Paul had reached in his earlier missionary work, and Karris questions why we should assume that all of Paul's letters must have been addressed to specific church situations (Karris 1991a, 82–123; 1991b, 127).

(3) Peter Lampe maintained that the purpose of the whole letter was to gain the confidence of the Romans so that they would support Paul's mission to Spain (Lampe 1991, 218). Paul does want their support (15:24, 28)—spiritual, material, or both. This reference, however, is too brief and casual and Paul's concern to clarify his understanding of the gospel for its own sake is too strong for the Spanish mission to be a major part of Paul's purpose (Klein 1991, 33).

(4) The collection that he was about to carry to Jerusalem was important to Paul because it grew out of his agreement with the Jerusalem leaders (Gal 2:10) and symbolized the oneness of Jewish and gentile believers. Jacob Jervell argues that the prominence of Jewish issues in Romans—the status of the law (7:7), whether Israel has an advantage (3:1), the ultimate fate of Israel (11:1, 11-12) and others—shows that the content of Rom 1:18–11:36 is the defense Paul expects to make in *Jerusalem*. He presents it to the Romans because he wants them on his side when he goes to Jerusalem (Jervell 1991, 56, 62–64).

It is certainly the case that Paul wants the Roman church to pray for his Jerusalem mission, to pray that the unbelieving Jews will not harm him and that Jewish Christians in Jerusalem will be willing to accept his offering (15:30-31). Paul is intently looking over his shoulder at Jerusalem as he writes to Rome, and that undoubtedly affects the content of the letter, but the prominence of Jewish issues is also explained by his own origin in Judaism and by the gentile-Jewish conflict in the Roman church. And that brings us to Rome.

The intended visit. Although Paul's past longing to visit Rome has been thwarted (in chap. 1 he does not say why), he now intends to come for the purpose of exercising his apostleship by preaching the gospel and gaining a harvest of obedient faith (1:5-7, 13, 15). The Romans fall within his obligation to preach to all categories of people (1:13-15). He modestly—or prudently—suggests also that he expects to receive a spiritual blessing from them (1:11-12).

How does this eagerness to preach in Rome square with Paul's statement in 15:20 that it has been his intention to preach where Christ has not already been named? This principle of action he now offers as the explanation for why he has not been able to come to Rome (15:22). He was preaching where the gospel had not been heard. But since Christ has been named in Rome and the church has been established independently of Paul, how can he now come to preach in Rome since he does not want to build on another's foundation (15:20)?

Most scholars have taken his statement in 15:20 to be a fixed policy. And if that is the case, there seems to be a conflict between that policy and his present hope to preach in Rome. Can the conflict be resolved?

According to Günter Klein, Paul's non-interference policy does not renounce all missionary activity in already Christianized areas. He will not build on another's foundation, but if there is a church that in Paul's view lacks an apostolic foundation, he is free to preach there. What is at stake is whether the church in Rome has actually been founded on Christ (see 1 Cor 3:10-11). Paul will preach in Rome because the Roman church lacks the fundamental kerygma (proclamation) and grounding in Christ (Klein 1991, 38–43).

This is an attractive theory that could explain much in Romans. But if Paul's posture in principle were that he could preach wherever a church was not founded on the apostolic preaching of Christ, and if Rome were such a church, he could have gone to Rome at any time. He need not have waited until he had evangelized the East (15:19-22).

Peter Stuhlmacher deals with the issue by connecting Paul's eagerness to preach in Rome (1:15) with his *past* desire in 1:13: he *had* intended to come and preach, but having been prevented, that is no longer his hope, and he will be satisfied with the mutual sharing of faith described in 1:11-12. That is not in conflict with the noninterference policy (Stuhlmacher 1991, 236–37).

But Paul's concrete elaboration of his strong sense of obligation to preach to all and the use of the present tense in 1:14 make it difficult to relegate his eagerness to preach in Rome in 1:15 to the past.

Karl Donfried has suggested the most convincing approach (Donfried 1991c, 45). Paul is not stating an unexceptionable policy in 15:20 but simply explaining why he has not been able to come to Rome. It has been his first responsibility to preach to those who have not heard the gospel. But now that he has completely evangelized the East—according to his understanding of his calling—and has no further place to work there, he is free to come to Rome where the gospel has already been heard. The purpose of Paul's visit will be to preach in Rome.

The visit and the letter. For the Hellenistic world generally and for Paul in particular a letter is understood as a substitute or surrogate for the presence of the sender and also the recipient. Paul states at one point that what he says by letter when absent, he does when present (2 Cor 10:11). In a somewhat formal and indirect way a letter represents what happens in face-to-face human meetings: greeting-dialogue-farewell (Funk 1967; Petersen 1985, 53–55). The purpose of the letter then is the same as the purpose of the visit: to preach the gospel—in light of the Roman situation, his own situation, the intended missions to Jerusalem and Spain, and in light of the capacity of the gospel to generate a certain logic or structure of thought irrespective of a particular situation.

The specific setting in the Roman church. This now needs further attention. The following scenario has been gaining increasing acceptance as the situation in the Roman church that Paul was addressing.

The Roman writer Suetonius (ca. 75–160) reports that the emperor CLAUDIUS expelled the Jews from Rome (in 49) because of rioting instigated by Chrestus. Chrestus is probably a corruption of Christus, and Suetonius may have thought that Christ was there in Rome at the time. These disturbances in the Jewish community probably refer to the conflict between law-abiding Jews and Jews who had come to believe in Jesus as the Messiah and had freed themselves from the Law of Moses. Among the Jews forced to leave the city would have been a number of Jewish Christians. There is no evidence that Claudius's edict of expulsion was ever rescinded, but it was probably allowed to lapse after his death in 54, and that would have made it possible for Jews who had left Rome to return. We can imagine that many Jewish Christians availed themselves of the opportunity. Jewish Christians were then returning to a Christian community that had for several years been entirely—or almost so—in the hands of gentile Christians. Differences would have been present, and tensions would have developed. Paul's purpose is to interpret the gospel so as to present the theological basis upon which these groups with different experiences and theological positions can live with mutual acceptance and love as one body in Christ (12:3-8; 14:1; 15:7-10). How are the gentile majority and Jewish minority to relate to each other (e.g., Donfried 1991c, 48–49; Wiefel 1991, 92–96; Ziesler 1989, 11–12; Dunn 1988, xlviii–xlix, liii; Wedderburn 1991, 55–56)?

The composition of the Roman Christian community needs to be further examined. The Jewish quarrels that Claudius addressed show that Christianity was in Rome by the 40s. We do not know who the first missionaries were, but the fourth-century writer "Ambrosiaster" suggests that they were Jewish Christians faithful to the Law of Moses, and that may well be correct. It could be that the absence of a central governing council for Roman Jews made it easier than it might have been for Christian missionaries to win converts from individual synagogues (Wiefel 1991, 108). By the time of Paul's letter, we may suppose that there were at least five groups in the Roman Christian community, representing at least three different theological positions: (1) Jewish Christians who were faithful to the Law of Moses; (2) Jewish Christians who were law-free; (3) gentile Christians who were law-abiding because of deep attachment to the synagogue prior to their conversion to Christianity; (4) gentile Christians who were law-free; (5) gentile Christians who stretched Paul's belief that salvation is by grace and not by works of the law to mean that the Christian stands under no moral obligation. Paul appears to assume that the Roman church was composed primarily of gentiles (1:5-6, 13-15; 9:3-4; 10:1-3; 11:13, 17-18, 24, 28, 30-31; 15:15-16, 18). But that it also contained Jewish members is seen in 15:7-12; 16:3, 7, 11. It would seem probable that the various house churches were marked and divided by these differing theological and ethnic characteristics.

We may also observe other social differences. Chapter 16 suggests that women had important places of leadership. If the Roman Christian community reflected the general population, it would have contained about two-thirds slaves and freedpersons and one-third free. Probably a majority of the members would have been from the lower socio-economic strata and a small minority from the upper classes (Lampe 1991, 222–30).

The letter is pervaded by Paul's concern about Jewish-gentile relationships (1:16; 2:12-16, 25-29; 8:33; 9:1–11:32; 15:8-12). His defense of the law and affirmation of God's faithfulness to Israel (3:1-8; 3:31; 7:7a, 10a, 12, 14a, 16; 11:1-2, 11, 23, 28-29) bespeak his own conviction about the continuity of the Christian community with Israel (4:11-12; 11:17-18). And he hereby supports the commitments of law-abiding Jewish Christians and gentile Christians who had firm attachments to JUDAISM as well as opposes the antinomian position (that faith has no moral requirements) of some. At the same time his proclamation of the gospel and his critique of the law (3:19-30; 4:1-5; 6:14; 7:1-6, 7b-9; 9:30–10:4) expound his own conviction about salvation by GRACE, not works of the LAW, and support the position of law-free gentile and Jewish Christians as well as confront his law-affirming Jewish Christian opponents.

The discussion up to this point may be summarized in the following way. Paul purposes to offer the Romans a universally valid gospel that is the power of God for the salvation of all humankind and in fact of the whole cosmos. This gospel, which has been worked out through his own experiences, is addressed to Rome for the sake of the gospel's own truth and for the well-being of the Romans. That is, Paul hopes to win converts to the Christian faith (1:5-6, 14-15) and to strengthen the faith of believers (15:14-15). And because of the all-encompassing capacity of the gospel, it can be the key for resolving the gentile-Jewish tension in the Roman church. At the same time Paul also wants to win the Romans' assent to his understanding of the gospel in the interest of gaining their support for his trip to Jerusalem and his Spanish mission.

Three additional topics that bear on the question of the letter's relationship to its historical situation call for brief discussion.

Historical setting and theological structure. Neither all of the elements in Romans nor the way they are related or structured can be accounted for—at least not exhaustively—by the historical situation. For example, it cannot be demonstrated, as is sometimes suggested (Campbell 1991, 252–53, 258–60), that the purpose of the gospel is the transformation of Jewish-gentile relationships.

It is clear from the syntactical indications of purpose in 3:25-26 that the *purpose* of the gospel is the demonstration of God's righteousness and the justification of believers. The new equality of Jews and gentiles (3:28-30) is the result of carrying out this purpose. It will also be argued in the commentary that justification and faith (3:21–4:25) have a structural relationship to life and freedom (5:1–8:36) that grows out of the inner logic of Paul's gospel and not out of the Roman situation.

Historical setting and letter type. The evidence of a certain sub-type of the letter genre in the first century augments the probability that Romans does both respond to a specific historical situation and also transcend that situation. A letter belonging to the sub-genre known as the letter-essay is addressed to a real situation and has the framework of a regular letter (greeting and closing), but what is framed inside is more nearly a treatise than a personal message. This type of letter has an instructional purpose that reaches beyond the immediate addressees (Stirewalt 1991, 147–48; Donfried 1991d, 121–25; Dunn, lix).

Paul apparently felt free to mix genres, and evidence of this is seen in the fact that what is framed inside the greeting and closing of Romans displays certain characteristics of the *logos protreptikos* or "speech of exhortation." This type had the purpose of winning the hearers to a particular way of life or thought and had the following parts: (1) a critique of other ways of life or thought (Rom 1:18–3:20); (2) a positive presentation of the true way (Rom 3:21–15:13); (3) a personal appeal (15:14-33) (Aune 1991, 278–82, 295–96).

Historical setting and diatribe style. Karl Donfried has acknowledged that the claim that Romans was addressed to a specific situation would be undermined if it could be shown that the diatribe exercised a pervasive influence on the letter. However, Donfried has argued that the diatribe was not a definite genre but rather a series of rhetorical devices, that it did not seriously influence Romans, and that it does not in fact bring into question the historical specificity of the letter to the Romans (Donfried 1991d, 112–19; 1991b, lxx). We need to consider Stanley Stowers's work on the relationship of Romans to the diatribe.

The most distinctive feature of the diatribe is its dialogical nature. If the objections of the one who questions the speaker/writer in the dialogue grow out of a misunderstanding of the *subject matter*, then these objections do not need to be explained by the *situation* of the letter. The objector is a literary, not a historical, figure (Stowers 1981, 2). Is that the case for Romans?

With regard to the social setting an older scholarship held that the diatribe was a type of popular moral or philosophical propaganda directed to the masses by wandering preachers with the intention of converting the former. Stowers' own view is that the setting from which the diatribe emerged is the philosophical school (Stowers 1981, 18, 35, 44–48, 75–76).

The diatribe was not a fixed form or technical genre but was a distinct style though subject to variation. It was first of all the record of a school lecture or discussion and not a literary tractate (Stowers 1981, 29, 44, 47–48, 75).

The dialogue proceeded by address from the teacher, objections from the students, and response to the objections. When there were no real questions or objections, the teacher manufactured them. The mode of discussion was not polemical, for the teacher was not trying to damage the student/opponent or his credibility. He did want, however, to expose and indict his error and lead him to truth. The goal was not simply to impart knowledge but to transform the student. The concern of Paul's questioning objections throughout Romans is what is to become of the law if JUSTIFICATION is by faith and not works (Stowers 1981, 20, 40, 56, 76–77, 105–106, 117, 166).

What gives the diatribe its rhetorical effect is the interplay between two audiences: the real one and the one that provides the fictitious objectors (Stowers 1981, 106, 140). We might imagine that the real audience identifies sympathetically with the indictment of the fictitious one because it thinks it is not being indicted. Then when it discovers that it is, there is no escape.

In summary fashion we may note that the following diatribal features appear in Romans: (1) address to the imaginary questioner or interlocutor as distinguished from the real addressees (2:1-5, 17-24; 9:19-21; 11:17-24; 14:4, 10); (2) objections to or false conclusions drawn from the writer's position (3:1-9; 7:7, 13-14); (3) dialogical exchange between writer and questioner (3:27–4:2) (Stowers 1981, 79, 119, 128–29, 134, 155, 164).

In Stowers's view, these similarities show that Paul was dependent on the diatribe in Romans though he adaptively made it his own. The diatribe element in Romans is not an accident, not Paul's preaching style unconsciously coming through, but is rather central to his message and his self-presentation as a *teacher* (Stowers 1981, 176–79).

Stowers concludes that the objections and false conclusions that Paul cites in Romans do not reflect specific positions of the addressees of the letter. The dialogical interaction grows out of Paul's theological argument and represents what is typical for Paul. But the typical is addressed to a specific historical situation of whose pedagogical needs Paul has some knowledge (Stowers 1981, 180).

The issue of rhetoric having now been introduced, a somewhat more comprehensive look at the relationship of Romans to Greco-Roman rhetoric is in order.

Romans and Rhetoric

The term "rhetoric" refers both to the use of and critical reflection about persuasive language. It has been strongly recognized in recent years that rhetoric as spoken or written discourse is a matter of argumentation and persuasion and not of stylistic ornamentation. Style, of course, is a part of rhetoric, but for the best speakers and critics style should serve argument and not be gratuitous ornamentation. The speaker/writer hopes to modify a situation of exigence or urgency by using discourse to change human attitudes or action (Mack 1990, 14–15; Kennedy 1984, 25, 34–35; Wuellner 1991, 128; 1987, 449). When "rhetoric" is used to refer to reflection about discourse, it deals with the rules that a society agrees are acceptable for debate and argumentation (Mack 1990, 16, 19).

Rhetoric emerged in the Greek city-states during the sixth and fifth centuries B.C.E. By the first century B.C.E., it pervaded the Greco-Roman world, permeating both the system of education and public discourse (Mack 1990, 25, 28). Rhetoric would have been a part of the cultural air breathed by Paul and the Evangelists (Kennedy 1984, 9–10).

While Donfried considers the indispensability of rhetorical criticism on Romans an open question (Donfried 1991b, lxxi), Wuellner clearly believes it is the necessary wave of the future. Studies of the literary form of the letter can illuminate the letter frame but not the structure and nature of the body. Rhetorical criticism will allow us to grasp the structure of the argument found in the letter body as addressed to a particular situation. Rhetorical criticism will enable us also to comprehend the letter as a social act inseparable from other social relationships as well as to appreciate the role of rhetoric in appealing to our emotions and imaginations and not just to our rationality (Wuellner 1991, 129–32; 1987, 453, 461; Jewett 1991, 266).

Ancient rhetoricians identified three species, genres, or types of rhetoric on the basis of the kind of judgment the speaker is seeking. Each may take a positive or negative form. (1) In forensic or judicial rhetoric the speaker is trying to persuade the audience to make a judgment about past events. It may take the form of prosecution or defense. (2) In deliberative rhetoric the attempt is to move the audience to take some action in the future. It may take the form of exhortation or dissuasion. (3) In epideictic or demonstrative rhetoric the writer wants the audience to accept or reaffirm some value or point of view in the present. It may take the form of praise (encomium) or blame (invective) (Kennedy 1984, 19–20). This present-time perspective is a frequent but not necessary characteristic of epideictic (Beale 1978, 223).

It seems reasonably obvious that Romans belongs primarily to the epideictic genre. Paul wants to persuade the Romans to accept and/or reaffirm his understanding of the gospel and salvation right now in the present. Some would say that Romans is thoroughly epideictic (Wuellner 1987, 460) on the ground that the moral teaching in Romans (12:1–15:13) has to do with belief and attitude and not with action (Kennedy 1984, 154). It is true that Paul praises such attitudes or dispositions as humility (12:3), love (12:9), and self-consistency (14:5, 22-23). But his exhortations about paying taxes (13:1-7) and eating and drinking (14:15, 20-21) pertain to specific actions and refer to possible future behavior and so take certain parts of the letter over into the sphere of deliberative rhetoric.

It has recently been argued that the main defining feature of epideictic rhetoric is "rhetorical performative." Epideictic participates in or performs the action to which it refers, and brings the audience to participate in the community act that is the speech (Beale 1978, 225–26, 236). This accords well with Paul's claim in Romans that the gospel which he presents in the letter is the power of God.

For Further Study

In the *Mercer Dictionary of the Bible*: GRACE; JUSTIFICATION; PAUL; RIGHTEOUSNESS IN THE NT; ROMAN EMPIRE; ROMANS, LETTER TO THE; ROME; SALVATION IN THE NT; SIN.

In other sources: C. K. Barrett, *A Commentary on the Epistle to the Romans*; C. E. B. Cranfield, *A Critical and Exegetical Commentary on the Epistle to the Romans*, ICC; K. P. Donfried, ed., *The Romans Debate*; J. D. G. Dunn, *Romans 1–8* and *Romans 9–16*; H. Y. Gamble, *The Textual History of the Letter to the Romans*; E. Käsemann, *Commentary on Romans*; S. K. Stowers, *The Diatribe and Paul's Letter to the Romans*; A. J. M. Wedderburn, *The Reasons for Romans*.

Commentary

An Outline

In the Greco-Roman period there was no sharp distinction between a private, personal letter and a public, literary one (epistle). The most ordinary personal letters were shaped by stylized letter-writing conventions. Paul's letters were personal in that they were written to real household churches, but they were meant to be read publicly in the whole assembly and perhaps circulated in other cities (Stowers 1989, 18–19).

The structure and content of Romans conforms broadly to the shape of the Greco-Roman letter form: greeting, prayer or thanksgiving, body, and closing. The outline above includes both greeting and thanksgiving in the opening. Items II–VII form a connected argument and should all be regarded as parts of the body. Especially should the ethical part not be excluded from the body since it has both a logical and syntactical ("therefore") relationship to the preceding theological parts—which themselves contain ethical implications. The personal statements in 15:14-32 close the body of the letter while 15:33–16:27 is the closing for the letter as a whole.

For the conventional term "greetings" (*chairein*) in the Greco-Roman letter Paul has substituted his theological term "grace" (*charis*, 1:7). Paul also preserves a characteristic of the semitic letter when he adds a peace wish to the greeting: grace to you and peace (1:7). Instead of the conventional "farewell" at the end Paul uses a benediction such as *The grace of our Lord Jesus Christ be with you* (16:20b) (Stowers 1989, 21–22).

The Greco-Roman letter genre was constituted by adding an initial greeting and final closing, as a frame, to the form of a proper speech as defined by the rhetoricians (Kennedy 1984, 141). The structured argument of Romans, then, can be illuminated by displaying its relationship to the speech form. This form had the following parts although speeches would not necessarily have all the parts.

(1) The *proem* or *exordium* (introduction) seeks to obtain the attention and good will of the audience.

(2) The *narration* provides the facts or background information.

(3) The *proposition* or *thesis* states the major contention to be proved and is followed immediately by a justifying reason. The thesis is the transition from exordium and/or narration to the proof.

(4) The *proof* or *confirmation* contains the arguments to support the thesis. Arguments could be creatively invented or could be "non-technical" proofs drawn from the traditional stock of laws, contracts, scripture, witnesses, and the like. The distinction between invented and non-technical proofs seems not to have been a firm one. The kinds of material available were classified as historical examples, analogies, and fables.

(5) The *refutation* neutralizes opposing views.

(6) The *epilogue* or *peroration* summarizes the argument and seeks to arouse the emotions of the audience to take action or make a commitment (Kennedy 1984, 23–24; Jewett 1991, 272–74; Mack 1990, 32–40; Wuellner 1991, 133–46).

Because the theological argument of Romans is complex and because the letter's theological intention is the chief item of debate within contemporary Romans scholarship (Donfried 1991a, lxxii), it seems well to begin the commentary proper by presenting a tentative "rhetorical-theological" overview of the letter as a whole.

The greeting (1:1-7) has already taken on a rhetorical function since it contains brief narration about both Paul himself and the SON OF GOD who is the content of the gospel. The rhetorical exordium corresponds to the letter thanksgiving in which Paul seeks the good will of the Romans by thanking God for their faith which is proclaimed worldwide and by expressing his strong desire to see them. This also continues the narration about Paul.

Paul's thesis (1:16-17), which is the letter theme, is that the gospel is the power of God unto salvation for all who believe. This claim is grounded on the justifying reason that in the gospel the righteousness of God is revealed. The commentary will show that the thesis truly is a transition closely connected syntactically to both exordium-narration and proof.

The rhetorical proof (1:18–15:13) corresponds to the letter body except for the body's concluding personal statement (15:14-32). Several fundamental proofs are offered for the power of God's righteousness.

(1) It is demonstrated in God's wrath that delivers rebellious human beings to the ruinous consequences of their own actions (1:18–3:20).

(2) It is seen in God's providing justification equally for Jews and gentiles (3:21–4:25). This section displays Paul's use of Abraham as a historical example.

(3) God's power is manifested in God's liberating deliverance from the victimizing power of Adam (5:12-21), sin (6:1-23), the law (7:1-25), and flesh and death (8:1-39). Justification opens up freedom as a new quality of life, a relationship to be examined in the commentary.

(4) God's righteousness will finally be able to save all Israel despite the rebellion of the latter (9:1–11:36). In this section we find Paul using analogies with the potter and his clay (9:19-24) and with the olive tree (11:17-24) in order to clarify the human situation (Jewett 1991, 272–74).

(5) The ethical section is also a proof because it is God's power that enables ethical renewal (12:1–15:13).

Paul has taken the refutation of opposing views up into his proof by his employment of the diatribe style. At certain points he mentions objections to or false conclusions drawn from his positions and then refutes these mistakes (3:1-9; 3:31; 4:1-2a; 6:1-3, 15-16; 7:7, 13-14; 9:14-15, 19-20; 11:1-3, 11; 11:19-20) (Stowers 1981, 119–22).

The rhetorical peroration corresponds to the personal conclusion of the letter body (15:14-32). Here Paul compliments the Romans for their spiritual achievements yet affirms his right to instruct them. This moves into a favorable evaluation of his own ministry, which in turn melds into a brief narration (recall the exordium) of the scope of his past mission. Then he "narrates" the future as his hope to visit the Romans on his way to Spain and his present need to go to

Jerusalem first. Finally he makes an emotional appeal for their prayers.

The letter closing (15:33–16:27) continues the rhetorical function of the peroration—to cement personal connections.

Letter Opening, 1:1-15

Paul's Greetings to the Saints in Rome, 1:1-7

Paul's greeting expands the simplest conventional greeting form (Theon to Tyrannus, greetings): *Paul to God's beloved in Rome, grace and peace from God our Father and the Lord Jesus Christ*. The Romans are designated as saints, set apart for God.

Paul introduces two expansions into the greeting. (1) He identifies himself as set apart for the GOSPEL, as the OT prophets had been set apart or elected to preach (Isa 49:1; Jer 1:5), and identifies himself as an apostle. A NT apostle is one sent with an authoritative commission to represent the sender. For Paul the commission is from the risen Lord to preach to the gentiles (1:5; Gal 1:15-16). According to Acts 1:21-22 to be an APOSTLE one must have been a follower of the earthly Jesus and a witness to his RESURRECTION. Paul did not meet the first of these criteria, but he was fully convinced that his having seen the risen Lord and having been commissioned by him was quite enough to make him an apostle equal in authority to the others (Rom 1:1, 5; 1 Cor 9:1; 15:8-11; Gal 1:15-16).

(2) In addition Paul defines the gospel in terms of a Christological confession that he probably received from the tradition existing before or alongside him. This confession portrays Jesus' mission as moving in two stages (not two natures): (a) according to the flesh—in his historical phase—he was the descendant of David; (b) then he was appointed or installed (*not* declared to be who he already was) SON OF GOD in power in the spiritual realm by the resurrection of the dead. Notice it is not by *his* resurrection from the dead but because he anticipates the future general resurrection of the dead. The CHRISTOLOGY of this early confession is broadly adoptionistic. Jesus was not eternally Son of God but became Son at a certain point. However, there is no assertive denial of his pre-existence.

Paul provides a frame for this confession. He introduces it as a confession about the Son, thereby anticipating its second part, and he concludes by naming the Son, Jesus Christ our Lord, the one to whom the believer owes total obedience. For Paul the term Son of God connotes Jesus' close bond with God and his role

as redeemer, but it is probable that no Pauline passage clearly connects pre-existence with the title Son. In Rom 1:3, 9 the content of the gospel is the Son while in 1:16-17, it is the righteousness of God. This shows that for Paul the inner meaning of christology is the standing of human beings before God.

Paul's Thanksgiving for the Roman Community, 1:8-15

Paul first of all thanks God for the faith of the Roman Christians and assures them of his prayerful concern for them. Apparently in his enthusiasm he forgets to follow up "first" with a "second." (On Paul's desire to visit Rome see Introduction: Occasion and Purpose, The Intended Visit.)

Paul wants to preach in Rome because his obligation to preach is unlimited. He must preach to those who have been cultivated by the use of the GREEK LANGUAGE and those who are barbarian. He is a debtor to both wise and foolish. Hence he is eager to proclaim the gospel in Rome. In the thematic statement that follows—his thesis—he begins to explain further the reason why.

Theme: The Gospel of Righteousness as Power, 1:16-17

Paul wants to preach in Rome because he is not ashamed of the gospel. "I am not ashamed" might have a psychological tone. He is not tempted to think he will be shamed for having trusted something unreliable. Or the term might be confessional and be roughly equivalent to "I confess" or "I acknowledge" (see Mark 8:38). Paul is not ashamed of the gospel because it is the power of God for salvation. The gospel proclaimed is not words *about* God's power but *is* God's power in action (see 1 Cor 1:18, 21, 24). Salvation—ultimate well-being—is characteristically future for Paul (5:9-10) but can also be past (8:24) and present (1 Cor 1:18; 2 Cor 2:15).

The righteousness of God means God's action in being faithful to God's COVENANT intention, and faith is the human appropriative response to this. Righteous or righteousness when attributed to human beings refers to being in a right relationship. But see the commentary on 3:21-31 for a fuller discussion of these important terms. Paul finds the essence of the gospel to have been expressed in Hab 2:4—the one righteous by faith shall live. Paul is able to do this by changing the meaning of the prophetic passage. The Greek text of the Habakkuk passage should probably be translated "the one righteous by my (God's) faithfulness shall live." And the Hebrew text of the prophet should probably be translated "the righteous one shall live by his (own) faithfulness." But for Paul the meaning is that the one righteous by faith (in Paul's sense of faith) shall live.

The strong interconnections linking the end of the thanksgiving, the thesis as transition, and the beginning of the letter body are noteworthy. Verses 16-18 are closely tied to v. 15 by a fourfold use of the word *for* (i.e., "because"; vv. 16a, [16b], 17a, 18a), and this formation overarches the formal distinctions involved. Verse 15 belongs to the thanksgiving, vv. 6-17, to the theme or thesis, and v. 18, to the beginning of the body. The causal sequence binds these three together.

Verse 16a states why Paul is eager to preach in Rome (v. 15): because he is not ashamed of the gospel. Verse 16b states why he is not ashamed of the gospel: because it is the power of God. *Gospel* has to be understood as the subject of *is* in v. 16b. Verse 17a explains why the gospel is the power of God: because the righteousness of God is revealed in it. Verse 17a is dependent on v. 16b because the *it* of v. 17a has to have *gospel* as its antecedent. The gender agreement of *it* is with *gospel*, not with *salvation* or *power*.

In the light of both terminology and concept, v. 18a would seem to be parallel to v. 17a: wrath is conceptually related to righteousness (both refer to God's actions), and righteousness in v. 17a and wrath in v. 18a both have the same predicate: *for . . . the righteousness of God is revealed* is parallel to *for the wrath of God is revealed*. Therefore both would be dependent on v. 16b and would thus express causes for the gospel's being the power of God: because righteousness is revealed in it and because wrath is revealed.

Although the terminology and parallelism seem to support that conclusion, some of the conceptual content points in another direction. Righteousness and wrath have a different *temporal* qualification here. The righteousness of God has been manifested in the *present* eschatological moment—now (3:21). But 1:18-32 shows that the wrath of God has been happening *since creation* (1:20). Therefore, although it goes against the parallel structure (meanings and interpretations are rarely, if ever, certain), 1:18 is best referred back to v. 15 as another cause for Paul's wanting to come to Rome: because the WRATH OF GOD is being revealed. He hopes that his coming with the gospel—God's power—will save some from that wrath. Thus Paul has both positively and negatively stated

reasons for coming—to bring the gospel and to save from wrath. And since the letter is a substitute for his presence, these are also his reasons for writing.

The Revelation of God's Righteousness, 1:18–4:25

Righteousness as Wrath, 1:18–3:20

1:18-32. Against the gentiles or all humankind. The wrath of God is being revealed against the ungodliness and wickedness of *all* human beings. This is not unjust of God. All are without excuse (v. 20) regardless of their religion or culture because God has made God's eternal power and deity known and perceptible in the created order since the beginning. But human beings in the interest of having finite gods (idols) that they can manipulate (vv. 23, 25) have refused to thank and honor God and have suppressed the truth of God which they have (vv. 18, 21, 25). The result is that the senseless human mind has become darkened and futile (vv. 21b, 22b). Thus, the human situation is that universal knowledge of God is a possibility only in principle—a possibility "before the fall" so to speak and still a latent possibility. The actual situation in historical existence is that people do not have knowledge of God (vv. 21b, 22b; 1 Cor 2:10-14). But the possibility in principle is enough to hold people responsible (v. 20), for the lack of knowledge results from their *choice* not to have it.

The wrath of God here is God's reaction to humankind's rejection of the truth and knowledge that God has plainly revealed in creation. It is not just a cosmic principle of retribution working automatically in the moral universe (Dodd 1954, 21–24) but God's personal action, God's giving people up (vv. 24, 26, 28) to the consequences of their rebellion.

This giving up has three manifestations.

1. God gave them up to the dishonoring of their bodies in homosexual relationships (2:24-27). HOMOSEXUALITY then is not in Paul's view so much SIN itself as a consequence of sin, and yet it is evil for Paul in that it is destructive of the human self.

Present knowledge makes it difficult to agree with Paul that sinful rebellion is the sole or even a primary cause of homosexuality. But Paul's apparent underlying principle may be right. Rebellious rejection of God deforms the inner depth of human life where the roots of all sexuality lie.

Some Greek moralists defended pederasty (sexual relations between adult men and young boys) as superior to heterosexuality. Among the arguments were: (1) it contributes to the wisdom of youth; (2) it is more masculine; and (3) it is more "according to nature" (Scroggs 1983, 44–49). Other moralists condemned pederasty with such arguments as: (1) it is effeminate; (2) it lacks mutuality and permanence; (3) it is exploitative; (4) it is the expression of insatiable lust; (5) it is contrary to nature (Scroggs 1983, 49–65; Furnish 1979, 62–66).

Paul essentially agreed with the opponents of pederasty. He held homosexuality to be generated by insatiable lust—consumed with passion (v. 27). And he believed that it was chosen—they exchanged (v. 26). And perhaps most emphatically he held it to be contrary to nature, against God's created intention as an order immanent in the world and humankind (Cranfield 1980, 125–26; Käsemann 1980, 48).

People will debate whether homosexuals are more lustful than heterosexuals. That homosexuality is simply chosen and not biologically or socially determined is too facile an assumption. What about "contrary to nature"?

For Paul and the ancient world generally there is no such thing as a homosexual nature or orientation. There is one nature—what we would call a heterosexual one. Thus what Paul is condemning as unnatural is homosexual acts by people whom he takes to have a heterosexual nature. His underlying principle, then, is that people when they act sexually should do so in accordance with their nature. If Paul then could be confronted with the reality of a homosexual nature, he would not be consistent with himself if he claimed that homosexual acts by people with a homosexual nature are contrary to nature.

2. God gave them up to a base mind—a mind that cannot tolerate crisis and that collapses under testing (v. 28). The wrath of God is that God ratifies the darkened thinking that people visit on themselves (vv. 21b, 22b) and turns it into a destiny that they cannot escape on their own.

3. God gave them up to improper conduct (v. 28). The vices that Paul then lists as illustrative of this conduct are behaviors that destroy the coherence of the social order and turn it into a tissue of conflict and reciprocal hostility (vv. 29–32).

2:1-16. Against the Jews—or all humankind. In v. 1 Paul addresses every person who judges another, and he tells such a person that he or she is without excuse because in judging another, one condemns oneself. This is because the judge is guilty of the same offens-

es. Who is the "man" whom Paul addresses here in the second person as the guilty judge?

In v. 1 Paul has shifted from the third person description of 1:18-32 to second person address—you, O man, the judge. The *you* is not the real letter audience—usually designated as "brother/brothers" (cf. 1:13; 16:17) by Paul—but the imaginary questioner of the diatribe. Such a shift of addressee along with a strong indictment, as here, is typical of the diatribe style. Paul indicts the false conclusion that some are in a position to judge others. This address to "you" personalizes and concretizes the "them" of 1:18-32. Yet despite the slight distance created by the insertion of the imaginary questioner the real audience is still in view (Stowers 1981, 81–86, 91, 96, 106, 110–12). Who is it?

The initial *therefore* in v. 1 suggests a close relationship between 1:18-32 and vv. 1-16. In the former he is describing primarily the situation of the gentiles, but the allusion to *Israelite* IDOLATRY in 1:25 (see Ps 106:20; Jer 2:11) shows that he has Jews also in mind. Thus the *you* in v. 1 includes everybody.

However, as the gentile is primarily in view in 1:18-32, the Jew is primarily in view in vv. 1-11, and for these reasons: (1) He is explicitly referring to the Jew in 2:17-29, and 2:1-11 is similar to 2:17-29 in that both criticize inconsistent behavior. (2) The standard of judgment in 2:1-16 is Jewish in nature—works or deeds in obedience to the law (vv. 6, 12-13). (See Pss 18:20-24; 62:12; Prov 24:12; Job 4:9-10; Sir 16:12-14.) (3) Rom 2:4 seems to criticize the Jewish attitude described in Wis 3:9-10; 4:15; 11:9-10, 23; 12:8-11, 19-22; 15:1-6; 16:9-10. These passages suggest that Israel will be judged but with mercy, and Israel will accept the opportunity to repent. The gentiles, on the other hand, are judged without mercy and do not accept the opportunity to repent. Paul's position is that Israel has not repented but is as guilty as the gentiles.

While the wrath of God that Paul describes in 1:18-32 is the historical anticipation of the final judgment, vv. 5-10 speak about that future day of wrath and retribution itself. God will repay people according to their works (*erga*). Those who do good will receive ETERNAL LIFE, but those who do evil will get anguish and fury. This is the situation for both Jew and Greek (vv. 9-11).

The term "works" (v. 6, author trans.) has a very specific meaning for Paul and can hardly be thought to mean something like acts of *faith* or looking beyond human achievement (Barrett 1957, 45–48). Works of the law are human achievements, and here Paul seems to allow that some will be justified by doing the law (v. 13). This appears to contradict his statements elsewhere that no one can be justified by works of the law (3:20, 28; 4:2-5; 9:30–10:3).

On the other hand, here in vv. 6-13, Paul may be speaking hypothetically, speaking from the Jewish point of view for the sake of argument. If the law is the medium of the divine-human relationship, as Judaism says, then only obedient works count for salvation. Since the Jews have not been obedient, they are out on their own terms. But Paul's own real position is that the law is not and cannot be the medium of the divine-human relationship (3:21). For Paul it is in fact possible to be perfectly obedient to the law (Phil 3:6), but fallen human beings will turn that righteousness of the law into a claim of self-salvation rather than accepting righteousness as a gift from God (Phil 3:4b, 6, 9; Rom 9:30–10:3). The righteousness of the law is not the righteousness of God.

To underline the equality of Jew and gentile Paul states that while the gentile does not have the law as the Jew does, gentiles—or some gentiles— nevertheless do by nature what the law requires and thus show that the work of the law is written on their hearts (vv. 14-15). No one, regardless of religion or culture, is without moral sensibility.

Paul is not necessarily expressing the Greek belief that the reason of every person is stamped by the divine cosmic reason. He may rather be stating that the transcendent will of God encounters gentile as well as Jew in concrete situations (Käsemann 1980, 63–64) and is affirmed from within.

Whether the gentile is obedient to this inner law is judged by CONSCIENCE. For Paul and the ancient popular philosophy from which he learned the concept of conscience, the latter is the self in its *judging* mode. Conscience does not *determine* what is right or wrong but is the self judging itself on the basis of a standard of right that is independent of conscience. Here the standard is the law written on the heart, and it is distinct from conscience, whose judging function is expressed in the conflicting thoughts which accuse or excuse.

The statement about the law on the heart in vv. 14-15 should probably be taken as a parenthesis. If it is, then v. 16 flows from v. 13 in a smooth and natural way. The doers of the law will be justified (v. 13) on the day when God carries out the judgment (v. 16). The operation of conscience then (vv. 14-15) is something that goes on in history prior to the judgment day

and perhaps anticipates it. But if 2:14-15 is not taken as a parenthesis, it interrupts the flow and makes the operation of conscience coincident with and a kind of ratification of God's final judgment. That is probably not what Paul wanted to say. For Paul conscience has a relative authority and should be heeded (1 Cor 8:7-12). But it is not infallible and is subject to correction by God's judgment (1 Cor 4:4-5).

2:17-29. Religion, obedience, and circumcision. Here Paul explicitly addresses the Jew: the Jew who has persuaded himself that because he knows the law he has a secure relationship with God on which he can depend and a right to instruct others about how to live in the light. But this Jew who knows the law and the will of God and preaches against theft and adultery does the very things he condemns. Paul indicts this discrepancy between religious claims and moral performance. Again only obedience counts if the Jew is faithful to his own position.

It occurs to Paul that some Jew will say: we have circumcision that counts for us with God. Paul rejoins that circumcision is a benefit only if you obey the law, but disobedience renders it void. You have been disobedient, so circumcision is of no value. Moreover, real circumcision is a matter of the heart. The uncircumcised person who keeps the law is better than the circumcised person who breaks it. True Judaism is an inward and spiritual matter.

3:1-8. Then has the Jew any advantage? We more-or-less expect Paul to say "no." He has argued that the Jew—despite knowing God and the law, despite being mercifully given the opportunity to repent, despite offering moral instruction to others and having the gift of circumcision—is as disobedient and as subject to wrath as the gentile. So what advantage has the Jew? Paul surprises us with "much in every way." The Jews were entrusted with the oracles of God. Paul does not say that the law (*nomos*) is an advantage but that the oracles (*logia*) are. The Jewish scripture is more than law. The Jews know from scripture that if some of them were unfaithful God is still faithful. Paul uses three terms in this context to express the reliability of God—faithfulness (*pistis*, v. 3), righteousness (*dikaiosynē*, v. 5) and truth (*alētheia*, v. 7). This knowledge is the Jews' advantage.

All of this seems to mean that our unrighteousness brings out the righteousness of God. That will prompt some diatribal objector to ask then whether God is not unjust to condemn us. Paul replies "absolutely not" (v. 6, author trans.), for how could God judge the world if he were unjust. Paul's answer could mean that since God is surely judge of the world, he must be just. Or it might mean that God could not be a just judge if he did not take into account the intention of people—to do evil—and not just the result—the confirmation of God's righteousness.

The fact that human unrighteousness leads to the faithfulness of God might also prompt some people to the closely related assertion—which Paul says some people slanderously attribute to him—let us do evil in order that the good might come. Paul does not really deal with this problem here; he dismisses it contemptuously. But he raises the issue again in 6:1 and then gives a substantive theological-ethical response.

3:9-20. Are we Jews then any better off? The meaning of the verb translated "are we better off?" is very problematical, and only the briefest account of the possibilities can be given (see the longer commentaries). The verb could have three possible meanings: (1) Are we making a defense? (2) Are we excelled, at a disadvantage? (3) Are we better off, at an advantage? The first two possibilities seem ruled out by what precedes. The third makes most sense in context even though the middle voice of the verb with this sense is not attested elsewhere. But there are cases of other verbs in the middle voice with an active sense.

Paul's answer to the question is also ambiguous. It could mean either "not absolutely" or "absolutely not." The latter seems more probable in context. Thus question and answer should read: Are we Jews any better off? Absolutely not!

Romans 3:1 and 3:9 then stand in a paradoxical relationship to each other. The Jews have an advantage but are no better off. Their knowledge of God's faithfulness from scripture does not mean that they are any less sinful than the gentiles. The Jews are no better off because all people, Jews and gentiles, are equally under the power of sin. When Paul uses "sin" in the singular, as here, it means, not an act, but a power that controls human beings, especially since he speaks of people as being *under* it. And yet Paul can also speak of sins in the plural to mean acts (4:7; 7:5; 11:27). Sin as power produces sin/sins as dispositions and acts.

Not even one person is righteous. Paul quotes scripture to illustrate and confirm this universal sinfulness. The sin/sins that he details embrace both dispositions and actions. They are both religious and moral. Humankind is without understanding (v. 11). Religiously speaking people do not fear or seek God (vv. 11, 18). Morally speaking they show no kindness but rather

deceive, curse, poison, and shed the blood of their neighbors (vv. 12-15).

Interestingly, none of these OT passages comes from the books of the law. They are primarily from Psalms but also from Ecclesiastes and Isaiah, and yet Paul comprehensively includes them under the category of law (v. 19). The accusations against all Jews and Greeks in vv. 10-18 are the accusations of the law (v. 19), for the purpose of the law is precisely accusation—to stop every mouth (undermine every self-defense) and hold the whole world accountable to God. Proper works of the law are implicitly defined as fear of God and concern for the neighbor—the opposite of the offenses here condemned. But none can be justified by such works because the law's purpose is to hold people guilty, knowingly guilty. The law brings knowledge of sin (v. 20); it does not bring obedience.

But the law can make people aware of their sin only because they have in fact sinned, violated the law, and the law also has a role in the latter connection. The knowledge of sin that the law gives is the knowledge that comes from *doing* it. That is, the claim that the law gives knowledge of sin for Paul means that the law makes people sin (Rom 7:5, 7-8; see commentary on Rom 7).

Since the theme of the works of the law has been introduced by Paul and since Paul's interpretation of Israel's law is one of the most hotly contested issues in Romans scholarship (Donfried 1991a, lxii, lxxi), it seems well to look at the debate at this point.

Excursus: The Law in Paul

In recent years, certain claims have been made that minimize Paul's differences with his ancestral religion and his critique of the law and thus challenge the so-called "Lutheran" interpretation of Paul. Some of these arguments for the "non-Lutheran" Paul will be presented here.

1. Palestinian Judaism in Paul's time had no legalistic merit doctrine of salvation. Election into the covenant people—getting in—and ultimately salvation are by God's grace. E. P. Sanders states that obedience is *either* a response to electing grace *or* a meritorious means of salvation. The correct interpretation of the Jewish sources is that obedience to the law is a response to grace and a means of staying in the covenant, not a way of earning salvation. Thus Paul is not attacking the righteousness of the law on the grounds that it leads to self-righteousness and pride (Sanders

1977, 81–83, 420, 422, 426; Dunn 1988, lxv; Ziesler 1989, 42–43).

2. The works of the law that Paul does oppose are not meritorious acts that earn salvation but such sociological boundary markers as circumcision, sabbath observance, and food laws that mark Israel off from other peoples and give her a sense of privilege or special status. Such an attitude fails to see that what God demands is the obedience of the heart (Dunn 1988, lxv–lxxi, 124, 137, 191–92, 382, 627).

3. Paul did not reject the law as the way to salvation because of any inherent flaw in the law itself, but because of two other factors that grow out of Paul's Christian theological standpoint. (a) Salvation is for all and therefore cannot be by the law because only the Jews have the law. Salvation by the law would exclude the gentiles. (b) Salvation cannot be by the law because dogmatically, as a matter of definition, it comes through Christ, through faith in Christ (Sanders 1977, 489–90, 496–97; 1983, 20, 27, 31–35, 47, 155).

The following counterarguments can be made.

1. Let it be gladly affirmed that grace is an important theme in first-century JUDAISM. That, however, does not mean that Judaism was not legalistic. The two modes of obedience—obedience as response to grace and obedience as a meritorious condition for salvation—are by no means an "either/or" but rather a highly ambiguous "both/and." It is not possible to separate the two experientially, and theo-*logically* grace as enabling power and salvation by works—theological legalism—go hand in glove. By theological legalism is meant the religious belief that human behavior, obedience, performance of God's requirements, counts with God as a condition for salvation.

In Leviticus Israel's salvation depends on the grace of atonement provided by God (17:11). On the other hand, Israel must maintain herself in life in the land by obedience to the law (18:5; 20:22; 23:11; 26:3-39). Similarly in Deuteronomy God chooses Israel out of God's love and not because of Israel's merit, and God graciously intervenes in history on Israel's behalf (1:30-32; 7:7-8; 8:17; 9:4; 10:15). Israel's OBEDIENCE then is the appropriate response to GRACE (5:6-21; 6:20-25; 7:6; 8:4; 14:1-2; 26:5-11; 27:9-10). On the other hand, Israel maintains herself in the land and purges her guilt by right actions (4:1, 5; 6:18; 7:12; 8:1; 11:26-28; 16:20; 21:9). This legalistic strand can be seen in many places (Job 34:11; Pss 18:20-24; 62:12; Prov 24:12; Jer 17:10; Hos 12:2; Tob 4:9-10; Sir 16:12-14): performance issues in salvation.

Stating this point is not a chauvinistic effort to make Christianity look better than Judaism. The NT also has its legalistic strand. For example, despite Paul's strong polemic against JUSTIFICATION by works, his appeal to judgment on the basis of deeds (Rom 14:11; 2 Cor 5:10) is legalistic. Even more strongly in Matthew, while grace is a reality (13:16, 17, 20, 23, 37-38) that enables the response (7:16-20; 12:33-37; 13:23), human beings must achieve salvation by their own efforts (5:20; 6:14-15; 7:24-25; 16:27; 18:35). Given the legalistic strand in the daughter religion (Christianity) it would be strange indeed if it were not in the parent (Judaism). The paradoxical theo-logic running through all this material is that God's grace as forgiveness and power enables people to do what *they* must do to be saved.

2. Returning to Paul, acts performed to express Jewish separateness, like circumcision, cannot be neatly distinguished from meritorious acts to gain salvation since God could be expected to approve such boundary markers. Moreover, Paul does not say that people seek the righteousness of the law—perform works of the law—in order to mark themselves off as distinct but in order to have something of their own to trust (Rom 9:30–10:3; Phil 3:4, 9): a righteousness of their own based on the law. This boasting or trust in self (3:27) is not before other people but before God (10:2). And while works of the law include cultic boundary markers (Gal 2:11-16), they also include strictly religious attitudes and moral acts as the commentary on 3:19-20 showed. Works of the law for Paul are cultic, religious, and moral acts performed in order to gain a standing with God based on one's own achievements.

3. Paul did not reject the law as the way to salvation *because* salvation by law would have excluded the gentiles. It would not have excluded them, because all are under the law already. There is an obvious sense in which the Jews have the Law of Moses, and the gentiles do not. But there is a running subtext in Paul that reveals that in the actual struggles of existence the gentiles are as much under the law in principle as the Jews. For example, what the law requires is written on the hearts of gentiles (2:14-15). It is the purpose of the law to hold everyone accountable, all the world; therefore all are under the law (3:19-20). The "all" of 3:19-20 are the same as the "all" of 3:9: Jew and gentile. Since the whole church—Jew and gentile—is said to have died to the law (7:4), all must have been under the law. In 5:12-14 the command to Adam is equiva-

lent to law, and ADAM symbolizes the whole human race.

4. Nor did Paul reject the law as the means of salvation because by definition salvation is through faith in Christ. He rather rejected it because there is a substantive opposition between the righteousness of the law and the righteousness of faith. The righteousness of faith is not relatively better but is a qualitatively different antithesis. The righteousness of faith is willing to receive from God while the righteousness of the law asserts itself against God and is an instance of living according to the flesh (see commentary on 9:30–10:3).

5. The pursuit of salvation or justification by works of the law is not just a failure to see that God requires the obedience of the heart but is a deformation of the heart, a rupture of the wholeness of the self, in which three different levels of self-awareness are both in conflict with each other and out of touch with each other. These levels are: (1) I am righteous and wise (Rom 3:27-28; 1 Cor 1:29; 3:18-21). (2) Why then do I compulsively pursue righteousness and wisdom (Rom 10:2-3; 1 Cor 1:20-22; Gal 1:13-14; Phil 3:4-6, 8-9)? (3) My righteousness and wisdom are really foolishness and wickedness—trash (Rom 3:10, 20, 23; Phil 3:6, 8-9; 1 Cor 3:19) (see Via 1990, 29–33).

6. Paul makes positive statements about the law: it is connected with faith (9:30-32) and promises and promotes life (7:10, 14a, 16b, 22-23). But he also makes negative statements: the law causes sin (7:5, 7-10). This is only an apparent contradiction because Paul is not stating opposing things about the law under the same category but is distinguishing yet relating two different categories—intention and result. Paul's basically consistent position, which accounts for most of his statements on the law, is that the law intends faith and life, but human beings as flesh try to use the law to save themselves with the result that they subvert the law's original intention and produce sin. Romans 5:13-14 and 5:20 are in conflict with the generally consistent position (see commentary).

7. God's original intention for the law is subverted not only because human beings as flesh try to make themselves secure through a righteousness of their own (Rom 8:3, 7; Phil 3:4, 9-10) but also because the law as a personified power deceives people (Rom 7:10-11). Paul associates the law with sin and death (1 Cor 15:56) and death with the demonic cosmic powers (1 Cor 15:24-26; Rom 8:38). Thus by implication the law is a demonic power that seduces people into the false belief that it is the source of salvation (7:10;

9:30–10:3) (Via 1990, 38–44, and commentary on 8:31-39).

Righteousness as Justification by Faith, 3:21–4:25

3:21-26. Righteousness, faith, and grace. But *now*— now when the *future*, final, eschatological revelation has become a *present* reality—God has manifested his righteousness apart from the law. Righteousness, faith, and grace will be distinguished for analysis, but for Paul they are inseparable parts of the divine-human transaction. Although manifested apart from the law, Paul shows (for example, in 1:17: 4:1-25; 10:5-13) how this righteousness is continuous with the law and prophets that bear witness to it. Righteousness must come apart from the law since the law has left all people sinful without distinction. Sin as falling short of the glory of God may refer to humankind's loss of the image of God (1 Cor 11:7). (On sin, see commentary on 1:18-32; 5:12-21; 7:1-25.)

Paul's understanding of righteousness is derived from OT and Jewish usage. In the OT we may discern three senses: (1) God's righteousness is God's character or nature—readiness to be faithful to the covenant relationship. (2) God actively manifests this character by intervention in human affairs to establish life. This manifestation of righteousness is salvation (Isa 46:12-13; 51:5-6; 61:11; 62:1-2; Ps 98:2-3). (3) Since God's righteousness or salvation can be received by people, it is also referred to as *theirs* (Isa 62:1-2; 54:17).

Paul essentially repeats these three usages. (1) Righteous is something God is (Rom 3:26)—God's character. (2) This character is revealed in action: God's righteousness is manifested (1:17; 3:21). (3) People who receive God's righteousness exist in the righteousness of faith—the state of human beings who have a right relationship with God (Rom 4:3, 5; 9:30). The righteousness of the law is the attempt of human beings to establish a relationship with God based on their own works (Rom 10:3; Phil 3:9; Williams 1980, 259–65; Wedderburn 1991, 116–23).

God's manifestation of his covenant righteousness occurs as the justification of the believer (3:22, 24, 26). In Greek the righteousness family of words and the justification family have the same root (*dikai-*). Justification is God's establishment of the new right relationship. It is not making the sinner *ethically* righteous in either action or intention. Nor is it treating the sinner *as if* he or she were ethically righteous—a legal fiction. Justification is rather a *relational* term, and its social setting is the law court. To justify is to acquit. Paul's usage begins in the law court but surpasses that frame of reference, for the OT forbids that a guilty person be acquitted (Isa 5:22-23; Prov 17:15) and asserts that God will not acquit the wicked (Exod 23:7). But that is exactly what Paul says God has now done: God justifies, acquits, pronounces not guilty the one who is sinful, ungodly, guilty (vv. 23-24; 4:5). This is not a legal fiction but a relationship that is real. The guilty person has with the judge the relationship of a not guilty person that cannot be broken (8:33-36). The unacceptable one is accepted.

Faith is the human acceptance or reception of God's justifying action (vv. 22-25). It is the opposite of works: that is, it is receiving from God rather than depending on one's own righteousness (9:30-32). Faith involves two closely connected moves: (1) It is will-ingness to believe that the proclaimed death and resur-rection of the Son of God constitute God's saving action. (2) It is a surrender to this divine action and a reversal of self-understanding based on it, a renuncia-tion of boasting or self-trust. The two acts of faith merge into one because Paul came to know Jesus as Lord and Son of God in coming to understand himself as having nothing on which to depend for salvation (Phil 3:6-11; Gal 2:19-20) (Bultmann 1951, 300–301).

Faith as response to God's justifying act is a *human* decision. It is acceptance of the preached word *as* word of God (1 Thes 2:13); therefore faith involves a committed interpretation of the human word that is the vehicle of God's righteous action. That faith is a hu-man decision for which people are responsible is seen in the fact that Paul puts his readers under the *impera-tive* to have and live by faith (1 Cor 7:29-31; 2 Cor 5:20; Rom 11:20-22). Yet faith is not a posture human beings produce in themselves but one that God gener-ates in them through the power of the preached word (Rom 1:16; 10:8, 17). Faith is given—"graced" (Phil 1:29). Both sides are seen in Phil 2:12-13: *you* work out your *own* salvation *because God* is working in you.

Faith in Jesus (Christ) (vv. 22, 26) is more literally translated "faith of Jesus Christ," and it has been argued that it means the "faithfulness of Jesus Christ" that is the medium of the divine activity rather than the faith of the believer in the divine activity (Hays 1981, 168, 196; Williams 1980, 271–76; Cousar 1990, 39). Actually the expression and its contexts (see also Gal 2:16) are ambiguous and it could mean one as

well as the other, or both. It is not possible to deter-mine that one of these meanings is the only right one.

Grace for Paul is both God's act in which God gives faith as response to the saving event and the act that is the saving event itself. These are two sides of the same event. Grace underlines the *gift*—unde-served—character of the event. Grace as event and gift extends what Paul has expressed in his understanding of the righteousness of God as the justifica-tion—acquittal—of the sinner: justification by grace. The eventful gift is the redemption accomplished in the sacrificial death of Christ Jesus.

The term "redemption" (*apolytrōsis*) was used for the liberation of slaves or prisoners of war and could be an allusion to the deliverance of Israel from Egyp-tian slavery. Therefore, it images Jesus' death as a liberation from sin.

The background of "sacrifice of atonement" by his blood has several facets. The term "sacrifice of atone-ment" (*hilastērion*) is generally used in the LXX (and in Heb 9:5) to refer to the mercy seat, which was the cover of the ark of the covenant in the holy of holies in the Temple (Exod 25:21). This is where God's presence is manifested (Exod 25:22; Lev 16:2) and where the blood of the sin offering is sprinkled to atone for sin (Lev 16:11-16). Closely associated with the sin offering is the ritual in which the scapegoat bears away Israel's sins into the wilderness (Lev 16:20-22). Romans 3:25 probably makes some refer-ence to this material although "mercy seat" is too restricted a meaning, especially since *hilastērion* could mean "expiation" more broadly (4 Macc 17:22).

In Isa 53:6, 10, 12 the death of God's servant is a sin offering and a bearing of Israel's sins. It is difficult to believe that the NT text makes no allusion to this, even though Jewish sources did not interpret the Isaiah text as teaching expiatory vicarious suffering (Williams 1975, 111, 120).

In 4 Macc 17:22 (see also 1:11; 6:28-29) the deaths of the Jewish martyrs are interpreted as a *hilastērion* that preserves and purifies Israel. This Hellenistic-Jew-ish text was probably influenced by the classical Greek notion of a hero or heroine dying for the city, father-land, family, or piety. Either directly or through such a Jewish source as 4 Maccabees this idea reached early Christianity (Williams 1975, 111, 120, 145–63, 230, 233). It should be pointed out that Rom 3:25-26a or 3:24-26 is probably a pre-Pauline confession.

The term *hilastērion* can mean either *propitiation* (a human act to appease or placate God—primarily in nonbiblical sources) or *expiation* (a divine act to deal with sin—primarily in the LXX). In Paul there is a hint of the idea of propitiation. The death of Jesus does after all avert the wrath of God (Rom 5:8-9). But the overall context in Paul shows that expiation is much the stronger sense: it is what God does to cover and forgive human sin. This interpretation is supported by several points.

(1) In speaking of Christ's death for human beings Paul does not say that it was *in place of* us (*anti*) (to appease God's wrath) but rather *for our sakes* or *in behalf of* us (*hyper*) (to affect us: Rom 5:8; 1 Cor 15:3; 2 Cor 5:14; Gal 3:13).

(2) Christ does not die in our place. Rather *our* old self also must die, and Christ's death is for us in that it draws us into itself and enables us to die to the old person we were (Rom 6:4-6; 7:4, 6; 2 Cor 5:14-15).

(3) It is humankind that needs to be reconciled, not God. We are the enemy, not God (Rom 5:10; 2 Cor 5:18-19).

(4) The cross confronts us as word (1 Cor 1:18) and as sacrament (Rom 6:4-6; 1 Cor 10:16; 11:26). The cross as word becomes effective by creating faith in us (Rom 10:8-9, 17). The cross as word, then, is toward us and affects us. It is not directed toward God.

In vv. 25b-26 the purpose of God's expiating act is to demonstrate God's own righteousness. God needs to make this active move because in the past God has passed over (not forgiven) former sins in God's restraint or inactivity (see Isa 63:15; 64:10-12). That is, God has not dealt with the sinful situation of the past (Williams 1975, 21-34). Perhaps the main reason for seeing the past as negative or neutral (unforgiven) is that it is contrasted with the present which is positive: righteousness is *now* demonstrated. The manifested righteousness has a dually stated purpose: in order for God (1) to be righteous, and (2) to justify the one who has faith in Christ (or the one redeemed by Christ's faithfulness). Since the latter purpose is positive, the fact that the former is mentioned at all probably (or possibly) means that it is a negative contrast. That is, the demonstration of God's righteousness entails judgment or justice as well as acquittal. This judgment is not in addition to justification by grace but is included within it. When one accepts the *undeserved* gift of a new standing with God, no longer under condemnation (8:33-34), then one must acknowledge—judge—oneself as *undeserving*.

In recent years René Girard has developed a complex theory to explain the origin and structure of both societies and religions. In his view societies project their internal, reciprocal violence and hostilities onto a sacrificial victim or scapegoat in order to remove from the society the violence that would otherwise destroy it. By deciding unanimously to kill the scapegoat, the society's violence and the guilt for it are transferred to the sacrificial victim. Thus social conflicts are eliminated or curtailed and the community can exist in accord. The victim is regarded as both guilty and sacred. The community conceals from itself the fact that it is really the violent and guilty party. The great difference that the biblical tradition inserts into this picture is that guilt is shifted away from the victim and back onto society where it belongs (Girard 1986, 27, 38, 101–103, 109–10, 117; 1989, 3–4, 7–8, 53, 94–96, 104).

Whatever one may think of the generalizability of Girard's theory, the structure of Romans, with its own modifications and transformations, reflects Girard's depiction of the development of religion and society. In the letter the whole human community is portrayed as totally divided (1:18-32) and involved in ruinous, reciprocal violence (3:10-18). In this situation God acted redemptively through the sacrificial death of Christ (vv. 21-26). Paul understands the social violence as sin (3:9), and the way to freedom from the violence of sin is to die sacramentally with the sacrificial victim (6:4-6). This communal participation in baptism creates a unified community—one body in Christ (12:5). But the redemption, both individual and communal, is never complete; and the individual is exhorted to keep redemption in process by the continual appropriation of the death to sin (6:11-12); and the church is exhorted to continue cementing communal bonds (12:3, 6, 9).

3:27–4:2. Boasting, faith, and the validity of the law. This section is a diatribal exchange in which Paul deals with the impact of justification by grace on the continuing validity of the law (Stowers 1981, 164–65). The dialogue is generated by the interlocutor's question about what has happened to boasting if justification is through faith.

To boast is to put one's confidence in or to affirm one's confidence in. It is virtually synonymous with to trust in (*peithō*) (Phil 3:3). The object of this confidence can be God (Jer 9:24) or Christ (1 Cor 1:31; 2 Cor 10:17; Gal 6:14; Phil 3:3), on the one hand, or one's own achievements—wisdom, power, righteousness (Jer 9:23; 1 Cor 1:29; Phil 3:3, 9), on the other hand (Bultmann 1951, 242–43; Käsemann 1980, 69–70). Paul's questioner wants to know what has become of our basis for having confidence in our own righteousness based on the law. What becomes of boasting?

Paul answers that it has been excluded on the law or principle of faith. The word translated "law" here is Paul's normal word for law (*nomos*). But it could mean principle, norm, or order. On the other hand, Paul could be understood as saying *law* of faith. That is, boasting is excluded on the basis of the Law of Moses understood, not as demanding works, but as intending faith (see commentary on 9:31-32). There is *one* God, of Jew and gentile; therefore, there is *one* condition for justification, for both Jew and gentile. It is faith.

Paul's questioner then asks: do we overthrow the law, since justification by faith rules out works performed in obedience to the law as a way to justification. Paul answers: absolutely not, we rather establish the law.

The interlocutor then wonders how justification by *faith* can uphold the law since ABRAHAM belongs to the law but was justified by *works* and thus has something of his own to boast about. JUDAISM understood Abraham as the prime example of the devout Jew who was received as righteous because of his faithful obedience to the law (Jub 23:10; 1 Macc 2:52; Kidd 4:14) (Dunn 1988, 196). Paul replies that whatever boastful claims Abraham might have been able to make, they would have no standing with God.

In the remainder of chap. 4 Paul proceeds to develop the point that justification does not overthrow the law because justification by faith is already in the law in the case of Abraham. Clearly Paul understands the law as including much more than demands, and he is going to interpret Abraham very differently than his fellow Jews did.

It is true that Paul affirms the continuity between Israel and Christianity in Rom 4 (Dunn 1988, 197). Paul does this, however, by Christianizing Abraham. He does not say: proper Christian faith is like the faith of Abraham, the father of Israel. He rather says: Abraham, the father of Israel, already had Christian faith. That is, Paul finally defines Abraham's faith as *resurrection* faith. Since Paul's strategy is to use Abraham to prove that the Christian gospel of justification by faith does not overthrow but rather establishes the law, he logically has to argue that Abraham already had the faith of justification by faith.

4:3-15. Abraham's faith is reckoned as righteousness. For Paul it was not Abraham's works but his *believing* God that was reckoned to him as righteousness. Paul interprets the faith and righteousness attributed to Abraham in Gen 15:6 as being qualitatively the same as the righteousness of faith that Christians have.

In vv. 4-5 Paul makes a clear distinction between the self-understanding that accompanies works and the one that accompanies faith. The person who does works for salvation regards these works as meritorious; that is, the reward from God is a debt or obligation (*opheilēma*) which God owes to the worker. But the one who simply accepts in faith the new relationship that God establishes, knows herself or himself as *ungodly*, not deserving.

Verses 7-8 connects the *reckoning* of righteousness with not *reckoning* sin in Ps 32:1-2 (Ps 31 in LXX). Thereby Paul identifies justification with the forgiveness celebrated in the Psalm. But this LXX quotation is the only place where Paul uses this common verb for "forgive" (*aphiēmi*).

Paul goes on to underscore the non-meritorious quality of Abraham's righteousness by pointing out that his faith was reckoned as righteousness *before* he was circumcised. Then he was circumcised as a seal of the righteousness. Therefore, Abraham can be the father of the gentiles, who have faith but are not circumcised, and of the Jews, who are circumcised but also follow the example of Abraham's pre-circumcision faith.

4:16-25. Abraham's faith as faith in the resurrection. The specific promise of God that Abraham believed and as a result had his faith reckoned as righteousness was the promise that he would have many heirs. The promise was given at a time when he was old and Sarah was barren and they had no legitimate heir.

The fact that Paul describes the God in whom Abraham believed as the one who gives life to the dead and calls into existence the things that do not exist shows that Paul is interpreting Abraham's experience of God in the light of the Christian experience of the God who raised Jesus from the dead (v. 24). The Abraham story may also have contributed to his understanding of Jesus' death and resurrection. The dialectical interaction between the two is seen in the fact that the discussion of Abraham moves immediately into the kerygmatic (preaching) statement about Jesus' death and resurrection for our justification.

Paul's appropriation of the Abraham story is a clear case of his Christian understanding governing his reinterpretation of the pre-Christian past.

We could say that Paul posits a "resurrection situation" in Abraham's history and a corresponding faith arising from it. The resurrection situation is what the Christians' and Abraham's situations have in common—the promise of life in the midst of death.

The broader import of Rom 4 is that for Paul the death-resurrection-faith situation is a possibility—in principle and in actuality—at any point along the line of the history of God's saving acts. Not only Abraham but also other Israelites had the kind of faith Abraham had (4:11-12). Yet Paul can speak of the time before Christ as the time before faith came (Gal 3:23-25). These two points of view can be reconciled by pointing out, with Käsemann, that salvation history is not uninterrupted but contains discontinuities (Käsemann 1971, 88). The "before faith came" does not mean there had been no instances of Christian faith before Christ but that these instances had come intermittently, separated by gaps. There were times of faith before Christ but also times before faith came.

Romans 4 constitutes a certain modification—or deconstruction—of Paul's customary position. Generally faith in Christ (Rom 3:22; Gal 2:16) or in his death and resurrection (Rom 10:9; Gal 2:20; 3:1-2, Phil 3:9) is the condition for salvation. Being in a right relationship with God comes through faith in Christ (Rom 10:10). Faith in Christ is *in itself* the way to, or the consequence of (Phil 1:29), salvation. But in Rom 4, faith in Christ is not itself the way to justification. Rather faith in Christ has become a paradigm or model for other analogous situations that are not specifically faith in Christ but are qualitatively similar to it. If that were not Paul's real point, he would not be able to show that the faith of justification was present in Abraham and thus does not overthrow the law.

The medium for this shift in Paul's position is the hermeneutical move of interpreting X *as* Y; that is, interpreting Abraham's faith in God's promise (X) *as* the Christian's faith in the death and resurrection of Jesus (Y). The substance of the shift is that faith in Christ has ceased to be the focus and has been replaced in the center by the category of having righteousness reckoned to one. This is what happened for both Abraham and the Christian believers—the reckoning of righteousness. What the two have in common is that faith is reckoned as righteousness (vv. 22-24a).

The focus or fundamental category is having faith reckoned as righteousness, and the faith in which righteousness—a right relationship with God—becomes a reality has a certain character. Having this faith is the

content of salvation, and this content is what Paul wants to define here. But the faith in which righteousness becomes a reality does not have to be faith in Christ. It has to be *like* faith in Christ. It has to be holding in hope to God's promise of life in the face of the impossible. Faith in Christ is the paradigm for faith as righteousness but not the only actual access to the right relationship.

Life as Liberation from Victimizing Powers, 5:1–8:39

Romans 5:1 is an important transitional verse. *Since we are justified* sums up 3:21–4:25, and *peace* encompasses the new *life* of *freedom* that 5:1–8:39 will unfold. Paul makes the discussion in Rom 5–8 engage issues connected with the Jewish-gentile conflict in the Roman church—for example, the ethical dimension of the gospel (6:1-4, 12-13; 8:13) and the role of the law (chap. 7). That historical connection, however, is not the generating source of Rom 5–8, for both the juxtaposition of 5–8 to 1:18–4:25 and the content of 5–8 flow theo-*logically* from the content of 1:18–4:25. For Paul the new relationship with God—JUSTIFICATION—issues in a new quality of life—FREEDOM; and yet that freedom is experienced ambiguously. Therefore, it is necessary to explicate the powers that assail the life of freedom: ADAM, SIN, the LAW, flesh, and death. But Paul's real interest is in affirming deliverance from the destructive powers. In his paradoxical and dialectical way Paul both declares that the liberation has occurred (6:6-8; 7:6; 8:1-2) and expresses the hope that it will occur (5:5; 8:20-25). In the ending of each of the major sub-divisions of this section he affirms that life has come to believers in and through Christ (5:21; 6:23; 7:25a; 8:39).

Justification and liberation are not identical with each other, but they do merge into each other in the process of SALVATION. Justification gives the sinner the new *relationship* of a sinless person, no longer under condemnation. The new relationship confers upon the believer's life a new center—Christ (2 Cor 5:15)—rather than oneself. Thus the believer no longer lives toward achieving his or her salvation through good works. Since it was this misguided effort that brought one under the power of sin and the law (7:13-25), the justification that provides the new relationship is also a deliverance into a new kind of life. Proceeding from the other direction, it is the liberation from the power of sin and death—the overwhelming ruinous drive to manipulate all reality—that makes it possible to accept the new relationship. Faith is a gift.

Justification and liberation are immanent in each other, but they are not identical. By analogy the relationship of justification is the shape of the new life, and freedom from the powers is the content that is shaped. Moreover, justification sees the guilty sinner as freely and responsibly rejecting God and pronounces him *not guilty*. The *justified* sinner is still *sinner*. Deliverance sees the sinner as the victim of superhuman powers and frees her from these powers. The liberated sinner has a new character, is on the way toward not being sinner. Justification and liberation continue to interact with each other in salvation understood as an ongoing process (2 Cor 3:18; 4:16).

Transition from Justification to Peace and Life, 5:1-11

Romans 1:18–4:25 is unified on the basis of its depiction of the negative (wrath) and positive (justification) sides of God's righteousness. Romans 5:12–8:39 coheres on the basis of its portrayal of the interconnected destructive powers—Adam, sin, law, FLESH, DEATH—and the proclamation of God's liberation from these through Jesus Christ. Romans 5:1-11 points transitionally in both directions.

Our transitional passage looks backward to justification and grace (vv. 1-2, 9), Jesus' death for sinners (vv. 6-9), salvation (vv. 9-10), and wrath (v. 9). It points forward to the hope of sharing eschatological glory (v. 2; 8:18, 21), suffering (v. 3; 8:18), ethical concerns (v. 4; 8:4-5, 13-15), and the death of Christ (vv. 6-9; 6:3; 7:4, 25a; 8:3).

According to some manuscripts Paul says "since we are justified by faith, therefore *we have* (indicative mood) peace." According to other manuscripts (slightly better) he says "since we are justified by faith, therefore *let us have* (subjunctive mood) peace." In terms of the larger context of Rom 5–8, either is compatible with Paul's thought. He can refer to God's salvation in human beings as an accomplished reality (6:3-4) or he can put believers under the imperative to make it a reality (6:11-13). Justification and peace are related as cause and effect—justification, therefore PEACE. They are not identical.

Peace does not mean the subjectivity of peace of mind. Its background is the Hebraic concept of *shalōm*—total well-being. Within the context of Romans, it refers to the reconstitution of the deformed self (1:21-23, 24-28; 3:23) and the restructuring of a society torn by reciprocal hostility and violence (1:29-32; 3:10-18).

Having strongly criticized boasting (trusting) in our own works, Paul proposes boasting in the hope of sharing God's glory as the fitting Christian posture. More than that, believers boast in their afflictions. Suffering is not a contradiction to standing in grace but the condition in which grace is effective (Dunn 1988, 264). We boast in our suffering because suffering leads through endurance and character—the quality of being proved by testing—to HOPE. And hope does not disappoint us because—it would seem—of our strength of character. But Paul surprises us. Hope does not disappoint us because the LOVE of God has been poured in our hearts by the Holy Spirit. It is God's love for us, not our love for God, which the HOLY SPIRIT has established in our hearts, the inner core of our being.

The Spirit for Paul is the power of God that makes God's reality and action present in human experience. In this context the action of God that the Spirit makes present is the love God demonstrated by sending God's Son to die for humankind. Our radical undeservingness of this love Paul underscores by means of a vivid contrast. While a person will hardly die for another who is righteousness (correct according to law or moral principle), a person perhaps would dare to die for someone who is good (more than correct). But Christ died for us ungodly sinners who are neither righteous nor good.

As in 3:24-25, the consequence of Jesus' saving death is expressed as justification (v. 9)—a new relationship. This is paralleled in v. 10 by defining the new situation as RECONCILIATION. This category takes its meaning from the reality of personal, group, and national hostilities, and it draws out the significance of peace with God in v. 1. In reconciliation hostility is overcome, and here it is human beings, not God, who are the enemy that needs to be reconciled. Justification and reconciliation overlap in meaning. Reconciliation is neither identical with nor the consequence of justification. Each describes the new situation that results from Christ's death, with reconciliation underlining the personal element in the relationship between God the judge and the justified sinner (Cranfield 1980, 265–67; Dunn 1988, 259).

Now that justification and reconciliation are a present reality through the love of God, total salvation in the future is assured. Paul typically, but not always, uses the term salvation for the future completion of redemption.

Freedom from Adam, 5:12-21

With this section the theme of sin takes on a new intensity and a somewhat different focus. Prior to this, sin is seen as universal but primarily as a matter of individual responsibility. Now with the role of Adam the supra-individual cause of sin comes clearly into the picture. Romans 6:1-23 then treats sin as a concrete everyday problem and struggle in the life of the believer. Chapter 7 deals with the relationship of sin to the law and chap. 8, with its connections to flesh and death. Yet throughout the discussion all these destructive powers are interconnected.

Adam is not the originating *source* of sin, but he is the agent through which sin as a demonic personalized power entered the world and infected all humankind and brought death in its wake. And yet death spread to *all* because *all sinned*. Paul maintains the paradox that sin and death are both freely chosen and fated, but the fated side is emphasized in vv. 12-21.

Structurally v. 12 is the first member of a comparison between ADAM and Christ, the second member of which occurs only at v. 18b: *as* through the one man Adam sin came (v. 12), *so* through the other one's act of righteousness justification came (v. 18b). Verses 13-17 is a parenthesis clarifying the difference between Adam and Christ, and v. 18a essentially repeats v. 12 as a preparation for the second member in v. 18b (Cranfield 1980, 272–73).

For Paul the presence of the law makes sin a transgression, makes it guilt-laden, causes it to count or incur wrath (vv. 13-14; 4:15). Adam's sin was such a guilty transgression because God's command to him not to eat from the tree (Gen 2:16-17) was the functional equivalent of law. But Paul holds here that between Adam and Moses' giving of the law, since there was no law, although people sinned and died, this sin was different from Adam's and was not counted. That declaration contradicts Paul's more general position in two ways. (1) There are many indications in Paul elsewhere that the whole human race has always been under the law in principle (see excursus on the law in the commentary on 3:9-20). Thus there could be no time when sin was not counted. (2) For Paul death is the wages or *result* of *sin* (Rom 6:23; 8:5-6); therefore, since Paul grants that death did in fact rule from Adam to Moses (when there was allegedly no law) and holds in 6:23 that death is the wages of sin, he cannot say consistently in v. 13 that sin is not counted. The reality of death shows that sin did count.

If Adam was not the originating *source* of sin, he is nevertheless the *cause* of the plight of all other human beings. His sin causes the sin (v. 19), death (vv. 15, 17), and condemnation (vv. 16, 18) of all others.

Adam and Christ are alike in that in each case what the one does affects the many—all others—and each of them represents the whole (or potentially the whole) of humankind. On the other hand, while Adam began a history, the history of sin, Christ reversed that history. Thus Adam represents humankind as sinful and Christ, humankind as righteous. And the righteousness of Christ does not just balance the sin of Adam and its consequences. It much more overbalances them, producing justification and life (vv. 15b, 16b, 17b, 18b, 19b).

In v. 16b the word signifying the opposite of condemnation should be translated justification, as it is. But in Greek it is not Paul's usual word for justification (*dikaiōsis*) but rather the cognate term *dikaiōma*, which ordinarily means requirement or righteous deed. *Dikaiōma* has a more normal meaning in v. 18 where it is used of Christ's righteous deed as a synonym for his obedience (v. 19).

Paul probably believed Adam to have been the first historical man, a difficult belief in the modern world. Nevertheless, Adam is also profoundly employed by Paul as a symbol for what the human situation always is in historical existence. In Rom 7 Paul can use the Adam story to express his own implication in sin and also to say what is true typically for other individuals. At the same time Adam symbolizes the whole of humankind, the structural human situation, the totality that overwhelms the individual. As Paul Ricoeur puts it, Adam is the always already there of evil in every situation into which the individual enters (Ricoeur 1969, 241, 243, 251, 257–58).

It has been held that Paul bases the participation of all humans in Adam on the physical-psychic solidarity of the human race and that he thinks of the participation of all in Christ in an analogous way. There is only the slightest hint of the role of faith. All share in Christ's work as a matter of the unity of the race (Best 1955, 35–37).

But Paul does *not* treat the effects of Adam's and Christ's actions in an analogous way. When he speaks of our involvement with Adam, he uses the past (aorist) tense and indicative mood—signs of factuality (vv. 15a, 17a, 19a, 21a). But when he speaks of the effect of Christ's obedient righteousness, although he once states that grace has already abounded (v. 15b), he characteristically here speaks of our involvement in Christ by using the future tense or subjunctive mood (vv. 17b, 19b, 21b)—signs of possibility. And he implies that this possibility—not a natural fact—will become a reality when it is *received* by faith (v. 17b).

Paul concludes the Adam section by stating that the law slipped or stole in *in order that* (probably a purpose rather than a result clause) the trespass might increase or become greater. This contradicts Paul's more typical position that sin is the *result rather than* the *purpose* of the law (see excursus on the law in commentary on 3:9-20). But the good news is that when sin increased, grace super-abounded; and the purpose of this grace is that it might reign through righteousness to produce eternal life. Grace, righteousness and eternal life are compactly distinguished and related. Grace (the gift and act of God) establishes righteousness (a right relationship with God) that issues in eternal life.

Freedom from Sin, 6:1-23

In Rom 6:1 Paul has his diatribal questioner draw a false conclusion, phrased as a question: What then shall we say? If grace superabounds where sin increases, should we not remain in sin in order that grace might abound? Paul answers "absolutely not" (author trans.). He then spends this chapter giving his reasons why the believer should not continue in sin. Thus he takes up in a substantive way the question that he summarily dismissed in 3:8. Sin in Rom 6 is both a personalized power (vv. 6-7, 12, 16, 20) and deeds of rebellion (vv. 12, 19, 21).

What are the reasons for not remaining in sin? It has been argued that since Paul rejects the law as a standard for performing good works that merit salvation and since he does not appeal to the inherent authority of the law, he has no logical basis for claiming that the believer must not continue in sin (Knox 1954, 471). Paul, however, does have powerful arguments of a different kind to justify his contention that the believer should live an ethical life. It is not Paul's position that the believer in consequence of his or her renewal will necessarily live an ethical life but rather that the morally responsible life is now a possibility that ought to be enacted—and for good reasons.

6:1-14. Sin and baptism. Paul tells the Romans that Christians should not sin because in BAPTISM they have shared in Jesus' death and potentially in his resurrection. Jesus' death was a victory over sin (v. 10); therefore, our baptismal participation in his death frees us from sin (vv. 6-7). We should enact in our daily ethical lives what we have become in baptism—freed from sin. The believer should not continue in sin because to do so shatters wholeness or integrity, ruptures the correspondence between what we are in baptism and what we are in our daily lives. Sin violates the newness (v. 4) and life (v. 13) that have been created in us in consequence of the death of our old self (v. 6).

Baptism has a real effect. It is not just a pointer to a faith experience that happens independently of baptism. It is a symbol in which the meaning or effect is actualized in and through the symbol. Since in baptism we are united with Christ's death (v. 5), the benefits of that death are extended to us, and we are freed from sin (v. 7). Baptism does something.

This freedom from sin, however, is not a fixed, inalienable condition or possession. It is a reality but a reality that is a possibility that must be appropriated by the believer. You must become what you are. The believer is placed under the imperative to understand herself as dead to sin and alive to God (v. 11) and to yield her members to God and not to sin (v. 13).

The movement of this section is from indicative affirmations about the reality of freedom from sin (vv. 1-10) through imperative calls to appropriate this reality-possibility (vv. 11-13) and back to the affirmation in v. 14 that sin will not lord it over you because you are not under law but under grace. Since the law is the power of sin (1 Cor 15:56), if it is done away with (v. 14b), sin is reduced in power (v. 14a).

It is important that for Paul while the believer has already shared in Christ's *death* through baptism (vv. 4a, 5a, 6a, 7) sharing Christ's *resurrection* is "*reserved*" (Käsemann 1980, 166–67) for the future (v. 5b). Through sharing Christ's death a new quality of life is possible in this life (vv. 4, 6), but we are not yet raised with Christ (Phil 3:10). This means that salvation is never possessed but is a continuing process in which grace and faith interact (2 Cor 3:18; 4:16).

It has often been held that the MYSTERY RELIGIONS of the ancient world (the worship of Attis, Osiris, Dionysus, etc.) focused on a dying-rising deity with whom the worshiper could attain unity and deification through ritual acts. By means of the cultic celebration the worshiper passed from death to life with the deity. This influenced Paul's view of baptism.

It has been questioned, on the other hand, whether any sources truly substantiate the idea that the mysteries were in existence in Paul's time, and real differences have been pointed out between Paul's understanding of baptism and the mystery rites.

For example, the mystery rites were believed to be effective in themselves, automatically, while for Paul baptism is effective only when appropriated by faith. Or in the mysteries the worshiper is absorbed into the deity while in Paul the believer retains his or her identity but has a new relationship with God (Best 1955, 47–48; Wagner 1967, 117–18, 195, 198, 202, 212, 217).

Whatever the chronological relationship between Paul and the mysteries and however many very real differences there were between them, they had one important thing in common. Redemptive power extends from the deity to the worshipers by means of symbolic acts. This is also true in Judaism where, for example, the liberating power of the EXODUS is re-experienced through the celebration of PASSOVER.

6:15-23. Sin and death. Paul begins his discussion of the second reason for not remaining in sin by repeating the initial words from 6:1: *What then?* Should we sin because we are not under the law but under grace? And again: "Absolutely not." The central point is that one should not sin because sin produces death.

Paul interweaves four kinds of material in this section: theological reflection, indicative affirmations about their being set free from sin, the imperative to be righteous, and observations about the Romans' past way of life.

Paul's theological reflections deal with the paradoxical interaction of freedom and slavery. A person is the slave of whatever lord or power he or she obeys. But the choice to acknowledge and obey *no* lord is not a human possibility. As finite creatures human beings must obey some higher power. The only choice is whether one will obey sin or obey God (or righteousness) (vv. 16, 18, 22). To be free from sin is to be the slave of God or righteousness. But to be free from sin is at the same time to be free for God and obedience, which one was not when one was a slave of sin (v. 20). Real freedom for Paul is slavery to the power that can give life (v. 22). Romans 6 emphasizes that freedom from sin is *slavery to God* which is *freedom for God* and obedience. But 1 Cor 3:21-23 adds that one who belongs to Christ and God is grounded in a reality beyond the world. On the basis of this ground the believer is also free *for the world*, free to engage in the totality of the world's reality without being enslaved by it.

Paul declares to the Romans that they have in fact been liberated from sin (vv. 18, 22). But as is typical of him, he also places them under the imperative to make that freedom/slavery—which is both a reality and a possibility—into an actuality. Present your bodily members as slaves to righteousness which leads to sanctification (v. 19c).

Käsemann has argued that for Paul the righteousness that God establishes in believers includes obedience. The ethical imperative does not stand alongside the indicative statements about the reality of justification or righteousness but coincides with them or is integrated into them (Käsemann 1980, 174–75). SANCTIFICATION is the believer's being for God in his or her everyday existence in the secular world (183), and for Käsemann justification includes sanctification; they coincide (174, 183). Or he can say that gift (justification) and task (sanctification) coincide (175). Obedience must verify the gift (174). Christ is no longer the Lord of the one who does not obediently serve him (175). If one fails at the task, he or she loses the gift.

Käsemann's interpretation ignores the fact that for Paul it is the *ungodly* or *sinful* person who is justified (3:23-24; 4:5). The person who is justified is still sinful. The justified believer who performs acts deserving of condemnation is still justified by God and is still the object of the crucified and risen Christ's intercession (8:33-34). Nothing can separate us from the love of Christ (8:35-39).

At the same time it is certainly the case with Paul that the proper and intended result of justification is sanctification. Righteousness is toward or into sanctification (v. 19; but also, see commentary on 14:10-12).

The one who is justified by grace without regard to his or her religious or moral achievements is nevertheless not to continue in sin because to do so: (1) causes the self to be divided against itself and (2) produces death. The juxtaposition of these two reasons implies that one dimension of death is self-division. The other—and more fundamental—dimension of death is that it is hostility to and estrangement from God (8:6-8). To go on in sin is to be both against God (vv. 16, 18, 22; 8:7) and against oneself (6:2, 4, 6; 7:5, 9; 8:10). The fundamental sinful reality is being against God (1:21a, 23, 25), and being against oneself is its consequence (1:21b, 24b, 27). Death is the slave wages paid by sin when one serves sin.

The free gift of God is life—a new relationship of reconciliation with God, the reconstitution of a shattered society and the reuniting of the divided self.

Freedom from the Law, 7:1-25

7:1-6. A death frees from the law. Paul introduces this topic by stating a broad principle (v. 1) which he illustrates (vv. 2-3) and then extends into its theological application (vv. 4-6). The connections of the parts are far from obvious or smooth, but the whole thing may hold together better than it appears to. And the main point is clear: the believer has been freed from the law.

The principle taken literally is a truism. A person is freed from obligation to the law by his or her own death. In the illustration a wife is freed from the legal requirement to be faithful to her husband by her husband's death. Thus one person is freed from the law by the death of another (vv. 2-3).

The theological application (7:4-6) makes metaphorical use of both preceding motifs, one's own death and the death of another. Under the conditions of fallen existence—the flesh—sinful passions aroused by the law worked in our members to produce death. But believers have been discharged from the law by dying to it. They are dead as far as the law's enticement to earn salvation by works is concerned. The old self has died through the body of Christ—probably a reference to Christ's death. The believer participates in the redemptive effects of Christ's death by dying with him (6:4; 2 Cor 5:14-15).

7:7-25. The law, sin, and internal conflict. First Corinthians 15:56 states concisely that the law is the power of sin, and Rom 7 probes that relationship in an elaborate way. Both sin and the law are personified by Paul as cosmic powers, suprahuman persons. Sin has dominion, reigns, enslaves (Rom 6:6-7, 12-14, 16, 20). It lies dead, revives, deceives, and kills (vv. 8-9, 11). Similarly, the law comes in (5:20; 7:9), arouses sin (vv. 5, 7), takes us captive (v. 6), and promises life but deceives by serving up death (v. 10).

Sin uses the law (vv. 8, 13). But the law as the instrument of sin is so closely tied to sin as a power, sin as the initiator of sinning, that the law itself can appear as the initiator. Sin employs the law, but the law is the power (7:5; 1 Cor 15:56) that brings latent sin to active life (v. 9). Therefore, the law itself can be spoken of as the provoker that causes sin (v. 7) and that, installed in the flesh, works against God's redemptive intention (vv. 22-23).

The law provokes or arouses sin (vv. 7-14), and existence under the law is rent by internal conflict (vv. 15-25). Paul makes use of the Adam myth to interpret his own experience as typical of humankind. There are three questions (which interpenetrate each other) to be pursued in interpreting this passage.

1. What phase of Paul's life is he talking about when he speaks of himself as engaged in all kinds of covetousness and torn asunder by conflict between intention and result?

He can hardly be referring to his Jewish life because as a Jew he saw himself as blameless regarding the righteousness of the law (Phil 3:6). It can also be argued that his description ill fits his Christian life. While there are other places where he attributes conflict to the Christian life (8:10), in such places the redemptive forces are victorious (8:11, 16). But in Rom 7 the law and sin seem to have the upper hand. Moreover, the structure of Romans suggests that he is not talking about Christian experience in this chapter. Just as 1:18–3:20 provides a negative foil for 3:21–5:11, and 5:12-21 provides a negative foil for 6:1-23, and 9:1–10:21 does for chap. 11, so 7:1-25 provides a negative foil for 8:1-39 (Käsemann 1980, 205, 210).

The most likely possibility is that since Paul as a Jew felt blameless (Phil 3:6), Rom 7:7-25 is describing his past Jewish life from the standpoint of his Christian faith. Looking back on his pre-Christian past he sees that he was in fact sinful and self-divided, but prior to his conversion he was unconscious of his true condition. Here he is describing the human situation as fallen—fleshly—and under the power of sin (v. 14), a part of cosmic fallenness (1:18–3:20; 8:22-23) (Bultmann 1951, 246–49; Käsemann 1980, 192, 199).

The chief problem with the immediately preceding interpretation is that the past tenses with which Paul has been describing his experience in vv. 7-13 are replaced by the present tense when he begins to speak about his inner conflict (vv. 14-24). Must we not then say that the present tense verbs present his pre-Christian and unconscious self-dividedness as if it were present and conscious. Does not the present tense in fact extend the inner conflict into the present of Paul and his Christian readers? Believers are only in the process of being renewed (2 Cor 3:18; 4:16). As long as they bear the image of the old Adam (1 Cor 15:39) and do not have Christ fully formed in them (Gal 4:19), which means as long as time lasts (Phil 3:10-11), they struggle with sin and self-division.

2. What exactly is the nature of the sinful covetousness or desire that Paul describes or in exactly what sense does the law provoke sin?

The most obvious answer is that the law provokes acts of covetousness. That wrong acts are in view is supported by the fact that the passions of sin aroused by the law are plural (7:5). Also the reference to members of the body and fruit for death (7:5) alludes to the similar language in 6:19, 21 where sin is rebellion upon rebellion.

The law is not sin, yet Paul would not have sinned but for the law. The very prohibition against coveting generated every coveting in him (vv. 7-8). The dynamic is that the law as a demand for obedience is a reminder of human limitations and thereby provokes in people a will not to submit (8:7).

At the same time vv. 9-10 seems to be a transition to sin in a different sense incited by the law (Theissen 1987, 209–10). *Sin* (v. 9) is closely related to the fact that the law promises life but causes death (v. 10). The law promises life, and under the conditions of fallen existence (in the flesh) people assume that life is attained by doing the law (10:5). They attempt a righteousness of the law that is a righteousness of their own (10:3; Phil 3:9), a human righteousness that puts God in their *debt* (Rom 4:4). This also is a refusal to submit to God (10:3). The law incites sin in the sense of offering a means to establish one's own righteousness, which is a rejection of God's righteousness.

Perhaps the connecting link between these two dimensions of sin is the function that Paul assigns to the law in 3:19—to shatter every self-defense and hold people accountable. The law provokes sin in the sense of overt acts of disobedience. Then people, knowing from the law that they are accountable and without a word to say, attempt to establish their own righteousness by obedience to the law and to put God in their debt.

3. What is the nature of the inner conflict Paul describes in vv. 15-24? Its nature is governed by the two dimensions of sin that Paul has brought to light. It is not an either/or but a both/and.

Paul in anguish declares that he does not do what he intends but rather does what he hates. He can will the good, but he cannot do it (vv. 15, 18-19). He rather does evil.

This self-division is in some part moral. The law was for Paul as a Jew, and still is in some sense, an ethical standard (13:8-10; 1 Cor 7:19). Paul wills to do the moral good that the law requires but finds that he lacks the resources and does the opposite.

With this sense of failure—at some level of consciousness—he then tries to use the law to establish righteousness and life for himself. Here the conflict is existential. He agrees that the law is good and spiritual (vv. 14, 16). He appropriates its promise to give life (v. 10a) but discovers that it gives death instead (v. 10b). The good he wills is life—salvation—but the evil he achieves is death, because he pursues his own righteousness rather than accepting God's.

We have seen that broadly speaking Paul evaluates the intention of the law positively but sees its results in the context of fallen human existence as negative. This paradoxical view of the law is seen in Rom 7. The law is not sin but is holy, just, good, spiritual, and promises life (vv. 7, 10, 12, 14, 16). Yet the law is the cause of sin (vv. 8-9) and deception and finally issues in death (v. 10). This ambiguity is seen compactly in vv. 22-23. He delights in the law in his inner person or mind—the law in its redemptive intention. But at war with this law there is another law, the law of sin in his members, the law misunderstood as demanding works. This law takes him captive.

Paul calls out in his wretchedness—the wretchedness of his pre-Christian but also Christian existence—and asks who will deliver him from this body of death, the death of self-division. And now in his explicit Christian voice he offers his thanks to God through Jesus Christ for deliverance (v. 25a). But in the last sentence of this discussion he returns with great realism to the self-dividedness that even existence in faith never escapes during this historical life: I serve in my mind the law of God, but in the flesh—the condition of fallenness—I serve the law of sin (v. 25b).

Freedom from Death and Flesh, 8:1-39

8:1-11, Law, flesh, death, Christ, and Spirit. The affirmation that there is therefore now no condemnation for those in Christ is based on the rescue from the law accomplished by Christ (7:25a) despite the continuing struggle of the life of faith (7:25b). The ground of this absence of condemnation is further specified as our liberation from the law of sin and death by the law of the Spirit. The law of the Spirit and the law of sin and death could mean two principles of reality or two ways of understanding the Law of Moses—in terms of its intention (to give life and the Spirit) and in terms of its result (to cause death).

The law is a *power* that overpowers human beings and entices them against their wills into sin. But the ambiguity of the law expresses itself in yet another way. The law is also *weak*. Its weakness is its inability to do what God intended it to do—give life and faith. This weakness was caused by the flesh—human being in its fallenness—which is also a power. But God has done what the law could not do by sending his own Son.

The sending is probably not thought of as a sending from a preexistent heavenly state. There is no reference to a preexistent mode of being or activity, as in Phil 2:6; Col 1:15, 17; 1 Cor 8:6; Heb 1:2. The sending is more like an earthly appointment, as in the commissioning of the prophets (Isa 49:1, 5-6; Jer 1:5, 7) or the sending of the son to the vineyard in the parable of The Wicked Tenants (Mark 12:6; Fuller 1978, 41-44). That Jesus was sent in the *likeness of sinful flesh* does not mean that Paul questions Jesus' real humanity. Jesus was a man of flesh (1:3) and suffered the human condition under the power of wrath or curse (Gal 3:13) and the law (Gal 4:4). But Paul's insertion of the word *likeness* suggests that in the case of Christ the sin that is endemic to the flesh was overcome (2 Cor 5:21).

The purpose of sending the Son is that the law's requirement (*dikaiōma*) might be fulfilled in us who walk according to the Spirit. This requirement is probably the faith that the law intends. But the reference to walking also includes the ethical life that both the law and faith have in view.

For Paul flesh is not a *part* of human being but the *whole* self from a certain point of view. Paul has deepened and developed the OT notion of flesh as weakness (Ps 56:41; Isa 31:3; Davies 1948, 18–20) and given it a range of meanings. The flesh is the visible or physical (1 Cor 15:39; 2 Cor 12:7) and as such is weak and perishable in comparison with God (Gal 4:13; 1 Cor 15:50; 2 Cor 4:11). Yet it is the sphere of human existence created by God in which believers and all others live, and it is not judged to be evil (Gal 2:20; Phil 1:24). But the concept takes on a darker connotation when it is denied that believers still live in the flesh (Rom 7:5; 8:9). Then flesh becomes fully evil, virtually identical with sin. The mind of the flesh is hostile to God, refuses to submit, and those in the flesh cannot please God (vv. 6-8). The mind of the flesh prefers its own righteousness to God's (10:1-3). Observe that when the flesh is physical it is not evil, and when it is identical with sin it is not physical. The flesh as evil is a stance of the whole self. It is the self as trusting in itself or in some other aspect of finite reality. Paul's term for mind here (*phronēma*) does not just mean thought but the orientation or direction of one's whole existence (Käsemann 1980, 219).

This direction of one's existence *is* death. Death is not a punishment added to this hostility to God, but death is already present in it.

The power that liberates from flesh and death Paul refers to interchangeably as the Spirit, Spirit of God, Spirit of Christ, and Christ in you (vv. 9-10). The tension and ambiguity of existence in faith are still in view: although *your* body is dead because of sin, the Spirit of *God* is life because of the new relationship that is righteousness. Clearly here the Spirit of the one raising Jesus from the dead is the power of God operative in human existence to give life to dying bodies.

The body for Paul, like flesh, is not a *part* of a human being but is the *whole* self or person from a certain point of view. The body is the person in his or her physicality as a part of the material world (1 Cor 12:12-26; 13:3; 2 Cor 10:10; Gal 6:17). This shades off, however, into the body as the whole person, something one *is*, not something one has (Rom 6:12; 12:1). More specifically the body is the self in its *relatedness* in principle to other dimensions of reality (Bultmann 1951, 192–96, 201–203; Käsemann 1969, 135; 1971, 17–23).

In the relationship of self to self the body is perhaps most characteristically the self as the object of the self's will (Rom 6:12-14; 12:1; 1 Cor 9:27; 13:3; Phil 1:20). But the body as having deeds of its own is also subject (Rom 8:13). In fact the parallelism between body and spirit in 1 Cor 6:15, 17 shows that the body has a spiritual dimension. It is the place where death and resurrection with Christ is both understood and actualized (2 Cor 4:7-12).

A part of the meaning of body is its identity with flesh (1 Cor 6:16; 2 Cor 4:10-11). As such it is the self as the object of the world's physical violence (Gal 6:17; 2 Cor 11:23-29) and the self as sexually related (1 Cor 6:16). But the body is also the self as intended for the Lord (1 Cor 6:13, 15). The body can be given over to the power of death (Rom 7:24; 8:10-11), but the body is also the vehicle of eternal life (1 Cor 15:44), the spiritual body, the self fully assimilated to the realm of the Spirit. Here its fleshly physicality is explicitly denied (1 Cor 15:44-50). The *identity* of the self in relation to God and self is maintained in the resurrection, but *not* its *physicality* (Via 1990, 68–70).

8:12-17. Life in the Spirit as an obligation or task. In the previous section the Spirit's overcoming of the believer's death and self-division is spoken of as an assured reality. But in this passage the transformation of death into life is a task and obligation of the believer. It is in some way not certain that the believer will carry out this task.

Paul says: *If you live according to the flesh*—and you *will* (a condition determined as true)—*you will die*. But immediately thereafter he also states: *If by* (or in) *the Spirit you put to death the deeds of the body*—and you *will* (again a condition determined as true)—*you will live*. Each of these conditions is stated as equally possible. Paul perhaps leans toward the latter since he moves on to affirmative statements about the leading and witness of the Spirit. Body here is the equivalent of flesh in its evil sense (see Gal 5:16-17, 19).

Thematically for Paul (eternal) life is the gift of GRACE (Rom 1:16-17; 5:21; 6:23), but in 8:13 life is conditioned on the believer's putting an end to sinful acts. The believer must do what God has done in him or her.

The role of the Spirit here is to make being a child of God a *present* reality. The Spirit bears witness to our spirit that we are in fact God's children. The human spirit here is not a fragment or apportionment of the divine Spirit, but the strictly human spirit. The Spirit in bearing witness with our spirit is not talking to itself; rather, divine and human spirits are distinguished.

The human spirit is not a *part* of the self but the *whole* self from a particular standpoint. The spirit is the self as knowing subject. As spirit the self knows itself (1 Cor 2:11) and knows the public world and other people (1 Cor 16:18; 2 Cor 2:13; 7:13). Perhaps most importantly, as Rom 8:16 shows, the human spirit is the self in its openness to the testimony of God's Spirit (Via 1990, 70–73).

If we are children of God, we are fellow heirs with Christ, provided we suffer with him in order that we might be glorified with him. This note of suffering becomes the theme of the next section.

8:18-27. Suffering the wait for redemption. Present suffering cannot be compared to the overcompensating GLORY to be revealed—glory being Paul's term for the full manifestation of eschatological redemption. Glory is the substance of resurrection existence that believers will finally share with Christ (8:17; 2 Cor 3:18; 4:17; Phil 3:20-21).

Just as human beings struggle and groan against the power of sin, law, flesh, and death, so the nonhuman creation waits and longs for release from the decay and futility that God has allowed the cosmic powers to impose on the world. The human and non-human creation form a solidarity—they struggle and groan together—so that neither will be fully redeemed apart from the other (cf. Gen 3:17-19; 4 Ezra 7:11-14). In 8:14-16 being a child of God is a *present* reality. But in vv. 22-23 while the Spirit gives a *foretaste* of this reality, full adoption as a child of God is identified with the resurrection of the body and is projected into a future for which we wait. Yet we wait with the hope in which salvation resides. Although we do not yet see our full redemption, hope is confident about the future which is in God's hands.

8:28-30. God's predetermining purpose. According to some manuscripts (reliable and diversified) Paul states that *all things* work toward the good—a happy outcome—for those who love God. According to other manuscripts (reliable but less numerous and less diversified) he says that *God* works with all things toward the good for those who love God. Whichever reading one takes, Paul has God's sovereign intention in view. Things do not work on their own. The *all things* probably refers especially to the suffering struggle in which believers are engaged.

The good is worked for those *who are called according to [God's] purpose*. These people God foreknew and predestined. God's redemptive intention is always there ahead of us. The eternal purpose of God becomes concrete historical reality in calling and justification, which have already happened. But here Paul goes further and also affirms our glorification—our final resurrection existence—as a part of the salvation that has already happened. This is in tension with his general tendency to reserve glorification for the future.

8:31-39. The certain security of the believer. What then shall we say? What is the outcome of our being already glorified (8:30)—despite being not yet glorified (8:17; Phil 3:21)? The outcome is that nothing can undo our redemption. Even if we do something deserving of condemnation, God's giving his Son for us guarantees our justification against which no charge can stand. Christ who died and was raised is interceding for us at God's right hand. This mythological image gives concrete expression to the never ending validity of Christ's death for us. Nothing can separate us from the love of Christ (v. 35) or, interchangeably, from the love of God in Christ (v. 39).

Our own deeds that are worthy of condemnation cannot separate us (vv. 31-37). Neither can the afflictions and reversals of the historical process separate us (v. 35). Nor can anything that life or death, present or future, might hand out separate us (v. 38). Not even cosmic fate can pull us away from the love of God. That is what Paul means by the principalities and powers (vv. 38-39). Paul presupposed the worldview of his time, which held that there are personal, hostile, supernatural powers that victimize and control human beings. Christ has overcome them (Via 1990, 40–44).

God's Word and the Destiny of Israel, 9:1–11:36

This section is not a parenthesis or excursus in which Paul merely indulges his Jewish patriotism by claiming for Israel a permanent place in the purpose of God. Paul rather addresses here an issue that grows essentially out of the preceding discussion. Can the word of God be trusted? For Paul the gospel of the righteousness of God as justification by faith is the fulfillment of God's promise to save Israel (Rom 4:13, 16, 20). *Israel* is the people of the COVENANT, the LAW, the sonship, the promises (9:4-5). But when the promises were fulfilled in the manifestation of God's justifying RIGHTEOUSNESS the result has been that most Jews are not justified believers while most believers are gentiles. Is justification by faith apart from the law then a nullification of God's promise to save Israel? Is God's promise unreliable? Has the word of God failed (9:6)?

Paul develops a three-fold argument to show that the word of God has *not* failed. This demonstration is of great theological importance to Paul, for if God's promising word to Israel is not reliable, then God's word is not reliable for anyone.

God's Rejection of Israel, 9:1-29

9:1-5. Paul's deep sorrow about his people. Paul is in anguish because most of his kinspeople according to the flesh—the Israelites—stand outside the realm of salvation. He would give up his own salvation for them if that were possible. It is ironical that Israel is mostly lost, for these are the very people who have had the tokens of salvation—sonship, the covenants, the law, the patriarchs, the promises. And from Israel the Christ is physically descended. To the word "Christ" (NRSV *Messiah*) Paul adds *who is over all, God blessed forever. Amen.*

How God is related to Christ here is a difficult interpretive problem (for various possible readings see Cranfield 1981, 464–70; Metzger 1975, 520–23) because the lack of punctuation in the original manuscripts leaves the relationship ambiguous. The two main alternatives are as follows: (1) Understand God as in apposition to Christ and read "Christ, who is God

over all." (2) Put a period rather than a comma after Christ thus separating God from Christ in an independent doxology and read " . . . Christ. God who is over all be blessed." Probably syntax and Pauline style favor the first. But the Pauline theological pattern seems to favor the second. Nowhere else does Paul directly identify Christ with God, and in 1 Cor 15:24, 27 he clearly subordinates the Son to God the Father.

9:6-29. The sovereign electing will of God. God's word promised salvation to Israel (Rom 4:16-18) (see commentary on Rom 11 for Paul's ambiguity regarding the constitution of the saved Israel). But most of Israel is not saved. Does that mean that God's word has failed? *No.* Here Paul gives his first argument to support the reliability of God's promise. It has never been the case that all of Abraham's descendants are saved. God's dealings with Israel have been consistent, for God has always distinguished among the descendants of ABRAHAM between the physical descendants and the children of the promise who alone are the children of God. Everything depends on God's electing will; nothing depends on human position or performance. Paul makes much use of the OT throughout this section.

For example, when twin sons were born to the patriarch ISAAC and his wife REBECCA, before they were born or had done anything good or bad, God chose JACOB and rejected ESAU. Only God's decisive action counts, not human works. This action of God can be spoken of as his promise (vv. 6-8), his calling (vv. 11-12), or his purpose of ELECTION (v. 11). All of these are expressions of his will (v. 18). God's will prompts God to show MERCY toward some (vv. 15-16) and to harden the hearts of others (vv. 17-18).

If then everything comes from God in deciding salvation or rejection and nothing from human beings—Paul's diatribal questioner will ask—how can God find fault since no one can resist his will (v. 19)? Paul's answer is that people have no more right to question God than the clay has to question the potter who molds it. But Paul does go on to say that in all of this God's purpose has been to create vessels of mercy destined for glory from among both gentiles and Jews.

The salvation of the gentiles Paul grounds on the promise in Hos 1:10; 2:1, 23 that God will make his people from those who are *not* his people. Paul, however, has changed the meaning of the OT text, for in HOSEA, the "not my people" refers to unfaithful, sinful Israel and not to the gentiles. Paul grounds the salvation of the relatively few believing Jews on the prediction that he attributes to Isaiah (but which actually amalgamates Isa 10:22-23 and Hos 1:10) that only a REMNANT of the huge number of Israelites will be saved.

God's word has not failed because from the beginning (with Abraham) until now the identity of Israel does not depend on birth (not all of Abraham's descendants are children of God) nor on performance of works, but solely on who God says it is by the exercise of his sovereign electing will. The failure of most of Israel to be saved is determined by God's doing, and God has been consistent.

Israel's Rejection of Righteousness through Faith, 9:30–10:21

It is then highly paradoxical when Paul states as his second argument against the failure of God's word that Israel has missed out on salvation because *Israel* has rejected God's way of dealing with humankind. Everything depends on God; everything depends on Israel.

9:30–10:4. Israel's pursuit of righteousness by works. Paul notes an irony. The gentiles, who did not pursue righteousness, attained righteousness by faith. Israel, on the other hand, did pursue the law that affords righteousness. This pursuit of the law was not a mistake in itself, for the law can lead to righteousness.

The law as limit (Rom 7:7) and as accuser (3:19) makes people aware of their finitude and guilt and thus should point them in faith to God as the source of salvation. But under the conditions of fallen existence the law enticed Israel to attempt her own salvation. That is, Israel wrongly thought that the law called for works rather than faith. Thus Israel failed to attain the *law*. This shows that the real intention of the law was faith.

Paul acknowledges Israel's zeal for God but denies that her zeal is enlightened. In ignorance of the righteousness that comes from God Israel sought to establish her own righteousness by means of the law. What is wrong with the righteousness of the law for Paul is that it asserts itself to establish a right relationship with God rather than receiving the relationship from God. It does not submit (*hypotassō* in the passive) *to God's righteousness* (10:3). This is parallel to Paul's statement in 8:7-8 that *the mind that is set on the flesh is hostile to God [and] does not submit* (hypotassō in the passive) *to God's law*, that is, to the intention of the law to evoke faith. The parallelism between the two passages shows that pursuing the righteousness of the law is an expression of the mind of the flesh in its hostility to God.

Paul then says "for Christ is the end (*telos*) of the law, leading to righteousness for every believer" (author trans.). The *for* (*gar*) does not express the reason for what Paul has just said. That is, Christ's being the end of the law is not the reason for Israel's not submitting. Rather it is the reason for something that Paul implies but does not state: Israel *should have* submitted to God's righteousness, *for* Christ is the end of the law (Williams 1980, 283–84).

Christ is the end of the law (10:4) in two senses, corresponding to Paul's dialectical—yes and no—understanding of the law. Christ is the *fulfillment* of the law's intention—to evoke faith and give life. But Christ is the *termination* of the law from the standpoint of its result—its being understood as a demand for works that produces death.

There is a difference between the attitude that Paul criticizes here—trusting in one's *obedient* works of the law as able to establish one's own righteousness with God—and the attitude he criticizes in 2:17-24—trusting that one is secure with God because one knows God's will in the law and approves what is excellent while at the same time *disobeying* the law. It should be remembered that Paul regards *all* people as under the law in principle; therefore, these sinful postures toward the law are not peculiarly Jewish but rather characteristically human.

10:5-13. Word, faith, and resurrection. Here Paul draws a line through the OT distinguishing between what is invalid and valid in the Jewish scriptures. To MOSES in Lev 18:5 he attributes the view that the righteousness of the law promises life to those who live by achieving obedience (v. 5; see Käsemann 1980, 285). *But* (adversative *de* indicating a contrast, v. 6) the righteousness of faith—replacing Moses as the speaker in Deut 30:11-14—calls, not for the achievement of obedience, but for believing and confessing the word. Paul interprets this word in Deuteronomy as the saving proclamation of Jesus' lordship and resurrection.

The very surprising thing about Paul's interpretation of Deut 30:11-14 is that the "word" in the Deuteronomy passage means the "law" (30:11, 14)—just as Leviticus speaks about the law—and not the righteousness of faith. Paul has read a fully Christian understanding of word back into the Deuteronomy passage, but his interpretation is not wholly arbitrary. "Word" in Deuteronomy does mean "law," but it also means the effective preaching about the God of Israel who gives life by bringing people through death (Deut 32:1-3, 6-13, 19-35, 36-43; esp. 32:39). This theme would have had a close affinity with Paul's preaching of the death and resurrection of Jesus. Thus while Paul clearly over-Christianized Deut 30:11-14, we can understand why he saw a connection between his preaching and the message of Deuteronomy. As in Rom 4 so also here he finds moments of the gospel in the OT.

Judaism prior to and in Paul's time used Deut 30:11-14 to speak about the inaccessibility of WISDOM. Wisdom is accessible only to God, but God has brought her near in the law (Bar 3:29–4:1). Paul may have Baruch as well as Deuteronomy in mind. In Rom vv. 6-8 Paul uses spatial imagery—up, down, near—of both the resurrected Christ and the preached word. Thus Christ and the word are in effect made identical. The word of the righteousness of faith says: Do not seek the risen Christ in a cosmically distant place but seek him in the near word which enters your heart and brings you to faith.

Paul personifies the righteousness of faith and has it speak of the nearness of the resurrected Christ in vv. 6-9. Righteousness first speaks of the nearness of Christ in negative terms (not far) and then in positive terms. But the fact that the category of nearness holds together the negative and positive ways of speaking suggests that they both have the same subject. Speaking negatively righteousness says: Do *not* seek the risen Christ up there in heaven to bring him down or down there in the abyss among the dead to bring him up (vv. 6-7). Then when righteousness speaks of the nearness of Christ positively or directly, it replaces the risen Christ with the preached word (v. 8). Righteousness does not say that Christ is near but that the word is near, on your lips and in your heart.

It is evident from the negative expression of Paul's theme (Christ is not far) that his point is the nearness of *Christ*. Therefore, it makes no sense to speak of the nearness of the *word* if the word does not represent Christ. Thus when Paul replaces Christ with the word, puts the word in Christ's place, he is interpreting the risen Christ *as* the power of the proclaimed word about Christ to bring people to faith (vv. 8, 17). Faith calls upon the Lord who is present in the heart by means of the word. Everyone who calls upon this Lord will be saved.

10:14-21. Preaching, faith, and understanding. Paul unfolds a series of stages that are necessary to lead to salvation: the sending of preachers, preaching, hearing, believing, and calling upon. Paul then affirms, by appealing to the predictions of scripture rather than to historical evidence, that preachers have been sent, have preached, and have been heard. But not all of Israel has obeyed or believed what was heard (v. 16). Paul then at v. 19 introduces a new category into his series—understanding. Did Israel not understand? He answers the question by again appealing to the OT. The gentiles who were not seeking God have found God. Evidently Paul means to say that the gentiles at least have understood. But Israel has been disobedient and contrary.

Paul's point is less than clear, and his answer to the question whether Israel understood and his view about how understanding is related to believing (faith) can be interpreted in two ways.

(1) Paul distinguishes faith from understanding and means to say that since the gentiles understood the gospel surely Israel understood it although they did not (all) believe it.

(2) For Paul faith and understanding overlap extensively. Understanding is the intellectual element of faith itself and like faith shapes human existence (Rom 12:1-2; 2 Cor 3:12-18). Thus Israel no more understood than she believed, and that is made all the more ironical by the fact that the gentiles did understand and believe. This seems to be the more probable interpretation.

Paul has argued that only a few Jews are believers: (1) because God alone has decreed who among the descendants of Abraham shall be the spiritual Israel and (2) because Israel in the interest of self-assertion has neither believed nor understood. The relationship between these two opposing explanations can be understood in at least two ways.

1. The relationship is radically paradoxical. From one side God's act of will determines everything, and from the other side it is totally a human decision. If this is not seen as a hopeless contradiction, both sides are taken as necessary to account for the mystery of human destiny while acknowledging that there is no way to explain how they meet and interact.

2. There is finally an insoluble paradox, but to some extent the divine and the human can be seen as fusing and their point of contact, as definable. This presupposes that the divine and human are to some degree commensurate and comparable.

In 1 Cor 1:18 and 2 Cor 2:14-16 the divine, initiating activity occurs in the preaching of the gospel and thereby creates a situation in which a decision is inescapable for those who hear. Some respond with a "yes" and gain life while others respond with a "no" and inherit death. These are human decisions. The opposite destinies of the gentiles and Israel depend on how *they* decide (vv. 19-21; cf. 9:30-32). Yet the divine action in preaching made the decisions inescapable and necessary, determined that the decisions would in fact be made. Therefore, the yes leading to life and the no leading to death are at the same time in some sense divine actions or divine determinations.

The Final Salvation
of All Israel, 11:1-36

Paul's third argument in favor of the reliability of God's promise to Israel is that in the end God will save all Israel.

11:1-6. The present salvation of a remnant. Paul himself—a saved Israelite—is proof that God has not abandoned God's historical people. Beyond that there is now, as in the past (Elijah's time), a REMNANT chosen by grace, not rewarded for works.

11:7-10. Election and hardening. Israel (as a whole) did not attain the right relationship with God (9:31-32) that it sought, but the elect attained it. The rest were hardened. Note that Israel contains both the elect and the hardened. Paul reiterates the point made in 9:14-18 that both the election of the saved and the hardening of the lost are God's doing. Using scripture Paul underlines the assertion that the failure of the hardened to see and to understand God's intention was visited upon them by God. The wrong choice establishes an inescapable destiny.

11:11-16. The stumbling of Israel and the salvation of the gentiles. Israel has stumbled but not so as to fall, that is, not so as to be finally lost. Israel's stumbling, her temporary rejection of and by God, has provided the opportunity for the salvation of the gentiles. The purpose of the gentiles' salvation is to make Israel jealous, and that will lead to the salvation of *some* Jews by means of Paul's apostolic ministry. Evidently Paul's point is that Israel's seeing the gentiles' attaining the salvation promised to Israel will make her want to claim her own lost heritage. If Israel's rejection has had beneficial results for the gentiles and the world, how much more consequential will be her inclusion. It will bring about—or be brought about by—the resurrection from the dead.

In v. 16 Paul states a principle that will turn out to have far-reaching implications (see commentary on 11:25-32). In the OT (Num 15:17-21; Lev 23:14) a holy

offering to God from the first fruits released the rest of the harvest for general or *non-holy* uses. Paul reversed this and stated that the holiness of the first fruits makes the whole *holy*. But the principle is the same in both cases, and it is reiterated with the root and branches image. What is true for the part is also true for the whole to which the part belongs. What is actual in the part—first fruits and root—is latent or potential in the whole—the full lump or harvest and the branches. The part represented by the first fruits and root is probably Abraham and/or the believing Israelite remnant through the centuries. The whole imaged in the full harvest and the branches is all Israel. Before drawing out the implications of this (in 11:25-32) Paul continues—in 11:17-24—his specific address to the gentile Christians in Rome, which he began at v. 13.

11:17-24. The relationship of saved gentiles to the historical Israel. Here Paul takes the root and branches image of 11:16 and develops it into an allegory of the history of salvation in which the people of God throughout history are portrayed as a cultivated olive tree (vv. 17, 24) or its root (v. 18), unbelieving Israelites are represented as branches cut off from this tree, and believing gentiles are imaged as *a wild olive shoot* grafted into the tree.

Several indications of diatribe style are seen here. (1) The gentile Christians are identified with the personified *wild olive shoot*. (2) This olive shoot is the diatribal interlocutor who raises an objection (v. 19). (3) Paul issues admonitions and warnings (Stowers 1981, 99–100).

Olive cultivation of the time included both grafting wild shoots into cultivated trees and cultivated shoots into wild trees (Cranfield 1981, 565–66; Dunn 1988, 661). Paul's meaning depends less on particular agricultural practices than on his metaphorical use of them. He does seem to want to suggest that there is something unnatural—unexpected—about finding gentiles among the Israelite people of God (v. 24).

In this passage the believing community, which extends from Abraham down into the church of Paul's time, does not exist because individual believers decide to get together and form it. Rather the historical community is always there prior to the individual, and individuals are saved by being placed in the community by God. The root (the historical believing community) supports the grafted in shoots, not vice versa.

The gentile Christians are not to think themselves superior to the Jews (branches) who have been cut off. The latter were cut off because of their unbelief, and the gentile Christians are in only because of their faith. They are dependent on both the prior existence of the tree and God's gift of faith. But *they* have a responsibility to continue in faith. If they let thinking highly of themselves replace awe and faith, God will cut them off also.

However strongly Paul affirmed in 8:31-39 that nothing can separate believers from the love of God, here he allows that believers may in fact renounce faith and be cut off. From the standpoint of God's intention salvation is certain. From the standpoint of possible human lack of resolution, salvation is not so certain. And yet since faith is *God's* work in believers as well as the latter's own decision, can faith finally be renounced?

Paul makes a transition to the next section by reminding the gentile Christians that if they have been unnaturally grafted into the saved community, how much more will God graft the cut off natural branches (Jews) back into the tree.

11:25-32. The mystery of Israel's final salvation. Having pronounced severe judgment on the Jews (chap. 2) and declared that most of them now stand outside of salvation (9:30-10:3; 10:18-21; 11:7-10), Paul here affirms that once the hardening of Israel allows the full number of gentiles to come in, then all Israel will be saved. By *the full number of the Gentiles* he probably means all the elect among the gentiles or gentiles as a whole. By *all Israel* Paul probably means Israel as a whole but not necessarily every single Jew. That would be consonant with the contemporary Jewish understanding of "all Israel" (Mishnah, *Sanh* 10). Paul anticipated this development in 4:16 where he says that grace is to avail for *all* the seed of Abraham— those who belong to the law and those who share the faith of Abraham.

Evidently Paul believes that the salvation of Israel will be accomplished by the eschatological return of Christ (vv. 26-27), whose preaching will bring Israel to faith. Faith is the only way that either gentiles (1:16-17; 3:21-26; 9:30-31) or Jews (1:16-17; 3:19-20; 4:12; 10:6-10, 13; 11:5-6) have ever come to salvation. So will it be at the end.

It is not possible that all Israel would not be finally saved because in choosing the patriarchs God has irrevocably called all Israel. The call, the covenant, the promises (9:4-5) cannot be nullified (vv. 28-29).

Paul concludes his argument and his vision of the future with the affirmation that God has consigned all to disobedience in order that he might have mercy on all. Mercy can be fully appropriated only when sin has been fully experienced and acknowledged (3:19-20; 7:7, 13, 15, 24-25). This belongs to the purpose of God. When Paul reaches this stage of his argument, it is no longer just that all Israel will be saved. It is now that *all human beings* will finally be the recipients of God's mercy (v. 32).

This vision of the future moves Paul to praise God for God's riches, wisdom, and inscrutable ways whose depths are unknowable to humankind and to give God glory.

In the course of Rom 9–11 Paul's thought about ELECTION undergoes a decided change. He moves *from* a quantitative division of human beings in which some are chosen and others are rejected (9:6-18) *to* a qualitative division in which rejection (disobedience) and election (mercy) are two stages through which *all* pass (v. 32). It is impossible to say how conscious Paul might have been of the shift.

This change is mediated by the principle articulated in 11:16 that what is actual in the part is latent in the whole. Some Jews and some gentiles have actual faith; therefore, all Jews and all gentiles have latent faith and ultimately will have actual faith (v. 32). Romans 11:16 in the context of Paul's thought leads by an inevitable logic to v. 32—the salvation of all human beings as the recipients of God's mercy.

The change in point of view leaves some tensions in Paul's theological argument. In 2:4, 17-18, 22-24 he criticizes Jews who presume upon the kindness of God and assume that their relationship with God is secure whether or not they are obedient. He implicitly condemns the assumption that being a member of the covenant people (9:4-5) places one among the elect (11:5-7). And yet he himself takes the position that belonging to the covenant people constitutes an irrevocable call (11:28-29) to salvation.

The affirmation of the salvation of all stands in tension with Paul's frequently expressed clear belief that God will execute a final judgment that will leave some outside of God's kingdom in final death (6:23; 14:10-12; 1 Cor 6:9-10; 2 Cor 5:10; Gal 5:19-21; 6:7; Phil 3:18-19; 1 Thes 5:3).

Perhaps both sides of these tensions are necessary to disclose the mystery of human destiny as Paul sought to grapple with it and to express the uncertain certainty of existence in faith. Paul's logic leads to the affirmation of universalism, the salvation of all people. But it would be presumption and an offense against God's sovereignty to tell God that God *will* save all human beings individually. The final judgment motif protects against that presumption. Yet the sweep of Paul's argument makes it impossible to assert that any particular individual will not be saved. One is assured of the final salvation of all (11:32) but must not assume one's own security (2:4, 17-18, 22-24). One is assured of the final victory of God's intention to save all (11:32) and redeem the cosmos (8:18-25), but in the course of the historical process one is not sure whether one belongs to the true believing remnant (11:5-7). The believer hopes (8:24-25; Phil 3:10-14)—with confidence (Rom 5:3-5).

God's Mercy (Righteousness) and the Behavior of Believers, 12:1–15:13

The *therefore* of 12:1 demonstrates a close relationship between Paul's theological interpretation of salvation in chaps. 1–11 and the ethical exhortation which he is going to give in 12:1–15:13—salvation, and for that reason, moral action.

Ethical Renewal as the Appropriation of Mercy, 12:1-2

Paul uses the expression *the mercies of God* (v. 1) to summarize the meaning of the gospel as he has developed it in Rom 1–11. The word for *mercy* here (*oiktirmos*) is different from the root for mercy which he used prominently in chaps. 9–11 (*eleeō* and *eleos*), but the two are synonymous (9:15).

Mercy represents the event of grace which changes human existence and *enables* the ethical posture which is called for. This *enablement* generates and implicitly contains a *motive* or justifying reason for the action or disposition required. The motive is wholeness or integrity: to be and act in accord with the new self or life which one has become through the mercies of God.

The required ethical stance is a *result of* the new life and is not identical with the latter (1 Cor 5:7; Gal 5:25), but it is the expected and appropriate result. The relationship of new life to ethical behavior is paradoxical. The new life given through God's mercy in justification and liberation is a reality and not just a possibility. Yet the very existence of the imperative—*become what you are by presenting your bodies as living sacrifices*—shows that the new life is not quite real but is a possibility to be realized in the process of moral action (Via 1990, 50–51).

Body for Paul means the *whole self* in its *relatedness* to the multiple dimensions of reality. By use of the cultic terms *sacrifice* and *service* (*latreia*) Paul extends worship to include the behavior of the body-self in all of its life relationships in a way pleasing to God.

The ethical imperative is extended in the call to *not be conformed to this world but [to] be transformed by the renewing* of the mind. One's whole existence is changed by the reshaping of the mind. This entails a move from the old age of sin and law to the new eschatological time. Mind here means the power of critical judgment, the ability to test and differentiate (Käsemann 1980, 330), and also suggests moral perceptiveness (Cranfield 1981, 609).

The transformation of the self by the renewal of the mind is something that the believer is to do. It is his or her own responsibility: transform yourself. This possibility, however, has been enabled by God's enacted mercy.

The renewal of the mind reverses the situation of a person in sin and under the wrath of God as portrayed in 1:18-32. Paul's use of cognate terms makes this clear. Humankind tested reality and chose (*dokimazō*) not to have God in its knowledge (1:28a). In consequence God gave it up to a mind that cannot cope with the tests of reality (an *adokimos* mind) (1:28b). But now in the eschatological time of salvation the realizable purpose of the mind's renewal is that it might discover or discern (*dokimazō* again) the will of God. For Paul the ethical norm is the will of God. That will, however, has not been exhaustively given in ethical rules but must be newly discovered in the changing situations of life.

Love in One Body in Christ, 12:3-21

The quality of *sober judgment*, which is to characterize the believer, Paul borrows from the Greek philosophical tradition where it connotes moderation, restraint, or a sense of proportion. For Paul, however, the content of this moderation will be drawn from the renewal of the mind through the gospel and the believer's sense of his or her place in the Christian community, imaged in this passage as one body in Christ.

The application of moderation that Paul makes here is the avoidance of excessive self-estimation. The key to this is the unity and diversity of the community. The church is *one* entity, not because of good feelings the members have for each other, but because they are all grounded together in a single reality that transcends them all—the crucified-risen Christ in his self-identification with his people. Common participation in Christ enables risky involvement with one another.

But as in the human body, so in the one body in Christ the members have different functions. Each member has a gift (*charisma*) given by grace, and each gift includes a role or calling and a function: a servant serves, a teacher teaches, et cetera. That these gifts are *different* from each other is a consequence of *God's grace*. Therefore, no one gift in its difference can be regarded as more or less important than another.

An additional check on over self-estimation is the suggestion that God has given each person a measure of faith that accords with that person's capacities. One's self-evaluation is to be in line with the measure of faith one has been given (v. 3b). The gift of grace then that comes with faith confers both a calling and a limit (Käsemann 1980, 334). Each gift is to be exercised by carrying out the function that is proper to it, and one should not attempt more functions than one has been given. The teacher, for example, exercises his or her calling by teaching and should not think of himself or herself too highly by claiming the functions of other callings.

That love should *be genuine* takes on here (v. 9) a thematic significance. Heretofore in Romans Paul has used the term *agapē* of God's love (5:5, 8; 8:39) in its surprising concern for the radically underserving. Now Paul uses *agapē* for the love that believers should extend both to fellow members of the body (vv. 9-10) and to enemies on the outside (vv. 14, 20). The love that believers have received they are to share.

For Paul love as an ethical disposition and mode of action means to seek the good or advantage of the other person rather than one's own. Paul expresses this in a number of places and with different vocabulary (15:1-2; 1 Cor 10:24, 33-34; 13:5; Phil 2:4; 1 Thes 5:15). This central ethical norm is an open or formal one. What constitutes the good of the other is left undefined and is to be determined in differing social contexts (Via 1990, 60–63). In this particular passage seeking the advantage of the other takes such expressions as showing honor (v. 10), meeting physical needs (v. 13), emotional identification (v. 15), living in harmony (v. 16), and renouncing vengeance (vv. 19-20). Love does not passively accept evil but overcomes it (v. 21).

The State and Taxes, 13:1-7

Paul calls on every person [to] *be subject to the governing authorities*. Paul's terms (*exousia*—13:1; *archōn*—13:3) are subject to varying interpretations. Some think that he has in mind primarily or exclusive-ly human officials (Cranfield 1981, 656–59) while others hold that the terms refer both to the civil rulers and the cosmic or angelic powers that act through them (esp. Cullmann 1957, 63, 66, 98). Probably both dimensions are in view with the emphasis being on the human.

The political rulers have authority at all because it has been delegated to them by God, the ultimate source of authority, for the purpose of preventing wrongdoing and promoting the common good (vv. 1b, 4). Since God has appointed the rulers, to resist them is to resist God.

A part of the believer's responsibility is to pay taxes, both direct (taxes—*phoros*) and indirect (revenue—*telos*). The admonition to pay taxes and to show respect and honor to all to whom they are due may mean that Paul is addressing an actual situation in the Rome of the fifties—unrest about the collection of indirect taxes (Wedderburn 1991, 62).

Paul offers here—explicitly or implicitly—four reasons for being subject to the authorities. (1) It should be done out of respect for the authority of God (vv. 1-2). (2) One should obey in order to escape punishment from the rulers, which is also an instrument of the wrath of God (vv. 2b-5). (3) One should obey for the sake of conscience. This assumes that those addressed know that they have an obligation to obey and would have a painful conscience if they did not (v. 5b). (4) Paul implies that one obeys and pays taxes in order to promote the good of the socio-political order (v. 4).

Paul affirms that God's governance of the world requires the political order in *principle*, but since he can also be critical of *particular* government officials in *particular* circumstances (1 Cor 2:8; 6:4), he is not saying that the believer is obligated to support any and every particular political system.

Since Paul's admonition to obey *the governing authorities* and pay taxes (vv. 1-7) is surrounded (12:9; 13:8-10) and framed by his affirmation of the love principle, these two motifs interpret each other. Paying taxes is seen as an expression of love—the seeking the advantage of the other that flows from receiving the undeserved love of God. And in the exhortation to pay taxes love is seen to have expressions that are public, political, and unsentimental.

Love as the Fulfillment of the Law, 13:8-10

If the believer pays all of his or her debts—respect, honor, taxes—the only remaining—and continuing—obligation is the obligation *to love one another*. That obligation can never be exhausted. Love to the neighbor is the fulfillment and summing up of all the individual commandments in the law. This probably does not mean that all the commandments of the law are still to be obeyed as such but now with a loving attitude. It rather means that love to the neighbor has superseded the many individual commands of the law because it actualizes what the law has always intended—not to do any harm to the neighbor. And yet the OT commandments of God retain a certain relative validity for Paul (7:7-12; 1 Cor 7:19; 7:7-12) in that they suggest how love can be made concrete. The individual laws are traces of God's will (Via 1990, 63–65). And Paul uses an OT command—"love your neighbor as yourself" (Lev 19:18)—to disclose the full intention of the whole law.

The Pressure of the Imminent End, 13:11-14

Paul reminds his readers to wake up because salvation is nearer than when we first believed. Salvation here means the return of Christ, the final judgment, and the eschatological completion of redemption, the resurrection of the body. Having moved from dealing with a specific ethical issue (political involvement) and a broad ethical norm (love for the neighbor) Paul now interprets the situation of believers in the temporal process both theologically and ethically by using the imagery of *night* and *day*. The night is far advanced and day has drawn near. Believers live in this in-between time that is no longer darkest night but is not yet quite day. Yet the day—the last day—is near enough to put pressure on the believer to live as if it were day. Cast off the works of darkness—drunkenness, debauchery, quarreling—and walk (live) as in the day. The principle is that the believer is to live in a way that is appropriate to his or her situation in the temporal process of salvation. The problem is that while the present situation of salvation is ambiguously neither night nor day, the moral demand is to live unambiguously as in the day.

That the believer is not yet fully in the day is underscored by the imperative to *put on . . . Christ* (v. 14). If one is told to put on Christ, then one has not yet put him on. But Paul can also tell baptized believers that they have already put on Christ (Gal 3:27) and are already "children of the day" (1 Thes 5:5). Living in the day and putting on Christ as the power of new life is both an actualized reality (1 Thes 5:4-5; Gal 3:27) and an unactualized reality (Rom 13:11-14)—the possibility of actualization through moral living.

Eating and Drinking among the Weak and the Strong, 14:1–15:13

This passage seeks to promote mutual acceptance (14:3-4, 13; 15:7), peace and harmony (14:19; 15:5), and mutual upbuilding (14:19) between two groups in the church at Rome that hold different opinions and apparently live in some tension with each other.

Paul designates them as the *weak in faith* (14:1) and the *strong* (15:1) and includes himself among the strong (15:1). The weak are vegetarians (14:2) who observe certain holy days (14:5) and apparently reject the drinking of wine (14:21). The strong eat anything (14:2, 21), consider all days alike (14:5), and drink wine (14:21). The meat avoidance seems not to be a matter of rejecting meat from animals sacrificed to idols, as at Corinth (1 Cor 8:1, 4, 7, 10), but rather to be a vegetarian rejection of all meat.

Regarding the history-of-religious sources of these differences the strong would be Christians of either gentile or Jewish background who had accepted a law-free position similar to Paul's that permitted their behavior on these issues. The weak are more difficult to categorize. Jews observed holy days, the SABBATH and other festival times, but Jews did not characteristically reject wine drinking. And while certain animals were forbidden as food (Lev 11), and Judaism permitted animals had to be slaughtered in the proper cultic manner (Lev 17:14; Deut 12:16, 23), Judaism did not reject the eating of meat in principle (Lev 11:1-3; Deut 12:15). On the other hand, some gentile religions did teach vegetarianism (e.g., Orphics and Pythagoreans).

Yet there is some evidence (Dan 1:12, 16; *Testament of Isaac* 4:5, 6, 41) that certain Jewish groups living under the pressure of a gentile environment did adopt vegetarianism and teetotalism (Wedderburn 1991, 33–34). Moreover, since 15:7-13 makes the point that the purpose of Christ's mission was to save both Jews and gentiles, it seems probable that the two groups designated as the weak and the strong were primarily, though not exclusively, respectively Jewish Christians and gentile Christians. Paul offers three perspectives for their living together in peace.

14:1-12. The theological perspective. That the weak person is weak specifically *in faith* suggests that he or she feels that faith alone is not sufficient for salvation but must be supplemented by the behaviors at issue here (Dunn 1988, 798). Interestingly Paul does not go on to condemn this position though he distinguishes himself from it (15:1—*we . . . are strong*).

The strong are not to treat the weak with contempt; the weak are not to condemn the strong. The important thing is that each should be convinced in his or her *own* mind that he or she is doing the right thing (v. 5).

The basis for this mutual acceptance is that both groups do what they do to honor the Lord. Moreover, all persons must finally *stand before the judgment seat of God* and give an account of themselves to God (vv. 10-12). Being accountable to the judgment of God lifts one above the position of being judged by a fellow human being. It is a Pauline paradox that God confronts us as both gracious redeemer (3:21–4:25) and demanding judge (1 Cor 6:9-11; 2 Cor 5:10; Gal 5:16-24).

14:13-23. The ethical perspective. Paul clearly believes that certain *ethical* acts and dispositions are inherently wrong (1:28-32; 1 Cor 6:9-10; Gal 5:19-21). But he rejects the Jewish distinction between cultic cleanness and uncleanness that rests on the belief that certain *physical* objects (like foods, Lev 11) or processes (like menstruation, Lev 15:19; marital sex, Lev 15:18; or childbearing, Lev 12:1-5) are inherently unclean (Via 1985, 88–96). Thus when he that *nothing is unclean in itself* (v. 14, emphasis added) Paul means nothing like food or drink. But such things are unclean to those who think they are unclean (v. 14b).

Paul is concerned that the strong should not cause harm to the weak who think that meat and wine should be avoided. Since meat and wine are not unclean in themselves (vv. 14, 20), he will not deal with the issue in terms of such unexceptionable rules as: do not eat meat, do not drink wine, observe the sabbath.

Paul rather applies the love principle (v. 15)—seek the good of the other—to this situation. It *is* wrong to eat meat or drink wine *if* it causes the ruin of a brother or sister for whom Christ died. It is all right to eat or drink if your faith's self-understanding allows it (vv. 22-23). But the person of weak faith believes it is wrong. If by your example you entice your weak brother or sister to eat meat or drink wine, you cause his ruin, cause her to fall or stumble (vv. 15, 20, 21). That is, you cause the weak one the inner pain of doubt and self-judgment because he or she will be going against what his or her own faith permits (vv. 22-23). The weak sin if they eat meat, not because it is wrong in itself, but because it violates what their faith allows; it violates the unity of their being. The strong do wrong if they cause this to happen to the weak.

Paul calls for mutual acceptance, but he really asks more of the strong than of the weak because they are capable of more. The strong have the freedom to eat meat and drink wine or not without suffering internal disruption. The weak do not have that much freedom. If they want to avoid inner conflict, they are free only not to eat or drink. So the strong are called on to give up their freedom to eat or drink in those situations where it causes harm to the neighbor.

15:1-13. The christological perspective. Here the strong are specifically asked to bear the weaknesses of those who are not strong and not to please themselves. This appeal is based on the model of Christ who *did not please himself*.

The weak and strong are admonished to accept each other as Christ accepted both of them. Christ became a servant in order to confirm God's faithfulness to his promises to Israel's forefathers and to bring the gentiles to glorify God.

Concluding Personal Statement, 15:14-32

Paul's Feelings about the Roman Church and His Self-Evaluation, 15:14-21

Paul is satisfied with the spiritual stature of the church at Rome but also claims justification for having written to them boldly on the ground that God's grace has made him *a minister . . . to the Gentiles* (v. 16). Paul describes his preaching of the gospel as priestly activity, and the offering he makes to God through the gospel is the gentiles. The term he uses of himself as *a minister* (v. 16, Gk. *leitourgos*) means priest in Neh 10:39; Isa 61:6; Sir 7:30; Heb 8:2. The verb *hierougeō* (serve as a priest) underscores this.

Paul believes that his work for God is something to boast about (v. 17). The word he uses for boasting (*kauchēsis*) is the same word that he uses for the boasting that is excluded by justification by grace in 3:27. But here in v. 17 he is proud, not of his attainments, but of what Christ has achieved through him.

For further discussion of this section see Introduction: Occasion and Purpose, The Intended Visit.

Travel Plans, 15:22-29

On this passage see the discussion of Paul's plans to visit Jerusalem and Spain in Introduction: Occasion and Purpose.

Emotional Appeal for Their Prayers, 15:30-32

This last part of the concluding personal statement (body closing) fulfills the rhetorical function of making an emotional appeal to the Roman church for their prayerful concern about Paul.

Closing, 15:33–16:27

For the issues raised by chap. 16, see above, Introduction: Manuscript Evidence and Destination. And for the structure of the Closing, refer to the outline at the beginning of the commentary. Only a few brief comments will be made here.

It could be that Paul intended to end the letter with the grace benediction in 16:20b and that Paul's scribe *Tertius* (16:22), added the greetings from Paul's associates, requiring a repetition of the grace benediction in 16:24. Manuscripts differ on the placement of this benediction (Gamble 1977, 91–94).

Among those for whom Paul requests greetings are *Andronicus and Junia*(s) (16:7) whom Paul designates as fellow Jews and as persons who are well known among the apostles. The Greek name Iounian, as far as spelling is concerned, could be the accusative case of the male name Iounias (Junias) or the accusative of the common Roman female name Junia. But apart from this verse there is no evidence for a male name Junias (Cranfield 1981, 788). The name should be read as the female Junia, and it should be recognized that there were women apostles.

The final doxology (16:25-27) is probably a post-Pauline addition. Such terminology as *the eternal God* (*tou aiōniou theou*), *the only wise God* (*monō sophō theō*), and *the mystery . . . made known* (*mystēriou . . . gnōristhentos*) is not characteristic of Paul. Especially strange is the idea of the gospel as a mystery kept secret through the ages but now made known through the prophetic writings (Kümmel 1965, 223). Paul's own position in Romans is that the righteousness of faith, recently made manifest through the redemption in Christ Jesus (3:21-26), was already proclaimed in the law (10:6-8), and actualized by Abraham (4:3-8).

Works Cited

Aune, David E. 1991. "Romans as a *Logos* Protreptikos," in Donfried 1991a.

Barrett, C. K. 1957. *A Commentary on the Epistle to the Romans*, BNTC.

Beale, Walter H. 1978. "Rhetorical Performative: A New Theory of Epideictic," *Philosophy and Rhetoric* 11/4 (Fall 1978): 221–46.

Best, Ernest. 1955. *One Body in Christ*.

Bornkamm, Günther. 1991. "The Letter to the Romans as Paul's Last Will and Testament," in Donfried 1991a.

Bultmann, Rudolf. 1951. *Theology of the N.T.*, vol. 1. 1967. "Glossen im Römerbrief," *Exegetica*.

Campbell, William S. 1991. "Romans III as a Key to the Structure and Thought of Romans," in Donfried 1991a.

Cousar, Charles B. 1990. *A Theology of the Cross, Overtures to Biblical Theology*.

Cranfield, C. E. B. 1980. *A Critical and Exegetical Commentary on the Epistle to the Romans*, 2 vols., ICC.

Cullmann, Oscar. 1957. *The State in the N.T.*

Davies, W. D. 1948. *Paul and Rabbinic Judaism*.

Dodd, C. H. 1954. *The Epistle of Paul to the Romans*.

Donfried, Karl P. 1991a. *The Romans Debate*, rev. ed. 1991b. "Introduction 1991: The Romans Debate since 1977," in Donfried 1991a. 1991c. "A Short Note on Romans 16," in Donfried 1991a. 1991d. "False Presuppositions in the Study of Romans," in Donfried 1991a.

Dunn, James D. G. 1988. *Romans 1–8*. 1988. *Romans 9–16*.

Fuller, Reginald H. 1978. "The Conception/Birth of Jesus as a Christological Moment," *JSNT* 1 (1978): 37–52.

Funk, Robert W. 1967. "The Apostolic Parousia: Form and Significance," *Christian History and Interpretation*.

Furnish, Victor Paul. 1979. *The Moral Teaching of Paul*.

Gamble, Harry. 1977. *The Textual History of the Letter to the Romans*. 1985. *The N.T. Canon*, GBS/NT.

Girard, René. 1986. *The Scapegoat*. 1989. *Violence and the Sacred*.

Hays, Richard B. 1981. *The Faith of Jesus Christ*, SBLDS 56.

Jervell, Jacob. 1991. "The Letter to Jerusalem," in Donfried 1991a.

Jewett, Robert. 1991. "Following the Argument of Romans," in Donfried 1991a.

Karris, Robert J. 1991a. "Romans 14:1–15:13 and the Occasion of Romans," in Donfried 1991a. 1991b. "The Occasion of Romans: A Response to Professor Donfried," in Donfried 1991a.

Käsemann, Ernst. 1969. *New Testament Questions of Today*. 1971. *Perspectives on Paul*. 1980. *Commentary on Romans*.

Kennedy, George A. 1984. *N.T. Interpretation through Rhetorical Criticism*.

Klein, Günter. 1991. "Paul's Purpose in Writing the Epistle to the Romans," in Donfried 1991a.

Knox, John. 1954. "The Epistle to the Romans," *IB*.

Kümmel, Werner Georg et al. 1965. *Introduction to the N.T.*, 14th rev. ed.

Lampe, Peter. 1991. "The Roman Christians of Romans 16," in Donfried 1991a.

Mack, Burton L. 1990. *Rhetoric and the N.T.* GBS/NT.

Manson, T. W. 1991. "St. Paul's Letter to the Romans—and Others," in Donfried 1991a.

Metzger, Bruce E. 1975. *A Textual Commentary on the Greek N.T.*

Nygren, Anders. 1949. *Commentary on Romans.*

O'Neill, J. C. 1975. *Paul's Letters to the Romans.*

Petersen, Norman R. 1985. *Rediscovering Paul.*

Ricoeur, Paul. 1969. *The Symbolism of Evil.*

Sanders, E. P. 1977. *Paul and Palestinian Judaism.* 1983. *Paul, the Law, and the Jewish People.*

Schmithals, Walter. 1975. *Der Römerbrief als historisches Problem.*

Scroggs, Robin. 1983. *The N.T. and Homosexuality.*

Stirewalt, Martin Luther, Jr. 1991. "The Form and Function of the Greek Letter-Essay," in Donfried 1991a.

Stowers, Stanley Kent. 1981. *The Diatribe and Paul's Letter to the Romans.* 1989. *Letter Writing in Greco-Roman Antiquity.*

Stuhlmacher, Peter. 1991. "The Purpose of Romans," in Donfried 1991a.

Theissen, Gerd. 1987. *Psychological Aspects of Pauline Theology.*

Via, Dan O. 1985. *The Ethics of Mark's Gospel.* 1990. *Self-Deception and Wholeness in Paul and Matthew.*

Wagner, Günther. 1967. *Pauline Baptism and Pagan Mysteries.*

Wedderburn, A. J. M. 1991. *The Reasons for Romans.*

Wiefel, Wolfgang. 1991. "The Jewish Community in Ancient Rome and the Origins of Roman Christianity," in Donfried 1991a.

Williams, Sam K. 1975. *Jesus' Death as Saving Event*, HDR 2. 1980. "The Righteousness of God in Romans," *JBL* 99/2 (June 1980): 241–90.

Wuellner, Wilhelm. 1987. "Where Is Rhetorical Criticism Taking Us?" *CBQ* 49/3 (July 1987): 448–63. 1991. "Paul's Rhetoric of Argumentation in Romans," in Donfried 1991a.

Ziesler, John. 1989. *Paul's Letters to the Romans.*

First Corinthians

Marion L. Soards

Introduction

First Corinthians is considered one of Paul's four *great* letters (along with Romans, 2 Corinthians, and Galatians) in part because of the actual length of this letter in comparison to the other writings attributed to Paul in the NT; but even more, 1 Corinthians is regarded as a great epistle because of the range of the topics and the depth of the reflections that it contains. The "great letters" are regarded by all students of Paul's writings as the central documents for the interpretation of the apostle's theology, and 1 Corinthians is particularly significant for its treatment of important aspects of basic Christian faith and practice.

Authorship

Since the writing of *1 Clement* in the late first century the letter we refer to today as 1 Corinthians has been attributed to the apostle Paul (see *1 Clem* 47.1-7). No one has ever seriously questioned whether Paul wrote this letter. Even the most radical critics, F. C. Baur and his so-called Tübingen School, accepted 1 Corinthians as authentic. From time to time isolated scholars have raised questions about the unity of the letter, sometimes suggesting either that the epistle as we know it was composed from parts of several letters by Paul that were assembled by a later editor or that it contains a significant number of major and minor glosses that were written into the letter by later scribes. Such broad theories have not attracted a following, though scholars regularly question the authenticity of a few verses of the letter. (We shall consider these verses as we work through the sections of the letter in the commentary that follows.)

Paul and the Corinthians

First-century CORINTH existed because the city had been reconstructed by order of Julius Caesar in 44 B.C.E., long after the Romans destroyed old Corinth in 146 B.C.E. In antiquity Corinth lay in a particularly crucial location on the isthmus that connected the mainland of Greece with the Peloponnesian peninsula that separated the Corinthian Gulf of the Adriatic Sea on the west from the Saronic Gulf of the Aegean Sea on the east. The new city was reestablished as a strategic military and economic outpost for Rome. The population of new Corinth was originally composed of Italian freedmen, given their freedom as a reward for military service. Other merchants and traders looking for new and rich opportunities joined the former soldiers, so that the new city had a complex, cosmopolitan population despite an initially shallow culture. The goods of the East and the West moved through Corinth's harbors and across the short roadways connecting them. The city was an exciting place—genuinely pluralistic with a penchant for SYNCRETISM; fortunes and fame were made and lost in Corinth.

From PAUL's letters to Corinth and from a judicious reading of Acts, especially Acts 18, we can reconstruct a portrait of Paul's experiences in Corinth and of his dealings with the members of the Corinthian church. Apparently, shortly after Paul arrived in Corinth he sought out the Jewish quarter of the city where he met Prisca and Aquila (see PRISCILLA AND AQUILA), a Jewish couple recently arrived in Corinth as part of the emperor Claudius's expulsion of certain Jews from Rome. Historians conclude that Prisca and Aquila were Jewish Christians, indeed that the Jews expelled from Rome were the Christian Jews who created a disturbance in the capital of the ROMAN EMPIRE by preaching the gospel of Christ among the Jews. This couple shared both their faith and their trade of tentmaking with Paul, and we learn as no surprise that Paul lived and worked with this couple in Corinth.

In the time that followed, Paul, Prisca, Aquila, TIMOTHY, SILAS, and perhaps others who remain unnamed, preached to Jews in the SYNAGOGUE that Jesus was the Christ. The success of this mission is clear from the memory that Crispus, the leader of the synagogue, and his household became Christians. Severe opposition arose, however, so that the mission moved out of the synagogue into the house next door that belonged to a God-fearer named Titius Justus (Acts 18:7). According to Acts many Jews and God-fearers came to believe through the preaching of Paul and his colleagues. This work in Corinth lasted for eighteen months before the unbelieving Jews launched a united attack against Paul and his colleagues. They brought him before the Roman tribunal of the proconsul Lucius Junius Annaeus GALLIO, whose term of office extended either from 1 May 51 to 1 May 52 or 1 May 52 to 1 May 53 C.E. Gallio refused to hear the case, which produced a sharp outcry and demonstration by Paul's Jewish adversaries.

According to Acts, Paul stayed in Corinth "many days longer" (18:18 RSV), although eventually he departed from Corinth with Prisca and Aquila. After a time of travels, Paul and his companions settled in EPHESUS for over two years. From Ephesus Paul wrote a series of letters to the Corinthians, and he even had conversations with representatives of the Corinthian congregation who visited him in Ephesus. From 1 Cor 5:9 we see clearly that prior to the writing of 1 Corinthians Paul had already written at least one other letter to the Corinthians. Scholars debate whether that earlier letter is completely lost or whether it may, in part, be preserved in 2 Corinthians. Whatever the case, we should understand that our canonical work, 1 Corinthians, is at least the "second" letter to the Corinthians. At the time that Paul wrote our 1 Corinthians, he had been in Ephesus for an extended period, for he mentions his plans to leave Ephesus in 1 Cor 16:5-9.

The Situation and the Problems

As Paul lived and worked in Ephesus, he learned of the situation in Corinth both from visitors and from a letter that the members of the Corinthian congregation sent to him. First, near the beginning of the letter, in 1:11, the apostle mentions *Chloe's people* with whom he has been in conversation. This designation indicates members of the household of Chloe and could be a reference to family members, slaves, or both. Later, near the end of the letter, in 16:17, Paul names *Stephanus and Fortunas and Achaicus* who had visited him, and so, made up for the absence of the other members of the congregation. We cannot determine whether the early reference to *Chloe's people* are to be identified with the three men (apparently the letter delegation)

named toward the end of the letter, but we do see that Paul had firsthand observations concerning the circumstances in Corinth. In the course of the letter Paul refers explicitly to matters of which he learned from his visitors—see 5:1-2 (and perhaps the material in 5:3-6:20). Second, at 7:1 Paul refers directly to the letter with the phrase *Now concerning the matters about which you wrote*. Subsequently he uses the phrase *now concerning*, still apparently referring to the letter from the Corinthians, in 7:25, 8:1, 12:1, and 16:1. The items considered in relation to the letter from Corinth include sex and marriage, food offered to pagan idols prior to being sold in the market for consumption, the GIFTS OF THE SPIRIT, and the method for the collection that Paul was assembling for the poor in Jerusalem.

Behind all the issues Paul addresses in 1 Corinthians lies a preoccupation of the Corinthians with wisdom. The wisdom with which they were concerned was not mature or reasonable judgment, but special information that gave those "in the know" special status in relation to others who did not share those data. The Corinthians wanted involvement with supposedly deeper meanings and lofty unseen things. Some of them apparently thought of their life in Christ as if it were participation in MYSTERY RELIGIONS. Paul pejoratively calls such wisdom "human wisdom" (1:20; NRSV *wisdom of the world*), and he contrasts it with God's powerful wisdom, shown in the cross of Christ, in order to castigate the Corinthians for their inappropriate attitudes and behaviors.

Paul's remarks reveal that he understands the preoccupation with wisdom to result from the basic will of the Corinthians to boast. By claiming to have wisdom the Corinthians elevate themselves above others who do not share their information. Indeed, the will to boast of one's status through possession of wisdom was so great one group of Corinthians even compared their wisdom over against another's, to establish their spiritual superiority (or the other's inferiority). Throughout this letter Paul criticizes the particular actions of the Corinthians, but above all he denounces the will to boast. The will to be superior and to brag about it was the fundamental problem that generated the other symptomatic problems in Corinth.

Date

Since we know from the mention of Gallio in Acts 18 that Paul was active in Corinth sometime between 1 May 51 and 1 May 53 C.E., by taking 1 May 52 as a starting point and by tracing Paul's travels up to the time he arrived in Ephesus (Acts 18–19), we can safely understand that Paul arrived in Ephesus in late 52. He labored in Ephesus until the spring of 55. Moreover, from 1 Cor 16:5-9 we learn that Paul wrote 1 Corinthians toward the end of his Ephesian sojourn, so that this letter was most likely written early in 55 (or, less likely, very late in 54).

Primary Themes

First Corinthians presents a kaleidoscope of themes, touching on various aspects of basic Christian faith and practice. Among the prominent topics treated are the forming of factions in the church, the value of human wisdom versus divine wisdom or power, the nature of spirituality, blatant forms of misconduct, sex and marriage, social status, the eschatological character of Christian existence, food offered to pagan gods prior to sale in the marketplace, the nature of Christian freedom, orderly worship, the gifts of the Spirit, the church as the BODY OF CHRIST, the superior way of love, TONGUES and PROPHECY, resurrection, the collection for the SAINTS in Jerusalem, and Paul's future plans. In the course of reflecting on these topics, Paul comments on a number of items of concern for people today—to name but a few: the essence of the GOSPEL, the shape and substance of Christian ministry, Christian involvement in lawsuits, appropriate and inappropriate sexual relations, DIVORCE, SLAVERY, the role of women in the life of the church, charismatic practices, the reality of Jesus' resurrection, and Christian giving.

For Further Study

In the *Mercer Dictionary of the Bible*: CORINTH; CORINTHIAN CORRESPONDENCE; EPISTLE/LETTER; ESCHATOLOGY IN THE NT; GIFTS OF THE SPIRIT; LOVE IN THE NT; MEAT SACRIFICED TO IDOLS; PAUL; RESURRECTION IN THE NT; SUFFERING IN THE NT; WISDOM IN THE NT.

In other sources: C. K. Barrett, *The First Epistle to the Corinthians*, HNTC; J. M. Bassler, "1 Corinthians," *WmBC*; R. B. Brown, "1 Corinthians," BBC; H. Conzelmann, *1 Corinthians*, Herm; G. D. Fee, *The First Epistle to the Corinthians*, NICNT; R. A. Harrisville, *1 Corinthians*, AugCNT; E. Fiorenza, "1 Corinthians," *HBC*; J. Murphy-O'Connor, "First Letter to the Corinthians," NJBC, *1 Corinthians*, and *St. Paul's Corinth*; W. F. Orr and J. A. Walther, *1 Corinthians*, AncB; C. H. Talbert, *Reading Corinthians*; M. E. Thrall, *First and Second Letters of Paul to the Corinthians*.

Commentary

An Outline

Salutation, 1:1-3

The letter opens with a fairly standard greeting, presenting the normal three elements an ancient reader would have expected at the beginning of a letter: sender(s), recipients, and a greeting. Although standard, these verses are pregnant with theological significance through Paul's adaptation or modification of the basic letter form.

Senders, 1:1

In naming the senders, Paul refers to himself as *an apostle*. For modern readers this word has become a technical title, so that we miss Paul's point that he is a "sent one," which is the literal sense of the word "apostle" (ἀπόστολος) in Greek. Not only is Paul one who is sent, he was sent in behalf of Christ Jesus. Moreover, his being sent came about through God's will, not by Paul's own choice. Thus, Paul says he was *called*, meaning that God intervened in his life and established the priority of God's own will. Furthermore, Paul does not write alone, for he works in conjunction with others whom God also directs into action. Here, Paul names *Sosthenes* as his coauthor. Remarkably, Sosthenes is the name of the leader of the Jews who brought charges against Paul before Gallio in Corinth (Acts 18:17). If the Sosthenes named here is the same person about whom we read in Acts, he surely experienced a radical change of heart and a reorientation of his life.

Recipients, 1:2

Paul refers to the Corinthians in a nuanced fashion. They are a *church* (ἐκκλησία). The Greek word can mean "church," or "congregation," or "assembly." In Greco-Roman literature it indicated a political assembly, but as Paul would have known the word from its use in the Greek translation of the Hebrew Bible, ἐκκλησία was used for the Hebrew word קהל that named the children of Israel both in their EXODUS wanderings and in their worshipful assemblies at the Temple. Paul says the church is *the church of God*—that is, God has priority in the formation of the congregation, so that only secondarily does the apostle refer to the geographical location of the church *in Corinth*. Moreover, he declares the Corinthians are *sanctified in Christ Jesus*, indicating that the Corinthians were made holy by Christ—not by their own efforts. The Corinthians are (literally) "called saints," as Paul was (literally) "called apostle." Paul and the Corinthians share the experience of God's calling them and actually naming the purpose of their lives. Furthermore, Paul refers to the Corinthians as being saints *together with all those who in every place call on the name of our Lord Jesus Christ, both their Lord and ours*. With these phrases Paul recognizes the common bond of the Corinthians with all other Christians. They are not an isolated holy group simply set apart from the world; rather, the Corinthians (and Paul and Sosthenes) live in a dependent relationship to Christ that establishes a mutuality that transcends the normal boundaries of human relations.

Greetings, 1:3

The greeting pronounces *grace* and *peace* upon the Corinthians *from God our Father and the Lord Jesus Christ*. Thus, we see the true source of GRACE and PEACE. Grace is a divine gift that produces the divine result of peace in the lives of those who experience it.

Thanksgiving, 1:4-9

Scholars have long recognized that as a formal element of Paul's letters the thanksgiving (or, thanksgiving-prayer) serves several purposes. First, the thanksgiving terminates the opening portion of the letter. Second, it signals the basic theme or themes of the letter that will follow. Third, the thanksgiving can sometimes even outline the major topics to be treated in the epistle. Here, for example, Paul acknowledges God's grace as active among the Corinthians to the end that they are *in every way . . . enriched in* [Christ Jesus], *in speech and knowledge of every kind*. Among the Corinthians the real gifts of "speech" and "knowledge" are at the heart of their problematic thoughts and actions. At once Paul names the genuine strengths and weaknesses of the Corinthian church. The members experience the endowments of grace, but, as the remainder of the letter reveals, their concern with and use of these gifts is completely out of hand.

The Corinthians' Endowments, 1:4-7a

Paul acknowledges and qualifies the spiritual gifts with which the Corinthians have been blessed. The goal of God's gifts of speech and knowledge relates to the testimony about Christ that comes to confirmation among the Corinthians. As God endows the Corinthians with spiritual gifts, God demonstrates the reality of God's gracious work in Christ. The Corinthians experience grace unto the glory of Christ, not for their own aggrandizement. God's authority is recognized in the words *the grace of God . . . has been given you*; God gave grace, the Corinthians merely (though really) received it.

The Lord's Faithfulness, 1:7b-9

The true status of the Corinthians becomes clear in these verses; they are *waiting* for the revelation of the Lord Jesus Christ. *Already* they experience grace, but *not yet* is the Lord fully present. The Corinthians live in relation to a promise. The full experience of God's grace lies beyond the present in the future, and the sole basis of hope in that future is that *God is faithful*. The grace that the Corinthians experience in the present is not the guarantee of their hope for the future; rather, God who grants grace now is himself the hope of the future. Grace is no guarantee; it is a sign of God's goodness, a manifestation of God's faithfulness, which itself underwrites the future. God called the Corinthians into communion with Jesus Christ and, in turn, with one another. The fellowship they experience is not of their own doing; it is God's work. The church is not theirs; it is God's—by will and by work. The Corinthians are called into the community of faith created by God's grace at work in the Lord Jesus Christ. Seeing this much should inform the Corinthians who they are as a church; and so, they should see how they are to live.

Body of the Letter, 1:10–15:58

The Gospel and Wisdom, 1:10–4:21

This first major portion of the body of the letter is a coherent reflection treating basic matters of Christian belief and the particular situation in Corinth. Paul argues against an understanding of the gospel as a kind of esoteric or mysterious wisdom teaching, especially a teaching that would elevate those who have the information above the masses to whom the teaching would not be available.

1:10-17. Factions in the congregation. At the outset Paul takes up the issue of factions (*divisions*, v. 10; *quarrels*, v. 11) in the Corinthian church. He expresses his astonishment at the situation and implies his disapproval of the matter, but he does not yet offer a full resolution to the problem. Paul's choice of vocabulary (*appeal*, v. 10) indicates his earnestness in admonishing the Corinthians, and his reference to *the name of our Lord Jesus Christ* expresses the means and authority of his appeal. Paul's goal for the Corinthians is that they will be united in thought and disposition.

As Paul talks about the factions in Corinth, he identifies the groups in relation to prominent persons: PAUL, APOLLOS, Cephas (PETER), and CHRIST. It is not clear whether he means to name three or four groups, for it is not certain whether there is a "Christ party" or whether Paul means that all, regardless of their relationship with Paul, Apollos, or Cephas, are related to Christ. At root the problem is that the Corinthians have turned relationships into status-giving identities or positions. Paul works to inform the Corinthians that they have direction in life, they do not merely have positions to defend or declare. The three rhetorical questions in v. 13 are answered "yes," "no," and "no." The first question about the division of the church names the problem, and the following two questions make it clear that the situation is absurd.

At first reading, the statements in vv. 14-16 seem to display a shockingly cavalier regard for BAPTISM. There is certainly sarcasm in the remarks as Paul attempts to jolt the Corinthians out of their boastful comparisons concerning their status in the church. Yet, as one sees by continuing to read Paul's words in v. 17, he is able to relativize the importance of baptism (which the Corinthians value as giving them special identities and status) because he understands his call as a call to preach. Baptism is a part of the larger picture of Christian faith and practice, but for Paul proclama-

tion of the gospel is the cutting edge. Given the particular problem in Corinth with its baptismal parties and boasting, Paul is genuinely thankful that baptism per se was not his primary ministry. Further clarification comes in his words contrasting "wisdom" and the CROSS. The good news of God's saving work in the cross of Christ is not a slick message that is sold through elegant packaging. Sheer manipulative eloquence is not a medium that can bear the weight of the message of the cross. Above all, the shocking claim that God saves humanity in the cross of Jesus Christ demonstrates that God works in defiance of this world's norms.

1:18-25. God's peculiar, powerful way. God works in a most peculiar way—not only in defiance of the standards of this world, but also in such a powerful way that it incapacitates, reverses, even turns upside down the values (objectively established) of this world. Paul declares this way of God's working as a fact. In v. 18 Paul sets up a rhetorical contrast scheme that drives home the heart of the gospel as he understands it. In relation to the theme of "the word of the cross," that is, the proclamation of the saving death of Jesus Christ, Paul refers to humanity in two groups. On the one hand, there are those who regard the word of the cross as *foolishness*; Paul says they are perishing. On the other hand, there are those who are *being saved*. The passive voice of the verb indicates that God is doing the saving here. Moreover, in the scheme of this contrast with *perishing* versus *being saved*, one finds *foolishness* contrasted with *the power of God*. The natural opposite of *foolishness* in this context would be *wisdom*. Remarkably Paul says that it is what God does, not what humans know, that saves. God acted in the cross of Christ and it produces a division among humanity that itself implies God's power.

To make this argument Paul quotes Isa 29:14, although he changes the verb in the quotation from "conceal" to *thwart* (v. 19). With this slight alteration Paul makes the citation fit more exactly the context to which he writes. As the apostle offers a scriptural precedent for the way God works through the cross of Christ, he does more than prooftext his point. His use of scripture shows that he understands scripture to be absolutely authoritative, absolutely essential for comprehending God's ways, but of an ultimately penultimate significance. God's work in Christ directs the use of the Bible; the Bible does not control God.

The argument here locates where the wisdom of the merely human wise one, scribe, and debater originate—in *this age*. God's "age," however, exposes the shallowness and inaccuracy of merely human wisdom. Even the loftiest theology that is disengaged from the primary revelation of God in Jesus Christ is *foolishness*. Humans do not reason their way to God; God saves humanity (and the world!) by the cross of Christ, which is, by this world's standards, *foolishness*. Christ preached as crucified brings a crisis of separation. Denial of the saving significance of the cross reveals that one is in bondage to "this world," whereas "those who believe" are shown to be called by God, to be grasped by the power of God—a demonstration that Christ is God's "wisdom." Verse 25 summarizes the whole section saying that God's wisdom or power expressed in the cross of Christ renders worldly wisdom into foolishness as a demonstration of the reality of the power of God.

1:26-31. Before and after God's call. In these theologically loaded verses, Paul calls the Corinthians to consider themselves both *before* (or, at) the time of their call and *after* (or, in) their calling. Before their calling Paul suggests that in a variety of ways the Corinthians were for the most part nobodies; after being called by God, however, the Corinthians are instruments of God's power with Christ Jesus as the source of their lives. To make this argument Paul engages in a careful, deliberate play on the LXX version of Jer 9:22-24. The reference to scripture is clear in v. 31, but already in vv. 28-29 the language echoes Jeremiah, especially in the reference to "the wise" and "wisdom" and to "the powerful" and "the strong." Paul's contrast scheme is designed to humble the Corinthians in order to heighten their appreciation for the saving work of God in Jesus Christ. Paul tells the Corinthians that in light of what God has done in Jesus Christ the only legitimate boasting that Christians do is about what God has done—not about what humans know, do, are, or achieve.

2:1-5. Paul's apostolic ministry and message. This section is an exposition of Paul's *apostolic* message and ministry. It comes in two moves: First, vv. 1-2 demonstrate the continuity between the form and content or the style and substance of the apostle's proclamation. Second, vv. 3-5 demonstrate the continuity of the message and the demeanor of the preacher or messenger. Paul's language is intensely personal. The statements make clear that his approach and practice of ministry were deliberate. The statements are, nevertheless, ambiguous. Paul is not saying, "I preached only the cross instead of the cross plus something more." Rather, he insists that he laid aside all other devices for persuasion and proclaimed the cross without frills.

Paul's portrait of himself refers to *weakness* and explains this idea by using the traditional Jewish image of *fear and trembling*—a reference to the reverent recognition of the reality of God! Paul says that his message was such that his speech allowed the Spirit and God's power to show themselves as they worked through his message. The Corinthians came to believe, not by showy human effort, but by the very working of God's power. Although humans are God's agents, God alone is the one who saves humanity.

2:6-16. Meditation on the operation of revelation. These verses are an excursus on the wisdom of God and the spiritual discernment of Christians, or a meditation on the operation of REVELATION. Interpreters ask whether Paul contradicts himself here. Does he have a two-leveled message with one word for some and a "deeper" teaching for others? No. One should recall that Paul designated his message "the word of the cross" (1:18 RSV). Clearly he interprets the saving significance of the cross throughout his letters by regularly applying the meaning of the cross to the lives of his readers. The cross is not only something that happened to Jesus. Paul declares that by the mysterious grace of God the cross affects, or effects (!), the lives of Christians. Paul does not have a special teaching for some. He can, however, explicate more to some than to others because of the differing degrees of their own spiritual maturation. This situation seems to be the basis for Paul's distinction between the "mature" and the "spiritual" on the one hand and the "unspiritual" or "natural" on the other.

Paul declares that God's wisdom is not available simply to inquiring minds. Paul refers to the scriptural precedent for this teaching, although it is impossible to identify precisely the passage he cites. His "quotation" in v. 9 seems to be a pastiche from perhaps Ps 3:20; Isa 52:15; 64:3-4; 65:16-17; Jer 3:16; Sir 1:10; and *AscIsa* 11.34. The depths of God's will and work come to humanity only as God chooses to reveal them through the Spirit. Paul explains the necessity of divine revelation through an argument on the principle of "like by like"—saying that a person is the only one who knows the inner secrets of himself or herself. It is likewise with God. Paul states that an unspiritual human is unable to receive the things of the Spirit of God because these things are only discernible by the Spirit. Moreover, in vv. 12 and 16 Paul boldly declares that Christians have the *Spirit that is from God* and *the mind of Christ*, so that they have God's wisdom imparted to them through the Spirit.

3:1-17. Working toward unity and edification. Paul ties together what he has said to this point in vv. 1-4 in order to show why he did not impart God's wisdom to the Corinthians. The chief implication of his remarks is that the Corinthians are immature, as is seen in their factionalization. Notice, however, that Paul at least regards the Corinthians as *infants* (v. 1) so that he does not completely deny they are persons of faith. Paul's words would prove insulting, nevertheless, for he repeatedly says the Corinthians are *of the flesh*. Although the Corinthians value wisdom and declare their status as mature believers or "spiritual ones," Paul refutes their claims.

Then, Paul takes up a series of metaphors in order to instruct the Corinthians. The entire set of remarks is aimed at correcting the Corinthians' misunderstandings and at directing them toward unity and mutual edification. In vv. 5-9 Paul offers a lesson by taking himself and APOLLOS as examples. Paul and Apollos are cast as field servants who serve the higher authority of their Lord. Their assignments are different, though they are both merely functionaries. The reality of divine farming is that God does the growing while the field hands simply execute God's will. As servants Paul and Apollos are equal and they get paid according to their labor. The NRSV provides a helpful translation of v. 9. Other translations may read "we are God's fellow workers" (RSV), an idea that makes little sense in the context of the previous lines; but the NRSV more accurately renders the ambiguous Greek as *we are God's servants, working together*. God's servants labor together; they do not form competitive groups, for they are united in their efforts under the sole authority of God. Paul recognizes God's authority over the apostles and over the church in Corinth, which he calls *God's field*.

At the end of v. 9 Paul shifts metaphors. Not only are the Corinthians *God's field*, they are also *God's building*. With that image established, Paul assumes the point of view of a sophisticated master builder and tells of the foundation he laid, the foundation of Jesus Christ. That foundation cannot be changed, although now others may erect an edifice on the foundation. Yet, Paul declares that even in the activity of building on the foundation of Jesus Christ, not all buildings are equal. Verse 12 catalogues a variety of building materials. Then, the following discussion promises a testing

of the materials, an eschatological testing in the future, promised *Day* (of the Lord). Those who built on the foundation of Jesus Christ may anticipate reward or loss in accordance with the quality and durability of the material they used. Paul means to admonish the Corinthians to a careful selection of materials, that is, to a way of life as a church that is fitting for the foundation of Jesus Christ. Christian works may not bring salvation—God accomplished that in the cross of Christ—but what Christians do with their lives makes a difference in God's eyes. As Paul applies the metaphor of *God's building* to the Corinthian situation, he informs them of their identity as God's Temple as they experience the indwelling of the Holy Spirit among them. Finally, Paul plainly warns that a just reward will be given to any who *destroy* God's Temple. Behavior that destroys the church will ultimately be destroyed by God.

3:18-23. Evaluating by God's standards. In these verses Paul returns to the original issues he identified and began to discuss at 1:18-25, namely, the contrast between God's mysterious saving activity in the cross of Christ and the elitist attitude of the Corinthians that resulted from their preoccupation with "wisdom." Paul identifies the behavior of the Corinthians for what he perceives it to be, sheer self-deception. By focusing on their own knowledge as a key to their spiritual standing, they have shunned the amazing power of God. Paul calls for the Corinthians to take a proper attitude toward wisdom: in comparison with the saving power of God it is of little value. In order to establish his point Paul cites Job 5:13 and Ps 94:11 (93:11 LXX). Here Paul is essentially underscoring his argument with prooftexts. The citation from JOB is very loosely related to the original text; literally the LXX refers to God as "the one who takes the wise ones in [their] prudence," whereas Paul names God as "the one who catches the wise ones in their craftiness" (v. 19b NASV). Paul comes closer to the psalm text in v. 20, simply altering the word "humans" in the psalm to read *wise*.

Having scored his basic point and documented it from the LXX Paul continues by informing the Corinthians that they do not claim enough. By dividing themselves into cliques or factions they fail to embrace the larger reality that God has called into being through the saving and unifying cross of Christ. The Corinthians belong to Christ, and because Christ belongs to God all that belongs to God belongs to Christ; so that all this is available to the Corinthians as they are faithful followers of Christ. In and through Christ God unifies a redeemed creation, and the Corinthians are called to a new life in that grand unity.

4:1-5. God as the only real judge. Nothing about Christian life leads to boasting. Paul illustrates why. He also identifies Christ as the only real or true judge. The lines begin by informing the Corinthians how they are to regard Paul, Apollos, Cephas, and all other early Christian workers. They are merely *servants* and *stewards*, called to serve Christ as agents of the proclamation of the mysteries of God's GRACE. Only one key quality must characterize stewards, trustworthiness or, more literally, faithfulness. God requires that Paul and the others be faithful executors of the charge with which they have been entrusted. What the Corinthians think of God's stewards is actually of little or no importance. In fact, Paul says the opinions God's stewards have of themselves is irrelevant. Why? Because of one simple fact: The Lord is the one who does the judging. In a sense Paul is freed by the Lord's being his sole judge, for he needs neither to worry about what others think nor even to be obsessed with evaluating his own performance. Paul is free to strive to be faithful, not worrying about his success, for in the end Christ will judge him (and all others) and then God will mete out whatever praise is appropriate.

The promise of judgment comes in striking eschatological form. The language is that of apocalyptic eschatology. Paul expects the coming of Christ in the end. That coming will create a separation of "light" and "darkness," apocalyptic language for good and evil. Christ's final judgment will be universal, disclosing and exposing all things, even *the purposes of the heart*. Then, in the end the focus turns to God who enacts the results of the judgment that Christ effected.

4:6-13. Exposing inappropriate boasting. Paul has illustrated matters with reference to himself and Apollos, but what he has said was intended to apply to the Corinthians, as is clear from v. 6. This verse, while stating that Paul wanted the Corinthians to draw a lesson from his discussion of himself and Apollos, is difficult to comprehend precisely. The grammar seems to suggest that Paul wants the Corinthians to learn for two purposes: (1) so that they will understand and apply the saying, *"Nothing beyond what is written"* (v. 6); and (2) so that they will not form factions because of arrogant prejudices. While these purposes are plain, exactly what lesson Paul would have the Corinthians gain from his metaphors about farming and building is not immediately apparent; and the meaning of the quoted saying itself is not clear. By *what is written*

Paul most likely is referring to the scripture he quoted in the sections prior to the metaphorical arguments in 4:1-5. If that is the case, we can return to Paul's basic point in 3:18-23, namely, by forming factions the Corinthians defy the unity that God in Christ is creating and to which the Corinthians themselves are called.

Paul's argument in the ensuing verses comes in two strokes. Verse 7 lays the basis for an attack on the Corinthians' practice of judging, comparing, and boasting. Verses 8-13 form the attack. At the outset in v. 8 Paul is quite sarcastic, mocking the Corinthians for their pride, or false pride as Paul would see it. In the face of Corinthian arrogance Paul counters with the example of the apostles themselves. Paul insists that God uses the real oppression of the apostles to a positive end. He then contrasts the state of the apostles with the claimed status of the Corinthians to show that something is wrong in their lives. His rhetoric is patterned: we . . . you; we . . . you; you . . . we. Paul's wording draws the attention of the Corinthians away from themselves and creates focused emphasis on the sufferings of the apostles. Thus, he lays out the nature of a genuine apostolic style of ministry characterized by "weakness."

This line of argument raises a question: What is the purpose of the suffering that the apostles endure? The last two clauses of v. 13 speak to this question, but they are notoriously difficult. The NRSV translates the verse, *We have become like the rubbish of the world, the dregs of all things, to this very day.* Thus, the translators take Paul's statement to indicate that the apostles have become "rubbish" and "dregs" in their sufferings, that is, Paul offers two negative descriptions in apposition. Orr and Walther (1976), however, suggests translating v. 13, in part, "until now the dirt scoured from the world, that which cleanses all"; so that Paul's phrases are read as a negative image that is superseded by a contrasting positive one. Remarkably, the Greek word (περικαθάρμα) translated as "rubbish" or "dirt scoured" occurs in Prov 21:18 (LXX) and means "expiation" or "ransom," and the Greek word (περίψημα) translated as "dregs" or "that which cleanses" occurs in Tob 5:19 and means "ransom" or "scapegoat." Rather than ending with two negative images in apposition ("rubbish," "dregs") or in a negative image that is superseded by a contrasting positive one ("dirt scoured," "that which cleanses"), Paul may ultimately define the positive meaning of the genuine suffering he and the others apostles endure. Thus, perhaps one should translate v. 13: "Being slandered, we call out, having become like an expiation for the world, a ransom for all until now." If this reading is correct, then, Paul is not saying that Christian suffering is a bad fate that can be endured; rather, Christian suffering plays a vital role in reconciliation.

4:14-21. A paternal appeal and threat. Paul's tone changes as he explains his motives for writing and issues an appeal to the Corinthians. The apostle employs the image of a "father" in relation to the congregation. Paul cites the special relationship he has with the Corinthians, and he recognizes this intimate association to be the natural result of his having founded the church through the preaching of the gospel of Jesus Christ. Paul works with the image of a father in terms the Corinthians would easily comprehend. As the father of the Corinthian church Paul is an example whom the Corinthians are to imitate. They are urged to take on Paul's *ways in Christ Jesus*. In order to direct the Corinthians Paul sends his "beloved and faithful child" Timothy, who in the pattern of relations named here would be a sibling to the Corinthians. Paul's call to imitation may seem egotistical, but we see later in 11:1 that Paul is urging the Corinthians to Christlike living (*Be imitators of me, as I am of Christ* [11:1]). The call here is an appeal for the Corinthians to take up or return to the standards of life that informed all of the congregations Paul founded.

Again, the Corinthians are called away from idiosyncratic, arrogant behavior as Paul reminds them they are part of the larger church that God in Christ is calling into being. Then, with the directions given, Paul continues in vv. 18-21 to write as a father to rowdy children as he issues a clear, pointed parental threat.

Specific Problems and Questions, 5:1–11:1

This lengthy and important part of the letter takes up a remarkable complex of materials that may be viewed as three major clusters of material: First, 5:1–6:20 treats a set of concrete misunderstandings. Paul has taught and written the Corinthians, but they have not accurately interpreted his remarks. Second, 7:1-40 deals with the topics of marriage, divorce, and social status. Again, the behavior of the Corinthians indicates that they have not taken the teachings of Paul to heart for the living of everyday life. Third, in an extended and spiraling segment of this section of the letter, 8:1–11:1, Paul discusses Christian rights and responsibilities in order to correct and direct the activities of the Corinthians.

5:1-13. Shocking sexual immorality. Verses 1-5 identify an incident of sexual immorality in the Corinthian congregation, wherein literally "someone has his father's wife." Paul declares his shock and announces that he has already passed judgment; he instructs the church about what to do and tells them why.

The problem is unclear in many ways. The situation is most likely that a man is living with his former stepmother. From Paul's discussion the man's father is quite likely dead. In turn, the language related to Paul's judgment, his instructions to the Corinthians, and his explanation are difficult and produce a number of challenges for interpretation.

First, Paul's directions concerning the action the Corinthians are to take are worded ambiguously. Yet, since Paul wrote to the "holy ones in Christ Jesus" (author trans.) at 1:2 and since he believes in the presence and the active power of the Risen Lord, one should probably take 5:4-5 to read, "When you are assembled in the name of the Lord, and I am with you in spirit along with the power of our Lord Jesus, give this one to Satan . . . " (author trans.).

Second, what is Paul's purpose in telling the Corinthians, literally, "Give this one to Satan unto destruction of the flesh, in order that the spirit may be saved in the day of the Lord?" What does "unto destruction of the flesh" mean? Whose "spirit" is it that "may be saved"? There are no easy solutions, but one should avoid interpretations that attribute to Paul ideas such as that Christians receive an indelible character in BAPTISM or that salvation comes by death.

In vv. 6-8 Paul turns on the community and their problem of boasting. The arrogance mentioned in v. 2 is a theme. Here Paul criticizes the Corinthians' boasting by using the image of leaven in relation to his directions for expulsion of the flagrantly immoral member. Paul's point is that a little undesirable boasting goes a long way. He advances his argument by employing the Jewish ritual of PASSOVER housecleaning to insure the full removal of all "leaven," that is, immorality and boasting.

Paul continues by declaring the motivation for Christian purity and discipline, namely, Christ, the paschal lamb. This traditional image registers the reality of the saving significance of Jesus' death and reminds the Corinthians that what God has done in Christ calls forth an altered manner of living for those who hear and believe the message of Christ.

A new, related line of thought comes in vv. 9-13. Paul refers to a former letter he says the Corinthians badly misunderstood. Paul means for the Corinthians to dissociate themselves from immoral persons in the church, not from those outside. Paul says that God attends to those outside the church. The directions not to eat with the immoral probably assume the context of the LORD'S SUPPER, which will occupy Paul in detail in chap. 11. Here, v. 13 is crucial. This verse is a quotation of Deut 17:7, although Paul uses the second person plural form of "drive out" rather than the second singular of the LXX. Thus, Paul tailors the biblical word to the Corinthians' situation, so that v. 13 helps one to comprehend Paul's difficult directions in 5:4-5. By expelling the immoral member from the church, the Corinthians assure that he comes under God's judgment. His condition is not, therefore, hopeless, but hopeful. The church, as those called by God in Christ, cannot tolerate such immorality; but if the church does allow such behavior, the sinner has no cause for change and no hope of reconciliation to God. God, on the other hand, can judge and call the sinner to the righteousness of faith.

6:1-11. Going to judgment before non-Christians. Having raised the issue of the relations of Christians both to other Christians and to those outside the church, Paul's mind seems to move to the matter of how Christians relate to one another outside the life of the church. Paul's discussion focuses on the issue of Christians suing each other in pagan courts of law. One cannot determine how Paul knows about this problem, nevertheless, he discusses the matter in some detail. Interpreters regularly refer to these verses as an excursus, although the discussion is not simply a digression from the main lines of thought.

Paul views Christians taking one another into pagan courts over lawsuits as an example of the degree of the Corinthians' lack of understanding, or better, lack of love, as will become clear later in the letter (chap. 13). The image of the "saints" judging the world adapts a motif of Jewish apocalyptic eschatology found in DANIEL, ENOCH, and the WISDOM OF SOLOMON. Does this statement contradict what was said about the church's capacity to judge in 5:9-13? No, for the judgment in view here is an anticipation of future judgment. Paul's argument is from greater to lesser, from future to present. If Christians will judge the world in a great apocalyptic future judgment, then, Paul argues, they should certainly be capable of exercising judgment over their own affairs here and now. Paul admonishes the Corinthians to take the full extent of life in Christ's community seriously.

In vv. 7-8 Paul advances his argument by declaring bluntly that the will to assert one's own rights at the expense of others—and at the expense of the general image of the community—is defeat. Verses 9-11 offer a catalogue listing in an illustrative, not exhaustive, manner certain characteristics and conditions that will not gain entry into the kingdom of God. The section becomes a brief meditation on "unrighteousness" (ἄδικος). The NRSV translation of *wrongdoers* (for ἄδικοι) rightly catches Paul's focus on actions, but this accurate translation runs the danger of minimizing Paul's point throughout this discussion that improper behavior results from a faulty theological attitude. Verse 11 is the most important statement in the section. From a frank recognition of the character of "some" of the Corinthians before their conversion, Paul elaborates why they now are—and, in turn, ought to be—different. They are *washed, sanctified,* and *justified* (v. 11); that is, Paul locates the Corinthians theologically, identifies them in relation to Christ, and recognizes the priority of God in their salvation and, now, in the conduct of their lives. In hearing this line, the Corinthians would likely think of their baptism, the gift of the Holy Spirit, and their new, right relationship with God. All of this transformation that the Corinthians have experienced comes, as the passive verbs show, through the work of God in Christ.

6:12-20. The character of Christian freedom. These nine verses form a complex segment of the letter. One finds here quotations from the Corinthians and a citation of the LXX. The verses are largely cast in the diatribe style of popular Hellenistic philosophy. One also encounters traditional elements of early Christian "doctrine." All of this material is woven together in service to Paul's deliberate line of argumentation.

Paul builds and argues a case in vv. 12-17 in response to the thinking and declarations of the Corinthians. As the NRSV and other translations recognize by placing the statement *All things are lawful for me* in quotations, Paul employs a pattern of rhetoric wherein he quotes the position of those with whom he is in imaginary dialogue in order to respond to their thinking. The conversation goes back and forth:

[Corinthians] *"All things are lawful for me,"*
[Paul] *but not all things are beneficial.*
[Corinthians] *"All things are lawful for me,"*
[Paul] *but I will not be dominated by anything.*
[Corinthians] *"Food is meant for the stomach and the stomach for food,"*
[Paul] *and God will destroy both one and the other.*

The Corinthians' slogan literally says, "All things [are] to me permissible." They may have learned this statement from Paul himself, for he never denies its validity; rather, he qualifies the idea with his argument. For the Corinthians, what they know or think they know has given them an abstract principle that can and has produced less than desirable results. Paul concretizes this idea. Freedom, according to Paul, is characterized by pursuing what it best; freedom does not lead to a new form of slavery. The Corinthians mistakenly claim an inner freedom that places them above the mundane realities of the world, and they are eager to demonstrate their liberation.

If Paul's remarks about the Corinthians' attitude toward food and sexual activity is accurate, the will to display freedom had gotten completely out of hand (although one should not forget that Paul creates deliberate distortions in his arguments in order to score his points). The Corinthians seem to assume that freedom means they are at liberty to gratify their every appetite. Paul expresses mild shock that from the notion that all foods are fit for consumption by those who are aware of their freedom, some in Corinth engage in casual sex with prostitutes in celebration of their freedom.

Paul's critique calls the Corinthians into a responsible relationship to "the Lord." Freedom, Paul tells the Corinthians, is "for the Lord," not merely for personal pleasure. To make his point with all possible force, Paul alludes to Gen 2:24 in v. 16b. On the one hand, he uses scripture to denounce involvement with prostitutes; on the other hand, the citation sets up a crucial statement of the nature of the spiritual union of Christians with the Lord.

In vv. 18-20 Paul's rhetoric takes the form of a clear frontal attack. He directs the Corinthians to *Shun fornication!* Then, he informs the Corinthians that their *body* is *a temple of the Holy Spirit within [them]*. Paul bluntly tells the Corinthians, *You are not your own.* Why? Because they *were bought with a price.* The language is a metaphorical reference to redemption as "ransom," and it alludes in an undeveloped way to the death of Jesus.

That the Corinthians belong to God is the ultimate qualification of their freedom. One should see that throughout this section Paul jabs his readers with the rhetorical refrain, *Do you not know . . . ?* The implication is that the Corinthians do not know what they ought to know. Paul writes to factor into the Corinthians' thinking new information that should correct their ignorance.

7:1-7. General remarks on marriage. Paul's statements in these verses are more often misunderstood than grasped and appreciated for what they say. At the outset, one should recognize that in v. 1 Paul is taking up the letter sent to him from Corinth with its variety of inquiries. Paul refers to the letter and, then, as the quotation marks in the NRSV around the words *"It is well for a man not to touch a woman"* recognize, he quotes a line from the letter. It is the position of some of the Corinthians that "It is well for a man not to touch a woman." Obviously the point was debated, for now the Corinthians have written to get Paul's own thinking on this point. Paul's position comes in v. 2. In Greek Paul uses an imperative in this statement, so that literally he declares, "Because of instances of sexual immorality, let each man have his own wife and let each woman have her own husband" (author trans.). This position is often called a concession, but the imperative force of the declaration calls that description into question.

From this opening exchange with the Corinthians Paul continues in v. 3 working with the assumption that people are already married. If so, then Paul instructs the husbands to give the wives their due and, likewise, the wives to give their husbands their due. At issue are so-called conjugal rights, which Paul assumes do exist. Verse 4 offers the social or anthropological assumptions behind Paul's directions. Remarkably, at this point Paul assumes a genuine mutuality in marital relations. The *authority* over each spouse's body is attributed to the other marital partner. There is little to no historical or cultural precedent for what Paul says here.

In v. 5 Paul initially encourages sexual union in the context of marriage, but he does allow for abstinence for special times of devotion *to prayer.* Some of the Corinthians seem to assume that ascetic restraint is a clear indication of spirituality, but Paul does not follow their line. Refraining from sexual union in a marriage is not the path of spirituality, although Paul allows for limited abstinence in special circumstances. When in the following verse Paul says, *This I say by way of concession, not of command,* he is merely qualifying his previous statement in v. 5 that allowed for sexual continence for prayer. In other words, Paul himself does not think that married persons need necessarily to refrain from sexual activity *by agreement for a set time* in order to devote themselves to prayer.

The heart of Paul's thinking about marriage and sex in marriage comes through in v. 7. Chastity, the capacity not to marry, freedom from a desire for sex in the context of a marriage, is a spiritual gift from God. For Paul, not marrying is preferable only if the capacity to remain single is given by God, but the gift of chastity is not universal and it is not necessary. Paul's own prejudices come out clearly in his remarks here, for he understands the gift of remaining unmarried to be an opportunity for freedom from marital responsibilities. Paul develops this dimension of this thinking later in 7:32-35.

7:8-9. Directions to the unmarried. Having discussed marriage, the advisability of sexual union in marriage, and the spiritual gift of remaining single, Paul turns directly to the unmarried members of the Corinthian congregation. He declares that he himself considers it better to remain unmarried than to marry, and his manner of expression shows that Paul is offering his own thinking on this subject. Later in this chapter he explains that he is of this opinion because of the eschatological character of the time in which he believes he and the Corinthians live. Nevertheless, Paul informs the unmarried members of the church that they should marry in certain circumstances. Paul reasons here from the assumption that the capacity to remain unmarried is a spiritual gift. The translation of this line in the NRSV and other translations, *But if they are not practicing self-control, they should marry*, is easily misunderstood. Paul is not saying, "If you cannot control yourself, get married." In Paul's well-known list of the fruit of the Spirit at Gal 5:23 one finds the noun "self-control" (ἐγκράτεια), so that although Paul uses the verbal form of "self-control" here (ἐγκρατεύεσθαι meaning "to practice self-control"), he is referring to a Spirit-empowered directing of one's self. If an unmarried person in Corinth does not have the Spirit-given ability to be chaste, then Paul says that person should marry.

7:10-11. Directions to the married. In turn, Paul writes again to the married. As he begins his remarks, Paul makes plain that he is not simply giving his own opinion; instead, he is delivering a word from the Lord to the Corinthians. The tradition to which Paul refers may lie behind the materials in passages such as Mark 10:2-9 and Luke 16:18 or Matt 5:32. This dominical word is a firm denial of the validity of DIVORCE. The NRSV correctly places v. 11 in parentheses. The statement is not an exception clause, however; rather, it provides directions in the event that persons practice divorce despite the word from the Lord. Remarkably Paul does not turn the Lord's word into a new law.

Moreover, facing the possibility of a divorce that is obviously contrary to the advice from the Lord, Paul does not denounce the divorced person. He has other advice. Paul's comments at this juncture once more assume that in marriage both wives and husbands have responsibilities and can take initiatives.

7:12-16. Regarding "mixed" marriages. Having directed remarks to unmarried Christians and to Christians married to each other, Paul writes *to the rest*, that is, to those Christians who are married to *unbelieving* partners. Paul works from the assumption that divorce is contrary to the teaching of the Lord (7:10-11); yet, he recognizes that the involvement of an *unbelieving partner* in a marriage creates a different set of circumstances. Paul's advice to the Christian partners is that they remain in their marriages if their non-Christian spouses agree. Paul's reasoning supports or maintains Christian freedom, although the ideas of reconciliation and peace are the foundations of his thought. Peace, not the conflict of a divorce, is the characteristic of Christian life.

Verse 14 is enigmatic. Paul probably assumes that non-Christian spouses are involved in pagan religions and makes these statements to recognize that no pagan deity plays a part in the Christians' dealings with pagan spouses. Thus, his reference to the children of "mixed" marriages aims at illustrating the ultimate power of the Lord. Christians are not defiled by pagan spouses, rather the Christian's presence in the family and the Spirit's presence in the life of the believer actually sanctifies the relationship. In turn, v. 16 summarizes the reason Paul advises Christians to remain married to pagans. Critical editions of the Greek text suggest the two sentences are questions, not assertions as the NRSV translates. The basic sense of the sentences is clear whether the words are taken to declare or to inquire, and what Paul says may seem peculiar at a glance. One sees clearly from Paul's total writings that he does not think humans ever save themselves or one another, God does the saving through Christ; so these lines are best understood to say that God may work through a Christian spouse to save an unbelieving partner.

7:17-24. God's gifts and the Corinthians' calling. The reference *to the rest* in v. 12 probably indicates that having addressed the question of how men and women are to relate in terms of sex, Paul thinks he is done with that topic. Nevertheless, he sums up the matter and elaborates a bit in this next segment of the letter. Paul tells the Corinthians they are to live according to the gift the Lord gave them in the state in which they were called. Paul applies this idea to CIRCUMCISION and to SLAVERY. The concluding lines of this section reiterate the basic idea that the Corinthians are to remain before God in the state in which God called them. How is a modern reader to take this notion? Some observations may aid comprehension. One should notice that Paul offers an off-balance contrast in v. 22:

    (A) a Christian slave is the Lord's free person
    in the Lord;
    (B) a free person is the Lord's slave.

The idea of being *in the Lord* transcends simple social conventions. Moreover, Paul's thought here is completely relativized in relation to his thoroughgoing apocalyptic eschatology as is clear from 7:31b, *For the present form of this world is passing away.* For Paul, God saves regardless of worldly social status, and remaining in the social state in which one was called demonstrates that it is not something that humans do that effects salvation; indeed, worldly social change is not equivalent to salvation.

Finally, the calling of Christians by God creates real freedom. All who are called are freed, in spite of social circumstances, to obey God (v. 19). The saving work of God actually eliminates the boundaries of sacred and profane, for God's saving work knows no confines.

7:25-40. Issues and eschatology. These verses are a contorted series of statements about "virginity," the eschatological nature of the time, and the death of a spouse. An amazing variety of issues are treated in rapid succession. Verses 25-28 are difficult, in part, because of the uncertain (for us) identity of the VIR-GINS. Verse 25 clearly states that Paul is offering his opinion, not a word from the Lord, but he suggests his opinion is informed and valuable. Paul's thinking is determined by his eschatological conviction that the worldly future is to be but a brief span of time. Therefore, Paul advises the virgins to stay as they are, as everyone else should; but Paul says if the virgins marry they do not sin.

Paul's eschatology becomes more explicit in vv. 29-31. All of human existence is relativized in light of the conviction that God's work is bringing this world to its end. The passage should be taken in relation to Paul's earlier teaching about freedom and the aim of Christian life to glorify God. Paul's point: The time left is short, so live it fully for God. In turn, vv. 32-35 are well intended (v. 35) but odd advice. Paul's atti-

tude is decidedly ascetic. There are certainly other possibilities that simply do not occur to Paul. The apostle seems capable of understanding marriage only as a responsibility that will create anxiety. Paul writes out of his own Spirit-endowed gift of singleness with little understanding of the broad range of possible relationships in marriage. The idea that the love and mutual support of a marriage might actually foster more effective Christian living does not appear to cross Paul's eschatologically riveted thinking.

The enigma of the virgins comes around again in vv. 36-38, although the NRSV resolves the matter (rightly) by rendering the Greek *fiancée* rather than "virgin." The language of these lines reflects the male-dominant character of the first-century culture in which Paul wrote. Although the focus and the language are somewhat different from the earlier discussion in 7:8-9 and 7:25, Paul's thinking is consistent: if passions are strong, then marry; whoever marries does well, but whoever is able to remain single does better.

8:1-13. Eating meat sacrificed to idols. Paul takes up a theme here that, despite the seeming lack of coherence, continues through 11:1: Christian rights and responsibilities, especially regarding "knowledge" and "freedom" in relation to idol sacrifices. As the opening words show, Paul is again responding to an issue brought to his attention by the Corinthians. He probably quotes the Corinthians' own position as the NRSV recognizes with the quotation marks around *"all of us possess knowledge."* Paul's critique of this declaration follows as he contrasts "knowledge" and "love." Paul remarks that knowledge is of no value in itself. The appropriate criterion is not knowledge but love for God. To focus on knowledge demonstrates an inadequate understanding. What really matters is to be known by God; and the evidence of God's knowing a believer is the believer's love for God. God's will and work must be the first priority of a believer, not a self-inflated estimation of the value of what one knows.

In v. 6 Paul offers a confessional statement that seems creedal in character. This "creed" assumes a Christian perspective and focuses on creation, call, Christ, and redemption. From the discussion one sees that the Corinthians had turned the confession into a speculative thesis that led to an artificially sophisticated lifestyle that easily denied the reality of *idols.* Paul, by contrast, takes pagan gods and lords more seriously than do the Corinthians. Later, at 10:20, Paul relates such gods and lords to demons, so that he considers them to be dangerous entities.

Verse 7 explicitly refutes the Corinthians' claim concerning knowledge. Every believer does not share the conviction that idols are not real. Paul's concern is to correct the arrogant behavior of those denying idols toward "weak" believers who assume the idols are real. Those who deny the idols insist their knowledge frees them to eat meat that had been previously sacrificed to idols (as most meat for sale had been), despite the objections of other believers who believed in idols and were scandalized by the eating of idol meat. Paul teaches that freedom is not abstract, but concrete. Real freedom is being freed from the necessity to assert only, or primarily, one's own rights. Knowledge alone is dangerous. What ultimately matters is that believers will the well-being of others rather than simply insist on their own rights and privileges.

9:1-27. Illustrative observations on the "rights" of an apostle. This chapter may appear to be an intrusion into the discussion of idols and eating idol meat, but Paul simply takes himself and the matter of his rights as an apostle as an illustration of a proper demeanor for Christians. Paul declares his freedom in a rhetorical question. Then, he explains the real meaning of freedom in his own life. Paul reminds the Corinthians that he could make claims as others do (vv. 4-5) or as soldiers, planters, and shepherds (v. 7). Moreover, he recognizes that God ordained that the apostles be able to derive their living from the work they do as ministers. To underscore this point Paul offers a midrashic exposition on Deut 25:4 in vv. 9-11. Yet, he continues by stating that he does not use the right of support by the churches, lest his taking pay for his ministry be misunderstood as bilking the congregation (v. 12). Paul elaborates the matter of his right to support by referring to the practice of supplying the needs of those in Temple service from the proceeds given to the Temple. Then, in v. 14 he cites a word from the Lord (cf. Luke 10:7) to the effect that *those who proclaim the gospel should get their living by the gospel.* Yet, Paul explains that he does not take his rightful support. Amazingly, Paul's reward is that he takes no reward! Paul preaches because he was commissioned to do so, but by not taking his due he gives up his own rights as an offering to God.

In vv. 19-23 Paul describes the style of his ministry and its motivations. He reiterates his freedom and declares that while he is free from all, nevertheless, he enslaves himself to all. Paul reports that he varies his personal behavior depending upon his audience. In relation to Jews who are *under the law* (v. 20) Paul takes on their patterns of living, although he himself is not under the law. In relation to those *outside the law* (v. 21) he lives as they do, but he is not free from God's law because he lives under "Christ's law." Paul says he varies his behavior in order to "win" both Jews and those outside the law. Paul strives to become all things to all people in all ways so that he may serve as God's agent in saving "some." Paul's remarks in v. 23 show that the power of the gospel presides over Paul; it is the senior partner in a partnership. Thus, the gospel is not relativized to worldly social conditions that are no more than contemporary social structures and sensibilities; rather, the apostle himself becomes relativized in order to preserve the integrity of the gospel.

Paul brings his discussion of apostolic rights to a conclusion in vv. 24-27. He takes up a set of athletic images as metaphors, explaining and advocating discipline. Paul's metaphors are inexact and should not be allegorized. First, Paul writes of *runners.* Basically he seeks to admonish the Corinthians to an active and disciplined life. Appropriate Christian living takes definite direction. With that point in mind Paul shifts to the image of boxing. He says he does not "fan the air" in the style of an untrained fighter; he works like an expert pugilist whose punches count because they hit their mark. Paul is focused through discipline.

Paul's final comments on boxing are almost shocking. He reveals that his opponent is himself. Surely this is a lesson for the Corinthians whose attitude leads to the kind of easy, self-indulgent living that merely presumes upon God's grace and does not relate in obedience to God's saving acts. Paul explains that he "blackens the eye of [his] body" (v. 27, author trans.) lest he be disqualified himself—a strong word of warning to the readers.

10:1-13. Relating the Exodus experience to Christian life. Having raised the frightening, serious matter of disqualification, Paul moves immediately to deliver a midrash on the EXODUS that is laced with scriptural allusions. Paul applies the Exodus story to the Corinthian situation as a further word of warning. Then, he specifies the heart of his concern by again taking up the matter of eating meat that had been offered to idols. Paul returns to the Corinthians' slogan about freedom and offers further rebuttal, clarification, and directions.

Verses 1-5 form the midrash. One finds here allusions to the book of Exodus, selected Psalms, the Wisdom of Solomon, and Numbers. Paul's style of biblical interpretation may strike modern readers as strange, but this manner of interpreting the biblical materials is neither unique nor was it unusual in Paul's day. Indeed, both PHILO and the RABBIS developed the idea of a peripatetic or divine rock. Paul may simply be "christianizing" a standard theme of Jewish wisdom teaching, or he may appropriate images and ideas from developed wisdom traditions in his own creative reflection. The idea of Christ's preexistence is inherent in Paul's comments, although preexistence per se is not the focus of the discussion.

The application of the Exodus imagery is made through typological analogy (see τυπικῶς in v. 11). The typological analysis and application lay the foundation for the stark warning that comes in v. 5, where *nevertheless* says a great deal. Indeed, in spite of the ancestors having been *baptized into Moses* (v. 2) and having participated in an archetypal LORD'S SUPPER, God was not pleased with most of them and they were overthrown in the wilderness. Thus, according to Paul, baptism and participation in the Lord's Supper are not unequivocal assurances against negative divine judgment. The sacraments are not magical charms that guarantee an absolute claim on salvation.

Verses 6-13 make further application of the midrash by adding and applying other Exodus materials to the exhortation. Primarily the story is brought to bear on the Corinthians in relation to the issue of idolatry, especially in relation to the theme of idol-meat. Verse 6 introduces the application in a general manner. Verse 7 applies the scriptural lesson directly to the issue of idolatry and in doing so quotes a portion of Exod 32:6 verbatim. Finally, vv. 8-10 form a trilogy of negative directions against immorality, testing the Lord, and grumbling. These verses also report the terrible results of such wrongful behavior—the death of *twenty-three thousand . . . in a . . . day* (v. 8, although in Num 25:9 one reads that "twenty-four thousand" died). Verse 11 explains the application, and one should notice two items. First, Paul's exegesis clearly reveals that he understands the scriptures to be typological as a result of the Christ-event. Second, Paul locates himself and the Corinthians at the juncture of the ages, as the NRSV recognizes with the correct translation, *they were written down to instruct us, on whom the ends of the ages have come.* This line is generally mistranslated and misunderstood as a reference to either a general summary of all previous times or epochs (*ends of the ages* [v. 11]) or a general summary of all previous nonepochal time ("end of the age"). But, these under-

standings fail to take seriously Paul's apocalyptic eschatological temporal dualism. From this perspective Paul understands that he and the Corinthians live at the point where "the present evil age" (Gal 1:4) and the "new creation" (2 Cor 5:17) are both *already* and *not yet* present. They live between the cross and the coming of Christ at a time when the ages are mingled. In this interim the old is already dying and the new is already being born, though the old has not yet passed away and the new has not yet fully arrived.

Verse 12 issues a sobering warning, probably because of Paul's convictions about the danger of the volatile times, that recognizes the continuing threat of opposition to God. More directly, v. 13 declares that the real crisis (temptation) besetting the community is indeed manageable and conquerable. Paul proclaims the theological basis of such management: God is faithful. God provides the antidote to the temptation. While there is no avoidance of the problem, mixed with the problem in this mingling of times is God's saving provision. Paul's confidence is in God's sustaining grace. Although one can imagine different ways in which Paul would name this divine provision—the Spirit, Christ, the power of God—the apostle does not name God's grace; rather, he declares God's faithfulness. Above all, Paul establishes here the necessity of the relationship of the Corinthians to God who saves.

10:14-22. Directions against idolatry. Paul elaborates and makes even more direct application of his warning to the Corinthians. He understands himself to be building on his preceding remarks and inferring conclusions in relation to them as is evident in his first word in this section, *Therefore*—or better, "On account of" (Διόπερ). Paul tells the Corinthians to *flee from the worship of idols.* Then, he states in eucharistic metaphors the unified nature of Christian life (vv. 15-16). By analogy to Israel Paul identifies the demonic forces associated with pagan religion and, in turn, with sacrificial food (vv. 17-20). One should note that Paul's reference is to the food, not to the act of eating. Then, Paul doubly reiterates the exclusive nature of Christian life in terms of the elements of the Lord's Supper, mentioning the cup before the bread. Finally, he instructs the Corinthians through two rhetorical questions. Paul informs them that their *eating,* an insistent practice of personal freedom, may and does provoke God. Thus, the apostle contrasts human and divine strength in such a way that he issues an indirect threat.

10:23–11:1. Further clarification of the nature of Christian freedom. Verses 23-24 repeat the Corinthians' slogan from 6:12, but this time there is no *for me* with the words *All things are lawful.* As in chap.ᵓ 6 Paul states and qualifies this slogan twice. First, he repeats and qualifies exactly as in 6:12, *but not all things are beneficial.* Then, he repeats the slogan and qualifies it in relation to edification or "building up." This reasoning recalls 3:10-15, so one sees that, above all, Paul desires the unity of the church. Paul builds on these qualified statements by declaring a maxim, *Do not seek your own advantage, but that of the other.* In other words, he teaches them to live so that each may say, "Not my good but your good be done."

Verses 25-30 make practical application of this principle. In fact, one sees Paul pluck a principle out of the thin air of abstraction and put it down with the power of particularity in the actual affairs of the Corinthians. In so doing, the principle of Christian freedom is maintained; but, the matter of one's conscience is not raised as governing one's actions! Rather, the conscience of others is brought in relation with one's freedom so that freedom is interpreted as an established opportunity for putting others before one's self.

In 10:31–11:1 Paul sums up and concludes by again declaring the goal of Christian life to be the *glory of God* in all that believers do. Paul continues to make matters concrete by reference to his own attitude, aim, and style of ministry. He calls for the Corinthians to imitate him as he imitates Christ. Thus, he issues a call to Christlikeness.

Orderly Worship and Spiritual Gifts, 11:2–14:40

This third major section of the body of the letter contains reflections on a variety of topics that are particularly interesting for contemporary Christian practices. Here, Paul discusses the role of women in worship, the celebration of the Lord's Supper, charismatic gifts and practices, and the essential traits of Christian life and relationships.

11:2-16. Keeping church customs. The section opens with a commendation that may or may not be in response to a claim the Corinthians have made about their own preservation of tradition as Paul delivered it. Verse 3, however, follows by taking exception to a practice Paul views as outside the boundaries of normal church *custom* (cf. v. 16). Paul begins his argument by articulating a scheme of priority of authority. There are three distinct and related statements, but the scale here is not a simple stepladder or hierarchy:

Christ	>	the head	>	of every man
the husband	>	the head	>	of his wife
God	>	the head	>	of Christ

One should notice, above all, that the scheme begins with the authority of Christ and ends with the authority of God. While the notion of the husband having authority over his wife offends progressive sensibilities, Paul's point here is to recognize the authority of Christ over humanity and the ultimate authority of God. The scheme is a Stoic-like system of "natural order" that values order over chaos. Verses 4-6 unpack one line of argumentation concerning this scale in relation to the worship activities of praying or prophesying, specifically focusing on the practice of women wearing head coverings.

There are immediate problems for interpretation: Which instances of *head* are literal and which are metaphorical? Are all uses of *head* literal, all metaphorical, or is there some mix? Clearly the first occurrence of *head* in both v. 4 and v. 5 are literal because of the issue of covering and not covering. But, what of the second use of *head* in each verse? Are they metaphors for Christ and husband respectively, or are they literal? (The third mention of *head* in v. 5 in the NRSV is a supplying of the word by the translators. In Greek the perfect passive participle ἐξυρημένη "having been shaved" is simply preceded by the definite article τῇ, probably meaning "the woman," not "her head"; so that the line reads "it is one and the same thing as her having been shaved.") From what follows in v. 7, the explication of a man's not covering his head in terms of his existing as the image and the glory of God and the woman' covering her head in terms of her being the glory of man, one sees that the dishonored "heads" of vv. 4-5 are metaphorical.

The strange sense of the argument begins to make sense when one sees that Paul understands *nature* (v. 14) to *give indication* of the God-ordained pattern of life. Nevertheless, there are several problems raised by these verses that are not easily resolved: (1) How can a woman, veiled or otherwise, pray or prophesy if she is to be silent in the church as 14:33-35 indicates? (2) Has not Paul confused nature and humanly determined fashion? Are male and female hairstyles given by nature or set in style? (3) How is one to understand the amount of energy Paul invests in this section, vv. 2-16? Does the show of creative effort indicate the severity of the problem? Or, is Paul simply biased? (4) What kind of attitude do these lines reflect—Greek, Jewish, or Christian? It is easier to raise difficult questions than to find gratifying answers. One needs to follow the remaining course of the argument.

Verses 7-12 continue the argument from the perspective of a set of biblical texts. Verse 7 restates the idea with which Paul is working, bringing in the language of Gen 1:26-27; yet, the idea clearly controls the exegesis. Then, vv. 8-9 extend the argument by taking recourse to the creation story of Gen 2:18-22.

Verse 10 is an enigma. The opening words, *For this reason*, can relate either to previous or to ensuing comments. The words probably refer to what went *before* (vv. 8-9 or vv. 2-9), since still another *because of* ends the line. Thus, because of the relationship of men and women, women ought to have *a symbol of authority* on their heads, and this wearing of a symbol is related to *the angels*.

What does Paul mean by *because of the angels*? The statement is obscure. Perhaps he is thinking of the fallen angels of Genesis 6 who took human women for wives; or, perhaps he means the angels who were thought to be protectors of the order of creation and who are present, according to early Christian thought, in the assembly of Christians at worship.

Verses 11-12 form a statement in peculiar juxtaposition to what Paul has said to this point. One should note the all-important phrase *in the Lord*. This location allows the balanced statement in v. 12 to be made. Paul understands the situation concerning men and women as he did the issues of circumcision and slavery in chap. 7. *In the Lord* one recognizes the eschatological abrogation of sexual distinctions, but as Christians await the Day of the Lord they are not to act as if the Day has already come. One remains in the state in which one was called as the only valid demonstration of freedom.

Verses 13-16 put the issue before the Corinthians for a last time and from another angle. Paul calls for the Corinthians to judge the matter of a woman's being unveiled at prayer. The basis of the evaluation is the teaching of nature; Paul understands that nature indicates God's will and how one is to style one's self as a copy of nature. Paul surely did not reflect on this weak example or argument, for what he attributes to nature is merely human fashion, reflecting culture, not necessarily God—unless Paul thinks somehow that culture derives from nature and, in turn, that fashion ultimately goes back to God. Strikingly, in denouncing his opposition Paul cannot cite revelation or the Lord; rather, he is reduced to custom for his standards and authorization. The issues here may elude resolution,

although one should not fail to see that v. 16 recognizes the potential denial of Paul's argument.

In sum, at its root the alteration of custom often (although not always) stems from individualism, that is, the claiming of personal rights in the name of the Lord—a problem already identified by Paul. Christians, Paul tells the Corinthians, are "not to confuse a direct desecularization that is carried on by ourselves with the eschatological desecularization brought about by Christ, but to maintain the imperceptibility of this unworldliness—by dint of Christians wearing their hair normally and clothing themselves in normal ways" (Conzelmann 1975, 191).

11:17-22. Problems in the assembly. Paul identifies and criticizes a problem or problems arising when the Corinthians *come together*. Paul says their gathering is not for the better but for the worse. The results of the congregational assembly are negative. Paul recognizes divisions among the members of the church. Oddly, he rationalizes this problem by explaining that factions are necessary in order that those who are approved may be recognized. It is debatable whether he is being sarcastic or whether he discerns God creating confusion in Corinth.

Verse 20 broaches the matter of the LORD'S SUPPER, declaring that at their assemblies the Corinthians do not eat a meal that can be so named. Then, vv. 21-22 identify individualistic self-gratification—in the extreme—as the social reality that Paul opposes. But, he puts a theological twist on his denunciation by showing that self-interest undermines community. Thoughtlessness toward others causes humiliation and, as becomes clear in what follows, is antithetical to love. From Paul's rhetorical questions in v. 22 one must ask whether the Corinthians are interpreting divisiveness as a pluralism that deserves praise. If so, Paul's remarks indicate that unity is essential and without it diversity is meaningless.

11:23-26. Recalling the origins of the Lord's Supper. These four verses recapitulate the early Christian tradition concerning the institution of the Lord's Supper. Paul reiterates this tradition as the foundation of his ensuing teaching in vv. 27-34. In light of the Corinthian situation he explicates matters related to the tradition but does not explain or theologize the tradition directly.

These verses are enormously important for the church in belief and practice, and must be studied along with parallels in Mark 14:22-24, Matt 26:26-28, and Luke 22:17, 19-20 for full appreciation of the tradition. A full-scale comparative analysis is not attempted here.

Verse 23 claims the Lord as the ultimate source of this tradition since the words go back to the Lord whom Paul understands to be raised and who is alive in the Spirit. Paul's language concerning *receiving* and *handing on* is technical vocabulary in both Greek schools and Jewish synagogue thought. This manner of speaking establishes both the authority and reliability of the teaching. Remarkably, nothing in the tradition necessitates the PASSOVER setting found in the Gospels, but mention of the betrayal shows the fixed nature of this tradition and points to its association with the larger PASSION NARRATIVE.

Verse 24 narrates the first act. Thanksgiving and breaking of bread are Jewish table customs that were performed by the head of a household or a host. The words *this is my body* refers to the bread alone. Brokenness is not in view here. The emphasis is on the phrase *that is for you*, words that recognize the vicarious nature of Jesus' death. Some interpreters contend this clause is inherently sacrificial in focus, but that is not necessary. The words translated *do this in remembrance of me* are ambiguous in Greek, though they clearly interpret the ritual. In Greek the phrase literally says "do this unto my memory." Does this mean (1) that as Christians do and remember what Jesus said that they perceive the power and presence of Christ, or (2) that as Christians do these things, God's memory of Christ or Christ's own memory of his disciples is jogged toward realization of the parousia. Both interpretations are suggested by scholars, although the first option finds the most support.

Verse 25 narrates the second similar act. The focus is the cup, not its contents. This observation helps one see that the interpretation attaches to the administration of the Supper, not the elements themselves. Moreover, the acts stand separately as well as together as sacramental communications. One should notice that the COVENANT is related to the cup. The blood defines or establishes this covenant. The type of covenant is not determined by the statements, though the relationship of the covenant to blood recalls, in the context of 1 Corinthians (see 5:7), the motif of the paschal lamb. The motive of remembrance anticipates repetition of the acts.

Verse 26 extends the repetition theme and brings together the bread and cup in the declaration, *you proclaim the Lord's death until he comes*. These words hold open God's future in relation to the Lord's death

as they refer to the Lord's coming. This note places the whole observation of the Lord's Supper in the larger conceptual framework of apocalyptic eschatology and takes the Supper as prescribed foundational behavior for life between the cross and the coming.

11:27-34. Proper and improper attitudes at the Supper. These verses are concerned with one's attitude toward the Supper. They give advice for eliminating an improper disposition at the celebration. The final lines, vv. 33-34, are practical and elucidate the more abstract materials in vv. 27-32.

Verses 33-34 begin *So then*, and aim at correction or circumvention of the previously named problem(s). Note the advice:

(1) *When you come together to eat, wait for one another*—from 11:21 one knows that the Corinthians individually or in small groups are going ahead with their meals.

(2) Parenthetically, Paul separates satiation of hunger from the community meal or celebration—cf. 11:22.

(3) Paul's advice aims at preventing condemnation ensuing from the inappropriate gathering in which the Corinthians are already engaging—cf. 11:17-19.

Thus, 11:33-34 and 11:17-22 form a bracket or INCLUSIO around Paul's reflections and directions on the Lord's Supper in the material between 11:23-32. This fact grants a perspective from which to view vv. 27-32. First, a pair of negative observations: (1) Paul is not directly or indirectly concerned with the nature of the sacramental elements; (2) the matter at hand is not one's personal piety or lack thereof. A second, positive observation is that Paul's concern is for an appropriate attitude that fosters appropriate behavior.

Verses 27-32 take up the issue of appropriate attitudes and behavior. Eating and drinking in an unworthy way is eating and drinking with an attitude of self-centeredness, individualism, or arrogance. Even hyperpious individualism would fall under the rubric *unworthy*. Unworthy participation—coming to the Supper without regard for the result of Christ's reconciling work that draws the Christian community into a new selfless relatedness—makes one *answerable for the body and the blood of the Lord*. To deny the reconciling, unifying effects of Christ's death casts one into the role of those who crucified Jesus. Thus, one must examine one's self to insure the appropriate Christ-like attitude and, then, in a spirit of self-giving and interrelatedness one eats and drinks. Otherwise, Paul says, one participates in the Supper unto judgment, that is, one casts one's self outside the pale of redemptive reconciliation into the context of God's eschatological wrath.

Verse 29 mentions *discerning* the body. This statement should not be reduced to an abstract level. Rather, to discern the body (notice the absence of blood) means to comprehend and appropriate into one's own life the transforming significance of Christ himself. *Body* metaphorically identifies the Christ-event with its power to transform lives and create the new Christian community of reconciliation. Furthermore, v. 30 is Paul's explanation of illness and death in the Corinthian community. He speaks from the perspective of his belief in Christ's real presence in the *remembrance* of the Supper. Surely his explanation is descriptive and dramatic, not a declaration. Finally, v. 31 mentions judgment—not eschatological, but present judgment in this world as in v. 30. This explains the importance of the Corinthians' heeding Paul' directions.

12:1-3. The nature of Christian enthusiasm. This section addresses a new topic, namely, *spiritual gifts* or the gifts of the "spiritual ones." The language at the outset of the discussion is ambiguous in Greek, but the basic sense of Paul's remarks comes through however one decides to translate the Greek word πνευματι-κοί—translated *spiritual gifts* in the NRSV. A note in the NRSV indicates the possible translation "spiritual persons." One should notice that throughout the remainder of the section Paul continues the discussion by referring to spiritual gifts (χαρίσματα, an unambiguous designation); so the initial reference (to πνευματικοί) is most likely to "spiritual persons."

Verse 1 shows that the Corinthians brought this topic to Paul's attention. Paul's stated wish may imply that the Corinthians do lack adequate information. Then, vv. 2-3 identify the problem as the practice of ecstasy. Ecstasy may be contrasted with enthusiasm to explicate Paul's point here. Ecstasy is the effort to "stand outside" oneself, to grasp or be grasp by a vital power that provides one with an extraordinary experience. Enthusiasm is the result of one's being indwelt by the power of God, so that one's quality of experience is transformed. At a glance it is hard or impossible to distinguish the frenzy of ecstasy from the empowering of enthusiasm, but according to Paul genuine enthusiasm affirms the lordship of Jesus whereas the practice of ecstasy generates behavior contrary or hostile to the affirmation of Jesus' lordship. The recognition of the lordship of Jesus is the criterion that forms the parameters of legitimate enthusiasm.

One should notice that Paul assumes the reality of extraordinary spiritual experiences. He battles a particular theological explanation given to the experiences, not the experiences per se. The situation seems to be that the Corinthians are taking spiritual gifts as the grounds for comparison that leads to ranking of gifts and boasting. The more flamboyant gifts according to the Corinthians, are to be cherished and more highly esteemed. Some people apparently become so elevated in their spirituality that they have no use for, indeed they even express disdain for, the all-too-human Jesus who suffered the disgrace of dying on the cross. Paul will have none of this kind of spiritual expression.

12:4-11. Unity and diversity of gifts. This section argues concerning the spiritual gifts that there is a unified purpose in a variety of expressions because of the common divine origin of one's gift. The gifts Paul discusses here are not natural, birthright propensities.

In vv. 4-6 there are three parallel statements based on an underlying triad of Spirit/Lord/God. In relation to each of these three "persons" Paul recognizes variety. There are varieties of gifts of grace and there is one Spirit; there are varieties of services and there is one Lord; there are varieties of activities and there is one God. Diversity in the human sphere exists, relates to, and is unified by unity in the sphere of the divine. By drawing these phrases together Paul creates the theological matrix for valid interpretation of the phenomenon of *spiritual gifts*. Ultimately all gifts extend from God and are given for the good of the church. These gifts are not rendered according to the disposition of those who receive them. They are given and established under the Lordship of Jesus the Lord.

Verses 8-10 catalogue gifts without offering an exhaustive inventory. The list seems, in light of the rest of the letter, particularly relevant to the situation in Corinth. In this list, *discernment of spirits*, that is, the capacity to judge rightly for which Paul calls throughout the letter, is itself recognized to be a charismatic reality (v. 10).

12:12-31a. The body of Christ. In three striking movements these verses introduce (vv. 12-13), develop (vv. 14-26), and apply (vv. 27-31) Paul's best-known ecclesiastical metaphor: *body of Christ*. Scholars debate the exact background from which Paul may have drawn inspiration for developing this memorable image for the church. His contemporaries, certain Stoic philosophers, spoke of the cosmos in its unity as a body, and Jewish wisdom thinking often reflected upon the idea of corporate personality among a whole people. While Paul's image is not unique, his thinking does not exactly match any background, and his use of the image of "body" is extraordinary. One should notice that this metaphor applies both to the local church and to the church universal (see Romans 12). Furthermore, philosophically, being a "body" is the very basis of human relation; and, in context, as Paul speaks of "body" he refers to the absolute antithesis of that over which the Corinthian pneumatics were in orbit, namely, "spirit."

The metaphor BODY OF CHRIST serves to explicate a powerful thesis, *So it is with Christ!* Christ means variety but essential unity. From the outset of this discussion it is clear that this metaphor is possible because of the unifying work of the Spirit. The emphasis on unity cuts sharply across all social boundaries. Then, as Paul develops the metaphor, he ponders the significance of "body" from alternating points of view. First, vv. 14-19 approaches the metaphor from the perspective of *differentiation* of body members. Paul elaborates this perspective and articulates the necessity of differences. He states that such differences are by divine design and volition and, then, concludes by summarizing the necessity of differences. Second, vv. 20-26 return to the perspective of *unity*. Again, Paul elaborates his thought and declares that unity reflects divine design. Paul declares that unity is necessary, relating his thought to the motif of mutual care in the church. Paul concludes this phase of the meditation by summarizing the value of relatedness in the church.

Verses 27-31a apply and explain the metaphor in specific relation to the Corinthians' situation. Paul delineates the godly order of spiritual gifts, probably placing speaking in TONGUES last in order to devaluate the desirability of this flamboyant gift. Paul pursues the theme of the necessity of differentiation or variety of gifts in rhetorical questions (vv. 29-30). Then, in v. 31a he states his desire for the Corinthians. Even though the gifts are granted by God, Paul advises, the Corinthians to aspire toward the "greater" gifts!

12:31b–14:1a. The superlative way of love. These verses are often referred to as an excursus on love, and there are good reasons for this description. From Paul's admonition to aspire for the greater gifts—literally, he says, "Earnestly seek the higher gifts of grace" (v. 31a)—Paul declares that he shows the Corinthians *a still more excellent way* (v. 31b). The transition from v. 31a to 31b is awkward, and the material that follows in 13:1–14:1a is remarkable. First, it intrudes. 1 Cor 12:31a flows well into 14:1b; and the theme of

love in chap. 13 relates only indirectly to the particular situation being addressed to this point in the epistle. Second, the material on love seems to be a self-contained, quite polished unit. Third, there are comparable Greek and Hellenistic-Jewish parallels to this meditation on love found in such diverse materials as Tyrtaeus, Plato, Maximus of Tyre, and especially 3 Ezra 4:34-40. Fourth, the chapter seems unconcerned with Christ. This array of observations produces a variety of suggestions; but, in any case the material seems to be an originally independent piece (or, originally independent pieces) of developed tradition that Paul inserted into this context and applied to the Corinthian situation. Paul is likely to have worked minor adaptations on this material in order to fit it into this letter, and it is not impossible that the piece, although originally independent, was composed by Paul himself.

Verses 1-3 establish the necessity of love, for love alone confers worth to all other spiritual gifts. The mention of *tongues* has immediate relevance to the Corinthian situation, and the *gong* and *cymbal* are naturally associated with pagan religious ecstasy; so that Paul's words form a poetic critique of the Corinthians' behavior as one knows it from the previous chapters. Yet, in the next lines *prophetic powers* names a gift highly regarded by Paul. Thus, even manifesting a gift Paul values is useless without love, so one sees here no simple condemnation of those who have values different from the apostle and his cohorts. In turn, the reference to FAITH in v. 2 seems odd. In this line *faith* seems to be something akin to "miraculous power," a traditional definition, rather than Paul's own understanding of faith as "fruit of the Spirit" (Gal 5:22; 1 Cor 12:9).

A minor textual problem makes it uncertain whether Paul says that without love it is no gain to hand over one's body "in order to boast" (13:3) or "in order to be burned" (see NRSV mg.). Whichever reading is original, the sense of Paul's statement is that either the pride or the selflessness of sacrifice is worthless without the authenticating motivation of love. Paul's twin verdicts here are that without love *I am nothing* and *I gain nothing*. Whatever characterizes human lives and whatever achievements humans attain are ultimately judged by the presence or absence of love.

A change of style occurs in vv. 4-7. The content and style are those of Jewish parenesis, and the form is didactic (instruction) not hymnic (praise). The phrase "Love *is*" supplies the verb in English which is absent in Greek, but the translation accurately captures the descriptive intention of the lines. In brief, vv. 4-6 create a listing that is epitomized in v. 7. Love is presented as the essential Christian characteristic: Love is selflessness and is not self-centeredness. Love is patient and kind. It is not jealous, boastful, arrogant, rude, irritable, and resentful. The lines critique the Corinthian situation elegantly but abstractly. Then, with a shift from the nature of love to the activities of love, one finds that love does not insist on its own way or rejoice at wrong; rather, love rejoices in the right, bears all things, believes all things, hopes all things, and endures all things. In short, love defines and directs Christian life.

Once again the style shifts in 13:8–14:1a. Now instead of pithy wisdom sayings one encounters elaborated arguments. The preceding verses of this meditation on love took the position that charismatic gifts are worthless without love, but now love and the charismatic gifts are set over against each other with the end of establishing the enduring, eternal, eschatological nature of love. Verse 8 opens with a contrast between love and prophecy, tongues, and knowledge—declaring the enduring quality of love and indicating that prophecy, tongues, and knowledge will come to an end or will cease. One recalls 1 Cor 7:31 where Paul said *the present form of this world is passing away*; so that one infers that prophecy, tongues, and knowledge belong to this world, not to God's new creation. Thus, v. 9 can identify the basis for the cessation of knowledge and prophecy—they are imperfect.

Verse 10 declares the eschatological end of imperfection and promises survival of that which is perfect, so that one recalls 1 Cor 3:10-15. This point is dramatized through the metaphor of putting away childish things. Immaturity gives way to maturity. Moreover, the ensuing metaphor of seeing in a mirror *dimly* articulates a contrast between current existence and the promised eschatological vision of seeing *face to face*. In these metaphors Paul states the idea of knowledge seen in earlier chapters. Current knowledge is labeled *partial*, whereas eschatological knowledge is promised to be *full*. Here, Paul writes that all full eschatological knowledge, as well as current partial knowledge, is based on our being fully known by God, so that one learns again of God's genuine priority in salvation. As stated in chap. 1, what matters is not what humans comprehend but what God has done and will do.

Finally, 13:13–14:1a heightens and concludes the previous lines of thought. There is a slight contrast between these statements and what went before, for now one hears of the three highest gifts—faith, hope, and love. Faith was mentioned in 13:2, but it is not clear that the same sense of "faith" is intended here. Nevertheless, faith becomes the foundation for Christian life. In turn, hope emanates from faith (13:7); but as the lines continue one sees that the point here is to establish the superiority of love, as stated in 12:31b. Interpreters debate whether 13:13 means that (1) faith, hope, and love are and remain valid eternally or (2) faith, hope, and love are now valid, but only love will endure eternally. In either case, one should see the superior and eternal character of love. The supreme characteristic and motivation—now and forever—for Christian life is nothing other than love.

14:1b-40. Practicing the gifts and maintaining orderly worship. This chapter returns to the direct consideration of spiritual gifts that was left off after 12:31a. Paul's general concern is with orderly worship, but there are bends and turns to the argumentation that are hard to follow and highly debated.

At the outset (vv. 1b-5) Paul compares and contrasts only two of the gifts, *tongues* and *prophecy*. His discussion makes clear that so-called TONGUES are unintelligible assertions (glossolalia), not foreign languages. He declares his own strong preference for PROPHECY over tongues. In his consideration of these two gifts Paul informs the readers that those who speak in tongues do not address people but God, and no human understands them because they utter the mysteries of the Spirit; whereas those who prophesy speak to humans for the edification, encouragement, and consolation of their hearers. Paul tells the Corinthians that tongues edify the one speaking and prophecy edifies the whole church. Paul states that he wants all to speak in tongues, but even more he desires that all prophesy. Paul's concern is not so much with the content of tongue-speech and prophecy as with the mode and orientation of these utterances. Paul declares the superior merit of an utterance that is oriented away from one's self to speech, even spiritual speech, that merely serves one's self.

In vv. 6-12 Paul shifts into a diatribe style of disputation, issuing a series of rhetorical questions in various forms that are followed by illustrative analogies and a concluding exhortation. Verse 6 begins with a false first person statement, declaring an irreality to make the point that giving one's self to the practice of glossolalia necessarily precludes one from engaging in sensible, understandable communication. Paul refers to the flute, harp, and trumpet and the muted playing of such instruments to illustrate the unintelligibility and inferiority of speaking in tongues (vv. 7-8). Tongues are no more useful than indistinct music, for one is as good as *speaking into the air* (v. 9).

Paul continues to illustrate his point with a similar analogy indicating the pointlessness of speaking in a foreign language to those who do not understand the language (vv. 10-11). Finally, v. 12 redirects the energies of the Corinthians. Paul calls for them to excel in edification as genuine manifestation of the Spirit. He reiterates his earlier point (see 12:31a) that the Corinthians are to seek the preeminent gifts, not merely the flashy ones. While the point is clear, Paul's phraseology is not, for his sentence could mean either "Seek spiritual gifts that edify the church in order to excel" or "Seek to excel in the spiritual gifts that edify the church." Given the thrust of the general argument against self-directed spiritual practices, the second option is preferable over the first.

Paul continues (vv. 13-19) by explaining his position. He offers an argument against a sheer enthusiasm that would be indistinguishable from ecstasy. In genuine enthusiasm one's mind stays engaged. A Christian caught up in the Spirit does not unplug the mind and feel a lot. Rather, the concern for others, both Christians and non-Christians—named here as "outsiders," or more literally, "the uninitiated"—orients the enthusiast and grounds enthusiasm in sensible reality. Paul reports his own practice of tongues and his clear preference for prophecy. He speaks in tongues and is thankful to God for it, but in church he prefers that which makes clear sense to others. One suspects that Paul must, therefore, have practiced glossolalia privately, though he does not impose such a restriction on the Corinthians' speaking in tongues. Nevertheless, the degree of Paul's preference of prophecy over tongues is clear from the numbers he articulates: five words with the mind are better than ten thousand words in a tongue—odds of two thousand to one. The reason for this preference is that in church prophecy benefits others whereas tongues edify only the self.

A further section of the reflection follows in vv. 20-25 with language and concerns reminiscent of 2:6 and 3:1. Paul calls the Corinthians away from childishness—perhaps meaning a fascination with things that dazzle—to maturity. He literally calls for them to "become perfect" or "complete ones," and in an aside he expresses his desire that they be naive in terms of evil. In v. 21 the apostle cites Isa 28:11-12 as a text on the topic of tongues. The citation is a very loose paraphrase that alters vocabulary, word order, subjects, and verbs alike, as is necessary since the original passage in Isaiah referred to foreign languages, not to glossolalia. Nevertheless, Paul finds in Isaiah a scriptural precedent for his position, and the citation leads into his next statements.

Verses 22-25 are striking. The individual sentences are clear, but the sequence of thought is nevertheless hard to follow. Verse 22 states a principle, claiming to do exegesis of the cited biblical passage ("then" or "thus"; Gk. = ὥστε). From the citation Paul concludes that tongues are a *sign* to unbelievers, not to believers; yet, prophecy speaks to believers, not to unbelievers. The way forward in this application should be clear, but it is not. From this lead, given that the whole church assembles and all speak in tongues and the uninitiated or unbelievers enter, one would expect that the uninitiated would be struck by the *sign* (and moved to believe?); but, instead Paul says that the uninitiated will say that the tongue-speaking believers are raving mad. Furthermore, given that all believers prophesy and the uninitiated enter, one expects that the uninitiated would not perceive; but, instead Paul says the uninitiated will be convicted by all, held accountable by all, and they will worship God and say that God is truly among the believers. Some sense for this strange sequence of statements comes clear if, for Paul, *sign* in v. 22a means "that which is obscure," not that which indicates something. Yet, v. 22b remains cryptic. In any case, Paul is marshaling still another argument for the preferance of prophecy to tongues.

In vv. 26-33a Paul delineates regulations for orderly assembly and worship. He names certain elements of worship: HYMNs, lessons, revelations, tongues, and interpretations. All of these must produce edification. Thus, Paul restricts the practice of tongues to two or three tongue-speakers per assembly. Moreover, he allows tongues only if someone is present who can interpret the tongues, for otherwise glossolalia is unintelligible, useless, and so, not permissible. Similarly, two or three prophets may speak in a single assembly, and curiously some prophecy is recognized to be more urgent than other prophecy. Here, v. 32 is difficult. Paul means either "each prophet controls the spiritual gift he or she possesses" or "one who prophesies is subject to evaluation by other prophets who are present." Given (a) that 12:10 recognizes *discerning the spirits* as an identifiable gift of the Spirit and (b) the emphasis on mind and Spirit in 14:13-19 and (c) the expectation that tongue-speakers can limit their expression to instances when interpreters are present, the first option seems most likely. Most importantly, however, Paul articulates the central theological position that underlies what he has said and will say, namely, *for God is a God not of disorder but of peace.*

No verses cause more difficulty in the late twentieth century than vv. 33b-36. The problems are complex for exegetical and sociological reasons. Thus, some preliminary observations are in order.

First, the phrase *the churches of the saints* in v. 33b is peculiar, for in the context of the undisputed Pauline letters there is no such designation. Rather, churches are referred to as the church(es) of God or Christ and as the church(es) of a region or city. Thus, divine proprietorship and geographical setting are the normal ways of identifying Pauline congregations.

Second, the command to silence in vv. 34-35 seems to contradict the expectation in chap. 11 of women praying and prophesying, albeit they should be veiled.

Third, the verb *to speak* in vv. 34-35 is *not*, as some commentators suggest, equivalent with "to chatter" as an activity distinct from other sensible speech or prayer or prophecy. Through the rest of chap. 14 *to speak* refers to inspired speech (cf. vv. 2, 3, 4, 5, 6, 9, 11, 13, 18, 19, 21, 23, 27, 28, 29, 39).

Fourth, the issue in chap. 11 is somewhat different in focus. There the focus was on "men and women," but here, as v. 35 makes clear, the issue concerns "husbands and wives."

Fifth, at 11:6 one finds that it is "shameful" (αἰσχρόν; NRSV *disgraceful*) for a woman to be shorn, whereas in 14:35 it is *shameful* (αἰσχρόν) for a wife to speak in church.

Sixth, some few and inferior manuscripts transpose vv. 34-35 to a position after 14:40. While the manuscript evidence is not strong, it shows both (a) scribal grappling with the illogical intrusion of these verses in the discussion of worship from the perspective of tongues and prophecy (two specific forms of verbal expression) and (b) the scribal recognition of a naturally smoother transition from 14:33a to 14:36.

Seventh, a very similar position is articulated in 1 Tim 2:11-12.

What can be made of the evidence? Because of the unusual character of the language and the textual problems associated with these verses, a strong case can be mounted that this section of the letter is an interpolation, perhaps of an early scribe's marginal gloss. Or, the shift of focus from men and women to husbands and wives may provide a key, indicating that

Paul is advocating the preservation of traditional Jewish patterns of family relations. This understanding is problematic since Paul is writing to Corinth, which is not a Semitic social context. Or, the speaking of the wives to which these verses refer may be simply a specific instance of enthusiasm that amounts to no more than the importing of pagan ecstasy into the context of Christian worship, so that Paul's advice applies only to a single situation and is not meant to be followed elsewhere. Still other solutions, none entirely gratifying, are offered by various interpreters. The lack of specific information about the situation(s) Paul faced in Corinth may make it impossible for later readers of the letter to understand these lines—even if they do come from Paul. Of late, however, the increasing tendency among both conservative and radical scholars is to regard the verses as an interpolation into Paul's original text.

In any case, the fact that the argument in v. 33b and v. 36 is based purely on custom, not on revelation or a word of the Lord, gives the statements a restricted force. Moreover, it is astounding that these verses (coupled with 1 Timothy 2) became the church's norm when one finds in 11:11-12, Gal 3:28, and in the frequent mention of prominent Christian women ministers in Paul's letters both declarations and assumptions about women taking active roles of leadership in the life of the church.

Finally, in vv. 37-40 Paul boldly confronts the Corinthians. He states a criterion that puts the burden of proof on anyone wishing to disagree. Agreement, by contrast, would verify one as a prophet or a spiritual one. It is not clear how Paul relates his teaching to a *command of the Lord*, although the point of discussion is concerned with the issue of prophecy, not with the immediately preceding matter of wives speaking in church (see v. 39). The passive form *is not to be recognized* in v. 38 suggests God's involvement in the life of the church. Ultimately tongues are permissible but prophecy is preferable and all is to be decent and orderly. Such are God's ways, and such is God's will.

The Truth of the Resurrection, 15:1-58

The letter moves toward its conclusion with the long, crucial discussion of the resurrection in chap. 15. In general this section is a long defense of the truth of the resurrection and its intrinsic importance for all of Christian belief and life.

15:1-11. Back to the basics. Paul takes the Corinthians back to the basics, to the very foundation of their faith. In vv. 1-2 he identifies what follows in vv. 3-11 as *the good news that I proclaimed to you*, and he qualifies this gospel with the phrases *which you in turn received, in which also you stand*/have stood, and *through which also you are being saved*. Then, he recognizes the troubling possibility that the Corinthians may have believed *in vain*. It is a moot point whether Paul refers to a reality or an irreality when he says the Corinthians may have believed *in vain*.

Verses 3-8 communicate the foundational content of the teaching of Paul in Corinth. Interpreters generally recognize that in these verses there are one or two early Christian confessional formulae to which Paul adds his own commentary. When the apostle says he delivered this tradition to the Corinthians *as of first importance* (ἐν πρώτοις), he may mean either that he delivered this teaching logically "above all" or temporally "in the first instance." The lines, in either case, state Paul's starting point.

Paul recalls the substance of his primary teaching in a complex that finds its structure in a series of "that" (ὅτι) clauses: *that Christ died . . . that he was buried . . . that he was raised . . . that he appeared*. These phrases form the backbone of the confessional material in vv. 3-5, and there is additional information both embedded in this basic framework and attached to it in vv. 6-8. Thus, some interpreters suggest perhaps two "competitive" confessions are amalgamated and adapted—although no polemical note occurs in the lines and the phrase *that he appeared* is merely extended through the ensuing series of *he appeared . . . then he appeared* statements in vv. 6-8.

Of interest and importance is the material that is embedded in vv. 3-5. First, in v. 3 one learns of Christ's vicarious, sacrificial, atoning death (*for our sins*) that occurred as part of God's will and work (*in accordance with the scriptures*). In v. 4 one learns of the timing of Jesus' resurrection (*on the third day*), which also occurred as part of God's will and work (*in accordance with the scriptures*); and in v. 5 one learns of the initial appearance to *Cephas*, a partial explanation of the prominence of PETER in the life of the early church. One also learns of the subsequent appearance to *the twelve*, an odd note since for a time after the demise of Judas Iscariot there were only eleven disciples in the inner group. Nevertheless, one sees the early presence and importance of *the twelve*. Thus, one finds here evidence of the early interpretation of Jesus' death and resurrection and an indication of the early church's recognition of authorizing appearances that ac-

tually identified and formed the structures of the church.

The additional information in vv. 6-8 reports the appearance to *five hundred [believers] at one time* and declares that most of them were *still alive* at the time Paul wrote. These lines both document the reality of the appearances by taking them out of the realm of private hallucination and register the point that even those who saw the risen Lord die. Moreover, the mention of JAMES (the brother of the Lord) recognizes and perhaps explains his prominence in the early church; indeed, the remark may explain his being a believer since he was not a disciple of Jesus. Commentators remark, "James' new status as a believer offers an indirect proof that there was nothing he could remember from his acquaintance with Jesus in the family that would make such belief impossible" (Orr and Walther 1976, 322). But, the facts of James' coming to leadership in the early church cut two ways: That *James* did not believe before and without this appearance is a direct proof that there was nothing he knew from the family or from his acquaintance with Jesus that compelled him to believe in Jesus!

The mention in v. 7 of the appearance to *all the apostles* seems to name a central criterion, perhaps *the* criterion, for apostleship from Paul's perspective. Then, v. 8 tells of the final appearance of the risen Lord, this one to Paul. This appearance occurred after the appearances to the others, but at the time of Paul's writing to Corinth, this last appearance had taken place about twenty years earlier. Paul's language is that of violent metaphor. He literally says he was born as of an abortion. Thus, he aims at communicating the abnormal manner in which he became an apostle.

In turn, vv. 9-11 explicate Paul's point so that there is no need to speculate about the sense of his metaphorical language. Paul tells of his behavior that should have disqualified him as an apostle. Then, he grounds the reality of his calling in the reality of God's transforming grace. The degree of the power of God's grace is clear in that Paul was not merely redirected, so that his own zeal took new directions; rather, God's grace grasped his life and made it into something new and different. Throughout this section, Christ's death, burial, resurrection, and appearances are taken in their full soteriological force; they are not reported as isolated propositions.

15:12-19. Controversy in Corinth. These verses move from the foundational issues to a controversy in the Corinthian church, and the verses declare in a tough-minded logic the invalidity of the Corinthians' position. The problem is that some of the Corinthians said *there is no resurrection of the dead*. Perhaps they meant (1) there is no resurrection at all, or (2) they advocated "immortality" rather than "resurrection," or (3) they denied a future resurrection and claimed a fully realized this-worldly resurrection (as in 2 Thess 2:1-2 and 2 Tim 2:17-18). Option two is not likely given the full discussion by Paul. Option one makes the plainest sense of the words; but given the Corinthians' penchant for enthusiasm, sacramentalism, and the futuristic christocentric argument that follows in this chapter, option three may be preferable.

This whole section resists viewing Christ's resurrection in isolation as a mythic theme or as an eternal timeless truth. Paul's argument exposes the errors of the Corinthians' denial of a future resurrection of the dead. Paul argues a tight logical loop: *Christ is raised* > the gospel is preached > the Corinthians have faith > the dead in Christ are raised > *Christ is raised*. To falsify one element of this loop is to invalidate the whole, and to invalidate the loop exposes the testimony of the apostles as false testimony about God. If, moreover, the testimony about God's gracious saving work is false, then, the dead are lost and Christians have no hope, but are to be pitied as deluded.

15:20-28. Christ, the resurrection, and the end. These verses form a remarkably rich section of Paul's reflections and teachings about resurrection (see RESURRECTION IN THE NT). One encounters quotations of and allusions to several passages from the LXX, and Paul employs other traditional materials in formulating his argument. Despite the seemingly straightforward nature of the lines, they are subtle. In vv. 20-22 Christ is presented as the one through whom there is a resurrection of the dead, but one should notice that *all will be made alive in Christ* (emphasis added). Resurrection is reality in Christ, but the resurrection of others—dead or living—is cast as a future phenomenon. Moreover, commentators debate who the *all* of v. 22 are—the "all" who die in Adam certainly refers to all humanity; but does *all* [who] *will be made alive in Christ* indicate all humans or merely all believers? The matter cannot be settled simply from the words in these verses or even from examining these lines in the context of the entirety of 1 Corinthians. Paul's remarks in 1 Thess 4:13-18, 5:1-11, Phil 2:5-11, and Rom 9–11 are critical parallels for interpretation.

Verses 23-28 delineate the events of the end, though Paul is probably not concerned here with a strict chronological ordering. Rather, all Paul's teaching follows from Christ's having been raised by God. In rapid succession these lines tell of the PAROUSIA (Christ's so-called second coming), the destruction of the forces set in opposition to Christ, Christ's delivery of the kingdom to God, Christ's reign that is now underway, and death as the last enemy of Christ. The implication of Paul's scenario is that Christians necessarily face death as an inevitable foe until Christ's achieves the end. Though Christ reigns and defeats his foes, including death, one should not miss the thoroughly theological cast of Paul's teaching. As v. 27 makes clear, God and God's power are active in Christ's accomplishing that good of which Paul tells and even predicts. Finally, v. 28 clarifies the ultimate purposes of God's power at work in Christ: *so that God may be all in all!*

15:29-34. Arguments against misunderstanding. Paul offers another set of arguments against the Corinthians' denial of resurrection. He makes statements and asks questions in a loose sequence, with all that he says aimed to refute and reverse the Corinthians' position. In form and thrust the argument is similar to vv. 12-19.

Through rhetorical questions Paul attempts to bring the thinking of the Corinthians into proper line. First, in v. 29 he uses two questions about a practice of the Corinthians to expose the inconsistency between their activities and the denial of the resurrection. Exactly what Paul means by referring to people *who receive baptism on behalf of the dead* is not clear. Dozens of theories have been proposed, and none is fully satisfactory. Whatever Paul means we should (1) note that he does not criticize or deny the practice but uses it to score his point: The dead will rise; and (2) resist any interpretation that bases its understanding on either the idea of necrobaptism or a doctrine of baptismal regeneration, for elsewhere Paul demonstrates no such thinking (compare 1 Cor 1 and Rom 6).

Verses 30-31 pose another question: Why would Paul jeopardize himself for a hopeless lie? He would not, but he does risk his very life for the sake of calling the Corinthians and others to believe the gospel truth of Jesus Christ's death and resurrection. Thus, the resurrection is no lie. In turn, v. 32 uses another question to illustrate the serious degree of Paul's perils in ministry. One cannot know whether Paul's reference to fighting with beasts is literally true or hyperbolically metaphorical, although the difficult phrase *with merely human hopes* (κατὰ ἄνθρωπον) may signal the metaphorical nature of the remark. Nevertheless, even if he speaks in picture language Paul means to identify the seriousness of the threat he faced. Paul cites Isa 22:1-3b to establish the necessity of the truth that the dead are raised. The apostle's remarks have been labeled "opportunistic," but when read in their specific context the statements are in no way unscrupulous.

Paul quotes a well-known Greek proverb from the poet Menander in v. 33 to make the point that association with those in Corinth who deny the resurrection presents a danger to those forming such affiliations. This proverb leads into a blunt upbraiding in v. 34. The call to sobriety is plain enough, and such language was standard rhetoric for urgent eschatological exhortations in early Christianity; literally Paul says, "Sober up righteously and by all means don't sin!" He avers that some have an active lack of knowledge about God (ἀγνωσία, usually translated "no knowledge"). There is a difference between ignorance that actively disregards the truth and naivete that is simply as yet uninformed.

15:35-49. Pondering the reality of resurrection. Paul offers another complicated segment of his argument that quotes the LXX; alludes to stories from Genesis; and develops analogies related to seed, fleshes, body and glory, and Adam. The lines open in the style of a diatribe with a dialogical argument. Verse 35 states the question from Paul's supposed opponent, and v. 36 issues the first, scoffing reply that leads into an analogy on seed. Paul's point becomes clear in v. 38: God is sovereign and supreme in relation to all creation.

This argument in v. 38b sets up the analogies following in vv. 39-41, which themselves lead to the summary application of all the analogies in vv. 42-44. Paul's point is that the resurrection or "spiritual" body is a kind of its own, unique as are other bodies; but the spiritual body is like all other bodies in that it is given by God (v. 38a).

The series of arguments concludes with a discussion using Adam typology (vv. 45-49). Paul uses this new style of reasoning and this fresh illustration to underscore three items: (1) The spiritual body will be distinctive; (2) God gives the spiritual body; and (3) the resurrected *will* have/be/get this body in the future as they are transformed by God from being like Adam to being like the risen Christ.

15:50-58. Concluding comments. Verse 50 introduces a new idea or line into the reflection. Naturally, from Paul's statement that *flesh and blood cannot inherit the kingdom of God*, one would ask, "Then how?" Paul assumes that unstated question and uses the following lines to answer the query.

The anticipated transformation of *flesh and blood* into the God-given spiritual body is *a mystery*. This mystery is not known by reason but, if at all, by God's revelation of this truth. Thus, Paul scores the point that the transformation of earthly existence into spiritual reality is purely God's work. Paul writes in traditional terms and language of divine transformation, using mysterious images designed to inspire awe and confidence. He continues by extending his reasoning in a didactic fashion. Verse 53 gives a prophecy that *will* be fulfilled. Paul offers a prooftext for his point from Isa 25:8, and to amplify his position Paul adds the words *in victory* to Isaiah's *death has been swallowed up*. The victory is God's, through Christ, and this divine victory has implications for Christian hope and life (v. 54). Paul continues in v. 55 with a quotation from Hos 13:14, and again he adapts it to suit the context. Both quotations from the LXX relate to the statement made earlier in 15:26.

Verse 56 is Paul's own exegesis of the quotations from the prophets, as is clear from the mention of "law" at the end of the line. Paul continues with a doxological declaration of the meaning of all that he has written (v. 57). Then, v. 58 builds a final admonition (*Therefore*) on the tradition. This statement is not a mere work ethic, but an assurance of the Lord's preserving of vital Christian efforts (cf. 3:10-15). Thus, Paul argues for the reality of resurrection, basing his argument on God's work in Christ and calling for the Corinthians to embrace his teaching as the basis for their future hope and current living.

Parenesis, 16:1-18

Chapter 16 concludes the letter, offering a parting report about the apostle's personal appointment book and expressing his ultimate regard for the church in Corinth.

Future plans, 16:1-12

16:1-4. The collection. Paul may or may not be responding to an inquiry at this point, but the words *Now concerning* identify a topic that was likely brought to Paul's attention by the letter or the delegates from Corinth. Paul moves to discuss the collection he was assembling for the poor saints in Jerusalem. One sees that giving in the church had not yet been systematized. There was no standard timetable and there was no formula for how much one should give. Tithing apparently was not yet an idea in the church. Paul does, however, say that he did not wish to do fund-raising when he arrived in Corinth. Moreover, he wanted the giving to be done naturally and willingly, so that generosity was more charismatic than duty-bound. Similarly, Paul's plans for delivering the collection were open to development or to the guidance of the Spirit.

16:5-9. Paul's travel plans. Paul's travel plans seem cryptic to twentieth-century readers, but they are related to the seasonal conditions of travel in the first-century Mediterranean world. Paul intended to spend the winter, the season when travel was impossible, in Corinth; then, when spring came and travel was possible he could go either East or West as the Spirit directed. Paul refers to his stay in Ephesus, indicating success and opposition; yet, he sees that the end of that stay is at hand. In speaking of his work in Ephesus, Paul says, *a wide door for effective work has opened to me.* The form of the statement shows that Paul understood both opportunities and successes in ministry to be the results of God's own involvement in his life and work.

16:10-12. Mentioning fellow workers. Paul refers to Timothy and Apollos as he moves toward the end of his letter. Timothy was apparently working on or was about to work on some commission, probably from Paul, and apparently the Corinthians requested Apollos to come to them. But, Paul says this development (literally) "was not the will." Whose will, Apollos's or God's? The sentence is ambiguous. In any case, Paul and Apollos could and did discuss the matter, plainly disagreed with each other, but continued to relate without friction.

Principles for Life, 16:13-14

These two verses are a bit of stock parenesis. The tone is traditional and eschatological. The Corinthians are admonished to *watch.* They are told to stand courageously "in their faith"—the foundation of their existence—and they are to do everything *in love*—the chief criterion for all Christian living (see chap. 13).

Saluting Special Persons, 16:15-18

Paul passes out praise for the prominent Christian workers in Corinth. The *household of Stephanas* (see STEPHANAS) especially shows spiritual gifts and should be rightfully acknowledged, not because of status, but because of the presence and the power of the Lord at work in their lives. Moreover, the Corinthians who visited Paul in Ephesus (*Stephanas and Fortunatus and Achaicus*) are praised for representing the Corinthians and bringing Paul encouragement on the mission field. Paul declares that these persons who have served faithfully are worthy of recognition.

Closing, 16:19-24

Paul passes greetings in vv. 19-24. He mentions *the churches of Asia*, conceiving the distinct assemblies in a region (see ASIA) as a network of congregations. *Aquila and Prisca* (see PRISCILLA AND AQUILA) send greetings through Paul to the Corinthians. Paul offers a generally greeting, and, then, he mentions an enigmatic form of greeting, the *holy kiss.* Though many have guessed what this *holy kiss* was, no one really knows.

The last lines are Paul's autograph. A scribe had written for Paul to this point, but now Paul takes pen in hand and gives the letter a truly personal touch. As he writes he couples a curse (ἀνάθεμα) on those who oppose the Lord with an eschatological cry for the Lord to come (μαράνα θά), a cry that shows the proper attitude toward the Lord. Although the anathema is in good Greek and the eschatological call is Aramaic transliterated into Greek, the words form a sound pair that contrast spiritual discord and spiritual concord. The last line of the letter is remarkable, for Paul ends with an unusual passing of his love to all the Corinthians in Christ Jesus.

Works Cited

Conzelmann, Hans. 1975. *1 Corinthians.* Herm.

Orr, William F., and James Arthur Walther. 1976. *1 Corinthians.* AncB.

Second Corinthians

W. Hulitt Gloer

Introduction

While no Pauline Letter demands more from its readers, none rewards its readers more fully than 2 Corinthians. Forged in the crucible of controversy, it has been called the "paradise and the despair of the commentator" (Martin 1986, x). Writing with an unmistakable intensity and urgency, Paul sets before his readers an unusually vivid picture of himself in this most personal of all his letters. At the same time he sets before us a most powerful portrayal of the nature of the gospel and the lifestyle of all who would be its ministers. In 2 Corinthians we discover the essence of what Paul understood the gospel and the nature of ministry to be.

First-Century Corinth

First-century CORINTH was a teeming urban center of relatively recent vintage. Once the chief city of the Achaian League, it had been destroyed by the Romans in 146 B.C.E. Recognizing its strategic military and commercial significance, Julius Caesar refounded the city in 44 B.C.E. and populated it with Roman freedmen. Beginning in 27 B.C.E. it functioned as the capital of the Roman province of ACHAIA. Archeological and literary evidence suggests that the city grew rapidly during the first century and was home to tens of thousands by the time of Paul's arrival.

Located on a narrow isthmus connecting the Peloponnesus with the mainland of Greece and separating the Gulf of Corinth and the Saronic Gulf, Corinth was situated at the crossroads of trade and travel. It controlled all trade and travel between the Peloponnesus and the mainland, and with its two harbors, one leading to Asia (Cenchreae) and one leading to Italy (Lechaeum), it controlled the safest and most direct trade route between Italy and ASIA.

As a result of its location, the city played host to tradespeople from all over the world and grew rich from taxes levied on the movement of goods it supervised and controlled. Its coffers were further lined as a result of banking, the production of bronze, an active terra-cotta industry, and the production of pigments, lamps, and small bone implements. In addition to all this, every two years Corinth played host to the Isthmian games, which brought to it people from all over the Mediterranean world.

Corinth was a microcosm of first-century religious life. Pagan cults of every stripe were represented: Apollo, Athena, Poseidon, Hera, Heracles, Jupiter Capitolinus, Asklepius, Isis, and Serapis. The city was especially well known as a center for the worship of Aphrodite whose temple stood high above the city atop the Acrocorinth, and throughout the Roman world the mention of Corinth elicited images of sexual license and excess. Philosophers of all persuasions plied its streets, and the presence of a Jewish colony is well attested. Paul's proclamation of the gospel added yet another ingredient to this diverse religious mix.

The Corinthian Church

PAUL founded the Corinthian church during his initial eighteen-month visit to the city during his second missionary journey (Acts 18:1-18). The fact that this visit coincides in part with the term of the Roman governor GALLIO (who ruled July 51–June 52 C.E.) suggests that Paul probably first arrived in Corinth early in 50 C.E.. During his stay he preached Christ crucified (1 Cor 2:1-2), and his preaching was accompanied by "a demonstration of the Spirit and of power" (1 Cor 2:4; cf. 2 Cor 12:12). While he began his ministry in the SYNAGOGUE, opposition from the Jews eventually compelled Paul to move next door to the home of Titius Justus. An effort on the part of the Jews to bring charges against Paul for preaching an unlawful religion was rejected by Gallio, after which Paul stayed in Corinth for "many days" continuing his ministry.

While the church was born as a result of Paul's preaching in the local synagogue, it is likely that its membership was made up of both Jews and gentiles (1 Cor 1:22-24). Sociologically the membership seems to have been reflective of a cross section of the urban society from which it was drawn. Some of its members represent positions of high social standing: Crispus (Acts 18:8; 1 Cor 1:14) was a synagogue ruler who had a house; SOSTHENES (Acts 18:17; 1 Cor 1:1) was a synagogue ruler; Erastus (Rom 16:23) was the city treasurer; GAIUS (Rom 16:23; 1 Cor 1:14) had a house large enough to accommodate the whole church. Many, perhaps most of its members, however, did not enjoy such a position in their society and seem to have been drawn from the lower classes (1 Cor 1:26-29).

Paul's Continuing Ministry to the Corinthians

While the NT contains two Corinthian letters, a careful reading of the CORINTHIAN CORRESPONDENCE suggests that Paul may have written as many as five letters to the church in Corinth. The following scenario, based on the Corinthian correspondence and the Acts narrative, details Paul's continuing ministry to the church after his initial visit and the place of the letters in that ministry.

Leaving Corinth after the founding of the church and an eighteen-month ministry there, Paul returned to JERUSALEM by way of EPHESUS and then proceeded to ANTIOCH. After a brief stay in Antioch he returned to Ephesus for an extended ministry of two and one-half years from autumn of 52 to spring of 55 (Acts 18:18ff.). While in Ephesus he wrote his first letter to the Corinthians urging them not to associate with Christians who were immoral, greedy, idolaters, slanderers, drunkards, or swindlers. This letter, which we will call *Corinthians A*, is the "previous" letter mentioned in 1 Cor 5:9.

Subsequently, Paul learned from visitors from Corinth of factiousness in the church (1 Cor 1:11), and received a letter from the Corinthians asking for advice and counsel regarding a number of issues (1 Cor 7:1ff.). He responded to the oral report and the letter by writing *Corinthians B* (our 1 Corinthians, 54 C.E.). Paul sent TIMOTHY on a special mission to Corinth (1 Cor 4:17; 16:10), and Timothy returned with news of a crisis fomented by a ringleader who had launched a personal attack on Paul (2 Cor 2:5-11; 7:8-13). Paul made a *painful visit* to Corinth to deal with the crisis (2 Cor 2:1). He was humiliated and returned to Ephesus (spring 55) where he wrote a "tearful" or "severe" letter (*Corinthians C*) calling on the Corinthians to

take action against the one who had offended him thereby demonstrating their influence in the matter and their affection for him (2 Cor 2:3-4; 7:8, 12). He sent this letter (which is either lost or partially preserved in 2 Cor 10–13) with TITUS (summer 55).

Anxious to learn of the Corinthian's response to his "severe letter," Paul left Ephesus hoping to meet the returning Titus in Troas. Though he found an "open door" for ministry there, when Titus did not appear, anxiety prompted Paul to leave for MACEDONIA in hopes of intercepting Titus there (2 Cor 2:12-13).

Upon meeting Titus in Macedonia and learning that the crisis was over and the rebellion quelled (2 Cor 7:6-16), Paul wrote *Corinthians D* (our 2 Corinthians) either in part (chaps. 1–9) or, less likely, in its entirety (in which case chaps. 10–13 are aimed at clearing up any remaining pockets of resistance) and sent it from Macedonia with Titus and two other brothers (2 Cor 8:16–9:5; fall 55).

Sometime later Paul learned of a renewed crisis in Corinth prompted by the arrival of "false apostles" who challenged his authority and introduced a rival teaching (2 Cor 10:10; 11:27; 12:6-7). He then wrote *Corinthians E* (2 Cor 10–13) to answer the accusations of the *false apostles* (2 Cor 11:13), dispel suspicions, and warn the Corinthians of a planned third visit when he would demonstrate his authority in no uncertain terms (2 Cor 12:14; 13:1-4, 10; 56 C.E.). This third visit is probably reflected in Acts 20:2-3.

Paul's Opponents in 2 Corinthians

Paul's polemic in 2 Corinthians is directed at a group he refers to as *super-apostles* (11:5; 12:11), *false apostles, deceitful workers* (11:13), ministers of Satan in disguise (11:14-15), *fools* (11:19), and *peddlers* of the word (2:17) who preach a *different gospel* about *another Jesus* that results in a *different spirit* (11:4). While he gives no systematic description of their teaching and practice, careful reading suggests they are outsiders (11:4) who have invaded Paul's mission field attempting to take credit for what he has done (10:13-18). Arriving with *letters of recommendation* (3:1), they claim to have a special relationship with Christ (10:7), a superior apostolate (11:5; 12:11), superior knowledge (11:6), and superior rhetorical abilities (11:6; 10:10). Flaunting their Hebrew pedigree (11:22), they refer to themselves as *ministers of righteousness* (11:15) and *of Christ* (11:23) who carry out their mission on the same basis as Paul (11:12). They place great significance in *visions and revelations*

(12:1), and emphasize the importance of *signs and wonders* as the true signs of apostleship (12:11-13; 5:12).

These *super-apostles* criticize Paul, charging that he acts in a "worldly manner" (10:2), that Christ does not speak through him (12:3, 19), that he does not perform the SIGNS AND WONDERS that are the true signs of an apostle (12:12), that he lacks a commanding presence (10:9-10), is unimpressive as a speaker (10:10; 11:6), and has an inferior knowledge (11:6). Furthermore, they suggest that Paul is bold when absent but that this boldness disappears when they are face to face (10:1), that his unwillingness to receive support from the Corinthians indicates a lack of love for them (11:7-11), and that he has been duplicitous with regard to his travel plans (1:17ff.) and the Jerusalem collection (12:14-18).

Efforts to identify these opponents have focused in three basic directions. While some have identified them as Judaizers, the absence of the kind of polemic found in Galatians makes such an identification questionable. Others have identified them as Gnostics and while they exhibit some traits characteristic of later GNOSTICISM, these traits are also common to Hellenistic thought in general, including Hellenistic JUDAISM. It is probably best to see them as Jewish-Christian propagandists who have been influenced by the HELLENISTIC WORLD and have incorporated into their own understanding of apostleship certain Hellenistic ideas such as a stress on rhetorical skills and a fascination with signs and wonders, visions and revelations.

In essence, there are two fundamental differences between Paul and his opponents in Corinth. The first relates to the nature of the GOSPEL itself. From Paul's perspective, his opponents preach *a different gospel* presenting a different Jesus by which *a different spirit* is received (11:4). Thus, the very nature of the gospel is at stake in the controversy reflected here.

The second difference relates to the nature of apostleship and the criteria by which it is evaluated. Paul's opponents present a triumphalist perspective in which the apostle is authenticated by his or her impressive bearing, commanding presence, eloquent speech, the performance of signs and wonders, the reception of visions and revelations, and displays of apostolic power. In such a view there is no place for weakness and suffering.

Paul, on the other hand, presents a perspective in which it is precisely in our weakness and suffering that the power of God is made manifest for all to see, in

which the true apostolic ministry is recognized by its fruits (3:2-3), and in which one shares in Christ's sufferings (4:8-12; 11:23-28). Those who preach the gospel of Christ crucified as Lord will exemplify in their ministry both the weakness in which Christ was crucified and the power exercised by Christ as risen Lord (4:7-12; 12:9-10; 13:3-4).

Thus, while in no way denying the importance of power and authority, Paul understands that these do not inhere in the apostle. They depend wholly on the activity of God who chooses to allow his power to rest upon the servant in his/her weakness and thereby to manifest that power (12:9-10). Such a perspective set Paul in direct opposition to the cultural conventions of his day, conventions that undergirded his opponents' view and must have made that view seem reasonable and very attractive to the Corinthians.

Authenticity and Integrity

The authenticity of 2 Corinthians has never been seriously questioned. The internal evidence supporting Pauline authorship is so strong that it is accepted without debate. The writer claims to be Paul and the letter is unmistakably Pauline in vocabulary, style, tone, and character.

The integrity of 2 Corinthians, however, has been the subject of much debate especially with regard to the relationship between chaps. 1–9 and 10–13. Because of the marked difference in tone that characterizes these two sections, there is widespread consensus that these two sections of our canonical 2 Corinthians represent two separate letters. Chapters 1–9 are confident, conciliatory, and full of praise for the Corinthians. They appear to be a response to a crisis resolved, a crisis precipitated by the actions of an individual. Chapters 10–13, on the other hand, are characterized by anxious pleading, defensiveness, and sharp attacks on rival apostles who are undermining Paul's ministry in Corinth. In short, chaps. 10–13 reflect a crisis brought about by a group of intruders referred to as *false apostles* that is far from being resolved, and the scathing rhetoric of these chapter is quite unexpected after the tactful, carefully reasoned remarks of chaps. 1–9.

Proponents of the unity of the letter (see, e.g., Hughes) point to the fact that there is no manuscript evidence that any part of our canonical 2 Corinthians ever circulated independently or as a part of another letter. They argue that the supposed differences between chaps. 1–9 and chaps. 10–13 are overdrawn and can be explained without resorting to a partition theory. After writing chaps. 1–9 Paul received distressing news of a deteriorating situation in Corinth and then penned chaps. 10–13 before sending chaps. 1–9, or chaps. 10–13 are addressed to a recalcitrant minority in Corinth, or the dramatic difference in tone can be attributed to the ups and downs of the apostles' mercurial temperament.

Proponents of a two-letter theory fall into two camps. On the one hand there are those who argue that chaps. 10–13 are to be identified with the "tearful" or severe letter mentioned in 2 Cor 2:3-4, 9, and 7:8, 12 which was written before chaps. 1–9 (see, e.g., Talbert). Those who hold this view suggest that certain things in chaps. 10–13 seem to precede chaps. 1–9: 12:11 precedes 3:1 and 5:12; 13:2 precedes 1:23; 13:10 precedes 2:3, 4, 9; 10:6 precedes 2:9 and 7:15. Furthermore, in 3:1 and 5:12 Paul speaks of commending himself *again* suggesting that he is thinking of his boasting in chaps. 10–13, and his announcement in 10:16 that he is looking forward to preaching *in lands beyond you* makes more sense if he is writing from Ephesus than from Macedonia from which he writes chaps. 1–9.

Others argue that the identification of chaps. 10–13 with the "tearful" or severe letter is too problematic. First, chaps. 10–13 make no reference to the one thing that we are certain must have been in the "tearful" letter, namely, the demand that a certain offender be punished (2:5-6; 7:12). Second, chaps. 10–13 promise an imminent visit and are written so as to make the impending visit more productive (10:2; 12:14; 13:1-2), but the "tearful" letter was sent so that Paul would not have to make a painful personal visit (1:23; 2:1). Third, when Paul describes what the "tearful" letter has achieved (7:5-12) there is no mention of the subject that dominates chaps. 10–13, the threat to the Corinthians' faith and to Paul's apostleship posed by the false apostles. Fourth, 12:18 assumes that Titus has made at least one visit to Corinth to assist in the collection, thus presupposing 8:6a or 8:16-19. Fifth, Paul is aware in chaps. 10–13 of suspicions that he is collecting money for the Jerusalem church under false pretenses (12:14-18) and that there are rumors of deceit and fraud (14:16-17), yet there is no suggestion of such suspicions in chaps. 8 and 9, but rather a confidence that the process he is engaged in will prevent any such suspicions from arising (8:20).

Factors such as these have led to an emerging consensus among recent commentators that chaps.

10–13 represent a separate letter written sometime after chaps. 1–9 when Paul had received news of another crisis in Corinth (Barrett, Bruce, Danker, Furnish, Kruse, Martin). The two letters probably became joined early in the manuscript tradition by an editor who removed the closing of one and the opening of the other in a kind of redactional activity employed by editors of other ancient letters. This is the view adopted in this commentary.

Noting a certain redundancy in Paul's discussion of the collection in chaps. 8 and 9, Paul's use of Greek particles in 9:1 (*peri men gar* similar to the *peri de* used to introduce new topics in 1 Corinthians), the fact that 9:2 is addressed to *Achaia* rather than Corinth, and the different reasons given for the sending of *the brothers* in 8:20 and 9:3-5, some have argued that these two chapters do not belong together and that chap. 9 represents a separate letter. However, given that Paul is not above redundancy, that there is no evidence that *peri men gar* would be recognized as a formal introduction, that 1:1 indicates the letter is also addressed to the churches of Achaia, and that the two reasons given for the sending of *the brothers* are not incompatible, it seems best to see chaps. 8 and 9 as a single, integrated treatment of the collection. Furthermore, when Paul mentions *the brothers* in 9:3, 5 he assumes his readers know about whom he speaks, yet they are only identified in 8:6, 16ff.

Noting a somewhat abrupt transition and a seeming lack of thematic continuity between chap. 7 and Paul's introduction of the collection in chap. 8, and pointing out that while in chap. 7 Titus has just returned from Corinth and in chap. 8 he is preparing to leave for Corinth, some have argued that chap. 8 does not go with chap. 7. Careful reading of the text, however, reveals that the two chapters are linked by the repetition of key terms (earnestness/zeal [*spoudē*], 8:7, 11 and 7:11, and boasting [*kauchēseōs*], 8:24 and 7:14), and an emphasis on Paul's love for the Corinthians and his request for their affection in return (6:11-13; 7:2; 8:7-8). The allusions to Titus are understandable if chaps. 1–9 were written after Titus's return from Corinth with good news and in preparation for his upcoming trip to Corinth in connection with the collection. This commentary assumes that chaps. 8 and 9 stand together with chaps. 1–7.

Some have argued that 2:14–7:4 constitutes an interpolation because the lengthy defense of Paul's apostleship that is contained in these verses seems to interrupt the flow of thought between 2:13 and 7:5.

While in 2:12-13 Paul is discussing his travel plans with regard to Corinth, in 2:14 he launches into a lengthy discourse concerning apostleship that continues until 7:4. In 7:5 he returns to the subject of his travel plans. However, Paul's references to *Macedonia* in 2:13 and 7:5 would be unduly repetitive if they stood side by side. Furthermore, there is a strong verbal linkage between 7:4 and 7:5-7 as three of the words employed in 7:4 are repeated in some form in 7:5-7 (*paraklēsis, chara/charēnai, thlipsis/thlibomenoi*). There is thematic continuity as well as the idea of comfort in affliction found in both 1:1–2:13, and 7:5-16 runs like a thread through 2:14–7:4. We shall assume, therefore, that chaps. 1–7 are a unity consisting of an apology (2:14–7:4) framed by two sections of itinerary (1:18–2:13 and 7:5-16).

Finally, much attention has also been focused on 6:14–7:1. It has been argued that Paul's admonition against being mismated with immoral and idolatrous pagans can be seen as a self-contained unit that interrupts the flow of thought of the surrounding context. Furthermore, when these verses are removed, 6:13 joins easily with 7:2. Thus, these verses have been seen as an interpolation. Some have held that these verses represent a fragment of the lost letter to the Corinthians mentioned in 1 Cor 5:9 in which Paul had charged them not to associate with Christians who were living an immoral lifestyle.

Noting the presence of eight key words not found elsewhere in the NT and the presence of certain elements that resemble the language and thought of Qumran (the dualistic antitheses, the reference to Beliar, the idea of community as a temple, the conflation of OT citations, and the general emphasis on separation), others have argued that the passage is a non-Pauline fragment that has been incorporated into the text by a later editor.

While these verses contain features characteristic of Qumran, these features were not peculiar to Qumran. Furthermore, Paul is perfectly capable of digressing and these verses may represent an intentional digression (known in classical rhetoric as an apostrophe). In this case while pleading for a mutual openheartedness Paul reflects that the reason for the lack of openheartedness among the Corinthians lies in their unwillingness to break with idolatrous associations as he had charged them to do in 1 Cor 10:14ff. ("Therefore, my beloved, flee from idolatry . . . ").

Literary Form

Our canonical 2 Corinthians falls naturally into four sections after the pattern of a typical first-century letter. A *salutation* in which Paul includes a brief self-description (1:1-2) is followed by a *thanksgiving* that functions to introduce the main theme(s) and express Paul's perspective on the theme while inviting the readers to share in that perspective (1:3-11). The *body* of the letter follows and falls into three main sections. In 1:12–7:16 Paul defines the nature of his ministry. In 8:1–9:15 he challenges the Corinthians to complete their participation in the collection for the saints in Jerusalem. In 10:1–13:10 Paul defends his ministry in response to the criticisms of *super-apostles* who are seeking to undermine his authority. Finally, the *closing* of the letter consists of final exhortations and greetings followed by a benediction (13:11-13).

For Further Study

In the *Mercer Dictionary of the Bible*: ACHAIA; APOSTLE/APOSTLESHIP; CORINTH; CORINTHIAN CORRESPONDENCE; EPISTLE/LETTER; GNOSTICISM; HELLENISTIC WORLD; MACEDONIA; OPPONENTS OF PAUL; ROMAN EMPIRE; SATAN IN THE NT; SUFFERING IN THE NT.

In other sources: W. Baird, *1 Corinthians/2 Corinthians*; C. K. Barrett, *A Commentary on the Second Epistle to the Corinthians*; G. R. Beasley-Murray, "2 Corinthians," *BBC*; E. Best, *Second Corinthians*, Interp; H. D. Betz, *2 Corinthians 8 and 9*; F. F. Bruce, *I and II Corinthians*, NCB; F. Danker, *II Corinthians*; V. Furnish, *II Corinthians*, AncB; P. E. Hughes, *Paul's Second Epistle to the Corinthians*, NICNT; C. Kruse, *2 Corinthians*; R. Martin, *2 Corinthians*, WBC; J. Murphy-O'Conner, "The Theology of the Second Letter to the Corinthians," *RE* 86/3 (1989); C. H. Talbert, *Reading Corinthians*; F. Young and D. Ford, *Meaning and Truth in 2 Corinthians*.

Commentary

An Outline

Salutation, 1:1-2

As a typical first-century Greek letter, 2 Corinthians begins with the identification of the author and the recipient(s) followed by a short greeting. Writing to a congregation where his apostleship was being challenged, PAUL includes a brief self-description that functions as a clear statement of his apostolic authority. He is *an apostle of Jesus Christ*, that is, Christ's commissioned representative, not by human appointment but by *the will of God*. With these words Paul sets the stage for the defense of his apostleship that will occupy much of what follows. At issue in Corinth is the nature of authentic apostleship, and it is to address this issue that Paul writes. The mention of TIMOTHY indicates that Timothy endorses what is written.

The letter is addressed to the Corinthian church and *all the saints throughout Achaia*, the Roman province of which Corinth was the capital including, for example, the Christians at Cenchreae (cf. Rom 16:1). As *saints* ("holy ones") they are set apart for obedience to the will of God, and if Paul is an apostle by the will of God this means allegiance to him and the gospel he proclaimed to them. Therefore, what is at stake in Corinth is not so much the apostleship of Paul but the genuineness of the faith of the Corinthians.

In 1:2 Paul combines the conventional Greek greeting (*grace*) with the traditional Hebrew greeting (*peace*) and indicates that these gifts come from God through Jesus Christ.

Thanksgiving, 1:3-11

In these verses, which take the form of a typical Jewish benediction ("Blessed be . . . "), Paul introduces the central theme of the letter: *the consolation of God in the midst of affliction and suffering*. He gives thanks to God for the fact that both he and the Corinthians have experienced God's consolation in the midst of affliction. This God is the *father of mercies* (i.e., the most merciful Father, one whose outstanding characteristic is mercy; cf. Ps 86:5, 15; Mic 7:18) and *God of all consolation* (i.e., encouragement and cheer), a description of God that goes back to the OT (Ps 103:13, 17; Isa 51:12; 66:13). Paul has experienced the reality of God's consolation in the midst of affliction so that he will be able to console others in their affliction with the same consolation with which he has been consoled, that is, the consolation of God (v. 4). In short, Paul's ability to console others is a direct result of God's prior work in his life. Furthermore, God's consolation for us in our affliction is sufficient, that is, abundant, even as Christ's sufferings for us are sufficient, indeed abundant. Thus, we can count on God's consolation to be abundant even as we have counted on Christ's sufferings to be abundant (v. 5).

In vv. 6 and 7 Paul writes that his afflictions and consolations would doubly benefit the Corinthians. First, whether he is afflicted or consoled, the result is the same: their comfort. Second, the Corinthians can also experience this consolation if they *patiently endure* the kinds of afflictions Paul is experiencing. This "endurance" is not Stoic resignation nor the power of positive thinking. It is the obedient faith of those who trust in God's power to sustain and deliver his people in affliction. Paul knows that those who share in his experience of suffering will also share in his consolation precisely because where God is at work there is consolation in the midst of affliction.

In vv. 8-11 Paul explains why he is so sure about the reality of God's consolation by recalling for his readers a recent example of his affliction. The occasion and nature of this affliction in Asia is unknown (some have identified it with the experience mentioned in 1 Cor 15:32). Whatever it was, his suffering was so severe that he saw no way out but death; and, helpless in the face of this *deadly . . . peril*, Paul was forced to trust no longer in himself but in God who raises the dead.

Paul sees his deliverance from this death as a type of the resurrection. Just as Christ was called in his death to trust in God who raises the dead, so Paul was called in the face of death to trust this God whose deliverance of Paul became a demonstration of his power. In short, it is Paul's suffering that becomes the revelatory vehicle by which the power of God is made known so that it is precisely in his suffering that the legitimacy of his apostleship is demonstrated. In his affliction and consolation he becomes an embodiment of that truth first seen in Christ's death and resurrection, that God's power is made known and perfected in our weakness (cf. 12:9).

Paul concludes his thanksgiving by calling for the continuing prayers of the Corinthians so that many will join in thanking God for his suffering and deliverance, for it is precisely in this that the power of God is made known. To all who would deny his apostleship on the basis of his suffering, Paul announces that it is in his suffering that his apostleship is authenticated.

Defining the Nature of His Ministry, 1:12–7:16

Responding to Charges, 1:12-14

Paul moves to respond to charges of vacillation in his relationship with the Corinthians because he has postponed a promised visit. His CONSCIENCE is clear because his actions have been motivated by *the grace of God* and not by *earthly wisdom* (lit. "the wisdom of the flesh"). He has acted with *frankness* and *godly sincerity* and is not hesitant to write openly about his recent change of plans in the hope that the Corinthians will hear him out and understand him fully.

Reaffirming His Credibility, 1:15-22

The charge of vacillation (v. 17) stems from a change in Paul's travel plans. While he had originally planned to visit Corinth after passing through MACEDONIA (1 Cor 16:5), he later indicated that he would visit Corinth both before and after passing through Macedonia (vv. 15-16). But after the first of these projected visits he decided not to make *another painful visit* (2:1) and sent a stinging letter instead (2:3-4). Thus, the charge of vacillation, of making *plans according to ordinary human standards* (v. 17, lit. "according to the flesh"), of being ready to say "yes, yes" and "no, no" at the same time.

Paul's questions in v. 17 are constructed in Greek so as to require "no" for an answer. He responds by saying that just as God is faithful to his people, so he has been faithful to the Corinthians (v. 18). He is concerned, however, lest questions about his credibility lead to questions about the credibility of the gospel. He insists there is no equivocation in this gospel (v. 19). Indeed, all the promises of God find their *yes* in Jesus (v. 20) and it is through him that we are able to say *amen* to the glory of God. It is this God who has established Paul, his colleagues, and the Corinthians in Christ, anointing them with his Spirit which functions as both God's seal (the mark of his ownership) and *a first installment* guaranteeing their full participation in the blessings of the age to come (vv. 21-22).

Explaining His Actions, 1:23–2:4

Having argued that his change of plans was a result of his faithfulness to God and to the Corinthians, Paul explains that his change of plans was to spare the Corinthians *another painful visit* (1:23; 2:1). Instead, he wrote them *out of much distress and anguish of heart and with many tears* to let them know of his abundant love for them (2:4).

Restoring the Offender, 2:5-11

The circumstances surrounding Paul's painful visit to Corinth and prompting the severe letter are implied in vv. 5-11. During his *painful* visit to Corinth a member of the Corinthian church had acted in some way so as to injure Paul and, by derivation, the whole congregation (v. 5), and the congregation had neither supported Paul nor reprimanded the offender. Rather than make a return visit Paul had written the severe letter *to test* the obedience of the whole congregation (v. 9). This letter had prompted the majority to take sufficient disciplinary action against the offender (v. 6), and Paul, whose concern is reconciliation rather than retaliation, calls for forgiveness (v. 7) and love (v. 8) to be extended to the repentant offender lest their disciplinary action fail to be redemptive. Failure to respond in this way would be to fall prey to Satan's designs of destroying the love and forgiveness that are to characterize God's people as the sign of God's redemptive work (v. 11).

Going to Macedonia, 2:12-13

Anxious for news of the Corinthian's response to his severe letter (2:3-4), Paul left EPHESUS and went north to Troas, the embarkation point for Macedonia, hoping to intercept the returning Titus there. Though a *door was opened* for him as he preached the gospel there, his anxiety was so great that he left Troas and crossed the Aegean Sea hoping to find Titus in Macedonia.

Being Led in Triumph, 2:14-17

Interrupting the account of his movements, Paul launches the most detailed defense of his apostleship to be found in any of his letters, a defense that runs through 7:4. In v. 14 he employs a striking image of apostolic service that sets the tone for all that follows. In the Greek term *thriambeuein* (translated *leads us in triumphal procession*) Paul's readers would recognize an allusion to the Roman "triumph" in which a victorious general would parade through the streets of Rome leading a long procession of captives whose afflictions and sufferings became a demonstration of the power and glory of the conqueror.

While it is possible Paul sees himself as a partner with Christ in his triumph, it seems more likely that in this context Paul sees himself as a captive of Christ whose ministry, beset by afflictions and sufferings as it is, becomes a demonstration of Christ's power and glory. This image becomes a graphic expression of the significant role suffering plays in apostolic ministry, a significance rejected by Paul's critics in Corinth. Yet it is precisely through Paul's ministry of suffering that God *spreads in every place the fragrance that comes from knowing him* (v. 14), that is, through Paul's ministry the knowledge of God is spread abroad and the suffering apostle becomes *the aroma of Christ* (v. 15).

Paul knows that not all will respond positively to this understanding of the nature of ministry even as all do not respond positively to the word of the cross. In fact, Paul describes the reaction to this understanding

of ministry in terms of the same twofold response described for the word of the cross in 1 Cor 1:18-25. For those who acknowledge that God reveals himself in Paul's suffering, this aroma is the fragrance of life. For those who reject it, the fragrance is the smell of death. To those being saved, suffering is an appropriate expression of apostleship. To those who are perishing, it is foolishness (vv. 15-16).

This reflection on the nature of apostolic ministry prompts Paul to ask, *Who is sufficient for these things?* (v. 16). Who, that is, is adequate for such a ministry? While his answer does not come until 3:5-6, in 2:17 he makes it clear that the "sufficient one" is not a *peddler of the word*, that is, someone who preaches and teaches for his or her own gain, even adulterating the message to make it more marketable. Those who are "sufficient" speak in Christ as persons of sincerity, as persons who speak for God (saying what God wants said), and as persons who speak as if standing in the presence of God (i.e., with God as judge, cf. 5:10).

Acknowledging His Commendation and Competence, 3:1-6

Paul raises two questions in v. 1 that are intended to distinguish him from those who have come to Corinth bearing letters of recommendation. The implied answer to both is "no." He need not commend himself and does not need letters of recommendation because the Corinthians themselves are his letter of recommendation, authored by Christ, *written . . . with the Spirit of the living God . . . on tablets of human hearts* (vv. 2-3; for the background of this image see Jer 31:33; cf. Ezek 11:19-20; 36:26-27). This letter is *to be known and read by all*.

In short, the Corinthians owe their very lives as Christians to the ministry of Paul and to deny his apostleship would be tantamount to denying their conversion. Their experience legitimates Paul's apostleship. Indeed, there is no better evidence of the validity of Paul's ministry than the existence of the Corinthian church.

The Corinthian church is itself the basis for Paul's confidence (v. 4), but he is quick to point out that his competence for this ministry is not in himself but from God *who has made us competent to be ministers of a new covenant*, a covenant not of letter but of spirit *for the letter kills, but the Spirit gives life* (v. 6). Thus, Paul sets up a contrast between the old covenant and the new, and implies that his ministry is an essential part of the dawning of the new age promised in Jer

31:33 and Ezek 11 and 36. This new spiritual covenant served by his ministry is the subject of 3:7-18.

Ministering under the New Covenant, 3:7–4:6

In a *midrash* on Exod 34:29-35 Paul develops further the contrast introduced in 3:6. In 3:7-11 he employs the rabbinic principle of arguing from the lesser to the greater (*qal wa-homer*) to demonstrate the surpassing glory of this new COVENANT and the ministry that accompanies it. While the old covenant is *chiseled in letters on stone tablets* (cf. 3:3 and Exod 31:18), the new is written *on tablets of human hearts* (3:3). While the old covenant results in *condemnation*, the new results in *justification* (3:9). While the ministry that accompanies the old covenant is *the ministry of death* (3:7), the ministry of the new covenant is *the ministry of the Spirit* (3:8) that *gives life* (3:6). While the old covenant has been *set aside* (3:11), the new covenant is *permanent* (3:11). While the old covenant came with *glory* (3:7, 9, 10, 11), the new covenant has come with *greater glory* (3:8, 9, 10, 11) so that *what once had glory has lost its glory* in the light of the new that has come.

As a minister of this new covenant, Paul acts *with great boldness* (3:12), unlike Moses who put *a veil* over his face to conceal the temporary character of the glory of the old covenant (3:13). In 3:14 and 15 this *veil* becomes a metaphor for the spiritual blindness that lies over the hardened minds of those who continue to live under the old covenant. When they turn to the Lord, however, this veil is removed and they are able to see *the glory of the Lord* as it is revealed in Jesus, and beholding him to be *transformed into the same image from one degree of glory to another* (3:18).

Paul reaffirms the fact that he is engaged in this ministry of the new covenant as a result of *God's mercy* (4:1; cf. 3:5). Therefore, he does not *lose heart* despite the suffering he may experience. The nature of this ministry is then described both negatively and positively. Those engaged in this ministry do not resort to methods that bring shame when exposed. They do not engage in deceptive methods for their own advantage and they do not adulterate the message to make it more palatable. Rather they commend themselves to the conscience of everyone in the sight of God by *the open statement of the truth* (4:1-2).

If Paul's message is veiled, it is veiled only to unbelievers who lack the enlightenment of the Spirit and have been blinded by *the god of this world*. In this blindness they see only Paul's suffering and are blind to the power of his message (4:3-4).

Paul's message does not center on himself. He preaches nothing but *Jesus Christ as Lord* and unlike those who would exploit the congregation, he postures himself as their "slave" (4:5). The basis for both his message and the manner of his ministry is to be found in his own experience of discovering *the light of the knowledge of the glory of God* [i.e., all that God is and wills] *in the face of Jesus Christ* (4:6).

Recognizing Treasure in Clay Jars, 4:7-15

In v. 7 Paul employs another powerful image for the apostolic ministry. *We have this treasure in clay jars.* In the ancient world treasure was often buried in clay jars. The jar was fragile and expendable and often had to be broken so that the treasure inside could be revealed. So the treasure of apostleship is carried within the life of a fragile human being *so that it may be made clear that this extraordinary power belongs to God and does not come from us* (v. 7). In the weakness and the brokenness of the vessel the power of God is made manifest, and, therefore, weakness and suffering are integral to authentic apostolic ministry.

In support of this view Paul presents a list of the tribulations accompanying his ministry in vv. 8-10. He is *afflicted, perplexed, persecuted,* and *struck down,* and in these sufferings he is carrying in his own body the death (lit. "dying") of Jesus. But he is *not crushed, driven to despair, forsaken,* or *destroyed* because the power of God sustains him, and, therefore, the life of Jesus is *made visible in [his] mortal flesh.* In short, Paul's apostolic sufferings are a manifestation of Jesus' death and resurrection, and his suffering to bring the gospel to the Corinthians assures them of life in Christ (vv. 11-12).

So Paul does not *lose heart* even though his ministry is beset by suffering. He has the same spirit of faith as the Psalmist who wrote, *"I believed, and so I spoke."* The quotation is taken from Ps 116, a hymn of thanksgiving for deliverance from death. What Paul believes that enables him to speak is the gospel that *the one who raised the Lord Jesus will raise us also with him, and will bring us with you into his presence* (v. 14).

Living in the Light of the Future, 4:16–5:10

In v. 16 Paul picks up on the theme of future glory as a reason that he does not *lose heart* amidst the suffering of his apostolic ministry. The contrast between present, momentary affliction, and future, eternal glory is a reason for apostolic confidence. While the *outer nature* (i.e., mortal existence) is passing away, the *inner nature* (i.e., identity as children of God) is being renewed day by day (4:16), and the affliction we encounter serves to prepare us for *an eternal weight of glory beyond all measure* (4:17). Thus, we are able to look beyond present, temporary, and seen affliction to the future, eternal, not-yet-seen glory that lies ahead (4:18).

In 5:1-5 Paul employs a series of metaphors to describe the resurrection life. In 5:1 he contrasts the transience of our *earthly tent* (a common idiom for life in the body) with the permanence of our *building from God*, a *heavenly dwelling* which is *eternal, not made with hands*. In 5:2-3 he employs the image of putting on a garment over a garment already being worn. Similarly in 5:4 he pictures the putting up of another tent around one already inhabited. In both cases, Paul's desire is to receive the new garment or tent without having to give up the old one so as not to be *naked* (5:3) or *unclothed* (5:4), that is, to avoid the threat of nonbeing (death).

So in this life we groan, longing for the mortal to be swallowed up by life, knowing that the Spirit of God that we have already received is the guarantee of the reality of this resurrection life (5:5).

In 5:6-8 Paul introduces yet another metaphor, that of being *at home* and *away from home*. To be *at home in the body* (i.e., mortal existence) is to be *away from the Lord*. It is to walk *by faith* and not *by sight*. While he prefers to be *away from the body and at home with the Lord*, his eschatological hope is the foundation of his confidence (5:6, 8). This eschatological hope is more than just a source of confidence. It is also a challenge to right living. Since we all must appear before the *judgment seat of Christ*, our aim, whatever our state, must ever be to please him (5:9-10).

Being Ministers of Reconciliation, 5:11–6:10

In 5:11-15 Paul discusses the motivation for his ministry. He carries out his apostolic ministry *knowing the fear of the Lord*, knowing, that is, that he will give an account for his service *before the judgment seat of Christ* (5:10). His motives and actions lie open before God and the Corinthians, who he hopes will listen to their consciences rather than to his critics (5:11). Paul's intention in writing is not self-commendation. His aim is to provide the Corinthians a basis for re-

sponding to his critics who boast in external appearances rather than the things of the heart (5:12).

In 5:13a Paul responds to charges that he is either mad (in which case he responds that his behavior is determined by his faithfulness to God) or that his ministry is not truly apostolic because it does not give sufficient evidence of ecstatic experiences (in which case he responds that such experiences are between him and God, and are not to be worn on one's sleeve as evidence of one's apostleship). Whatever his behavior, whether he is *beside* himself, or in his *right mind*, it is for God and his glory, and for the benefit of the Corinthians. Paul's primary motivation is *the love of Christ* (Christ's love for him), a love demonstrated in the fact that *one has died for all; therefore all have died*, died, that is, to a sinful, self-centered existence so that they might live a Christ-centered life (5:14-15).

The new life in Christ is characterized by two things. First, there is a new way of knowing (5:16) in which we no longer evaluate either Christ or others *from a human point of view* (lit. "according to the flesh," i.e., knowledge without reference to God and God's purposes). Second, there is a new way of being, *a new creation* (5:17). The old self-centered humanity *has passed away*; the new Christ-centered humanity *has come* (cf. Paul's treatment of the two humanities in Rom 5:12ff.). *All this is from God who reconciled us to himself through Jesus Christ* (5:18).

Reconciliation, a major soteriological motif in Paul (cf. Rom 5:10; Col 1:21ff.; Eph 2:11-22), is summarized in 5:18-21.

First, it is initiated and accomplished by God (5:18, 19).

Second, it is accomplished *through* (5:18), *in Christ* (5:19) who was made *to be sin* (5:21). While this phrase has been interpreted to mean (a) that God caused him to assume our sinful nature or (b) that God allowed him to be condemned as a sinner, it is probably best to understand it to mean that (c) God made him a sin offering. In any case, God has so acted that *in him* [Christ] *we might become the righteousness of God*, that is, sinners are given a righteous status before God through the righteous one who absorbed their sin and its judgment in himself.

Third, all who are reconciled become ministers of *reconciliation* (5:18), charged with announcing the *message of reconciliation* (5:19) as *ambassadors for Christ* (5:20).

This message contains the plea to *be reconciled to God*, a plea addressed in this case to the Corinthians whose alienation from Paul has become a denial of the reality of the gospel of reconciliation in their lives. This reconciliation is a relationship with God and others that must be continually reaffirmed and realized. Thus, quoting Isa 49:8, Paul exhorts the Corinthians not to accept the reconciling grace of God in vain by acting in a way that is contrary to their experience of God's grace for every day is the *today* of salvation.

Paul has attempted to live and minister so as not to hinder the message he proclaims. In 6:4b-5 he presents a catalog of afflictions that he has borne with *great endurance* (cf. 11:23-33 for a second and more detailed listing). In 6:6-7 he lists moral and spiritual characteristics necessary to conduct his ministry. These are the *weapons of righteousness for the right hand and for the left*. In 6:8-10 he gives seven pairs of antithetical ways of viewing his ministry that contrast the visible appearance and essential reality of that ministry. Those who evaluate on the basis of human standards will have one perception of Paul's ministry. Those who judge according to the standards of the new creation will have quite another perception.

Appealing to the Corinthians, 6:11-13

In all his dealings with the Corinthians Paul has spoken frankly with a heart wide open to them. If there is any lack of openness between Paul and the Corinthians, the fault lies with them (vv. 11-12). So as a father speaking to his children (cf. 1 Cor 4:14-15), Paul appeals to them to open wide their hearts to him (5:13).

Calling for a Holy Life, 6:14–7:1

These verses (seen by many as an interpolation: see "Integrity," above) are a digression suggesting that one reason for the Corinthians' alienation from Paul is that they are still accommodating too much to the pagan environment in which they live (a problem amply attested in 1 Corinthians). The passage begins with an exhortation not to be *mismatched with unbelievers*. The term *mismatched* means "unequally" or "unnaturally" yoked, such as harnessing an ox and an ass together (a practice prohibited in Deut 22:10). This is followed by five rhetorical questions presupposing a negative answer illustrating the incongruity of a believer being yoked to an unbeliever. Righteousness, light, Christ, believers, and God's temple have nothing in common with lawlessness, darkness, Beliar (an evil spirit in intertestamental literature, under, or identified with, Satan), unbelievers, and idols (6:14b-16a).

Verses 16b-18 characterize the church as God's *temple* and depict the nature of that community with a series of OT quotations (Lev 26:12; Isa 52:11; a combination of Ezek 20:34, Isa 43:6, and 2 Sam 7:14). The section closes with an exhortation in 7:1 to be a holy people in reverent fear of their God (cf. 5:10).

Continuing the Appeal, 7:2-4

In v. 2 Paul repeats his plea of 6:13. The basis for that appeal is found in vv. 2b-3. He has been totally honest in all of his dealings with the Corinthians, and his purpose for writing is not condemnation but an expression of his life-and-death commitment to them. Verse 4 is an expression of his confidence in the Corinthians.

Rejoicing in Reconciliation, 7:5-16

In v. 5 Paul resumes the account of his movements begun in 2:12-13. The affliction he had experienced in Troas (2:13) continued in Macedonia as he awaited Titus's return from Corinth with a report of their reception of his severe letter (2:3-4). On receiving Titus's report his regrets about sending the letter vanished (v. 8) and he was *overjoyed* (v. 4) because it had led the Corinthians to a *godly grief* that led them to repentance and salvation rather than a *worldly grief* which leads only to death.

As a result of his letter the Corinthians had (1) rallied to Paul's side and reaffirmed their solidarity with him (vv. 5-6); (2) acted to discipline the offender, realizing that the offender's actions not only injured Paul but ultimately the whole congregation (2:5-7; 7:11-12); and (3) lived up to Titus's expectations of them based on Paul's boasting about them as Titus witnessed their obedience to Paul's apostolic leadership (vv. 13-15).

Paul concludes this section with another affirmation of his *complete confidence* in the Corinthians (v. 16; cf. v. 4) that serves to set the stage for the request he is about to make in chaps. 8 and 9. Such expressions of confidence typically functioned to undergird the subsequent request by creating a sense of obligation through praise.

Challenging the Corinthians to Complete the Collection, 8:1–9:15

Chapters 8 and 9 focus on Paul's collection for the saints in Jerusalem (see 1 Cor 16:1-4 and Rom 15:25-27). Having expressed his *complete confidence* in the

Corinthians (7:16), Paul calls upon them to fulfill their obligation to this collection.

Excel in Giving, 8:1-8

Paul challenges the Corinthians to follow the example of the Macedonian churches. Using the ancient rhetorical technique of comparison to evoke competition between two individuals or groups, Paul seeks to motivate the Corinthians by alluding to the generosity of the Macedonians. Though experiencing *a severe ordeal of affliction* and *poverty*, they have voluntarily given generously, even *beyond their means*, out of the overflow of their gift of themselves to the Lord and to Paul (vv. 1-5). So Paul encourages the Corinthians to demonstrate their commitment to the Lord and to him as he sends Titus to complete their gift to the collection (v. 6). Playing on their pride, he calls upon them to excel in this *generous undertaking* as they excel in everything else (v. 7). Here is an opportunity for them to demonstrate the *genuineness* of their love as the Macedonians have done (v. 8).

Follow Christ's Example, 8:9-15

In these verses Paul challenges the Corinthians to fulfill their obligation on the basis of the example of Christ who *though he was rich, yet for your sakes he became poor, so that by his poverty you might become rich* (v. 9) Paul advises them to match the eagerness they had previously shown with the necessary action to complete their gift (vv. 10-12). They are encouraged to give (1) according to their means and (2) in keeping with the principle of equality (vv. 13-15) whereby those who have share out of their abundance with those who have not so that there is a *fair balance*. Citing Exod 16:18 Paul finds scriptural support for this practice in the story of the gathering of the manna in the wilderness (v. 15).

Receive the Representatives, 8:16–9:5

Paul is sending a delegation to receive the contribution of the Corinthians. The delegation includes Titus (8:16-17), the brother *who is famous among all the churches for his proclaiming the good news* and who has been appointed by the churches to travel with them perhaps as a kind of independent auditor (8:18-19), and *our brother whom we have often tested and found eager in many matters* (8:22). These arrangements have been made so there can be no charges of deceit leveled against Paul or this project. The purpose for the delegation is clearly stated in 8:20-21:

We intend that no one should blame us about this generous gift that we are administering, for we intend to do what is right not only in the Lord's sight but also in the sight of others.

Titus comes as Paul's representative, while the other two come as representatives of the churches (8:23). Paul encourages the Corinthians to show them proof of their love and the reason for Paul's boasting about them. In other words, complete the collection (8:24).

9:1-5 extend and support the commendations in 8:16-24 (for the view that chap. 9 represents a separate letter, see "Integrity," above), and together with 9:6-15 provide the conclusion for Paul's treatment of the collection in 8:1–9:15. The subject of Paul's *boasting* about the Corinthians is given in 9:1-2. He has boasted to the Macedonians about the eagerness of the Corinthians to participate in the *ministry to the saints*. They have been ready to participate *since last year*. This boasting has *stirred up most* of the Macedonians, and Paul hopes that his boasting about the Macedonians in 8:1-5 will stir up the Corinthians.

In 9:3-5 Paul gives a second reason for sending *the brothers* (Titus and the two unnamed brothers of 8:16-24; the first reason was given in 8:20-21). They will *arrange in advance* for the *bountiful* gift the Corinthians have promised so that neither the Corinthians nor Paul will be humiliated when he arrives with representatives of the Macedonian churches because the Corinthians, about whom Paul has been boasting, are not prepared with their gift.

Give Bountifully and Cheerfully, 9:6-15

Paul concludes his appeal on behalf of the collection by challenging the Corinthians to "sow bountifully" so that they may *reap bountifully* (v. 6; cf. Gal 6:7-8). To "sow bountifully" is to give *not reluctantly or under compulsion* but "cheerfully" (v. 7; cf. 9:5 and LXX of Prov 22:8a). To *reap bountifully* is to be *enriched in every way* (v. 11) by the God who is able *to provide you with every blessing in abundance*, not to be self-sufficient, but so that *having enough of everything, you may share abundantly in every good work* (v. 8).

In v. 9 Paul quotes from the description of the man who fears the Lord in Ps 112:9, whose *righteousness* [i.e., acts of piety, esp. almsgiving] *endures forever*.

The generosity of the Corinthians in sharing in the collection will supply the needs of the saints (v. 12) and will be a sign of their obedience to the gospel that will bring glory to God (v. 13). It will result in thanksgiving to God (v. 11b); in fact, it will overflow *with many thanksgivings to God* (v. 12b) because God is the ultimate source of both the spirit of generosity and the abundance from which the Corinthians are able to give.

All of our giving is done in light of and in response to God's *indescribable gift* (v. 15) for which Paul gives thanks as he closes this discussion. Romans 15:25-27 (probably written from Corinth after 2 Corinthians), suggests that the Corinthians heeded Paul's appeal with regard to the collection.

Defending His Ministry, 10:1–13:10

Because of the abrupt change of tone, there is a widespread consensus among NT scholars that chaps. 10–13 represent a separate letter. While some identify it as the "tearful" or "severe" letter referred to in 2:3-9 and 7:8-12 that was written before chaps. 1–9, a growing number of commentators—including the present one—argue that it was written some time after chaps. 1–9 in response to a fresh outbreak of trouble in Corinth precipitated by the arrival of *false apostles* (11:13) who were attempting to undermine Paul's ministry there (on the relationship between chaps. 1–9 and chaps. 10–13, see "Integrity," above). In any case, these chapters contain a passionate and vigorous defense of Paul's apostolic ministry.

Responding to Criticism, 10:1-11

Paul appeals to the Corinthians on the basis of *the meekness and gentleness of Christ* and in light of a series of criticisms leveled at him by his unnamed opponents in Corinth.

The first criticism, as reflected in vv. 1 and 10, is that while Paul is bold from a distance, he is weak and unimpressive in person. The charge probably reflects on his oratorical skills (cf. 1 Cor 2:3-4; 2 Cor 11:6), his physical appearance, and his behavior on the painful visit when in the face of opposition he left Corinth and, rather than returning in person, fired off the severe letter. Paul responds with the veiled threat in vv. 2 and 11, that he is prepared to back up his strong words with action if necessary when he arrives in Corinth.

The second charge is that he acts *according to human standards* (v. 2, lit. "according to the flesh"). This may mean either that he acts according to egocentric, worldly motives or that he acts without spiritu-

al power. Paul responds that while he lives as a human being, he wields weapons with *divine power* (vv. 3-4a). Employing military images, he describes these weapons as capable of destroying *strongholds* (i.e., *arguments and every proud obstacle raised up against the knowledge of God*), taking captives (i.e., *every thought captive to obey Christ*) and punishing *every disobedience* (vv. 4b-6). While he wields these weapons in *the meekness and gentleness of Christ* (v. 1), this must never be confused with weakness. He will wield them in Corinth if necessary but hopes that the Corinthians will not force a showdown.

In response to the claims of his opponents, Paul reminds the Corinthians that he too belongs to Christ (v. 7) and that the Lord has given him the apostolic authority (v. 8) for the purpose of building up rather than tearing down.

Seeking the Lord's Commendation, 10:12-18

In v. 12 Paul focuses specifically on his opponents, ironically stating that he does not "dare" to compare himself with those who nonsensically measure themselves by one another and make themselves the measure of genuine apostleship. In reality no comparison is possible, for Paul sees them as *false apostles* who serve Satan rather than Christ (11:13-15). Unlike Paul, his opponents *boast beyond limits*, demonstrating the kind of excessive self-praise characteristic of the sham philosopher (v. 13). Furthermore, they boast *in the labors of others* (v. 15) and take credit for *work already done in someone else's sphere of action* (v. 16).

The clear implication is that Paul's opponents have invaded the sphere of action assigned to Paul and are seeking to take it over for themselves. In so doing they are not building up but destroying the Corinthian congregation (v. 8; 13:10). Paul, on the other hand, keeps within the field assigned to him (v. 13) preaching the gospel in places where it was not already known (cf. Rom 15:20-21). It was in keeping with that charge that Paul had come to Corinth as the first to preach the gospel there (v. 14). Corinth was, therefore, in his jurisdiction, and he now hoped to proclaim the good news in the lands beyond Corinth without boasting of work already done (v. 16).

Citing Jer 9:24 (LXX), Paul asserts that if any boasting is to be done it is to be boasting in the Lord, *For it is not those who commend themselves* [as do his opponents] *that are approved, but those whom the Lord commends* (v. 18). Once again Paul needs no letter of recommendation, for the very existence of the

Corinthian church is evidence of the Lord's commendation, the only commendation that matters.

Playing the Fool for Love:
the Fool's Speech, 11:1–12:13

This passage has been called Paul's "fool's speech" on the basis of Paul's introduction of it as *a little foolishness* (11:1) and his comment at the end, *I have been a fool* (12:11). The necessity of defending his apostolic status in the face of the boasting of his opponents forces Paul to engage in the kind of self-commendation he has just repudiated in 10:12-18. That such boasting is foolishness is clear; that it is necessary at this point is also clear, lest he lose the Corinthian congregation to even greater fools.

Careful reading of this "fool's speech" reveals that it is a devastating attack on Paul's boastful opponents. His emphasis throughout on the foolishness of such boasting (11:1, 17, 21; 12:1, 11) becomes an indictment of his opponents who practice such boasting. Furthermore, by boasting of humiliating experiences rather than of glorious accomplishments, he reveals the great gulf that separates his understanding of apostleship from theirs.

Having invited his readers to bear with him in *a little foolishness* (11:1), Paul explains that it is motivated by his concern for the Corinthians. Comparing himself to the father of a bride who has been betrothed, he sees his role as that of guarding his daughter's virginity between the time of the betrothal and the consummation of the marriage (11:2). He fears that the Corinthians are in danger of being led astray from *a sincere and pure devotion to Christ* by *super-apostles* who have come to Corinth preaching *another Jesus*, a *different Spirit* and a *different gospel* (11:3-5).

Paul emphasizes that he is in no way inferior to these *super-apostles*—an ironic designation of his opponents that makes light of their pretentious claims. Apparently Paul was being unfavorably compared with them on several accounts.

First, his style as a public speaker had been criticized because it lacked the rhetorical sophistication displayed by his opponents (11:6). This may also lead to the suggestion that he lacked the knowledge that according to his opponents an apostle should have. While not disputing his critics' evaluation of his eloquence, Paul will not allow their evaluation of his knowledge, a knowledge that has been made evident to the Corinthians in every way. In short, he is *not in the least inferior* to the *super-apostles*.

Second, in a culture where many considered it degrading for a philosopher to work, Paul's insistence on supporting himself while in Corinth with his refusal to accept support from the Corinthians had been seen as an indication of an inferior status and even as a lack of love for the Corinthians. Paul responds that his behavior was certainly not an indication of a lack of love; rather he has acted so as not to burden them (11:7-11). Finally, Paul will have nothing of his opponents' claim to an equal status with him (11:12). Disguising themselves as apostles of Christ, they are in reality *deceitful workers, false apostles, ministers* of Satan (11:13-15).

In 11:16 Paul repeats his plea of 11:1 asking indulgence for his foolish boasting. Nevertheless he will engage in the foolishness of boasting according to human standards as his opponents do (11:16-18). With powerful sarcasm he indicates that this is possible because in their "wisdom" the Corinthians *put up with fools* who would exploit them (11:19-20), something that he was *too weak* to do (11:21).

Paul begins his boasting by establishing that while his ethnic and religious credentials are no less Jewish than his opponents (11:22), his credentials as a minister of Christ are superior (11:23a). Ironically, the evidence he brings to support his claim is not a list of glorious triumphs but of the trials and hardships he has suffered as an apostle (11:23b-33). While some have understood this litany as an attempt at one-upmanship (the opponents bragged about what they had suffered for Christ, so Paul recounts what his service to Christ had cost him), the irony that pervades the context suggests that it is better seen as a kind of parody of the opponents' exalted claims. While they boast of things that demonstrate their strength, Paul boasts of things that show his weakness (11:29a-30) for in his weakness the transcendent power of God is made known (4:7-15; 12:9).

The incident at DAMASCUS (11:32-33) illustrates *danger in the city* (11:26). It stands as an example of Paul's weakness especially when viewed against the backdrop of the Roman *corona muralis* (wall crown) that was presented for valor to the first soldier to ascend the wall of an enemy city. The marked contrast between such a courageous ascent and Paul's inglorious descent of the city wall would not be missed by the Corinthians and could only have been seen as another evidence of his weakness and humiliation.

In response to the claims of his opponents, Paul finds it necessary to boast about *visions and revela-*

tions (12:1). Using the third person (a reflection of his reticence about boasting of his own experiences), Paul tells of being *caught up to the third heaven* (considered in some Jewish cosmologies to be the highest heaven), which is here synonymous with Paradise. He says nothing of what he saw, and what he heard he cannot repeat because it was either inexpressible or impermissible to repeat (12:2-4).

While such experiences have a personal benefit for the one who experiences them, they have no real benefit for others. Therefore, Paul chooses to boast of his *weaknesses* (12:5-7) because he had learned that it is in weakness that God's power is made manifest. Paul had learned this from his experience of the *thorn . . . in the flesh* that had been given him to keep him from *being too elated*.

While the *thorn* has been the subject of much speculation, it is probably best understood as a physical illness or infirmity that left Paul open to public ridicule (cf. Gal 4:13-14). Paul's persistent plea for its removal was greeted by the promise of God's sufficient grace and the knowledge that God's *power is made perfect in weakness* (12:8). If this is the case, then it is not in our strength but in our weakness that God's power is revealed, and, therefore, it is in our weakness that we should boast (12:9). It is as we suffer *weaknesses, insults, hardships, persecutions, and calamities* that we become the showplace of God's power (12:10).

Thus, while Paul's vision had provided nothing that could be uttered for the benefit of others, the thorn in the flesh communicated the grace and power of God each day. In his weakness, therefore, Paul embodied the folly of the cross that reveals the power of God (1 Cor 1:18-31; 2 Cor 4:7-12).

Paul concludes his "fool's speech" by reasserting that he is in no way inferior to the *super-apostles* (12:11). He has performed the signs of a *true apostle* (12:12). His ministry was of both word and deed and had included *signs and wonders and mighty works* (cf. Rom 15:18-19). He has held back nothing from the Corinthians except that he has not asked them for support, and ironically he asks to be forgiven for not exploiting them as his opponents have (12:13).

Anticipating His Third Visit, 12:14-21

As Paul anticipates his third visit to Corinth, he makes it clear that he will continue his practice of not burdening the Corinthians. As a genuine apostle, he does not want what the Corinthians have but the Corinthians themselves. He cares for them as a parent for a child (v. 14) knowing that apostolic authenticity is demonstrated when one is willing *to spend and be spent* for the Corinthians (v. 15).

Verses 16-18 suggest that Paul has been charged with defrauding the Corinthians with regard to the collection for the saints in Jerusalem. Perhaps his critics were saying that while Paul asked for no money for himself, he was actually using the collection to line his own pockets. He responds by pointing to the exemplary behavior of his representatives (*Titus* and *the brother*). Just as they had not taken advantage of the Corinthians, neither had he.

Paul's concern is not for his own reputation but for the building up of the Corinthians (v. 19). As he approaches his third visit, he fears (1) that he may not find the Corinthians to be as he wished and that they might not so find him; (2) that there will be quarreling, jealousy, anger, selfishness, slander, gossip, conceit, and disorder; and (3) that the congregation will still be plagued by impurity, sexual immorality, and licentiousness (vv. 20-21).

Warning the Corinthians, 13:1-4

Citing Deut 19:15 Paul views his upcoming third visit as a third witness against his opponents and their followers. He had previously warned them on his second visit and then by means of the severe letter. When he arrives he will not be lenient but will vigorously assert his apostolic authority. He will give compelling evidence that Christ speaks through him in powerful action with regard to the unrepentant. Such powerful action is modeled after the pattern of Christ who was *crucified in weakness, but lives by the power of God* (v. 4).

This does not mean that the crucifixion represents weakness and the resurrection power; the cross is the supreme expression of God's power (1 Cor 1:24) and the resurrection shows that what appears to be weakness (the crucifixion) is in truth the power of God (see Rom 1:4). Similarly the apparent weakness of Paul—his unimposing presence (10:10) and his suffering service (6:4-10; 11:25-29)—is in fact the sign that God's power is at work in his ministry (12:10). Since Paul shares the suffering of Christ (Phil 3:10; Gal 2:10), he is "weak in him" (v. 4); since he shares the power of Christ's resurrection (Phil 3:10), he will exercise the power of Christ when dealing with the Corinthians (Baird 1988, 108).

Challenging the Corinthians, 13:5-10

Paul challenges the Corinthians who question whether Christ speaks through him to examine whether Christ lives in them (v. 5). While Paul hopes that they will recognize the authenticity of his apostleship and thus his authority (v. 6), his overarching concern is that the Corinthians will do what is right, regardless (v. 7). He is happy to appear weak so long as the Corinthians are strong (v. :8) and prays that they will *become perfect* (v. 9; lit. "upright again").

In v. 10 Paul states the purpose for his writing. He has written so that when he comes he might not have to be severe in using the apostolic authority that had been given to him for the building up of the church.

Closing 13:11-13

Closing Exhortations and Greeting, 13:11-12

These verses contain the briefest of paraeneses (cf. Rom 12:9-13; 1 Cor 16:13-15; 1 Thes 5:12-22). Attention to Paul's fourfold admonition will allow the Corinthian church to become what God intends and will assure the Corinthians of God's presence.

Benediction, 13:13

This is the fullest Pauline benediction to be found in any letter. It is distinguished from others by its clearly trinitarian form. The grace of the *Lord Jesus Christ* expresses and leads us to know the love of *God* whose *Spirit* produces communion with God and with one another.

Works Cited

Baird, William. 1988. *1 Corinthians/2 Corinthians*.
Ralph P. Martin. 1986. *2 Corinthians*. WBC.

Galatians

Charles H. Cosgrove

Introduction

Galatians is addressed to a group of gentile-Christian congregations founded by PAUL and located in central Asia Minor (modern Turkey). The date and place of composition are uncertain. Paul's so-called third missionary journey (ca. 52–56) is a possibility, in which case he may have composed the letter in EPHESUS, CORINTH, or in some part of MACEDONIA.

The Occasion of the Letter

Since Paul's founding visit, the Galatians have been influenced by certain persons who Paul claims are *confusing* them and wanting *to pervert* the gospel (1:7; cf. 5:10, 12). These persons may be Jewish-Christian teachers from JERUSALEM who disagree with Paul about the nature of the GOSPEL for the gentiles. They insist above all on CIRCUMCISION (5:2-6; 6:12-13), and will be referred to here as "the Circumcisers."

To judge from Paul's argument, the Circumcisers have urged the Galatians to accept the Law as a way of promoting the power and wondrous works of the Spirit (3:5). Paul's letter is an effort to refute this teaching and persuade the Galatians to return to the way of life in Christ that Paul first taught them.

Paul's Argument

Paul makes his appeal in three stages. The first stage is an "apostolic autobiography" (1:11–2:21) in which Paul claims that his apostolic authority and his gospel preaching come directly from God, the implication being that the Galatians had better listen to him. At the same time Paul depicts himself as the only apostle who has consistently defended the gentile cause in the gospel. The Galatians can trust him. Thus the primary aim of the apostolic autobiography is to encourage the Galatians to trust Paul, so they will accept his interpretation and logic in the central argumentation of the letter.

The second phase of Paul's appeal (3:1–4:31, with a certain anticipation in 2:15-21) consists largely of theological argument from scripture and Christian tradition. Paul argues that the Galatians enjoy eschatological life (manifest in the wondrous power of the Spirit, 3:5) solely because they believed Paul's gospel and not because of any relationship they may now have with the Law of Moses. In fact, if they practice works of the Law, they will put themselves under a curse and forfeit the blessing they now experience in Christ.

The third phase of Paul's appeal is an apostolic exhortation (5:1–6:10). Paul defines the relationship between the Law and FREEDOM in the Spirit. He admonishes the Galatians in a way that suggests their ethical life has been deteriorating—as if their adoption of the Law might itself be the cause of an increase among them of *works of the flesh*. In this way the exhortation functions as an implicit argument against Law-keeping.

Galatians and Anti-Judaism

In our time all Christian commentary proceeds in the shadow of the Holocaust, hence a word is in order about the impression Galatians gives today of sanctioning "anti-Judaism." For Paul, as for most Jews in his day, JUDAISM was defined by the Law, but in Galatians Paul says that all those "in the Law" are in slavery. That amounts to a harsh attack on Judaism, even if Paul was in some sense seeking to redefine Judaism on the basis of his conviction that the Messiah had come with a new revelation about the Law.

As part of the Christian Bible, Galatians has an anti-Jewish ring that is amplified by the political power of Christianity in the world. But when Paul wrote Galatians, the letter represented a critique that barely tinkled within the world of ancient Judaism; it certainly did not pose any social or political threat to Jews. As an ancient Jewish scholar Paul had every right to reinterpret Judaism by his own lights, and

Jews and Christians of all ages have every right to quarrel with him about that reinterpretation. They also have an opportunity to learn from him.

For Further Study

In the *Mercer Dictionary of the Bible*: CIRCUMCISION; FREEDOM; GALATIA; GALATIANS, LETTER TO THE; JERUSALEM COUNCIL; LAW IN THE NT; NT USE OF THE OT; OPPONENTS OF PAUL; PAUL.

In other sources: H. D. Betz, *Galatians: A Commentary on Paul's Letter to the Churches of Galatia,* Herm; F. F. Bruce, *The Epistle to the Galatians: A Commentary on the Greek Text,* NIGTC; C. H. Cosgrove, *The Cross and the Spirit: A Study in the Argument and Theology of Galatians*; R. B. Hays, *The Faith of Jesus Christ: An Investigation of the Narrative Substructure of Galatians 3:1–4:11,* SBLDS; D. Lührmann, *Galatians: A Continental Commentary*; F. J. Matera, *Galatians,* SP; R. C. Tannehill, *Dying and Rising with Christ,* BZNW.

Commentary

An Outline

I. The Opening, 1:1-5
II. A Thanksgiving Parody, 1:6-10
III. The Letter Body, 1:11–6:10
   A. Apostolic Autobiography, 1:11–2:21
   B. Central Apostolic Argument, 3:1–4:31
   C. Apostolic Exhortation, 5:1–6:10
IV. A Personal Postscript, 6:11-18

The Opening, 1:1-5

Instead of simply stating his name as "sender," Paul opens the letter by elaborating on his apostleship, declaring that he became *an apostle* directly through *Jesus Christ and God the Father*. What Paul means is that God has given him a direct commission to preach the gospel to the gentiles (1:16; cf. Rom 1:1-6, 13-14; 15:15-18), and in that commission God has also revealed the gospel to him (1:11-12). Being an apostle and knowing the gospel go together in Paul's self-understanding because he attributes both to the same source and revelatory moment.

The point of stating and defining his apostleship in the letter opening is to establish (probably by way of reminder) two things. First, the Galatians must heed what Paul says because he is God's messenger to them, the unspoken insinuation being that the Circumcisers have not gotten their message from God. Second, and by obvious implication, Paul's teaching is true because he got it straight from God.

Paul encapsulates that teaching in several brief expressions. He identifies God as *the Father, who raised* [Jesus] *from the dead* (v. 1), and he calls Jesus *the Lord,* who *gave himself for our sins to set us free from the present evil age.* The idea that the gospel means liberation from an EVIL cosmic condition (in which human beings are trapped) recurs elsewhere in the letter. That liberation, in Paul's understanding, comes to pass through Jesus' death, about which he will have more to say in 2:15-21, 3:10-14, and 6:14-15.

A Thanksgiving Parody, 1:6-10

In Paul's other letters rather elaborate "thanksgiving statements" follow his epistolary openings. But not in Galatians. Instead of celebrating their increasing growth and steadfastness in the gospel, Paul berates the Galatians for abandoning the gospel and turning to *another gospel.* He even goes so far as to pronounce a "curse" on anyone who might preach a gospel other than the one that he himself first taught the Galatians.

In the ancient Mediterranean world, it was widely assumed that the utterance of a curse, especially by a person who enjoyed special connections with the divine world (as Paul claims he does), could bring harm (including the possibility of death) to its object. Thus Paul is not simply expressing his own depth of concern; he is implementing his apostolic power (cf. 1 Cor 5:3-5) in a spiritual attack on his opponents (whom he later suggests—3:1—have themselves practiced witchcraft on the Galatians).

The Letter Body, 1:11–6:10

Apostolic Autobiography, 1:11–2:21

1:11-24. Paul's call and commission. In vv. 11-12 Paul claims that he did not receive his gospel *from* any human beings; it came directly *through a revelation of Jesus Christ.* This probably means a REVELATION by God of the risen Jesus. In 1 Cor 15:8 Paul reports that the resurrected Christ appeared to him, and in v. 16 he says that God "revealed his Son *in* me." We don't know exactly how Paul experienced this revelation (which may also be what he has in mind in 2 Cor 12:1-4), but clearly he understood it as a miraculous event in which God commissioned him to preach the gospel of Christ to gentiles without the requirement that they receive CIRCUMCISION and practice the Law of Moses. Admittedly, Paul does not say anything about the Law in vv. 11-24, but his insistence that he has always preached the same gospel (see esp. the stories that follow in 2:1-21) indicates that by *the gospel* he always means a gospel that does not require Law-keeping from gentiles.

According to some interpreters, the Circumcisers claimed that Paul received his apostolic commission from the Jerusalem apostles. In that case (so the argument goes) he would be obliged to conform his preaching to the Jerusalem version of the gospel, which the Circumcisers purport to represent. This conjecture seems very likely, considering the oath Paul takes in v. 20. But even if the Circumcisers did not claim that Paul stood under the authority of Jerusalem, Paul might well have made the argument he develops in the narrative of vv. 13-24. For that narrative backs up his claims to apostolic authority (vv. 1, 11-12) on the basis of which he instructs the Galatians about the gospel and the law, interprets scripture, and tells them how to live their lives in Christ.

Paul begins by describing his *earlier life in Judaism*, which provides a contrast to his life after receiving his call from God. It also implies that he knows more about the Law than the Circumcisers themselves do (see v. 14). Next Paul explains that after receiving his apostolic commission from God he had no contact with any of the apostles in Jerusalem. Instead he went directly to *Arabia* and then *returned to Damascus* (v. 17), which indicates that his call-revelation occurred in DAMASCUS. The point of vv. 13-17 is to refute any actual or potential claim that he received his knowledge of the gospel or any kind of commission from the Jerusalem church.

But three years later, Paul says, he did go up to JERUSALEM, evidently for the first time after receiving his call. His purpose was "to *see* Cephas" (v. 18, author trans.), Cephas probably being PETER. Paul uses a word in v. 18 (*historēsai*) that typically means to "inquire" or to "see someone about something." This shows that Paul is no longer at this point arguing that he didn't learn anything from any of the other apostles. When he says that he went up "to *see* Cephas" and that he didn't see any of the other apostles except JAMES (v. 19), he is making it clear that he had no meetings with

the Jerusalem apostles that might be construed as occasion for any apostolic commissioning. Perhaps Paul finds it important to stress the unofficial nature of his meetings with Cephas and James because he has not yet arrived at the point in his life story where he began his apostolic ministry. His first mention of "preaching the gospel" appears only after the story of his first visit to Jerusalem, which was followed by trips to *Syria and Cilicia* (v. 21). Anyone who had been told (evidently correctly) that Paul began his apostolic ministry only after his first visit to the Jerusalem church might have inferred that the Jerusalem apostles commissioned him for this work. Paul makes it clear that he was party to no official meetings of the Jerusalem apostles, and he certifies this with an oath (v. 20).

2:1-10. God leads the Jerusalem apostles to confirm Paul's gospel. In vv. 1-11 Paul describes his first official meeting with the Jerusalem apostles. Whatever the Galatians may have been told about this meeting, Paul maintains that by the end of it, thanks to his own witness (v. 2), the chief Jerusalem apostles had come to full agreement with him about the nature of his apostleship and about the gospel for the gentiles (vv. 7-9).

Cephas, James, and JOHN may have invited him or even "summoned" him to Jerusalem. But Paul says that he went up in obedience *to a revelation* (v. 2), as if to ward off any impression that he was following directives from Jerusalem. At Jerusalem he presented his gospel, apparently in both public gatherings of the church and in private conferences with church leaders (v. 2). He did so, he says, in order to make sure that he had not been laboring for nothing (v. 2). But, as it turned out, *even Titus, who was with me, was not compelled to be circumcised, though he was a Greek* (v. 3). Verses 1-3 suggest that if the Jerusalem leaders had rejected Paul's understanding of the gospel for the gentiles and had insisted that TITUS be circumcised, then Paul would have accepted this as God's will. That seems surprising in the light of how Paul has argued thus far and how he continues to underscore his independence from Jerusalem in what follows. But it is nonetheless the impression Paul leaves, perhaps as if to say, "There came a time when God (to whom I am alone obedient) told me to go to Jerusalem and submit my gospel to the test of the Jerusalem authorities, and the result was, in God's providence, that the Jerusalem apostles approved my gospel." Nevertheless, the Jerusalem apostles were really only "seeing" and "recognizing" the activity of the divine "grace" already at work in Paul apart from any agency or authorization on their part (vv. 7-9).

But there were some *false believers* (v. 4) who *slipped in to spy on the freedom we have in Christ Jesus.* This FREEDOM must be the practice of living "free" from obedience to the Law. One guesses that the "false" believers saw Paul and BARNABAS breaking the Law (perhaps in their dietary practice) or discovered that Titus was not circumcised, and then denounced Paul and his party before the Jerusalem apostles (in order to *enslave us,* Paul says). But, as v. 5 describes it, Paul and his company stood heroically steadfast "in order that the truth of the gospel might be preserved for you" (RSV)—"you" being the Galatians, whom he has not yet even met! The rhetorical point of v. 5 is to imply that even before the Galatians became Christians, Paul was on their side. From first to last he remains the hero of the gentile cause.

By contrast the pillar apostles couldn't have been more affirming of Paul. Not, Paul says, that he cared anything about their status. He, like God, doesn't pay attention to such things (v. 6). But, we might add, Paul is in fact only too pleased to point out that the pillars affirmed his gospel. So he trades on their prestige at the same time that he denies owing them any obedience or special regard.

The pillars recognized that the same God who entrusted Cephas with the *gospel for the circumcised* (v. 7, meaning a gospel for the Jews) also entrusted Paul with the *gospel for the uncircumcised* (v. 7, meaning a gospel for the gentiles). The *gospel for the uncircumcised* is a Law-free gospel, and Paul probably assumed that since there is only "one" gospel, Jewish Christians are also not *required* by the gospel to keep the Law. The pillars at Jerusalem may have understood the agreement about the gospel (vv. 6-10) to mean that Jewish Christians must keep the Law while gentile Christians are not obliged to do so. That would explain how the controversy at ANTIOCH (2:11-21) could have arisen after the agreement made in Jerusalem. The understanding achieved at Jerusalem involved a fundamental misunderstanding between the two parties.

2:11-21. Paul champions the gentile cause at Antioch. In a story about the church at Antioch Paul again portrays himself as the hero who defends the gentile cause in the gospel. As he recounts it, Jewish and gentile Christians were accustomed to eating together in the Antioch church, evidently without observing any of the Jewish dietary laws. But when a certain group *from James* came, all the Jewish Christians (except for Paul but including Cephas, and even Barnabas) abandoned table fellowship with the gentiles. Paul accuses these Jewish Christians of *hypocrisy* (v. 13), meaning they acted in a way inconsistent with what they knew and affirmed to be the *truth of the gospel* (v. 14).

We should not assume that the party *from James* carried the same message to Antioch that the Circumcisers later brought to Galatia, except in the general sense that both groups promoted the Law and linked it positively with life in Christ. The Galatians were in a position to discern points of correspondence between the Antioch incident and their own situation. We can only guess about these similarities.

Paul accuses Cephas of "compelling" (v. 14) the gentiles to *live like Jews* (i.e., by practicing the Law). Cephas, Paul says, knows better than to pressure the gentiles into Law-keeping, for he himself lives *like a Gentile and not like a Jew.* And this way of living—which Cephas's present behavior so glaringly contradicts—is in accord with the truth of the gospel. That means that in Paul's understanding neither Jewish nor gentile Christians are obliged to keep the Law. Considered in the context of the Antioch incident, it also means that when Jewish and gentile believers are together, Jewish Christians ought to live as gentiles.

The theological rationale for Jewish-Christian freedom from the Law is found in a dense and obscure argument presented, ostensibly, as the speech Paul made at Antioch. Since it was a customary practice of the time to compose speeches in the course of a historical narrative, we need not assume that Paul reproduces in vv. 14b-21 exactly what he said at Antioch. That helps explain why it is difficult to see the immediate relevance for the Antioch controversy of everything he says in these verses.

According to Paul, Jewish Christians "know" that they owe their righteousness before God to the "faith of Jesus Christ" (v. 16; NRSV mg.). Paul does not say how they know this. The Galatians are to take his word for it, Paul himself being a Jewish Christian. The phrase, "the faith of Jesus Christ," is the most natural way to translate the Greek expression found here, which may refer to Christ's own faith or, more likely, to "Christian faith" as an eschatological way of salvation. The traditional translation, *faith in Christ* forces the Greek and should be avoided unless there is no other coherent way to interpret the phrase. In 1:23 Paul says that he preaches *the faith.* In 3:23, 25 he speaks of faith as a transcendent reality that comes into the world, like Christ himself. And in 3:22 he speaks of "what was promised from the faith of Jesus Christ" (author trans.). These texts suggest that "the faith" and "the faith of Jesus Christ" are names Paul uses for the way and means of salvation that God has brought in Christ.

In v. 20 Paul speaks of "the faith of the Son of God" (NRSV mg.), meaning the faith Jesus himself exercised, which may also be the sense of "the faith of Jesus Christ" in v. 16. In either case—whether the expression means Jesus' own faithfulness or stands in a larger sense for the way of salvation in Christ—the faith of Jesus Christ, according to Paul, effects what the works of the Law could not: it alone makes Jewish Christians righteous before God.

In his discussion of salvation, Paul uses a verb (*dikaioun*) that is used in the SEPTUAGINT in the passive voice to render Hebrew expressions that mean "be righteous" or "become righteous." It makes sense to follow this usage in translating the passive form of the verb (*dikaiousthai*) in Paul. Thus, we may render v. 16, "we know that a person does not become righteous by works of the Law but by the faith of Jesus Christ." The passive form occurs three times in v. 16. It is also found at v. 17, 3:11, 3:24, and 5:4.

Does righteousness (or JUSTIFICATION) by this faith imply that Jewish Christians are not obligated to keep the Law? In v. 17 Paul links seeking to be righteous in Christ with a way of living that leaves Christians open to the charge that they are sinners—sinners because they do not keep the Law. Presumably the party from James leveled this charge at the Jewish Christians at Antioch. Paul's answer to this charge is that if seeking to be righteous in Christ makes Jewish Christians sinners, then Christ himself is an agent of sin. That is, the rhetorical question in v. 17 is a *reductio ad absurdum*. As an argument it has force only if one already accepts Paul's premise that seeking to be righteous in Christ rules out seeking to be righteous by the Law. The party from James no doubt sees righteousness in Christ and righteousness in the Law as compatible. Paul doesn't. He "knows" that God commissioned him, a Jew, to evangelize and live among gentiles, without imposing the Law on them. This probably explains why he is so certain about the distinction between the righteousness provided in Christ—which both Jews and gentiles have—and the righteousness of the Law (which, according to Phil 3:6, he once had). According to v. 18, Paul would make himself a sinner before God only if he were to reinstate the requirements of the Law (*the very things that I once tore down*). The same

holds for the Jewish Christians at Antioch, who have in fact reinstated those requirements, thus making themselves sinners before God by abandoning the righteousness they have in Christ—a righteousness constituted in part by their table fellowship with gentile Christians.

Verses 19-20 take another approach. In Christ, believers "die" to the Law, just as they die *with Christ* to the present world order (6:14; cf. Rom 7:4-6). They die *through the law* (v. 19) because Christ's death took place through the Law, namely, through the *curse of the law* (3:13). Thus, to be a Christian is to be *crucified with Christ*, which transfers one to the sphere of being in Christ. Only by dying with Christ does one come to experience eschatological life, signified in v. 19 by the Hellenistic Jewish expression *live to God* (cf. 4 Macc 7:19; 16:25). It follows from this interpretation of Christ's death that Christians are righteous because Christ lives through them and that they owe no obedience to the Law because they have died to it.

Paul closes off this argument with another *reductio ad absurdum*. If righteousness before God could be achieved through the Law, *then Christ died for nothing* (v. 21). Paul's point is that since Christ obviously did not die for nothing, righteousness must not be "from the Law." But this argument does not refute the view that righteousness before God depends on both the Law (as norm) and Christ (as source of atonement and moral power in the Spirit), which may be the theological opinion of the party from James (and the Circumcisers at Galatia).

Central Apostolic Argument, 3:1–4:31

3:1-5. Faith mediates the Spirit. With this paragraph Paul addresses the Galatians directly, suggests they have been *bewitched*, and gives some important clues about what he understands the "other gospel" (1:7) in Galatians to be. The passage moves from a question about the past to an inference about the present. The Galatians know that they received *the Spirit* (when Paul first preached to them) because they heard and believed, not because they began practicing the Law (v. 2). *Therefore*—the Greek text of v. 5 contains the illative particle *oun*—they should draw the same conclusion about the basis of their present experience of the Spirit: "Does the one who supplies you with the Spirit and works miracles among you do so because of the works of the Law or because you heard and believed [the gospel]?" (author trans.). The implied answer is that God's present provision of the Spirit and its mighty works has nothing to do with whether or not the Galatians keep the Law. Or, as vv. 3-4 suggest, if the Galatians continue on their present course with the Law they will end up with the flesh and, presumably, lose the Spirit (see FLESH AND SPIRIT).

This is the first argument aimed directly at the Galatians in their own situation, and it suggests that the Circumcisers told the Galatians that doing the Law mediates the power of the Spirit.

3:6-14. Faith brings the Spirit as the blessing of Abraham. In vv. 6-14 Paul develops a somewhat intricate argument to show that the blessing of the Spirit comes through the death of Christ alone, apart from the Law. First, he cites a scripture text that makes "faith" a basis for "righteousness" (Gen 15:6 quoted in v. 6) and concludes from this that *those who believe* (lit. "those from faith") are Abraham's children (v. 7). He then uses this bit of exegesis to interpret another, more famous, scriptural promise about all the gentiles (or "nations") being blessed through Abraham (Gen 12:3; cf. 18:18). By associating Gen 15:6 and Gen 12:3, Paul is able to draw the conclusion he needs to make his point: the blessing of Abraham on the gentiles belongs to those who share Abraham's faith, that is, to gentiles like the Galatians (v. 9).

But what is the blessing of Abraham? Since Paul seems to interpret this blessing in an all-encompassing sense in Rom 4:13 (as "inheriting the world"), we should perhaps not limit it in any way here. But the explicit content that Paul identifies as the substance of the promise to Abraham is *the Spirit* (v. 14). And we should note here the following implication of this identification: The blessing of Abraham is fulfilled among the Galatians in their present experience, namely, in God's ongoing gift of the Spirit to them, which includes *miracles* (v. 5).

Verses 10-14 develop the argument from Abraham in a way that relates that blessing to two of the letter's central themes: the Law and the cross of Christ. While it was a well-established Jewish tradition, based in the Bible, that faithfulness to the Law brings God's blessing, Paul radically disjoins the two. Those who *rely on* the Law fall *under a curse*, the Law's own curse upon the unrighteous (v. 10). This happens because "in the Law (i.e., in the sphere of the Law) no one is righteous before God" (v. 11a, author trans.; on the translation "no one is righteous," see the comments on 2:16). Paul does not attempt to prove this by arguing that no one can keep the Law perfectly. Instead he quotes the words of Hab 2:4 as proof that no one in

the Law is righteous before God. *"The one who is righteous will live by faith,"* Paul declares (v. 11b), citing a version of Hab 2:4 that does not contain the possessive pronoun "his" (as the Hebrew scriptures do) or "my" (as the LXX does) before the word "faith." Nor does Paul mark it as a quotation from scripture by introducing it with a phrase such as "as it is written." He apparently expects the Galatians to recognize the words, probably because he himself made this text central to his foundation teaching (cf. Rom 1:17).

Scripture prophesies that the righteous person will *live by faith* (v. 11b). The Law, by contrast, *does not rest on faith* (v. 12a). As proof Paul now cites another scripture text, again without identifying it as such: "The one who does them [the works of the Law] will live by them" (v. 12b; author trans.). This is a paraphrase of Lev 18:5, a passage sometimes echoed in Jewish formulations of the Law's promise of life (cf. Neh 9:29; Ezek 20:13; Luke 10:28; CD 3:16; PssSol 14:3). The Circumcisers might have quoted this text to the Galatians as proof that doing the Law mediates eschatological life (the ongoing power of the Spirit). By contrasting Hab 2:4 and Lev 18:5, Paul demands that the Galatians choose between *faith* (meaning "Christian faith") and *works of the Law*, which comprise two ways of relating to God. The Circumcisers no doubt integrated these two ways by combining faith with works of the law. If so, Paul sharply distinguishes what they join. Nevertheless, nothing in the contrast itself, but only the preceding argumentation (in vv. 1-5 and vv. 6-9) and the weight of Paul's apostolic authority, are likely to persuade the Galatians to treat Hab 2:4 (and not Lev 18:5) as the definitive biblical word for the new age.

In v. 13 Paul declares that Christ *redeemed us from the curse of the law by becoming a curse for us.* According to the Law-text cited here (Deut 21:23), victims of crucifixion are an abomination (or "curse") in God's sight. Paul equates this curse with the curse of the Law already mentioned in v. 10. The death of Christ lifts this curse *for us*, a phrase that refers to those under the Law's curse and therefore may refer strictly to Jews.

With the transference of the curse to Christ the blessing of Abraham in Christ can flow to the gentiles (v. 14a) so that *we might receive the promise of the Spirit through faith* (v. 14b). Paul doesn't explain how the lifting of the curse from the unrighteous in the Law lets the blessing flow to the gentiles, with the reciprocal effect that "we" (which must mean we Jews who believe in Christ) receive the promise of the Spirit by faith. The Galatians are to take Paul's authoritative word for it. But they may also find his interpretation appealing, since it implies that Jewish Christians (such as the Circumcisers) enjoy the life of the Spirit solely by faith and only because God has first given this blessing to gentiles (such as the Galatians)!

3:15-18. Christ the sole heir of Abraham. Paul supplements his argument about how the blessing of Abraham (the Spirit) comes by comparing the Abrahamic covenant to a will. Even in human affairs it is illegal to add a codicil to a covenant (or a "will") once it has been ratified. God ratified the covenant with Abraham, in which God promised the inheritance to Abraham's offspring, long before God gave the Law. Therefore God could not, with justice, add the Law as a kind of later codicil, thus making the inheritance conditional upon keeping the Law. Since the very idea that God might attempt such an unfair thing is blasphemous, Paul qualifies his argument from the outset by explaining that he is going to speak "like a (mere) human being" (which is what v. 15 literally says).

The aim of vv. 15-18 is to reinforce Paul's contention that the Law has no say about the promise God made to Abraham, which Paul has already indicated is the *promise of the Spirit* (v. 14). God's promise to Abraham concerned an inheritance for a single *offspring* (v. 16), Paul says, quoting God's promissory words, *"And to your offspring,"* in Gen 13:15 (cf. Gen 12:7). In fact, the word *offspring* can be used in both the collective and the singular sense. In Gen 13:15 it is used as a collective (meaning "descendants"), but Paul interprets it as singular and takes it as referring to Christ. This exegetical move makes Christ the sole heir of the promise, thus excluding all those "in the Law" along with everyone else in the world! In 3:22-29 Paul explains how others come to be included with Christ as heirs of the promise.

3:19-22. The purpose of the Law. After disconnecting the Law from the promise and attributing to the Law the power only to curse and not to bless, Paul must explain why God gave the Law in the first place. He offers a brief and rather obscure answer to this question in vv. 19b-20. The Law was given "for transgressions" (v. 19b, author's trans.), which may mean to inhibit them. But, in view of Rom 5:20, it might mean "to create them" by making sin legally punishable as transgression. The remainder of vv. 19-20 poses an exegetical conundrum that continues to vex interpreters. Paul is perhaps arguing that the Law came

only indirectly from God and therefore enjoys a lower status than the covenant with Abraham (which God made directly with Abraham).

In vv. 21-22 Paul seeks to dispel any impression that he views the Law as an opponent of the promise. The opponent is sin, which dominates all things (v. 22). The Law was never endowed with any power to *make alive,* hence it is not able to produce righteousness in a sin-enslaved world (cf. 1:4, *the present evil age*).

3:23-29. Becoming heirs with Christ. Having offered a brief defense of the Law in order to defend his own interpretation of its place in history, Paul now takes up an unfinished line of argument begun in 3:15-18. How can anyone become an heir of the promise to Abraham if Christ himself is the sole heir (3:15; cf. 3:19)?

Those under the Law are enslaved to sin. During this enslavement the Law serves as a kind of "guardian" (*paidagōgos*) until the arrival of Christian faith (3:23-25). In the Greco-Roman world the *paidagōgos* had charge of a boy during his minority, that is, until the boy came into his inheritance (see the comments on 4:1-11). Thus, being under the Law's guardianship, Paul says, coincides with the time of *waiting* for the inheritance. But now that *faith* has arrived (v. 25), this time of waiting under the guardianship of the Law is over.

The arrival of *faith* with Jesus Christ has transformed the Galatians into God's children (lit., "sons of God"). Through baptism they have "put on Christ" (RSV) and become "one" in Christ (vv. 27-28). That makes them part of the "one offspring" of Abraham, and in this process of unification with Christ they become heirs of the promise given to Christ alone (v.29).

4:1-11. The limited time of the Law. In 4:1-11 Paul explains what he meant by saying (in 3:23-25) that being under the Law is like being under a guardian. To be an heir during one's minority (childhood) is to be in a position no better than a slave, without access to the goods of one's inheritance. During this time the heir (typically a male) is under various overseers until a time set by his father. In the same way, Paul says, Jews and gentiles alike lived in a period of minority until the time of fulfillment set by God. But now that the *fullness of time* [has] *come* (v. 4), those redeemed by God through divine *adoption* receive the goods of the *inheritance,* namely, the Spirit itself (vv. 6-7).

In vv. 8-11 Paul equates serving the Law with bondage to the *elemental spirits* of the world. Many

Jews in Paul's day attributed cosmic wisdom to the Law. Perhaps the Circumcisers taught the Galatians that by observing the Jewish calendar, informed by the Law's cosmic wisdom, Christians may live safely and prosperously in the present age (see v. 10). Paul calls this a path to cosmic bondage. Accepting the Law only brings the Galatians right back to the situation of futility in which Paul found them, when they were *enslaved to beings that by nature are not gods* (v. 8).

4:12-20. A "pathos" appeal. In 4:12-20 Paul makes an emotional appeal, what ancient rhetoricians called an argument from "pathos." He reminds the Galatians of the kindness and honor they bestowed upon him during his first visit (vv. 13-16), and wonders whether his letter, with its blunt truthfulness, will make him their enemy (v. 16). He attributes ulterior motives to the Circumcisers (v. 17) and describes himself, by contrast, as a mother who is perplexed by the fact that she is in labor pangs all over again with the same child (vv. 19-20)!

4:21-31. The law bears children for slavery. Before issuing apostolic exhortation to the community, Paul presents an allegorical interpretation of the story of Abraham's two wives and two sons. Paul identifies the slave wife HAGAR with the covenant of the Law from Mount SINAI. The Law, as a slavewoman, bears children for slavery. These enslaved children comprise the present Jerusalem, which stands for the Jewish people as a whole. The freewoman SARAH (who represents God's covenant with Abraham) stands, allegorically, for the heavenly Jerusalem, where the free children of the Spirit are born. This Jerusalem is *our mother* (v. 26), Paul says, including himself and the Galatians (v. 28) among her children.

The Mosaic covenant and the Abrahamic covenant are not only distinct, their children are at odds with each other: *But just as at that time the child who was born according to the flesh persecuted the child who was born according to the Spirit, so it is now also* (v. 29, quoting Gen 21:9), a citation that the Galatians are likely to construe as a call to expel the Circumcisers from their midst.

Apostolic Exhortation, 5:1–6:10

5:1-12. Stand fast in freedom. The logically inseparable themes of SLAVERY and FREEDOM have been running through the letter since the beginning (see 1:4; 2:4-5; 3:13, 22-25; 4:1-11, 21-31). According to Paul, Christ's death liberates people from slavery to sin. It redeems those under the Law from the Law's curse on

the unrighteous. At the same time it also establishes freedom from the Law as a way of righteousness, an idea first broached in chap. 2 (2:4-5; 2:15-21). In v. 1 Paul calls the Galatians to stand fast in this (threefold) freedom to which Christ has set them free. He follows up this basic exhortation with a series of warnings (vv. 2-6). Accepting circumcision removes one from the sphere of Christ's blessing (v. 2). It also obligates a person to keep the entire Law (v. 3), which the Galatians may not realize if the Circumcisers have so far insisted only on circumcision and the Jewish calendar (cf. 4:10 and 6:12-13). In v. 4 Paul reiterates the point of v. 2, telling the Galatians that by becoming "righteous in the Law" (author trans.; on this translation, see the comments on 2:16) they lose Christ and fall from grace.

Next Paul describes his own view of Christian existence in ways that prepare for the ethical exhortation to follow. *For through the Spirit, by faith, we eagerly wait for the hope of righteousness* (v. 5). The words *hope of righteousness* probably mean the hope of salvation that belongs to righteousness and not the hope of becoming righteous. Thus far Paul has described the ethics of this righteousness only once. In 2:17 the expression *our effort to be justified in Christ* describes the way of life that Paul has adopted by giving up the practice of the Law in order to be in communion with gentile Christians. In v. 6 he defines the ethics of this righteousness as *faith working through love*. Paul would probably call the originally integrated community life at Antioch (2:12a) an expression of this love-working faith. In 5:13–6:10 he elaborates on his view that "love" is the basic form and guiding principle of righteousness in Christ.

Verses 7-12 resemble the "pathos appeal" of 4:12-20 in emotional tone and strategy. Paul celebrates the Galatians' beginnings in Christ, expresses confidence about their future, and blames the Circumcisers for the Galatians' defection from *the truth*. It may be that one of the Circumcisers is *confusing* the Galatians by telling them that in other churches Paul himself preaches circumcision (vv. 10-11).

5:13-26. Love as the way of freedom in the Spirit. Verses 13-26 show how the theme of *love* is related to basic themes of the earlier argumentation, namely, *freedom, the Law, the cross*, and *the Spirit*. Believers have died in Christ to the Law as a way of righteousness (2:17-20). The resultant freedom in Christ is to take ethical form as serving one another in love (v. 13). This is what it means to "walk by the Spirit" (v.

16 RSV; cf. v. 25). Opposed to this way of living is what Paul terms *the flesh* and its desires (v. 17), which he personifies as a kind of independent power. The passions of the flesh produce the *works of the flesh* described in vv. 19-21. These passions are in opposition to the Spirit, which produces the *fruit* described in vv. 22-23. The opposition of the flesh and the Spirit hinders Christians from doing what they *want* (v. 17). That means that the choice created for them by their freedom is to follow one of these two powers (cf. v. 13). If they *live by the Spirit* (i.e., yield to its desires, following the principle of love), they will not satisfy the passions of the flesh (v. 16).

Walking by the Spirit in love fulfills a basic intent of the Law (v. 14). In saying this Paul cites Lev 19:18, *You shall love your neighbor as yourself.* Early Christians identified Lev 19:18 as a summary of the Law, having learned to do so from Judaism (and especially from Jesus' own prophetic Jewish teaching). Paul is not saying that Christians must show love because the Law tells them to, but that the love commanded by the Spirit is in continuity with a basic interest of the Law itself. Dying with Christ (see the comments on 2:19-20) crucifies the flesh with its passions and cravings (v. 24). This enables believers to fulfill this way of love, which is embodied in the *fruit of the Spirit* (vv. 22-23). And, with a touch of wry humor, Paul comments that *there is no law* against such things as *love, joy, peace, patience, kindness,* and so forth.

6:1-10. Concluding exhortations. The ethical exhortation in vv. 1-10 presents additional and more specific admonitions. The community is to treat those who sin with gentleness and humility, renouncing spiritual rivalry (vv. 1-5). By bearing one another's burdens they will *fulfill the law of Christ* (v. 2). Paul does not define this law. Perhaps he expects the Galatians to recognize it as something he taught them about during his first visit. The law of Christ is probably the way of Christ exemplified in Christ's self-giving love (the way of Christ *who . . . gave himself for me,* 2:20; who "did not please himself," Rom 15:3; and who "became poor" for the sake of others, 2 Cor 8:9).

In vv. 7-10 Paul takes up the themes of the flesh and the Spirit once more (cf. 5:13-26), encouraging the Galatians to *sow to the Spirit* in order to inherit *eternal life* (cf. 5:21). Paul defines *sowing to the Spirit* in ethical terms as *doing what is right* (v. 9), which

means *work for the good of all, and especially for those of the family of faith* (v. 10). The Greek expression behind *work for the good* is typically used in Hellenistic Jewish Greek to designate assistance to the poor, and this nuance (which echoes 2:10) should be heard in v. 10 as well.

A Personal Postscript, 6:11-18

The concluding postscript indicates that Paul followed the custom of having a trained writer (an *amanuensis*) take down the letter. But now at the end, as was also common, Paul inscribes something in his own (evidently clumsy) hand (v. 11). In this last word to the Galatians, Paul claims that the Circumcisers themselves don't even keep the Law (v. 13). Perhaps the Circumcisers think that only certain requirements of the Law (above all regarding CIRCUMCISION but apparently also the Jewish calendar; see 4:10) are obligatory for gentile Christians. In that case, Paul may be alleging, the Circumcisers prove themselves unfaithful to the very Law they are promoting. For circumcision (as Paul says in 5:3) obligates one to keep the entire Law, not just certain parts of it.

Paul also accuses the Circumcisers of seeking to avoid suffering for the cross (v. 12) and being interested only in their own glory ("boasting" in the Galatians' circumcised flesh, v. 13). He contrasts himself with them by declaring that he boasts only in *the cross of . . . Christ* (v. 14). The cross, Paul says, means death to the world (v. 14) and establishes a *new creation* in which *neither circumcision nor uncircumcision* counts for anything (v. 15; cf. 5:6). In Christ's death the present world itself also dies, at least as far as those in Christ are concerned. This implies that the community of those in Christ is the locus of the new creation.

Righteousness in this new creation constitutes itself in the erasure of distinctions between Jew and Gentile, male and female, slave and free (6:15; 3:28). These distinctions represent hierarchies by which the present age is ordered. But they come to an end in the death of the present world through Christ's crucifixion. Thus Paul closes his letter on a revolutionary note, declaring that the new social order, which embodies the apocalyptic hope of new creation, has already dawned in Christ. And the church is to be the place in the world where this new social order is sown.

Ephesians

Frank Stagg

Introduction

Ephesians is the most comprehensive writing in the NT on the church, both goal and instrument in God's *eternal purpose* to create in Christ Jesus *one new humanity*. It was *through the cross* that God broke down *the dividing wall* between Jew and gentile, replacing *hostility* with *peace*.

Opening with a doxology praising God for carrying through his redemptive purpose which antedates *the foundation of the world* and prayer for the illumination and empowering of the readers, the letter continues with an exposition of the origin, nature, and mission of the CHURCH, with a call to unity, freedom from old vices, and practice of virtues proper to God's people.

Authorship and Destination

PAUL as author is explicit in the first word of the text, supported by autobiographical references to bonds, afflictions, and *chains* (3:1, 13; 4:1; 6:20). Matters of style, word usage, and theology leave scholars divided as to whether authentically from Paul, a pseudonym, or an insoluble problem (see Tolbert 1990 and Kümmel 1975, 357-63). It does follow that the letter is from Paul or from some cogent, unknown writer with amazing insight into Paul's mind and experience.

No theory of destination is compelling. The superscription "To the Ephesians" was probably added when letters of Paul were first collected and published as a corpus. MARCION (ca. 140) listed this letter as "To the Laodiceans," probably influenced by Col 4:16. The words *in Ephesus* (1:1) are absent from the earliest known manuscripts (including 𝔭46, Vaticanus, and Sinaiticus), and were unknown to Tertullian and Origen, in which no place name appears. Nothing in the letter implies Ephesus. TYCHICUS, bearer of the letter (6:21), may have been authorized to insert a place name if the letter was to be read in various churches, but this is speculation.

Date

If not from Paul, there are no criteria for dating the letter. If from Paul, either his Caesarean or Roman imprisonment is likely. If, as held here, Ephesians is Paul's response to his eviction from the Temple and arrest in JERUSALEM, the likely date is around 60 C.E.

Relationship with Colossians

About one-third of Colossians appears also in Ephesians. Verbal parallels are found throughout the letter with the exception of 2:6-9, 4:5-13, and 5:29-33. Whether by common authorship or not, it is generally recognized that Ephesians is dependent upon Colossians and not vice versa. Both letters feature Christ and the church, differing in focus. In Colossians, Christ is the head of the church; in Ephesians, the church is the body of Christ. These two foci are not mutually exclusive or improbable for the same author, different situations calling for different emphases.

Occasion and Purpose

The theme that dominates Ephesians, God's purpose to reconcile Jews and gentiles to himself and to one another, in Christ Jesus and through the cross, also runs through Paul's undisputed writings, and it is emphatic in Romans and Acts. A flood of light falls upon Romans and Ephesians as well as Acts if it is perceived that Romans was written on the eve of Paul's visit to Jerusalem (cf. 15:25) and Ephesians after his eviction from the Temple and arrest leading to years of imprisonment in CAESAREA and ROME.

The *dividing wall* seen as *broken down* (2:14) seems to echo Paul's eviction from the Temple when charged that he has "actually brought Greeks into the temple and has defiled this holy place" (Acts 21:28). A wall separated the Court of the gentiles from that of the Jews, with plaques warning that anyone of another nation caught beyond that wall would be responsible for his death which would follow. That wall stood materially until the destruction of the Temple by Roman armies in 70 C.E.; but to Ephesians, that wall was in effect already broken down in that what it represented was rejected.

Before reading Ephesians, it is illuminating to read in Acts 20–28 Paul's last-recorded visit to Jerusalem and also Paul's own compulsion to make that visit as anticipated in 1 Cor 16:1-4, 2 Cor 8-9, and Rom 15:22-33 (see Stagg 1990, 259—78).

Wanting to go to Spain by way of Rome, Paul felt compelled to go first to Jerusalem with an offering called a *koinōnia* from MACEDONIA and ACHAIA for the poor among the *saints* in Jerusalem (Rom 15:26). Paul's strategy was to get gentile churches to give not only money but themselves to the Jews (2 Cor 8–9) and to get the Jewish saints in Jerusalem to accept not only the money but the gentile Christians who gave it (Rom 15:31). Thus, Paul's mission to Jerusalem intended both to provide relief for the poor and to unite Jew and gentile in Christ. Instead, the mission led to his eviction from the Temple and the closing of Tem-ple doors not only to gentiles but also to a Jew such as Paul (Acts 21:30).

Paul was held prisoner for two years in Caesarea and under house arrest in Rome for at least two years (Acts 28:30). It is plausible that sometime during those years he looked back upon that traumatic experience in Jerusalem and wrote his classic on the Church. At the heart of Ephesians is the vision of "the broken wall" (Barth 1959). Along with the sign of the veil in the Temple "torn in two, from top to bottom" (Matt 27:51) stands that in Ephesians of "the broken wall." Much of the gospel is dramatized in these two signs.

For Further Study

In the *Mercer Dictionary of the Bible*: BAPTISM; CHURCH; COLOSSIANS, LETTER TO THE; EPHESIANS, LETTER TO THE; EPHESUS; MARCION; PAUL; RECONCILIATION; ROMAN EMPIRE; SLAVERY IN THE NT; SATAN IN THE NT. In other sources: M. Barth, *The Broken Wall*; *Ephesians*; W. G. Kümmel, *Introduction to the N.T.*; N. H. Keathley, ed., *With Steadfast Purpose*; J. A. Robinson, *St. Paul's Epistle to the Ephesians*; A. Van Roon, *The Authenticity of Ephesians*.

Commentary

An Outline

> I. Salutation, 1:1-2
> II. Doxology and Prayer, 1:3-23
> III. The Unity of All Humankind in Christ, 2:1–3:21
> IV. Practical Exhortations, 4:1–6:20
> V. Personal Words and Benediction, 6:21-24

Salutation, 1:1-2

The greeting is similar to that in Colossians, the most striking difference being the absence of a place name, except in later manuscripts. There is no compelling explanation for this absence. Origen took the phrase *tois ousin* ("those being") in an ontological sense, that is, "the saints who truly are!" The NRSV mg. reading is possible, "saints who are also faithful."

Doxology and Prayer, 1:3-23

1:3-14. Doxology. These twelve verses consist of one sentence in the Greek text. They fall into three strophes, each ending with *to the praise of his glory* (vv. 6, 12, 14). A trinitarian motif may be implied, for the first strophe praises *the God and Father of our Lord Jesus Christ*, the second praises *Christ*, and the third praises the *Holy Spirit*. This could argue for a post-Pauline development, but it is anticipated in 2 Cor 13:13. No formal doctrine of trinity appears, for the letter begins and closes with *God our (the) Father and the Lord Jesus Christ*, with no reference to the Holy Spirit.

The first strophe (vv. 3-6) traces our calling to a holy and blameless life and destiny as God's children to God's having elected us *before the foundation of the world*. ELECTION and destiny do not imply unilateral determination; they simply mean that God calls us before we are able to answer.

The second strophe (vv. 7-12) is laden with heavy theological terms about God's accomplishments *in Christ*. *Redemption* is liberation from the bondage of sin. This liberation is effected through Christ's *blood*, his life given for us. *Forgiveness* is not indulgence; it is not only acceptance of the sinner but overcoming of *trespasses*, all traceable to God's *grace*. In Christ is seen God's *plan for the fullness of time*, that is, *to gather up all things in him*.

The third strophe (vv. 13-14) praises the *Holy Spirit*, the present possession of whom gives us the *pledge* (*arrabōn* = a down payment making a transaction binding) of our full redemption as God's people.

1:15-23. Prayer. This is one long sentence in Greek. It is a prayer that the readers be illuminated so as to know *the hope* implied in God's call, *the riches* of the *inheritance* God has offered, and the *power* which is inherently God's and which expresses itself in overcoming all resistance. It is the prayer that the readers experience within themselves the very power that *raised [Jesus] from the dead.*

The Unity of All Humankind in Christ, 2:1–3:21

Chapters 2–3 form the theological base for the CHURCH as the new humanity composed of Jew and gentile, God's new creation in Christ. With this is Paul's understanding of his own ministry to the gentiles and his prayer for his readers.

2:1-10. From death to life. Two foci appear: *You were dead. . . . But God . . . made us alive together with Christ* (vv. 1, 4-5). The emphasis is upon God's act of GRACE in giving new life to gentiles; but the *You* (v. 1) is expanded to *All of us* (v. 3), Jew and gentile alike, dead in sin until brought to life by God's grace.

In fact, several contrasts appear in this passage: Jew and gentile once dead, now made alive; Jew and gentile once divided, now together; not our work, but God's work; not by good works but for good works.

Trespasses (*paraptomasin*) refer to willful acts of disobedience. *Sins* (*hamartiais*) may refer to failure or "missing the mark," but even this term implies guilt. Sin is not only an act of disobedience, it results in spiritual death (Rom 6:23).

Paul shared the widely held view that powerful, evil spirits under an evil ruler (SATAN) are behind human sin, but this does not imply that we are mere victims and not *disobedient* sinners. He also saw that Jews as well as gentiles followed *the desires of flesh and senses*; but again, they were not merely victims. *Flesh* stands for disposition and life apart from God, with no special reference to the literal flesh (cf. Gal 5:19-21 for "the works of the flesh" as nonsensual as well as sensual). Also, Jews as well as gentiles are seen as *by nature children of wrath* (v. 3). This does not imply that they were mere victims of Adam's sin or of God's anger. "Wrath" to Paul was not God's anger so much as God's letting us follow our own choices even if they lead to our self-destruction (cf. Rom 1:18-32). Sinners "by nature" means that Jew and gentile alike are sinners in their natural state.

But God introduces the positive side of "from death to life." Salvation for gentile and Jew is new life and new life together, grounded in God's rich *mercy*, out of his *great love*, and by his *grace*. Sin and death are the works of Jew and gentile. Life, including life together with God and with one another, is God's act out of his love, mercy, and grace.

Verse 5 may intend that God makes each Jew and gentile alive *with Christ*. Probably it intends that "in the Christ" (so in p^{46}, Vaticanus, et al.), God makes Jew and gentile alive with one another. This parallels the picture in v. 6 (obscured in NRSV): "both raised together and seated together in the heavenlies in Christ Jesus" (author's trans.). This is the major theme of Ephesians. Overcoming hostility between Jew and gentile will *show the immeasurable riches of his grace in kindness toward us in Christ Jesus* (v. 7).

Salvation is *by grace* through the *faith* that is trust; and though not of our own doing, it is *for good works.* Jew and gentile as a new creation is in eternal design and achievement God's *poiema, what he has made us*!

2:11-22. One fresh humanity in Christ. Continuing his "before and after" theme, Paul contrasts the gentile status before Christ and now. They once were called *"the uncircumcision"* by those called *"the circumcision"* (v. 11). Paul himself had once built his faith and practice upon such an arbitrary and superficial distinction. He now exposes it in three Greek words: "in flesh, handmade." It is "in flesh," thus superficial; it is "handmade," thus artificial—a little skin removed with a knife.

The gentile's real privation was not genetic or cultic; it was the alienation from God and thus alienation from the people of God. The privation was not "uncircumcision" or being born gentile; it was being *without Christ*. It was in being *in the world* (a world like this) *without God*. Paul's word is *atheoi*, literally "atheists." Gentiles were not atheists in a philosophical sense; they were strangers to the true God, thus *strangers to the covenants of promise, having no hope.* They had their gods and their hopes; but they did not have "the hope of glory" (Col 1:27).

Verse 13 introduces the mighty newness *in Christ Jesus*. Those once *far off have now been brought near by the blood of Christ.* Again, the union of Jew and gentile in Christ is the overriding theme of Ephesians.

Verses 14-22 comprise the heart of Ephesians. This paragraph seems to look back on Paul's trauma of eviction from the Temple in Jerusalem, charged with having taken uncircumcised gentiles beyond the dividing wall separating the Court of the gentiles from that of the Jews (Acts 21:27-30). Although the wall stood materially until destroyed by Roman soldiers in 70 C.E., Paul saw that Christ Jesus had already in effect broken it down, rejecting the principles upon which it had been built.

Christ himself (*autos*) *is our peace*! This means peace with God, but the emphasis is upon peace between Jew and gentile, for *in his flesh he has made both groups into one*. Jesus not only rejected in words the holiness code that superficially ruled some "clean" and others "unclean" (cf. Mark 7:23); he rejected that code in his actions, touching a leper (Mark 1:41) and eating with "tax gatherers and sinners" (Luke 15:1-2). He defined his true family in terms not of flesh but of obedience to the will of God (Mark 3:35).

Christ broke down the separating wall when he *abolished the law with its commandments and ordinances* (v. 15). He not only rejected such ordinances as kosher foods and purification rites but also the holiness code that rested upon externals (e.g., Lev 15:19-20; 21:18-24; Deut 23:1-6). He followed the tradition already found in such scriptures as Ps 24:3-6 and Mic 6:8. His holiness code had to do with moral and ethical principles and the attitudes and dispositions behind such principles and actions. When one holiness code replaced another, the dividing wall was broken down. (see HOLY SPIRIT).

Peace was made when Christ created in himself *one new humanity in place of the two* (v. 15). "Fresh" is a better rendering of *kainon* than "new." The church, the body of Christ, is not simply novel; it is a fresh kind of humanity where worldly criteria that separate are replaced by principles that unite. The old humanity was bent on excluding; the new humanity seeks to include.

The *one body* in which Jew and gentile are reconciled (v. 16) is the CHURCH. This is achieved *through the cross*, where the principle of self-serving is overcome by that of self-giving. The Jew-gentile hostility, like every hostility, was based on the self-serving principle. The CROSS is the ultimate in the self-denial which is salvation (Mark 8:34-35; John 12:24-26). The "enmity" (KJV; NRSV *hostility*) that is slain at the cross is life centered upon itself, the sin behind all sins.

The *peace* proclaimed to those *far off* and those *near* is peace between gentile and Jew; but it is first of all peace with God and peace with and within themselves (v. 17). This peace occurs when the love that serves and includes replaces the selfishness that exploits and excludes.

Jews and gentiles now have the same *access* to the Father, through Christ and *in one Spirit* (v. 18). Gone are the old courts, walls, barriers, and doors segregating Jews from gentiles, men from women, and priests from laypersons, as was built into the architecture of the Temple and imposed upon people. The "broken wall" and the "rent veil" mean now that all in Christ and by faith may enter the "Holy of Holies" into the very presence of *the Father*.

Using a political model, gentiles *are no longer strangers and aliens*, foreigners merely tolerated in another's land. They are *citizens with the saints and also members of the household of God* (v. 19). In Christ, Jews and gentiles alike are at home in God's house, unlike Temple discrimination.

The model having the church built upon *the foundation of the apostles and prophets* (v. 20) is seen by some as impossible to Paul, for whom the only possible foundation is Jesus Christ (1 Cor 3:11). The point is weighty and, to many, decisive against Pauline authorship of Ephesians. On the other hand, models are flexible; and different models are not necessarily competing. Ephesians holds to the centrality of Christ, whatever is intended here. *The foundation of the apostles and prophets* is ambiguous. This may intend either the apostles and prophets themselves as the foundation, or the foundation upon which they built. Christ is the unrivaled creator and lord of the church, the model here being *cornerstone*, not a mere ornamental stone but a keystone holding walls together.

Unlike the old Temple with dividing walls and veil, Jews and gentiles in Christ now form a new *holy temple*, built together into *a dwelling place for God* (vv. 21-22). God dwells in the fellowship of His people.

3:1-13. Paul's ministry to the gentiles. In 3:1 Paul began to pray, and then he paused to describe his role in ministry to the gentiles before resuming his prayer in 3:14 (each unit introduced with *Toutou charin*, "because of this"). In effect, vv. 2-13 form a digression, although highly relevant and instructive.

Identifying himself as *prisoner for Christ Jesus for the sake of you Gentiles*, Paul breaks off to give the background against which his prayer is best understood. NRSV obscures by seeing "this cause" (KJV; NRSV *reason*) as explaining Paul's imprisonment rather than why he presumes to pray for the gentiles.

To understand why Paul thus prays for the gentiles requires that they understand his special commission as minister to the gentiles. The explanation revolves around *the mystery* given him *by revelation* and his commission to proclaim the good news of God's eternal purpose to unite Jews and gentiles in Christ.

The commission given Paul translates *oikonomian*, a term for stewardship or management of a house. "Dispensation" (KJV) is misleading when confused with modern dispensational ideas. Paul simply means that the REVELATION given him carries with it a stewardship obligation to proclaim it (see 3:9). *Diakonos* (servant or minister) carries the same idea in v. 7. By the grace of God, Paul has received this revelation and the commission to proclaim it.

Paul calls this revelation a *mystery*, about which he has written briefly (v. 3), presumably in the early part of this letter (see also Col 1:26-27). This mystery is now an open secret, known first to God alone, and then revealed to his servant who is to proclaim it to Jews and gentiles. It is not apparent who were the *holy apostles and prophets* to whom this mystery was revealed. This understanding was offered the Twelve, but for the most part they resisted it (cf. Mark 9:38-41; Acts 1:6; 10:1–11:3; Gal 2:11-14). STEPHEN, PHILIP, and unnamed men from CYPRUS and CYRENE anticipated Paul in this VISION (Acts 6:8–8:1; 8:4-40; 11:20).

Verse 6 states the basic provision of the *mystery*, the union of Jew and gentile in Christ. NRSV interprets, but obscures some powerful wordplay: *gentiles have become fellow heirs, members of the same body, and sharers in the promise* (v. 6). The Greek text has it "heirs with and bodied with and partakers with." The second of these terms is possibly a new coinage, *syssōma* (synsomatic). These three terms strain to stress the oneness of Jew and gentile in Christ.

Verses 7-9 stress the marvel of Paul's part in showing forth the mystery. Of this mystery he became a *servant* (*diakonos*), and this by the *gift of God's grace* given him by the "energizing of his power" (author trans.). Seeing himself as *the very least of all the saints*, he marvels at the grace given him "to proclaim to the gentiles the untraceable (*anexichniaston*) wealth of Christ" (author trans.). He might strike its trail but could not trace it out, so vast it was.

In bringing to light this mystery, hidden in God for ages, *the wisdom of God in its rich variety* now could be made known to *the rulers and authorities in the heavenly places* (v. 10). This "multicolored (*polypoikilos*) wisdom of God" is seen at last *through the church!* Even the heavenly creatures do not understand God's wisdom until the emergence of the church, God's new creation out of hitherto hostile Jews and gentiles.

This great achievement was "according to the purpose of the ages" (NRSV *the eternal purpose*). God has had one plan through the ages, in Christ Jesus thus to unify Jew and gentile in giving them *access to God in boldness and confidence through faith* (vv. 11-12). Now that his readers see that Paul sees his mission to the Jews as God's gracious gift to him, they have no reason to *lose heart* over his sufferings.

3:14-19. Paul's prayer resumed. After several digressions in which Paul describes the mystery he is commissioned to proclaim, with its special relation to gentiles, Paul resumes the prayer begun in 3:1, repeating "For this cause" (*Toutou charin*).

A play on the words *Father* (*patera*) and *family* (*patria*) serves further to stress the theme of oneness. The intention may be "every fatherhood" rather than *family*, God seen as the archetype of all fatherhood. Either way, all peoples are seen as deriving from the same divine fatherhood, thus all "families" are united under "the Father of our Lord Jesus Christ." Although this sexually exclusive language is problematic today, the concern of Ephesians was elsewhere, to overcome ethnic bias.

The prayer is that they be strengthened in their *inner being* as Christ dwells within them. Salvation does not come as an abstraction; it comes only as Christ becomes a transforming presence within the inner self.

Paul next prays that not only may they be *rooted and grounded in love* (v. 17) but that they may be empowered *to comprehend, with all the saints* (v. 18) the love of Christ in its full magnitude: breadth, length, height, and depth. *The love of Christ* may be intended objectively, love *for* Christ, or subjectively, the love Christ has *for us*, presumably the latter. Such understanding is not for "loners," but for those who learn *with all the saints*.

To know the love of Christ is to know *that which surpasses knowledge* (v. 19). Again, here is a play on words, knowing which surpasses knowledge! To "know" the love of Christ is experiential knowledge, and it surpasses cognitive knowledge.

A reply to gnostic claims may appear in v. 19. Christ's love surpasses *knowledge* (*gnosis*) from which gnostics took their name and of which they were so proud. Again, in Christ gentiles and Jews *may be filled with all the fullness* (*plērōma*) *of God*. In Col 1:19, "all the fullness of God" was pleased to dwell in Christ, not in a gnostic hierarchy of eons or emanations. Also, where one is "in Christ" and Christ dwells in that one, that one is *filled with all the fullness of God* (v. 19; cf. Col 2:10).

3:20-21. Doxology. Paul could not talk about God's grace and his marvelous "plan of the ages" without breaking into prayer and praise. He praises God for his power working within us, achieving *far more than all we can ask or imagine!*

Practical Exhortations, 4:1–6:20

Although theology continues, this section is primarily practical, with attention to the individual life, the life and work of the church, and guiding principles for the extended family: wives/husbands, children/parents, slaves/masters.

4:1-6. Basis for unity. In his capacity as *the prisoner in the Lord*, Paul calls for life worthy of *the calling* by which the readers were *called*. Salvation in Christ is our *calling* (*klesis*) or vocation. Initiative always is with God: creation, revelation, redemption. Calling and ELECTION refer to the same thing, divine initiative. God's calling opens the option, it does not dictate the response.

Those in Christ ought to be characterized by *humility and gentleness, with patience.* Humility was despised in the Greek world, proper to slaves alone. In the NT, servanthood and humility are seen as virtues, exemplified in Jesus and proper to his followers (John 13:4-5; Phil 2:3ff.).

Bearing with one another in love, is best rendered "holding back" or "forbearing," recognizing the fact that we tend to antagonize one another and strike back. It is *love* that gives us the disposition and strength to hold back.

Love demands more than simply holding back; it requires that we make every effort "to guard" (*terein*) *the unity of the Spirit in the bond of peace* (v. 3). Though unity is the divine provision, it is not unilaterally bestowed. It belongs to Christian vocation. *Peace* like *shalom* is well-being under the sovereignty of God.

Seven (the number for perfection) unities are named, in three groups: *one body, one Spirit, one hope; one Lord, one faith, one baptism; one God and Father of all* (vv. 4-6). The *one body* is the church, the body of Christ. Only context is clue to whether Spirit or the human spirit is intended. The *one hope* is "Christ in you" (Col 1:27). The one Lord is Christ. *One faith* is not one creed but one trust or faith commitment. *One baptism* is not only the one initiation rite but the commitment it signifies. *One God* is not only

affirmation of the MONOTHEISM basic to OT and NT, but also the ultimate ground for the unifying of humanity.

4:7-16. Diversity in unity. The ascended Christ as prime minister of the church gives gifts of grace, varying with the individual, designed to equip all the saints for ministry. The receiving church is to be the serving church, both means and goal in the purpose of God.

The quotation, apparently from Ps 68:18, is freely adapted. The psalm celebrates the triumph of "the God of Sinai" as he came into "the holy place" and "ascended the high mount," that is, "the sanctuary," the "temple at Jerusalem." He did so "leading captives" and "receiving gifts," changed here to *gave gifts.* In Ephesians, Christ both *ascended* and *descended*, the order unclear. The descent may be the incarnate experience leading to his death, the ascent being the resurrection and ascension. What is clear is that the descending and ascending one is the same. Christ is not dead but alive; not absent but present; not ghostly but embodied; not passive but active in the life and ministry of the church, his body.

Verses 11-16 form a classic statement as to the ministry of the church. Christ is *the Minister.* He gives to the church its various ministries, *some . . . apostles, some prophets, some evangelists, some pastors and teachers.* This catalogue is illustrative rather than complete, as comparison with other catalogues shows (Rom 12:6ff.; 1 Cor 12:28). There is no mention of bishops, presbyters, or deacons! These, too, although unmentioned here, belong to the equipping ministers of the Church. They are servants, not rulers.

The function of equipping ministers is *to equip the saints for the work of ministry* (v. 12). All in Christ are *saints*, ones set apart in Christ (with no implication of special sanctity). All are called to ministry. The whole Church is in intention the ministering body of Christ. Ministries vary with the gifts present in the members of the Body. The total ministry includes Christ, the equipping ministers, and all the saints.

The Church is intended to be both servant and minister and the goal of all ministry, itself "a perfect man, unto the measure of the stature of the fullness of Christ" (v. 13, author trans.). Unity and maturity are marks proper to the body of Christ, with each member functioning in terms of its role, and all members blended into one growing body. The saints are not to remain *children*, vulnerable to deceit; but they are to reach maturity and unity in variety. *Speaking the truth in love* could be rendered "holding the truth in love" or "being true in love."

4:17-24. Former vices to shun. Those *in the Lord* are no longer to live like *gentiles*, seen here as pagan (the readers were ethnically gentiles). The gentile plight was living *in the futility of their minds*. Alienated from God, their minds were not only uninformed but *darkened*, incapacitated and immoral. Those in Christ are called to a new quality of life, new and constantly *renewed*, a new creation in *the likeness of God in true righteousness and holiness*.

4:25–5:2. Sins of the spirit that destroy unity. A catalogue of wrong feelings, attitudes, and dispositions is matched in each case with positives. *Falsehood* is to be replaced with *the truth*. Since we are *members of one another*, in being true or false to others, we are that to ourselves. *Be angry but do not sin?* How? Anger is recognized as a reality; it is what we do with it that matters. To *let the sun go down on your anger* is to *make room for the devil*. It is to let anger eat away at us, even while we sleep. Stealing is to be replaced with honest work, providing not only for ourselves but *to have something to share with the needy*.

Evil talk is any talk that is like inedible fruit (*sapros*; cf. Matt 12:33, where "bad fruit" is not rotten but the wrong kind). In its place is to be talk *useful for building up* and for *giving grace*. There is no place for bitterness, wrath, anger, wrangling, slander, and malice. Instead, we should be kind, tenderhearted, and forgiving. All this follows, if as imitators of God, we *live in love, as Christ loved us*. This is the fragrant *sacrifice* to be offered to God.

5:3-20. Sins of sensuality that corrupt and degrade. Gross acts of sensuality like *fornication, impurity,* and *greed*, seen as pagan, are to be so far removed that they are not even mentioned among the *saints*. Even *obscene, silly, and vulgar talk*, making light of sensuality, is *out of place*.

The warning in v. 5 is severe (cf. 1 Cor 6:9-10). The Greek text may be imperative, "This know ye, knowing" or indicative, "This ye know, knowing." The warning that *no fornicator or impure person, or one who is greedy* (worship of things seen as a form of idolatry) will inherit the kingdom of Christ is not softened. This is impossible to assimilate into the soteriology that equates salvation with what is perceived as confessional orthodoxy. For the most part, it is ignored as are such warnings as attributed to Jesus (cf. Matt 7:15-27; 25:31-46). Verse 5 is weighted on the side of orthopraxy rather than orthodoxy.

Light and *darkness* are the themes through vv. 6-14. The gentile readers were once *darkness*, but now they are *light* and *the children of light* (v. 8; cf. Matt 5:14-16). As in biblical usage generally, light and darkness are moral and ethical terms, not cognitive. A benighted person is evil, not necessarily ignorant; and an enlightened person is good, not simply informed. To walk in darkness is to live in evil. To walk in light is to live in goodness.

Light and darkness are disclosed by their *fruit*. The fruit of light includes what is *good and right and true* (cf. Gal 5:22). Darkness, in fact, is *unfruitful* in that it bears no edible fruit.

It is the function of light to give light, exposing darkness and turning darkness into light (vv. 13-14). The darkness to be exposed are the *shameful* acts of darkness. The children of light are to be in action what they are in nature. The DEAD SEA SCROLLS belonged to a priestly group who saw themselves as "the sons of light," but they were hiding their light in their withdrawal at QUMRAN. Jesus countered as he addressed an ordinary group, saying: "You are the light of the world . . . let your light shine before others" (Matt 5:14-16).

Although light and darkness are moral and ethical terms, they are not indifferent to wisdom or foolishness. The children of light are to be *wise* and not *foolish* (vv. 15-17). For example, getting drunk with wine is not simply evil; it is foolish. Getting *filled with the Spirit* and "singing songs to God in praise and thanksgiving" (cf. Col 3:16) is both good and wise.

5:21–6:9. The extended family. This passage is a domestic code for the extended family: wife-husband, child-parent, slave-master. Parallels with commonalities and differences are found in Col 3:18–4:1; 1 Pet 2:13–3:7; Titus 2:1-10; and 1 Tim 2:1ff., 2:8ff.; 3:1ff., 3:8ff.; 5:17ff.; 6:1-2. The code in Ephesians seems to be built upon that in Colossians.

The extended family in the Greco-Roman world gave rise to codes designed to regulate relationships within domestic and civil structures of society, traceable in Aristotle (*Politics* 1.3) and Philo (*Hypothetica* 7.14). No direct dependence upon such codes is traceable here, but some influence is probable. The NT codes offer moral and ethical principles that should humanize and Christianize these relationships (Stagg and Stagg 1978, chap. 8).

Ephesians 5:21 is linked grammatically to what precedes, but in intention it governs what follows: *Be subject to one another out of reverence for Christ*. This applies to all who are in Christ; it is egalitarian; and it follows Jesus' basic law that, contrary to the pagan disposition to rule, his followers are to find their greatness in servanthood (Mark 9:33-37; 10:35-45). All codes must be subordinated to this principle.

All codes are historically conditioned, as here. Jewish and Roman law decreed that the husband was head of the family; and both laws gave slave owners legal authority over slaves. These were legal realities, whatever their injustices. The early church had no worldly power sufficient then to change such structures and laws. It did have the disposition to bring them under the claims of Christ.

Codes at best intend to articulate and apply values and principles in a given historical situation. They are never one and the same as such principles, and they are not failsafe. For example, kindness is a principle, universally and eternally valid. How kindness is expressed can never be defined in any code. Because all codes are historically conditioned and by nature not one and the same as that which they seek to apply, they are not to be uprooted from one situation and imposed upon another. Codes, like wineskins (Mark 2:22), are to be replaced as necessary if the "wine" of principle or value is to be preserved.

5:22-33. Wives-husbands. *Wives, be subject to your husbands* (NRSV) is a questionable translation, for there is no verb in the Greek text of v. 22. *Be subject* translates a participle in v. 21, and this carries over to v. 22, with imperatival force. In form it is middle voice and probably middle in force, "subject yourselves" instead of passive, "be subject." If middle voice, at least wives are recognized as responsible and competent to shape their side of the marital relationship, not subordinates to be commanded. If applied, v. 21 would call upon the husband to do likewise, with mutual choice of voluntary submission, each to the other.

In affirming husband as *head of the wife*, the code follows the legal structures then obtaining, not the ideal cited by Jesus from Gen 2:24: " 'For this reason a man shall leave his father and mother and be joined to his wife, and the two shall become one flesh.' So they are no longer two, but one flesh" (Mark 10:7-8). Significantly, the code itself gives way to the principle of Jesus in v. 31!

Christ as *head* and *Savior* of the church is the model here for wives as subject to their husbands. *In everything* heightens the demand over that in Col 3:18. Husbands normally were providers and protectors of the family, but surely a husband is not "savior" of his wife in the sense that Christ is Savior of the church. Many husbands are not themselves "saved," much less saving. The code is best understood within its own limits as historically conditioned. To absolutize the code as binding on wives today is to open the door to any abuse of which fallible husbands are capable and often disposed.

The appeal to "love" as the controlling principle in the husband's relationship with his wife follows what Jesus verified as "the first" commandment of all (Mark 12:29). A husband is to love his wife *as Christ loved the church and gave himself up for her.* Should a wife love a husband any less?

At this point, the focus turns to the church itself. What is intended by *cleansing her with the washing of water by the word* is difficult. Taken literally, this serves as a text for baptismal regeneration, as problematic as the contention that circumcision was a means to salvation, rejected outright in 2:11ff. *By the word* (NRSV) translates *en remati*, literally "in a word." This may imply a baptismal confession of the name of Christ (cf. 1 Cor 6:11), but this is speculation.

That a husband should love his wife "as his own body" may be understood two ways. He may love her the way he loves himself, or in loving her he does love himself, since the two have become one flesh.

Verse 31 recaptures the mutual and egalitarian ideal of v. 21. All are to be *subject to one another out of reverence for Christ*, and husband and wife are to become *one flesh.* It follows that husband should *love his wife* and wife should *respect her husband* (v. 33), but surely a wife should love her husband and a husband should respect his wife.

6:1-4. Children-parents. The code here differs somewhat from that in Colossians. In both letters, both parents are to be obeyed by their children; but "in everything" drops out in Ephesians! Instead, many manuscripts have *in the Lord*; but this phrase is absent in some strong Greek and Latin manuscripts and several early church fathers. Thus Ephesians does not impose obedience unconditionally, a significant factor today when many children are abused by their fathers and/or mothers.

Ideally, obedience to parents is *right*, for parental responsibility requires corresponding authority. Authority is forfeited when abused.

The text here builds upon the fifth commandment (Exod 20:12; Deut 5:16), *the first commandment with a promise.* Significantly, the egalitarian principle is in force here, for mothers and fathers are to be obeyed alike in the Decalogue and in Ephesians.

What precisely is intended by the promise *live long on the earth* is unclear. If individual longevity is the promise, it is unclear why many obedient children die young and many disobedient ones live long. In the Decalogue the promise may be long life "in the land" for a nation obedient to parents, not individuals.

Verse 4 goes beyond Colossians in adding a positive to the negative in discipline. Fathers are not only to refrain from provoking their children to anger, but also to *bring them up in the discipline and instruction of the Lord.*

Not including mothers here is in keeping with the distrust of mothers in much of the ancient world, · deeming them unfit to teach even their own children. Such distrust of women does not accord with the manner of Jesus. Neither does it agree with the recognition that Timothy's "sincere faith" was in his maternal heritage, a faith that lived first in his maternal heritage, "a faith that lived first in your grandmother Lois and your mother Eunice" (2 Tim 1:5), not from his Greek father (Acts 16:1). Of course, there is no evidence today that mothers are less competent than fathers in teaching or parenting.

6:5-9. Slaves-masters. This part of the code parallels that in Colossians, with no significant variations. Slavery as such is not challenged, for whatever reason. What does concern the code is the quality service given by the slave, service which is a credit to a follower of Christ. As *slaves of Christ* they are to render service in deed and in spirit worthy of a servant of Christ. Ultimate reward is from the true Master, under whom the distinction between *slaves* and *free* persons is transcended (v. 8; cf. Gal 3:28).

Without condoning slavery, *masters* are warned that they are answerable to the ultimate "Master" for how they relate to those whom they hold as slaves.

6:10-20. The whole armor of God. This section sees the Christian as embattled, threatened by *cosmic powers* seen as *spiritual forces of evil in the heavenly places* (vv. 10-17), and also by human forces to whom the gospel is to be preached with boldness (vv. 18-20).

The present world retains the language about demonic forces, and there is yet sincere belief in the reality of such threats; but nothing today compares with fear in the ancient world of such powers believed to inhabit the stars, mountains, trees, and human beings. The word "disaster" preserves the belief that human sufferings are traceable to some star god. Modern space travel and even mining of mountains would be problematic to the ancient world, for fear of disturbing cosmic powers.

The *whole armor of God* implies nothing of worldly militarism. All the armor is defensive except the *shoes* that *will make you ready to proclaim the gospel of peace* (v. 15) and *the sword of the Spirit, which is the word of God* (v. 17; cf. Rev 1:16).

Defensive armor includes *the belt of truth.* The injunction anticipates our "fasten your seatbelts!" In a world like this, the Christian pilgrimage can be a rough ride. "Truth" is our defense, and it requires no defense. *The breastplate of righteousness* is a reminder that although we are not saved by our goodness, righteousness belongs properly to followers of Jesus. *Faith* is more than a shield, but it is that. *Salvation* is more than security, but it is that too.

Prayer rightly includes self, but there is a special duty to pray *for all the saints.* Paul includes himself in his prayer requests, but it is not a self-serving request. Imprisoned for preaching a gospel inclusive of Jew and gentile, he prays that he have the "boldness" to speak *the mystery of the gospel,* the very gospel for which he is *an ambassador in chains.* No threat is to silence him or cause him to modify his proclamation of "the mystery of the gospel" (cf. 3:1-6).

Personal Words and Benediction, 6:21-24

Tychicus is apparently the bearer of the letter (no postal system then for civilians). His further mission is to inform the readers more fully as to Paul's situation. This is for their encouragement in difficult times.

Peace, love, faith, and *grace* are primary in the benediction, as a reminder of what is received from *God the Father and the Lord Jesus Christ* and also of that by which *the whole community* is to be characterized. The final appeal is for *an undying love for our Lord Jesus Christ.*

Works Cited

Barth, Marcus. 1959. *The Broken Wall.* 1974. *Ephesians.* AncB.

Kümmel, W. G. 1975. *Introduction to the N.T.*

Robinson, J. A. 1904. *St. Paul's Epistle to the Ephesians.*

Roon, A. Van. 1974. *The Authenticity of Ephesians.*

Stagg, Frank. 1990. "Paul's Final Mission to Jerusalem," in *With Steadfast Purpose,* ed. N. Keathley.

Stagg, Evelyn, and Frank Stagg. 1978. *Woman in the World of Jesus.*

Tolbert, Malcolm O. 1990. "Ephesians, Letter to the," MDB.

Philippians

Charles H. Talbert

Introduction

Philippians is one of thirteen letters attributed to PAUL in the NT. It belongs to the group of nine Pauline letters addressed to seven churches that is arranged in order of descending length. It is to devotional literature what Romans is to doctrinal and 1 Corinthians to ethical writing. The Marcionite prologue to Paul's letters (late second century) gives perhaps the oldest Christian view of the letter.

> The Philippians are Macedonians. They persevered in faith after [they] had accepted the word of truth and they did not receive false apostles. The Apostle praises them, writing to them from Rome from the prison, by Epaphroditus.

Genre

Philippians is both like and unlike ancient non-Christian letters (Soards 1990, 660). Like them, it begins with a salutation (A to B, greeting) followed by a prayer form (thanksgiving and petition), moves to a body, and ends with a conventional closing (e.g., greetings). Unlike them, its components are Christianized, for example, Salutation—*Grace and peace from God our Father and the Lord Jesus Christ* (1:2); Closing—*The grace of the Lord Jesus Christ be with your spirit* (4:23).

Author and Recipients

The letter's claim to be by Paul is universally accepted today. It is addressed to Christian converts in the Macedonian city of PHILIPPI. That church, founded during Paul's second missionary journey (Acts 16:9-40), stayed in close contact with the apostle (2 Cor 11:8-9; Phil 4:15-16; Acts 20:1-2, 3-6). It was basically gentile Christian in composition.

Integrity

There is diversity of opinion about whether or not Philippians is a unity. Some take 3:1b–4:3 as a fragment of a second letter. Others regard 4:10-20 as one note; 1:1–3:1 + 4:4-7 as another; and 3:2–4:3 + 4:8-9 as a third. If so, then these different letters were collected, edited, and published as one when the Pauline letter collection was made near 100 C.E. Still others believe that Philippians can best be explained as one letter. One's position on the matter of integrity affects one's decisions about other issues.

Date, Locale, and Occasion

If Philippians is not a unity, then its different components may come from different locales at different times and have different purposes. (1) If three independent letters are assumed, then 4:10-20 may be the earliest, written from an alleged imprisonment in EPHESUS, on the third journey, to thank the Philippians for their gift; 1:1–3:1 + 4:4-7 (perhaps 4:21-23) may be next, also from an Ephesian imprisonment, calling for unity and joy; while 3:2–4:3 + 4:8-9 may be the latest, written shortly after leaving Ephesus, perhaps from CORINTH, warning about false teachers (Koester 1976, 665–66). (2) If there were two original letters, then 1:1–3:1a + 4:4-23 may have been written from prison in Rome (Acts 28), Ephesus (an alleged imprisonment on the third journey), or CAESAREA (Acts 23:23–26:32) to thank the church for its gift and to exhort them to Christian unity; 3:1b–4:3 may have come from a time when Paul was not in prison, close to that of Galatians and warning about similar problems with false teaching (Michael 1928). (3) If the letter is a unity, it was written from prison in Rome, Ephesus, Caesarea, or elsewhere (2 Cor 11:23—Paul was imprisoned a number of times before the Caesarean imprisonment of Acts 23; *1 Clem* 5:5—Paul was imprisoned seven times) to serve multiple functions: giving thanks for a gift, encouragement to unity, warning about heresy, information about travel plans (Hawthorne 1983, xxix–xlviii).

Although no consensus exists, this commentary assumes the unity of Philippians, for which a good case has been made by Garland 1985, Kurz 1985, and Watson 1988. Again, although consensus does not exist and certainty is impossible, this reading of Philippians assumes a Roman origin, near the beginning of Paul's imprisonment there. The only serious obstacle against this ancient view, the great distance between Rome and Philippi that allegedly renders the travel undertaken and proposed difficult, is removed by the comment of Philostratus (*Life of Apollonius* 7.10), that the distance from Puteoli (near Rome) to Corinth (fairly close to Philippi) was crossed in five days. The similarities with Romans and Galatians are then explained by locating Philippians early in Paul's imprisonment in Rome. (For an outline of Paul's life and the place of his letters in it, see Soards 1990, 660.)

For Further Study

In the *Mercer Dictionary of the Bible*: PAUL; PHILIPPI; PHILIPPIANS, LETTER TO THE; PRISON EPISTLES.

F. W. Beare, *A Commentary on the Epistle to the Philippians*, HNTC; W. G. Doty, *Letters in Primitive Christianity*; D. Garland, "The Composition and Literary Unity of Philippians: Some Neglected Factors," *NovT* 27 (1985): 141–73; G. F. Hawthorne, *Philippians*, WBC; H. Koester, "Philippians, Letter to the," *IDBSupp* 665–66; W. S. Kurz, "Kenotic Imitation of Paul and of Christ in Philippians," in *Discipleship in the New Testament*, ed. F. Segovia, 103–26; R. P. Martin, *Carmen Christi: Philippians 2:5-11 in Recent Interpretation*; J. H. Michael, *The Epistle of Paul to the Philippians*, MNTC; S. K. Stowers, *Letter Writing in Greco-Roman Antiquity*; C. H. Talbert, "The Problem of Preexistence in Philippians 2:6-11," *JBL* 86 (1967): 141–53; D. Watson, "A Rhetorical Analysis of Philippians and Its Implications for the Unity Question," *NovT* 30 (1988): 57–88.

Commentary

An Outline

Introduction, 1:1-11

Salutation, 1:1-2

The letter's beginning adopts and adapts the customary form of ancient letters: A to B, greeting. PAUL is the author but TIMOTHY (Acts 16:1-3; 19:22) is included to lay the foundation for his future visit (2:19-23) and to demonstrate Paul's humility (2:3-4; 3:17). The letter is sent *to all the saints in Christ Jesus* in Philippi; we would say to all the Christians there. *With the bishops and deacons* might better be translated "overseers and helpers" to convey the idea that they

are not officials in the second-century sense but administrative functionaries manifesting the gifts of service (Rom 12:7—ministry [διακονία]; 1 Cor 12—helpers) and oversight (Rom 12:8—the leader; 1 Cor 12:28—administrators). These functionaries would be addressed because, in part, Philippians is a response to a gift sent to the prisoner Paul by the church and doubtless supervised by these overseers and helpers. The greeting of v. 2 invokes *God our Father* (Matt 6:9; Luke 11:2; Rom 8:15; Gal 4:6; 2 John 3) and the *Lord Jesus Christ* (Rom 15:6; 2 Cor 1:3; 11:31; Col 1:3), making it distinctively Christian.

Prayer, 1:3-11

Ancient letters often used a prayer form after the salutation. A THANKSGIVING (vv. 3-6) and a petition (vv. 9-11) are joined by an expression of personal affection (vv. 7-8). Thanksgiving and petition are organized in similar ways: reference to prayer followed by its two objects, ending with an eschatological note, the *day of Jesus Christ*. In this section one hears themes that will recur throughout the letter: Paul's joy, the Philippians' gift, the completion of salvation at the last day, Paul's imprisonment, and Christian growth.

1:3-6. Thanksgiving. Paul gives thanks for two things: (1) either for his every remembrance of them or for their every remembrance of him (the Greek allows either; so does the context), which is always in every prayer, for all of them, with joy (vv. 3-4); and (2) for their sharing in the gospel, that is, their gift to him in prison (v. 5; 4:10). The thanksgiving ends with a reference to their eschatological hope, the day of Christ, when God's saving activity in them, begun in the past, will find its completion (v. 6).

1:7-8. Expression of personal affection. Paul's hope for the Philippians verbalized in v. 6 is grounded both in their sharing in God's grace (v. 7, here, ministry as in 1 Cor 3:10; Gal 2:9) and in Paul's deep affection for them (v. 8).

1:9-11. Petition. Paul asks for two things for the Philippians: (1) that their love *may overflow* with knowledge and full insight (1 Cor 12:8, 10) so that they may *determine what is best* (vv. 9-10a), and (2) that, at the day of Christ, they *may be pure and blameless, having produced the harvest of righteousness*. The petition, like the thanksgiving, ends on the note of eschatological hope, the day of Christ.

Body of the Letter, 1:12–4:20

The body of Philippians unfolds in a concentric pattern: A (1:12-26), B (1:27–2:16), C (2:17–3:1a), B' (3:1b–4:9), A' (4:10-20).

Paul's Rejoicing, 1:12-26

This section, A in the pattern, is held together by an INCLUSIO: spread/progress (προκοπήν) in v. 12 and v. 25. It consists of two units, vv. 12-18 and vv. 19-26, the first focused on Paul's rejoicing in the present, the second on his rejoicing in the future.

1:12-18. Paul's rejoicing in his present status. Being a prisoner and having heard that some preach out of bad motives does not keep Paul from rejoicing for two reasons: (1) because his imprisonment, rather than hurting the Christian cause, has advanced it among pagans (vv. 12-13; the *imperial guard* could refer to soldiers, members of the court, or officials of a government house, none of which were restricted to Rome) and Christians (v. 14); and (2) because even those seeking to afflict Paul advance the Christian cause (vv. 15-18; these opponents, whose message is acceptable but whose motives are questionable, are not those of 3:2-19, whose message is erroneous).

1:19-26. Paul's rejoicing in the future. Whether he dies as a martyr or is released from prison will not keep Paul from rejoicing for two reasons: (1) because if he dies as a martyr, Christ will be honored and he will be with Christ (vv. 19-23; cf. 2 Cor 5:8); and (2) because if he is released, it will mean *fruitful labor* for him and glory for Christ (vv. 22-26; cf. 2 Cor 5:9).

Paul's Exhortations, 1:27–2:16

This section, B in the pattern, consists of three paragraphs, 1:27-30, 2:1-13, and 2:14-16. The focus of the first is on the church's relation to the world while that of the second is on the community's inner life. The third offers general exhortations to round off the two prior paragraphs.

1:17-30. The church's relation to the world. Verse 27a is best translated: "Live, as citizens of heaven, worthily of the gospel of Christ." Just as the Philippians strove to live as citizens of Rome, worthily of their privilege in a Macedonian context, so the Philippian Christians, as citizens of heaven (3:20), are to live in line with their citizenship in this present evil age. Verses 27b-30 give two specific examples of what this means.

1:27b. Christian unity. To live in line with their heavenly citizenship in relation to the world means maintaining Christian unity. Military (*standing firm*) and athletic (*striving side by side*) metaphors describe the desired unity on behalf of *the faith of the gospel*. Paul calls for a new Macedonian phalanx and a new Olympic team of athletes to be formed, composed of Philippian Christians who manifest the same unity as successful military units and athletic teams do.

1:28a-30. Christian fearlessness. Living worthily of their heavenly citizenship means also fearlessness in the face of pagan hostility (v. 28a). Two bases for such fearlessness follow: (1) it is a sign to pagans of the ultimate outcome of history (v. 28b); and (2) not only faith in Christ but also suffering for Christ is a gift from God, as Paul's example shows (vv. 29-30; 1 Thes 2:2).

2:1-13. The community's inner life. This section is held together by an inclusio: the theme of vv. 1-2 echoed in v. 13. The section focuses on the inner life of the community. It is composed of three subsections, vv. 1-2, vv. 3-11, and vv. 12-13, each consisting of injunctions and their bases. All call for Christian unity.

2:1-2. Relate to one another as you are related to by God. Verse 1 offers four bases: "Since there is [1] *encouragement in Christ*, [2] *consolation from* God's *love*, [3] *sharing in the Spirit*, and [4] *compassion and sympathy* shown by God to us." The "if" clauses should be translated "if (and there is)" or "since." Verse 2 follows with four injunctions: (1) *be of the same mind*, (2) have *the same love*, (3) be *in full accord*, and (4) be *of one mind*. Relate to one another in a way that is consonant with the way God relates to you.

2:3-11. Relate to one another as Christ related to God. Verses 3-4 offer two injunctions: (1) *Do nothing from selfish ambition or conceit, but in humility regard others as better than yourselves*; and (2) *Let each of you look not to your own interests, but to the interests of others.* The problems Paul addresses were recognized by the philosopher Epictetus to be indigenous to the human condition. He said: "It is a general rule—be not deceived—that every living thing is to nothing so devoted as to its own interest" (*Discourse* 2.22.15).

The basis for these injunctions is in vv. 5-11. Verse 5 is missing a verb in the second half of the sentence. Translated literally, it reads: "Think this among yourselves, which also _____ in Christ Jesus." Different verbs may be supplied—either "was" or "think." This explains the difference in modern translations. If "think" is supplied, then the result is: "Let your bearing towards one another arise out of your life in Christ Jesus" (NEB). If "was" is supplied, then one finds: "The attitude you should have is the one that Christ Jesus had" (TEV). The RSV second edition reflects the former; the RSV third edition employs the latter. In terms of meaning, the former would mean, "Relate to one another as you relate to Christ" (i.e., with humility and submission); the latter, "Relate to one another as Christ related to God" (i.e., with humility). The former is an appeal to experience, the latter an appeal to tradition. The latter seems to fit the context better.

Verses 6-11 are almost universally regarded as an early Christian HYMN taken up and employed by Paul as the basis for his call to humility. The hymn divides into two parts, vv. 6-8 where Jesus is the subject of the action, and vv. 9-11 where God is the subject. In the first part, Jesus *humbles* himself, even to the point of death. In the second part, God exalts Jesus, giving him the name and position of Lord. Modern interpreters of the hymn disagree over whether vv. 6-8 refer to preexistence (v. 6), INCARNATION (v. 7), and death on the cross (v. 8), or only to Jesus' human existence as an antitype of Adam's experience in Gen 1–3: being in God's image (v. 6a; Gen 1:27); not trying to be like God (v. 6b; Gen 3:5); being obedient to God (vv. 7-8; Gen 2:16-17; 3:11). Either way, it is Jesus' humility that serves as the basis for the injunctions in vv. 3-4. Relate to one another as Jesus related to God, with humility.

2:12-13. Relate to one another, in obedience to Paul, as the God who indwells you enables you. In vv. 12-13 the two bases are split, v. 12a being the first, v. 13 the second. The injunction comes in v. 12b. It reads: *Work out your* [plural] *own salvation with fear and trembling.* This is not a call to personal salvation by works (Eph 2:8-9); the Philippians' salvation is assumed. Nor is it a call for individuals to grow spiritually (as in 3:12-15); it speaks rather about corporate wholeness. In Pauline thought, salvation involves not only individuals but also human community (Eph 4:1-16). Since groups as well as individuals sin, groups as well as individuals need to be delivered from sin. Moreover, groups as well as individuals need to grow spiritually. Here the community that has experienced God's saving power is asked to work out that initial deliverance from sin in all of the community's life. With a sense of seriousness, work out the implications of your corporate salvation in the many relationships of the community's life. The bases are two: (1) *For it is God who is at work in you* [plural], *enabling you* [plural] *both to will and to work for his good pleasure* (v. 13); and (2) *just as you have always obeyed me, not only in my presence, but much more now in my absence* (v. 12a).

2:14-16. General exhortations. Having exhorted the Philippians to right relations with the world (1:27-30) and proper relations within the community (2:1-13), Paul ends this section with the general exhortation *Do all things without murmuring and arguing*, that is, with cheerful obedience (v. 14; cf. 1 Cor 10:1-12; Exod 14:12; Num 16:41, 49). Two reasons for such behavior follow: (1) it benefits the world (vv. 15b; cf. Matt 5:14-16), and (2) it will benefit the Philippians (vv. 15a, 16a) and Paul (v. 16b).

Paul's Plans: Travelogue, 2:17–3:1a

Just as in 1 Cor 4:17-19 and 2 Cor 8:16-19, information about the travel plans of Paul and his coworkers appears in the middle rather than at the end of the letter (Rom 15:14-29). This paragraph functions as C, the centerpoint, in the concentric pattern of the letter's body. It consists of three parts: (1) about TIMOTHY (vv. 19-23), (2) about PAUL (v. 24), and (3) about EPAPHRODITUS (vv. 25-30). It is held together by an inclusio: "rejoicing" in 2:17-18, echoed in 3:1a.

2:19-23. Hope plus commendation. Paul hopes to send Timothy to see the Philippians soon to gather news about them. He will send Timothy because there is no one like him *who will be genuinely concerned* for their welfare. Others *are seeking their own interests* (2:4). Paul will send his best.

2:24. Paul's hopes for himself. In 1:24-25 Paul concluded that, since his remaining in the flesh was better for the Philippians, he expected to live and be released from prison. Here, in v. 24, he voices his *trust in the Lord that I will also come soon.* If he is to be released, it will be not because he wishes it but because God enables it.

2:25-30. Decision plus commendation. When the Philippians sent their latest gift to Paul (4:10), they not only sent it by Epaphroditus, but sent Epaphroditus himself to stay with Paul and assist him in his ministry while the apostle was in prison (vv. 25, 30). Epaphroditus became ill and nearly died (vv. 27, 30). Even though he survived, he became emotionally distraught, longing for home (v. 26). Paul, therefore, determined to send him back to Philippi. Lest the Philippians be unhappy with him on his return for not finishing his mission, Paul commends him for his labors and asks that he be welcomed and honored (v. 29).

Paul's Exhortations, 3:1b–4:9

This section is B' in the letter body's pattern, corresponding to Paul's exhortations in 1:27–2:16. The section begins with an introduction, 3:1b, and ends with a conclusion, 4:9. In between are two panels, each with three parts. Panel One appeals to apostolic example against error and consists of 3:2-11, 3:12-15, and 3:16–4:1. Panel Two utilizes apostolic teaching for the church's benefit and consists of 4:2-3, 4:4-7, and 4:8.

3:2–4:1. Panel one: apostolic example. In this segment of text Paul uses his own example to argue against three distortions of religious existence: legalism (vv. 2-11), perfectionism (vv. 12-15), and libertine behavior (3:16–4:1). Debate rages about whether these three issues reflect one, two, or three groups of opponents. Issues one and two could be explained by opponents who were either Jews or Jewish Christians. Issue three, if representative of the same group as one and two, requires a legalistic, perfectionistic, libertine opposition, perhaps Jewish-Christian GNOSTICISM. Unanimity reigns only on the conclusion that the opponents of chap. 3 are not the same as those of 1:15-18. In 1:15-18 Paul expressed reservations about his opponents' motives, not their message. In chap. 3 Paul defends against a wrong message.

3:2-11. Against legalism. A warning is issued, using terms of disparagement for the opponents: *dogs* (Rev 22:15; Matt 15:21-28), *evil workers* (Rom 2:17-

24), *those who mutilate the flesh* (Rom 2:25-29). Christians are the true *circumcision* (Col 2:11). Paul then uses his own situation as a paradigm. He has every reason for confidence in the flesh—to trust human achievement to gain God's approval. A list of seven Jewish virtues is given (vv. 5-6), beginning with *circumcised on the eighth day* (Lev 12:3) and ending with *as to righteousness under the law, blameless.* Yet he regarded (perfect tense) them all as loss because of Christ (v. 7) and regards (present tense) everything as loss *because of the surpassing value of knowing Christ Jesus my Lord* (v. 8).

Paul's motivation for considering all things as rubbish is threefold : (1) *in order that I may gain Christ* (v. 8c; cf. Matt 13:44-45); (2) *in order that I may . . . be found in him* (Gal 3:27; Eph 4:24) with a righteousness not from law but from either the faith of Christ or faith in Christ (v. 9; Rom 3:21-22; 10:1-13; Gal 2:15-16); and (3) *I want to know Christ and the power of his resurrection and the sharing of his suffering by becoming like him in his death* (2:8; cf. Rom 6:5, 10), *if somehow I may attain the resurrection from the dead* (vv. 10-11; cf. Rom 6:8; 8:17). These three reasons are different aspects of the same reality—trusting Christ for one's relation with God instead of reliance on one's own achievements. Legalism, reliance on one's own productivity and achievements to gain a relation to God, is ruled out of order for the Philippians by Paul's example.

3:12-15. Against perfectionism. *Not that I have already obtained this or have already reached the goal* (v. 12). Paul claims to have experienced neither complete victory over sin nor the resurrection from the dead, as some perfectionists in the early church did (sinlessness—1 John 1:8; resurrection—2 Tim 2:18). Rather, like a long-distance runner, he presses on towards the goal (v. 14; cf. Eph 4:12-13; Heb 12:1-2). In Pauline thought, SALVATION involves three tenses: past ("We were saved"—Rom 8:24); present ("We are being saved"—1 Cor 15:2); and future ("We shall be saved"—Rom 5:9). It is inappropriate, then, to claim in the present what only belongs to the future. The paragraph concludes with the exhortation: *Let those of us then who are mature be of the same mind* (v. 15). Paul's example is again appealed to, this time against perfectionism.

3:16-4:1. Against libertine behavior. This unit is held together by an inclusio: 3:16, *Only let us hold fast to what we have attained*, and 4:1, *Stand firm in the Lord in this way*. Verse 17 begins with an explicit appeal to the Pauline example. *Brothers and sisters, join in imitating me, and observe those who live according to the example you have in us* (1 Cor 4:16; 11:1; 1 Thes 1:6; 2 Thes 3:7, 9). On the mission field, new converts need an embodied gospel. The apostle offers them himself and those who follow his example. Unlike those who make their belly their god (cf. Rom 16:18), with their minds set on earthly things (v. 19; 1 Cor 6:12-20), Christians are citizens of heaven whose bodies will be transformed at the PAROUSIA to be like their Savior's glorious body (3:20-21; 1 Cor 6:14). This eschatological hope is the basis for Christians' standing firm in the Lord (4:1). Paul's point here is captured by the early Christian author of the *Epistle to Diognetus*:

> For the distinction between Christians and other men is neither in country nor language nor customs. For they do not dwell in cities in some place of their own, nor do they use any strange variety of dialect, nor practice an extraordinary kind of life. . . . Yet while living in Greek and barbarian cities . . . following the local customs . . . they show forth the wonderful and confessedly strange character of the constitution of their own citizenship. They dwell in their own fatherlands, but as if sojourners in them; they share all things as citizens, and suffer all things as strangers. Every foreign land is their fatherland, and every fatherland is a foreign country. . . . They pass their time upon the earth, but they have their citizenship in heaven (5:1-2, 4-5, 9; Lake 1970, 2:358–61).

Throughout the section, 3:2–4:1, Paul's example has been held up as a norm for the readers. "Keep your eye on the goal if you can see it. If not, keep your eye on one who knows the way to the goal and who is going there" (Robertson 1917, 118).

4:2-9. Panel two: apostolic instruction. In this segment of text Paul deals with three topics: (1) a specific need for Christian unity in the Philippian church (vv. 2-3); (2) the call for perpetual joy (vv. 4-7); and (3) an appeal to meditation on what is noblest and best (v. 8).

4:2-3. Christian unity. Two women in the Philippian church, Euodia and Syntyche, are urged to be of the same mind (1:27; 2:2; 3:15). An unnamed loyal companion, an individual, or perhaps the church as a whole, is urged to help the women agree (v. 3). They are worth the effort because they have *struggled beside me in the work of the gospel, together with Clement and the rest of my coworkers* (v. 3). Paul here makes no gender distinctions in ministry (cf. Rom 16:1-2, 7), just as he makes none in church membership (Gal 3:27-28).

4:4-7. Perpetual joy. The apostle asks for perpetual joy: *go on rejoicing in the Lord always* (v. 4). What follows are two injunctions and two promises.

Injunction: *Let your gentleness be known to everyone* (4:5a)

Promise: *The Lord is near* (4:5b).

Injunction: *Do not worry about anything, but in everything by prayer and supplication with thanksgiving let your requests be made known to God* (4:6).

Promise: *And the peace of God . . . will guard your hearts and your minds in Christ Jesus* (4:7).

"If anything is big enough to worry about, it is not too small to pray about" (Baille 1962, 47). Neither the hostility of others nor adverse circumstances need interrupt Christians' joy because of the resources provided by God: his nearness (either spatially, Ps 34:18, or temporally, 1 Thes 4:17; 1 Cor 15:52), his answers to prayer (cf. Ps 84:11; Jas 4:2; Matt 7:7), and his peace (cf. John 14:27).

4:8-9. Meditation on what is noblest and best. Just as the ancient Jew meditated on God, his acts and his precepts (Josh 1:8; Ps 1:2; 63:6; 77:12; 119:23, 48, 78, 97, 99, 148; 143:5), so the Christians are to think about things that are uplifting and ennobling. *Whatever is true, whatever is honorable, whatever is just, whatever is pure, whatever is pleasing, whatever is commendable, if there is any excellence* [and there is], *and if there is anything worthy of praise* [and there is], *think about these things.* The entire section of exhortations, 3:1b–4:9, ends with a generalizing command and a promise:

Command: *Keep on doing the things that you have learned and received and heard and seen in me* (4:9a; cf. 3:17)

Promise: *and the God of peace will be with you* (4:9b). The apostle's concern is that his converts live according to what he taught and modelled. In this respect Paul mirrored the views of the philosophical schools of his time. The philosopher's word alone, unaccompanied by the act, was regarded as invalid and untrustworthy (Chrysostom, *Discourse* 70.6). Being a disciple meant imitating a teacher's acts and words so as to become like him (*Discourse* 55.4-5). "Plato, Aristotle, and the whole company of sages . . . derived more benefit from the character than from the words of Socrates" (Seneca, *Epistle* 6:5-6). Paul's appeal both to his words and to his deeds would have been what the Philippians expected from their apostle.

Paul's Rejoicing, 4:10-20

This section is A' in the body's pattern, corresponding to 1:12-26. It falls into two parallel panels (vv. 10-14 and 15-18) in which a rejoicing Paul (v. 10) thanks the Philippians for their gifts to meet his need, past (vv. 15-18) and present (vv. 10-14). The section concludes with a promise (v. 19) and a doxology (v. 20).

4:10-14. Panel one: present generosity. This panel is organized in terms of basically the same three components that will be found in panel two: (1) thank you, (2) but, (3) nevertheless.

4:10. Statement of the Philippians' act of generosity in the present. Now that an opportunity has presented itself for the Philippian church to give Paul material assistance again, they have done so. Paul rejoices in their concern for him.

4:11-13. Not that (οὐχ ὅτι) Paul speaks out of great want. He has learned *to be content* (αὐτάρκης) *with whatever I have* (v. 11). He knows how to deal both with plenty and with deprivation (v. 12). The Greek term translated *content* was widely used in Stoic circles to refer to a state of being independent of external circumstances. Epictetus, for example, praised Agrippinus, a distinguished Roman Stoic of the mid-first century C.E. because: "His character was such . . . that when any hardship befell him he would compose a eulogy upon it; on fever, if he had a fever; on disrepute, if he suffered from disrepute; on exile, if he went into exile" (*Fragment* 21). The Stoic discovered within himself the resources to allow contentment no matter what situation might arise. For Paul the resources came from his relation to Christ. Verse 13 might better be translated: "I have the strength for everything (poverty or plenty) in union with the one who infuses me with power" (cf. 2 Cor 12:9-10; Col 1:29). Paul's independence of circumstances came through his dependence on the Lord (cf. Heb 13:5-6).

4:14. Nevertheless the Philippians did well in sharing in Paul's distress. Even though he could have done without their gift, yet Paul affirms their care and concern shown for him by their contribution.

4:15-18. Panel two: past generosity. Three similar components to those in vv. 10-14 make up the second panel, vv. 15-18.

4:15-16. Statement of the Philippians' acts of generosity on two or more occasions in the past. Although Paul refused to allow the Corinthian church to give him money in order to avoid any charges of self-interest on his part (1 Cor 9:3-18; 2 Cor 12:13), he accepted aid from the Philippian church more than once prior to the present gift.

4:17. Not that (οὐχ ὅτι) Paul seeks the gift in and for itself. Paul does not want his acknowledgment of the Philippians' past generosity to be interpreted as his desire for more from them. It is what they gain by it that he seeks (cf. 2 Cor 8:1-5).

4:18. A pleasing sacrifice. Commercial language used in v. 18a indicates that this part of the letter is Paul's receipt for the Philippians' gift (*paid in full*). Sacrificial language in v. 18b points to their gifts as their participation in the Christian liturgy of life (2:17; Rom 12:1-2).

4:19-20. A promise and a doxology. The conclusion to the two panels, 4:10-14 and 15-18, comes in the form of a promise and a doxology.

4:19. A promise. Verse 19 is a promise or a petition depending upon which textual variant is chosen for the main verb: *my God will fully satisfy every need* (future tense) or "may my God fully satisfy your every need" (aorist optative). The NRSV reflects the better textual alternative. Paul speaks as a prophetic figure, certain that God will act in a certain way because of who he is. *My God will fully satisfy every need of yours.* What follows is better rendered: "in a glorious manner in Christ Jesus." (Hawthorne 1983, 208). As in 2 Cor 9:6-11, Paul believes God gives prosperity to his children to enable their generosity.

4:20. A doxology. *To our God and Father be glory forever and ever. Amen.* For similar doxologies to end a letter, compare Rom 16:25-27; 2 Pet 3:18b; Jude 24–25. The letter ends (v. 20) as it began (1:2) with a reference to God the Father.

Conclusion, 4:21-23

The conclusion to a Pauline letter often contained one or more of the following: a peace wish, greetings, reference to the holy kiss, a grace or benediction. Two of these components are found here: greetings (vv. 21-22) and a grace (v. 23). *Caesar's household* refers to that body of officials and servants involved in imperial administration. They would be found in most of the great cities of the empire, for example, Rome and Ephesus. That the saints of Caesar's household greet you (v. 22) indicates how far the gospel had penetrated Roman society. Without Paul's imprisonment (1:12-13), would this have happened?

Works Cited

Baille, John. 1962. *Christian Devotion.*

Garland, D. 1985. "The Composition and Literary Unity of Philippians: some Neglected Factors," *NovT.*

Hawthorne, G. F. 1983. *Philippians.* WBC 43.

Koester, Helmut. 1962. "Philippians, Letter to the." IDBsup.

Kurz, W. S. 1985. "Imitation of Paul and of Christ in Philippians," in *Discipleship in the New Testament.*

Lake, Kirsopp. 1970. *The Apostolic Fathers.*

Michael, J. H. 1928. *The Epistle of Paul to the Philippians.* MNTC.

Robertson, A. T. 1917. *Paul's Joy in Christ: Studies in Philippians.*

Soards, M. 1990. "Paul." MDB.

Watson, D. 1988. "A Rhetorical Analysis of Philippians and Its Implications for the Unity Question," *NovT.*

Colossians

Frank Stagg

Introduction

Colossians is a creative response to heresy. Instead of merely condemning it, PAUL exposed its fallacies and countered with a fresh statement of the Christian calling. Paul clarified his own theology and the moral and ethical practice it implied as he met what apparently was a strange new syncretism of pagan, Jewish, and Christian thought and practice.

Authorship

Whether Colossians is from Paul or his followers is debated. Arguments relate to style, word usage, and theology as compared with the undisputed letters of Paul. Variances are real, but theories accounting for them are not compelling. Extensive use of traditional materials (hymnic, paraenetic, domestic codes) plus Paul's dependence upon scribal help (cf. Rom 16:22) may account for the variants (Cannon 1983, chaps. 2–4). Seeming linkage with Philemon (probably the letter out of LAODICEA, 4:16) argues for Paul as author.

Time and Place

Paul's many imprisonments (2 Cor 11:23), leave uncertain the place from which he wrote Colossians. Options generally considered are ROME, CAESAREA, and EPHESUS. Evidence is not compelling for any one of these. Fortunately, this does not vitally affect interpretation. Date is tied to place; mid-fifties to early sixties, if written from Caesarea or Rome.

Occasion and Purpose

The threat at COLOSSAE was for Paul a *philosophy and empty deceit* (2:8), falsifying the nature of Christ, human nature, and the world, with dire implications for faith, worship, and practice. It subordinated Christ to a hierarchy of spiritual beings, teaching the worship of angels, ascetic disciplines, and bondage to a religious calendar. Paul contended for the all-sufficiency of Christ, the fullness of God embodied, creator, redeemer, and sustainer.

The heresy behind Colossians can be identified only as reflected in the letter. It had strong affinities with what appeared later as GNOSTICISM, with a mixture of pagan, Jewish, and Christian elements. It assumed a DUALISM of spirit and matter, the former good and the latter worthless or evil. This low view of matter could lead to rigid ASCETICISM or permissiveness. Such dualism posed the problem of how an evil creation could come from the goodness of spirit. The gap was bridged by a theory of a series of aeons or emanations called the pleroma or "fullness," issuing from God and ending with a demiurge (worker) as agent in creation.

The church in Colossae seemingly was founded out of a pagan past (1:21, 27; 2:13) by EPAPHRAS (1:7f.; 4:12f.), as yet not visited by Paul (1:4, 7-9; 2:1). Paul's appeal is that they continue in the tradition already received, that represented by the Christian hymn quoted in 1:15-20.

For Further Study

In the *Mercer Dictionary of the Bible*: CHRISTOLOGY; COLOSSAE; COLOSSIANS, LETTER TO THE; DUALISM; EPISTLE/LETTER; GNOSTICISM; PAUL; PRISON EPISTLES; SALVATION IN THE NT; WOMEN IN THE NT.

In other sources: G. E. Cannon, *The Use of Traditional Materials in Colossians*; E. Lohse, *Colossians and Philemon*, Herm; R. P. Martin, *Colossians: The Church's Lord and the Christian's Liberty*; R. McL. Wilson, *Gnosis and the New Testament*.

Commentary

An Outline

Salutation, 1:1-2

Paul alone in Colossians appears as an *apostle*. It was under this authority that Paul warned his readers against new traditions that threatened the authentic faith of the church, which had been proclaimed by Paul's *beloved fellow servant* Epaphras (v. 7).

TIMOTHY alone is associated with Paul in the salutation, though eight others are named later. Possibly Timothy served as scribe, even sharing in the composition, Paul taking the pen only at 4:18.

Grace . . . and peace was a familiar Christian greeting, modeled on current usage but changing the Greek "greeting" (*charein*) to grace (*charis*). *Peace*, like the Hebrew *shalom*, is well-being under the rule of God.

Thanksgiving and Prayer, 1:3-14

1:3-8. Faith, love, hope. This triad, in this order, appears in 1 Thes 1:3 and 5:8, possibly Paul's first letter. To Paul faith was primarily trust. Love (*agape*) is a disposition to relate to others for their good, whatever the cost to self, with no self-serving motive (1 Cor 13:5). *Hope* is eschatological, *laid up for you in heaven* (v. 5; see also 1:27). It sustains and gives meaning to life, overcoming the futility of fate in angel worship.

From Epaphras they had received *the word of the truth, the gospel* (v. 5) and had *truly comprehended the grace of God* (v. 6). The *truth* they received should not be lost to some new tradition presented as *philosophy* (2:8). The gospel derives from *the grace of God*, excluding the need for alleged merits like ascetic practice, angel worship, or worldly regulations (2:6-23).

Paul sees the gospel validated through its worldwide acceptance (not provincial) and its fruitbearing (v. 6; see Gal 5:22-23). It yields a new quality of life (see Matt 7:16-20).

1:9-14. Wisdom and fruitful lives. Along with Paul's confidence in the Colossians is concern that they be *filled with the knowledge (epignosin) of God's will in all spiritual wisdom and understanding* (v. 9). Paul's *epignosis* (thorough knowledge) may be his answer to the *gnosis* (knowledge) sought by the Gnostics, their claim to a higher revealed knowledge of their origin and destiny. Paul stands in the Hebrew tradition of *knowledge* as acquaintance with God (v. 10). Such saving knowledge includes a knowledge of God's will, validated by obedience and fruit, the resulting quality of life. This is not human achievement but the working of God's *glorious power* (v. 11).

The community of the DEAD SEA SCROLLS saw themselves as "the sons of light," as did the later Gnostics; but Paul sees all God's people as children of light. Like a new Exodus, God has *rescued us from the power of darkness and transferred us into the kingdom of his beloved Son* (v. 13). *Redemption* is not paying off God. It is God's act of liberation (*apolytrosis*) by *the forgiveness of sins* (v. 14).

Preeminence of Christ, 1:15-23

1:15-17. Creator of the universe. An early Christian hymn may be preserved in vv. 15-20, even though there is no agreement as to its extent or structure, whether in two strophes or more. Christ is seen as creator of all that is (vv. 15-17), head of the church (vv. 18-20), and redeemer and sustainer of his people (vv. 21-23).

Christ is *the image [eikon] of the invisible God* (v. 15). When we see him, we see "the Father" (John 14:9). "Jesus" means "YHWH Savior," and as "Emmanuel" he is "God with us" (Matt 1:21, 23). New Testament writers would never have said that Jesus is "the second person of the trinity," for this says too little and implies division in deity.

That Christ is *the firstborn of all creation* must be harmonized with the claim that he is *before all things* (v. 17). *Firstborn (prototokos)* indicates not time but primogeniture, the rights of the firstborn.

That *in him all things in heaven and on earth were created* (v. 16) counters the claim that created matter is worthless or evil. It reflects the idea that people are ruled by a hierarchy of spiritual beings, called *thrones or dominions or rulers or powers* (v. 16). Ancient people thought the stars were inhabited by angels or demons and that these determined human fate ("disaster" implies that a star is against us). Christ is creator, but he is not created. He is *before all things* and the power holding together all things (v. 17).

1:18-20. Head of the church. Paul made much of the CHURCH as the body of Christ (1 Cor 12:12-30; Rom 12:1-8; Eph 1:22-23). Against the threat at Colossae, he changed the focus to Christ as the head of this body. He is *the beginning (archē)*, understood absolutely as in John 1:1 or as the originator of the church. He also is *the firstborn [prototokos] from the dead*. As in v. 15, *prototokos* means primogeniture, rights over creation (v. 18).

That all the *fullness (pleroma) of God* dwells in Christ (v. 19) strikes at the heart of the Colossian heresy. *Pleroma* was a term for all the spiritual beings (æons or emanations) supposedly between God and the universe, bridging the gap between spirit and matter. For Paul there is no gap, for in Christ is the fullness of deity, and he is the creator (cf. 2:9).

The "fullness of deity" was pleased not only to dwell in Christ but also *to reconcile to himself all things* (v. 20). Creator and redeemer are the same, and redemption includes all creation (cf. Rom 8:19-23). Rejected is the gnostic idea that spirit and matter are by nature antithetical. Estrangement is moral, and Christ brings about reconciliation by moral means, *making peace through the blood of his cross*. Language here is to be taken seriously, not literally. The cross as timber has no blood, but RECONCILIATION comes through the self-giving of Christ, ultimately in giving his life on the cross. Christ's death becomes effective in our salvation not as an external transaction but only as we are crucified with him (cf. Gal 2:19-21; Rom 6:5-11).

1:21-23. Redeemer and Preserver. The Colossians probably were gentiles (1:27), alienated from God and with a mind-set hostile to God, reflected in their evil works. That was "once," but "now" they have been reconciled to God. God in Christ is the agent in reconciliation, not the problem. Reconciliation has to do with relationship, but salvation in its fuller dimensions intends a new quality of life, holy and blameless and irreproachable. Salvation is not God's unilateral action: it requires the faith that endures (v. 23).

Paul's Apostolic Ministry, 1:24–2:7

1:24-25. The sufferings of Christ. It is a bold claim, yet Paul declared that in his ministry he completed things lacking in the sufferings of Christ. He did so as a part of Christ's *body, that is, the church*. The human

body was a primary model for the church to Paul (see 1 Cor 12:12-26; Rom 12:5), one body comprised of many members. Not only does Christ suffer for the church, but it suffers for him. What is done to the church is done to Christ (see Matt 25:40, 45; Acts 9:4). Paul's sufferings included "chains" and more (4:18; 2 Cor 11:23-29).

1:26-29. God's open secret. The *mystery* long hidden but now revealed is summed up as *Christ in you*. As apostle to the gentiles, Paul gave himself to both Jews and gentiles, all alike in sin and called to a new relationship and quality of life in Christ. "You" is plural in v. 27, *Christ in you* all! This eternal purpose of God, overcoming the estrangement between Jews and gentiles as well as that between Jew and gentile and himself, is the revealed *mystery* (Eph 3:9) as well as *the hope of glory*. Life together in Christ is a glorious hope and the only hope offered us by the God of glory.

2:1-7. Faithfulness to heritage. The concern of this unit is that those at Colossae and Laodicea hold fast to the *treasures of wisdom and knowledge* which already they have in Christ, not letting anyone *deceive* them with *plausible arguments*, that is, the art of persuasion. The heresy threatening them made bold claims to something superior, but it was in fact inferior, false, and empty. Although Paul warns his readers of this subtle threat, he affirms them for their *morale and . . . firmness* and encourages them to remain true to their heritage of faith. Here and throughout Colossians, the basic theme is the all-sufficiency of Christ. They need only to hold to and cultivate what already they have been taught.

Warnings against Entrapments, 2:8-23

This unit is the heart of Colossians, exposing the nature of the threatening heresy and pointing to Christ as the *fullness of deity* (v. 9) and as providing for our *fullness in him* (v. 10).

2:8. Captured by human traditions. Paul uses a rare word (*sulagogein*) for capturing and taking booty. This implies the self-serving motive of those who seek to entrap others as well as the fraud suffered by the victims of *human tradition* posing as *philosophy* but in fact only *empty deceit*. Paul's term for this fallacy is *the elemental spirits of the universe*. "Elements" (*stoicheia*) was a term used variously, including what were thought to be the elements of the cosmos (earth, fire, water, air) and the stars thought to be composed of these elements. The stars were thought to be inhabited by angels who controlled the universe and the fates (dis-aster) of humans.

2:9-10. The fullness of deity. Paul takes the gnostic *pleroma (fullness)* and applies it to Christ. In him *the whole fullness of deity dwells bodily.* The KJV "Godhead" intended what we mean by "godhood" (NRSV *deity*), but it mistakenly came to stand for "persons of the godhead." The NT knows only one God, and the fullness of deity came bodily into the world in Christ (John 1:1, 14).

Fullness also is offered us in Christ. Salvation is seen as becoming fully human: nothing more, nothing less, and nothing other. Christ, who is above *every ruler and authority*, is our sufficiency for our own fulfillment as human beings.

2:11-15. The old and the new. "A circumcision made without hands" (RSV) is the inward "circumcision" of the heart (Rom 2:29). Just as in literal CIRCUMCISION some flesh is removed, so there is *the circumcision of Christ* (i.e., made by Christ) that removes *the body of the flesh* (i.e., sinful nature). Literal circumcision serves here as a paradigm for the cleansing that comes under the lordship of Christ.

Literal BAPTISM also serves as a paradigm for what could be called "a baptism not made with hands." Literal baptism is no more saving than literal circumcision, but each dramatizes something that is saving. "Fullness of life" comes not by religious rites but by the very power that raised Christ from the dead.

New life comes when God forgives us all our trespasses. We are freed from all legalism, whether the cultic laws of Judaism or regulations imposed by *rulers and authorities.* Christ has set aside the record against us with its *legal demands . . . nailing it to the cross* (v. 14). In Christ we are free from the tyranny of rules and from "rulers and authorities" themselves.

2:16-19. Food laws and calendars. God alone is our ultimate judge (1 Cor 4:1-5), and we are judged by his requirements, not those of other people. The Colossians are not to let Gnostics or others judge them by food laws or religious calendars (v. 16). Jesus freed us from calendars (Mark 2:27-28) and kosher laws (Mark 7:15, 19). Such arbitrary rules are but a *shadow.* Christ is the *substance.*

The imperative in v. 18, *Do not let anyone disqualify you,* could be rendered, "do not let anyone award you a prize unjustly." Paul's opponents offer the prize for those who qualify by *self-abasement and worship of angels* instead of *holding fast to the head,* that is, Christ. Such is an empty prize. The true prize is

growth that is from God, attained only as the body of Christ holds fast to the head.

Dwelling on visions translates difficult syntax. This may be a quotation from the mystery religions, including the Greek *embateuon* ("setting foot upon"; NRSV *dwelling on*), a term used for entering a sanctuary in initiation rites where *visions* were sought (Lohse 1971, 118–20). Paul warns against such *visions* as displacing what God has done in Christ.

2:20-23. Impotence of rules. Since *the elemental spirits of the universe* are but human creations, why be subservient to their rules? We belong not to *the world* but to Christ.

Rules like *Do not handle, Do not taste, Do not touch* relate only to such things as perishable food, not to lasting significance. They are merely human rules. They may have the appearance of wisdom as they impose devotion, self-abasement, and ascetic practice, but they are powerless to check *self-indulgence.*

Moral and Ethical Admonitions, 3:1–4:1

3:1-4. Heavenly vs. earthly claims. That Christians *have been raised with Christ* means that they are under the claim of heaven, the world *above, where Christ is, seated at the right hand of God,* the place of honor and power. Although they have *died* and *been raised,* Christians yet live *on earth,* caught between two claims, those from above taking precedence.

We are to live now a life suited to heaven, not to get there but because already we belong there in Christ. The life above is assured by Christ's present enthronement and by his promised return in glory. Life on earth for those in Christ may have the appearance of dishonor and defeat (e.g., Paul's *chains* [4:18]), but its true honor will be revealed eschatologically when Christ is revealed in his glory.

3:5-11. What to put off. Five *earthly* sins are listed, four as sexual abuses: *fornication, impurity, passion, evil desire.* The fifth is more deadly: *greed (which is idolatry).* The material as such is not evil; it is God's creation. It is materialism that is evil. When it owns us, it becomes a god and we idolaters. The *wrath of God* (v. 6) coming upon this is the outworking of God's moral law (Rom 1:18-32). It is reaping what we sow (Gal 6:7-8).

A second list of five *earthly* things are antisocial vices: *anger, wrath, malice, slander, and abusive language.* Anger in itself is not the problem; it is what we do with it or let it do with us. *Wrath* here is anger become chronic. Malice, slander, and abusive language intend harm to others. In the new life, worldly distinctions are transcended, for in Christ *there is no longer Greek and Jew, circumcised and uncircumcised, barbarian, Scythian, slave and free.* Greek stands for gentile. *Scythian* was a term for that ethnic group as more savage than *barbarian*, a questionable stereotype. This enlarges upon Gal 3:28 but significantly drops "no longer male and female" (see 3:18-19).

3:12-17. What to put on. Five virtues to put on displace the evils to put off. These have to do with conduct serving others, unlike the self-serving vices. Forbearance (RSV) or bearing with one another (NRSV) is holding back from one another when tempted to retaliate. Unlike indulgence, forgiveness is creative. It seeks to free from sin as well as restore relationships.

The main adornment for *God's chosen ones* (God chooses us first) is *love.* This fruit of the Spirit (Gal 5:22), abiding and greatest gift of Cod's grace (1 Cor 13), *binds everything together in perfect harmony.*

The *peace of Christ* is not the world's "peace" (John 14:27). Augustus Caesar boasted of *Pax Romana,* but the peace of Rome was imposed by military might. *Pax Christi* is inner peace, attained by the cross, not by the sword.

The *word of Christ* is to dwell in each Christian, and all are to *teach and admonish one another in all wisdom.* Nothing here excludes women or laypersons from teaching or admonishing. *Psalms, hymns, and spiritual songs* imply the full range of songs to God, not precise distinctions.

3:18–4:1. Domestic relationships. This is the first appearance in the NT of an early domestic code (also in Eph 5:22–6:9; 1 Tim 2:8-15; 6:1-2; Titus:1-10; 1 Pet 2:13–3:7; see Stagg and Stagg 1978, 187–204).

Wives, be subject to your husbands mistranslates the middle imperative *hypotassesthe.* The text reads, "Wives, subject yourselves." This at least recognizes the right of a wife to order her own life *as is fitting in the Lord.* From the NT as a whole, more is to be said. Codes are historically conditioned, never final or complete. Husbands are to love their wives and not mistreat them; but silence here does not imply that wives are not to love their husbands or may mistreat them.

The code for children and parents rightly implies that parental responsibility requires the child's obedience; but when the code is absolutized, problems arise. The code here does not cover the problems of child abuse, a modern scandal.

Slaves are to give a quality of service that is a credit to them and to Christ, not for self-serving purposes or because the master deserves it. Masters themselves are reminded that they must answer to the master in heaven (see PHILEMON, LETTER TO for another approach to slavery).

Closing Appeals and Greetings, 4:2-18

4:2-4. Prayer. Paul's prayer request was not that the doors of his prison be opened for his release but that *a door for the word* be opened, that he might *declare the mystery of Christ,* the very gospel for which he was in prison. Paul was not imprisoned for preaching Jesus as the Christ, for others did that without arrest. It was because he preached that "in Christ" there was no Jew and Greek that he was evicted from synagogues and Temple and imprisoned. If given an open door, he would preach *clearly* the very gospel for which he suffered chains.

4:5-6. Outsiders. The Colossians are urged to conduct themselves wisely toward outsiders and to make their speech gracious, *seasoned with salt,* appealing as well as informed and honest.

4:7-17. Colleagues. *Tychicus* seemingly was the bearer of the letter, commissioned to add his report to the letter. *Onesimus* is doubtless the runaway slave of Philemon. Once estranged from *Mark* (Acts 15:37-40), Paul now warmly commends him. *Aristarchus, Mark,* and *Jesus Justus* are the only Jews now with Paul, a price paid for his gospel of no distinction between Jew and gentile in Christ. This letter and one *from Laodicea* (probably Philemon) are to be exchanged, with *Archippus* charged to "fulfil the ministry" (RSV) already given him, possibly the release of Onesimus (Knox 1959, chap. 3).

4:18. Paul's autograph. Paul now takes the pen for his autograph. Remembering his *chains,* they should also remember the *mystery of Christ* (4:3) for which he was in chains.

Works Cited

Cannon, George E. 1983. *The Use of Traditional Materials in Colossians.*

Knox, John. 1959. *Philemon among the Letters of Paul.*

Lohse, Eduard. 1971. *Colossians and Philemon.*

Stagg, Evelyn, and Frank Stagg. 1978. *Woman in the World of Jesus.*

Wilson, R. McL. 1968. *Gnosis and the New Testament.*

First Thessalonians

Linda McKinnish Bridges

Introduction

First Thessalonians deserves careful reading. Dwarfed by the giant literary shadows of Romans, Galatians, and the Corinthian letters, 1 Thessalonians has often been overlooked by Pauline scholars. Yet, this small but significant letter offers the reader an opportunity to explore an early sample of Christian literature (certainly the earliest in our CANON), to hear the burning theological and ethical issues of a young, inexperienced Christian community in THESSALONICA, and to see the passion and tender care given to them by their extraordinary leader, the apostle PAUL.

The Writer

That Paul wrote 1 Thessalonians is not contested. The literary style, vocabulary usage, and parallels in Acts point to Paul as the author. *When* he wrote the letter, however, is much more difficult to establish.

Some scholars date the letter around 40 C.E. (Luedemann 1984; Donfried 1985; Richard 1990; Jewett 1986), while others situate the writing around 50 C.E. (Koester 1982; Malherbe 1983, 1987). The reason for lack of consensus is that a detailed itinerary of Paul's missionary activity is impossible to reconstruct from either Luke's story of Paul in MACEDONIA (Acts 17–18) or Paul's own letter to the church in Thessalonica. Neither writer wrote for the sole purpose of relating travel itineraries; therefore, exact dates are conjectures, at best.

Just as the exact date of the writing is difficult to determine, so is the precise setting and surrounding circumstances. Not only are Luke's and Paul's accounts sketchy, sometimes they do not agree. The reader, therefore, must be familiar with both accounts in order to establish background information for the Thessalonian letter.

The Acts Account. How did Paul arrive in Thessalonica? According to the Acts account, Paul was impris-

oned in PHILIPPI at the beginning of the mission to Europe (Acts 16:19-24). Paul, along with SILAS and TIMOTHY, then left Philippi, traveled through AMPHIPOLIS and Appolonia and then arrived in Thessalonica. When they arrived, Paul went into the synagogue, as was his custom, and proclaimed Jesus as Messiah (17:3).

How long did Paul stay? Paul stayed in Thessalonica for three Sabbaths (three weeks). As a result, some Jews, a number of gentiles, and many women were converted. Their success angered the Jews, however, and a hostile crowd attacked the home of a new convert, Jason. Jason and other believers were dragged to the city magistrate. Paul, although not present, was charged with treason (17:7). Paul and his colleagues secretly left Thessalonica by night. They traveled to Beroea, where the Thessalonican Jews continued to agitate the crowds. Silas and Timothy remained in Beroea, and Paul went on to ATHENS alone.

When did Paul write the letter? Acts does not give us information about any of Paul's letters. From the Acts account, however, we surmise that Paul wrote a letter after visiting the community of believers in Thessalonica.

The Account from 1 Thessalonians. How did Paul arrive in Thessalonica? Paul does not give details of his initial arrival in Thessalonica. We must learn that information from Acts 17.

How long did Paul stay? In the Acts account, we read that Paul stayed in Thessalonica for three weeks. In Paul's letter, however, the visit appears longer. Again, the details are sketchy. We do know that Paul was in the city long enough to establish his trade of tentmaking and to provide a model of behavior for the Christians (2:9-10). We also know that on several occasions Paul received gifts sent from Philippi by a traveling courier (Phil 4:15). Philippi was about 100 miles distant. The time spent in travel would have taken longer than three weeks (4:15).

When did Paul write the letter? First Thessalonians does not give a date. The letter was written after Timothy reported his visit to Paul. No other churches are mentioned in the letter. We can surmise that Paul wrote 1 Thessalonians shortly after leaving the city of Thessalonica, perhaps in CORINTH in 50 C.E., in the company of Timothy and Silas.

The Letter

Traditionally scholars have viewed 1 Thessalonians according to its thematic structure. The letter has been divided into the categories of thanksgiving, personal remarks, and ethical and doctrinal teaching. Recently, scholars have proposed new readings of 1 Thessalonians, using the exegetical methods of structuralism (Malbon 1983), feminist reading (Gaventa 1990), and Graeco-Roman rhetorical conventions (Wanamaker 1990).

Although various methods are used to outline and interpret the epistle, 1 Thessalonians, nonetheless, remains a letter. This epistle is an authentic piece of correspondence between two parties, Paul and the church at Thessalonica. Unfortunately we only have clear access to one part of the conversation—Paul's. To hear the voice of the other party, the novice Christians in the church at Thessalonica, we must listen carefully.

The Community

Paul's letter was not intended to be a systematic theological treatise. Paul wrote to a community, composed predominantly of gentile believers who were struggling with their new faith (see the description by Blevins 1990, 909, of the setting of the community). Paul does not present dogmatic rules for life; nor does he prescribe a quick fix for their theological anxiety. Rather, in this letter Paul shares himself and pastoral words of comfort with "the beloved ones" in Thessalonica (2:8).

The occasion for the letter comes from the community. Timothy returns to Paul from Thessalonica with a good report and with a list of questions from the community. These questions, either in written or oral form, articulate the basic concerns of the community. The questions also reveal a troubled congregation. Paul writes to comfort them.

As we read Paul addressing the concerns of the Thessalonian church in this intimate letter, we can also hear the anxious voices from the church. The community is experiencing persecution (1 Thes 1:6; 2:14-16). They are concerned about the recent death of church members (4:13-18). They remain confused about the meaning of an incalculable PAROUSIA (5:1). The community in Thessalonica also question Paul's style of leadership (2:1-12). Sexual ethics are also a major concern (4:1-8).

For Further Study

In the *Mercer Dictionary of the Bible*: APOSTLE/APOSTLESHIP; EPISTLE/LETTER; ESCHATOLOGY IN THE NT; PAROUSIA; PAUL; THESSALONIANS, LETTERS TO THE; THESSALONICA.

In other sources: E. Best, *The First and Second Epistles to the Thessalonians*; L. McK. Bridges, "Paul as a Nursing Mother," *Lectionary Homiletics* (Nov 1993); R. Collins, *The Thessalonian Correspondence*; Beverly Gaventa, "The Maternity of Paul," in *The Conversation Continues*, ed. R. Fortna and B. Gaventa; R. Jewett, *The Thessalonian Correspondence: Pauline Rhetoric and Millenarian Piety*; H. Koester, "I Thessalonians—Experiment in Christian Writing," in *Continuity and Discontinuity*, ed. F. Church; A. J. Malherbe, *Paul and the Thessalonians: The Philosophic Tradition of Pastoral Care*; E. S. Malbon, "'No Need to Have Any One Write?' A Structural Exegesis of 1 Thessalonians," *Semeia* 26 (1983): 57–83; I. H. Marshall. *1 and 2 Thessalonians*; L. Morris, *The First and Second Epistles to the Thessalonians*; J. M. Reese, *1 and 2 Thessalonians*; C. Wanamaker, *The Epistles to the Thessalonians: A Commentary on the Greek Text*.

Commentary

Greeting the Church, 1:1

Paul begins the letter with the familiar, traditional epistolary greeting (cf. Rom 1:1-7; 1 Cor 1:1-3; 2 Cor 1:1-2; Gal 1:1-4). *Silvanus*, the SILAS of Acts 15:22, and *Timothy*, Paul's missionary colleague, were probably the couriers of the Thessalonian letter. They transported the letter from CORINTH to THESSALONICA.

Paul does not identify himself as servant as he does in the greeting of Romans, or as an apostle as seen in 1 and 2 Corinthians and Galatians. Perhaps Paul's position as leader is not as unstable in the Thessalonican church as it would later become in the other churches. The liturgical prayer, a traditional Pauline greeting, offers *grace . . . and peace* to the church.

Encouraging the Church, 1:2-10

Central to the skill of a good communicator is the ability to make contact with the audience. Paul, an excellent communicator, gains the attention of the listeners by talking directly to them. He praises them and their accomplishments. In this tribute, the themes of the entire epistle are also introduced.

1:2-4. Praise. Paul offers thanks for the believers. The tone of praise is repeated in 2:13-14, 2:20, 3:6-10, and 4:1. A familiar triad—faith, love, and hope—describe the people (1 Thes 5:8; Rom 5:1-5; 1 Cor 13:12-13). The church at Thessalonica is noted for their work that comes from their faith, their labor that proceeds from their love, and their steadfastness that follows their hope (v. 3). Paul also gives thanks because he knows that his friends, "the beloved ones,"

have been called by God (v. 4). Paul continues to offer tribute for the "beloved ones" throughout the epistle (see 2:19-20; 3:6-10).

The language used in these verses instills community and intimacy. The presence of the second personal pronouns, the use of familial term, "brothers" (ἀδελ-φοί), translated inclusively as *friends* (NRSV), and the use of the word calling or ELECTION (ἐκλογήν) in v. 4 are used to create intimacy between the speaker and the audience.

1:5-7. Paul's ministry of imitation. Paul encourages the readers to imitate him. At first glance, the injunction sounds self-serving. Paul, however, was not establishing his life as the authoritarian model for morality for the community. Rather, Paul is saying, "imitate me as I imitate Christ." See the further development of the idea of imitation in 1 Thes 2:13-16 and 2 Thes 3:6-9.

Verses 6b-8 clarify the metaphor of imitation. To imitate Paul means to be willing to experience the joy of the Spirit even in times of distress (v. 6b). The persecution may have been emotional or physical suffering, or both. To break from the past, either from the Jewish tradition or gentile cultic worship, required emotional anguish for the neophyte Christians. Persecution may have also been more visible, like political oppression or economic hardship.

Paul's understanding of imitation suggests that believers are to become an example to others as he had been an example to them. As Paul had been instrumental in bringing the Thessalonians to faith, so should the community of faith, in turn, be responsible for spreading the gospel (vv. 7-8).

1:9. Ethics. The community received Paul and his gospel. That reception was manifested in clear and visible ways. The believers left their former way of life; they turned from idols to embrace a new life-style with Christ. Paul clarifies this new ethical behavior in 4:12.

To leave a cultic life-style and embrace the strict, ethical admonitions of Paul was no easy task for the novice, Thessalonian Christian. Religious cults were popular in the city of Thessalonica. Archaeological evidence points to the presence of the cults of Serapis, Dionysus, Cabirus, and Samothrace in Thessalonica. Sexual symbols, mystical rites, and frenzied, orgiastic worship characterized the cults.

1:10. Eschatology. The theme of eschatology is briefly introduced here, foreshadowing further development in 4:13. The community of believers have not only left their former life-styles, they are waiting patiently for the return of Christ.

Notice the didactic use of the relative clauses. The community "waits for God's son *who* is from heaven, *who* was raised from the dead, and *who* is Jesus, our deliverer" (author trans.). With characteristic literary flair, Paul packs a thought unit, using every opportunity to teach the gospel, even through a preponderance of relative clauses.

Serving the Church, 2:1–3:10

Soon after Paul's arrival in Thessalonica he incurred much agony (ἀγῶνι) in opposition (see Acts 17:1-9). Paul had also endured much agony in his previous missionary stop in PHILLIPI (Phil 1:30). Paul ministered in the face of considerable obstacles. His motives for ministry were pure, and the opposition unwarranted.

As a Nursing Mother, 2:1-9

Paul, who is perhaps being maligned by opponents in the church, uses literary energy to explain his innocence. Paul's ministry is not to please people, as he has perhaps been accused. Paul did not minister to the Thessalonians with words of flattery, nor with the motive of greed. Nor did Paul come looking for glory from them or others.

How did Paul come to the people? Although he could have come as a heavy, apostolic tyrant or dictator, "throwing his weight around" in the congregation, he chose to come gently, as a nursing mother, ὡς ἐὰν τροφὸς θάλπῃ τὰ ἑαυτῆς τέκνα (vv. 6-7). This striking contrast of images provides a vivid picture of Paul's relationship with the people. As a mother would nurse her child, giving of her life, sharing her time, being accessible, providing life-sustaining nourishment whenever needed, so does Paul care for the people of Thessalonica. The maternity of Paul challenges the contemporary abuses of pastoral leadership.

As an Encouraging Father, 2:10-16

A second familial metaphor describes how Paul serves the church. Paul responded to them as father, πατήρ (vv. 10-11). Paul's images of pastoral leadership do not come from Roman military structure or the ancient business world, but from the arena of the household. Verse 12, which continues the thought of vv. 10-11, describes the role of the father: to exhort or teach, to encourage or cheer, to witness or affirm. The father in the first-century home was the primary parent responsible for moral guidance. Paul's maternal and paternal images form a unified image that challenges contemporary views of pastoral leadership and power in the church.

Some scholars view vv. 13-16 as an interpolation, added later and not written by Paul. Most argue for the interpolation view because of the anti-semitic tone of the passage. Others argue that although it was written by Paul, vv. 13-16 provide a digression, or interruption of his train of thought.

I suggest, however, that the unit vv. 13-16 is not an interpolation. Rather, these verses are used by Paul to support and expand the familial metaphor given in vv. 10-12. Verses 10-13 illustrate the role of the fatherly pastor. Just as the role of the first-century father was to encourage the children, so Paul encourages the people (v. 13). Paul likewise takes on the role of teacher as he reminds the Thessalonians to imitate him (v. 14). Finally, Paul affirms the congregation by reminding them of his own personal suffering. Paul is fulfilling the role of the traditional Jewish father who brings the memory of past experiences as lesson to be learned for the present (v. 16).

As an Orphan, 2:17–3:10

Paul loves the people of Thessalonica, and he is not ashamed to show his emotion for them. In their absence, he feels like an orphan (ἀπορφανισθέντες), like a child without parents. Again, this potent image reinforces Paul's style of leadership. Paul has not only given these people the gospel, he has given them *himself* (2:8). They have become family to him. The community of believers becomes his *crown of boasting* (2:19-20).

Paul sent Timothy back to the Thessalonians as Paul's official courier (3:2). Paul received a glowing report. Paul is encouraged (3:6).

Praying for the Church, 3:11-13

We already know that Paul prays for this church as seen in 1:2. Verses 11-13 give us some of the content of those prayers.

The verses are linked by verbs found in the optative mood, a grammatical expression for prayer: *may . . . direct* (v. 11), *may . . . make you increase and . . . abound in love* (v. 12). Paul prays so that the church might be blameless and holy (v. 13).

Teaching the Church, 4:1–5:22

Commonly called the paranesis, which means teaching or exhortation, this section deals with ethical behavior in the community. Paul's concern for the ethics of the congregation has already been foreshadowed in 1:9 and reinforced in Paul's prayer in 3:12-13.

Theology and Praxis, 4:1-2

Paul understands that loving God, a horizontal relationship, also means loving the community, a vertical relationship. A sense of urgency is heard in Paul's voice as he begs (ἐρωτῶμεν) the members of the church to have their walk with others parallel their talk about Christ (v. 1). Ethics, for Paul, is not a philosophical abstraction. Rather, Paul summarizes Christian behavior by giving practical guidelines for holy living.

Sexual Ethics, 4:3-8

Paul does not mince words when he says: *Abstain from fornication* (v. 3). In v. 4, Paul exhorts the believer to control one's own "vessel" (σκεῦος). Some English translations, however, render this Greek word as *wife*. For example, the RSV translates v. 4a as, "each one of you know how to take a wife for him." This biased translation limits the exhortation to married men and misses the force of the paragraph. To control one's own sexual urges is the point of this verse. The reason for sexual discipline relates to issues of justice for the entire community, not only within marriage (v. 6). To exploit another person sexually damages both individuals and the life of the community suffers. Paul acknowledges that to live a life with sexual limits is not easy. This is God's way, however, and the HOLY SPIRIT has been given for assistance (vv. 7-8).

Relationships, 4:9-12

Paul begins a new thought unit with the words, *Now concerning.* The new topic continues to highlight the horizontal mandate of the gospel—*love one another* (v. 9). Four verbal infinitives provide the grammatical structure for this section: to love more, to be quiet, to mind your own affairs, and to work with your own hands. Some of Paul's converts may have been refusing to earn their own keep. Some of the church members may have also stopped working thinking that Jesus would return soon. Paul urges them to wait quietly, while working and relating to people.

Return of Christ, 4:13–5:11

A new topic begins in v. 13. Paul addresses directly the questions given to Timothy by the congregation. Their dilemma is this: The church members have had relatives to die since Paul's last visit. They understood that Paul taught the imminent return of Christ, the PAROUSIA. Then their relatives began to die, and the parousia had not yet happened. They are confused. They are also grieving. They grieve over the loss of their loved ones. They also grieve because their teacher is not present with them in their time of mourning.

In response, Paul makes two important points. One, Paul says that those who have died will not be disadvantaged at the parousia (4:13-18). God will take care of them. Reunion with them and union with Christ will occur in the end. Two, the exact time of Jesus' return cannot be determined in advance (5:1-11). Therefore, the Thessalonians should relax and be comforted.

Paul's initial reaction is to comfort his grieving friends (5:11). To do so he recalls a word from the Lord (4:15). He uses powerful, visual images—"the archangel's voice," "a trumpet," "the clouds"—to describe the majestic event that is to come. The most comforting point is found in the tiny Greek word σύν (together with) in v. 17. Paul wants the community to know that we will be all *together with* the Lord (v. 17).

This epistle draws the confused, grieving believers in Thessalonica closer *together with* Paul, their teacher and friend. Paul promises that the return of Christ will bring a grand reunion, where loved ones will be brought *together with* one another (2:17–3:10).

Final Instructions, 5:12-22

Last-minute imperatives of ethical behavior are given in the closing of 1 Thessalonians. Paul earnestly begs that the believers recognize and respect their leaders (vv. 12-13). Paul encourages the community to consider those who are idlers (ἀτάκτους), faint-hearted, and weak with generous and forgiving grace (v. 14). Do not return evil for evil (v. 15).

The imperatives also guide the liturgical life of the congregation. *Rejoice* (v. 16). *Pray* (vv. 17-18). Do not restrain the Holy Spirit (v. 19). Do not despise prophecy (v. 20). *Test everything* (v. 21). Keep away from evil (v. 22).

Blessing the Church, 5:23-28

Using the grammar of prayer, the optative mood, Paul offers a concluding prayer for the Thessalonians. The ethical behavior of the Thessalonians remains a primary focus (see the prayer in 3:11-13). Energy for the task, however, comes not from the believer but from God.

Paul's understanding of apostolic authority surfaces in the conclusion (see 2:1–3:10). Paul not only offers prayers for the people, but he is also eager to receive them (v. 25) The *holy kiss* (φιλήματι ἁγίῳ) became a liturgical gesture in the second or third centuries (v. 26). The letter is to be read aloud in the meetings of the church (v. 27). The ending of the letter echoes the beginning with the word *grace* (χάρις, 1:2 and 5:28).

Works Cited

Blevins, James L. 1990. "Thessalonians, Letters to the," in *MDB*.

Donfried, K. P. 1985. "The Cults of Thessalonica and the Thessalonian Correspondence," *NTS* 31:336–56.

Gaventa, Beverly, 1990. "The Maternity of Paul: An Exegetical Study of Galatians 4:19," in *The Conversation Continues: Studies in Paul and John in Honor of J. Louis Martyn*, ed. Robert Fortna and B. Gaventa.

Jewett, R. 1986. *The Thessalonian Correspondence: Pauline Rhetoric and Millenarian Piety*.

Koester, H. 1982. *Introduction to the New Testament. 2: History and Literature of Early Christianity*.

Luedemann, G. 1984. *Paul, Apostle to the Gentiles: Studies in Chronology*.

Manson, T. W. 1953. "St. Paul in Greece: The Letters to the Thessalonians," *BJRL* 35:428–47.

Malbon, E. 1983. "'No Need to Have Any One Write?' A Structural Exegesis of 1 Thessalonians," *Semeia* 26:57–83.

Malherbe, A. J. 1983. "Exhortation in First Thessalonians," *NovT* 25:238–56. 1987. *Paul and the Thessalonians: The Philosophic Tradition of Pastoral Care*.

Richard, E. 1990. "Contemporary Research on (1 & 2) Thessalonians," *BTB* 20:107–15.

Wanamaker, C. 1990. *The Epistles to the Thessalonians: A Commentary on the Greek Text*.

Second Thessalonians

Linda McKinnish Bridges

Introduction

Although 2 Thessalonians continues the conversation with the church in THESSALONICA, this epistle must be read separately. It is not simply the second half of 1 Thessalonians. Let 2 Thessalonians be 2 Thessalonians!

To note the dissimilarities between the two letters helps to separate the readings. Second Thessalonians does not contain the personal warmth and affective language as seen in 1 Thessalonians. Absent in 2 Thessalonians is the frequent use of first- and second-person pronouns. Although a basic epistolary structure remains the same, the syntax and style is more complex in 2 Thessalonians, using more relatival clauses and dependent phrases. Furthermore, while 1 Thessalonians addresses many concerns of the community, 2 Thessalonians focuses on one issue, namely, how to be faithful in persecution.

The Writer

Did PAUL write 2 Thessalonians? Although scholars generally conclude that Paul wrote 1 Thessalonians, consensus has not yet been reached regarding the authorship of 2 Thessalonians. The authorship question, first raised at the turn of the century, still lingers.

Wolfgang Trilling (1981) and others, for example, oppose Pauline authorship on the basis of a study of vocabulary and style. On the other hand, Robert Jewett (1986) and others, argue for Pauline authorship on the basis of vocabulary and style. Both arguments are compelling. Although Pauline authorship was not questioned in the first few centuries of the church, recent linguistic analyses show significant variation in Greek syntax between the two letters. Paul either wrote in a totally new style when he composed the second letter, or another person used Paul's apostolic authority to gain a hearing for 2 Thessalonians.

Questions regarding the author, however, do not diminish the powerful voice of the letter, either for first-century or twentieth-century readers. The writer, whether Paul or another, writes a real letter to real people with real problems. We listen in on the conversation.

The Letter

Traditional, first-century, epistolary conventions are seen in 2 Thessalonians. This carefully constructed letter includes a greeting, body, and closing. Particular attention is given to chap. 2, the central chapter. This crucial section introduces the primary focus of the letter—the community's response to the PAROUSIA of Christ.

Which letter was written first? The question is valid, for canonical sequence has more to do with length of the letters than with chronological concerns. Some scholars, H. Grotius 1679, J. Weiss 1937, T. W. Manson 1953, and others, posit that 2 Thessalonians was actually written first. They assume Paul wrote 2 Thessalonians while in ATHENS. TIMOTHY delivered the letter to the church, as Paul later records in the second letter (1 Thes 3:1-6). First Thessalonians, Paul's second letter, was written from CORINTH and composed after Timothy returned from his previous visit.

Contemporary scholarship remains divided on the issue of the sequence of 1 and 2 Thessalonians. Robert Jewett (1986) presents a cogent argument for canonical sequencing. By contrast, Charles Wanamaker (1990) offers a detailed argument for the reversal.

The question of sequence is valid; the answers, however, remain questionable. For our purposes here, we follow the traditional sequencing and assume that 2 Thessalonians was written after 1 Thessalonians. The second letter continues the conversation with the community. The style of conversation, however, is strikingly dissimilar.

The Community

At least three problems concern this community of believers. One, they are theologically confused (2 Thes 2:2). They think *that the day of the Lord* has already come. Paul describes what will take place before Christ comes to assure them that the parousia, or coming of Christ, has not happened yet.

Two, some members of the community have become social problems and economic burdens for the church. These people, believing that Christ had already come, have become lazy (3:6). They are not working. They depend on others for their economic support.

The third problem, related to the first two, has to do with false teachers in the church. OPPONENTS OF PAUL and his teachings have infiltrated the life of the community (1:4-12). They have introduced faulty theologies and weak ethics. They have also brought suffering and persecution to the members of the community who do not heed their teachings.

Who are these false teachers? We know more about what they said than where they came from. Various options regarding the identity of the opponents have been given, such as gnostic infiltrators, millenarian radicals, or enthusiastic revivalists. We, however, can only guess at their identity and place of origin.

Could it be that these opponents were members from the church in JERUSALEM? The chasm between Paul's ministry and the intended ministry goals of the Jerusalem church was great. The Jerusalem church often sent missionaries to check on Paul's work (Acts 15:22f.; Gal 2:4-10). It is not unlikely that a group of anti-Paul, energetic, Judaizers from Jerusalem also entered Thessalonica causing disruption and distressing the Thessalonican Christians. They contradict Paul's teachings, assuring the neophyte Christians that the *day of the Lord* has already come (2:2).

Furthermore, these opponents oppose Paul's ethical teachings by encouraging the Thessalonican community to relax, not bother with working (3:12). The opponents demand conformity, and the community labors under great pressure and persecution (1:4-12). To this community of new believers in Thessalonica, who have been influenced by these infiltrators, Paul says, "Be faithful, don't give up, hang in there."

For Further Study

In the *Mercer Dictionary of the Bible*: ESCHATOLOGY IN THE NEW TESTAMENT; MAN OF LAWLESSNESS; PAUL; THESSALONIANS, LETTERS TO THE; THESSALONICA.

In other sources: *See also* "1 Thessalonians," above; J. Bailey, "Who Wrote II Thessalonians?" *NTS* 25 (1978–1979): 131–45; E. Krentz, "Traditions Held Fast: Theology and Fidelity in 2 Thessalonians," in *The Thessalonian Correspondence*, ed. R. Collins; M. J. J. Menken, "The Structure of 2 Thessalonians," in *The Thessalonian Correspondence*, ed. R. Collins; R. Russell, "The Idle in 2 Thess. 3:6-12: An Eschatological or a Social Problem," *NTS* 14 (1988): 105–19; D. Schmidt, "The Authenticity of 2 Thessalonians: Linguistic Arguments," *SBLSP* 1983.

Commentary

An Outline

I. Greeting the Church, 1:1-2
II. Thanking the Church, 1:3-12
III. Warning the Church, 2:1-17
   A. The Coming of Christ
      and the Person of Lawlessness, 2:1-12
   B. The Gathering of Christians, 2:13-17
IV. Teaching the Church, 3:1-15
   A. The Prayer for Discipline, 3:1-5
   B. The Discipline in the Community, 3:6-15
V. Blessing the Church, 3:16-18

Greeting the Church, 1:1-2

Note the similarities between the epistolary greeting in 1 and 2 Thessalonians. Three major characters are introduced—PAUL, SILVANUS, and TIMOTHY. Traditionally we focus on the missionary activities of Paul, often to the exclusion of Paul's colleagues. It is important to note, however, that the missionary activity of the early church was not accomplished through the efforts of one, but of many. Paul worked with BARNABAS, JOHN MARK, LYDIA, Phoebe, and a host of others, some of whom are not even mentioned in the letters. Together, they planted churches and nurtured young congregations in the faith.

Thanking the Church, 1:3-12

Paul's letters exhibit liturgical qualities. The depth of emotion is best revealed in the Greek syntax. This section, although containing ten verses in English, is constructed from only two Greek sentences, vv. 3-10 and 11-12. The Greek embedded clauses and phrases give power and personal drama to the moment of thanksgiving.

The thanksgiving section, while liturgical in tone, also has a rhetorical function. The use of second-person pronouns and words of praise urges people to stop and listen to the important points of the presentation. Likewise, the first-century reader hears Paul's affective language and is compelled to listen. While listening to Paul's praise (vv. 3-4), they are also introduced to the main themes of the letter (vv. 5-11).

Two themes are introduced in this section and then further clarified in the body of the letter. First, the theme of *the day of the Lord* is introduced in vv. 5-10 and then discussed in greater detail in 2:1-12. Likewise, the theme of the community is introduced here and is given fuller treatment in the paranetic section of 2:13–3:15.

1:3-4. Praise and prayer. The church is congratulated on their faithful persistence in spite of local opposition. In a spirit of prayer, Paul praises the congregation for their faith in God and love for one another. The Thessalonican church has become a model of faith for other churches (v. 4).

1:5-10. Reversal of fortunes. The *day of the Lord* will bring both reward and punishment. This theology of suffering includes rewards for those who have been faithful and affliction for those who have caused the persecution. This reversal of fortunes, repaying those who caused affliction with affliction, belongs to God's righteous judgment (vv. 5-7). Those who have been faithful, even in persecution, will be able to relax when Jesus returns. To be able to relax at *the day of the Lord* stands in sharp contrast to those who, not knowing God and not obeying the gospel of Christ, will be given punishment. The punishment will be total separation from the face of the Lord and from the glory of his strength (vv. 7-9).

1:11-12. Praise and prayer. The section closes with a prayer (vv. 11-12) just as it began with a spirit of prayer (1:3-4). Attention shifts, however, within the INCLUSIO from the explanation of *the day of the Lord* to the response of the community to Christ's coming. With an understanding of *the day of the Lord*, expressed with apocalyptic images and predicted reversal of fortunes, the community is still faced with the question, "How are we supposed to live in the meantime?" It is this question that lingers in the minds of the young believers. Living in the meantime requires intercessory prayer by Paul and ethical behavior by the Thessalonian Christians (v. 12).

Warning the Church, 2:1-17

The predominant theme of 2 Thessalonians, subtly introduced in the thanksgiving section of chap. 1, is given full treatment in chap. 2. The parousia (παρουσίας), the coming of the Lord, and our coming together with him (ἐπισυναγωγῆς) are crucial concerns of the community.

Perhaps the young Christians have been asking particular questions concerning the manifestation of Christ, when and how it might occur. Paul responds by describing not only the details of Christ's coming but also our "assembling" with him.

The Coming of Christ and the Person of Lawlessness, 2:1-12

The believers at Thessalonica were confused, literally "shaken in their mind and continually disturbed" (v. 2, author trans.). Someone, somewhere told the congregation that the parousia had already occurred. It is not clear how they received this information, perhaps by a supposedly spirit-inspired utterance, an oral report, or maybe a letter purported to be written by Paul. By whatever means, the young Christians have been deceived.

The purpose of this section is to prove that *the day of the Lord* positively could not have already arrived. Verses 3-7 detail the events that must precede the Lord's coming, and vv. 8-12 point to the events that have not yet happened.

Paul warns that the day of the Lord will not come unless the APOSTASY comes first and the person of lawlessness, the son of destruction, is revealed. Who is this person of lawlessness? This person represents for both the first and twentieth-century reader the epitome of EVIL. The person of lawlessness opposes God, proclaiming to be God.

By wrapping the abstract concept of evil into human form, the readers can visualize its reality and menace. Many comparable historical figures, like Antiochus Epiphanes, Pompey, Gaius Caesar, probably entered the mind of the first-century reader. The first-century reader, most likely, expected a future historical figure to appear whose power could only be restrained by the preaching of the gospel. Full victory over such a person, which also signals victory over pervasive evil, is only possible in the parousia (v. 8).

What about the people? The person of lawlessness deceives the people. Those who have been deceived, therefore, receive not the love of truth and ultimately perish (vv. 10-11). This rather harsh language describes why some people have chosen to reject the gospel. Perhaps Paul is describing the opponents, those people who saw the radical freedom of Christians as a direct threat to their own religious traditions.

Obviously, *the day of the Lord* has not yet come, Paul asserts. In other words, it is going to become much worse before it becomes better.

The Gathering of Christians, 2:13-17

In tones of worship and praise, Paul gives thanks for God's initiative in calling the young Christians into salvation. The appropriate response to the glory of God in Christ is clear to the young Christians in Thessalonica: *Stand firm and hold fast to the traditions that you were taught by us* (v. 15). Capsuled in elegant, apocalyptic descriptions, complemented by beautiful, liturgical phrases, and supplemented by deep, theological insights stands the core of Paul's thought—ethical behavior. It makes a difference how you live. Talk about the end of time does not make much sense unless one also talks about what the parousia means for the gathered people of God in the present. Paul introduces the concept here of the community's response to the coming of Christ and then gives greater detail in the final chapter.

Teaching the Church, 3:1-15

A small word of transition, *finally* (λοιπόν), marks this new section. This word is used often to signal a change of thought and to mark the beginning of the ethical or paranetic portion of the letter (cf. 1 Thes 4:1; 2 Cor 13:11; Phil 4:2). The chapter begins with praise and prayer and concludes with specific instructions for ethical behavior.

The Prayer for Discipline, 3:1-5

Prayer is crucial for Paul. Prayer is also reciprocal between leader and people. Just as the Thessalonians need prayer, so does Paul. The ultimate goal of righteous living for Paul is not for self-glory. Rather, one is to live righteously so that the gospel of Christ, the word of the Lord, might run on ahead and triumph (v. 1). The progress of the gospel can be encouraged by one's life. Not all people, however, will contribute to the progress. Some are not responsive to the word of God (v. 2).

Paul refers to those people who oppose the progress of the Christian mission as the "out-of-place ones" (ἀτόπων). These opponents are consistent dialogue partners throughout this letter, as well as 1 Thessalonians (see 1 Thes 2:13-16). Paul speaks to them and against them as he communicates to the entire church.

The opponents are also a convenient literary foil to show the young believers how not to act. Paul condemns the behavior of the opponents while at the same time he exhorts the others to obedience.

The Discipline in the Community, 3:6-15

Unlike the paranetic section in 1 Thessalonians that contains many instructions (see 1 Thes 4–5), 2 Thessalonians is concerned with only one issue. Its solitary position makes the single exhortation clear and dramatic: Keep away from every friend who is living in *idleness* (ἀτάκτως) (v. 6).

The word *idleness* (see also 1 Thes 5:14 and 2 Thes 3:6, 7) can denote either undisciplined or disorderly actions or persons, or idle or lazy individuals. In the Thessalonian correspondence, the word seems to denote idle behavior that leads to disorderly lives.

Members of the congregation have not been working. They are living in irresponsible idleness. By depending on the wealthier members of the congregation to provide their economic sustenance, they are creating havoc in the community.

Paul reminds them that he and the ethical tradition that he taught does not advocate laziness (v. 8). His own life is an example. Paul did his missionary work without payment (see 1 Thes 2:9; 1 Cor 9:1-18; 2 Cor 11:7). According to the law of Moses and to traditional religious practices, he could, however, have demanded a salary.

A maxim summarizes Paul's position in v. 10: "If you don't work; you don't eat." The instruction given by Paul is plain and simple. The believer is to work, eat one's own bread, and not meddle in the affairs of others. The church is to take special notice of those who cannot obey this instruction. The church is instructed to isolate the person until the behavior is modified. Ostracizing deviant persons becomes necessary for the preservation of the larger community. Notice, however, that the idle person who is undergoing rehabilitation is still to be considered as friend, not enemy.

Blessing the Church, 3:16-18

Second Thessalonians concludes with a prayer of blessing. Paul notes that he is writing this letter with his *own hand* (v. 17). For some scholars, this is a critical clue that this letter may not have been written by

Paul, but rather by someone who needed Paul's authority to gain a hearing in the church. Another position is to see v. 17 as Paul's own personal, written signature to a letter actually written by an AMANUENSIS, or secretary. Paul, or his authority, is an important component of the conversation to the Thessalonians.

As the letter began, so it ends. *Grace* (χάρις), the beginning and ending of the life of an individual believer and the community of faith, also becomes the beginning and ending of a letter written by a faithful follower of the gospel, Paul, to a group of young believers in Thessalonica.

Works Cited

Grotius, H. 1679. *Operum Theologicorum.*

Jewett, R. 1986. *The Thessalonian Correspondence: Pauline Rhetoric and Millenarian Piety.*

Manson, T. W. 1953. "St. Paul in Greece: The Letters to the Thessalonians," *BJRL* 35:428-47.

Trilling, W. 1972. *Untersuchungen zum zweiten Thessalonicherbrief.*

Wanamaker, Charles. 1990. *The Epistles to the Thessalonians: A Commentary on the Greek Text.*

Weiss, J. 1959. *Earliest Christianity: A History of the Period A.D. 30–150.* Vol. 1. Trans. F. C. Grant.

First and Second Timothy and Titus

E. Glenn Hinson

Introduction

First and Second Timothy and Titus, referred to since 1703 as the PASTORAL EPISTLES, pose one of the intriguing dilemmas of NT scholarship. Claiming both strong internal and external support as the work of the PAUL, they display enough peculiarities by comparison with other letters bearing his name that many question whether Paul could have written them.

The Problem of Authorship

Five issues have been raised regarding Paul's authorship: (1) Vocabulary, grammar, and style differ from those found in Paul's other letters, especially Romans, 1 and 2 Corinthians, and Galatians. (2) The doctrine of the Pastorals differs from Paul's in some ways. (3) The ecclesiastical organization depicted in them is unlike that existing in Paul's lifetime. (4) The heresy attacked is late. (5) The historical data presented in the letters do not square with the framework of Paul's life sketched in Acts.

Theories about Authorship

Scholars have offered a number of theories about authorship. (1) Some scholars attribute the letters to an admirer of Paul responding to a different set of problems and circumstances, dating them variously as early as 90 to 100 C.E. and as late as 140 to 150 C.E. (against MARCION). (2) Others have developed a "fragments hypothesis." A pious follower of Paul had fragments of letters by Paul which he incorporated into these letters, mostly into 2 Timothy. (3) Still others have argued for the genuineness of 2 Timothy and disputed that of 1 Timothy and Titus.

Paul as Author

Those who sustain Paul's authorship of the Pastoral Epistles make the following responses to the arguments against it: (1) Variations in vocabulary, grammar, and style can be explained by (a) the use of a secretary to whom considerable freedom was given, (b) Paul's aging, (c) natural variations in the vocabulary and style of any writer in different contexts writing to different addressees (individuals in this case), and (d) incorporation of formal elements such as hymns, catalogues of virtues and vices, codes for Christian conduct, and confessions of faith. (2) The doctrine agrees with that of Paul's other letters for the most part. Where it varies, it is not post- but *pre*-Pauline, found in hymns or confessions cited in the letters. (3) The ecclesiastical organization of the Pastorals is that of the twofold office of presbyter-bishops and deacons, as in Philippians, and not the threefold office of IGNATIUS (d. 110–117). The roles of Timothy and TITUS, moreover, do not fit the model of bishops in the second century. (4) The heresy attacked in the Pastorals was not second-century GNOSTICISM or Marcionism but some sort of Judaistic, possibly Essene, aberration. Even if it had a gnostic cast, this does not require a post-Pauline date, for the date of Gnosticism has been moved back to Paul's day. (5) Although the historical setting does not fit the scheme of Acts, Luke did not tell the complete story of Paul's life. There is strong early Christian tradition favoring Paul's release after trial, travels, and reimprisonment. In addition, (6) some have questioned whether early Christians accepted the custom of writing under an assumed name as readily as sometimes assumed by scholars who consider the Pastorals pseudonymous.

Purpose

Those who question whether Paul wrote the Pastorals usually envision them as anti-gnostic or anti-Marcionite. The author used basically the same approach Ignatius, Bishop of Antioch, did in the early second century, that is, strengthening ecclesiastical organization. The names of Paul and his disciples, Timothy and Titus, gave an authoritative ring to the proposal. If there were genuine "fragments" which could be incorporated into the letters, they would add further certification. If the pious forger made up personal reminiscences, he did so deliberately to enhance the Pauline nuances.

Those who interpret the Pastorals as Paul's own must try to interpret them as they project themselves. First Timothy presents itself as the instructions of an old soldier to his young aide-de-camp about mission work—public worship, ministry, behavior in the church, and so on. Second Timothy is much more personal, Paul's last will and testament during his second imprisonment and plea for Timothy to join him. Titus contains directions for a seasoned missionary about his work on the island of Crete. Opponents do not figure very prominently in the letters, but they may have been Judaizers with some gnostic tendencies as in Paul's other writings.

Date

If by Paul, the Pastorals would have to have been written during a period after his release from prison in Rome about 62 C.E. If by some later author, they should not be dated later than the last decade of the first century.

For Further Study

In the *Mercer Dictionary of the Bible*: PASTORAL EPISTLES; CHURCH; PAUL; TIMOTHY; TITUS.

In other sources: W. Barclay, *The Letters to Timothy, Titus, and Philemon*; C. K. Barrett, *The Pastoral Epistles in the New English Bible*; E. G. Hinson, "1–2 Timothy and Titus," *BBC* 11; J. N. D. Kelly, *A Commentary on the Pastoral Epistles*.

Commentary

An Outline

Greeting and Affirmation of Apostolate, 1:1-2

The letter opens with a strong assertion of apostleship as in Romans and Galatians. Paul addresses Timothy in an intimate way as his legitimate child in faith.

General Orders to Timothy, 1:3-20

A military motif prevails throughout this letter. As a commander to his aide, Paul orders TIMOTHY to stay at his post in EPHESUS and to put a stop to teaching other than Paul did and to wrangling about the Law. The goal is agape-love that comes from a pure heart, good CONSCIENCE, and authentic faith. Some have gone astray by ignoring these and plunging into meaningless speculation, wanting to be teachers of the Law but not understanding what they were doing.

Paul agrees with the Judaizers, or Jewish Gnostics, that the Law is good if properly applied. Its proper use is to show what is wrong, as a catalogue of vices based on the TEN COMMANDMENTS confirms, and not what is right. We learn what is right from the gospel with which Paul was entrusted. The gospel is what reveals God as God truly is.

Frequently a target of attacks from Judaizers, the old apostle cannot help lapsing into a defense (vv. 12-17). Paul is "exhibit A" of the grace of God to which the gospel bears witness. What else could Paul do but give thanks to Christ for appointing him as apostle despite what he had once been—a blasphemer, persecutor, and bad-mouther. He was no better than a pagan. Yet the grace of God overflowed with the faithfulness and love that are in Christ. Yes, Paul has to agree with the saying, *Christ Jesus came into the world to save sinners* (v. 15; cf. Luke 19:10), for he was the prime example. Why? So that Christ might display his incredible patience as an example for future believers.

In typical Pauline fashion these thoughts touch off a doxology (v. 17). Praise of God as the only God may be the apostle's way of negating the emperor cult that burgeoned under Nero.

Paul reinforces his general orders with an appeal to their close ties as father and son in faith (vv. 18-20). Yet the command is clear. Timothy, selected by prophets for the job (cf. Acts 13:1-3), must wage a good battle in Ephesus. He has the qualities Paul wants for the whole community, faith and a good conscience. At least *Hymenaeus and Alexander* have suffered shipwreck in the faith and Paul has *turned them over to Satan*. This phrase probably referred to a formula used in cutting them off from the community (cf. 1 Cor 5:5) with physical illness as a possible consequence.

Orders Concerning the Churches, 2:1–6:2a

Paul next issues more specific orders about the church in Ephesus. He addresses the three major areas of concern for young churches—public worship, the ministry, and behavior of their members.

Public Worship, 2:1-15

Appropriately his directions concerning public worship begin with insistence on prayer for all persons and not just for believers (vv. 1-7). The main point is the universality of the prayer. By contrast with some sects in JUDAISM such as the ESSENES, Christians should entreat God on behalf of the emperor and all persons in authority so that they may live peacefully in their own religious commitment.

Paul predicates this appeal on MONOTHEISM. The one and only God wants all persons to be saved and converted to the truth of Christianity. A snippet from an early Christian hymn or confession of faith buttresses the point. Not only is there one God but also one mediator between God and humankind, the man Christ Jesus, who gave himself as *a ransom* not just for the few but *for all*. The gospel cannot be narrowed to an elect. It is for everyone.

Predictably, mention of the universal gospel touches Paul's defense mechanism. It is to this that God appointed him as preacher and apostle and teacher of the gentiles.

To counter the debates that fractured the assembly, Paul appealed for tranquillity in the conduct of worship (vv. 8-15). *Men should pray* with pure lives and *without anger* or disputes. Early Christians, like both Jews and Gentiles, prayed standing, with eyes open

and hands lifted toward heaven. Paul was underscoring character and conduct. They should lift up *holy hands* and leave tempers and taunts behind. We relate to God better with peaceful expressions.

Women, likewise, should do things that would promote harmony in the worship services. One dimension would be to dress modestly. Early Christian women tried to set themselves apart from their contemporaries by simplicity of habit—shunning costly clothing, jewelry, elaborate hair styles (cf. 1 Pet 3:1-6). Instead of majoring in dress, they majored in good deeds.

Another dimension for promotion of harmony would be humility in conduct. Although in the church Paul wanted equality (Gal 3:28), practical realities forced women to accept subordinate roles in public worship (cf. 1 Cor 15:34-35). Context may well have dictated concessions at EPHESUS for the sake of preserving peace.

Paul argues like a RABBI in support of the subordinate role for women. (1) God created man before woman (v. 13; cf. Gen 2:22). (2) The serpent deceived Eve and not Adam (v. 15; cf. Gen 3:1-6). The statement that "woman will be saved through bearing children" (RSV) is difficult, maybe impossible, to interpret. A simple interpretation is probably best, that the gift of women through bearing children offsets her failure if she has other Christian qualities—faith, love, purity, and modesty.

The Ministry, 3:1-16

Paul speaks first about the office of presbyter or bishop. The office (Gk. *episkopos*) may have derived from the "superintendent" (*mebaqqer*) of the ESSENES. The term was used interchangeably with the word presbyter (Titus 3:5-7). From this brief instruction one can surmise that presbyter-BISHOP superintended the churches (v. 5), taught, watched over the charities, and led in public worship. The chief concern in this passage, however, was character and not duties.

The phrase "husband of one wife" (RSV) has been interpreted in several ways: (1) faithful to one wife, (2) monogamous, (3) never remarried even after death of a spouse, (4) never divorced, and (5) necessarily married. The first two are the more likely, although in the NRSV, *married only once*, favors the first, second, and third options.

Paul envisioned the church as an extended family and the presbyter-bishop as the head of it. The bishop needed, therefore, the qualities of a good father. How he presided over his own family would give a good clue to his ability to lead this larger family. In a mission situation such as Timothy served in Ephesus, moreover, the bishop should not be a newly baptized Christian and should have a good reputation with outsiders. These early communities became victims of Christian failing and the attacks of adversaries in times of persecution. *Devil* here probably means "Satan," however, rather than human adversary.

The office of DEACON (vv. 8-13), unlike that of bishop, probably did not have a direct antecedent in JUDAISM except in the servant model of JESUS. The qualifications listed would indicate that deacons shared leadership in worship, visited the sick and imprisoned, played a leading role in the LORD'S SUPPER or Agape meals, handled money for the poor, and taught. They needed careful scrutiny regarding their ministry. Like bishops, they needed to demonstrate in their families the character and gifts of leaders.

There is much debate concerning the reference to women in v. 11. Does it mean women deacons, wives of deacons, or women in general? The last two interpretations have had few advocates. In favor of women deacons are: (1) the reference to Phoebe as a deacon in Rom 16:1; (2) the absence of "their" which one would expect if Paul meant wives; (3) the nature of the virtues listed; and (4) the use of *likewise* to break the train of thought. In favor of wives of deacons are: (1) the brevity of the statement; (2) the way it is sandwiched between statements about male deacons; (3) the discussion of ministry of women in connection with *widows* in 5:3-16; and (4) the likelihood that a more definite term than *women* would have been used if women deacons were meant. The weight of argument slightly favors women deacons. The qualifications suggest a role similar to that of deacons. Women deacons in the late second century assisted in the baptism of women, visited the sick, discharged a ministry of prayer, and did other diaconal tasks.

Paul interjects another personal note explaining why he was writing (vv. 14-16). If Paul is delayed, Timothy should go right ahead with his task, for he knows very well what to do in the CHURCH.

Mention of the church brings to Paul's mind a hymn about Christ as *the mystery of our religion* (v. 16). The hymn emphasizes the universality of God's saving plan to which the church bears witness.

Behavior in the Church, 4:1–6:2a

At this point Paul turns to a series of miscellaneous orders concerning behavior in the church at Ephesus.

He refutes the false ASCETICISM of the Judaizers regarding prohibition of marriage and abstinence from certain foods. He instructs Timothy to avoid debating and instead to focus on his own personal piety, remembering especially the spiritual gift he has received for ministry. He follows this with directives about the proper behavior of groups within the Christian family—older and younger persons, widows, presbyters, slaves, and masters.

Casting his refutation (4:1-5) in the form of a prophecy, Paul cites some specific errors, all of which sound like the kind of teachings which would have originated with the ESSENES. They either spent a lot of time talking about demons or evil spirits or, alternatively, teaching things inspired by them. Having bad consciences as a result, they prohibited marriage and observed certain food laws. Paul rebuts these two practices by citing the OT concept of creation and the Christian concept of thanksgiving. Everything God created is good. Giving thanks further validates it for believers.

By contrast with the false ascetics, Timothy should be a good MINISTER of Christ (4:6-10). For this Paul prescribes three ingredients. First, he should nourish himself on the sound teaching that he received under Paul's tutoring and avoid the speculative interpretations of scriptures the ascetics propounded. In Titus 1:14 Paul called these "Jewish myths" and human concoctions.

Second, Timothy should train himself spiritually. Using an athletic metaphor (cf. 1 Cor 9:24-27; Phil 3:12), the apostle underscores how important this is for a minister. If physical exercise is of great benefit, how much greater must be spiritual exercise, for it bears not merely on the present life but also on the life to come. The promise of ETERNAL LIFE is what Christians strive to attain because they have placed their hope in the living God, the Savior of all persons, as believers amply attest. The main accent falls once again on the universality of God's saving work.

Third, combining command and personal plea, Paul directs Timothy's attention to his spiritual gift as the ground on which he can do what ministry requires (4:11-16). Timothy, now in his thirties, should stop hiding behind the excuse, "I'm too young." He should be an example of believers in all dimensions of Christian life—speech, conduct, love, faith or faithfulness, and sexual purity. A weighty expectation! Until Paul could get there, he should continue with the key duties—reading OT scriptures, preaching, and teaching new converts. The wherewithal for all of this would come from his charisma.

How Timothy received this "spiritual gift" is somewhat unclear. Obviously God gave it, but was Paul (as in 2 Tim 1:6) or the "presbytery" the means? As in 1:18, prophets discerned Timothy's spiritual gifts. It would be unlikely, therefore, that Paul or the presbyters would be required to convey the Spirit he already possessed. Laying on of hands accompanied and confirmed what prophetic utterance indicated, that is, Timothy's God-given capacity for ministry. This aspect Timothy must not forget. The gift of God would assure his progress.

Paul sums up his urgent charge. Timothy must pay heed both to himself and to what he teaches, for the stakes are high. He has responsibility both for his own spiritual welfare and for that of the people who listen to him.

This comment opens the way for a transition to the four groups within the household of faith for whom Timothy is responsible: young and old, widows, presbyters, and slaves. Concerning the first group (5:1-2), the apostle emphasizes the familial approach. Timothy should treat older men and women like fathers and mothers, younger men and women like brothers and sisters. Obviously with the latter he had to be circumspect about sex.

Widows (5:3-16) must have constituted a considerable segment of the Ephesian community and their numbers posed a problem. The main objective of this directive was to enroll on the church's charitable list only those whose needs and manner of life established them as genuinely bereft. Paul lists two basic requirements: (1) need and (2) record of Christian service *before* being widowed.

Regarding need, Timothy should see first whether personal family members, children or grandchildren, could care for the widows, thus relieving the overburdened extended family. An allusion to the fifth commandment undergirds the point. A Christian who does not watch out for members of his or her own family is worse than an unbeliever, for Christian faith makes it a principle (v. 8).

Paul's "real widow" would be truly dependent on God, praying night and day. The early churches, of course, knew some not like that, the kind who abandoned themselves to pleasure and comfort, perhaps even prostitution.

As a safeguard against such self-indulgence, Paul established three practical tests: (1) age over *sixty*,

(2) *married only once*, and (3) having good reputation for charitable works. "Wife of one husband" (RSV) probably means a single marriage, but the same possibilities exist here as for presbyters and deacons (3:2, 12; Titus 1:6).

Emphasis on reputation for charity suggests that some widows functioned as deacons. Paul lists four specific items that perhaps hint at duties of women deacons. They reared children, practiced HOSPITALITY, washed the feet of the saints, and relieved the sick. As a catchall, Paul adds, widows should have devoted themselves to every sort of good deed.

In vv. 11-15 Paul explains why younger women should not be enrolled as widows, indicating three sets of problems: (1) sexual passion, (2) idleness, and (3) gossiping. He uses very strong language. Their strong sex drive may cause them to violate their pledge to Christ as their bridegroom, made either when baptized or when enrolled as widows. Moreover, they may become troublemakers within the Christian community. Consequently Paul urges in no uncertain terms the remarriage of young widows. Confronted here with a specific problem, he proposes marriage, child-bearing, and care of a home as the way to safeguard the church's reputation. Paul knew that the mission could not afford scandal.

Once again returning to the problem of overtaxed social aid, Paul urges any faithful woman to take needy widows into her household. Some early manuscripts read "believing man," but wealthy women often headed households (e.g., LYDIA in Acts 16:14, 40).

Elders (5:17-25) should be understood in the nontechnical sense of "older men" here to avoid dividing them into two classes. Most leaders, if not all, came from this group. *Honor* would have a dual meaning, both respect and pay, as quotations from the OT would imply. At this early stage pay consisted of gifts of food and necessities rather than MONEY. The older leaders would receive twice the allotment for widows and others on the charitable roll.

Where leaders required discipline, Paul had two bits of advice: (1) Do not accept an accusation against a presbyter unless two or more witnesses confirm it. (2) Reprove the offender publicly, either before the elders or the CONGREGATION. Here Timothy must not let personal bias intrude, a point underlined with an oath.

The best DISCIPLINE is, of course, preventive. Thus Paul counsels Timothy not to baptize or ordain anyone hastily. Laying on of hands accompanied both BAPTISM and ordination. Since Timothy played a key role in choosing people, he must take care lest he be implicated in their offenses. The goodness and wickedness of people are sometimes evident, sometimes not.

Thrown in (v. 23) is a little aside about Timothy's personal health. The ancients ascribed medicinal value to wine.

Slaves (6:1-2a) also constituted an important element of the Christian community. Here Paul distinguished the motives of slaves under pagan and under Christian masters. Slaves should treat pagan masters respectfully to avoid bringing reproach on the name of God and Christian teaching. They should show still greater respect for Christian masters because they are *believers and beloved.* Many slaves must have chafed more under Christian than under pagan owners!

Final Orders to Timothy, 6:2b-19

The apostle shifts from orders concerning behavior in the church to warn about the profit motive in religion (vv. 2b-10), deliver a personal charge to Timothy, and give a special word to the wealthy.

Early Christianity attracted some, like SIMON MAGUS (Acts 8:18-24), who tried to turn it into a profit-making enterprise. Paul suspected that the wranglers at Ephesus were inspired by such motives. They could not square these with the teachings of Jesus. Religion, Paul had to admit, is immensely profitable, but not in the way these people pursued it. Rather, Christians must seek contentment with food and clothing, the necessities. People who crave wealth are headed for destruction, for obsession with money is the root of all evils. That is what has caused many to end up in heartache already.

Timothy (vv. 11-16) should shun this and aim at genuine virtue. In what has the ring of a baptismal or ordination charge Paul challenges his favorite son in faith to keep the pledge he made at baptism, a solemn commitment before God and Jesus Christ. Like a good soldier, Timothy must fight valiantly and discharge the orders given him until Christ returns.

Allusion to the appearance of Christ again touches off a doxology, this time mixing Jewish and Greek elements, probably from an early Christian HYMN. The words throw out a stout challenge to the emperor cult. Christ alone rules, possesses immortality, dwells in unapproachable light, and is thus due honor and dominion.

ʼAs for the rich (vv. 17-19), who would have been in a minority in early Christian communities, Timothy must charge them not to trust in their wealth but only in God and to be generous. Paul wants them to consider their wealth a stewardship that would give them a solid foundation in eternity. The Christian's goal is not wealth but "real life."

Closing Charge and Salutation, 6:20-21

Paul ends as he began. Almost plaintively, he commands his sometimes vacillating aide to keep the orders given, that is, the true Christian faith. In sum, avoid silly speculation, so-called knowledge, which has led others astray.

An Outline

Second Timothy
I. Greeting and Affirmation of Apostolate, 1:1-2
II. Recollections and Personal Encouragement, 1:3–2:13
III. Counsels for Timothy, 2:14–4:8
IV. Farewell and Concluding Benedictions, 4:9-22

Written after Paul's reimprisonment in ROME, 2 Timothy is his last will and testament (cf. 4:6-8). It sounds two notes: (1) how much PAUL expects of Timothy and (2) what he hopes Timothy will do as his successor in mission.

Greeting and Affirmation of Apostolate, 1:1-2

This greeting differs only slightly from that in 1 Timothy. As one might expect of someone anticipating his death, Paul throws in a hopeful note. He is *an apostle* through God's will according to *the promise of life* attested in Christ's resurrection.

Recollections and Personal Encouragement, 1:3–2:13

Paul initiates his last will and testament with some remembrances that would offer encouragement to his successor (1:3-5). As in other letters, he begins with a prayer of THANKSGIVING to God, whom he served with the same clarity of purpose as his Jewish forbears did. He prayed night and day for his son in the faith, Remembrance of Timothy's tears at their parting aroused a longing to see him. Paul recalled the sincere faith that both Timothy's Jewish grandmother LOIS and his Christian mother EUNICE had exhibited. So Paul was confident he would find the same in Timothy.

His imprisonment notwithstanding, Paul directed Timothy to have confidence in God (1:6-14). Timothy should *rekindle the gift* God had given as indicated by Paul's *laying on of . . . hands* (cf. 1 Tim 4:14). God did not equip him with a spirit of timidity but of power, love, and self-control. He, therefore, should not hesitate to offer his witness to Christ or to defend Paul. As Christ and Paul had suffered, so too should Timothy suffer for the gospel in the power of God.

Mention of God's power stirs up in Paul's mind a HYMN or confession of faith (1:9-10). The first stanza praises God for God's saving work in Christ, calling humankind on the basis of MERCY rather than merit. The second stanza praises Jesus Christ as the one through whom God carried out the eternal plan. The third stanza declares what Christ did—abolished death and brought life and immortality through the gospel.

The word *gospel* triggers an instinctive apology on the part of the aged apostle (1:11-14). It is to this that God appointed Paul as preacher, apostle, and teacher (cf. 1 Tim 1:11) and it explains his suffering. Yet he has no regrets. He has complete confidence in God, that God will see to it that he keeps his pledge.

Paul appeals to Timothy to look to him as an example of reliable teaching he had heard from him that is grounded in faith and love in Christ. Timothy must guard the truth of the gospel committed to him. Although some have detected in the reference to a deposit a succession theory like that of *1 Clem* 42:2-4; 44:2, the statement here does not have to do with succession of bishops. It is about preservation of truth. The ultimate guardian is the HOLY SPIRIT indwelling us.

Paul recounts briefly his own sad plight (1:15-18). All the Christians from the province of ASIA living in Rome had deserted him, notably *Phygelus and Hermogenes*. Well, there was an exception, *Onesiphorus,* an Ephesian who had sought Paul out and done everything he could to aid him. The prayer for his household would seem to indicate that he may have given his life to help Paul.

Having built a foundation for faithfulness from the example of Timothy's family and himself, Paul comes to the main point. His dear child in faith must be strong and endure suffering (2:1-7). What he had heard from Paul, he must hand on to other faithful persons who will have the ability to teach others. Here again is an embryonic form of succession but of doctrine and not of office.

Paul invokes three images of perseverance: the soldier, the athlete, and the farmer. The soldier models stalwart endurance of hardships, non-entanglement, and desire to please. The athlete image emphasizes the need for *discipline*. The farmer image underlines the importance of hard work. Paul underscores his point with a sort of "Are you listening?"

Ultimately the apostle directs Timothy to the example of Christ (2:8-13). The gospel itself, briefly summarized (cf. Rom 1:3-4), is the reason for faithfulness. It is for the sake of the gospel that Paul suffers imprisonment. Though he is fettered, the word of God is not. The apostle has endured what he has for the sake of those God has chosen to take part in the eternal purpose. Their eternal glory, the antithesis of suffering, is the object of God's plan.

Reflections on God's assurances brings another hymn or confession of faith to mind (2:11-13). The first stanza has an exact parallel in Rom 6:8, suggesting a baptismal context. BAPTISM entails dying and rising with Christ. The second stanza echoes Jesus' words about endurance (Matt 10:22; 24:13; Mark 13:13) and promises participation in Christ's messianic kingdom. The third stanza warns against denial (cf. Matt 10:33). However shaky our faith, God is always faithful.

Counsels for Timothy, 2:14–4:8

Having laid his foundation, Paul turns to more specific directions about the Ephesian problem. His main counsel is to avoid getting entangled in meaningless debates and to discipline those who need it with humility and gentleness. Timothy has to set the example.

By way of contrast with the wranglers Timothy should avoid destructive debating and be a constructive workman (2:14-26). Constant disputation only upsets hearers. Timothy should model constructiveness, steering clear of harmful chatter that spreads through the body like cancer. Prime examples of the type Timothy should shun are *Hymenaeus* (2:17; cf. 1 Tim 1:20) and *Philetus,* who taught that the *resurrection has already taken place.* Some early gnostic groups taught that the resurrection took place in baptism, possibly on the basis of Paul's own teaching (cf. Rom 6:4).

Paul uses two metaphors to draw the line between himself and the wranglers: (1) the solid *foundation* of a strong building (2:19) and (2) the varied utensils in a household (2:20-21). God has established the foundation and inscribed it. God knows his own in an intimate way, and everyone claiming the Lord's name should avoid wrong. Why would any other type be in the church? Because it is a mixed body, like a large household. The key issue is not type of utensil or vessel, but the purity of each.

The apostle once again places the weight of responsibility on Timothy's shoulders (2:22-26). He should flee uncontrolled impulses and aim at the Christian virtues especially suitable in these circumstances, thus putting himself in the company of authentic believers. In handling the disputants he should do two things: (1) stay out of arguments; and (2) treat them with patience and kindliness. The accent falls on gentleness in handling opponents. The aim is to rescue the offenders from the Devil's snare and bring them back to the authentic Christian message.

Paul interjects a kind of apocalyptic warning (3:1-9). Jewish apocalypticists expected dire happenings in the *last days*. To describe these, Paul lists a catalogue of vices similar to the one used in Rom 1:29-31 but not dependent on it. The first two vices—*lovers of [self]* and *lovers of money*—epitomize the whole list. They are arrogant persons who act insensitively toward other persons and toward God. Timothy must shun them.

Paul describes a subtle method of operation. They preyed especially on women burdened by an extreme sense of guilt, always seeking a solution to problems but never able to arrive at the truth. Such charlatans, however, Paul assures Timothy, will not succeed. They will fail like the Egyptian magicians, JANNES AND JAMBRES, who tried their occult powers against MOSES. Everybody will be able to see their counterfeit faith, as they saw the Egyptian magicians' (Exod 8:16-19).

Operating on the assumption that he would have to maximize his plea, Paul invokes again his personal example and Timothy's training (3:10-17). Timothy had shared Paul's missionary labors and knew the price he had paid. He should not be surprised, for the faithful always suffer while the evil imposters get worse and worse. This called for steadfastness. Bedrock for Timothy would be confidence he could place in persons he learned from (his grandmother and mother) and in scriptures.

Scriptures, learned from infancy, furnished the ultimate ASSURANCE. Verse 16 could be translated either "Every scripture is inspired and profitable" or "Every inspired scripture is also profitable" with the latter more likely (ERV, NEB, et al.). The doctrine of inspiration allows room for human agency, but it emphasizes scriptures as the one fully reliable means of REVELATION. They serve, therefore, as the basis of Christian teaching, reproof of SIN, correction, and constructive education in Christian life. Religious leaders like Timothy can count on them.

The apostle buttresses his appeal to example with a solemn exhortation to preach the gospel (4:1-8). With a solemn OATH, he pleads with his sometimes timid colleague to stand fast and do his duty with patience and care. This is urgent because an apocalyptic situation seems at hand when novelty will have more followers than the truth at the time when Paul senses that the end is near. His life about to be poured out on the altar, Paul counts on Timothy.

In this poignant passage the apostle had to reassure himself as much as Timothy. He had *fought the good fight, finished* the race, and *kept the faith* (4:7). Now he could look forward to receiving his eternal reward given to all who have loved Christ's coming.

Farewell and Concluding Benedictions, 4:9-22

The remainder of 2 Timothy consists of personal notices and instructions (vv. 9-18), greetings (vv. 19-21), and a benediction. Scholars who hold the "fragments hypothesis" ascribe all or most of this passage to Paul.

At this point Paul needed Timothy desperately. Demas, his fellow worker during his first imprisonment (Col 4:14; Phlm 24), had deserted him. Crescens and TITUS had taken mission assignments in GALATIA and Dalmatia. LUKE was now the only one with him. Paul, therefore, needed as much help as possible, even John Mark, with whom he must have become reconciled after their rupture (Acts 15:38). MARK would replace TYCHICUS, whom Paul sent to Ephesus with the letter.

Winter approaching (v. 21), Paul wanted Timothy to bring warmer clothing, the heavy blanket-like cloak he had left in Troas with Carpus. He also needed the books, especially the parchments, containing important writings—perhaps parts of the OT, collections of testimonies, and other documents.

Paul could not help inserting a warning about *Alexander the coppersmith*, perhaps the person "turned over to Satan" (1 Tim 1:20) but the name was a common one. Paul was confident God would pay him back, but he knew the danger Alexander posed to Timothy.

After this brief digression the apostle recounts his own sad circumstances. During his first defense, meaning either his first trial or a preliminary hearing in Rome, all deserted him. Yet he would not hold that against them and prayed they not be held accountable in the Judgment. The Lord, God or Christ, stood by him and rescued him from extreme danger. The very thought evokes from Paul a confession of faith and doxology.

The concluding paragraph adds a greeting to long-time missionary associates *Prisca and Aquila* (Acts 18:2, 18; 1 Cor 16:19; Rom 16:3f.) and to Onesiphorus's *household*, a note suggesting Onesiphorus was dead. Paul throws in a couple of other tidbits about mutual acquaintances and passes on some greetings from others. The fact that he mentions them need not be seen as a conflict with the fact that all deserted him in his first defense (v. 16). These persons did not qualify for a formal defense.

An Outline

Titus
I. Greetings and Affirmation of Apostolate, 1:1-4
II. Instructions for the Community, 1:5–2:15
III. Instructions Regarding the World, 3:1-11
IV. Some Final Instructions, 3:12-14
V. Concluding Salutation and Benediction, 3:15

PAUL did not have as intimate personal ties with TITUS as with TIMOTHY, but he counted heavily on him for effective mission work. Titus had handled the Corinthian problem more effectively than Timothy (2 Cor 8:6; 12:18). At Paul's request (3:12) Titus evidently joined him in ROME. Before writing 2 Timothy Paul sent him to Dalmatia (2 Tim 4:10). From there he went to CRETE.

The letter to Titus has essentially the same objectives as 1 Timothy: to instruct an associate about the ordering of church life and about defense of the mission against agitators. It is both personal and official, intended to be read publicly.

Greetings and Affirmation of Apostolate, 1:1-4

OPPONENTS OF PAUL's mission turned up wherever Paul and his associates worked. Consequently the apostle had constantly to assert his commission. His commission had three aims: to enhance the faith of the elect, to bring them to godly knowledge of the truth, and to share the hope of ETERNAL LIFE. This hope never disappoints because God never lies and has revealed it at the right time through preaching. It is this that God entrusted to Paul.

The greeting to Titus is a bit stiffer than those to Timothy. Titus is an authentic child in a common faith, rather than "beloved" (2 Tim 1:2).

Instructions for the Community, 1:5–2:15

The bulk of the letter gives instructions about the ordering of church life with some warnings about disturbers thrown in. Predictably the qualifications of presbyter-bishops gets attention first (1:5-9). The APOSTLE had left Titus in Crete to set up proper organization and to appoint qualified persons to continue the mission. As in other areas, Paul specified an urban pattern.

Qualifications for presbyter-bishops (NRSV *elders*) correspond closely with that for bishops and deacons in 1 Tim 3. Here too Paul envisioned the church as a family. Success in heading his own household would provide a good clue to management of an extended family. The BISHOP is God's steward. He should be mature, unselfish, and other-directed, able to preach healthy doctrine and refute those who oppose it.

Worthy leadership will be essential in order to counter those who stand opposed to what Paul has taught. Judaistic leanings of the troublemakers are quite clear. Some belonged to the "circumcision party" (cf. Gal 2:12; Col 4:11) and taught Jewish myths. Evidently they also adhered to Jewish dietary laws. They may also have engaged in some kind of magical rites.

Paul had no patience for them because they upset whole families for base motives. The Cretan poet Epimenides characterized them correctly (1:12). Titus must silence them, reprove them sharply, act forcefully to put a stop to them.

Here the apostle offers an antidote to the Cretan troublemakers, exemplary behavior within the Christian community (2:1-10). For this Titus himself offered the key. He had to teach healthy doctrine. Paul directs Titus's attention to four groups—older men, older and younger women, younger men, slaves.

For *older men* (2:1-2) Paul lists essentially the same qualities as he demands of presbyter-bishops and deacons. Christianity does not have two standards of behavior.

For *older women* (2:3-5) he lists qualities similar to those he gives for women deacons or wives of deacons in 1 Tim 3:11. In Crete they would have a special responsibility for the Christian education of younger women, for whom Paul's main concern was strong and stable families. Love of women for husbands and children is the key to the family. As in social codes in other letters of Paul (Col 3:18; Eph 5:22), Paul enjoins wives voluntarily to accept the authority of their husbands lest Christianity's reputation suffer harm in societies that were not yet ready for equality of male and female (Gal 5:28).

For *younger men* (2:6-8) the apostle uses more decisive directions. Titus should set the example of gentlemanly behavior Paul expected. How these individuals behaved would silence the kind of criticism that arose so easily from pagan lips or from the troublemakers in Crete.

For *slaves* (2:9-10) Paul prescribes acceptance of their status and exemplary service. Christians should not act like typical slaves, talking back and stealing. Rather, they should model reliability so as to make the message of the Savior God noble and attractive to all.

The allusion to God as Savior causes Paul to lapse into a HYMN or confession of faith on God's saving grace as the basis for Christian behavior (2:11-14). GRACE was manifested at a definite moment in history, in the birth of JESUS of Nazareth. It instructs us to lay aside irreligious and worldly behavior, to live godly lives, and to await the consummation of the Christian hope. The signal for the latter will be the return of Christ. Christ came to do two things: liberate us from sin and prepare us to be God's own people. Christ's death furnished the ransom price needed to free us from evil, and it laid a foundation for the church.

At this point (2:15) Paul interjects a general charge to Titus. He must not act indecisively but with full authority, that is, Paul's.

Instructions Regarding the World, 3:1-11

Whereas in chap. 2 Paul gave directions on behavior within the Christian community, in chap. 3 he widens them to the larger world in which Christians live. He wants the Christians of Crete to be model citizens—obedient to their rulers (cf. Rom 13:1-7), honest, and courteous to all (vv. 1-2). They were not always like that (v. 3), but God pulled off a mighty work of recycling.

In support of this plea the apostle cites an early Christian baptismal hymn on regeneration and renewal. Whatever the human situation prior to the Christian era, God decisively changed it in the coming of Christ. Out of goodness and generosity God saved us in one decisive intervention in human history. God acted out of MERCY and not on the basis of our righteousness. We, however, appropriated this mercy through BAPTISM and the gift of the Spirit, which God poured out upon us generously through Jesus Christ. The purpose of the whole divine act is that we may become heirs of eternal life after God has rightwised us. The formula *The saying is sure* (v. 8) looks backward rather than forward.

Concluding the main body of the letter (vv. 8b-11), Paul takes one last shot at the troublemakers. Titus must be insistent on what Paul has said so that believers may apply themselves to good deeds beneficial to humankind. Contrariwise, he must avoid divisive debates deadly for Christian witness. He should shun the factious person after one or two warnings (cf. Matt 18:15-17). If such a person refused to relent, he or she would be self-condemned.

Some Final Instructions, 3:12-14

Paul intersperses in his conclusion some personal notes with his final instructions. When he dispatched *Zenas . . . and Apollos* with the letter, he had evidently not yet decided whether to send *Artemas* and *Tychicus*. He intended to do so soon, however, and to meet Titus in *Nicopolis* where they would *spend the winter*. Zenas and Artemas are not mentioned elsewhere in the NT. Thinking of the needs of these missionary travelers, Paul throws in a final comment about the need for consistent charity, the distinguishing mark of early Christians.

Concluding Salutation and Benediction, 3:15

Paul closes this letter as he did those to Timothy with concluding greetings and a benediction. Probably written earlier, this greeting is more optimistic than 2 Tim 4:9-22.

Philemon

Charles H. Cosgrove

Introduction

Paul writes to PHILEMON on behalf of Philemon's slave ONESIMUS, who has become a convert through Paul's own witness. By comparing the names in Philemon with those in Col 4:7-17, we may conclude that Philemon is a member of a house church at COLOSSAE. While PAUL addresses almost every sentence directly to Philemon, as if the letter were for him alone, he also identifies the church as recipient (along with APPHIA and ARCHIPPUS).

Date and Place of Writing

Although Paul does not state his location at the time of writing, except to indicate that he is in prison (v. 10), he probably writes from EPHESUS around 52–54 C.E. (see Harrison 1950).

The Occasion of the Letter

We know from v. 16 that Onesimus is Philemon's slave. Paul writes in order to persuade Philemon to act graciously toward Onesimus in the wake of some alleged (and unnamed) misdeed by the slave (see v. 18).

Since Paul addresses the letter not only to *Philemon* but *to the church*, he probably intends for it to be read aloud in the assembly. The CONGREGATION is supposed to "overhear" Paul's words to Philemon, which makes the slave-owner accountable not only to Paul but to them as well.

Traditionally it has been assumed that Onesimus is a fugitive slave, and interpreters have reconstructed his story more or less as follows. Once there was a slave named Onesimus who ran away from his master Philemon, and (somehow or other) came in contact with Paul, founder of the CHURCH to which Philemon belongs. Under Paul's influence Onesimus came to faith in the God of Jesus Christ and decided to do the right thing by returning to his master.

The difficulty with this reconstruction is that it fails to provide a plausible explanation of how the runaway slave happens to wind up in Paul's company. It strains credulity to think this is sheer coincidence.

Some have therefore suggested that the fugitive Onesimus grew remorseful and deliberately sought out his master's friend, Paul, in the hopes that Paul might be willing to smooth things over with Philemon. Paul nowhere indicates that Onesimus has had a change of heart about running away.

The suggestion that Onesimus intentionally went to Paul for help is, nevertheless, a step toward a better reconstruction. We should abandon the assumption, nowhere confirmed by the letter itself, that Onesimus is a fugitive slave. It happens that in Roman case law, which was widely respected even outside of ROME, there are precedents establishing the propriety of a slave seeking out a third party, usually an esteemed "friend of the master" (*amicus domini*), in order to resolve a difficulty with a master. If a slave left the household in order to speak with this third party (who may have been in another city), the slave was not considered a runaway.

It is probable that Onesimus, fearing reprisal from his master for some alleged misdeed, sought out Paul as an *amicus domini* who might mediate between him and Philemon. In that case, Paul's letter and his upcoming visit (v. 22) are actions of mediation on behalf of Onesimus.

For Further Study

In the *Mercer Dictionary of the Bible*: ONESIMUS; PAUL; PHILEMON, LETTER TO; PRISON EPISTLES; SLAVERY IN THE NT.

In other sources: J. M. G. Barclay, "Paul, Philemon, and the Dilemma of Christian Slave-Ownership," *NTS* 37 (1991): 161–86; P. N. Harrison, "Onesimus and Philemon," *ATR* 32 (1950): 268–94; John Knox, *Philemon among the Letters of Paul*; L. A. Lewis, "An African-American Appraisal of the Philemon-Paul-

Onesimus Triangle," in *Stoney the Road We Trod: African-American Biblical Interpretation*, ed. Cain Hope Felder; J. B. Lightfoot, *St. Paul's Epistles to the Colossians and to Philemon*; E. Lohse, *A Commentary* on the Epistles to the Colossians and to Philemon; N. R. Petersen, *Rediscovering Paul*; B. M. Rapske, "The Prisoner Paul in the Eyes of Onesimus," *NTS* 37 (1991): 187–203.

Commentary

An Outline

I. Opening, 1-3
II. Thanksgiving, 4-7
III. Letter Body: Appeals for Onesimus, 8-22
   A. First Appeal: "For Love's Sake," 8-10
   B. Second Appeal: For Usefulness' Sake, 11-14
   C. Third Appeal: The Rights
     of Apostolic Paternity, 15-16
   D. The Fourth Appeal: "Receive Him as Me," 17-20
   E. A Statement of Confidence
     and Final Instructions, 21-22
IV. Closing, 23-25

Opening, 1-3

Paul, writing from PRISON (cf. vv. 9-10, 13) and naming *Timothy* as coauthor, identifies himself as a *prisoner* (δέσμιος) *of Jesus Christ*. Later in the letter he will voice his wish that Onesimus continue to serve him in the "bonds" (δεσμοῖς) of the gospel (vv. 10-13). The literal chains of Paul symbolize the metaphorical chains that bind Paul as Christ's *prisoner*. Onesimus is also in chains, namely, the metaphorical chains of (literal) slavery to Philemon—and may be clapped into literal chains upon his return. If he has been serving with Paul in the chains of the gospel, he is also, like Paul, Christ's prisoner. Thus at the very beginning of the letter Paul hints that Onesimus shares Paul's status. This hint prepares for v. 17, where Paul says, "Receive him as . . . me" (RSV).

Paul describes Philemon as "our beloved coworker." He next names *Apphia our sister*, and after her *Archippus*, "our comrade in arms." We know practically nothing about these three persons, although ARCHIPPUS appears in Col 4:17. APPHIA might be the wife of Philemon or of Archippus, if she is married to either of them. *Your house* (v. 2), in which the CHURCH meets, may be the house of Philemon or Archippus. The singular *your* would most naturally be taken with the last person named (Archippus), but it could also refer to Philemon as the one most directly addressed throughout the letter.

After naming the recipients Paul gives one of his customary liturgical greetings (v. 3).

Thanksgiving, 4-7

Paul constructs an elaborate epistolary THANKSGIVING in vv. 4-8. In the presence of those gathered to hear the reading of the letter, Paul thanks God for Philemon's many virtues. This is an example of what the Latins called a *captatio benevelentiae*. We might say that Paul "butters up" Philemon before bringing up the matter of Onesimus.

As Petersen (1985, 72) points out, the rhetorical function of the thanksgiving is to inaugurate the basic strategy of persuasion that governs the letter as a whole. Paul's *I hear* therefore *I . . . appeal* (vv. 5, 9) means "you have refreshed the hearts of the saints with your faith and love, now refresh my heart also" (author trans.; cf. vv. 7 and 20). Philemon is about to learn how he can continue to be his virtuous self and refresh Paul's heart.

Letter Body: Appeals for Onesimus, 8-22

For analysis we can divide the body of the letter into five parts: an opening expression of apostolic authority and general introductory appeal (vv. 8-10), followed by three additional appeals (vv. 11-14, 15-16, and 17-20), a closing statement of confidence (v. 21), and an announcement of an impending visit (v. 22).

First Appeal: For Love's Sake, 8-10

"For love's sake," Paul says, he is appealing rather than commanding, but the command is rhetorically present nonetheless in two ways. First, by calling the content of his appeal "what is necessary," Paul rules out the possibility that Philemon can act honorably without doing what Paul requests. Second, as Petersen (1985, 65) rightly notes, Paul's appeals are a convention used by persons in authority (esp. royalty) to express commands. The language of request functions as a command when the one who requests has the authority to command. Paul includes a reminder of his authority in v. 8 ("Although I have the boldness in Christ to command you," author trans.) and again in v. 9, where he refers to himself by means of a term πρεσβύτης, which carries the general meaning of *old man* and the specialized technical meaning of "ambassador," which best seems to fit here. In 2 Cor 5:20 (cf. Eph 6:20) Paul uses a cognate verbal form to depict himself as God's ambassador. There, too, he describes his ambassadorial mode of discourse as *appeal*.

In v. 10 Paul discloses the purpose of his letter as an appeal for Onesimus. It becomes clear in what follows that Onesimus, whether justly or unjustly by Greco-Roman convention and law, is in trouble with Philemon. Paul does not need to point this out, nor does he anywhere in the letter dispute any complaint that Philemon may have against Onesimus. He tacitly presumes Philemon's interpretation of what has happened, and so his appeal "for my child, whom I have fathered in my chains" (author trans.) sounds initially like an appeal for mercy. The expression "for love's sake" (author trans.) in v. 9 has already prepared Philemon to hear the appeal in this way. Nevertheless, in what follows Paul progressively displaces his argument from love with arguments from usefulness and paternal apostolic rights.

There is, in fact, already a hint of these subsequent arguments when Paul says in v. 10 that he "fathered" Onesimus. This metaphor means that Paul, as apostle, converted Onesimus and now enjoys fatherly apostolic rights over him (cf. 1 Cor 4:14-15; 2 Cor 6:13; 12:14-15). Hence, in calling Onesimus his "child" Paul implicitly lays claim to Onesimus and, in effect, disputes Philemon's prior claims on Onesimus.

Second Appeal: For Usefulness' Sake, 11-14

Having hinted at his rights to Onesimus, Paul goes on in vv. 11-14 to suggest that he might retain the "use" of Onesimus. "Onesimus," a common slave name, means "useful," and it is a synonym of that word (εὔχρηστος) used in v. 11. Onesimus, Paul says, was once *useless* (ἄχρηστον) but now he is *useful* (εὔχρηστον), both to Philemon and to Paul. This is how one talked about slaves in the Greco-Roman world: as property valued for their instrumentality. Since Onesimus suggests servile identity, we should bring this out in English by calling him Useful.

Although Paul calls Useful his child, his argument from usefulness in these verses treats Useful as chattel. Even though Paul has already spoken of himself as a *prisoner*, this does not put him on the same level with Onesimus. Paul's bondage to Christ gives him considerable authority, whereas Useful's status as a slave makes him powerless.

Paul's evaluation of Useful as formerly *useless* probably expresses what he takes to be Philemon's

own opinion. We don't know how or for exactly what reasons Philemon may have regarded Useful as a worthless slave. In any case, Paul adopts the perspective of the slave owner. The only question is whether the property called Useful will revert to Philemon or be retained by Paul. The decision is to be made in the interests of usefulness, not those of Useful himself.

Nevertheless, Useful is not merely property to Paul. Paul calls him *my own heart* (lit. "inward parts," the locus of deepest affection). Paul had wished to hold on to his beloved child, so that Useful might "serve" him "in the bonds of the gospel" (v. 13, author trans.). But, he says, "I didn't want to do anything without your opinion" (author trans.). The word "opinion" can mean *consent*. It is not, however, an unambiguous term for consent. By choosing this word rather than, say, "assent" or "agreement," Paul manages to be courteously deferent to Philemon without giving away the right to hold on to Useful. As he goes on to say, the reason he is sending Useful back to Philemon (along with the letter) is so that Philemon can do the right thing ("what is good") voluntarily and not by compulsion. All of this suggests that if Paul did not send Useful back, Philemon would have no choice but to accept the loss of Useful. As it now stands, he can make Paul a gift of Useful.

Third Appeal:
The Rights of Apostolic Paternity, 15-16

Paul suggests that divine PROVIDENCE has separated Useful from Philemon for a time. He states the aim of this providence in terms of Philemon's and not Useful's interest. The separation is, "perhaps," so that Philemon *might have him [Useful] back forever, no longer as a slave but more than a slave, a beloved brother . . . both in the flesh and in the Lord.* As a follower of Christ, Onesimus *is* a brother, whether Philemon receives him as such or not. Do Paul's appeals oblige Philemon to give Onesimus his freedom? Paul's suggestion in vv. 15-16 clearly implies this, for brotherhood may exist in the Lord between master and slave, as Paul's letters otherwise suggest, but brotherhood cannot exist in the flesh between master and slave. To put it differently, if Paul had meant to restrict brotherhood to a "purely spiritual" plane, leaving social relations undisturbed, he should have written simply *in the Lord* and not added *in the flesh* as well. So there is scarcely any room to doubt that Paul is appealing for Useful's freedom.

Verse 16 seems therefore to undermine the argument that Paul has been building since v. 10. That argument, at least in part, treated Useful as property and focussed delicately on the question of whose property Useful really is. Verse 16 declares Useful *no longer a slave but . . . a brother*, thus effectively undercutting either Paul's or Philemon's "ownership" of Useful. Useful is no longer to be slave to Paul or Philemon. He is now *brother* to Philemon and, we can add, recalling v. 10, *child* to Paul.

The effect of Paul's rhetoric, however, is in fact to undercut all of Philemon's authority over Useful while maintaining Paul's apostolic fatherly authority over the former slave. Thus Paul comes out ahead, and Useful comes under a new patriarchal authority. Although Philemon gets his property *back forever,* his property is no longer property and he really ought to send Onesimus back to Paul.

Verses 15-16 displace the argument begun in v. 10, which treated Useful as disputed property, with an argument that treats him as a person. This implicit recognition of him as a person scarcely acknowledges that Useful has any rights in Christ. While naming Useful's new status in Christ, Paul does not make it the basis of his mandate that Philemon free Useful. In v. 16 he does not say, for example, that Philemon should receive Useful as a brother *in the Lord* and therefore also *in the flesh.* He leaves it to his hearers to construe the relationship between *in the Lord* and *in the flesh.* Later Christian readers must do the same. We must also confront the fact that in Philemon the mandate for Useful's freedom rests on Paul's authority and not on any stated principle of the gospel. It is the apostle-patriarch Paul who decides Useful's fate, and Philemon is expected to obey not because the gospel requires him to accept Useful as *a beloved brother . . . in the flesh* but because Paul does. Thus Paul acts as a kindly monarch, God's own vice-regent, and Useful is entirely dependent on Paul's paternalistic favor.

By basing Useful's fate on his own decision as father and not directly on the gospel, Paul avoids the general question of Christian slave-ownership. If that question posed a dilemma for Paul, he never treats it as such in this letter.

Fourth Appeal: "Receive Him as Me," 17-20

The fourth appeal contains the first formal imperative in the letter. Referring to the fact that he is Philemon's partner, Paul tells Philemon to receive Useful as if he were Paul himself. Now, in effect, Useful becomes Paul's ambassador and is therefore elevated above Philemon. At the same time all Useful's debts are canceled by Paul's promise (witnessed by an autograph, v. 19) to settle accounts with Philemon. Since Philemon owes Paul his own self, a fact that Paul mentions by saying he's not going to mention it, this settling of accounts really takes place in the letter itself. Paul is calling in part of the debt Philemon owes him, a debt that can, of course, never be fully paid since Philemon owes Paul everything—just as Useful now does. Thus, before any detailed calculation of Useful's debts is made, Useful is in the clear with Philemon, and Philemon and Useful are *both* hopelessly in debt to Paul.

In v. 20 Paul says that he wants to "profit in the Lord" from Philemon, a statement that recalls his "suggestion" that Philemon might grant him the "use" of Useful (vv. 11-14). Then, echoing the language of his opening thanksgiving, Paul urges Philemon to "refresh" his "heart" (again, the word is "inward parts") in Christ.

A Statement of Confidence and Final Instructions, 21-22

If there was ever any doubt that Paul's suggestions through appeal were commands requiring OBEDIENCE, v. 21 dispels it. Paul says that he is confident of Philemon's *obedience* and knows that Philemon will *do even more* than what Paul has requested.

Paul closes the body of the letter with a request that the church *prepare a guest room* for him, informing them that he intends to pay them a visit. He asks for their prayers to help make this possible. An unspoken purpose of these requests is no doubt to back up the letter with a promise of his personal apostolic presence.

Closing, 23-25

Paul concludes the letter with greetings from EPAPHRAS, MARK, Aristarchus, Demas, and LUKE. We may assume that these persons are esteemed by Philemon (and the Colossian church) and that Paul mentions them as further witnesses to Philemon's handling of the case of Useful (vv. 23-24). A liturgical blessing brings the letter to a close (v. 25).

Works Cited

Harrison, P. N. 1950. "Onesimus and Philemon," *ATR* 32:268–94.

Petersen, Norman R. 1985. *Rediscovering Paul: Philemon and the Sociology of Paul's Narrative World.*

Hebrews

Marie E. Isaacs

Introduction

The King James Version confidently designates this work as "The Epistle of Paul to the Hebrews." Modern scholarship, however, has shown this to be improbable on all counts. It is more a sermon than a letter, almost certainly not by the apostle Paul, and written to a Christian congregation rather than to the Jewish nation. About little else can we be certain, however. We know virtually nothing about the circumstances that led to Hebrews's composition, original destination, date, or authorship. What evidence we have is largely to be inferred from Hebrews itself—and that is far from unambiguous.

A Sermon

Only in its final greetings (13:22-25) does Hebrews resemble a first-century letter. Otherwise, from its opening prologue (1:1-4) to its closing warnings (12:29), it exhibits all the features of an expository sermon. (Some scholars think the sermon extends as far as 13:21.) Thus the work is highly rhetorical throughout, especially in those passages where the preacher interrupts his theological exposition and addresses the audience directly (see 2:1-4; 3:7-4:13; 5:11-6:20; 10:19-39; 12:1-29).

Although Ps 110 seems to be the homily's main text, it is by no means its only one. Thus the author of Hebrews uses a number of OT passages (mostly drawn from the Pentateuch and the Psalms) in his attempt to draw out the implications of Christ's death and ascension for the particular situation of the group to whom he is writing. Like all Christian preaching, Hebrews tries to grapple with contemporary experience on the one hand, and inherited religious tradition on the other, in order to make sense of them both.

The Situation Addressed

From the work itself we can infer a number of things about the congregation. It was a group whose knowledge of the Christian message had not come firsthand from the earthly JESUS but via the preaching and teaching of the earliest disciples (2:1-3). Although the preacher accuses them of spiritual immaturity (5:12-14), they were not recent converts. In fact theirs was an admirable record of fidelity even in the face of persecution and suffering, which they had encountered in the past (10:32-34; cf. 12:4). Now, however, that enthusiasm was on the wane.

Exactly what has caused this crisis of confidence we cannot say. Various suggestions have been made: the delayed PAROUSIA, the outbreak of the Jewish war against Rome in 66 C.E., the Neronian persecution in 64 C.E., the fall of the Jerusalem Temple in 70 C.E., and so forth. What is clear is that they were a congregation in danger of drifting (2:2; 3:12; 4:11), tempted to go backward rather than forward. Many commentators have interpreted this to mean that they were tempted to revert to their original ancestral faith, JUDAISM. There is nothing in Hebrews that would suggest that the preacher is inveighing against Judaism, however. Rather, he finds examples of both fidelity (11:1-40) and infidelity (3:7-19) among the people of God in the past, and uses these by way of warning and encouragement to God's people in the present.

It is impossible to be sure as to the location of this particular group. JERUSALEM, ALEXANDRIA, CORINTH, SYRIA, and Asia Minor have all had their proponents. The current favorite is ROME, although this suggestion too is not without its difficulties. Both religiously and culturally its members seem to be Christian converts from the Greek-speaking Judaism of the dispersion. That of itself does not tell us where they were currently located, however.

As to Hebrews's date, it could have been written any time between the 60s and the 80s C.E.. It is first attested by Clement of Rome at the end of the first century. He cites parts of it, but not by name or title.

Central Theme

The main aim of this sermon is clearly pastoral. The author calls it *a word of exhortation* (13:22). The fundamental message to the group addressed could be summed up as:

Don't give up! See in Jesus, seated at the right hand of God in heaven, the assurance that God's sovereignty will ultimately reign on earth. In the meantime, understand that the Christian's pilgrimage to final salvation inevitably involves suffering, just as surely as Jesus' own route to God was via the cross.

In conveying this message Hebrews expounds biblical texts that enable the author to interpret salvation as the process whereby access to God is achieved. To this end he focuses upon divinely appointed places of rendezvous between God and the people. In Jewish tradition these were, par excellence, the promised LAND of CANAAN (cf. 3:1–4:13; 11:1–12:3), and the cult place, where God was approached via sacrifice (cf. 4:14–10:8). In neither territory, Hebrews argues, has but a partial encounter with God occurred, since the barrier of sin, which hindered true access to God, remained. Hence, the only one who truly entered into the presence of God, that is, heaven, was Jesus. He was the *pioneer* who entered into the promised land (2:10; 12:2), the Melchizedekian high priest who has entered the superior Holy of Holies (8:1–10:18), namely, heaven itself. And that by virtue of his death, which, by analogy, was the expiatory sacrifice that enabled the HIGH PRIEST to gain access to God. Other NT authors describe the work of Christ in sacrificial terms. Hebrews, however, is unique in comparing it to the sin offering of the Day of Atonement. Moreover, nowhere else in the NT do we find Jesus' death and entry into heaven depicted in priestly terms.

Author

From the second century, Christian tradition attributed Hebrews to Paul. Not until the fourth century was the Western church convinced, however. Even in the East there were those who were aware that there were problems, on stylistic grounds alone, of ascribing it to the APOSTLE. Hence, Clement of Alexandria suggested that Hebrews was originally written by Paul in Aramaic and then translated into Greek by Luke. Most NT characters have been suggested as the author of Hebrews, including BARNABAS, APOLLOS, and even a wom-an—Priscilla. Perhaps we should leave the last word on the identity of the author of Hebrews to Origen. "As to who actually wrote the epistle God alone knows the truth of the matter" (Eusebius, *EccHist* 6.12-14).

Nonetheless, from Hebrews itself we can deduce quite a lot about its author. There is nothing to suggest that the work was originally written in Aramaic or Hebrew. Its author (as well as presumably his audience) was, therefore Greek rather than semitic-speaking. Hence he uses the LXX version(s) of the OT. Indeed, in places (eg. 1:6,7) his argument would have made no sense had he been using the Hebrew of the MT. He also seems to be at home not only with the scriptures themselves, but also with accepted Jewish exegetical methods and traditions current in the first century.

Scholars are divided as to how far Hebrews has been influenced by current Hellenistic philosophy. Most agree that at the very least he draws upon the same wealth of literary vocabulary, and moved in the same circles of educated thought, as diaspora Jews such as PHILO of Alexandria, and the authors of the *Wisdom of Solomon* and the *Epistle of Aristeas*. Undoubtedly, he was trained in the rhetorical skills that loomed so large in the higher education of the Greco-Roman world of his day.

Equally evident is that the author stood firmly within first-century Christian tradition. Thus his homily—for all its unique features—is built upon two major tenets of Christian faith, which he assumes that his readers share: (1) that Jesus is now exalted in heaven; and (2) that his death was the means whereby that exaltation was achieved. He not only reaffirms these beliefs; he reinterprets and extends them to meet the needs of the situation of his audience. In so doing he has created a new and powerful theology of access to God, which has spoken to generations ever since.

For Further Study

In the *Mercer Dictionary of the Bible*: ATONEMENT, DAY OF; EPISTLE/LETTER; EXPIATION IN THE NT; HEBREWS, LETTER TO THE; HELLENISTIC WORLD; HIGH PRIEST; JUDAISM; MELCHIZEDEK; RESURRECTION IN THE NT.

In other sources: H. W. Attridge, *The Epistle to the Hebrews*, Herm; F. F. Bruce, *The Epistle to the Hebrews*, NICNT; J. Héring, *The Epistle to the Hebrews*; F. L. Horton, *The Melchizedek Tradition: A Critical Examination of the Sources to the Fifth Century AD and the Epistle to the Hebrews*; G. Hughes, *Hebrews* and Hermeneutics: The Epistle to the Hebrews as an Example of Biblical Interpretation; P. E. Hughes, A Commentary on the Epistle to the Hebrews; M. E. Isaacs, Sacred Space: An Approach to the Theology of the Epistle to the Hebrews; W. G. Johnsson, "The Pilgrimage Motif in the Book of Hebrews," JBL 97 (1971): 239-51; E. Käsemann, The Wandering People of God; H. Koester, "'Outside the Camp': Hebrews 13.9-14," HTR 33 (1962): 299-315; W. L. Lane, Hebrews, WBC; B. Lindars, The Theology of the Letter to the Hebrews; H. Montefiore, The Epistle to the Hebrews, BNTC; D. Peterson, Hebrews and Perfection: An Examination of the Concept of Perfection in the Epistle to the Hebrews; R. Williamson, "The Eucharist and the Epistle to the Hebrews," NTS 21 (1975): 300-12; R. McL. Wilson, Hebrews, NCC.

Commentary

An Outline

I. Prologue: The Exaltation of Jesus, the Son of God, 1:1-4
II. He Excels the Very Angels, 1:5–2:18
  A. Scriptural Proof of the Son's Incomparable Status, 1:5-14
  B. A Warning Aside: Heed the Christian Message, 2:1-4
  C. The Sovereignty and Solidarity of the Son of Man, 2:5-18
III. Fidelity and Infidelity, 3:1–4:13
  A. Jesus the Faithful Son Contrasted with Moses the Faithful Servant, 3:1-6
  B. A Warning Example: The Faithlessness of the Wilderness Generation, 3:7-19
  C. Beware Lest You Fail to Enter God's Promised Rest, 4:1-11
  D. A Coda : The Penetrative Power of God's Word, 4:12-13
IV. Jesus the High Priest, 4:14–10:18
  A. Merciful and Compassionate, 4:14–5:10
  B. An Exhortatory Aside: Grow Up! There Can Be No Going Back, 5:11–6:20
  C. According to the Order of Melchizedek, 7:1-28
  D. The Sacrificial Work of Christ, 8:1–10:18
V. An Exhortation to Persevere in the Faith, 10:19–12:29
  A. Perseverance: Some Encouragements and Warnings, 10:19:39
  B. The Faithful of the Past, 11:1-40
  C. The Faithful Endurance Required Now, 12:1-29
VI. Epistolary Exhortation and Conclusion, 13:1-25
  A. Christian Holiness and Its Obligations, 13:1-6
  B. The Implications of Jesus' Sacrifice, 13:7-19
  C. A Closing Benediction, 13:20-21
  D. A Farewell Note, 13:22-25

Prologue: The Exaltation of Jesus, the Son of God, 1:1-4

Hebrews opens with a prologue that extols the Son as God's supreme agent of REVELATION, creation, and salvation. These claims are put forward as commonly accepted Christian tradition. The tone, therefore, is confessional rather than argumentative.

1:1-2b. The Son, as God's definitive spokesman, supersedes all his predecessors. The genuine inspiration of the OT and its prophetic voice is not in dispute. Reference to the plurality and diversity of revelation in the past (*in many and various ways*), therefore, should not be understood pejoratively (*contra* NEB in fragmentary and piecemeal fashion). Nonetheless, it gives way to the single, definitive word articulated in Jesus.

Son is the name he has inherited (unlike Phil 2:11 where it is "Lord"). It signals his superior status to *prophets* (v. 1) and *angels* (v. 4) alike. This theme is developed in 1:5–2:18 concerning angels, and in 3:1-6 it is taken up with regard to MOSES (counted among Israel's prophets in Jewish tradition).

1:2c-3b. The Son as agent in creation. Here terms and functions, previously ascribed in Judaism to divine wisdom (Job 28:23-28; Prov 8; Sir 24:3-24; Wis 7:1–8:1), are applied to the Son. Thus he is God's agent in bringing *the worlds* (lit. "the ages") into being, and in the ongoing work of sustaining the universe. We find the selfsame functions ascribed by PHILO (the Alexandrian Jewish rabbi and older contemporary of the apostle Paul) to God's word ($\lambda \acute{o} \gamma o \varsigma$). In most respects Philo's *logos* is but wisdom ($\sigma o \phi \acute{\iota} a$) in another guise.

Like wisdom in Jewish writings (cf. Wis 7:25f.), so the Son in Hebrews is described as God's *reflection*. Like *the word* in Philo (cf. On *Planting* 18) he is the *exact imprint*. The language of the divine wisdom/word is applied to the Son somewhat obliquely, however. Thus, unlike Paul in 1 Cor 1:24, 30, Hebrews does not directly describe Jesus as God's wisdom. Nor, unlike the prologue of John's Gospel, is he identified with the preexistent *logos* who became flesh.

The closest parallel in the NT to these verses is Col 1:15-20. It is possible that both Colossians and Hebrews are drawing upon an early Christian HYMN or confession. If so, Hebrews does not use it to stress the Son's preexistence so much as to assert his preeminence. Above all, the prologue is concerned to affirm the sovereignty of Christ in his postexistence.

1:3c-4. The Son as agent of salvation. Unique to Hebrews is the analogy that it draws between the death and ascension of Jesus and the actions of the Levitical high priest on the Day of Atonement (see Lev 16 and ATONEMENT, DAY OF). Thus the CROSS is likened to the sacrificial offering that was the essential prerequisite for entry into the shrine's inner sanctum, and heaven becomes that inner sanctum, the Holy of Holies in which Jesus is now situated.

This theme, developed at length in 4:14–10:18, is announced at the very outset: *When he had made purification for sins, he sat down at the right hand of the Majesty on high* (v. 3). The motif of session (sitting at the right hand of God) alludes to Ps 110:1, one of the most widely cited texts in the NT. It is used throughout this homily (1:13; 8:1; 10:12-13; 12:2) to affirm that Jesus is now in heaven, seated at God's right hand. A psalm that originally celebrated the enthronement of a Davidic king as God's son and viceroy is seen to find its fulfilment in the exalted Christ.

He Excels the Very Angels, 1:5–2:18

A discussion of Jesus' status vis-à-vis the angels arises out of the session theme of the prologue. From his heavenly location should not be inferred that Jesus is one of the angels, however. As Son he has a different status from the other occupants of heaven.

Scriptural Proof of the Son's Incomparable Status, 1:5-14

Seven OT texts are cited as confirmation. They are used to advance a carefully constructed argument:

1:5. Jesus is not an angel. He is Davidic Messiah, SON OF GOD. Ps 2:7 and 2 Sam 7:17 (texts that addressed the Davidic king as Son of God) are cited as twin testimonies to this.

1:6. Jesus receives homage. Jesus is the one who receives rather than pays homage, since he is God's *firstborn* (a term used of the Davidic king in LXX Ps 88 (MT 89):17).This is confirmed by Deut 32:43 (to be found only in the LXX).

1:7. Angels are changeable. Using the LXX Ps 103:4, Hebrews can claim that scripture shows that angels are so unstable that God can reduce them to the elemental forces of wind and fire, if he so chooses. (The MT Ps

104:4 says something quite different, i.e., that God can use winds and flames as his messengers.)

1:8-12. The Son, on the other hand, exercises eternal sovereignty. Ps 45:6-7 (LXX Ps 44:6-7), originally addressed as an encomium to the Davidic king, is here applied to Jesus. In both its Hebrew and Greek versions there are ambiguities in this psalm. Hence v. 6 (=Heb 1:8) can either be translated as, "Thy throne O God is forever," or "God is your throne forever," or "Your throne is a throne of God forever." Whether or not the original psalmist addressed Israel's king as "God" (cf. Exod 7:1; Ps 82:6), or Hebrews so designates Jesus, is far from certain. What is clear is that the emphasis here is upon the eternal sovereignty exercised by the Lord's anointed on God's behalf (1:9; cf. Isa 61:1). With the citation (vv. 10-12) of Ps 101:26-28 (MT 102:25-27), the permanence and stability of this rule is contrasted with the impermanence and instability of the created order.

1:13-14. Jesus is now enthroned in heaven. The section concludes with the text first cited in the prologue, Ps 110:1. Christ's heavenly session demonstrates his sovereignty over all things, angels included.

A Warning Aside: Heed the Christian Message, 2:1-4

This is the first of a number of instances where the author interrupts his exposition to address his audience directly. Here it is to issue a warning against the dangers of drifting away from the Christian faith.

The rhetorical question in v. 3 introduces an *a fortiori* argument. If the revelation mediated by angels is to be heeded, *how much more* so should the message of salvation, which was originally proclaimed by the Lord and validated by his original disciples? *The message declared through angels* (v. 2) probably reflects the tradition that had grown up in Judaism that angels were present when Moses was given the Law on Mount Sinai (cf. also Acts 7:28, 35; Gal 3:19). *Signs, wonders and various miracles,* together with the gifts of the *Holy Spirit,* act as corroborative testimony. Here the empowering work of the Spirit is to the fore (cf. also 6:4; 10:29). Elsewhere (3:7; 9:8; 10:15) the emphasis is on the HOLY SPIRIT as the source of scripture's inspiration.

The Sovereignty and Solidarity of the Son of Man, 2:5-18

2:5-9. The sovereignty of the son of man. Psalm 8:4-6 (MT vv. 5-7) is cited to show that God originally entrusted the exercise of sovereignty over the created order, not to angels, but to Man (=Adam; cf. Gen 1:26-30). The NRSV *human beings, mortals* (together with the plural verbs and pronouns) brings out well the corporate emphasis. This translation, however, obscures the singular *Man, Son of Man* of the original text. Whereas the psalmist was indeed using this language in a corporate rather than a titular sense, it was precisely the singular of the original that enabled Hebrews to see in the exaltation of one man, Jesus, the fulfilment of God's purposes for all humanity.

The MT of the psalm marvels that we should be made "a little lower than God" (*Elohim*). Following the LXX, however, Hebrews has *for a little while lower than the angels. Little while* is given a dual interpretation: (1) Applied to the earthly Jesus it refers to the interlude between his death and his heavenly exaltation. (2) Applied to the present it refers to the equally brief interlude between Jesus' heavenly enthronement and his exercise of sovereignty on earth. As yet the latter awaits its fulfilment until his return (see 9:28). In the meantime Jesus is the pioneer; the Son who leads *many sons* (NRSV *many children*) to their destiny of sovereignty (v. 1).

2:10-18. Jesus' solidarity with his followers. Three additional OT texts are used (vv. 12-13) to confirm this. As fellow members of the assembly (ἐκκλησία) of God he addresses them as his siblings (Ps 22:22), united with him in their praise of and trust in God (Isa 8:17), and counted as his (God's) children (Isa 8:18).

The chapter concludes with a statement of the genuine humanity of Christ. Unlike angels, he was subject to human limitations—including temptation (*testing*), suffering, and death. Therefore his help is directed, not towards angels in whose heavenly domain he now resides, but to human beings whose frailty he shared throughout the span of his earthly life. It is precisely Jesus' common humanity that qualifies him to act as *a merciful and faithful high priest* on our behalf.

Fidelity and Infedility, 3:1–4:14

Picking up the word *faithful* from 2:17, the homily now moves to the topic of fidelity and infidelity. This section is predominantly an exhortation to remain steadfast and not to lose hope.

Jesus the Faithful Son Contrasted with Moses the Faithful Servant, 3:1-6

Both envoys (cf. v. 1, *apostle*) of God are comparable in their fidelity. Both were "faithful in my (i.e.,

God's) house." This is an allusion to Num 12:7 (LXX). Unlike the MT of this verse ("He is entrusted with all my house"), which points up Moses' status as Israel's supreme leader, the LXX stresses his constancy. He alone of all the wilderness generation continued to have faith in God's purposes for his people (=his *house*, household). On the other hand, Moses' status is lower than that of Jesus, and may be likened to that of a servant rather than the son of the house.

A Warning Example: The Faithlessness of the Wilderness Generation, 3:7-19

3:7-11. Israel's loss of faith in the past. In contrast to Moses' fidelity is the loss of faith on the part of those he sought to lead. Verses 7-11 cites Ps 94 (MT 95):7-11, which recalls Israel's resolve, in the face of the hardships of the wilderness, to turn her back on the promise of a homeland, and to return to a life of bondage in Egypt (cf. Num 14:1-35). The psalm also contains an allusion to an incident (Exod 17:1-7; Num 20:2-13) in which the people's complaint at their lack of water gave rise to the place names *Meribah* (=strife or contention) and *Massah* (=proof or test). The LXX translates rather than transliterates these Hebrew names. Hence they become: *as in the rebellion*, and: *as on the day of testing* (v. 8). The psalmist saw Israel's demand for water as putting God to the test—itself a demonstration of her loss of faith. By altering the punctuation and adding *therefore* (v. 10) Hebrews makes *forty years* refer, not to the duration of God's anger, but to the length of time Israel had been privileged to experience God's works (v. 17 reverts to the more usual reading). The effect of this is to heighten the enormity of the people's ingratitude.

3:12-4:11. A commentary on Psalm 95. Here the preacher applies the psalm to the present situation of his Christian audience. He draws an analogy between the experience of the wilderness generation and that of the group he is now addressing. Like their predecessors, they too are living through testing times. Unlike them, however, they should stand firm and not lose hope in the promises of God's future. They should take warning from the fate that befell the faithless of the past, whose punishment was that they were forbidden to enter the promised land of Canaan.

Like the psalmist, the author of Hebrews confines himself at this point to the threat of disinheritance. *They will not enter into my rest.* He does not mention that, in the case of CALEB, JOSHUA, and those Israelites under twenty years of age, God relented, in response to Moses' pleading (see Num 14:29ff.). To have done so would have detracted from the main purpose of this particular sermon. The preacher wants to use the words of the psalm as an exemplary warning to his own generation of the dangerous consequences of abandoning their faith.

Beware Lest You Fail to Enter God's Promised Rest, 4:1-11

By *enter* and *rest* Hebrews is not simply referring to Israel's possession of the land of CANAAN. He is well aware that that was achieved under Joshua (cf. 4:8). In Jewish tradition however, the land had come to represent more than a place of rest from Israel's wanderings (cf. Deut 3:20; Josh 1:3), or from the assaults of her enemies (cf. Deut 25:19; Josh 11:23). The land, more specifically Jerusalem (cf. Ps 132:14) and its Temple (cf. Deut 12:18), came to be thought of as God's abode or resting place. Thus *rest*, understood as the presence of God (cf. Exod 3:14; LXX Deut 33:14), could be a metaphor for salvation. Clearly that is how it is understood by the author of Hebrews.

Linking the psalm's noun *rest* with the verb "to rest" found in (LXX) Gen 2:2 enables Hebrews to move from the idea of salvation as the possession of the LAND to its depiction as the attainment of heaven itself. Salvation is thus to be in the presence of God in heaven, there to share that "rest" that he himself enjoyed on the seventh day, having created the universe. *Sabbath rest* (σαββατισμός) is the word coined by Hebrews (4:9) to characterize salvation as heavenly rather than earthly in its locus. Understood thus, the promised "rest" was not obtained when JOSHUA (v. 8) entered Canaan. (Chapter 11 reverts to this theme. The land sought in faith by Israel's patriarchs was not the earthly Canaan but a heavenly inheritance.)

What is more, neither the promise nor threat of this particular word of God was intended for the wilderness generation alone. Hence the psalmist (assumed by Hebrews to be DAVID) could and did address both to the *today* of his own time. Had the promise been fulfilled in Joshua's day there would have been no need for the psalmist of a later generation to have repeated it. For Hebrews this demonstrates that the promise is still outstanding (vv. 7-10). Thus he uses the psalm to challenge his contemporary audience to seize the *today* of God's word, lest they fail to become heirs of salvation. Like the wilderness generation, they stand on the brink of entry. They are *in the process of entering* God's rest. The NRSV *enter* (v. 3) obscures the

continuous force of the Greek at this point. The recurrent warnings in this section (3:12-14; 4:1,11) remind the readers that, even for them, salvation *remains* (3:9) to be attained in the future.

A Coda: The Penetrative Power of God's Word, 4:12-13.

The homiletic exposition of Ps 95 concludes with a coda in praise of the word (λόγος) of God. Clearly this is not a reference to Jesus, but to God, speaking through the scriptures that have just been cited. The Bible is seen as no dead letter of the past, but *living and active*; of continuing and contemporary relevance.

The image of divine judgment as a sword is a traditional one (cf. Isa 34:5-6). Wis 18:14-16 depicts the word as a warrior, wielding the divine sword of judgment against Israel's enemies at the EXODUS (cf. Eph 6:17; Rev 1:16; 2:12; 19:15). *Spirit* and *soul, joints* and *marrow,* and *thought* and *intentions* are used as three pairs of synonyms to emphasize the penetrative power of God's word and its ability to bring judgment even to the seemingly impenetrable.

Jesus the High Priest, 4:14–10:18

In this central section the principal soteriological model employed is that of the high priest, and the role he played in the Day of Atonement ceremonies. In this analogy, the death and ascension of Jesus represent both the offering and the offerer, the expiatory sacrifice that was the essential prerequisite for entry into the Holy of Holies and the high priest who was thus enabled to enter into the presence of God on the people's behalf.

Not only are comparisons made but contrasts are also drawn. Thus Jesus is superior both to the Day of Atonement's sacrificial victim, and its high priest. Furthermore, the cult place that Christ has entered far excels even the Holy of Holies, since it is nothing less than heaven itself. When in 8:7-13 and 9:15-22 Hebrews moves from the image of Jesus as expiatory sacrifice to one whereby he is seen as a COVENANT offering, we find a similar stress on his supremacy over what has gone before. His was a superior sacrifice that inaugurated a new and better covenant.

Merciful and Compassionate, 4:14–5:10

Hebrews 4:14-16 acts as a transition from the theme of access to God in terms of entry into the promised land (3:1–4:13), to its depiction in terms of the Jewish cult that dominates 4:14–10:18. Christ's priesthood, hinted at 1:3 and first stated at 2:17, *a merciful and faithful high priest*, is now pursued.

By way of encouragement to hold fast to their faith, the readers are once more reminded that Jesus is now in the presence of God in heaven. Earlier images of heaven as a royal court where Christ is enthroned now give way to its depiction as the inner sanctum of Israel's cult place. Thus it contains a *throne of grace* (4:16), i.e., the *mercy seat* located in the tabernacle's Holy of Holies (cf. 9:5). This is a reference to the lid or covering of the ark, upon which the victim's blood was sprinkled by the high priest on the Day of Atonement. Since the effect of this action was expiatory, the ARK could be spoken of as the place where mercy was dispensed. In the light of Jesus' expiatory work, Christians should be confident (NRSV *approach . . . with boldness*; cf. 3:6; 10:19) that they may approach God.

The source of Jesus' compassion as HIGH PRIEST lies in his genuine humanity—*one who in every respect has been tested as we are* (4:15). This picks up the theme of testing from 3:8 where it referred to the wilderness generation's desire to put God to the test. Thereby their own faith was tested and found wanting. By contrast, Jesus' response to testing was quite different. He was *without sin*.

Excursus: Priesthood in Postexilic Israel.

With the demise of the Davidic monarchy in postexilic Judaism, it was the institution of priesthood that came to the fore. Hence the covenant made by God with LEVI came to be seen as analogous to the one he made with Moses (cf. Jer 33:14-26—a passage regarded by many scholars as a postexilic interpolation). Like the Davidic covenant (2 Sam 7:12-16), the Levitical one was portrayed as permanent (Num 25:11-13; Sir 45:6-21)—*forever*.

The dominance of the priestly model of leadership in the postexilic period is evident from the second century B.C.E., with the installation of the Hasmonean high priesthood. In 140 BCE, Simon Maccabeus claimed the dual role of high priest and ethnarch both for himself and in perpetuity for his heirs (cf. 1 Mac 14:41). JOSEPHUS tells us (*Ant* 13.301) that by the time of John Hyrcanus (130–104 B.C.E.) the Hasmoneans had adopted the title "king" as well as high priest.

The QUMRAN community seems to have come into being originally as a protest, not against Hasmonean claims to (non-Davidic) kingship, but to their right to the high priesthood. According to the Covenanters,

although of the tribe of Levi, they were not descended from the Zadokite line (cf. *1QpHab* 12:7-8; 10:10; *CD* 12:2). They therefore regarded Hasmonean incumbency of the office to be invalid. The restoration of the true Zadokite line became part of their eschatological vision of the cult in the future. Thus, unlike Hebrews, the Qumran Covenanters looked forward to the purification of Judaism's Levitical high priesthood, rather than to its replacement by something wholly other—a Melchizidekian order.

5:1-4. The Aaronic priesthood. The major qualifications for the Aaronic priesthood are: (1) Common humanity. The priest must be part of what he represents. Hence he is *chosen from among mortals* (v. 1). (2) He should display a tolerant understanding towards those who err (v. 2), since he himself has human weaknesses (cf. 4:15) that require that he offer sacrifice, not only for the people, but for himself (v. 3). Here Hebrews has in mind the Day of Atonement ritual, where the two separate offerings were clearly distinguished (cf. Lev 9:7; 16:6-17). Later (7:27; 9:7) he is to assert the superiority of Christ's priesthood over that of the Levitical order, not least in his sinlessness (cf. 4:15), which precluded the need for two sacrifices and two entries into the Holy of Holies. (3) Priesthood requires a call and appointment that has God rather than oneself as its instigator (v. 4). "Appointed" (RSV) is preferable (as in 7:28 and 8:3) to the NRSV *put in charge of* (v. 1). 5:5-10 applies these qualifications to Jesus in inverse order:

5:5-6,10. His is a divine appointment. He has not only been called by God as his Son (Ps 2:7; cf. Heb 1:5); he has also been designated *a priest forever according to the order of Melchizedek* (Ps 110:4). In their original setting both Pss 2 and 110 were addressed to a Davidic king. Although Israel's preexilic kings could and did exercise what were later to become the exclusive functions of the priesthood (cf. 2 Sam 6:13-18; 24:17; 1 Kgs 3:15), since they were of the tribe of JUDAH rather than Levi, they were not priests. Hence the Psalmist addressed the Davidic king as of *the order of Melchizedek*, rather than Levi. Hebrews can therefore appropriately designate Jesus, the Davidic Messiah, as priest. In what sense he is *after the order of Melchizedek* will be developed in chap. 7.

Although Ps 110:1 is widely used in the NT, it is striking that Hebrews is the only Christian writer before JUSTIN MARTYR in the second century to use verse 4. Even those Qumran writings that feature MELCHIZEDEK (*11QMelch*; *1QapGen*) make no use of it.

5:7-10. Jesus shares human weakness. He is thus part of the humanity he represents. Unlike the Levitical high priest, however, in the case of Jesus it is not sin that is the common bond between representative and people; it is suffering and mortality (cf. 2:14-15). *Having been made perfect* (v. 9) is not a reference to moral perfectibility, and should not be understood as parallel with, *He learned obedience through what he suffered* (v. 8). That would be to suggest that Jesus' death was designed to correct his prior disobedience, whereas Hebrews stands firmly within the tradition that regarded him as sinless (cf. 2 Cor 5:21; 1 Pet 2:22; 1 John 3:5). His suffering is certainly portrayed as educative—but not in a punitive sense. Rather, it developed (cf. Luke 2:52) and expressed his filial obedience to God.

The language of *perfection* (τελείωσις) and its cognates (τελείουν and τελειωτής) in Hebrews, whether applied to Jesus or his followers, never loses the sense of achieving an end or goal (τέλος). In terms of the Jewish cult that end was access to God, symbolized by the entry of the high priest into the Holy of Holies. *Perfection* (cf. 7:11) for the Christian author of Hebrews is the attainment of that goal in terms of entry into heaven. It is, moreover, a process (*being made perfect*) that includes not only the end, but the means to that end. In the case of Jesus, his passion was the path to his perfecting (cf. 2:10; 5:9; 7:28). His disciples also, if they follow Jesus the *perfecter* (12:2), may achieve access to the presence of God, that is, heaven (cf. 10:4; 12:23), although, unlike Christ, for them that lies in the future.

Verse 7 is unlikely to refer to Jesus' prayer in Gethsemane (cf. Matt 26:36-46 ‖ Mark 14:32-42 ‖ Luke 22:40-46), since there his petition, "Remove this cup from me," was not granted. Here, however, *his prayer was heard*. Far from being a fearful entreaty, this prayer exudes the confidence that is the hallmark of the truly *reverent*. It displays that frank expression of emotion (*loud cries and tears*) that, according to Jewish tradition, characterized the prayer of the righteous. Thus Philo can say of Moses' prayer: "But the man of worth has such courage of speech that he is bold not only to speak and cry aloud, but actually to make an outcry of reproach, wrung from him by real conviction, and expressing true emotion" (*Who Is the Heir of Divine Things* 19). As vv. 6 and 10 make clear, this is the confidant prayer of Jesus, the Melchizedekian high priest, which accompanied the offering of the sacrifice of his own life.

An Exhortatory Aside: Grow Up! There Can Be No Going Back, 5:11-6:20.

Before further developing the theme of Jesus' Melchizedekian high priesthood, Hebrews urges his readers to become more mature (v. 1 *maturity* is preferable to NRSV *perfection*).

5:11-6:3. In spiritual matters they are mere babes. They have yet to progress beyond the ABCs of the faith. These are listed in vv. 1-2. *Repentance from dead work*s = behavior that will ensue in spiritual death. There is nothing here to suggest the contrast that we find in Paul between faith and works. *Contra* NRSV, *instruction on baptisms* (6:2) is unlikely to refer to Christian baptism since: (1) The NT word for baptism is neuter, whereas here it is masculine, and (2) it is in the plural. If it were baptism we would expect the singular. It is better understood, therefore, as referring to purificatory rites of ablution in general.

Similarly, we should not confine *laying on of hands* to any one specific Christian rite of initiation. In biblical tradition it occurs in a whole variety of different contexts as the mode whereby power was transferred and blessings bestowed (Lohse 1974). *Resurrection of the dead* refers to the general resurrection that lies in the future (see 11:19) rather than to the resurrection of Christ that has already taken place. Only once in Hebrews (13:10) do we find a reference to Jesus' resurrection.

All these beliefs and practices can be found in JUDAISM. Nonetheless, for the author of Hebrews, convinced as he was that Judaism's scriptures are *about Christ* (6:1), they may be described also as Christian *basic teaching*. This is therefore no call to reject the inspiration of the past in order to embrace Christianity, but a call to see in Jesus the true fulfilment of God's previous revelation.

6:4-12. Hope versus despair. Here the hopelessness that comes from giving up one's Christian discipleship is contrasted with the hope that is held out to those who remain steadfast. It is impossible for renegades to be readmitted to the community of faith once they have left (6:4-6; cf. 10:26-31), not because they have committed postbaptismal sin. Nor because there is a special category of "mortal" sins for which there can be no forgiveness. Like Num 15:30-31, Hebrews believes that there can be no expiatory sacrifice for one who *acts high-handedly*, that is, for one who refuses to accept the very jurisdiction of God. To *fall away* in this context means to deliberately place oneself outside the new covenant community. To abandon Christian discipleship is to ally oneself with that very rejection that originally brought about Christ's crucifixion. As the rest of this homily goes on to assert, that sacrifice was unique and cannot be repeated.

All this is merely by way of warning. So far the recipients have remained loyal (v. 9). So they are not only warned; they are encouraged (vv. 10-12) to look forward in hope rather than go back via a path that can only lead to a dead end.

6:13-20. God has confirmed his promise by an oath. Christian hope is grounded in the twofold character of God's word: (1) the *promise* that is the believer's inheritance, and (2) the *oath* that guarantees the promise (v. 17). Hebrews cites the example of ABRAHAM. God's promise that he would father a great nation (Gen 12:1-4) was emphatically renewed (by God swearing an oath) after the patriarch had demonstrated his willingness to sacrifice his son (Gen 22:16-18). Both promise and oath are to be trusted (v. 18, *two unchangeable things*), but the word accompanied by the oath is the superior, definitive, last word of God.

This argument paves the way for chap. 7. It enables the author to claim that Melchizedekian high priesthood is superior to the Aaronic order since it was confirmed by an oath. Although v. 16 acknowledges the problem, unlike some Jewish authors (cf. Philo, *Allegorical Commentaries* 3.207), Hebrews does not discuss how it is possible for God to swear by himself.

According to the Order of Melchizedek, 7:1-28

In order to pursue the analogy of Christ's death and ascension in priestly terms, it is essential for the author to establish the non-Levitical order of his priesthood. Jesus could not at one and the same time be Davidic Messiah of the tribe of Judah (vv. 13-15) and Aaronic high priest of the tribe of Levi.

7:1-3. The order of Melchizedek. In the two references to MELCHIZEDEK in the OT (Gen 14:17-20; Ps 110:4) Hebrews finds a type of priesthood that is non-Levitical. In vv. 1-2 he focuses on two things mentioned in Gen 14: (1) Melchizedek's blessing of Abraham, and (2) his receiving tithes from the patriarch. In these actions is to be found evidence of Melchizedek's superiority (vv. 4-8).

Melchizedek was probably originally a Canaanite priest-king. Little more can be said of this figure from the mists of Israel's prehistory. Perhaps precisely because of this he came to exercise the creative imagination of both Jewish and Christian writers.

Verse 2 reflects first-century Jewish exegetical belief that the *zedek* of the priest-king's name was derived from the Hebrew *sedeq* (righteous-ness) and therefore meant *king of righteousness*. In fact it may have had its origins in Zedek, the name of a Canaanite deity, and meant "Zedek's king." By the time of Hebrews, Melchizedek had become associated in Jewish thought with the city of *Salem* (=Jerusalem), whose name was supposedly derived from the Hebrew *shalom, peace.*

The Qumran Covenanters were also interested in Melchizedek (cf. *1QapGen* 14; *11QMelch*). Their interest in him was not as a priestly figure but as a heavenly being, whom they thought would come in the final jubilee year to exercise judgment on God's behalf.

From scripture's silence as to Melchizedek's origins and final destiny v. 3 infers that he was *without father, without mother, without genealogy, having neither beginning of days nor end of life.* He therefore typifies a kind of priesthood that is neither inherited nor bequeathed. Jesus' resurrection, *the power of an indestructible life* (v. 16), demonstrates that he *remains a priest forever* (v. 3 = Ps 110:4), and therefore has no successor (cf. 7:24). From this the reader might be led to think that Melchizedek was the model for Christ. Yet, as v. 3 shows, for Hebrews it is Melchizedek who resembles the SON OF GOD rather than *vice versa.*

7:4-10. Melchizedek is superior to both Abraham and Levi. Abraham acknowledged this in receiving his blessing and giving him tithes. And Levi, although as yet unborn, did likewise, since he may be regarded as seminally present (= *in the loins of*) in his great grandfather.

7:11-19. Failure of Levitical order. The Levitical order failed to effect access to God, which was its whole purpose. Therefore it has been superseded by a new priesthood. Hebrews (vv. 12, 18) is aware that to abrogate the Aaronic office is effectively to overthrow the Mosaic Law that legislated for its provision. Apart from a brief mention at 10:1, however, the issue of the Law is not pursued further. The discussion is confined to priesthood.

7:20-28. The superiority of Jesus' high priesthood. Psalm 110:4, initially introduced at v. 17 to stress the eternity (*forever*) of Christ's priestly order, is now used to assert that Melchizedekian priesthood is God's final word—*The Lord has sworn and will not change his mind.* Just as 6:13-20 argued that in the case of Abraham God's promise was even better when con-

confirmed by an oath, so here the asseveration that prefaced the address to a Davidic king in Ps 110 is seen to confirm that it is Melchizedekian rather than Levitical priesthood that is God's definitive word. This priesthood is *the guarantee of a better covenant* (cf. 8:7-13; 9:15-27).

7:23-25. Christ's priestly ministry is singular and permanent. It is therefore better than that of AARON, since it requires no line of succession (cf. 7:3). The ministry of the ascended Christ is that of *intercession* (cf. Rom 8:34) rather than sacrifice. The latter was but the means whereby Jesus entered heaven.

7:26-28. He was a high priest who was sinless. Unlike the Aaronic high priest, who needed to offer two sacrifices and therefore make two entries into the Holy of Holies on the Day of Atonement, Jesus had no need of personal expiation. He entered the presence of God but once. He *has been made perfect* (v. 28) does not imply his own need of moral perfectibility. Rather, the language of "perfection" in Hebrews refers to the process whereby he achieved the goal of entry into heaven (see note on 5:9).

The Sacrificial Work of Christ, 8:1–10:18

At this point the cultic imagery is expanded to make way, not only for Christ as priest, but Christ as sacrificial victim, whose death was the essential prerequisite for his access to God. This is worked out in terms of Jesus as (1) the new covenant sacrifice (8:7-13; 9:15-22), and (2) the superior Day of Atonement offering.

The whole purpose of expiatory sacrifices in the Jewish cultic system was to remove the barrier of sin which separated the profane from the holy. They were the divinely appointed means whereby the worshiper could approach God. Above all this was exemplified in the Day of Atonement ceremonies. Using this model, Hebrews compares the death of Christ to that offering, and his ascension to heaven with the entry of the high priest into the Holy of Holies. Thus the goal of all sacrifice has been achieved, making the cult itself redundant.

8:1-6. Jesus is now in the presence of God. With yet another allusion to Ps 110:1, *seated at the right hand*, the preacher brings us back once more to this *the main point* (v. 1) of his sermon. He cites (v. 5) Exod 25:40 (LXX), *"See that you make everything according to the pattern that was shown you on the mountain,"* to claim that the plans of the tabernacle shown to Moses by God were but a shadowy copy (NRSV, v. 5, *a sketch and shadow*) rather than the real thing. That superior reality, which now replaces the earthly shrine, is heaven itself—*the sanctuary and the true tent* which Christ has entered.

Hebrews 8:6 at once concludes this section on Jesus as *minister* in the superior shrine, and introduces the new theme of him as *the mediator of a better covenant*.

8:7-13. The promise of a new covenant. Here the Mosaic covenant on Mount Sinai (see Exod 19) is contrasted with that promised by JEREMIAH (31:31-34). COVENANT, especially as developed in Deuteronomistic circles in the years leading up to the EXILE, became the term that encapsulated Israel's faith that she had been chosen as God's people. The bond between God and Israel was not thought of as a contract between two equal partners. Nonetheless, it was bilateral in nature. God's commitment to his people carried with it a solemn obligation to serve him alone and to be obedient to his commandments. It was because of Israel's lamentable failure to fulfil her side of the obligation that Jeremiah looked forward to a new covenant.

8:8-12. The prophecy of Jeremiah. This is cited from the LXX (=Jer 38:31-34). Hebrews goes further than Jeremiah, however. He suggests that failure to keep the covenant was not merely weakness on the people's part; it was inherent in the Mosaic covenant itself, as the very mention of *a second* one demonstrates. *For if the first had been faultless, there would have been no need to look for a second one* (v. 7).

What lies at the heart of Jeremiah's promise of a new covenant is the same notion of adoption that lay behind the Mosaic covenant. To this, however, the prophet has added some striking new features: (1) *I will put my laws in their minds and write them on their hearts* (v. 10). It is this interiorization of the will of God that leads to radical obedience. (2) With the universal knowledge of the Law's demands will come the redundancy of its teachers and interpreters. *For they shall all know me from the least of them to the greatest* (v. 11).

8:13. The new covenant. This new covenant has been inaugurated by the death of Christ. It heralds a new order (a theme that runs throughout 7:1–10:18) that makes what went before *obsolete, growing old* and *soon to disappear*. For Hebrews, the new covenant is thus part of the new age that, like the promised land, has yet to be attained. It is the promise held out to the believer of God's future, to be experienced in the present as hope.

9:1-10. The inadequacy of the earthly cult. The author returns to the theme that dominates this central section—the Day of Atonement.

9:1-5. The layout and contents of the shrine. Clearly, the simple twofold division of the wilderness TABERNACLE (Exod 25-26) rather than the more complex structure of the Jerusalem Temple (see TEMPLE/TEMPLES) is in mind. In the former was an outer tent (*the first one*), *the Holy Place* (v. 2), beyond which was an inner sanctum, *the Holy of Holies* (v. 3).

In the accounts in Exodus (25:1–31:11; 36:2–39:43; 40:1-15; 40:16-38) the only furnishing in the Holy of Holies was the ARK. The final fate of the ark remains unknown. It was probably removed and/or destroyed by the Babylonians when they sacked the Temple (cf. Jer 3:14-17). JOSEPHUS (*BJ* 5.219) tells us that in the Temple of his day the inner sanctum was completely empty. In Hebrews's account the ark is made to contain within it certain sacred objects: the *tablets of the covenant* (cf. Deut 10:2; 1 Kgs 8:9; 2 Chr 5:10); the urn containing the *manna* (cf. Exod 16:33-34); and *Aaron's rod* (cf. Num 17:16-24). Furthermore, unlike Exod 30:1-10; 38:25-28, Hebrews (v. 4) locates the *altar of incense* inside rather than outside the Holy of Holies.

9:6-10.The regulations for worship on the Day of Atonement. These are briefly alluded to. Two points are emphasized: (1) The Holy of Holies was the exclusive domain of the high priest, who was permitted to enter on but one day of the year. (2) Expiatory sacrifice was the *sine qua non* without which even he was not permitted access. He in fact made two sacrifices and two entries into the inner sanctum. First he offered a bull to expiate for the sins of himself and his household (cf. Lev 16:6,11). Then he sacrificed a goat to purify both the people and the cult place (cf. Lev 16:16). *Sins committed unintentionally* (v. 7), reminds us that Israel's sacrificial system (including its "sin" and "guilt" offerings) was largely intended to expiate unwitting rather than "high-handed" sins (see Num 15:30-31).

The sins of the people were laid upon the head of a second goat (the "scapegoat") by the high priest. Since nothing that is sinful can be offered to God, this animal was not sacrificed, but driven out live into the wilderness (cf. Lev 16:20-22). Nowhere in the NT is Jesus depicted as the scapegoat. The emphasis rather (v. 14) is upon Jesus as the spotless victim.

The Mosaic ritual itself (= *the first tent*, v. 8) was a parable in action (= *symbol*, v. 9) of the fact that it provided no definitive, lasting access to God. Even during the period of its dispensation (=*standing*, v. 8), it could only deal with external rather than internal purification. It could not cleanse the *conscience* (v. 9). That had to await the sacrifice of Christ (= *the time . . . to set things right*, v. 10).

9:11-14. The superiority of Christ as priest and victim. This lies in the fact that Jesus has entered the presence of God, not through the sacrifice of an animal, but through the superior offering of himself. Verse 13 alludes to another of Israel's expiatory rites—the ceremony of the red heifer (Num 19:2-20) in which the animal was burned with cedar wood, along with hyssop and scarlet "stuff" (cf. Heb 9:19). The resultant ashes were then mixed with water and sprinkled upon the people (see HEIFER, RED).

It is the contrast between the exterior and the interior that is drawn at this point in the homily. Judaism's expiatory rites could only cleanse what is outside (= the *flesh*, v. 13), whereas Jesus' sacrifice dealt with the interior sense of guilt (= *conscience*), that inner accuser that condemns a way of life that leads to death. (*Dead works*, v. 14, should not be understood in the Pauline sense of "works of the law" over against faith.)

By capitalizing *Spirit* the NRSV gives a trinitarian interpretation to v. 14. It is better understood, however, as a reference to Jesus' own spirit or person, which is *eternal* by virtue of his resurrection (cf. 7:16).

9:15-22. The new covenant and its sacrifice. This resumes the theme of 8:7-13. Now the death of Christ is likened, not to the Day of Atonement offering, but to the sacrifice that accompanied the ratification of the Mosaic covenant (Exod 24:1-8). Apart from Luke 20:20 and 1 Cor 11:25, Hebrews is the only NT work to depict Jesus as the *new* covenant victim. (Mark 14:24 || Matt 26:28 mentions covenant but not new covenant.) Unlike them, however, Hebrews does not place this within the context of the last supper. In fact, Hebrews displays no interest in the Eucharist whatsoever.

9:15. The death of Jesus ratifies a new covenant. *Redeems* (cf. 9:12) conjures up a picture of God's manumission of his people from slavery in Egypt. The bondage envisaged here, however, is that of sin.

9:16-17. A testator must first die before a will can take effect. This argument depends upon the double meaning of διαθήκη, the LXX's translation of the Hebrew word for *covenant (berith)*. In secular Greek it means "will" (cf. Gal 3:15-17).

9:18-22. A death was also necessary to ratify the Mosaic covenant. Whereas in Exodus the covenant offering was concerned with consecration, here it is interpreted as expiatory. This is probably because the Day of Atonement, rather than the inauguration of the covenant, dominates Hebrews's thinking. The one becomes interpreted in terms of the other. Thus, unlike the biblical account, not only the people, but the book (v. 19) together with the contents of the tabernacle (v. 21) are sprinkled with the blood of the covenant victim. Hebrews 9:19 also contains elements drawn, not from the covenant, but from the ceremony of the red heifer (see note on 9:13).

9:23-28. Christ's death as the means whereby he entered heaven. Once more we are back with the dominant motif of the Day of Atonement. Hebrews 9:23-24 is another *a fortiori* argument. If the contents of the material shrine needed cleansing, *how much more* the *heavenly things themselves*. The latter is probably a metaphor for that which is interior, namely, the CON-SCIENCE. Thus this section looks back to 9:11-14 and forward to 10:1-10, which focus upon the internal as opposed to the external.

9:25-28. Levitical sacrifices and the death of Christ. The repetitive character of Levitical sacrifices is contrasted with the *once for all* (vv. 26, 27, 28) of the death of Christ. A *reductio ad absurdum* argument is employed to show that if this were not the case Jesus would have had to die repeatedly. As we all know, however, humans die but once! Jesus' return will not be to atone for sin, but to bring final salvation. Throughout Hebrews salvation is held out as a future hope—not a present possession.

10:1-18. The sacrifice to end all sacrifices. This passage functions as both a recapitulation of the argument of 8:1–10:18 and as its climax. Thus it reiterates:

(1) 10:1-3. Christ's sacrifice needs no annual renewal. Sacrifices of the cult, on the other hand, had to be repeated. This proves that they, together with the Mosaic Law that legislated for them, were not God's final revelation (*true form*) but only a precursor (*shadow*). Far from absolving guilt (*consciousness of sin;* cf. 9:14), they merely acted as its constant reminder.

(2) 10:4-10. Unlike animal sacrifice, that of Jesus was a voluntary self-offering. Ps 40:6-8 is cited (vv. 5-7) in its LXX form (=Ps 39:7-9). *A body you have prepared for me* (v. 5) is the LXX translation of the obscure Hebrew phrase, "Ears you have dug for me," which the NRSV of Ps 40 freely renders, "You have given me an open ear." This is used to echo the Psalmist's insistence upon the supremacy of obedience over sacrificial offerings *per se* (v. 9). Above all, Jesus' death is seen as superior to that of animals, since they had no option. Putting the psalm on the lips of Jesus (v. 5; cf. 2:12-13) is not to claim his preexistence, but to identify his death with the superior self-offering spoken of by the psalm.

(3) 10:11-18. Since it was effective, it does away with all further need of sacrifice. Having offered the definitive sacrifice, Jesus is now enthroned in heaven (Ps 110:1). His enemies have as yet to be subjugated on earth (cf. 2:8; 9:28). Nonetheless, he has gained access to God (= *perfected*) not only for himself but ultimately for his followers (= the *sanctified*). His death has thus fulfilled the two promises that lay at the heart of Jeremiah's new covenant: (a) a genuine change in humanity that affects the interior and not simply the exterior; and (b) the removal of sin. With this achieved, there is no further need of a sacrificial system at all.

An Exhortation to Persevere in the Faith, 10:19–12:29

The sermon proper is concluded by a series of encouragements and warnings aimed at a readership who may be tempted to abandon their discipleship in the face of present hardships. Once more the theme of pilgrimage (cf. 3:1–4:14) is taken up.

Perseverance: Some Encouragements and Warnings, 10:19-39

10:19-25. Trust in the faithfulness of God. An appeal to the fidelity of the Christian is grounded in a belief in the fidelity of God: *He who has promised is faithful* (v. 23). Heb 10:19-20 is best understood as an allegorization of the *curtain* that divided the Holy of Holies from the rest of the shrine. It now represents the death (= *flesh*) through which Jesus passed in order to gain access to God.

10:26-31. Go forward rather than back. The warning of 6:4-6 is renewed. *Anyone who has violated the law of Moses dies without mercy* (v. 28) alludes to Deut 17:8. Here what is condemned is not every breach of the Law, but idolatrous APOSTASY. What makes that unforgivable is that it constitutes a refusal to accept God's jurisdiction. That is as true of the new covenant as it was of the old. To go back on Christian discipleship is to spurn the Son of God, to treat the cross as if it were merely a profane death, rather than a sacred sacrifice that inaugurated a new covenant, and thus to outrage the spirit of God that mediated that grace (v. 29).

10:32-39. Be encouraged by your own past good record. *Enlightened* (v. 32) became a metaphor for BAPTISM from the second century onwards. Here, however, it is used as an image of spiritual conversion in general. The references to public ridicule (= *exposed to abuse*), *persecution*, and the *plundering of . . . possessions* (vv. 32-34) are too vague and general to enable us to pinpoint either the date or destination of this epistle. Habakkuk 2:3-4 (LXX) is cited (vv. 37-38) to affirm, by way of encouragement: (1) that Jesus will shortly return (*in a very little while*); and (2) that his readers will not be among those who renege on their commitment.

The Faithful of the Past, 11:1-40

The theme of faith is now picked up from the Habakkuk quotation cited at the end of chap. 10. *By faith* is the repetitive refrain by which a list of various heroes and martyrs of Israel's past are introduced as exemplars of faith. Nowhere in the biblical accounts themselves are their exploits attributed to faith.

Such listings of the achievements of people and events of the past in order to bolster up the resolve of the faithful of the present seem to have been traditional. Thus Wis 10 appeals (although not by name) to ADAM, ABEL, NOAH, JACOB, JOSEPH, MOSES, and the EXODUS generation as examples of those who triumphed over adversity with the aid of God's wisdom. An even closer formal parallel is PHILO (*On Rewards and Punishments* 11-14), in his definition and exposition of hope. He, however, confines himself to types in general of those who have exemplified hope. Hebrews, on the other hand, cites particular individuals and events that have demonstrated faith, i.e., a belief and trust in God's as-yet-unseen future, which was to find its fulfilment in Jesus.

11:1-3. What is faith? Commentators disagree as to the meaning of two crucial words in v. 1. The NRSV choice of *assurance* for ὑπόστασις and *conviction* for ἔλεγχος find no parallel in first-century Greek usage. It is therefore preferable to translate v. 1: "Now faith is the *title deed* of things hoped for, *the evidence* of things not seen."

Faith is not purely subjective. It is trust in the reality of God's consummation of his purposes in the future. Our ancestors "received confirmation" (v. 2, lit. "testimony," *contra* NRSV, *approval*) of God's promises. In their case, that final salvation was as invisible as

was the material, visible world, before God brought it into existence through his divine command (v. 3).

11:4-7. Abel, Enoch, and Noah. Genesis 4:3-10 does not explain how or why Abel's was the superior sacrifice. Here (v. 4) it is ascribed to his faith. Hebrews 11:5 follows the LXX of Gen 5:21-24 and understands the enigmatic, "and he was not because God took him" of the MT, as implying that Enoch was translated to heaven (cf. *1 Enoch* 12.3; 15.1; *2 Enoch* 27.8; 71.14; *Jub* 4.23; Philo, *On the Changing of Names* 38; Josephus, *Ant* 1.2.4). Noah (cf. Gen 6:13-22) believed in God's warning of the impending flood (v. 7, *events as yet unseen*).

11:8-12. Abraham and Sarah. The story of Abraham's migration in response to God's call (Gen 12:1-8) enables Hebrews to link faith with obedience (v. 8). Like that of his successors ISAAC and JACOB, Abraham's sojourn in Canaan was but temporary (v. 9; cf. Gen 17:8; 23:4), since God's promise was not of an earthly but of a heavenly reality (v. 10). (The theme of the heavenly city will be resumed at 12:12.) Unlike those traditions that looked forward to the descent of the heavenly Jerusalem to earth (e.g., *4 Ezra* 13:36; Rev 21:2, 10), for Hebrews the land/city that is the true destination of pilgrimage is wholly transcendent.

11:13-16. The goal of faith. The true goal of faith is a heavenly rather than an earthly homeland. This recapitulates the main point of the chapter. None of these heroes of the past lived to see God's promises fulfilled. They lived in the faith that a *better country, a heavenly one* was to be theirs in the future.

11:17-22. Isaac, Jacob, and Joseph. Abraham was willing to offer his *only son* Isaac since he had faith in God's power to raise the dead (v. 19). A belief in a future resurrection of the dead was widespread in the first century. It is not, however, attributed to Abraham in the biblical account.

The NRSV translation *figuratively speaking* (v. 19) is to be rejected. Rather, as in 9:9, it means a *symbol* of future salvation: "Isaac's rescue from virtual death on the sacrificial pyre is symbolic of the deliverance that all the faithful can expect" (Attridge 1989, 336). Isaac's blessing of his sons (Gen 27:27-29, 39-40) is also seen to have a future reference (v. 20).

By adopting the LXX of Gen 47:31, "bowing in worship over the top of his staff" (v. 21), Jacob's blessing of his sons (Gen 48:8-22) is seen as an act of homage to God. (The MT, "Israel bowed himself on the end of his bed," means rather that he was prostrated by old age.)

11:23-27. Moses. Even Judaism's supreme agent of revelation (cf. Exod.33:11; Num 12:1-8) was motivated by a vision of the future. It was this, rather than fear (v. 27), that led him to leave Egypt. (His murder of an Egyptian overseer [Exod 12:11-12] is not mentioned.)

Abuse suffered for the Christ (v. 26) could either have Jesus the Messiah, or Moses the Lord's *anointed* (cf. LXX Ps 88:51-52 [MT 89:50-51]) as its referent. Probably both are intended. Thus, Moses, in obedience to and solidarity with the reproach that will be endured by the future Christ, accepted his fate as an exile. This glimpse of the future motivated his endurance.

11:28-31. The Passover, the Exodus, the fall of Jericho, and Rahab. These (cf. Exod 12:21-30; 14:21-31; Josh 6:12-21; 2:1-21; 6:22-5) all similarly reflect a faith in the future.

11:32-8. Other heroes and martyrs. Beginning with various military and political leaders of the postsettlement period (vv. 32-34), the list now includes not simply the victors, but the persecuted, many of whom lost their lives (vv. 35-38). *Women received their dead by resurrection* (v. 35), probably refers to the miracles performed by ELIJAH (1 Kgs 17:17-24) and ELISHA (2 Kgs 4:18-37). The picture of torture and death in vv. 36-38 has probably been colored by the stories of the Maccabean martyrs (see 2 Macc 6:18-31; 7; 4 Macc 6–12).

11:29-40. A summary. Their faith was to find its fulfillment in Christ. They awaited a *better* resurrection. This was what inspired them to endure—even in adversity.

The Faithful Endurance Required Now, 12:1-29

12:1-3. Look to the example of Jesus, the pioneer and perfecter of faith. The array of *witnesses* paraded in chap. 11 find their climax in Jesus. He has not only blazed the trail (= *pioneer*); he has reached its goal (= *perfecter*)—heaven. In their preparation for and participation in the contest (cf. *race*) of faith, Christians should take courage from his example.

12:4-13. View suffering as God's fatherly discipline. The readers, unlike Jesus, have not yet had to face a martyr's death. Their present *trials* (v. 7) should be seen as a sign of their true membership of the household of God. Far from being evidence of God's displeasure, they are signs of his fatherly care (cf. Wis 11:9-10). The educative value of suffering (cf. Prov 13:24; 22:15; Wis 3:3-5; Rom 5:3-4; 1 Cor 11:32) is

confirmed by way of a citation (vv. 5-6) from Prov 3:11-12 (LXX). Painful though their present plight might be (v. 11; cf. the athletic imagery of vv. 1-2), its aim is educative rather than punitive.

12:14-17. Take warning from the example of Esau. Hebrews 12:14-15 appeals for harmony (= *peace*) within the Christian community. See . . . *that no root of bitterness springs up and causes trouble* (v. 16) alludes to Deut 29:17 (LXX)—a passage which, in its original context, warned against APOSTASY from the covenant community. Similarly, the author of Hebrews is concerned that his readers should not abandon their Christian commitment. Otherwise they could become like Esau (cf. Gen 25:27-34; 27:30-40), who sold his birthright cheap. The biblical account has no reference to Esau's belated and futile repentance. In introducing it (v. 17), Hebrews echoes the previous warning (6:4-6; 10:26-31) that repentance for the apostate is impossible.

12:18-24. The heavenly Zion contrasted with Mount Sinai. Although not explicitly named, vv. 18-21 clearly alludes both to the site (Mt. Sinai) and the events that surrounded the ratification of the Mosaic covenant and the giving of the Law. In his summary the author of Hebrews combines features drawn from Exod 19:12-19; 20:18-21 with those of Deut 4:11-12; 5:23-27 in order to stress the distance imposed upon the people by the very awesomeness of that theophanic revelation. Mount Sinai's site was so sacred that not so much as an animal was permitted to set foot upon it. Unlike the Exodus account, Hebrews will not even exempt Moses from the taboo. He, too, was terrified.

Verses 22-24 contrasts this with Mount Zion. This is not to be identified with the Jebusite stronghold captured by David (cf. 2 Sam 5:6-9), which became the capital city, Jerusalem. For Hebrews, heaven, not earth, is God's abode. This *heavenly Jerusalem*, unlike Mount Zion, may be *touched* (cf. v. 18).

Even so, that salvation has yet to be achieved by the believer. As yet only Christ has attained it. "You have approached" is a better translation than the NRSV *you have come* (v. 22). Meanwhile, the author has a proleptic vision (v. 23) of that future heavenly Jerusalem, peopled by the faithful of all ages, who, having been perfected through the work of Christ, will finally make up the completed assembly of the people of God. Chief among their number is Jesus. The blood of his new covenant sacrifice speaks of forgiveness and reconciliation, unlike that of Abel (cf. Gen 4:10-11) which cried out for vengeance.

12:25-29. A final solemn warning. The awesome responsibility of having access to God is to be taken seriously. The theme of the infidelity of the wilderness generation (cf. 3:7–4:13) is once more touched upon (v. 25). Part of an oracle, originally a promise to the postexilic remnant of the restoration of the Jerusalem Temple, is cited: *"Yet once more I will shake not only the earth but also the heaven"* (v. 26 = Hag 2:6). Here it is used, however, as an assurance of the replacement of all that is earthly and transient (= *what is shaken*, v. 27) by the heavenly and permanent (i.e., what *cannot be shaken*, vv. 27, 28). Verses 28-29 conclude with a call to worship. The offering now acceptable to God is that of gratitude and reverence on the part of the worshiper.

Epistolary Exhortation and Conclusion, 13:1-25

An abrupt change in tone and style signals the beginning of the author's epistolary conclusion. Here he appends a number of injunctions concerning the implications of his sermon for Christian living.

Christian Holiness and Its Obligations, 13:1-6

The ethical hallmarks that should characterize the new covenant community are briefly listed: (1) *Mutual love* between its members. (2) Hospitality. Probably this refers also to fellow Christians; visitors, who are *strangers* to the particular community. Heb 13:2 alludes to Abraham and Sarah's unrecognised guests (Gen 18:2-15). (3) Empathy towards those who have been imprisoned or otherwise maltreated (NRSV *tortured* is too specific) for their faith. (4) Marital fidelity and sexual chastity. (5) An absence of material greed. This is reinforced in v. 5 by the citation of a combination of Deut 31:6,8 and Josh 31:8, and in v. 6 by LXX Ps 117 (MT 118):6. These texts exhort reliance upon God.

The Implications of Jesus' Sacrifice, 13:7-19

Between an injunction to remember leaders—past (v. 7) and present (vv. 17-19)—is now placed a parenthetical summary of the epistle's main argument. Its condensed style makes this passage initially difficult to follow. Once "unpacked', however, it becomes clear. What is being said is: (1) The gracious act of God (= *grace*) in the death and exaltation of Jesus is superior to the Mosaic cult (=*regulations about food*, v. 9). (2) Christians have an expiatory sacrifice (= *an altar*) which, like those offered on the Day of Atonement, was not eaten (v. 10). Just as the carcases of these animals were *burned outside the camp* (v. 10; cf. Lev 16:27), so Jesus was disposed of *outside the city gate* (v. 12; cf. Mark 15:20 = Matt 27:31). (3) Therefore, look beyond the fate of Jerusalem and its sanctuary, which is but transitory. Follow instead the way of Jesus. *Abuse* (cf. 11:26) will be the necessary lot of those who journey with him to the heavenly city (vv. 13-14). (4) Now, the only sacrifice required of the Christian is the praise of God in worship and the performance of good works in life (vv. 15-16).

A Closing Benediction, 13:20-21

This takes the form of a prayer for the recipients, and a doxology in praise of Christ.

13:20. Led up from the dead. "Led up from the dead" is a better translation than the NRSV *brought back*: Hebrews presents Christ's victory over death as exaltation rather than resurrection. In keeping with Jewish traditions of the Messiah as the shepherd of God's flock (cf. *PsSol* 17:40), Jesus is the *great shepherd of the sheep* (cf. John 10:11,14; 1 Pet 2:25; 5:4).

A Farewell Note, 13:22-25

Here more practical matters are dealt with. The author describes what he has written as a *word of exhortation* (v. 22)—the usual designation of a sermon (cf. Acts 13:15). The mention of *Timothy* (v. 23) led later interpreters to link Hebrews with PAUL (cf., e.g., Rom 16:21; 2 Cor 1:1; 1 Thes 1:1), and to conclude that the apostle was its author. It is unclear whether Timothy *has been set free* (v. 23) means from prison, or from some task that has, until recently, detained him. Equally ambiguous is *those from Italy* (v. 24). This could mean that Italy was the place from which Hebrews was written. It could, however, designate Italians who were sending their greetings home, in which case Italy would be its destination. Given these ambiguities (and that some scholars do not attribute vv. 21-25 to the original author), it is impossible to determine from these verses either the epistle's origin or destination.

Works Cited

Attridge, H. W. 1989. *The Epistle to the Hebrews*, Herm.

Lohse, Eduard. 1974. "The Laying on of Hands." TDNT 9:431-34.

James

R. Alan Culpepper

Introduction

James is an eminently practical letter, manifesting a passionate concern for the role of faith in the concrete circumstances of life. Rather than deal with SANCTIFICATION, James challenges believers to control their tongues. Rather than debate the meaning of JUSTIFICATION, James calls on Christians to treat the POOR and the rich with equal respect. James, therefore, shuns abstract arguments and pointedly calls for PURITY and faithfulness in all areas of life.

Literary Character

Although James begins with an epistolary greeting, it lacks other characteristics of the letter form. Instead, one finds a series of exhortations with affinities to Jewish wisdom materials and Greco-Roman philosophical, ethical instruction: lack of topical continuity, eclecticism, repetition of motifs, and admonitions that do not apply to a single audience or situation.

Some fifty to sixty imperatives have been counted in James's 108 verses. Lists of traditional virtues and vices are featured (3:16-17). Occasionally, various maxims are gathered around one topic, as in Jas 5:13-18, where prayer is discussed from several perspectives. In Jas 2 one finds the only sustained argument in the letter, on the dangers of partiality and the relationship between FAITH and works. More often, however, the reader of James finds a series of different maxims or exhortations, often organized by a mnemonic device called *catchword linkage*. Sayings are strung together in such a way that a significant term in one saying also appears in the following saying. For example, note the succession of linking terms in Jas 1:2-6: *trials* (v. 2)–*testing* (v. 3); *endurance* (v. 3)–*endurance* (v. 4); *lacking* (v. 4)–*lacking* (v. 5); *ask* (v. 5)–*ask* (v. 6). The exhortations in James are carefully selected; it is not just a random collection of sayings. At the same time, the paraenetic character and catch-word linkage employed in James make it difficult to reduce the letter to an orderly topical outline.

Social Setting

James is concerned about oppression of the poor by the rich and reciprocal hostility from the poor. The Christians meet in assemblies (2:2) led by *elders* (5:14), and one might be expected to aspire to the role of teacher (3:1). Some justify their lack of faithfulness by boasting Pauline slogans (2:14-26), and echoes of words of JESUS recur frequently. Envy and malicious talk are constant threats to the fabric of community life (4:2, 11). Laborers work for unfair wages (5:4). Life itself poses trials for the believers, who are encouraged to endure hardship patiently, anoint the sick with oil, and replace oaths with prayer.

James 1:1 contains the address and greeting: *To the twelve tribes in the Dispersion: Greetings*. Three interpretations of this address have been advanced: (1) all Jews living outside of Palestine; (2) Christendom conceived as the fulfillment of Israel; and (3) Jewish Christians living outside of Palestine who still looked to Jerusalem for leadership. The first has largely been abandoned because the epistle is clearly from a Christian leader to other Christians. The figurative interpretation is held in one form or another by all who claim that the epistle is pseudonymous and hold to a late date. The third position is compatible with the view that the epistle derives directly or indirectly from James, the brother of Jesus and leader of the Jerusalem church.

Authorship and Date

Among the factors that must be accounted for are the following: JAMES does not claim to be an APOSTLE, only *a servant of God and of the Lord Jesus Christ* (1:1). There is no claim to a familial relationship with Jesus. In fact, there are only two references to Jesus in the entire letter (1:1; 2:1). Although James seems to know both the tradition of the sayings of Jesus and some of the tenets of Paulinism, it does not quote any other NT book and is not quoted elsewhere in the NT. At most, one may argue that Jude 1 echoes Jas 1:1. James is also written in excellent Greek and reflects both Hellenistic and Jewish Christian features.

The traditional view is that James was written by James the Just, the brother of Jesus, prior to his death in 62 C.E. Alternatively, some scholars maintain that James is a pseudonymous work, written in the name of James late in the first century. It has also been suggested that the letter was originally a Jewish document that was subsequently reworked by a Christian, but this position has failed to gather much support.

A mediating position seems to be gaining favor. It holds that James contains material from the teachings of James in Jerusalem that was later compiled or edited by someone else. It was then sent to Jewish Christians who had been dispersed from Jerusalem during the turbulent events of the 50s and 60s. On this reading, James gives us a glimpse of the early Palestinian church just before it was dispersed by the war of 66–74 C.E. (see Davids 1982).

For nearly two centuries the early church was remarkably silent about James. The first clear reference to the letter appears in Origen (third cent.), who referred to it as scripture and attributed it to James the Just. In his "Preface to the New Testament" in 1552, Luther concluded, "Therefore St. James' epistle is really an epistle of straw, compared to these others, for it has nothing of the nature of the gospel about it." His reasons for discrediting James were that it opposed Paul in "ascribing justification to works" (*Luther's Works*, 35:396) and because of its apparent lack of organization.

Nevertheless, evidence for the origin of the material in James in the early days of the church (before the composition of the Gospels or the collection of Paul's letters) seems strong. The absence of anything peculiar to James the Just is also significant. The epistle preserves the traditional, ethical concerns of early Jewish Christianity, but drops its emphasis on the Law, circumcision, and dietary restrictions. At the same time, it embraces and endorses the authority of James and combats a misinterpretation of Paul. The letter, therefore, appears to be the work of one who gathered up the teachings of the early church in Jerusalem, attached the name of the late head of the church (since it contained his teachings), and sent it to Jewish Christians who had been dispersed as a result of the anarchy in Judea in the 60s.

For Further Study

In the *Mercer Dictionary of the Bible*: FAITH AND FAITHLESSNESS; JAMES, LETTER OF; GENERAL LETTERS; JAMES. In other sources: P. H. Davids, *The Epistle of James: A Commentary on the Greek Text*, NIGTC; M. Dibelius, *James*, Herm; D. E. Hiebert, *The Epistle of James: Tests of a Living Faith*; S. Laws, *A Commentary on the Epistle of James*, HNTC; R. P. Martin, *James*, WBC; D. P. Scaer, *James, the Apostle of Faith: A Primary Christological Epistle for the Persecuted Church*; H. S. Songer, "James," *BBC*.

Commentary

An Outline

Introductory Address and Greeting, 1:1

James, the brother of Jesus and leader of the early church, greets the Jewish Christians dispersed from Jerusalem.

The Obedience of Faith, 1:2-27

The first chapter is composed of a series of ethical instructions. A definition of pure religion concludes the chapter.

Testing Produces Joy, 1:2-4

Appropriately, the first word is one of encouragement for those who face trials. The term *trials* (*peirasmos*) can mean either (1) temptation to do evil, or (2) trial or stress. Here it means the latter. The main thrust of these verses is that trials are an opportunity for joy and growth. Stubbornly refusing to give in to anxiety, despair, or grief is both the test and the testimony of authentic faith. These verses echo the saying of Jesus in Matt 5:11-12 (= Luke 6:22-23) and call not just for brave endurance but for joy in the midst of trial.

Prayer Produces Wisdom, 1:5-8

Two new concepts are introduced in these sayings: WISDOM (cf. 3:13-18) and double-mindedness (4:8). Wisdom is the ability to transcend our circumstances and see life from God's perspective.

Care must be taken to let James be James. Do not read James's words with Paul's meanings. By *faith* James does not mean a saving belief but loyalty and commitment under trial, faithful living. By *wisdom* James means God's gift of discernment and empowerment, something akin to Paul's understanding of the role of the Spirit, or being "in Christ." Unlike the rabbis, James does not depend on the study of TORAH for wisdom but on prayer. If wisdom is a gift from God, it is natural to insist that the Christian ask for it (Luke 11:13 = Matt 7:7-8). By *double-mindedness* James does not mean doubt but divided loyalty or conflict of interest.

Verses 7 and 8 have been handled variously by the translators: as distinct but related statements (KJV), as subject and predicate (RSV), or as appositional (NEB, JB, NIV, GNB, NRSV).

The doubter is a "two-souled person" who is unwilling to trust God completely, contrary to the SHEMA that calls for the faithful to love God with all their heart, soul, and might (Deut 6:4-5). The double-mind-

ed vacillate; they are uncommitted, refuse to take sides, and do one thing wishing they were doing another. When James encourages us to ask without doubting, he is not talking about drumming up a particular kind of feeling when we pray but about living out a steadfast trust in God.

Wealth Is Transient, 1:9-11.

These verses introduce James's concern for poverty and WEALTH. This theme too is deeply rooted in the teachings of Jesus, especially in Luke. The humble person is a Christian, but does James think of the rich person as a Christian or not? In contrast to the NEB, JB, and GNB, it is doubtful that James considered the rich man to be a brother also.

James contrasts the humble, lowly person with the arrogant, godless person. *Rich* and *poor* are not exclusively economic terms but carry contrasting connotations of pious humility and wicked arrogance. Here the social location of James's readers must be kept in mind.

Boasting usually carries a negative connotation in the NT, but it can also mean rejoicing and glorifying God. The reversal of fortunes is a common biblical theme (e.g., Luke 12:13-21; 16:19-31). The humble should rejoice because God has chosen them and will exalt them. Both the present grace of God and its future fulfillment call for exultation. James challenges us to see life from the vantage point of the fulfillment of God's redemptive work.

The lowly will be exalted and the wealth of the rich will pass away. The only thing that is worthy of our glory and praise is the completion of God's work. Wealth is meaningless in the face of death (Isa 40:6-7; Ps 103:15). James returns to the dangers of wealth in 2:5-7, 4:13-16, and 5:1-6.

Sin Results in Death, 1:12-16

This unit deals with both trials and temptations. Verse 12 returns to the theme of enduring trials (cf. 1:2-4). It offers two good reasons for enduring trials: (1) one who endures is blessed, and (2) that one will receive *the crown of life*, eternal life. The term for standing the test is one that was also used in connection with the testing of coins to determine whether they were genuine. The goal for the Christian is keep faith genuine in the midst of life's tests. The reward is salvation.

Verse 13 is the first instance of diatribe style: entering dialogue with an imaginary opponent. Does

God test persons of faith or tempt us to sin? Commentators are divided on the issue of whether the term *peirasmos* has the same meaning in v. 13 as it has had previously (i.e., "trial") or whether it now means "temptation." If the meaning is temptation, then v. 13 is the beginning of a new section that is joined to v. 12 by catchword linkage. Trials are to be endured, but temptations are to be resisted. Still, the two cannot be completely separated; some temptations may call for endurance also.

James warns us that we cannot blame our sin on God. God is not tempted, and God tempts no one. Neither does James introduce the notion of the demonic here (cf. 3:15; 4:7). Instead, he requires us to face our own culpability. James emphasizes the human side of sin. Whatever the origin of the temptation, we are the ones who choose to sin.

The EVIL we do begins with the desire we enjoy. The imagery is drawn from hunting and fishing. The fish is lured, and the prey is enticed to a trap (2 Pet 2:14, 18). The image is also used of the harlot enticing to FORNICATION. Hiebert (1979, 105) comments: "Temptation has its source not in the outer lure but in the inner lust."

Evil is seldom born full-grown. James therefore unveils the process of its growth. Sin always has the insidious power to grow into something we never intended. At its birth SIN is hardly recognizable, but when it has grown up it is death. Many people would like to sin and then be done with it; but sin, once born, always grows up. The problem with sin, therefore, is not that we may get caught but that sin itself kills.

God Gives Perfect Gifts, 1:17-21

These verses speak of God's good gifts and our need to receive them with gladness. Verse 17 sets forth the principle of God's goodness and changelessness. If God is good and cannot change, then God cannot entice people to evil. There is no variation in God's goodness either. It does not wax or wane. As the creator of the stars, God is the "father of lights." The technical terms in v. 17b, which have been translated variously, can all refer to astronomical phenomena. God neither changes nor is changed.

Verse 18 supplies an illustration of God's goodness. The issue is whether it refers to God's giving life in creation or in redemption. The reference to our being *a kind of first fruits of his creatures* tilts the matter in favor of God's activity in redemption. God's work, therefore, stands in opposition to sin. Sin brings

death; God brings forth new life. The new life begins in God's resolute will. The instrument of regeneration is the gospel message, but Christians are responsible for demonstrating the reality of the new life by the way they live. Our changeless, steadfast, creative God gives only good gifts, the chief of which is salvation; but this is just the beginning of God's work.

The cluster of three related, short sayings on receiving the word (vv. 19-21) is typical of Jewish wisdom (e.g., Prov 13:3; 15:1; 29:20; Eccl 7:9; Sir 5:11; 6:33). The reference to being *quick to listen* indicates a ready, responsive attitude. It is probably tied to hearing the preached word. *Slow to speak* counsels against hasty, ill-considered reactions. *Slow to anger* guards against a flash of temper, but it does not mean that anger has no place in Christian life.

Verse 21 begins with the common image of taking off clothes, which was often used to speak of repentance and BAPTISM (Rom 13:12; Eph 4:22; Col 3:8; 1 Pet 2:1). The word *all* reminds us that God is never satisfied with partial purity. Then, receive God's word with meekness—which means not weakness but humility. *The implanted word* is not inborn or "engrafted" (KJV). It is the seed planted in us through the word of God or the preaching of the gospel (compare Jesus' seed PARABLES). Salvation is still future, but *the implanted word* has the power to bring it about. Like sin, the word grows in a dynamic process. Rather than death, however, it results in salvation.

The Obedient Persevere, 1:22-25

These sayings continue James's refrain that the only faith that makes any difference is the faith that is obedient to God's direction. In the previous section he said that we should be quick to receive the word. Now he tells us what he means by that: be quick not only to listen but to obey. Hearing and doing was a common theme both in Jewish wisdom and in the teachings of Jesus (Deut 6:4-5; Matt 7:24-27; Rom 2:13). Having stated the principle in v. 22, James illustrates the point in vv. 23-24, and then draws a positive conclusion (v. 25). The illustration of the mirror was common in ancient ethical teachings (cf. 1 Cor 13:12). Mirrors were made of polished copper or bronze and were neither common nor very clear. The person who hears the word and does not seize the opportunity to respond with obedience is like the person who gets a chance to see what he or she looks like and then forgets.

By *the perfect law, the law of liberty* (v. 25), James probably means the higher standard of righteousness in the teachings of Jesus. Literally, James enjoins the reader to be not a "forgetful hearer but a workful doer." The beatitude then pronounces blessing on the doer *in their doing.*

The Obedient Care for the Oppressed, 1:26-27

These verses aptly sum up most of the message of the letter. The Christian is instructed to control the tongue, care for others, and resist temptation. Here is the positive side of hearing the word.

James echoes the prophets' critique of religion that is vain and futile. Some persons may do all the right, religious things, but if they *do not bridle their tongues,* their religion is futile. These persons are not hypocrites who pretend in order to deceive others; they themselves are deceived. They think they are religious but show no inner character that is consistent with the religion they profess.

Verse 27 offers a penetrating definition of pure religion that stands in contrast to the vain religion James has just described. The language is drawn from the practice of ritual cleanness. *Pure and undefiled* here means that which is free from moral pollution and corruption in the presence of God—the Father of those who are hurt by an abusive tongue, the Father of the widows and orphans also. *Orphans and widows* were traditional examples of the powerless and neglected (Isa 1:10-17; Deut 14:29; 24:17-22; Jer 5:28).

James spotlights both the personal and the social elements of true piety in v. 27: care for the helpless and moral purity, or as one commentator put it, "charity" and "chastity."

The Obedience of Faith in Worship and Works, 2:1-26

Chapter 2 offers the most sustained argument in the letter. Essentially it has two parts, one dealing with showing partiality and one demanding works of faithfulness.

The Heresy of Partiality, 2:1-13

Most commentators treat v. 1 as a prohibition, but it may also be an opening question (NRSV). The author gives an illustration of partiality in the context of a meeting of the church either for worship or to hear a legal case. The term for partiality or favoritism literally means "face receiving."

Two men enter the assembly. We are not told whether they are Christians or visitors. The rich person is distinguished by his rings and fine clothing. By contrast the POOR person (a *ptōchos*—one almost has to spit to say the word!) has dirty or shabby clothes and no rings. Both enter. How does the church respond? They do not see the persons. Instead, they take note of the clothing. The man in fine clothing is shown to a prominent seat. The poor man is told to stand out of the way or sit at someone's feet.

Verse 4 issues the first of the condemnations by means of a question that expects an affirmative answer. Yes, they have made judges of themselves, and they have *become judges with evil thoughts* (cf. Lev 19:15; Luke 18:6). Distinguishing between persons robs Christian community of its distinctive character.

Verses 5-7 expose the awful consequences of such partiality. God has chosen *the poor of the world* (cf. Deut 4:37; 7:7; 14:2; 1 Cor 1:26). God has refused to favor the wealth of the rich and has thereby nullified social distinctions. The role reversal is dramatic. In God's eyes it is not a person's *face* but one's *faith* that matters. The oppressed are favored and exalted. They will be *rich in faith,* heirs of the inheritance coveted by others. Verse 5 contains the only reference to the *kingdom* in James; it is promised to those who love God (1:12).

Two penetrating questions follow. James charges that the church shows favor to the rich, but it is the rich who oppress them. The next charge is the most devastating: the rich also blaspheme the excellent name that was invoked over you—which is probably an allusion to the name of Christ invoked in the context of BAPTISM. By siding with the rich, the church has taken the side of oppressors and blasphemers. Care must be taken today, of course, to distinguish the first-century connotations of rich and poor. These verses should not be treated as a general condemnation of wealth or as a blessing of poverty. The issue here is partiality, not possessions.

The argument of vv. 8-13 is that the law commands love of neighbor. Therefore, anyone who shows partiality has violated the law, and anyone who has violated any part of the law has violated the whole law. Love of neighbor (Lev 19:18) was viewed as the essence of the law. *Royal law* (v. 8) may mean the supreme law, God's law, or the OT law as interpreted by Jesus. Partiality, therefore, is a serious offense, not something to be tolerated or excused. Love, on the other hand, is partial to the needy and the neglected.

One cannot despise or dishonor another person by showing partiality and still please God. The principle of the unity of the law was taught by the rabbis. Since every commandment expresses the lawgiver's will, the violation of any commandment is an offense against the lawgiver. To drive home the point, James appeals to two central laws of the Decalogue, ADULTERY (IN THE OT) and MURDER. One who violates any commandment is a transgressor of the whole law.

Verse 12 draws the practical conclusion: speak and act as persons who are about to be judged by the law of FREEDOM (cf. 1:25). As elsewhere in James, an eschatological urgency is brought to bear on the ethical dimensions of life. The closing verse of this section reflects the paradox of judgment under the gospel. No MERCY will be shown to one who shows no mercy (Matt 5:7; Luke 16:19-31). Mercy does not triumph at the expense of JUSTICE, but the cross is the greatest testimony to the triumph of mercy.

The Relationship of Faith and Works, 2:14-26

James is apparently confronting a situation in which people in the church were professing faith in Christ but felt no need for moral purity or ethical living. Faith alone was regarded as essential, while works were unnecessary. James is not addressing the question of how one "gets saved." He is concerned about Christians who have grown complacent about living faithfully.

The argument takes the form of a question: *What good is it . . . if you say you have faith but do not have works?* (v. 14). In this hypothetical instance the person's faith is confirmed only by the claims he or she makes for it. This kind of argument by constructing an imaginary dialogue was characteristic of a diatribe between CYNICS and STOICS, but may have been common in synagogue sermons as well. The second question, *Can faith save you?* (v. 14) expects a negative answer. The question is deliberately provocative. One hardly wants to admit that a person of faith will not be saved. The implications are disturbing. The question, therefore, forces reflection on the nature of faith. Underlying James's attack may be his concern over misinterpretation of Paul's insistence that we are saved by faith alone.

Verses 15-16 give an illustration, and v. 17 draws the obvious conclusion. The illustration has parallels with Matt 25:35-45 and 1 John 3:17. A Christian meets a brother or sister who is in need of food and clothing, but all the Christian does is extend sympathy and best wishes. But prayer and sympathy are of little value when one refuses to share the basic necessities of life with those in need. The question, "What good

is it?" echoes v. 14. The obvious conclusion is that faith without works is dead. James is not arguing for the superiority of works over faith but for the inseparability of faith and works. An authentic faith will make a difference in how a person lives.

Verse 18 is difficult, and no solution to its difficulties is entirely satisfactory. An imaginary speaker interjects a comment, but is the speaker James's ally or his opponent, and how far does the comment extend? Is the comment only *"You have faith and I have works,"* or does it extend through v. 19? The problem is that the comment seems to express James's point, not that of an opponent. Although no satisfactory solution is evident, the gist of the objection is that faith and works may be separated, and it is this separation that James disallows. Works demonstrate the existence of a vibrant faith.

Even orthodox belief is no substitute for a living faith. Verse 19 seems to be part of James's response to the interlocutor, pointing to the intellectual content of faith: *you believe that.* The affirmation that *God is one* was the central affirmation of Jewish worship (Deut 6:4). Knowledge, even confession, without commitment is of no value. *Even the demons believe!*

The rhetorical question in v. 20 sets up an appeal to biblical characters: ABRAHAM and RAHAB. The question plays on the contrast between *works* (*ergōn*) and *barren* (*argē*). Abraham demonstrated faith by offering ISAAC. Verse 23 cites Gen 15:6, just as Paul does in Rom 4:3. The next statement, *You see that a person is justified by works and not by faith alone* (v. 24), seems to be a rebuttal to Rom 3:28: "For we hold that a person is justified by faith apart from works prescribed by the law." The difficulty is largely resolved when one pays close attention to the different problems JAMES and PAUL were addressing, and the difference in the meaning of the terms in each context. Paul was arguing that one is justified by reliance on God's grace rather than by works of the law. James was addressing complacent Christians, arguing that intellectual belief in God is of no value unless it gives rise to deeds that demonstrate one's faith.

Even recognizing these differences, it still appears that James is responding to Christians who are misinterpreting Paul and quoting Pauline slogans. James uses language that echoes Paul's teaching (the formula, *by faith alone* (v. 24), occurs elsewhere only in Paul's letters); appeals to Abraham as Paul does in Rom 4; quotes Gen 15:6 as Paul does in Rom 4:3; and his affirmation reverses the points of Paul's affirmation in

Rom 3:28. James was probably not responding directly to Paul, however, but to distortions of his teachings.

Rahab was a popular heroine in contemporary literature (Matt 1:5; Heb 11:31). She was considered to be a model of the ideal proselyte. Verse 26 concludes the chapter with an analogy: *faith without works* is as dead as a *body without . . . spirit* (cf. v. 17).

The Obedience of Faith in Words and Wisdom, 3:1-18

James 3 treats two subjects of vital importance to Christian living: controlling the tongue (vv. 1-12) and recognizing true wisdom (vv. 13-18).

The Power of Words, 3:1-12

The tongue can easily serve as a barometer of character and spiritual maturity (Matt 12:34-37), so control of one's speech is not optional for Christians. The chapter begins with a specific warning that *not many . . . should become teachers*. The reason given is that teachers will be judged more strictly than others.

As sensitive as James is to the many subtle forms of sin that can insinuate themselves into the life of a Christian, it still holds out the ideal of perfection. By steadfastness "you may be perfect" (1:4, NRSV *mature*), and faith is perfected by works (2:22). An echo can again be found in the sermon on the mount: "You, therefore, must be perfect, as your heavenly Father is perfect" (Matt 5:48). James does not require perfection but uses it to underscore the difficulty of complete mastery over one's speech.

Two metaphors drive home the point that a small member can control the whole body: *bridle* and *rudder*. Although the metaphors lend themselves to the positive sense that one small member could actually harness and control the whole body, James emphasizes the difficulty of harnessing the tongue rather than its power to subdue a wild or undisciplined body. The paragraph reaches a pointed conclusion in v. 5a. The tongue's influence does not correspond to its size. James paints graphic, disturbing pictures of the tongue's potential for perversity and leaves it up to each individual to decide what to do about the problem of unrestrained speech.

The third metaphor introduces the tongue's potential for destruction: a spark can destroy a whole forest. Verse 6 is so difficult to translate that commentators have often suggested the text is corrupt. The NRSV, however, renders it intelligible by simply reversing the sequence of the second and third clauses and translat-

ing the verb as passive (*is placed*). The tongue can stain, defile, or render a person unclean before God.

The phrase *the cycle of nature* is peculiar. It reflects the view that life is an eternal, cyclical procession. The phrase had entered into common usage, however, and James uses it without adopting the philosophy it once conveyed. The tongue not only exposes the whole realm of evil within us; like a spark it sets on fire the whole arena of human life. Consequently, the tongue can ignite far greater EVIL than we may ever intend. The source of the tongue's iniquity is finally revealed: hell itself.

The progressive growth of evil can be charted through this tangled verse. GEHENNA, place of torment and home of demons, the inexhaustible source of iniquity, lights the fiery tongue. The tongue introduces the whole world of evil into our bodies and puts to flame the whole order of life. Paul would have introduced a list of vices; James paints a graphic picture of the most destructive fire imaginable.

Verses 7 and 8 advance James's series of hyperboles on the evils of the tongue by comparing its untamed and poisonous nature to that of wild beasts. The second point of comparison follows quickly: the tongue is *full of deadly poison*. Few things evoke fear more quickly than the sight of a scorpion or a poisonous snake. The hissing tongue is full poison (Ps 140:3; Rom 3:13). Who can still claim, "but words will never hurt me"?

Having condemned the wild, poisonous nature of the tongue, James finally gives specific examples. The tongue is fickle. James did not know the idiom "forked tongue," but it expresses the tongue's inconsistency. The tongue is used both to curse and to bless, and that *ought not to be so*. This admonition may refer to casual cursing, but James may be referring to the church's worship, and specifically to preachers who both praise God and invoke curses on others in God's name. One cannot bless God and curse those made in his image. Such speech is evidence of the double-mindedness James condemns (1:8; 4:8).

Two further metaphors follow, illustrating the incompatibility of blessing and cursing. Springs were vital to life in Palestine. Yet, in the same area one found both fresh and bitter water—but never from the same opening. Each spring was known for the water it produced. Similarly, a fig tree cannot produce olives, nor can a grapevine produce figs (cf. Matt 7:16). Verse 12 ends abruptly. The shorter text reads: *No more can salt water yield fresh*. The longer text draws the statement in line with the previous metaphors: "Thus no spring can yield both salt water and fresh water." The longer text, however, says no more than v. 11, while the shorter text maintains that one product cannot become another.

The Wisdom from Above, 3:13-18

Verses 13-17 form a unit that contrasts the evidences of wisdom from above with earthly wisdom. Verse 18 provides a transition to the sayings on conflict that follow in 4:1-12.

The unit begins with a question that invites self-examination. An imperative follows. If one has both wisdom and discernment, then let that person demonstrate spiritual maturity not in devastating arguments but in the good works that come from *gentleness born of wisdom* (v. 13). If faith results in works (2:14-26), so too true wisdom is manifested in one's conduct and manner of life. True wisdom produces humility not arrogance.

Verse 14 conveys the implication that the church is plagued by bitter jealousy and ambition. These may be especially evident in its teachers and would-be leaders. James echoes words of Jesus again at this point: these sins come from the heart (cf. Matt 15:19). The admonitions that follow may stand in coordinate relationship to one another ("do not boast about it or deny the truth," NIV) or causal relationship ("do not be arrogant and so lie against the truth," NASB).

Verse 15 explains why boasting is excluded. Ambition and arrogance are the fruit of a kind of wisdom, but not the true wisdom that comes down *from above*. True wisdom is one of God's good and perfect gifts (1:17). Nevertheless, the wisdom of the arrogant and ambitious who create dissension in the church is indeed inspired: it is inspired by the devil. The three adjectives form a crescendo of sinful alienation from God. Such wisdom is *earthly, unspiritual, and devilish* (v. 15).

Verse 16 pushes the argument one step further: if counterfeit wisdom is exposed by jealousy and selfish ambition, these in turn give rise to disorder and every kind of evil. True wisdom bears seven identifying marks (v. 17):

1. *Pure.* Like the works of God, the life of his people should be morally perfect and undefiled.

2. Ready for peace (*peaceable*). The wisdom from above is therefore diametrically opposed to the divisiveness of the earthly, sensual, and demonic inspiration of the arrogant and ambitious.

3. *Gentle* or "considerate" (NEB, NIV). In a position of strength, the wise person is considerate of those who might otherwise be dominated or manipulated.

4. Compliant (*willing to yield*). In a position of weakness, the wise one is reasonable, yielding, and obedient.

5. *Full of mercy and good fruit.* True wisdom results in the true religion (acts of mercy, 1:27) and true faith (acts of charity, 2:15-17).

6. *Without a trace of partiality* or "unwavering" (NASB). The sense is either that true wisdom does not "make a distinction" or that it is not fickle and inconsistent—like the tongue that both blesses and curses (vv. 9-12).

7. Sincere. Having nothing to hide, wisdom is *without . . . hypocrisy*, genuine. It can be taken at face value.

The aphorism in v. 18 closes this section on the contrasting effects of the two wisdoms. Its interpretation hinges on two issues: (1) is *the harvest of righteousness* (a) an appositional genitive (in which case the fruit is righteousness) or (b) a subjective genitive (in which case righteousness produces its own fruit); and (2) is the fruit *sown in peace* (a) *by* or (b) *for* those who make peace? The similarity to the blessing of the peacemakers (Matt 5:9) is unmistakable. Peace and righteousness are mutually dependent; each requires the other. The mark of true wisdom is, therefore, its capacity to produce peace and righteousness. Peacemaking and jealousy are antithetical; one creates unity, the other division.

The Obedience of Faith in Community, 4:1–5:6

As with most of James, the section that follows is composed of loosely related instructions for ethical living. Various divisions of the chapters have been proposed. Here Jas 4:1–5:6 is viewed as a series of exhortations on living faithfully in community. Three of the chief dangers to the communities of faith are dissension (4:1-12), presumption (5:1-6), and inappropriate use of wealth (5:1-6).

Faith as a Response to Dissension, 4:1-12

This section is an extension of the previous one in that it exposes the consequences of earthly wisdom: the quarrels that destroy (vv. 1-3), the world that corrupts (vv. 4-6), the humility that restores (vv. 7-10), and the judgment on those who judge (vv. 11-12).

The first verse raises two questions. The first diagnoses the situation; the second challenges the readers to accept James's diagnosis of the cause of quarreling and infighting. The wars and fightings are generally understood as metaphorical references to quarrels and factions within the community. The second question suggests that the quarrels are caused by "pleasures" that war in your members. The thought that our pleasures are the cause of fighting among members of the Christian community places pride, ambition, and vanity in their true context.

The charge *you . . . murder* seems so harsh as a charge concerning the church that Erasmus (1519 ed. of Greek NT) proposed that the text was corrupt and that "you envy" (*phthoneite*) should be read instead of "you murder" (*phoneuete*). This conjecture was accepted by Calvin and the KJV, but is now generally rejected. There is no manuscript support for the conjecture. On the other hand, murder is often connected metaphorically with sins of the tongue.

The tragedy is that by fighting we do not obtain what we desire. On the other hand, we have only to ask God for what we need. God is the giver of every good and perfect gift (1:17). Again, we ask but we do not receive because we do not ask rightly. James does not say that we are asking for sinful things, but we are asking sinfully. We are not praying for forgiveness or righteousness, but to further our own interests. We may ask for good things for the wrong reasons. This does not mean, of course, that all unanswered prayer is due to praying wrongly.

Using a term that evokes echoes of Hosea's condemnation of Israel, James charges that such Christians are adulterers and adulteresses (v. 4). *World* is used here in the hostile sense found in the Johannine literature (1 John 2:15-17). God and the world are set in opposition to one another, so that friendship with one means hostility toward the other (Matt 6:24; Luke 16:13). The desire for pleasure divides and distorts our entire existence. This forced choice means that neutrality toward God is impossible.

Verse 5 announces a quotation from scripture, but the remainder of v. 5 cannot be found anywhere in the OT. Psalms 41:2 and 83:3 come as close as any reference, but James may paraphrase material such as Gen 6:3 or Exod 20:5. The first part of v. 6 promises that God does not readily give us up. Instead, he gives more grace. God helps wavering Christians!

There are ten imperatives in vv. 7-10. Together they provide an expanded definition of repentance.

1. *Submit . . . to God*. The imperatives that follow explain this first, basic demand. It is a military term meaning to put oneself under the command of a superior.

2. *Resist the devil*. The second command is the counterpart to the first. The first requires the second. Again, James uses a military metaphor: to stand against.

3. *Draw near to God*. This is a cultic term for worshiping God.

4. *Cleanse your hands*. This is the language of ceremonial cleansing (Exod 30:19-21; 2 Cor 7:1).

5. *Purify your hearts*. Again, ceremonial language. To cleanse one's heart means to cleanse one's entire inner being (cf. Ps 24:4).

6. *Lament* (lit. "be wretched"). True repentance is accompanied by remorse.

7. *Mourn*.

8. *Weep* (Luke 6:25; Mark 14:72).

9. *Let your laughter be turned to mourning and your joy to dejection*.

10. *Humble yourselves*. Any other road to exaltation is the result of sinfulness.

True repentance, however, does not lack for results. Three promises follow the ten imperatives: (1) the devil *will flee from you*; (2) *God will draw near to you*; and (3) God *will exalt you*.

Verses 11-12 form a conclusion to Jas 3:1–4:12 in that they return to the sins of speech and dissension within the community. Verse 11 begins with the only imperative in these two verses. The command is not to disparage or belittle one another. The present tense implies that such disparagement is currently taking place. The issue is not whether what is being said is true or not. James leaves no room for those who would justify their damaging words by saying, "Well, I am just telling the truth." The rest of vv. 11-12 gives a theological justification for this command: (1) The one who disparages or judges a brother disparages or judges the law: "inasmuch as ye have done it unto the least of these my brethren ye have done it unto God's law" (cf. Matt 25:40).

The command not to slander appears both in the OT (Lev 19:16) and in the NT (Rom 1:30; 2 Cor 12:20). (2) Breaking the law highhandedly implies that we are not bound by the law. (3) If we place ourselves above the law, as judges, we have usurped God's prerogative. We have taken God's place as the lawgiver. Are we able to give a better law or a more righteous judgment? God is the only one who is able to save and to destroy. Breaking the law by disparaging others is therefore a disparagement of God. It is blasphemy. The conclusion of v. 12 puts us in our place again: *So who, then, are you to judge your neighbor?*

Faith as a Response to Presumption, 4:13-17

This section turns again to the rich and the results of love of the world. James has in mind here the merchants in particular, the small businessmen who worked ambitiously and industriously, traveling to whatever place held the prospect of profit. James does not condemn their business dealings as dishonest. What he condemns is the presumptuous disregard of God's sovereignty as they make their plans. The businessmen are merely an illustration of the attitude that ignores God in our daily affairs. Their plans assume that they are in full control of their lives. First, they do not know the future. Second, their lives are mortal and transitory. James is not saying that it is wrong to make plans, only that we ought to live our lives under God's sovereignty.

The saying "If the Lord wills" (RSV) is common in hellenistic writings. It may express either genuine or superficial piety. James, therefore, may intend a bit of irony. If the pagans at least say, "If God wills," then should not Christians recognize their finiteness and place the planning of their lives under God's sovereignty? By placing our lives under God's will we also have a sure defense against dread, despair, and fear of the future. In contrast, those who worship God on Sunday and live in complete disregard of God's sovereignty the rest of the week show an attitude of sinful arrogance.

Verse 17 is a maxim or proverb, such as James quotes in 2:13 or 3:18. If we know what is good and do not do it, we sin. The word order emphasizes that such compromise is nothing less than sin. Sin is not related just to certain absolutes, therefore, but also to the level of our spiritual maturity and discernment.

A Warning to the Rich, 5:1-6

With this paragraph James shifts both his target and his tone. He offers a sharp, prophetic warning to the rich landowners who oppress the poor. These are apparently not members of the community because he never calls them brothers (as in 5:7-11). He does not call them to repent; he laments the judgment on them. His primary concern, however, is to dissuade Christians from falling into envy towards the power and privilege of the wealthy.

The call to weep and howl (RSV) depicts a scene of utter despair and misery. The present participle vividly describes the scene as already occurring. In vv. 2-3 James describes the effects of the judgment upon the wealth of the rich. Perfect tense verbs are used, as though the judgment had already been accomplished.

1. Their wealth is ruined, decayed, *rotted*. We may have a list of three types of wealth: foodstuffs, garments, and metals.
2. Their garments are *moth-eaten*.
3. Their *gold and silver have rusted*. These metals, of course, cannot rust. So James is either thinking of the coins of the time that had so much alloy that they did rust, or else he is describing the corruption of riches by a power greater than rust.

Moreover, the rich will be condemned by their wealth. The rust will bear witness against them that they did not use their wealth responsibly. The rust that eats at the metals in an awful turn of events will eat at their flesh. The final irony of this verse is that they have been storing up treasure *in the last days*. While they should have been preparing for the Lord's coming by righteous living, they have hoarded their goods and oppressed the poor. The goods they hoarded now condemn them (Matt 6:19-21; Luke 12:15-21; 16:19-31).

Verse 4 describes the charges against landowners. The charges, though, are brought by the wages they have wrongfully held back from those who labored in their fields. Jewish law required that laborers be paid at the end of each day, since some depended on the day's wage for food. The harvest, of course, was a time of great income for the landowner, but he defrauds the poor who work his fields. These cries rise to the Lord, the Lord of Hosts! (cf. Isa. 5:7-9). The wealth of the rich has been gained at the expense of the poor.

The rich have lived a life of ease and pleasure, supported by the suffering and oppression of others. They have fattened their hearts (cholesterol!) like fatted calves that continue eating even on the day of their slaughter. Now the day of the Lord has come, and they themselves are the fatted calves. Yet they live in complete disregard for the imminence of the Judgment.

Verse 6 states the third and most serious offense. These landowners have condemned and killed the righteous. They have killed the righteous sufferer, perhaps by means of judicial proceedings. Some see it as an allusion to the crucifixion of Jesus or the martyrdom of James the Just. Neither is really called for, however. "The righteous" is probably a collective term (NIV).

The Obedience of Faith in Patience, Oaths, and Prayer, 5:7-18

The remaining verses of the letter can be divided into four sections: a call for patience (vv. 7-11), rejection of profanity (v. 12), the power of prayer (vv. 13-18), and restoring the wayward (5:19-20). The main themes of the letter are found in this closing section: rich—poor, the need to control speech, concern for harmony within the community, and the need for endurance.

A Call for Patience, 5:7-11

The word for patience means literally to have a long temper, or we might say "a long fuse." James turns from condemnation of the rich in 5:1-6 to concern for the community. Although the poor may be abused by the rich, James calls on Christians to be patient. Some have understood *the coming of the Lord* as a reference to God's coming in judgment, as in the OT prophets, but most interpreters are convinced it is a reference to the PAROUSIA of the risen Lord.

James draws an illustration from the life of the small farmer. The farmer awaits the "precious fruit from the earth" (RSV). His livelihood depends on the harvest. He plants his carefully saved seed, hopes, waits, and stretches his resources and rations—everything depends on the harvest. *The early and late rains* are characteristic of the climate of the east end of the Mediterranean. The early rains came in October and November, the late rains in April and May. Without the early rains the crops would not survive; without the late rains the harvest would be small.

Verse 8 draws the conclusion: "So you be patient also." The best response to impatience is new resolve. The basis for such resolve is offered by the promise that the coming of the Lord is "at hand" (RSV).

Discouragement and impatience can easily lead to grumbling, and grumbling to disunity. James therefore warns the Christians not to "moan" about one another. Even if some complaining about the rich might be tolerated (vv. 1-6), the Christians should not turn their impatience against one another. Both hope and judgment are expressed by the rest of v. 9. Don't complain about one another lest you be judged also. The judge is standing at the doors even now (Mark 13:29; Rev 3:20). He is coming to judge both the rich and the poor. Wait on his judgment and do not incur condemnation at the last minute by sowing dissension within the community of believers.

Christians are not in a unique situation just because they have suffered. The prophets suffered too. The Christians will do well to take the prophets as an example of suffering and patience. They too spoke in the name of the Lord. Verse 11 turns to a specific example of patience: Job. Actually JOB does not seem all that patient in the OT book, so James may be referring to contemporary tradition regarding Job. This is the only reference to Job in the NT, and James speaks of Job's endurance or steadfastness rather than his patience. The main point is that Job remained faithful in spite of his suffering. The issue is whether we will endure and not lose faith.

The Lord is full of compassion and mercies. The one who is patient and endures trial faithfully will see the good that the Lord is doing.

Rejection of Oaths, 5:12

This verse appears with little context. It may be that James has in mind again the dangers of the tongue and the ways it disrupts community. Harold Songer (1972, 136) finds the sequence of admonitions meaningful: "Suffering Christians (vv. 7-11) must guard their speech and not grumble (v. 9) or swear (v. 12) . . . but pray (vv. 13-18) and confess their sins (v. 16)."

This verse is closely paralleled by Matt 5:33-37 (cf. Matt 23:16-22). James's concern is not oaths sworn in court but the practice of using oaths in everyday discourse. This practice had developed to the point that some oaths were binding, while other, similar formulas were not. One could give the appearance of swearing a sacred oath, therefore, but actually use a defective form with no intention of being bound by it. Jesus and James both condemn such hypocrisy. If this is the central concern, then James is saying that Christians should always speak in such a way that no one would ever doubt our word. Oaths would then no longer be needed.

The Power of Prayer, 5:13-18

Following the warning against swearing in the previous verse, James turns to the positive admonition to be diligent in prayer. The section opens with three questions: Is anyone *among you suffering*? Is *any cheerful*? Is *any among you sick*? The answers give his response: Let him *pray*. Let him *sing praise*. Let him call for the *elders of the church*. Prayer is not just an aid in time of distress; it is the appropriate response to every circumstance in life.

The first question seems not to have illness in view but rather distress, misfortune, or calamity. In the NT the term for singing is used of singing praises to God in public worship (1 Cor 14:15; Eph 5:19). Don't forget God in the good times.

Is any sick? The term can denote any illness or weakness, here apparently a serious illness. *The elders of the church* were probably the senior, respected men of the community. Prayer is primary. The anointing with OIL is mentioned in a participle. There is no instruction to consecrate the oil. It is the common term for olive oil, which was at times used medicinally (Mark 6:13; Luke 10:34). Here it is an external sign of the inward power of prayer. James is apparently describing a common practice of the church rather than prescribing a new procedure. James does not prescribe this procedure for every illness, nor does he assure that we will always be cured or spared from death. Obviously that is not the case. Instead, James is describing a procedure by which one in need is upheld by the church and God's mercy and healing power is invoked.

The last part of v. 15 forms a transition to James's closing emphasis—rooting sin out of our lives. Sin and sickness were closely connected in popular thought. James does not contend that sickness is always the result of sin, but he allows that it may be. Prayer can deal with both sickness and sin. In times of need we are to pray for God's care and deliverance.

James exhorts Christians to confess their sins to one another. He does not say the sick person is to confess his or her sins to the elders. He seems to have in mind open, public confessions of specific sins in the context of worship and prayer for one another. Apart from confession we cannot experience forgiveness. Excesses are to be avoided, of course. In some instances specific, public confession would not lead to restoration or harmony.

The latter part of v. 16 states the theme of the whole section. The entreaty or petition *of the righteous [person] is powerful and effective.* The prayer of ordinary persons has great power when God makes it effective. James is not just talking about the prayer of saints. He illustrates the power of prayer by appealing

to the example of ELIJAH. The period of three and a half years is based on a rabbinic estimate of the time of the drought based on 1 Kgs 18:1. Elijah is the fourth OT character James has used, following Abraham (2:21-24); Rahab (2:25); Job (5:11). James takes pains to say that Elijah was human and subject to the same suffering the rest of us endure. Legend emphasized the effectiveness of Elijah's prayer. James argued that it wasn't Elijah; it was the power of prayer at work.

Concluding Exhortation: Restoring the Wayward, 5:19-20

A Christian's responsibility for sinners does not stop with prayer. James closes the letter by calling on us to take responsibility for erring Christians. To wander *from the truth* means to turn aside from God's will and live in moral corruption. James is not talking about converting an unbeliever but restoring an erring brother or sister. He does not specify how this restoration takes place. Death is the final result of sin. If we minimize the gravity of the erring one's position, we also minimize the significance of restoration.

One who restores another also covers a multitude of sins. The term to *cover* comes from the OT and means to secure their forgiveness (Ps 32:1; 85:2). Some commentators take this to mean that the agent of restoration has secured forgiveness for his or her own sins, but the idea that meritorious works bring forgiveness cuts against the NT emphasis that sin is forgiven by grace.

This last admonition, to be active in turning others from sin, captures the purpose of the letter. So, with no closing greetings, it ends abruptly, leaving us to consider its claim upon our lives.

Works Cited

Davids, P. H. 1982. *The Epistle of James: A Commentary on the Greek Text.* NIGTC.
Hiebert, D. Edmond. 1979. *The Epistle of James: Tests of a Living Faith.*
Luther's Works. Ed. Theodore G. Tapert. 1955–1958.
Songer, Harold S. 1972. "James." *BBC.*

First Peter

J. Ramsey Michaels

Introduction

First Peter is one of two NT letters bearing the name of the apostle PETER. Nothing in the letter itself identifies it explicitly as the "first" of the two. In the NT it is given the title "First Peter" or "the First Epistle of Peter" because of 2 Pet 3:1, where that work refers to itself as "this second letter," and perhaps also because in "Second Peter" the apostle is represented as expecting his own death very soon (2 Pet 1:14). First Peter presents itself not as the beginning of an ongoing correspondence, but as a once-for-all directive from the apostle to a large number of Christian congregations spread over five Roman provinces of Asia Minor (1:1).

Authorship and Genre

The authorship of 1 Peter is disputed because its elegant Greek style is believed to be inconsistent with the tradition that Simon Peter was an uneducated Galilean (Acts 4:13). Defenders of Petrine authorship, such as E. G. Selwyn and Peter Davids, have resorted to the theory that Peter's coworker *Silvanus* (5:12) was responsible for putting some of Peter's ideas into good Greek style. This in effect makes Silvanus the real author of the letter. More likely, Silvanus (or Silas) was simply the messenger who delivered the letter to its Asian destination, just as he helped deliver the decree of the JERUSALEM COUNCIL to ANTIOCH according to Acts 15:22-32.

A better theory is that 1 Peter was a semiofficial communication from the church at ROME. Like *1 Clement* at the end of the first century C.E., 1 Peter claims to be written from a congregation in *Babylon* (5:13), which by the latter half of the century had become a designation for the city of Rome (cf. Rev 17:4-5, 18). If Peter was the Roman congregation's resident apostle at the time, it is not surprising that a circular letter from Rome to Christians scattered throughout the Asian provinces might have been written under his supervision and authority. If so, the letter's style can be attributed to an anonymous learned scribe without resorting to theories about Silvanus.

The appropriateness of a circular letter from *Babylon* (5:13) to the Diaspora, or *Dispersion* (1:1) is unmistakable, for Babylon was the city that had first scattered the Jews from their homeland in 587/6 B.C.E. Peter is drawing an analogy between the Jewish community scattered throughout the world and the worldwide Christian community of his day (5:9). The church at Rome is telling its sister churches in the provinces that they all share a common lot as *aliens and exiles* in the ROMAN EMPIRE (1:1; 2:11), and that they must know how to respond to slander, hostile questioning, and even persecution, whether from the populace or the imperial authorities.

Another major objection to the traditional view that Peter wrote 1 Peter is the assumption, itself based on tradition, that the apostle Peter died in the persecution under Nero in 64 C.E., a decade before Jews and Christians began referring to Rome as "Babylon." The traditions about Peter's death are relatively late, and the later they are the more detailed and specific they become (as, e.g., in *ActPet* 30-41). John 21:18-19 may or may not suggest that Peter was martyred, but in any case gives no information as to when or under what circumstances. The same is true of the reference to his death in 2 Pet 1:14. What is usually considered the earliest explicit reference to Peter's martyrdom merely states that Peter "suffered not one or two, but many trials, and having thus given testimony went to the glorious place which was his due" (*1 Clem* 5.4).

Although there is no consensus on the authorship of 1 Peter, the letter is well known and well attested in the ancient church (POLYCARP, PAPIAS, IRENAEUS, Tertullian, Clement, and Origen; see Michaels 1988, xxxi–xxxiv). The burden of proof still rests with those who want to assign it to someone other than Peter.

Integrity

Many questions have been raised in the past about the integrity of 1 Peter. The apparent sharp break between 4:11 and 4:12 has suggested to some that a letter consisting of 1:1–4:11 dealt with persecution as a rather remote possibility, and that 4:12–5:11 was added as a postscript when the persecution suddenly broke out. Alternatively, some have argued that 1:3–4:11 was not a letter at all but a baptismal sermon, or even a baptismal liturgy, later framed into a letter by the addition of 1:1-2 and 4:12–5:14.

In keeping with more recent literary approaches to the NT, the tendency in the past two or three decades has been rather to interpret 1 Peter as a literary unit, and in most instances as an actual letter. Although there has been continued recognition of rhetorical forms in 1 Peter such as "household duty codes" (2:18– 3:7), and even of possible hymnic or creedal fragments (e.g., 1:18-21; 2:21-25; 3:18-22), these are now generally discussed under the heading of Peter's "sources" (along with the OT and the sayings of Jesus), not as generic features which somehow call into question the work's integrity or its identity as a real letter.

For Further Study

In the *Mercer Dictionary of the Bible*: ESCHATOLOGY IN THE NT; ETHICS IN THE NEW TESTAMENT; GENERAL LETTERS; PERSECUTION IN THE NT; PETER; PETER, LETTERS OF; ROME; SUFFERING IN THE NT.

In other sources: W. J. Dalton, *Christ's Proclamation to the Spirits: A Study of 1 Pet 3:18–4:6*; P. H. Davids, *The First Epistle of Peter*, NICNT; J. N. D. Kelly, *A Commentary on the Epistles of Peter and of Jude*, HNTC; J. R. Michaels, *1 Peter*, WBC, and *Word Biblical Themes: 1 Peter*; E. G. Selwyn, *The First Epistle of St. Peter*; C. H. Talbert, ed., *Perspectives on First Peter*, NABPR/SSS 9.

Commentary

An Outline

> I. Greetings, 1:1-2
> II. The Identity of the People of God, 1:3–2:10
> A. The Great Salvation, 1:3-12
> B. The New Way of Life, 1:13-25
> C. The Chosen Community, 2:1-10
> III. The Responsibilities of the People of God, 2:11–4:11
> A. Respect for Everyone, 2:11-17
> B. Slaves and Masters, 2:18-25
> C. Wives and Husbands, 3:1-7
> D. Seeking Peace, 3:8-12
> E. The Hope of Vindication, 3:13–4:6
> F. Christian Community, 4:7-11
> IV. The Responsibilities of Elders, 4:12–5:11
> A. The Fiery Ordeal, 4:12-19
> B. Elders and Their Congregations, 5:1-11
> V. Conclusion, 5:12-14

Greetings, 1:1-2

Peter, like PAUL, identifies himself as *apostle of Jesus Christ*, but writes to a far larger audience than Paul. While Paul wrote only to individual congregations, or (in one instance) "the churches of Galatia" (Gal 1:2), Peter's audience encompasses five Roman provinces roughly equivalent to present-day Turkey. He addresses his readers as Christian believers chosen by the God of Israel and thereby alienated from the religion and culture of the ROMAN EMPIRE. Like the Jews, they are a Diaspora (cf. Jas 1:1), a chosen people scattered throughout the empire. Peter attributes their conversion to God's foreknowledge and the purifying work of the HOLY SPIRIT. Like the Jews in Moses' time who promised to obey God as the blood of sacrificial animals was sprinkled over them (Exod 24:3-8), these Christians have obediently accepted the blood of Jesus Christ poured out for them. Peter wishes them abundant *grace and peace*.

The Identity of the People of God, 1:3–2:10

The Great Salvation, 1:3-12

A long introductory "blessing" embraces the present experience and future hope of Christians, setting both against the background of biblical (and extrabiblical) prophecies out of the Jewish past. The whole section is loosely held together by relative pronouns (e.g., vv. 6, 8, 10, 12), as Peter moves back and forth between praise of God and the instruction of his readers.

1:3-9. Salvation as revelation and joy. Peter praises God for the power evident in raising Jesus Christ from the dead, and for the mercy evident in giving Christians (himself included) a new birth as children of God with a sure promise of eternal salvation (v. 3). Shifting from *us* to *you*, he assures his readers that God will keep them safe through whatever persecutions they may now be facing (vv. 5-6). His knowledge of their actual circumstances in the Roman provinces seems general and rather limited, yet he is confident that whatever is happening to them now is God's way of testing their faithfulness, as gold is tested and purified *by fire* (v. 7; cf. Ps 66:10 and Wis 3:5-6). He is confident that their faith will turn out stronger than ever, bringing them *praise and glory and honor* at the time "when Jesus Christ appears" (v. 7b).

Peter's mention of the "appearing," or "revealing," of Jesus in v. 7b reinforces and personalizes his reference to *salvation ready to be revealed in the last time* (v. 5b; cf. 1:13; 4:13; 5:4). "Salvation" *is* JESUS, now invisible, but soon to become visible in power and splendor. To be saved is to see him when he appears, and know the joy of his presence (vv. 6, 8). Until then, one must love him and trust in him sight unseen (v. 8). *Indescribable and glorious joy* (v. 8; cf. 4:13b) is still future, reserved in HEAVEN for all who love Jesus even though he is now hidden from human view (cf. 1 Cor 2:9; 2 Tim 4:8).

1:10-12. Salvation's witnesses. Salvation to Peter is the "end," or goal, of Christian faith (v. 9), not its beginning, but he reminds his readers that this future salvation and the sufferings that made it possible were prophesied long ago (v. 10). By mentioning both *prophets* (v. 10) and *angels* (v. 12b), Peter places his audience at the end of time, and at the center of the universe. The ancient Jewish prophets were already Christians in that the *spirit of Christ* (v. 11) was speaking through them about the *sufferings* intended for Christ (i.e., his death on the cross), and the "glorious events" to follow: his resurrection from the dead, his journey to heaven (cf. 3:19, 22), and his final "appearing" again on earth. Not even the prophets understood when or how this would all take place. They tried to find out, but God told them it was not for them or for their time. Instead, Peter claims, it is for our benefit today (cf. Matt 13:17 = Luke 10:24). The Holy Spirit sent from heaven has made the good news known through missionaries in Asia Minor, and even God's angels long to look down from heaven on the wonders of human salvation (v. 12b).

The New Way of Life, 1:13-25

1:13-21. Hope and holiness. *Therefore* in v. 13 introduces a call to action on the basis of the salvation just described. Yet Peter cannot stop celebrating the salvation itself. The section begins, like the preceding one, with *hope* (v. 13; cf. 1:3), and ends on the same note (v. 21). Peter keeps weaving into his call to

action reminders of what God has done and will do for Christian believers (compare such phrases as *the grace that Jesus Christ will bring you when he is revealed*, v. 13; the holy one *who called you*, v. 15; and all of vv. 18-21). Consequently, the call to action is general, not specific. The imperatives of hope (v. 13) and godly fear (v. 17) have more to do with attitudes of mind than with behavior, and are directed not toward other people but toward God. Only the command to *be holy* (vv. 15-16) focuses on day-by-day Christian living. To be holy as God is holy (cf. Lev 19:2, which Peter cites) was traditionally understood as a religious or cultic goal, but Peter identifies holiness here as something expressed in *conduct* (v. 15). "Holy conduct" for Peter is something that runs counter to the values of Roman society (i.e., *the futile ways inherited from your ancestors* [v. 18]), but only in later sections of his letter (e.g., in 2:11–3:12), will he define it more concretely.

In vv. 18-21 Peter resumes his celebration of God's saving work through Jesus Christ. He describes Christian salvation here as "redemption" (*ransom*) or release from slavery by the payment of a price. The price is not *silver or gold* (cf. Isa 52:3), but something far more precious—the blood of Christ understood as a ransom (cf. Mark 10:45; Titus 2:14). Drawing on the Exodus story (e.g., Exod 12:1-7), Peter compares the blood of Christ to *that of a lamb without defect or blemish* (v. 19; cf. Exod 12:5), and places Christ's death in the context of God's eternal plan, from *before the foundation of the world* to *the end of the ages* (v. 20). By the shedding of Christ's blood (cf. v. 2) and his *resurrection . . . from the dead* (cf. v. 3), the readers of this letter have become for the first time "believers in God" (v. 21)—the God of Israel—and sharers in Israel's redemption. The implication is clear that these Christian readers are gentiles by birth and not Jews.

1:22-25. Undying love. Peter now brings his argument to a focus in a single ethical command: *love one another deeply from the heart* (v. 22b). The love command proper is framed by references to purification through OBEDIENCE (v. 22a; cf. vv. 2, 18-19), and spiritual rebirth (v. 23; cf. v. 3). The key word is *deeply* or "constantly" (cf. 4:8). Love among Christians should be as strong and as lasting as their faith *tested in the fire* (cf. v. 7). Theirs is an undying love because they have been reborn by the planting of *imperishable seed*—that is, by the preaching of the Christian gospel understood as *the living and enduring word of God*

(vv. 23-25). Peter drives home his point with a citation of Isa 40:6b, 8: all humanity fades away like the grass and the flowers, but *the word of the Lord endures forever*. To Peter the word of the eternal God, the message spoken by Jesus the Lord (cf. Mark 13:31), and the good news about Jesus announced by his followers (cf. v. 12) all amount to the same thing—an eternal Word summoning those who hear it to eternal and genuine love for each other.

The Chosen Community, 2:1-10

2:1-3. Growing toward salvation. For the time being, Peter continues on the theme of hearing the word of God, without exploring further the love command. With the image of rebirth still in mind, he compares his readers to *newborn infants* (v. 2), urging them to do what comes naturally to babies—that is, to long for the *pure, spiritual milk* consisting of *the Lord* (v. 3) and the Lord's message. This means rejecting all other spiritual food as impure: all the *malice* and *guile*, all the *insincerity, envy, and all slander* evident to Peter in Roman society (v. 1). *Milk* here is not elementary Christian instruction intended to give way later to "solid food" (as, e.g., in 1 Cor 3:2, and Heb 5:12-13). It is not teaching or instruction at all, but the very life of God given in *mercy* (1:3; 2:10b) to those who are reborn, in the same way a mother nourishes her children. "Milk from the breasts of the Lord" later became a striking metaphor in the collection of early Christian hymns known as the *Odes of Solomon* (see, e.g., *Odes* 4.10; 8.14; 14.2-3; 19.2; 35.5; 40.1, in *OTP* 2:725–71). Like babies, Christians need this *pure, spiritual milk* in order to grow. The end of the growth process is *salvation* (v. 2b)—the salvation Peter had said is now *ready to be revealed* in Christ (cf. 1:5). Here as in chap. 1, salvation is the assured and appropriate outcome of a faithful life.

2:4-10. Becoming the people of God. In vv. 4-10, Peter's metaphor shifts from that of growth to that of building under construction (cf. Eph 2:21; 4:12, 16). At the same time his attention shifts from Christians as individuals to their corporate identity as a people. As more and more of them come to Christ in the course of the Christian mission (v. 4)—by "tasting" Christ's mercy (2:3)—they are being built into a kind of temple (*a spiritual house, to be a holy priesthood*, v. 5).

From Isa 28:16, a text Peter assumes is referring to Christ as *a stone, a cornerstone chosen and precious* (v. 6), he draws the implication that Christians too are *living stones* (v. 5) out of which God is building this new "temple." He plays on a contrast almost universal in his time between honor and shame. His text from Isaiah concludes that those who trust in the great cornerstone *will not be put to shame* (v. 6b), and Peter applies this to Christians because they have believed in Jesus (v. 7a). Theirs is the "honor," while "shame" is reserved for those who reject Jesus (vv. 4, 7b; cf. Ps 118:32). God's CORNERSTONE becomes for them *a stone that makes them stumble, and a rock that makes them fall* (cf. Isa 8:14). To this fate, Peter says, God has appointed them (v. 8b), just as surely as God has "appointed" Jesus Christ the cornerstone of faith.

Christian believers, on the other hand, are *God's people*, and the recipients of God's MERCY (v. 10). Although they are gentiles, whatever was true of the Jewish people is now true of them. They are *a chosen race, a royal priesthood, a holy nation*, and *God's own people* destined for vindication (v. 9a; cf. Exod 19:6; Isa 43:20-21). The last of these phrases refers not to the present but to the future, like Peter's references to future salvation in 1:5, 9, and 2:2. Although God has called these gentile Christians "out of darkness" (cf. 1:14, 18) to *marvelous light* (v. 9b), the *marvelous light* of salvation has not quite dawned (cf. *1 Clem* 36.2). They must still undergo suffering for a while longer (cf. 1:6-7). Living as they do between the darkness of their gentile past and the light of God's future, these Christians have the responsibility of praising the God of Israel both with their words and their lives. Like Israel itself (cf. Hos 1:6-9), they were once *not a people* and once *had not received mercy*. Now they are *God's people*, now they have *received mercy* (v. 10; cf. 1:3), and they await their inheritance.

The Responsibilities
of the People of God, 2:11–4:11

The expression *Beloved, I urge you* introduces a new section in which Peter will enlarge on his readers' responsibilities to the society in which they live. This section extends all the way to 4:11 (note the repetition of *Beloved* in 4:12 and *I exhort* [lit. "I urge"] in 5:1).

Respect for Everyone, 2:11-17

Building on the designation *exiles* back in 1:1, Peter now focuses on the potential hostility between Christians and a culture where they are *aliens and exiles*. Their struggle is both inward and outward. It is first a struggle between the *soul* of Christian believers (i.e., their new life destined for salvation) and certain *desires of the flesh* within them carried over from their pagan past (v. 11), but it finds outward expression in social conflicts and tensions between Christians and their unbelieving neighbors in the Roman Empire (v. 12). Peter's main concern is with this social dimension of his readers' life in Christ. The conflict in which they find themselves is to be won not by aggressive behavior in society, but by "conducting themselves honorably" among those who ridicule or mistreat them (v. 12; cf. 2:15, 20; 3:6, 11, 17).

Peter writes in the spirit of Paul, who had urged Christians in Rome not to "be overcome by EVIL, but overcome evil with good" (Rom 12:21). He also echoes Jesus in the SERMON ON THE MOUNT: "Let your light shine before others, so that they may see your good works and give glory to your Father who is in heaven" (Matt 5:16). Peter has adapted the saying—or one like it—to the social situation of Christians in the empire. Their task in such circumstances is to live in such a way that those who denounce or accuse them will come to appreciate, even worship, the God of Israel. Peter's advice is much like that of the Jewish (or Jewish-Christian) TNaph 8.4: "If you work that which is good, my children . . . God shall be glorified among the Gentiles through you, and the devil shall flee from you." The main difference is that Peter's vision—here as elsewhere—is focused on the coming day *when Jesus Christ is revealed* (cf. 1:7, 13), here understood as a day of judgment or reckoning (v. 12). His hope is that opponents of the Christian movement will see the error of their ways and turn to God, so that on that day they will "give glory to God" and share in the honor in store for those who believe (cf. 1:7, 2:7a). Yet he knows that a different outcome is also possible—not honor but shame (cf. 2:7b)—and he will look more closely at such a scenario later in his argument (cf. 3:16; 4:17-18).

"Good conduct among the gentiles" is defined in vv. 13-17 in relation to Roman imperial authority, and in vv. 18-25 and 3:1-7 in relation to the family or household. For this reason, 2:18–3:7 is commonly viewed as a "household duty code" comparable to other such codes in contemporary Greek and Roman literature (cf. Col 3:18–4:1; Eph 5:21–6:9). Peter does not distinguish sharply between responsibility to the state and responsibility within the family. Both involve a command to defer to the authority of others (vv. 13, 18; 3:1, 5). By giving this command its widest possible application in v. 13 (lit. "every human creature"), Peter makes it clear that he is not urging some kind of abstract subjection to institutional authority (as in the

NRSV, *every human institution*), but voluntary deference or respect to individuals simply because God created them. It is in this context that he commands respect for the emperor and the local magistrates who represent him (compare the similar transition in 1 Tim 2:1-2 from "all people" to "kings and all who are in authority").

Unlike Paul in Rom 13, Peter makes no claim that God put the emperor in power or that imperial authority is God's authority. The emperor should be respected *for the Lord's sake*, not because he is divine but because he is human (cf. v. 17, *Honor everyone. . . . Honor the emperor*). His job is to maintain order in society by punishing wrongdoers and rewarding those who do good (v. 14). Peter is confident that the emperor will honor those who honor him, and that if Christians in the provinces "do right," they will silence even their most vocal critics (v. 15). At the same time he insists that they must have their priorities straight. He reminds them that they are "free" in Jesus Christ—not free of all obligation to the empire, but certainly free of its values (i.e., *the futile ways inherited from your ancestors*, 1:18). Because God has set them free, they are at the same time God's *servants* (v. 16). Their reverence for God and their love for each other (cf. 1:22) take precedence even over the respect they owe the emperor and *everyone* (v. 17).

Slaves and Masters, 2:18-25

Peter now shifts attention from all Christians as "servants of God" to those who were actual slaves in Roman households (οἰκέται, lit., "household servants," v. 18), but within a few verses he shifts back again to all the readers of his letter. The household serves as an appropriate context in which to introduce the sobering thought that all Christians may soon have to suffer for their faith in Roman society. Unlike Paul (Col 4:1; Eph 6:9), Peter addresses only slaves, not slaveowners, because he wants to make a point about suffering, and slaves are the ones who suffer. What counts with God is not suffering as such, or even the patient endurance of suffering, but *suffering unjustly* (v. 19) or "doing right and suffering for it" (v. 20). Endurance of suffering is a virtue only when suffering is undeserved, like the suffering of JESUS (vv. 21-23). This is the case when slaveowners are harsh or cruel (v. 18).

It is difficult to specify a point at which Peter widens the application of his words from household servants in particular to Christian believers in general.

He allows the former to be stand-ins for the latter because he does not want to temper the optimism about the empire expressed in vv. 13-17. But his readers could hardly miss the point. What could happen to Christian slaves at the hands of a cruel master could happen to any Christian if the mood of the populace took an ugly turn. Christ died for all believers, not just slaves (v. 24). All of them, not just slaves, are called to follow in his footsteps (v. 21). All were *going astray like sheep*, and all have *returned to the shepherd and guardian of your souls* (v. 25).

Because he has all believers in view, Peter puts his emphasis as much on verbal as on physical abuse. Actual physical suffering was not yet widespread among Christians, but they knew what it was to be denounced, ridiculed, and accused of crimes against the social order (cf. 2:12, 15). Peter wants to make sure they do not retaliate in kind. In language drawn from Isa 53, he describes Christ's behavior at his arrest and trial, accenting the fact that "no deceit was found in his mouth" (v. 22; cf. Isa 53:9b). "Deceit" to Peter is not deception, but malice or ill will of any sort (cf. 2:1). He elaborates Isaiah's words with the observation that Christ never denounced his accusers, and never threatened them with divine vengeance, as martyrs were said to have done in the time of the MACCABEES (cf. 2 Macc 7; 4 Macc 9–10). He simply left them to God, and to the prospect of God's righteous judgment (v. 23; cf. 1:17; 4:5).

Still drawing on Isa 53, Peter takes the opportunity to insist that Christ's suffering was more than an example. Adopting the confessional "we" and "our" from Isa 53, he includes himself with his readers (for the first time since 1:3) as sharers in a common salvation. Christ on the cross took "our" sins away (cf. Isa 53:4, 12b). He did not merely atone for sins or secure forgiveness; he actually carried the sins in his body to the cross and left them there (v. 24). With "our" sins gone, "we" are free to live for what is right, even in the face of hostility and slander. Peter quickly shifts back to his customary "you" as he reflects on his gentile readers' "healing" or conversion from paganism (vv. 24b-25; cf. Isa 53:5b-6). Without mentioning Christ's resurrection explicitly, he describes the Christ of the cross as now alive from the dead, carrying out the role of SHEPHERD over his flock (for the risen Christ as shepherd, cf. Mark 14:27-28; John 10:15-17; Heb 13:20-21). Later he will explain how Christ functions as shepherd over his congregations through the ministry of elders (5:2-4).

Wives and Husbands, 3:1-7

3:1-6. Advice to wives. Just as Peter, in addressing slaves, gave special attention to those who served cruel or hostile masters (2:18), so in addressing wives he focuses on those who are married to unbelieving husbands (v. 1). His goal is that husbands might be *won over* not with words but by reverent and pure conduct (v. 2; cf. 2:12). Taking over certain stereotyped denunciations (by Jewish, Greek, and Roman teachers alike) of some women's flamboyant tastes, he adapts them to this purpose. What counts as lavish *adornment* in God's sight is not hairdo or jewelry or clothes (extravagant or otherwise), but rather *the inner self with the lasting beauty of a gentle and quiet spirit* (v. 4). Peter associates flamboyant dress with flamboyant behavior and domestic rebellion, and modest dress with modest behavior and domestic peace. He knows nothing of the Christian "Total Woman" of the 1970s, for whom big hair and excessive makeup became the badge of wifely submission!

Peter does command wives to defer to their husbands' authority, and he does so even when the husband does not *obey the word* (i.e., not a Christian believer, v. 1). But a woman does not carry out this command by denying or concealing who she really is. Her obligation to defer to an unbelieving husband does not extend to adopting his religion—as Roman society expected—for the *conduct* to which she is called includes reverent fear toward her God (v. 2). Her role models are the *holy women* of Israel's past (probably SARAH, REBEKAH, RACHEL, and LEAH) who *hoped in God* (v. 5), and in particular Sarah, who once called Abraham *lord* (v. 6)—even though she laughed when she said it (Gen 18:12)!

Peter is probably aware not only of the irony of Sarah's laughter, but of the deeper irony of using Sarah and the *holy women* as examples in the first place. The women he is addressing here are not married to godly patriarchs like ABRAHAM, ISAAC, and JACOB, or anyone like them. They would have found it truly laughable to call their unbelieving husbands "lord" as they called Jesus "Lord," or "obey" them as they "obeyed" God (cf. the accent on "obedience" in 1:2, 14, 22). Yet by faith they are "Sarah's children." Peter's argument is from the greater to the lesser: if Sarah called Abraham "lord" (even in her laughter), Sarah's children should at least show deference and respect to their less than ideal marriage partners. The real social setting in which these wives lived emerges in Peter's final words of advice: *do what is good, and never let fears alarm you.* The appropriate submission of a wife to her husband is defined by "doing good" (i.e., doing the will of God, cf. 2:15), not the other way around. This means there is always a possibility that the unbelieving husband might not be *won over* by the *purity and reverence* of her life, or even be willing to tolerate her alien religion—hence the comforting but ominous last command to the wives, *never let fears alarm you* (v. 6b; cf. Prov 3:25).

3:7. Advice to husbands. Peter has a few words for husbands as well. If a wife must accept her husband's authority, the husband has a corresponding obligation to *show consideration* and *honor* to his wife—first, because she is physically *weaker* than he, and second, because a Christian husband and wife are together *heirs of the gracious gift of life.* Because society's expectation was that a wife would adopt her husband's religion, the likelihood was that the wife of a Christian husband had become a Christian too. If so, husband and wife are partners in faith and prayer—a kind of church in miniature. If not, the Christian husband must understand and honor his wife simply as God's creature (cf. 2:13, 17a), and as someone weaker than he, knowing that God values weakness above strength (cf. 5:5-6; 1 Cor 1:26-29; 12:22-24).

Seeking Peace, 3:8-12

Peter now generalizes from the advice just given about specific relationships in 2:18–3:7. He urges his readers to show kindness in all their dealings with each other (v. 8), and to seek peace even toward those who do not share their faith, but who ridicule and insult them (v. 9). In particular, he urges them not to trade insults with their oppressors, but always to speak words of kindness and blessing (vv. 9-10; cf. the appeal to Christ's example in 2:22-23). Drawing on words from Ps 34:12-16, Peter concludes that God will reward such an attitude on the part of his people and punish those who oppress them (vv. 10-12). Like the married couples in the preceding paragraph, they will find that God answers their prayers (v. 12).

The Hope of Vindication, 3:13–4:6

3:13-17. Encouragement "just in case." On the basis of the psalm just quoted, Peter urges his readers to maintain integrity before Christ their Lord in situations where they might have to face opposition and hostile questioning, whether from fellow citizens or the ruling authorities (vv. 14b-15). His confidence in such cases is that those who denounce them will be *put to shame* (v. 16), probably on the day of reckoning (cf. 2:12) when God comes to judge the world (cf. 3:12). Like those "persecuted for righteousness' sake" in the SERMON ON THE MOUNT (cf. Matt 5:10), faithful Christians are *blessed* (v. 14a), for their lot will be infinitely *better* on the day of judgment than that of their oppressors (v. 17).

3:18-22. The victory Christ won. Peter again introduces Jesus Christ as his example, picking up where 2:21-25 left off. There he had spoken of Christ's behavior in his PASSION (2:23), of his actual death (2:24), and (implicitly) of his resurrection (2:25). Now, illustrating the notion of suffering for "doing good" (3:17), Peter refers to Christ's death, RESURRECTION (vv. 18b, 21b), and journey to heaven (vv. 19, 22)—all the "glorious events" the prophets had only partially understood (cf. 1:11). Possibly he and his readers were familiar with a three-part confession of faith about Jesus Christ *put to death in the flesh / made alive in the Spirit / gone into heaven*—a symmetrical expression consisting of three participles in Greek, each with the same ending (-θείς).

The third of these participles (πορευθείς, *gone* in the phrase, *gone into heaven,* in v. 22) is anticipated already in v. 19 with the claim that Jesus *went* (πορευθείς) *and made a proclamation to the spirits . . . who in former times did not obey, when God waited patiently in the days of Noah* (vv. 19-20a). This suggests that throughout vv. 19-22 Peter is elaborating the third element in the three-part confession—Christ's journey to heaven. Building on Jesus' analogy between *the days of Noah* and the present (Matt 24:37 = Luke 17:26), Peter links the evil or unclean spirits Jesus faced in his ministry of exorcism with the state of the world just before the flood. He focuses especially on the illicit union described in Gen 6:1-4 between "sons of God" (usually understood as evil angels) and women on earth. According to some Jewish traditions, this union produced "giants" who would "be called evil spirits upon the earth" (*1 Enoch* 15.8). Peter's point is that the victory over demons which began in Jesus' earthly ministry was completed after his resurrection, in the course of his journey to heaven. This victory established Jesus' lordship over all *angels, authorities, and powers* (v. 22)—even those that are hostile—and so reinforces Peter's assurances to his readers (vv. 13-17) that they have nothing to fear from those who question or denounce their Christian way of life.

One difficulty with the passage is the apparent statement that the disobedient spirits were *in prison* (Gk. ἐν φυλακῇ, v. 19b). If they were in prison, what did Christ announce to them? Their release? This would not have been good news! Their salvation? Nothing here or in any other NT text suggests that evil spirits will be saved. Their subjection to him? If they are already in prison, what would further subjection mean? For these reasons, it is possible that ἐν φυλακῇ should be understood as "in refuge" or "in hiding," rather than *in prison*. According to *1 Enoch* evil angels are said to be chained or imprisoned (cf. also 2 Pet 2:4; Jude 6), but not evil spirits, and the word φυλακή is not used. In Revelation, the only other NT use of φυλακή in connection with evil spirits, Babylon is doomed to be "a haunt of every foul spirit" (Rev 18:2). Such a translation suggests that Peter viewed the "disobedient spirits" as free and very active in the world until Jesus tamed them by his resurrection (vv. 18b, 21b) and journey to heaven (vv. 19, 22). At that point their safe havens (whether on earth, under the earth, or in the air) were no longer safe from his universal lordship, and in the course of his journey he invaded their haunts and announced their subjection.

Within his reflection on Christ's journey, Peter extends the analogy between Noah's day and his own by comparing the waters of the flood to Christian BAPTISM (vv. 20-21). Like NOAH and *a few* others then, Christians are *saved through water* now, not in the sense of being washed clean from their sins, but because they have already been purified through Christ's death and resurrection (cf. 1:2, 22; see also Josephus's explanation of John's baptism, *Ant* 18.117).

4:1-6. Sharing in victory over sin and death. The triumphant tone of 3:22 is at once muted by a reminder that no one can share in Christ's resurrection and victorious journey without first preparing for the same kind of suffering he experienced (cf. 2:21-25). Christ is the one who *has finished with sin* (v. 1b) in that he did away with it *once for all* (3:18a) by his death on the cross (cf. 2:24). Now he has nothing more to do with sin (cf. Heb 4:15; 7:26; 9:28), and the same must be true of his followers (vv. 2-3). They must make an absolutely clean break with the immoral culture out of which they came (cf. 2:1, 11). If they do, they can expect to be ridiculed and slandered (lit., "blasphemed"), just as Christ was before he suffered (v. 4; cf. 2:23a). But like Christ, they too can expect vindication from God, *who stands ready to judge the living and the dead* (v. 5; cf. *the one who judges justly*, 2:23b).

As a postscript to the paragraph, the set phrase *the living and the dead* reminds Peter that God's vindication of the righteous did not begin with Jesus, but embraces many who died long before his coming (cf. Heb 11). They too heard God's *gospel* (cf. Heb 4:2, 6), accepted it, were condemned for it, but have the sure hope of resurrection from the dead. Peter echoes here the thought that "the souls of the righteous are in the hands of God and no torment will ever touch them. In the eyes of the foolish they seemed to have died . . . but they are at peace. For though in the sight of men they were punished, their hope is full of immortality" (Wis 3:1-4, RSV).

Christian Community, 4:7-11

A series of short generalized commands (vv. 7-11a) leading up to a doxology (v. 11b) gives the impression that Peter is now bringing his letter to an end (cf. Paul in 1 Thes 5:12-24). His reminder that *the end of all things is near* (v. 7) follows appropriately the reference to God as *him who stands ready to judge the living and the dead* (4:5). The prospect, however remote, of official persecution requires unity and cohesion among Christian believers, and Peter sees the source of this unity in worshipping and ministering congregations. In contrast to 2:18– 3:7, his focus is on congregations rather than households, and mutuality is at the heart of all his commands: mutual love (v. 8), mutual HOSPITALITY (v. 9), and mutual ministry (vv. 10-11). There are no fixed roles here comparable to slaves and masters or wives and husbands. There are no offices, no clergy-laity distinctions, no leaders or followers. All believers have a responsibility to love, show hospitality, and MINISTER to each other. Precisely who ministers to whom is determined not by status or seniority, but solely by *the manifold grace of God* (v. 10). By repeating the word *God* three times in v. 11a, Peter drives home the point that all ministries are from God, and therefore accountable to *him who stands ready to judge the living and the dead* (4:5).

The Responsibilities of Elders, 4:12–5:11

The address *Beloved* in 4:12, as in 2:11, introduces a new section of the letter. The accompanying appeal, however, does not follow immediately as it does in 2:11, but is deferred until 5:1, where it turns out to be directed to *elders* in particular. The whole section from 4:12 through 5:11 has much the same function as 4:7-11—to build congregational unity in the face of impending trouble—but it does so at greater length, and with a more specific audience in view. Having spoken generally to all the congregations reading his letter, Peter now turns his attention more specifically to those ruled (like his own congregation in Rome) by elders on the basis of seniority. This means that 4:12-19 is something of a digression, laying a basis for the appeal to elders in 5:1-11 by reiterating and reinforcing the themes of 2:11–4:6.

The Fiery Ordeal, 4:12-19

4:12-16. True suffering and true joy. The reiteration carries a new note of urgency, echoing the concern early in the letter about *various trials* testing believers as fire tests gold (cf. 1:6-9). Peter now urges joy in suffering, not because suffering is a good thing in itself or a reason for joy, but because those who suffer for Christ are sharing in Christ's own experience. Consequently, when Christ's glory is revealed, they will rejoice all the more (v. 13; cf. 1:6, 8). Those who are ridiculed for his sake are *blessed* (v. 14a; cf. 3:14), not because they are suffering but because they are suffering for the right reasons (cf. Matt 5:11). At such times the Spirit of God (and the coming glory) rests on them just as Jesus said it would (cf. Luke 12:11-12). Many manuscripts add that if the Spirit is blasphemed (cf. Luke 12:10), the guilt of blasphemy rests not on those who are ridiculed, but on their oppressors (v. 14b KJV).

Such promises do not apply to those who suffer for the wrong reason. Christians who are accused of crimes against Roman society, or even of antisocial behavior that is not explicitly criminal (e.g., as "busybodies" [KJV], or self-appointed guardians of public morality), must make sure that such charges are untrue (v. 15). Only when they have no reason to be ashamed of their actual conduct are Christians free to *glorify God* in the face of hostile questions (cf. 2:12, 15, 19-20; 3:15-16). This, to Peter, is what it means to suffer *as a Christian*.

4:17-19. Judgment at the house of God. Peter's imagery for divine judgment centers on the Christian community as the "house," or temple, of God (cf. 2:5). His point of departure is Ezek 9:6 (LXX), where God orders the judgment on Jerusalem to begin "from my sanctuary" and "from the men who are elders, who are inside the household." Peter refers to the house or sanctuary here and to the "elders" in 5:1-5. To him the judgment of God (cf. 1:17; 2:23; 4:5) is one universal judgment, and is now under way. If a *fiery ordeal* is breaking out even among God's people, how much worse is the fate in store for the "disobedient" (vv. 17-

18; cf. 2:8)? This could have led to a kind of vengeful joy in the punishment of the wicked, but it does not. Instead, Peter reminds his readers of the common humanity they share even with their oppressors (cf. 2:13). The judge to whom believer and unbeliever alike are accountable is also the creator who made them all. Peter urges continued trust in that *faithful Creator*, and a renewed commitment *to do good* in the face of unjust suffering (v. 19; again cf. 2:12, 14-15, 20; 3:6, 11-12, 13, 17).

Elders and Their Congregations, 5:1-11

5:1-4. Elders. Peter now resumes the appeal begun in 4:12. For the benefit of congregations ruled by elders, and in keeping with the notion that judgment begins from the elders in "the house of God" (Ezek 9:6), he reminds elders of their responsibilities (vv. 1-4). This he does as an *elder* himself (v. 1), whether as a leader in his own congregation at Rome, or as one of the Twelve chosen by Jesus (cf. 1:1) and therefore an *elder* to all Christians everywhere (cf. v. 9b, *your brothers and sisters in all the world*). He shares with the elders to whom he writes a special responsibility to testify to Christ's sufferings—which he has done repeatedly in this letter (cf. 1:11; 2:21-25; 3:18; 4:1, 13)—and a special hope of reward when Christ's glory is revealed (v. 1b; cf. v. 4). Peter urges elders to be good shepherds over *the flock of God* (v. 2; cf. Acts 20:28), not for financial gain or even "their own satisfaction on the job, but as glad volunteers in God's service" (Kelly, 201). They must lead by example instead of lording it over their respective congregations (lit. "lots" or "assigned portions"), so that *the chief shepherd*, Jesus Christ (cf. 2:25), will reward them when he appears in glory (v. 4).

5:5-11. Their congregations. Peter turns his attention briefly to the *younger* (v. 5a), adapting to his purpose a formalized code of behavior similar to the household codes of 2:18–3:7 (cf. Titus 2:1-6; *1 Clem* 1.3). His actual interest is not in those who are young in age, nor in some subordinate order of ministry, but simply in all who are not elders. He quickly moves from the elder/younger distinction to a strong emphasis on mutuality reminiscent of 4:7-11: *And all of you must clothe yourselves in humility in your dealings with one another* (v. 5b). Such words, like those of 4:7-11, are relevant to all congregations whether ruled by elders or not.

The theme of humility before God continues in the next few verses, as Peter reflects on Prov 3:34 LXX:

God opposes the proud, but gives grace to the humble (v. 5c; cf. Jas 4:6). The call to humility, with its promise of exaltation or vindication (vv. 6-7, 10-11; cf. Matt 23:12; Luke 14:11; 18:14), frames a related call to resist the devil (vv. 8-9; cf. Jas 4:7-10). Despite Christ's victory over the evil spirits (3:18-22), the devil remains on the loose *like a roaring lion* (v. 8), ready to *devour* those who are unprepared (cf. *JosAsen* 12.9). To Peter, being "devoured" by the devil does not mean persecution as such, or even martyrdom, but APOSTASY or loss of faith. Resisting the devil and trusting God are not two commands but one (cf. Jas 4:7). He reminds his readers that the conflict they face is worldwide (v. 9), and that God's *eternal glory* is their destiny (v. 10; cf. *his marvelous light* in 2:9). Their sufferings are indeed few and brief (v. 10; cf. 1:6) when weighed against that glory to come (cf. Paul in Rom 8:18 and 2 Cor 4:17).

Conclusion, 5:12-14

Peter ends with a word acknowledging *Silvanus*, probably not as scribe or coauthor, but as the bearer of the letter to the Asian provinces (v. 12a). The expression *through Silvanus* is echoed in Ignatius's letters, where the proposition "through" consistently has this meaning (e.g., *Phld* 11.2, *Smyrn* 12.1, Rom 10.1). Playing down the letter's scope (*this short letter*, cf. Heb 13:22), Peter nevertheless claims that it is *true grace of God*, for which those who read it must "stand" (v. 12b). With greetings from a sister congregation *in Babylon* where he resides (probably Rome), and from Mark (cf. Col 4:10, Phlm 24), his associate whom he calls his *son* (v. 13), Peter urges that his greeting (*Peace to all of you*) be passed along through the Asian congregations as through a family, *with a kiss of love* (v. 14; cf. 1:22; 2:17; and 4:8).

Works Cited

Kelly, J. N. D. 1969. *A Commentary on the Epistles of Peter and Jude*.

Michaels, J. Ramsey. 1988. *1 Peter*. WBC.

Second Peter

Edwin K. Broadhead

Introduction

Second Peter was accepted into the NT CANON as one of the GENERAL LETTERS—apostolic letters addressed to the CHURCH as a whole. Nonetheless, 2 Peter has proven elusive and problematic. The enigmatic nature of this text was recognized early within church history, and numerous questions remain unanswered. These problems will be identified and addressed by giving attention to the role of 2 Peter in canonical perspective, in historical perspective, and in contemporary perspective.

Second Peter in Canonical Perspective

Origen (ca. 185–254 C.E.) provides the first written acknowledgement of the existence of 2 Peter (in Eusebius, *EccHist* 6.25.8, 11), yet he also expresses doubts about its authenticity. EUSEBIUS (ca. 260–339 C.E.) himself was hesitant to accept the letter. Jerome (ca. 346–420 C.E.) wholly endorsed the letter and assigned it to apostolic authorship. He supposed the difference in style between 1 and 2 Peter could be explained by Peter's use of two different scribes. Probably based on Jerome's endorsement, 2 Peter gained wide acceptance within the Latin and Greek churches. When the canon of the NT was fixed in the fourth-century church, the place of 2 Peter was established.

Second Peter presents itself as an epistle with an apostolic foundation and a postapostolic focus. While other general letters tend to limit apostolic attestation to the opening and closing lines, 2 Peter insists throughout upon its apostolic foundation. In addition to the apostolic address (1:1) the letter recalls the presentation of the apostolic preaching (1:12) and makes plans for its preservation (1:13-15). Peter's role as an eyewitness and his experience of the TRANSFIGURATION are recalled (1:16-18). The continuity and vitality of interpretation are confirmed (1:19). A prior letter is recalled (3:1), and the christological foundation is confirmed on the witness of the apostles (3:2). The witness of PAUL is recalled (3:15-16), and the testimony of scripture is evoked (3:16).

The primary concern of this letter is for the time after the death of the apostles. The departure of the earliest leaders will bring a time of crisis (3:4). This period will be marked by eschatological doubt (3:3-13) and moral failure (2:2, 9-22). The destruction of the world and its judgment lie close at hand (3:5-13). The letter warns against these troubles (2:1; 3:3) and seeks to prepare the reader to face this forthcoming crisis (1:12-15; 3:17-18).

This trauma involves the activity of false teachers from within the Christian tradition (2:1-3, 15; 3:16). They will take advantage of the newly converted and the unstable (2:14, 18-22). The letter prepares its readers for this postapostolic trauma through warning about the future (2:1; 3:3) and remembrance of the past (1:12-15; 3:1-2).

Several issues shape this apostolic challenge. The apostolic faith is foundational. This faith is based upon knowledge of Jesus Christ as Lord and Savior (1:1, 14, 16; 2:1, 20; 3:2, 18). The apostle is an eyewitness to the work of Jesus (1:16-18) and continues to receive REVELATION from Christ (2:14). This apostolic faith is based on the prophetic tradition (1:19-21; 2:3; 3:2, 13). The readers of the letter share in this faith (1:1-2, 12; 3:1-2, 17-18).

The scriptures provide a sure witness and warning for the recipients of the letter. The scriptures are understood as a body of literature which believers hold in common. Among the writings considered as scripture are the prophetic warnings (1:19-21; 2:3; 3:2, 13), the stories and sayings of the OT (2:4-9, 15-16, 22a; 3:5-6, 8), the writings of Paul (3:15-16), and other writings (3:16).

Attention is given as well to the formulation of the faith. The reader is warned against clever myths (1:16) and esoteric interpretation of prophecy (1:21). More importantly, the letter seeks to restore ethical stability (1:3-11; 3:11, 14, 17-18) in the face of moral failure (2:9-22). At the heart of the letter lies a warning against eschatological delusion: the promised judgment and renewal of the earth will not fail (3:4-13).

Second Peter thus presents a strategic approach to the problems at hand. The warning against false teachers is framed as a final letter of challenge from one of the last of the apostles. With prophetic foresight, the apostle warns the readers of the trauma that will engulf believers in the postapostolic age. False teachers practicing corrupt ethics and preaching a failed eschatology are countered by the sure foundation of the apostolic faith, the words of scripture, the consistent righteousness, and the sure hope of the believer.

Within this canonical perspective 2 Peter presents itself as a general epistle based on a final apostolic testimony. From this standpoint, the letter is seemingly addressed to a specific group of Christians by Peter near the time of his death (in ROME ca. 64–65 C.E.).

Second Peter in Historical Perspective

Second Peter presents a quite different image in historical perspective. Current knowledge about language, theological development, and church history raise serious questions about the relationship of 2 Peter to the apostolic era and to the other writings of the NT.

Second Peter is only formally related to 1 Peter. The greeting (1:1), the blessing (1:2), and the benediction (3:18) are on the same model as those of 1 Peter. Beyond this, 2 Peter is framed as the second letter from the apostle (3:1). This formal framework does not bear up in the substance of the letter. Differences in language and style were noticed as early as Jerome (*Ep* 120.11), and modern statistical analysis confirms this. The style of 2 Peter tends to be more formal and grandiose than 1 Peter. The two letters share few themes or concerns in common.

In reality, the epistle closest to 2 Peter is JUDE. Indeed, large parts of Jude are found in 2 Peter:

2 Pet 1:2	=	Jude 2
2 Pet 1:12	=	Jude 5a
2 Pet 2:1-3	=	Jude 4
2 Pet 2:6	=	Jude 7
2 Pet 2:10b-15	=	Jude 8–12a
2 Pet 2:17	=	Jude 12b–13
2 Pet 2:18	=	Jude 16
2 Pet 3:2-3	=	Jude 17
2 Pet 3:14	=	Jude 24
2 Pet 3:18b	=	Jude 25

Beyond this, various elements of organization and numerous themes are shared in common between Jude and 2 Peter.

This common ground has been explained through three theories: (1) Jude is a reduction of 2 Peter; (2) Second Peter is an expansion of Jude; (3) Jude and 2 Peter are two different applications of one traditional work. The third opinion is the most likely. The relatively low level of precise verbal agreement in the common material speaks against direct dependence of one letter upon the other. Both works may be based on an apostolic testimony that circulated in a variety of forms. The letter of Jude, employing a midrashic approach with various allusions to the OT and to apocryphal writings, represents a more Jewish form of the tradition. Second Peter shows less interest in the Jewish traditions and structures and represents a more Hellenized form of the apostolic testimony.

Of primary concern for most interpreters is the relationship of 2 Peter to the apostolic era and to Peter. The language and conceptualization of the letter seem far removed from the world of a Galilean fisherman. The desire to escape the corruption of the world and participate in the divine nature (1:4) is more akin to Hellenistic thought than to the Palestinian world of Peter. Common authorship of 1 and 2 Peter is unlikely. Various images in the letter point to a postapostolic period. While the crisis is foreseen as a future event (2:1; 3:3), it is addressed as a present reality (2:10; 3:4, 16). The death of the earliest leaders is seemingly acknowledged (3:4). The apostolic experience of faith is now expressed in more fixed and formulaic terms (1:1; 3:2). The tension between Paul and Peter is absent (3:15). A fixed body of scripture is assumed, and includes Paul's writings (3:16). The proper interpretation of scripture has become an issue (1:20-21). The remembrance of JESUS has been framed primarily as *power* and *majesty*, and it has been focused in one event—the Transfiguration (1:16-18). Second Peter is almost unknown in the first and second century, and its apostolic origin is questioned from the beginning. The letter first emerges in the manuscripts from Egypt, and it is accepted last among the Syrian church.

Second Peter also stands at a distance from the major lines of NT thought. The experience of faith has been formulated as apostolic commands (3:2). The CHRISTOLOGY posed here tends to focus on formal titles (1:11; 2:20; 3:18), to be docetic in outlook (1:1, 3), and to emphasize power and glory (1:3, 16-17). FAITH is framed as revelation (1:14) and recognition (1:3, 8,

12; 2:20; 3:18). Missing are the teachings of Jesus, the cross and the resurrection, and the experience of GRACE and RECONCILIATION. The outlook is closer to Hellenism than to Palestinian Judaism. The moral demands likely reflect the virtues of Hellenistic Judaism. The expected collapse of the universe is similar to Stoic thought. The heresy addressed sounds similar to the developing gnostic tendencies of the late first and early second centuries. This outlook is also evident in the language of 2 Peter. There are fifty-seven words in 2 Peter not found elsewhere in the NT; thirty-two of these are not found in the Greek OT (i.e., LXX) either. Fifteen of these thirty-two words are found in other Jewish Hellenistic writings. Three words in 2 Peter have no parallel in Greek literature. Thus, the historical perspective makes doubtful the identity of 2 Peter as an epistle from the apostolic age.

A more likely framework for 2 Peter is the literary form known as the "Testament" (see TESTAMENTS, APOC-RYPHAL). In this literature a heroic figure gives words of instruction and warning before departing. Without exception, these texts are composed after the death of the hero to recall and preserve the impact of the leader. Often these texts are used to address particular problems faced by a later generation. The pattern for Peter's Testament may be drawn from the story of MOSES in Deuteronomy. Told that his death is imminent, Moses ascends the mountain to see what lies ahead (Deut 3:23ff.). Moses' mountaintop experience with God is remembered (Deut 4:9-14). The earlier COMMANDMENTS are recalled (Deut 4:13). Warnings to OBEDIENCE are issued, and the people are instructed in how they should face the trials of the future without their leader. This Mosaic model is taken up in the writings of Josephus (*Ant* 4.8.2) and in the *Testament of Moses*. Examples of the Testament form may be found in the OT, in Jewish literature, and in the NT.

Seen from a historical perspective, 2 Peter belongs to the postapostolic stage of church history in which the teaching and authority of the apostles was brought to bear against contemporary controversies. From this historical perspective, 2 Peter is a Testament framed in the form of a letter. It seeks to draw upon the apostolic era to address a postapostolic situation, likely between 90 and 110 C.E. Likely addressed to a general audience, the author and place of composition are unknown.

Second Peter in Contemporary Perspective

Second Peter continues to hold value in a contemporary perspective. Second Peter provides key historical insights into the postapostolic age and the development of the institutionalized church. Seen in terms of its own context and purposes, this letter provides crucial information about the controversies which underlie the formation of the CHURCH.

Beyond this, 2 Peter offers a theological contribution. This epistle provides a primary example of how the Christian church handled the literature and the traditions which it inherited. The traditions of the OT, of Judaism, and of apostolic Christianity converge within this text. Of key interest is the manner in which the early church appropriated these traditions for its own age and task. Beyond this, the interaction of the church with the world is modeled. The ongoing dialogue of Judaism and Christianity with the Hellenistic environment echoes through this epistle. Second Peter also demonstrates the in-house arguments that form the matrix of early church history. The definition of scripture, the naming of heresy, and the fixing of church patterns are all underway in this letter.

Thus, 2 Peter provides information on how early Christianity handled its heritage, articulated its identity, and found its way in the world. The church, which lives yet between the age of the apostles and the day of judgment, has much to learn from this work.

For Further Study

In the *Mercer Dictionary of the Bible*: EPISTLE/LETTER; ESCHATOLOGY IN THE NT; GNOSTICISM; JUDE, LETTER OF; LORD IN THE NT; PAROUSIA/SECOND COMING; PETER; PETER, LETTERS OF; SAVIOR IN THE NT; TESTAMENTS, APOCRYPHAL. In other sources: R. Bauckmam, *Jude, 2 Peter*, WBC; C. Bigg, *A Critical and Exegetical Commentary on the Epistles of St. Peter and St. Jude*, ICC; J. Calvin, "2 Peter," *Calvin's Commentaries*; L. Johnson, *The Writings of the New Testament*, 442–52; E. Käsemann, "An Apologia for Primitive Christian Eschatology," in *Essays on New Testament Themes*, 169–95; K. Schelkle, *Die Petrusbrief, der Judasbrief*, HTKNT 13/2; W. Schrage and H. Balz, *Die katholischen Briefe: Die Briefe des Jakobus, Petrus, Johannes, und Judas*, NTD; R. Summers, "2 Peter," *BBC*.

Commentary

Salutation, 1:1-2

Typical of ancient letters, 2 Peter opens with mention of the sender and the receiver and with a word of greeting. The apostolic nature of the letter is established from the beginning in the titles associated with the author: *servant and apostle of Jesus Christ*. The author names himself as *Simeon Peter*. Simeon represents an unusual spelling based on the Hebrew form and is found elsewhere in the NT only in Acts 15:14. Many interpreters see here an attempt to convince the reader of the ancient and apostolic nature of the letter.

The recipients of the letter are specified only as fellow believers. Later they are identified as the recipients of a prior letter (3:1). The word of greeting is framed upon 1 Pet 1:2b, and it enhances the apostolic appearance of the letter. Three elements within the salutation, however, point to a postapostolic period: faith is understood more as a possession than an experience (v. 1); Jesus is seemingly addressed as *God* (v. 1); and the title of *Savior* is applied to Jesus. While these elements have parallels within the NT, they typify the later, more marginal stages of NT thought.

The reference to the believer's *knowledge* (ἐπίγνωσις) *of God and of Jesus* may be a subtle rebuke of the false teachers. They are, perhaps, among those who claim a special knowledge (γνῶσις) of the divine, later known as Gnostics. If so, the greeting already sets the true knowledge of believers over against that of false teachers (see KNOWLEDGE IN THE NT).

Theological Exposition, 1:3-11
The Gift, 1:3-4

The body of the letter opens with a brief theological exposition that sets the background for the apostolic challenge. The reader is first reminded of all that has been given to believers. The knowledge and the promises of Christ provide life and deliverance. The gift is understood primarily in terms of knowledge. While the basis of this message is primitive Christianity, the language and concepts are those of Hellenism.

The Demand, 1:5-7

Demand is built upon gift. The believer is to support the gift of faith with a life of virtue. This list combines normative biblical values (*faith, mutual affection, love*) with ethical categories common to popular Greek philosophy (*knowledge, goodness, self-control, endurance*). Again, a basic NT pattern is expressed in the concepts of Hellenism.

The Result, 1:8-11

The result is focused, both in its positive and its negative aspects. At the center of this discussion echoes the theme of knowledge. Depending on how one practices morality, the *knowledge of . . . Jesus Christ* may be cultivated or lost. The discussion alternates between gift and demand. BAPTISM, calling, and ELECTION form the basis of the Christian life; these may be lost through moral neglect. Entrance into the kingdom is a gift; it may be forfeited. The reduction of the kingdom of God wholly to the kingdom of Christ is further evidence of a later stage of Christian thought.

The Author's Situation and Purpose, 1:12-15

The situation of the author clarifies the purpose of the letter. The apostle has received revelation of his imminent death (v. 14). While the apostle remains, his purpose is twofold: to remind the readers of the apostolic faith (v. 13) and to prepare them for the postapostolic period (v. 15). These two goals shape the remainder of the letter.

The Apostolic Foundation, 1:16-21

The Certainty of the Witness, 1:16-18

The author assures the readers of the validity of the tradition they have received. Not *cleverly devised myths*, but the apostolic message provides the foundation of their faith. Perhaps the author seeks to counter the timeless mythical structures of Hellenistic thought with a salvation-history focus on God's activity. Here the authority of the entire apostolate is confirmed through the use of the plural (*we* is used twice in v. 16; in v. 18; and in v. 19). This authority is based on eyewitness experience, and the TRANSFIGURATION of Jesus is recalled as an example. Those who preach the future coming of Christ are qualified to do so by their experience of his past revelation in honor and glory. The faith of the postapostolic church is founded on its sure witness to God's saving activity within history.

The Certainty of the Message, 1:19-21

Further confirmation is provided by the certainty of the message. Behind the prophetic and apostolic word stands the activity of the HOLY SPIRIT. As God spoke on the mount of Transfiguration, so God speaks through the prophecy that the church possesses. This tradition is confirmed over against all alternatives as the message for the church.

The Coming Crisis: Ethics, 2:1-22

The apostolic heritage is now applied to the postapostolic situation. Apostolic instruction is set against false teachers in two specific areas: ethics and eschatology.

The Appearance of False Teachers, 2:1-3

Emphasizing the continuity between OT and apostolic tradition, the *false prophets* of the OT reemerge within the postapostolic church. Their leadership is set against that of apostolic tradition—*the way of truth* (v. 2). Their teaching will be marked by subtlety, destructiveness, immorality, heresy, and deceptive words. Both their appearance and their judgment have been prophesied.

Old Testament Lessons, 2:4-10a

The continuity of OT and apostolic traditions is filled out through three examples: the fallen angels (drawn from apocryphal sources such as *EthEnoch* 20:2; *SibOr* 4:185); Noah's generation (Gen 6:6-8; 8:18); *Sodom and Gomorrah* and *Lot* (Gen 19:16, 24,

29). The point of these examples becomes clear in 2:9-10a: God is able to preserve the godly and to judge the unrighteous. Second Peter applies this truth directly to the situation of the postapostolic church.

The Character of the False Teachers, 2:10b-22

A full range of vocabulary and imagery describes the opponents' moral failure. Evocative similes are employed: irrational animals, cursed children, waterless springs, storm-driven mists, and slaves of corruption. Numerous descriptions clarify their immorality: bold, willful, slanderous, revelers, blots, blemishes, adulterous, insatiable, greedy, cursed, bombastic, and licentious. The OT story of BALAAM (vv. 15-16) and two graphic proverbs describe those who follow their path (v. 22).

The Coming Crisis: Eschatology, 3:1-13

The second heresy addressed by the letter is the failed eschatology of the false teachers. A similar pattern of argument is followed.

The Appearance of Scoffers, 3:1-4

The warnings of 2 Peter are grounded upon four foundations: the word of *the holy prophets*, the commandments of Jesus, the teaching of the apostles, and a previous letter. The specific threat addressed in the remainder of this epistle is the loss of faith in the return of the Lord. In this threat both ethical and eschatological failure are combined (v. 3). The death of the fathers (v. 3) points to the end of the apostolic era. Historically, this transition meant that expectation of the return of Christ faded into the distance and with it the threat of imminent judgment. The author of 2 Peter fights against this tendency.

The Apostolic Answer, 3:5-13

The early church sought in various ways to deal with the delayed PAROUSIA of Christ. A unique approach to this problem is given in 2 Pet 3:5-13. Four arguments are given against those who have abandoned the apostolic tradition of the imminent parousia. First, the word of God does not fail. Upon the dynamic of God's word the ancient world was both founded and judged by water. Upon the same divine word, the present world will undergo a judgment of fire. A second answer, based on Ps 90:4, argues that God's time is relative. A third response sees purpose behind the delay: God has allowed time for REPENTANCE and salvation. The fourth reply focuses the unexpected nature of the judgment; the lack of present signs is no indication of its failure or its lack of intensity. The apostolic reply concludes with an appeal that again unites ethics and eschatology: the certainty of judgment should produce lives of holiness and godliness. As with the OT models, both destruction and renewal are envisioned. Here the renewal extends beyond the interests of the individual or even of the church to include the entire creation.

The Challenge to Endure, 3:14-18a

In view of the coming trauma, believers are challenged to wait with upright behavior. The delay is to be seen as a particular moment of grace within God's salvation history. The reader is warned that attempts to twist the apostolic message are not new: Paul's letters and other scripture suffer the same abuse. In light of the ethical and eschatological crisis, the believer has received an apostolic warning. Rather than fall away or turn back, the believer is to *grow in the grace and knowledge of . . . [the] Savior Jesus Christ.*

Final Benediction, 3:18b

Even the final words of the apostolic message recall its focus. Over against the unstable ways of the false teachers, believers are to give glory to Jesus Christ, both in their present living and until the day of judgment.

First, Second, and Third John

John B. Polhill

Introduction

The three Johannine Epistles can be classified in two ways. Along with the Petrine Epistles, James, and Jude, they belong to the category of "general" or "catholic" epistles. They have also traditionally been grouped with the Gospel of John and Revelation in the "Johannine corpus." Their affinity with the fourth Gospel is unmistakable. The relationship to Revelation is more remote.

Literary Form

In form, all three have traditionally been denoted epistles. This is most accurate for the latter two. Second John follows the standard conventions of first-century epistles and is addressed to a Christian congregation. Third John is a private epistle from a church leader to an individual. The writer of both identifies himself as *the elder* (2 John 1; 3 John 1).

First John is anonymous. It does not have the usual form of an epistle: no address, no conclusion, none of the conventions of a Greek letter. It is still probably best described as general epistle—a written communication, probably to a group of churches by a church leader concerning matters of mutual concern. The language and thought are so close to that of the other two that it was probably also written by "the elder."

Authorship and Date

Who was this *elder*? Tradition identifies him with the apostle JOHN, who is said to have lived to a ripe old age, ministering in Ephesus. This view identifies John with the BELOVED DISCIPLE and sees him as author of the Gospel and Epistles of John. A second view builds upon a tradition from POLYCARP that there were two Johns in Ephesus, the apostle and a disciple of the apostle known as the Elder John (EUSEBIUS, *EccHist* 3.39.4-6). Many would see this "elder John" as "the elder" of the three epistles. A third view emphasizes the communal aspect in the Johannine Epistles and sees the entire Johannine corpus as coming from a "Johannine School" of thought. The traditions in which this community grounded itself are taken back ultimately to the beloved disciple of the fourth Gospel.

Although some argue otherwise, the majority of scholars place the epistles in a Johannine milieu according to one of these three views. They are usually placed in Asia Minor around the last decade of the first century. Throughout this commentary, the writer will be designated as John or the elder with no distinction implied between the two.

Life Setting

All three epistles depict a CHURCH in conflict. False teachers have separated from the church. The elder accuses them of three errors. First, they have an inadequate view of the INCARNATION, failing to give full due to the humanity of Jesus (1 John 2:22; 2 John 7). Second, they have a deficient view of SIN, failing to keep God's commandments while at the same time claiming to be above sin (1 John 1:8, 10; 2:4). Finally, they have a failure in FELLOWSHIP, not loving their Christian brothers and sisters (1 John 2:9; 4:20).

These separatists have often been identified with GNOSTICISM, and more specifically with Cerinthus, a Gnostic precursor whom IRENAEUS depicts as an opponent of John in Ephesus. There are problems with this identification, however, since Cerinthus does not seem to have held all the views applied to the false teaching in 1 John, nor are all Cerinthus's main views attacked in the epistles. That the elder was fighting some sort of incipient Gnosticism seems likely. Later Gnostics often maintained a spiritual perfectionism that saw itself as above sin. They were elitist and tended to disdain others (lack of love), and they held a docetic CHRISTOLOGY, denying the humanity of Jesus.

For Further Study

In the *Mercer Dictionary of the Bible*: ATONE-MENT/EXPIATION IN THE NT; BELOVED DISCIPLE; EPIS-TLE/LETTER; GNOSTICISM; INCARNATION; JOHN; JOHN, GOSPEL AND LETTERS OF; LIGHT/DARKNESS IN THE NT; LOVE IN THE NT; RIGHTEOUSNESS IN THE NT.

In other sources: R. E. Brown, *The Epistles of John*, AncB; R. A. Culpepper, *1 John, 2 John, 3 John*, Knox Preaching Guides; I. H. Marshall, *The Epistles of John*, NICNT; S. S. Smalley, *1, 2, 3 John*, WBC.

Commentary

An Outline

Prologue, 1:1-4

With its reference to *what was from the beginning* and *the word of life*, the prologue to 1 John is reminiscent of the fourth Gospel's prologue (John 1:1-18). There are differences, however. In 1 John *the beginning* probably refers to the tradition of the Christian witness to Christ rather than to the preexistence of the Word. There is also a stronger emphasis on the eye-witness TESTIMONY to the real humanity of Christ: *what we have seen with our eyes, what we have looked at and touched with our hands* (v. 1). Already John focuses on the false teachers. In response to the innovations of the false teachers, John calls his readers back to their roots—to the original apostolic testimony to Christ, to the word of the gospel they first heard. He especially concentrates on the false teachers' inadequate CHRISTOLOGY, as he expands on the "word made flesh" of the fourth Gospel's prologue (John 1:14).

Of particular concern to John is the unity of his community. It is a triangular fellowship—among Christians with both *the Father* and *Son* (v. 3). This emphasis persists throughout 1 John, particularly in the motif of "abiding." John expresses his personal purpose for writing in verse 4—*that our joy may be complete*. John is concerned with restoring the joy of the

fellowship, which has been threatened by the withdrawal of the false teachers from the community.

Part One: God Is Light, 1:5–3:10

First John is difficult to outline, because its themes are constantly repeated. The division followed here is based on the recurrence of the phrase *this is the message* in 1:5 and 3:11. In 1:5 the message is defined in terms of light, in 3:11 in terms of love.

The Johannine Epistles are marked by dualistic language. There is either darkness or light, no in-between. One belongs either to the realm of light or to that of darkness. Darkness is marked by sin, falsehood, hate, and death. Life is characterized by righteousness, TRUTH, love, and life. The first main division contrasts these two realms. The contrast is explicit in the first two subdivisions: those who walk in light are cleansed from sin (1:5–2:2); they keep the commandments (2:3-11). The light and darkness imagery is not explicit in the following sections but is implicit in the dualistic contrasts. The world is to be shunned as the world of darkness (2:12-17). The true confession in the Son is contrasted with the lie of the false teachers (2:18-27). Finally, *the children of God*, children of light, are contrasted with the children *of the devil* (2:28–3:10).

Dealing with Sin, 1:5–2:2

John's first subject is the place of sin in the believer's life. His basic premise is that God is wholly light (v. 5). Since sin is darkness, there is no room for sin in the lives of those who have FELLOWSHIP with God. Yet, sin is a reality even for believers, and God has provided means for dealing with it.

This section is constructed in a series of six antitheses, expressed in conditional sentences ("if anyone should . . . "). There are three negative statements describing those who walk in the darkness of sin (1:6, 8, 10). Alternating with these are three positive statements, treating the believer's relationship to sin (1:7, 9; 2:1-2).

The negative statements are best seen as describing the false teachers. They are not walking in the light but continue to sin (v. 6). This is so because they claim to have no sin, and this is sheer self-delusion (v. 8). They even claim to have never sinned (v. 10), and this makes God a liar, who throughout scripture asserts the sinfulness of all humanity (cf. Prov 20:9; Ps 14:2-3). Much like later Gnostics, John's opponents seem to have claimed a spiritual perfection in which they either viewed themselves as above sin or considered moral behavior a matter of indifference. John did not agree with this spirit/flesh DUALISM, but rather saw one's behavior in the flesh as indicative of one's spiritual state.

In three positive antitheses, John presents his readers with a realistic program for dealing with sin. His conviction is that sin has no place for those who walk in the light. The atoning blood of Christ has cleansed them of sin (1:7). If they do sin, however, they should confess it, and God will forgive and cleanse them (1:9). In such a case, the believer has an ADVOCATE to intercede with the Father (2:1). (Note the term "paraclete" applied to Jesus in his intercessory role. In the Gospel of John, the term is used of the Spirit.) The word "just" refers to the righteousness of Christ which qualifies him as intercessor for our unrighteousness. Christ is further described as the atonement (*hilasmos*) for our sins, a term with sacrificial overtones (cf. *blood* in 1:7). John is a realist. The goal of every Christian is to have fellowship with God, to walk in his light, to be free of sin (2:1). But we still live in an imperfect world where temptation is a reality. When we do sin, we have forgiveness through Christ.

Keeping His Commandments, 2:3-11

This section can be divided into two subsections. The first (vv. 3-6) is closely related to the previous treatment of sin, as it deals with keeping the commandments. The second (vv. 7-11) moves the thought forward to the supreme command to love. In both sections the argument is built around a recurring participial construction ("the one who says, loves . . . ").

Verse 3 begins with the theme of "being known" by God. This is an experiential knowledge, closely related to the theme of "abiding" that permeates this section: the truth is *in* a person (v. 4); we are *in him* (v. 5); one claims to *abide in him* (v. 6). For John, salvation is a relationship—to be personally known by God; to live in him and in the Son; to live in a community of love with fellow Christians. In this section John depicts the keeping of the commandments as a mark of this relationship to the Father. Probably he has in mind the whole moral tradition of the Johannine

community. Verse 6 focuses on the specific example of Christ. In contrast to the false teachers, who seem to have put little stock in Christ's human life, John presents it as a model for Christian living.

Verse 7 moves to a particular COMMANDMENT—that of love. It is both old and new. It is old because the Christians have heard it from the beginning of their Christian life (v. 7). It is also the *new commandment* that Christ gave (John 13:34; 15:12). Verses 8-11 reflect the close relationship of light and love. Because God is both light and love, to walk in his light is also to walk in his love. John again looks to the false teachers. They are likely the ones who *hate* (v. 11). Johannine dualism allows no in-betweens: To fail in love is to hate. Throughout the epistle love applies to love between Christian brothers and sisters. John is concerned with the conflict in his own community and does not address the Christian's relationship to outsiders—except, that is, the false teachers. Once they belonged to John's community; now they have left (2:19). They have no love for their former sisters and brothers in Christ.

Shunning Worldliness, 2:12-17

With vv. 12-14 one comes upon the address that was lacking at the epistle's beginning. The section raises many questions. Who are the *little children*, *fathers*, and *young people*? Elsewhere in 1 John *little children* addresses the whole community, and indeed the things said about the little children (forgiveness of sin, knowledge of the Father) apply to every Christian, but who are the fathers and young people? Do these terms designate age, or office, or stages in Christian maturity? Why does v. 14 virtually repeat vv. 12-13? For emphasis? The main function of the section seems clear. These are words of assurance to the Johannine Christians that they need not shrink from the disdain of those who have left nor doubt their own status with God. Their roots are firm: their sins are forgiven, they know the Father and the Son, and they have conquered the devil (*evil one*).

Verses 15-17 link up with the reference to conquering the devil in v. 14. In Johannine thought the devil holds sway over the world (John 12:31; 16:11). To *love the world* is to place oneself under his dominance. John does not depict the world as EVIL in itself; on the contrary, Christ died for the world, God sent his Son to save it (1 John 2:2; John 3:16). In the Johannine dualism, however, one cannot live within the world's sphere of POWER and God's at the same time. Verse 16 aptly summarizes the world's enticements—physical appetites, things which please the eye, boasting in self-achievement. To center oneself on these rather than on God is to invest in the transient.

Making the True Confession, 2:18-27

The reference to the world's *passing away* in 2:17 serves as a transition to the announcement that it is the *last hour* in v. 18. The term *antichrist* seems to have originated in Johannine circles, but the idea of false prophets and messiahs coming in the last days before Christ's return was well established in early Christianity (cf. Mark 13:22; 2 Thes 2:8). Usually ANTICHRIST is depicted as a single figure, but John speaks of many of them because he identifies antichrist with those who separated from his community (v. 19). For John the separation proves they never really belonged in the first place. They are guilty of the cardinal lie, denying that JESUS is the Christ (v. 22). This is the primary doctrinal error of the separatists. They held an inadequate view of the INCARNATION, emphasizing Christ's divinity and neglecting his humanity. The example of his life (2:6), his mediatorial role (2:1f.), and his atoning death (5:6) held no importance for them. Because they did not have the Son, neither did they have the Father nor the *eternal life* which is in him. It is not so for John's *little children*. They have the anointing of the Spirit (v. 20). They make the true confession and have both Son and Father (v. 23). Theirs is the life eternal (v. 24). John was concerned lest the separated group lead his community astray (v. 26). He thus assures them they need no experience in the Spirit that they had not already received, no teaching other than what they had been given from the beginning (v. 27).

Living as Children of God, 2:28–3:10

John returns to the theme of the last days, continuing his note of assurance in v. 28. His *little children* will have boldness to appear before the Lord at his return because they abide in him. The mark of their abiding is their righteous living. Since God is righteous, their righteousness is a sign that they have been begotten by God and are his true children (v. 29). The style of this section is again antithetical, constructed with the phrase "everyone who. . . ." It is interrupted in 3:1-2 by an encomium on being a child of God. Because God has begotten us in his love, we are now his children (3:1). Our final state does not yet appear, but John assures us we will be like Christ, *for we will see him as he is* (3:2).

Returning to the "everyone who . . . " style, 3:3 urges that those who share this hope of glory maintain their conformity to Christ even now by sharing in his purity. This links with the reference to doing righteousness in 2:29 and contrasts with the reference to *commits sin* in 3:4. Those who live in sin and iniquity will not share in Christ's coming. Christ came to take away sin (cf. John 1:29). Sin finds no place in him, and the sinner has neither seen nor known him (3:6). In fact, those who sin are the children of sin's originator, the devil (3:8, 10). Here again John's dualistic treatment of sin appears. The one abiding in Christ does not sin (3:6). The one begotten of God *cannot sin* (3:9). One must bear in mind John's treatment of sin in the life of the believer (2:1-2). He was well aware of that reality and faulted those who claimed to be sinless (1:8, 10). Many have noted that John used the present tense throughout this section, indicating a continual state of sinning: the one who abides in Christ does not "live in" sin. One must be careful not to water down John's point. Christ and sin are incompatible. The one who abides in Christ must seek to perfect that relationship by conquering sin.

Part Two: God Is Love, 3:11–5:12

The same themes recur in 1 John 3:11–5:12 that are found in 1:5–3:10—right living, the right confession of Christ, love. The balance differs. Whereas God's righteousness dominates the first part, God's love commands the last half of the epistle. The word used for love throughout 1 John is *agape*, a rather bland word in secular Greek, which often meant little more than "like, prefer." The NT writers seized the word and filled it with new meaning in the light of God's gift of love in Christ. No one does this more profoundly than John.

Loving in Deed and Truth, 3:11-24

Using his normal antithetical style, in vv. 11-18 John contrasts love and hate. CAIN's murder of ABEL is held up as the archetype of all hatred. Cain's disposition is traced to the devil, and his motivation is linked to his jealousy over his brother's righteous deeds (v. 12). Thus, in dualistic fashion, John makes of a single piece hatred, unrighteousness, murder, and the devil. Ultimately, death is added to the fabric. To hate is to murder, and no murderer has a share in eternal life (v. 15). This is the way of the unrighteous world which, like Cain, abhors the righteous. Christians should thus not be surprised when they encounter the world's hatred (v. 13; cf. John 7:7; 15:18, 19).

If the way of hatred is death, the way of love is life, life in God's own Son who laid down his life for us. This is how we *know* what love is (v. 16). How we *demonstrate* that love abides in us is in concrete deeds of charity to needy brothers and sisters (v. 17). Love is not a feeling or a profession for John. It is active, expressed in concrete deeds (v. 18; cf. Jas 1:22). Perhaps such lack of concern for the needy was the clearest evidence of the lovelessness of those who had separated from John's community.

Verse 19 introduces the theme of confidence before God's judgment. It is closely connected to v. 18, because it is this active, charitable love that gives such confidence. John assures his readers that even should they experience qualms of GUILT at their own imperfection in love and righteousness, God knows the hearts of those who truly abide in his love (v. 20). Indeed, because we abide in him, God hears our prayers and grants our requests (v. 22). Verses 22b-23 summarize the three main traits of the one who abides in God, the three which run like a thread throughout the epistle: keeping God's commandments, loving one another, and believing in the Son. There is also a witness that God abides in his children—the HOLY SPIRIT (v. 24). The mention of the Spirit serves as a transition to the next section.

Testing the Spirits, 4:1-6

The early CHURCH was alive with spiritual experience, but it soon became apparent that not all such experience came from God. It became necessary to *test the spirits* (v. 1). Much like PAUL (1 Cor 12:3), John laid down the basic confession of Jesus Christ as the main test (v. 2). But John adds a qualifying clause: they must confess Jesus Christ as having *come in the flesh*. He has the Christology of the separatists in mind, their failure to acknowledge the significance of Jesus' humanity. Theirs is not God's Spirit, but the spirit which opposes God, that *of the antichrist* (v. 3; cf. 2:18, 22).

Verses 4-6 contrast *the Spirit of God* and *the spirit of the antichrist* (vv. 2-3). John's *little children* may take assurance that the victory is theirs, because God's Spirit is more powerful (v. 4; cf. 2:14). One certain contrast is that *the world* listens to the message of false spirits; it does not heed God's Spirit (vv. 5-6a). This is perhaps indicative that the separatists who had *gone out* into the world (2:19) were having more

success in spreading their message than John. It certainly reflects John's conviction that *the world* is under the sway of the evil one and naturally heeds the spirit of deceit rather than *the spirit of truth* (v. 6).

Being Perfected in God's Love, 4:7-21

First John 4:7-21 is the most profound treatment of God's love in the NT. Verses 7-11 depict the priority of God's love. Verse 12 is transitional, introducing the main themes of the following verses: abiding in God's love (13-16), and being perfected in God's love (17-21).

True love, perfect love, begins with God (v. 7-11). The main thrust of this section is that John's readers should *love one another*. This exhortation begins and ends the treatment (vv. 7, 11). In between John establishes the basis of all love—God's love. It is significant that throughout this section John addresses his readers not as *little children* but as *beloved* (3:21; 4:1, 7, 11); that is, as those who have received God's love. Within the Christian community all love begins with God. *God is love* (v. 8). The evidence of God's love is his sending his Son into the world to die as a sacrificial atonement (*hilasmos*; cf. 2:2) for our sins so that we might have life (vv. 9-10; cf. John 3:16). Through acceptance of God's sacrificial love in Christ, the believer is begotten of God and comes truly to know him (v. 7). It is not a matter of the believer's striving after God and finding him but of God reaching down in love; he loved us first (v. 10; cf. v. 19). There is thus a triangle of love which begins with God's love, is manifested in the love of Christ, and comes to life in the believer who accepts God's sacrifice of love in Christ. But this love is not genuine until it becomes a quadrangle, reaching out to others (vv. 7, 11).

The theme of abiding in God (vv. 13-16) is closely related to that of being "begotten" by (*born of*) God and "knowing" him in v. 7. "Abiding" is a favorite Johannine term. It describes the intimate, mystical relationship between Father, Son, Spirit, and believer. The evidence of this relationship is the presence of the Spirit in the believer's life (v. 13; cf. 3:24). The basis of the relationship for the believer is confessing that Jesus is the Son of God sent to save the world (vv. 14-15; cf. vv. 9-10). The stuff of the relationship is love—God's active love in the believer's life. God is love; abiding in love and abiding in God are one and the same (v. 16).

Verses 17-20 treat the "perfection" or "completion" of God's love in the believer. The very concept of perfection points to the relational character of love. It grows in proportion to the depth of one's abiding in God. It models itself after the example of Christ's sacrificial love (v. 17). As it deepens, fear is dispelled, for there is *no fear* in a genuine relationship of love (v. 18). Abiding in God's love, the believer has no room for fear, only for confidence on the day of judgment (v. 17). This confidence is only justified when love is perfect, and love is perfect only when it reaches out to others. Just as God loved us first and reached out to us, so must his love in us reach out to others (v. 19). Love is tangible (cf. 3:17-18). To claim love for an invisible God, a love that cannot be visibly demonstrated, is a sham. The arena for showing one's love for God is the visible world of the brother or sister in need (v. 20). As John has said before, none of this is new (2:7-8). It is *the commandment* of the Lord (v. 21; cf. John 13:34, 15:12).

Finding Life in the Son, 5:1-12

The concluding section of the body of 1 John is a final word of ASSURANCE to John's readers that they have obtained life in the Son (v. 12). Three characteristics in them demonstrate this (vv. 1-5), and three witnesses confirm it (vv. 6-12).

Verses 1-5 are a final summary of the three traits that mark one as begotten of God. First, they *love God*, and because they love the Father they love his children as well (v. 1). Second, they keep God's *commandments,* and this is not burdensome because God gives them the power to conquer the world (vv. 3-4; cf. Matt 11:30). Finally, they have the right faith, believing and confessing Jesus as the Christ, *the Son of God* (vv. 1, 5).

Verses 6-12 point to the witnesses that confirm that there is life in the Son. Verse 6 is a crux of interpretation: the proper confession of Jesus affirms that he came through *the water and the blood*. Do these refer to the INCARNATION, the water and blood of childbirth? Do they refer to his atoning death, the water and blood that flowed from his side at the CRUCIFIXION (John 19:34)? Or does the water refer to his BAPTISM and the blood to his atoning death? The last seems the more likely. The separatists from the community may have held a view much like that of Cerinthus, who maintained that the divine Spirit descended on the man Jesus at his baptism and departed before the crucifixion. It was the coming of the Spirit that counts, not the life of the man nor his death. No, replies John. He came by water and by blood, by his divine Spirit and by the outpouring of his human blood in his atoning death. The Spirit associated with his baptism and the blood of his crucifixion are thus two witnesses to who Christ is. The inner testimony of the Spirit is a third (v. 8). Finally, there is a fourth witness, *the testimony of God* (vv. 9-12). What is this witness of God? Is it his giving of his Son, as v. 11 seems to indicate? Or, is it his raising him from the dead and thus assuring the life that is in the Son?

Epilogue, 5:13-21

In vv. 13-21 John brings together themes which have run throughout the epistle. Verses 13-15 are words of assurance. Verse 13 gives John's main purpose in writing—that his readers might fully know that they *have* ETERNAL LIFE through their faith in the Son (cf. John 20:31). The false teachers may have raised doubts for some. John assures they need not fear for their salvation—they already have life in Christ. (Note the Johannine "realized eschatology.") Verses 14-15 give the further assurance that God answers their prayers. There is a qualification: the petitions must be *according to his will* (3:22 should also be read with this qualifier).

Verses 16-17 treat intercessory prayer of one Christian for another. John's readers are assured that God hears and grants such requests. But there is a sin for which John does not recommend intercession—the sin "unto death" (*mortal sin*). It is not altogether clear what he had in mind. Perhaps it was the sin of those who had left the community and rejected the significance of Christ's atoning death.

In vv. 18-19 John returns a final time to the subject of sin in the Christian. The one *born of God* does not live in the realm of sin, the world dominated by the evil one. Instead, children of God belong to God and Christ (the most likely referent for *gennetheis* in v. 18) keeps them from the devil's clutches.

The false teachers may have claimed special knowledge. John assures his readers that the SON OF GOD has come and given them insight into the truth (v. 20). He is himself the truth (John 14:6) and the only way to knowledge of the one true God (cf. John 1:18, 17:3).

Why John concludes with an abrupt command to shun idols is anybody's guess. The warning may be quite literal. The Greek world, and Ephesus in particular, was filled with idols. The reference may be figurative, as it often is in the NT. The error of the separatists with their proud claims to sinless perfection was itself a form of self-idolatry.

Salutation, 1-3

Second John follows closely the customary Greek letter form. The sender is *the elder*. The recipient is *the elect lady,* which most likely refers to a sister CHURCH. The church is one within the Johannine community, as the elder's implicit authority and the customary Johannine language would indicate (e.g., *all who know the truth . . . that abides in us*). In place of the usual Greek word of salutation, *chairein,* the NT writers characteristically substitute *grace* (*charis*) and add the Hebrew greeting *peace*. John adds a third greeting *mercy* (cf. 1 Tim 1:2; 2 Tim 1:2). At the end he tacks on two more distinctly Johannine blessings—*truth and love.*

Body of the Letter, 4-11

Reminder of Love Commandment, 4-6

The main body of 2 John is divisible into three parts: vv. 4-6, 7-9, and 10-11. In the first part (vv. 4-6) John reminds the sister church of the Lord's *new* commandment of love. John's main concern in the letter is to warn the congregation of the false teachers, and as is clear from 1 John, one of their primary faults was their lack of love. Another was their moral deficiency; so John reminds the congregation that genuine love

for God is demonstrated by living according to the *commandments* (v. 6).

False Teachers Described, 7-9

In vv. 7-9 John focuses on the false teachers more directly. Once a part of the community, they have now *gone out* into the world (cf. 1 John 2:19). They belong to the deceiver, *the antichrist* (cf. 1 John 2:18, 26). They do not confess that Jesus Christ has come in the flesh; that is, they have a deficient view of his humanity (cf. 1 John 2:22f.; 4:2f.). John describes them as "progressives." They have gone out into the world and "gone ahead" in their theology, departing from the true teaching of Christ (v. 9). Johannine theology could itself be described as "progressive" in the sense of "advanced." The trouble with the separatists was in having gone too far in their accommodation to the world.

Warning Not to Receive False Teachers, 10-11

The false teachers do not yet seem to have reached the *elect lady,* and in vv. 10-11 John advises the congregation to shun them altogether should they arrive. They are not to accept them in their homes, not even to greet them. This should be understood in light of early Christian HOSPITALITY. Itinerant missionaries depended on local Christians to provide their basic needs as they traveled. In the case of false teachers, to show them the customary hospitality would only further their cause.

Conclusion, 12-13

As with the salutation, the conclusion to 2 John closely follows conventional letter form with its exchange of greetings. Even in the note that he had more to write but hopes to share it in person, the elder is following literary convention.

Like 2 John, 3 John is quite brief, the length of a single PAPYRUS page. It too follows customary epistolary form. Unlike 2 John, it is written to an individual. It makes no mention of false teachers, but it does have an ironical relationship to 2 John. The refusal of hospitality *the elder* recommended to the "elect lady" (2 John 1) is now experienced by the elder himself.

Salutation, 1-2

The writer again identifies himself as *the elder* and addresses *Gaius*. We know nothing else of GAIUS. He may have been a member of Diotrephes' church (v. 9) or, as is more likely, one nearby. The prayer that all be well and the recipient *in good health* (v. 2) is a standard feature of private letters in John's day.

Body of the Letter, 3-12

The body of the letter falls into 3 parts: Gaius's hospitality (vv. 3-8), Diotrephes' opposition (vv. 9-11), and a commendation of *Demetrius* (vv. 11-12).

Gaius's Hospitality, 3-8

Verses 3-4 commend Gaius for the good report "the brothers" have given him, that he is walking in the truth. Most likely, this refers to his giving hospitality to "the brothers" (vv. 5-8). These were probably co-workers of John, itinerant missionaries who had been provided for by Gaius while they were working in his region. On returning to John's church, they had reported Gaius's generosity to the congregation. The passage reflects the early Christian practice of providing for traveling missionary workers. They were given food and lodging and on their departure enough provision to take them to their next stopping place. They refused help from non-Christians, depending wholly on the Christian community. Verse 8 states a basic principle of Christian missions—those who give support to missionaries participate in the ministry.

Diotrephes' Opposition, 9-11

Verses 9-11 reflect a breakdown in this arrangement. John had written a letter to *the church*, presumably regarding the provision of hospitality for his co-workers, but an individual in the congregation named *Diotrephes* had opposed him. Diotrephes' opposition was expressed in four ways: he spoke idle, gossipy words against John; he refused hospitality to the traveling Christian workers; he forbade others to give them

hospitality; he expelled any member who did offer them support. We know nothing else of Diotrephes. John does not accuse him of any doctrinal or moral failure; so he doesn't seem associated with the separatists. We don't know from what he derived his POWER over the CHURCH, whether from office or personal prestige. John accuses him of liking *to put himself first* (v. 9).

The whole situation betrays a power struggle. Diotrephes may have been exerting the autonomy of his congregation against the authority of the elder John. The situation may reflect a transition stage in church organization. The old order of centralized apostolic authority was dying out. Whatever the situation, the irony is that Diotrephes was following the elder's own advice (cf. 2 John 10). The elder's emissaries were certainly not false teachers, but Diotrephes may have turned John's prohibition of supporting false teachers into a blanket principle covering all itinerant workers. Verse 11 is best understood in this connection. For John there is no greater work than loving one's fellow Christian. Refusing hospitality was an unloving, evil work, and evil workers have *not seen God*. Here John comes close to linking Diotrephes with the separatists.

Commendation of Demetrius, 11-12

The commendation of *Demetrius* (v. 12) is probably linked to the problem with Diotrephes. DEMETRIUS may have been the bearer of 3 John, and Gaius's accepting him and furnishing hospitality the whole purpose for John's writing.

Conclusion, 13-15

Third John's conclusion follows conventional epistolary form. The claim to have more to write and the desire to talk face-to-face are literary conventions (cf. 2 John 12). In this instance, however, John's desire for a visit may have been substantive. The problem with Diotrephes may have urged the elder to come *soon* (v. 14) and deal with the matter personally (cf. v. 10).

Jude

Watson E. Mills

Introduction

Jude ranks, along with 2 and 3 John, among the most neglected and least well known of the twenty-seven books of the NT. The neglect of Jude is especially deplorable since Jude is a crucial document from a period of Christian history when rigid lines were being drawn between orthodoxy and heresy. In the strongest terms, the book of Jude posits a definite relationship between belief and practice.

Jude is included in a division of the NT CANON known variously as the GENERAL LETTERS or sometimes the "apostolic epistles" (James, 1, 2 Peter, 1, 2, 3 John, and Jude). These letters are said to be "catholic" (or universal) in their appeal since the letter opening does not name a single, specific recipient as do most of Paul's letters. The universal letters rather are addressed to all Christians everywhere (cf. 1 Pet 1:1). Yet despite this tradition, it would appear that the words of warning in Jude are directed to a very specific, though unnamed, community of Christians. In fact, the author appears to know the specific situation so well, that he is even aware of the movements of the "opponents" (see below, Opponents).

Authorship

The JUDE referred to in v. 1 is almost certainly JUDAS, the brother of Jesus, whose brother JAMES is James "the Just," a leader of the Jerusalem church. Both names were common in the early Christian community. For instance, the two disciples Judas Iscariot and Judas son of James; Judas Barsabbas (Acts 15:22-33); and, in the Maccabean era, Judas Maccabeus.

Jude is the short form for Judas (and is used only here in the NT for Ἰούδας, otherwise translated Judas) and James is the English form for Jacob. In the NT there are several men by each name. There is only one combination of brothers by those names, however—the James and Jude who are listed as two of the four brothers of Jesus (Matt 13:55; Mark 6:3). While most modern commentators agree on the referents, they disagree as to whether the author was the Jude referred to, or someone who used his name. The hypothesis that the author used the name of Jude has prevailed in many recent commentaries (Barnett, Grundmann, Reicke, Schelkle, Sidebottom), if only because arguments for a date too late for Jude's lifetime are held by the commentators.

We know little about Jude the brother of Jesus. He was one of four brothers of Jesus (with James, Joseph, and Simon), probably younger than James (Matt 13:55; Mark 6:3). Apparently, like Jesus' other brothers, Jude did not become a follower of Jesus during Jesus' earthly ministry (John 7:5) but only after the resurrection (Acts 1:14). According to 1 Cor 9:5, the brothers of the Lord became traveling missionaries, and, presumably, Jude is included in that reference. His missionary work was probably among the Jews, but not necessarily limited to PALESTINE. Julius Africanus (Eusebius, *EccHist* 1.7.14) says that the relatives of Jesus spread the gospel throughout Palestine, starting from Nazareth and Cochaba (in TRANSJORDAN). According to the *Acts of Paul* (*NTApoc* 2:388), Judas, the Lord's brother, befriended Paul in DAMASCUS—a tradition based only on identifying the Judas of Acts 9:11 with the brother of the Lord.

The fact that the writer refers to himself as Jude the *brother of James* (v. 1) and not the brother of Jesus could be a telling argument against the hypothesis of pseudonymity. Such a description is much more easily explicable on the hypothesis of authenticity. The humility that prompted this description must in itself be regarded as a mark of genuineness, matched by his more eminent brother's similar behavior (Jas 1:1).

Date, Relationship to 1 Peter, Recipients

Many of the scholars who doubt the traditional authorship do so on the grounds that the content of the letter suggests it is of a late composition. Bo Reicke (1964), for example, settled on a date of 90 C.E. Verse 3 supposes that the faith is already becoming a systematic body of doctrine, and vv. 17, 18 speak as if the generation of the apostles has died out. If Jude was indeed the younger brother of Jesus then is it not impossible that he was alive well into the latter part of the first century. J. A. T. Robinson argues that if *James* (v. 1) had already died, the author would have given some epithet such as "blessed" or "good" or "just" in referring to him. In the absence of any such reference Robinson holds that Jude must be dated before James's death in 62 C.E.

The date of the writing is inevitably related to the question of the relationship between Jude and 2 Peter. Except for a few opening and closing words, virtually all of Jude is included in 2 Peter:

Jude		2 Peter
2	=	1:2
3	=	1:5
5a	=	1:12
5b-19	=	2:1-3:3
24	=	3:14

Not only is the material common to the two letters, but each reflects a similar organizational approach. Both letters (1) warn against false teachers; (2) use three illustrations of God's judgment, two of which are identical (*angels* and *Sodom and Gomorrah*; (3) use BALAAM as an example of false teachers; (4) characterize the false teachers as those who are defiant toward divine authority; (5) use materials from apocryphal writings; and (6) use the same strong metaphors to characterize the false teachers (i.e., irrational animals, doomed to eternal darkness; spots and blemishes; arrogant boasters, etc.).

These literary similarities may be explained in one of three ways: (1) Second Peter borrowed heavily from Jude; (2) Jude borrowed heavily from 2 Peter; (3) both 2 Peter and Jude used a common source either oral or more probably written, but in either case no longer extant.

Since the early nineteenth century, a majority of scholarly opinion has favored the priority of Jude (option 1 above). Essentially the evidence is that (1) it is far more likely that the writer of 2 Peter would incorporate Jude into 2 Peter than that Jude would have lifted one chapter out of 2 Peter and presented it as a separate epistle; (2) the unknown writer of 2 Peter made use of the epistle from Jude, the brother of James and Jesus, to lend authority to his letter; (3) the

writer of 2 Peter removed from Jude the explicit references to apocryphal books (*1 Enoch* in Jude 6, 14, and 2 Peter 2:4) and the identifiable materials of apocryphal books (the *Assumption of Moses* in Jude 9 and 2 Peter 2:11) to make his letter more acceptable to Christian readers.

There is nothing to indicate to whom the letter was written, or where the writer was situated, except that the author is addressing Christian people (v. 1) who are apparently beset by the same kind of problems that have plagued the recipients of 2 Peter. This reality may well suggest an identity of the two groups, but in no way proves it.

Opponents

The most universally held opinion is that these false teachers were Gnostics. Indeed, GNOSTICISM was a very widespread threat to the mainstream of Christian thought by the late first and early second centuries. By that time it was firmly entrenched in the Mediterranean world—Palestine, ASIA, Africa, and ROME. Some scholars, however, contend that this letter comes too early for it to contain specific refutations of a fullblown Gnosticism such as that found in the second century. Moreover, if it were a refutation of Gnosticism, it is surprisingly timid in its denunciation. Bauckham (1983) suggests the opponents were itinerant charismatics who have caused trouble for the Christian community elsewhere (Matt 7:15; 2 Cor 10-11; 1 John 4:1). Whoever they were, the "opponents" were not just casual passersby, but rather active members of the Christian community who were involved directly in its various functions, and thus had a fertile ground and opportunity to promulgate their heretical teachings.

Purpose and Structure

The purpose of the letter is to demonstrate how these false teachers pose a threat to the Christian community and how the readers must carry on the fight for the faith.

The statement of the theme (vv. 3-4) contains two parts: (1) an appeal to Jude's readers to carry on the fight *for the faith* and (2) the background to this appeal, that is, specific references to the false teachers, their character and their judgment. Similarly the body of the letter contains two parts that correspond to this division: (1) the background (vv. 5-19) establishes that these false teachers are condemned and that their judgment has been prophesied in the Hebrew Bible since the days of Enoch. Thus these false teachers constitute a genuine and serious threat to the churches. Thereby the way is prepared for the second, and central, part the of body of the letter; (2) the appeal (vv. 21-23) calls on his readers to fight for the faith.

Jude cites a series of four "texts" although they are not actual quotations so much as textual allusions. The arrangement is such that each text is followed by an interpretative section:

Text	Interp.	Location	Drawn from
one		vv. 5-7	three types from
	one	vv. 8-10	the Hebrew Bible
two		v. 11	three types from
	two	vv. 12-13	the Hebrew Bible
three		vv. 14-15	the Book of Enoch
	three	v. 16	
four		vv. 17-18	the Apostles
	four	v. 19	

The first two "texts" are summary references to two sets of three OT types (vv. 5-7, 11). It is evident from the way he quotes the material in two of these instances (Prov 25:14 and Isa 57:20) that here Jude is depending upon the text of the Hebrew Bible and not that of the LXX as has been often supposed. The writer then quotes a prophecy of *Enoch* (vv. 14-15) and a prophecy *of the apostles* (vv. 17-18). Each is followed by a passage of interpretation (vv. 8-10, 12-13, 16, 19) which, by pointing to the character and behavior of the false teachers, identifies them as those to whom this type of prophecy applies. In text one, a secondary text (v. 9) is introduced in the course of the passage of interpretation.

Ellis (1978) has demonstrated that vv. 5-19 are actually cast in the form of a midrash. The term "midrash" is used in this instance to describe Jude's exegesis of the scriptures and other ancient materials and his application of these results to a specific historical situation. The term does *not* imply that Jude's midrash bears any close resemblance to the highly developed and stylized forms of later rabbinic midrashim.

The function of this section is to provide the background for the ultimate purpose of the letter: the appeal for its readers to *contend for the faith* (v. 3).

The midrash demonstrates the clear danger that these false teachers bring to the church, and prepares the way for the clarification and expansion of the purpose of the letter (vv. 20-23) already hinted at in v. 3.

In vv. 20-23 the author brings his readers to a dramatic conclusion, the urgency and relevancy of which has been heightened. Jude issues the call for his readers to fight to keep the faith.

For Further Study

In the *Mercer Dictionary of the Bible*: ENOCH, FIRST; ENOCH, SECOND; GENERAL LETTERS; GNOSTICISM; JAMES; JUDE, LETTER OF; PETER, LETTERS OF.

In other sources: R. J. Bauckham, *Jude, 2 Peter*; J. D. Charles, "Jude's Use of Pseudepigraphical Source-Material as Part of a Literary Strategy," *NTS* 37 (1991): 130–45; J. N. D. Kelly, *A Commentary on the Epistles of Peter and Jude*; B. Reicke, *The Epistles of James, Peter, and Jude*; E. M. Sidebottom, *James, Jude, and 2 Peter*.

Commentary

An Outline

I. Greeting, 1-2
II. Purpose, 3-4
   A. Appeal, 3
   B. Background, 4
III. Development of the Background, 5-19
   A. Description of the False Teachers as Sinners, 5-10
   B. Description of How These False Teachers Are Leading Others into Sin, 11-13
   C. A Prophecy Adapted from Enoch, 14-16
   D. A Prophecy Adapted from the Apostles, 17-19
IV. The Appeal, 20-23
V. Closing Doxology, 24-25

Greeting, 1-2

This section follows the form of the Jewish letter with the parties formula (from sender "X" to recipient "Y") and salutation or greeting. The authority rests upon the term "servant" (δοῦλος) not upon identification of the writer with Jesus' blood line. *Those who are called* reflects the fact that "the called" (κλητοῖς) has become a technical term within the Christian community, indicating those who have responded to the gospel. The tripartite formula *called, beloved,* and *kept* could possibly reflect an understanding of the servant songs of Isaiah (41:9; 42:1; 42:6). Jude omits "grace" (χάρις) in the salutation. The *mercy, peace, and love* offered here is also found in 1 and 2 Timothy.

Purpose, 3-4

The present less-finished treatise has been substituted for the one planned because of the danger of the present situation, that is, there are those present who refuse to follow the teachings of the faith and are ready to lead others in this heretical vein. The writer is thinking not so much of any creed or dogma, but rather an erroneous and unacceptable mode of conduct. There is a contemptuous ring in the phrase *certain intruders* who *have stolen* their way into the community. This threat is real; the author calls his readership to their responsibility to face up to this threat.

Development of the Background, 5-19

Description of the False Teachers as Sinners, 5-10

Next, the author describes the certainty of the judgment upon any who fail to live out the faith. Examples from the Hebrew Bible make it abundantly clear that status alone is no guarantee of a saving relationship with God. These false teachers, and any who follow them, are sinners and must face the consequences of their actions.

Description of How These False Teachers Are Leading Others into Sin, 11-13

Here the author points out, rather graphically, how as in the cases of CAIN, BALAAM, and KORAH, these false teachers are trying to lead others into immorality and away from their calling. These false teachers are motivated by jealousy and pride—a pride so great that it cannot tolerate any knowledge or power greater than its own.

A Prophecy Adapted from Enoch, 14-16

Jude quotes Enoch's prophecy as dramatic evidence of the impending punishment upon the false teachers. Apparently the Book of Enoch was well known in the first century, and Enoch himself was remembered as one "who walked with God" (Gen 5:22, 24). Here the Lord has come to bring judgment upon the ungodly, their character, their behavior. *Grumblers* (see Exod 16:2, 9) calls to mind the experience of the Israelites as they wandered aimlessly in the wilderness. These false teachers are chronic faultfinders, who, while incessantly complaining about others, follow their own lustful desires without regard for others.

A Prophecy Adapted from the Apostles, 17-19

Taken from the words spoken earlier by the apostles (though the specific tradition quoted remains unknown), this apostolic prophecy is expressed as a warning. That such persons as these would appear among the faithful is itself a sign that the "end times" are near. These false teachers cause serious divisions within the community by setting themselves up as superior to ordinary Christians. Jude maintains it is *these ungodly people* who are *devoid of the Spirit*.

The Appeal, 20-23

All that has come before has pointed the reader to this final appeal. Here Jude offers an exhortation to the faithful, a kind of "Christian antidote" to countermand the work of the false teachers. This appeal to action begins *But you, beloved* to heighten the contrast between the faithful and the false teachers. The contrast is further sharpened when he adds praying *in the Holy Spirit* as a quantifier for the faithful. This theme calls to mind a similar note found in the writings of Paul (Rom 8:26; 1 Cor 12:3; Gal 4:6; Eph 6:18). The referent here is in no way equivocal since the false teachers are without the Spirit. Jude offers these specific ingredients for his "antidote": (1) *build yourselves up on [the] most holy faith*; (2) *pray in the Holy Spirit*; (3) *keep yourselves in the love of God*; (4) *look forward to the mercy of our Lord Jesus Christ.*

Verses 22-23 abruptly shifts the focus to the way in which in the readers should respond toward those have been taken in, to greater and lesser degrees, by the false teachers. The text here is uncertain and it is not immediately clear whether Jude refers to two or three groups of individuals. The NRSV follows ℵ and A (three groups) while the NEB follows B and Clement of Alexandria. If we are to understand three groups, Jude's advice becomes progressively more drastic: (1) those who have not made up their minds—they must be convinced by argument; (2) those who are already involved with the false teachers—spare no effort in trying to rescue these (*save others by snatching them out of the fire*, v. 23); (3) those who have strayed so far they are only to be pitied—these must be feared by the faithful so as to avoid contamination.

Closing Doxology, 24-25

Beyond the responsibilities of the recipients is the sure presence of God's support and protection that in effect guarantees that their efforts to avoid spiritual heresy will not be in vain. These closing words call to mind an eschatological celebration of worship. The believers celebrate the final consequence of God's purposes, that is, they are found to be a suitable sacrifice before God.

Works Cited

Barnett, A. E. 1962. "The Epistle of Jude. Introduction," *IB*.

Bauckham, Richard J. 1983. *Jude, 2 Peter*. WBC.

Ellis, E. Earle. 1978. *Prophecy and Hermeneutic in Early Christianity*.

Grundmann, W. 1974. *Der Brief des Judas und der zweite Brief des Petrus*. THKNT.

Robinson, J. A. T. 1976. *Redating the New Testament*.

Reicke, Bo. 1964. *The Epistles of James, Peter, and Jude*. AncB.

Schelkle, K. H. 1980. *Die Petrusbriefe, der Judasbrief*. HTKNT.

Sidebottom, E. M. 1967. *James, Jude, and 2 Peter*. NCB.

Revelation

Mitchell G. Reddish

Introduction

Few writings have captured the imagination of as many people as has the book of Revelation. Artists, musicians, and writers have been intrigued by its rich imagery and symbolism and have mined its treasures as inspiration for their own works. Examples include Olivier Messiaen's musical composition *Quartet for the End of Time* and Handel's *Messiah*; Dürer's woodcuts and Michelangelo's *Last Judgment* in the Sistine Chapel; William Blake's *America, a Prophecy*; and Ernesto Cardenal's *Apocalypse*. People in despair and in crisis situations have turned to Revelation for comfort and hope, finding assurance in the book's confident assertion that God is in control of the universe and that good will ultimately triumph over EVIL. Its hymns, prayers, and words of praise have greatly enriched the church's liturgy.

In spite of its tremendous influence, Revelation remains for many readers a mysterious, enigmatic, even frightening work. The bizarre symbolism and repetitive structure of the book have caused many readers to abandon hope of making sense of John's message. On the other hand, some people claim to possess the key to unlocking the mysteries of this work, viewing it as a book of predictions of soon-coming world events. Armed with fanciful interpretations often more bizarre than the images of the book itself, these individuals transform John's writing into a propaganda sheet for their own futuristic views. Both reactions to the book—bewilderment and sensationalism—need to be avoided. Properly understood, Revelation contains a message of hope and comfort, as well as a call to faithfulness, that is still as valid to the CHURCH of today as it was to the church of the first century.

Literary Form

The Book of Revelation exhibits characteristics of several literary types. The work contains the major elements of ancient letters: greeting (1:4-5a), blessing or thanksgiving (1:5b-6), body (1:7–22:20), and closing (22:21). Embedded within the work are also seven messages to local churches, each cast in a form similar to a letter. Some scholars have argued that Revelation should be understood as prophetic literature. Indeed the author calls his writing a *prophecy* (1:3; 22:7, 10, 18, 19) and refers to the prophets as his brothers (22:9, NRSV *comrades*). Other scholars have viewed Revelation as modeled after the form of ancient Greek drama.

As valid as these insights may be, most scholars agree that Revelation is best understood as belonging to the literary form of an apocalypse, a type of writing popular in certain Jewish and Christian circles. The name of the genre is derived from the opening words of Revelation in which the author calls the contents of his work an *apocalypsis* (revelation). Ancient apocalypses were writings that purported to contain revelations of cosmic secrets, mediated to human recipients by supernatural beings either directly or in visions or dreams. The contents of the revelations usually consisted of both eschatological and otherworldly information. Although the social setting for many of the ancient Jewish and Christian apocalypses is unclear, apocalypses seem to have been produced in response to some sort of crisis situation (political, military, social, theological), either real or imagined. APOCALYPTIC LITERATURE was written to offer its readers a message of hope and comfort by providing an alternative view of reality from that dominant in the current sociohistorical setting. Apocalyptic writings assured their readers that, in spite of how the situation appeared, God was in control of history and the universe. Eventually God would triumph, rewarding the faithful and destroying evil.

Several literary and theological characteristics, while not definitive of the genre, are commonly found in apocalypses. Among the literary characteristics are pseudonymous authorship, historical reviews in the form of *ex eventu* prophecy ("prophecy" after the event has happened), mythological and symbolic language, visionary and auditory revelations, and rapture experiences. Theological characteristics include a dualistic theology (God versus the powers of evil), a dualistic view of history (two ages: the present, evil age and the glorious age to come), expectation of the imminent end of this age, and a deterministic understanding of world events.

Provenance and Social Setting

Evidence from Revelation indicates that the author and his audience were residents of Asia Minor, located in present day Turkey. The author states that he received the revelation contained in the Apocalypse while he was on the island of PATMOS, located off the coast of Asia Minor in the Aegean Sea. In addition, churches in seven cities of Asia Minor are recipients of special messages in Revelation.

John states he is on Patmos *because of the word of God and the testimony of Jesus* (1:9). Whereas this could mean John went to the island to share the Christian faith with the people there, the usual understanding is that John was banished by the Roman authorities to Patmos for being a Christian. Some islands in this area were used by the Romans as penal colonies, although there is no evidence that Patmos was ever so used. Similar phrasing elsewhere in the book supports the understanding that John's presence on Patmos was due to persecution (cf. 6:9; 12:11; 20:4).

The social and political setting reflected in Revelation is one of persecution and even martyrdom. Not only has John been banished because of his faith, but he also knows of other Christians who have been killed, even singling one out by name, *Antipas* (2:13; see also 2:9-10; 6:9-11; 16:6; 17:6; 18:24; 19:2; 20:4). Martyrdom is a major interpretive key for Revelation, with martyrs receiving special praise and reward. Calls to faithfulness and endurance resound throughout the book. Whereas some persecution seems to be based on Jewish hostilities (2:9-10), the majority derives from the Roman government. Enforcement of emperor worship and punishment of those who refuse is a major cause of the persecution (chap. 13).

This sociopolitical setting of suffering and persecution has been questioned by scholars who correctly point out that evidence for such persecution is meager or even nonexistent. No empire-wide persecution against Christians occurred in the first century. Furthermore, the portrayal of the emperor Domitian as a cruel despot by Roman and early Christian writers is likely due more to bias and imagination than to historical fact. Yet even if this is true, the author of Revelation was aware of some cases of persecution and martyrdom, no matter how limited in scope or duration. From his vantage point as a recipient of such persecution, the situation did indeed seem perilous. Reality is a matter of perspective, and from the perspective of John and his audience persecution was a present experience and a future threat. Although all Christians in Asia Minor might not have viewed the social and historical situation as life-threatening, John certainly did. Thus the setting for Revelation can be correctly labeled a persecution setting, even if that persecution was not widespread.

Date and Authorship

The writing of Revelation is commonly placed during the time of Domitian, emperor of Rome 81–96 C.E. The statement of IRENAEUS (ca. 140–ca. 202 C.E.) that the VISION of the Revelation was seen at the end of the reign of Domitian is the earliest external evidence attesting the date of Revelation (*AdvHaer* 5.30.3). Several writers in the following centuries also support a Domitianic dating for the book. Other early writers mention the reigns of Claudius, Nero, and Trajan as the setting for Revelation. Internal evidence lends additional support to the claim of Irenaeus. In Revelation *Babylon* (14:8; 16:19; 17:5; 18:2, 10, 21) is used as a symbolic name for ROME, a practice that would be appropriate only after 70 C.E. As Babylon had destroyed Jerusalem in the sixth century B.C.E. and had persecuted the people of God, Rome had also destroyed Jerusalem (70 C.E.) and was now persecuting God's people. A further indication of dating appears in the use of the Nero *redivivus* myth in chaps. 13 and 17. This belief in the return of Nero was popular during the last half of the first century, following the death of Nero in 66 C.E. Since the internal evidence coheres with Irenaeus's dating of the book during the time of Domitian, most scholars place its composition around 95 C.E.

The author of Revelation identifies himself as *John* (1:9). Christian writers as early as the second century identified this John as the disciple of Jesus. This identification is almost certainly ruled out, however, by the way in which the author refers to *the twelve apostles* as the *foundations* of the new Jerusalem (21:14). The writer is looking back on a venerated group of heroes of the faith. Furthermore, the author never claims apostolic authority for his writing. He describes himself simply as *your brother who share with you in Jesus the persecution and the kingdom and the patient endurance*" (1:9). Whereas the majority of Jewish and Christian apocalypses were written pseudonymously, such does not seem to be true of Revelation. The writer of the Apocalypse apparently does not claim to be anyone other than who he is: John, a Christian leader who has received a revelation from God while on the island of Patmos. John was obviously well known to the Christians in Asia Minor and knew the churches and their backgrounds intimately (2:1–3:22). Since he referred to his message as a *prophecy* (1:3), he viewed himself as a Christian prophet and had possibly functioned in this role among the Christians in Asia Minor. His extensive use of the Hebrew Bible and the many semitisms in his Greek suggest that he was a Jewish Christian, likely originally from Palestine.

Literary Structure

The literary structure of Revelation has been the focus of much debate among interpreters. All commentators recognize the importance of the number seven as a structuring device in the book—seven messages, seven seals, seven trumpets, seven bowls. How are these series of sevens related? The seven messages in 2:1–3:22 have sometimes been viewed as disconnected to the remainder of the work. A close examination, however, reveals otherwise. The clearest example of such connections occurs in the introductions to each of the seven messages, which borrow phrases from the description of the exalted Christ in chap. 1. Furthermore, the themes of persecution, faithfulness, endurance, rewards for the righteous, and the new Jerusalem, which are prominent in the seven messages, are also the major themes in the remainder of the book.

Some interpreters see the four series of sevens as consecutive series; that is, John presents in chronological order his vision of coming events. A progression is certainly intended in the events described, as evidenced by the opening of the seventh seal that introduces the seven trumpets. Yet the progression is not strictly linear. Rather, later events sometimes recapitulate earlier events. For example, the plagues and calamities of the seven trumpets describe in a new way the punishments and judgments of the end times depicted by the seven seals. Instead of a straight linear progression, the structure of Revelation presents a movement that is spiral. Earlier events are presented in different forms and use different images. As in certain musical pieces, a theme is played, then variations of that theme occur, each variation moving the piece forward. In Revelation, the movement of the work is from John's historical situation to the arrival of the new Jerusalem, the fulfillment of God's ultimate plan for creation. Within that overall forward movement, however, are numerous instances of overlapping and parallel scenes.

Interpreting Revelation

Fascinated and intrigued by the often bizarre imagery in Revelation, interpreters throughout the centuries have attempted in various ways to understand this writing. One of the more popular approaches today understands the book as a catalogue of unfulfilled prophecies of the final days of history. Proponents of this view believe that they are now living in the last days and that informed readers can see predictions in Revelation being fulfilled in current world events. Wars, natural disasters, societal ills, and economic catastrophes are all interpreted as signs of the end times. The beasts and other symbols of evil are identified as actual persons and institutions now in existence or soon to appear. According to this view, John was not addressing the concerns of his own time and situation, but was speaking about the events unfolding today. One of the major problems with this method of interpreting Revelation is that it divorces the work from its first-century historical context. The message of Revelation would have been virtually incomprehensible and meaningless to the Christians of Asia Minor to whom it was addressed. Another problem with this approach is that it fails to take seriously the apocalyptic genre of Revelation with its extensive use of ancient myths and symbols.

A proper interpretation of the Apocalypse must take account of the sociohistorical context and the literary genre of the work. In addition, the function of the language of Revelation needs to be understood. The language of the book is primarily pictorial and symbolic. It is not propositional language. The message of Revelation cannot be condensed into neat, concise theological statements. The language of Revelation is evocative, powerful, emotive language, more akin to poetry than to prose. The Book of Revelation should overwhelm the reader (or hearer) with visual and auditory symbols. Revelation needs to arouse the imagination. It must be experienced, not deciphered. A skilled exegete can explain the origin of many of John's symbols and images by pointing to the Hebrew

Bible, Jewish APOCALYPTIC LITERATURE, and ancient myths as the sources for much of the writing. A scholar can also help us understand how John's original readers may have understood the book's message in their sociohistorical context. As helpful and necessary as these insights are, however, they do not exhaust the meaning of the Apocalypse. The symbols in the book are multivalent and open-ended. They continue to speak to new generations of perceptive readers who realize that the monstrous evils of pride, idolatry, abuse of power, and dehumanization represented by the beasts of Revelation continue to appear in ever new forms, manifesting themselves in individuals and institutions. Likewise, the images of hope and assurance that empowered and comforted John's first-century audience still function in that manner for modern readers.

For Further Study

In the *Mercer Dictionary of the Bible*: APOCALYPTIC LITERATURE; CHURCHES OF REVELATION; LAMB OF GOD; MYTH; NT USE OF OT; REVELATION, BOOK OF; PERSECUTION IN THE NT; SYMBOL; VISION.

In other sources: G. R. Beasley-Murray, *The Book of Revelation*, NCB; I. T. Beckwith, *The Apocalypse of John*; J. L. Blevins, *Revelation as Drama*; M. E. Boring, *Revelation*, Interp; G. B. Caird, *The Revelation of St. John*, HNTC; A. Y. Collins, *The Apocalypse, N.T. Message, Crisis and Catharsis: The Power of the Apocalypse*, and "Revelation, Book of," *AncBD* 5:694-708; E. Schüssler Fiorenza, *The Book of Revelation*, and "Revelation: Vision of a Just World," *ProcI*; C. J. Hemer, *Letters to the Seven Churches*; R. L. Jeske, *Revelation for Today*; J. P. M. Sweet, *Revelation*, WPelC; L. L. Thompson, *The Book of Revelation*.

Commentary

An Outline

Prologue, 1:1-8

The first two verses serve as a title to the work and describe it as a revelation (Gk. *apocalypsis*) from God mediated to John by a heavenly messenger, dealing with soon-occurring events. This description contains many of the elements of the literary genre of an apocalypse as defined by scholars. Indeed, the genre derives its name from the opening word of v. 1 in the Greek text. Although God is the ultimate source of the revelation, it comes to John from Jesus through an ANGEL. John is described as one *who testified to the word of God and to the testimony of Jesus Christ* (v. 2). Testifying, or bearing witness (*martyreō*), is an important theme in Revelation (cf. 1:5, 9; 2:13; 3:14; 6:9; 11:3; 12:11, 17; 17:6; 20:4). One of the purposes of the writing was to call all Christians to be faithful witnesses. The benediction in v. 3 (the first of seven benedictions in the work) indicates that John intended his work to be read aloud to the Christians in Asia Minor as they gathered for worship. Like other apocalyptic writers, John saw himself as living in the final days of history.

These verses comprise an epistolary introduction, describing both the sender and the recipients of the message. *The seven churches* (v. 4) refer to the churches in the Roman province of Asia mentioned in 1:11 and 2:1–3:22. Although addressed to these seven churches specifically, the work is intended for all Christians because the number seven often symbolized completeness or totality. The description of God as the one *who is and who was and who is to come* (vv. 4, 8), an adaptation of Exod 3:14, affirms the continuing presence of God in the lives of believers. Note the change in structure at the end of this trilogy. John does not describe God as the one "who will be" but uses a more dynamic phrase, the one *who is to come*. God is active, not static. *The seven spirits* before God's throne symbolize the power and presence of God active throughout the world (cf. 5:6; Zech 4:1-14), later expressed in Christian theology by the doctrine of the HOLY SPIRIT. The titles attributed to Christ—*the faithful witness, the firstborn of the dead, and the ruler of the kings of the earth*—would have been especially appropriate to John's first-century readers who were faced with persecution and martyrdom. If they too are faithful witnesses, refusing to concede to the divine claims of earthly rulers, they will share in Christ's resurrection.

After the doxology to Christ in vv. 5b-6, John, in language borrowed from Dan 7:13 and Zech 12:10, delivers a prophetic pronouncement of the coming of Christ. The coming, or PAROUSIA, of Jesus Christ, which symbolizes the fulfillment of God's goal for the universe, is portrayed in the subsequent visions (19:11-21), is divinely promised (22:7, 12, 20), and is the final plea of the book (22:17, 20). The prologue closes with a threefold declaration from God, giving divine assurance of the authenticity of John's revelation. This is one of only two places in the book where God speaks directly (cf. 21:5). The ascription *the Alpha and the Omega*, the first and last letters of the Greek alphabet, identify God as the beginning and the end of all history. God is the creator and the consummator of the universe.

The Commissioning of John, 1:9-20

Like many of the Hebrew prophets, particularly ISAIAH and EZEKIEL, John relates a dramatic experience of being commissioned as a PROPHET. *In the spirit* means overcome by the Spirit of God, perhaps in a trance. This phrase identifies John's experience as a visionary experience. *On the Lord's day* probably refers to Sunday, the day of Christ's resurrection. The selection of these particular seven churches to be recipients of the revelation to John is not clear. Perhaps they were the churches with which John was most familiar.

John's vision of the SON OF MAN combines features from the "Ancient One" in Dan 7:9 and the mighty figure of Dan 10 (cf. also Ezekiel's vision of God in 1:26-28). The phrase *one like the Son of Man* (v. 12, lit. "one like a son of man," i.e., one in human form) is also drawn from Daniel (7:13). The exalted Christ stands among the churches, a symbol of power, majesty, and judgment.

Overwhelmed by the spectacle, John falls to his feet (cf. Dan 10:8-9). Both the description of the Son of Man and his first words to John (*I am the first and the last*) indicate his unity with God. He is the resurrected Christ who has conquered death and the place of the dead (*Hades*). For John's readers faced with the possibility of death, that claim would indeed be comforting. The imagery of *the seven stars* in Christ's right hand is perhaps drawn from contemporary depictions of the emperors holding the seven planets or stars in their hands, symbolizing their power over the world. For John, Christ and not the emperor is sovereign. Christ identifies the stars as *the angels of the seven churches*. These angels are the guardian angels of the churches, but even more, they are the heavenly counterparts of the churches. (Cf. the assertion in Dan 10 that nations have such heavenly guardians/counterparts.) When the angels receive the message, the churches do also. The imagery of *the seven lampstands* is derived from Zech 4 where a seven-branched lampstand represents the presence of God (cf. Exod 25:31-40). For John *the seven lampstands are the seven churches* (v. 20), in the midst of whom Christ stands to strengthen and uphold them.

The Messages to the Seven Churches, 2:1–3:22

Often called letters, these messages are cast more in the form of court decrees or proclamations. With slight variations, the messages follow a typical pattern: address to the angel of the church, description of Christ (in terms borrowed from the attributes of the Son of Man in chap. 1), words of praise and/or admonition and condemnation, exhortation, a call to hear, and a promise to the ones who conquer. The information stated or implied about each of the churches bespeaks John's deep familiarity with each of the cities (see Hemer 1986; see also CHURCHES OF REVELATION).

2:1-7. Ephesus. EPHESUS, a seaport and major trading center, was the most important city in Asia Minor. The city was renowned for its temple to the goddess ARTEMIS (cf. Acts 19:21-41), and was also one of the centers of the imperial cult in Asia Minor. Christianity had been established early in Ephesus and had prospered (cf. Acts 18:24–19:41). Christ praises the church at Ephesus on two accounts: its patience and endurance, apparently in the face of some sort of persecution, and its faithfulness in discerning good from evil, truth from falsehood. The latter commendation includes the church's wisdom in rejecting the works of the NICOLAITANS, a group mentioned more fully in the letter to the church at Pergamum. The Ephesian church, apparently in its zeal to preserve the integrity of its faith and root out evil, has become overzealous and forgotten that love is the first responsibility of Christians. The church is admonished to repent of this error or Christ will come in judgment on the church. To *remove your lampstand from its place* means that the people will no longer be a part of the body of Christ. As in all the letters, a closing promise is given to those who conquer, that is, the faithful believers. The promises in all the letters are variations of the same theme—the faithful are assured of participation in the kingdom of God. The *paradise* imagery in v. 7 is found in many apocalyptic writings. The world to come will be a restored and transformed Garden of Eden where the faithful will enjoy a blessed existence.

2:8-11. Smyrna. Like Ephesus, SMYRNA was an important seaport, located approximately thirty-five miles north of Ephesus. It was a city loyal to Rome. In 195 B.C.E. the city erected a temple to the goddess Roma and in 26 C.E. was given the right to build a temple in honor of the emperor TIBERIUS. Nothing is known of the beginnings of Christianity in Smyrna. During the reign of Trajan (98–117 C.E.), IGNATIUS, bishop of ANTIOCH, was martyred. On his way to Rome to be executed, Ignatius stayed in Smyrna, and later on the journey wrote a letter back to the church there and one to Polycarp, bishop of Smyrna. Around 156 C.E. Polycarp himself suffered the fate of martyrdom (see POLYCARP, MARTYRDOM OF). Christ issues no criticisms of the church at Smyrna, only encouraging and extolling the Christians there. Although outwardly poor and afflicted, they are rich in faith and in spirit. The church is suffering persecution from Jews in Smyrna, who because of their attacks on God's people no longer deserve to be called Jews but *a synagogue of Satan*. This statement should not be generalized to mean that John condemns all Jewish people. His harsh words here are aimed only at those who were persecuting the church. John warns the church at Smyrna that more persecution is to be expected. They are to remain faithful, however, even if martyrdom is required. The faithful will receive eternal life, symbolized by the *crown of life*. In Greek athletic contests, the victors were awarded a crown or wreath. To be exempted from *the second death* is another metaphor for ETERNAL LIFE (cf. 20:6, 14).

2:12-17. Pergamum. The capital of the Roman province of Asia, PERGAMUM was home to numerous temples, among them the spectacular temple to ZEUS and the famous ASCLEPION, devoted to Asclepius, the god of healing. Pergamum was an important center for the imperial cult also, having been the first city in the province of Asia to erect a temple to the deified Augustus. The references to *Satan's throne* and *where Satan lives* (v. 13) likely refer to the imperial cult, although some commentators see them as references to the temples of Zeus or Asclepius. The Christians in Pergamum are commended for their faithfulness even in the face of martyrdom. Strong in resisting this external threat, they have been weak in resisting internal threats to their faith. Some in their group have accepted the false teaching of BALAAM, a Mesopotamian diviner who was blamed for leading the Israelites into idolatry and sexual immorality (see Num 22–25, 31). The Nicolaitans at Pergamum are accused of a similar heresy. They eat food sacrificed to idols and practice FORNICATION. They were likely libertine Christians, similar to those in CORINTH (1 Cor 8–10), who believed it was acceptable to eat meat that had been ritually slaughtered and offered to pagan gods or even to the emperor. Whether fornication here is to be understood literally as sexual immorality or figuratively for participation in pagan cults (as often in the Hebrew Bible) is unclear. The faithful will receive MANNA and a white stone. In some Jewish traditions the miracle of the manna in the wilderness (Exod 16:13-36) was expected to be repeated in the messianic age. White stones were used to indicate acquittal in a jury trial and also served as admission tickets to certain events. Either meaning could apply here.

2:18-29. Thyatira. THYATIRA was the least important of the seven cities whose churches are sent messages in Revelation. LYDIA, the dealer of purple cloth whom PAUL met in PHILIPPI (Acts 16:11-15), was originally from Thyatira. The city was home to a large number of trade and craft guilds, organizations that served both social and religious functions. The church at Thyatira is praised highly for its works and for its increasing faithfulness. Like the church at Pergamum, the Thyatirans have not been diligent enough, however, in resisting false teachings and practices. A woman referred to as *Jezebel* (cf. the stories of JEZEBEL in 1–2 Kings) was serving as a prophet and teacher in the church. Her practices were similar to those of the Nicolaitans at Pergamum. Perhaps she was claiming that Christians could participate in the religious rituals and practices of the trade guilds without compromising their faith. Having been warned previously, perhaps by John, she has persisted in her practices. Now she and her followers will be punished by God. The *bed* upon which the woman is to be thrown (v. 22) is likely a sickbed. *Adultery* here is almost certainly figurative. The woman and her followers may have claimed to be so "spiritual" and so in touch with the supernatural world that they could fathom even *'the deep things of Satan'* (v. 24). On the other hand, this phrase may be John's sarcastic parody of their claim to be in touch with the deep mysteries of God. In language borrowed from Ps 2, the faithful are promised that they will triumph over evil and rule with Christ, *the morning star* (v. 28; cf. 22:16).

3:1-6. Sardis. The city of SARDIS had once been the capital of the ancient kingdom of Lydia and a wealthy city. Under Roman rule it was still a prosperous commercial center but did not match its former glory. Sardis was located on an almost impregnable acropolis. On two occasions in its history, however, the city had been conquered due to the lack of diligence on the part of its defenders. John may be alluding to these events in the city's past when he tells the church that it must *wake up* (vv. 2-3) and be diligent in its work. The church in Sardis receives only mild praise (v. 4). The majority of the message to the church is an admonition to wake up and be more alive. The church suffers from lethargy and apathy. Outwardly it appears vital, but its inward condition is critical. The church is on the point of death. If the church does not change, then Christ will come in judgment on them. Their lack of watchfulness will prove disastrous, for Christ *will come like a thief* (cf. Matt 24:42-44; 1 Thes 5:2). The faithful at Sardis will be clothed in white garments, a symbol of purity, and their names will not be removed from *the book of life*. Ancient cities kept registries of their citizens. The book of life is the list of heavenly citizens (cf. Exod 32:32; Dan 12:1). The promise of Christ to confess the name of the faithful before God echoes a similar saying in the Gospels (cf. Matt 10:32; Luke 12:8).

3:7-13. Philadelphia. Founded in the second century B.C.E. by either Attalus II Philadelphus or his older brother Eumenes II (who succeeded one another as kings of Pergamum), the city of PHILADELPHIA and the surrounding area were subject to frequent earthquakes. In 17 C.E. Philadelphia (as well as Sardis) suffered major destruction from an earthquake. Philadelphia, like Smyrna, was visited by Ignatius on his way to martyrdom and the church there received a letter from Ignatius. The *key of David* imagery is borrowed from Isa 22:22. Here, Christ, as the holder of the key, grants or withholds entrance into the KINGDOM OF GOD. The church at Philadelphia receives no condemnation, only commendation, exhortation, and promise. The *open door* (v. 8) provided by Christ leads to God. Access to God is at the heart of the struggle for this church. The local Jews were perhaps denying the validity of the Christians' approach to God and excluding them from the synagogues (v. 9). The words of Christ offer them assurance that they do indeed have access to God, an access that cannot be denied. Even their Jewish opponents will eventually have to admit that the Christians are indeed beloved by God. The faithful will be preserved from the *hour of trial that is coming*, a reference to the eschatological woes that will come in judgment upon the earth. These cataclysmic events are described in detail in the remainder of the book. The conqueror will become *a pillar*, that is, will have a secure place in the presence of God.

3:14-22. Laodicea. Located in the Lycus River valley, the city of LAODICEA was founded by Antiochus II around the middle of the third century B.C.E. and named after his wife Laodice. Because of its location at an important crossroads, Laodicea became a major commercial center. The church at Laodicea is mentioned in Col 4:13-16. Nothing worthy of praise is found among the Laodicean Christians. They receive only criticism from Christ, who condemns them for being ineffective, describing them as neither cold nor hot. This imagery was likely suggested by the beneficial hot springs at nearby Hierapolis and the pure, cold water at COLOSSAE. Laodicea, on the other hand, was plagued with a bad water supply that was both lukewarm and foul. The emetic quality of the water at Laodicea provides the background for the description of Christ who is nauseated by the Laodiceans and spits (or vomits) them from his mouth (v. 16). Although the Laodiceans think they are successful and self-sufficient, they are in reality *wretched, pitiable, poor, blind, and naked* (v.17). To correct their bankrupt spiritual condition, the Laodiceans must turn to Christ. The offer of white robes, symbols of PURITY, is particularly appropriate at Laodicea for the city was famous for its clothing industry, and particularly for its black wool. The salve for their eyes likewise draws upon local information. Laodicea was famous for an eye salve manufactured there. The memorable image of Christ knocking at the door and inviting those inside to eat with him is a promise of Christ's presence, both now and particularly at the messianic BANQUET in the coming age. Those who conquer are promised a share in Christ's reign in the coming kingdom (cf. 22:5).

The Heavenly Throne Room, 4:1–5:14

Chapter 4 begins a new section in the Apocalypse. Whereas chaps. 2 and 3 dealt primarily with the immediate concerns of John's readers, the remainder of the book, while still addressing the first-century situation, is more eschatological in orientation. A characteristic of many apocalypses is the otherworldly journey in which the author claims to have been taken away to another domain (heaven, the underworld, the extremes of the earth) and shown the secrets of those places. Chapter 4 begins in that fashion, but the motif of a journey is not carried through. John's "visit" to the heavenly regions is a visionary experience and not a physical journey.

4:1-11. The throne of God. The open door (cf. 3:8) leads to God's dwelling place. God and his throne are described in images drawn from Ezekiel's vision of the throne-chariot of God (Ezek 1–2; cf. Dan 7 and Enoch's vision of God's throne room in 1 Enoch 14:8-24). The vision is intended to overwhelm and awe the reader with a sense of the majesty and mysteriousness of God. The scene serves as a forceful reminder that God, and not the Roman emperor or any other power, is sovereign over the universe. God, and God alone, is worthy of worship. The *twenty-four elders* seated on thrones constitute the heavenly council. Who they represent is not clear. The most popular suggestion is that they represent the twelve patriarchs of Israel and the twelve disciples of Jesus. The *sea of glass, like crystal* (v. 6) likely draws from the mythological imagery of the sea as representative of chaos, the untamed part of creation, threatening to overcome the created order. Here the sea is still a potential threat, but it has been subdued (the sea is smooth like crystal, instead of turbulent). In the *new heaven* of chap. 21, the sea no longer exists. The *four living creatures* (John has creatively transformed Ezekiel's imagery) lead the heavenly entourage in continual worship of God. Liturgical elements are prevalent in Revelation.

5:1-14. The lamb and the scroll. John then sees *a scroll* in the hand of God. The SCROLL is sealed to guarantee its authenticity and to keep secret its contents. The scroll contains the destiny of the world, the purposes and plans of God for all creation (cf. Ezek 2:9-10; Dan 10:21). As in many apocalyptic writings, in Revelation the course of history is already determined. The heavenly council is at an impasse because no one in the universe has been found who is able to break the seven seals and open the scroll. The dramatic tension of the scene is heightened by the reaction of John, who begins to weep because no one is *worthy to open the scroll*. Then one of the elders informs him that indeed there is one who can open the scroll—the Messiah, described as the Lion of the tribe of JUDAH (Gen 49:9) and the Root of David (Isa 11:1, 10).

Christ stands among the elders as a slain *Lamb*. Whether the specific referent for this metaphor is the sacrificial lamb of the Jewish cultus, the PASSOVER lamb, or the imagery of Isa 53, sacrifice is certainly a part of the message of this slaughtered Lamb figure. But there is a deeper meaning in the imagery. The slain Lamb is the crucified Christ, that is, the martyred Christ. This Lamb is more than victim, however. He is also a powerful, conquering Lamb, similar to the great horned sheep in *1 Enoch* 90:9-42. In fact, as the book of Revelation emphasizes, martyrdom is the means of conquering for both Christ and his followers. The *seven horns and seven eyes* on the Lamb emphasize his strength and wisdom—all-powerful and all-knowing. When the Lamb takes the scroll, the twenty-four elders and the four living creatures fall down in worship before him and once more break forth in song, praising the Lamb for the redemption he has effected for those *from every tribe and language and people and nation* (v. 9). Like the Israelites in Exod 19:6, the redeemed community is to be *a kingdom and priests serving our God* (v. 10). Soon the twenty-four elders and four living creatures are joined by a countless multitude of angels singing in full voice a resounding chorus of praise to the Lamb. Next the whole universe joins in the doxology of adoration and praise, not just for the Lamb but for *the one seated on the throne* as well. Christ is not just the agent of God, but is one with God. For that reason the worship and honor that are due God are appropriate for the Lamb as well.

The Seven Seals, 6:1–8:5

The Lamb proceeds to open the seals on the scroll one by one, unleashing a series of destructive events on the earth. Series of cataclysms such as these are a stock element of many apocalyptic writings (cf. 2 Esdr 4:51–5:13; 6:11-28; 8:63–9:13; 2 Bar 27:1-15; *TMos* 10:4-6; Mark 13:3-27 par.). Often called the eschatological woes, these events are presented as signs of the end times and serve as a part of God's punishment of the earth. As mentioned earlier, the events associated with the seven seals, as well as the other calamities in the book, should not be taken literally, nor assumed to be presented in chronological order. The destructive punishments unleashed by the seven trumpets and seven bowls are different representations of the same eschatological occurrences.

The First Six Seals, 6:1-17

6:1-8. The first four seals. The opening of the first four seals lets loose on the earth the four horsemen of death and destruction, one of the most memorable of the images in the entire Apocalypse. The symbolism of the riders on four different colored horses (*white, red, black,* and *pale green*) is adapted from Zech 1:8-11 (four horsemen are sent out by God to patrol the earth) and Zech 6:1-8 (chariots with four different colored horses are sent out over the earth). The first four seals are opened with a dramatic flourish—the seal is opened and one of the four living creatures cries, *"Come!"* The first rider, on *a white horse,* symbolizes warfare and conquering. White is an appropriate color, since victorious military commanders often rode a white horse in a triumphant procession. "Wars and rumors of wars" (Mark 13:7) are often associated with the end times. When the second seal is opened, a rider on *a red horse,* symbolizing violence and bloodshed, marches across the stage of history, leaving in its path disorder, violent death, and the absence of peace. The opening of the third seal brings forth the rider on *a black horse,* representing famine. The prices for the wheat and the barley are so exorbitant that the average person could not afford to buy food. Luxury items, olive oil and wine, would not be affected however. While the poor starve, the wealthy can continue their indulgent, selfish lifestyle. The fourth rider appears on *a pale green horse.* He is identified as *Death* (the Gk. word can also mean "pestilence") and is accompanied by *Hades,* the place of the dead. Together they wreak destruction upon the earth in a variety of forms (cf. Ezek 5:15-17; 14:21). Their destruction is not complete, however, for they kill only a fourth of the inhabitants of the earth.

6:9-17. The fifth and sixth seals. The opening of the fifth seal reveals to John the souls of the martyrs under the heavenly altar. Their location under the altar derives from their lives having been poured out as a sacrifice. The cry of the martyrs (*How long?*) is a cry for justice, for divine vindication. The cry is both one of personal vengeance and a cry for God to avenge the cause of justice and righteousness. How long will the forces of evil continue to dominate? How long will God allow the people of God to suffer? In outward appearances, the death of the martyrs seemed in vain. Their God was powerless to save them. The forces of evil had conquered. The prayer of the martyrs is that God will reverse the judgment of the world so that the purpose of their dying, as well as the sovereignty of God, might be revealed. The martyrs are each given *a white robe,* symbols of purification and victory, and told to wait until the number of martyrs would be complete. This idea of a predetermined number of righteous who must die before the end arrives is found in other apocalyptic writings (cf. *1 Enoch* 47:3-4; 2 Esdr 4:33-37). The deaths of the martyrs are not meaningless. Their deaths help fulfill the predetermined number and thus hasten the coming of the end when God's justice will be established.

A series of new cataclysms breaks forth when the sixth seal is opened. Described in traditional apocalyptic language, the cosmic disturbances and catastrophes bring judgment upon all the earth, particularly upon the rich and the powerful (v. 15). The punishment is so severe that the people cry out for mercy, asking who is able to withstand such judgment.

Interlude, 7:1-17

Before the seventh seal is opened, the action pauses. In the midst of all the punishment and judgment, John stops to give a word of assurance to God's people. The two visions that comprise this interlude reassure the faithful that they will be saved from the punishments that will affect the earth.

7:1-8. The sealing of the 144,00. vision John sees four angels hold back the winds that are set to unleash destruction on the earth. Another angel commands them to delay their punishment until God's servants have been given a mark on their foreheads for protection. Ezekiel 9:3-4 is the source for this imagery of a mark on the forehead for protection (cf. also the mark on the doorposts that saved the people of God from the plague of the death angel in Exod 12:21-32). Those who are thus protected comprise a throng of 144,000, with 12,000 taken from each of the twelve tribes of Israel. The number 144,000 should be understood figuratively. As a multiple of 12 and 10, both of which often symbolized completeness, 144,000 also represented completeness. But who comprises this complete group? Although some interpreters have argued that the 144,000 are Jews or Jewish Christians, in Revelation neither of these groups receives preferential treatment. Just as the numerical size of the group should not be understood literally, neither should the description of the group as being drawn from the twelve tribes. Instead the imagery depicts the church as the new people of God, the new Israel (cf. Jas 1:1). Although it is possible that the groups in the two visions both symbolize the complete number of God's people, the 144,000 more likely represent a complete subgroup—the martyrs (see the further descriptions of this group in 14:1-5). John gives special attention to them because they must bear the ultimate witness to their faith.

7:9-17. The great multitude. In contrast to the 144,000 in the first vision, the people who comprise the group in the second vision are too numerous for anyone to count. Whereas the first group was solely martyrs, the second group includes all the people of God, *from every nation, from all tribes and peoples and languages* (v. 9). They have *come out of the great ordeal* (v. 14), that is, the persecution that precedes the end. In a paradoxical metaphor, John says that they have washed their robes *in the blood of the Lamb* and made them white. Christ's sacrificial death has purified the people and rendered them righteous. This innumerable crowd of the faithful is in heaven, where they wave palm branches, symbols of joy and celebration, and sing a song of praise to God. Once more the heavenly chorus composed of the angels, the twenty-four elders, and the four living creatures join in with their doxology to God. The interlude ends with a comforting description of the existence awaiting the faithful. Neither hunger, nor thirst, nor scorching heat will afflict them for the Lamb will care for them. The Lamb, paradoxically, will be their shepherd who provides for their needs. Suffering and pain will be absent, for *God will wipe away every tear from their eyes* (cf. 21:3-4).

The Seventh Seal, 8:1-5

A climactic moment has been reached. The seventh seal is opened. One expects a final vision of what is to come. Instead, a short period of silence follows the opening of the last seal. The silence is not only for dramatic effect, but also indicates reverence, awe, and anticipation. The opening of the seventh seal does not yield the expected end but inaugurates a new series of woes, the seven trumpets. Before the trumpet series begins, another angel appears. Standing before the heavenly altar, the angel mixes incense with the prayers of the people and offers them on the altar. Although not restricted to them, the prayers of the martyrs under the altar in 6:9-11 would certainly be included in this offering. The prayers of the people are prayers for justice and the coming of the kingdom of God. *The smoke of the incense, with the prayers of the saints, rose before God* (v. 4), indicating that God hears the people's prayers. The angel takes fire from the altar and casts it down upon the earth, resulting in thunder, lightning, and an earthquake. The prayers of the people have been effective. The judgment on the earth has begun, as the blowing of the seven trumpets will make clear.

The Seven Trumpets, 8:6–11:19

The blowing of *the seven trumpets* sets forth a new series of eschatological woes on the earth. What was begun with the opening of the seven seals is portrayed here in a different set of images. The two series overlap rather than succeed one another. There is a progression from the seals to the trumpets, however. Whereas the destruction wrought by the opening of the seals was basically limited to humanity, the destruction from the trumpet blasts affects the entire universe: the earth (8:7), the oceans (8:8-9), fresh water (8:10-11), the heavenly bodies (8:12), and persons (9:1-20). A further advance is noted in the extent of the destruction of human lives. When the fourth seal is opened, Death and Hades kill one-fourth of the population. In contrast, the trumpet punishments affect one-third of the world. Again, one must remember that this is poetic, not mathematical, language. The numerical statements convey that the destruction is not yet complete. The trumpet judgments are dependent on the Egyptian PLAGUES in Exod 7–10. Plagues of hail and fire (8:7), water turning to blood (8:9), darkness (8:12), and locusts (9:1-11) match the Egyptian plagues.

The First Six Trumpets, 8:6–9:21

8:6-11. The first three trumpets. The first trumpet blast sends fire that scorches the earth, affecting a third of the plant life. The second trumpet causes *something like a great mountain* (8:8) to fall into the sea, turning the water to blood. Not only are the fish in the sea killed but ships are also destroyed. The plague from the third trumpet blast is an extension of the second one. Whereas the second trumpet blast affected only the salt water, the third affects fresh water, turning them poisonous. *Wormwood*, the name of the star that poisons the water, is a popular name for any of several related plants. The wormwood mentioned several places in the Bible is probably a small shrub with hairy, gray leaves that was known for its extremely bitter taste. This latter characteristic explains why in the Bible "wormwood" is used figuratively for bitterness and sorrow. The plant is not actually poisonous, but John intensifies its effect.

8:12-13. The fourth trumpet. The results from the blowing of the fourth trumpet provide a good example of why the imagery in Revelation cannot be taken at face value. If a third of the sun and moon were darkened, then the length of a day and a night would not correspondingly be shortened by one third. John's imagery is not limited by reality or scientific accuracy, however. Between the sounding of the fourth and fifth trumpets, an announcement is made by an eagle flying through the sky. The announcement serves as a preview of what is to come and as a warning to the inhabitants of the earth. The first three trumpets have unleashed their punishments, but even more terrifying are the calamities yet to come. This announcement is a dramatic technique that heightens the suspense of John's vision.

9:1-11. The fifth trumpet. After the eagle warning, the fifth angel blows his trumpet and a fallen star takes a key and opens the bottomless pit. The star is an angel, as is often the case in APOCALYPTIC LITERATURE (cf. *1 Enoch* 86, 88). *The bottomless pit*, or abyss, is the place where demons or fallen angels were imprisoned. (Cf. *1 Enoch* 1–36, known as the "Book of the Watchers." This work, elaborating on the tradition in Gen 6:1-4, describes the rebellion against God of a group of angels. As punishment they are consigned to the abyss, described as a desert place and a place of burning fire.) The pit is the reservoir of EVIL. When the shaft to the pit is opened, smoke billows out and blocks the sun. Out of the smoke comes a swarm of locusts who look *like horses equipped for battle* (v. 7). The imagery of destructive horse-like locusts is drawn from Joel 1:1–2:11. The plague of locusts in Joel is also accompanied by darkness throughout the land. Locusts were (and still are) a devastating terror in the Near East. Swarms of locusts can destroy an entire

region due to their numbers and their voracious appetite. John is even more creative than Joel in his description of the locusts. Not only do they have the appearance of horses, they wear

what looked like crowns of gold; their faces were like human faces, their hair like women's hair, and their teeth like lions' teeth; they had scales like iron breastplates, and the noise of their wings was like the noise of many chariots with horses rushing into battle. (vv. 7-9)

The surreal locusts of John's vision are told not to harm the vegetation. Instead their task is to torture the wicked of the earth, those *who do not have the seal of God on their foreheads* (v. 4). They do not kill, but only inflict agonizing torture with their scorpion tails for five months, a limited amount of time. These demonic locust figures are grotesque and frightening representations of evil. They symbolize war, destruction, and chaos, but on a much grander scale than anything seen before. These evil forces, released in the last days, serve God's purposes by inflicting pain and punishment on the wicked. Evil itself, however, after this final resurgence will eventually be defeated by God. The idea of the last assault of evil is given in a different form in 19:11–20:15. The name of the leader of the locust monsters is given in Hebrew (*Abaddon*) and in Greek (*Apollyon*). The word *Abaddon* means "destruction" and is used figuratively in the Hebrew Bible for death or the place of the dead (see Job 26:6; 28:22). *Apollyon* is from a Greek word meaning "to destroy." (Some scholars have seen here a reference also to Apollo, whose symbol was a locust and of whom Domitian claimed to be an incarnation. See Beasley-Murray 1974, 162–63.)

9:12-21. The sixth trumpet. The sixth trumpet, which is the second woe foretold by the eagle, brings forth another invading army, cavalry from the *river Euphrates*. This woe is set in motion by the command of a voice from the heavenly altar, the place where the prayers of the people have been poured out (8:3-5) and from underneath which the cries of the martyrs have been heard (6:9-11). The sixth trumpet, then, is in part a response to the prayers of God's people. It is part of God's punishment of the wicked and the vindication of the righteous. As with the earlier punishments, this one is limited. Only a third of humankind is killed. The EUPHRATES River was the eastern boundary of the ROMAN EMPIRE. On the other side were the Parthians, the dreaded enemy of the Romans. The Parthian cavalry may have provided the rudimentary image for John, but John's army is no earthly force. Like the locust plague of the fifth trumpet, the cavalry is a grotesque, supernatural force that will wreak destruction. Their appearance is frightening; their effect is devastating. John envisions God using these demonic agents to carry out God's will. The angels who lead the destruction are *bound* (v. 14), that is, they are part of the fallen angels who were bound and thrown into the pit according to apocalyptic writings (see comment on 9:1).

The EXODUS motif that is so prevalent in Revelation explains the statement that, even after these plagues, the remainder of the people do not repent. The people of the world will follow in the footsteps of the PHARAOH. They will continue their idolatrous and rebellious ways.

Interlude, 10:1–11:13

As was the case between the sixth and seventh seals, so between the sixth and seventh trumpet blasts John inserts an interlude to provide reassurance to the faithful that they will not be harmed by the eschatological woes. This interlude, like the earlier one, contains two visions.

10:1-11. The mighty angel with the little scroll. John sees a mighty angel coming down and standing with one foot *on the sea* and one *on the land*. The physical description of the angel owes much to the description in Dan 10 of a similar heavenly being and the description of God in Ezek 1:26-28. This scene draws also upon the vision in Dan 12 in which two angels appear to Daniel, "one standing on this bank of the stream and one on the other" (12:5). The angel speaks like a roaring lion, causing the seven thunders to break forth. The seven thunders deliver a message that John is able to understand and that he is about to write down when he is told to seal up the message, that is, keep it secret. The reader is left puzzled and curious about the contents of the message from the seven thunders. The secrecy motif heightens the drama, but it plays a more important role. The refusal to reveal the message of the seven thunders is a way of saying that even such revelatory visions as John experienced and wrote down for his readers are incomplete. God's purposes and plans are not all revealed, because God is beyond full comprehension by mortals. The ineffable MYSTERY of God remains intact.

The angel *raised his right hand to heaven and swore by him who lives forever and ever* (vv. 5-6; cf. Dan 12:7) that there would be no more delay. The

time for the fulfillment of God's purposes is near. John believed that he and the church of his time were living in the last days. The final onslaught of evil was breaking forth upon the world. Soon God would act decisively and would triumph over the evil forces. This word would have been a message of great comfort to John's readers who were facing persecution and perhaps martyrdom. The cry "How long?" has been answered: "No more delay!"

The voice from heaven speaks once more to John, commanding him to take the open scroll from the angel's hand and *eat it*. A similar episode is reported by Ezekiel as part of his experience of being called to be a prophet (2:8–3:3). For John, eating the scroll is a reinforcement of his commissioning to the role of the prophet. The scroll is *sweet as honey,* but makes his *stomach . . . bitter* (v. 10). This scroll, like the scroll in chaps. 4–5, contains God's plan for all creation, the message John is to make known as a prophet of God. Eating the scroll is symbolic of taking in the message, of "consuming" God's word, so that God's message is now John's message. The scroll is both bitter and sweet, because both judgment and mercy, punishment and blessing, are a part of the divine plan. A close parallel with the scroll is found in Dan 12. There Daniel is told to keep the book sealed "until the time of the end" (12:4). Now, however, the book is unsealed because *there will be no more delay* (v. 6). The long-awaited time of God's vindication has arrived.

11:1-13. The measuring of the Temple and the two witnesses. The second vision of the interlude begins with John being given a measuring rod and told to go and measure the Temple. Only the inner courts are to be measured. The measuring is a sign of protection. Whereas the inner court is preserved, the outer court will be trampled by the nations. Many scholars have postulated that this was an earlier prophecy that was put forth by ZEALOT defenders of Jerusalem prior to its destruction by the Romans in 70 C.E. After the outer part of the Temple was captured by the Romans, the defenders barricaded themselves in the inner courts. If the suggestion by some interpreters is correct, this prophecy would have been a prediction by the Zealot defenders that even though the Romans might trample the outer courts, God would not allow the inner sanctuary to fall to them. Sadly, they were in error. John has perhaps taken this earlier prophecy and adapted it for his purposes. The Temple has already been destroyed by the time John writes, so his concern is not with the actual Temple in Jerusalem. Rather, for John the people of God are now the Temple. The church is what is marked for protection. This vision then serves as a word of encouragement and assurance to the faithful. The unrighteous will be "trampled" (v. 2) during the time of the eschatological woes, but God's people will not be harmed. The period of the trampling will be forty-two months, three and one-half years. In Daniel three and a half years (or "times") is the predicted length of time before the end arrives (7:25; 12:7). The figure should not be pressed. As half of seven, a number for completeness or totality, three and one half represents incompleteness, a short period of time.

The introduction of the *two witnesses* (v. 3) seems disconnected to the vision of the Temple. The abruptness of their appearance supports the contention that the measuring of the Temple is an earlier tradition that John has reworked. The two witnesses are given authority to prophesy for 1260 days (three and one half years), the same amount of time mentioned in v. 2. To prophesy is to proclaim God's message to the world, to be faithful witnesses of God and Christ. The content of their message is likely indicated by their garb, *sackcloth.* Since sackcloth was worn as a sign of penitence, the prophecy of the two witnesses is a call to repentance. The two witnesses are further described as *the two olive trees and the two lampstands that stand before the Lord* (v. 4). In Zech 4 the image of two olive trees is used for ZERUBBABEL the governor and JOSHUA the high priest, both of whom are viewed as messianic figures. The two olive trees provide oil for the lampstand. John applies both images, the olive trees and the lampstands, to the two witnesses. For John, however, the two witnesses are not messianic figures. They are further described in terms reminiscent of ELIJAH and MOSES (11:6; cf. 1 Kgs 17:1; Exod 7:8–11:10).

The two witnesses must give the ultimate testimony—their lives—when they are attacked and killed by the beast *from the bottomless pit.* This beast John will describe more fully in the coming chapters. The place where they are killed is *prophetically called Sodom and Egypt, where also their Lord was crucified* (v. 8). Jerusalem, like Sodom and Egypt, has become for John a symbol of rebellion against God. Jerusalem is representative of the entire world that rejects God and the prophets of God. John's portrayal of Jerusalem as the place where the prophets are killed is not an anti-Jewish statement. In the Hebrew Bible, Jerusalem is often condemned for its disobedience to God and its rejection of God's spokespersons. John is simply

adapting that tradition here. Of course, for him that condemnation of Jerusalem is even more pointed because Jerusalem was the place of Jesus' martyrdom. Even after death, the two witnesses are treated shamefully, their bodies allowed to lie on the streets to be the subject of taunts and ridicule.

God will not allow his prophets to die in vain, however. After a short span of time (*three and a half days*), they are resurrected and ascend into heaven in the sight of their enemies. Following their ascension, a great earthquake strikes the city, killing seven thousand people. Those who are left *were terrified and gave glory to the God of heaven* (v. 13). The witness of the two martyrs produces results. Their testimony in word and in blood leads to repentance by the people.

The Seventh Trumpet, 11:14-19

Verse 14 serves as a reminder of the action of the work prior to the interlude. The lengthy interlude had interrupted the three woes that were announced by the eagle (8:13). Verse 14 ties the earlier section with what is to follow. The third woe, though announced, is not described. It is hinted at in the first part of v. 18 (*the nations raged, but your wrath has come*). The seventh trumpet blast brings the action to an end. God's purposes have been fulfilled. The heavenly voices declare the completion of God's plan when they announce, *The kingdom of the world has become the kingdom of our Lord and of his Messiah* (v. 15). God's reign no longer lies in the future, but is a present reality. In a way, the seventh trumpet blast is anticlimactic. After all the destruction and punishment leading up to the last days, John provides no description of God's new order. It is completed. Instead of a picture of the kingdom of God, John lets his readers hear the celebration that takes place over God's victory. The twenty-four elders sing a song of triumph, saying, *We give you thanks, Lord God Almighty, who are and who were, for you have taken your great power and begun to reign* (v. 17). God is no longer described as the one who is and who was and who is to come. The last element is no longer needed. God has already come; the future has become the present. John could have ended his message here. The consummation of the kingdom has been achieved. John has more to reveal, however. He will present new images of punishment and salvation, eschatological woes and eternal reward.

Chapter 11 ends with a brief glimpse into the heavenly Temple in which the ark of the covenant is seen. The ARK had sat in the Holy of Holies in Solomon's

Temple, a visual reminder of the presence of God in the midst of the people. The ark of the covenant was probably carried away or destroyed when the Babylonians captured Jerusalem in the sixth century B.C.E. When God's kingdom has arrived in its fullness, John sees the ark in the heavenly Temple, a symbol of God's presence with the people.

The Great Conflict, 12:1–14:20

Chapters 12–14 portray the life-and-death struggle of the church with the evil forces aligned against it. For John and his readers, evil is incarnated primarily in the Roman emperor and his claims to divinity. This confrontation with the imperial cult is the major focus of this section. But John realizes that the conflict he and other Christians are facing is larger than what it appears. John sees this struggle in the context of the great cosmic conflict between the forces of good and evil. The evil powers have always rebelled against the sovereignty of God and attempted to thwart God's purposes. The suffering of the Christians of John's day was not isolated or insignificant. John paints their trials on a cosmic canvas, one that stretches back in history to primeval times. The struggles in which the church is engaged is simply another chapter in the ancient story of chaos versus order, obedience versus disobedience, rebellion versus loyalty. By giving his readers a new perspective on their ordeal John gave meaning to their suffering. Their persecution and martyrdom were not in vain. By their patient endurance and faithful witness, they were contributing to the overthrow and defeat of the powers of evil. John also offers assurance to his readers by revealing to them the ultimate outcome of this cosmic conflict of which they are a part.

The Vision of the Great Dragon, 12:1-18

Chapter 12 draws heavily upon ancient mythology for its images, adapting a popular cosmic combat MYTH found in many cultures of the ancient world. The closest parallel to the story told by John is the Greek version of the myth which tells of the birth of Apollo, son of Zeus and Leto. Python, the great dragon, pursues the pregnant goddess Leto, seeking to kill the unborn Apollo and his mother. Leto is carried away to safety to an island where Poseidon, god of the sea, hides her by sinking the island under the sea. When Python's search is unsuccessful, he finally gives up and goes away. The island is raised and Leto gives birth to Apollo, who goes and kills Python. John

adapts this universal myth to convey the story of the defeat of the forces of evil by Jesus. John's use of this myth may have been particularly significant for his readers who were confronted with the claims of the imperial cult. Several of the Roman emperors used this myth for their own propaganda purposes, presenting themselves in the role of Apollo, the destroyer of evil. John and his readers know otherwise, however. Christ, not the emperor, is the real victor over the malevolent forces of chaos, darkness, and wickedness. As such, Christ and not the emperor is the one worthy of obedience and worship.

12:1-6. The woman, the dragon, and the child. The woman is presented as the cosmic queen, *clothed with the sun, . . . the moon under her feet, and . . . [wearing] a crown of twelve stars* (the zodiac). The *great red dragon* has *seven heads and ten horns, and seven diadems on his heads* (v. 3). In the Babylonian story of creation TIAMAT, the monster of the deep, also has seven heads. LEVIATHAN, the serpent-like monster of chaos in Hebrew folk-lore, also had many heads (cf. Ps 74:14). The *ten horns* (cf. Dan 7:7) symbolize the monster's power, the crowns his dominion. He is a powerful figure, as evidenced by his knocking a third of the stars out of the heavens (a traditional motif in many of the ancient myths). The application of Ps 2:9 to the child—he *is to rule all the nations with a rod of iron* (v. 5)—identifies him as the Messiah. The dragon fails in his attempt to kill the child, who is snatched away and taken to God. In John's story the birth and ascension of Christ are compressed into a single event. The woman escapes to the wilderness and is protected there by God for 1,260 days, the same three-and-a-half-year period John has mentioned before (see 11:2-3).

12:7-12. Michael and the dragon. Verses 7-12 appear to be an insertion into the cosmic combat myth. In reality they contain simply another version of the same struggle. That John is adapting a Jewish story here is evidenced by the role played by MICHAEL. He is the hero of the story, the one who defeats the dragon and his angels. The story of the ouster from heaven of rebellious angels is found in several Jewish sources (cf. *1 Enoch* 6–16) and has been popularized in John Milton's *Paradise Lost*. The great dragon is identified as *that ancient serpent, who is called the Devil and Satan, the deceiver of the whole world* (v. 9). In the Hebrew Bible Satan (literally the "accuser" or "adversary") is not the leader of the forces of evil who are arrayed against God. Rather Satan is the accuser of the righteous, the "prosecuting attorney" who brings charges against God's people. In later nonbiblical Jewish writings, likely due to the influence of the Zoroastrian religion of Persia, Satan (or Belial, or Beliar, or Azazel, or Semyaza) begins to be seen as the leader of the demonic forces of evil. Satan is portrayed as the archenemy of God. That understanding of the role of Satan was taken over by NT writers and is evident in Revelation also (see SATAN IN THE NT).

The ancient Jewish myth that John is using would have portrayed Michael as the one who defeats Satan and casts him out of heaven. John alters that story. Satan has been overthrown *by the blood of the Lamb and by the word of their testimony* (v. 11), that is, the testimony of the martyrs. For John the defeat of Satan is not a primeval event, but one that occurs in the death and exaltation of Christ and continues in the faithful witness of the martyrs who give their lives for the sake of God. John is saying to the persecuted church that their deaths have meaning. The faithful are contributing to the overthrow of the forces of evil. Their deaths may look like defeat, but John gives them a new vision in which death is victory.

12:13-18. The pursuit of the woman. Thrown out of heaven, Satan turns his attack upon the woman on earth. The woman, however, is given divine protection. She is *given the two wings of the great eagle* and carried off to the wilderness where she is protected during the coming period of trouble (cf. Exod 19:4, "I bore you on eagles' wings and brought you to myself"). Unable to defeat the woman, the dragon then goes off to make war on her children, the faithful witnesses (v. 17). The woman is a multivalent image. She is at the same time Mary (mother of Jesus), Israel (from whom the Messiah comes), the church, and the people of God of all ages, whose "children" are still being persecuted. John is adapting a universal myth here for his Christian message. Exact correspondence between the characters in the myth and the Christian story is not possible. One should not press for consistency in the role of the woman in the story.

The Two Beasts, 13:1-18

Whereas chap. 12 depicted the heavenly battle with Satan, chap. 13 reveals the earthly counterpart of that struggle. Thrown down to earth, the dragon stands poised to unleash his fury against God's faithful.

13:1-10. The beast from the sea. The first beast arises from the sea, the primordial realm of chaos and rebellion. The description of the beast is dependent on the four beasts from the sea in Dan 7, whose characteristics are merged into this one beast. John makes clear the source of this beast's power: *the dragon gave it his power and his throne and great authority* (v. 2). In awe and fear of this great beast, the people follow after the beast and worship him. Who is this beast? Even though the term is not used in Revelation, he is the ANTICHRIST, the eschatological opponent of Christ and his followers (see Reddish 1990, 34.) The Antichrist has taken on a particular identity for John. As the clues John gives elsewhere make clear, the beast is the ROMAN EMPIRE, and particularly the emperors themselves (see chap. 17). The many heads symbolize the various emperors who have ruled over the empire. The statement that one of the heads of the beast *seemed to have received a death-blow, but its mortal wound had been healed* (v. 3) is a reference to the Nero *redivivus* myth. Nero occupied a special place in the minds of the Christians, for Nero had instigated the first persecution against Christians when he blamed the fire in Rome on them in 64 C.E. Later, Nero committed suicide by stabbing himself in the throat. The rumor soon spread, however, that Nero was not really dead or that he would come back to life and rule over the people again. By saying that this mortal wound had been healed, John is warning the church that Nero's persecution has returned in the present emperor, Domitian.

For forty-two months (three and a half years) the beast wages war against God's people. Without attributing evil to God, John states that the beast *was allowed to make war on the saints* (v. 7). Satan and his cohorts may have the upper hand at the moment, but ultimately God will assert control and the beast will be allowed to persecute the saints no longer. Those who succumb to the lures of the beast and worship it are the ones whose names are not written in *the book of life*, the register of the citizens of heaven (cf. 3:5). The last part of v. 10 is a refrain that sounds throughout the Apocalypse: *Here is a call for the endurance and faith of the saints.*

13:11-18. The beast from the earth. The second beast, also called *the false prophet* (19:20), is a beast from the land who deceives the people and enforces worship of the first beast. He performs SIGNS AND WONDERS like prophets of God, but he is a *false* prophet. Those who refuse to worship the first beast are killed. Those who comply, who pay homage to the first beast, receive a mark on their right hands or on their foreheads. This "mark of the beast," a parody of the sealing of the 144,000 in chap. 7, allows them to buy and sell in the marketplace. The mark of the beast requires wisdom, John says, for the number of the beast is the number of a person. That number is 666. The ancient practice of *gematria*, the assigning of numerical values to words, is at work here. In the ancient world, letters were used for numbers. (In our alphabet, A=1, B=2, C=3, etc.) One could easily convert a person's name into a number. Since the numerical value of several names could equal 666, the identification of the person John had in mind is not certain. The most likely referent for John's 666 number code, however, is Caesar Nero, whose name in Hebrew equals 666. The beast is not Nero, for he is dead. But Domitian, the current emperor, is a reincarnation of Nero. (Some commentators have argued for the symbolic meaning of 666. Since six is one less than seven, the perfect number, then 666 represents triple imperfection or evil.)

The background for this chapter is obviously emperor worship. The first beast who is worshiped represents the Roman emperor. Who, then, is the second beast? He represents everyone who encourages and supports emperor worship (local magistrates, imperial priests, provincial councils). By depicting the emperor and the promoters of the imperial cult as beasts who operate under the authority of the great dragon, John pulls back the curtain and reveals to his readers the true identity of those who are persecuting them. The imperial cult is an instrument of Satan, for it usurps the worship that belongs only to God.

Interlude, 14:1-20

Once more John pauses in the midst of scenes of suffering to offer words of encouragement and assurance. Twice already John has reassured his readers that the faithful will receive divine protection during the coming trials. This protection is protection from the effects of God's punishment, not protection from persecution and death. John is fearful that many of his Christian comrades may have to bear witness through death. Even if that happens, however, they can be assured that God will not abandon them. They will still share in God's new kingdom. That is the assurance that the marks of protection convey.

14:1-5. The Lamb and the redeemed. These verses reveal the ultimate destiny of the faithful. Chapter 13 portrayed the apparent defeat of God's people who died a martyr's death. The opening section of chap. 14 reverses that judgment, depicting the faithful not as defeated but as triumphant. John sees Christ (the Lamb) standing on Mt. Zion, the center of the messianic kingdom. With him are the 144,000 that were introduced in chap. 7. Like the heavenly chorus in 5:8-10, the 144,000 sing a new song of praise to God, a song that no one else could learn. While it is tempting to interpret the 144,000 as symbolic of all the redeemed of humanity, a closer reading of the description of them suggests that they are specifically the martyrs, the ones who have been the victims of the beasts in chap. 13. These with the Lamb *have not defiled themselves with women, for they are virgins* (v. 4). This description is figurative, not literal. One of the regulations for HOLY WAR required sexual abstinence before battle (cf. 1 Sam 21:4-5). John uses this requirement for ceremonial purity to symbolize moral and religious purity. The 144,000 have not been defiled by idolatry or by the enticements of the great whore of Babylon (chap. 17). They *follow the Lamb wherever he goes*, even unto death. They are described as *first fruits*. This is sacrificial language, appropriate for those who have sacrificed their lives for God. Finally, *in their mouth no lie was found*. The martyrs maintained their witness even under persecution, refusing to proclaim Caesar as lord.

14:6-13. The message of three angels. The central section of this chapter presents three angels who move across the stage, each proclaiming the coming judgment of God. The message of the first angel is a call to repentance and a warning of the impending judgment. The second angel issues a proleptic announcement of the fall of Babylon (Rome). The third angel pronounces judgment upon those who have succumbed to the power of the beast and its cult. Once more a call for the endurance of the saints is sounded (v. 12). The second beatitude of Revelation pronounces blessings upon those *who from now on die in the Lord* (v. 13). Those who are called to die as martyrs can face their ordeal with the knowledge of the glorious rest that awaits them. After death, they will no longer have to endure trials and persecutions.

14:14-20. The final judgment of God. This section depicts the final judgment of God in imagery that is borrowed from Joel 3:13. The first scene shows the harvesting of the earth, like wheat that is cut with a sickle (cf. Matt 13:24-30). John does not make clear whether this harvesting is a complete gathering of all people, the wicked for punishment and the righteous for rewards, or whether, like the second scene, this one portrays only the judgment of the unrighteous. Either of these options is preferable to the attempt by some commentators to argue that the first scene depicts only the ingathering of the faithful, whereas the second scene (vintage), portrays the punishment of the wicked. In Joel both images are used to show God's judgment against the wicked. In both scenes in chap. 14 an angel from the presence of God (*the temple . . . the altar*) gives the comand for the divine judgment to begin. The imagery of blood flowing *as high as a horse's bridle, for a distance of about two hundred miles* (v. 20) conveys the magnitude and severity of God's punishment on the wicked.

The Seven Bowl Plagues, 15:1–16:21

The seven seals and the seven trumpets have already disclosed the eschatological woes that are to strike the earth. John now introduces a different series, this one composed of seven bowls, that will present a different perspective on these calamities. Like the seven trumpet plagues, the bowl plagues are modeled after the PLAGUES on Egypt in the book of Exodus.

The Martyrs on the Heavenly Shore, 15:1-4

Verse 1 gives a brief announcement of the new series of seven plagues that are soon to break forth. These will be the last plagues, *for with them the wrath of God is ended* (v. 1). Before beginning the bowl plagues, John presents another vision of the faithful whom he sees standing beside *a sea of glass mixed with fire* (v. 2). This is the sea that stands before the throne of God (4:6). Here the sea also connotes the RED SEA of the Exodus tradition. As the Israelites traveled safely through the Red Sea and arrived in the Promised Land, so the faithful in John's vision have passed through their Red Sea (persecution and martyrdom) and now stand on heaven's shore. Moses and the Israelites sang a song of THANKSGIVING and praise after reaching the distant shore (Exod 15:1-18.) Likewise the victorious martyrs now sing *the song of Moses . . . and the song of the Lamb* (v. 3).

The Seven Angels with Bowls, 15:5-8

John sees seven angels who are to inflict the seven plagues come out of the heavenly Temple. Each is given a bowl containing the wrath of God that is to be poured out on the earth. The imagery of the bowls is likely ₁a composite of two ideas from the Hebrew Bible. Bronze basins or bowls were used by the priests to carry away the ashes from the altar after sacrifices were offered (Exod 27:3). In John's vision the angels

who are given the bowls have just exited the Temple where the heavenly altar is located (cf. the angel with the censer at the altar in 8:3-5). The bowls are *full of the wrath of God* (v. 7). Several passages in the Hebrew Bible speak of the cup of God's wrath (Isa 51:17; Ps 75:8; Jer 25:15-29; 49:12) that God's enemies drink, symbolizing God's punishments on them.

The Pouring of the Seven Bowls, 16:1-21

16:1-7. The first three bowls. In response to a command by a voice from the Temple, the seven angels pour out their bowls of judgment on the earth. The bowl plagues are very similar to the trumpet plagues, both of which draw upon the plagues inflicted on Egypt. The pouring out of the first bowl results in painful sores on *those who had the mark of the beast and who worshiped its image* (v. 2). This plague is similar to the sixth Egyptian plague (Exod 9:8-12). The second and third bowl plagues, like the second and third trumpet plagues, affect first the sea and then the fresh water. Here both are turned to blood, which is seen as fitting because the wicked had *shed the blood of saints and prophets* and now they must drink blood (v. 6). John proclaims that God is a God of justice. The people deserve the punishment they receive. The altar (the angel attending the altar, or the souls of the martyrs under the altar?) agrees in the assessment that God's judgments are true and just. The result of the second bowl plague is more severe than the result of the second trumpet plague. With the latter, only one-third of the earth is affected. With the former, *every living thing in the sea died* (v. 3).

16:8-11. The fourth and fifth bowls. The pouring of the fourth bowl on the sun brings about a scorching heat on the earth. Like the Egyptian PHARAOH, the people are obstinate in their rebellion against God and refuse to repent. The first four plagues have already affected all parts of the cosmos (land, waters, sea, and the sun). The focus of the fifth plague is narrower than that of the previous four plagues. The fifth bowl is poured *on the throne of the beast.* The ROMAN EMPIRE receives special punishment because it is responsible for leading many people into idolatry. Reminiscent of the ninth plague on Egypt (Exod 10:21-29), the fifth bowl plague produces an agonizing darkness over the whole land. Once more John states that the people do not repent of their evil ways. Some people are so hardened against God that nothing is able to bring them to repentance.

16:12-16. The sixth bowl. The sixth bowl plague has many similarities with the sixth trumpet plague in 9:13-19. Both describe invading armies from across the Euphrates who invade the west. In both scenes John is making use of the Roman fear of a Parthian invasion. John sees *three foul spirits like frogs* (v. 13) coming out of the mouths of the dragon, the beast, and *the false prophet* (that is, the second beast). The imagery of the frogs comes from the second Egyptian plague (Exod 7:25–8:15) in which the land is overrun by an abundance of frogs. John has greatly modified the imagery, however. These are no ordinary frogs. They are demonic spirits who gather together the kings of the earth for the great eschatological battle. The place where they are assembled *is called Harmagedon* (v. 16, or, ARMAGEDDON). The name Harmagedon is likely derived from Hebrew words meaning "mountain of Megiddo." Megiddo was an important city guarding the pass through the JEZREEL Valley in Israel. Several important battles had been fought at Megiddo throughout Israel's history. Thus the name Megiddo would have connoted a battlefield for people familiar with Israel's past. John is not predicting a literal battle that is to take place at Megiddo. *Harmagedon* is figurative language. It symbolizes the final attempt by the forces of evil to defeat God. John does not give any description here of the confrontation. He will do that in a later chapter (19:11-21). Instead, he gives an admonition from Christ: *"See, I am coming like a thief! Blessed is the one who stays awake and is clothed, not going about naked and exposed to shame"* (v. 15). This call to watchfulness is a warning about being unprepared for the coming of Christ which will occur unexpectedly. The wise person will live in anticipation and preparedness.

16:17-21. The seventh bowl. The emptying of the seventh bowl into the air brings down the curtain on the eschatological drama. A loud voice from the Temple announces, *"It is done!"* (v. 17). A cataclysmic earthquake, accompanied by lightning and thunder, rips through the earth, destroying *the great city . . . and the cities of the nations* (v. 19). The great city is called *Babylon,* but in reality is Rome. It is singled out for special mention because of its role in the persecution of God's servants and its idolatrous and blasphemous claims. The following chapters will present a fuller description of the downfall of Rome. The plague of hail that also occurs when the seventh angel pours his bowl is a part of the Exodus motif that is so strong in this section of the Apocalypse.

The Fall of Babylon, 17:1–19:10

For John, Rome represented the ultimate rebellion against God. The divine claims of the emperor, the imperial cult, and the persecution of God's people were all components of Rome's sinfulness and resistance to God. John goes to great lengths in this section to expose the true character and identity of this "great city" and to show reactions both on earth and in heaven to the city's demise.

The Great Whore, 17:1-18

Invited by an angel to see the judgment that befalls the great city, John is carried away *in the spirit* (in a vision) into a wilderness. John introduces a new imagery for Rome. The city is portrayed as a *great whore* who rides on a scarlet beast *full of blasphemous names* who has *seven heads and ten horns.* The beast is the same as the one John described in 13:1-10 and represents the Roman Empire. The blasphemous names refer to the divine claims made for the emperors. The woman riding on the beast is dressed in luxurious clothes and adorned with expensive gold and jewels. In her hand she holds a golden cup full of filth, representing her idolatry and wickedness. To the world, Rome appeared to be a dazzling, enticing city. John unmasks the true identity of the city. It is a repulsive, drunken prostitute. Like prostitutes in ancient Rome who wore their name on a headband, the woman bears her name stamped on her forehead. The use of sexual imagery for IDOLATRY is prominent in biblical traditions (cf. Rev 2:20-22). The most damning indictment of the city is the statement that the woman is *drunk with the blood of the saints and the blood of the witnesses to Jesus* (v. 6).

The angel describes the beast as the one who *was, and is not, and is about to ascend from the bottomless pit and go to destruction* (v. 8). This description is a parody of God, *who is and who was and who is to come.* In addition, the description is a reference to Nero who lived, then died, and was expected to return to lay claim to the throne once more (see 13:3). Through the voice of the angel, John tells his readers that the vision of the woman and the beast has more than a surface meaning for those who are wise enough to understand. As the woman represents Rome, the beast upon which she rides symbolizes the Roman Empire. The seven heads of the beast have a dual meaning. They represent seven mountains (Rome was known as the city of seven hills) and seven kings (the emperors). John's explanation of the beast has intrigued commentators for centuries. Who are the specific emperors John has in mind when he says that *five have fallen, one is living, and the other has not yet come; and when he comes, he must remain only a little while* (v. 10)? What about the beast who *is an eighth but it belongs to the seven* (v. 11)?

Scholars have given various answers to these questions. The problem is that by the time of John there had been more than seven emperors. Where does John start? Whom does he omit? Rather than attempt to decipher the listing of emperors, one should interpret the number seven as symbolic. The number seven is derived from the ancient myth of a seven-headed monster. That myth, not the actual number of emperors, controls John's imagery. The seven-headed beast symbolizes all the emperors up to and including Domitian. *Five have fallen*, meaning that Rome has already seen the majority of its rulers; *one is living* (Domitian); and the seventh will last only a short time (because the end is near). The claim that the beast is the eighth, but also part of the seven, is another reference to the Nero myth. Domitian (one of the seven) is, figuratively, the reincarnation of Nero.

The ten horns represent the rulers of other nations who are cohorts of the beast. They will join forces in the war against the Lamb. Their power is limited (*for one hour*), however. They will meet their defeat at the hands of Christ and his faithful followers (cf. 19:11-21). Verses 15-18 present a surprising development. The beast and the ten kings turn on the great whore and destroy her. They unwittingly become agents of God in inflicting punishment on Rome for its arrogance, idolatry, persecution, and greed.

Laments on Earth, 18:1-24

Chapter 18 is similar in form to a funeral dirge. It is composed of several laments over the fall of Babylon (Rome). Examples of these abound in the writings of the prophets in the Hebrew Bible, from which John has freely borrowed in constructing the present songs of doom (cf. Isa 13; 23–24; 34; Jer 50–51; Ezek 26–27). An angel first announces the fall of the city, an event John narrated earlier in 17:15-18. The destruction of the city will be complete. It will become a place haunted by demons and foul animals. Not only has Rome committed evil itself, but it has lead astray other nations, kings, and merchants who have drunk her wine and committed fornication with her.

In this chapter, the chronological perspective shifts. In vv. 2-3, Babylon has fallen. In vv. 4-8, the fall has not yet occurred and the people of God are given advance warning to leave the doomed city before its destruction occurs. Even though for John the destruction is future, he is so certain of God's ultimate triumph that he can speak of it as an accomplished fact. A similar chronological shift occurs several times in the following verses. The command to come out of the doomed city, modeled after Jeremiah's words in Jer 51:45, has a figurative meaning as well as perhaps a literal one. The people are to come out, or separate themselves, from the idolatry and wickedness of the city. God's people are called to reject the values and lifestyle of Rome and its followers. Rome's arrogance and pride are aptly stated in v. 7, *"In her heart she says, 'I rule as a queen; I am no widow, and I will never see grief'."*

Verses 9-20 report the laments of three groups of people who witness the fall of the great city (cf. Ezek 26–28). Each of these groups (kings, merchants, and mariners) has profited from its association with Rome. They weep and mourn because the fall of Rome means economic and political ruin for them. The wealth and extravagance of Rome is indicated by the vast amount of goods sold by the merchants. The last item in the list of v. 13 is rather jarring and indicates the depth of Rome's depravity: *cattle and sheep, horses and chariots, slaves—and human lives.*

After the laments are finished, an angel takes up a huge millstone and throws it into the sea, stating that such will be the fate of Babylon. This imagery of destruction is adapted from Jer 51:63-64 where the prophet is told to take the scroll on which his oracle against Babylon is written, tie a stone to it, and throw it into the Euphrates River, saying, "Thus shall Babylon sink, to rise no more." The totality of Rome's destruction is expressed in vv. 21-23. No music will be heard, no artisans will be found, no sounds of millstones or bridal parties will be heard, and no light will shine any longer. The city will be desolate. Rome has deserved this punishment, for in the city *was found the blood of prophets and of saints, and of all who have been slaughtered on earth* (v. 24). The destruction of the city is divine retribution for the suffering and persecution that Rome had inflicted on God's people.

Celebration in Heaven, 19:1-10

Strictly speaking, this section is an audition, rather than a vision. Each part of this section describes what

John has heard. The fall of Rome brings about a reaction of celebration in heaven. The heavenly multitude sings praises to God because God has exacted judgment on Rome. Their song is a song of victoiy. The cry of the martyrs (6:10) has been answered and God has avenged *the blood of his servants* (v. 2). The songs of the heavenly chorus are not primarily songs of gloating, but celebrations of justice and vindication. The *twenty-four elders and the four living creatures* join in the worship and praise of God. Then a heavenly voice invites all God's people to join in the celebration. Heaven and earth are united in glorious peals of praise to God as Hallelujahs! reverberate throughout all creation. (This chapter is the only place in the NT where the word HALLELUJAH occurs.)

The final hallelujah song in this section offers praise not for the destruction of Rome but for *the marriage of the Lamb* (v. 7). The bride of the Lamb is the church. In the Hebrew Bible the metaphor of Israel as the bride of God is found often (see esp. Hos 1–3). Since Christians saw themselves as the new Israel, the application of the bride imagery to the church was a natural one. In the NT the author of Ephesians gives an extended application of this metaphor (Eph 5:23-32; cf. 2 Cor 11:2). The bride is dressed in *fine linen, bright and pure*, which is interpreted as the righteous deeds of the saints. The contrast between the church and Rome is unmistakable. Rome is the great prostitute, drinking from a cup of abominations and impurities. The church, on the other hand, is the pure bride of Christ, adorned in fine, bright linen.

The fourth beatitude of Revelation (v. 9) declares: *Blessed are those who are invited to the marriage banquet of the Lamb.* Who are the guests? They too are the church. One cannot press John's imagery for consistency. John's language is poetic, imaginative language, not analytical or scientific language. In John's creative presentation, the church can be both the bride and the wedding guests. The imagery of a wedding and a wedding feast convey the mood of the kingdom of God. God's kingdom is filled with joy and celebration, happiness and intimacy.

In response to all that he has heard, John falls down in worship before his angel guide. The reaction of the angel is quick and decisive: *"You must not do that! I am a fellow servant with you and your comrades who hold the testimony of Jesus. Worship God!"* (v. 10). The words of the angel were apt words for John's readers as well. Tempted to compromise their faith and participate in emperor worship, they should hear these words as a warning. No one, not even the angels and certainly not the beastly emperor, is worthy of worship. Worship belongs to God alone.

The Final Victory, 19:11–20:15

Several times John has either intimated or directly stated that the decisive victory over evil has been accomplished. In this section he gives the final and most complete portrayal of the defeat of all the forces aligned against God. Like all of the Apocalypse, the scenes here are not literal predictions of coming events, arranged in chronological order. Instead, John presents the reader with powerful images of judgment, punishment, and the righteousness of God.

19:11-16. The triumphant Christ. This passage portrays the coming of Christ as judge and warrior. Heaven opens and John sees a rider on *a white horse.* (This horse and rider should not be confused with the one that appeared at the opening of the first seal in 6:1-2.) The rider is Christ, *called Faithful and True* (cf. 3:14, *the faithful and true witness*). His eyes are *like a flame of fire* (cf. 1:14; 2:18). His many diadems are evidence of his royal position. His name *that no one knows but himself* (v. 12) signifies the mystery of Christ who surpasses all human understanding. His robe is dipped in blood, like that of God the Divine Warrior in Isaiah 63 whose robe is stained with the blood of his enemies. *His name is called The Word of God* (cf. John 1:1, 14; and esp. Wis 18:14-16). The sword from his mouth, his ruling with a rod of iron, and his treading the wine press (v. 15) are all images of judgment upon the earth. In case any doubt exists concerning the identity of this splendid figure, emblazoned on his robe and on his thigh are the words *King of kings and Lord of lords.* Christ is accompanied by the armies of heaven, also riding white horses. Although some commentators understand the heavenly armies to be composed of angels, the forces here are probably identical with the *called and chosen and faithful* of 17:14, the martyrs. They do not engage in actual combat (notice they wear festal garb, not battle vestments), but they accompany Christ to share in his victory. They are witnesses of their own vindication.

19:17-21. The final battle. An angel calls to the birds and invites them to *the great supper of God* to eat the bodies of God's enemies who will be killed (cf. Ezek 39:17-20). This is a grotesque counterpart to 19:9. Like the redeemed who are invited to the marriage supper of the Lamb, the wicked of the earth will also participate in a great feast. The difference is that they will be the main course! In the final battle the beast and false prophet are captured and thrown into *the lake of fire that burns with sulfur* (v. 20). The lake of fire is GEHENNA, the place of torment for the wicked. The remainder of the forces arrayed against Christ are killed *by the sword that came from his mouth* (v. 21). The identification of Christ's weapon as the sword of his mouth (i.e., the word of God) should be a caution to anyone who is tempted to interpret the battle imagery of Revelation literally.

20:1-6. The millennial reign. As a result of the battle, Satan is bound by an angel and thrown into *the bottomless pit* (see 9:1; cf. Isa 24:21-22). There he is to remain for a thousand years. The imprisonment of Satan is certain, for he has been bound with a chain, locked in the pit, and a seal placed over the door. All the evil forces have now been removed from the earth.

The millennial reign of Christ and his followers now begins. The concept of an interim earthly rule prior to the consummation of the KINGDOM OF GOD in heaven is found in several apocalyptic writings. The idea apparently developed from the attempt to combine the older prophetic idea of a this-worldly kingdom of God centered in Israel that would occur in the last days with the apocalyptic notion of a new heaven and new earth as the locale for God's kingdom. The interim reign of the messiah, followed by the otherworldly kingdom of God, preserves both concepts. The length of this interim reign varies in different traditions. John pictures it lasting for *a thousand years*; in 2 Esdr 7:28 the messianic reign lasts 400 years. Among the many other limits set for this reign are 4,000 years, 600 years, 60 years, 365 years, or even 365,000 years.

According to v. 4 the millennial reign is not for all believers, but only for the martyrs. This interim period is a special reward for those who have given their lives for the sake of God's kingdom. The rest of the dead (righteous and unrighteous) will not be raised until the end of the millennium. The first resurrection is only for those who have paid the ultimate price for their witness. They are the *firstfruits* (14:4) of the harvest. The remainder of the faithful will be united with them after the second resurrection. The millennium should not be taken literally. Instead it should be seen as powerful imagery offering reassurance that God knows and values the tremendous sacrifices that some believers are called upon to make for the sake of God's kingdom.

20:7-10. The final conflict. Satan is loosed from his imprisonment after the millennium is ended and mounts one last assault on the people of God. Why, in John's scheme, Satan must be released after he has been bound is not clear. Perhaps it is John's way of emphasizing the formidable power of evil. Even when it appears that evil has been contained and is no longer a threat, it has the capacity to rebound and wreak havoc in one's life. A more mundane reason for having Satan released is so John could introduce one more image in his apocalyptic drama, the figures of *Gog and Magog*. Satan is joined by Gog and Magog, representing *the nations at the four corners of the earth* (v. 8). The symbolism of Gog and Magog is taken from Ezek 38–39 where Gog, the leader of the land of Magog, leads a group of nations in an attack on Jerusalem. John adapts that tradition, making Gog as well as Magog the names of nations. Satan and his army attack the people of God, described as *the camp of the saints and the beloved city* (v. 9). God intervenes, however, destroying the rebellious forces of Satan. Satan is thrown into the lake of fire, there to be *tormented day and night forever and ever* (v. 10), along with his cohorts, the beast and the false prophet. Finally, and definitively, Satan is defeated.

20:11-15. The last judgment. The final judgment takes place in front of the *great white throne* of God. The earth and heaven flee from God's presence because as part of the old, rebellious order no place exists for them anymore. A new heaven and new earth will be needed. All people stand before the throne, while two types of books are brought and examined. In one book, *the book of life* (cf. 3:5; 13:8; 17:8), are recorded the names of all the people of God. It is the heavenly register of the redeemed. In the other books are recorded all the deeds of humanity. The imagery here appears in conflict. If one's name is in *the book of life,* how can one also be judged by works? If one's name is not in the book of life, can one be saved by works? The resolution of this tension lies in the creative juxtaposition of these two images. John is reminding his readers that salvation is a matter of God's grace, not their achievement (the book of life). On the other hand, one's actions do matter. They are an indication of the seriousness of one's commitment to God. Grace and works are held together in this scene in creative tension. No one escapes God's judgment. Even Death, the last enemy and the destroyer of life, is not exempt. *Death and Hades* (the place of the dead), along with *anyone whose name was not found written in the book of life*, are cast into the lake of fire, the second death.

The New Jerusalem, 21:1–22:5

All of John's visions have been leading up to this final section. The eschatological woes, the punishments, the words of assurance, the last judgment, all are left in the shadows of this final spectacular scene of God's glorious kingdom. As has been the case throughout the Apocalypse, John draws heavily upon motifs and images from the Hebrew Bible and apocalyptic traditions. The reader must keep in mind that John's language is imaginative and symbolic. A literal reading of the text produces a distorted understanding of John's message. The imagery of *the new Jerusalem* and *the new heaven and the new earth* are symbols of life lived in intimate communion with God.

New Heaven and New Earth, 21:1-8

Not only do earth and heaven give way for a new heaven and new earth (cf. Isa 65:17; 66:22), but the sea no longer exists in John's vision of the new world. The sea is a symbol of chaos, rebellion, and evil. John sees the new Jerusalem coming down out of heaven. This is no human construct. Its origin is from God. The city is *prepared as a bride adorned for her husband* (v. 2). John has earlier painted a graphic picture of another city, "the great city," Rome. The new Jerusalem is in direct contrast to that city. Rome was portrayed as a prostitute; the new city is like a bride. The hallmark of this new city is that God dwells here with God's people. Nothing separates the people from their God, not physical distance, not emotional nor physical pain.

God speaks directly in vv. 5-8, declaring that the re-creation of all things is completed. The end has arrived through the actions of the one who is Alpha and Omega, beginning and end. The faithful (the conquerors) are assured that they will inherit the blessings of God and will be God's children. The wicked, however, are excluded from God's kingdom. The list of those who will be cast into the lake of fire is probably traditional, but some of its elements would have had special significance for John's situation. The cowardly and the faithless are those who did not resist the beast of Rome; the liars are those who confessed the emperor as lord (cf. 14:5).

The Holy City, 21:9-27

An angel comes and takes John up to a high mountain from which he can view the new Jerusalem. The city has *twelve gates* named for the *twelve tribes of Israel* and *twelve foundations* named for the *twelve apostles*. This symbolizes the city as the total people of God. The measurement of the city reveals that it is a cube, symbolizing the perfection of the city. In the Greek text the measurements are multiples of twelve (twelve thousand stadia), symbolizing the enormity and completeness of the city. The city is built of precious metals and jewels (cf. Isa 54:11-12). Much of this description is borrowed from other traditions, including the listing of the precious stones on the breastplate of the high priest (cf. Exod 28:17-20). The presence of these stones support the claims made earlier that the people of God are a priestly people. The gates of the city are made of pearls and the streets are made of gold. The total effect of the description is to overwhelm the reader with the magnificence and glory of this dwelling place for God's people.

No need exists in the city for a temple, symbolic of the presence of God, because in the new Jerusalem God and the Lamb dwell with the people. Likewise no sun or moon are needed because the glory of God and Christ shine throughout the city. The glory of the city is such that it will draw nations and kings into it. It is a place of safety where the gates of the city need never be shut (v. 25). It is also a place of purity and righteousness into which everyone and everything that is unclean are forbidden to enter.

The River of Life, 22:1-5

John's description of the new Jerusalem is heavily dependent on Ezekiel's vision of the restored Jerusalem (chap. 47). In Ezekiel, as well as in other writings (particularly in APOCALYPTIC LITERATURE), future hope is expressed in terms of a restored Garden of Eden. That imagery is prevalent in these verses in the tree of life and in the river that flows through the city. John borrows from Ezekiel the idea that the leaves of the tree will be for healing. The most revealing characteristic of life in the new Jerusalem is that God's servants *will see his face* (v. 4), a feat not possible before (cf. 1 Cor 13:12; Matt 5:8). This act expresses intimacy, fellowship, and complete knowledge. Life in God's new kingdom is eternal, for *they will reign forever and ever* (v. 5).

Epilogue, 22:6-21

The book concludes with a series of warnings, exhortations, and assurances. The identity of the speaker is not clear in all cases. Verses 7, 12, 16, and 20 come from Christ. Verses 6 and 10 may be from Christ or an angel. In v. 6 the speaker declares the message of John to be authentic because its ultimate source is God. Verse 7 presents a blessing for those who hold fast to the message John has revealed in this writing.

Once again (cf. 19:10) John falls down to worship his angelic guide and is strongly rebuked (vv. 8-10). Worship should be directed to God alone. Apocalyptic writings often claim to have been written by venerable figures of the distant past, but their message has only recently come to light. To explain why the works, if ancient, had not been known earlier, a command to secrecy is often included. The works have been sealed up until the last days, which are the present time (cf. Dan 8:26; 12:4, 9). John does not use an ancient pseudonym. He writes in his own name for his own time. There is no need to seal up his message, *for the time is near* (v. 10). In fact the end is so near that little time is left for people to change their ways (v. 11).

Christ declares that he is coming soon to bring punishment and reward (v. 12). He applies to himself the same titles that have been used in the book for God (cf. 1:8; 21:6). The final blessing of the book is pronounced upon *those who wash their robes*, that is, those who have been redeemed by Christ's death (cf. 7:14). While the redeemed may enter the new Jerusalem, the wicked (*dogs* was a derogatory term often applied to the godless) must remain outside. Once more the authenticity of the message is declared (v. 16). In v. 17 the Spirit and the bride (the church) respond to the promise that Christ is coming by issuing their own invitation, *"Come."* (In the Gk. text, *come* is singular, indicating that the invitation is addressed to Christ and not to people in general.) Everyone is urged to join in extending the invitation, and finally the invitation is opened to all who want the water of life to come (cf. John 7:37-38).

Verses 18-19 contain a curse formula to safeguard the accuracy and authenticity of the work. Formulas of this nature, found in many ancient writings, were an attempt to prevent copyists from altering the text. John believes that his message is a true word from God and wants to preserve its integrity. For the third time in this section, Jesus exclaims, *"I am coming soon"* (v. 20). This time John answers in words that are both a shout of jubilation and a prayer for fulfillment: *Amen. Come, Lord Jesus!*

The book ends with an epistolary conclusion similar to those in Paul's letters.

Works Cited

Beasley-Murray, George R. 1974. *The Book of Revelation*, NCB.

Hemer, Colin J. 1986. *The Letters to the Seven Churches of Asia in Their Local Setting.*

Reddish, Mitchell G. 1990. "Antichrist," MDB.